COOKING A TO Z

Jane Horn
Editor/Writer

Janet Fletcher
Contributing Writer

Gary Hespenheide
Designer

CALIFORNIA
CULINARY
ACADEMY

Jane Horn, a free-lance food writer and cookbook editor, holds a degree in communication from Stanford University. In addition to *Cooking A to Z*, she has worked as either author or editor (or both) on a number of other cookbooks, including *The New Harvest* (101 Productions), a guide to exotic and specialty produce; and *California Fresh*, published by the Junior League of Oakland-East Bay. In the California Culinary Academy cookbook series, she coauthored *Chicken & Other Poultry* and was contributing writer for *Microwave & More*, which explores timesaving cooking methods and equipment. She has also written a weekly newspaper food column.

Janet Fletcher is a free-lance food and wine writer and editor. She holds a degree in economics from Stanford University and attended the Culinary Institute of America in Hyde Park, New York. She has cooked in several west coast restaurants, including the highly acclaimed Chez Panisse, and now writes a weekly restaurant column for the Oakland *Tribune*. In addition she writes magazine articles and produces newsletters, brochures, and promotional literature for clients in the food and wine industry. She coauthored *Appetizers & Hors d'Oeuvres* and *Italian Cooking* and was contributing writer for *Cookies,* all part of the California Culinary Academy cookbook series.

The California Culinary Academy   In the forefront of American institutions leading the culinary renaissance in this country, the California Culinary Academy in San Francisco has gained a reputation as one of the most outstanding professional chef training schools in the world. With a teaching staff recruited from the best restaurants of Western Europe, the Academy educates students from around the world in the preparation of classical cuisine. The recipes in this book were created in consultation with the chefs of the Academy. For information about the Academy, write the Office of the Dean, California Culinary Academy, 625 Polk Street, San Francisco, CA 94102.

Copyright © 1988
Chevron Chemical Company
All rights reserved under international and Pan-American copyright conventions.

3 4 5 6 7 8 9
88 89 90 91 92 93

ISBN 0-89721-147-2

Library of Congress Catalog Card Number 87-072103

 Chevron

Chevron Chemical Company
6001 Bollinger Canyon Road, San Ramon, CA 94583

CONTRIBUTORS

Cakes, Pastries, and Breads
Tina Salter

Cooking Technique
Daniel Strongin

Equipment
Bill Hughes

Food Processor
Greg Patent

General Recipe Development
Susan Walter

Ice Cream and Frozen Desserts
Leonard D. Grotta

Jams, Jellies, Preserves, and Condiments
Katie Millhiser

Microwave Cooking
Lorinda Moholt

Additional Recipes and Text
Bruce Aidells
John Phillip Carroll
Ron Clark
Hallie Donnelly
Olivia Erschen
Lonnie Gandara
Michael Goodwin
Jay Harlow
Faye Levy
Susan E. Mitchell
Julie Renaud
Cynthia Scheer
Vicki Barrios Schley
Angelo Villa
Charlotte Walker
Naomi Wise

Consultants
Ron Clark
Joyce Jue
Julie Renaud

Ortho Books

Publisher
Robert J. Dolezal

Editorial Director
Christine Robertson

Production Director
Ernie S. Tasaki

Managing Editor, Cookbooks
Sally W. Smith

Systems Manager
Katherine L. Parker

National Sales Manager
Charles H. Aydelotte

Address all inquiries to
Ortho Information Services
P.O. Box 5047
San Ramon, CA 94583

Illustrator
Edith Allgood

Copy Chief
Melinda E. Levine

Copyeditors
Andrea Y. Connolly
Judith Dunham

Proofreader
Lorna Cunkle

Editorial Assistants
Karen K. Johnson
Kass Kapsiak
Tamara Mallory
Raymond F. Quinton

Layout Editor
Linda M. Bouchard

Typographer
Robert C. Miller

Indexer
Elinor Lindheimer

Production by
Studio 165

Separations and Printing by
Toppan Printing Co., Ltd.
    Tokyo, Japan

Special Thanks to
Joanne Bautista
John A. Brown Kitchenwares
Vivianne Coles
Cuisinarts
Peggy Fallon
Jane Frorath
Sylvia Hajak
Robert L. Iacopi
Rebecca Johnson
Sam Kellogg
Tricia Reuter O'Brien
Darryl Salter
Paula Schlosser
Mark Zielinski

PHOTOGRAPHY

Recipes
Kevin Sanchez, photographer
Susan Massey-Weil, food stylist
Liz Ross, photographic stylist
Chris Coughlin, photographer's assistant

Technique
Marshall Gordon, photographer
Kathleen Prisant, food stylist
Diana Torrey, stylist's assistant

**Equipment;
Author, Chefs (at left)**
Kit Morris, photographer
Carol Haagens, photographer's assistant

Additional Photographers
Patricia Brabant, pp. 7, 78, 81, 82, 86, 112, 125, 126, 127, 161, 162, 163, 164, 165, 186, 239, 260, 400, 421, 423, 431, 437, 454, 483, 484, 486, 495, 498; Victor Budnik, pp. 312, 313; Ed Carey, pp. 133, 206, 237, 270, 273, 328, 388, 582 (left); David Fischer and Patrick Lyons, pp. 25, 75, 111, 231, 563, 611; Joel Glenn, pp. 114, 122, 233, 358, 445, 447, 485, 595, 602; Dennis Gray, pp. 53, 134, 194, 199, 201, 202, 253, 450, 467, 527, 598; Michael Lamotte, pp. 6, 13, 14, 26, 27, 28, 39, 42, 56 (left), 61, 64, 92, 139, 141, 143, 144, 146, 147, 150, 159 (right), 169, 182, 185, 188, 234, 286, 293, 298, 300, 341, 395, 397, 424, 427, 458, 463, 496, 509, 514, 528, 541, 565, 631; Fred Lyon, pp. 46, 176, 219, 221, 265, 280, 335, 346, 357, 452, 453, 510, 519, 531, 581, 591, 597, 609, 610; Doug Manchee, page 131 (right); Bob Montesclaros, pp. 68, 174, 198, 296, 350, 417, 472, 474, 476, 513, 533, 557; Allan Rosenberg, pp. 91, 179, 181, 374, 491, 614, 618, 623, 624, 625, 629, 630; Tom Tracy, page 303; Jackson Vereen, pp. 224, 295, 392, 532, 536, 537, 538, 542, 544, 546.

Additional Stylists
Allison Anthony, Roz Baker, M. Susan Broussard, Sandra Cook, Joanne Dexter, Olivia Erschen, Amy Glenn, Sandra Griswold, Carol Hacker, Karen Hazarian, Robert Lambert, Sandra Learned, Bunny Martin, Cherie Miller, Amy Nathan, Janet Nusbaum, Jan Rhodes, Cynthia Scheer, Sara Slavin, Carla Tavaras, Kathleen Volkmann, Doug Warne, Maria Winston.

PREFACE

Cooking A to Z is a practical, comprehensive culinary reference book. It is also a collection of more than 600 specially selected recipes covering the basics and more. And it is a beautiful book that anyone who loves food will read with pleasure.

If you are a novice cook, through this book you can learn the fundamentals — the terms, techniques, and equipment you need to prepare any recipe with success. *Cooking A to Z* will also guide you through the constantly changing marketplace: it tells you how to shop for and cook with fresh ingredients and processed foods; how to stock pantry and cupboard; and how to identify, select, and care for kitchen equipment. More experienced cooks will appreciate the convenience of finding all the basic food and cooking information in one up-to-date volume, as well as a wealth of reliable and creative recipes. With so much to offer, *Cooking A to Z* will prove invaluable to cooks and (noncooking) food enthusiasts alike, both as a workbook and as a source of hours of fascinating reading.

The information presented on these pages reflects the expertise of consultants drawn from all aspects of cooking. Equipment entries offer the most current information on the range of basic culinary tools and appliances. You will learn how to use the equipment, how to decide whether or not it should be part of your personal *batterie de cuisine*, and which pieces are interchangeable. Each of the equipment entries is accompanied by a photograph that clearly shows the item. Cooking terminology, the culinary shorthand that is the foundation for every recipe, is fully explained; terms are often illustrated. More than 35 sets of step-by-step photographs, plus detailed text, demonstrate important techniques such as boning, beating egg whites, carving, filleting, and decorating cakes. For each ingredient, you are provided with specific information for use,

availability, selection, and storage. Throughout the book you will find over 75 special features that offer highlights and tips. The recipes are wide ranging, from sauces to cookies to roasts, and include exciting ways to use familiar ingredients and those that are new to you.

You will refer to this book when you come across something you don't know in a recipe, or when you hear of a recipe and want to know what it is or how to prepare it. For instance, perhaps you recently tasted the following dessert: an apple tart composed of a pastry base with a filling of sliced apples, finished with an apricot glaze and presented in a pool of custard sauce. Open *Cooking A to Z* and look up: *apple, tart, tart pan, tart pastry, glaze,* and *custard.* You will find information on selecting, storing, and using apples; on what a tart is and how to make one; on what a tart pan is and what different kinds there are; on the types of tart pastry and which one to use; on the definition of *glaze* and several representative types of glazes; and on custards and how to make a custard sauce. You will find a number of recipes for tarts, as well as one for apple pie (just in case, even after learning all about tarts, you still prefer pie).

Cooking A to Z is organized alphabetically; the encyclopedia format makes it easy to locate any subject. You can also use the thorough index. While each of the almost 500 entries tells a complete story, many will also direct you elsewhere in the book for further information or additional recipes. Hundreds of full-color photographs of both recipes and techniques complement the clear, straightforward text and also make browsing a pleasure.

Whether this is your first cookbook or the latest addition to an extensive culinary library, *Cooking A to Z* will prove indispensable, so give it a good spot on your shelf or kitchen counter.

A popular Chinese restaurant dessert, meltingly tender Chinese Almond Cookies, uses both almond extract and whole blanched almonds to impart nutty flavor. The recipe is on page 145.

ACHIOTE

The hard, brick red seed of the annatto tree is called achiote. The seeds are valued more for the golden yellow color they impart to other foods than for their flavor, which is somewhat dusty.

Use   The seeds, typically, are soaked in water or heated in oil or lard, then discarded, and the oil or water is used to color food. Latin American cooks often add ground achiote to the water when cooking rice; and they use it in spice pastes for stews and sprinkle it on meats before roasting. The seed is also used commercially in this country to color butter, margarine, and cheese.

Availability   Check Latin American, Caribbean, and Philippine markets for achiote. It is available as whole seeds, ground powder, paste, and liquid extract.

Selection   Achiote seeds should have a lively brick red color; a brownish color indicates age.

Storage   Both seeds and powder should be stored in a tightly covered jar in a cool, dark place. Seeds will keep indefinitely; powder will keep up to six months. The paste should be refrigerated after opening; it will keep indefinitely.

Preparation   To color cooking fat, heat 2 parts oil or lard with 1 part achiote seed over moderately low heat until fat turns a golden orange (5 to 10 minutes). Cool, strain into a jar, and refrigerate. To prepare seeds for grinding, cover with water, bring to a boil and simmer 5 minutes, then remove from heat and let soak until cool. Drain and grind with a mortar and pestle, clean coffee grinder, or electric minichopper.

ACIDULATED WATER

The flesh of certain fruits and vegetables, such as apples and pears, will darken when exposed to air unless used immediately after cutting or unless they are dropped into acidulated water, a dilute solution of 5 or 6 parts water to 1 part acid. Typically the acid is lemon juice or vinegar.

ADJUST, TO

In cooking, this term means to taste a dish after it has cooked for a while, or just before serving, and then add more seasoning if needed.

AL DENTE

The literal meaning of this Italian term is *to the tooth*. It describes the consistency of pasta and vegetables when cooked just to the point of doneness. At this stage food still offers some resistance when chewed (the technical term is *percussion*) and has developed a fuller and richer flavor than when raw.

ALLSPICE

The allspice berry resembles an oversized, reddish brown peppercorn. Its flavor and aroma suggest a pungent and spicy blend of cloves, cinnamon, and nutmeg.

Use   Allspice adds zest to both savory and sweet dishes, including stews, sauces (particularly tomato-based ones), marinades, relishes and preserves, cooked fruit, and baked goods of all kinds. It combines well with other spices. One of the pickling spices, it is sometimes part of the French blend *quatre épices* (four spices) used in pâtés. If necessary substitute a mixture of equal amounts of cloves, cinnamon, and nutmeg for allspice.

Availability   Buy it packaged or bulk, whole or ground.

Selection Packaged seasonings lose quality after a while; try to buy from a store that restocks its spice section fairly often.

Storage Keep in an airtight container away from light and heat. Ground spice stays pungent up to six months, whole berries even longer.

Preparation Grind whole berries in a pepper mill, clean coffee grinder, electric minichopper, or with a mortar and pestle.

> ### Recipes and Related Information
> *Carrot Spice Cake, 86; Honeyed Chicken With Apricots, 557.*

ALMOND

Encased in a light-tan pitted shell, the almond is a white, oval, flat nut covered with a brown skin. Both bitter and sweet varieties exist. Raw bitter almonds contain toxic prussic acid, which is harmful except in small amounts, and so only sweet almonds are sold in the United States. Because the acid is destroyed by heat, commercial processors can use oil from the more intensely flavored bitter nut for extracts and liqueurs. For more flavor, European recipes may add a touch of bitter almond to the sweet almond.

Use Extremely versatile, the almond is used as both ingredient and garnish. It adds texture and crunch to poultry, fish, rice, sauces, vegetables, salads, breads, desserts, cake and pastry fillings, and candy.

Availability Almonds come packaged in cans or clear bags, or in bulk; in the shell or shelled; unblanched or blanched; whole, chopped, sliced, or slivered.

Selection Buy nuts that are as fresh as possible.

Storage Unshelled nuts can be stored in a cool place for up to six months. Shelled nuts will keep in an airtight container in the refrigerator for several months or in the freezer for up to six months (thaw before using).

Preparation See NUT.

ALMOND PASTE AND MARZIPAN

Made from finely ground blanched almonds, sugar, and egg whites, marzipan and almond paste can be molded to form flowers, stems, leaves, and other fanciful shapes, or rolled out into sheets to decorate cakes and pastries. They have been used for making confections for centuries. They were originally two distinct products, but now have become essentially interchangeable, both in use and in name. If a difference must be stated: Marzipan is cooked and firmer and more pliable than almond paste, which is not cooked. They can be found in better supermarkets or gourmet shops, or you can make your own (see right).

To roll out either almond paste or marzipan, dust work surface lightly with confectioners' sugar and roll out with a rolling pin. Tint almond paste or marzipan by kneading in a few drops of food coloring. Pale tints are usually the most appetizing on pastry.

▣ HOMEMADE ALMOND PASTE
2 cups very finely ground blanched almonds
2¼ cups sifted confectioners' sugar
1 to 2 egg whites, beaten until foamy
Fondant (optional)

1. Combine almonds and sugar in a bowl. Stir well to blend. Gradually stir in enough egg whites to moisten almond mixture. Gather mixture into a ball; knead until smooth. Wrap well and refrigerate. Keeps for 1 week.

2. To make almond paste more pliable and easier to roll out, work a little fondant into it. Fondant is a sticky white icing available at bakeries or stores that sell cake-decorating supplies (see page 96). To roll out almond paste, dust work surface with confectioners' sugar.

Makes about 1 pound.

Food Processor Version Use metal blade to process almonds and sugar until almonds are very finely ground. Add 1 unbeaten egg white and process 20 seconds. If paste does not form a ball, add more egg white.

▣ HOMEMADE MARZIPAN
2 cups sugar
¾ cup water
3½ cups very finely ground blanched almonds
2 egg whites, beaten until foamy
Confectioners' sugar, for dusting

1. Combine sugar and the water in saucepan. Cook to 240° F (soft-ball stage; see CANDY AND CONFECTION, Stages of Sugar Syrup). Remove from heat; stir until cloudy. Then stir in almonds.

2. Stir in egg whites and cook over low heat until mixture firms slightly. Dust work surface with confectioners' sugar. Knead marzipan until pliable. Wrap well and store in refrigerator for up to 1 month.

Makes 1¾ pounds.

Food Processor Version Use metal blade to grind almonds in 2 batches. Add to recipe as directed. Process cooked mixture until pliable (30 to 45 seconds).

> ### Recipes and Related Information
> *Almond Meringue Cake, 361; Almond Torte 89; Apricot-Almond Squares, 143; Chinese Almond Cookies, 145; Panforte, 186; Raspberry-Almond Tart, 496; Ricotta Cheesecake, 119; Your Own Bridge Mix, 59.*

Green-tinted marzipan was rolled out and then applied to a leaf mold. The marzipan takes the shape of a leaf, even the detailing of the veins. After removal from the mold, it can be placed on a cake for decoration.

ANGELICA

A large perennial herb native to the northern hemisphere and New Zealand, angelica is valued principally for its roots and stalks.

Use Fresh angelica is eaten as a vegetable in the world's northernmost regions, such as Iceland, Norway, and Siberia. Because of its pungent flavor and alleged digestive properties, angelica root is used in the production of cordials and liqueurs, such as Benedictine and Chartreuse. The leaves and stalks may be used to flavor custards. When processed commercially, the green celerylike stalks are generally candied in sugar syrup for decorative use in breads, cookies, cakes, and fruitcakes. Candied angelica is expensive, and occasionally counterfeits made of dyed substitutes appear in the market.

Availability Fresh angelica is not grown commercially in the United States. Some home gardeners cultivate it, and it may be found wild. Angelica stalks candied in sugar syrup are available packaged or in bulk from specialty food markets or a bakers' supply outlet.

Storage Keep fresh stalks in a plastic bag in refrigerator crisper and use within a couple of days. Store candied angelica in a cool, dark place for two to three months, or freeze indefinitely.

Preparation Wash and trim fresh angelica. Halve lengthwise to be sure hollow stalks are clean. Cut stalks in smaller lengths and steep in milk for custards, or dice and candy in sugar syrup. Candied angelica can be marinated in brandy or liqueur for several hours before using.

Recipes and Related Information
Candied Fruit, 93; Candy, 93.

ANISE

An annual herb in the parsley family, anise yields small, pungent leaves and greenish gray seeds; both have a licoricelike flavor.

Use Add anise leaves sparingly to salads and vegetable dishes. Anise seed (also spelled *aniseed*) is popular in German and Scandinavian cookies, cakes, and breads, and in Italian twice-baked cookies (*biscotti*). Add it to pickles, cabbage slaw, or ground-pork mixtures. Anise oil is used as a flavoring agent in cough medicines.

Availability Whole anise seed is packaged in glass jars. It is rarely available ground but may be ground at home. Anise leaves are not available commercially.

Selection Packaged seasonings lose quality after a while; try to buy from a store that restocks its spice section fairly often.

Storage Keep in an airtight container away from light and heat. Anise seed will stay pungent up to one year.

Preparation Leaves are used whole; rub them lightly between the fingers to release oils. Seed may be used whole, or ground in a pepper mill, clean coffee grinder, electric minichopper, or with a mortar and pestle.

■ BISCOTTI

Almost every Italian bakery sells several varieties of dry *biscotti*, twice-baked (*bis cotto*) cookies that are meant to be dunked in coffee or wine. They keep for weeks in an airtight container; offer them with afternoon tea or coffee or with a late-night glass of sweet wine. Note that the dough must chill at least overnight.

¼	cup dried currants
2	tablespoons Marsala
½	pound unsalted butter, softened
2	cups sugar
4	eggs
1	teaspoon vanilla extract
1	tablespoon anise-flavored liqueur
4	cups flour
1	teaspoon baking powder
1	teaspoon baking soda
½	teaspoon salt
2	teaspoons grated lemon rind
1	teaspoon anise seed
½	cup half-and-half
1	cup coarsely chopped, toasted walnuts
1	cup coarsely chopped, toasted hazelnuts

1. Put currants in a bowl with Marsala; soak for 20 minutes.

2. Cream butter; add sugar gradually and beat until light. Add eggs one at a time, beating until light and fluffy. Add vanilla, liqueur, and currants with their soaking liquid.

3. Sift together flour, baking powder, baking soda, and salt. Stir in lemon rind and anise seed. Add to creamed mixture alternately with half-and-half. Stir in walnuts and hazelnuts by hand. Cover and chill dough for at least 2 hours or overnight.

4. Divide dough into quarters and place each quarter on a length of waxed paper. Form into a roll about 15 inches long and 1½ inches thick. Wrap in waxed paper, then in aluminum foil. Chill overnight (dough can be frozen at this point for up to 1 month; bring frozen dough to refrigerator temperature before proceeding).

5. Preheat oven to 350° F. Unwrap rolls and place them on ungreased baking sheets. Bake until very lightly browned (20 to 25 minutes). Carefully transfer rolls to a cutting board and cut on a 45-degree angle into slices about ½ inch thick. Place slices cut side up on baking sheets and return to oven. Bake until golden (8 to 12 minutes). Cool cookies thoroughly on racks. Store in airtight containers.

Makes about 4 dozen cookies.

Food Processor Version As a timesaver, use standard shredding disk to process nuts.

Recipes and Related Information
Florentine Grape Coffee Cake, 279; Spiced French Honey Bread, 304.

APPLE

The sweet, round, thin-skinned fruit of a tree that grows in temperate zones, the apple is presumed a native of southwest Asia. Of the thousands of classified varieties, fewer than 20 are commercially important in the United States. Skin color of most varieties is green, yellow, or red; the moist, crisp flesh is white to creamy white, sometimes with yellow, green, or red tints.

Use Raw apples are commonly eaten out of hand or in fruit salads. Apples may be stewed and puréed for applesauce, baked whole, or used as an ingredient in a wide variety of baked desserts. Cooked apples are a popular garnish for savory pork dishes; they also figure in some classic French chicken and veal preparations. Apples may be pressed for juice, which, in turn, may be fermented into cider or distilled into brandy (also known as applejack and Calvados).

Availability Early varieties such as the Gravenstein and Astrachan are harvested in July and August. Late varieties begin in September and continue through November. Controlled-storage apples are available the rest of the year. Fresh apples are sold in bulk, overwrapped trays, or plastic bags. Cooked apples are available as canned or bottled applesauce or as canned apple-pie filling. Sliced apples are also available dried.

Selection Choose firm apples without bruised spots. Scald (irregularly shaped tan or brown area) has tougher texture than unblemished skin but does not seriously affect eating quality.

The following are suggested pairings of apple varieties and uses; eating apples such as Golden Delicious, Granny Smith, or Newtown pippin are fine eaten out of hand but also are good, all-purpose cooking apples. These groupings are offered for optimum flavor; or use what your recipe suggests.

For Eating Try Golden Delicious (gold), Granny Smith (green), Jonathan (brilliant red), McIntosh (red to green), Newtown pippin (green), Red Delicious (red), Stayman (red), or Winesap (red).

For Pies and Applesauce Use tart or slightly acidic varieties: Gravenstein (yellow-green with red stripes), Grimes Golden (gold), Jonathan (brilliant red), McIntosh (red to green), Newtown pippin (green), Northern Spy (red); Rhode Island Greening (green), Stayman (red), Winesap (red), and York Imperial (red).

For Baking Use firmer-fleshed varieties preferably over 3 inches in diameter: Northern Spy (red), Rome Beauty (red), Winesap (red), York Imperial (red).

Storage Refrigerate apples until use; hardy varieties will last a month or more. Dried apples will keep indefinitely when stored in a plastic bag in the refrigerator.

Preparation Peel apples or not, as desired. For cooked dishes, halve or quarter apples and remove core. To core whole apples, use an apple corer, or use a small, sharp knife to cut all the way around the core and lift it out.

Homey Apple Crisp (see page 10) is an early American baked fruit dessert with a sweetened crumb topping. Whipped cream or vanilla ice cream is the perfect, cool complement to the warm, fragrant fruit.

Cut full triangles for the base of the charlotte shell and blunt-tipped triangles for the sides. If possible, set a side piece on each bottom piece.

▪ APPLE CHARLOTTE

A combination of puréed apples and crisp fingers of buttered bread, Apple Charlotte is baked and served warm. Although a charlotte can be prepared in any appropriately sized mold or baking dish, a round, tinned-steel charlotte mold with its flat bottom, slightly flaring sides, and heart-shaped handles is traditional.

> **Good-quality, firm-textured bread (French, brioche, bakery white)**
> 1 **cup butter, melted**
> **Sugar, for dusting mold**

Basic Glaze (see page 250; use apricot preserves)

Apple Purée

> 5 **pounds tart apples (Granny Smith or pippin), peeled, cored, and sliced**
> ¼ **cup butter**
> ¼ **cup water**
> 1 **teaspoon vanilla extract**
> **Sugar, to taste**

1. Prepare Apple Purée. Preheat the oven to 400° F. Cut bread into ¼-inch-thick slices and remove crusts.

2. Lightly butter a 4-cup charlotte mold or soufflé dish; dust with sugar. Cut bread to fit mold (see photograph at left). Dip slices in melted butter and line bottom, then sides of pan.

3. Fill lined pan with cooled purée and cover with another layer of butter-dipped bread.

4. Bake until golden brown and firm to the touch (30 to 40 minutes). Remove from oven and cool 5 minutes before turning out onto a serving platter. Brush well with glaze. Slice into wedges and serve.

Serves 6.

Apple Purée   In a large pan, cook apples with butter, the water, and vanilla over low heat, stirring occasionally. As apples begin to soften, mash them with a wooden spoon and stir until a *very* thick purée forms (about 1 hour). Stir continually or the mixture will scorch and stick to pan. Add sugar to taste (take into account that the mold is dusted with sugar and the bread shell is brushed with a sweet glaze, so you may want to leave apples somewhat tart for a contrast of flavors); let cool.

▪ NUTTY BAKED APPLES

A delicious stuffing of chopped nuts, brown sugar, and butter transforms plain apples into a satisfying and homey cold-weather dessert.

> 6 **large baking apples**
> ⅓ **cup finely chopped walnuts, pecans, or blanched almonds**
> ⅓ **cup firmly packed brown sugar**
> 2 **teaspoons butter or margarine, softened**
> 1 **teaspoon grated lemon rind**

1. Preheat oven to 375° F. Core apples and remove about 1½ inches of peel around stem ends. Arrange in a buttered, shallow baking dish just large enough to hold all the apples.

2. In a small bowl mix nuts, brown sugar, butter, and lemon rind. Fill each cored apple with an equal amount of the nut mixture. Add water to the dish to a depth of about ¼ inch.

3. Bake apples, uncovered, basting occasionally with liquid from bottom of dish, until tender when pierced with a fork (40 to 45 minutes).

4. Serve hot or at room temperature.

Serves 6.

Microwave Version   Core large cooking apples (or firm, just barely ripe pears) and prick skin in 3 or 4 places. Fill core with a mixture of butter, brown sugar, walnuts, and raisins. Fit snugly in a casserole, cover, and cook according to the following timetable:

Number of Apples	Cooking Time (100% Power)	Standing Time
1	2–4 minutes	3 minutes
2	4–6 minutes	3 minutes
3	6–8 minutes	3 minutes
4	9–10 minutes	3 minutes

▪ APPLE CRISP

Humble and homey, a crisp is a baked dessert of fruit with a crumb topping of butter, flour, and sugar. Crisps are at their best served hot or warm; they can be prepared ahead and baked during the main part of the meal.

> 5 **large tart apples (2 to 3 lb), Granny Smith or pippin**
> ½ **to 1 teaspoon vanilla extract, ground cinnamon, grated lemon rind, or brandy, to taste**
> **Sugar, to taste (depending upon tartness of apples)**
> **Whipped cream or vanilla ice cream, for accompaniment**

Crisp Topping

> 2 **cups flour**
> 1 **cup granulated or firmly packed light brown sugar**
> 1 **cup unsalted butter**

1. Preheat oven to 350° F. Peel, core, and slice apples. Place apples in a shallow, 2-quart ovenproof dish. Sprinkle flavoring of choice over apples and then sugar (see Note).

2. Sprinkle Crisp Topping over apples, covering them completely with crumbs. Bake until crumbs are golden and apples are tender when pierced with the tip of a sharp knife (about 30 to 45 minutes). If top browns before apples are cooked throughout, cover with aluminum foil and lower temperature to 325° F.

3. Serve hot or at room temperature with whipped cream or vanilla ice cream.

Serves 6.

Note If a thicker syrup is preferred, toss apples in 1 to 1½ tablespoons flour before adding flavoring and sugar.

Crisp Topping Into a medium mixing bowl, sift flour; blend in sugar. Cut in butter with a pastry blender or fingertips until mixture resembles coarse crumbs.

Oat or Nut Topping For a dense crust add ½ to 1 cup quick-cooking rolled oats or ¼ cup chopped nuts (walnuts, hazelnuts, or almonds) to topping with the flour. For a lighter, crunchier crust, use only 1 cup flour mixed with 1 cup oats.

Rhubarb Crisp For apples and flavoring, substitute 2 pounds rhubarb (use stalks only, not leaves), cut into 1-inch pieces and sprinkled with 1 teaspoon cinnamon and 2 tablespoons flour.

▣ APPLESAUCE

Ground cinnamon, nutmeg, or fresh lemon juice can be added to the apples for extra flavor.

> **6 medium-sized tart cooking apples (about 2 lb)**
> **¼ cup sugar**
> **¼ cup water**

1. Peel, core, and cut apples into chunks. Place apples in a 2-quart saucepan with sugar and the water.

2. Bring to a boil, cover, reduce heat, and cook, stirring occasionally, until apples are very tender (15 to 20 minutes).

3. Stir with a fork until mixture has a saucelike consistency. (Put through a food mill or process until smooth in a food processor, if desired.)

4. Serve warm, at room temperature, or chilled.

Serves 6.

Microwave Version Place 6 apples, pared, cored, and cut into 1-inch chunks, in a 2-quart casserole. Add ¼ cup water, ¼ to ½ cup sugar (depending upon tartness of apples), and a sprinkling of cinnamon, nutmeg, or allspice to taste, if desired. Stir and cover. Cook at 100 percent power (7 to 9 minutes) until tender, stirring after half the cooking time. Mash with a fork for chunky applesauce or purée in a blender or a food processor for a smooth-textured sauce.

Recipes and Related Information
Apple Butter, 320; Apple Dumplings With Nutmeg Sauce, 193; Apple Filling, 627; Apple Pie, 437; Apple Turnover, 626; Corer, 156; Pecan Applesauce Cake, 87; Red Cabbage With Apples, 75; Walnut-Apple Strudel, 222.

APRICOT

The apricot is the round, thin-skinned fruit of a tree native to China. Most varieties range from about 1 inch to 2 inches in diameter, with a deep gold skin and flesh. The moist, juicy flesh surrounds a dark, almond-shaped pit.

Use Fresh apricots are eaten out of hand. Apricots may be poached for fruit salads or compotes, baked in pies or tarts, stewed with meats, or cooked with sugar for jam or preserves. Dried apricots are often used to add sweetness and texture to stuffings, fruit breads and fruitcakes, or as part of a pastry filling.

Availability The fresh crop is harvested in May, June, and July. Canned and dried apricots are available all year.

Selection Choose fragrant apricots with a red blush; ripe apricots give slightly to pressure. Avoid any that are hard and greenish yellow, or dull, soft, or mushy.

Storage Use ripe apricots immediately or refrigerate for up to two days in a plastic bag. To ripen firm apricots, store in a closed paper bag in a warm room. Dried apricots will keep indefinitely stored in a plastic bag in the refrigerator crisper.

Preparation To peel fresh apricots, drop into boiling water for 10 seconds, then transfer with a slotted spoon to ice water. Skin will slip off easily. Halve and pit.

Recipes and Related Information
Apricot-Almond Squares, 143; Apricot and Curry Chutney, 323; Apricot Filling, 627; Apricot Preserves, 319; Basic Glaze, 250; Broiled Duck Breasts With Apricot-Mustard Glaze, 475; Honeyed Chicken With Apricots, 557; Winter Fruit Compote, 186; Your Own Bridge Mix, 59.

ARROWROOT

A fine, dry white powder, arrowroot is valued for its thickening ability and neutral flavor. It is processed from a tropical rhizome occasionally eaten as a starchy vegetable in China and the Caribbean.

Use Arrowroot powder is used as a thickening agent for soups, sauces, stews, and desserts. It imparts a sheen to fruit glazes and sauces. The powder is ideal for thickening egg-bound sauces and other sauces that shouldn't be allowed to boil, because it thickens at a lower temperature than flour and cornstarch and, unlike those two agents, doesn't need to be cooked to remove rawness.

Availability Packed in boxes; it is less widely available and more expensive than cornstarch.

Storage Will keep indefinitely in a closed container in a cool, dry place.

Use a sharp knife to slice off artichoke stem and kitchen scissors or a paring knife to trim away thorny leaf tips. Rub cut surfaces with lemon juice to prevent browning.

Preparation To use arrowroot powder for thickening, dissolve 1 part powder in 3 parts cold water before adding to sauce or stew. One tablespoon of arrowroot has the thickening power of approximately 3 tablespoons flour or 4½ tablespoons cornstarch. Avoid arrowroot in dishes that must stand more than 10 minutes or be reheated; it will not hold.

ARTICHOKE

A Mediterranean native, the artichoke was introduced to the New World by French settlers in Louisiana and, later, by Spanish settlers in California. The edible parts of this tall plant are the green, globelike buds, which give the most commonly available variety its name—Green Globe. Small young buds about the size of a large walnut are tender enough when cooked to eat whole. Large mature buds develop a fuzzy interior choke that must be removed. The Jerusalem artichoke resembles the regular artichoke in flavor but is a member of the sunflower family.

Use Whole cooked artichokes are eaten hot, lukewarm, or chilled, most often with a dipping sauce. Hot artichokes are often accompanied by melted butter; lukewarm or chilled artichokes by a mayonnaise or vinaigrette. Large artichokes can be filled with seafood or bread-crumb stuffings. Whole bottoms can be stuffed and baked or garnished with poached eggs. When sliced and sautéed, the bottoms can be used as a garnish for pasta, pizza, or omelets. Small artichokes can be fried whole, pickled, or steamed and marinated for a salad garnish. Steamed and halved, small artichokes can be added to braised chicken, veal, lamb, or seafood dishes.

Availability They are sold fresh, canned, marinated, or frozen. Fresh artichokes are generally available year around, but late fall and early spring are peak harvest times. Bottoms and hearts are available in cans or marinated in jars; artichoke hearts are available frozen.

Selection Look for compact, heavy, plump globes that yield slightly to pressure and have large, tightly clinging, fleshy green leaf scales. Avoid browning (indicates old age, injury, or frost) and light weight.

Storage Refrigerate fresh artichokes in a plastic bag for up to four days.

Preparation See Preparing Whole Artichokes.

▪ PREPARING WHOLE ARTICHOKES

Trim off thorny tips of outer leaves with scissors or paring knife. Snap or cut off smallest, toughest leaves close to stem. Rub freshly cut parts with lemon to prevent discoloration. Slice stem off to form a flat bottom. Set artichoke, stem side down, on a steamer above at least 1 inch of boiling water. Cover and steam until bases are tender (30 to 60 minutes, depending on size). Artichokes are now ready to eat or to be used in one of the following preparations.

Microwave Version Outside leaves of microwaved artichokes will be tougher than if cooked conventionally. Wash artichokes. Trim stems and thorny tips of outer leaves. Slice away about 1 inch off of top. Rub cut edges with lemon juice to prevent discoloration. Securely wrap each artichoke in waxed paper or parchment paper. Cook according to the following timetable:

Number of Artichokes	Cooking Time (100% Power)	Standing Time
1	5–8 minutes	5 minutes
2	8–10 minutes	5 minutes
4	12–14 minutes	3 minutes

Artichoke Bottoms Use large artichokes only. After steaming remove all leaves and scrape away choke, leaving a shallow cup that can be used to hold hot savory ingredients such as poached eggs or oysters. Leave artichokes slightly underdone if filled bottoms will be reheated with other ingredients.

Artichoke Cups Use large artichokes only. Carefully spread outer leaves to expose heart. Remove small heart leaves and scrape out fuzzy choke with a spoon. Fill hollow with a sauce for dipping outer leaves or a salad such as shrimp with herbed mayonnaise.

Cream of Artichoke Soup If you have a lot of leftover leaves from preparing artichoke cups or bottoms, make them into a cream soup. Simmer in chicken stock until quite tender, purée in a food processor or food mill, strain out fibers, add milk or cream, and thicken with a flour and butter roux.

Marinated Artichokes Cut cooked artichokes into quarters or smaller wedges. Remove chokes and heart leaves. Trim tops of outer leaves down to entirely edible parts (pull off a leaf and test it). Marinate in a mixture of 3 parts olive oil, 2 parts water, 1 part vinegar or lemon juice, and salt and pepper to taste. Fresh or dried herbs, blanched whole garlic cloves, or red pepper flakes may be added to marinade. Store in refrigerator; artichokes will keep for weeks in the marinade.

▪ ARTICHOKES WITH DIPPING SAUCES

Eating artichokes is an informal affair; there is no substitute for fingers. Pull off leaves one at a time, dip into sauce, and use your teeth to scrape off meat inside the base of each leaf. Discard small, fibrous heart leaves and cut out fuzzy choke. Eat base with knife and fork, dipping chunks into sauce. Have available plenty of napkins and a large bowl for discarding leaves.

1 medium to large artichoke per person
2 tablespoons dipping sauce per person

Curried Mayonnaise

   1 **tablespoon vegetable oil**
  ¼ **teaspoon curry powder**
  ¼ **cup mayonnaise**
     Fresh lemon juice, to taste

Herbed Vinaigrette

     Pinch *each* salt and freshly ground pepper
   1 **tablespoon tarragon-flavored wine vinegar**
   4 **tablespoons olive oil**
   1 **tablespoon minced fresh herbs (tarragon, basil, dill, or chervil)**

Lemon Butter

  ¼ **cup butter**
  ½ **lemon, juiced**
     Pinch freshly ground pepper or dash Louisiana-style hot sauce (optional)

Trim and steam artichokes (see Preparing Whole Artichokes on opposite page). Serve warm, tepid, or cold with dipping sauce of choice.

Serves 2 to 3.

Curried Mayonnaise In a small skillet heat oil over low heat. Add curry powder and cook 2 to 3 minutes. Allow to cool, then stir into mayonnaise. Add lemon juice to taste. Flavor will improve if sauce is made several hours ahead and allowed to stand until needed.

Herbed Vinaigrette Blend salt and pepper with vinegar. Whisk in oil and blend in herbs. Taste for seasoning and adjust to taste. This sauce does not keep well (herbs can become bitter), so make it the same day it will be used.

Lemon Butter Melt butter, and add lemon juice and pepper (if used). Pour into warm individual bowls.

■ STUFFED ARTICHOKES

The most dramatic Italian vegetable dish is probably stuffed artichokes, their leaves bulging with well-seasoned bread crumbs. In this recipe, anchovies add bite to the stuffing mixture. Tomato sauce keeps the artichokes moist during baking and makes an excellent dip in which to dunk the filled leaves.

   2 **medium, cooked artichokes (see Preparing Whole Artichokes, opposite page; slice a ¾-inch piece off the top before cooking)**
 1½ **cups seasoned bread crumbs**
   1 **hard-cooked egg, chopped**
   2 **anchovy fillets, finely chopped**
     Salt and freshly ground pepper, to taste
   2 **teaspoons olive oil**
   1 **cup Basic Tomato Sauce (see page 516) or canned tomato sauce**
  ¼ **cup freshly grated Parmesan cheese**

1. To make a cavity for stuffing, gently pull out tender center leaves of cooked, cooled artichokes with a teaspoon; scrape out fuzzy choke.

2. Preheat oven to 350° F. Combine bread crumbs, egg, anchovies, and salt and pepper to taste.

3. Stuff prepared filling into center cavity of artichokes; fill between leaves with a teaspoon. Drizzle 1 teaspoon olive oil over each artichoke.

4. In a greased, shallow, 9-inch baking dish, pour ½ cup tomato sauce. Stand artichokes in dish and pour rest of sauce over them. Sprinkle with cheese, and cover with aluminum foil.

5. Bake for 20 to 30 minutes. Remove foil for last few minutes of cooking and allow sauce to thicken. Artichokes are done when hearts can be pierced easily with a metal skewer or long-tined fork.

Serves 2.

Steaming is a particularly good method for cooking artichokes because it locks in both flavor and nutrients. For more information on steaming, see page 554.

> ### *Recipes and Related Information*
> *Artichoke Frittata, 204; Fennel and Artichoke Salad, 218; Jerusalem Artichoke, 324; Pheasant Brochettes With Baby Vegetables, 296.*

A smooth, buttery sauce is an easy way to transform asparagus into a festive dish. Hollandaise Sauce (see page 516) and asparagus are a classic pairing.

ARUGULA

Also known as rugola, rocket, Italian cress, and roquette, arugula is a delicate salad green popular in Mediterranean countries. When young its slender, dark green leaves are tender and nutty, with a subtle peppery flavor; mature arugula has an unpleasantly hot, mustardlike character. The four-petaled, white blossoms are edible.

Use   Arugula is enjoyed as a salad green, alone, garnished with the delicate flowers, or in combination with other greens. As part of a sandwich filling, it lends an appealing nutty flavor; small whole leaves can be added to potato or lentil soup at the last minute.

Availability   It is sold loose or in clear bags, and is at its best in spring and fall.

Selection   Buy fresh greens that are not limp and do not show any signs of decay.

Storage   Keep in a plastic bag in refrigerator crisper for several days; wash just before using.

Preparation   Trim away roots; wash leaves well and dry thoroughly.

ASPARAGUS

The asparagus plant is a member of the lily family. Its edible part is the long, slender shoot, which can range from pencil thin to about one half inch thick. Mostly asparagus is harvested green. White asparagus is harvested when the tip just breaks the ground; lack of exposure to the sun keeps the spear pale.

Use   Steamed or boiled asparagus is served at room temperature or chilled as a salad, often with mayonnaise, vinaigrette, or other salad dressing; served hot, it is generally dressed with butter or oil or Hollandaise sauce and offered as a first course or side dish. Asparagus tips are a popular garnish for salads, soup, rice, and pasta dishes; for omelet and quiche fillings; and for Asian stir-fries.

Availability   Asparagus is available fresh, frozen, or canned; whole spears or tips. The fresh crop is harvested between March and June.

Selection   Choose bright green or white spears that are brittle, not limp, have tightly closed tips, and stalks that are at least two-thirds green.

Storage   Refrigerate spears, upright, with stem ends in water; or wrap cut ends in wet paper towels or cloth, cover with a plastic bag, and refrigerate. Refrigerated asparagus keeps up to one week.

Preparation   Break asparagus spears by hand where they snap easily. Alternatively, use a small knife or vegetable peeler to remove tough outer peel at stem end; tips are tender and do not require peeling. Leave whole or cut diagonally into 1- to 2-inch pieces.

Cooking   See BOIL, STEAM, STIR-FRY.

■ ASPARAGUS WITH LEMON, TOMATO, AND ONIONS

When asparagus and new onions turn up in Italian markets at the same time, the chefs of Bologna prepare this dish and put it in their windows.

  1½ **pounds medium asparagus**
    2 **small, sweet new onions** *or*
      4 green onions, minced
    2 **tablespoons fresh lemon juice**
   ½ **cup extravirgin olive oil**
      Grated rind of 1 lemon
    2 **tablespoons snipped fresh chives**
    2 **tomatoes, peeled, seeded, and diced**
      Salt and freshly ground pepper, to taste

1. Bring a large pot of salted water to a boil. Add asparagus and cook until barely tender (about 5 minutes). Transfer with tongs to a bowl of ice water. When cool, drain and dry well. Transfer to a serving platter with all tips facing the same direction.

2. Combine onion, lemon juice, olive oil, lemon rind, and half of the chives. Whisk well, then stir in tomatoes. Season to taste with salt and pepper. Spoon sauce over asparagus, then garnish with remaining chives. Serve at room temperature.

Serves 4.

Food Processor Version   Use metal blade to process onion, cut in 1-inch pieces, 10 seconds. Add lemon juice, olive oil, lemon rind, and half the chives; process 5 seconds. If you have a French-fry disk, process tomatoes, halved and squeezed to remove excess juice, into dressing in work bowl.

Recipes and Related Information
Beef With Asparagus, 558; Cream of Any Vegetable Soup, 563; Pasta Primavera, 414.

AVOCADO

The avocado is the pear-shaped fruit of a tropical tree. Some varieties, such as the common Fuerte, have a thin, dark green skin; others, such as the Hass, have a thick, rough, pebbly skin that changes from green to black as they ripen. The yellow-green flesh surrounds a large dark seed; when ripe, the flesh is smooth and buttery with a nutty flavor.

Use   Avocados are generally eaten raw as a salad or first course. Halved avocados can be stuffed with seafood or eaten plain with lemon or vinaigrette. Sliced avocados add a buttery texture to green salads, seafood salads, sandwiches, and omelet fillings. They are commonly used to garnish Mexican tostadas, tacos, and other Latin American dishes, and are the major ingredient in guacamole. Seasoned mashed avocado makes a rich, creamy smooth, and delicious sandwich spread.

Availability   The supply of winter varieties peaks in January; summer varieties appear in the market from June through late August. Because the fruit can be held on the tree for months without becoming overripe, avocados are generally available the year around.

Selection   Choose avocados with full necks and with flesh that gives slightly to pressure. Dark-skinned varieties should be very dark; light-skinned varieties should have a soft, dull-looking skin with a velvety feel.

Storage   If using within a few days, ripe avocados will keep at cool room temperature; or store in refrigerator for up to one week. Ripen at warm room temperature, preferably in a dark spot; ripening takes from three to five days (refrigeration will slow process). To ripen quickly, place in a paper bag. To store partially used avocados, rub cut surfaces with lemon juice, cover tightly with plastic wrap, and refrigerate.

Preparation   Cut avocado in half, lengthwise, around seed. Twist halves apart. To remove seed, either slide tip of a spoon gently underneath and lift it out or carefully strike seed with a sharp knife, embedding knife in seed. Rotate knife to lift out seed. To slice or cube avocado, hold one half, cut side up, in one hand and use a large spoon to scoop flesh out of skin in one piece. Put half, pit side down, on a cutting surface and slice or cube. Sprinkle cut surfaces with lemon or lime juice to keep them from browning.

▪ GUACAMOLE

Avocado is used extensively in Mexico. Often just sliced and served as a garnish, it provides one of the important textural contrasts so typical of the cuisine. Certainly its best known and most popular use is in guacamole.

Guacamole is a versatile dish. In Mexico it is most often served on lettuce as a salad or side dish, but it is used also as a garnish for tacos, burritos, tostadas, or *flautas* and, of course, as a dip accompanied by fried tortilla wedges or assorted raw vegetables.

> 2 **large avocados**
> 2 **teaspoons fresh lime or lemon juice**
> ¼ **cup sour cream (optional)**
> 1 **small clove garlic, crushed**
> 1 **small tomato, diced**
> 1 **canned jalapeño chile, seeded and finely chopped (optional)**
> ¼ **cup finely minced onion**
> **Few sprigs cilantro, coarsely chopped**

1. Halve avocados; remove pit, scoop out pulp, and mash with a fork.

2. Add lime juice, sour cream (if used), garlic, tomato, jalapeño (if used), onion, and cilantro, mixing after each addition.

Makes approximately 2½ cups.

Food Processor Version   Use metal blade to process garlic and 1 small onion until finely chopped (10 to 15 seconds). Add avocado and process to desired consistency. Add lime or lemon juice, sour cream, jalapeño, and cilantro sprigs; process 5 seconds. Stir in tomato.

Quick Guacamole   Follow Guacamole recipe through step 1. Mix mashed pulp with ⅓ cup prepared salsa. *To make in a food processor:* Use metal blade to process avocados to desired consistency. Add salsa and process a few seconds to combine.

Makes approximately 2 cups.

Recipes and Related Information
Avocado Bacon Burger, 44; Avocado, Jicama, and Grapefruit Salad, 281; Guacamole Burger, 44.

B

BAIN-MARIE

A hot water bath or bain-marie provides a constant, even source of heat to delicate foods such as custards, cheesecakes, and sauces. Restaurant kitchens use a bain-marie to hold sauces at serving temperature for long periods of time. The home cook will also use a
water bath for this purpose, but more typically will use it to insulate oven-cooked foods. The cooking dish is set in a larger pan filled partway with water that is almost, but not quite, boiling and then placed in the oven. Any pan can be used as the bottom container, as long as it is large enough to hold the cooking dish with a few inches of clearance on all sides. Roasting pans or cake pans, found in most home kitchens, are commonly used for this purpose. A large saucepan is suitable for stove-top service. A double boiler is a form of bain-marie.

Recipes and Related Information
Cheesecake, 117; Custard, 168; Sauce, 512.

BAKE, TO

The process of baking, as well as that of roasting, its twin, involves cooking raw food in an oven with currents of dry, hot air. For all practical purposes, to bake and to roast mean the same thing. See ʀᴏᴀsᴛ.

BAKE BLIND, TO

To bake a pastry crust for a pie or tart, partially or completely, before it is filled. To keep pastry from puffing up during baking, it is pricked evenly with a fork, lined with aluminum foil or parchment paper, filled with dried beans or metal or ceramic pie weights, then baked until set (10 to 15 minutes). Foil and beans are removed and pastry is returned to oven until it is partially or completely baked, as needed.

Partially baked crusts are used for some custard and cream fillings, which tend to be soggy or undercooked if filled raw. Fully prebaked shells are used to hold an uncooked filling (fresh fruit), a cold filling (mousse, Bavarian cream, pastry cream), or a filling that is cooked on top of the stove and added later (lemon curd, pudding).

Recipes and Related Information
Cake and Pastry Tools, 92; Pie and Tart, 434.

BAKER'S PEEL

Professional bakers use wooden shovels called peels to slide yeast breads and pizzas into the oven and to retrieve them when done. The amateur pizza maker can find scaled-down peels in cookware stores. Use the peel for the final rising of pizza and bread dough, after
first sprinkling with cornmeal to prevent sticking. To transfer pizza or loaf to oven, give peel a few preliminary shakes to make sure the pizza glides freely, then set far edge of peel at far edge of baking surface (either baking stone or baking sheet); give peel a sharp jerk, and slowly pull back as pizza or loaf slides off.

Baker's peels are made of smooth, pale basswood and are commonly available in three sizes: 12 by 14 inches, 14 by 16 inches, and 16 by 18 inches. Buy the size that fits your oven and suits your needs. If you make single loaves, or pizzas for one or two, the smaller ones are sufficient. Giant breads need a giant board. If you have two ovens and bake several pizzas or breads at one time or in succession, and if you plan on cutting and serving on the peels, consider buying several. They also make wonderful bread and cheese boards.

After using, wipe peel clean with a damp cloth; scrape off any pieces of food. Don't wash under running water or wood will warp and eventually split.

Recipes and Related Information
Baking Stone and Tile, 24; Pizza, 445; Yeast Bread, 613.

BAKING PANS, FOR BATTER AND DOUGH

Selecting bake ware can be confusing. Often the same baking pan is sold under different names and in a variety of materials. As a primary guideline, consider the function of the pan, and then buy the one that will do the job best, regardless of what it is called. See ᴍᴀᴛᴇʀɪᴀʟs ғᴏʀ ᴄᴏᴏᴋᴡᴀʀᴇ for more information.

Increasingly, professional-quality bake ware is available for home use. Although these pans usually cost more, in the long run they will prove their worth and justify their higher price. The superior materials and craftsmanship mean a better-looking, higher-quality final product. Professional pans have a longer life expectancy as well.

Should you purchase every pan described here? Hardly. Before buying, ask yourself the following questions. What do I bake most often? What is the yield of favorite recipes?

Bake ware is available for home use in a range of shapes, sizes, and materials. Shown top row, from left: ring mold, angel food cake pan, miniature savarin rings, panettone pan, charlotte mold, loaf pans, brioche molds, cake pans. Middle row, from left: savarin mold, ladyfinger pan, madeleine pan, muffin and popover pans, flan rings, tart pans, quiche pan. Bottom row, from left: pizza pans, Kugelhopf pan, baking cloche, bundt pan, cake pans, pie tins, baking sheet, and baking pan.

Do I need more than one of each pan? What are the dimensions of my oven? How much storage space do I have? Then purchase what best suits your needs.

ANGEL FOOD CAKE PAN

This pan with high sides has a center tube that promotes even distribution of heat and supports the delicate air-leavened batter as it rises. As angel food cakes must cool upside down, these pans usually have small metal feet spaced around the rim or a tube higher than the pan sides for added stability and to allow air circulation. Pans are typically 10 inches in diameter by 4 inches tall and are made of aluminum, often with a nonstick coating. They have a 9-cup capacity. Most have removable bottoms.

BABA MOLD

These small, thimble-shaped, aluminum molds are used for baking the sweet, yeast-leavened French cake known as baba. The molds are as tall as they are wide—2¼ inches. Miniature savarin rings are often substituted for baba cups (see Savarin Mold).

BAGUETTE PAN

Adapted from professional bake ware, these black steel or stainless steel troughs hold the long, slender loaves of crusty bread known as baguettes during their final rise and in the oven. Most bread recipes yield two loaves, so that is the configuration commonly found in cookware stores;

other sizes are available by special order. Pans are 17 inches long, with 2-inch-wide troughs. Some have a vented band between each pair of troughs for circulation of heat.

BAKING CLOCHE

Commercial bakery ovens produce breads with superior crusts by injecting a fine spray of water into the oven cavity. The bell-shaped stoneware baking cloche re-creates this environment for home-baked breads. To use, the porous dome is first soaked in water. The dough is set on the base, which has been sprinkled with cornmeal to prevent sticking, then covered with the dome, and put in the oven. Steam forms within the dome and blankets the dough. If you bake bread often and have a lot of storage space (dome is 10 inches high and base is 11 inches in diameter), you may want to buy one. A covered, unglazed clay casserole will work as well; only the shape is different.

BAKING PAN AND BAKING SHEET

Baking pans have straight sides, ¾ inch tall or higher, all the way around. Baking sheets have a low lip on one or more edges for easy handling. Baking pans are designed to contain runny batters. Baking sheets, also called cookie sheets, work for any freestanding baked product—stiff cookie doughs, rolls and free-form yeast breads, biscuits, cream puffs, and meringues, for example.

Both pans and sheets are kitchen workhorses. Sheets are used to support bottomless flan rings and delicate tartlet pans. Pans set under pies keep ovens clean by catching bubbling juices. They can help organize setup by serving as a catchall for ingredients and equipment.

Buy baking pans or baking sheets of the heaviest weight and best quality available. Aluminum and heavy-gauge black steel are good choices. A typical baking pan measures 11 by 16 by 1 or 2 inches. A standard jelly-roll pan measures approximately 11 by 15 by ¾ inches. Bak-

ing sheets vary in size, but a 14- by 17-inch sheet should fit most home ovens. Consider buying several sheets if you have two ovens, or if you bake in big batches.

A relative newcomer, the air-cushioned cookie sheet, sandwiches a layer of air between two sheets of aluminum. Inspired by the professional baker's trick of double sheeting—baking on two stacked sheets as a way of controlling heat distribution—this design keeps dough from browning too quickly on the bottom. Sheets measure 9½ by 14 inches and 14 by 16 inches. An air-cushioned jelly-roll pan is also available.

BRIOCHE PAN

An egg-rich French yeast bread with a characteristic top-knot of dough, a brioche is traditionally made in a flared, fluted tinned steel mold.

Molds range from individual ones, 3½ inches in diameter by 1½ inches high, to those sized to serve a whole dinner party, 8 inches by 2½ inches. Brioche pans also make charming soup bowls or containers for condiments and preserves.

BUNDT PAN

These deep tube pans are used to bake the popular, densely textured bundt cakes. Pan sides have curves and indentations that produce a cake with an attractive, sculptured exterior. The center tube allows heat to reach more of the batter and also shapes the cake into a ring, which is easier to slice. Typically, these pans are made of cast aluminum with a nonstick interior coating and measure 10 inches in diameter by 3½ inches high, with a 12-cup capacity. Also available is a tray of six miniature bundt cake molds. Each mold holds 1 cup of batter.

CAKE PAN

Every kitchen probably has at least one of these baking pans. They are basic equipment and very versatile. Round pans are used for layer and other types of cakes and for breads; square and rectangular ones for sheet cakes, bar cookies, and breads. Most recipes call for round or square pans 8 or 9 inches by 1½ inches high. The standard rectangular pan is 9 by 13 by 1½ to 2 inches. Deep cake pans with 3-inch sides, formerly only available from restaurant suppliers, are now sold at well-stocked cookware stores. Also called cheesecake pans, these produce a cake with more volume than one baked in a shallower pan, because the batter has more surface to grab on to as it rises. Often the cake is sliced horizontally to produce additional layers.

The best-quality cake pans are made of heavy-gauge aluminum. If square or rectangular, they have sharply angled corners that make a more professional-looking product. Other materials are tinned steel, black steel, stainless steel, and ovenproof glass. Round pans often have removable bottoms.

PAN SUBSTITUTION

Whenever possible, use the size and shape pan recommended in the recipe you are using. Measure pan depth on the outside of one side, bottom to top; measure length and/or width across top of pan between inside edges. If you do not have the right size pan or wish to vary the shape, you can consult the chart below to find a reasonable substitute. Choose a pan that has the same volume and similar depth as the pan in the recipe. The depth may vary up to ½ inch as long as the volume remains the same. The volume of a pan is measured by the amount of liquid it holds when filled to the rim. (This does not refer to the amount of batter the pan holds.) You may need to bake your cake, pie, or bread a little longer if you choose a deeper pan than the one recommended.

Pan Measurements Sides × Depth	Shape of Pan	Volume of Pan
2¾″ × 1⅜″	Muffin cups	Scant ½ cup
9″ × 1¼″	Pie plate	1 quart (4 cups)
8″ × 1½″	Round	1 quart (4 cups)
8″ × 8″ × 1½″	Square	1½ quarts (6 cups)
7″ × 11″ × 2″	Rectangular	1½ quarts (6 cups)
4½″ × 8½″ × 2½″	Loaf	1½ quarts (6 cups)
10″ × 2″	Deep-dish pie	1½ quarts (6 cups)
8″ × 2″	Round	1½ quarts (6 cups)
9″ × 1½″	Round	1½ quarts (6 cups)
8″ × 8″ × 2″	Square	2 quarts (8 cups)
9″ × 9″ × 1½″	Square	2 quarts (8 cups)
5″ × 9″ × 3″	Loaf	2 quarts (8 cups)
9″ × 2″	Round	2 quarts (8 cups)
9″ × 3″	Bundt	2¼ quarts (9 cups)
9″ × 4″	Kugelhopf (tube)	2¼ quarts (9 cups)
8″ × 3¼″	Tube	2¼ quarts (9 cups)
9″ × 9″ × 2″	Square	2½ quarts (10 cups)
9½″ × 2½″	Springform	2½ quarts (10 cups)
9″ × 13″ × 2″	Rectangular	3 quarts (12 cups)
10″ × 2½″	Springform	3 quarts (12 cups)
10″ × 3½″	Bundt	3 quarts (12 cups)

CHARLOTTE MOLD

Like jelly-roll and bundt pans, this round mold with slightly flared sides gets its name from what is traditionally baked in it. A charlotte is a type of sweet dessert with an outside shell of bread or cake fingers and a center of cooked fruit or chilled cream. The pan is well-suited for making any molded dish: baked entrées, soufflés, and bombes (molded ice cream), for example. The mold is of tinned steel, with heart-shaped handles and a lid. The better ones still come from France. Sizes range from ¾- to 8-cup capacity.

CORN-STICK PAN

Making cornbread in corn-shaped, cast-iron molds adds a homey, country touch. These pans make seven corn sticks and need seasoning so they won't rust. In addition to the traditional ears of corn, molds now come in many designs.

CRUMPET AND ENGLISH MUFFIN RINGS

Crumpets are flat, round, griddle-cooked English yeast breads made in molds because the batter is too liquid to hold its shape. English muffins are similar to crumpets but are made with a stiffer batter, so using rings is optional. The stainless steel, 4-inch by 1-inch rings are packaged in sets of four. If you don't make these breads often enough to warrant the purchase of special equipment, use well-scrubbed tuna fish cans, with tops and bottoms removed.

FLAN FORM

See Tart Pan.

KUGELHOPF PAN

This turban-shaped tube pan is used for *Kugelhopf,* a sweet yeast bread studded with raisins and almonds. It most closely resembles a bundt pan, with swirls and ridges molded into the sides. A 9-inch pan with a 9-cup capacity is standard. Materials used are tinned steel, black steel, aluminum, and ovenproof glass. Some have nonstick interiors. This attractive pan can do alternative service as a mold for layered salads.

LADYFINGER AND LANGUES-DE-CHAT PAN

Strictly speaking, ladyfinger molds have straight sides, and those for making the crisp French cookie known as *langue-de-chat* (cat's tongue) have slightly pinched middles, but they look enough alike to be used interchangeably. The tinned steel trays have 10 molds, each about 3¾ inches tall and about 1 inch wide. Both ladyfingers and langues-de-chat can also be formed without a mold, using a pastry bag and plain tip; directions are usually given in the recipe.

LOAF PAN

Another kitchen essential, loaf pans are multipurpose—for breads, pound and fruit cakes, meat loaves, and pâtés. The standard loaf pan for bread is 5 by 9 by 3 inches. Smaller pans measure 4½ by 8½ by 2½ inches. Miniatures are about 2 inches wide by 4 to 5 inches long. Other pans are longer, or shallower, or narrower, or taller, but whatever their proportions, all are rectangular. They are made of tinned or black steel, aluminum, ovenproof glass, or ceramic. Some have a nonstick interior finish.

Crinkle-Edged Loaf Pan   This rectangular pan with accordion-pleated ends resembles a stretched brioche mold. Several sizes are available.

Pullman Pan   Because it bakes with a lid, this specialty bread pan produces a loaf with a dense texture and thin crust. Used for sandwiches or canapés, it is known as a pullman loaf or *pain de mie.* Long and narrow, this pan usually measures 4½ by 12½ by 4 inches.

MADELEINE PAN

This tinned-steel tray has slightly elongated, shell-shaped molds used to prepare madeleines, the buttery, French sponge cookie-cakes. Full-sized madeleines are 3 inches long; miniature madeleinettes measure 1⅝ inches.

MUFFIN PAN

The standard muffin pan has 6 or 12 cups, each 2¾ inches wide at the top and 1½ inches deep. Large cups produce a product 4 inches in diameter by 2 inches deep. These come in 2-, 4-, and 6-cup trays. Miniatures (also called gems) are bite-sized, a mere 1⅞ inches across by ¾ inch deep. Gem trays have 12 or 24 cups. Buy a muffin pan made of a heavyweight metal of good quality, whether aluminum (coated or uncoated), tinned steel, or cast iron. Muffins and cupcakes will rise higher and bake more evenly if you do.

PANETTONE PAN

Tall and cylindrical with straight sides, this mold is used for an Italian holiday fruited yeast bread. Although not authentic, the bread will taste just as good if baked in a coffee can, charlotte or soufflé mold, or even a tall tube pan. The panettone pan is 7½ inches in diameter, with 4-inch sides.

PIE PAN

American pie pans have sloping sides, in contrast to European tart pans, which have straight sides. As with any bake ware, heavyweight metal pie pans produce a more evenly browned product, but ovenproof glass and ceramic make good, versatile pans as well. Standard sizes are 8, 9, and 10 inches in diameter by 1 inch deep; consider buying one in each size. Deep-dish pans are 1½ to 2 inches tall.

A note on recipe style: Some directions call for pie pans or tins, others for pie plates. Generally, the former are metal, the latter glass or ceramic. Regardless, use what you have as long as it's the correct size.

PIZZA PAN

Pizza is more popular than ever. In addition to the familiar round metal pans, several other choices are available to the home pizza maker.

Deep-Dish Pizza Pan Aficionados of thick Chicago-style pizza can try their hand at home with the same high-sided pan that restaurants use. Made of aluminum or black steel, the round pan measures 15 by 2 inches. Some even come with a metal gripper, for purists the only way to rush the pizza from oven to table. Aluminum pans will darken and season with use, which will improve their heat conductivity and produce an even better crust. Wash black steel and darkened aluminum with warm sudsy water and wipe dry. Don't scrub to remove baked-on food or the seasoning will wear away.

Perforated Pizza Pan As dough bakes, it produces steam. Unless this moisture is drawn away, the crust will be soggy instead of desirably crisp. One solution is to use this aluminum pan pierced with hundreds of holes that allow steam to escape and heat to penetrate crust. The pan does wonders for frozen pizza as well and is dishwasher-safe. It is available in 13-, 14-, and 15-inch rounds; buy the size that fits your oven.

POPOVER PAN

The pan for the American cousin to Yorkshire pudding must absorb heat well. Popover batter needs a quick shot of heat to convert its moisture to steam, which then forces batter to expand into a light, airy bread. Cast iron is the traditional material, but tinned and black steel are good alternatives. Most pans have 6 cups. Popovers can also be made in individual porcelain custard cups (see MOLD).

QUICHE PAN

Although many baking dishes can be used to prepare the savory custard pie known as quiche, the one most associated with it is a fluted, straight-sided ceramic or metal pan with a removable bottom. Quiche pans are usually 10 to 12 inches in diameter by 1½ inches tall. Quiches are often baked in shallower tart pans if they are to be used as a first course. A porcelain dish is an attractive choice if you are serving the quiche in its pan.

RING MOLD

The center hole of this pan is larger than that of a tube pan. It is typically made of aluminum, comes in a range of sizes, and is suitable for breads, cakes, molded rice, and gelatin desserts.

SAVARIN MOLD

A savarin is a sweet, yeast-leavened French cake similar to a baba, but is larger and baked in a shallow ring mold, as opposed to the tumbler-shaped cup used for the baba. After baking, the cake is drenched with liqueur, painted with an apricot glaze, and served with a mound of whipped cream, custard, or fresh fruit placed in the center. The mold, 7 to 10 inches in diameter, is made of tinned steel. As a variation, miniature savarin rings for single servings are also available (see Baba Mold).

SPRINGFORM PAN

Most cheesecake recipes call for this round baking pan with high sides, but it is also used for other dense cakes that need special handling to be unmolded. A clamp releases the sides from the base, ensuring that the cake can be removed intact from the pan. Sizes range from 6 to 12 inches, in half-inch increments. Standard height is 2½ inches, and most are made of tinned steel.

TART PAN

Tarts are baked in shallow, fluted, straight-sided pans that usually have removable bottoms or in bottomless metal bands called flan forms or rings, which are set on baking sheets for support. Tinned or black steel are the most common materials. Round tart pans range from 8 to 12 inches in diameter and are 1 to 2 inches deep. Other sizes include a 14-inch square and an 8- by 12-inch rectangle. Flan forms, which are round, rectangular, or scalloped, come in sizes corresponding to tart pans. Tartlet pans are miniature tart pans; some are shaped like diamonds, ovals, circles, or rectangles, with fluted, rounded bottoms. Boat-shaped tartlet pans are called barquette tins.

TUBE PANS

These cake pans have a center tube that supports delicate batters as they rise in the oven. This design also gives a boost of heat to the core of the cake, which promotes more even baking. Angel food cakes, bundt cakes, and yeast breads such as *Kugelhopf* are baked in tube pans. Most of these pans can hold a large amount of batter, anywhere from 9 to 12 cups. Some have a nonstick interior, although these should also be greased and floured if that step is called for in the recipe.

Recipes and Related Information

Angel Food Cake, 82; Apple Charlotte, 10; Babas au Rhum, 623; Baking Stone and Tile, 24; Cake, 77; Cheesecake, 117; Christmas Panettone, 628; Classic Brioche, 622; Cookie, 139; French Baguettes, 617; Kugelhopf, 628; Ladyfingers, 84; Madeleines, 147; Muffin, 374; Old-Fashioned Buttermilk Corn Sticks, 270; Pie, 431; Pizza, 445; Plump Popovers, 29; Quiche Lorraine, 443; Savarin, 623; Tart, 431; Yeast Bread, 613.

Currant-studded Irish Soda Bread (see page 24) is distinctively marked with a cross-shaped surface. Like all quick breads, it is quickly assembled. Serve it sliced and spread with fresh butter and homemade marmalade.

BAKING POWDER

A chemical leavening agent used for making baked goods, baking powder is a carefully balanced mixture of an acid or acid-reacting salt, or a combination of acid-reacting salts, and sodium bicarbonate. Most baking powders also contain a small amount of dry starch, such as cornstarch, to prevent absorption of moisture. In the presence of moisture or heat, the acid acts upon the alkaline component—sodium bicarbonate—to produce carbon dioxide gas. Single-acting baking powders release gas quickly upon contact with moisture. Double-acting baking powder, the most widely used today, releases a small amount of gas upon contact with moisture but requires heat for full reaction.

Use Baking powder leavens a variety of commercial and home-baked goods. It gives volume and an appetizing texture to cakes, quick breads, muffins, biscuits, pancakes, waffles, crackers, and cookies.

Availability Baking powder is packaged in tins.

Storage Keep in an airtight container in a cool, dry place. Routinely replace old baking powder every three to four months.

Preparation Baking powder is usually sifted with the other dry ingredients of a recipe to disperse it evenly before adding it to a batter. Because baking powder is activated in part by liquid, baking powder batters should be baked immediately after liquid is added.

Recipes and Related Information
Baking Powder Biscuits, 49; Baking Soda, 23;
Leaven, 338.

BAKING SODA

Also known as sodium bicarbonate or bicarbonate of soda, baking soda is a chemical leavening agent used for a variety of baked goods. In combination with an acid ingredient, such as buttermilk or molasses, it releases carbon dioxide gas and causes expansion of a batter.

Use Because it is an alkaline substance, baking soda is used to neutralize and leaven batters with acid ingredients. It also absorbs odors; an open box in the refrigerator will keep air fresh. A tablespoon of baking soda dissolved in 2 cups warm water is an effective cleanser.

Availability Baking soda is packaged in boxes.

Storage Keep in a cool, dry place.

Preparation If used in excess, baking soda can impart a soapy taste to a finished product. To avoid unpleasant flavors, the rule of thumb is to use no more than 1 teaspoon of soda per cup of acidic liquid. If additional leavening power is needed, it should come from baking powder. This explains why many recipes call for baking powder in addition to baking soda. Baking soda is usually sifted with the other dry ingredients of a recipe to disperse it evenly before adding it to a batter. Because baking soda is activated immediately by liquid, batters leavened only by baking soda should be baked immediately after liquid is added.

■ IRISH SODA BREAD

This currant-studded bread is really a giant biscuit. It is immediately recognizable because of its distinctive cross-shaped surface. This design is formed by marking an *x* on the top of the dough before baking. It makes an inviting breakfast when slathered with butter and marmalade—and also goes well with a main-dish soup. It's as easy to make your own spread as it is to make a quick bread; see page 320 for a recipe for Classic Orange Marmalade.

> 2¾ **cups unbleached flour**
> ¼ **cup wheat germ**
> 3 **tablespoons sugar**
> 1 **teaspoon** *each* **baking soda and baking powder**
> ½ **teaspoon salt**
> 3 **tablespoons cold butter or margarine**
> ½ **cup dried currants or raisins**
> 1¼ **cups buttermilk**
> 2 **teaspoons milk**

1. Preheat oven to 375° F. In a large bowl stir together flour, wheat germ, sugar, baking soda, baking powder, and salt. Cut in butter until mixture is the consistency of coarse crumbs. Stir in currants.

2. Add buttermilk and stir only enough to moisten dry ingredients.

3. Turn dough out onto a floured surface and knead lightly until it is smooth enough to shape into a flattened ball about 1½ inches high. Place on a greased baking sheet and brush with milk. With a floured knife cut an *x* into top of loaf (cutting from center to within about 1 inch of edge) about ¼ inch deep.

4. Bake until loaf is golden brown (40 to 45 minutes). Test by inserting a wooden skewer in thickest part.

5. Slide loaf onto a wire rack to cool slightly. Cut into thick slices and serve warm or at room temperature.

Makes 1 loaf.

Food Processor Version Use metal blade to process flour, wheat germ, sugar, baking soda, baking powder, salt, butter, and currants (10 seconds). Transfer to bowl and mix in buttermilk as directed.

> ***Recipes and Related Information***
> *Baking Powder, 23; Biscuit, 49; Leaven, 338.*

BAKING STONE AND TILE

A commercial brick baker's oven produces light, wonderfully crispy breads, cookies, and pizzas because its porous stone floor and side walls absorb moisture from the dough and distribute heat efficiently. To achieve similar results with a home oven, use round or rectan-gular baking stones made of smooth, unglazed, high-fire stoneware or unglazed, square quarry tiles. The former, also sold as pizza stones, are sold at cookware stores; the latter can be purchased from suppliers of floor tile. Buy enough individual tiles to cover oven rack or floor.

Stones are available in 13- and 15-inch rounds or 12- by 15-inch rectangles. Some are packaged with a stainless steel rack for carrying and serving. Which size should you buy? First of all, the one that fits your oven. Then, the size and shape that accommodate what you bake most often. Round stones are best suited for single pizzas or breads. Up to four small pizzas or several loaves can fit on a rectangular stone at one time, and they needn't be round.

To be effective, stone must preheat with oven, usually at 400° F or higher, on lowest rack. Pizza or loaf is transferred to stone with a wooden paddle (baker's peel). After baking, stone stays in oven to cool. If stone is used frequently, store it on oven rack.

Baking stones are fragile and apt to crack if exposed to sudden changes of temperature. Clean by wiping with a damp cloth, not in the dishwasher, as the porous material will absorb soap or detergent. With use, pale color will darken and stain, a superficial change that in no way affects performance.

> ***Recipes and Related Information***
> *Baker's Peel, 18; Pizza, 445; Yeast Bread, 613.*

BAMBOO SHOOT

The young, spring shoots of the tropical bamboo plant are a popular Asian vegetable. The ivory-colored shoots are conical, usually about 3 inches wide and 4 inches long, and covered with a multilayered brown husk. When harvested they may be sweet, but they quickly become bitter when out of the ground. Lengthy boiling in the husk removes the bitterness. Flavor of the cooked, husked shoot is mild and refreshing; texture is fibrous and crisp.

Use Bamboo shoots add texture and sweetness to Asian soups, stews, and stir-fried dishes. Japanese diners prize fresh bamboo shoots as a first sign of spring.

Availability   Water-packed, canned bamboo shoots are available whole or sliced. Occasionally "fresh-cooked" bamboo packed in water in plastic bags is exported to the United States. Sun-dried bamboo shoots are sometimes available in Asian markets.

Storage   Once opened, canned bamboo shoots will stay fresh for 1 week to 10 days if stored properly; place in fresh water in a covered container, refrigerate, and change water daily. Store fresh bamboo shoots in water, cover the container, refrigerate, and change water daily. Bamboo shoots may be covered with water and frozen for several months, but they will lose some crispness.

Preparation   Rinse canned bamboo shoots well, washing off any grainy white calcium (a residue from commercial processing) caught in the ridges. If a canned flavor persists, blanch briefly in fresh water before using. Fresh-cooked bamboo packed in water should be parboiled 15 minutes.

Recipes and Related Information
Mu Shu Pork, 378; Pork and Cabbage Wontons, 192; Shanghai Spring Rolls, 389.

BANANA

The common yellow banana is generally about 7 to 9 inches long and about 1½ inches in diameter. The red banana is shorter and slightly fatter. When ripe, the flesh is moist, slightly sticky, soft, and sweet. Unripe bananas are hard, rather dry, and starchy.

Use   Ripe raw bananas are eaten out of hand, or sliced and used in fruit salads or as a topping for breakfast cereals. Bananas are baked as a dessert or blended with other ingredients to flavor cakes, quick breads, puddings, pies, or ice cream. Use slightly underripe bananas for baking with butter and brown sugar; save overripe bananas for cakes and breads.

Availability   Fresh bananas are sold all year.

Selection   Choose plump, well-filled fruit with unblemished skin and no signs of decay.

Storage   Bananas continue to ripen after harvest. Ripe yellow bananas have a solid yellow skin with brown speckles. Ripe red bananas have dark red skin with black speckles and feel slightly soft. With both varieties, the skin will continue to darken as the banana ages. To ripen bananas further after purchase, store at room temperature. A bright yellow fruit with a green tip will reach ideal ripeness in two to three days. After ripening, bananas may be refrigerated for several days.

Preparation   Peel. For use in fruit salads, sprinkle bananas with lemon or lime juice to prevent browning.

■ BANANAS FOSTER

This impressive flaming dessert from New Orleans is simple but must be prepared at the last minute in small batches; do not attempt it for a large dinner party. Flaming desserts are easier to prepare over a gas burner (see the directions in step 2). If you are cooking on an electric burner, heat the rum in a small saucepan until it just begins to boil. Then pour it over the bananas and use a match to ignite it. The liqueur and rum can also be warmed in a microwave oven. Use 100 percent power and heat 30 to 45 seconds.

    2   tablespoons unsalted butter
    2   tablespoons light or dark brown sugar
        Pinch ground cinnamon
        Pinch freshly grated nutmeg
    2   small, firm bananas, cut in half lengthwise
    ¼   cup Drambuie liqueur
    ¼   cup dark rum
    2   scoops vanilla ice cream

1. In a 10-inch omelet or sauté pan over medium heat, melt butter. Add sugar, cinnamon, and nutmeg; mix well. Add bananas and sauté until they begin to soften (about 1 minute on each side).

2. Pour in liqueur and rum. Turn up heat and tilt pan to ignite liquor. Shake pan slightly to prolong flames. When flames burn out, place 2 banana halves on each serving plate. Place a scoop of ice cream between the banana halves and spoon the sauce over all.

Serves 2.

Recipes and Related Information
Banana Cream Pie, 440; Banana Split, 311; Toasted Coconut-Banana Bread, 491.

BARD, TO

To cover meats, poultry, or fish with thin slices of fat—usually bacon or pork fat—before cooking (see photograph, page 593). This technique developed as a way of keeping faster-cooking, lean parts moist and juicy until fattier areas are done, or to keep roasts with little internal fat moist. For example, the breast meat of chicken or turkey is lower in fat than the dark meat of the legs or thighs and thus is finished sooner. Barding the breast will keep it from drying out before the bird is fully cooked. Veal is another meat that also benefits from barding or the application of another type of baste.

Barding and larding are similar techniques in that they both use applied fat to maintain or add moisture; they differ in where the basting fat is placed. Barding adds surface fat. Larding bastes by inserting strips of fat into the meat's interior mass (see LARD).

Bananas Foster makes an impressive grand finale to any meal. The bananas may be cut in chunks, as shown here, or halved, as in the recipe at left. Other fruits, such as fresh peaches, pears, or papayas, can be substituted for the bananas; you can also pour the delicious sauce over angel food cake.

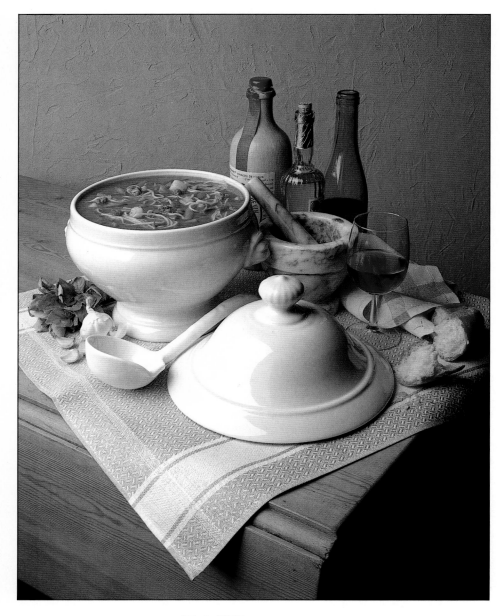

Beef Soup au Pistou gets its name from the pungent paste of puréed basil and garlic that is stirred into the soup just before the tureen is brought to the table.

BASIL

A native of India, basil is cultivated as an annual culinary herb in temperate climates. Its soft green leaves are intensely aromatic, with a pungent, licoricelike flavor.

Use   Fresh basil flatters tomato salads and sauces. It is the principal ingredient in Italian pesto and French *pistou,* which are used as a pasta sauce and soup garnish respectively. Fresh basil leaves enhance mixed green salads, pasta and pizza, Mediterranean squash and eggplant salads and cooked dishes, vegetable soups, egg dishes, veal, lamb, fish, and chicken. To substitute dried basil for fresh, see HERB.

Availability   Fresh commercial garden basil is most plentiful in summer. Fresh hothouse basil is available all year. Dried basil is packed in airtight jars or tins.

Selection   Choose fresh, aromatic bunches that aren't limp and don't show signs of decay. Packaged seasonings lose quality after a while; try to buy from a store that restocks its spice section fairly often.

Storage   Fresh basil will last three or four days if wrapped first in damp paper towels, then in plastic wrap, and refrigerated. To freeze fresh basil, snip leaves finely and freeze in plastic bags. To dry fresh basil, hang bunches upside down in a warm, dry place. Store dried basil in a cool, dark place in an airtight container. Replace every six months.

Preparation   Wash leaves and dry thoroughly. Use whole or mince. Leaves cut with a knife discolor quickly; use only in cooked dishes. For uncooked dishes, tear leaves by hand.

■ BEEF SOUP AU PISTOU

This traditional French soup is usually made without meat, but ground beef makes it even better. The word *pistou* refers to the pestolike paste of basil and garlic that flavors the soup.

> 2 tablespoons olive oil
> 1½ pounds lean ground beef, crumbled
> 1 large onion, thinly slivered
> 1 clove garlic, minced
> 1 large can (28 oz) tomatoes, coarsely chopped; reserve liquid
> 3½ cups Beef Stock (see page 560) *or* 2 cans (14½ oz each) regular-strength beef broth
> 2 cups water
> 2 teaspoons salt
> ¼ teaspoon freshly ground pepper
> 2 medium potatoes (about 1 lb), cut in ½-inch cubes
> 1 pound green beans, cut in 1-inch pieces
> ¼ pound vermicelli, broken in half
> ½ cup finely grated Gruyère or Swiss cheese
>   Grated Gruyère or Swiss cheese, for garnish

Pistou

> ¼ cup olive oil
> 3 cloves garlic, minced
> ½ cup loosely packed, fresh basil leaves *or* 2 tablespoons dried basil and ½ cup loosely packed, chopped parsley
> ¼ teaspoon *each* salt and sugar
> 1 tablespoon red wine vinegar

1. In a 5- to 6-quart kettle, heat oil. Add ground beef and cook over medium heat, stirring often. As meat begins to brown, stir in onion and continue cooking until onion is soft. Stir in garlic. Add tomatoes and their liquid, broth, the water, salt, pepper, and potatoes.

2. Bring to a boil, cover, reduce heat, and simmer for 1 hour. Meanwhile cook green beans uncovered in a large quantity of boiling, salted water until they are tender-crisp (6 to 8 minutes). Drain and rinse immediately with cold water to stop cooking; drain and set aside.

3. After soup has cooked for 1 hour, add vermicelli and boil gently, uncovered, stirring occasionally, until pasta is just tender (10 to 12 minutes). Add green beans and cook just until beans are heated through.

4. Add the ½ cup Gruyère cheese, about 2 tablespoons at a time, stirring after each addition until cheese melts.

5. Place Pistou in a warm tureen, add soup, and stir until soup and Pistou are well blended. Serve at once, garnishing each serving with additional grated cheese to taste.

Makes about 16 cups, 6 to 8 servings.

Pistou In blender or food processor, combine olive oil, garlic, basil, salt, sugar, and vinegar. Whirl until smooth.

Makes about ⅓ cup.

▇ PESTO

A summer sauce, pesto is made when basil is abundant and inexpensive. Its pungent aroma is unforgettable, whether it's tossed with hot linguine or stirred into steaming minestrone. For Genoese sailors long at sea, a fragrant *pasta al pesto* is the traditional welcome home.

> 2 **cups loosely packed, fresh basil leaves,**
> ½ **cup light olive oil**
> 2 **tablespoons pine nuts, toasted**
> 4 **large cloves garlic, minced**
> 1 **teaspoon coarse salt**
> ½ **cup freshly grated Parmesan cheese**
> 2 **tablespoons freshly grated Pecorino Romano cheese**
> 3 **tablespoons unsalted butter, softened**

Put basil, olive oil, pine nuts, garlic, and salt in a blender or food processor. Blend or process until smooth. Transfer to a bowl and stir in Parmesan, Pecorino Romano, and butter.

Makes 1 cup.

Make-Ahead Tip Pesto may be made up to 1 week ahead, covered with a thin film of olive oil, and refrigerated in an airtight container. Pesto may be frozen for up to 1 month, covered with a thin film of olive oil; if you plan to freeze it, make pesto without garlic and stir in minced garlic just before using. It is also possible to freeze pesto in ice-cube trays; each cube will provide sauce for 1 portion of pasta. In this case, wait to incorporate Parmesan, butter, and garlic until you are ready to serve it.

Recipes and Related Information
Northern-Style Tomato Sauce, 412; Osso Buco, 58; Pizza Margherita, 446; Tomatoes With Mozzarella and Basil, 507.

BASTE, TO

This term, usually associated with meats and poultry, means to brush on or pour liquid over foods while they are cooking to keep them moist and flavorful and to develop an attractive finish. Usually the basting liquid is a combination of pan drippings and fat. Seasonings or other ingredients may be added to enhance taste.

Recipes and Related Information
Bulb Baster, 67; Cake and Pastry Tools, 89.

BATTER

A batter is a mixture of flour and a liquid, such as milk, beer, or wine, plus eggs and other leavening or flavoring ingredients. The proportion of flour to liquid determines the thickness and end use of the batter, although by definition all batters must be thin enough to pour or drop from a spoon. Pourable batters, which have an equal amount of flour and liquid, are used for pancakes, popovers, and cakes. Thicker drop batters contain twice as much flour as liquid and are the basis for muffins, drop biscuits, fritters, and coatings for fried foods.

Batter coatings act as a puffy, protective barrier between oil and food. Coatings also improve the taste, appearance, and texture of fried foods. Quick-cooking foods that can hold their shape, such as fish, boned poultry, vegetables, and fruits, give the best results when dipped in batter and fried. *Frittered, French-fried,* and *batter-fried* are all terms used for batter-coated foods.

Batters have a wonderful flavor, but are not as convenient a coating for fried foods as a simple dip in flour or crumbs. It is a messy process, and one that allows little time between setup and cooking—once a food has been dipped in the batter, it must be fried at once, or batter will slide off. Although batter-coated foods cook quickly, preparation takes time. Most batters should rest at least 30 minutes to 1 hour before use to allow flour to blend completely with liquid, to give leavening a chance to activate, and to allow gluten to relax. But, this isn't always necessary, and usually a recipe will guide you. Remember to dry food thoroughly before coating or batter won't adhere. Dusting with flour (or confectioners' sugar in the case of fruit) is often recommended as a first step. Flour dries the surface of the food and gives the batter something to cling to.

For all batters, be sure the oven or frying fat is heated to the proper temperature. Deep-fried batter-coated foods cook at approximately 365° F. Test temperature with a deep-fat thermometer (see THERMOMETER); another test is to drop a cube of bread in the hot fat and slowly count to 60. The fat is ready to use if the bread is golden brown. For more information about cooking oils and frying, see DEEP-FRY and FRY.

Basting adds moisture and flavor to food. The best basting brushes are made of natural boar bristles. Make sure the bristles are securely attached to the handle.

3. Dip food into batter and fry until golden (about 2 minutes per side). Serve immediately sprinkled with kosher salt.

Makes 2 cups batter.

■ BASIC FRITTER BATTER FOR FRUIT

This batter is similar to the basic version, but uses milk instead of wine and is sweetened to complement fruit.

> 1 **cup flour**
> **Pinch salt**
> 2 **tablespoons sugar**
> 2 **eggs, separated**
> ½ **cup milk**
> 2 **tablespoons butter, melted**
> **Oil, for frying**
> **Slices or pieces of fruit such as banana, pineapple, apple, papaya**
> **Confectioners' sugar, granulated sugar, cinnamon sugar, fruit sauce, or melted preserves, for topping**

1. Follow directions for Basic Fritter Batter (at left), substituting milk for wine.

2. Serve immediately sprinkled with confectioners' sugar, granulated sugar, or cinnamon sugar, or drizzled with fruit sauce or melted preserves.

Makes 2 cups batter.

■ TEMPURA BATTER

Use light, crispy tempura batter to coat firm-textured seafood such as prawns, sea bass, and sole, and pieces of carrot, broccoli, zucchini, eggplant, and sweet potato.

> 1 **cup flour**
> 2 **teaspoons baking powder**
> 1 **teaspoon salt**
> 1 **cup ice water**
> 1 **egg, beaten**
> **Oil, for frying (preferably peanut oil)**

Dipping Sauce

> ¾ **cup Chicken Stock (see page 560)**
> 4 **tablespoons Japanese soy sauce**
> 3 **tablespoons mirin (sweet sake) or dry sherry**

1. In a small bowl sift together flour, baking powder, and salt. Place the ice water in a medium bowl; whisk in beaten egg. Add sifted dry ingredients and whisk together lightly just to combine (do not overmix—even if small lumps of flour are left in batter).

2. Use batter immediately. Make sure food to be dipped is dry. To fry at an even rate, cut food into pieces of the same size. Serve with Dipping Sauce.

Makes about 1½ cups batter.

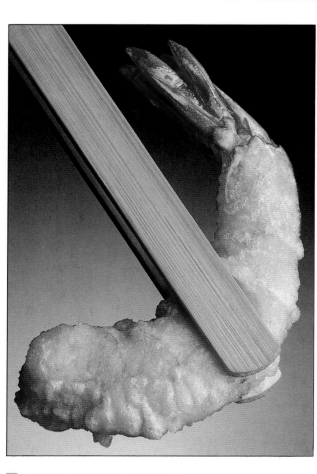

Light, crispy tempura is probably the dish that most readily comes to mind when Westerners think about Japanese food. Always serve tempura immediately after frying. If left to stand, it becomes soggy.

■ BASIC FRITTER BATTER

Fritters are best served immediately after frying. To hold until the entire batch has been cooked, lay fritters on a wire rack and set in a 350° F oven. To keep warm for up to 20 minutes, hold in a 200° F oven. Use this batter for all kinds of vegetables, meats, and fish, cut in slices or bite-sized pieces. Note that the batter must chill for two hours before using.

> 1 **cup flour**
> 1 **tablespoon sugar**
> **Pinch salt**
> 2 **eggs, separated**
> 1 **cup white wine**
> 2 **tablespoons butter, melted**
> **Oil, for frying**
> **Diced vegetables, meat, or fish**
> **Kosher salt, to taste**

1. Into a medium bowl sift flour, sugar, and salt. In a blender or food processor combine egg yolks, wine, and melted butter until smooth. Cover and refrigerate for 2 hours.

2. When ready to cook fritters, heat oil to 360° F to 375° F in a Dutch oven, heavy deep skillet, or other frying kettle. Meanwhile, beat egg whites to soft peaks; fold into chilled batter.

Dipping Sauce In a small saucepan combine Chicken Stock, soy sauce, and mirin; bring to a boil. Remove from heat and cool.

Makes about 1 cup.

▉ PLUMP POPOVERS

Steam forming in this egg-rich batter billows each popover into a hollow puff that is virtually all crust—the better to lavish with butter and jam. You can make the batter ahead. Complete step 1, cover batter, and refrigerate for up to a day. When ready to bake, stir batter well and proceed with step 2.

    1 cup milk
    3 eggs
    1 tablespoon sugar
    2 tablespoons butter or margarine, melted
       and cooled, or vegetable oil
    1 cup flour
    ¼ teaspoon salt

1. In blender or food processor combine milk, eggs, sugar, butter, flour, and salt. Whirl until smooth and well combined, stopping motor once or twice and using a rubber spatula to mix in flour from sides of container.

2. Preheat oven to 400° F. Generously grease standard muffin or popover pans or custard cups. Pour batter into pans, filling about half full.

3. Bake until popovers are well browned and firm to the touch (35 to 40 minutes). Avoid opening oven until end of baking time. Serve hot.

Makes 10 to 12 popovers.

> ### Recipes and Related Information
> *Biscuit, 49; Cake, 77; Deep-fried Zucchini Blossoms, 238; Muffin, 374; Waffle and Pancake, 598.*

BATTERIE DE CUISINE

Loosely translated, this French phrase means the *artillery of the kitchen*—all the pots and pans, utensils, and basic equipment used for cooking.

Although it is always fun to buy culinary paraphernalia, most cooks function extremely well with a collection of well-chosen, high-quality equipment that suits their particular needs. The following is a checklist of basic equipment (for specific information, consult the entries listed in Recipes and Related Information, at right).

Bake Ware Baking pans and sheets, brushes, cake pans, cooling rack, loaf pan, muffin pan, pastry blender, pie pan, rolling pin, sifter, springform pan, tube pan.

Cookware Double boiler, saucepans, sauce pot, sauté pan, skillets, steamer, stockpot.

Knives Boning knife, chef's knife, paring knife, serrated bread knife, plus chef's fork, kitchen scissors, and knife sharpener or sharpening steel.

Machines Coffee grinder or electric minichopper, food processor, electric mixer.

Measuring Tools Dry and liquid measuring cups, measuring spoons, scale, thermometers (deep-frying, instant read, freezer, oven), timer.

Ovenware Baking dishes, casseroles, broiler pan and rack, roasting pan and rack.

Small Equipment Bulb baster, cheesecloth, citrus reamer, citrus stripper and zester, colanders and sieves, cutting board, food mill, funnel, garlic press, graters, kitchen twine, lacers and skewers, ladle, mixing bowls, molds, mortar and pestle, parchment paper, peeler, pepper mill, skimmer, spatulas, spoons (slotted and wooden), tongs, turners, whisk.

> ### Recipes and Related Information
> *Baking Pans, 18; Cake and Pastry Tools, 89; Casseroles and Baking Dishes, 103; Cheesecloth, 119; Chopping and Cutting Board, 129; Citrus Reamer, 131; Colander, Strainer, and Sieve, 137; Cookware, 151; Food Processor, 240; Gadgets, 258; Grater, 281; Knife, 328; Measure, 353; Mixers, 369; Mixing Bowl, 369; Mold, 369; Needle and Fastener, 384; Spatula, Scraper, and Turner, 548; Spoon, Ladle, and Scoop, 551; Thermometer, 575; Timer, 579; Tongs, 582; Whisk, 608.*

BAY

The evergreen bay shrub—also known as laurel—is a native of southern Europe. Its thick, glossy, dark green leaves are an important culinary herb. They contribute a pungent aroma to stocks, soups, and stews.

Use Add bay leaves with restraint to flavor meat stocks, marinades, vegetable or dried bean soups, pot roast, roast chicken, and tomato or béchamel sauces. Remove leaves before serving. Whole bay leaf is a common component of bouquet garni. Add a pinch of ground bay leaf to stuffings, soups, or stews.

Availability Dried bay leaves are packed in jars, tins, or plastic bags. Ground bay leaf is packed in jars or tins. Fresh bay is rarely available commercially.

Selection Packaged seasoning loses quality after a while; try to buy from a store that restocks its spice section fairly often.

Storage Keep dried and ground bay leaves in airtight containers in a cool, dark place for up to one year.

BEAN

All beans are members of the legume family, one of the world's most important food groups. Their genus is *Phaseolus*. Most beans consist of a pod with a single section that holds one row of seeds. Some varieties are cultivated more for their edible pod than for their seeds; others have tough, stringy pods and are cultivated primarily for their seeds, which may be used either fresh or dried. There are hundreds of varieties of fresh and dried beans. Those described here are among the most common.

Use   Beans with edible pods are enjoyed as a salad and as a side dish. French cooks serve tiny *haricots verts* both cold and hot—cold, with vinaigrette or mayonnaise; hot, with melted butter or olive oil. Chinese cooks often stir-fry beans with bits of seasoned minced pork or with oyster sauce. Italians add edible-podded beans to vegetable soups or sauté them with *pancetta* (unsmoked bacon). Indian cooks braise green beans with coconut and spices.

Shell beans may also be eaten as a cold salad or a hot side dish. They add body and flavor to soups and stews.

Availability   Fresh beans are available in bulk at produce markets and supermarkets. See specific beans for season. Dried beans come packed in plastic bags and are sold in bulk. Some beans are canned as well.

Selection   See specific beans.

Storage   Refrigerate fresh beans with edible pods in a perforated plastic bag for up to three or four days. Store fresh shell beans with inedible pods similarly and use within two or three days; shell just before using. Store dried beans in an airtight container in a cool place; they will keep up to one year.

Preparation   Varies depending upon bean; check specific entries for preparation information. Most dried beans (except lentils) require soaking before cooking. Cover with plenty of cold water and soak eight hours or overnight. Or use a quick-soak method: Boil beans and water 2 minutes; cover and let stand 1 hour. Discard water before proceeding with recipe.

Cooking   See Timetable for Cooking Beans on opposite page, and BOIL, SAUTE, STEAM, STIR-FRY.

AZUKI BEAN

Also spelled *adzuki,* this small, red bean is available dried, packed in plastic bags, from Asian markets. Chinese and Japanese cooks use these soft, slightly sweet beans in steamed rice dishes. Azuki beans are also boiled, mashed with shortening, and sweetened with sugar to make red bean paste, used by Asian cooks in a variety of sweet dishes, from jellies and puddings to stuffed pastry. The paste is available canned in Asian markets. Leftover bean paste will keep for months if refrigerated in a covered jar or plastic container.

BLACK BEAN

Also known as turtle beans, black beans are highly important to the various cuisines of Latin America and the Caribbean. These small, jet-black beans come to market dried, packaged in plastic bags or sold in bulk. Use within one year of purchase. Cooked black beans are also available canned in some parts of the country. They have an earthy, meaty flavor and a mealy texture. Black beans are used in soups, stews, salads, and bean dips. They go well with pork, rice, and greens.

BROAD BEAN

See Fava Bean.

CANNELLINI BEAN

See Kidney Bean.

CHINESE LONG BEAN

Also known as yard-long beans or asparagus beans, these thin, pliable green beans do grow to exceptional lengths, usually about 18 inches. Asian cooks use young, tender long beans in stir-fries. Mature long beans yield edible seeds similar to black-eyed peas. Long beans are available fresh in Asian markets in late summer and fall. Select thin, firm beans without wrinkles or spongy parts.

Long beans may be steamed or stir-fried; substitute them for green snap beans in any recipe, although their flavor is slightly milder and they have a crunchier texture. To prepare, trim ends and cut beans into small pieces.

CRANBERRY BEAN

Fresh cranberry beans have inedible whitish green pods with red striations and measure about 3 inches long and ½ inch wide. The shelled beans also have mottled reddish markings. The beans are occasionally available fresh in the summer; select firm, full pods with no signs of drying. To prepare fresh beans, open pods and remove beans. Dried cranberry beans are packaged in plastic bags or sold in bulk; use within a year of purchase. Canned cranberry beans are available in some parts of the country.

Add cranberry beans to stews and soups, especially Italian minestrone, or boil and serve as a side dish.

Recipes: Cranberry Bean Minestrone, 564.

FAVA BEAN

Also known as broad beans or horse beans, fava beans have pods that range from 4 to 18 inches long. When young and small, the whole pod may be eaten raw with oil and salt. More mature pods should be shelled; the moist green beans inside have a tough skin that should be peeled. Fresh fava beans are available in late spring and early summer. Select heavy, full pods that have good color and are without blemishes. To prepare, open pod and remove beans; use thumbnail to split and remove skin on each bean. Dried fava beans are packaged in plastic bags or sold in bulk. Cooked beans have an assertive, almost bitter flavor and a mealy texture.

Add fava beans to soups and stews or enjoy as a side dish dressed with butter or oil. Boiled favas may also be eaten cold or at room temperature as a salad dressed with vinaigrette.

■ BRAISED FAVA BEANS

A Sicilian specialty, these well-seasoned beans make a delightful hors d'oeuvre when wrapped up in cool lettuce cups, or serve them as a side dish to accompany a roast. Note that the beans need to soak overnight.

- 1 **pound dried fava beans**
- 1 **cup chopped yellow onion**
- 3 **tomatoes, coarsely chopped**
- ½ **cup tomato purée**
- ½ **cup coarsely chopped Italian parsley**
- ½ **cup coarsely chopped celery**
  Salt and freshly ground pepper, to taste
  Red pepper flakes (optional)
  Lettuce leaves
  Olive oil, for garnish
  Parsley sprigs, for garnish
- 4 **ounces Parmesan cheese, sliced paper-thin, for garnish**

1. Put beans in a large pot; add water to cover and soak overnight. The next day, add onion, tomatoes, and tomato purée. Bring to a boil, reduce heat to maintain a simmer, and cook until beans are just tender. There should be almost no water left.

2. Cool beans to room temperature, then add parsley, celery, salt, pepper, and hot pepper flakes (if used) to taste. Form cups with lettuce leaves and fill with beans; garnish with a drizzle of olive oil, a parsley sprig, and a slice of Parmesan cheese.

Serves 12.

Food Processor Version Use metal blade to chop parsley; set aside. Cut 1 stalk celery into 1-inch chunks and turn motor on and off to chop; set aside. Cut 1 large onion into eighths and process with metal blade, turning motor on and off 3 or 4 times; set aside. Process tomatoes with metal blade as for onion.

FLAGEOLET

A popular French shell bean, the *flageolet* has an inedible green pod about 3 inches long and small, light-green, kidney-shaped seeds. Fresh flageolets are occasionally available in the summer; look for well-filled, pliable pods that contain even-sized beans and do not show evidence of drying. To prepare, pull on tip of pod to split it open; remove beans. Dried flageolets are packaged in plastic bags or boxes or sold in bulk. Canned French flageolets are available in specialty food markets.

Braised flageolets are the traditional French accompaniment to leg of lamb. They may also be added to soups and stews or eaten cold as a salad with lemon and oil.

TIMETABLE FOR COOKING BEANS

To cook green beans (Chinese long bean, haricot vert, runner bean, snap bean): Steam in a small amount of boiling, salted water in a covered saucepan until tender (2 to 10 minutes, depending upon size and age); or cut in pieces and stir-fry in a skillet in 1 to 2 tablespoons vegetable oil until tender-crisp (2 to 5 minutes, depending upon size and age). Add salt or other seasoning just before serving and toss to blend. *To cook dried beans:* For all types except split golden gram (mung), cook as directed in a proportion of 3 parts water to 1 part beans; use a 4-to-1 ratio of water to beans for split golden gram (mung).

Type of Bean	Soak	Time
Azuki	Overnight or quick-soak	Boil 10 minutes; cover and simmer 1½ to 2 hours
Black	Same	Boil 10 minutes; cover and simmer 1 to 1½ hours
Cranberry	Same	Boil 10 minutes; cover and simmer 1½ to 2 hours
Fava	Same	Boil 10 minutes; cover and simmer 2 to 2½ hours
Flageolet	Same	Boil 10 minutes; cover and simmer 1½ to 2 hours
Great Northern	Same	Boil 10 minutes; cover and simmer 1½ to 2 hours
Kidney	Same	Boil 10 minutes; cover and simmer 1½ to 2 hours
Lentil	No soaking	Bring to boil; cover and simmer 20 to 25 minutes
Lima	Overnight or quick-soak	Boil 10 minutes; cover and simmer 1 to 1½ hours
Mung	Soak 1 to 4 hours	Bring to boil; cover and simmer 30 minutes
Navy	Overnight or quick-soak	Boil 10 minutes; cover and simmer 1½ to 2 hours
Pinto	Same	Boil 10 minutes; cover and simmer 1½ to 2 hours
Red	Same	Boil 10 minutes; cover and simmer 1½ to 2 hours
Soybean	Same	Boil 10 minutes; cover and simmer 1½ to 2 hours
Split golden gram (mung)	No soaking	Bring to boil; cover and simmer 20 to 30 minutes

FLAGEOLETS WITH HERBS

Small, pale green flageolets are used frequently in French cuisine, particularly as a flavorful accompaniment to roast leg of lamb. Note that the beans must soak overnight, or quick-soak 1 hour (see Preparation).

    2 cups (about 1 lb) dried flageolets or
         small navy beans
   10 cups water
    1 bay leaf
    4 carrots, sliced
    1 onion, sliced
    2 cloves garlic, quartered
  1½ teaspoons dried rosemary
    1 teaspoon dried thyme
    2 tablespoons olive oil
    2 cups Beef Stock (see page 560)
    2 teaspoons salt
    1 teaspoon freshly ground pepper

1. Soak beans as directed on page 30, using 6 cups water. Add the remaining water, bay leaf, carrots, onion, garlic, rosemary, thyme, and oil.

2. Increase heat, and boil 10 minutes; reduce heat, and simmer 1½ hours; drain. Add stock, salt, and pepper, and continue cooking 30 minutes.

Serves 8 to 10.

GREAT NORTHERN BEAN

The Great Northern is a large white shell bean with a mild flavor. Dried Great Northern beans are packaged in plastic bags or sold in bulk. Use within a year of purchase. Cooked Great Northern beans are also available in cans and jars. Use in soups, stews, baked bean dishes, and salads.

GREEN BEAN

See Snap Bean.

HARICOT VERT

The haricot vert is an exceptionally slender, stringless green bean. Although long popular in France, this sweet, tender bean has only recently been commercialized in America. Now specialty markets generally have fresh haricots verts from July through September. Choose firm pods, ⅛ inch or less in diameter, with solid green color. To prepare, remove stem ends. Store beans in a perforated plastic bag in the refrigerator crisper; use within one or two days of purchase. Steam briefly, then sauté in butter or oil, and serve hot, or dress steamed beans with vinaigrette and serve at room temperature or chilled.

ITALIAN ROMANO (GREEN) BEAN

See Snap Bean.

KIDNEY BEAN

The kidney bean is the kidney-shaped seed of a common shell bean. Both red and white varieties exist, although the white kidney bean is more commonly called a *cannellini* bean. Dried red and white kidney beans are packaged in plastic bags or sold in bulk; use within a year of purchase. Canned kidney beans are widely available. The meaty flavor and mealy texture are appealing in soups, stews, chili, and salads.

RED BEANS AND RICE

This is the traditional Monday-night dinner of New Orleans. The custom probably began because folks had spent all their money on the weekend and needed a cheap but substantial way to feed themselves. Although it is an inexpensive meal, it does not lack in flavor and appetite appeal, and it makes an ideal dish for informally entertaining a large group. Note that the beans first have to soak overnight, and then when cooked should be refrigerated at least overnight.

    1 pound dried red beans
    4 quarts water
    2 meaty ham hocks
    8 cups Beef Stock (see page 560) or
         Chicken Stock (see page 560)
    4 bay leaves
   ½ teaspoon thyme
    1 teaspoon cayenne pepper
    1 teaspoon freshly ground pepper
    1 pound andouille (sausage)
   ¼ pound tasso (sausage), chopped (optional)
    2 cups chopped onion
   ½ cup chopped celery
    1 green bell pepper, chopped
    1 bunch green onions, chopped
    1 tablespoon minced garlic
    8 chaurice sausages (approximately 2 lb) or
         other fresh, hot sausages
       Salt and freshly ground pepper, to taste
       Red wine vinegar, to taste (optional)
    4 cups cooked rice
       Hot-pepper sauce, to taste

1. Wash beans and soak overnight in the water. The next day drain beans and wash well under cold running water. Place beans, ham hocks, and stock in a heavy, 6- to 8-quart stockpot or Dutch oven. Beans should be covered by about 2 to 3 inches of liquid; add more if necessary. Bring to a boil and skim any scum that collects on the surface. Reduce heat to simmer and add bay leaves, thyme, cayenne, and pepper. Simmer for 30 minutes while you prepare vegetables.

2. Chop ¼ pound of the *andouille* into ¼-inch pieces. Place in a 12-inch cast-iron frying pan (or other heavy frying pan) with *tasso* (if used). Fry for 5 minutes to render fat and brown meat. Add chopped onion and celery and cook until vegetables are soft (about 10 minutes). Add bell pepper, green onions, and garlic. Cook an additional 5 minutes, then add to simmering pot of red beans. Continue to cook beans until they are soft and some begin to break apart (about 1 hour). Allow beans to cool; refrigerate, covered, overnight or for up to 4 days.

3. When ready to serve, bring beans to a simmer. Place *chaurice* whole in a heavy frying pan, cover, and fry over medium heat for about 15 minutes, checking sausages frequently and turning them as they brown. Meanwhile, slice remaining andouille into ¼-inch slices and add to beans. Cook in beans for about 10 minutes. Taste beans for salt and pepper and correct if necessary; add a little vinegar (if desired). To serve, place about ½ cup hot rice in center of each plate, spoon beans over rice, and accompany with 1 chaurice. Serve with hot-pepper sauce.

Serves 8.

Food Processor Version   Use metal blade to process vegetables, one after the other. Cut 2 large onions into eighths, put in work bowl, and turn motor on and off 3 to 4 times. Cut 1 stalk celery into 1-inch chunks and process same way. Cut bell pepper into 1-inch pieces and process same way. Cut green onions into 1-inch pieces and process 5 to 10 seconds.

LENTIL

The flat, disklike seeds of a leguminous plant, lentils are native to Asia Minor. Today lentils are marketed only dried, either packed in plastic bags or boxes or sold in bulk. Lentils are available in several different colors, including yellow, pink, and greenish brown. Store all varieties in a cool, dry place and use within a year.

Add lentils to soups and stews; boil until tender, drain, and dress with vinaigrette for a cool salad; or boil until tender, drain, and reheat with oil, butter, or bacon fat for a side dish.

LIMA BEAN

Also known as butter bean, the lima bean is a relatively large, kidney-shaped, light-green bean in an inedible green pod. Limas are occasionally available fresh in summer; choose solid-green, pliable pods without evidence of drying. To prepare, pull on string to open pod and remove beans. Limas are also available canned, frozen, and dried; dried limas are packed in plastic bags or sold in bulk. Store fresh limas in a plastic bag in refrigerator crisper; use quickly. Use dried limas within a year of purchase.

Add limas to soups and stews; boil until tender, drain and dress with butter or oil, and serve hot; or boil until tender, drain and dress with vinaigrette, and serve at room temperature or chilled as a salad.

■ **SUCCOTASH**

The name succotash derives from an Indian word, *m'sickquatash,* meaning corn not crushed or ground. Colonists learned from Native Americans the land-saving practice of planting corn and beans together, then training the bean vines up the corn stalks. At the harvest they simply combined the two in cooking. Today we usually make succotash with corn and lima beans, but many New England cooks prefer cranberry beans, and the Pennsylvania Dutch often add green bell peppers, tomatoes, and other vegetables. Some early recipes also called for fowl or meat plus potatoes or turnips, thus making more of a stew. This modern recipe is simple, colorful, and delicious, and it is very good made with frozen vegetables.

The classic Monday-night dinner of New Orleans, Red Beans and Rice, is embellished with Louisiana sausages and smoked meats. The hot sausage here, called chaurice, is flavored with fresh onions, parsley, and chiles and lightly smoked. Also pictured is tasso, a Cajun seasoning meat, which is more spicy and smoky than ham. If tasso is unavailable, you can use a smoked ham.

> ¼ **cup butter**
> 2 **cups fresh corn kernels or frozen corn kernels, thawed**
> 2 **cups cooked lima beans**
> ¼ **teaspoon salt**
> ¼ **teaspoon freshly ground pepper**
> ½ **cup whipping cream**
> 2 **tablespoons chopped parsley**

1. In a medium saucepan over medium heat, melt butter. Add corn, beans, salt, and pepper; stir to combine.

2. Add cream and simmer gently, uncovered, for about 5 minutes.

3. Stir in parsley and serve.

Serves 6.

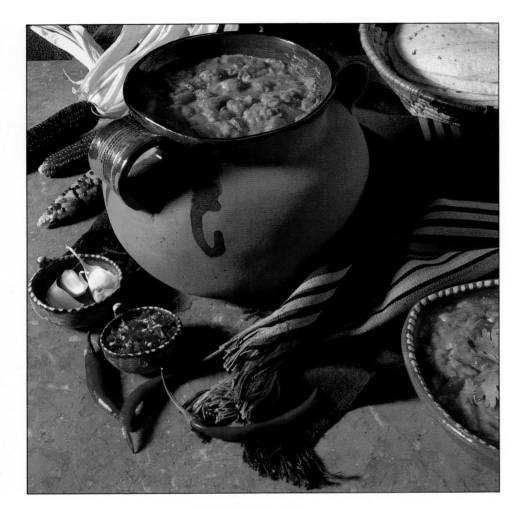

"Never saw a man so tired he couldn't eat some beans," said the old prospector in Treasure of Sierra Madre. *Probably he was thinking of that southwestern indispensable, Frijoles, shown here, and its variation, Refried Beans.*

MUNG BEAN

The small cylindrical seed of a leguminous plant, the mung bean is most commonly green, but brown and black varieties exist. When shelled and split in half, the green mung bean yields a rectangular yellow bean called the split golden gram or *moong dal*. Both mung beans and split golden gram are highly valued by Indian cooks as a source of protein. Sprouted mung beans, an even finer source of protein, are used frequently in Asian cooking.

Fresh mung bean sprouts are widely available all year. Select firm white sprouts without brown areas. Refrigerate in a plastic bag and use immediately. If not using right away, blanch bean sprouts in boiling water for 30 seconds, then transfer to ice water. Refrigerate, covered with water, and change water daily. Blanched bean sprouts will stay fresh for five or six days. Mung bean sprouts are also available canned; rinse under cold water before using. Dried mung beans are packaged in plastic bags or sold in bulk. Use within a year of purchase.

Use whole mung beans in soups, stews, and pilafs. Mung bean sprouts add texture to salads, stir-fries, and omelets. Mung bean starch is the basis for the transparent "cellophane" noodles used by Chinese cooks. Indian cooks use mung bean flour for breads and sweets.

NAVY BEAN

The navy bean is a small, oval, white bean so named because it has long been a staple of the diet of the U.S. Navy. Dried navy beans are packaged in plastic bags or sold in bulk. Use within a year of purchase. Navy beans are also widely available canned; they are the variety used for most canned and home-cooked versions of pork and beans or baked beans. Use navy beans in soups, stews, and salads.

■ BOSTON BAKED BEANS

In colonial times, it was customary to begin cooking baked beans early Saturday, so they would simmer quietly all day and evening and be ready for an effortless Saturday supper, Sunday breakfast, or noontime dinner. Today, beans are no longer considered strictly Sabbath food (although they still take all day to cook). If you wish, add a little catsup to the recipe; it's not traditional, but it adds color and tang. Otherwise, pass catsup at the table.

> 2 cups (1 lb) dried navy beans
> 1½ teaspoons salt
> 3 tablespoons *each* molasses and brown sugar
> 1 tablespoon dry mustard
> ¼ cup catsup (optional)
> 1 onion, peeled and left whole
> ¼ pound salt pork

1. Pick over beans to remove pebbles or bits of dirt, then rinse well in a colander. Place in a large pan, add 1 teaspoon salt and enough water to cover beans by about 3 inches. Bring to a rolling boil over high heat, and boil for 2 minutes. Remove from heat, cover pan, and let stand 1 hour.

2. Uncover pan, bring back to a boil, reduce heat, and simmer until beans are tender (1 to 1½ hours). Add more water if necessary to keep beans well covered.

3. Drain well, reserving liquid. In a bean pot or casserole of about 2½-quart capacity, combine molasses, brown sugar, mustard, catsup (if desired), and ½ teaspoon salt. Add drained beans, and stir in enough reserved cooking liquid to cover beans; mix well. Push whole onion down one side of beans. Cut several gashes in salt pork and bury it on the other side.

4. Cover pot, place in oven, and turn heat to 350° F. Bake until beans are bubbling (about 1 hour). Reduce heat to 250° F and bake for 6 to 8 hours more, stirring every hour or so. As beans cook, they will absorb liquid; continue adding reserved cooking liquid (or water), a little at a time, to keep them moist but not soupy. Baked beans are done when thick, fragrant, and a deep brownish red. They can remain in a 200° F oven for 1 or 2 hours longer if you wish; just remember to add liquid occasionally so they do not dry out. Beans also reheat well the next day. Remove and discard onion before serving. Serve with sliced salt pork if you wish.

Serves 4 to 6.

PINTO BEAN

The pinto bean is the mottled oval seed of a common shell bean. Dried pinto beans are sold in plastic bags or in bulk; use within a year of purchase. Canned pinto beans are also widely available. Pinto beans appear in many southwestern and Mexican soups, stews, and chilis.

▦ FRIJOLES

Homemade beans do taste better than beans from a can. Note that the beans have to soak overnight, or quick-soak 1 hour (see Preparation).

    1 pound dry pinto beans
   16 cups cold water
    1 large onion, coarsely chopped (about 1½ cups)
    1 tablespoon (about 2 cloves) minced garlic
    ¼ teaspoon red pepper flakes
    1 medium onion, finely chopped (about 1 cup)
    3 tablespoons bacon fat or lard
    1 large tomato, peeled, seeded, and
      coarsely chopped (about 1 cup)
      Salt and freshly ground pepper, to taste

1. Soak beans overnight in 8 cups of the cold water.

2. Drain and add 8 cups fresh water, the coarsely chopped onion, garlic, and red pepper. Bring to a boil, lower heat, cover, and simmer until beans are tender (about 90 minutes).

3. In a medium skillet over moderate heat, sauté finely chopped onion in bacon fat until wilted; add tomato and sauté until soft. Place ½ cup drained beans in small bowl and mash well with a fork. Add mashed beans to skillet along with a little of their liquid (about ¼ cup); stir over low heat until a thick paste.

4. Spoon contents of skillet into bean pot. Simmer, stirring frequently, until liquid thickens (about 30 minutes). Season to taste with salt and pepper.

Serves 6 to 8.

Texas Jalapeño Pinto Beans Complete steps 1 through 3. Spoon contents of skillet into bean pot and add canned or pickled jalapeño chiles to taste—up to an entire 4-ounce can for a very, very spicy dish. Continue with step 4.

Refried Beans Complete steps 1 and 2. Drain cooked beans, reserving liquid. Mash well with a fork or a potato masher (not a food processor). In a large, heavy skillet, heat 3 tablespoons of rendered bacon fat with 4 tablespoons of lard until aromatic and almost smoking. Very carefully add mashed beans (they will spatter) and lower heat. Cook over medium-low heat, stirring frequently, until fat is absorbed. Thin to desired consistency with some of the reserved cooking liquid, stirring it in by tablespoons. Add ¼ pound Monterey jack cheese, coarsely grated, and cook about 15 minutes longer, until cheese is completely absorbed. Season with salt and pepper.

RUNNER BEAN

Also known as the scarlet runner bean, the runner bean has a flat, broad, green pod and small scarlet seeds. The edible blossom may be red or white. The runner bean is available fresh in summer and fall. Choose firm pods that have solid color, do not show signs of drying, and have beans that are not too pronounced. Steam and serve hot, with butter or oil, or cold with vinaigrette. Add to vegetable soups or mixed vegetable salads. To prepare, cut along each side of bean to remove strings and ridges. Slice across pod on the diagonal between each seed.

SNAP BEAN

Immature *Phaseolus vulgaris*, at the stage when entire pod is edible, is called snap bean. Snap beans include the common green or string bean, the Italian Romano bean, the yellow wax bean, and the purple-podded bean. Snap beans are available fresh, frozen, and canned. Some fresh varieties are available the year around, but the supply peaks in summer. Choose fresh snap beans that are firm, with smooth pods, and do not show signs of browning or drying. To prepare for cooking, remove strings and brown tips (see GADGETS, Bean Slicer). Snap beans may be steamed, braised, sautéed, stir-fried, or pickled. Serve hot, with butter or oil, or cold as a salad. They may be added to soups or hot, mixed vegetable combinations.

SOYBEAN

Fresh soybean pods are dark green with a soft outer fuzz; inside are two or four small oval beans. Soybeans can be yellow, green, brown, black, or mottled. When cooked their texture is firm, their flavor mild.

Because of their high protein content, soybeans are a valuable food source. They are made into a wide variety of products, from bean curd (tofu) to soy milk to soy sauce to soy flour.

Shell and boil fresh soybeans as you would English peas, or substitute soybeans for lima beans or fava beans in recipes that have a comparable flavor and texture. Dried soybeans can be sprouted for use in salads, stir-fries, and sandwiches, or boiled and served hot as a side dish. The salted black beans widely used in Chinese cooking are soft black soybeans that have been cooked, inoculated with a mold, and brined for about six months. Salted black beans are used to flavor steamed fish, pork ribs, clams, and many other dishes.

Fresh soybeans are available occasionally in Japanese markets and specialty markets in summer and fall; dried soybeans can be bought in bulk at Asian markets and health-food stores. Salted black beans are sold in Chinese markets in cans or small bags usually labeled "salted black beans." Do not confuse them with the uncooked variety, which is sold in similar packages.

Choose firm, well-filled soybean pods, without brown edges or spots.

Keep in a plastic bag in refrigerator for one to two days. Dried soybeans and salted black beans that are kept in an airtight container keep indefinitely in a cool, dry place.

Recipes: Bean Curd, 36; Flour, 234; Sauce and Condiment (Commercial), 523.

SPLIT GOLDEN GRAM (MOONG DAL)

See Mung Bean.

STRING BEAN

See Snap Bean.

TURTLE BEAN

See Black Bean.

WAX BEAN

See Snap Bean.

BEAN CURD

Also marketed under its Japanese name, *tofu*, bean curd is a highly nutritious soybean product that has been made in east Asia for over 2,000 years. Tofu is made from soybeans that are soaked, then puréed, and cooked to create soy milk. Soy milk is then mixed with a coagulant similar to the rennet used in making cheese. As curds form, they are shaped and pressed in rectangular molds to form tofu. Its texture is smooth, moist, and silky; its basic flavor is bland, but it readily absorbs other flavors.

Use   Tofu is an important source of protein for billions of people. It is eaten cold with a variety of seasonings and dipping sauces; it is also deep-fried, stir-fried, braised, stuffed, steamed, grilled, and poached in soups. Delicate Japanese-style tofu is suitable for soups and simmered dishes; Chinese-style tofu contains less whey and therefore is firmer and better for stir-frying, deep-frying, braising, and grilling.

Bean curd is used increasingly in non-Asian processed foods, from salad dressings to nondairy ice creams. The latter may be suitable for low-cholesterol and lactose-free diets; however, these products are generally not low-calorie as they are high in sugar and vegetable oil. Check package label for ingredients.

Availability   Both types of fresh tofu are sold packed in water in sealed plastic tubs or in sealed foil packages. The foil packages do not require refrigeration, until opening. Deep-fried bean curd is available in bulk or in sealed plastic bags. Japanese markets may also carry freeze-dried and charcoal-grilled tofu in cakes. The skin that forms on the surface of hot soybean milk is dried and sold as sheets, rolls, or sticks and is used as a meat substitute in some vegetarian dishes.

Storage   Fresh bean curd is highly perishable and should be used within two or three days of purchase. Refrigerate unused portion, covered with ample water, in a covered plastic container; change water daily.

Preparation   Rinse tofu briefly under cold running water. Cube, dice, or slice as recipe directs.

 FRIED TOFU

Serve deep-fried tofu as a hot appetizer with a dipping sauce or use it as a meat substitute in such dishes as Mu Shu Pork (see page 378). The first step, pressing the tofu, may not be necessary if the tofu is firm enough; remember to drain it thoroughly. Softer, Japanese-style tofu will have to be pressed.

> **7 ounces firm Chinese-style tofu**
> **Oil, for deep-frying**

1. Drain tofu well. Wrap in a clean kitchen towel or several thicknesses of paper towel, place on a plate set in a sheet pan, and invert another plate on top. Place a 1-pound weight on top plate. Let stand 30 minutes, then unwrap and drain. Tofu will exude a lot of liquid. (This may be done ahead of time and the tofu refrigerated.)

2. Slice pressed tofu into squares, triangles, or other shapes about ⅜ inch thick. In a wok or other deep pan, heat oil to 350° F. Fry tofu pieces a few at a time, until puffy and golden brown (6 to 8 minutes).

Serves 4 to 6 as an appetizer.

BEARD, TO

Also called debeard; to pull out the byssus of a mussel, the bristly, beardlike hairs that are connected just inside the hinge of the shell (see photograph, page 536). Mussels attach themselves to rocks and each other with these threads. The byssus must be scrubbed from the outer shell and pulled from the inner shell before cooking. Mussels die soon after bearding, so preparation should follow immediately.

BEAT, TO

To mix ingredients by stirring rapidly in a circular motion by hand or with an electric mixer in order to make smooth (batters) or to lighten with air (egg whites and whipping cream).

BEEF

Technically, beef is any meat from a full-grown ox, bull, cow, or steer. In practice, however, almost all commercial beef comes from steers (castrated males). Ox meat is too tough, bulls are too unruly, and cows fatten too slowly to be suitable for commercial beef production.

The American beef industry is continually trying to improve the breed of cattle used for beef. Through selective breeding and cross-breeding for flavor, yield, disease-resistance, efficient feed-to-muscle conversion, and other characteristics, today's beef cattle are very different from the cattle brought to the colonies by seventeenth-century English settlers.

Most beef cattle today are black Angus or Hereford, although the French Charolais is gaining popularity. Crosses with Brahman bulls and Texas longhorns are also commercial successes.

WHAT DETERMINES QUALITY OF BEEF CATTLE

Diet is a major factor in determining the quality of meat on beef cattle. Grain-fed or grain-finished cattle develop more intramuscular fat (marbling), and therefore more flavorful and more tender meat, than do grass-fed cattle. Some experts claim that corn-fed cattle are superior in flavor to those fed a grain diet that also includes oats, barley, or sorghum. However, even grain-fed cattle have some hay or straw in their feed for roughage.

Age at time of slaughter is another determinant of quality. Young animals have tender meat but lack flavor. Older animals have more flavor but tougher meat. Most beef cattle today are slaughtered when they reach about 1,000 to 1,200 pounds, which generally takes 11 to 16 months.

How beef is treated after slaughter also affects its quality. Beef that has been allowed to hang, or age, on the carcass for two to six weeks at a cold temperature in a humidity-controlled room will be more tender than fresh beef. Under these controlled conditions, excess moisture in the meat evaporates and enzymes begin to break down the muscle fibers, thus tenderizing the meat. Few retail meat markets offer aged beef to consumers. Most aged beef is destined for restaurants.

WHAT MAKES BEEF CHOICE

The quality (how tender, juicy, and flavorful the meat is) of any piece of meat depends on its location on the animal and on the "grade" assigned to each meat carcass.

The choicest cuts of all meats come from the parts of the animal that do the least work. Just as in humans, the hard-working lower leg of an animal develops a strong, tough muscle, full of sinewy fibers and connective tissues, while the well-protected and rarely exercised little muscle right in the middle of the back (the filet mignon, on a steer)

remains tender. The tougher cuts can be just as tasty and nutritious as the tender ones if they're cooked by a method that tenderizes them.

GRADES OF BEEF

All meat sold in the United States is checked by government inspectors for wholesomeness. The United States Department of Agriculture also inspects most meat to determine its grade. The "quality" of beef that determines its grading by the USDA is based on its tenderness, juiciness, and flavor. The top grades for beef are USDA Prime, Choice, and Good. However, in most of the country, grading is voluntary, and only about 50 percent of American beef is graded. The major difference between grades is the degree of marbling.

Marbling is the small, paper-thin veins of fat that crisscross a piece of meat. Hard-working muscles, such as the flank and shin, have very little marbling; tender cuts, such as the rib and the loin, are finely marbled all over.

Prime, the highest grade of meat, containing the greatest degree of marbling, is produced in very limited quantities, and is generally sold at premium prices to finer restaurants and specialty meat markets. Prime cuts, because they are already expensive, also tend to receive the longest aging.

Choice is the grade generally sold at retail stores. It is preferred by consumers because it contains sufficient marbling for taste and tenderness and is less costly and less fattening than Prime.

Good, a lower-priced grade of meat, has less marbling than USDA Choice. It is as nutritious as the other grades, but less juicy and flavorful. Some supermarket chains sell it under their own quality designation rather than a USDA grade name. It is also used commercially for many canned meat items.

Use Beef is a major protein source in many of the world's cuisines. Some best-loved beef dishes include: Italian carpaccio, raw beef sliced paper-thin and served with a mustard sauce; French *boeuf bourguignonne*, beef stewed in Burgundy wine; Russian beef stroganoff with mushrooms and sour cream; English roast prime ribs of beef with Yorkshire pudding; and, of course, American hamburgers.

Availability Many retail stores have adopted the National Livestock and Meat Board's recommendations for standardizing meat labels (see Cuts of Beef). The names of the retail cuts vary sharply from region to region and store to store: London broil, for instance, may be flank steak in one market, a thick-cut top round steak in another. With the new form of labeling, the primal cut (chuck or rib, for example) is listed on the label along with the kind of meat (beef, pork, or other), and the retail cut, so that a well-informed consumer can best determine how to cook a particular piece of meat (see Cooking). The following are beef products also available in markets.

CUTS OF BEEF

Chuck
1. *Stew*
   Ground beef
2. *Chuck roast*
   Blade roast and steak
3. *Boneless shoulder pot roast and steak*
   Arm pot roast and steak
4. *Cross-rib roast*
   Short ribs

Rib
1. *Standing rib roast*
   Rib steak
   Rib-eye (Delmonico) roast and steak
2. *Short ribs*

Short Loin
1. *Top loin steak*
   Club steak
2. *Top loin steak*
   T-bone steak
   Filet mignon
   (tenderloin)
3. *Top loin steak*
   Porterhouse steak
   Filet mignon

Sirloin
1. *Pinbone sirloin steak*
   Boneless sirloin steak
2. *Flatbone sirloin steak*
3. *Wedgebone sirloin steak*
4. *Tip steak*
   Tip roast
   Cube steak
   Kebabs

Foreshank and Brisket
1. *Stew*
2. *Shank crosscuts*
3. *Fresh brisket*
   Corned brisket

Short Plate
1. *Short ribs*
   Stew
2. *Stew*
   Skirt steak rolls
   Ground beef

Flank
1. *Flank steak*
   Flank steak rolls
   Ground beef

Round
1. *Boneless rump roast*
2. *Round steak*
   Top round steak
   Bottom round steak and roast
   Eye of round
   Cube steak
3. *Tip roast*
   Tip steak
   Cube steak
   Kebabs
4. *Heel-of-round roast*
   Ground beef

The tenderness of a cut depends upon what part of the animal it came from. Therefore, the cut should determine the cooking method. Tender cuts are usually cooked by dry-heat methods such as roasting, broiling, and grilling. These cooking methods enhance flavor but tend to toughen meat fibers. Less tender cuts require moist-heat cooking methods (stewing and braising); the cooking liquid tenderizes the meat and breaks down tough connective tissue. The gelatin that dissolves out of the connective fibers helps to thicken and enrich the cooking liquid. Marinating, pounding, cubing, and grinding can also be used to tenderize tough cuts. Commercial tenderizers such as papain, which partially predigest raw meat, are also used by many cooks; however, these tenderizers may affect both the flavor and the chewy, dense texture of beef. Some of the tougher cuts used for stir-frying and grilling are tenderized by slicing thinly and marinating.

There are eight primal (wholesale) cuts on a side of beef.
Chuck, Foreshank and Brisket, Short Plate, Flank, and Round The chuck and all the primal cuts on the lower half of the steer provide the lower-priced, less tender meats. Except for steaks cut from the flank, which are often grilled or used for kebabs and stir-fry dishes, these cuts are best suited to cooking in some sort of liquid. Cuts for pot roast include the chuck, the blade roast, the shoulder, the arm, the cross-rib roast, the brisket, the flank, and nearly all parts of the round, from the relatively tender top round to the medium-tough bottom round to the very tough eye of round. Stewing cuts include the entire chuck, the top of the foreshank, the short plate, and most of the round. The most popular cut for well-marinated *fajitas* (Tex-Mex marinated barbecued steak) is the skirt steak, but the flank and brisket are other good choices.

Ready-to-cook beef kebabs are usually cut from the round, but the long, thin kebabs favored in Thai cooking are sliced from the flank. In areas where Asian cooking is popular, flank steak—which at least has little waste—has become as expensive as porterhouse.
Rib, Short Loin, and Sirloin These primal cuts contain the tenderest meat, and are usually the most costly. From this area come the expensive steaks and roasts which are cooked by dry heat: rib roast, filet mignon, and rib, club, T-bone, porterhouse, and sirloin steaks. There is also a portion of the blade chuck roast that is actually an extension of the tender rib-eye muscle, and it, too, can be cooked as a steak. The top round is also sold as a roast or a steak for dry-heat cooking, but is not tender enough for all tastes, and many people prefer to braise this cut. Short ribs are suitable for moist-heat cooking methods.

Beef Jerky Thinly sliced lean dried beef, beef jerky doesn't require refrigeration. It is a good source of protein and has excellent keeping qualities. The original beef jerky was sun-dried or smoked over campfires. Most commercial beef jerky today is highly seasoned first, then oven-dried. It is available in supermarkets and sporting-goods stores. Latin American markets carry a version of beef jerky called *carne seca.* Armenian *bastourma,* available in Middle Eastern markets, is a similar, highly spiced sun-dried beef.

Chewy beef jerky can be eaten as is, diced and simmered in soups or stews, or soaked to soften, then added to eggs or hash. Store jerky in an airtight container at room temperature for up to three months, or refrigerate or freeze indefinitely.

Beef Marrow Beef bones yield a buttery edible marrow that adds richness and juiciness to dishes as it melts. The leg bones contain the most marrow. Have the butcher saw bones into chunks to make it easier to remove the marrow. To cut out raw marrow, use a small, sharp knife: Cut around the marrow and then pry it out. To store, wrap marrow and refrigerate for up to three days or freeze for up to two months. To use, chop and add to hamburgers, meat loaves, stuffings, and dumplings; chopped marrow is an ingredient in Bercy Butter, a classic garnish for grilled steak.

Corned Beef This preparation gets its name from the Old English word *corn,* for a small kernel or a grain of salt. Corned beef is brined beef, generally made with brisket or plate. Pickling spices, garlic, and sugar are usually added to the pickling medium. Most commercial varieties also contain saltpeter (sodium nitrate or potassium nitrate) for preservation and color retention. Some specialty markets offer their own fresh corned beef; it must be simmered in water until tender. Most supermarkets offer ready-to-eat corned beef, either canned or in a plastic package, in a large piece, or sliced for sandwiches.

Use corned beef in thick rye-bread sandwiches, in potato salad, in hash, as part of a dinner with potatoes and cabbage. Fresh corned beef in brine will keep for weeks in the refrigerator but gets saltier with time. Cooked corned beef may be refrigerated, well wrapped, for one or two weeks.

Pastrami A corned beef, pastrami is usually made with beef plate that is rubbed with black pepper and other spices, then smoked. It is a popular Jewish delicatessen item, usually steamed and sliced thin for thick rye-bread sandwiches. Some supermarkets also carry large chunks of pastrami packaged in plastic or sliced pastrami for sandwiches, also packed in plastic.

Because of its high fat content, pastrami is best served warm. Steam and slice thin. Leftover pastrami will keep, well wrapped, in the refrigerator for several days.

Selection The most tender cuts of beef come from the muscles that were rarely used, such as those in the loin and the rib. More active muscles—such as the shank, shoulder, tongue, and leg (or "round")—are tougher.

To select flavorful beef, look for marbling (intramuscular fat), which is a natural baster. Consumer concern about dietary fat has led to a demand for lean beef, but the most flavorful beef is well marbled. The beef's external fat should be creamy white, not yellow; the muscle should be red and firm. Avoid meat that is mushy or reddish brown. See also Grades of Beef.

Storage Large cuts of beef deteriorate less quickly than small cuts, such as stew meat or ground beef. However, all beef should be refrigerated or frozen immediately after purchase.

To refrigerate beef, remove store wrapping and rewrap loosely in waxed paper to allow for some air circulation. Set beef on a plate in the coldest part of the refrigerator. Use ground beef within one or two days, steaks within three or four days, roasts within one week.

To freeze beef, remove store wrapping and rewrap in moistureproof freezer paper; freeze immediately. To stack steaks or chops, put a double thickness of waxed paper between layers. Label and date packages with indelible ink. Thaw the oldest packages first. Transfer meat to refrigerator for slow thawing. Use thawed meat immediately; do not refreeze. Large roasts and steaks may be frozen for up to nine months, beef cubes for up to four months, ground beef for up to three months.

Preparation Most beef comes ready to cook from the butcher. Sometimes you may want to trim away some external fat, or slash the layer of fat on a steak to prevent it from curling as it broils or grills. Tough cuts can be made more tender if they are marinated, pounded, cubed, or ground. Commercial tenderizers, which partially "predigest" raw meat, are employed by many cooks, although these tenderizers may affect both the flavor and the characteristic chewy, dense texture of beef (see MARINATE, POUND).

Cooking Selecting the right cut of beef for a dish and applying the right cooking method to a given cut are essential to a successful result. Tender cuts of meat take well to quick, dry-heat cooking—roasting, broiling, panfrying, and grilling. Tougher cuts require slow, moist-heat cooking—stewing and braising.

Certain relatively tough cuts of beef are also used for stir-frying (usually following a brief marination period) and, after more marination, for barbecuing. In both cases, the meat seems tender because it is sliced very thinly across the grain (before cooking for stir-frying, and after cooking for barbecuing).

See BRAISE, BROIL, GRILL, PAN-BROIL, PANFRY, ROAST, STEW, STIR-FRY.

Tender, juicy strips of porterhouse steak need only the simple finish of an herb-seasoned butter, here flavored with fresh chives and parsley.

DRY-HEAT COOKING

These cooking methods—roasting, broiling, grilling, and pan-frying—do not include any added moisture. Sometimes fat is brushed or set on lean cuts to keep them from drying out during cooking. Sheets of beef fat can provide effective basting (see BARD) for lean beef roasts. Ask your butcher for thin sheets of exterior beef fat (not crumbly kidney fat). Arrange a single thickness of fat over top of roast and tie in place with string. As the roast cooks, the melting fat keeps the meat moist and juicy. The following recipes are for the more tender cuts of beef.

■ LONDON BROIL

Flank steak, a cut of meat from along the flank or underside of the beef, is traditionally used for this dish. A lean cut, it benefits from scoring and a flavorful marinade. The steak must marinate at least six hours, or overnight.

    1 flank steak (about 1½ lb)
    1 clove garlic, minced
    1½ tablespoons vegetable oil
    ½ tablespoon red wine vinegar
      Salt and freshly ground pepper, to taste

1. Score steak lightly and place in a shallow 9- by 12-inch nonaluminum pan. Sprinkle with garlic, oil, and vinegar. Turn to coat both sides and marinate in the refrigerator, loosely covered, 6 to 24 hours.

2. Preheat broiler. Drain marinade. Place steak on a rack in a shallow pan on top shelf of oven and broil 5 minutes on first side. Turn and broil 5 minutes on second side.

3. Place on a cutting board and slice across grain into diagonal strips about ¼ inch thick. Season with salt and pepper and serve immediately.

Serves 6 to 8.

■ ROAST PRIME RIB OF BEEF WITH YORKSHIRE PUDDING

Many family celebrations wouldn't be complete without this traditional dish that suggests everything bountiful and delicious. The Yorkshire Pudding is flavored with drippings from the roast. It cooks during the last half hour or so of the roast's cooking time.

    1 prime rib of beef (4 rib, about 11 lb)
    1 tablespoon salt
    ½ teaspoon freshly ground pepper
      Horseradish Cream Sauce (see page 305),
      for accompaniment

Yorkshire Pudding

    1 cup flour
    1 teaspoon salt
    2 eggs
    ½ cup milk
    ½ cup water
    2 tablespoons hot beef fat

Gravy

    2 tablespoons hot pan juices
    1½ tablespoons flour
    1½ cups Beef Stock (see page 560)

1. Preheat oven to 400° F. Rub beef with salt and pepper. Place beef in a roasting pan, fat side up, and roast 15 minutes per pound, approximately 2½ hours (or until internal temperature 125° F for rare, 135° F for medium-rare, or 140° F for medium).

2. Remove from oven. Reserve 2 tablespoons of pan juices; discard the rest.

3. Let meat rest 15 minutes. Remove roast to a carving board and carve.

4. Serve with Horseradish Cream Sauce, Yorkshire Pudding, and Gravy.

Serves 8.

Yorkshire Pudding

1. While meat is roasting, whisk together flour, salt, eggs, milk, and the water. Let rest 30 minutes.

2. Twenty minutes before roast is done, remove 2 tablespoons hot beef fat from roasting pan to a 10-inch cast-iron skillet and heat in oven 10 minutes.

3. Pour prepared Yorkshire Pudding batter into hot skillet and bake in 400° F oven until puffy and golden brown, about 25 minutes. (Pudding can be baked on same rack as roast if there is room, or on another rack, in another oven, or in oven used for meat while roast is resting.)

4. Remove, cut in 8 pieces, and set aside on platter to serve with meat.

Gravy Pour the reserved 2 tablespoons pan juices into a 1-quart saucepan over low heat. Stir in flour and cook 2 to 3 minutes. Whisk in stock and cook until slightly thickened (about 5 minutes). Serve over Yorkshire Pudding and prime rib.

■ BEEF TENDERLOIN

This method of roasting is useful for many tender cuts of beef that have little exterior fat and minimal marbling. Chateaubriand, which may be prepared in the same manner, is traditionally served surrounded with vegetables such as broiled tomatoes, small potatoes, and parsley sprigs, and accompanied with a sauce such as Béarnaise (see page 518).

    3 tablespoons vegetable oil
    2 tablespoons Dijon mustard
    2 tablespoons brandy
    1 teaspoon salt
    ¼ teaspoon freshly ground pepper
    2 pounds beef tenderloin, trimmed of
       exterior fat and any silvery membrane

1. In a small bowl mix together 1 tablespoon oil, mustard, brandy, salt, and pepper. Rub tenderloin with mustard mixture and rest 30 minutes.

2. Preheat oven to 400° F. Pour remaining oil in a Dutch oven or heavy cast-iron skillet and heat over medium-high heat. Brown tenderloin on one side (about 5 minutes). Turn meat and brown other side (about 5 minutes more).

3. Roast tenderloin in pan 25 to 30 minutes (or until internal temperature is 125° F for rare, 135° F for medium rare, and 140° F for medium). When done, let meat rest 15 minutes before carving.

4. To serve, cut the meat into ½-inch-thick slices.

Serves 6 to 8.

■ BROILED PORTERHOUSE STEAK
WITH SAVORY BUTTER

Place steaks on a lightly greased rack over a broiling pan; do not salt before starting to cook. To add flavor, if desired, rub steak with a cut clove of garlic or herbs of choice. In this recipe, delicious fresh chives and parsley flavor the butter that melts into a classic, thick steak.

    ⅓ cup butter or margarine, softened
    1 teaspoon fresh lemon juice
    ¼ teaspoon dry mustard
    1 tablespoon snipped fresh chives
    ¼ cup finely chopped parsley
    1 porterhouse steak (1½ to 2 lb), 1½ inches thick

1. Beat butter in a medium bowl until fluffy; gradually beat in lemon juice until well combined; then blend in dry mustard. Mix in chives and parsley, distributing evenly.

Shape butter into a roll about 1 inch in diameter; enclose in plastic wrap and refrigerate until firm (about 1 hour).

2. Preheat broiler. Trim excess fat from edges of steak; slash remaining fat at about 1-inch intervals. Place steak on greased rack of broiler pan about 4 inches from heat.

3. Broil, turning once, for 6 to 8 minutes on each side for rare (increase time for medium or well-done). When turning steak to broil second side, dot with about 1 tablespoon of butter mixture.

4. Place broiled steak on a carving board. With a short pointed knife, cut around the T-shaped bone; remove bone. Cut the smaller loin portion of the steak across the grain into several slices. Then slice the remaining meat across the grain about ¼ inch thick. Serve slices from each portion on warm dinner plates. Accompany with slices of herb butter.

Serves 2 to 3.

■ STEAK AU POIVRE

Club steaks are traditionally boneless, cut from the loin, and often called New York strip steaks. A variation of this recipe may be made with green peppercorns.

    6 club steaks (about ¾ lb each)
    6 tablespoons black peppercorns, crushed
    3 tablespoons vegetable oil
    3 tablespoons unsalted butter
       Juice of 1 lemon
    1 teaspoon Worcestershire sauce
    4 to 5 sprigs parsley, minced
    1 tablespoon snipped fresh chives
    4 tablespoons Cognac (optional)
    1 to 2 teaspoons salt

1. Coat both sides of steak with pepper, pressing firmly into meat. Let stand 30 minutes.

2. In a large, heavy-bottomed skillet, sauté first side of steaks in oil over medium-high heat until well browned (about 5 minutes); turn and sauté 3 minutes on second side. Remove steaks to a serving platter and keep warm.

3. To make sauce, add butter, lemon juice, Worcestershire sauce, parsley, and chives to skillet; whisk to combine. If using Cognac, pour into a small saucepan, heat slowly to warm, then ignite. Let Cognac cook until flame dissipates (about 3 minutes). Carefully pour Cognac over butter-lemon mixture in skillet and whisk together. Season with salt and pour over reserved steaks.

Serves 6.

Steak Diane Prepare steaks as for Steak au Poivre through step 2 but without peppercorn marinade. For sauce, use 3 tablespoons butter, juice of 1 lemon, 2 tablespoons snipped fresh chives, and 4 tablespoons Cognac (if desired). Prepare as in step 3 and season to taste with salt and freshly ground pepper before serving.

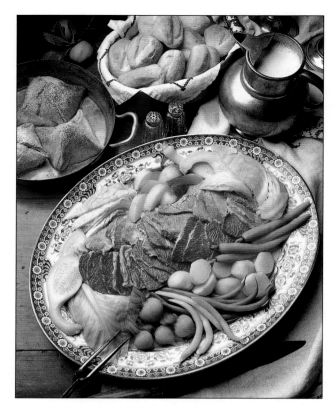

Making New England Boiled Dinner is slow, relaxed cooking, which can take care of itself while you attend to other matters. Once done, the meat can be kept warm for a couple of hours, or it can be reheated. The vegetables can be trimmed ahead of time, but should be cooked just before serving, so they retain their fresh color and shape.

MOIST-HEAT COOKING

Cooking with liquid will tenderize even the toughest cut of meat and draw out its flavor during the long, slow process. Braising and stewing are the methods used to tenderize lean, flavorful, but relatively tough cuts such as round, chuck, or brisket.

■ NEW ENGLAND BOILED DINNER

Just about every culture has its boiled dinner, dating back to the days when most cooking was done in a single pot slung over the fire. Since it's worth having leftovers for sandwiches or corned-beef hash, this recipe calls for a generous amount of corned beef.

> 5 to 6 pounds corned-beef brisket
> 8 to 12 small beets, tops removed
> 8 to 12 small boiling potatoes, peeled
> 8 to 12 small boiling onions, peeled
> 8 to 12 carrots, scraped
> 6 small turnips, peeled
> 1 head green cabbage, cored and quartered
>   Mustard, for accompaniment

Horseradish Sauce

> 1 cup chilled whipping cream
> 4 to 5 tablespoons prepared horseradish
> 3 tablespoons cider vinegar
>   Salt and freshly ground pepper, to taste

1. Rinse corned beef under running water and place in a large, deep pot. Cover with cold water and bring just

to a boil over high heat; skim off any scum that rises to the surface. Reduce heat to low, partially cover pot, and let simmer gently for 3 hours. (At this point meat may sit in the hot cooking liquid for another hour or two if you wish to delay serving. Bring back to a simmer before continuing with the vegetables.)

2. About an hour or so before you wish to serve, place beets in a medium saucepan, cover with water, and boil until tender when pierced (30 to 40 minutes). Drain; peel when cool enough to handle. Return peeled beets to saucepan, add a few ladlefuls of the corned-beef broth, and keep warm over low heat.

3. While beets are boiling, drop potatoes into simmering corned-beef pot and cook for 10 minutes. Drop in onions, carrots, and turnips, and simmer until vegetables are quite tender when pierced (about 30 minutes more). Add cabbage wedges and simmer exactly 3 minutes.

4. Remove meat from pot, slice thinly, and arrange on a large warm platter. Surround meat with vegetables from pot. Drain beets, and place in another serving bowl.

5. Serve with mustard and Horseradish Sauce.

Serves 6 to 8.

Horseradish Sauce   Whip cream until it stands in stiff peaks. Fold in horseradish and vinegar, and season with salt and pepper.

■ BASIC BOEUF EN DAUBE

France's ubiquitous wine-based beef stews are justly popular nearly everywhere that beef is eaten. Try the variation or make up your own: blanch seasonal vegetables until tender and add just before serving, vary the cooking liquid, or sprinkle with fresh herbs from your garden.

> ¼ pound sliced bacon
> 3 pounds beef round or chuck, in stewing pieces
> 2 large onions, minced
>   Cooking oil, if necessary
> 2 tablespoons Cognac, Armagnac, or brandy
> 2 pounds carrots, peeled, trimmed, and
>   sliced thickly diagonally
> 4 cloves garlic, crushed and peeled
> 3 veal bones *or* 1 calf's foot (optional)
> 1 bouquet garni
> 3 cups dry red wine
> 1 cup Beef Stock (see page 560) or
>   canned beef bouillon (preferably low-salt)
>   Salt and freshly ground pepper, to taste
> 6 to 8 small boiling potatoes, scrubbed or
>   peeled (optional)
> 6 slices French bread and 1 clove garlic,
>   halved (optional)

1. Cut bacon slices horizontally into 1- by ¼-inch strips. In a very large, heavy skillet, sauté bacon until lightly browned but not crisp. Remove bacon with a slotted spoon; drain on paper towels and reserve.

2. Reheat bacon fat, and, over high heat, brown about one third of the beef. (If beef is crowded, juices will be released and meat will boil rather than brown.) Remove with a slotted spoon to a large, heavy casserole or Dutch oven, and brown remaining beef in two more shifts, transferring it to the casserole when brown. Over moderate heat, sauté minced onion in skillet until wilted (add vegetable oil to skillet if necessary), and transfer to casserole.

3. In a small saucepan over low heat, warm Cognac. (Have a long match ready.) Warm casserole over low heat. Pour Cognac into casserole, warm for a minute, and, very carefully (making sure nothing flammable is near the stove), set Cognac aflame. When flame dies down, add reserved bacon, carrots, garlic, veal bones (if used), bouquet garni, wine, and stock. Stir, carefully season to taste, cover, and simmer very slowly until beef is very tender (2 to 2½ hours) or slowly bake in oven at 250° F.

4. Meanwhile, boil potatoes, if used, in salted water to cover until tender (25 to 30 minutes). When stew is done, remove and discard veal bones and bouquet garni. Degrease stew (see DEGREASE). If desired, liquid may be poured off into a saucepan and boiled over a high flame until reduced by half, and/or it may be thickened and enriched with beurre manié made of 3 tablespoons butter and 3 tablespoons flour (see page 517). Return liquid to the stew along with potatoes, if used. Correct seasonings and reheat gently for a few minutes.

5. Toast French bread, if used, and rub while hot with cut sides of garlic. Float toasts on top of stewing liquid. Serve stew hot in widemouthed soup bowls; top each bowl with a piece of garlic toast from the main serving dish.

Serves 6.

Boeuf Bourguignonne (Burgundy Beef Stew) Decrease carrots to about ½ pound (2 or 3 large carrots), and add 1 pound of small white boiling onions, peeled and trimmed. Trim 1 pound of fresh mushrooms, wipe clean with a mushroom brush or slightly damp paper towel, and cut in quarters. In a heavy skillet, rapidly sauté mushrooms in 2 tablespoons of butter and 2 tablespoons oil until lightly brown. Add mushrooms to the stew 10 minutes before serving, and garnish stew with 2 tablespoons minced parsley. Omit potatoes and toast; serve stew over a bed of cooked, lightly buttered noodles.

Serves 4 to 6.

OTHER WAYS WITH BEEF

Whether sliced paper-thin, cut into strips, chopped, or ground, and whether served raw or cooked, beef stars in scores of international favorites, from the all-American burger to sophisticated carpaccio and the pastry-wrapped beef piroshki and baked empanada.

■ STEAK TARTARE

Beef of the best quality tastes delicious cooked or raw, as this well-known dish attests.

    1 pound raw, freshly ground, top-quality beef
        fillet, sirloin, or round steak
    2 egg yolks
    2 anchovies, chopped
    2 tablespoons capers
    1 shallot, minced
    4 sprigs chopped parsley
    ½ teaspoon dry mustard
    ½ teaspoon salt
    ¼ teaspoon freshly ground pepper
        Juice of 1 lemon
    2 teaspoons Cognac (optional)
        Buttered toast, for accompaniment

In a medium bowl mix beef, egg yolks, anchovies, capers, shallot, parsley, mustard, salt, pepper, lemon juice, and Cognac, if used. Serve on buttered toast.

Serves 4 to 6 as an entrée, 8 to 10 as an appetizer.

■ NORTH BEACH GARLICKY MEAT LOAF

This richly seasoned meat mixture captures the flavors of San Francisco's North Beach area, home to many wonderful Italian restaurants and cafés. Leftover meat loaf makes delicious sandwiches on a flavorful, homestyle bread. Do not slice the loaf until needed; it slices best when cold.

    1¼ cup dry bread crumbs
     5 tablespoons grated dried cheese
        (Parmesan cheese or a mixture of Parmesan,
        Romano, and dried Jack cheeses)
     5 tablespoons minced parsley
    1½ to 2 tablespoons finely minced garlic
    1½ pounds ground beef
     ½ teaspoon *each* salt and freshly ground pepper
     2 eggs
     ¼ cup (approximately) water
        Catsup, for coating

1. Preheat oven to 350° F. Mix bread crumbs, cheese, parsley, and garlic. Add meat, and salt and pepper, and mix together. Pour in eggs and a little of the water; knead mixture to an even consistency, adding more water if mixture seems dry.

2. Mold into a greased loaf pan, top with a very thin coat of catsup, and bake for 70 minutes.

Serves 6.

North Beach Meatballs Preheat oven to 450° F. Make meat mixture. Wet hands and roll mixture into 1½-inch meatballs. Place meatballs on a large, lightly greased baking sheet and bake for 20 minutes. Serve while still sizzling hot. (Meatballs may also be reheated in meatless tomato sauce of your choice and used to dress pasta.)

Serves 12 as an appetizer.

TIPS

ABOUT GROUND BEEF

As any supermarket shopper knows, ground beef, unlike other ground meats, comes in several grades and prices, determined by the amount of fat ground with the meat. The cheapest grade—usually just called ground beef—contains fully 30 percent fat (as much as sausage!). It's often identified as chuck, but other parts may be included in the grind. This grade can be used in dishes (such as spaghetti sauce) where the meat is browned first, and the fat poured off; however, considering the loss of nearly a third of the meat's volume, its economy is moot. It can also be used in meat loaf recipes that contain a high proportion of bread crumbs (which will absorb the fat) if calories and cholesterol aren't a problem. The middle grade—often called lean ground beef, lean ground chuck, or ground round—contains about 20 percent fat, and is the normal grade used for hamburgers, meat loaf, meatballs, and more elaborate ground-beef dishes. The leanest grade—usually identified as ground sirloin or extra-lean ground beef—contains approximately 15 percent fat. Although somewhat dry when cooked, it's the dieter's favorite for hamburgers.

◼ ALL-AMERICAN HAMBURGER WITH INTERNATIONAL TOPPINGS

The debate still rages over whether hamburgers should be panfried or broiled, rounded or flattened—these issues remain emphatically a matter of personal taste, and of experimentation. Rather than being served on the traditional hamburger buns, hamburgers may be accompanied by toasted English muffins, sourdough French rolls, or whole wheat pita bread. Burgers may also be topped with any Compound Butter (see page 68); anchovy butter and butter made with Roquefort or blue cheese are especially apt.

  1¼ **pounds lean ground beef**
      Salt and freshly ground pepper, to taste
    2 **to 4 tablespoons seasoning of choice, or a combination of the following: Worcestershire sauce, steak sauce, barbecue sauce, liquid smoke flavoring, salsa**
    4 **hamburger buns, split (or other bread of choice)**
      Catsup, mayonnaise, mustard, sweet pickle relish (as desired)
    1 **sweet red onion, thinly sliced**
    1 **ripe tomato, sliced**
      Pickles, thinly sliced (optional)
      Shredded lettuce (optional)

1. Preheat broiler according to manufacturer's directions. As broiler heats, season meat with salt and pepper, and mix in any of the other suggested seasonings, if desired. Shape into 4 patties. (For thin hamburgers, place patties between 2 sheets of waxed paper and flatten with a rolling pin.)

2. Place patties on a lightly greased rack of broiler pan and broil 4 inches from heat until desired doneness is reached. The timing will vary with the thickness of the hamburgers. See BROIL, Timetable for Broiling Meat, for approximate broiling times.

3. During the last 3 minutes of cooking, place buns, cut side up, on rack with burgers to brown.

4. Spread hamburger buns with condiments of choice. Place burger on lower half of bun, and top with onion, then tomato, then pickle slices and lettuce, if desired.

Serves 4.

Avocado Bacon Burger   Gently fry 4 slices bacon until crisp, pouring off fat as it accumulates. Set cooked pieces aside to drain on paper towels. While burgers cook, peel, pit, and slice 1 small avocado and dribble a little fresh lime or lemon juice on slices. Top each burger with one slice of onion (if desired), one of bacon, one of tomato, and several slices of avocado.

Cheeseburger   Proceed as above, but during the last 1½ minutes of cooking, place a ¼-inch-thick slice of cheese (Cheddar, Monterey jack, or Swiss) on top half of each bun as it toasts under broiler; broil until cheese bubbles and melts. Do not let cheese burn.

Fast-Food Burger Dressing   Vigorously stir together 3 tablespoons catsup with 3 tablespoons mayonnaise. Stir in 1 tablespoon, or to taste, sweet pickle relish. Dress buns with catsup mixture. Top burger or cheeseburger with slices of sweet onion and tomato, and shredded lettuce.

Guacamole Burger   Peel, pit, and mash 1 small avocado (about 1 cup mashed flesh). Combine avocado with 1 small tomato, chopped, or ¼ cup Mexican salsa; 1 tablespoon fresh lime (or lemon) juice; 1 tablespoon grated onion; and salt, pepper, and cayenne pepper or bottled salsa jalapeño, to taste. Top each burger with onion and tomato, if desired, and a dollop of guacamole.

Little Italy Burger   In a medium frying pan, heat 1 tablespoon olive oil. Add one-half red and one-half green bell pepper, sliced; 1 medium red onion, sliced; and 2 cloves of garlic, minced. Sauté until limp. Stir in ½ teaspoon dried oregano leaves, crumbled, and 1 tablespoon minced parsley. Divide the mixture over 4 burgers.

Mushroom Cheeseburger   In a medium frying pan, melt 1 tablespoon butter. Add ¼ pound mushrooms, sliced; 2 cloves of garlic, minced; and 1 shallot, minced. Sauté until mushrooms have yielded liquid and are turning brown at the edges. Prepare broiled cheeseburgers and top each burger with the mushrooms.

Pan-fried Hamburger   Barely grease a large, heavy skillet (such as cast-iron) with a little vegetable oil. Heat empty skillet over a high flame until it begins to smoke. Add patties and sear on one side; whether thick or thin, use timing guidelines for 1-inch patties (see page 63). Turn and sear the other side. For medium or well-done hamburgers, lower heat to moderate after 2 minutes, and continue cooking until hamburger is cooked as desired. While hamburger cooks, lightly toast buns in toaster.

Philly Cheeseburger   Substitute split French rolls for buns. Make the Little Italy Burger dressing (see above). Follow directions for Cheeseburger (see above), topping the upper half of each roll with 2 slices of provolone cheese. Dress the lower half of the roll with sweet pickle relish, add hamburger, and top burger with Little Italy Burger dressing, and cover with the half of the roll with the melted cheese.

Ranchero Burger   Top each of 4 slices French bread with 2 slices Monterey jack cheese; broil 1 minute. Top cheese with a slice of tomato, a cooked burger, a fried or poached egg, and sliced ripe olives or chopped chives. Cover each sandwich with a second slice of bread. For more zest, add chopped chiles or salsa.

Russian Burger   On each broiled hamburger place 1 tablespoon sour cream or yogurt. Top each with 2 teaspoons red, black, or golden caviar. Sprinkle chopped green onions or chives over caviar. May be served open-faced on slices of dark rye bread.

CARPACCIO

To make the Italian dish carpaccio, lean raw beef is sliced and pounded tissue-thin, then dressed with Parmesan and a piquant vinaigrette. To make slicing easier, put meat in freezer until it is very cold but not frozen.

> 1½ pounds beef tenderloin, trimmed of all fat
> 1½ cups peeled, seeded, and chopped fresh tomato
> ½ cup minced Italian parsley
> ¼ cup minced fresh oregano
> ¼ cup minced fresh basil
> ⅓ cup fresh lemon juice
> 3 to 4 tablespoons olive oil
> 3 tablespoons freshly grated Parmesan cheese
>   Salt and freshly ground pepper
> 2 tablespoons snipped fresh chives (optional)

1. Cut beef into 10 thin slices, approximately 2½ ounces each. Put each slice between two sheets of plastic wrap or waxed paper and pound with a mallet or the bottom of a skillet until beef is paper-thin.

2. In a bowl combine tomatoes, parsley, oregano, basil, and 1 tablespoon each of lemon juice and olive oil. Marinate at room temperature for at least 10 minutes or up to 1 hour.

3. To serve, arrange tenderloin slices on individual plates or large platters. Scatter tomatoes around them. Drizzle with remaining olive oil and lemon juice. Dust with Parmesan. Sprinkle salt and pepper over all and garnish with chives, if used.

Serves 10.

CORNED-BEEF HASH

Hash means a hodgepodge or jumble; in cooking it describes chopped food, usually meat with potatoes, which is browned in a skillet until crusty. It's a delicious way to use leftover cooked meat—here you use corned beef, but roast beef works well also. Allow a good 30 to 40 minutes to cook hash, since it must crust on the bottom twice before a final crust forms and the hash is turned out onto a platter. Chop meat and potatoes coarsely; if you use a food processor, don't chop too fine.

> 2 to 3 cups chopped cooked corned beef
> 2 to 3 cups chopped boiled potatoes
> 1 onion, finely chopped
> ¼ teaspoon freshly ground pepper
> 4 tablespoons butter or shortening
> ⅓ cup whipping cream

1. In a large bowl, mix beef, potatoes, onion, and pepper. In a 10-inch skillet (preferably well-seasoned cast-iron) over medium-low heat, melt butter. Spread meat mixture evenly over the bottom, forming a thick cake. Press down firmly all over with the back of a spatula. Cook about 10 minutes, giving pan a sharp jerk now and then to prevent sticking.

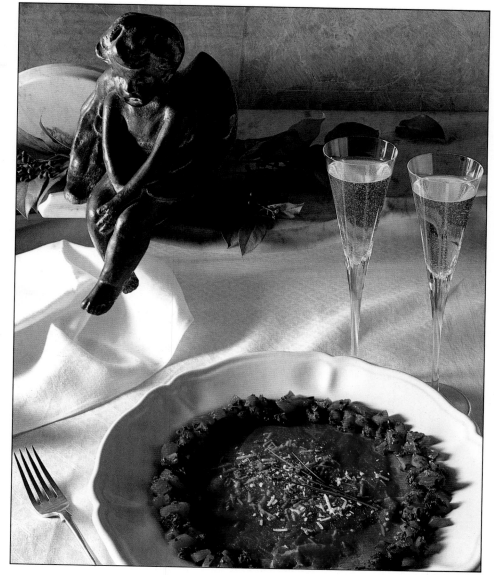

2. Scrape all over bottom of pan with a spatula to loosen the crust, and stir it into the hash. Again press firmly all over to make a flat cake, and cook 10 minutes more, giving pan a sharp jerk now and then to prevent sticking.

3. Pour cream over hash, then scrape up crust again and stir to incorporate cream. Flatten hash with a spatula and cook another 10 minutes, giving pan a few sharp jerks now and then to keep hash from sticking.

4. To serve, you may cut into wedges, flipping each piece over on a plate, crusted side up. Or, you may unmold the whole hash by flipping it from the skillet onto a platter. While this looks impressive, remember the skillet is hot and heavy, and you must work fast, so unmolding is a little tricky. It is easier if you get a friend to help you.

Serves 4 to 6.

Red-Flannel Hash   Add 2 cups diced cooked beets to the hash mixture and fry as directed.

Created at Harry's Bar in Venice, Carpaccio is an easy and elegant first course of thin-sliced beef. Here, it is ringed with herbed tomatoes and garnished with coarsely grated Parmesan cheese.

Fondue is not just party food. It makes a novel supper when served with a salad or vegetable casserole and warm French bread. Complement the meat with one or more dipping sauces.

2. To eat, skewer meat with a fondue fork or bamboo skewer, dip into hot oil for 1 to 3 minutes (depending on the degree of doneness desired), and then dip into selected sauce.

Serves 4.

Dijon Mayonnaise Dipping Sauce Whisk 2 tablespoons Dijon mustard into ¼ cup homemade mayonnaise (see page 519).

Horseradish–Sour Cream Dipping Sauce Stir ¼ cup prepared horseradish into 1 cup sour cream.

Piquant Parsley Dipping Sauce Combine ½ cup olive oil, 2 tablespoons red wine vinegar, 1 tablespoon capers, 1 teaspoon anchovy paste, 1 bunch parsley, finely chopped, and 1 clove of garlic, finely chopped.

■ BEEF AND MUSHROOM PIROSHKI

The unusual, luscious filling of these savory Russian turnovers is especially designed to restore moisture to cooked beef. They can also be made with raw lean ground beef, if desired. The dough, too, is unusual, but not difficult to work with. As with nearly all pastries and turnovers, filled, unbaked piroshkis may be frozen until ready to use, but they shouldn't stand for too long at room temperature lest the dough grow soggy.

>   4 **tablespoons butter**
>   3 **medium onions, minced (about 3 cups)**
>   ¼ **pound mushrooms, wiped clean and**
>   **chopped in fine dice**
> 1½ **cups finely diced rare roast beef** *or*
>   **¾ pound lean ground beef**
>   1 **teaspoon salt**
>   ½ **teaspoon freshly ground pepper**
>   ¼ **cup sour cream, at room temperature**
>   2 **hard-cooked eggs, chopped fine**
>   ¼ **cup finely minced fresh dill** *or*
>   **2 tablespoons dried dill, crumbled**
>   1 **egg, lightly beaten with 3 tablespoons water**

Sour Cream Pastry

> 1¾ **cups flour**
>   ½ **teaspoon salt**
>   ½ **teaspoon baking powder**
>   4 **tablespoons butter, chilled and cut**
>   **into small pieces**
>   1 **egg**
>   ½ **cup sour cream**

1. Prepare and chill pastry dough.

2. In a large skillet, melt butter. Add onions and sauté, stirring over moderate heat, until wilted. Add mushrooms, and continue stirring until lightly browned. If using raw ground beef, add it to skillet and sauté, stirring and breaking up with a fork, until it loses its redness.

■ BEEF FONDUE

Fondue pots for cooking meat are traditionally made of thin metal. The pot is placed over an alcohol burner or candle to maintain the temperature of the oil. The Mongolian hot pot is similar, although there the cooking liquid is stock. Meat for fondue is seared in hot oil; therefore it requires a tender cut that is best cooked rare. Generally, serve approximately ½ pound meat per person.

> 2¼ **cups vegetable oil**
> 1½ **tablespoons red wine vinegar**
>   ½ **teaspoon salt**
>   ¼ **teaspoon freshly ground pepper**
>   2 **pounds top round of beef, cut in 1-inch cubes**

1. In a large bowl mix ¼ cup of the oil, the vinegar, salt, and pepper; toss with beef. Place remaining oil in a 2-quart fondue pot or saucepan. Heat oil on stove to approximately 360° F. If using range top, transfer to fondue pot over alcohol or canned heat burner; place at the table. Arrange meat and dipping sauces (see below) around fondue pot.

3. Remove from heat, stir in roast beef, if used, salt, pepper, sour cream, chopped eggs, and dill; cool.

4. Preheat oven to 400°F. On a floured surface, roll out pastry to a large, very thin sheet. Using a 4-inch cookie cutter, cut pastry into rounds. (For larger piroshki, called pirogi, mark dough with an 8-inch pie plate and cut with a knife. Double quantity of filling for each pirogi.) Gather trims into a ball, wrap, and chill.

5. Dough shrinks after cutting; reroll each round. Place 1½ to 2 tablespoons of filling (for small piroshki) on half the circle of dough. Brush rim of circle with egg-water mixture, fold dough over to enclose filling, and seal by squeezing edges with fingers or by pressing with tines of a fork. Brush top with egg mixture. Repeat until all pastry circles have been filled. Roll out chilled dough trims, cut another set of rounds, and fill.

6. Bake on a lightly greased baking sheet 25 minutes (35 minutes for large piroshki). Serve immediately.

Makes about 18 small or 8 large piroshkis.

Sour Cream Pastry

1. *To make in food processor:* Mix all ingredients until blended thoroughly. *To make by hand:* Mix together flour, salt, and baking powder. Cut in butter until mixture forms a coarse meal. Blend in eggs and sour cream.

2. Set mixture on a lightly floured board or a sheet of waxed paper. Gather together and knead just until smooth and elastic. Flatten into a pancake, wrap in plastic wrap, and chill at least 2 hours, or overnight.

Recipes and Related Information

Beef Soup With Noodles, 390; Beef Soup au Pistou, 26; Beef Stock, 560; Beef With Asparagus, 558; Classic Beef Consommé With Vegetable Julienne and Madeira, 562; Fajitas, 292; Green Onions in Silky Beef, 285; Joe's Special, 203; Lasagne With Meat Sauce, 414; Moussaka, 209; Pinto Bean Chili, 429; Rolled Beef With Prosciutto, 57; Santa Maria Barbecued Beef, 291; Sautéed Beef Steaks Marchand de Vin, 533; Singapore Satay, 292; Stuffed Green Peppers Mexicana, 426.

BEET

The beet is a root vegetable that thrives in cool climates. The common table beet is bulb-shaped with paper-thin, dark skin, dense, wine-red flesh, and edible green leaves with red veins and stems. Other, less common table varieties have golden or white flesh. A special horticultural variety is grown for its leafy tops rather than the swollen root. Yet another variety, the sugar beet, is rarely eaten, but is processed for sugar.

Use Cooked, peeled beets are eaten hot or cold, whole, or cut in pieces. They are served cold as a salad or salad garnish, or hot as a side dish with butter or a sweet-and-sour sauce. Beets may be pickled or made into relish. They are the principal ingredient in borscht, served hot or cold. Beet greens, when young and tender, may be added raw to a salad. Older greens must be cooked and may then be eaten cold, with lemon and oil, or hot, with butter or oil. Besides being delicious, the greens are an excellent source of vitamin A, calcium, and iron. They should not be discarded unless they are ragged or wilted.

Availability Beets are sold fresh, canned and pickled. Fresh beets are available all year, but peak months are June through October.

Selection Choose smooth, firm beet roots; small ones are generally sweeter. If green tops are still attached, they should look fresh, not wilted.

Storage Beets may be stored up to six months in a cool root cellar or storage shed; cut green tops off one inch above the root. Refrigerate for up to one month. Store greens in plastic bags in the refrigerator for three to five days; wash just before using.

Preparation *Roots:* Cut off beet greens 1 inch above crown. Scrub roots gently; do not break skin.

Greens: Wash greens well and dry. Young, tender leaves may be eaten raw as a salad. For older greens, separate stems from leaves.

Cooking See BAKE, BOIL, SAUTE (GREENS), STEAM.

■ HARVARD BEETS

The natural sweetness of the beets may require adjusting the amount of vinegar in the recipe to suit individual taste.

> 2 **bunches beets (about 1 lb each)**
> 3 **tablespoons sugar**
> ¼ **cup cold water**
> 2 **teaspoons cornstarch**
> 5 **tablespoons apple cider vinegar**
> **Juice and grated rind of 1 medium orange**
> 1 **tablespoon unsalted butter**
> **Salt and freshly ground pepper, to taste**

1. Remove stems from beets, leaving about ½ inch. In a 3-quart saucepan place beets and cover with water. Bring to a boil, reduce heat, and simmer until beets are easily pierced with a knife (approximately 30 minutes, depending on size of beets). Drain in a colander and cool for about 20 minutes. Trim stems and root tip from each beet and slip off skins. Slice beets ¼ inch thick.

2. In the same saucepan combine sugar, the cold water, cornstarch, vinegar, orange juice, and rind. Cook over low heat, stirring constantly until mixture is clear and thickened (4 to 5 minutes). Add sliced beets and butter. Stir to coat beets. Cook until hot (6 to 8 minutes). Season to taste with salt and pepper.

Serves 4 to 6.

Beets with their greens and young turnips make a distinctive winter salad. Serve as a first course before a hearty roast.

■ WINTER SALAD OF BEETS AND TURNIPS

Beet greens are mixed with beets and turnips for a hearty first course. Note that beets must bake for 1½ hours.

- **3 or 4 medium beets with greens attached**
- **7 or 8 small turnips**
- **2 tablespoons** *each* **fresh lemon juice and red wine vinegar**
- **1 tablespoon Dijon mustard**
- **½ tablespoon anchovy paste**
- **½ cup plus 2 tablespoons olive oil**
- **3 tablespoons freshly grated Parmesan cheese**
  Salt and freshly ground pepper, to taste
- **½ head** *each* **green-leaf and romaine lettuce, washed and dried**
- **2 tablespoons minced parsley**

1. Preheat oven to 375° F. Remove beet greens and stems and set aside. Wash beets and put them in an oven-proof bowl or baking dish. Add water to come halfway up sides of beets, then cover tightly with a lid or aluminum foil and bake until beets can be easily pierced with a knife (about 1½ hours). Remove from oven and let cool. While beets are still warm, peel them and slice into rounds, then into thin matchsticks.

2. Wash beet stems and greens, then separate stems from greens. Bring a large pot of salted water to a boil and blanch greens for 30 seconds. Transfer greens

with a slotted spoon to a bowl of ice water. Drain and pat thoroughly dry. Boil stems 1 minute in same water; transfer to ice water and, when cool, drain and dry them. Coarsely chop both beet greens and stems.

3. In a large bowl, combine lemon juice, vinegar, mustard, and anchovy paste. Whisk in the ½ cup olive oil. Stir in 1 tablespoon of the Parmesan. Add beet greens and stems and marinate 15 minutes.

4. Bring another large pot of salted water to a boil. Wash turnips, then boil until tender. Very small turnips may take only 10 minutes, larger turnips up to 45 minutes. Drain and dry. While still warm, peel turnips, slice into rounds, then into thin matchsticks. Very small turnips may be left whole or halved.

5. Add beets, turnips, and remaining 2 tablespoons oil to marinating beet greens; let marinate 20 minutes. Add salt and pepper to taste. Line a serving platter with green-leaf and romaine leaves. Top with salad. Combine remaining Parmesan and parsley and sprinkle over salad.

Serves 4.

Recipes and Related Information
Budapest Borscht, 76; Red-Flannel Hash, 45.

BELGIAN ENDIVE

Also known as French endive, or Belgian or witloof chicory, Belgian endive is the blanched shoots of a chicory root. To produce blanched (white) shoots, the roots are dug up and removed to a cool, darkened location or to forcing beds where they are covered with sand. The resulting shoots, harvested when 4 to 6 inches long and about 1½ inches wide, are made of compact, tightly furled, white leaves shading to yellow or light green tips.

Use   Belgian endive is eaten raw as a salad green or is braised in butter or cream sauce as a vegetable side dish. Braised with ham slices and cream sauce, it is a main course. Belgian endive leaves are perfect edible containers for cheese spreads or all kinds of hors d'oeuvres.

Availability   Fresh Belgian endive is sold in late fall and winter.

Selection   Choose bright white Belgian endive heads that are firm and unblemished.

Storage   Keep endive in a plastic bag in the refrigerator. Use within three or four days.

Preparation   Cut away bitter core with a knife. Rinse with cold running water. To braise, cook heads whole in butter in a covered pot, adding lemon juice to prevent discoloration. For salads, use raw leaves whole or cut into rings or strips.

Cooking   See BOIL, BRAISE.

◼ BRAISED BELGIAN ENDIVE

Small heads of lettuce can also be braised.

    8 small Belgian endives
    3 tablespoons unsalted butter
    ½ cup Chicken Stock (see page 560)
       Juice of 1 lemon
    2 tablespoons parsley, minced
       Pinch sugar

1. Trim dry ends from endive. Remove any brown or shriveled leaves. In a heavy-bottomed, 10-inch skillet, place endives, butter, stock, lemon juice, parsley, and sugar.

2. Simmer over medium heat 8 minutes; turn and simmer 7 minutes more. Endive will be tender when pierced with a knife.

Serves 4.

BIND, TO

To cause ingredients to thicken and form a cohesive mass by adding another ingredient, called the binding agent. For example, Hollandaise sauce and mayonnaise are bound by egg yolks, puddings by tapioca, Bavarian cream by gelatin, some cream soups by potato, and many sauces, soups, and stews by flour, cornstarch, crackers, or bread crumbs.

BISCUIT

A biscuit is a quick bread made with a soft dough (3 parts flour to 1 part liquid), rather than the fairly moist batter used for quick loaf breads and muffins.

The ideal biscuit is uniform in shape, with straight sides and a level top, and has doubled its height during baking. The crust is crisp, tender, and golden brown, with lighter sides. The crumb is generally creamy white and fine grained, and pulls off in flaky sheets.

When shaping biscuits, use a floured, sharp-edged cutter or knife and cut by pressing downward. A dull edge will pinch top and bottom together, and the biscuits won't rise properly. Twisting the cutter produces lopsided biscuits.

Drop biscuit dough, too sticky to roll, is spooned directly onto an ungreased baking sheet. For dumplings, dough is dropped into boiling water or stock, or on a simmering stew, and gently steamed. Deep-dish fruit cobblers use either rolled or dropped biscuit dough for a top crust.

Biscuits are at their best served hot from the oven. If they must be reheated, wrap them in aluminum foil and heat in a 350° F oven for 10 minutes. To freeze, let cool and protect with freezer wrap, or tray-freeze: Set biscuits on a baking sheet, freeze just until firm, then package in plastic freezer bags labeled with the date. Frozen biscuits will keep for two to three months. Thaw in wrapping at room temperature; if wrapped in aluminum foil, place in a low oven.

◼ BAKING POWDER BISCUITS

Although biscuits are traditionally shaped with a round biscuit cutter, the dough can also be cut with a knife into squares, rectangles, or diamonds. Whichever tool you use, flour the cutting edge so the dough will release easier.

    2 cups flour
    4 teaspoons baking powder
    ½ to 1 teaspoon salt, to taste
    6 tablespoons solid vegetable shortening
    ¾ cup milk
       Flour or beaten egg, for topping (optional)

1. Preheat oven to 425° F. Butter and flour a baking sheet or line with baking parchment.

2. Mix flour, baking powder, and salt; then sift into a medium bowl. With a pastry blender or with fingertips, cut vegetable shortening into dry ingredients until mixture is the consistency of fine crumbs. Pour in milk all at once and stir to mix. As soon as mixture holds together, turn out onto a floured work surface and knead lightly.

3. Roll or pat dough to a thickness of ½ to ¾ inch (depending on use); cut into 2½-inch rounds with a floured cutter.

4. For crustier biscuits place rounds about 1 inch apart on prepared baking sheet. For softer sides set touching or ¼ inch apart. Finish with a dusting of flour (for a soft surface) or brush with a beaten egg for a shiny surface. Bake until golden brown (12 to 15 minutes). Biscuits are best served hot from the oven.

Makes about 16 biscuits.

Drop Biscuits Prepare as for Baking Powder Biscuits with these changes: Increase shortening to ½ cup and milk to 1 cup. For pebbly biscuits, scoop out a tablespoon (or more) of dough with a floured spoon, drop batter onto a baking sheet, leaving a few inches between each biscuit, and dust each with flour. For a smoother surface, scoop out batter with floured hands, roll lightly between hands to the size and shape of an egg, dip all sides in flour, and place on baking sheet; do not crowd. Bake until puffed and golden brown (10 to 12 minutes).

Cheese Biscuits Add 1 teaspoon dry mustard to dry ingredients. After fat has been cut in, add ½ cup grated Cheddar or Swiss cheese and ¼ cup freshly grated Parmesan cheese and combine.

Herb Biscuits Add 1½ teaspoons crushed dried dill or other herb and 1 teaspoon freshly ground pepper to dry ingredients.

TIPS

MIXING BISCUIT DOUGH

When mixing the dough be gentle and work quickly, or the biscuits will be tough. On the other hand, don't undermix the dough. Kneading further distributes the leaven and develops the gluten in the flour just enough to support the biscuit as it rises. Undermanipulated biscuits are squatty and will have yellow spots in the crumb and brown spots on the crust—the result of undissolved or poorly distributed leaven. With experience you will sense when the dough is ready.

▣ BLUEBERRY COFFEE CAKE

Dust confectioners' sugar over this almond-crusted fresh blueberry cake to dramatize its luscious appearance.

¼ **cup** *each* **sliced almonds and firmly packed brown sugar**
1½ **cups flour**
¾ **cup granulated sugar**
1 **tablespoon baking powder**
½ **teaspoon salt**
¼ **teaspoon freshly grated nutmeg**
⅓ **cup butter**
1 **cup fresh blueberries**
1 **egg**
½ **cup milk**
1 **teaspoon vanilla extract**
  Confectioners' sugar, for dusting

1. Preheat oven to 350° F. Generously grease a 9-inch tube pan with a capacity of 6 to 7 cups. Combine almonds and brown sugar; sprinkle mixture in pan; set aside.

2. In a large bowl mix flour, granulated sugar, baking powder, salt, and nutmeg; cut in butter until mixture resembles coarse crumbs. Lightly stir in blueberries.

3. In a small bowl beat egg lightly with milk and vanilla. Stir milk mixture into blueberry mixture just until combined. Spread batter gently in prepared pan.

4. Bake until coffee cake is well browned and a long skewer inserted in thickest part comes out clean (45 minutes to 1 hour).

5. Let stand in pan for about 5 minutes, loosen edges, and invert onto a serving plate. Serve warm or at room temperature, dusted with confectioners' sugar.

Serves 6 to 8.

Recipes and Related Information
Blueberry Buttermilk Pancakes, 600; Blueberry Muffins, 375; Fruit Cobbler, 51.

BOIL, TO

The process of heating a liquid to the boiling point (212° F at sea level). When it reaches the boiling point, all of the liquid will be in motion, with bubbles constantly rising and breaking on the surface.

Once water reaches 212° F, its temperature won't increase, but it will be more agitated and will evaporate faster. The following terms should help you create a type of boil by identifying the appearance of the surface of the water.

Shake   Surface begins to shake, but bubbles have not yet appeared (for stocks).

Smile   Small bubbles begin to pop up on the surface (for delicate sauces, poaching, stocks).

Simmer   A continuous stream of small bubbles slowly rises to the surface (for slow cooking; soups, stews).

Moderate Boil   Water surface is agitated but not rolling on top of itself (for most cooking).

Rolling Boil   A great deal of turbulence is produced as bubbles form rapidly and rise to the surface, but break before reaching the surface (for green vegetables, pasta, reducing liquids).

BOILING VEGETABLES

An American cookbook from the turn of the century directed that string beans (cut in pieces) needed to boil one to three hours to tenderize. Few of us have probably been subjected to three-hour beans, but vegetables boiled to a dull, mushy, nutrient-depleted mass most likely were typical fare as we grew up. Today's emphasis on fresh, quality ingredients has resulted in a greater understanding of how to cook these foods to preserve their appearance, flavor, and nutrition.

Boiling is one of the principal cooking techniques for fresh vegetables. There are two approaches: using a large amount of water or using very little (usually ½ to 1 inch or enough water to cover). Green vegetables cooked uncovered in a pot full of water will keep their color better than if boiled in a small amount of liquid, but can lose important nutrients. When cooked in 1 or 2 inches of water in a covered pan, these vegetables retain nutrients but can turn dull and unappealing.

The challenge is to prepare vegetables so that nutrients are conserved and visual appeal maintained; most recipes will provide specific cooking instructions. In general, to avoid loss of nutrients, cook as briefly as possible in a small amount of water. To hold color, add a little salt to the water and begin cooking uncovered to allow gases that have a negative effect on color to escape, then finish in a covered pan; or lift cover several times during cooking to release gases. Bring water to a boil first, then add vegetables; quickly return to a boil and cover. Remember that vegetables cut in pieces of similar size will cook more evenly. To preserve the color of green vegetables, it's best to cook them uncovered in a large amount of boiling, salted water. Bring salted water to a boil and add vegetables. Stir vegetables until water returns to a boil, then let boil until done. Drain immediately and serve.

Cooking time depends upon freshness and maturity of vegetables and whether they are whole or cut up, and is usually measured from the point at which water returns to a boil after vegetables have been added. As a measure of comparison, broccoli spears will boil tender-crisp in about 7 to 10 minutes; florets need only 3 to 5 minutes to be ready. A head of cauliflower should cook 15 to 20 minutes; florets 5 to 10 minutes; slices only 3 to 5 minutes.

BONE, TO

A basic preparation technique used to separate the flesh of meat, poultry, and fish from the bones, and to trim away sinews, gristle, and fat in order to make eating easier and more enjoyable. All cooks, even those who prefer to have the butcher perform this service for them, should learn how to bone certain cuts, such as chicken breasts. Whole and bone-in poultry and other meats are less expensive per pound and will allow the cook last-minute flexibility when deciding what to prepare. Boned breasts are well suited to poaching, sautéing, and frying. Boneless legs and thighs are elegant when served with a savory stuffing. See FISH, for a discussion of filleting. See DISJOINT for a description of cutting up a whole chicken.

You will bone with less damage to the piece of meat if you use your hands to learn, by feel, the anatomy of the animal. That way you will get to know where the bones and joints are and then be able to cut in order to expose them. These preliminary cuts are exploratory ones that show you where subsequent cuts should be made. Use a sharp knife and a cutting board. Remember to wash the preparation surface thoroughly before and after it comes in contact with raw poultry.

BONING A CHICKEN BREAST

For a whole breast, remove skin and place breast skin side down. With tip of knife cut through membrane covering breastbone. Pick up breast with both hands and press back on ribs to break them away from breastbone, which will pop out. Pull out breastbone, including cartilage.

Cut away ribs by using tip of knife to make shallow cuts as close to rib bones as possible. Or, slip fingers between ribs and meat and work meat free from bones. Work wishbone free with fingers. Split breast in half, removing tough membranes lying along breastbone.

Locate white tendon on smaller muscle of each breast half. Place tendon side down on work surface and hold end with fingernail. With knife held vertically, scrape from end of tendon inward, removing meat from tendon. Trim into neat fillet shape.

BONING A CHICKEN LEG AND THIGH

Do not separate leg and thigh. With boning knife, cut along thigh bone, to expose it, and then down drumstick.

With hand, push meat away from bone. Then hold by exposed end of thigh bone so that leg and thigh hang down. Cut meat away from bone by making little cuts around the bone. Continue around knee joint to free leg bone.

If a larger piece of meat is desired, pound to flatten before stuffing. To separate into boneless leg and thigh, cut through at point where thigh and leg bone are joined.

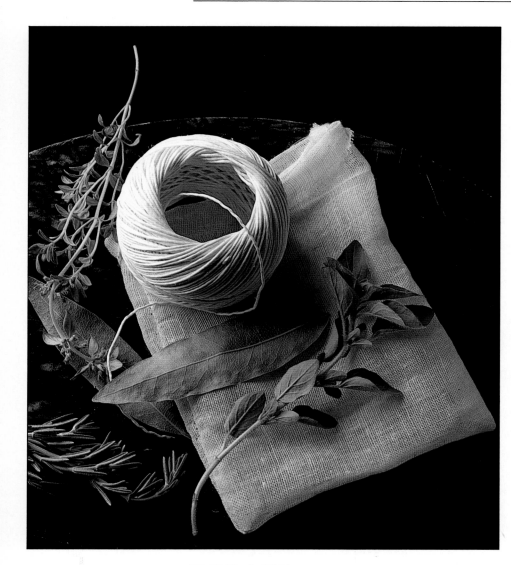

Bouquet garni is a classic seasoning mixture made of fresh herbs that are tied in a bundle or wrapped in cheesecloth. The herbs will vary depending on usage and the cook's preference.

BORAGE

A hardy, highly ornamental, annual herb native to southern Europe and North Africa, borage has a stout stem, bristly gray-green leaves, and delicate, star-shaped, blue-violet flowers. The leaves have a cucumberlike flavor.

Use   Young borage leaves may be eaten raw as a salad or added to salads. Older leaves may be cooked and served like spinach. Fresh borage flowers make a colorful garnish for salads or iced drinks; dried borage flowers may be added to potpourri; candied flowers are used to decorate cakes and desserts.

Availability   Found in specialty markets from May through October.

Selection   Choose fresh leaves that are not limp and do not show any signs of decay.

Storage   Keep leaves and flowers loosely in plastic bags in the refrigerator. Use within a couple of days.

BOUQUET GARNI

A bundle of aromatic herbs and vegetables, bouquet garni is used to flavor soups, stocks, poaching liquids, stews, and braised dishes. It is always removed after cooking. The herbs are tied together with a string or gathered together in a cheesecloth bag to facilitate their retrieval from the finished dish. Traditional bouquet garni herbs include bay leaf, thyme, and parsley, although other herbs and vegetables such as tarragon, chervil, peppercorns, celery, and leeks may be included to enhance the flavor of a particular dish.

For a small bouquet garni, tie together with string three sprigs fresh parsley, two sprigs fresh thyme, and one bay leaf. If using dried or loose herbs, wrap all ingredients in a square of cheesecloth and tie with a string.

Recipes and Related Information
Bay, 29; Cheesecloth, 119; Herb, 299; Parsley, 406; Stock and Soup, 558; Thyme, 578.

BOWL CHOPPER

The bowl chopper is easy to recognize. It has a single stainless steel blade which is curved along the bottom at the cutting edge, and an easy-to-grip wooden knob as the handle. It chops and minces like a chef's knife, food processor, or electric minichopper, and is efficient for small tasks—a few tablespoons of garlic, herbs, or onion. Although it can be bought separately, most often it is paired with a small hardwood bowl whose curve matches the curve of the chopping blade.

A bowl chopper has homey appeal and is also practical. The bowl keeps the food contained so that it doesn't hop around when hit by the blade. Consider buying a chopper and matching bowl if you cook for one or two persons most of the time.

Select a blade that fits its bowl, or it won't be as effective. After each use, rinse the chopper in warm, sudsy water and wipe dry. Don't wash bowl; wipe away remaining food. Periodically treat wood with mineral oil. To protect blade, store chopper in bowl.

A *mezzaluna* is a large, double-handled, curved chopper, used on a flat chopping surface. A more serious piece of kitchen equipment than the bowl chopper, it has been referred to as the Italian chef's knife.

Recipes and Related Information
Food Processor, 240; Knife, 328.

BRAISE, TO

Braising is a combination of cooking methods designed to render tough cuts of meat and fibrous vegetables succulent and tender. Usually, food is first sautéed or browned for color and flavor, then cooked slowly in a small amount of liquid in an airtight pot. This creates a moist, steamy cooking environment that gently breaks down hard-to-chew connective tissue and muscle and releases the food's own juices. The browned meat is often set on a bed of chopped aromatic vegetables (*mirepoix*), which later may be puréed, mixed with pan juices, and used as a sauce. About ¼ to ½ inch of liquid—water, stock, wine, hard cider, tomato purée—is added to the bottom of the pot, which is tightly covered to prevent evaporation. Cooking is completed either on top of the stove or in the oven. Stewing is almost identical to braising, but uses smaller pieces of meat and requires more liquid.

Any casserole with a tight-fitting lid is suitable for braising. It is important that the vessel be of a material that conducts heat evenly and efficiently to prevent scorching and hot spots. The pot should not be much larger than the meat plus its liquid, so that the heat will be directed to the meat rather than the empty spaces.

The best foods for braising are shoulder cuts of beef (often called chuck), lamb, veal, and pork. Other good cuts are beef brisket, beef round, beef rump, veal shanks, and lamb shanks. Boneless cuts that are rolled and tied in a neat cylinder are ideal for braising because they are easy to carve. Whole chickens and Rock Cornish game hens are also delicious when braised.

BRAISING VEGETABLES

Although vegetables are commonly part of a meat or poultry braise for their wonderful flavor, they are also braised alone and served as a side dish. Root vegetables and leafy greens are superb when braised. Butter, or butter with some water, stock, or wine, plus seasonings, is a typical mixture for braising vegetables. Sugar is frequently added for flavor and to help develop a shiny syrup. Browning vegetables adds to their taste, but isn't always called for in many braised vegetable recipes. Often the first step is to toss vegetable pieces briefly in hot oil or melted butter; more liquid is then added and the vegetables cooked until tender. Alternatively, after slowly cooking in a small amount of liquid just until tender, vegetables can be finished in butter and seasonings for a short period of time until coated. Sometimes all ingredients are added at once.

Cooking times depend upon the size and shape of vegetables, their freshness, and maturity. As a rough guideline and comparison for other vegetables, celery hearts should braise for 10 to 15 minutes; Belgian endive needs about 15 to 20 minutes; blanch whole leeks to tenderize, then braise anywhere from 15 to 25 minutes, depending upon thickness; braise halved leeks 10 to 15 minutes without blanching (they will separate if precooked); braise carrots until tender and glazed with the reduced cooking liquid, anywhere from 8 to 15 minutes depending upon size of the pieces; braise greens just until wilted along with some sautéed onions and a small amount of liquid.

■ ROLLED BEEF WITH PROSCIUTTO

Braciole is the Italian word for boneless meat cutlets, which are almost invariably stuffed, rolled, and tied. Here, in a Roman version, the cutlets are wrapped around a filling of prosciutto and celery, then gently braised with tomatoes and aromatic Italian mushrooms.

> 1 pound bottom round of beef
> 1½ ounces dried porcini mushrooms
> ⅓ pound prosciutto, sliced paper-thin
> 1 cup coarsely chopped celery leaves
> 3 to 4 tablespoons olive oil
> 1 tablespoon minced garlic
> 1 cup minced onion
> 2 cups peeled, seeded, and diced tomatoes, fresh or canned
> Salt and freshly ground pepper, to taste

1. Have butcher slice meat into eight 2-ounce slices, or freeze it briefly and slice it yourself with a sharp knife. Place slices between 2 sheets of lightly oiled waxed paper and pound with a mallet or bottom of a skillet until they are paper-thin. Soak *porcini* mushrooms in hot water to cover for 1 hour.

2. Place beef slices on a flat surface. Divide prosciutto slices evenly among them and sprinkle chopped celery leaves over prosciutto. Roll each beef slice into a neat bundle and tie securely with kitchen string.

3. Heat 3 tablespoons oil in a heavy skillet over medium-high heat until a light haze forms. Brown beef rolls on all sides, in batches if necessary, then set aside. If necessary, add a little more oil to coat surface of pan, then add garlic and onion and sauté over moderate heat until softened but not browned.

4. With a slotted spoon, remove mushrooms from soaking liquid and squeeze dry. Strain liquid through cheesecloth to remove any grit or sand. Add mushrooms, tomatoes, and reserved soaking liquid to skillet. Season with salt and pepper to taste. Return meat to skillet and bring sauce to a simmer. Cover, reduce heat to maintain a slow simmer, and cook 2 hours. Check meat after 1 hour, adding a little water if sauce has reduced too much. When meat is quite tender, transfer rolls to a warm serving plate, cut strings carefully with a small knife, and cover with sauce.

Serves 4.

Food Processor Version Use metal blade to process 3 to 4 cloves of garlic for 10 seconds. Cut 1 large onion into eighths and add to work bowl. Turn motor on and off 3 or 4 times. Scrape bowl and pulse 2 to 3 more times until onion is minced.

Serve Osso Buco with buttered fettuccine and a tiny spoon for scooping the soft marrow out of the veal shank bones. The hollow bone gives the dish its name.

▉ OSSO BUCO

Meaty veal shanks turn fork-tender when braised slowly with wine and vegetables, and they yield a delectable dividend: a nugget of marrow in each hollow bone (*osso buco*).

> 3 **veal shanks, each sawed into 6 to 8 pieces about 2½ inches long**
> **Salt and freshly ground pepper**
> 2 **cups flour, for dredging**
> ½ **to ¾ cup safflower oil**
> 1¼ **cups dry white wine**
> 2 **cups Brown Veal Stock or Beef Stock (see page 560) or canned stock**
> 4 **sprigs fresh thyme**
> ½ **cup parsley sprigs and stems**
> 3 **bay leaves**
> 1 **cup whole fresh basil leaves**
> 5 **tablespoons butter**
> 1½ **cups chopped onion**
> 1 **cup diced celery**
> 1 **cup diced carrots**
> 1 **tablespoon minced garlic**
> 2 **cups peeled, seeded, and chopped tomatoes**

Gremolata

> 2 **tablespoons finely minced Italian parsley**
> 1 **tablespoon grated lemon rind**
> 1 **teaspoon finely minced garlic**

1. Salt and pepper shanks well, then dredge lightly in flour and shake off excess. In a large Dutch oven over medium-high heat, heat oil. Add shanks and brown well on all sides, in batches if necessary. Transfer shanks to a plate as they are browned.

2. When all shanks have been browned, pour off excess fat, add wine to Dutch oven, and bring to a boil. With a wooden spoon, scrape up any browned bits clinging to bottom of pot. Add stock and simmer 2 minutes. If using canned beef stock, dilute with water to taste, to reduce strength and saltiness.

3. Place thyme, parsley, and bay leaves in a cheesecloth bag. Add to pot along with basil. Return shanks to pot and set aside.

4. In a large skillet over moderate heat, melt butter. Add onion, celery, carrots, and garlic, and cook until vegetables are slightly softened (about 5 minutes). Add tomatoes and simmer 5 minutes. Transfer mixture to Dutch oven, cover tightly, and bring to a simmer over moderately high heat. Reduce heat to maintain simmer and cook gently for at least 2 hours. (Dish may also be baked in a 325° F oven for 2½ to 3 hours; bring it to a simmer on top of stove first.) Check occasionally to make sure liquid has not reduced too much; add a little wine, stock, or water if necessary.

5. When meat is fork-tender, transfer shanks to a warm serving platter. Place pot briefly over high heat to reduce sauce slightly. Add Gremolata during final 30 seconds, then spoon sauce over meat.

Serves 8.

Gremolata In a small bowl combine parsley, lemon rind, and garlic; mix to blend well.

Food Processor Version Use metal blade to process 3 or 4 cloves garlic for 10 seconds. Cut 2 large onions, 2 celery stalks, and 2 medium carrots into 1-inch pieces. Add half to work bowl. Turn motor on and off 3 to 4 times to chop coarsely. Add to skillet in step 4. Repeat with remaining onion, celery, and carrot and add to skillet.

▉ GAME HENS COQ AU VIN

Classic coq au vin uses an old rooster. The tender game hens are a tasty alternative and speed the cooking time considerably.

> 2 **Rock Cornish game hens (1 to 1½ lb each), cut into serving pieces**
> **Salt and freshly ground pepper**
> ½ **cup butter**
> ¼ **cup brandy**
> 4 **cups (approximately) dry red wine**
> **Bouquet garni (3 sprigs parsley, 1 bay leaf, 1 teaspoon dried thyme, 1 teaspoon dried marjoram, wrapped in 4-in. square of cheesecloth)**
> 3 **slices (each ½ in. thick) salt pork**
> 12 **small boiling onions, peeled**
> 12 **mushroom caps**
> **Beurre manié (3 tablespoons each flour and butter kneaded together)**

1. Wash game hens and pat dry; season with salt and pepper. In a large, heavy-bottomed sauté pan over medium-high heat, melt butter. Add game hens and sauté until golden brown (about 5 minutes per side). Drain fat from pan.

2. Pour brandy over game hens and flame it. When flame dies down, add enough red wine to cover hens. Add bouquet garni and cook, covered, over medium heat until game hens are tender when pierced with a fork (about 30 minutes).

3. After 15 minutes, brown salt pork in a medium, heavy-bottomed sauté pan over medium-high heat. Add onions and sauté until a rich brown color (about 10 minutes). Add mushrooms and continue cooking until just tender (about 1 minute). Set aside.

4. When chicken is tender, remove bouquet garni. Add vegetables. Drop beurre manié into sauce and whisk to blend; cook over medium heat until sauce has thickened.

Serves 4.

■ LEEKS BRAISED WITH TASSO

This dish demonstrates a typical and flavorful use of the Cajun seasoning meat called *tasso,* which imparts a smoky tang to the leeks and adds a contrast of color. Tasso is usually made from lean pork shoulder cut into chunks. It is richly seasoned with cayenne. Smoked ham can be substituted for tasso, but it is less smoky.

   3 **medium-sized leeks**
   1 **carrot, diced**
   2 **shallots, finely chopped**
   2 **cloves garlic, minced**
  ¼ **pound tasso, finely chopped**
   2 **cups Beef Stock (see page 560)**
   2 **tablespoons butter**

Split leeks and wash thoroughly. Place in a heavy pan over medium heat with carrot, shallots, garlic, tasso, stock, and butter. Cover, reduce to simmer, and cook until leeks are tender when pierced (30 to 40 minutes). Remove to a warm serving dish and reduce liquid until it turns syrupy. Pour over leeks and serve.

Serves 4 to 6.

BRAZIL NUT

The Brazil nut is the fruit of the tall bertholettia tree, which grows wild in Paraguay and Brazil. The tree yields 3- to 4-pound pods with thick shells that must be broken open with a machete. Inside are 12 to 20 three-sided Brazil nuts, with a dark brown shell that is rough and hard and has sharp edges. The large kernel inside has a thin brown skin and ivory meat; it is oily, with a flavor reminiscent of hazelnut and coconut.

Use Shelled Brazil nuts are used in candies, cakes, and salted nut mixes. They add texture and nutty flavor to stuffings, chicken salad, and grain dishes.

Availability Whole shelled nuts are packed in cans or plastic bags, or are sold in bulk. Unshelled nuts are available in bulk.

Selection Buy as fresh as possible.

Storage Keep unshelled nuts in a cool place for up to six months. Shelled nuts go stale quickly; store them in an airtight container in the refrigerator and use within three months. Shelled nuts may be frozen for up to six months, although they will lose some crispness.

Preparation See NUT.

■ YOUR OWN BRIDGE MIX

Trail mixes, party mixes, bridge mixes, cocktail mixes—whatever the name, they are an addicting munchie, and best when you make your own. Fill small bowls with this nutty mix, which is naturally sweetened with raisins and dried apricots and spiked with wine. Place the bowls strategically around the room: on the bar, on the mantel, on the piano, or wherever guests are likely to gather. This recipe yields a large batch, enough for a crowd; store any extra in an airtight container.

   1 **pound Brazil nuts, unskinned**
   1 **pound almonds, unskinned**
   1 **pound blanched cashews**
  ½ **pound shelled pine nuts**
  ¼ **pound muscat raisins or seedless dark raisins**
  ⅓ **pound golden raisins**
  ⅓ **cup Marsala or sweet vermouth**
  ½ **pound shelled pistachio nuts**
  ¼ **cup shredded unsweetened coconut**
  ¼ **cup lightly salted sunflower seeds**
  ¼ **cup finely minced dried apricots**
     Kosher salt
     Worcestershire sauce (optional)

1. Preheat oven to 350° F. In separate batches, toast Brazil nuts, almonds, cashews, and pine nuts on cookie sheets until lightly browned and fragrant. Set nuts aside to cool.

2. In a medium saucepan combine muscat and golden raisins with Marsala. Bring to a boil, reduce heat, and simmer gently until liquid has evaporated (20 to 30 minutes). Set aside to cool.

3. Combine cooled toasted nuts with raisins, pistachios, coconut, sunflower seeds, and apricots. Add salt and Worcestershire sauce (if used) to taste.

Makes about 10 cups.

HOW TO BREAD FOOD

Holding food with fingers, dip food in flour and turn to coat on all sides; shake off excess flour.

Dip food in egg mixture, coating evenly with liquid. Do not get liquid on fingers. Remove food with a slotted spoon or wire skimmer, allowing excess liquid to drip off.

Set food in crumbs. Shake dish to coat food with some crumbs. Turn food and pat with fingers to firmly set top crumbs. Turn again and pat to set crumbs on other side; shake off excess.

BREAD, TO

To coat with bread or other crumbs, mostly to foods that will be fried. During cooking, the crumbs form a pleasantly crunchy crust that acts as a protective barrier between food and cooking oil. Often a layer of flour and then egg precedes the crumbs. The flour dries the outside of the food and gives the egg something to adhere to. The egg acts as glue for the crumbs. To develop an attractive, crisp crust, it is important to shake off excess coating before applying the next. The above directions will ensure that the crumbs coat the food and not your hands by keeping your hands free of egg wash, a very effective binder.

Recipes and Related Information
Deep-fry, 174; Fry, 254.

BROCCOLI

A vegetable in the cabbage family, broccoli has a thick, rigid, green stalk, grayish green leaves, and a flowering dark green or purplish green head. All parts are edible.

Use   The flowering heads of young broccoli may be eaten raw, dressed with vinaigrette, or accompanied by a dipping sauce. More mature broccoli is generally boiled or steamed and eaten cold as a salad or hot as a side dish. It is flattered by cheese sauce and cream sauce. Chopped broccoli may be made into soup, soufflé, or baked pudding. A variety of Chinese broccoli with more leaf than flower is used in Chinese stir-fried dishes.

Availability   Fresh and frozen. Fresh broccoli is sold all year, with peak supplies in fall through winter. Frozen broccoli is available whole or chopped.

Selection   Choose broccoli with tightly closed florets that do not show signs of yellowing. Avoid spears with tough, woody stems and wilted leaves.

Storage   Keep broccoli in a plastic bag in the refrigerator for three or four days. It also freezes well.

Preparation   Wash carefully. Trim butt end. If desired, peel tough green outer skin of stalks down to moist, pale green part. Flower heads cook more quickly than stalks; to cook heads and stalks evenly, split stalks lengthwise in halves or quarters, slicing all the way up to but not through flower heads.

Cooking   See BOIL, STEAM, STIR-FRY.

■ **BROCCOLI SAUTEED WITH GARLIC**

Italian vegetables are often parboiled—partially cooked in water until almost tender—then sautéed in olive oil or butter, sometimes both.

> 1 **bunch of fresh broccoli or**
>   **1 package (10 oz) frozen sliced broccoli**
> 2 **cloves garlic, minced**
> ¼ **cup olive oil**
>   **Salt, to taste**

1. Slice off and discard ends of fresh broccoli stalks; peel stalks if broccoli is tough. Split stalks in half or into quarters with florets left attached, or slice whole stalks horizontally into bite-sized pieces. Steam or drop into boiling salted water and cook until just fork-tender. Drain well. (Cook frozen broccoli according to package directions until barely tender.)

2. Over medium heat, sauté garlic in olive oil until golden. Add broccoli and salt and sauté about 3 to 4 minutes.

Makes 4 servings.

A quick, easy-to-make white sauce combined with grated Parmesan cheese transforms blanched broccoli into a golden gratin.

◼ BROCCOLI GRATIN

A gratin is a popular way of preparing any vegetable that tastes good with cheese. The vegetable is cooked until tender, then baked with cheese sauce—try one flavored with grated Parmesan. Gratins can be made with one vegetable or with a mixture of cooked vegetables or vegetable purées.

> ¾ **pound broccoli**
> **Pinch salt**
> 1 **cup Cheese Sauce (see page 513), finished with 1 egg yolk**
> 2 **tablespoons grated Parmesan cheese**

1. Preheat oven to 425° F. Divide broccoli into medium florets. (Reserve stalks for soup.)

2. In a large saucepan boil enough water to cover broccoli generously and add a pinch of salt. Add broccoli and boil, uncovered, until just tender when pierced with a sharp knife (about 5 minutes). Drain broccoli, rinse with cold water, and drain thoroughly.

3. Butter a 4- or 5-cup shallow baking dish.

4. Arrange broccoli in one layer in baking dish. Spoon sauce over broccoli, covering it completely. Sprinkle with cheese. Broccoli can be kept, covered, up to 1 day in refrigerator.

5. Bake until hot (about 5 minutes if broccoli and sauce were hot, or about 15 minutes if they were cold).

6. If surface is not brown by the time mixture is hot, broil for about 1 minute. Serve hot.

Serves 4.

Recipes and Related Information

Beef With Asparagus, 558; Cream of Any Vegetable Soup, 563; Vegetable Purées, 487.

BROCCOLI RAAB

This leafy green member of the cabbage family figures prominently in Italian cooking. It has slender but firm stalks about 12 inches long, bright green leaves with jagged edges, and small green florets with yellow flowers. Its flavor is pleasantly bitter. It is marketed under a variety of similar names, including *cima di rapa, cima di rabe, broccolirab, broccoli di rape, rape, raab,* and *rapini.*

Use   Broccoli raab may be steamed and served cool or chilled, as a salad with lemon and oil. Italian cooks briefly boil broccoli raab, then sauté it with oil and garlic for use as an accompaniment to pork roast. Alternatively, it may be very slowly sautéed in oil without preblanching.

Availability   Fresh broccoli raab is most widely available fall through spring.

Selection   Choose stalks with dark green, fresh-looking leaves and sturdy stems.

Storage   Keep in a plastic bag in refrigerator crisper for three to four days.

Preparation   Trim away any large wilted or bruised leaves; peel tough outer layer of stalk or cut away tough stem ends entirely.

Cooking   See PARBOIL, SAUTE, STEAM.

■ ROMAN-STYLE BROCCOLI RAAB

The full flavor of broccoli raab stands up to garlic and cheese and is an excellent foil for pork or tomato-sauce dishes. Substitute Swiss chard if broccoli raab is not available.

>   2 **pounds broccoli raab**
>   ¼ **cup olive oil**
>   ½ **tablespoon minced garlic**
>   **Coarse salt and freshly ground pepper**
>   3 **tablespoons fresh lemon juice**
>   2 **tablespoons grated Romano cheese**

1. Wash broccoli raab and trim away any woody stems. Bring a large pot of salted water to a boil. Blanch broccoli raab 2 minutes. Drain and refresh in a bowl of ice water. Drain again and gently towel-dry.

2. Heat olive oil in a large skillet over moderate heat. Add garlic and sauté, stirring constantly, for 1 minute. Add broccoli and cook, turning often with tongs, until greens are coated with oil, hot throughout, and tender (about 2 minutes). Season to taste with salt and pepper; add lemon juice. Transfer to a warm serving platter. Sprinkle with cheese and serve at once.

Serves 4.

BROIL, TO

A cooking method which uses dry, radiant heat. It is appreciated for its convenience, speed, and simplicity. The goal for all broiled foods is to have the surface perfectly browned when the interior is cooked to taste. For a moist and tender final product, a delicate balance must be maintained between rapid surface cooking and slower internal heat transfer. The farther food is from the heat source, the more time it can stay under the broiler before overcooking. Thus larger pieces of meat, requiring a longer broiling time than thin fillets or skewered foods, may need to be set on a low oven rack to ensure a nicely browned surface and properly cooked interior.

Experiment with your broiler's temperature controls and rack settings. With experience you will develop an understanding of how to control the variables of this technique. As a general rule of thumb, however, place food about 4 to 6 inches from the broiler element. Broiled items should be uniform in size and at room temperature, so all will cook evenly and quickly.

SOME HINTS TO KEEP IN MIND

- Always preheat your broiler. If it's electric, have the door ajar when the unit is in operation.
- Line the inside of the broiler pan with aluminum foil to ease cleanup.
- Trim excess fat from meats and poultry before broiling since fat can ignite from high heat. For the same reason, drain off oil-based marinades and pat meat dry.
- Use tongs, not a fork, to turn meat; pricked meat loses its juices and becomes dry.
- Broiling *Fish:* Broiled fish is done when the meat is opaque and no longer clings to the bone. Cook 8 to 10 minutes per inch of thickness.
- Broiling *Meat:* See Timetable for Broiling Meat, opposite page. Any timetable should be considered merely a guideline, because so many variables should be taken into account when computing broiling time—shape of meat, amount of fat and bone, whether it was at room temperature, accuracy of your oven. Other ways than time for judging doneness include color of meat and touch. A few minutes before the estimated end of cooking time, make a small cut in the meat (near the bone if it has one; near center if boneless) to view the inside. Another way, used by professional chefs, takes into account how meat changes consistency as it cooks (see GRILL, When Is It Done?). When broiling steak, trim away most fat, leaving about ¼ inch; slash fat to keep from curling. For very thick steaks, use an instant-read thermometer to judge internal temperature. Very lean meats such as veal benefit from a baste or marinade to keep them moist.
- Broiling *Poultry:* See Timetable for Broiling Meat, opposite page. Broiled poultry is done when a meat thermometer inserted in the thickest part of the flesh reads 170° F to 175° F, or when the juices run slightly pink, or when the flesh springs back slightly when touched.
- Broiling *Vegetables:* Because they lack fat to keep them from drying out, baste vegetables with fat (oil or butter) or marinate them before broiling. Also ahead of time, blanch fibrous vegetables, such as leeks or celery, to soften slightly. Don't use the most intense heat, as vegetables may char before they cook completely. Broil until tender when pierced and slightly streaked with brown. Suggested for broiling: Japanese eggplant, leek, mushroom, onion, peppers, squash, tomato.

BROWN, TO

To expose food to high temperature in order to deepen surface color and intensify flavor. This is done under a broiler, in the oven, or by cooking in fat on top of the stove. Browned foods, properly cooked, have a crisp and pleasing texture without being brittle and burnt.

BROWNIE

How to define a brownie? Most often it's described as a square of rich, thin chocolate cake. Technically, however, it's a bar cookie, and it isn't always chocolate. Even the dictionary hedges in its definition of this extraordinarily popular sweet; Webster's describes it as "usually" chocolate and "often" made with nuts. What about texture? Brownie lovers argue whether the best is fudgy and chewy, or light and cakelike.

Actually there isn't a single, standard brownie recipe. There are numerous approaches, which have all evolved from the many techniques of making cakes. What is important is the final product, not what you had to do to make it or whether you've chosen to use solid chocolate, chocolate syrup, or cocoa powder to infuse the batter with its characteristic flavor.

Traditionally brownies are flat and square, although few of us would refuse one cut in a wedge or something even more unorthodox. The texture is either moist, chewy, and dense, or moist and cakey. Most often they are brown, but butterscotch brownies (blondies) are golden, those made with white chocolate quite pale, and marbled ones two-tone. The addition of chopped nuts is common, but controversial. Even more contentious is the inclusion of fruit, which some recipes may suggest.

In sum, a brownie is square or rectangular, made of chocolate, with nuts or other additions, and has a moist texture. But not always.

Note   These delicate formulations are created to produce a particular result. Varying proportions of ingredients, size of pan, and, most important, oven temperature and baking time even slightly will alter the final product. So, if you find *the* brownie recipe, follow it to the letter each time and you will be rewarded batch after batch.

CUTTING BROWNIES WITH PRECISION

Although even brownie crumbs taste wonderful, these bars look best when cut cleanly. For best results, refrigerate brownies in the pan to firm the chocolate before cutting. Turn out onto a dry, clean work surface and cut upside down to keep the top from crumbling. Use a sharp, serrated knife; for very fudgy brownies, dip knife in hot water before cutting. Wipe after each cut to prevent dragging. For brownies made in a square pan, cut in half each way, then halve each half. For larger rectangular pans, mark cuts lightly on the surface of the brownie using a ruler and sharp knife, and then cut along these lines. To make straight cuts, lay the ruler along the marked line and use the ruler's edge to guide the knife. If the brownie is especially moist, wipe the knife blade between cuts.

TIMETABLE FOR BROILING MEAT

A timetable such as this one can help you estimate how long a particular cut will take to broil to a particular degree of doneness. Keep in mind that the times are approximate and are based on a preheated broiler and meat at room temperature. Depending upon thickness and tenderness, cuts cook from 2 to 6 inches from the heat. Thicker cuts (1 inch thick or more) need to broil farther from the heating element and will need the longer cooking time. See also TEMPERATURE, Guide to Internal Temperatures.

Type of Meat	Thickness	Total Cooking Time (in minutes)		
		Rare	Medium	Well Done
Beef				
Flank steak	1 inch	4–5	6–8	
Hamburger	1 inch	3–5	9–11	13–15
	2 inches	4–6	11–13	15–17
Rib eye	1 inch	3–5	6–7	10–12
	2 inches	5–7	6–7	12–14
T-bone, porterhouse, club steak	1 inch	5–6	9–11	13–16
	2 inches	7–8	11–13	15–18
Tenderloin	1 inch	3–5	6–7	
	2 inches	5–7	9–11	
Top sirloin steak	1 inch	5–6	9–11	13–16
	2 inches	7–8	11–13	15–18
Lamb				
Loin chop	1 inch	5–7	8–10	12–14
	2 inches	7–8	10–12	14–16
Rack chop	1 inch	5–7	8–10	12–14
	2 inches	7–8	10–12	14–16
Shoulder chop	1 inch	5–7	8–10	12–14
Pork				
Loin chop	1 inch	8–10	12–14	
	2 inches	10–12	14–16	
Shoulder chop	1 inch	8–10	12–14	
	2 inches	10–12	14–16	
Tenderloin		10–12	14–16	
Poultry				
Boned breast				5–10
Chicken, turkey (bone-in pieces)				50–70
Halved game hen				12–15
Small whole bird				25
Veal				
Loin chop	1 inch	8–10	12–14	
Rack chop	1 inch	8–10	12–14	

Children of all ages love brownies, those ultimate bar cookies. Chewy or cakelike, nutty or plain, solid or layered, there's a brownie recipe to please every taste.

STORING AND FREEZING BROWNIES

Because brownies are so moist, they keep extremely well. When cool, remove bars from pan and wrap individually or leave in pan, tightly covered. Store in a cool, dry place. Moist, dense brownies will keep up to one week, drier, cakelike brownies one to two days. In warm weather you may want to store brownies in the refrigerator, where they will keep for three to four days. For longer storage wrap well and freeze for up to two months. Thaw slowly at room temperature.

◼ CLASSIC FUDGE BROWNIES

These brownies have a moist texture and an intense, chocolate flavor. For a taste of mocha, try the Espresso Brownies variation.

    4 **ounces unsweetened chocolate, chopped**
  ½ **cup butter**
    3 **large eggs**
1⅓ **cups sugar**
    2 **teaspoons vanilla extract**
  ¾ **cup flour**
      Pinch salt
    1 **cup chopped pecans or walnuts**

1. Preheat oven to 350° F. Line bottom of an 8-inch-square cake pan with parchment paper; butter pan and dust with flour.

2. In a small, heavy-bottomed saucepan, melt chocolate and butter over low heat. Let chocolate mixture cool and continue with step 3.

3. In a large bowl beat eggs and sugar until thickened and lemon-colored; blend in vanilla. Sift flour and salt together and fold in; blend in chocolate mixture, then nuts.

4. Spread into prepared pan; bake until toothpick inserted near edge comes out clean (30 to 35 minutes).

5. Cool in pan. Refrigerate at least 2 hours before cutting. Serve chilled or at room temperature.

Makes 16 brownies.

Espresso Brownies Add 1 teaspoon instant coffee powder to chocolate-butter mixture as it melts.

◼ WHITE-CHOCOLATE AND CHIP BROWNIES

The cocoa butter in white chocolate makes this brownie even richer; the color—dotted with dark bits of chocolate chips—makes it elegant.

    3 **ounces white chocolate**
  ½ **cup butter or margarine**
1½ **cups flour**
  ½ **teaspoon baking powder**
  ¼ **teaspoon salt**
    3 **eggs, at room temperature**
1½ **cups sugar**
    1 **teaspoon vanilla extract**
    1 **package (6 oz) semisweet or milk chocolate chips**
  ½ **cup sliced almonds**

1. Preheat oven to 350° F. Line bottom of a 9- by 13-inch pan with parchment paper; butter pan and dust with flour. In a small, heavy saucepan, melt white chocolate and butter over low heat; stir well to blend. Remove chocolate mixture from heat and let cool while continuing with step 2.

2. In a medium bowl combine flour, baking powder, and salt; set aside.

3. With an electric mixer beat eggs and sugar at high speed until thick and lemon-colored. Blend in vanilla. Gradually add white chocolate mixture, then flour mixture; beat well until combined. Stir in chocolate chips and ¼ cup almonds.

4. Spread batter in prepared pan, and sprinkle with remaining ¼ cup almonds. Bake until edges begin to pull away from sides of pan and center is nearly set when tested with a toothpick (30 to 35 minutes).

5. Let cool in pan on a wire rack for 10 minutes, then cut into bars. Remove from pan when cool.

Makes 3 dozen bars.

CAKE-LOVER'S BROWNIES

Not as dense and gooey as fudgy brownies, these bars have more in common with a rich chocolate cake.

> 4 ounces unsweetened chocolate, chopped
> ½ cup butter, softened
> ¾ cup sugar
> 3 eggs
> 1 tablespoon vanilla extract
> ½ cup flour
>   Pinch salt
> 1 cup chopped pecans or walnuts
> ¼ cup chocolate chips *or* ½ cup raisins (optional)

1. Preheat oven to 350° F. Line bottom of an 8-inch-square cake pan with parchment paper; grease and flour.

2. In a double boiler over hot, but not boiling, water, melt chocolate; remove from heat and cool.

3. In a medium bowl cream butter and sugar until the consistency of whipped cream. Add eggs, one at a time, beating well after each addition. Stir in vanilla.

4. Sift flour and salt, and fold into egg mixture; gently blend in chocolate, then nuts and chocolate chips (if used). Spread into prepared pan; bake until toothpick inserted 2 inches from edge comes out clean (25 minutes; center may still look a little soft). Cool in pan.

5. Refrigerate at least 2 hours before cutting. Serve chilled or at room temperature. Best eaten within 2 days.

Makes 16 brownies.

BUTTERSCOTCH SAUCEPAN BROWNIES

The pecan-studded batter for these buttery blond brownies can be mixed in one saucepan to simplify preparation.

> 1 cup flour
> ¾ teaspoon baking powder
>   Pinch salt
> ⅓ cup butter or margarine
> 1 cup firmly packed brown sugar
> 1 egg
> 1 teaspoon vanilla extract
> ½ cup chopped pecans

1. Preheat oven to 350° F. Line bottom of an 8-inch-square cake pan with parchment paper; butter pan and dust with flour. In a medium bowl thoroughly combine flour, baking powder, and salt; set aside.

2. In a 2-quart saucepan melt butter over medium heat. Add brown sugar, stirring until sugar dissolves and mixture bubbles. Remove from heat and let stand 5 minutes to cool slightly.

3. Beat in egg and vanilla, then gradually stir in flour mixture. Stir in pecans. Spread batter in prepared pan.

4. Bake until edges begin to pull away from sides of pan and center is nearly set when tested with a toothpick (25 to 30 minutes).

5. Let cool in pan on a wire rack 10 minutes, then cut into bars. Remove from pan when cool.

Makes 18 bars.

MARBLED CREAM CHEESE BROWNIES

Two batters—one made with cream cheese, the other with melted semisweet chocolate and chopped nuts—are swirled together to make these unusual brownies.

Cream Cheese Mixture

> 2 tablespoons butter or margarine, softened
> 1 small package (3 oz) cream cheese, softened
> ¼ cup sugar
> 1 egg
> 1 tablespoon flour
> ½ teaspoon vanilla extract

Chocolate Mixture

> 4 ounces semisweet chocolate
> 3 tablespoons butter or margarine
> ½ cup flour
> ½ teaspoon baking powder
> ¼ teaspoon salt
> 3 eggs
> ¾ cup sugar
> 1 teaspoon vanilla extract
> ½ cup chopped walnuts

1. Preheat oven to 350° F. Line bottom of an 8-inch-square cake pan with parchment paper; butter pan and dust with flour.

2. *For Cream Cheese Mixture:* In a medium bowl beat butter and cream cheese until well mixed. Add sugar and beat well. Add egg and beat until fluffy. Blend in flour and vanilla; set aside.

3. *For Chocolate Mixture:* In a small, heavy saucepan melt chocolate and butter over low heat; stir well to blend and set aside to cool. In a small bowl combine flour, baking powder, and salt; set aside. In a medium bowl beat eggs at high speed with an electric mixer until light-colored. Gradually beat in sugar, then vanilla. Gradually add flour mixture, mixing until well combined. Blend in chocolate mixture. Stir in walnuts.

4. Spread half of Chocolate Mixture in prepared pan. Pour Cream Cheese Mixture over it, lightly spreading to pan edges. Cover with remaining chocolate mixture. Swirl a thin spatula through all 3 layers to create a marbled effect.

5. Bake until edges begin to pull away from sides of pan and center is nearly set when tested with a toothpick (40 to 45 minutes).

6. Let cool in pan on a wire rack 5 minutes, then cut into bars. Remove from pan when cool.

Makes 18 bars.

Brussels Sprouts With Fresh Chestnuts is at its appealing best during the winter months, when chestnuts are in season.

BRUISE, TO

To partially crush a food—such as a clove of garlic—with the heel of a knife or with a mortar and pestle to release flavor. Bruising also facilitates removal of garlic's papery peel. When used for a sauce, berries are often bruised so they will absorb sugar more easily.

BRUNOISE

A mixture of aromatic vegetables cut in an even, fine dice, *brunoise* is used to flavor soups, stews, and sautés. Commonly included are onions, celery, carrots, and leeks, and less often turnips and parsnips; the choice is up to the cook. *Mirepoix* is a similar vegetable mixture used in the same way, but cut in coarser pieces.

BRUSH, TO

To apply a coating with a brush. Most often what is spread on is a flavoring agent, such as a glaze or a basting liquid; a fat, such as butter or oil; or a protective layer, such as an egg wash or aspic. A natural-bristle brush is recommended, as plastic bristles will melt and distort upon contact with heat.

Recipes and Related Information
Baste, 27; Cake and Pastry Tools, 89; Glaze, 268.

BRUSSELS SPROUT

The Brussels sprout is a member of the cabbage family, native to northern Europe. Instead of one large head, the plant produces numerous small heads arranged in neat rows around a thick stalk.

Use   Cooked Brussels sprouts may be eaten cold as a salad but are generally eaten hot as a side dish, dressed with butter, oil, or meat-roasting juices. Their nutty flavor is flattered by sliced almonds, braised chestnuts, and cream sauces.

Availability   Fresh and frozen. The domestic fresh crop is harvested from mid-August through the first week of May. Imported Brussels sprouts from Mexico are available in late spring and summer. Brussels sprouts are generally removed from their stalk and sold in bulk (by the pound) or in cardboard buckets overwrapped with cellophane. However, they are increasingly coming to market still attached to their stalks. These sprouts have superior flavor; remove the heads from their stalk just before cooking.

Selection   Choose Brussels sprouts that are small and odorless, tightly closed, and bright green, without yellowing or loose leaves around base.

Storage   Refrigerate fresh Brussels sprouts in a plastic bag for three to five days.

Preparation   Wash; trim stem ends and remove wilted or discolored leaves. Cut an *x* in stem ends for faster and more even cooking.

Cooking   See BOIL, SAUTE, STEAM.

▪ BRUSSELS SPROUTS WITH FRESH CHESTNUTS

The European custom of roasting chestnuts and selling them on street corners is a romantic tradition that dates from antiquity. Brussels sprouts and chestnuts make a classic pairing for a holiday side dish.

> 2 **pounds fresh chestnuts** *or*
>   **1 can (16 oz) chestnuts, drained**
> 2 **pounds fresh Brussels sprouts**
> 2 **cups Beef Stock (see page 560)**
> ¼ **teaspoon salt**
>   **Freshly ground pepper**

1. On the rounded side of each chestnut, make a deep *x* through outer shell and inner shell underneath. Place chestnuts in a 2-quart saucepan, cover with water, and boil for about 15 minutes; drain. Peel shell and inner skin. (If chestnuts are too hot to handle, cool briefly, but not for more than 1 or 2 minutes or they will be hard to peel.)

2. Trim the Brussels sprouts of dried stems and leaves. Cut an *x* into stem end of each so that they will cook more evenly and be less apt to separate.

3. In a large skillet combine stock and Brussels sprouts, and bring to a boil. Reduce heat and simmer 15 minutes. Add cooked chestnuts, salt, and pepper to taste, and cook 10 minutes more.

Makes 8 servings.

BULB BASTER

Bulb basters look like over-sized eyedroppers and work in the same way. They are used to keep meats moist and flavorful by drenching them with pan juices or other liquid.

Their shafts are made of either nylon or stainless steel, both with a remov-able rubber bulb. Metal basters come with a long-handled cleaning brush to push out any food trapped in the narrow tip. Some are also packaged with a hollow metal injecting needle for internal basting and flavoring, which screws onto the shaft. Most basters measure about 10 inches from tip to top of bulb.

Nylon basters are considerably cheaper than metal ones; they also let you see how much liquid is drawn up into the shaft. Metal, however, is more durable and should last a lifetime. Both materials are safe to be put in a dish-washer. Remove bulb to clean. To reassemble, wet edge of shaft and bulb will slide on easily.

BURNET

A perennial herb native to Europe, burnet has rounded, toothed leaves that grow close to the ground, a tall flower stem, and rose-colored flowers. The leaves have a mild, cucumberlike flavor.

Use Add whole burnet leaves to salads or float in iced drinks. Mince and add to mayonnaise or when using fines herbes. The leaves are a refreshing addition to salads, iced drinks, and herb vinegars.

Availability Fresh burnet can be found in specialty markets from May through October.

Selection Buy burnet that looks fresh and sprightly, without signs of wilting or decay.

Storage Keep in a plastic bag in refrigerator crisper for one or two days.

Preparation Wash just before using.

BUTTER

A solid fat, butter is made by agitating or churning cream (the fatty portion of cow's milk). It takes about 10 quarts of milk to yield 1 pound of butter. Most of the butter available commercially is sweet cream butter made from fresh (not sour) cream; it may be salted or unsalted. Sour cream butter, churned from cream that has been allowed to mature and sour slightly, is now hard to find commercially due to changing tastes; however, many who have grown up on sour cream butter prefer its pronounced flavor. It is probably still made for home use by many of those who keep dairy cows.

Although some consumers and cookbook writers use the term sweet butter to refer to unsalted butter, that term is misleading. A supermarket package labeled sweet cream butter may or may not be salted. If the butter does contain salt, it will be listed as an ingredient on the la-bel. Unsalted butter is usually identified as such on the label. Salt adds flavor to butter and prolongs its refriger-ated shelf life. However, many cooks prefer the delicate, fresh taste of unsalted butter. Vegetables sautéed in un-salted butter with a pinch of salt have a different flavor than those sautéed in salted butter. Because it is more perishable, unsalted butter is more expensive. Except in certain delicate cookies and pastries, it is rarely essential to the success of a dish.

Whipped butter is sweet cream butter, salted or un-salted, which is whipped with air or inert gas to make spreading easy.

Use Butter adds flavor and richness to a variety of cooked foods and prepared dishes. Pouring melted butter on cooked vegetables; spreading softened butter on breads, muffins, biscuits, or other baked goods; swirling butter into a soup; and dotting butter on the top of a casserole before baking are all ways to use the nutty fla-vor of butter to enrich a dish.

It is the base of several important sauces, garnishes, and frostings. Both the classic Hollandaise sauce and its variations and the classic beurre blanc (white butter sauce) and its variations are butter-based sauces for sa-vory foods. Compound Butters are classic garnishes for grilled meats, poultry, and fish. Butter provides the basis for buttercream frosting and hard sauce, the traditional accompaniment for steamed puddings.

Butter is also valued as a cooking medium. Cooking fish, meat, poultry, eggs, bread, vegetables, and batters in butter adds flavor and an appetizing brown surface.

As an ingredient in baked goods, butter adds tender-ness and flavor and prolongs shelf life. Butter can also help leaven a baked product. Thoroughly creaming but-ter for a cake batter traps air and moisture; when cake is baked, hot air and steam expand and so does the cake. Similarly, layers of butter folded into a puff pastry dough will release steam in the oven, causing the pastry to rise.

Clarified butter has a clearer taste than whole butter and is preferred for light sauces. As it doesn't burn easily, it is often used for sautéing.

Availability In retail markets butter is packaged in ¼-pound sticks or 1-pound blocks, wrapped in pure vegetable parchment or parchment-laminated metal foil to prevent absorption of other flavors or odors during storage. For added protection, it's usually packaged in waxed-paper cartons. Whipped butter is most commonly sold in 8-ounce tubs.

Selection High-quality butter should have a sweet, not stale, aroma. It should have a semisoft consistency at room temperature and should not sweat, which would indicate excessive water content. It should melt smoothly on the tongue without leaving a deposit. Salted butter should not taste oversalted.

Storage Salted butter will keep for several weeks in its original package in the coldest part of the refrigerator. Unsalted butter loses its delicate flavor after a week or two of refrigeration. Keep partially used butter in a covered dish in the refrigerator to prevent absorption of other odors. Store only what will be used within three days in the butter-storage compartment of the refrigerator. Butter freezes well—up to one month in its original package and up to nine months in freezer paper.

▉ BROWN BUTTER (BEURRE NOISETTE) AND BLACK BUTTER (BEURRE NOIR)

The nutty flavor of both of these butter sauces complements poached fish, fried eggs, brains and other variety meats, green beans, cauliflower, and asparagus. To make Brown Butter, cook clarified butter over low heat until amber and fragrant. For Black Butter, cook clarified butter until very dark brown, almost black.

▉ CLARIFIED BUTTER

Also known as drawn butter, clarified butter is butter with the milk solids removed. The clear yellow fat that remains can withstand high heat without burning. It will keep several weeks in the refrigerator or longer in the freezer.

To clarify butter: In a heavy pan, melt 1 pound of butter over low heat. Skim off froth and carefully pour clear yellow liquid from pan, leaving milky residue behind. Discard residue.

Makes about 1½ cups.

▉ COMPOUND BUTTERS

Compound butters (also known as composed butters or flavored butters) are a mix of softened butter plus flavoring used as a sauce on grilled meats, fish, and poultry. They are also wonderful for basting. Compound butters freeze well, up to two months wrapped in waxed paper. Shape butter into a block or roll before chilling or freezing. To use, cut desired amount off block and store remainder.

Prepare butters as follows: In a medium bowl combine ingredients either by hand or with an electric mixer until well blended. Use immediately, or wrap in waxed paper.

Ancho Chile Butter
Adds heat to grilled meat, fish, or poultry. *Makes ½ cup.*

- 2 large dried ancho chiles (or use New Mexico, pasilla, or California variety)
- ½ cup butter

Cover chiles with boiling water. When they are rehydrated, drain and finely chop in a food processor or blender. Mix with butter.

Bercy Butter
Classically used for grilled beef and fish. *Makes ½ cup.*

- ½ cup dry white wine
- 1 tablespoon minced shallots
- 1 tablespoon minced parsley
- 1 tablespoon fresh lemon juice
- ¼ cup cubed poached marrowbone
  Salt and freshly ground pepper, to taste

Boil wine and shallots until reduced to about 3 tablespoons; cool, then mix with parsley, lemon juice, marrowbone, salt and pepper.

Garlic Butter
Spread on bread or melt on meat, fish, or vegetables. *Makes ½ cup.*

- 5 cloves garlic, peeled
- 2 cups water
- ½ cup butter, softened

Boil garlic in the water about 5 minutes. Drain, cool, then crush garlic and mix with butter.

Herb Butter
Pair with fish, poultry, or vegetables. *Makes ½ cup.*

- 4 tablespoons herbs of choice (chives, oregano, parsley, thyme, tarragon)
- ½ cup butter, softened

Maître d'Hôtel Butter
Classically served with grilled meats, fish, or vegetables. *Makes ½ cup.*

- 2 tablespoons chopped parsley
- 1 teaspoon fresh lemon juice
- ½ cup butter, softened

Nut Butter
Use as a garnish for soups or toast, or as a sauce for fish or poultry. *Makes ¾ cup.*

- ½ cup finely chopped, toasted hazelnuts, almonds, or pistachios
- ½ cup butter, softened

Orange Butter

Use with fish, poultry, vegetables, breads, pancakes, or waffles. *Makes ½ cup.*

  2 teaspoons freshly squeezed orange juice
    Grated rind of 1 orange
  ½ cup butter, softened

Red Pepper Butter

Use with fish and poultry. *Makes 1 cup.*

  2 shallots, finely chopped
  2 large red bell peppers, peeled, seeded, and finely chopped
  1 tablespoon balsamic vinegar
  1 tablespoon butter
  ½ cup unsalted butter, softened

Cook shallots, red pepper, and vinegar in 1 tablespoon butter until peppers soften; cool, then mix with butter.

Recipes and Related Information

Beurre Blanc, 518; Broiled Porterhouse Steak With Savory Butter, 41; Buttercream Frosting, 248; Butter Curler, 69; Hollandaise Sauce, 516.

BUTTER CURLER, MOLD, PADDLES, PRINT

Butter doesn't taste any better when it's curled, rolled, or pressed out of a mold, but it's certainly prettier and more fun to use. For all the butter shapes, store and serve over ice. Some of these shapes are tricky to produce. You may want to practice with each of these tools before attempting anything elaborate for a special dinner party. If you have time, prepare the shapes in quantity and freeze, well-wrapped. Then use the amount you need and leave the rest for another occasion.

BUTTER CURLER

The curved stainless steel blade has one notched edge that produces shell-like, ribbed curls of butter. To use, dip blade in warm water and draw across a block of butter that is soft enough to peel without falling apart, yet cold enough to hold its shape, but not shatter, when pressed.

BUTTER MOLD

Use this wooden cup to shape rounds of butter charmingly imprinted with a bird, flower, or other motif. Immerse mold in ice water for about 10 minutes. Fill cavity of mold with softened butter and refrigerate until butter firms. Press out butter by pushing down on plunger.

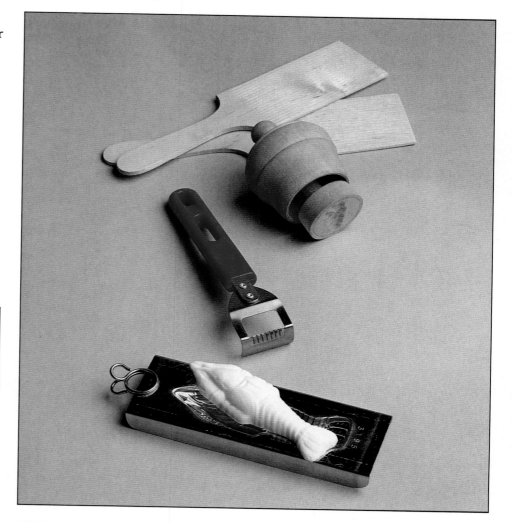

BUTTER PADDLES

To make butter balls, soak wooden paddles in water for about 10 minutes. Set a lump of cold butter about the size of a large marble on the ribbed surface of one paddle. Lay the other paddle, ribbed side down, on butter at a 90-degree angle and rotate until a ridged ball is formed.

BUTTER PRINT

This wooden or ceramic disk embosses a design on single servings of butter. Dip print in ice water, then press on a slightly softened pat or round of butter.

Whether rolled into balls, curled, or molded, shaped butter adds a decorative note to the table. Shown from top to bottom are: butter paddles, wooden mold with grape design, butter curler, metal mold with fish pattern.

BUTTERFLY, TO

This butcher's technique involves halving food horizontally, without cutting all the way through it, so that the two halves can be opened like the wings of a butterfly or the pages of a book. Often this is the first step when preparing a roast that is to be stuffed and rolled.

Braised Chinese Cabbage and Garlic, a richly seasoned vegetable side dish, is shown in a special earthenware casserole known as a clay pot or sand pot. This type of pot has been used in China for centuries for slow, gentle cooking over very low heat.

CABBAGE

One of the oldest vegetables cultivated by man, cabbage grows well in almost any climate and is appreciated in almost all of the world's cuisines. The cabbage or brassica family is quite large and includes such common vegetables as cauliflower, broccoli, mustard, kale, horseradish, radish, rutabaga, and turnip.

The members of the brassica family that go by the name cabbage are many and varied. Most are characterized by large round heads of tightly packed leaves, although some varieties are elongated, flattened, or loosely packed. Most varieties are white to light green, although red varieties exist.

Use   Raw and cooked cabbages are employed in many countries throughout the world. Raw cabbage can be shredded, dressed, and eaten as a salad, as in American cole slaw. It can be steamed, sautéed, braised, or baked, added to soups and stews, stuffed whole, or creamed. Steamed cabbage leaves can be filled with a stuffing, rolled, and braised. Thai diners often use whole cabbage leaves as a wrapper for spicy salads. Cabbage also makes a popular pickle: German sauerkraut, Japanese cabbage pickle, and the spicy Korean kimchee are all variations on the same theme.

Availability   Fresh cabbage is in the produce section all year, except for savoy cabbage, which is plentiful from fall until spring. Chinese cabbage is available at Asian markets, specialty produce markets, and well-stocked supermarkets. This entry details specific varieties of commercial importance.

Selection   See specific cabbages.

Storage   Western varieties may be stored in a plastic bag in the refrigerator crisper for at least two weeks. Chinese cabbage keeps, under similar conditions, for up to one week. Do not wash cabbages before storing.

Preparation   This varies depending upon variety; check specific types for preparation information.

Cooking   See BOIL, BRAISE, SAUTE, STEAM, STIR-FRY.

CHINESE CABBAGE

Several varieties of Chinese cabbage are available on the commercial market. Some form relatively compact, elongated heads. Others are open, leafy, flowering cabbages.

Bok Choy   This elongated, non-head-forming cabbage has long white ribs with dark green leaves; it resembles chard. Choose bok choy (also known as *pak choy* or *pak choi*) that has good color and firm white ribs; avoid wilting leaves. To prepare, trim stem and discard any discolored or ragged leaves. Bok choy is usually sliced across the ribs and stir-fried, but it may be eaten raw as a salad. A miniature version called baby bok choy or *bok choy sum* is occasionally available in specialty markets; it is particularly attractive when braised whole.

Napa Cabbage   Also called Chinese cabbage or celery cabbage, Napa cabbage has elongated, tightly furled leaves with wide white ribs and soft, pale green tips. Mild in flavor, it may be eaten raw or cooked. Choose heads that are heavy for their size, without bruised or ragged leaves; avoid very large heads, which may be bitter. To prepare, trim away any brown or bruised leaves. Slice and add raw to salads, or use in soups and stir-fries.

BRAISED CHINESE CABBAGE AND GARLIC

Braised and simmered dishes allow you to put together a Chinese dinner at a leisurely pace. The cabbage simmers unattended for the last 15 or 20 minutes, allowing plenty of time to prepare the rest of the meal. Lily buds are the dried, unopened buds of a tiger lily. Soaked in water and drained, they add a pleasant texture and slightly tart and tealike flavor to certain Chinese dishes. They are available at Asian markets, as are Chinese clay pots (see CASSEROLES AND BAKING DISHES, Chinese Clay Pot).

    ½ cup dried lily buds
       Oil, for stir-frying
    1 large head garlic, separated into cloves
       and peeled
    1 medium carrot, peeled and sliced
       on the diagonal
    1 tablespoon minced fresh ginger
    1 pound bok choy or other large-ribbed Chinese
       cabbage, cut crosswise into 1½-inch slices
    2 or 3 green onions, trimmed and
       cut into 2-inch lengths
    1 cup Rich Chicken Stock (see page 560) or
       duck stock, salted to taste
    1 tablespoon black soy sauce

1. In a small bowl soak lily buds in lukewarm water until soft. Drain, squeezing out excess liquid. Cut or pinch off hard ends, and set lily buds aside.

2. Have ready a 1½-quart or larger Chinese clay pot (see CASSEROLES) or other flameproof, covered casserole. If using a clay pot, preheat it with hot water and dry it. Heat a wok or skillet over medium heat. Add a tablespoon or so of oil, and stir-fry garlic cloves and carrot until lightly browned. Add ginger and stir-fry until fragrant. Transfer contents of wok to casserole. Add a little more oil to wok, and stir-fry cabbage and green onions until just heated through. Transfer to pot. Add stock, soy sauce, and lily buds to wok and bring just to a boil. Pour over vegetables in pot.

3. Place casserole over medium-low heat, bring to a simmer, and cover. Simmer 15 to 20 minutes. Serve directly from pot.

Serves 6 to 8 with other dishes.

GREEN CABBAGE

The most common cabbage in American markets is the large round-headed variety with pale green or green leaves overlapping tightly around a central core. Select head cabbage that is heavy for its size, without drying around the core. To prepare, discard any wilted or damaged outer leaves and remove core with a sharp paring knife. Cabbage may be shredded and eaten raw as a salad or coleslaw; it may be steamed, braised, added to soups, or preserved as sauerkraut. The whole head may be blanched, then stuffed between the leaves and braised, or hollowed, stuffed, and baked. Individual leaves may be blanched to soften, then stuffed and braised. See Cabbage Preparation, page 76.

QUICK BUTTERED CABBAGE

This simple, basic technique is useful for cooking all green vegetables. They should be cooked until tender with just a touch of crispness; the easiest way to check is by tasting. When cooked in this way, cabbage remains bright green and has a delicate flavor. Serve it with any meat or poultry, or even with seafood.

    1 medium (about 2 lb) green cabbage
    ¼ cup butter
       Salt and freshly ground pepper, to taste

1. Cut hard core from cabbage and discard. Rinse cabbage and cut in thin strips.

2. In a large saucepan boil enough lightly salted water to cover cabbage generously. Add cabbage and boil, uncovered, until just tender (about 5 minutes); check by tasting.

3. Drain cabbage, rinse with cold water, and drain thoroughly. Gently squeeze dry in a colander. Cabbage can be kept, covered, for 1 day in refrigerator.

4. Melt butter in a large skillet over medium heat. Add cabbage, salt, and pepper. Cook, stirring, until butter is absorbed (about 3 minutes). Taste and add more salt and pepper, if needed.

Serves 4 to 6.

STEAMED CABBAGE WEDGES

A very simple but delicious and attractive preparation for cabbage, the wedges can be dressed with a flavored butter, such as lemon butter, and served with a poultry or meat stew. See BUTTER, Compound Butters, for a selection of recipes for flavored butters. See STEAM for more information about steaming vegetables.

    1 medium (about 2 lb) green cabbage

1. Trim any battered outside leaves from cabbage. Cut head in half lengthwise; cut each half into wedges, each including part of core. Steam until just tender (5 to 8 minutes).

2. Transfer wedges to a cutting board, cut away core, and transfer intact to plates (slide knife blade under wedge to lift it in one piece).

Serves 4 to 8.

Microwave Version For 1 pound of cabbage, prepare for cooking as directed in step 1. Place in a glass container and add 2 tablespoons water. Cook at 100 percent power 5 to 7 minutes. Let stand 2 minutes before dressing with lemon butter; serve.

■ BOHEMIAN CABBAGE ROLLS

Plump cabbage-wrapped packets of ground ham and pork are steamy and delicious. Serve with fluffy white rice.

        1 egg
      ⅓ cup whipping cream
      ¼ cup soft bread crumbs
      ¼ teaspoon salt
      ⅛ teaspoon *each* ground allspice, dill, and
            white pepper
        2 cups ground smoked pork picnic shoulder
            or leftover ham
      ½ pound ground pork
        1 large (2½ to 3 lb) green cabbage
            Paprika
            Flour
        2 tablespoons butter or margarine
        1 medium carrot, thinly sliced
        1 medium tomato, peeled and chopped
        1 medium onion, finely chopped
      ½ cup *each* dry white wine and tomato juice
            Sour cream and chopped parsley, for garnish

1. Preheat oven to 375° F. To prepare filling, beat egg with cream; mix in bread crumbs, salt, allspice, dill, and pepper. Lightly combine with ground meats; set aside.

2. To prepare cabbage, cut out core and carefully separate outer 6 leaves (reserve remainder for salad or other uses). Cut out thickest part at base of each leaf. Place leaves loosely in a large, deep frying pan; add just enough water to cover bottom. Cover and steam just until leaves are wilted and bright green (2 to 3 minutes). Remove cabbage from pan and drain.

3. Divide filling among the 6 prepared cabbage leaves. For each cabbage bundle, fold in sides, roll up loosely, and fasten with a toothpick (see Cabbage Preparation, page 76). Sprinkle cabbage rolls lightly with paprika, then coat with flour.

4. Pour out water from pan in which cabbage was steamed; in same pan brown cabbage rolls lightly on all sides in butter. Transfer rolls to a 2- to 3-quart casserole as they brown. Surround with carrot and tomato.

5. In same pan cook onion until it begins to brown. Mix in wine and tomato juice. Bring to a boil and cook, stirring, 3 minutes. Pour over cabbage rolls. (At this point casserole may be covered and refrigerated overnight.)

6. Bake, uncovered, for 1 hour. Uncover and continue cooking for 15 minutes longer. To serve, spoon vegetables and sauce over cabbage rolls, and top with a dollop of sour cream and a sprinkling of parsley.

Serves 6.

Food Processor Version   With slicing disk slice carrot and set aside until needed. Cut onion into quarters, put in work bowl, and with metal blade, turn motor on and off 3 or 4 times; remove from work bowl and set aside.

To grind meat: Cut lean pork and smoked pork into 1-inch pieces. Pulse motor about 10 times to chop. Add egg, cream, bread crumbs, salt, and spices. Process 5 seconds to combine.

Microwave Version   *To wilt leaves:* Place 6 cabbage leaves in a dish in the microwave oven; cover and cook at 100 percent power for about 2 minutes. Let stand, covered, if additional time is needed to soften the leaves; drain any liquid.

■ STUFFED WHOLE CABBAGE

Instead of stuffing individual cabbage leaves, try stuffing the whole head and cutting it into wedges to serve. When cabbage is sliced, the filling contrasts attractively with the subtle green of the leaves.

        1 large (2½ to 3 lb) green cabbage
        1 small onion, diced
        1 clove garlic, minced
        2 tablespoons vegetable oil
        4 tablespoons unsalted butter
      ½ pound ground veal
      ½ pound ham, minced
        3 sprigs parsley, minced
      ½ teaspoon salt
      ⅛ teaspoon freshly ground pepper
        1 egg
      ¼ cup Beef Stock (see page 560)
      ½ cup soft bread crumbs
      ½ cup whipping cream

1. Remove tough outer leaves from cabbage, reserve 2 or 3 to cover top, and discard remainder. Slice off top of cabbage and scoop out interior, leaving a shell about ¾ inch thick and a cavity approximately 4 inches in diameter (see Cabbage Preparation, page 76). Place cabbage in a 4-quart saucepan; cover with boiling water, reduce heat, and simmer until just tender (about 20 minutes). Drain upside down in a colander; let cool.

2. Preheat oven to 350° F. In a large skillet sauté onion and garlic in oil and 2 tablespoons butter over medium heat until soft but not browned (about 5 minutes). Add veal and ham, and sauté, stirring constantly and breaking up clumps as they form, until thoroughly cooked (about 10 minutes).

3. Mix in parsley, salt, pepper, egg, Beef Stock, bread crumbs, and cream. Cook briefly (2 to 3 minutes), stirring to combine. Stuff filling into hollowed cabbage. Cover stuffed cabbage with reserved cabbage leaves.

4. Grease a 3-quart casserole with remaining 2 tablespoons butter and set stuffed cabbage in dish. Cover casserole tightly with lid or aluminum foil and bake 90 minutes. Remove from oven, let rest 10 minutes, discard loose top leaves, and cut into 6 to 8 wedges to serve.

Serves 6 to 8.

CHOUCROUTE GARNI

Alsace is a region of France near Germany. Alsatian food often reflects both French and German cuisines. *Choucroute* is French for sauerkraut: the word gives this dish its name—sauerkraut with accompaniments. This recipe is easily made ahead for a gathering. Bring the piping hot casserole to the table and serve guests some meat, potatoes, and sauerkraut. Accompany with a glass of Riesling or dry white wine. Many cooks reserve duck, goose, or chicken fat to use here in place of vegetable oil.

      1 **tart apple, diced**
      2 **medium onions, diced**
      4 **tablespoons vegetable oil**
     ½ **cup parsley, minced**
      4 **slices bacon, diced**
     10 **juniper berries, crushed**
      1 **teaspoon thyme**
      1 **bay leaf**
     1⅔ **cups Chicken Stock (see page 560)**
     1⅓ **cups Riesling or dry white wine**
      3 **to 4 skinless ham hocks**
      2 **pounds sauerkraut, rinsed**
     12 **small potatoes**
      6 **veal sausages**
      3 **smoked pork chops or pork steaks**

1. In a 6-quart Dutch oven, sauté apple and onions in oil over medium heat until soft (10 minutes). Stir in parsley, bacon, juniper berries, thyme, bay leaf, stock, wine, and ham hocks. Cover and simmer 45 minutes.

2. Rinse sauerkraut in colander under cool water; pat dry. Scrub potatoes and cut each in half. Add sauerkraut, potatoes, and veal sausages to Dutch oven. Stir to combine, cover, and simmer another 15 minutes.

3. Remove pork chop meat from bone and cut into 2-inch cubes. Stir in pork cubes, cover, and cook another 40 minutes. Make sure each portion has a serving of meat, potatoes, and sauerkraut.

Serves 8 to 10.

Recipes: Crispy Coleslaw, 506; New England Boiled Dinner, 42.

RED CABBAGE

Ranging from reddish purple to dark purple, the firm, round red cabbage has tightly packed, overlapping leaves around a white central core. It is available the year around. Select compact cabbages that feel heavy for their size and do not have wilted outer leaves. To prepare, discard any damaged outer leaves and remove core with a sharp paring knife. Red cabbage may be pickled or eaten raw as a salad, braised, steamed, or sautéed. Adding vinegar or lemon juice to the cooking water (about 1 tablespoon per cup of water) will help preserve the bright color.

RED CABBAGE WITH APPLES

Apples and cabbage are a traditional pairing of flavors, sparked by a sweet-and-sour mixture of cider vinegar and brown sugar. Serve this alongside bratwurst or with any pork or beef dish.

      2 **tablespoons vegetable oil**
      1 **onion, coarsely chopped**
     ¼ **cup cider vinegar**
      2 **tablespoons brown sugar or honey**
         Salt and freshly ground pepper, to taste
      1 **green apple, cored and thinly sliced**
      1 **small red cabbage, coarsely shredded**

1. In a large frying pan, heat oil. Add onion and sauté until softened (5 minutes). Add vinegar, sugar, and salt and pepper to taste; stir to mix.

2. Add apple and cabbage. Bring liquid to a boil, reduce heat to medium, cover, and cook until cabbage wilts (about 10 minutes). Stir occasionally to coat cabbage with vinegar-sugar mixture.

Serves 4.

Microwave Version Prepare cabbage for cooking. Place shredded cabbage in a glass container and add 2 tablespoons water. Cover and cook at 100 percent power for 6 to 8 minutes. Add to recipe in step 2, after apple has cooked. Toss to coat with vinegar-sugar mixture.

Red Cabbage With Apples is part of a traditional German wurst supper. Shown with the cabbage dish are pan-fried bratwurst, sautéed onion, Spätzle (see page 190), and dark pumpernickel bread.

CABBAGE PREPARATION

Coring cabbage   *Insert a sharp knife at edge of core, angled so knife tip points to center of cabbage head. Cut completely around core.*

Cabbage shell   *Remove any damaged outer leaves. Slice off about one fourth of top of cabbage. With a spoon scoop out center of head, leaving enough cabbage leaves to form a shell with walls about ¾ inch thick.*

Cabbage rolls   *Cut away a V-shaped piece from thickened base of each cabbage leaf. Lay leaves on work surface, with edges curling up. Set filling in center of leaf, fold in sides, then roll up from bottom to close package.*

■ BUDAPEST BORSCHT

Developed in Eastern Europe, Budapest Borscht is a combination soup and stew and makes a substantial winter food. Serve with homemade whole-grain bread as a colorful first course or light supper.

1½	**pounds red cabbage**
5	**beets**
5	**small boiling potatoes**
6	**plum tomatoes**
1½	**tablespoons vegetable oil**
1	**onion, diced**
2	**cloves garlic, finely chopped**
6	**cups water**
½	**cup red wine vinegar**
1	**tablespoon honey**
3	**tablespoons parsley**
1	**teaspoon thyme**
1	**bay leaf**
1½	**teaspoons dried dill**
1	**tablespoon Hungarian paprika**
2	**teaspoons kosher salt**
¼	**teaspoon freshly ground pepper**
½	**cup sour cream, for garnish**
4	**tablespoons fresh dill, for garnish**

1. Slice cabbage into ¼-inch strips. Peel beets with a sharp knife and cut into julienne strips. Peel potatoes and cut in half. Peel and seed tomatoes; cut into quarters.

2. In a 4-quart saucepan, heat oil. Add onion and garlic. Sauté for 5 minutes. Add cabbage, beets, potatoes, tomatoes, the water, vinegar, honey, parsley, thyme, bay leaf, dill, paprika, salt, and pepper. Bring to boil and reduce heat. Simmer for 25 minutes. Serve with a dollop of sour cream and a garnish of chopped dill.

Makes 8 cups, 6 to 8 servings.

SAVOY CABBAGE

A large head-forming variety with crinkly, pale green leaves, savoy cabbage is especially popular among European cooks. It is milder and more tender than regular green cabbage, making it particularly suitable for salads. It may also be steamed, braised, stuffed, or added to soups. Savoy cabbage is available from fall until spring; select solid heads without signs of yellowing. To prepare, discard any ragged or discolored leaves and remove core with a sharp paring knife.

Recipes: Boiled Dinner Bolognese, 530.

■ RED-AND-GREEN CABBAGE SLAW

Bright with slivers of red and green peppers, this cabbage salad has a zippy oil and vinegar dressing.

1	**small savoy cabbage (about 1½ lb), thinly shredded**
½	**cup *each* seeded and slivered red and green bell pepper**
½	**cup *each* finely chopped parsley and thinly sliced green onions**
2	**tablespoons vinegar**
1½	**teaspoons salt**
½	**teaspoon celery seed**
½	**cup white vinegar**
⅓	**cup vegetable oil**

1. In a large bowl mix cabbage, pepper, parsley, and onion. For dressing, shake (in covered jar) or stir together sugar, salt, celery seed, vinegar, and oil until sugar dissolves.

2. Pour dressing over cabbage mixture; mix lightly. Cover and refrigerate 30 minutes to 3 hours.

Serves 6 to 8.

CAKE

Both in our culture and throughout the world, cakes have a wonderful, long-standing tradition. In all sorts of celebrations, cakes play a central role—whether it's a cupcake with a single shining candle or a multitiered, elaborately trimmed bridal confection.

Although storebought cakes and those made from a mix have a place in lives that are increasingly busy and hectic, there is no substitute for the pleasure derived from baking in your own kitchen with the freshest, best-quality ingredients. Baking is one of the most satisfying and enjoyable ways to put your creative powers to work—and a light, richly flavored homemade cake is always appreciated and admired.

TYPES OF CAKES

Cakes are made from a thin batter, which is a mixture of flour and a liquid in approximately equal amounts, plus eggs or other leavening or flavoring ingredients, and often fat. In this country cakes are classified either by how they are leavened or by whether or not the batter contains fat.

Cakes rise because steam and gases force the batter to expand in the presence of heat. The liquid in the batter converts to steam in the oven, and bubbles of gas develop during the mixing process and during baking. The bubbles are created in two ways. A leavening agent such as baking powder, baking soda, or yeast produces carbon dioxide in the presence of moisture. Other bubbles are created by beating air into the ingredients, as when sugar and butter are creamed, when sugar and eggs are beaten together, or when egg whites are beaten separately and folded into the batter.

Angel food cake, sponge cake, and meringues are lightened by an airy foam of beaten eggs. Cakes that depend chiefly on carbon dioxide are the familiar American layer cakes, cupcakes, and dense tube cakes, and the yeast-leavened European specialties—French baba and savarin, and the Alsatian *Kugelhopf*.

Recipes that use carbon dioxide (except for yeast cakes) almost always begin by vigorously beating together butter and sugar (creaming). These are known as butter, shortened, or creamed cakes—cakes made with fat. They include layer cakes, pound cakes, and fruitcakes.

As in all cooking, the lines between these categories often blur. Chiffon cake and génoise are hybrids. Like an angel food cake, a chiffon cake incorporates beaten egg whites, but it also uses baking powder and is made with vegetable oil, a fat. Génoise batter is lightened with a whole-egg foam and enriched with melted butter. Pound cakes, perhaps the classic shortened cake, traditionally used 1 pound each of butter, sugar, eggs, and flour, and were leavened only by creaming air into the butter-sugar mixture. Today we are less lavish with the rich ingredients and prefer a lighter textured pound cake, so baking powder appears in many of these recipes.

ABOUT FOAM AND BUTTER CAKES

All cakes are made from a thin, pourable batter. By varying the ingredients that make up the batter, their proportion, and the method of leavening, it's possible to produce many different types of cakes. The two main categories are foam cakes and butter cakes; chiffon cake and génoise combine characteristics of both (see Types of Cakes at left). For both foam and butter cakes, use a light touch when adding dry ingredients. Otherwise the delicate foam could be deflated and the cake will lose volume, or the creamed batter over-manipulated, resulting in a tough cake. If adding beaten egg whites to either type of cake, first fold in one third of the whites to lighten the batter; it will be easier to fold in the remaining whites if the two are of similar consistency (see FOLD). Finally, take your time; give each step the chance to do what it's supposed to do. If you proceed too fast, the ingredients may be insufficiently blended or not beaten to full volume.

FOAM CAKES

These cakes have a high proportion of eggs, sugar, and liquid to flour (more liquid per cup of flour than butter cakes). Generally they do not have fat unless you place génoise and chiffon cakes in this category, and they often are. Foams are made of egg whites only (angel food cake), which produce a delicate, airy, mildly flavored cake, or whole eggs (sponge cake and génoise), which make a richer cake because the yolks are included.

Keep the following points in mind when making a foam cake:

- Air trapped in beaten eggs—whole, yolks and egg whites beaten separately, or whites only—is the primary leavening for foam cakes. The more air in the batter, the higher and lighter the cake will be. Beat the eggs properly and handle the fragile foam very gently so it won't deflate.
- Eggs will beat to their maximum—three times original volume—if at room temperature (about 70° F).
- For angel food cakes and whenever beating egg whites, keep the bowl, whites, and utensils completely free of fat. That means avoiding drops of yolk in the whites or using a mixing bowl that isn't scrupulously clean. Fat inhibits development of foam, which results in less volume. A copper bowl and balloon whisk are ideal utensils, but a stainless steel bowl and an electric mixer with wire beaters are fine. Avoid plastic or glass bowls. See EGG, Beating Eggs.

BUTTER CAKES

Always appreciated for their tenderness, good flavor, velvety crumb, and thin, golden brown crust, butter cakes use fat for moisture and richness, and as a means of incorporating air into the batter. When making a butter cake, remember the following:

- Fats cream best at 70° to 75° F. Soften chilled butter or shortening at room temperature at least 30 minutes before using.
- When creaming, beat fat briefly to make it pliable before adding sugar; cream fat and sugar until a pale, ivory color and the consistency of stiffly whipped cream. Scrape down sides of bowl occasionally so all of the batter is incorporated. See CREAM.
- Make sure dry ingredients are well blended to disperse leavening agent. Sifting does this most efficiently, but you can also use a whisk or fork, or a food processor.

Tortes, or flourless cakes, are like a classic sponge cake, but part or all of the flour has been replaced by ground nuts, cookie or bread crumbs, or a combination.

INGREDIENTS FOR CAKES: WHAT EACH DOES

Cakes are balanced formulas and each ingredient plays a role in the cake-making process. Sugar and fat tenderize the toughening action of flour and eggs. Liquid ingredients balance dry. For each type of cake, certain ingredients must be included, but the proportions can vary somewhat without affecting the quality of the final product. New recipes are created just that way—by starting with a basic recipe and changing amounts slightly or by substituting one ingredient for another.

Flour, sugar, milk, butter, eggs, nuts, raisins, fruits, and spices are just some of the ingredients that are transformed into cakes and pastries of all sorts. Using the freshest, best-quality ingredients will make a noticeable difference in the final product.

Flour   Along with eggs, flour gives a cake its structure by forming an elastic network that traps expanding gas and steam. Use cake flour when indicated for a lighter, more tender cake. Sifting is recommended for most cakes, especially for more delicate ones such as angel food, sponge, and chiffon. Sifting results in a finer end product; it aerates the flour, removes specks of foreign material, and breaks up lumps. Cake flour should always be sifted; follow recipe directions about sifting before or after measuring. If you wish to substitute all-purpose flour for cake flour in a recipe, substitute 2 tablespoons cornstarch for the same amount of flour per 1 cup cake flour specified. It's unnecessary to sift all-purpose flour before measuring, although some older recipes may call for it. It's a good idea to sift after measuring to blend the flour with the other dry ingredients. For more information about sifting, see FLOUR.

Fat   From fat, a cake gets tenderness, richness, and fluidity. Select a fat that is plastic (pliable) and easily beaten. Butter is preferred for its flavor, but is limited in the range of temperatures at which it can be beaten. Hydrogenated vegetable shortening is plastic at a wider range of temperatures than butter, but is tasteless. Some recipes compromise by calling for half shortening (for its superior creaming ability) and half butter (for excellent flavor). Butter creams best at room temperature. Let chilled butter warm on the counter until it is cool to the touch, but soft enough that a finger pressed into the surface leaves an impression. When oil is specified, use a light one such as safflower oil. Lard should be avoided because it doesn't cream well.

Sugar   To balance the toughness contributed by flour and eggs, sugar is added to the batter to tenderize and, of course, to sweeten. When sugar is creamed with fat, its crystalline structure carries air into the mixture and contributes to the volume of a cake. Use granulated sugar unless otherwise indicated. Angel food cake recipes often specify superfine sugar which, like cake flour, is finely granulated and makes a finer crumb.

Eggs For foam cakes, eggs are the primary or only source of leavening and, along with flour, provide structure for all baked goods. They are a source of liquid and function as emulsifiers, which make the batter more uniform and stable. Unless otherwise directed, always use eggs graded large. Separate eggs when cold. Use whole eggs, egg yolks, and egg whites at room temperature. If desired, eggs may be measured by volume and weight. An egg is two-thirds white and one-third yolk. See EGG, Beating Eggs, for information about beating whole eggs, egg yolks, and egg whites.

Liquid In a cake batter, liquid adds moisture, which converts to steam with heat. Common liquids for cakes include milk, cream, sour cream, buttermilk, yogurt, fruit juices, and water. Recipes for foam cakes don't require liquids, other than what is provided by eggs or, in the case of chiffon cakes, by oil.

Acid Cream of tartar and lemon juice, both acids, help to stabilize an egg foam until it sets in the oven. Cream of tartar is commonly beaten into egg whites for this reason, especially if they are not whipped in a copper bowl. Acids help develop a finer texture and more tender crumb; for an angel food cake, they enhance its characteristic white color.

ABOUT CAKE PANS AND OTHER EQUIPMENT

By custom, an angel food cake has a hole in its center and a layer cake is round. We expect to see them that way and so most are, but angel food cakes in loaf form taste just as wonderful, as do square layers. The point is that any one of a number of baking pans will do a particular job well. Don't be compelled to buy every specialty pan you come across unless you have a lot of storage space, you bake a particular cake often, or different shapes appeal to you. Whichever you choose is up to you as long as the pan meets these criteria: it is of the proper volume and height for the recipe (regardless of shape); it is of good quality; it is made of a material that will conduct heat evenly and well. For information on specific pans and materials, see BAKING PANS, FOR BATTER AND DOUGH and MATERIALS FOR COOKWARE.

Other equipment useful for cake making includes such kitchen staples as wooden spoons, spatulas, measuring spoons and cups, mixing bowls, cooling racks, and a quality portable or stand electric mixer with a strong motor. Additional specialized tools, particularly those used for cake decorating—pastry bags, combs, turntables—are optional. See CAKE AND PASTRY TOOLS.

PREPARING PANS

Greasing and flouring baking pans aren't always necessary, but most recipes suggest that you do because it is less likely that the cake will stick. Some recipes call for greasing the bottom and sides, some only the bottom. Some recipes recommend adding a lining of parchment or waxed paper, others don't. Most call for dusting a pan with flour, but a few might suggest using sugar or crumbs. This powdery coat develops a thin, crisp crust and also keeps a cake from absorbing fat from the pan. Follow the directions in the recipe. If you are using a nonstick pan, grease and flour anyway if you are instructed to do so.

A few cakes need special treatment. Dense butter cakes such as pound cakes and heavy fruitcakes, which must bake slowly and for a long time, are baked in greased and paper-lined pans to protect the sides of the cake from overbrowning. Many bakers prefer parchment paper because it can withstand high oven temperatures and is very easy to peel off. Rich batters (those with a lot of sugar or eggs) and those with a large quantity of fruit should bake in greased and floured pans, even pans with nonstick interiors. Angel food cakes and chiffon cakes bake in ungreased pans so the delicate batter can cling to the sides as it rises.

When greasing pans, only a thin layer of fat is necessary, but it should be evenly applied. Use butter, solid shortening, oil, or vegetable cooking spray, and apply with a paper towel, pastry brush, or fingers. To make a paper liner, use bottom of cake pan as a guide, and trace around pan onto a piece of parchment or waxed paper. Cut paper to fit, and place it on the greased bottom of the pan. Grease the paper. If using paper, don't flour pan until after paper is in place. For dusting, place a few tablespoons flour, sugar, or other powder in greased pan, and tilt pan in each direction until entire surface is covered with a thin layer of flour. Invert pan and tap it on a counter or with your fist to remove excess flour (see PREPARING PAN FOR BAKING).

FILLING PANS

Cake batter should fill the pan from one-half to three-quarters full depending upon cake. The pan should never be so full that when the batter rises it overflows. For batters that rise high, such as angel food and sponge cakes, use deeper pans and less batter per pan. For heavier batters such as layer and pound cakes, pans are filled two-thirds to three-quarters full. When dividing a batter among several pans, as for layer cakes, use a ladle or spoon, rather than pouring from the mixing bowl, in order to maintain control and divide batter equally.

ABOUT BAKING CAKES

Place a cake in the oven as soon as possible. Leavening agents begin their action even before a cake is baked and need oven heat to finish the job or they will lose some of their power. Always bake in a preheated oven. Turn oven

SUCCESSFUL CAKE BAKING

If you are well organized and have thoroughly read the recipe before you begin, you will find baking a pleasure and will produce more successful baked products. Look up any unfamiliar terms or techniques. Assemble all of the equipment and ingredients in advance (a baking pan is a good catchall; the French call this process *mis en place*—all in place). Measure all ingredients precisely and carefully; have them at the specified temperature and in the condition indicated in the recipe. Finally, get into the habit of checking oven temperature and turning on the oven before you do anything else. Even the best bakers fail to achieve perfect results every time. Consult the following if you experience difficulties.

IF BUTTER CAKE BATTER CURDLES
- Each egg was not sufficiently mixed in before the next one was added.
- Batter was beaten at too high a speed. If it starts to curdle, ignore it or reduce the mixer speed to medium or medium-low and add 1 tablespoon flour per egg.

IF CAKE FALLS IN THE MIDDLE
- Batter was overbeaten, creating excess aeration which cake was unable to contain.
- Too much sugar was added to the batter.
- Too much baking powder was added.
- Too much liquid was added.
- Cake was undercooked.
- Oven door was opened before cake was set or cake was disturbed because oven door was closed with too much force.

IF CAKE PEAKS IN THE CENTER
- A hard (high-gluten) flour was used instead of soft flour (cake flour).
- Batter was overbeaten after flour was added. (This overactivates the gluten in the flour, creating a tough cake.)
- Oven was too hot. Cake rose too quickly.

IF CAKE IS TOUGH, FLAT, AND HEAVY
- Batter was underbeaten, causing insufficient aeration.
- Not enough sugar was added.
- Not enough baking powder was added.

on at least 10 to 15 minutes before you need to use it. Baking at the proper temperature and maintaining that temperature throughout the process are critical to the success of the final product. Cakes need to bake relatively fast to give their structure some rigidity. Without this framework, they would rise and then collapse because the leavening gases could not be maintained. Avoid opening the oven door during the first half of baking, which is the rising period. If the door is opened, the temperature will drop and the cake will fall; if you must open the door, do so quickly and close it gently without banging it shut.

Know your oven and how it bakes. Test it at several different temperatures with an oven thermometer to see if it is accurately calibrated. If it is off by 25° F or less, you can compensate by raising or lowering the oven temperature. If it is off by as much as 50° F, have it recalibrated. If you have two ovens and you often use both at one time for baking, you may find it convenient and helpful to leave an oven thermometer in each oven. See THERMOMETER.

In a standard oven, bake cakes on the center rack unless otherwise directed. Leave 1 to 2 inches between pans, and between pans and walls of oven. Try not to bake on more than one rack at a time; if you do, the goods baked on the bottom rack will tend to burn because they are close to the heating element and the heat will reflect from the pan on the upper shelf. If you are baking in quantity and need to employ more than one rack, use the middle rack and stagger the pans; once the cake is set rotate pans so they will bake evenly.

You can bake any of the recipes in this book in a convection oven, but you may need to adjust the oven temperature or baking time; see manufacturer's instructions.

USING A MICROWAVE OVEN
Baking cakes in a microwave oven produces mixed results. They won't brown and can bake unevenly; however, they can be moist, airy, and light, and they can have greater volume than those baked in a conventional oven because they don't develop a crust and therefore can rise more. The best cakes for baking in a microwave are rich cakes made with whole eggs, pudding cakes, and cakes made with oil. Boxed cake mixes also can be baked in a microwave with good results—just omit one egg when making the mix to improve texture and volume.

Round and ring shapes bake most evenly. Cakes often bake more evenly on the bottom when elevated on a plastic trivet or inverted glass dish. Rotating the cake dish once or twice, a quarter to a half turn, also facilitates even baking, especially in older ovens.

Experiment with several recipes to see if cakes from a microwave are to your liking; that's the best way to determine which ones are suited for this type of cooking.

WHEN IS THE CAKE DONE?
Experienced cooks rely not only on baking time to know when a cake is ready to come out of the oven, but also on how it looks, smells, sounds, and feels. A cake is done when it springs back lightly when touched in the center with a fingertip and when it begins to pull away from the sides of the pan. It will have developed an aroma, and the popping and sizzling of the batter will have slowed down (if these sounds have stopped completely, cake may be overdone). Start checking about 10 minutes before the end of the recommended baking time. A cake tester, toothpick, or wooden skewer should come out clean when inserted into the center of the cake.

COOLING AND TURNING OUT OF THE PAN
Cool the cake as directed in the recipe. Sponge cakes and butter cakes are often left to sit in their pans on wire cooling racks for 5 or 10 minutes before turning out. During this brief period they will continue to shrink from the sides of the pan. In addition, steam builds between cake and pan, which will help release the cake. Before unmolding, run a knife around the cake to loosen it from the sides of the pan, then sandwich it between two cooling racks and invert. Remove pan, sandwich cake gently between two racks, and flip again. Cool completely at room temperature before icing or storing.

Angel food cakes and chiffon cakes cool by hanging upside down in their pans. Set the angel food cake pan on its legs, or invert and place on the neck of a bottle or a funnel. Chiffon cakes in their pans can be inverted and set directly on a cooling rack because they don't rise as high as angel food cakes and won't be crushed by the rack.

STORING AND FREEZING CAKES

Cakes with fat, such as butter cakes and chiffon cakes, have the best keeping qualities; sponge cakes taste freshest when eaten the day they are baked or within a day or two. Ideally, cakes should be frozen unfrosted and unfilled, then frosted or filled after thawing. Butter-based icings can be frozen successfully for up to two months in rigid containers; thaw in the refrigerator, then bring to room temperature to make spreadable. If icing curdles during thawing, add a little hot, clarified butter and whip at high speed until it comes together. Icings based on egg whites or whipped cream do not freeze well. If you must frost a cake before freezing, select a butter-based icing. Always allow cake to cool completely before freezing. Certain spices, such as nutmeg and cloves, intensify in flavor when they are frozen, so use slightly less than the amount called for in the recipe.

Wrap cakes well with plastic wrap and aluminum foil, date, and freeze for time indicated. Cakes stored longer than the recommended period will suffer a loss of quality but will still be safe to eat. The freezing times are for goods stored at 0° F. Storing foods at temperatures higher than 0° F shortens the storage period considerably.

Angel, Chiffon, and Sponge Cakes Wrap first in plastic wrap and then airtight in a plastic storage bag: angel food cake—four to five days; chiffon cake—up to two weeks; sponge cake—two to three days. To freeze, follow directions for butter cakes. For added protection, store in a box or rigid container, sealing edges with freezer tape; label. Freeze unfrosted cakes up to six months, frosted cakes up to two months.

Butter and Pound Cakes Wrap well and store airtight, five to seven days. To freeze unfrosted, wrap, label, and date. Freeze for up to four months. To thaw, loosen wrapping and thaw at room temperature. To freeze a frosted cake, chill on a tray in freezer (uncovered) until firm. Wrap, label, and date. Freeze for up to two months. To thaw, remove wrapping and thaw at room temperature or in refrigerator.

Cheesecakes Refrigerate, loosely covered with aluminum foil, up to three days. To freeze, chill on a tray in freezer (uncovered) until firm. Wrap, label, and date. For added protection, store in a box or rigid container, sealing edges with freezer tape; label. Freeze for up to four months. Thaw in wrapping in refrigerator.

Fruitcakes Store in an airtight container; will keep up to three weeks when cut; freeze after that. To freeze, wrap, label, and date. Freeze for up to 12 months. Thaw in wrapping at room temperature.

FREEZING CAKE BATTER

As a timesaver, batter for butter cakes can be frozen, unbaked, for up to four weeks, and baked just as it comes from the freezer.

Prepare batter and spoon into pan in which it will be baked, first lining pan with heavy-duty foil. Freeze, uncovered, until solid (this usually takes 6 to 12 hours). Remove batter from pan, wrap it completely, label and date package, and return it to freezer. To bake, grease baking pan in which batter was frozen, peel away foil around batter, and place batter back in pan. Add at least 5 to 10 minutes to normal baking time; cake is done when a wooden pick inserted in center comes out clean.

Proper packaging is important for protecting batters during storage. Package materials must be resistant to both moisture and air. Aluminum foil is excellent; use either heavy-duty foil or a double thickness of regular foil. Heavy plastic bags designed for freezer storage are suitable for packaging cupcakes. Be sure to check the label on the package—if it does not say the bags are suitable for freezing, choose another bag.

Air pockets between food and package material collect moisture, resulting in frost and freezer burn. When wrapping frozen batters, press out as much air as you can and mold wrappings as close to food as possible. To extract air from plastic bags, insert a drinking straw in the opening, squeeze the opening shut around the straw, inhale to draw out air, and fasten tightly. Label and date all packages.

Most batters will keep up to four weeks at 0° F. If your freezer doesn't maintain a temperature of 0° F (and many combination refrigerator-freezers don't), do not keep the batter frozen more than two weeks.

CAKE DECORATION

Some cakes look and taste fine when unadorned. Others require a finish, whether simple or elaborate. The process of cake decoration ranges from the texturing of icing spread on a cake to the application of intricate patterns. When cakes are baked to celebrate an occasion or event, you can tailor their shape and decorations accordingly. Rectangular cakes are good picnic fare because they can be simply iced and easily carried. The same cake base can be baked in layers and elegantly adorned with buttercream rosettes or piped scrolls to serve at a dinner party. See FROSTING, ICING, AND FILLING for specific techniques.

FINISHING THE CAKE

The outside of a cake can be covered with one of the following treatments.

Almond Paste Almond paste or marzipan can be rolled out and used to form the top layer or outside covering of a cake. Almond paste can also be molded or shaped to form cake decorations (roses, flowers, leaves, stems, animals, fruits).

Confectioners' Sugar For a simple, quick finish, sift a light layer of confectioners' sugar over the cake. Create a design by laying a stencil, a fancy paper doily, a cutout snowflake, or strips of paper on the surface of the cake. Sift confectioners' sugar over the pattern, and carefully

With an easy-to-make paper piping cone (see page 246), you can decorate any cake, cookie, or pastry with all types of designs or messages. Lines 1 through 4 are typical borders. Line 5 shows a sample of script. Line 6 is a classic repeating design.

This slice of Devil's Food Cake with Chocolate Buttercream Frosting is an irresistible temptation. The recipe is on page 86.

remove pattern to reveal design. Powdered cocoa may also be used alone or in combination with confectioners' sugar to create contrasting designs.

Glazes A glaze is thinner than an icing. It is often poured over a cake rather than spread on. Cakes can be covered with a jelly glaze, a chocolate glaze, a confectioners' sugar glaze, or a fondant icing glaze.

Icing Applying icing in a smooth, flat layer is a common decorating technique. A textured surface (swirls, peaks, lines) can be created with a flat metal spatula or knife. Icing can also be applied in a smooth layer and textured with a comb scraper (serrated metal triangle) to create grooves. Of the many kinds of icings, some must be spread on with a spatula or knife, and others can be piped on with a pastry bag and tip.

TYPICAL CAKE DECORATIONS

These decorations are applied to the icing, glaze, or other surface covering on the cake to create patterns and add complementary flavor.

Chocolate Melted and tempered chocolate can be used in many ways. Make chocolate curls, rolls, and ruffles out of melted chocolate, wrap the cake in a paper-thin chocolate ribbon, or pipe chocolate through a pastry bag onto an iced or plain cake. See CHOCOLATE for directions; see FROSTING, ICING, AND FILLING for information on using a pastry bag.

Cookie Crumbs Finely crushed cookies can be patted around the sides of the cake to add flavor, color, and texture to the icing.

Fresh Fruit Either whole or sliced fresh fruit can be arranged decoratively on top of a cake. Fresh fruit is usually brushed with a thin jelly glaze to make it shine.

Miscellaneous Decorations Candied (glacé) orange, lemon, or citrus peel (chop candied peel, or cut in julienne strips, or dip pieces in melted chocolate); dried fruits (raisins, currants); crystallized violets, roses, or mimosas (available from well-stocked cookware shops or stores specializing in equipment for cake decorating); candied coffee beans; silver balls, gold leaf, and crystal sugar; preserved ginger; a cloth or paper ribbon tied around the cake after icing is firm; fresh flowers or leaves (free from harmful sprays).

Nuts Finely chopped, coarsely chopped, slivered, or sliced nuts, nut halves, or whole nuts can be used. Whole or halved nuts can be dipped in caramel or chocolate. Nuts taste and look best when lightly toasted in the oven before they are used to decorate a cake.

Sauces Serve a sauce on the side or set cake slices in a pool of sauce. Chocolate sauce, fruit sauce, purée (raspberry or strawberry), and vanilla custard sauce (*crème anglaise*) are good choices.

SLICING AND SERVING

Let the cake cool before attempting to slice it. Use a sharp knife with a thin blade. For iced cakes, clean the knife after each cut to remove accumulated frosting. Angel food cakes and sponge cakes are pliable and hard to slice. For these cakes, a serrated knife works best. Cut with a sawing motion; don't press down as you slice or you will compress the cake.

A cake slice can be presented lying down on its side or standing up (when possible or when more attractive). Try to include part of the top decoration, if any, in each serving.

◼ ANGEL FOOD CAKE

This foam cake is pure white because only egg whites—no yolks, no fat—are used. Food for angels, indeed! If the idea of 14 egg whites overwhelms you, remember that they freeze well. Stockpile them in your freezer when preparing recipes that call for egg yolks only. See EGG, Storage for freezing information. Work quickly and gently when making an angel food cake. If the batter is overmixed, it will lose volume and the final product will be tough. Remember that the cake must cool upside down. For a light summer dessert, accompany cake slices with fruit sauce or sliced fresh fruit. Slices of angel food cake make delicious French toast.

    1½ cups sifted cake flour
    1¾ cups sugar
    14 egg whites
        Pinch salt
     1 teaspoon cream of tartar (optional)
     2 teaspoons vanilla extract
    ½ teaspoon almond extract
     1 teaspoon fresh lemon juice

1. Preheat oven to 300° F. Sift flour again into a dry mixing bowl. Sift sugar into a separate bowl and set both bowls aside.

2. In a copper or stainless steel bowl, beat egg whites to soft peaks; add salt when whites are just foamy (if bowl is stainless steel, add cream of tartar at this point as well). Gently fold in sugar with a rubber spatula; fold in flour in 2 batches, then add vanilla and almond extracts and lemon juice. When all is completely incorporated, pour batter into a 10-inch tube pan and smooth top.

3. Bake until cake is a pale, creamy brown color, top springs back when gently touched with finger, and a wooden skewer inserted in center comes out clean (about 1 hour). Cool upside down in pan. (If pan doesn't have its own feet, invert pan over the neck of a bottle or balance on 4 small ramekins.)

4. To serve, gently remove from pan, releasing sides with a knife. Decorate and serve as desired.

Serves 10 to 12.

ROLLING A SPONGE CAKE

Turn cake out onto kitchen towel lined with a piece of sugar-dusted parchment paper; carefully roll.

When cool, gently unroll and spread with filling, leaving a narrow margin of bare cake all around. If cake is covered completely, the filling will be forced out of the cake as it is rerolled.

Carefully roll again and decorate. For a special effect, shown here, roll part-way; pipe whipped cream rosettes along edge and top with raspberries. Dust with confectioners' sugar, if desired.

◼ BASIC SPONGE CAKE

This extremely versatile cake has a light, soft, and fine crumb. Sponge cakes depend on egg yolks and egg whites for leavening, each beaten and incorporated separately. Simple garnishes are best—such as fresh fruit, whipped cream, ice cream, or light frostings. To layer, halve cake with a serrated knife.

  6 eggs, separated
  1 cup sugar
  2 teaspoons vanilla extract
     Pinch salt
  ½ teaspoon cream of tartar (optional)
  1 cup cake flour, sifted

1. Preheat oven to 350° F. Lightly grease and flour an 8- or 9-inch-diameter cake pan. Line bottom with parchment paper.

2. In a large bowl beat egg yolks to break them up; add ¾ cup sugar and continue to beat until mixture falls from beater in a ribbon and leaves a slowly dissolving trail on surface (ribbon stage). Beat in vanilla.

3. In a separate large copper or stainless steel bowl, beat egg whites until just foamy; add salt (if bowl is stainless steel, add cream of tartar at this point as well). Beat whites to soft peaks; add remaining ¼ cup sugar and beat until stiff, glossy peaks form.

4. Fold flour into yolk mixture in three stages. Then fold in one third of whites to lighten. Very gently fold in remaining whites; fill prepared pan with batter.

5. Bake until pale gold color, top springs back when pressed gently with finger, and a wooden skewer inserted in center comes out clean (20 to 30 minutes). Cool in pan 10 minutes, then turn out onto rack and cool completely. Decorate as desired.

Serves 8.

Chocolate Sponge Cake Substitute ¼ cup cocoa powder for ¼ cup of the flour.

◼ BASIC SPONGE CAKE ROLL

Cake rolls are not difficult to prepare and decorate, and are always very pretty when served. Typical of sponge cakes, they are appealing when simply filled and dusted with confectioners' sugar or cocoa powder. For a more substantial filling, use any flavor of buttercream frosting.

  4 eggs, separated
  ⅔ cup sugar
  1½ teaspoons vanilla extract
     Pinch salt
  ¼ teaspoon cream of tartar (optional)
  ⅔ cup cake flour, sifted

1. Preheat oven to 350° F. Lightly grease and flour an 11- by 15-inch jelly-roll pan. Line bottom with parchment paper.

2. Prepare according to directions for Basic Sponge Cake through step 4. Fill prepared jelly-roll pan and bake until top springs back when gently pressed with finger (about 15 minutes). Cool in pan 5 minutes.

3. Turn cake out onto a kitchen towel covered with a sheet of parchment paper that has been dusted with confectioners' sugar, superfine sugar, or cocoa powder (depending on recipe). Remove paper from cake bottom and trim crusts all around. Carefully roll up in parchment, wrap with kitchen towel to secure, and cool completely on a wire rack.

4. Gently unroll, then spread with filling of choice to within 1 inch of edges. Reroll carefully; finish as desired.

Serves 6 to 8.

Chocolate Sponge Cake Roll Substitute 3 tablespoons cocoa powder for 3 tablespoons of the flour.

Elegant, sugar-dusted Ladyfingers are a classic example of the pastry maker's art. To shape them into even lengths, the cake batter is piped onto a baking sheet with a pastry bag.

LADYFINGERS

These soft, spongy fingers of cake are probably best known as the shell for Charlotte Russe (see page 170). They are also delicious eaten alone. Quick to make, they store well in an airtight container for one week. For longer storage and in damp, wet weather, they should be frozen.

   1 **cup cake flour**
      Pinch salt
   4 **eggs, separated**
  ½ **cup sugar**
  ¼ **teaspoon cream of tartar (optional)**
   1 **teaspoon vanilla extract**
      Confectioners' sugar, for dusting

1. Preheat oven to 350° F. Line a baking sheet with parchment paper; butter paper and lightly dust with flour. Sift flour and salt together and set aside.

2. In bowl of heavy-duty mixer or other medium bowl, beat yolks and ¼ cup sugar together until mixture falls from beater in a ribbon and leaves a slowly dissolving trail on surface (ribbon stage). In a copper or stainless steel bowl, beat egg whites to soft peaks (if bowl is stainless steel, add cream of tartar when whites are just foamy); add remaining sugar and beat until stiff peaks form.

3. Stir one-fourth beaten egg whites into yolk mixture to lighten; sift in half the flour and fold into batter. Add remaining flour, then most of remaining beaten egg whites. Fold in rest of whites and vanilla.

4. Fill a pastry bag fitted with a ½-inch plain tip half full with batter. Pipe 4-inch-long fingers onto paper-lined baking sheet, about 1 inch apart (see Note). Sprinkle with confectioners' sugar and bake until edges are just beginning to brown (15 to 18 minutes). Cool on wire racks.

Makes 3 dozen ladyfingers.

Note   If ladyfingers are to be used to line a charlotte mold, you can pipe fingers ½ inch apart so that as they bake they will expand and touch. To line mold, don't separate ladyfingers. Trim them to proper height, then lift in a sheet and set around inside of mold. For a variation, pipe rows of ladyfingers on the diagonal.

GENOISE

A sponge cake is leavened with a foam made of separately beaten egg yolks and egg whites, and without fat; a génoise uses whole eggs and is enriched with butter. It is the classic French cake, and the foundation for almost all of the French *gâteaux*. Eggs will beat to greatest volume if utensils and ingredients are at room temperature.

   4 **eggs**
  ⅔ **cup sugar**
   1 **cup cake flour, sifted twice**
      Pinch salt
   3 **tablespoons unsalted butter, melted and cooled**

1. Preheat oven to 350° F. Lightly grease and flour an 8-inch-diameter cake pan; line bottom with a circle of parchment paper.

2. *To prepare in a heavy-duty mixer:* In warmed bowl of mixer (fill bowl with hot water and drain), beat eggs at medium speed to break up; add sugar and beat until mixture falls from beater in a ribbon and leaves a slowly dissolving trail on surface (ribbon stage). *To prepare with a portable electric mixer or balloon whisk:* Beat eggs and sugar to ribbon stage in a large mixing bowl set over a pan of hot, but not boiling, water (make sure that pan does not touch water).

3. Gently fold in one third of flour, then another third. Mix some batter with melted butter; continue mixing until butter is incorporated, then fold into batter with last third of flour.

4. Pour batter into prepared pan and smooth surface, making a slight hollow in center. Bake until a pale gold color, the center springs back when gently pressed with finger, and a wooden skewer inserted in the center comes out clean (25 to 30 minutes). Cool in pan 10 minutes; turn out onto a wire rack to cool completely.

5. Slice horizontally into 2 layers with a long, serrated knife (see photograph at right). To moisten and flavor cake layers, brush with a soaking syrup (see SUGAR AND SYRUP), then fill with fruit, buttercream, or any of the frostings or icings in FROSTING, ICING, AND FILLING.

Serves 8.

LEMON CHIFFON CAKE

An American creation of the 1920s, the chiffon cake is a cross between a foam cake and a shortened cake. Because it uses oil instead of butter, it is extremely moist and stores well. Chiffon cake has a pleasing light texture and keeps its shape well, so it can travel to a potluck or picnic without damage. The cake tastes equally delicious if made with fresh orange juice and orange instead of lemon (see Orange Chiffon Cake variation). Glacé icing is extremely simple to prepare and apply.

> 2 cups cake flour
> 1½ cups sugar
> 1 tablespoon baking powder
> ½ teaspoon salt
> ½ cup vegetable oil
> ¼ cup fresh lemon juice
> ½ cup milk
> 1 teaspoon finely grated lemon rind
> 6 eggs, separated
> ½ teaspoon cream of tartar (optional)
> Citrus Glacé Icing (see page 250)

1. Preheat oven to 325° F. In a large bowl sift flour, sugar, baking powder, and salt. Add oil, lemon juice, milk, and grated rind.

2. In a copper or stainless steel bowl, beat egg whites to soft peaks (if bowl is stainless steel, add cream of tartar to whites when just foamy). Gently fold one third of whites into flour mixture to lighten, then gently fold in remaining whites.

3. Pour batter into 10-inch bundt or tube pan. Bake until wooden skewer comes out clean and top springs back when gently pressed with finger (about 1 hour). Cool upside down on wire rack.

4. When cool, remove from pan and decorate with Citrus Glacé Icing.

Serves 8 to 10.

Orange Chiffon Cake Substitute grated orange rind and fresh orange juice for the lemon rind and juice. Prepare icing with orange flavoring.

BASIC YELLOW LAYER CAKE

The American counterpart to the French génoise, the versatile layer cake appears at all celebrations. It can be dressed up or down, and is rich and moist. This is a butter or creamed cake, which means that fat and sugar are beaten together to incorporate air. The creaming step gives the cake its characteristic velvety texture. Remember that fats cream to best volume at room temperature. A chocolate variation follows. The batter can also be used for cupcakes. Fill and frost with any of the frostings in FROSTING, ICING, AND FILLING.

> 2½ cups cake flour
> 2½ teaspoons baking powder
> 1 teaspoon salt
> 1⅓ cups sugar
> ¾ cup solid vegetable shortening or butter
> 3 eggs
> 1 teaspoon vanilla extract
> ½ cup milk

1. Preheat oven to 350° F. Lightly grease bottoms of two 9-inch-diameter cake pans; line bottoms with circles of parchment paper; lightly grease and flour pans and paper.

2. Sift together flour, baking powder, and salt; set aside. In a large bowl cream sugar and shortening until combined. Add 1 egg; beat until light, fluffy, and a pale, ivory color. Add remaining eggs, beating well after each addition. If using a heavy-duty mixer, stop beating as soon as eggs are incorporated and mixture is light and fluffy. Blend in vanilla.

3. Remove beater from mixture. By hand, gently fold in sifted flour mixture in 3 stages, alternating with milk, and beginning and ending with flour.

4. Divide batter evenly between 2 prepared pans. Bake until golden brown, top springs back when gently pressed with finger, and a wooden skewer inserted in center comes out clean (20 to 25 minutes). Cool in pan 10 minutes, then turn out onto wire rack and cool completely. Decorate as desired.

Serves 8.

For an 8-Inch Layer Cake Use two 8-inch cake pans. Bake 25 to 30 minutes. Each layer can be split in half to make a 4-layer cake.

Basic Chocolate Layer Cake Substitute ½ cup unsweetened cocoa powder for ½ cup flour; sift cocoa powder and flour together to blend.

Basic Cupcakes Spoon batter into lightly greased and floured muffin pans or line pans with paper cupcake liners. Bake 15 to 20 minutes.

Makes 18 to 24 cupcakes.

Unlike American layer cakes, which are formed from two separately baked rounds, a layered génoise is created from a single layer sliced in half horizontally. Use a sharp, serrated bread knife, longer than the diameter of the cake, to make a clean slice.

This scrumptious Carrot Spice Cake is topped with Cream Cheese Frosting, partly piped on with a pastry bag, and walnut halves. The sides are covered with chopped, toasted walnuts.

3. Stir baking soda into buttermilk. Add ½ cup flour to egg mixture; then add ⅓ cup buttermilk mixture. Continue to add flour and buttermilk alternately, beating well after each addition. Stir in cocoa mixture.

4. Divide batter evenly between the 2 prepared pans. Bake until top springs back when gently pressed with finger and a wooden skewer inserted into center comes out clean (30 to 35 minutes). Cool in pans 5 minutes, then turn out onto wire racks and cool completely. Frost with Chocolate Buttercream.

Serves 8.

■ CARROT SPICE CAKE

For a simple finish to this delicious cake, follow the directions given in the recipe. For a more elaborate presentation, see photograph at left.

> 1⅓ cups unsalted butter
> 1¾ cups sugar
>   4 eggs
>   2 cups flour
>   2 teaspoons baking soda
>   1 teaspoon ground cinnamon
>   ½ teaspoon ground allspice
>   ¼ teaspoon freshly grated nutmeg
>   ¼ teaspoon ground cloves
>   3 cups (about 1 lb) grated carrots
> 1¼ cups chopped walnuts
>   ¼ cup golden raisins
>   ¼ cup coarsely chopped walnuts, for decoration

Cream Cheese Frosting

>   ¼ cup unsalted butter, softened
>   6 ounces cream cheese, softened
>   2 cups sifted confectioners' sugar
>   2 teaspoons fresh lemon juice

1. Preheat oven to 325° F. Lightly grease and flour a 9- by 13-inch baking pan.

2. In a large bowl cream butter to lighten; gradually add sugar and cream until light, fluffy, and a pale, ivory color. Add eggs, one at a time, beating well after each addition.

3. Sift together flour, baking soda, cinnamon, allspice, nutmeg, and cloves. Add to butter mixture and blend well. Stir in carrots, the 1¼ cups walnuts, and raisins.

4. Spread batter evenly in pan. Bake until top springs back when gently pressed with finger and a wooden skewer inserted into center comes out clean (45 to 55 minutes). Cool in pan on wire rack. Spread Cream Cheese Frosting on cool cake. Sprinkle the ¼ cup walnuts on top.

Serves 10 to 12.

Cream Cheese Frosting   Cream butter and cream cheese. Add confectioners' sugar and lemon juice; beat until smooth.

■ DEVIL'S FOOD CAKE

Perhaps this rich, dark chocolate layer cake got its name because it contrasts dramatically with the snowy whiteness of angel food cake. Split the layers, if desired, to create a four-layer extravaganza.

> ¾ cup unsweetened cocoa powder
> ¾ cup boiling water
> ½ cup solid vegetable shortening or butter
> 2 cups sugar
> 2 eggs
> 1 teaspoon vanilla extract
> ¼ teaspoon salt
> 1½ teaspoons baking soda
> 1 cup buttermilk
> 2 cups sifted cake flour
> 2 cups Chocolate Buttercream Frosting
>   (see page 248)

1. Preheat oven to 350° F. Lightly grease bottoms of two 8-inch-diameter by 2-inch-deep cake pans; line bottoms with circles of parchment paper; lightly grease and flour pans and paper. Stir cocoa into the boiling water until dissolved; set aside.

2. In a large bowl cream shortening and sugar together until light and fluffy. Add eggs, one at a time, beating after each addition. Beat in vanilla and salt.

PECAN APPLESAUCE CAKE

Chunks of homemade applesauce keep this cake moist for days. If you are looking for a healthier snack, replace the flour and sugar with whole wheat flour and honey.

    ½ cup unsalted butter or corn oil
    ½ cup firmly packed brown sugar
    2 eggs
    ½ cup honey
    ½ cup apple juice
    2½ cups sifted unbleached flour
    1½ teaspoons baking soda
    1 teaspoon salt
    ¼ teaspoon baking powder
    1 teaspoon ground cinnamon
    ½ teaspoon ground cloves (optional)
    ¼ teaspoon ground allspice (optional)
    ½ cup dried currants
    1 cup chopped pecans
       Pecan halves, for decoration

Chunky Applesauce

    4 apples
    ¼ cup sugar
    2 tablespoons water

Whipped Cream Icing

    6 ounces cream cheese, softened
    ⅓ cup firmly packed light brown sugar
    1 teaspoon vanilla extract
    1 cup whipping cream

1. Preheat oven to 350° F. Lightly grease and flour a 9- by 13-inch baking pan. Make Chunky Applesauce; cool to room temperature.

2. In a large bowl cream butter with brown sugar until light and fluffy. Add eggs and beat. Combine honey with apple juice; set aside.

3. Sift together flour, soda, salt, baking powder, cinnamon, and cloves and allspice (if used). Add to egg mixture alternately with honey–apple juice mixture, beating after each addition. Stir in currants, pecans, and Chunky Applesauce.

4. Bake until cake tester comes out clean (40 to 50 minutes). Cool in pan on wire rack.

5. Spread Whipped Cream Icing over top of cake. Decorate each serving with a pecan half.

Serves 10 to 12.

Chunky Applesauce Peel, core, and slice apples. In a medium saucepan combine apples with sugar and the water; cover and cook until apples are just tender but not mushy (do not overcook).

Makes 1½ cups.

Whipped Cream Icing Beat cream cheese with brown sugar until smooth. Add vanilla. Whip cream until it holds peaks, and gently fold into cream cheese mixture.

GINGER-PEACH UPSIDE-DOWN CAKE

Spicy gingerbread makes a delicious partner to peaches or nectarines in this unusual version of the classic American dessert—upside-down cake. The cake batter is spooned on a layer of sliced fruit. When turned upside down after baking, the fruit slices glow under a buttery brown-sugar glaze that drips delicately down the sides of the cake.

    1 cup firmly packed light brown sugar
    6 tablespoons unsalted butter, melted
    3 peaches or nectarines
    2½ cups flour
    2 teaspoons baking soda
    ½ teaspoon ground cinnamon
    2 teaspoons ground ginger
    ⅛ teaspoon freshly grated nutmeg
    ⅛ teaspoon ground cardamom (optional)
    ½ teaspoon salt
    ½ cup dark molasses
    1 cup boiling water
    1 scant cup unsalted butter, melted,
       or safflower oil
    1 cup granulated sugar
    2 eggs, lightly beaten
    2 teaspoons finely grated orange rind (optional)

1. Preheat oven to 350° F. Butter sides of a 10- by 3-inch springform pan. Stir brown sugar into the 6 tablespoons melted butter; spread evenly in bottom of pan. Peel and pit peaches; cut into ½-inch-wide slices. (If using nectarines, do not peel.) Arrange slices (packed closely together) in concentric circles on sugar in bottom of pan.

2. Sift together flour, baking soda, cinnamon, ginger, nutmeg, cardamom (if used), and salt; set aside. Combine molasses and the water in a bowl; set aside.

3. In a large bowl beat the 1 cup melted butter and granulated sugar until light. Beat in eggs and orange rind (if used). Add the molasses mixture. Stir in dry ingredients; beat until well blended. Pour batter into the peach-lined pan. Bake until cake tester comes out clean or cake springs back when lightly touched in center (about 1 hour). Cover top of cake with aluminum foil if it begins to burn at the edges.

4. Allow cake to cool in pan for 30 minutes. Invert cake on serving platter, remove cake pan, and allow glaze to drip down sides of cake. Serve while still warm or at room temperature with whipped cream.

Serves 10 to 12.

■ CHOCOLATE MARBLE CREAM CAKE

Here's a chocolate marble cake designed to be eaten with your fingers. It's perfect fare for picnics or box lunches.

    4 ounces semisweet chocolate, coarsely chopped
2¼ cups sifted cake flour
1½ teaspoons baking powder
   ¾ cup granulated sugar
   1 cup whipping cream
   2 tablespoons fresh lemon juice
   2 extralarge eggs
    Confectioners' sugar, for decoration

1. Preheat oven to 375° F. Lightly grease bottom of a 5- by 9- by 3-inch loaf pan. Line bottom of pan with parchment paper; lightly grease and flour pan and paper.

2. Melt chocolate in a bowl over hot, not boiling, water. When chocolate is just melted, remove from heat; cool 10 minutes.

3. Sift flour with baking powder twice; set aside. Combine granulated sugar, cream, and lemon juice in a medium bowl. Add eggs, one at a time, beating well after each addition.

4. Divide batter evenly between 2 medium bowls. Stir melted chocolate into half of batter. Stir half of flour into each half of batter. Fill loaf pan, alternating layers of chocolate and vanilla batter. To create a marbled effect, run a knife through batter in a figure-eight pattern.

5. Bake 20 minutes. Reduce oven to 350° F and bake until golden brown, top springs back when gently pressed with finger, and a wooden skewer inserted in center comes out clean (20 to 30 minutes). Turn out onto wire rack to cool. When cool, sift a light layer of confectioners' sugar on top.

Serves 8 to 10.

■ POUND CAKE

A very rich creamed cake, pound cake was originally made with 1 pound *each* butter, sugar, eggs, and flour. The eggs were the sole leavening. Today, a little baking powder is often added for additional lightness. If you prefer a less sweet version, omit the 3 tablespoons sugar.

  1½ cups flour
   ½ teaspoon baking powder
   1 cup butter
   1 cup plus 3 tablespoons sugar
   4 eggs

1. Preheat oven to 350° F. Lightly grease and flour a 4½- by 8½- by 3-inch loaf pan. Sift flour and baking powder together; set aside.

2. In a medium bowl cream butter and sugar together until light, fluffy, and a pale, ivory color. Add eggs, one at a time, beating well after each addition (if mixture begins to curdle, add 1 tablespoon flour).

3. Fold in flour and pour immediately into prepared pan. Bake until golden brown and a wooden skewer inserted into center comes out clean (25 to 30 minutes). Cool in pan 10 minutes, then turn out onto wire rack and cool completely. Serve sliced with fresh fruit or ice cream.

Serves 8.

■ RICH FRUITCAKE

Although the English may not have invented fruitcake, it is certainly associated with that country. There, fruitcakes are made for all sorts of celebrations, from Christmas to weddings to birthdays. Compared with an American version, this is more cakelike. It is dark, rich, and very traditionally English. The fruits mixed into the spiced batter are a combination of dried and candied—raisins and currants, glacé cherries, and candied citrus peel. For more flavor, let fruits macerate in either sherry or brandy several hours or overnight.

  2½ cups flour
   1 teaspoon baking powder
   ½ teaspoon *each* ground cinnamon and nutmeg
   ¼ teaspoon *each* ground allspice and cloves
  1½ cups dark raisins
  1½ cups golden raisins
  1½ cups dried currants
   1 cup glacé cherries
   ½ cup candied citrus peel
   ½ cup slivered or sliced almonds
   ½ cup sherry or brandy
   1 cup butter, softened
  1⅓ cups firmly packed brown sugar
   4 eggs
   ½ cup milk
    Grated rind and juice of 1 lemon

1. Preheat oven to 350° F. Lightly grease a deep, 8-inch-diameter cake pan; line with a double layer of parchment paper. Lightly grease and flour paper. Into a medium bowl sift flour, baking powder, cinnamon, nutmeg, allspice, and cloves; set aside.

2. In a large bowl combine dark raisins, golden raisins, currants, cherries, citrus peel, and almonds. Sprinkle with sherry and set aside (preferably several hours or overnight).

3. In a large bowl cream together butter and sugar until light, fluffy, and a pale, ivory color. Add eggs, one at a time, beating well after each addition. Fold in flour mixture alternately with milk. Drain fruit if any liquid is left and fold into batter.

4. Spoon batter into prepared pan. Bake 1 hour. Reduce heat to 300° F and bake until golden brown and a wooden skewer inserted into center comes out clean (1½ hours). Should cake begin to overbrown before it is done, cover with aluminum foil.

Serves 10 to 12.

■ ALMOND TORTE

In the winter this very moist cake is delicious with cooked fruit compotes. In the summer accompany it with fresh fruits and fruit sauces.

    1¼ cups flour
     1 teaspoon baking powder
    ¾ cup sugar
    ¾ cup butter
     1 package (7 oz) soft almond paste
     4 eggs
    ½ teaspoon almond extract
        Raspberry Sauce, for accompaniment
        (see page 522)

1. Preheat oven to 350° F. Lightly grease bottom of a 9-inch-diameter cake pan; line with a circle of parchment paper; lightly grease and flour pan and paper. Sift flour and baking powder together and set aside.

2. In a large bowl cream together sugar, butter, and almond paste until light and fluffy. Add eggs, one at a time, beating well after each addition; stir in almond extract. Fold in flour mixture.

3. Pour batter into prepared cake pan. Bake until golden and a wooden skewer inserted into center comes out clean (40 to 50 minutes). Cool 10 minutes in pan, then remove from pan and cool on rack to room temperature. Serve accompanied with Raspberry Sauce.

Serves 8.

Recipes and Related Information

Cheesecake, 117; Chocolate Ruffle Torte, 127; Gingerbread, 267; Greek Walnut Torte, 605; Lemon Roulade Charlotte, 171; Poppy Seed Cake With Cream Cheese Frosting, 454.

CAKE AND PASTRY TOOLS

Having every tool and utensil described here does not guarantee that your pie crust will be flaky or that your angel food cake will rise light and airy, but the better equipped you are, the easier baking will be. On the other hand, buy only what you need and have room to store.

BOWL SCRAPER

This thin, flat, flexible piece of nylon has one edge that is curved to fit the curve of a mixing bowl. Many cooks prefer it to a rubber spatula for getting at the last bit of batter left in a bowl or for scooping up frosting, cream puff paste, or other light mixtures. Usually either kidney-shaped or rectangular, it has a general overall measurement of 5¾ inches by 3¾ inches. It is dishwasher-safe.

Fresh fruit best complements the rich, buttery flavor of Almond Torte. Try a summery sauce of puréed and whole raspberries.

BRUSHES: PASTRY AND BASTING

Use a pastry brush if you need to apply a delicate jelly glaze to a fruit tart or cake; coat breads, rolls, and pastries with an egg wash, milk, or butter; or wipe away excess flour or other crumbs on a pie or a serving plate. These brushes tend to have short handles (1½ to 4 inches long), and the best are made of long-lasting boar bristles rather than nylon. They are either flat (½ inch to 4 inches wide) or round (usually about 1 inch in diameter). Round brushes and wide flat ones make fast work of buttering pans and wide sheets of filo dough. For laying on the thinnest glaze or liqueur bastes, some pastry makers use a brush made of goose feathers, which are braided at the ends to form a handle.

Brushes with longer handles are used for basting meats and poultry or for buttering pans. Handles average about 12 inches long and bristles are often offset, at an angle. This design lets the cook stand back at a safe distance from a hot oven or grill, yet still be able to reach the food.

Select a brush with bristles that fit deep into the handle and are connected securely to it so they stay on the brush and do not end up in the food. Some nylon and plastic brushes can go in the dishwasher. Natural-bristle brushes should be washed by hand with warm, soapy water right after using and air-dried.

CAKE COMB

The swirls and grooves that texture the frosting of many cakes are easily made with this tool, which is also known as a decorating comb or comb scraper. It is a rigid metal triangle with serrated teeth on all three sides; each row of teeth is of a different size. Made of stainless steel, the comb measures approximately 5 by 5 by 4 inches.

Many specialty tools are available to assist the home baker. Clockwise from bottom left are: pie weights, pastry bag and tips, dough scraper, cooling racks, pastry blender, pastry brushes, flour dredger, cardboard cake trays, cake tester, cookie press, pastry crimper and wheels, rolling pin, cookie cutters, and a marble board.

CAKE-DECORATING TURNTABLE

By elevating a cake above the counter, this device allows more room for your hand to maneuver. Because the platter rotates, you can apply frosting, chopped nuts, or other surface decoration more evenly and with a more professional-looking result. Plates come in 12-, 14-, and 16-inch rounds or 12- by 16-inch rectangles; all sizes sit on a 4-inch-high base. The better ones are metal, with a cast-iron base and an aluminum alloy disk. For the occasional user, a less expensive plastic version with a shorter base will serve the same purpose.

CAKE TESTER

A cake is considered done if crumbs or batter does not adhere to a tester inserted into the center. For this task you can use a special tool made of a rigid stainless steel wire with a plastic-coated loop handle, or, perhaps more handily, a toothpick, bamboo skewer, broom straw, or sharp knife.

CARDBOARD CAKE TRAYS

These are invaluable aids for cake-decorating. Set under cakes to give them support so they can be easily maneuvered, these trays are especially helpful when applying frosting or other finishing touches. The trays are coated and are available in standard cake sizes, in rounds, rectangles, and squares. Look for them at better cookware stores and at cake-decorating supply stores. You can make your own tray by cutting cardboard slightly smaller than the cake and wrapping it smoothly and tightly with aluminum foil.

COOKIE PRESS

With this hand-operated machine you can transform butter-rich spritz cookie dough into dozens of fanciful shapes. The body is an aluminum and chrome cylinder that you fill with chilled dough. A removable aluminum collar at one end holds one of over a dozen accompanying pattern disks; a mechanism at the other end—either a lever, screw, or plunger—forces the dough through the disk. A press can also function like a pastry bag if you use one of the decorating tips. Look for a cookie press that allows you to regulate the amount of dough ejected through the disk. Even with the best presses, it takes some practice to produce uniform results, but you can always recycle the rejects and try again. After use, wash each part thoroughly in warm, sudsy water, and dry immediately before storing.

COOLING RACK

Wire cooling racks allow air to circulate around baked goods as they cool so steam won't build up underneath and cause them to get soggy. Round racks are good for a single layer of cake; rectangular ones hold two layers, a sheet cake, several loaves of bread, or a big batch of cookies. A good assortment would be two or three round racks and two rectangular ones. Select rectangular racks as large as you can store; these allow you to cool several baking sheets' worth of cookies at a time. Buy racks made of sturdy, heavy-gauge wire strong enough to support cakes and breads without sagging. Larger racks should have feet in the center as well as the corners. Round ones measure 11½ inches in diameter; well-sized rectangular ones are 10½ by 17 inches and 13 by 19 inches.

DREDGER

A cup-shaped dredger is a handy way to coat a cake or pastry with confectioners' sugar, cinnamon sugar, or cocoa, or to flour a work surface. Flour dredgers have about a 2-cup capacity, with a perforated metal screw-on cover and a handle. Sugar dredgers are smaller, holding no more than ½ cup, have a mesh cover, and do not have a handle.

FLOUR SIFTER

See COLANDER, STRAINER, AND SIEVE.

ICING SPATULA

See SPATULA, SCRAPER, AND TURNER.

PASTRY BAG AND TIPS

With a pastry bag you can inscribe a cake with a special message or adorn it with chains of stars, shape delicate ladyfingers and elegant éclairs, or border a roast with a ribbon of mashed potatoes. To use, the cone-shaped bag is filled with batter or icing; when pressure is applied to the bag, the filling is pushed out through a decorative tinned or chromed steel tip held at the pointed end of the bag.

Pastry bags are made of lightweight nylon, canvas, or plastic-lined cloth. Nylon is preferred because it doesn't retain odors, is flexible, and is easy to care for. Most useful sizes are 12, 14, and 16 inches long. Smaller bags are better suited for small designs and for decorating cakes and cookies. Larger bags hold more and can pipe a larger

surface without needing a refill. They can be purchased alone or in a set with an assortment of the most common tips: *plain* for writing and for making lines, stems, dots, or line drawings; *open-star* for small or large rosettes, stars, and border designs; *closed-star* for rosettes and flowers; *leaf* for piping leaves; *slit* for ribbons. Hundreds of specialty tips can be bought singly or in sets. A plastic coupling unit allows you to change tips without switching to a new bag or to use tips that would otherwise not fit the bag. If you don't want to bother with the coupler, consider buying several sizes of bags and a selection of tips for each.

After use, wash pastry bag, tips, and coupling unit in hot, sudsy water; rinse well and air-dry completely or bag will mildew and tips rust.

For information on how to use a pastry bag, see FROSTING, ICING, AND FILLING.

PASTRY BLENDER

To cut fat into flour when making pastry or biscuit dough, most people use a pastry blender. This hand tool has six U-shaped, thin stainless steel wires that are held in place by a wooden or plastic handle. The wires evenly distribute the cold fat, which is worked until the flour-fat mixture is the desired consistency, usually described as coarse crumbs. The more rigid the wires, the better the tool will work. Make sure wires are fastened securely to handle.

PASTRY BOARD

For rolling out pastry and for making candies, you want a surface that stays cool. Marble is considered best because it naturally maintains a surface temperature 20° F cooler than air. It is nonporous and therefore won't absorb moisture from the dough and cause it to stick. Marble, however, is heavy and expensive. A less costly, less weighty, but quite effective alternative is a board made of a dense, white, synthetic polycarbonate. Like marble, this material stays cool; it has the additional attribute of being dishwasher-safe.

Portable marble boards weighing about 20 pounds are ½ inch thick and measure 18 inches square. Boards of synthetic materials come in many sizes; 16 by 18 inches and 16 by 20 inches are practical dimensions. Choose the largest board that will easily fit your work space and allows you to roll out dough comfortably.

PASTRY CLOTH

Made of canvas, pastry cloths are used as a surface for rolling out pastry. Some are printed with guides representing standard diameters of pie crusts; others are set in a frame that keeps the cloth taut and wrinkle-free. Before use, flour is rubbed into the weave, which creates a somewhat nonstick finish. Before storing, the cloth should be shaken out; occasional washing will keep it sanitary. Cloths measure 17 by 18 inches or 21 inches square.

Many European cookies are shaped by pressing soft dough into whimsical, charming carved wooden molds, like these Dutch ones.

PASTRY AND COOKIE CUTTERS

Anyone can be an artist with the help of these cutters. Buy ones with a thin cutting edge that will slice through dough without dragging. Sides should be strong enough so they do not bend under pressure or deform when squeezed. Make sure cutters are deep enough for the thickness of the dough they will cut; cookie dough is usually ⅛ to ¼ inch, biscuit dough usually ½ inch. Most cutters are tinned steel and should be dried thoroughly after washing so they won't rust.

Pastry Cutters   Also used for biscuits, they come in a graduated set and have plain or fluted edges. Special puff pastry cutters are available to stamp out pastry cases (vol-au-vents) for savory or sweet fillings or to roll out triangles for croissants.

Cookie Cutters   Hundreds of different cookie cutters are available, some with handles, some with a rolled edge, singly or in sets. Specialty cookie cutters include the following:

Cookie Boards   Springerle, the traditional German anise cookies, are formed by rolling the stiff dough over a wooden board incised with cutout figures of birds, flowers, animals, houses, and people, each separated by double lines. The lines are cutting guides for separating the cookies before baking them. Boards come in two-, four-, and six-cookie sizes and as individual boards that make a single, giant figure. Also available for springerle are rolling cookie cutters and incised wooden rolling pins. Multiple and single-cookie boards for the rich Dutch spice cookies called *speculaas* (see photograph at left) are similar to those for springerle. The large board makes 12 cookies.

Cookie Stamps   Some of these round or square forms are large and attractive enough to hang on the wall. Made of wood, glass, or ceramic, they have a pattern cut into the surface. After dusting with flour to prevent sticking, the stamp is pressed into a small ball of dough. The dough is flattened and impressed with the reverse of the incised design.

Rolling Cookie Cutters   These are like jigsaw puzzles. The shapes are mounted on a drum attached to a wooden handle. The drum is rolled across the dough with pressure; the raised design cuts an interlocking pattern so dough is not wasted.

Shortbread Molds   Ceramic shortbread molds are concave, with the traditional Scottish thistle carved in the center and fluting, said to represent the rays of the sun, trimming the rim. The rich shortbread dough fills the hollow space and bakes right in the mold. Another version, a shallow, concave wooden mold, shapes the cookie by having the dough rolled over it. The dough is trimmed of any excess, turned out of the mold, and baked. Shortbread can also be baked in a baking pan.

PASTRY CRIMPER

This tool looks like tiny, flat-headed tweezers and fits over the upper and lower edges of a double-crust pie. When pinched together, a crimper seals the edges and impresses a design into the dough. Made of stainless steel, it measures about ¼ inch wide and 1½ inches long.

PASTRY/DOUGH SCRAPER

Extend the life of a wooden work surface by scraping it clean with this rigid metal scraper rather than by soaking it in water. Use it also to turn dough, to cut dough into small pieces, or to manipulate dough that is too wet and sticky to handle easily. The dough scraper is a rigid, stainless steel rectangle, measuring 3 by 6 inches, with a plastic or metal handle. It can go in the dishwasher.

PASTRY AND PIZZA WHEELS

When selecting one of these rolling-bladed tools, make sure the wheel turns freely and that, if it is large, there is a guard to protect your fingers. Use wheels to cut anything flat—pastry, pizza, cookies, pasta dough, and ravioli. Wheels with a crinkled edge are known as pastry jaggers; they cut a pinked line and are usually used to fashion strips of dough for weaving into a lattice pie crust. The wheels are stainless steel, aluminum alloy, or wood (one version of a jagger), with a wood, plastic, or molded metal handle; diameters range from ½ inch to 3 inches.

PIE WEIGHT

To blind bake a pie or tart crust means to bake it without a filling. Pie weights, which are ceramic or aluminum pellets or beans, keep a crust flat as it bakes so that it doesn't puff up, deform, and shrink. Crust is first lined with aluminum foil or parchment paper and then filled almost full with weights. When crust is done, foil and weights are removed. One package of weights fills two pie crusts. Before there were weights, bakers used dried beans or rice, still good choices.

ROLLING PIN

A well-designed rolling pin is heavy, so it, rather than you, does the work of shaping pastry and bread dough into a smooth, flat, even sheet. A heavier pin requires fewer runs across the dough to do the job. There are several types. The *American* is the familiar wooden cylinder with a handle on each end. The *French straight* is a slender wooden dowel without handles; the *French curved* is also a wooden dowel without handles, but it tapers from center to each end. The *tutove*, which has a grooved, rigid nylon cylinder and handles, is a special tool used for rolling puff pastry. *Marble* rolling pins are specifically for pastry work because they keep dough cool, although they are very cumbersome and expensive.

Which rolling pin should you use? Choose one that you are comfortable with and that produces the desired results. The American type is probably easier to manipulate than the others, although some pastry chefs feel that a rolling pin without handles gives you a better sense of the thickness of the dough. Regardless of the design, select one of smooth hardwood that is heavy, well balanced, and of a length that is wider than the pastry so it won't leave ridges in the dough as you roll. A rolling pin with a handle rotates more smoothly if handles move on ball or nylon bearings. A 15-inch length is very versatile—long enough and heavy enough to do a good job.

During use, keep rolling pin and work surface well-dusted with flour to prevent sticking. Flouring the surface works better than covering the pin with a cloth stocking, which usually wrinkles and makes an unwelcome pattern on the dough. Always wipe wood clean with a soft cloth before storing.

> ### Recipes and Related Information
> *Biscuit, 49; Cake, 77; Cookie, 139; Frosting, Icing, and Filling, 244; Pie and Tart, 431; Pizza, 445.*

CANDIED FRUIT

Many types of fresh fruit are candied for use in cakes, pastries, and confections. Cherries, pineapple, citron, angelica, orange rind, and lemon rind are among those most readily available in candied form. The candying process involves cooking or steeping the fruit in a highly concentrated sugar syrup, then drying it. The sugar penetrates and preserves the fruit.

Use Candied fruits add festive color and a sweet note to breads, cookies, and cakes. Holiday fruitcakes are usually well endowed with liquor-soaked candied fruits. Because good candied fruits can be expensive, they are looked upon by many as an indulgence to reserve for holiday specialties.

Availability Specialty shops, candy stores, and some health-food stores offer a selection of candied fruits. Many supermarkets carry packages of mixed candied fruit the year around and offer a wider selection at Christmas time.

Selection Many packaged supermarket mixes depend heavily on artificial colors and preservatives; read the label for ingredients.

Storage Keep candied fruits in a cool, dark place for up to three months. They may be frozen indefinitely.

> ### Recipes and Related Information
> *Candy, 93; Christmas Panettone, 628; Divinity, 96; Rich Fruitcake, 88.*

CANDY, TO

To glaze or preserve by cooking in sugar syrup, or to coat with sugar. A favorite presentation for cooked yams, sweet potatoes, and carrots is to coat them with a mixture of butter and sugar. Citrus peels are candied and used to flavor or decorate baked desserts.

■ CANDIED CITRUS PEEL
When strips of peel are cooked in a sugar syrup, the peel becomes infused with sugar, which acts as a preservative. This is a two-day process; the peel must sit in its syrup at room temperature overnight and then be cooked again. However, you can candy up to six fruits' worth at a time. Increase the recipe accordingly. The candied peel will keep up to one month. Use a sharp knife to cut the candied peel into strips or sharp-edged aspic or truffle cutters to form decorative shapes.

    1 grapefruit, 2 oranges, *or* 2 lemons
    ½ cup sugar
    ¼ cup water
    1 tablespoon corn syrup
      Sugar, for dusting candied peel

1. With a paring knife or vegetable peeler, remove peel from fruit in strips, leaving some white pith, but no more than ⅛ to ¼ inch, attached. Reserve fruit, wrapped airtight, for another use.

2. Place strips in a medium, heavy-bottomed saucepan and cover with cold water; boil 5 minutes. Drain, rinse with fresh water, and repeat process; set drained strips aside in saucepan.

3. Meanwhile, in a small, heavy-bottomed saucepan combine sugar, the water, and corn syrup, stirring over low heat until sugar has dissolved; raise heat and boil 2 minutes.

4. Pour sugar syrup over drained peel and cook over very low heat 1 hour. Cool, cover, and let sit at room temperature overnight.

5. The next day, bring to a boil, reduce heat to very low, and cook 1 hour. Remove peel from syrup and drain on wire rack set over parchment paper or baking sheet. Let dry completely (on a damp or cool day, let dry in a gas oven or in a still-warm oven that has been recently heated and turned off).

6. Roll in sugar and serve as is, or cut up for use as a flavoring, or cut into decorative shapes for garnishes. Store in an airtight container between layers of parchment paper. Will keep 1 month.

> ### Recipes and Related Information
> *Candied Fruit, 93; Crystallized Flowers, 238; Glazed Carrots, 100; Lucia Buns, 99; Maple-Glazed Sweet Potatoes, 569; Sugar and Syrup, 567.*

PEANUT BRITTLE

Peanuts are synonymous with this hard, richly flavored candy, but other nuts, such as almonds, pecans, or hazelnuts—or a mixture—will be equally delicious.

        2 cups sugar
        1 cup light corn syrup
        ¾ cup water
        2 cups raw peanuts (whole or halved),
            skins removed
        2 tablespoons butter

1. Oil or butter a baking sheet. In a large, heavy-bottomed saucepan, combine sugar, corn syrup, and the water; stir over low heat until sugar has completely dissolved. Increase heat to medium and cook without stirring until a rich golden brown (300° F on a candy thermometer, hard-crack stage).

2. Immediately remove from heat, add nuts and butter, and stir until nuts are coated. Pour onto prepared sheet, spreading quickly with a buttered spatula to about ½-inch thickness. Cool, break into pieces, and serve. Or store airtight; brittle keeps for about 2 weeks.

Makes about 1½ pounds brittle.

FONDANT

Crystalline, creamy fondant is a foundation or base for other confections, including some frostings. When making fondant the goal is to develop sugar crystals that are fine enough that the candy won't have a gritty texture (see To Control Crystal Formation). After kneading, fondant should be stored for several days before using. Making fondant is hard work and many cooks prefer to purchase it ready-made from cake-decorating supply stores.

        2 cups sugar
        2 tablespoons liquid glucose (available at
            cake-decorating supply stores)
        ⅛ teaspoon cream of tartar
        ½ cup water
        ¼ to ½ teaspoon vanilla or almond extract (optional)

1. In a large, heavy-bottomed saucepan combine sugar, liquid glucose, cream of tartar, and the water and dissolve over low heat, washing down any crystals that may form on the sides of the pan with a brush dipped in hot water.

2. Bring to a boil and cook without stirring to 238° F on a candy thermometer (soft-ball stage). Immediately remove from heat and pour onto a marble slab or other smooth work surface. Cool undisturbed to 110° F. With a dough scraper or 2 metal spatulas that have been dipped in hot water, lift fondant from edges and push back to center.

3. Work fondant continuously, lifting and folding from edges to center, until it becomes white in color and smooth, pliable, and satiny. If desired, the final kneading can be done with buttered hands. If the fondant

becomes too stiff to work, cover with an inverted metal bowl and let sit briefly to soften; work again when ready.

4. Before using, let fondant ripen in an airtight container for several days to become more pliable. *To flavor:* Knead in vanilla or almond extract. *To tint:* Pierce mass and sprinkle a few drops of food coloring (pastel colors are most appropriate, so don't add too much coloring) into holes; let color seep into fondant, then knead to distribute evenly. Fondant keeps for up to 3 months if well wrapped and stored airtight in a cool place.

Makes ¾ to 1 pound.

DIVINITY

Divinity is creamy, like fondant, but is fluffier because the sugar syrup is beaten into whipped egg whites. If made with brown sugar, the candy is called seafoam. Wrapped airtight, Divinity will keep one to two weeks.

        3 cups sugar
        ¾ cup light corn syrup
        ¼ cup water
        2 egg whites
        1 tablespoon vanilla extract
        1½ cups chopped toasted nuts, chopped
            candied citrus peel, or chopped glacé cherries

1. Oil or butter an 8-inch baking pan or set out sheets of parchment paper. In a medium, heavy-bottomed saucepan combine sugar, corn syrup, and the water; stir over low heat until sugar has dissolved completely. Increase heat to medium and cook without stirring until 250° F on a candy thermometer (hard-ball stage).

2. While syrup is cooking, beat egg whites until soft peaks form. When sugar syrup reaches temperature, slowly pour in a thin stream onto egg whites, beating continuously at high speed. Fold in vanilla and nuts.

3. Continue to beat until mixture cools slightly; pour immediately into prepared pan or drop by tablespoonfuls onto parchment paper. Let stand until firm. If made in pan, cut into squares to serve.

Makes about 5 dozen candies.

CHOCOLATE FUDGE

In older cookbooks, fudge recipes are often named for one of the New England women's colleges, because making this candy was such a popular pastime with students at these schools—Smith, Vassar, and Wellesley all have their own versions.

        1½ cups sugar
        1 cup whipping cream
        1 jar (7 oz) marshmallow cream
        ¼ cup butter, cut in pieces
        1 pound semisweet chocolate, chopped
        1 teaspoon vanilla extract
        1 cup chopped nuts (optional)

1. Oil or butter an 8-inch baking pan. In a large, heavy-bottomed saucepan, combine sugar, whipping cream, and marshmallow cream; stir over low heat until sugar has dissolved completely. Increase heat to medium and cook without stirring until 238° F on a candy thermometer (soft-ball stage).

2. Remove from heat and add butter and chopped chocolate; stir until completely melted and smooth. Stir in vanilla and nuts (if used).

3. Pour into prepared pan and cool until firm. Cut in 1-inch squares and serve. Stored airtight between layers of parchment paper, fudge keeps for 2 to 3 weeks.

Makes about 5 dozen candies.

▓ CHOCOLATE TRUFFLES

Truffles are extremely easy to make because they have few ingredients and aren't dependent upon a temperamental sugar syrup for their base. Note that the truffle mixture must chill overnight before shaping.

   1¼ **cups whipping cream**
    1 **pound semisweet chocolate, chopped**
   ½ **cup unsalted butter, cut in small pieces**
     Unsweetened cocoa powder or chopped nuts, for coating

1. In a large, heavy-bottomed saucepan, bring cream to a boil. Add chocolate in small bits. Then add butter a little at a time. Stir until all is smooth. Cover and chill 8 hours or overnight.

2. If using cocoa, sift onto a plate. If using nuts, place in a layer on a plate. Scoop up chocolate mixture in teaspoonfuls. With hands, shape into ¾-inch balls (chocolate will melt a bit when handled). Roll in cocoa or nuts and set on another plate. Store, covered, in refrigerator until ready to serve. Truffles keep up to 1 month.

Makes about 6 dozen truffles.

Grand Marnier Truffles Before chilling and shaping chocolate mixture, add ¼ cup Grand Marnier and 1 teaspoon grated orange rind.

Recipes and Related Information
Icing Fondant, 251; Pralines, 424; Sugar and Syrup, 567.

CAPE GOOSEBERRY

Despite its name, the cape gooseberry is not a gooseberry at all, but a relative of the husk tomato (or tomatillo) and the ground cherry. It is also known as Chinese lantern, golden gooseberry, or strawberry tomato. Of Peruvian origin, it was later cultivated and highly regarded in South Africa, especially around the Cape of Good Hope. Today it is a commercial crop in New Zealand.

The small, golden, oval fruit is concealed by a brown, papery, outer husk, which must be removed. Its texture is firm and moist, its flavor mild.

Use Cape gooseberries are eaten raw as part of a fruit salad and cooked as an ingredient in a fruit compote. They may be added to stuffings of bread and fruit, made into jams or dessert sauces, used for pie and tart fillings, or added to gingerbread.

Availability Fresh cape gooseberries are available in specialty markets from March through June.

Selection Choose fruit with undamaged husks.

Storage Refrigerate in a plastic bag in crisper for up to two days.

Preparation Remove husk and rinse fruit. Slice, halve, or leave whole.

Perhaps not since the introduction of fudge has a confection appealed to the American sweet tooth as much as the French candy, truffles. Set in individual foil cups, they make a glamorous dessert.

CAPER

The small, unopened flower buds of a Mediterranean bush are called capers. They have a firm, almost crunchy texture and, depending on how they're packed, a piquant, salty or pickled flavor.

Use   Capers provide a piquant note to sauces, dressings, and salads. Their pungent bite is appreciated with smooth-textured foods such as smoked salmon, brains, and eggs; in creamy dishes such as Vitello Tonnato; and as a garnish for fried fish or veal.

Availability   Capers are generally pickled in vinegar and packed in jars. Some Italian markets carry salt-packed capers in bulk.

Capers vary considerably in size, depending on the variety and the stage of development at harvest. Many connoisseurs consider the smallest capers—the nonpareil variety from southern France—to be the finest, although larger capers are not necessarily stronger in flavor. The brining or salting process has a more important effect on flavor than does size. Try several brands to find one that you like.

Storage   Capers in vinegar keep for months in the original jar in the refrigerator. Salt-packed capers may be stored for several months at room temperature in an airtight container.

Preparation   Before using capers packed in vinegar, drain off liquid. Salt-packed capers should be rinsed and dried. Large capers may be coarsely chopped.

■ EGG AND CAPER SALAD

If you will be using Egg and Caper Salad as picnic fare, it's better to assemble the open-faced sandwiches at the picnic site. Pack the salad in a plastic container and bread and oregano sprigs garnish in plastic bags to keep them fresh. Remember to also bring a serrated knife to cut the bread into quarters.

    4 **eggs, hard-cooked**
    2 **stalks celery**
    2 **tablespoons mayonnaise**
    2 **tablespoons plain yogurt**
    1 **tablespoon Dijon mustard**
  ¼ **teaspoon kosher salt**
    1 **tablespoon capers**
    4 **slices whole grain bread**
  16 **small sprigs fresh oregano**

With a sharp knife, dice hard-cooked eggs and place into a 1-quart mixing bowl. Mince celery and add to eggs. Add mayonnaise, yogurt, mustard, salt, and capers. Stir to mix well. Place ½ cup on each slice of bread, garnish with sprigs of oregano, cut into quarters, and serve as open-faced sandwiches.

Serves 2 for lunch, 8 as part of a picnic.

Food Processor Version   Trim away leaves from celery, cut celery stalks into 3-inch lengths, and wedge tightly in feed tube with slicing disk in place; process. Remove disk, leaving celery in work bowl, and insert metal blade. Add eggs, mayonnaise, yogurt, mustard, salt, and capers. Pulse rapidly a few times to chop egg and combine mixture.

> ### *Recipes and Related Information*
> *Eggplant Relish, 208; Steak Tartare, 43;*
> *Tapénade, 399; Vitello Tonnato, 594.*

CARAMBOLA

Also known as star fruit or star apple, carambola is the waxy, yellow-green fruit of a tropical evergreen tree native to India and Malaya. It has five pronounced exterior ribs. Crosswise slices display a striking star pattern with five dark seeds in the center. Carambolas range from 2 to 5 inches long, depending on place of origin, and are usually about 2 inches wide. The flesh is watery and, depending on variety, can be sour or sweet.

Use   Carambolas are eaten raw in fruit salads or out of hand (discard seeds) with a sprinkling of lime juice. Carambola slices can be used to garnish salads or desserts or as an ingredient in fresh fruit tarts or sorbets. Indian cooks make pickles and chutney with carambola and add it to stews; they also make a refreshing drink with crushed fruit, sugar, and ice.

Availability   Peak season for fresh carambola is August to February.

Selection   Ripe carambolas have a golden color with some browning on the edge of the ribs. Green-tinged carambolas are better for cooking.

Storage   Refrigerate in a plastic bag in the crisper and use within three or four days.

Preparation   Peel is edible.

CARAMELIZE, TO

To cook sugar slowly until it melts and turns a deep, golden brown. Caramel syrup is used to coat molds for custards and ice cream, as a glaze for cakes and pastries, and to add flavor and color to soups, sauces, and stews. Caramelizing also refers to a type of browning that occurs during cooking.

> ### *Recipes and Related Information*
> *Caramels, 95; Crème Brûlée 170; Crème Caramel, 169;*
> *Sugar and Syrup, 567.*

CARAWAY SEED

A biennial plant of the parsley family, caraway is native to Asia Minor. It yields a hard brown seed, about ¼ inch long, that is curved and tapered at the ends. Caraway seed has a pungent, slightly sweet flavor akin to anise.

Use Caraway seed is frequently used in the cuisines of middle Europe (Germany, Poland, Austria, Hungary) and Scandinavia. It is kneaded into bread doughs, especially rye bread, and added to cheeses, to pork and sauerkraut dishes, to noodles and cabbage, to short ribs, goose, and other rich meats. It is also the principal flavoring ingredient in kümmel, a cordial.

Availability Caraway seed is sold whole, packed in jars or tins.

Selection Packaged seasonings lose quality after a while; try to buy from a store that restocks its spice section fairly often.

Storage Keep caraway seed in a cool, dark, dry place for up to one year.

CARDAMOM

Also spelled cardamon, cardamom is one of the most aromatic and pungent spices on the spice shelf. It is the dried fruit of a plant in the ginger family, native to India. The plant is low-yielding, and as the fruit must be snipped by hand with scissors, cardamom is necessarily expensive. The fragrant, hard black seeds are encased in a small round seedpod.

Use Indian cooks add cardamom to curries, rice pilafs, and stews for its special aroma and stimulating flavor. It is a common ingredient in an Indian *garam masala*. Scandinavian cooks use cardamom in sweet breads and buns, mulled wine, cakes, and braised meat dishes. In the Middle East, cardamom is used to flavor coffee. It adds an exotic fragrance and sweetness to applesauce and baked apples, poached fruits, and fruit pies.

Availability Whole cardamom pods are packed in jars or plastic bags or are sold in bulk. Whole cardamom seed and ground cardamom seed are packed in jars and tins.

Selection Packaged seasonings lose quality after a while; try to buy from a store that restocks its spice section fairly often.

Storage Keep in a cool, dark, dry place. Ground cardamom will stay pungent for three or four months, whole cardamom pods for about one year.

Preparation Crush whole cardamom pods gently and remove seeds. Add seeds whole to dishes, or grind in a pepper mill, clean coffee grinder, or electric mini-chopper, or with a mortar and pestle. Use sparingly.

■ LUCIA BUNS

Swedish bakers fashion these inventively shaped, cardamom-spiced rolls for December 13, Saint Lucia Day.

> 2 **packages active dry yeast**
> ½ **cup warm (105° to 115° F) water**
> 1¼ **cups warm (105° to 115° F) milk**
> ½ **cup butter or margarine, softened**
> ¾ **cup sugar**
> 1 **teaspoon** *each* **salt and ground cardamom**
> 2 **tablespoons grated orange rind**
> 6 to 6½ **cups flour**
> 2 **eggs**
> ½ **cup dried currants**
> **Raisins**
> **Candied cherries, halved**
> 1 **egg white, beaten with 1 teaspoon water**
> **Coarse sugar (pearl or decorating sugar, or crushed sugar cubes)**

1. Sprinkle yeast over the warm water in large bowl of electric mixer. Let stand until soft (about 5 minutes).

2. Stir in milk, butter, sugar, salt, cardamom, and orange rind, stirring until sugar dissolves. Add 3½ cups of the flour. Mix to blend, then beat at medium speed until smooth and elastic (about 5 minutes).

3. Beat in eggs, one at a time, beating until smooth after each addition. Mix in currants. Gradually stir in about 2 cups more flour to make a soft dough.

4. Turn dough out onto a board or pastry cloth coated with some of the remaining ½ to 1 cup flour. Knead until dough is smooth and satiny and small bubbles form just under surface (12 to 15 minutes). Add enough flour to keep dough from being sticky.

5. Turn dough in a greased bowl. Cover with plastic wrap and a towel; let rise in a warm place until doubled in bulk (1 to 1½ hours).

6. Punch dough down; turn out on a floured surface, cover with inverted bowl, and let rest for 10 minutes. Divide dough into 2 equal portions. Roll each into a 12-inch square. Cut each square in half to make two 6- by 12-inch rectangles. Cut each rectangle crosswise into 12 strips. Roll each strip into a pencil-thin strand 8 inches long.

7. On greased baking sheets cross 2 strands to make an *x*. Curl each end into a small coil. Place a raisin in center of half the coils; place a cherry half in remaining coils. Repeat until all dough is shaped into rolls. Brush rolls lightly with egg white mixture. Sprinkle with coarse sugar. Let rise until almost doubled (30 to 40 minutes). Preheat oven to 400° F.

8. Bake rolls until golden brown (12 to 15 minutes). Serve warm or at room temperature.

Makes 2 dozen rolls.

CARDOON

Although the cardoon resembles celery, it's actually a thistle, like the artichoke. It has foot-long, pale green stalks, a tender white heart, and a flavor reminiscent of both artichoke and celery. Cardoon is much appreciated by both French and Italian cooks.

Use   Cardoon heart (inner stalks) may be steamed or boiled, then drained and buttered or dressed with anchovy sauce, or baked with cheese sauce. Italian cooks steam it, then coat it with egg and bread crumbs, and deep-fry it. It is also a traditional component in an Italian *bagna cauda.*

Availability   Fresh cardoon is a winter vegetable. Peak season is October through December.

Selection   Choose bunches with sturdy, pale green stalks and fresh-looking leaves, and without signs of wilting or decay.

Storage   Refrigerate in a plastic bag in crisper for one to two days.

Preparation   Remove and discard tough outer stalks. Trim spurs and leaves from inner stalks. String outside surfaces of stalks as you would celery by scraping with a paring knife. Cut stalks into ½-inch or larger lengths and keep in water acidulated with vinegar or lemon juice to prevent discoloration before cooking.

Cooking   See BOIL, BRAISE, DEEP-FRY, STEAM.

CAROB

Also called St. John's bread, carob is the pod of a tree native to Syria. According to legend, carob sustained St. John in the wilderness. Although carob is unrelated to chocolate, it has a vaguely similar sweet flavor.

Use   Mediterranean children eat dried carob pods as a sort of candy. In the United States, the seeds are sold in health-food stores and enjoyed as an out of hand snack. The seeds are also ground to produce carob powder or flour, for use in beverages, cakes, cookies, and breads. Carob chips are used as a substitute for chocolate chips in cookies and health-food snacks. Because carob does not contain caffeine and has a naturally sweet taste, some consider it a nutritious alternative to chocolate.

Availability   Carob is sold in most health-food stores as whole seeds, unsweetened chips, toasted powder, or chunks sweetened with dates.

Storage   Refrigerate carob seeds. Store carob chips, chunks, and powder in an airtight container in a cool place; they will keep indefinitely.

CARROT

A root vegetable, carrots have feathery green tops; commonly cultivated varieties are a deep orange color and average about 7 to 8 inches long and ¾ inch in diameter; they get larger and less sweet with age. Baby carrots are increasingly available commercially and are especially attractive on raw vegetable platters.

Use   Carrots have the highest sugar content of any vegetable after beets. They are delicious raw—whole, in sticks, or grated in salads. Carrot sticks are a nutritious addition to a child's lunchbox or an appetizer assortment of raw vegetables. Steamed and buttered or sugar-glazed carrots are a common side dish. Carrots may be creamed or pickled, added to stews, baked in a pudding, made into soup, or added to soups; because of their natural sweetness, they are an essential ingredient in a good basic stock. One of the most popular American desserts— spiced carrot cake with cream cheese frosting—depends on grated raw carrots for its moist, appealing texture and distinctive flavor.

Availability   Fresh carrots are sold all year, in bulk or in plastic bags. Frozen and canned carrots are also available.

Selection   Choose small, slender carrots that are rigid, not rubbery. If tops are attached, they should be fresh looking and bright green. Avoid carrots that are split, pale, or deeply discolored around the stem, which indicates age.

Storage   Remove carrot tops, if attached. Store fresh carrots in a plastic bag in the refrigerator crisper. They will keep for several weeks but will gradually lose sweetness and rigidity.

Preparation   Peel if desired; trim ends.

Cooking   See BOIL, BRAISE, GRILL, STEAM.

■ GLAZED CARROTS
Baby vegetables are charming, especially when dressed up with a buttery glaze. This very simple preparation is one to remember for an impromptu dinner.

   16 **baby carrots, scrubbed and trimmed**
   ¼ **cup butter**
   2 **tablespoons brandy or fresh lemon juice**
   1 **tablespoon brown sugar or honey**

1. In a large skillet bring salted water to a boil. Add carrots, cover, and simmer until tender-crisp (10 to 15 minutes). Do not overcook. Drain.

2. Push carrots to one side and add butter, brandy, and sugar, stirring to combine. Sauté carrots over medium-high heat, shaking skillet, until carrots are well coated and lightly browned. Serve immediately.

Serves 4.

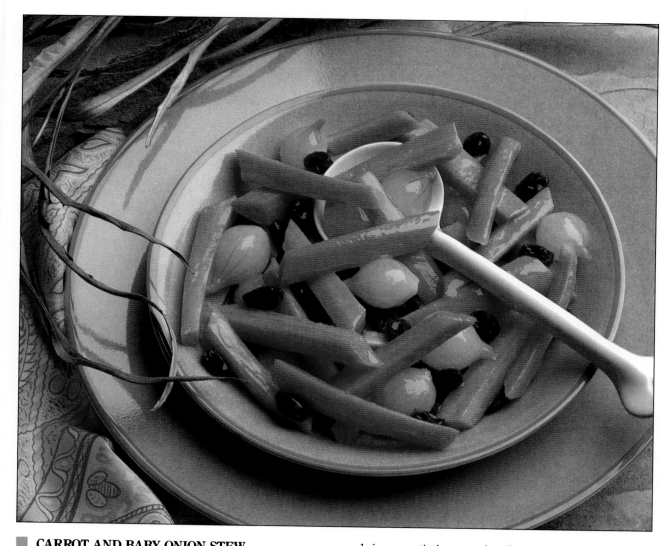

When combined with white wine and dark raisins, simple root vegetables such as carrots and baby onions become a sophisticated vegetable side dish.

CARROT AND BABY ONION STEW WITH RAISINS

Raisins and white wine give this vegetable stew a delicate, sweet-and-sour flavor. When the vegetables are tender, their cooking liquid becomes a buttery glaze. Serve this stew as an accompaniment to any roast, broiled meat, or poultry, especially beef, pork, chicken, and duck. Note that the stew can be prepared as much as two days ahead of serving and stored in the refrigerator until needed.

¼ **cup butter**
1 **pound carrots, quartered and cut in 2-inch pieces**
½ **pound baby onions, peeled (see Note)**
½ **cup dark raisins**
⅓ **cup dry white wine**
⅓ **cup water**
  Salt and freshly ground pepper, to taste
1 **bay leaf**

1. Melt butter in a large frying pan over medium heat. Add carrots and onions and sauté until lightly browned.

2. Add raisins, wine, the water, salt and pepper to taste, and bay leaf. Bring to a boil. Reduce heat to low, cover, and simmer, stirring occasionally, until vegetables are tender (about 35 minutes).

3. Raise heat to medium, uncover, and cook until liquid forms a syrupy glaze (about 10 minutes). If mixture is too watery and vegetables are beginning to fall apart, remove them carefully with a slotted spoon and boil liquid until it thickens; return vegetables to liquid and heat gently. Stew can be kept, covered, up to 2 days in refrigerator; reheat in a covered frying pan over low heat.

4. Taste and add more salt and pepper, if needed; best if served hot.

Serves 4.

Note To peel the baby onions, drop them into a saucepan of boiling water and boil 1 minute. Drain, rinse with cold water until cool, then peel with a paring knife.

Recipes and Related Information
Carrot-Raisin Salad, 507; Carrot Spice Cake, 86; Cream of Any Vegetable Soup, 563; Vegetable Purées, 487.

CARVE, TO

The process of cutting up a whole piece of meat into attractive, serving-sized pieces. The ritual of carving need not be an intimidating process. The proper equipment and a relaxed attitude will make all go much easier. Have on hand a carving knife with a long narrow blade about 8 to 10 inches long and 1 inch wide, made of a material that can be sharpened and that will hold an edge, such as high-carbon stainless steel. Also useful are a two-pronged chef's fork and a carving board with a well.

It's best to let roasts sit anywhere from 15 to 30 minutes, depending upon size, before carving. This resting period allows the juices to recirculate and the internal temperature to equalize. As a rule, carve only what is needed. The rest of the meat will stay moist if stored whole or on the frame. Save juices from meats for a sauce.

Arrange carved meat in an attractive manner on a serving platter, rather than randomly laying slices one on top of another. A garnish, whether the standard sprigs of parsley or a more imaginative choice, always enhances the visual appeal of the food when it is presented at the table. See GARNISH for examples of some basic plate decorations that are easy to master.

Recipes and Related Information
Beef, 37; Lamb, 335; Pork, 455; Poultry, 468; Veal, 591.

CARVING A TURKEY

Cut away trussing string and discard. Insert point of knife into bird where meaty part of leg meets breast; slice through skin down to the hip joint to expose joint. Stick knife directly into the joint and sever leg from body. Leg should fall away easily. Repeat on other side.

Turn leg skin side up; locate joint with knife and cut through to separate drumstick and thigh. Slice meat off drumstick and thigh. Remove wing by slicing through at corner of breast to expose shoulder joint; slice through joint. Remove other wing.

If carving at the table, remove breast meat by slicing at angle in slices about ¼ inch thick. If slicing in the kitchen, remove breast meat in one piece by inserting blade of knife flat along breastbone. Follow contour of bone with knife, and breast half will come away from frame. Repeat on other side. Slice breast meat.

CARVING A STANDING RIB ROAST

Place rib roast on cutting board fat side up. Remove feather bones by cutting down between bones and roast until bones fall away.

Separate meat from rib bones by making a clean vertical cut. Angle knife slightly toward rib bones, beginning at the small end, and continue cutting directly against the bones until you reach and are stopped by the backbone.

Using the rib bones as a guide, slice meat into serving pieces by making even, horizontal slices. Loosen the slices from the backbone and lift away by resting slice on knife and steadying with chef's fork.

CARVING OTHER MEATS

Carving a leg of lamb   This technique can also be used for veal or pork. Have butcher remove the hip bone. Slice away a small piece of meat from underside of leg to stabilize. Starting at narrow (shank) end, make vertical slices into the leg at regular intervals. Free slices by cutting horizontally along bone from shank end to hip joint (big end).

Carving a flank steak   To produce the most tender slices, carve across the grain of the meat and slice very thin. Lay the knife perpendicular to the grain and cut into the steak. Larger slices are produced by cutting diagonally. The more parallel the knife is to the meat— the more it is angled—the bigger the surface area of the slice.

Carving a boneless roast   Don't remove strings until you come to them; they help hold roast together. For a large roast, have it stand on end, then carve horizontally. Hold roast firmly in place with chef's fork below where you will cut. Slice into the meat with a steady sawing motion, keeping the knife as level as possible. For smaller roasts, carve vertically or on a slight diagonal.

CASHEW

The cashew nut is the seed of a tropical fruit called the cashew apple or pear cashew. The fruit itself is pear-shaped and soft like a peach, and may be white, red, or yellow. The kidney-shaped nut, encased in a shell, hangs outside the fruit. The shell is toxic and must be removed and the nuts cleaned before marketing. Cashews have a rich, buttery flavor and a crunchy texture.

Use   Roasted or fried cashews are enjoyed as a snack or predinner nibble. Chopped cashews may be added to cakes, cookies, pies, vegetable sautés, fruit chutneys, and relishes. Indian cooks add fried cashews to rice pilafs, breakfast cereals, and dumplings; they also use cashew nut butter, made from ground roasted cashews, as a thickener for curries.

Availability   Most cashews are roasted before being packed in jars or cans. They are available salted and un-salted. Health-food stores and specialty stores some-times carry raw (unroasted) cashews in bulk; they have a milder, less buttery character than roasted cashews.

Selection   Buy cashews that are as fresh as possible.

Storage   Keep roasted cashews in airtight jars or cans at room temperature for up to one month. They will keep longer if refrigerated or frozen. Raw cashews should be refrigerated or frozen if not used within a few days.

Preparation   See NUT.

CASSEROLES AND BAKING DISHES

Many of these pans are multipurpose. Primarily intended for slow cooking such as making stews and braises, which require extended cooking to tenderize tough cuts of meat, they are also suitable for roasting and for baking such combination dishes as layered entrées, vegetable accom-paniments, and fruit desserts. The more attractive ones can be presented at the table. Capacity ranges from as little as 2 cups to sizes for a crowd. Dishes are made in earthenware, porcelain, copper and other metals, and heat-resistant glass. Most casseroles are safe to use in the microwave oven. Some, however, have ingredients in the materials or glazes that make them unsuitable. To check, follow directions on page 364. See MATERIALS FOR COOKWARE for more information.

Casseroles are lidded pots, designed for slow, moist cooking in the oven; they are often suitable for use on top of the stove as well if they can withstand direct exposure to heat. The best are made of materials that absorb and hold oven heat evenly and efficiently, without scorching or producing hot spots. They have tight-fitting lids that trap steam, thus creating a moist interior that keeps food from drying out during the long cooking period. Because casseroles need little manipulation by the cook and must fit into the oven cavity, they have short handles or none at all. These versatile cookers are optimally effective when food fills most of their interior; the heat is then directed to the food and not to empty space. Buy several in sizes that match what you cook most often.

Casseroles and baking dishes are used for slow-cooked foods such as stews and braises, for roasting, and for baking. Some are multipurpose; they can go in the oven and can also withstand the direct heat of a burner. Clockwise from left to right are small and large covered roasters, electric slow cooker, marmite, bean pot, covered casserole, clay baker, gratin dish.

Baking dishes are low and fairly shallow in comparison with casseroles, don't have covers, and usually don't have handles either. They are suited for foods that need prolonged exposure to steady, even oven heat to evaporate liquid or to provide firmness in the case of fish, custards, egg dishes, rice and grains, vegetable side dishes, and baked entrées. Usually made of porcelain or earthenware, baking dishes can be utilitarian or dressed up enough to take to a dinner party.

CLAY BAKERS

Based on an ancient cooking method used by the Romans and Chinese, these earthenware casseroles are used for baking poultry, slow-cooking meats, and meat dishes. They allow food to bake in its own juices without added fat or basting. Because fragile pottery should not be subject to extreme temperature changes, they are put in a cold, not preheated, oven. Before filling with food, clay bakers without a glazed interior are first soaked in cold water. In the oven the water held in the porous clay converts to steam, which adds moisture to the cooking environment. Interior glazing makes the dish easier to clean, but eliminates its porosity. Never clean unglazed clay cookware with soap or detergent; it will be absorbed into the pores. After using, fill with hot water and let sit for a few hours, then scrub with coarse salt and a plastic sponge. Rinse and thoroughly air-dry. Don't be overly concerned with stains and dark spots, which naturally develop on this type of cookware.

Chinese Clay Pot   With its sand-colored, unglazed exterior and dark brown interior glaze, this pot is ideal for slow cooking over very low heat. The most common design, available in various sizes, is about two thirds as tall

as it is wide, with rounded or sloping sides. It may have one long handle or two short loop handles, and may or may not be reinforced with wire on the outside. A 3-quart pot, big enough to hold a whole chicken, is the most useful size. To safely use these fragile pots: Always heat the pot partially filled with liquid, never empty; heat gradually, first over low heat and then increase to medium heat if needed. If cooking on an electric burner, use a heat diffuser to raise the pot up off the heating coils. When a braising calls for an initial stir-frying or browning, do this step in a wok or skillet, not in the heat-sensitive clay pot. To avoid breakage, cool pot before putting on a wet or cold surface. Any heatproof casserole with a tight-fitting lid will work as well as a clay pot for Chinese-style braising. Do not use unglazed earthenware clay bakers for braising; they cannot stand direct heat.

DUTCH OVEN

The cast-iron forerunner of today's Dutch oven hung from a special hook in the large, open fireplaces of colonial American kitchens or was set on a stand over the fire. Cast-iron pots are still popular, but today the Dutch oven has come to mean any large, heavy, lidded pot intended for slow cooking. Other materials used are enameled cast iron, aluminum alloys, and stainless steel. Buy one with a heavy bottom and a tight-fitting cover. Standard size is 5 quarts.

ELECTRIC SLOW COOKER

Essentially an automatic casserole, the electric slow cooker provides slow, moist cooking through a steady, even transfer of heat from heating elements to food through a stoneware insert bowl (stoneware is an excellent absorber of heat). Because the food is cooked so gently and is tightly covered, there is little evaporation; thus meats and poultry are kept from becoming dry. The electric slow cooker is designed to cook throughout the day—8 to 10 hours. It is energy efficient, a boon to those cooks who work out of the home, and it functions at such a low temperature that it doesn't heat up the kitchen. Guidelines for converting conventional recipes to the slow cooker are provided by the manufacturer. Typically, a stew that requires an hour on top of the stove needs at least six hours in the slow cooker. Capacities range from a compact 1-quart size, for one or two people, to a 6-quart model suitable for large families and for entertaining.

ROASTING PANS AND RACKS

Whether you roast turkey or other meats frequently or only for holiday meals, a heavyweight roasting pan and rack should be considered basic equipment. Roasters are either rectangular or oval and one of two types: high-sided with a domed cover or shallow and open. Covered pans are most commonly used for roasting turkey or chicken. To keep the bird from cooking in its own fat, it is elevated on a rack or on ridges that are part of the bottom surface of the pan. The enclosed interior provides a moist, rather than dry, environment, so the bird actually steams rather than cooks in dry heat. These pans are made of many different materials, usually enameled steel or cast iron, and are sized to match common weights and sizes of poultry. The low and open roasting pan is the choice of most cooks because it is so versatile—for roasting and for casseroles, and for use as a bain-marie (hot water bath). It is sold under several names, sometimes called a roasting pan, lasagne pan, or cake pan. The best materials for the low roaster are aluminum, enameled steel, or copper.

Regardless of type, select a roasting pan that offers the most versatility. Don't buy an oversized pan unless you really need it. If you prepare large birds or roasts, select a pan as large as your oven will hold, but allow several inches of space all around for air circulation. It should be sturdy enough to support a large roast or turkey, but not so heavy that lifting is a struggle. The handles should be well attached and easy to hold; if they are extensions of the sides of the pan, they should be large enough to grip comfortably. For making gravy, be sure the pan can safely cook on the top of the stove as well. Some roasting pans can do double duty for broiling; however, the best broiler pans are still those that come with your oven.

A rack both provides open space beneath a roast so that heat can reach its underside and allows drippings to fall into the pan. Without a rack, the bottom of the roast will stew in the pan juices instead of staying dry and crisp. The most practical racks are collapsible for easy storage; they are made of chromed steel, sometimes coated with a nonstick finish, and are adjustable. Rigid racks are sturdy, but require more storage space when not in use.

SPECIALTY POTS

The shape of each of these three pots evolved to best prepare a particular dish, but all are considered slow cookers.

Bean Pot This pot has a narrow neck, a tubby, rounded bottom, a snug lid, and curved, lug handles. This ungainly but somehow appealing vessel is thought best for developing the characteristic flavor and consistency of that New England favorite—baked beans. Made of ceramic, bean pots come in 2-, 3½-, and 5-quart capacities.

Gratin Dish A gratin has a characteristic crisp, golden brown crust achieved by browning it in the oven or under the broiler. It cooks in a special shallow dish designed to expose a maximum amount of surface so that as much crust as possible is produced; it is the crust that makes a gratin, not what's underneath it. These oval pans often have little ear-shaped handles for transporting dish from oven to table. Sizes range from 4-inch, single-serving dishes to 14-inch dishes designed for multiple servings. They are available in porcelain, tin-lined copper, enameled cast iron, stainless steel, and ovenproof glass.

Marmite In French, *marmite* means casserole. Like the bean pot, this earthenware vessel is wider at the bottom than at the top. Certain soups and stews cooked in a marmite take their name from it; *petite marmite,* a hearty baked soup flavored with meat, poultry, root vegetables, and beef marrow, is one of the best known of these dishes. This pot has rustic charm and you will enjoy serving from it. Capacity ranges from 1½ to 6 quarts.

CAULIFLOWER

A member of the cabbage family, cauliflower is produced by blanching—wrapping the large green leaves around the developing head to block out sunlight. The result is a solid white head made up of small, tightly compacted white flowers on thick stems. Although most people eat only the florets, the entire plant is edible, including the leaves.

Use Cauliflower may be eaten raw, with oil and salt or a dipping sauce. It is a common addition to *crudités* assortments. Steamed or boiled cauliflower may be simply buttered, or dressed with cheese sauce, browned sliced almonds, or buttered bread crumbs. It may be cooked, cooled, and dressed with vinaigrette or mayonnaise. Cauliflower may be pickled, added to soups or stews, or fried tempura style.

Availability Fresh cauliflower is sold all year but is most abundant late fall until spring. Cauliflower is also available frozen.

Selection Choose cauliflower with fresh-looking green leaves, if they are still attached, and without brown spots on the head.

Storage   Refrigerate fresh cauliflower in a plastic bag in the crisper for up to four or five days.

Preparation   Wash thoroughly, trim stem end, and remove leaves (cook separately, if desired). Cook whole or use a small sharp knife to separate into smaller florets.

Cooking   See BOIL, STEAM.

▦ PAKORAS

Indian vegetable fritters or *pakoras* can be fried before guests arrive and reheated at the last minute in a 375° F oven for 10 minutes. Instead of wheat flour, Indian cooks traditionally use chick-pea flour. Because this flour is very difficult to find in this country, the recipe has been developed with all-purpose flour. You may substitute cooked potato cubes or shredded carrots for the cauliflower.

1	head cauliflower (about 1 lb), cut into florets
1	onion, minced
1	clove garlic, minced
2	tablespoons vegetable oil
2	teaspoons jalapeño chile, minced
4	sprigs parsley, minced
2	sprigs fresh mint, minced
1½	cups flour
1	tablespoon baking powder
1	teaspoon salt
1	teaspoon cumin seed
¼	teaspoon turmeric
¼	teaspoon freshly ground black pepper
⅛	teaspoon cayenne pepper
¾	cup water
½	cup milk
	Oil, for frying
	Cilantro Raita, for accompaniment (see page 522)

1. Cook florets in 3 quarts boiling water for 3 minutes. Remove with a slotted spoon, drain, and pat dry.

2. In a medium skillet sauté onion and garlic in oil over medium heat until softened (about 8 minutes). Stir in jalapeño, parsley, and mint; cook 2 to 3 minutes more. Reserve.

3. In a medium bowl combine flour, baking powder, salt, cumin seed, turmeric, black pepper, and cayenne pepper. Slowly stir in the water and milk to make a thick batter. Let rest 30 minutes.

4. Stir in reserved cauliflower and onion mixture. To deep-fry, heat 4 to 5 inches of oil in a 3-quart saucepan or wok to 375° F. Add batter, 1 teaspoon at a time, taking care not to crowd pan. Fry 3 minutes, carefully turn over with wire skimmer or slotted spoon, and fry second side 2 minutes. Remove from hot oil with skimmer and drain on paper towels. Cool briefly. Serve with Cilantro Raita.

Makes 36 to 40 pakoras.

CAVIAR

Although caviar refers traditionally to the roe of sturgeon, the word is being used increasingly to designate the roe of other fish such as salmon and whitefish.

Most sturgeon caviar comes from one of three varieties of sturgeon, whose principal home is the Caspian Sea bordering Russia and Iran. Beluga caviar from the beluga sturgeon is the most desirable; the eggs are gray to almost black, are the largest of sturgeon caviars, and have the most delicate taste. The eggs of the osetra sturgeon are golden yellow to brown and have a stronger flavor. The sevruga sturgeon yields the eggs with the strongest flavor; they are light to dark gray. Domestic caviar comes from Washington and Oregon sturgeon.

Although beluga caviar is generally the finest, quality depends to a large extent on the individual fish and on how carefully roe is processed. To prepare caviar, eggs are removed from the roe sac, inspected and cleaned, then pushed by hand through a screen or cotton sieve to separate them from membrane. The roe is then brined to flavor and preserve it before it is packed with salt in tins. The best caviar is *malossol,* Russian for *lightly salted.*

Pressed caviar is made from mature eggs, usually from sturgeon caught late in the season. The eggs are pressed together to make a strongly flavored concentrate. It is less expensive than other sturgeon caviars, and some prefer its full flavor.

Salmon caviar ranges from light orange to dark red depending on the salmon variety. The eggs are larger than sturgeon roe but are processed in a similar fashion.

Whitefish caviar, also called golden caviar, is from Great Lakes whitefish. The eggs are a bright yellow-gold and quite small.

Use   Caviar is enjoyed as an appetizer, with buttered toast or blini to support it. The best caviar does not require another garnish; roe of lesser quality may be served with lemon, sour cream, minced hard-cooked egg, or onion. Caviar may also be used as a garnish for pasta or raw oysters. It should never be cooked.

Availability   Sturgeon caviar is usually available fresh or pasteurized; it cannot be successfully frozen. Salmon caviar is available fresh, pasteurized, or frozen. Whitefish caviar is sold fresh or frozen. Caviar is always packed in tins or jars.

Selection   All fish eggs (except for pressed caviar) should be firm, crisp, and separate, not mushy or soupy. They should have a clean, fresh briny smell and flavor.

Storage   Pasteurized, vacuum-packed caviar does not require refrigeration until opening. After opening, refrigerate and use as soon as possible. Fresh caviar should be stored at 28° F, which is warmer than a freezer but cooler than a home refrigerator. For best storage, pack tin or jar in ice and store in coldest part of the refrigerator. If unopened, it will keep for up to one month. After opening, use within a couple of days. Pressed caviar should be stored and used similarly. Frozen caviar should be slowly thawed in refrigerator and eaten immediately.

Preparation   To serve, rest caviar tin or jar in a bowl of ice and open at the last moment. Pressed caviar should be removed from refrigerator half an hour before serving to facilitate spreading.

■ NEW POTATOES WITH CAVIAR
Caviar need not be expensive imported sturgeon roe (although it can be). Let your budget be your guide in selecting from among the variety of colorful caviars on the market (see left). The contrast of warm potato and ice-cold caviar makes a memorable mouthful. This recipe would be sophisticated picnic fare: To carry to picnic site, wrap potatoes in aluminum foil to keep them warm and pack caviar in ice. If desired, substitute sour cream for Lemon Crème Fraîche.

> 3 dozen tiny red-skinned new potatoes
> Olive oil
> Kosher salt
> Juice of 1 lemon
> 12 ounces assorted caviar (golden, red, and black)
> Lemon wedges

Lemon Crème Fraîche

> 1 cup whipping cream, buttermilk, or sour cream
> 2 tablespoons fresh lemon juice

1. Steam potatoes over boiling salted water until they are just tender when pierced. Dry them well; drizzle them while hot with olive oil, then sprinkle with salt and lemon juice. Cut off top of each potato about ¼ inch down; scoop out and discard some of the inside pulp, leaving a firm, thick-sided shell. Wrap potatoes in foil and place in a tightly sealed container.

2. At serving time, set out potato shells, caviars, crème fraîche or sour cream, lemon wedges, some tiny serving spoons, and plenty of napkins. Guests can fill their potato shells with crème fraîche or sour cream and the caviar of their choice, with a little lemon juice squeezed over the top.

Serves 12.

Lemon Crème Fraîche   In a small bowl or a jar, mix whipping cream and lemon juice and let sit at room temperature until mixture thickens to the consistency of sour cream. This will take 12 to 24 hours depending on the temperature of the room. Refrigerate after thickening; it will keep for several weeks.

Makes 1 cup.

CAVIAR FOR THE BUDGET CONSCIOUS

Serving good sturgeon caviar at a cocktail party is out of the question for most hosts and hostesses. Some people compromise by buying inexpensive lumpfish, but although it may look like the real thing, it is salty and indelicate and only serves to remind its eaters of what they're missing. Others may splurge on a little of the good stuff but have to spread it so thin that no one gets to enjoy it. Such economy combined with extravagance brings to mind the legendary Colette, who flatly stated (speaking of truffles), "If I can't have too many, I'll do without."

Now there's a better way. The golden caviar of Great Lakes whitefish is being sold across the country and at very reasonable prices relative to its quality. These tiny golden eggs not only look good but taste good if they've been well cared for.

Most golden caviar is flash-frozen after processing; otherwise, the eggs get soggy and collapse almost immediately. When you buy it, it should still be frozen, or you should ask how long it has been out of the freezer.

(Some markets take a tin or so out of the freezer each day to display on ice.) Don't buy a tin that has been out of the freezer more than one day.

Ideally, caviar should be stored at 28° F, which is colder than a refrigerator, but not as cold as most home freezers. When you bring caviar home, fill a bowl with ice, nestle the tin in the ice, and set the bowl in the coldest part of the refrigerator. (Make sure water cannot seep into the tin.) Then serve it within one or two days.

You can serve golden caviar just as you would black caviar. The only difference is that you don't have to scrimp! Spread it on warm buttered toast and serve with lemon. Spoon liberally onto blini (see page 602) with sour cream. Serve slices of small boiled potatoes topped with sour cream and caviar. Spoon a dollop of sour cream and some caviar atop crêpes (see page 602) and sprinkle all with dill. Spoon a little onto raw oysters on the half shell. Fill tiny Cream Puffs (see page 163) with sour cream, caviar, and chopped chives.

CAYENNE PEPPER
Finely ground red pepper from a variety of dried red capsicum peppers (chiles) is the source of cayenne pepper. Orange-red to red, depending on the chiles used to prepare it, it varies in intensity but is always hot.

Use   Cayenne pepper adds a spark of heat to foods. It is used in numerous cuisines to flavor just about everything, including dessert. Cooks add it to eggs, fish, vegetables, sauces, soups, stews, curries, chutneys, and chili. Just a pinch will heighten the flavor of almost any dish; before adding cayenne pepper to a recipe, see Preparation for a caution about variation in pungency.

Availability   Cayenne pepper is sold packed in jars or airtight bags.

Selection   Packaged dried seasonings lose quality after a while; try to buy from a store that restocks its spice section fairly often.

Storage   Keep in an airtight container in a cool, dry, dark place. Replace every six months.

Preparation   Because cayenne blends vary in pungency, use with restraint at first, then taste and adjust seasoning as desired.

Recipes and Related Information
Basic Crêpes, 602; Blini, 602.

Recipes and Related Information
Corn Maquechoux, 158; Stuffed Mirliton, 110.

CELERIAC

Grown primarily for its swollen root, celeriac is a type of celery. About the size of a baseball, the knobby, brown-skinned root has long, celerylike stalks that are usually removed in processing for the retail market. The appearance of this vegetable gave rise to its other common names: celery root, celery knob, and turnip-rooted celery. It has firm, crisp white flesh with a flavor that very much resembles that of celery.

Use   Celeriac may be eaten raw in salads or cooked in soups, stews, and casseroles. Boiled celeriac may be whipped with butter and cream, or mixed with whipped potatoes. Sliced celeriac may be baked in a cream or cheese sauce. French cooks cut raw celeriac into fine matchsticks and dress it with a mustard mayonnaise to make *céleri-rave rémoulade,* a salad popular with both home cooks and chefs.

Availability   Fresh celeriac is most readily found fall through winter.

Selection   Choose small to medium celery root that is firm, not spongy.

Storage   Celeriac will stay fresh in a plastic bag in the refrigerator crisper for up to one week.

Preparation   Peel with a small, stainless steel paring knife (carbon knives discolor celeriac). Plunge immediately into acidulated water to prevent discoloration. Slice, grate, or cube as recipe directs. Celeriac may also be washed and boiled in its skin, then peeled.

Cooking   See BOIL.

■ CELERY ROOT SALAD
Céleri-rave rémoulade

The unglamorous celery root, when peeled and shredded, can be transformed into an elegant salad, often served as a first course in French restaurants. A creamy dressing made of mustard and shallot coats the crunchy pieces. Use a food processor, if you have one, fitted with a shredding disk, for the tedious shredding job. A food processor also makes quick work out of emulsifying the ingredients for the piquant dressing.

> 1   **large (1 to 1½ lb) celery root**
> 2   **tablespoons fresh lemon juice**
> 1   **egg yolk**
> 2   **tablespoons tarragon wine vinegar**
> 1   **tablespoon Dijon mustard**
> ½   **teaspoon salt**
>   **Pinch cayenne pepper**
> 1   **shallot, finely chopped**
> ¼   **cup *each* olive oil and vegetable oil**
>   **Butter or Boston lettuce leaves**
>   **Chopped parsley, for garnish**

1. Peel celery root thoroughly, cutting out any deep bits of peel. Shred quickly, using a food processor or grater (you should have 5 to 6 cups). Immediately mix well with lemon juice to prevent discoloration. Cover and refrigerate for about 1 hour.

2. In a medium bowl beat egg yolk with vinegar, mustard, salt, cayenne, and shallot. Using a whisk or fork, gradually beat in oils, a small amount at a time, until dressing is thick and creamy.

3. Shortly before serving, mix celery root lightly with dressing to coat.

4. Serve celery root mixture on lettuce leaves, sprinkled with parsley.

Serves 6.

Food Processor Version   Use a metal blade to process egg yolk, vinegar, mustard, salt, cayenne, and 1 tablespoon oil for 1 minute. Slowly add remaining oil. Add shallot and process 10 seconds more.

> ***Recipes and Related Information***
> *Sherried Oxtail Soup, 501; Vegetable Purées, 487.*

CELERY

A member of the same vegetable family as carrots and parsley, celery has long, crisp stalks that may reach a foot in length. Some varieties are forcibly blanched and are white or very pale green throughout. Most commercial celery, however, has green outer stalks and pale green inner stalks furled around a central heart. Celery has pungent green leaves that are often removed in processing for the retail market.

Use   The crisp texture of raw celery is appealing in salads or as an hors d'oeuvre, often stuffed with a creamy cheese. It adds texture and flavor to soups, stuffings, and stews. Its flavor is important, if not essential, to stock-making. It is also a required ingredient in a classic French *mirepoix,* the mixture of diced aromatic root vegetables used to flavor sauces, soups, and stews. Braised celery hearts (the tender, innermost stalks) are a good companion to game, duck, or pork.

Availability   Fresh celery is sold the year around, either loose or packed in cellophane bags.

Selection   Choose celery that looks moist and crisp, and does not show signs of limpness or drying. Generally speaking, the darker the color, the stronger the flavor.

Storage   Refrigerate celery in a plastic bag in crisper for up to 10 days.

Preparation   Trim ends, remove leaves, and peel away any tough outer strings. Save leaves for use in stock.

Cooking   See BOIL, BRAISE, STIR-FRY.

■ BRAISED CELERY WITH WALNUTS

Although usually thought of as a salad vegetable in this country, celery is delicious cooked and served as a side dish. As celery is fibrous and won't cook tender with a brief sauté, it must first be parboiled to cook partway.

1 head celery, separated into stalks and washed
2 tablespoons butter
1 small onion, finely chopped
⅓ cup walnuts, coarsely chopped
Grated rind of 1 lemon

1. Cut celery diagonally into 1½-inch pieces. In a medium saucepan bring to a boil enough salted water to cover celery; add celery and parboil 5 minutes. Drain.

2. Meanwhile, in a large frying pan melt butter. Add onion and walnuts and sauté briefly. Add lemon rind and celery. Toss to coat celery.

Serves 4.

CELERY SEED

This tiny, pungent seed is the fruit of wild celery, which is also known as smallage.

Use Celery seed adds a celerylike flavor to soups, salad dressings, pickling mixtures, tomato juice, potato salad, cole slaw, stuffings, meat loaf, and shellfish stews. It is ground and mixed with salt to make celery salt.

Availability Celery seed is packaged in airtight jars or plastic bags.

Selection Packaged seasonings lose quality after a while; try to buy from a store that restocks its spice section fairly often.

Storage Keep in a cool, dry, dark place; replace celery seed once a year.

CHAYOTE

Also known as mirliton, vegetable pear, *chocho,* and christophine, the chayote is a pear-shaped, tropical squash native to Central America. It has been grown in North Africa and exported to Europe for years as a gourmet vegetable. Chayote is becoming increasingly available in markets throughout the United States. Its skin is smooth, thin, pale green to green with slight ridges; its flesh is moist and creamy white, with a delicate, slightly sweet flavor often compared to that of a cucumber. The single flat seed is edible with a nutty taste. On the average chayotes measure 4 to 6 inches in length and weigh about 1 pound.

Use Chayote may be used like any other squash: baked, steamed, boiled, stuffed, or fried. Its mild flavor is a good counterpoint to spicy stuffings and other spicy treatments, although it is often simply steamed and buttered or cooled and dressed in vinaigrette.

Availability Peak availability for fresh chayote is October through April. If you cannot find chayote, try a large pattypan squash.

Selection Choose small unblemished chayotes with dark green skins.

Storage Refrigerate in a plastic bag in crisper for up to two weeks.

Preparation Young chayotes with tender skins do not need to be peeled; peel mature squash. Halve or quarter and remove seed.

Cooking See BOIL, SAUTE, STEAM.

Céleri-rave rémoulade is the French name for this very popular salad made of shredded celeriac (celery root) tossed in a tangy mustard-shallot dressing.

■ STUFFED MIRLITON

The mild flavor of chayote takes well to the spicy stuffing given in this recipe from Louisiana, where the vegetable is known as mirliton.

> 2 **chayotes, cut in half lengthwise**
> 4 **cups water**
> ¼ **cup unsalted butter**
> ½ **pound andouille (sausage), chopped**
> 1 **cup chopped onion**
> ½ **cup chopped celery**
> ½ **cup chopped green bell pepper**
> 1 **tablespoon minced garlic**
> ½ **pound raw shrimp, shelled, deveined, and chopped**
> ½ **cup chopped green onions**
> ½ **teaspoon basil**
> ¼ **teaspoon thyme**
> ½ **teaspoon cayenne pepper**
> 1 **teaspoon Worcestershire sauce**
> ¾ **to 1 cup dry bread crumbs**
> **Salt and freshly ground pepper, to taste**

1. Place halved chayotes in a pan large enough to hold them in a single layer, cover with the water, and bring to a boil. Boil over medium heat until flesh of squash is tender (about 30 minutes). Remove from pan and cool under cold water. Remove seeds and scoop out pulp, being careful not to break through skin of chayotes. Chop pulp; reserve pulp and shells.

2. Preheat oven to 350° F. In a 12-inch frying pan over medium heat, melt butter. Add *andouille* and cook until slightly browned (about 5 minutes). Add onion and celery and cook until vegetables are soft (about 10 minutes). Add green pepper and garlic and cook for another 2 minutes. Add chopped shrimp and cook until shrimp turns pink (1 to 2 minutes). Add green onion, basil, thyme, cayenne, Worcestershire, and chopped chayote pulp. Add enough bread crumbs to bind the stuffing. Taste for salt and pepper; correct if necessary. Fill chayote shells with stuffing and bake for 30 minutes.

Serves 4.

Food Processor Version   Use metal blade to chop 1 medium onion and 1 stalk celery. Add to andouille. With metal blade process 1 small green pepper, cut in 1-inch pieces, and 3 cloves garlic; add to pan.

CHEESE

Despite their remarkable variety, almost all cheeses start out as coagulated milk. The milk is coagulated by adding bacteria that cause it to curdle—to separate into solid curds and liquid whey. The vast differences in taste and texture depend on three factors: the source of the milk, the treatment after coagulation, and the aging process.

Most of the world's cheeses are made from cow's, goat's, or sheep's milk. Italian buffalo-milk mozzarella is one notable exception. Not only do the different types of animals yield milk of very different character, but the flavor of the milk is affected by the season and the region. Summer milk from cows that have grazed on pastureland tastes different from—many say better than—winter milk from grain-fed cows. Microorganisms in a given region also contribute to the flavor of a cheese, which partly explains why cheeses made by the same methods in different regions will not taste the same.

PROCESSING

Cheeses may be made from whole milk, skimmed milk, or milk with added cream (such as the French double and triple creams). The higher the fat portion of the milk or milk and cream mixture, the creamier and smoother the final cheese.

Cheese may also be made from either pasteurized or unpasteurized (raw) milk. Pasteurizing kills bacteria that impart flavor to cheese, which is why many consumers claim that a raw-milk cheese has better flavor than the same cheese made from pasteurized milk. Raw-milk cheeses are strictly regulated because raw milk is a potential carrier of disease-causing bacteria. Raw-milk cheeses, both imported and domestic, must be aged at least 60 days. Many cheeses—such as Maytag Blue from Iowa and Parmesan and Fontina Val d'Aosta from Italy—are made from raw milk and meet this aging requirement. Others, such as French Camembert and Brie, are aged less than 60 days and must be made from pasteurized milk if intended for sale in this country.

Raw-milk cheeses depend on natural bacteria to produce lactic acid, which curdles the milk by coagulating its protein (casein). Pasteurized milk does not contain these acid-producing bacteria; they must be introduced with a culture or starter. Sometimes rennet, an enzyme extracted from the stomachs of young calves, is added to speed coagulation. For some cheeses, coloring is added at this point; to make blue-veined cheeses such as Gorgonzola, the milk is inoculated with mold spores.

After coagulation the curd is cut into smaller pieces to encourage draining of the whey—the liquid, noncoagulating portion. The size of the cut and the length of the draining period determine the texture and moisture content of the finished cheese. Curds cut into large pieces and left to drain briefly produce a moist, soft cheese. Smaller cuts and a longer draining period yield a firmer cheese. Sometimes the curd is cooked or briefly heated with the whey before draining; this process produces a firm hard cheese such as Gruyère.

Some curds are ladled into molds and allowed to drain naturally. Others are molded and pressed, either lightly or heavily, to establish a shape and expel even more whey. Pressed cheeses have a firmer, more solid texture than unpressed cheeses.

After molding, cheeses may be soaked in brine or repeatedly washed with water, brine, or alcohol. They may be sprayed with spores to produce an exterior mold; they may also be waxed, smoked, wrapped with herbs or leaves, coated with ashes, or soaked in oil.

Lastly, some cheeses are aged or ripened under controlled temperature and humidity. Aging develops flavor and causes moisture loss. Generally, the longer a cheese has been aged, the stronger in flavor and drier it will be. Young Parmesan can be sliced and has a smooth, nutty flavor; aged Parmesan, best for grating, has a sharp flavor.

TYPES OF CHEESE

To make sense of the enormous variety of cheeses, it helps to classify or categorize them in some way. One helpful system is to classify them by texture: Are they hard or soft? Sliceable? Spreadable? Another system is to classify them by the source of the milk: cow, sheep, goat. Some cheeses are traditionally grouped together because they're made by a common process, such as the blue-veined and *pasta filata* cheeses.

Some of the more traditional classifications are outlined below. Categories inevitably overlap, and placement of a cheese in a particular category is somewhat arbitrary. A cheese may be semihard when young but hard when aged. Blue cheeses may be classified by texture—Gorgonzola is semisoft, Stilton is semihard—but they are generally grouped together because of their color.

CLASSIFICATION BY TEXTURE: SOFT CHEESE

Soft-textured cheeses, also known as fresh cheeses, include such popular varieties as cottage cheese, cream cheese, and French *fromage blanc*. They are uncooked and unripened or barely ripened; they are often not molded, but simply spooned into tubs. Soft cheeses are usually very mild and creamy.

Use Fresh cheeses such as cream cheese may be spread on crackers or bread. Cottage and pot cheeses may be salted and eaten with crisp vegetables as a salad, or sugared and eaten with fruit for breakfast or dessert. Serve slightly chilled. *Mascarpone* or whipped, sweetened cream cheese may be used to fill crêpes or fruit tarts. Fresh cheeses may also be made into cheesecakes and cheese pies.

Selection Buy soft cheeses from a market that has a rapid turnover.

Storage Because of their high moisture content, soft cheeses are highly perishable; all should be refrigerated in a covered container and most should be eaten within one week.

Cheeses in This Category Cottage cheese, pot cheese, farmer cheese, cream cheese, Neufchâtel, Gervais, *fromage blanc*, ricotta, *stracchino, mascarpone.*

■ COEUR A LA CREME

This charming molded cheese dessert is traditionally made in a heart-shaped basket or porcelain dish that is pierced on the bottom so the mixture can drain as it sets. The molds are available at better cookware stores.

- 1 **pound cottage cheese**
- 1 **pound cream cheese, softened**
- 1 **teaspoon vanilla extract**
  Pinch of salt
- 1 **cup confectioners' sugar, sifted**
- 2 **cups whipping cream**
- 1 **pint whole strawberries *or* 1 cup Raspberry Sauce (see page 522), for garnish**

A simple, but appealing dinner finale in the European tradition features a variety of cheeses in wedges, slices, or balls, served with fruits, nuts, and crackers. Offer a selection of fruit liqueurs or serve a dessert wine such as a late-harvest Zinfandel, a port, or a Muscat Canelli.

1. Have ready a heart-shaped, 8-cup *coeur à la crème* mold. Dampen a towel and press into mold, leaving towel ends free.

2. Press cottage cheese through a sieve or whirl briefly in food processor; place in a 2-quart mixing bowl. Stir in cream cheese, vanilla, and salt. Add confectioners' sugar.

3. Whip cream to soft peaks; fold into cheese mixture. Pour mixture into prepared mold and cover with towel ends. Place mold in a shallow dish and chill 8 to 12 hours.

4. To unmold, fold back towel. Set serving plate over cheese and invert. Remove mold and towel from cheese. Garnish with whole strawberries or Raspberry Sauce.

Serves 8 to 10.

Recipes: Buttermilk Blintzes, 600; Cheese Roulade, 206; Figs With Flavored Ricotta, 220; Gnocchi Verde, 190; Marbled Cream Cheese Brownies, 65; New York–Style Cheesecake, 117; Ricotta Cheesecake, 119; Unbaked Cheesecake, 118.

BRIE IN PUFF PASTRY

Center wheel of Brie on top of smaller puff pastry circle. Brush water on pastry from cheese to pastry edge. Cover with larger circle of pastry and press gently on top piece of dough at edges to seal the two circles together. Freeze until dough is firm but not frozen (about 10 minutes).

Cut a scallop pattern around edge of dough. Cut a ¼-inch hole in center of pastry (do not puncture cheese). Roll a 1-inch by 1½-inch piece of foil into a tube; set in hole in pastry (will serve as a steam vent).

Brush pastry decorations with water and apply to top. Freeze 20 minutes. Remove from freezer. Brush top of pastry with egg wash. Bake 20 to 25 minutes at 425° F.

CLASSIFICATION BY TEXTURE: SOFT-RIPENED CHEESES

Soft-ripened cheeses have not been cooked or pressed. Instead they are cut in large curds and allowed to drain naturally. They are then sprayed with spores or washed with brine, water, or alcohol to promote development of a rind. Sprayed cheeses develop a powdery white rind; washed cheeses develop an orange-hued rind.

These cheeses ripen from the rind inward. When fully ripe, they have a smooth, almost spreadable texture and range in flavor from mild to quite strong.

Use Soft-ripened cheeses are delicious dinner cheeses, served after the main course but before dessert. They are traditionally offered with bread or crackers and wine. The rind is edible, although some prefer to cut it away. Serve soft-ripened cheeses at room temperature.

Selection These cheeses should give slightly to pressure. They should feel supple but not liquid. Avoid any that have a chalky white center (they are underripe) or a strong ammonia odor (they are overripe). The rind should be evenly colored and slightly moist.

Storage Keep them in the refrigerator, wrapped airtight in plastic; change wrapping every few days. Use within a couple of weeks.

Cheeses in This Category Boursault, Brie, Brillat-Savarin, Camembert, *Caprice des Dieux, Carré de l'Est, Chaource,* Coulommiers, Liederkranz, Limburger, Muenster, Pont l'Eveque.

◼ BRIE OR CAMEMBERT IN PUFF PASTRY

Soft-ripened cheeses, such as a round of Brie or Camembert, are a special treat when baked in puff pastry (see photographs at left). Wedges of the pastry served with a glass of wine and fresh fruit are delicious after dinner. You can enclose any size wheel of Brie or Camembert in puff pastry. Allow 2 ounces of cheese per person for a small serving. One recipe of puff pastry can easily enclose a 1-pound wheel of cheese. You can make circles of puff pastry from 1½ pounds virgin puff pastry and use trimmings to decorate the outside of the pastry.

> 1½ recipes (2 lb) Classic Puff Pastry
>   with 6 turns (see page 482)
> 2 wheels (8 oz and 4 in. diameter each)
>   Brie or Camembert, well-chilled, *or*
>   1 wheel (16 oz and 8 in. diameter)
> 1 egg, lightly beaten with 1 teaspoon water

1. Roll out Classic Puff Pastry a little less than ¼ inch thick. Chill sheet of dough until firm. If using two 4-inch wheels of cheese, cut out two 6-inch circles and two 7-inch circles of puff pastry. If using one 8-inch wheel, cut out one 10-inch circle and one 11-inch circle. Cover and refrigerate 30 minutes. Gather scraps of dough into a ball; refrigerate 30 minutes.

2. Roll out trimmings of dough as thin as possible (less than ⅛ inch thick) ; freeze until very cold but not frozen. Use pastry cutters or a sharp knife to make cutouts for decorating top of puff pastry (stems, leaves, flowers, grapes, etc.). Freeze decorations until firm. Freeze wheels of cheese no longer than 20 minutes.

3. Place two 6-inch circles (or one 10-inch circle) of puff pastry on a parchment-lined baking sheet. Place a wheel of cheese in center of each. Brush water around the border from cheese to edge of pastry. Cover each wheel with a 7-inch circle of puff pastry dough (or an 11-inch circle if using larger wheel). Press down on dough around base of cheese with fingertips to seal edges of dough together. Firm dough in freezer 10 minutes.

4. When dough is well chilled but not frozen, cut a scallop pattern at edge of pastry with a sharp knife. Create a hollow aluminum foil tube (a chimney) by wrapping a 1-inch by 1½-inch strip of foil 2 or 3 times around a pencil; butter exterior of foil tube and remove pencil. Cut a ¼-inch hole in center of top layer of pastry and fit buttered tube into it. This will allow steam from inside pastry to escape. Brush cutout decorations with water and apply in an attractive pattern on top. Return to freezer for 20 minutes. Preheat oven to 425° F.

5. Remove pastry rounds from freezer, and brush top of each with egg wash (take care not to drip any down sides of pastry). Bake until golden brown (20 to 25 minutes). Cool for 30 to 45 minutes before cutting. If served immediately, cheese will run out after pastry is cut. Cut each pastry into 4 (or 8 if using a large wheel) wedges.

Serves 8.

CLASSIFICATION BY TEXTURE: SEMISOFT CHEESES

The cheeses in this category have generally been pressed but not cooked. Ranging in flavor from very mild to strong, they have a soft texture but can be sliced. Many of these cheeses were originally made by European monks and are known as monastery cheeses.

Use Serve semisoft cheeses as part of a cheese board, with bread or crackers and wine. Bring to room temperature before serving. Because they can be sliced, they may be used for sandwiches. Because they melt well, they may be used in grilled sandwiches or as a topping for many types of casseroles.

Selection Choose semisoft cheeses that give slightly to pressure. They may smell strong, but they should not smell rank or ammoniated.

Storage Keep semisoft cheese in the refrigerator, wrapped airtight in plastic; change wrapping every few days. Semisoft cheeses keep for up to one month.

Cheeses in This Category   Bel Paese, brick, Esrom, Gouda, Havarti, Livarot, Monterey jack, *morbier*, Oka, Port Salut, *reblochon*, Saint Paulin, Samsoe, Sonoma jack, *taleggio*, Tilsit.

Recipes: Cheese Roulade, 206; Chiles Rellenos, 428; Refried Beans, 35; Tiropita, 223.

CLASSIFICATION BY TEXTURE: SEMIFIRM CHEESES

These cheeses have been cooked and pressed to eliminate excess moisture. They may or may not have a rind. Texture is firm but smooth and allows cheeses to be sliced; flavor ranges from mild to sharp.

Use   Serve semifirm cheeses as part of a cheese board, with bread or crackers and wine. Bring to room temperature before serving. Because they can be sliced, they may be used for sandwiches. Most semifirm cheeses also melt well and may be grated for use in a range of cooked dishes, such as omelets, soufflés, sauces, breads, puddings, pies, and casseroles.

Selection   Avoid semifirm cheese with a cracked rind or a dry, crumbly texture.

Storage   Keep in refrigerator, wrapped airtight in plastic; change wrapping every few days. For long storage, overwrap plastic with aluminum foil and store in bottom of refrigerator. Coating cut side of cheese with butter or hot paraffin before wrapping prevents drying and the development of surface mold. Semifirm cheeses keep for several months under these conditions. They may also be frozen for up to two months. Wrap tightly in plastic, then in foil, and freeze quickly. Thaw slowly in refrigerator.

Cheeses in This Category   Appenzeller, Asiago, Caerphilly, Cantal, Cheddar, Cheshire, Danbo, Derby and Sage Derby, Double Gloucester, Edam, Emmentaler, fontina, Gjetost, Gruyère, Jarlsberg, *raclette*.

▤ FONTINA FRITTERS

Golden brown outside and molten within, these fritters are a heavenly mouthful. The batter may be made ahead, but the cheese must be fried at the last minute. Serve with a crisp, white Italian wine, such as an Orvieto or a Soave.

> ¾ **pound chilled fontina, not too ripe**
> ¼ **cup dry white wine**
> 2 **eggs, separated**
> 1 **teaspoon minced garlic**
> 1 **teaspoon baking powder**
> 1½ **cups flour**
> 1 **teaspoon salt**
> 2½ **tablespoons olive oil**
> ½ **to ⅔ cup ice water**
>   **Vegetable oil, for deep-frying**
> ½ **cup minced fresh basil**
>   **Salt, to taste**

1. Cut cheese into 1-inch cubes. In a bowl whisk together wine, egg yolks, and garlic. Whisk in baking powder, flour, and 1 teaspoon salt. Whisk in oil, then add enough of the ice water to make a thick but pourable batter, about the consistency of pancake batter. Let rest at room temperature for 2 hours.

2. When ready to serve, heat 2 inches of vegetable oil in a frying pan to 360° F. Beat egg whites with a pinch of salt until stiff but not dry. Fold into batter along with minced basil.

3. Dip cheese chunks into batter. Allow excess batter to drip off; fry chunks in oil until uniformly golden. Drain fritters on paper towels and salt lightly. Serve fritters immediately.

Serves 8 with other hors d'oeuvres.

CLASSIFICATION BY TEXTURE: FIRM CHEESES

These pressed, cooked cheeses have been aged until dry and hard. When young, they can be sliced; when aged, they must be grated.

Use   Hard cheeses are rarely used as table cheeses, except when young. Young Parmesan, dry jack, and Asiago can be sliced and may be served after dinner with fruit or nuts. Dry, aged cheeses are designed for grating. Use

Dip cubes of fontina cheese in batter, then fry until crisp and brown. The piping-hot Fontina Fritters makes a fine appetizer, served with chilled white wine and herbed olives.

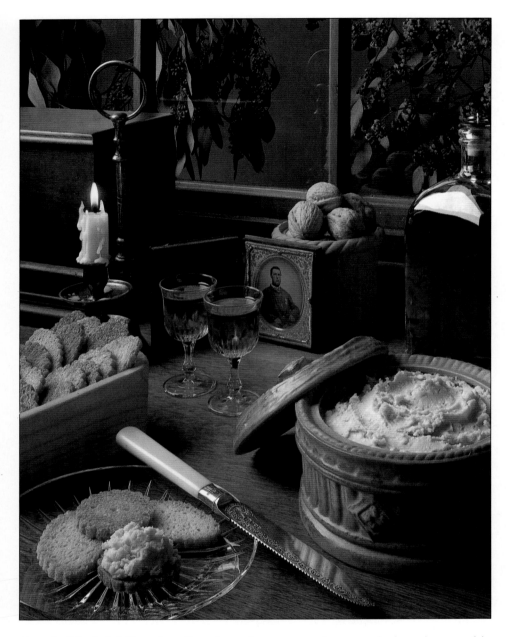

A crock of English Stilton cheese mixed with mellow port makes a royal spread for small toasts or crackers.

CLASSIFICATION BY PROCESS: BLUE-VEINED CHEESES

Inoculating cheese with mold spores will, with time, produce a blue-veined interior. Blue-veined cheeses are generally pungent; they range in texture from the moist creaminess of Gorgonzola to the firm, slightly crumbly Stilton.

Use Blue-veined cheeses are a pleasing addition to an after-dinner cheese board. Complemented by apples, pears, and walnuts, they should be served with crackers or bread and a rich red wine or port. Bring to room temperature before serving. Crumbled blue cheese makes a piquant addition to salads and salad dressings. Blue cheese may be whipped half and half with butter to make a cracker spread or a topping for grilled meats.

Selection Blue cheeses may smell strong but should not smell rank or ammoniated. If possible, sample before buying; avoid cheeses that are overly salty or chalky.

Storage Small pieces may be stored in the refrigerator, wrapped in plastic, for up to one month; change plastic wrap every few days. Large pieces or whole wheels keep longer if covered with a damp towel; cut cheese as needed and rewrap carefully.

Cheeses in This Category Bleu de Bresse, Danablu, Fourme d'Ambert, Gorgonzola, Maytag Blue, Oregon Blue, *Pipo Crem'*, Roquefort, Stilton.

◼ STILTON CROCK WITH PORT WINE

A wedge of blue-veined Stilton cheese and a decanter of port are a venerable British tradition, usually served in the drawing room at the end of a formal meal. This pair can also be packed into a handsome crock for a predinner spread, the flavors melding during the course of a week-long aging. If you are hosting a large party, you can order a whole wheel of Stilton (usually in 10- or 16-pound pieces). Slice off the top and scoop out the cheese, leaving a sturdy wall all around. Then mash the cheese with about one bottle of port, refill the wheel, and replace the cover for aging. It makes an impressive buffet centerpiece, especially at holiday time.

2 **pounds Stilton cheese**
⅓ **to ½ cup imported port**
   Crackers, for accompaniment

1. Trim any rind from cheese; place cheese in a bowl. Add port. With back of a wooden spoon, blend port and cheese. Pack into a 4-cup crock, cover with plastic wrap, refrigerate, and let age 1 week.

2. Bring cheese to room temperature and serve with crackers.

Makes 4 cups, or enough for 20 to 30 cocktail servings.

Recipes: Blue Cheese Soufflé, 205; Stilton Snow Peas, 419.

them in pasta, on soups, in casseroles, on pizzas, and in rice or egg dishes. Because hard cheeses go stale quickly after grating, it is preferable to buy them in blocks and grate them at home just before using.

Selection Firm cheeses should be hard but not dried out. If possible, sample before buying and reject any that taste overly salty or bitter.

Storage Because of their exceptionally low moisture content, hard cheeses store well. Follow storage and freezing advice for semifirm cheeses.

Cheeses in This Category Aged Asiago, *Grana Padano*, Parmesan, Pecorino Romano, Sapsago, Sbrinz.

Recipes: Gnocchi di Patate, 189; Pesto, 27.

CLASSIFICATION BY PROCESS:
PASTA FILATA CHEESES

A specialty of Italy, *pasta filata* (spun paste) cheeses are made by washing the curd in hot water or whey, then kneading and stretching it to the desired consistency and shape. The process produces a pliable cheese that can be molded by hand; occasionally these cheeses are formed into animal or pear shapes. The finished cheese should be smooth and elastic but not rubbery. Pasta filata cheeses are usually mild in flavor and are occasionally smoked.

Use   In Italy fresh mozzarella is drizzled with olive oil and served as a first course, often with sliced tomatoes or roasted peppers. Fresh or factory-made mozzarella may be used in baked pasta dishes, such as lasagne, or layered in vegetable casseroles.

Selection   Fresh mozzarella should be purchased and used within two or three days of its manufacture. Other pasta filata cheeses have a longer shelf life. Avoid any that have a rubbery texture.

Storage   Refrigerate, wrapped airtight in plastic. These cheeses keep for several weeks. Serve at room temperature.

Cheeses in This Category   *Cacciocavallo,* mozzarella, Provolone, Scamorza.

Recipes: Deep-fried Zucchini Blossoms, 238; Pizza, 445; Tomatoes With Mozzarella and Basil, 507.

CLASSIFICATION BY PROCESS:
WHEY CHEESES

Most cheeses are made from coagulated milk curds, but a very few are made from the liquid whey. To make a whey cheese, the whey is heated until its solid matter coagulates. The best-known examples are Italian ricotta, made from the whey drained from provolone and mozzarella, and Norwegian Gjetost.

Use   Ricotta may be sugared and eaten with fresh berries or sliced fruit. It may be salted and eaten as a salad with crisp vegetables, olives, and olive oil. Seasoned ricotta is used as a filling for baked pasta dishes, as a stuffing for breast of veal, and in cheesecakes.

Norwegian Gjetost is usually sliced thin and eaten with toast for breakfast or with spiced fruit cake.

Selection   Fresh ricotta is very perishable; it should be purchased and used within a few days of its manufacture.

Storage   Keep in a covered container in the refrigerator. It is moist and creamy, with a very mild, almost sweet flavor. Domestic factory-made ricotta has a slightly longer shelf life but lacks the creamy texture and pure flavor of the fresh version.

Gjetost, an unusual cheese, is made from whey heated slowly until the water evaporates and the natural sugars caramelize. Lactose and brown sugar may be added. The result is a golden brown cheese with a smooth, creamy texture and a pronounced caramel flavor. It stores well, wrapped in plastic and chilled; change wrap often.

OTHER CLASSIFICATIONS:
PROCESSED CHEESES

Most processed cheeses derive from a natural cheese that has been ground and mixed with emulsifiers to make it uniformly smooth, then is pasteurized and packed. Some processed cheeses contain preservatives and colorings. Products labeled cheese spread or cheese food may contain flavorings as well as liquid or powdered milk for added moisture and spreadability.

These cheeses generally have a mild flavor and a uniformly smooth texture. Although they keep well and are often conveniently packaged, they lack the distinctive character and complexity of natural cheeses.

OTHER CLASSIFICATIONS:
CHEESES FOR SPECIAL DIETS

Today's market is full of cheeses made to comply with special diets. Low-fat and low-salt or low-sodium cheeses are widely available and are identified as such on their labels. Because fat adds richness and texture to cheese, low-fat cheeses may lack the full flavor and good melting qualities of the comparable full-fat cheeses. Part-skim mozzarella, for example, does not melt as well as whole-milk mozzarella but may be preferred by those counting calories.

CLASSIFICATION BY MILK SOURCE:
GOAT CHEESES

Also known as *chèvre* (French for goat), goat's milk cheese has a distinctive chalky color and tangy flavor. Young, fresh goat cheese is mild and creamy. As it ages, it gets stronger and drier. Goat cheeses are made in a variety of shapes and sizes. They may be coated with ash or dried herbs or sprayed with mold spores to produce a rind.

Use   Goat cheeses are a pleasing addition to a cheese board; offer them with crackers or bread and wine. Small, round goat cheeses may be coated with soft bread crumbs and sautéed or baked until warm throughout. Goat cheese adds a creamy tang to stuffings, salads, pizza toppings, soufflés, and omelets.

Selection   Young, highly moist goat cheeses have a short shelf life. Buy them from a shop that has a rapid turnover and try to sample before purchase. Reject any that have a sour or ammoniated flavor.

Storage   Keep moist goat cheese in refrigerator, covered with plastic wrap; it will keep for one or two weeks. Change plastic wrap every few days. Aged goat cheese keeps slightly longer.

Cheeses in This Category   Banon, *bûcheron,* California chévre, *caprino,* Chabichou (or *Cabécou*), feta (some feta is made from sheep's milk or part sheep's milk), Montrachet, Sainte-Maure.

ENTERTAINING WITH WINE AND CHEESE

Cheese and wine are ancient foods that go back to the earliest days of agriculture. It is not surprising, then, that they pair very well. There is probably not a wine that cannot be matched to one cheese or another, nor a single cheese that cannot be served with some wine. But some combinations of wine and cheese go together better than others.

A wine and cheese buffet can make excellent party fare, as long as you avoid the familiar "Cheddar, Swiss, and Brie, burgundy and chablis." A good cheese board can consist of as few as three or four cheeses, or a dozen or more, depending on the number of guests. The key is to provide a variety of flavors and textures. Wines should also be chosen for variety, so that at least one wine will suit every guest's personal taste.

Here are some pointers on assembling a selection of wines and cheeses:

- For a party at which dinner will not be served, allow about ¼ pound of cheese per person and one bottle of wine for every three or four guests. Allow half as much for a before-dinner cocktail hour. Remember, cheese is filling; don't overwhelm appetites before dinner.
- Try for a balanced selection of cheeses by choosing one example from each category. To get you going, you might want to plan around one soft-ripening cheese (such as Brie, Camembert), one semisoft cheese (consider Port-Salut, Monterey jack), one firm cheese, either of the Swiss or Cheddar type, and one blue-veined cheese. With more guests, for variety add a stronger soft or semisoft cheese (two are Pont l'Evêque, Esrom), a hard cheese (such as quality Parmesan, aged Gouda), a goat's-milk cheese, a double- or triple-cream cheese (such as Boursault, Saint-André), an herbed or spiced cheese (including Havarti with dill or Cumminost), or whatever other types you like.
- Follow the same approach with the wines. Start with one dry red, say a Zinfandel or a lighter-style Cabernet, and one white wine that is slightly sweet, such as Chenin Blanc or Riesling. Next, add both a dry white (Chardonnay or Sauvignon Blanc) and a different style of red (such as Gamay Beaujolais). Unless the purpose of the party is to provide an opportunity for tasting as many wines as possible with a variety of cheeses, keep the wine selection simple.
- Serve an assortment of breads or crackers. Avoid highly seasoned crackers if you want the flavor of the cheese and wine to come through. With really fine cheeses, thin, unsalted crackers or matzos are best.
- Other nice accompaniments to a cheese board are crunchy raw vegetables, nuts, olives, and fresh fruits, especially apples and grapes. Some guests might also enjoy a few condiments like fancy mustards, chutney, and gherkins.
- To show cheeses at their best, serve them at room temperature. Provide plenty of knives or cheese slicers, at least one for each cheese, to facilitate serving.

▪ BAKED GOAT CHEESE SALAD

The richness of the goat cheese complements the pungent winter greens and a tangy wine vinegar. When baked, the cheese becomes creamy. This is a good company dish as the cheese must marinate one hour before baking, so preparation is completed before guests arrive.

1	small goat cheese log (about 5 oz)
9½	tablespoons olive oil
⅓	cup dry bread crumbs
1½	tablespoons red wine vinegar
¼	teaspoon salt
⅛	teaspoon pepper
¼	cup snipped fresh chives
10	to 12 cups washed, dried, and torn salad greens (endive, chicory, watercress, arugula)
½	red bell pepper, cored, seeded, and cut into thin strips
	Freshly ground black pepper
	French bread, for accompaniment

1. Slice goat cheese into ½-inch-thick rounds. Pour 4 tablespoons olive oil into a shallow bowl; place bread crumbs on a sheet of waxed paper. Dip goat cheese rounds into olive oil to coat completely, then into bread crumbs; shake off excess crumbs. Set breaded rounds on a tray and chill for 1 hour. Toward the end of chilling period (or about 30 minutes before serving), preheat oven to 375° F.

2. In a small bowl whisk together 3 tablespoons oil, vinegar, salt, pepper, and chives; reserve. Thirty minutes before serving, let salad greens come to room temperature, if chilled.

3. Pour remaining olive oil into an 8-inch square baking dish. Set chilled goat cheese rounds in dish and bake until a light golden crust forms (about 8 minutes). Turn with a spatula (handle rounds gently so that they don't break) and bake on second side for 2 minutes.

4. To serve, toss salad greens with two thirds of the dressing; divide among 6 individual salad plates. Remove cheese from baking pan and place one breaded round in the center of each nest of greens. Arrange red peppers around goat cheese, drizzle with remaining dressing, and grind black pepper over top. Serve immediately with French bread.

Serves 6.

Recipes: Deep-fried Zucchini Blossoms (goat cheese and sun-dried tomato variation), 238.

CLASSIFICATION BY MILK SOURCE: SHEEP'S MILK CHEESES

Sheep's milk cheeses have a sharp tang that immediately distinguishes them from cow's milk cheeses. Most sheep's milk cheeses are made in countries and regions that have too little pasturage to support cattle—such as Greece, Spain, the Pyrenees, and the Middle East.

Use Depending on their moisture content, sheep's milk cheeses may be sliced for use in sandwiches, snacks, and salads, or grated for use as a flavor accent on salads and cooked dishes.

Selection If possible, ask for a sample before buying. Sheep's milk cheeses may be sharp but should not be excessively salty or bitter.

Storage Keep them in plastic wrap in the refrigerator, changing the wrapping every few days. Highly moist cheeses deteriorate more quickly than varieties with low moisture.

Cheeses in This Category Feta (some feta is made from goat's milk), *kasseri*, Liptauer, *manchego*, *pecorino*, Romano, Ricotta Pecorino (also known as *ricotta salata*), Roquefort.

Recipes: Greek Salad, 507; Tiropita, 223.

CHEESECAKE

This rich, creamy confection has achieved an enduring popularity that seems to transcend food fads and concern for calories. A cheesecake is a cake or pie with a custard-like filling whose main ingredient is cream cheese, cottage cheese, ricotta cheese, or some combination, contained in a cookie or crumb crust, or baked without a crust.

In New York, "real" cheesecake is a tall, dense, lemony, cream cheese–based cake. Elsewhere, preference might be for something lighter, perhaps flavored with liqueur or finished with a coat of sour cream or a layer of fresh fruit. Then there's marble, mocha, pumpkin, savory, chocolate chip, Italian, no-bake, and many, many others.

PREPARING CHEESECAKE

Regardless of the version you prefer, there are a few points to remember that apply to all. Packaged cream cheese usually contains gum, which makes a cake denser. Natural cream cheese, available at cheese and specialty food stores and well-stocked supermarkets, is free of gum and will produce a lighter-textured cake. Whichever type you favor, have the cream cheese at room temperature before using; it will mix easier and blend more quickly with the other ingredients.

Most recipes specify using a springform pan, whose sides release for easier removal of the cake. If the cheesecake is to bake in a hot water bath (bain-marie), wrap the outside of the pan with foil. The foil acts as a barrier to keep the water from seeping through the seams of the pan and into the cake, making it soggy. An alternative is to use a cheesecake pan, which is a deep layer-cake pan preferred by commercial bakers. Because it is made in one piece, it stays watertight, but for that reason the cake is more difficult to unmold.

■ NEW YORK–STYLE CHEESECAKE

This is always a dense, rich cake, served in thin slices because it is so filling. To suit today's taste for lighter desserts, cottage cheese has been added, but the texture is classic. Serve it as it comes from the oven or top with a lemon or raspberry glaze. The thick batter may strain the motor of some portable electric mixers. Use a heavy-duty mixer if possible; first beat by hand completely or partway to soften and blend the ingredients, then finish mixing with the machine.

> 1 pound whole-milk cottage cheese
> 1½ pounds natural cream cheese,
>   at room temperature
> 1½ cups sugar
>   Grated rind and juice of 1 lemon
> 5 eggs
> ¼ cup cornstarch
> 1 pint sour cream
> 2 tablespoons vanilla extract

Lemon Custard Glaze (optional)

> 1 egg
> 2 egg yolks
> 6 tablespoons sugar
> ¼ cup fresh lemon juice
> 1 teaspoon finely grated lemon rind
> 4 tablespoons unsalted butter, softened
>   Cookie crumbs (optional)

Raspberry Glaze (optional)

> 1 package (10 oz) frozen raspberries
> 2 tablespoons sugar
> 1 tablespoon cornstarch
> 2 teaspoons raspberry liqueur or kirsch

1. Preheat oven to 300° F. Butter bottom and sides of a 10-inch springform pan.

2. To refine texture of cottage cheese, force cheese through a wire-mesh sieve or purée in a blender or food processor. In a large bowl blend softened cream cheese and cottage cheese purée with a heavy-duty mixer and paddle attachment, or by hand with a wooden spoon. Add sugar and lemon rind; mix well to incorporate.

3. Add eggs, one at a time, beating well after each addition. Sift in cornstarch; beat to combine. Stir in sour cream, vanilla, and lemon juice. Pour into prepared pan and bake 50 minutes (it will be pale yellow—not at all brown—set around the edges, and still wobbly under the surface in the center). Turn off oven, leave door slightly ajar, and allow cheesecake to cool completely. When cool, spread with either glaze (if desired) or leave plain; refrigerate at least 6 hours, or overnight. Before serving, bring cake to room temperature. To slice cleanly and evenly, use a sharp, thin- and narrow-bladed knife. It may be necessary to dip blade in hot water and wipe clean after each slice, so knife draws easily through cake without drag.

Serves 12 to 16.

Lemon Custard Glaze In a medium stainless steel bowl, combine egg, egg yolks, sugar, lemon juice, and lemon rind. Immediately place over a pot of boiling water (double-boiler fashion) and whisk egg mixture until it thickens to the consistency of mayonnaise (do not boil or mixture will curdle). Remove from heat and immediately whisk in butter. Spread on cake while custard is still warm. If desired, sprinkle cookie crumbs around border of cake to decorate top.

Raspberry Glaze Thaw raspberries; drain, reserving juice. In a small saucepan combine juice with sugar, cornstarch, and about half of the berries. Bring to a boil, stirring, and cook until thickened and clear. Strain to remove seeds. To strained sauce add liqueur and reserved berries. Cool to room temperature, then spoon on cake, letting some glaze spill over top onto sides, if desired.

TIPS

WHAT CAUSES CRACKS?

Probably the most frequent complaint by home bakers about cheese-cakes is that they often crack. Usually this is the result of baking at a temperature that is too high, which causes the outside of the cake to set before the interior has had time to expand and settle. Cheesecakes should bake slowly; check the accuracy of your oven frequently with an oven thermometer. Creating humidity inside the oven will keep the surface of the cake moist and also combat cracking. To do this set a pan of water on the rack below the cheesecake, or bake the cake in a hot water bath.

Overbeating dense batters can also cause cracks. When too much air is incorporated into the mixture, it will rise, then collapse and split. If using a heavy-duty mixer, beat with the flat paddle and not the whisk. A food processor fitted with the steel blade will work well. You may need to process in two batches, depending on the size of the work bowl. You can also beat by hand. A final recommendation: If cracks appear despite all precautions, ignore them. The cake will taste just as wonderful and disappear just as fast as one that is crack-free.

A specialty of southern Italy, Ricotta Cheesecake has a ricotta filling encased in pastry. Raisins, pine nuts, almonds, and a hint of chocolate enrich the filling.

▦ UNBAKED CHEESECAKE

This mildly flavored cheesecake benefits from the addition of one of the fruit variations. Because the filling sets with gelatin, only the crumb crust needs to be baked.

    1 **pound natural cream cheese, at room temperature**
    ½ **cup superfine sugar**
    2 **tablespoons vanilla extract**
       Grated rind and juice of 2 lemons
    3 **egg yolks**
    1 **envelope unflavored gelatin**
    1 **cup whipping cream**
    3 **egg whites**
    ¼ **cup granulated sugar**

Graham Cracker Crumb Crust

    2 **cups fine graham cracker crumbs**
    2 **tablespoons granulated sugar**
    ¼ **cup melted butter**

1. Preheat oven to 350° F. Butter bottom and sides of a 10-inch springform pan. Prepare Graham Cracker Crumb Crust.

2. In a large bowl beat cream cheese until smooth; add sugar, vanilla, and lemon rind, and beat well. Add egg yolks, one at a time, beating well after each addition. In a small saucepan dissolve gelatin in lemon juice over low heat. Pour into cream cheese mixture.

3. Whip cream to soft peaks and fold into cheese mixture. Whip egg whites to soft peaks; add ¼ cup granulated sugar and beat briefly just to incorporate sugar. Stir one third of beaten egg whites into cream cheese mixture; gently fold in remaining whites.

4. Pour filling over cooled crust. Smooth surface with a spatula. Refrigerate until set (2 to 3 hours, or overnight). To serve, decorate top and sides with whipped cream or one of the fruits suggested in the variation.

Serves 8 to 12.

Graham Cracker Crumb Crust In a medium bowl combine graham cracker crumbs and sugar; add melted butter and mix thoroughly. Press into prepared pan. Bake 10 minutes. Cool on a wire rack.

Food Processor Version Use metal blade to process cream cheese, lemon rind, vanilla, and superfine sugar until smooth, scraping work bowl as necessary. Add all egg yolks at once and process 15 seconds. With motor running, pour dissolved gelatin through feed tube and process 10 seconds. Transfer to large mixing bowl and complete recipe as directed.

Fruit Cheesecake Mix in any of the following fruits with whipped cream in step 3: 1 pound fresh ripe, pitted cherries poached in ½ cup water and puréed in food processor or blender; or 1 cup dried apricot purée (soak in water for several hours or overnight, then poach in soaking water until tender, about 15 minutes; sweeten to taste and purée); or 1 package (10 oz) frozen raspberries, thawed, drained, puréed, and strained through a fine sieve to remove seeds.

■ RICOTTA CHEESECAKE

Cheesecakes in southern Italy are made with ricotta, raisins, and pine nuts, and are commonly flecked with chocolate and flavored with rum. This version incorporates crunchy pine-nut brittle, a delicious candy to savor on its own. Offer this rich *torta* in the afternoon with a glass of Marsala, or serve it as the luscious finish to a light meal. Note that the raisins must macerate in the rum for 1 hour.

1	cup superfine sugar
3	tablespoons water
5	tablespoons pine nuts
4	tablespoons golden raisins
2	tablespoons rum
3¼	cups flour
1	tablespoon baking powder
½	cup firmly packed dark brown sugar
1¼	cups ground almonds
4	tablespoons chilled unsalted butter, cut in small pieces
1	egg
1	teaspoon vanilla extract
1½	pounds whole-milk ricotta cheese
1	teaspoon grated lemon rind
2	ounces milk chocolate, coarsely chopped

1. In a 1-quart saucepan heat ¼ cup superfine sugar and the water over high heat. When mixture boils and sugar dissolves, add pine nuts. Continue cooking, swirling pan often, until sugar turns light brown. Turn mixture out onto an oiled baking sheet and let cool. Break up into small chunks. Combine raisins and rum in a small bowl and set aside for 1 hour.

2. *To make dough in a food processor:* Combine flour, baking powder, brown sugar, and almonds; process 5 seconds. Add butter and process until mixture resembles coarse meal, about 10 seconds. Whisk egg and vanilla together, then add to food processor with motor running. Process just until dough nearly holds together. Turn dough out onto a board, gather into a ball, and wrap in plastic. Do not knead or work dough, even if it doesn't hold together well. Refrigerate at least 1 hour. *To make*

dough by hand: Stir together flour, baking powder, brown sugar, and almonds. Cut in butter with a pastry blender until mixture resembles coarse crumbs. Whisk egg and vanilla together, then add to flour mixture. Toss lightly with a fork, just until dough holds together. Gather into a ball and wrap in plastic; refrigerate 1 hour.

3. In a large bowl combine ricotta, remaining sugar, lemon rind, raisins, and rum. Add chocolate bits and pine-nut brittle; mix well.

4. Preheat oven to 350° F. Line bottom and sides of a 10-inch springform pan with aluminum foil. Place a little more than half the pastry dough on bottom of pan, patting it into place and pushing it up sides. Spoon in ricotta filling. Roll out remaining pastry into a 10-inch round and lay over top of filling. Bake until top colors slightly (50 to 55 minutes).

5. Transfer cheesecake to a rack and cool in pan. Release sides of springform pan and gently peel back foil from sides. Lift bottom of cake gently with a spatula and pull out foil. Serve barely warm or at room temperature.

Serves 12.

Make-Ahead Tip Pastry dough may be made 1 day ahead and refrigerated. If stored airtight, brittle can be made up to 2 weeks ahead.

CHEESECLOTH

Soft, lightweight, and porous, cheesecloth is woven of natural cotton, which won't fall apart in hot liquids or add flavor to food. It is used as a neutral, porous wrap. Flavoring infusions such as bouquet garni and mulling spices are bundled in cheesecloth so they can be easily dropped into and retrieved from soups, stews, and beverages. Delicate poached foods such as whole fish and pasta rolls are wrapped in this material to preserve their shape while they cook. Some baked goods, such as fruitcakes, which benefit from slow soaking in liquor, are swaddled in alcohol-soaked cheesecloth to season. It also serves as a flexible strainer for stocks and other liquids.

Cheesecloth is sold in both coarse and fine weave. Each has its place in the kitchen. Coarse cheesecloth resembles bandage gauze. Inexpensive and widely available in supermarkets and cookware stores, it can be cut, used, and thrown away without too much concern for cost. Better quality, fine-mesh cheesecloth is harder to find and seems expensive in comparison with the coarse type, but because it can be washed and reused, it lasts longer.

CHERIMOYA

A heart-shaped fruit native to Ecuador and Peru, the cherimoya is now cultivated in southern California. Its dull green skin has thumbprintlike indentations edged in brown. The fruit inside is creamy white with large black seeds; it has a creamy, custardlike texture and a flavor reminiscent of banana, pineapple, and pear. Its other common names—custard apple and sherbet fruit—attest to its flavor and texture. Cherimoyas range in weight from ¼ pound to 2½ pounds.

Use   Cherimoya is refreshing when eaten chilled "on the half shell." The flesh is scooped out with a spoon and the seeds discarded. The peeled, diced fruit may be added to fruit salads or puréed for sherbet, ice cream, or daiquiris.

Availability   Fresh cherimoyas are in season from November through May. Because they must be hand-pollinated and handpicked and because the trees are low-yielding, cherimoyas are always expensive.

Selection   Choose green cherimoyas that give slightly to pressure; brownness indicates overripeness.

Storage   Hard cherimoyas may be ripened at room temperature. Ripe cherimoyas should be refrigerated and used within one or two days.

Preparation   Scoop from skin and remove seeds.

CHERRY

Although wild cherries are a prehistoric fruit, cherry cultivation probably originated in Asia Minor. Today cherries are cultivated throughout the world's temperate zone. Most of the many cherry varieties can be classified as either sweet (for eating raw) or sour (for cooking). The most commercially important sweet varieties in America are the yellow-orange Royal Ann and the dark red Bing; other varieties include Black Republican, Black Tartarian, Chapman, Lambert, early Burlat, and Schmidt. The most important sour varieties in America are red Montmorency and English Morello.

Use   Sweet cherries may be eaten out of hand or added to fruit salads, fruit compotes, tarts, or ice cream. They may be preserved in brandy for use as a garnish for ice cream or cake. Sour cherries are best for pies, cobblers, preserves, jams, dessert sauces, and pickles. Vinegared sour cherries are a piquant garnish for pâtés and other cold meats. Sour cherries are also used for commercial maraschino liqueur and syrup and for distilling.

Availability   Depending on the variety and the area, fresh sweet cherries are available late spring through August. June is the peak month for most varieties. Sour cherries are harvested from mid-June to mid-August but are rarely available fresh outside the immediate area of cultivation. Most domestic sour cherries are canned whole, in light or heavy syrup, often identified as cherry-pie filling. Wild cherries called *amarena* are imported from Italy packed in syrup or brandy. Dried sour cherries and wild cherry preserves are occasionally available in Greek markets.

Selection   With the exception of Royal Anns, dark color is the best indication of good flavor. Cherries should have a bright, glossy, plump appearance and fresh-looking stems. Avoid soft cherries or any with brown discoloration.

Storage   Handle fresh cherries carefully; refrigerate and use within a few days of purchase. Transfer leftover canned cherries to a covered plastic container; refrigerate for up to two weeks.

Preparation   For compotes and fruit salads, remove fresh cherry stems; remove pits with a cherry pitter, if desired. Fresh sour cherries should be pitted before cooking.

■ SOUR-CHERRY PIE

A lattice-top cherry pie shows off the ripe, red fruit to perfection. A cherry pitter (see opposite page) will make quick work of ridding the cherries of hard-to-remove pits.

- 1 **9-inch double-crust Flaky Pastry or Egg Pastry (see pages 434, 435)**
- 1¼ **cups sugar**
- 5 **tablespoons flour**
- ⅔ **cup cherry juice or other red fruit juice**
- ½ **teaspoon ground cinnamon**
- ⅛ **teaspoon almond extract**
- 1 **tablespoon fresh lemon juice**
- 5 **cups pitted tart red cherries**
- 1 **egg white, lightly beaten**
- 1½ **tablespoons unsalted butter**

1. Preheat oven to 425° F. Roll out pastry for bottom crust and line a 9-inch pie plate. Roll out remaining pastry to form top crust or lattice top (see page 433).

2. In a saucepan combine sugar, flour, cherry juice, cinnamon, almond extract, lemon juice, and cherries. Cook over low heat, stirring frequently, until mixture thickens; set aside to cool.

3. Brush inside of bottom crust with egg white to moistureproof the crust. Pour in cooled filling. Dot with butter.

4. Moisten edges of bottom crust and cover with top crust or lattice top; finish edges. Bake for 20 minutes. Lower heat to 400° F and continue baking until crust is golden brown (40 minutes). Cover edges of crust with strips of aluminum foil, if necessary, to prevent excessive browning.

Serves 8.

■ CHERRY CLAFOUTI

Buttery pastry, sweet red cherries, and custard are baked together to create a French *clafouti*, a type of custard tart. A clafouti can be made from a batter, something like a fruit-dotted puffy pancake or popover, or with a pastry dough that is covered with fruit. If made with a batter, the dish is served from its baking pan. When baked in pastry, it is served in wedges. This version is a combination of a soft filling contained in a tart pastry crust. Although cherries are traditional, when the fresh fruit is unavailable, you can substitute sliced fresh kiwis, poached pears or peaches, or fresh berries. Boysenberries, loganberries, or olallieberries make delicious clafouti.

    1 (9½-in.) Sweet Tart Pastry (see page 441)
    ½ cup milk
    ½ cup whipping cream
    2 whole eggs
    2 egg yolks
    ½ cup sugar
      Pinch freshly grated nutmeg
    1 tablespoon kirsch
    1 egg white, lightly beaten
    2¼ cups pitted sweet red cherries
    ¼ cup confectioners' sugar

1. Place pastry dough on a lightly floured surface and roll out to form a circle ⅛ inch thick and large enough to line a 9½-inch tart tin with removable bottom. Blind bake until partially baked (see page 18); cool in tart tin on a wire rack.

2. Preheat oven to 400° F. In a heavy-bottomed saucepan bring milk to a simmer over medium-low heat; add cream. In a mixing bowl whisk together eggs, egg yolks, sugar, and nutmeg. Add a little of the milk-cream mixture to gently raise the temperature of the eggs and keep them from curdling; stir well to blend. Blend in remaining milk-cream mixture; cool. Stir in kirsch. Set custard aside.

3. To prevent crust from getting soggy, gently brush tart shell with a thin layer of lightly beaten egg white. Arrange cherries (whole or cut in half; if halved, arrange cut side down) in an even layer over bottom of tart shell. Carefully pour custard over cherries (do not fill tart shell more than three fourths full).

4. Bake for 10 minutes at 400° F. Reduce heat to 325° F and bake until custard is set (about 35 minutes).

5. Sift confectioners' sugar over tart. Place under preheated broiler to caramelize sugar. Watch carefully—sugar burns easily. Serve slightly warm.

Serves 6 to 8.

Recipes and Related Information
Cherries Jubilee, 315; Fruit Cheesecake, 119.

CHERRY PITTER

Like a hole puncher, which this hand tool resembles, a cherry pitter makes quick work out of a most tedious chore—removing pits from cherries and olives. All the models are variations of a basic press system: the device holds the round or oval fruit in place while pressure is applied to a plunger that pushes out the pit. The simplest model handles one or two cherries at a squeeze and must be continually reloaded. If this procedure seems too time-consuming, look for an automatic pitter with a built-in container that can hold up to 3 cups of cherries. A funnel feeds the stored fruit to the pitter each time you press the plunger. It *is* child's play. If you have a junior chef who wants to help with meal preparation, this is exactly the type of repetitious work that young hands love to do.

Recipes and Related Information
Cherry, 120; Olive, 398.

CHERVIL

An annual herb native to Asia and Eastern Europe, chervil resembles a very delicate form of parsley. It has soft, feathery, green leaves atop slender stems and umbrella-shaped clusters of tiny white flowers. The leaves have a faint anise flavor.

Use   The aniselike flavor of chervil complements egg, tomato, and fish dishes. Add it to green salads and potato salads, cream soups, mayonnaise, and herb butters and sauces. Chervil is an ingredient in the classic French fines herbes mixture.

Availability   Fresh chervil, tied in bunches or packed in plastic bags, is occasionally available in specialty markets. Dried chervil is sold in airtight jars.

Selection   Buy chervil that is fresh-looking without signs of wilting or decay. Packaged seasonings lose quality after a while; try to buy from a store that restocks its spice section fairly often.

Storage   Keep fresh chervil in refrigerator, wrapped in damp paper towels then in plastic, for up to three days. Store dried chervil in an airtight container in a cool, dry, dark place.

Preparation   Mince fresh chervil leaves just before using. For cooked dishes, add chervil at the last moment; its delicate flavor dissipates with cooking.

Sidewalk chestnut vendors are a familiar winter sight in New York and the cities of Europe. They tuck the steaming nuggets into paper cones for shoppers and strollers, who probably appreciate the warmth as much as the rich, nutty taste. Chestnuts become harder to peel as they cool, so serve them hot from the cooking container or in a napkin-lined basket.

CHESTNUT

The chestnut is the fruit of a tree native to several continents. Chestnut trees flourished in America until the early twentieth century, when they were destroyed by a fungus blight. They still have not been reestablished, although efforts are being made.

The golden chestnut is encased in both a fine, reddish brown membrane and an inedible hard, brown shell. The shelled, cooked chestnut is simultaneously sweet and starchy, with a moist, crumbly texture.

Use   Fresh chestnuts may be roasted in their shells, then peeled and eaten whole as a snack. Peeled chestnuts may be simmered in stock or milk and served as an accompaniment to game or rich meats or made into soup. Whole chestnuts are often braised with red cabbage or Brussels sprouts. Cooked and puréed chestnuts may be seasoned with butter, salt, and pepper for a savory side dish, or sweetened with sugar and cream and used for dessert. French and Italian cooks use sweetened chestnut purée as a filling, garnish, or ingredient for a variety of desserts. Whole candied chestnuts are a popular Christmas confection in Western Europe and an autumn treat in Japan. Chopped candied chestnuts may be added to ice cream, dessert sauces, or confections. Americans add chopped cooked chestnuts to holiday poultry stuffings. Japanese steam autumn chestnuts with rice. In northern China, dried chestnuts are added to stews.

Chestnut flour, made from dried, ground chestnuts, is used in Europe for breads, soups, and desserts.

Availability   Fresh chestnuts are available in winter. Whole peeled chestnuts packed in water are imported from France. Unsweetened chestnut purée, packaged in cans and identified as *purée de marrons,* is imported from France and Switzerland. Sweetened chestnut purée, labeled as *crème de marrons,* is imported from France in cans and tubes. Also from France come whole candied chestnuts (*marrons glacées*) and chestnut pieces (*marrons débris*) in vanilla-flavored syrup, packed in cans and jars. Dried chestnuts are available in Italian and Chinese markets. Chestnut flour is sold in health-food stores and some Italian markets.

Selection   Choose glossy chestnuts that fill their shells and feel heavy for their size. Those with air pockets are likely to be older and dried out. Chestnuts can appear fresh and still be spoiled inside, so it's a good idea to buy a few more than you need.

Storage   Fresh chestnuts will keep up to one week in a cool place or up to two weeks in a plastic bag in the refrigerator. Unused chestnut purée or tinned candied chestnuts will keep in a covered plastic container in the refrigerator for several months. Dried chestnuts will keep in an airtight container in a cool place for two months or in the refrigerator or freezer indefinitely. Chestnut flour keeps one month in the refrigerator.

Preparation   To shell fresh chestnuts, cut an *x* in the flat side. Roast in a preheated 350° F oven for 10 minutes, then peel. Alternatively, blanch them in boiling water for 3 to 4 minutes. Remove from water one at a time and peel (easiest when chestnuts are hot).

■ ROASTED CHESTNUTS

Cook chestnuts at home in the oven as described below, or wrap them in heavy-duty aluminum foil and roast them outdoors over coals. You can also roast them on a grate in the fireplace or over an open fire, using a heavy, lidded skillet with a long handle or a popcorn popper; shake the pan repeatedly until the shells pop open.

> **2 dozen chestnuts**
> **Olive oil**
> **2 tablespoons water**

1. Preheat oven to 425° F. With a small, sharp knife, cut a cross in the flat side of each chestnut. Place chestnuts in a casserole with a tight-fitting lid; add a few drops of oil, toss nuts to coat lightly, add the water, and cover.

2. Bake until chestnuts feel tender when squeezed and peel easily (25 to 30 minutes). Remove to a napkin-lined basket or serve from the casserole.

Makes 2 dozen.

CHICORY

A variety of mostly perennial plants go by the family name *chicory*. Some chicory is grown for its leaves, some for its roots. Chicory grown for its roots is rarely seen in retail markets; the roots are dried, ground, and used as a coffee substitute or additive, popular in New Orleans.

The chicory family includes Belgian endive, escarole, and radicchio, as well as the salad green often labeled chicory in retail markets. The latter chicory is also sometimes labeled *frisé* or curly endive.

Because several of the major members of the chicory family are described in separate entries, this entry deals primarily with the salad green commonly called chicory. A head of chicory contains loosely grouped leaves that are frizzy and have spiky edges. Outer leaves are dark green; inner leaves are pale green, becoming yellow at the heart.

Use Chicory adds texture and a slightly bitter flavor to green salads. Because of its coarse texture, it is often mixed with other greens.

Availability Fresh chicory is sold all year but may be more abundant in early spring or late fall.

Selection Select chicory without evidence of wilting or browning on leaf tips.

Storage Keep chicory in a plastic bag in refrigerator crisper; use within two or three days.

Preparation Wash well just before using. Trim root end and discard any dark or ragged leaves.

CHIFFONNADE

A French term, *chiffonnade* refers to leafy greens and herbs cut into thin ribbons. A chiffonnade of basil, for example, can serve as a flavoring mixture or as a bed for other foods. Shredded lettuce or sorrel is a classic garnish for soups. To prepare a chiffonnade, trim leaves of their stems and any woody parts. Then roll leaves together into narrow tubes and slice into fine strips.

Chiffonnade is also a salad dressing that is based on a French dressing with the addition of chopped hard-cooked egg and strips of green bell pepper, chives, and other vegetables.

CHILL, TO

To make something cold by placing it in the refrigerator or by stirring it over ice water. Salads, gelatin-based dishes, pâtés, soups, mayonnaise-based sauces, custards, pastry dough, and fruit desserts are examples of foods that may require chilling.

CHIVE

A member of the onion family, chives grow in long, thin, hollow green shoots.

Use Snipped chives add a delicate onion flavor to soups, salads, vegetable dishes, eggs, fish, and cheese spreads. They are frequently used as a topping for baked potatoes, along with sour cream. Because of their delicate flavor, they are best as a raw garnish; if possible, add them to cooked dishes at the last minute. Chives are one ingredient in the classic French fines herbes mixture.

Availability Whole fresh chives are sold the year around, tied in bunches or packaged in plastic bags. Snipped freeze-dried chives are packed in airtight jars or tins. Snipped frozen chives are also available in supermarket freezer cases.

Selection Buy fresh shoots without evidence of wilting or decay. Dried seasonings lose quality after a while; try to buy from a store that restocks its spice section often.

Storage Wrap fresh chives in damp paper towels, then in a plastic bag, and refrigerate; use within three or four days. Store freeze-dried chives in an airtight container in a cool, dry, dark place and use within three months. Use frozen chives within six months.

Preparation Mince fresh chives with a knife or snip with kitchen scissors just before using. There is no need to reconstitute freeze-dried chives or thaw frozen chives before using.

■ CHIVE POTATO SALAD

In this version of a popular salad, tiny whole potatoes are tossed in a creamy dressing, punctuated by the oniony flavor and bright green color of fresh chives. Note that the potatoes cook a day in advance, and that, once tossed in dressing, they will keep another 24 hours.

> 2 **pounds small new potatoes**
> ¾ **cup Mayonnaise (see page 519)**
> ¾ **cup Crème Fraîche (see page 161) or sour cream**
> 1 **bunch fresh chives, snipped**

1. The day before the salad is prepared, peel off a strip of skin from around the middle of each potato. Bring a 4-quart pot of salted water to a boil. Add potatoes and cook, covered, until easily pierced with the tip of a sharp knife (20 to 30 minutes). Drain and cool completely. Refrigerate, covered.

2. The next day, combine Mayonnaise and Crème Fraîche in a medium bowl. Add potatoes and toss to cover with sauce. Sprinkle with snipped chives. Serve immediately or refrigerate, covered, up to 24 hours before serving.

Serves 6.

CHOCOLATE

The seeds of the tropical cocoa (or cacao) tree, called cocoa beans, are the source of chocolate. The seeds themselves are quite bitter; although the Aztecs enjoyed a beverage made from roasted ground cocoa beans mixed with hot water, today's taste demands further processing. Numerous advances in processing have led to a variety of chocolate products, from unsweetened cocoa to milk chocolate.

PROCESSING

The processing of chocolate begins with the harvest of the pods of the cocoa tree. Pods are broken open and seeds and pulp removed. Seeds are allowed to ferment for two to nine days to develop flavor; they are then dried, graded, packed, and shipped.

The chocolate manufacturer generally blends seeds from several sources to produce a consistent style and desirable flavor. After cleaning and blending seeds, the manufacturer roasts them to develop flavor and aroma. After roasting and cooling, seeds are shelled. The meat or nibs are saved; the shells are sold for animal feed or fertilizer. The nibs, which are slightly more than 50 percent cocoa butter, are then ground to produce chocolate liquor. The chocolate liquor is then used alone or blended with other ingredients to make specific types of chocolate or chocolate products (see Availability).

Use　Chocolate is little used in Asian cuisines, but it is undoubtedly one of the favorite flavors of the Western world. Indeed, in America chocolate ice cream is second only to vanilla. It is employed both as an ingredient and as a food in itself. Sweetened chocolate bars, either plain or flavored with milk, vanilla, nuts, or a variety of other flavorings, are a favorite snack food. Chocolate is used in countless candies and confections. It may be made into a syrup for use on ice cream and in sodas. Chocolate and chocolate products—in the form of either powdered cocoa or solidified bars—are an ingredient in frostings, cakes, cookies, pies, breads, puddings, mousses, ice creams, soufflés, and dessert sauces. It adds richness and mellow flavor to savory sauces and stews, such as Mexican mole and Sicilian caponata. Chocolate milk is a favorite of American schoolchildren, and hot chocolate or hot cocoa is a popular beverage in cold weather in many Western homes. Melted chocolate is used as a coating for dipped fruits, cookies, candies, and even pretzels.

Availability　Chocolate is sold in many forms. For the best flavor, choose a chocolate of high quality.

Chocolate-Flavored Syrup　This syrup is primarily corn syrup and cocoa with preservatives, emulsifiers, and flavorings. Chocolate syrup is packed in cans or plastic squeeze bottles.

Commercial Coating Chocolate (also known as *couverture*)　Professional confectioners use coating chocolate for dipping and for making chocolate curls, ruffles, and other garnishes. It has more cocoa butter than regular baking chocolate and thus melts and spreads well. In its original, unmelted form, coating chocolate contains cocoa butter made of stable fat crystals. If you melt and recool the chocolate without tempering it (carefully heating and cooling chocolate to a precise temperature), some of the fat crystals may recrystallize as unstable crystals. The unstable fat crystals rise to the surface of the chocolate and form dull gray streaks called fat bloom. Tempering melted chocolate promotes the formation of fat crystals and prevents the occurrence of fat bloom; this process also produces chocolate with a very shiny, unstreaked surface (see Working With Chocolate).

Couverture is not readily available to the home baker. It may be obtained from wholesale bakery supply houses and some mail-order suppliers, usually in 10-pound bars. If it is unavailable, use a good-quality semisweet or bittersweet chocolate with a high cocoa butter content. Many brands of European chocolate bars can be used in place of coating chocolate. See also Compound Chocolate Coating.

Compound Chocolate Coating　Although it has chocolate in its name, this is an imitation product. It may be simply melted and used directly for dipping or spreading.

Eating Chocolate　To make eating chocolate, cocoa butter and sugar are added to the chocolate liquor. Surprisingly, distinctions of bittersweet, semisweet, and sweet do not correspond to any fixed degree of sweetness; the amount of sugar in each depends on the formula of the individual manufacturer. According to U.S. Food and Drug Administration regulations, *sweet chocolate* may contain less than half the chocolate liquor required in bittersweet chocolate. Although different manufacturers use different formulations, *bittersweet chocolate* is usually the most intensely chocolate-flavored and the least sweet, with *semisweet chocolate* being sweeter, and *sweet chocolate* being sweeter still. The three are usually interchangeable in recipes.

Most bittersweet, semisweet, and sweet chocolate is sold in paper-wrapped bars. Semisweet chocolate is also made into chips and packed in bags; chips may be substituted for semisweet chocolate bars ounce for ounce. The chips, however, usually have a lower cocoa butter content than semisweet chocolate bars, thus their flavor is less intense and they melt less easily.

German's Sweet Chocolate　First made by a Mr. German, this type of chocolate has been popularized by the recipe for German's Sweet Chocolate Cake on the package. German's Sweet Chocolate is a proprietary name of the Baker Chocolate Company.

Milk Chocolate To make milk chocolate, dried milk solids are added to sweetened chocolate. It is widely used for candy bars and other confections but is rarely used in cooking. It should not be used in recipes unless specified.

Powdered Cocoa For powdered cocoa, enough cocoa butter is pressed out of the chocolate liquor to leave a press cake with a content of 10 to 24 percent cocoa butter. The cake is pulverized to make cocoa powder. *Dutch-process cocoa* is made by treating either whole nibs or chocolate liquor with an alkaline solution, yielding cocoa with a darker color and mellower flavor. *Instant cocoa* contains lecithin, an emulsifier that makes cocoa easier to dissolve in cold liquids. Many brands of instant cocoa also contain added sugar. Cocoa and instant cocoa are generally packed in airtight tins.

Solid Unsweetened Chocolate Chocolate liquor that has been poured into molds and solidified, solid unsweetened chocolate is usually sold in 8-ounce boxes, with the chocolate divided into tissue-wrapped 1-ounce squares for easy measuring.

White Chocolate Not technically chocolate at all because it lacks chocolate liquor, white chocolate is cocoa butter with added sugar, milk, and flavorings. It may contain lecithin and it usually contains vanilla or vanillin. It should not be substituted for chocolate in recipes.

Storage Keep solid chocolate, wrapped airtight, in a cool, dry place for up to four months. Chocolate kept in the refrigerator will sweat when brought to room temperature and may not melt properly. Chocolate stored in a warm place may develop bloom—a dusty white coating caused by melted cocoa butter rising to the surface. It is harmless and the chocolate may safely be used.

Cocoa will keep indefinitely in an airtight tin in a cool place. Store chocolate syrup in a covered container in the refrigerator; it will keep indefinitely.

WORKING WITH CHOCOLATE

Chocolate is an ingredient with many qualities and uses. Melted chocolate can be worked to create a variety of decorations (see photographs, page 126). The Chocolate Ruffle Torte on page 127 is an example of how chocolate ribbons and ruffles can be used.

All work with chocolate should be done at a cool time of the day in a cool room. Handle chocolate quickly and lightly to avoid melting. These techniques are not easy for people with hot hands.

To Melt Chocolate Chocolate is temperamental. It burns easily and should always be melted slowly. When melting chocolate by itself for any purpose, it is best to chop it into small pieces. Place chopped chocolate in the top of a double boiler or in a stainless steel bowl over a pan of hot (not boiling) water; adjust heat so water remains just below a simmer. Take care not to let water

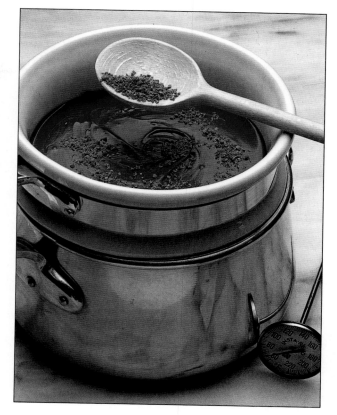

To keep its surface shiny and free of streaks, chocolate must be heated until it melts and then cooled to a specific temperature. This process is called tempering.

boil or allow steam to rise and settle in pan of chocolate. If there is a speck of water in the container used to melt the chocolate, the chocolate will tighten (seize) into an unmeltable mass. To salvage tightened chocolate, stir in 1 teaspoon of vegetable shortening per ounce of chocolate.

Chocolate will melt well in liquid (such as milk or cream) as long as there is at least 1 tablespoon of liquid per ounce of chocolate.

Chocolate can also be melted in a microwave oven. Put chocolate in a glass container and set oven on medium or high heat; chocolate will melt in 1 to 3 minutes, depending on volume.

To Temper Chocolate Coarsely chop chocolate to be tempered. In addition, finely grate a few ounces of unmelted semisweet or bittersweet coating chocolate. You will need 1 tablespoon grated chocolate for every 4 ounces of coarsely chopped chocolate. Melt chopped chocolate in a dry bowl set over hot water; stir until smooth. Do not allow chocolate to exceed 115° F (test with an instant-read thermometer). Remove bowl from hot water and set on a towel to steady it. Gradually stir in grated chocolate, a spoonful at a time, stirring until melted before adding another spoonful.

If the dipping chocolate is semisweet or bittersweet, cool to 86° to 90° F; if milk chocolate, cool to 83° to 88° F. Return bowl to warm water to maintain desired temperature. If temperature drops too much, mixture will be too thick to coat properly. If it rises above 90° F, it will have to be retempered.

MAKING CHOCOLATE RUFFLES

To make a thin chocolate sheet for a ruffle Refrigerate a piece of marble for several hours or place a rimmed baking sheet filled with ice on top of marble for 30 minutes to chill it. (Chocolate can be spread on the back of a baking sheet but ruffles will not look as shiny when finished.) Dry marble with paper towels. Pour a 1-inch-wide strip of melted and tempered chocolate on ice-cold marble. Use a flexible metal spatula and swift, smooth, even strokes to spread chocolate into a thin sheet about 3 inches wide and 10 inches long.

To form a fan-shaped ruffle When chocolate begins to set but is still pliable, slide a wide-bladed putty knife under right edge of chocolate. To form a fan-shaped ruffle, push chocolate toward left side of marble by moving putty knife from right to left (flexing wrist back and forth as you push). Use index finger and thumb of left hand to gather chocolate into a ruffle as you go along. Transfer ruffle to a waxed paper–lined baking sheet and immediately place in refrigerator.

For the Chocolate Ruffle Torte Make enough ruffles to cover the top of the cake in an overlapping design of rose petals. Rechill marble as necessary. Store ruffles between pieces of waxed paper in a pan in refrigerator until ready to place on cake, after cake has been wrapped with chocolate ribbon (see below). Cover top of pan with plastic wrap.

MAKING CHOCOLATE RIBBONS

Cut out a sheet of waxed paper that is slightly wider than cake is tall and as long as circumference of cake. With a flexible metal spatula, spread a thin layer of melted and tempered chocolate on waxed paper. When chocolate begins to set but is still pliable, place one end of strip against cake (with wet chocolate toward cake). Wrap rest of chocolate strip around cake so it rests smoothly against sides of cake. Press top edge of chocolate down onto top of cake. Chill in refrigerator until chocolate is firm and waxed paper peels away easily.

MAKING CHOCOLATE LEAVES

Choose thick, waxy plant leaves with visible veins. Paint melted and tempered chocolate evenly on undersides of leaves. Chill in refrigerator until chocolate is firm. Slide fingernail between leaf and chocolate near stem to loosen chocolate from leaf. Pull leaf away from chocolate. Use these delicate leaves to decorate all sorts of cakes.

MAKING CHOCOLATE CURLS

It is easiest to produce chocolate curls from a 4-ounce or larger bar of chocolate (at room temperature). Scrape long side of bar with a potato peeler. When chocolate is just the right temperature, this will produce chocolate curls. If chocolate is too cold, you will end up with short chocolate shavings or shredded chocolate.

CHOCOLATE RUFFLE TORTE

This stunning chocolate mousse torte requires some knowledge of the properties of chocolate and a little experience in working with melted chocolate. If you are a beginner to chocolate work, see Working With Chocolate.

- ¾ **cup unsalted butter, softened**
- ¾ **cup sugar**
- ¾ **cup (3 oz) finely ground almonds**
- 6 **ounces bittersweet chocolate, melted and cooled**
- 6 **egg yolks**
- 6 **egg whites**

Chocolate Mousse

- 1¼ **cups whipping cream**
- 6 **ounces semisweet chocolate, melted and cooled**
- ½ **cup water**
- 7 **tablespoons sugar**
- 4 **egg yolks**

Chocolate Ribbons and Ruffles

- 1 **pound semisweet chocolate**

1. Preheat oven to 350° F. Butter and lightly flour 2 round cake pans 2 inches tall and 8 inches in diameter (see Pan Substitution Chart, page 20, if you don't have pans this size). Line bottom of each with a circle of waxed paper.

2. In large electric mixer bowl, cream butter with half of the sugar until light. Add almonds and beat until light. Beat in melted chocolate.

3. Add egg yolks, one at a time, beating well after each addition; beat until light and fluffy.

4. Beat egg whites in a separate bowl until they begin to hold peaks. Gradually add remaining sugar and beat until stiff but still glossy.

5. Stir one fourth of egg whites into chocolate mixture to lighten batter. Gently fold in remaining whites. Whites should be completely incorporated but not deflated.

6. Divide batter equally between the 2 pans and gently smooth top of batter. Bake for 30 to 40 minutes, or until done. Cool in pans 10 minutes, then turn out onto wire racks to finish cooling. This cake tends to sink in the middle as it cools. Trim top with serrated knife to create even layers.

7. Place one layer on a cardboard cake circle that is ⅛ inch smaller than the cake. Spread half of the Chocolate Mousse over this layer. Set next layer on top of mousse. Spread remaining Chocolate Mousse on sides and top of cake. Refrigerate until mousse is firm (about 45 minutes).

8. Decorate cake with Chocolate Ribbons and Ruffles.

Serves 8.

Chocolate Mousse Whip cream until it holds soft peaks. Refrigerate. Melt chocolate; cool to tepid. Combine the water and sugar in saucepan. Bring to a boil to dissolve sugar. Boil 1 minute. Measure out ½ cup hot syrup. Place egg yolks in a deep, 4- to 5-quart stainless steel bowl. Whisk in hot syrup. Continue whisking in one direction (either clockwise or counterclockwise) over a double boiler until mixture holds soft peaks (5 to 7 minutes). Beat yolks off heat with electric mixer or by hand until they are cool. Stir in melted, tepid chocolate. Fold in one eighth of whipped cream. Gradually fold in remaining whipped cream. If you fold in cream too quickly, it will cause chocolate to harden and form chocolate chips.

Chocolate Ribbons and Ruffles Melt and temper (see page 125) 1 pound of semisweet chocolate. Follow step-by-step instructions on opposite page to form ruffles and ribbons.

Chocolate Ruffle Torte, adorned with pleats of rich chocolate, is a cake that borders on being a work of art. Inside the chocolate case are both chocolate cake and chocolate mousse—a chocoholic's fantasy.

CHOCOLATE-DIPPED FRUIT

When dipping fruits in chocolate, first dry the fruits completely. Any residual moisture will cause the chocolate to seize, or become stiff. Strawberries, glacé apricots, candied ginger, candied citrus peels, dried figs, and prunes look fabulous half-dipped. Fruits that tend to darken when exposed to the air, such as bananas, apples, and pears, are best totally coated. Moist fruits, such as orange sections, raspberries, and seedless grapes, should also be completely coated. The amount of chocolate required depends on the size of the pieces of fruit being coated. A dipping fork, with two or three thin prongs or a loop, is useful, although many professional candy makers use the tips of their fingers. Have ready a baking sheet covered with aluminum foil or parchment paper to set the fruit on after dipping. Fruits completely covered in chocolate can be refrigerated, loosely covered, up to 48 hours, or layered in a container between sheets of waxed paper or parchment paper. Partially covered moist fruits such as strawberries should be served within 12 hours.

- 1 orange, sectioned
- 1 apple
- 1 box (8 oz) raspberries
- 14 ounces semisweet chocolate, tempered (see page 125)

1. Section orange. Using a sharp knife, remove skin and white membrane of orange, exposing flesh beneath. Carefully cut out each section by cutting next to membrane from edge to core on each side of section. Place sections on paper towels to dry.

2. Wash apple and pat dry. Core apple and cut into 12 pieces. Pat sections dry. Wash and dry raspberries. Discard any that are moldy or bruised.

3. Using a dipping fork or 2 fingers, dip orange sections and apple slices into tempered chocolate. Coat fruit completely, lift from bowl of chocolate, shake gently to remove excess chocolate, and place on a baking sheet lined with aluminum foil or parchment paper. Dip raspberries in same manner, being extremely gentle. Store dipped fruit in the refrigerator if not serving immediately.

Makes about 4 dozen coated fruits.

STRAWBERRIES IN WHITE CHOCOLATE

White chocolate is very perishable due to the milk solids that are combined with sugar and cocoa butter to make this product. The best method for melting and tempering white chocolate requires a bain-marie (hot water bath). Water is boiled in a large pan while the chocolate is finely chopped and placed in a metal mixing bowl. The heat is then turned off under the water, and the bowl of white chocolate is placed in the hot water. The chocolate is stirred constantly as it melts, and the tempering process

continues as for semisweet chocolate (see page 125). Many American companies make a confectioners' coating, or summer coating, which is similar to white chocolate but uses vegetable fat instead of cocoa butter.

- 30 large strawberries, with long stems
- 10 ounces white chocolate

1. Wash strawberries and thoroughly pat dry. Temper chocolate according to instructions in the introduction and on page 125.

2. Hold strawberries by their stems. Dipping one at a time, lower tip of strawberry into chocolate to cover half of the fruit. Gently shake strawberry to remove excess chocolate and place on a baking sheet lined with aluminum foil or parchment paper. Repeat with remaining strawberries, setting berries about ½ inch apart on baking sheet. Place fruit in refrigerator if not serving immediately. Refrigerate for up to 12 hours. Because strawberries are perishable, they are best eaten within hours after dipping.

Makes 30 strawberries.

DIPPED AND STUFFED STRAWBERRIES

Strawberries in white chocolate are taken one delicious step further—they are filled with rich cream cheese.

- 20 large strawberries, with long stems
- ½ cup natural cream cheese
- 10 ounces semisweet or white chocolate, tempered (see preceding recipe)

1. Wash strawberries and thoroughly pat dry. Cut a slit in each strawberry from tip almost to stem. Gently pry slit apart until it is about ¼ inch wide at tip.

2. Taking about 1 teaspoon of cream cheese, fill opening. Smooth edges with a knife to conform to the contour of strawberry.

3. Dip as directed in step 2 of Strawberries in White Chocolate (preceding).

Makes 20 strawberries.

CHOP, TO

To cut food into small, but not necessarily even, pieces with a knife, a bowl chopper, in a food processor, or in an electric minichopper. Chopped pieces are larger than those that are minced or diced, and can be evenly or randomly shaped. See KNIFE, Cutting Techniques, for information on proper hand position when chopping with a knife and specifics on chopping particular foods. Also see specific entries on other chopping equipment.

CHOPPING AND CUTTING BOARD

A cutting surface must be soft enough to cushion the edge of a knife blade so that it will not dull the knife, but hard enough to resist splintering or otherwise disintegrating into the food. Wood is the favorite cutting surface of most cooks. Laminated hardwood cutting boards and end-grain butcher blocks are both excellent choices. Wooden boards have some disadvantages, however. They require a lot of care, including periodic sanding and oiling. They also tend to absorb odors from food and are harder to sterilize and deodorize than nonporous materials. For this reason, some cooks prefer a synthetic surface for cutting meats, poultry, and especially seafood. The best synthetic boards are made of a dense, opaque white polycarbonate and have a slightly uneven surface that gives under the knife blade much as wood does. They are easy to clean with dishwashing detergent (which should never be used on a wooden board). Do not confuse these boards with decorative boards of shiny, clear plastic or any other hard surface, which will dull knives.

Whether you use a wooden or synthetic cutting board, choose the largest size that will easily fit your work space. Nothing is more frustrating than trying to cut a lot of foods on a tiny board. Although sizes may vary from one manufacturer to another, boards are typically available sized 15 by 20 by ⅜ inches, 18 by 24 by ⅜ inches, and 16 by 9 by ⅜ inches.

HOW TO CLEAN WOODEN CUTTING SURFACES

After each use, scrape wooden boards clean with a metal dough scraper. Never soak with water. If a film remains, sprinkle with coarse salt and scour with a plastic or wire scrub brush; wipe with a clean, damp sponge. For minor stains, rub with the cut side of a lemon half. Deep stains can only be removed by sanding. Occasionally, sanitize the wood by cleaning with a solution of equal parts of bleach and water; rinse away solution with a clean, damp sponge. To keep wood from drying out and splintering, oil occasionally with mineral oil, or special wood oil available at hardware stores, home improvement stores, and better cookware stores.

> ***Recipes and Related Information***
> *Cake and Pastry Tools, 92; Knife, 328.*

CILANTRO

Also known as coriander or Chinese parsley, cilantro is a pungent herb often used in Latin American and Asian cooking. It has small, fragile green leaves and thin stems. Although cilantro resembles parsley, its slightly musty aroma and flavor are entirely different. The aromatic seeds, which have a sweet flavor far removed from the flavor of the leaves, are an important and ancient seasoning marketed as coriander seed.

Use Cilantro leaves and stems add pungent flavor to Latin American soups, salads, and stews; they are an aromatic, all-purpose garnish for countless Latin American dishes, used in much the same way minced parsley is in French or American cooking. Chinese steamed fish and shellfish, noodle dishes, soups, and stews are also commonly garnished with fresh cilantro leaves. Fresh cilantro is also used in Indian chutneys, Moroccan stews, and Thai salads.

Coriander seed is an ingredient in most commercial curry powders and pickling spice mixtures. Ground coriander is added to hot dogs and other sausages, to gingerbreads, coffee cakes, Danish pastry, and Swedish butter cookies, and to lamb, pork, chicken, and cheese dishes.

Availability Fresh cilantro, tied in small bundles, is available all year. Coriander seed is available whole or ground, in bulk or prepacked in airtight containers or plastic bags.

Selection Buy fresh-looking bunches without evidence of wilting or decay. Packaged seasonings lose quality after a while; try to buy from a store that restocks its spice shelves fairly often.

Storage Keep fresh cilantro, root ends down, in a jar of water. Cover with a plastic bag and refrigerate up to one week. Store coriander seed in an airtight container in a cool, dry, dark place. Replace ground coriander every six months. Whole coriander seed will last longer, anywhere from one to two years.

Preparation Trim root ends of fresh cilantro; mince or add whole to dishes. Toast whole coriander seed briefly in a dry skillet to bring out its flavor.

■ **CILANTRO CHUTNEY**

To prepare a fresh coconut, see page 132. Serve this refreshing sauce with all kinds of fish.

⅓ cup fresh lemon juice
2 cups cilantro leaves
½ cup peeled, chopped fresh coconut
⅓ cup finely chopped green onion
1½ tablespoons minced fresh ginger
1 tablespoon seeded, chopped red or green chiles
2 teaspoons sugar
1 teaspoon ground cumin
Kosher salt and freshly ground pepper, to taste

Place lemon juice and half the cilantro in a food processor fitted with a steel blade; purée. Add remaining cilantro, coconut, onion, ginger, chiles, sugar, and cumin; process until smooth. Taste and season with salt and pepper. Serve as soon as possible.

Makes 2 cups.

Recipes and Related Information
Cilantro Raita, 522; Cold Fillet of Sole With Cilantro, Lime, and Pomegranate, 232; Guacamole, 15.

CINNAMON

The most important baking spice in America, cinnamon is the dried bark of an evergreen tree. The cinnamon used by American bakers is *Cinnamomum cassia*, imported from Indonesia and China. It is a dark reddish brown and has a robust warm, sweet flavor. Another variety of cinnamon, *Cinnamomum zeylanicum*, comes from Sri Lanka and is considered by many to be superior. It is pale tan and has a delicate flavor that strikes most American palates as too subdued.

The cinnamon bark, left to dry in the sun, rolls up into tight curls, the form in which it is usually shipped.

Use Cinnamon is used throughout the world to flavor both sweet and savory dishes. American bakers use it in cakes, apple pie, sticky buns, and other sweet rolls. It flavors eggnog, mulled wine, and Mexican hot chocolate. Cinnamon is an ingredient in Chinese five-spice and Indian *garam masala.* Greeks add it to beef stews, ground lamb dishes such as moussaka and *pastitsio,* rice pudding, and pastries such as baklava and nut cake. Moroccans use it in carrot salad, the flaky pigeon pie called *pastilla,* couscous, and sweet puddings. Cinnamon also flavors the Vietnamese beef noodle soup called *pho* and a variety of Spanish and Portuguese custards and baked cakes, pastries, and breads.

Availability Cinnamon is available ground or in rolled sticks, in bulk or prepacked in airtight glass jars, tins, or plastic bags.

Selection Packaged seasonings lose quality after a while; try to buy from a store that restocks its spice shelf fairly often.

Storage Keep cinnamon in an airtight container in a cool, dry, dark place. Replace ground cinnamon every six months; stick cinnamon will stay pungent indefinitely.

Preparation Stick cinnamon is added directly to stews, syrups, or liquids as a flavoring agent but should be removed before serving. The most fragrant ground cinnamon is ground at home from the stick; break cinnamon stick into smaller pieces by hand, then use a clean coffee grinder or electric minichopper to grind to a powder just before using. To clean grinder, whirl a piece of bread in it briefly; the bread will pick up any powdery remains.

■ **CINNAMON TOAST**

This nursery and camp food is a perennial (although perhaps secret) favorite with most of us all of our lives. For a dressy version, use a rich sweet bread, such as leftover brioche, panettone, or raisin bread. For a different flavor, add a little grated nutmeg or grated lemon rind to the cinnamon-sugar mixture.

6 slices bread
Butter
Cinnamon Sugar (3 parts granulated or
light brown sugar to 1 part ground cinnamon)

1. Lightly toast bread. Butter one side and sprinkle with Cinnamon Sugar.

2. Toast under broiler to melt sugar. Serve immediately.

Makes 6 pieces of toast.

Recipes and Related Information
Baklava, 222; Braised Pork With Prunes, 458; Cinnamon Balls, 144; Cinnamon-Raisin Muffins, 375; Cinnamon Rolled Danish, 626; Fruited Coffee Ring, 493; Herb and Spice Blends, 301; Moroccan Pastilla, 221; Snickerdoodles, 145; Spice Doughnuts, 180; Winter Fruit Compote, 186.

CITRON

A citrus fruit, citron resembles a large, thick-skinned lemon. Among Western cooks, it is valued primarily for its thick peel, which is candied for use in fruitcakes and confections.

Use Minced citron may be added to puddings, fruitcakes, and hot cross buns, and to any recipe calling for candied fruit.

Availability Some health-food stores sell large pieces of candied citron in bulk. It is also available in specialty stores and through mail-order suppliers of candied fruit.

Minced candied citron packed in plastic tubs is sold in some supermarkets; it is also an ingredient in many diced candied fruit mixes. Most supermarket varieties contain preservatives.

Storage Citron obtained from health-food stores or mail-order services will probably be made without preservatives and should be stored in the freezer. Even supermarket citron containing preservatives should be refrigerated, covered, and used within six months.

Preparation Chop with a knife.

CITRUS REAMER

The intense, natural flavor of freshly squeezed citrus juice can't be matched by the bottled product. A citrus reamer is used to extract juice from the fruit. Many designs are available, but in fact all are essentially variations of a single idea— an upright, pointed, ribbed cone, shaped like half a lemon, which, when forced into the flesh of a lemon, lime, or orange, breaks it down and releases the juice.

At its most basic is the reamer made of wood with a handle. Juice, pulp, and seeds drip into a bowl. Slightly more elaborate in design, a plastic, metal, or ceramic reamer is attached to a base that is perforated to allow juice to drip through into a separate bowl while trapping pulp and seeds. This type often comes with its own container, which has a lip for easy pouring.

Both manual and electric machines are available to ease the chore of squeezing a pitcher full of juice. Some food processors offer optional reamer attachments. A long-popular, hand-operated model made of chromed steel features a reamer fixed to an upright support that rests on a horseshoe-shaped base. A lever works a hinged cap that fits over the reamer and the fruit set on it; the juice passes through a strainer and into whatever type of container has been set beneath it.

A citrus spout looks like a metal or plastic hose nozzle. Inserted into unpeeled fruit, it extracts drops, rather than spoonfuls of juice, useful for sprinkling on vegetables, fish, and salads. Fruit can be refrigerated with spout still inserted. In addition to convenience, this device is appealing because fruit that has not been cut open keeps fresher longer. Avoid spouts made of aluminum as they blacken the skin of the fruit at the contact point.

CLARIFY, TO

To make clear by removing impurities. Two foods that are clarified are butter and stock. To clarify butter, it is first melted; then the surface foam is skimmed off and the milk solids, which have settled to the bottom, are discarded. Stock is clarified by adding egg whites to lukewarm liquid; the whites coagulate and, as they rise to the surface, trap materials floating in the stock. The liquid is then skimmed and strained.

Recipes and Related Information
Clarified Butter, 68; Stock and Soup, 558.

CLOVE

In cooking, *clove* refers to both the dried bud of a tropical evergreen tree, which is the source for clove spice, and one section of a head of garlic or shallot. This entry discusses clove spice. Also see GARLIC and SHALLOT.

The dark, nail-shaped clove is picked by hand just before it opens and is then dried in the sun. Because of the labor involved, it is one of the world's most expensive spices but also one of the most aromatic, with a warm, sweet, almost peppery flavor. Eighty percent of the world's supply comes from Zanzibar, the remainder from Madagascar and Brazil.

Use Cloves add a sweet, pungent aroma to cakes, gingerbread, fruit pies, fruit compotes, and baked fruit. Whole cloves are used to stud hams before baking and to stud onions for flavoring stock. Mulled wine and hot chocolate are often scented with clove, as is Swedish Glogg. Around the world cloves are added to meat stews, such as German sauerbraten, and to such spice blends as Indian *garam masala*. Cloves are also commonly used in pickling and preserving mixtures.

Availability Cloves are available whole or ground, in bulk or packed in airtight jars, tins, or plastic bags.

Selection Packaged seasonings lose quality after a while; try to buy from a store that restocks its spice section fairly often.

Storage Keep cloves in an airtight container in a cool, dark, dry place. Whole cloves will keep indefinitely; replace ground cloves every six months.

Preparation Whole cloves may be added directly to a dish but should be removed before serving. To facilitate removal, whole cloves are sometimes wrapped in a cheesecloth bag or studded in an orange, onion, or other suitable flavoring ingredient.

Old-fashioned pomander balls are simply fruits studded with whole cloves, then dried. These natural air fresheners are as decorative as they are practical. They can be added to a Christmas punch, hung in the closet to repel moths, used as tree ornaments and place-card holders, stacked in a bowl as a centerpiece, or given as gifts.

COAGULATE, TO

To transform a liquid substance into a soft, semisolid mass. A prime example of coagulation in cooking is the thickening of eggs when heated. Custards, cream pie fillings, egg-based sauces, and coddled eggs use coagulated egg proteins as a way to thicken or set the mixture. The word has the same derivation as curdle—which means to form into solids and a liquid—but implies a stage where a mixture thickens but isn't lumpy. In one sense, coagulation is a controlled curdling, where proteins begin to solidify but are kept from separating by monitoring temperature and by gentle stirring.

> ### Recipes and Related Information
> Custard, 168; Egg, 194.

COARSE CRUMBS

This pastry term, specifically for making pie crusts and biscuits, describes the appearance of flour and fat—butter, lard, vegetable shortening, or a combination—when properly and sufficiently mixed. To achieve this texture, fat is cut in to the flour, or reduced to smaller and smaller flour-coated pieces, with a pastry blender, a fork, two knives, or skilled fingers, until the desired consistency is reached. Coarse meal and small peas are other common recipe descriptions for coarse crumbs.

> ### Recipes and Related Information
> Biscuit, 49; Cake and Pastry Tools, 91; Cut In, 171; Pie and Tart, 431.

COAT, TO

To cover with a dry ingredient such as flour, crumbs, sugar, or nuts, or a liquid such as sauce, glaze, aspic or gelatin, or a frosting. Typically, foods that are sautéed, fried, or broiled are given a dry coating, which adds texture and flavor, preserves natural juices, and serves as a protective barrier between food and cooking fat. Liquid coatings are decorative, keep foods moist, and add flavor.

COAT A SPOON, TO

To leave a velvety film on the back of a spoon dipped in soft custard; a test for the doneness of a soft custard (see CUSTARD). As an additional test, if a track made by running a finger down the coated spoon stays clear, the custard is ready and should be removed from the heat immediately or it will curdle.

COCONUT

Cultivated in Latin America, Africa, Indonesia, and other tropical areas, the coconut is the fruit of the towering coconut palm tree. The round nut has a hard, hairy brown shell, a thin brown skin, and firm, sweet, snow-white flesh.

Use   There are uses for almost every part of the coconut and the coconut palm. The hairy fibers on the shell are woven into mats and ropes or are made into brooms. The palm leaves are used to thatch roofs, the trunks for timber, and the sap of the tree is distilled for a beverage. Dried coconut meat is used in the manufacture of soaps and margarine. Coconut oil serves as a cooking oil and coconut shells as serving bowls.

The coconut palm is the main source of food in the Pacific Islands and is extremely important in Southeast Asia, India, and Latin America. Coconut milk and coconut cream are used in beverages, sauces, soups, and desserts. In Asia the grated fresh meat is an ingredient in vegetable, rice, and noodle dishes and in condiments such as Indonesian *sambals* and Indian chutneys. American cooks use sweetened coconut in pies, cakes, puddings, cookies, candies, and candy bars, and as a garnish for fruit salads and fruit compotes.

Availability   Whole fresh coconut is marketed all year, with peak supplies from September through January. Grated coconut is available in some supermarket freezer cases. It is also dried and packed, either sweetened or unsweetened, in plastic bags or tins. Grated coconut is also sold in bulk in many health-food stores.

Selection   The average coconut weighs about 1½ pounds and should sound full of liquid when shaken.

Storage   Unopened coconut will keep in the refrigerator crisper for up to one month. Once opened, the coconut meat should be used immediately. Any leftover meat, in pieces or grated, may be frozen with the liquid from inside the coconut for several months. Dried coconut will keep in an airtight container in a cool, dry place for several months.

Preparation   To open a whole coconut, puncture one or two of the round "eyes" near stem end with a screwdriver or ice pick. Let interior liquid drain out. (Leftover coconut may be frozen in this liquid.) Put whole coconut on a baking pan in a preheated 350° F oven for about 20 minutes; remove from oven and tap with a hammer in several places. It should crack open. Use a screwdriver to chip away shell from meat, or carefully pry them apart with a knife. Then use a small, sharp paring knife to peel away the thin brown skin. Grate a few chunks at a time in a hand grater, food processor, or blender.

Recipes: Cilantro Chutney, 130; Coconut Cream Pie, 440; Coconut Custard Pie, 440; Coconut Flake Crust, 436; Toasted Coconut-Banana Bread, 491; Your Own Bridge Mix, 59.

The meat, milk, and cream extracted from the tropical coconut are important ingredients in the cuisines of the Pacific Islands, Southeast Asia, India, and Latin America.

▨ COCONUT MILK AND COCONUT CREAM

Coconut milk and cream are used to enrich and flavor beverages, puddings, stews, rice dishes, and sauces. Coconut cream is available packed in tins in Asian and Latin supermarkets. Store leftover commercial coconut cream in an airtight container in the refrigerator for up to one week; homemade coconut cream should be used within a few hours. Both homemade and purchased versions may be frozen indefinitely. However, frozen coconut milk and cream never have quite the smooth texture of the fresh or canned versions.

To make coconut milk and coconut cream, blend 1 cup of freshly grated coconut with 1 cup of hot water in a blender or food processor. (If using dried coconut, substitute milk for hot water.) Let steep 30 minutes, then strain through a sieve, pressing down on pulp to extract as much liquid as possible. Repeat with the same coconut but use fresh water or milk. Discard pulp. The resulting liquid is a rich coconut milk. The richer liquid that rises to the top as the milk cools is coconut cream, which may be spooned off and used separately, or stirred into the milk to enrich it.

CODDLE, TO

To cook in water just below the boiling point. The most common application is coddling eggs for Caesar salad. Coddling warms the yolk so it will hold more oil in suspension when incorporated into the dressing. The egg is left in the hot water only long enough to coagulate the surface of the white and to warm the egg slightly.

Recipes and Related Information
Caesar Salad, 506; Egg, 194.

Call it what you wish—java, café, brew—there is nothing in the world quite as satisfying as a hot cup of coffee for starting out the day.

COFFEE

Native to Africa, the coffee tree produces small red berries containing two flat-sided oval beans. These beans, when cleaned, skinned, dried, and roasted, are the basis for one of the world's most popular beverages.

The best coffee beans are the fruit of *Coffea arabica*, a tree that flourishes at high altitudes in the tropics and subtropics. *Coffea robusta*, a disease- and frost-resistant tree that thrives at lower altitudes, yields lesser-quality beans that are the basis of most commercial blends.

Today Brazil produces about half of the world's crop, with the rest of Latin America accounting for one quarter and Africa for one sixth.

Use   Coffee is enjoyed as a beverage and as an ingredient in other beverages. It adds richness and mellow flavor to stews, barbecue sauces, and the classic southern red-eye gravy. It may be added to pumpernickel bread for flavor and color, to spice cakes and fruitcakes, to mousses, custards, ice cream, puddings, dessert sauces, and frostings. Some recipes call for brewed coffee, others for instant coffee, instant espresso, or coffee extract.

Availability   Coffee is sold as whole roasted beans, in bulk or bags; ground, in bulk, bags, or vacuum-packed jars or cans; or as instant powder or granules, in vacuum-packed jars or cans.

Selection   The best coffee is made from freshly roasted beans. If possible, buy coffee beans in small batches directly from the roaster or from a retailer with a rapid turnover.

Storage   To slow oxidation and loss of flavor, store whole beans and ground coffee in airtight tins in freezer. Whole beans should be used within one month, ground beans within one week. Store instant coffee in an airtight jar in a cool place.

PROCESSING AND ROASTING

After harvesting, most coffee berries are sun-dried and allowed to ferment for two to three weeks to facilitate removal of the pulp and thin skin surrounding the beans. In some countries with abundant water, the berries are processed by a wet method: They are washed first, then mechanically stripped of pulp; next the beans are fermented in concrete tanks for up to 24 hours, washed repeatedly, then dried—either in the sun or mechanically. Finally, the papery outer skin is removed. The wet method is costlier, but yields higher-quality beans.

Whether processed by the wet or dry method, all beans are then sorted by size and picked over by hand to remove faulty specimens.

Coffee beans are shipped green (unroasted) and roasted by the packer, the wholesaler, or, in some instances, the coffee retailer. The temperature of the roast determines the flavor of the beverage. The longer the bean is roasted, the darker and more strongly flavored the coffee made from it (see Coffee Roasts).

DECAFFEINATED COFFEE

Caffeine is removed from coffee by one of two processes: a water method or a solvent method. In the water method, unroasted coffee beans are soaked for several hours in a mixture of water and coffee components until 97 percent of the caffeine has been leached out. The beans are then dried and roasted. The soaking liquid is treated with methylene chloride, which draws out the caffeine and allows liquid to be reused on subsequent batches.

In a variation of the water method called Swiss water process, the unroasted beans are soaked in a water solution until about 97 percent of the caffeine has been leached out. The solution also leaches out soluble flavor components. To retrieve them, the liquid solution is filtered through charcoal that has been treated to trap the caffeine but allow most of the flavor components through. The filtered liquid is condensed and added back to the beans, which are then dried and roasted.

There are four different solvents used to remove caffeine from coffee: methylene chloride, ethyl acetate, carbon dioxide, and triglycerides. Solvent methods are quicker and less expensive and they disturb fewer of the flavor components. Nevertheless, many people concerned about solvent residues continue to prefer a water-process decaffeinated coffee.

INSTANT COFFEE

Instant coffee is made from brewed coffee from which the water is removed either by evaporation in a vacuum or by freeze-drying. It is quickly reconstituted with hot water.

GRINDING

Coffee beans must be ground before they can be brewed. Because ground coffee oxidizes (and therefore turns rancid) faster than whole coffee beans, it is advisable to employ a home grinder and grind beans just before using.

TYPES OF GRINDS

The type of coffee maker determines the optimum grind. The finer the grind, the more quickly water extracts the flavor. Consequently, fine grinds are best suited to coffee makers that complete their brewing cycle quickly, such as espresso machines, Italian stove-top steam-pressure pots, and open-pot Turkish or Greek coffee makers. A medium or drip grind is designed for drip pots and plunger pots. Coarse or regular grind is suitable for machines with slow brewing cycles, such as percolators.

COFFEE GRINDERS AND MILLS

A few models of electric drip coffee makers have a built-in grinding system, but most are freestanding machines, either manual, functioning like a pepper mill, or one of the two types of electric units.

Electric Coffee Grinder   This is the more elementary of the two systems. Stainless steel blades pulverize the whole beans as they rotate; the fineness of the grind is controlled by how long the push button governing the motor is depressed. Drawbacks include unevenly ground beans, blades that may jam if the container is packed too tightly, and small capacity. These grinders can, however, do double duty for grinding spices and nuts. If you use one to prepare more than just coffee, the container should be cleaned before storing so flavors don't transfer from one food to another. Use the brush that comes with the machine, or whirl a slice of soft bread until reduced to fine crumbs; bread will pick up leftover powder or oils.

Electric Coffee Mill   Variable settings and grinding disks rather than blades ensure a more precise, uniform grind each time. Most have two receptacles—a hopper for whole beans and a container for the ground coffee. Mills can hold and process more beans than a grinder, which means more coffee per operation.

BREWING

Although there are many brewing methods, each does essentially the same thing: infuses ground coffee with water in order to extract the flavor essences. This process can be as basic as pouring hot water over coffee grounds and then straining out the liquid. For many coffee lovers, however, brewing the "perfect cup" is a much more complex affair. For them it is a careful, studied pairing of bean with brewing system, filter with coffee maker.

Regardless of how much time and effort you care to put into your morning cup of coffee, the most satisfying beverage is the offspring of good beans and a good coffee maker. Understanding the brewing process is also important.

Studies have determined that for optimum flavor and body, water temperature should be slightly less than boiling, or about 200° F. Higher temperatures extract too much of the coffee solids, producing a bitter brew lacking aroma, which boils away with the steam. Coffee made with water that is too cool is thin and insipid. The ideal extraction is 20 percent of the coffee solids, a point that occurs when grounds have been in contact with 200° F water for about two minutes. If extraction is too fast, the result is weak, flat, and off-tasting. If brewing is too slow or too long, the product is bitter and sour.

Whatever method you prefer, always start with cold water. Then make sure that the water is heated to the proper temperature (at least 185° F), and that extraction isn't rushed or dragged out. Finally, make sure that hot water reaches all the grounds.

COFFEE STRENGTH

How strongly to brew coffee is entirely a matter of taste. The higher the proportion of grounds to water, the stronger the coffee. To make a medium-strong cup of infused or drip coffee, use 2 tablespoons grounds (1 coffee measure) to 6 ounces water. Reduce proportions of grounds for weaker coffee. For espresso, use 2 tablespoons of ground coffee to 3 ounces water.

BREWING METHODS AND COFFEE MAKERS

The design of the coffee maker determines how the coffee is to be brewed. The following is a general guide to the variety of coffee makers available in America and the brewing method required by each.

Espresso Makers: Manual and Electric   The stove-top espresso maker, also known as *la moka*, is a three-part cast aluminum or stainless steel coffeepot with a spout and handle. The bottom is filled with water; a small coffee basket filled with very fine grounds is set atop it; then the upper chamber is screwed on and the machine placed over heat. As the water boils, steam is forced up through the grounds and then condenses as coffee in the upper chamber. To produce the intensely dark, rich espresso favored by the French and Italians requires a more complicated espresso machine. Several home models exist, all based on the same principle—that of rapidly forcing a combination of steam and water through tightly packed, very fine grounds. Some have a steam nozzle to froth milk for Italian cappuccino and *caffè latte* or the French version of the latter, café au lait.

Stove-top espresso makers are relatively inexpensive and are available in 1- to 12-cup sizes. Cost of home espresso machines ranges from less than $100 to more than $500, and you get what you pay for. Cheaper models tend to have inexpensive gaskets, seals, and pump systems, and as a result break down sooner. If you are one of the growing number of coffee enthusiasts who want to enjoy espresso at home, invest in the best machine you can afford.

Filter Drip System: Manual and Electric   The manual filter drip system consists of a pot fitted with a paper-lined cone. The cone and carafe are either a single unit or two separate pieces. The grounds are placed in the paper filter, then hot water is slowly poured over the grounds and allowed to drip into the pot below. For optimum extraction, begin by wetting the grounds, making sure you've moistened them completely, then let them steep for about 30 seconds. Pour more water to the top of the filter and let drip through; repeat until you've brewed the number of cups you want. To keep coffee hot, set pot on a heat diffuser over a low flame.

The electric filter drip system is merely an automatic version of the above method. The machine heats cold water poured into a special reservoir to the proper temperature. Within moments, hot water begins dripping down through the grounds held in a paper-filter–lined basket; brewed coffee is deposited in the pot below, which sits on a warming plate.

Whichever system you use, always remove grounds from cone after brewing because they absorb aroma from the coffee.

TIPS

COFFEE ROASTS

A pale roast (also called light city roast) produces delicate, fairly acidic coffee because the heat was not strong or long enough to decompose or evaporate most of the acids in the bean.

A light medium roast (also called American or full city roast) is the one used in most of the nationally distributed, commercial blends.

A dark roast (also known as French or Viennese roast) produces a rich-tasting, full-bodied coffee. Although the nomenclature is not regulated, generally a Viennese roast is lighter than a French roast.

A very dark roast (also known as Italian or espresso roast) produces dark, shiny beans used in making the richly flavored, bittersweet Italian espresso.

Coffee lovers can choose from a wide variety of coffee-making equipment. Shown from left to right are: manual filter drip pot, coffee mill, coffee grinder, French plunger pot, electric drip coffee maker, manual and electric espresso makers, open pot (ibrik), percolator, and Italian filter pot.

Manual systems are sized from 1 to 12 cups. Cones are plastic or porcelain. One-piece drip pots are made of heat-resistant glass with a wooden grip at the center of the pot. Electric machines offer many options: 4-, 8-, 10-, and 12-cup capacities; two brewing cycles (1 to 4 cups and 5 to 12 cups) so that smaller amounts aren't brewed too quickly; a stop-drip valve that interrupts brewing briefly if carafe is pulled off the base; built-in grinders; and an electronic start feature that can be programmed to begin brewing automatically at a preset time. Bells and whistles don't brew a better cup of coffee, however; most of these models are comparable. Choose a coffee maker that is easy to use. That means the filter can be installed without effort and the water cannister is easily accessible. After that, get what appeals to you.

Italian Filter Pot   This pot, also known as the *napoletana* or *machinetta*, consists of two identical mug-shaped aluminum cylinders—one with a spout, the other without—and a coffee filter basket. The cylinder without a spout is filled with water and topped with a basket filled with grounds, then joined lip-to-lip with the spout, which faces downward. The machine is set over high heat, and when the water begins to boil, the entire apparatus is turned upside down by the handles. Hot water then drips down through the grounds and deposits brewed coffee in the lower cylinder (the one with the spout).

Open Pot   The open pot, also known as an *ibrik* or Greek or Turkish coffeepot, is undoubtedly one of the oldest coffee makers. Today's models resemble a tall, narrow mug with a long handle. Water and sugar are placed in the mug and brought to a boil; pulverized coffee is added and the mug is returned to heat. When mixture boils up, mug is removed from heat until froth settles. The procedure is repeated twice, then the mixture is divided among small cups.

Percolator   The pump percolator is the least desirable method for brewing coffee because the water gets too hot and only a little bit passes through the grounds at a time. The percolator consists of a pot with a basket that sits on a tube. The basket is filled with grounds and the pot with water. The pot is then set over heat or, if electric, is plugged in. The water is heated to boiling and is forced up the tube and into the basket, dripping back down into the pot repeatedly for up to 20 minutes. To compensate for the slow brewing process, the grind is usually coarse, which takes longer to extract.

Plunger The French plunger pot brews coffee by infusion. The pot is a glass cylinder with a fine mesh filter and plunger; the pot sits in a chromed metal frame that has a black, heat-resistant handle. Grounds and hot water are combined in the pot and allowed to steep for 3 to 5 minutes, with the plunger fully raised. Then the plunger is depressed, pushing grounds to bottom of pot and trapping them there. The clear coffee is poured into small cups. The result is the strong and flavorful *café filtre* often served in restaurants. This is a fast method that makes a good cup of coffee, but it isn't automatic because the water must be preheated and the coffee served immediately as it can't be held at serving temperature. The better models are expensive, but have a superior filter system and are extremely attractive. They are available in 4-, 8-, and 12-cup sizes.

Recipes and Related Information

Coffee Eclairs, 164; Coffee Fondant, 251; Coffee Ice Cream, 312; Country Ham Slices With Red-Eye Gravy, 462; Espresso Brownies, 64.

COLANDER, STRAINER, AND SIEVE

This family of equipment separates liquids from solids as in draining and rinsing a food, sifts flour and other dry ingredients, makes purées, and refines the texture of sauces and custards. Although thousands of seemingly different strainers and drainers are available, they are really all modifications of the same idea—a container with holes. They vary only in overall size, in the size of the openings, whether they are made of flexible mesh or more rigid material, and whether they can stand alone or need support of some kind. As a group they overlap one another in what they can do and are often interchangeable. A few, however, such as flour sifters or the cone-shaped chinois, are specialists. These designs have evolved to perform a particular separation better.

COLANDER

These freestanding metal or plastic bowls have relatively large holes that allow liquid to pass through quickly. They sit on a ring base or legs and have two handles. Some are made with a long handle and without bottom support and are used for draining over a pot or the sink. Colanders are best suited for rinsing food and draining cooked pasta and vegetables. Small handheld versions are useful for transferring cooked food from pot to plate. Buy a colander as large as will fit in your sink and on your shelf. They are made of stainless steel, enameled steel, nylon, tinned copper, and ceramic.

STRAINER AND SIEVE

These are made of fine to coarse wire mesh supported by some sort of rigid frame. The basic bowl strainer is a kitchen staple because of its versatility: it drains, separates liquid from solid, solid from solid, and refines. Job for job, however, it doesn't perform as well as the specialty strainers—flour sifter, tamis, drum sieve, and chinois—each of which is designed to excel at a particular task. How many strainers do you need? A bowl strainer is a must; have several in different sizes and gauges of mesh. Buy the others if you would use them often and if you have a place to store them when you're not. Always choose a strainer with stainless steel mesh and a nonrusting frame.

Are strainers and sieves different? Not really. A strainer can be called a sieve when it is used to separate coarse particles from fine or to reduce soft solids to smooth purées—a very minor distinction.

Chinois (China Cap) Part of the classic French *batterie de cuisine*, the cone-shaped chinois gets its name from its resemblance to a peaked Chinese hat. Made of very fine mesh and equipped with a handle, it does an excellent job of separating stock from flavoring ingredients. A colander draped with several layers of dampened

These straining, sifting, and refining tools are variations of a basic design—a container with holes. Shown clockwise from left to right are: small bowl strainers, rigid and wire mesh chinois, large bowl strainer, colander, drum sieve, flour sifter, flour and sugar dredgers.

cheesecloth can be substituted for the chinois. Another version is rigid rather than mesh, with hundreds of tiny holes, and is used in conjunction with a pointed wooden pestle or pusher to make purées. A jelly-making chinois comes with a stand so it does not need other support; others have a handle and a lip and are set over a bowl or pan. Typically, a chinois is 8 inches in diameter and 10 inches tall. The mesh is tin and the frame tin-plated steel; to avoid rusting, wash promptly and dry thoroughly.

Drum Sieve/Tamis   Traditionally the frame for both of these European tools was wood; now it is more often metal. The round or teardrop-shaped tamis is a baking tool—for dusting cakes and pastries with confectioners' sugar or cocoa, or work surfaces with flour. Drum sieves are round and are used for puréeing, for refining custards, and to sieve egg yolks. European in origin, these strainers are not very common in American kitchens.

Flour Sifters   Most recipes no longer insist that flour be sifted, but many home bakers still do (see FLOUR, Is Sifting Necessary?). Sifting lightens the flour, breaks up clumps, and is a way to blend dry ingredients so that they are evenly dispersed. Wire bowl strainers work well for this job, but flour sifters do it just a little better. Their cylindrical shape directs the flour downward into cup or bowl; a bowl strainer lacks this control and flour tends to drift onto the work surface. Sifters have a mechanism to push the flour through, although many bakers move the flour along by banging the side of the sifter with the heel of their hand. Hand sifters that have a rotary handle to force the flour against the wire mesh are easiest to operate. Electric sifters can clog and aren't recommended, nor are triple-mesh hand sifters as they can trap food between layers and are hard to clean. Buy a sifter that holds at least 3 cups of flour, or more if you bake often or in large quantity.

COMBINE, TO

To mix two or more ingredients until blended. Sometimes in cooking this term also means to put ingredients that will be blended in one bowl or pan as a preparatory step.

CONDUCTION

To transfer heat by direct contact, molecule to molecule. For example, the interior mass of a steak or a turkey is heated by conduction; the heat touches the outer surface of the food and then is slowly passed along from one molecule to another through the interior to the center. Liquid in a saucepan is heated by conduction; the flame heats the pan, which in turn heats the liquid. A metal spoon sitting in a bowl of hot soup gets hot because of conduction as the heat travels from the soup to the bottom of the spoon and then up to its handle.

Microwave ovens, to a great degree, depend upon conduction for cooking. Microwaves penetrate the outer surface of food only an inch or two; the food is then finished by conduction. Times required for cooking with a microwave often include resting periods after cooking so that interior heat has time to work its way to the center.

Some materials are better conductors of heat than others. Metals in general are good conductors, as is hot fat. Water conducts less well than fat because it is unable to be heated to as high a temperature. Wood is a poor conductor of heat, which makes it an excellent material for cookware handles and cooking spoons.

> ***Recipes and Related Information***
> *Convection, 138; Materials for Cookware, 351;*
> *Microwave Oven, 362.*

CONVECTION, CONVECTION OVEN

The process of transferring heat by the circulating motion of air or liquid (including fat) is called convection. As heat is applied to a liquid (water or fat, for example) or a gas (air), whether from a flame or coil underneath a pan or from the heating unit of an oven, the molecules closest to the heat source rise and those farther away sink. Moving currents are created when rising molecules cool and others heat up and so start to reverse their direction. (Once the hot gas or liquid touches the food, however, it is carried into the food by conduction.)

The convection oven creates extremely even oven heat because a fan in the oven cavity blows air over the heating element and keeps the hot air constantly moving. The circulating air results in even cooking, no matter how many pans are on a rack or how close they are to one another. Thus, these ovens are ideal for foods requiring hot, dry, circulating air—roasted and broiled meats and poultry, fish, and baked goods of all kinds.

A favorite with professional bakers since the early 1950s for its even browning and fast cooking, the convection oven cooks up to one third faster than conventional ovens and at lower temperatures for many foods. As a result, these ovens save energy as well as time. Unlike a microwave oven, this system does not need special utensils, and except for broiling, preheating is not required. Most home convection ovens are portable, designed to sit on a counter or recessed into cabinet space.

If you bake frequently or enjoy roasted or broiled meats, you will appreciate the unique capabilities of this type of oven. Options include dial or electronic touch controls, temperature probe, multistage programming, and dehydrator racks.

When determining time and temperature, follow the manufacturer's recommendations. As a general rule, to adapt a recipe written for roasting in a conventional oven, decrease roasting time by 30 percent and keep temperature the same. To bake a casserole, you should be able to keep heat and time about the same as a conventional oven. For leavened baked goods, you will need to decrease temperature by 50° F to 75° F; time may be slightly less.

Some cooks feel that although home convection ovens have their advantages, they do not perform as well as commercial models. Before buying a portable convection oven, you might want to talk to someone who already owns one and, if possible, try cooking with it.

Recipes and Related Information
Conduction, 138; Microwave Oven, 362.

COOKIE

Although American history has a decidedly English flavor, our word for cookies, the small, flat cakes that delight us from childhood on, derives from an earlier colonial influence: *koekje* is Dutch for "little cake." In England they are known as biscuits. Whatever they are called, these sweet baked treats are popular throughout the world in many forms and flavors.

Cookies fall into five basic categories, grouped primarily by the way they are shaped: drop, bar, molded and pressed, refrigerator, and rolled.

EQUIPMENT FOR BAKING COOKIES

One of the pleasures of making cookies is that they don't require lots of obscure or expensive ingredients or utensils. Nevertheless, baking will be easier and more fun if you are equipped with the basics.

Since making cookies is probably the most popular form of baking, have on hand several baking sheets. They should have a flat or barely turned-up edge so that the oven heat can reach every cookie evenly from all directions. Buy ones that are made of a heavyweight, heat-conductive material such as aluminum; they won't warp and will bake more evenly.

Insulated baking sheets have air sandwiched between two sheets of aluminum. The layer of air prevents cookies from burning on the bottom and promotes even baking. If you use an insulated baking sheet, you may find baking times increase slightly—generally requiring the maximum baking time given in the recipe.

Nonstick baking sheets are useful if they are made from heavy-gauge metal and coated with a top-quality nonstick material or silicone resin (see MATERIALS FOR COOKWARE, Nonstick Surfaces). When removing cookies from nonstick pans, use a spatula that won't scratch the surface.

Most bar cookies are baked in standard square or rectangular pans. The most frequently used sizes are an 8-inch square, a 9-inch square, and a 9- by 13-inch rectangle. The same baking characteristics can be found in these pans as in baking sheets of comparable materials. Bar cookies can also be baked in glass ovenware of the same dimensions as just specified.

Level wire racks enable cookies to cool quickly and evenly, with air circulating from all directions. Their shape doesn't matter, but having enough of them is a must if you bake often. Cookies are at their best if they can cool completely before you stack and store them.

Other equipment that is considered basic includes measuring spoons and dry and liquid measuring cups; a timer; a narrow metal spatula for leveling off dry ingredients and loosening edges of bar cookies from a pan; a wide, flexible metal spatula for transferring cookies from baking sheets; a rubber scraper for removing batter from a bowl or the blades of an electric mixer and for spreading batter in a baking pan; sifters and sieves for blending flour and other dry ingredients, for removing lumps from confectioners' sugar or cake flour, and also for sifting a decorative coating of confectioners' sugar or cocoa over the surface of baked cookies; rulers for measuring the dimensions of bar cookies to be cut uniformly, the thickness of a rolled-out dough, or the diameter of a roll of refrigerator-cookie dough; parchment paper; heavy-duty electric and portable mixers; food processor; blender; and specialty equipment such as cutters, molds, and a cookie press.

ABOUT MAKING AND BAKING COOKIES

Although making cookies is not a complicated procedure, any culinary undertaking goes more smoothly if you use the proper equipment and are organized. Read the recipe before you begin and have all equipment at hand and ingredients measured and in the form specified.

Grease pans only if the recipe calls for it. Use vegetable shortening or a nonstick vegetable spray (not butter). Another option is to line baking sheets with parchment paper. This method saves cleanup and permits easy transfer from baking sheet to cooling rack. Set unbaked cookies on cool baking sheets only. If you drop or set cookie dough onto a hot baking sheet, it will begin to spread or even bake before all the cookies are in place. If you are baking many cookies at one time, have several sheets available to use in rotation.

Good circulation of hot air in the oven is needed to bake cookies evenly. In general, use the middle oven rack, positioning a single baking sheet in the center of it. If you

Using whimsical, charming cookie cutters makes artists of us all. Who could resist these appealing sugar cookie rabbits?

have a wide oven, you may be able to place two narrow baking sheets side by side, but allow at least one inch of space between them, and between the baking sheets and sides of the oven. If time dictates baking two sheets of cookies at once, place one baking sheet on one side of the upper oven rack and the other baking sheet on the other side of the center rack. Halfway through the baking time, reverse the position of the two baking sheets.

Use a timer when baking cookies and know the idiosyncrasies of your oven. Many ovens have hot spots, or don't heat to the temperature they are set for. Test your oven frequently with an oven thermometer; if it is off, adjust the time or temperature accordingly. Check cookies for doneness toward the end of the low range of suggested cooking time, and then keep an eye on them until they are ready. They can quickly overbake.

COOLING AND STORING COOKIES

Some cookies are sturdy enough to be removed to cooling racks as soon as they come from the oven. Others are more delicate and must first cool slightly on the baking sheet. Each recipe should tell you how the cookies are to cool, but keep in mind that fragile cookies need very gentle treatment.

Cookies kept for short periods of time (up to one week) are best stored in a tightly covered tin at room temperature. Be sure the cookies have cooled completely before packing them in the container. If you are storing more than one kind of cookie, keep them separate. If placed together, crisp cookies will absorb moisture from soft cakelike cookies; before long all will be soggy. If cookies have icing or another topping, separate successive layers with sheets of waxed paper or kitchen parchment.

Cookies stored for longer periods of time (up to three or four months) can be kept in the freezer. Package each kind of cookie separately in an airtight enclosure of freezer wrap, freezer-weight plastic bags, heavy aluminum foil, or a foil-lined container. Rich, buttery, crisp cookies tend to freeze better than soft, moist, cakelike ones. Brownies are the exception; they can be frozen with great success. Thaw frozen cookies in their freezer wrapping or container at room temperature for 15 to 30 minutes. If cookies need frosting, glazing, or sprinkling with sugar, wait until they are thawed to add it.

DROP COOKIES

Made from a soft dough, drop cookies are extremely easy to prepare; they are often a child's first baking experience. They don't need to be molded, just pushed from a spoon onto a baking sheet.

To shape drop cookies, use two spoons. Scoop up the specified amount of dough with one, then use the other to help transfer the dough onto the baking sheet. Use both spoons to shape the spoonfuls of dough into a smoothly rounded mound. Some bakers prefer to use a very small ice cream scoop to make a uniform round. Try to make all the cookies the same size and shape so they will finish baking at the same time.

■ OLD-FASHIONED SOFT SUGAR COOKIES

Nutmeg and lemon rind punctuate the familiar flavor of these tender, cakelike cookies.

> 2½ cups flour
> 1 teaspoon *each* baking soda and freshly grated nutmeg
> ¼ teaspoon salt
> ½ cup butter or margarine, softened
> 1½ cups sugar
> 2 eggs
> ½ teaspoon *each* vanilla extract and grated lemon rind
> 1 cup sour cream
> Vanilla Granulated Sugar (see page 585), optional
> ¼ cup (approximately) raisins

1. In a bowl stir together flour, baking soda, nutmeg, and salt to combine thoroughly; set aside.

2. Preheat oven to 375° F. In mixer bowl combine butter and sugar, and beat until well blended. Beat in eggs, one at a time, mixing until fluffy after each addition. Add vanilla and lemon rind and mix to blend thoroughly.

3. Add flour mixture alternately with sour cream, mixing until smooth after each addition.

4. Drop by tablespoons, placed well apart, onto well-greased baking sheets. Sprinkle each cookie lightly with Vanilla Granulated Sugar (if used). Place one or more raisins in the center of each. Bake until cookies are golden brown (12 to 14 minutes). Remove at once to wire racks to cool.

Makes about 5 dozen 2¾-inch cookies.

■ TRADITIONAL RAISIN-OATMEAL COOKIES

Oatmeal, which replaces part of the flour, brings a chewy texture and nutlike flavor that are an unforgettable part of enjoying these cookies.

> 1½ cups flour
> 1 teaspoon baking soda
> ½ teaspoon ground cinnamon
> ¼ teaspoon *each* salt, freshly grated nutmeg, and ground cloves
> ¾ cup butter or margarine, softened
> 1½ cups firmly packed brown sugar
> 2 eggs
> 1 teaspoon vanilla extract
> 2 cups quick-cooking rolled oats
> 1 cup raisins

1. In a bowl stir together flour, baking soda, cinnamon, salt, nutmeg, and cloves to combine thoroughly; set aside.

A bar of delectable imported chocolate, coarsely chopped, transforms Favorite Chocolate Chip Cookies into luxurious Chocolate Chunk Cookies. You can bake these cookies to your taste—either crisp or chewy.

2. Preheat oven to 375° F. In mixer bowl combine butter and brown sugar, and beat until well blended. Add eggs, one at a time, beating well after each addition. Add vanilla and mix to blend.

3. Gradually add flour mixture until just blended. Stir in rolled oats and raisins.

4. Drop by tablespoons, placed about 2 inches apart, onto lightly greased baking sheets. Bake until cookies are lightly browned (about 10 minutes). Cool on wire racks.

Makes about 4 dozen 2½-inch cookies.

■ FAVORITE CHOCOLATE CHIP COOKIES

These cookies will be crisp if baked at the temperature specified in the main recipe, and soft and chewy if baked at the lower temperature suggested in the variation.

    1¼ cups flour
    ½   teaspoon baking soda
    ¼   teaspoon salt
    ½   cup butter or margarine, softened
    ½   cup firmly packed brown sugar
    ½   cup granulated sugar
    1   egg
    1   teaspoon vanilla extract
    1   package (6 oz) semisweet chocolate chips
    ½   cup chopped walnuts (optional)

1. In a bowl stir together flour, baking soda, and salt to combine thoroughly; set aside.

2. Preheat oven to 375° F. In mixer bowl combine butter and sugars; beat until fluffy and well blended. Beat in egg. Add vanilla and mix well.

3. Gradually add flour mixture until just blended. Stir in chocolate chips and walnuts (if used).

4. Drop by rounded tablespoons, placed well apart, onto lightly greased or nonstick baking sheets. Bake until cookies are well browned (12 to 14 minutes). Cool on wire racks.

Makes about thirty 2¾-inch cookies.

Chewy Chocolate Chip Cookies Bake cookies in a 325° F oven until they are a light golden brown (10 to 13 minutes). Cool on baking sheets for 3 minutes before removing to wire racks to cool completely.

Chocolate Chunk Cookies Omit semisweet chocolate chips. Coarsely chop a 3- to 4-ounce bar of semisweet chocolate, and fold it into cookie dough in step 3.

Peanut Butter–Chocolate Chip Cookies After beating butter and sugars, add ½ cup peanut butter (smooth or chunky). Beat well, then continue as for Favorite Chocolate Chip Cookies. Omit chopped walnuts.

TILE & LACE COOKIES

Making tiles   Remove warm cookies, one at a time, from baking sheet and immediately drape over rolling pin (for small cookies, use small rolling pin) or curl in metal baguette pan. When cool, transfer to wire rack. If using sliced almonds in dough, drape or roll cookies so nutty sides are up.

Making cigarettes   Roll each warm cookie around buttered handle of wooden spoon or cone. Remove when cool.

Making tulips   Let each lace cookie cool on baking sheet until just firm enough to handle. Drape, bumpy side down, over inverted 2½- to 3-inch-diameter drinking glass, pressing draped portions of cookie softly into a cup shape. When set, transfer to wire rack or carefully place on baking sheet.

■ LEMON ROOF-TILE COOKIES

A drop-cookie batter, baked wafer thin, produces cookies of remarkable flexibility. While still warm from the oven, they can be rolled or curled into a variety of whimsical shapes. Curved into distinctive U shapes or twirled into "cigarettes" or cones, French *tuiles au citron* are a classic accompaniment to homemade ice cream or sorbet. They can also be baked as large cookies, then shaped into stylized tulips as edible containers for a frozen dessert, or left flat, stacked, and filled with any flavor mousse or a lemon curd. Although crisp when they are freshly baked, they may absorb moisture from the air and soften after standing. You can restore their crispness by arranging the cookies in a single layer on a baking sheet and placing them in a 200° F oven for 20 to 30 minutes.

     ¼ cup blanched almonds
     ⅓ cup sifted cake flour
     ¼ cup butter or margarine, softened
     ½ cup sugar
     2 egg whites (about ¼ cup)
     ¼ teaspoon lemon extract
     1 tablespoon grated lemon rind
     ½ cup (approximately) sliced almonds (optional)

1. In blender or food processor, whirl blanched almonds until powdery. In a small bowl combine almonds with cake flour, stirring to blend thoroughly; set aside.

2. Preheat oven to 400° F. Grease baking sheets and dust with flour (or line baking sheets with lightly buttered parchment paper).

3. In mixer bowl combine butter and sugar; beat until light and fluffy. Beat in egg whites until well blended. Stir in lemon extract and lemon rind. Gradually add flour mixture, beating until smooth.

4. Drop batter onto prepared baking sheets by rounded teaspoons, about 2 inches apart, to make tiles as shown in top photograph, or cones or cigarettes as shown in middle photograph. Batter can also be dropped by level tablespoons, about 3 inches apart, to make tulips as shown in bottom photograph. Sprinkle each with sliced almonds (if desired) to cover sparsely. With small spatula or back of a spoon, spread batter to a 3-inch-diameter circle for tiles or cones or to a 4-inch-diameter circle for tulips.

5. Bake until edges of cookies are brown (4 to 6 minutes). Let stand on baking sheets until cookies are barely firm enough to handle but still pliable (30 seconds to 1 minute). Carefully remove with a spatula and shape into tiles, cones, cigarettes, or tulips as shown in Tile and Lace Cookies (at left), or transfer to wire racks to make flat cookies.

6. If cookies become too cool to shape, return to oven for a few seconds until they are pliable again.

Makes about 30 small or 16 large cookies.

■ PECAN LACE COOKIES

These cookies can be shaped and served in all the ways suggested for Lemon Roof-Tile Cookies (at left). Shaped into tulips, they are delectable filled with apple or butter-pecan ice cream and topped with hot caramel sauce.

     ¼ cup butter or margarine
     ¼ cup firmly packed brown sugar
     ¼ cup light corn syrup
     ⅓ cup flour
     ½ cup finely chopped pecans
     1 teaspoon vanilla extract

1. Preheat oven to 350° F. Grease baking sheets and dust with flour.

2. Melt butter in a 1½- to 2-quart saucepan over medium heat. Stir in brown sugar and corn syrup. Increase heat to high and bring mixture to a boil, stirring constantly until brown sugar dissolves.

3. Remove pan from heat. Stir in flour and pecans until well combined. Blend in vanilla.

4. Drop batter onto prepared baking sheets by rounded teaspoons, placed about 2 inches apart, to make tiles as shown in top photograph or drop by rounded tablespoons, placed about 3 inches apart, to make tulips as shown in bottom photograph. With small spatula spread batter into an even circle.

5. Bake until cookies are browned (6 to 8 minutes for small cookies, 8 to 10 minutes for large ones). Let stand on baking sheets until cookies are barely firm enough to handle (30 seconds to 1 minute). Remove carefully with a spatula and shape as shown in Tile and Lace Cookies (at left), or transfer to wire racks to make flat cookies. If cookies become too cool to shape, return to oven briefly.

Makes about 30 small or 8 to 10 large cookies.

BAR COOKIES

Like drop cookies, bars have a soft-dough base. They are even more straightforward to put together because the batter isn't shaped at all before baking, just spread in a pan; the cookies are cut apart when they've cooled.

Brownies are the ultimate bar cookie (see BROWNIE). They are addictive and in a class by themselves. But don't let their stellar reputation blind you to the appeal of other members of this cookie family, equally easy to make and wonderfully varied in flavor and appearance. In general, bar cookies need to cool in the pan on a wire rack until barely warm (usually 15 to 20 minutes) before cutting them into bars or squares. After you've cut the specified number of cookies, let them cool completely in the pan before removing them. Bar cookies look best if cut cleanly and uniformly. Use a ruler and mark where you will cut before doing so by scoring the surface with a knife.

Most bar cookies freeze well. The richer and more buttery they are, the better they will store in the freezer.

APRICOT-ALMOND SQUARES

A crisply toasted almond pastry and a moist, tart apricot filling characterize these elegant bar cookies.

1 cup dried apricots
½ cup unblanched almonds
½ cup butter or margarine, softened
¼ cup granulated sugar
1 cup flour
½ teaspoon baking powder
¼ teaspoon salt
2 eggs, at room temperature
1 cup firmly packed brown sugar
½ teaspoon vanilla extract
¼ teaspoon almond extract
  Confectioners' sugar

1. Preheat oven to 350° F. Place apricots in a small saucepan; cover with water. Bring to a boil over medium-high heat. Cover and simmer until tender (6 to 8 minutes). Drain and pat dry with paper towels. Cut into thin slivers and set aside.

2. Spread almonds in a shallow pan. Bake until toasted (8 to 10 minutes). Let cool; whirl in blender or food processor to form coarse crumbs.

3. In mixer bowl beat butter and granulated sugar until fluffy. Blend in ½ cup of the flour and ground almonds. Spread evenly over bottom of an ungreased, 9-inch baking pan. Bake 20 minutes; remove pan from oven.

4. While pastry is baking, in a small bowl stir together remaining ½ cup flour, baking powder, and salt to combine thoroughly; set aside.

5. In mixer bowl beat eggs and brown sugar at high speed until thick. Gradually blend in flour mixture, then vanilla and almond extracts. Stir in apricots. Spread over baked layer.

6. Bake until well browned (about 30 minutes). Cool about 10 minutes, then cut into squares. Sift lightly with confectioners' sugar. Remove from pan when cool.

Makes 3 dozen squares.

FRESH LEMON BARS

A classic among cookies, these refreshing bars have a special appeal for lovers of lemon meringue pie.

1 cup butter or margarine, softened
½ cup confectioners' sugar
1 teaspoon vanilla extract
2 cups flour
4 eggs
2 cups granulated sugar
  Grated rind of 1 lemon
6 tablespoons fresh lemon juice
¼ cup (approximately) confectioners' sugar, for topping

Tangy, layered Fresh Lemon Bars are simply prepared and simply delicious, which makes them an appealing dessert for entertaining.

1. Preheat oven to 350° F. Generously grease a 9- by 13-inch pan.

2. In mixer bowl combine butter, the ½ cup confectioners' sugar, and vanilla; beat until fluffy. Gradually add flour, mixing until well combined. Spread evenly in prepared pan. Bake for 20 minutes.

3. While pastry bakes, in a bowl combine eggs, granulated sugar, lemon rind, and lemon juice; stir to blend all ingredients (do not beat). Pour lemon mixture over baked cookie layer.

4. Return to oven and bake until topping is set and lightly browned (18 to 22 minutes).

5. Sift additional confectioners' sugar over warm cookies to generously cover top. Cut into bars. Remove from pan when cool.

Makes 3 dozen bars.

Festively wrapped in white tissue paper, sugar-dusted Mexican Wedding Cakes are given to guests at Oaxacan nuptials as keepsakes of the special day.

■ CLASSIC SCOTCH SHORTBREAD

The word *short* has a number of meanings. When the subject is cookies, it means crisp and tender, due to an abundance of butter. These traditional cookies are not overly sweet. If you prefer a sweeter flavor, sift an additional tablespoon of Vanilla Confectioners' Sugar (see page 585) over the cookies after you cut them into wedges. The cookies have the characteristic sandy texture.

   1 **cup flour**
   6 **tablespoons Vanilla Confectioners' Sugar (see page 585)**
   ½ **cup firm butter or margarine, diced**

1. Preheat oven to 325° F. In a medium bowl stir together flour and Vanilla Confectioners' Sugar to combine thoroughly.

2. Using a pastry blender or your fingers, cut or crumble in butter until all the particles are uniformly small and well coated with flour mixture. Use your hands to firmly press crumbly dough into a flattened ball.

3. Place dough in an ungreased 8-inch-diameter pan, preferably with a removable bottom. Press dough evenly and firmly into pan. Use your index finger to impress a row of uniformly spaced dimples around outer edge. With tines of a fork, score dough into 12 wedges; then pierce randomly between scores to keep cookies flat.

4. Bake until color is pale golden brown (30 to 35 minutes). Cool on a rack for about 10 minutes. Cut cookies into wedges along previous scorings. When cool, remove pan sides and cookies.

Makes 1 dozen cookies.

MOLDED AND PRESSED COOKIES

There is some art to these rich, buttery cookies, because they are handshaped or formed with a cookie mold. The simplest of these cookies are shaped into balls before baking. The more complex are formed into other shapes by hand, by forcing through a template of a cookie press, or by using a mold. Although the typically sweet, butter-rich dough used for molded cookies can withstand a certain amount of handling and still stay tender, these cookies will be best if your touch is light.

■ MEXICAN WEDDING CAKES

Rich with butter and ground nuts, these tender cookies are coated generously, while still warm, with confectioners' sugar, which seems to melt into the cookies. In the Mexican state of Oaxaca, they are festively wrapped in fringed white tissue and given as favors to wedding guests.

   2½ **cups flour**
    ¼ **teaspoon salt**
    1 **cup finely chopped pecans**
    1 **cup butter or margarine, softened**
    ½ **cup confectioners' sugar**
    2 **teaspoons vanilla extract**
   1½ **cups (approximately) confectioners' sugar**

1. In a bowl stir together flour, salt, and pecans to combine thoroughly; set aside. Preheat oven to 350° F.

2. In mixer bowl combine butter and the ½ cup confectioners' sugar; beat until fluffy. Blend in vanilla. Gradually add flour mixture, beating just until dough clings together.

3. Shape dough into 1½-inch balls. Place about 2 inches apart on ungreased baking sheets. Bake until firm and lightly browned (20 to 25 minutes).

4. Spread about ¾ cup of the remaining confectioners' sugar on a rimmed baking sheet. As cookies finish baking, remove them to sugar-lined baking sheet; generously sift some of the remaining confectioners' sugar over warm cookies, turning in sugar if necessary to coat all surfaces liberally. Transfer to wire racks to complete cooling.

Makes about thirty 1¾-inch cookies.

Cinnamon Balls To flour mixture add 1 teaspoon ground cinnamon. Shape dough into 1-inch balls; place about 1 inch apart on baking sheets. Bake 20 minutes.

Makes about forty-two 1¼-inch cookies.

CHINESE ALMOND COOKIES

When selecting from the varied attractions of certain Chinese take-out restaurants, many people find rich almond cookies, packaged to go in a waxed-paper bag, virtually irresistible. They are just as compelling when baked at home. Making the cookies with a combination of butter and lard brings together the best quality of each ingredient—the flavor of butter and the tender crispness that lard imparts to pastry. See photograph, page 6.

    2 cups flour
    ½ teaspoon baking powder
    ½ cup *each* butter and lard, softened
    1 cup sugar
    1 teaspoon almond extract
    ½ teaspoon vanilla extract
    2 egg yolks
    ⅓ cup (approximately) blanched almonds
    2 teaspoons water

1. In a medium-sized bowl stir together flour and baking powder to combine thoroughly; set aside. Preheat oven to 350° F.

2. In mixer bowl combine butter and lard; beat until fluffy. Add sugar and beat until well combined. Blend in almond and vanilla extracts, then 1 egg yolk. Gradually add flour mixture, beating until well combined.

3. Shape dough into 1-inch balls. Place about 1½ inches apart on lightly greased baking sheets. Slightly flatten each cookie with fingertips; press almond into center.

4. In a small bowl beat remaining egg yolk with the 2 teaspoons water until blended. Lightly brush top of each cookie with egg-yolk mixture.

5. Bake until cookies are golden brown and feel firm when touched lightly (15 to 18 minutes). Let stand on baking sheets for 1 to 2 minutes, then transfer to wire racks to cool.

Makes about forty-two 2-inch cookies.

SNICKERDOODLES

Charmingly old-fashioned, these cookies, covered with cinnamon sugar, recall long afternoons on a porch swing, sipping homemade lemonade.

    1⅓ cups flour
    1 teaspoon cream of tartar
    ½ teaspoon baking soda
    ⅛ teaspoon salt
    ½ cup butter or margarine, softened
    ¾ cup sugar
    ½ teaspoon vanilla extract
    1 egg

Cinnamon Sugar

    ¼ cup sugar
    2 teaspoons ground cinnamon

1. In a bowl stir together flour, cream of tartar, baking soda, and salt to combine thoroughly; set aside. Preheat oven to 400° F.

2. In mixer bowl combine butter and sugar; beat until fluffy. Blend in vanilla. Beat in egg until well combined. Gradually add flour mixture, beating until just well combined.

3. Drop cookie dough by rounded teaspoons, 6 to 8 at a time, into Cinnamon Sugar spread in a shallow pan. Roll cookies to coat well, shaping them into balls as you roll. Arrange balls about 1½ inches apart on greased baking sheets.

4. Bake until edges are golden brown (8 to 10 minutes). Transfer to wire racks to cool.

Makes about 3 dozen 2½-inch cookies.

Cinnamon Sugar   In a shallow pan mix sugar and cinnamon until thoroughly combined.

CHOCO–PEANUT BUTTER COOKIES

Speckled with grated semisweet chocolate, these peanut butter cookies give a classic recipe new flavor. You can also make these cookies with almond butter, with or without the chocolate.

    1½ cups flour
    2 teaspoons baking powder
    ⅛ teaspoon salt
    ½ cup butter or margarine, softened
    ½ cup peanut butter
    ½ cup *each* granulated sugar and
        firmly packed brown sugar
    1 teaspoon vanilla extract
    1 egg
    1 square (1 oz) semisweet baking chocolate, grated

1. In a bowl stir together flour, baking powder, and salt to combine thoroughly; set aside. Preheat oven to 375° F.

2. In mixer bowl combine butter and peanut butter; beat until fluffy. Add sugars and beat until well combined. Blend in vanilla, then egg, and beat until fluffy. Gradually add flour mixture, beating until well blended. Stir in chocolate.

3. Shape dough into 1-inch balls. Arrange balls about 1½ inches apart on ungreased baking sheets. Flatten each cookie with a fork, pressing tines once into dough and then crisscrossing the first pattern to make the characteristic crosshatch design.

4. Bake until cookies are lightly browned and feel firm when touched gently (10 to 12 minutes). Transfer to wire racks to cool.

Makes about forty-two 2-inch cookies.

Almond Butter Cookies   Substitute almond butter for peanut butter; omit chocolate, if desired.

**MAKING
MULTICOLORED
COOKIES**

*Checkerboards For each
log, arrange 3 strips of Light
and Chocolate Dough side by
side, alternating colors.
Stack three layers of strips as
shown in photograph (first
and third layer should be
identical, middle layer
should be opposite of top and
bottom); chill and slice.*

*Pinwheels Roll chilled or
frozen Light and Chocolate
Dough to 1-inch-thick
rectangles. Stack doughs and
tightly roll up, jelly-roll
fashion. Chill well, then slice
and bake.*

*Mosaics Cut logs of Light
and Chocolate Dough into
¼-inch-thick slices. With
same small decorative
cutter, remove center from
each slice. Place Light Dough
cutouts in chocolate slices
and Chocolate Dough
cutouts in light slices.*

REFRIGERATOR COOKIES

Long before there were cookie mixes or plastic-encased
rolls of cookie dough in the supermarket refrigerator case,
there were homemade icebox cookies. The rich dough can
be prepared ahead and stored for up to three days in the
refrigerator. The cold dough is sliced and baked; and it is
sturdy enough to be worked into eye-pleasing, two-color
checkerboards, pinwheels, and mosaics (see photographs
at left).

If making refrigerator dough is unfamiliar to you, keep
in mind the following: Because refrigerator cookies are
sliced thinly from a roll of dough, solid ingredients must be
either finely chopped or pliable enough so the dough can
be sliced easily without tearing. Always shape dough before chilling it. After beating in dry ingredients and other
added elements, dough will be quite soft and creamy.
Divide it roughly in half, then turn out each half onto a
square of plastic wrap or kitchen parchment. Using two
spatulas—and the wrap as a guide—coax dough into a
long, fat, sausagelike shape. While lifting and rolling, enclose dough in the wrapping. When dough is confined, you
will be able to use your hands to mold it into an even more
regular shape.

Keep wrapped dough in the coldest part of the refrigerator (or in the freezer—but keep track of the time, because it will begin to freeze after about 45 minutes). If
dough is very soft and you want to keep the round shape,
remove dough and smooth its contours once or twice during the chilling period.

To freeze dough for longer storage, enclose it in a mois-
ture-proof wrapping such as freezer wrap or heavy aluminum foil. (Cookies enclosed in waxed paper or plastic wrap
should be overwrapped in a sturdier material if you decide
to freeze part of the unbaked dough.) Well-wrapped cookie
dough can be kept frozen for up to a month. To thaw frozen dough, transfer it from freezer to refrigerator one to
two hours before you plan to slice and bake it.

■ MULTICOLORED
REFRIGERATOR COOKIES

With the photographs at left as your guide, you can combine tender, crisp chocolate and butterscotch doughs to
make checkerboards, pinwheels, or mosaic refrigerator
cookies. Note that the dough needs to be chilled or frozen
several times during the process for easier handling.

Light Dough

- 1⅓ cups flour
- ½ teaspoon baking powder
- ¼ teaspoon salt
- ½ cup butter or margarine, softened
- ¼ cup solid vegetable shortening
- ½ cup each granulated sugar and firmly
  packed brown sugar
- ½ teaspoon vanilla extract
- 1 egg yolk

Chocolate Dough

- 1 cup flour
- ¼ cup unsweetened cocoa
- ½ teaspoon baking soda
- ¼ teaspoon salt
- ½ cup butter or margarine, softened
- ¼ cup solid vegetable shortening
- ½ cup each granulated sugar and firmly
  packed brown sugar
- 1 egg

Light Dough

1. Combine flour, baking powder, and salt; set aside.

2. In mixer bowl blend butter and shortening. Add sugars
and beat until fluffy. Beat in vanilla, then egg yolk.

3. Gradually add flour mixture, beating until just blended.
Chill and shape dough as directed for the cookie style of
your choice.

Chocolate Dough

1. In a bowl stir together flour, cocoa, baking soda, and
salt to combine thoroughly; set aside.

2. In mixer bowl combine butter and shortening; beat to
blend well. Add sugars and beat until fluffy. Add egg and
beat until well blended.

3. Gradually add flour mixture, beating until just blended.
Chill and shape dough as directed for the cookie style of
your choice.

To Make Checkerboards

1. Transfer Light Dough to a large sheet of plastic wrap
or waxed paper. Using a spatula and the plastic wrap,
shape dough into a 2-inch-square log about 9 inches long.
Wrap tightly and refrigerate until firm (at least 2 hours,
or overnight; or place in freezer for 30 to 45 minutes).

2. Repeat shaping and chilling procedure described in
step 1 using Chocolate Dough.

3. To make long strips, slice Light Dough lengthwise into
halves or thirds. Separate layers and slice each lengthwise into halves or thirds. You will have 4 strips if you cut
dough into halves or 9 strips if you cut dough into thirds.

4. Repeat cutting procedure described in step 3 using
Chocolate Dough.

5. Following the photograph, place strips of Light Dough
and Chocolate Dough side by side to form 2 logs, alternating colors to make each layer. Wrap each log tightly in
plastic wrap, firmly pressing multicolored strips together.
Return to refrigerator for at least 3 hours, or overnight.

6. Preheat oven to 350° F. Remove one roll of cookie
dough at a time from refrigerator. Slice cookies to a
thickness of ¼ inch, and arrange slices about 1 inch apart
on ungreased baking sheets.

7. Bake until cookies feel firm when touched lightly (8 to 10 minutes). Transfer to wire racks to cool.

Makes about 6 dozen 2½-inch cookies.

To Make Pinwheels

1. Transfer Light Dough to a large sheet of plastic wrap or waxed paper. Using a spatula, flatten dough into a rectangle about 1 inch thick. Wrap tightly and refrigerate until firm (at least 2 hours, or overnight; or place in freezer for 30 to 45 minutes).

2. Repeat shaping and chilling procedure described in step 1 using Chocolate Dough.

3. Place Light Dough between 2 sheets of plastic wrap; roll into a 12-inch by 16-inch rectangle. Remove top sheet of plastic.

4. Repeat shaping procedure described in step 3 using Chocolate Dough.

5. Invert Light Dough over Chocolate Dough; peel off top sheet of plastic wrap. Starting with a 16-inch edge, and using bottom sheet of plastic and a spatula to guide dough, tightly roll 2 sheets of dough together, jelly-roll fashion. Cut roll in half to make two 8-inch-long rolls. Enclose each tightly in plastic wrap; refrigerate for at least 3 hours, or overnight.

6. Preheat oven to 350° F. Slice and bake until cookies are golden brown and feel firm when touched lightly (10 to 12 minutes). Transfer to wire racks to cool.

Makes about 5 dozen 3-inch cookies.

To Make Mosaics

1. Divide Light Dough in half. Transfer each half to a sheet of plastic wrap or waxed paper, and shape into a 2-inch-diameter log. Wrap each tightly and refrigerate until firm (at least 2 hours, or overnight; or place in freezer for 30 to 45 minutes).

2. Repeat shaping and chilling procedure described in step 1 using Chocolate Dough.

3. Preheat oven to 350° F. Cut 1 roll each of Light Dough and Chocolate Dough into ¼-inch-thick slices. Use a small decorative cutter to remove center from each cookie slice. Place light centers in chocolate slices; place chocolate centers in light slices. Repeat with remaining rolls of dough. Bake as for Checkerboards.

Makes about 6 dozen 2½-inch cookies.

ROLLED AND CUT COOKIES

These thin, crisp cookies are shaped by rolling out chilled dough and then cut with cookie cutters or around a hand-made pattern of your own design. Because they can be extremely decorative, they are popular for holidays. Plan to make these cookies when interruptions are few. Prepare the rich, buttery dough, and wrap and refrigerate it

on one day; then roll out, cut, and bake the cookies on the next. There are cookie cutters in just about every shape you can imagine. To custom-design your own, find a simple shape that you like, trace it onto heavy cardboard, cut it out, and use it as a pattern.

The dough should be firm, but not too hard or it will crack when it is rolled out. On the other hand, if it is too soft it will stick to everything. Roll out only a small amount of dough at one time to avoid letting unused dough get too warm. Don't use too much flour when rolling out the dough or the cookies will be tough. Lightly flour the rolling pin and use a pastry cloth, or roll the dough between two sheets of waxed paper. If the dough sticks to the cutters, flour the cutters lightly by spooning flour into a shallow dish and dipping cutters into it when necessary. Use a wide spatula or turner for transferring cookies to baking sheets and for removing from sheets to cooking racks.

■ TRADITIONAL SUGAR-COOKIE CUTOUTS

This classic cookie is rich, crisp, and faintly spiced with either ground mace or nutmeg—a perfect dough to cut into valentine hearts, Easter chicks, Halloween pumpkins, George Washington hatchets, or Christmas trees. If desired, use a pastry bag or piping cone to decorate them with Royal Icing (see page 250). Note that the dough must chill several hours or overnight.

> 1¾ cups flour
> 2 teaspoons baking powder
> ¼ teaspoon ground mace or nutmeg
> ½ cup butter or margarine, softened
> 1 cup sugar
> 1 teaspoon vanilla extract
> 1 egg
>   Vanilla Granulated Sugar
>   (see page 585), optional

1. In a bowl stir together flour, baking powder, and mace to combine thoroughly; set aside.

2. In mixer bowl combine butter and sugar; beat until light and fluffy. Blend in vanilla. Add egg and beat again until fluffy. Gradually add flour mixture, beating until just well combined.

3. Enclose dough in plastic wrap and refrigerate until firm (1 to 2 hours or overnight).

4. Preheat oven to 325° F. Work with about half of the dough at a time, keeping remainder in refrigerator. On a lightly floured board or pastry cloth, roll out dough to a thickness of about ⅛ inch. Cut with cookie cutters into rounds or other fancy shapes. Carefully transfer to lightly greased baking sheets. Sprinkle with Vanilla Granulated Sugar (if desired).

5. Bake until cookies are golden brown (10 to 12 minutes). Let stand for about 1 minute, then transfer to wire racks to cool.

Makes about 3 dozen cookies.

Decorating gingerbread people, a holiday tradition, is one of the pleasures of childhood that even the youngest artists can do.

RUGELACH

Although Jewish delicatessens sell Rugelach throughout the year, these cream cheese crescents are a Hanukkah tradition. They may be stuffed with nuts and raisins, as they are here, or with jam or poppy seed filling if preferred. They do not keep well and should be eaten within a few hours of baking.

> ½ cup raisins, coarsely chopped
> 1 tablespoon brandy
> 1 cup finely chopped, toasted walnuts
> ½ cup granulated sugar
> 1 teaspoon cinnamon
>   Confectioners' sugar, for dusting

Cream Cheese Pastry

> 1 package (8 oz) cream cheese,
>   at room temperature
> ½ cup unsalted butter, at room temperature
> ¼ teaspoon salt
> 1 tablespoon sugar
> 1 teaspoon vanilla extract
> 1 cup flour

1. In a small bowl combine raisins and brandy; let stand 30 minutes. Add walnuts, sugar, and cinnamon; stir to blend; set aside.

2. Preheat oven to 425° F. Divide Cream Cheese Pastry in half. On a lightly floured surface, roll each half into a thin round. With a sharp knife cut 10-inch-diameter circles from each round of dough by placing bottom of a 10-inch tart tin (or a 10-inch-diameter pattern cut from paper) on dough and cutting around it. Roll scraps from both circles into another thin round, and make an 8-inch-diameter circle.

3. Sprinkle surface of each 10-inch circle with ⅔ cup raisin-nut filling; use ½ cup filling for 8-inch circle (a few tablespoons of filling will be left over). Press filling lightly with your hands to make it adhere to dough.

4. With a floured knife cut 10-inch circles into 12 wedges and cut 8-inch circles into 8 wedges. Starting with wide edge, roll each wedge toward tip, encasing filling.

5. Arrange rolls on ungreased baking sheets. Place sheets in oven and immediately reduce heat to 400° F. Bake until lightly browned (12 to 14 minutes). Transfer to wire racks; when cool sprinkle cookies with confectioners' sugar.

Makes 32 cookies.

Cream Cheese Pastry   In a bowl beat cream cheese, butter, salt, sugar, and vanilla until light and smooth. Add flour and beat until just blended. Gather dough into a ball and enclose in waxed paper or plastic wrap; refrigerate several hours or overnight.

GINGERBREAD PEOPLE

These little cookie people, cut from a thick slab of spicy molasses dough, are wonderful for a children's party. Make a batch and allow children to decorate their own. School-age children can maneuver an icing-filled paper piping cone. Provide younger children with a confectioners' sugar glaze, sprinkles, and decorating sugar.

> ½ cup unsalted butter, softened
> ½ cup firmly packed brown sugar
> ½ cup molasses
> 1 egg
> 2½ cups flour
> 1 teaspoon baking soda
> ½ teaspoon salt
> 2 teaspoons ground ginger
> 1 teaspoon ground cinnamon
> ½ teaspoon freshly grated nutmeg
> ½ teaspoon ground cloves
>   Dried currants, for decorating
>   Royal Icing (see page 250)

1. In large mixer bowl cream butter; gradually add sugar and beat until light. Add molasses and egg and beat to blend well; set aside.

2. In a bowl stir together flour, baking soda, salt, ginger, cinnamon, nutmeg, and cloves. Gradually add flour mixture to butter mixture, beating until just blended. Gather dough into a ball and enclose in plastic wrap; refrigerate at least 1 hour.

3. Preheat oven to 325° F. On a lightly floured board, roll out gingerbread to a thickness of ¼ inch. Cut out cookies with a floured, 4½-inch-long cutter and transfer to greased baking sheets. Bake until cookies are lightly browned around edges and feel barely firm when touched gently (about 10 minutes). Transfer to wire racks. While each cookie is hot, press in currants to create eyes, mouth, and buttons. When cool, decorate with Royal Icing piped from a paper cone.

Makes about 1 dozen 4-inch-long cookies.

Recipes and Related Information
Baking Pans, 18; Biscotti, 8; Cake and Pastry Tools, 89; Linzer Hearts, 298; Macadamia Crisps, 346.

COOKWARE (POTS AND PANS)

In simplest terms, cookware permits controlled exposure of food to heat. The best pots and pans conduct heat evenly and efficiently and are most responsive to changes in temperature, usually due to their material and construction (see MATERIALS FOR COOKWARE). Size and shape are adaptations that have evolved over time for specific purposes; these features are subjective ones, having less to do with performance than with personal cooking styles or manufacturers' preferences.

Quality cookware is an investment that will return long-term dividends of reliability and durability. How do you judge quality? Price is a clue; better cookware costs more. But with proper care, each piece can be a one-time purchase. Resist the prepackaged appeal of a set. More than likely these collections include at least one pan that you wouldn't buy if you didn't have to. What appears to be a bargain, then, really isn't. If you don't need it, you don't want it. Resist, too, the seduction of surface flash—color and pattern don't keep a sauce from burning or make water boil faster. A material with good heat-conducting qualities offers those attributes. If it's pretty, consider its appearance a secondary bonus. Today's home cooks have come to appreciate and even prefer the clean, spare, utilitarian lines of commercial cookware, choosing a decorative pan only if it will go to the table.

BUTTER WARMER

This is a very versatile little pan, despite its single-purpose name. It is perfectly sized for melting jellies and preserves for glazes; warming syrups, single portions of soups, and baby foods; softening honey and ice cream sauces; and heating alcohol for flambés. Most hold about 2 cups. Choose one with a wide, stable, flat bottom. A pan this small should also have a long handle, so the cook's hand is at a distance from the burner. Most cookware lines offer a version, in the usual materials. Some are enameled steel or cast iron—decorative enough to come to the table.

CARAMELIZING POT

If you make sugar syrups and candies more than occasionally, you might consider investing in this heavyweight, straight-sided pot traditionally used for sugar work. Copper is the metal of choice because it is extremely sensitive to heat; this affords important control of sugar syrup, which can quickly deepen from brown to burned in a matter of seconds. Unlike most copper cookware, caramelizing pots aren't lined with tin: copper and sugar are compatible (other foods and copper are sometimes adverse) and the high temperatures that sugar work requires can melt tin. They come in 1- and 2-quart sizes and have a hollow, rolled handle and a pouring spout.

CHICKEN FRYER

An American invention, the chicken fryer is a deep, covered frying pan well-suited for frying, browning, and braising. With its short handle and lip (to more easily pour off accumulated fat), it resembles a cast-iron skillet, and is usually made of cast iron or enameled cast iron. To help control spattering, its sides are higher than those of a skillet; and its domed lid is useful for slow, covered cooking. Both are about 12 inches in diameter. Although extremely versatile, the chicken fryer isn't as popular as it once was; those who saw their grandmothers using one to make great fried chicken do know its value.

DEEP-FAT FRYER

A deep-fat fryer should be tall enough to hold at least several inches of fat with sufficient additional room for the hot fat to bubble up without spilling over when food is dropped in; the fryer should be wide enough so that food can float freely to an evenly browned crisp. Depth is more critical than surface area, as safety is a key issue for this technique; width is a convenience that allows more food to fry at a time. French-style models are deep and wide, with a narrow base and wider surface, and ear handles. American deep-fat fryers resemble oversized saucepans, with a single long handle. Four quarts is a standard size and is appropriate for most recipes; steel, enameled steel, and aluminum are the usual materials.

Basket inserts, useful for lowering food into the fat, then lifting it out again when done, are often packaged with the pot. These baskets are also sold separately, to use with a pot you already have. The handles on some models are designed to hold the basket up out of the pan

SAUTE PAN

Wide, straight-sided, and shallow, with an extralong handle, sauté pans are designed for quick cooking in a small amount of oil or butter over high heat. *Sauter*, in French, means to jump. Traditionally, the pan is moved rapidly back and forth to prevent food from sticking to it, so the food jumps about from the constant motion. More typically today, sautéed food is turned rather than tossed, but the process is still fast moving. Like the slope-sided skillet, this pan is useful for browning and stir-frying meats, poultry, and vegetables; unlike a skillet, this one offers more protection against spattering fat and liquid, and it is better suited for combination cooking—stews, fricassees, and braises, for example. Any heavyweight skillet can substitute for a sauté pan.

Most sauté pans have 2½-inch sides; sizes range from 2 to 7 quarts (3 to 5 quarts are the most useful sizes) and most come with covers. Look for a sauté pan made of a heavy-gauge metal that picks up and transmits heat evenly without burning or hot spots and that has a handle made of a material that stays relatively cool; if very large, a long handle and a lug handle on the opposite side ease lifting. Materials are copper, aluminum, stainless steel, enameled steel, and clad metals.

SKILLET (FRYING PAN)

While the straight-sided sauté pan developed out of French culinary tradition, the flare-sided skillet (also called a frying pan) has American roots. The two evolved as slightly different approaches to the same process—rapid stove-top cooking in fat of some sort. The skillet is a shallower pan, with less bottom surface, but still tall enough to contain liquid for a sauce or stir-fry. Cast iron is the traditional material: it is heavy, an excellent heat conductor, works equally well on top of the stove and in the oven (perfect for Pommes Anna), and with use develops a seasoning that functions like a nonstick finish. Unless the seasoning is maintained and the pan kept dry, cast iron can rust, however (see MATERIALS FOR COOKWARE).

Other materials include aluminum, stainless steel, enameled steel, enameled cast iron, and clad metals. A skillet with an applied nonstick finish, which permits frying with little or no fat, is extremely useful. These are generally inexpensive and are worth buying in addition to your other skillets. The most popular sizes for skillets are 10 and 12 inches in diameter; if you can store them, buy both sizes. If you cook for a large family, you may even want the 14-inch-diameter pan. Smaller pans (6, 7, or 8 inches) are commonly used for omelets.

Electric frying pans with automatic controls permit precise regulation of temperature; if you have extra storage room, they are good backups for stove-top skillets, especially when frying in quantity. Many are now available with nonstick finishes. Those made of heavyweight metal will perform better and last longer.

STEAMERS

Steaming apparatus come in all sizes and shapes, but the idea is always the same: to support the food over a quantity of boiling water, with room for the steam to circulate around the food. The size and configuration depend upon what is being steamed.

All-Purpose Steamer A traditional steamer is made of two (or more) stacked pots with bottoms that are perforated to allow the steam to rise from the lowest pot through the upper layers. Three quarts is a typical size. Steaming pots are larger—as much as 8 quarts—and have an insert that is perforated on the bottom. Like all steamers, they have tight-fitting lids that prevent steam from escaping. Blanching inserts have holes on the sides as well as the bottom. They are used to cook pasta as well as vegetables. Sometimes steaming pots are packaged with both inserts and sold as vegetable-spaghetti cookers. Many cookware manufacturers offer separate steaming and blanching inserts in a variety of sizes to fit their saucepans and stockpots.

Asparagus Steamer A specialty steamer, this is a tall, narrow pot with an insert to hold asparagus stalks upright; the stalks partly boil and partly steam. The insert, with handles, makes it easier to remove stalks and then drain them. Although definitely not a necessity, the asparagus steamer is convenient to use if you have the space to store it.

Chinese Steamer The Chinese steam with a rack of some sort: either a cross-shaped wooden or metal rack, a circular, stainless steel ring that looks a little like a cake cooling rack, or a perforated metal tray. These are usually set in a wok. Stacking steamer baskets of bamboo or metal are also used in Asian cooking; they allow you to steam several different items over one pot of water.

Couscousière To prepare couscous, a stew considered the national dish of Morocco and other north African countries, grains of semolina steam in a perforated pan set over the pot containing meat and vegetables (couscous can refer to either the stew and grain in combination or just the grain). The moisture given off in the lower pan rises up and cooks the grains, which should be light and fluffy. A *couscousière* consists of two stacked pieces, both bulbous in shape; the stew pot on bottom has considerably larger capacity than the upper grain steamer. It is made of aluminum and stainless steel, and, if you are fond of ethnic stews, is a great presentation piece at a meal for guests.

Folding Steamer Insert Almost any pot, narrow or wide, can be transformed into a steamer with this collapsible insert. Made of stainless steel, it is constructed of perforated, overlapping rectangles attached to a circular base, also perforated, which sits on three tiny legs. The device expands and contracts like the petals of a flower to fit most sizes of saucepan or saucepot. Inexpensive and compact, it has probably introduced more people to the pleasures of steamed food, particularly vegetables, than has any other piece of equipment. It has a 5½-inch base and when flat measures 9½ inches in diameter.

STOCKPOT

Tall, narrow stockpots are fixtures on restaurant ranges, sometimes kept simmering 24 hours a day to provide the liquid foundation for myriad sauces and soups. Their shape is well suited for slow, gentle cooking of liquids; less moisture is lost through evaporation in a deep pot than in one that is shallow and wide. The high sides also keep the flavoring elements—bones, meat, and root vegetables—immersed throughout cooking so that the gently bubbling water can slowly extract their essences into the broth. For the home cook, a stockpot is useful for making soup and stock and for cooking large amounts of food such as corn or lobster for a crowd. This pot uses less cooking surface than a saucepot of similar capacity, making room for other foods to cook at the same time. The pot isn't moved around on the stove, but may be carried when full, so it has two lug handles rather than one long handle.

Think big when choosing a stockpot—at least 8 quarts. Making stock is time-consuming; it's more efficient to produce it in quantity. Make sure the pot has a thick bottom; this extra weight prevents scorching of both ingredients and pot, and keeps the pot from warping. Stockpots are commonly made of aluminum, stainless steel, clad metals, and enameled steel.

WOK

The most famous symbol of Chinese cooking is the wok, and it is hard to imagine a more versatile or better-designed piece of cookware. Its round bottom allows food to be stir-fried or deep-fried with a minimum of oil. A steel or cast-iron wok is an excellent conductor of heat, making it possible to cook over a very small fire. With a cover and a steaming rack or basket, the wok becomes a steamer for everything from whole birds and fish to bite-sized pastries. You can simmer, braise, and even smoke foods in a wok.

Woks are available in many designs and materials. The traditional shape has a round bottom, for cooking over a gas flame (originally a charcoal brazier). Cooks with electric ranges should use a flat-bottomed wok for more efficient heating. A wok may have two metal loops as handles, two similar handles trimmed with wood, or one long wooden handle with or without a handle on the opposite side. A long handle is useful, especially for stir-frying, since it allows you to lift the wok with one hand to pour the contents out onto the serving platter without being spattered by oil.

Woks come in all sizes, from 9 to 30 inches in diameter. The 14-inch size is the most common for home use and is included in the standard wok sets sold in most cookware and department stores. The best material for woks is 14-gauge spun steel. Cast iron is also traditional, but many home cooks find it too heavy. Avoid those with nonstick surfaces that clean easily but do not allow foods to brown as well as steel or iron surfaces do. Stainless steel is pretty, but conducts heat poorly and food tends to stick to it. Anodized aluminum performs well but is very costly.

Among the essential wok accessories (included in most wok sets) are a wok ring, cover, Chinese-style wire strainer, ladle, and spatula. Optional accessories include steaming racks and bamboo steaming baskets (see Chinese Steamer), wire draining racks for fried foods, bamboo cleaning brushes, and extralong chopsticks for stirring while food cooks.

Like a cast-iron skillet, a steel wok must be carefully seasoned; see MATERIALS FOR COOKWARE.

COOL, TO

To bring hot food to room temperature (approximately 70° F). This is not the same as chilling food, which involves temperatures of 40° F or less.

COPPER EGG-WHITE BOWL

For centuries, cooks have recognized that egg whites beaten in an unlined copper bowl have appreciably more volume. Experiments suggest that copper binds with a protein in the whites to help create a more stable foam. This means that the beaten egg whites will keep their volume longer. For home use, the most popular bowls are 10 and 12 inches in diameter. They are deep, with a rounded bottom and sloping sides. Ideal for developing airy foam, this shape best accommodates a balloon whisk, whose bulbous, open design incorporates more air into a mixture than a narrow, more tightly constructed whisk. To use, the bowl is set on the counter and rotated as eggs are whisked, or is held against the body with one arm and secured by looping the thumb through a ring attached to the rim. Copper inserts are available for some heavy-duty portable electric mixers.

Recipes and Related Information
Egg, 196; Whisk, 608.

CORN

Also called maize, corn is not technically a vegetable, but a grass native to the New World. Of the hundreds of cultivated strains, most can be classified as either popcorn, field corn, or sweet corn. Popcorn is a type of corn whose kernels burst open when exposed to heat, revealing the familiar dry, white, puffy interior (see POPCORN). Field corn is used for animal feed or is dried for hominy; when ground, it yields hominy grits or *masa harina*. For a discussion of dried corn products (cornmeal, dried sweet corn, hominy, hominy grits, masa harina), see GRAIN. Corn marketed for the table, whether fresh, frozen, or canned, is sweet corn, which stores more sugar than starch; this entry will discuss sweet corn.

Sweet corn may be yellow or white, in full-sized ears or baby corn that may be eaten in its entirety. When sweet corn is picked, the sugar it contains begins rapidly converting to starch, so it is advisable to cook corn as soon as possible after purchase.

Use Fresh sweet corn on the cob can be steamed, boiled, oven-roasted, or grilled and eaten out of hand. Fresh corn kernels may be made into soup or added to soup; used in salads, vegetable sautés, fritters, and relishes; creamed or made into puddings or soufflés. In Peru, chunks of steamed sweet corn are added to stews and served with seviche.

Availability Fresh corn is sold almost the year around, with peak supplies in summer. Florida supplies most off-season corn in the United States. Frozen corn on the cob and corn kernels are also available. Corn kernels are canned, either water-packed or creamed.

Selection Choose ears that feel full and heavy for their size; kernels should be relatively small and milky when pierced, and silk should be moist, without any signs of drying or decay.

Storage Keep fresh corn in the refrigerator in a plastic bag and use as soon as possible. Do not remove husk and silk until ready to use. These natural wrappers will help keep the corn from drying out when exposed to the cold air of the refrigerator. Leftover frozen or canned corn may be stored in an airtight container in the refrigerator for up to three days.

Preparation Remove husk and silk from fresh corn if steaming or boiling. To oven-roast or grill, peel back husk but leave attached. Remove silk and replace husk, tying it shut at the tip with string. Soak in cold water 30 minutes to moisten husk, then roast or grill. Alternatively, remove husk and silk, wrap ears in foil with butter, and roast or grill. To prepare fresh corn kernels, remove husk and silk, then run a sharp knife down cob from tip end to stem to cut kernels away, or use a corn kernel remover, which automatically shears kernels from cob.

Cooking See BOIL, GRILL, STEAM.

◼ ELOTES
Corn on the cob with lime-chile butter

In this dish, corn on the cob (with husk intact) is roasted on the grill and seasoned with a surprising combination of lime and chili powder. These sour and piquant flavors actually bring out the sweetness of the corn. Elotes can also be cooked indoors if the weather turns bad.

> Fresh ears of corn (about 2 per person),
> silk removed, husks left intact
> ¾ to 1 cup butter, at room temperature
> ¼ cup (generous) fresh lime juice
> 2 to 3 tablespoons Texas chili powder or
> powdered hot chiles (such as New Mexico chiles)
> Salt, to taste

1. *To cook corn outdoors:* Prepare fire in grill. Drench corn with water until husks can absorb no more; twist shut. If fire is very hot, wrap ears in aluminum foil. Place corn on grill and roast for about 20 minutes, turning frequently, until tender. Keep warm until ready to serve. *To cook corn indoors:* Preheat oven to 400° F. Remove husks and smear ears with a small amount of butter. Wrap each ear in aluminum foil and roast in oven until tender (20 to 25 minutes).

2. As corn roasts, use a fork to beat together butter, lime juice, chili powder, and salt, adjusting proportions to taste. When ready to serve, remove husks and coat corn with the mixture.

Serves 6 to 8.

◼ CORN MAQUECHOUX

This Creole version of creamed corn is best served in summer when corn is sweetest, peppers are at their best, and fresh basil is abundant. With three colors of bell peppers—red, green, and yellow—plus the yellow corn, it makes a festive and flavorful accompaniment to fried or roast chicken.

> 3 tablespoons unsalted butter
> 1 cup finely chopped onions
> 2 shallots, finely chopped
> ½ cup chopped red bell pepper
> ½ cup chopped green bell pepper
> ½ cup chopped yellow bell pepper
> 3 to 4 cups fresh or frozen
> sweet corn kernels
> 2 tablespoons chopped parsley
> 4 tablespoons chopped green onion
> 1 cup whipping cream
> ¼ teaspoon dried thyme
> 1 tablespoon chopped fresh basil *or*
> ½ teaspoon dried basil
> ½ teaspoon cayenne pepper
> Salt and freshly ground black pepper, to taste
> Sugar, to taste

Melt butter in a heavy 3- to 4-quart saucepan over medium heat. Add onions and shallots and sauté until vegetables are soft but not browned. Add peppers and cook another 2 to 3 minutes. Add corn, parsley, green onions, cream, thyme, basil, and cayenne, and simmer for 10 to 15 minutes. Adjust taste with salt, pepper, and, if necessary, sugar.

Serves 4 to 6.

Food Processor Version Cut 1 medium onion into quarters and put in work bowl with metal blade in place; add shallots. Turn motor on and off 3 or 4 times to process. Cook as directed. Cut 1 *each* small green, red, and yellow bell peppers into 1-inch pieces. Process with metal blade, turning motor on and off 3 or 4 times. Cook as directed.

> ### Recipes and Related Information
> *Basic Fritter Batter, 28; Corn Kernel Remover, 159; Corn Relish, 322; Succotash, 33.*

CORN KERNEL REMOVER

If you love corn on the cob, corn salsas, chowders and soups, creamed corn, fritters, puddings, and all the many other wonderful ways there are to prepare corn when fresh and seasonally plentiful, this tool may prove handy even though it has limited uses. It does only what its name promises—cuts kernels off the cob—but it does it very well. The device consists of a plastic, metal, or wood trough with a fixed blade and movable teeth set across it; the corn slides along the trough and under the blade, which shears off the kernels. The teeth act like mashers if you want creamier corn; they can be moved away from the blade when not needed. This tool is not a year-round item in cookware stores; it's most available in summer months, when corn is at its most plentiful in the market.

> ### Recipes and Related Information
> *Corn, 158; Corn Relish, 322; Succotash, 33.*

CORNSTARCH

Derived from corn, cornstarch is a powdery white thickener. It gives a transparent sheen to sauces, syrups, and stews. Where appearance is important, as in a glaze for a fruit tart, it is preferred to flour, which produces a more opaque finish.

Use Cornstarch is used to thicken sauces, soups, stews, puddings, and syrups. It is a frequent ingredient in Chinese cooking to thicken sauces and to coat meats and fish before frying. Cornstarch also gives a light texture to baked goods. To substitute all-purpose flour for cake flour in baked goods, replace 2 tablespoons flour per cup with 2 tablespoons cornstarch.

Availability Cornstarch is widely available at supermarkets packed in boxes.

Storage Cornstarch will keep indefinitely in a cool, dry place.

Preparation To thicken a sauce, dissolve cornstarch in a small amount of cold water or stock before stirring into simmering liquid. Cook gently for a few minutes to remove the raw cornstarch flavor. Cornstarch-thickened sauces should not be boiled very long or they will separate. One tablespoon cornstarch has approximately the thickening power of 1½ to 2 tablespoons flour.

> ### Recipes and Related Information
> *New York–Style Cheesecake, 117; Sauce, 512.*

CRANBERRY

The small, tart red cranberry is the fruit of a low-lying vine native to North America and northern Europe. Wild cranberries were an important nutrient for Native Americans, who mashed them with dried meat and animal fat to make pemmican, a long-lasting food that nourished them through cold winters and extensive hunting expeditions. Today cranberries are cultivated commercially, with half the American crop grown in Massachusetts. Raw cranberries have a firm, crunchy texture and are very tart.

Use The naturally high acidity of the cranberry makes it excellent for relishes and jellies. It adds zest to salads, stuffings, cakes, muffins, quick breads, pies, and puddings. Cranberry juice is particularly refreshing and can be used in punches or cocktails. Cranberry relish, cranberry sauce, and other cranberry preparations are traditional dishes served on American Thanksgiving tables.

Availability Fresh cranberries are available from September to December, packed in plastic bags. Frozen cranberries, packed in plastic bags, are sold in most supermarkets all year. Canned cranberry relish and cranberry sauce are marketed the year around, as is bottled cranberry juice.

Storage Keep fresh cranberries in an unopened plastic bag in the refrigerator for up to four weeks. Store leftover fresh cranberries in an airtight container in the refrigerator. To freeze, wrap package in a plastic bag; freeze up to one year.

Cranberries were a staple in the diet of Native Americans during this country's early days. The berries were part of pemmican, a long-lasting dried food that nourished the Indians through the long, cold New England winters.

Preparation Wash berries and remove any stems; drain. It is unnecessary to thaw frozen berries before adding to batters or dishes that will be cooked.

■ WHOLE-BERRY CRANBERRY SAUCE

Although cranberries are synonymous with turkey, they are also delicious with roast pork, beef, and chicken. For a chunky sauce, cook 1 to 2 minutes more until the berries break down. For a smooth sauce, purée the berries in a blender or food processor for about 2 minutes.

 1 **package (12 oz) fresh or frozen cranberries (about 2½ cups)**
 1 **cup sugar**
 1¼ **cups water**
  Juice and grated rind of 1 orange

1. Wash cranberries and pat dry. In a 2-quart saucepan combine sugar, the water, orange rind, and juice; cook, stirring, over medium heat, until sugar dissolves. Add cranberries to sugar syrup, bring to a boil, and cook until cranberry skins start to break or pop (about 1 minute).

2. Remove cranberries from the heat and pour into a 3-cup bowl or storage jars with lids to cool. Sauce can be stored, covered, in the refrigerator for up to 10 days, or placed in airtight jars in the freezer for up to 3 months (leave ½-inch headspace between sauce and jar lid).

Makes 2⅓ cups.

Variation Stir 1 cup coarsely chopped, toasted walnuts into cranberry sauce after removing from heat.

Makes 2¾ cups.

> ### *Recipes and Related Information*
> *Cranberry Conserve, 320; Cranberry-Orange-Nut Loaf, 492.*

CREAM

If freshly drawn milk is left to settle, the high-fat portion rises to the top to form a thick layer of cream. The modern dairy skims cream using a centrifugal cream separator and markets it in several different versions.

Use The high fat content of cream gives it a rich buttery flavor and a velvety texture. Cream is used to enrich sauces, soups, stews, and hot and cold beverages. Poured over berries, sliced bananas, poached fruit, and hot and cold cereals, it is a sauce in itself. Brushing cream on just-baked breads and rolls gives them a soft, shiny crust. Adding cream to baked goods such as biscuits and shortcake provides added richness and tenderness. Cream contributes body to a variety of sweet and savory puddings, custards, and mousses, and is, of course, the basis for all ice creams and many other frozen desserts. Cream also adds richness and texture to such confections as caramels, truffles, toffee, and pralines.

Due to its high fat content, cream holds a shape when whipped. A dollop of whipped, lightly salted cream is used to garnish and enrich soups. Sweetened whipped cream garnishes pies and tarts, cakes, puddings, mousses, sundaes, fresh berries, and cooked fruit desserts. Whipped cream gives body to mousses and parfaits; it may be flavored with chocolate or vanilla and used as a filling for cream puffs, or folded into pastry cream and used as a filling for crêpes and cakes. Whipped cream is also spooned on top of coffee, hot cocoa, Irish coffee, and many other coffee drinks.

Half-and-half or light cream may be substituted for heavy cream or whipping cream in many instances, although they yield a lighter, less rich dish. Half-and-half and light cream are unable to hold a foam and cannot be substituted in a recipe that calls for whipped cream.

Crème fraîche, a cultured cream often used by the French in sauces, is made by adding natural ferments to pasteurized heavy cream. It may be used whenever sour cream is called for: in soups, doughs and batters, salad dressings, and sauces, for example. It may also be lightly sweetened and spooned over berries or fruit desserts.

The smooth texture and rich, tangy flavor of sour cream are appreciated in dips, salad dressings, cold soups, and frostings. Sour cream gives a tender crumb to baked items such as cakes and biscuits.

Availability Although raw (unpasteurized) dairy products are sold in some health-food stores, most commercial dairy products, including cream, have been pasteurized (see MILK) to destroy disease-causing organisms and extend shelf life. If the product is not labeled as raw or unpasteurized, it has been pasteurized. Some cream is ultrapasteurized to extend shelf life.

Half-and-half is usually homogenized (see MILK) to prevent milk and cream from separating, and light cream may be homogenized. Whipping cream is not homogenized because that would interfere with its whipping ability. Cream is available in the following forms:

Half-and-Half A mixture of milk and cream, half-and-half contains between 10.5 percent and 18.0 percent milk fat.

Light Cream, Coffee Cream, or Table Cream The milk fat content is between 18 percent and 30 percent.

Light Whipping Cream or Whipping Cream The milk fat content is between 30 percent and 36 percent.

Heavy Whipping Cream or Heavy Cream The milk fat content is at least 36 percent.

Sour Cream This cream product is made in one of two ways: either by adding lactic acid–producing bacteria to pasteurized cream and letting it culture for about 24 hours until it reaches 0.5 percent acidity, or by adding vinegar or another acidifier to pasteurized cream and letting it stand until it curdles. The former procedure produces cultured sour cream; the latter method, acidified sour cream.

Any sour cream must contain at least 18 percent butterfat and may contain rennet, emulsifiers, and stabilizers. The requirement drops to 14.4 percent butterfat if nutritive sweeteners or bulky flavorings are added.

Crème Fraîche This cultured cream is thickened, or curdled, by the action of the acid-producing bacterial culture. Crème fraîche is thicker than whipping cream but less thick than American sour cream. It has a smooth, pourable texture and a tangy, nutlike flavor.

Heavy whipping cream, light whipping cream, coffee cream, and half-and-half are packed in cardboard containers. All are available in supermarkets, although light whipping cream and coffee cream may not be sold in smaller markets. Whipped cream is also marketed in pressurized aerosol cans, although it may contain sweeteners, flavoring, or stabilizers. Check the label. Sour cream is widely available at supermarkets packed in plastic tubs. Crème frâiche can be easily made at home (see right) or may be purchased in selected supermarkets, specialty gourmet shops, and cheese stores, in bulk or packed in plastic containers.

Storage Cream is highly perishable. Make it one of the last purchases at the supermarket and refrigerate it at home as soon as possible. Pasteurized cream stays fresh for at least one week. Ultrapasteurized cream keeps for six to eight weeks in an unopened container; after opening, use within one week. Sour cream should be refrigerated and used within one week. Crème frâiche should be refrigerated, covered, and used within one week.

Preparation To produce a more stable foam, chill cream, bowl, and beaters before whipping. Generally, 1 cup whipping cream yields 2 cups whipped cream. Choose a bowl large enough to handle the increased volume comfortably but small enough to allow beaters to maintain good contact with cream. It is best to whip cream shortly before using. It also may be whipped ahead, covered, and refrigerated for several hours. Some liquid will probably separate from the mass, but it will reincorporate readily; at serving time, rewhip lightly.

When folding whipped cream into another, heavier mixture, it's sometimes easier to add the whipped cream in stages, to lighten the other mixture. Fold in about one-third whipped cream to blend, then fold in remainder. For information about proper folding technique, see FOLD.

Sauces, soups, and stews containing sour cream should not be allowed to boil or they may curdle. Unlike sour cream, imported crème fraîche and crème fraîche made with buttermilk do not curdle when boiled and may be added to simmered dishes. Crème fraîche made with sour cream or yogurt curdles when boiled.

■ CREME FRAICHE

Some buttermilk or leftover crème fraîche is added to the whipping cream to start the curdling action. Heat 1 cup whipping cream in a small saucepan to 95° F. Transfer cream to a clean jar with a tight-fitting lid. Add 1 tablespoon buttermilk and shake well. Let stand at room temperature until thickened (12 to 24 hours). Refrigerate. Save 1 tablespoon from each batch and use in place of buttermilk in future batches. Do not try to make crème fraîche with ultrapasteurized cream, because it does not contain enough bacteria to curdle.

Cream will whip to greatest volume if liquid, bowl, and beaters are first chilled. It is best to whip cream just before using.

Recipes and Related Information
Banana Cream Pie, 440; Candy and Confection, 94; Chantilly Cream, 252; Chocolate Marble Cream Cake, 88; Coconut Cream Pie, 440; Cream-Basted Fried Eggs, 200; Cream Biscuits, 50; Cream Sauce, 513; Horseradish Cream Sauce, 305; Horseradish–Sour Cream Dipping Sauce, 46; Lemon Crème Fraîche, 107; Parmesan Cream Sauce, 412; Sour Cream Pastry, 47; Whipped Cream Icing, 87; Whipped Crème Fraîche, 264.

CREAM, TO

In baking, to beat fat—butter or solid vegetable shortening—with sugar until soft, smooth, and light. This process traps air that expands in the oven to help create a baked product with more volume. Creaming is especially important for butter (shortened) cakes, which depend on this step for some or all of their leavening. For cookies, creaming serves to combine ingredients rather than aerate and is done to produce a smooth texture.

To incorporate the most air, butter should be at warm room temperature (75° to 79° F). Let refrigerated butter sit out on the counter for about 30 minutes before using. An instant-read thermometer is the most accurate gauge of temperature, but you can also judge by touch. If butter yields slightly to pressure, yet still feels cool, it's ready. Solid vegetable shortening is plastic (pliable) at a wider range of temperatures than butter, and so it needn't soften before using.

Beat fat briefly to make it soft and pliable before adding sugar, then beat them together until light—a pale, ivory color—and the consistency of whipped cream. Scrape down sides of bowl occasionally to incorporate fully both ingredients.

How long should you cream a mixture? You want to continue long enough to accomplish your purpose; if you are creaming to leaven a cake, you may be directed to continue for as long as 6 to 8 minutes. For other mixtures follow this rule of thumb: cream until color lightens, consistency becomes fluffy, and batter is less grainy from sugar when you rub it between your fingers.

Chocolate Eclairs are made from fingers of cream puff pastry filled with vanilla pastry cream and iced with Bittersweet Chocolate Sauce. The flavor of the pastry cream can be easily varied. The éclair recipe appears on page 164.

CREAM OF TARTAR

A by-product of wine making, cream of tartar is the acid salt of tartaric acid. The crystallized sediment that falls to the bottom of a wine cask after fermentation and the crystalline substance that collects on its sides are crude tartar. To refine it for commercial use, it is decrystallized in a basic solution, then recrystallized, then bleached and allowed to crystallize again. The layer of white crystals that forms on the surface of the cooling liquid is powdered to make commercial cream of tartar.

Use   Cream of tartar is a common ingredient in commercial baking powders, along with baking soda. In the presence of moisture, cream of tartar and baking soda react to produce carbon dioxide gas, thereby leavening the mixture or batter. Due to its acidity or low pH, a pinch of cream of tartar promotes coagulation in beaten egg whites if added partway through the beating process. Confectioners add cream of tartar to sugar syrup to impede crystallization, thereby yielding creamier, less grainy candies.

Availability   Cream of tartar is widely sold packaged in airtight jars or tins.

Storage   Keep in an airtight container in a cool, dry place; it will keep indefinitely.

Preparation   Sift with other dry ingredients before adding to a batter. Because the leavening action of cream of tartar commences immediately upon contact with moisture, work quickly after adding moisture to batter.

Recipes and Related Information
Baking Powder, 23; Egg, 196.

CREAM PUFF PASTRY

The French call this pastry *pâte à choux*, cabbage pastry. It is the base for such delicacies as cream puffs, éclairs, and profiteroles. During baking, the little mounds of cream puff dough grow into knobby-surfaced pastries that do indeed resemble cabbages. These crisp, puffy shells can be filled with a variety of creams and glazed with numerous icings. The usual fillings are pastry cream, Chantilly cream, ice cream, or mousse. The toppings range from a dusting of confectioners' sugar to a rich chocolate sauce or crunchy caramel glaze. The fully baked puffs can also be filled with savory mixtures and served as finger foods that are perfect for cocktails.

INGREDIENTS FOR CREAM PUFFS

The dough is quickly and simply made from a paste, called panada, of water, butter, salt, sugar, and flour. Eggs are added one by one, causing the pastry to inflate like a balloon in the oven. Like the batter for popovers—those other steam-leavened crispy, hollow shells—cream puff paste has an equal amount of flour and liquid. But cream puffs are much richer than popovers because the dough contains about eight times more fat. The fat also contributes tenderness, elasticity, and, with the water and egg, is a source for the steam-generating moisture that puffs the pastry as it bakes. Eggs add structure, richness, and liquid, and serve as an emulsifier to blend the liquid and fat into a smooth paste.

CREAM PUFF PASTRY BASICS

The technique for making cream puff paste is straightforward and simple (see Making Cream Puffs at right). The water, butter, salt, and sugar are combined in a heavy-bottomed saucepan and heated until the butter melts and the mixture just comes to a boil. At that moment the pan is removed from the heat and the flour is beaten in. With further beating the mixture thickens to a lumpy paste that later becomes smooth as each egg is incorporated. The paste has been beaten sufficiently when it pulls away from the sides of the pan in a ball. After the paste has cooled enough that it won't curdle the eggs (about 5 minutes), the eggs are added one at a time. The smooth, shiny finished mixture is a rich golden color and ready to be shaped as desired.

The most efficient way to create precise shapes is to pipe the cream puff paste onto parchment-lined baking sheets using a pastry bag with the tip specified in the recipe (see FROSTING, ICING, AND FILLING, page 244, for directions on using a pastry bag). If a pastry bag is not available, use two spoons and your fingers (dipped in egg wash or water) to roughly shape the paste.

Cream puff paste should be used while still warm. If you want to keep leftover paste, rub the surface with butter, cover, and refrigerate for up to 8 hours. To use, bring to room temperature and handle as you would fresh paste. Leftover paste does not puff as high as fresh paste and should be used only for small puffs, such as profiteroles or miniature éclairs.

■ CREAM PUFF PASTRY
Pâte à choux

This is the foundation for all types of classically shaped cream puff desserts—including éclairs, large and small cream puffs, profiteroles, and *gougères*. Unbleached white bread (hard) flour is best for making cream puffs. If hard flour is unavailable, substitute all-purpose flour.

For 1⅓ cups

- ½ cup water *or*
  ¼ cup water and ¼ cup milk
- 4 tablespoons unsalted butter, cut into pieces
- ½ teaspoon sugar
- ¼ teaspoon salt
- ½ cup unbleached white bread flour, sifted
- 2 eggs

For 2 cups

- ¾ cup water *or*
  ⅜ cup water and ⅜ cup milk
- 6 tablespoons unsalted butter, cut into pieces
- ¾ teaspoon sugar
- ¼ teaspoon salt
- ¾ cup unbleached white bread flour, sifted
- 3 eggs

For 2⅔ cups

- 1 cup water *or*
  ½ cup water and ½ cup milk
- 8 tablespoons unsalted butter, cut into pieces
- 1 teaspoon sugar
- ½ teaspoon salt
- 1 cup unbleached white bread flour, sifted
- 4 eggs

1. Preheat oven to 425° F. Place the water, butter, sugar, and salt in a 2½-quart saucepan; bring to a boil over low heat. The mixture should be heated slowly so butter is just melted when water reaches a boil. When mixture boils, remove from heat immediately and add flour all at once. Stir vigorously with a wooden spoon. Return to medium heat and stir until mixture pulls away from sides of pan and forms a ball (about 30 seconds), leaving a white film on pan.

2. Remove from heat; cool 5 minutes. Add eggs, one at a time, beating thoroughly after each addition. The paste should look smooth and shiny but be stiff enough to hold its shape when piped or dropped onto a baking sheet.

If paste looks dull and is very stiff, lightly beat another egg and add a little of it to paste; beat until mixture is smooth. Add more egg if needed.

3. Fit pastry bag with a ¾-inch plain ornamenting tip. Fill bag half full with cream puff pastry. Pipe or spoon cream puff pastry onto parchment-lined baking sheets into shapes specified in individual recipes. Bake as directed.

1⅓ cups yields 8 éclairs, 10 cream puffs, or 40 profiteroles; 2 cups yields 12 éclairs, 15 cream puffs, or 60 profiteroles; 2⅔ cups yields 1 gougère.

■ CREAM PUFFS

For a dessert, fill Cream Puffs with whipped cream or pastry cream and dust lightly with confectioners' sugar. Once shells are filled with cream, they must be refrigerated to avoid spoilage unless served right away. However, shells quickly lose their crispness in the refrigerator. To use as an hors d'oeuvre or first course, fill with a savory mixture such as creamed crab, herbed cream cheese, or sour cream and caviar. Fill no more than 2 hours prior to serving. Cream puffs are good choices for stand-up cocktail parties when you plan to pass all or most of the food. The pastry makes a neat little package that can be eaten with ease. Unfilled shells can be frozen, wrapped airtight, and reheated in a 400° F oven 5 minutes to crisp.

- 1⅓ cups Cream Puff Pastry (at left)
- 1 egg lightly beaten with 1 teaspoon water
- 2 cups Chantilly Cream (see page 252) *or*
  1½ cups Pastry Cream (see page 251) folded with 1 cup Chantilly Cream
- ¼ cup confectioners' sugar, for dusting

1. Preheat oven to 425° F. Line a baking sheet with parchment paper. Attach paper to baking sheet with a few dots of Cream Puff Pastry. Place Cream Puff Pastry in a pastry bag fitted with a ¾-inch tip. Pipe 2½-inch-diameter mounds of pastry about 2 inches apart on baking sheet (or drop mounds of pastry onto sheet using 2 spoons). Brush surface of each mound with egg-water mixture.

2. Bake at 425° F for 15 minutes; reduce heat to 400° F and continue baking 15 minutes longer. Make a few small slits in the side of each cream puff to allow steam to escape; turn off oven and return cream puffs to oven for 10 minutes. Prop oven door slightly ajar with a wooden spoon. Cool cream puffs on wire racks.

3. To fill cream puffs: Slice shells in half horizontally with a serrated knife. Remove any uncooked dough from inside. Place Chantilly Cream in a pastry bag fitted with a medium star tip. Pipe cream into bottom half of shell until cream extends 1 inch above the rim; cover with top half of shell. Sift confectioners' sugar over filled puffs. Serve immediately or refrigerate until ready to serve.

Makes 8 to 10 large puffs.

MAKING CREAM PUFFS

After adding flour to butter mixture in saucepan, cook, stirring vigorously, until mixture pulls away from sides of pan, forms a ball, and leaves a white film on saucepan.

This photograph shows how paste looks just after one egg has been added. Notice how paste separates into several lumps after the addition of an egg. When stirred vigorously the paste will return to a smooth consistency.

Cream puff pastry is ready to be piped or spooned onto a baking sheet when it reaches this smooth, shiny consistency. It should be stiff enough to hold its shape when piped.

To form éclairs, pipe 5-inch strips of paste 2 inches apart on a parchment-lined baking sheet (see Chocolate Eclairs, right). To form cream puffs, pipe 2½-inch mounds of paste 2 inches apart on baking sheet (see Cream Puffs, page 163).

■ CHOCOLATE ECLAIRS

Eclairs, fingers of cream puff pastry, are filled with flavored (chocolate, praline, or coffee) pastry cream and iced with a thin, shiny glaze. They are shaped by piping the pastry onto baking sheets with a pastry bag and plain tip (see photograph at left). Several delicious variations follow this recipe. Before using the Bittersweet Chocolate Sauce, cool to 90° F; then spread 1 to 2 tablespoons on top of each éclair or finish by dipping top of each pastry into the warm icing.

   1⅓ cups Cream Puff Pastry (see page 163)
     1 egg lightly beaten with 1 teaspoon water
   1½ cups Pastry Cream (see page 251)
     ½ cup whipping cream
     1 cup Bittersweet Chocolate Sauce (at right)

1. Preheat oven to 425° F. Place Cream Puff Pastry in a large pastry bag fitted with a ¾-inch tip. Cut a piece of parchment paper to fit a baking sheet; using a dark pen or pencil, draw along the long edges of the paper two parallel lines that are 5 inches apart; then turn paper over on baking sheet.

2. To form éclairs, pipe eight 5-inch strips of pastry, 2 inches apart, onto paper-covered baking sheet, using the lines on the paper as a guide. Brush éclairs with egg-water mixture. Run the back of a fork along top of each éclair to score top and keep it flat during baking.

3. Bake 15 minutes; reduce heat to 400° F and bake 15 minutes more. Remove éclairs from oven and make a few small slits along one side of each éclair to release steam. Turn off oven; return éclairs to oven for 10 minutes, keeping oven door slightly ajar with a wooden spoon. Cool éclairs on wire racks.

4. Prepare Pastry Cream and flavor as desired. Stir cold Pastry Cream until smooth. Beat whipping cream until it holds stiff peaks and fold into Pastry Cream.

5. Just before serving (no more than 2 hours before), place filling in a pastry bag fitted with a ¼-inch tip. Poke a hole in one end of éclair with the tip and fill with 3 to 4 tablespoons of the filling. If you don't have a pastry bag, use a serrated knife to slit each éclair along one side and then spoon filling inside.

6. To ice éclairs spread 1 to 2 tablespoons warm (90° F) Bittersweet Chocolate Sauce on top of each éclair, or dip top of each éclair in warm icing. To do as much as possible in advance (up to 4 or 5 hours before serving), ice éclairs before filling them. Store iced pastries in a cool, dry place; to keep them crisp, fill them carefully just before serving.

Makes 8 éclairs.

Caramel Eclairs   Dip éclairs in a sugar syrup that has been cooked to a medium caramel color (see SUGAR AND SYRUP); cool éclairs icing side down on a cold baking sheet. Fill with vanilla- or praline-flavored Pastry Cream.

Coffee Eclairs   Fill pastries with coffee-flavored Pastry Cream. Glaze with Glacé Icing flavored with coffee or chocolate (see page 250).

Double Chocolate Eclairs   Fill pastries with Pastry Cream flavored with chocolate. Glaze with Bittersweet Chocolate Sauce or chocolate-flavored Glacé Icing (see page 250).

Mocha Eclairs   Fill pastries with Pastry Cream flavored with chocolate and coffee (to make mocha). Glaze with Bittersweet Chocolate Sauce or Glacé Icing flavored with coffee or chocolate (see page 250).

■ ICE CREAM–FILLED PROFITEROLES

Tiny cream puffs filled with ice cream and topped with a deep, rich chocolate sauce are the classic dessert: profiteroles. The sauce is everything a chocolate sauce should be, it flows easily and coats well.

   1⅓ cups Cream Puff Pastry (see page 163)
     1 egg lightly beaten with 1 teaspoon water
     1 pint vanilla or coffee ice cream

Bittersweet Chocolate Sauce

     3 tablespoons water
     3 tablespoons sugar
     6 ounces semisweet chocolate, broken into pieces
     2 ounces unsweetened chocolate, broken into pieces
     1 cup whipping cream

1. Preheat oven to 425° F. Line baking sheets with parchment paper. Attach parchment to baking sheet at corners with dots of Cream Puff Pastry. Place Cream Puff Pastry in a pastry bag fitted with a ½-inch tip. Pipe forty-eight 1-inch-diameter mounds of pastry onto paper-lined baking sheets (at least ½ inch apart). Brush each puff with egg-water mixture, flattening the top slightly.

2. Bake 10 minutes; reduce heat to 400° F and bake until crisp and brown (about 10 minutes). Remove from oven and poke a ⅛-inch hole in bottom of each puff with tip of knife or tiny pastry tip. Turn off oven; return puffs to oven until dried out (5 to 10 minutes); prop oven door slightly ajar with a wooden spoon. Cool cream puffs on wire racks.

3. To fill pastries: Place a baking sheet in freezer. Slice each puff in half horizontally. Form 48 tiny mounds (1 rounded teaspoon each) of ice cream on cooled baking sheet. Flash-freeze. Cover ice cream mounds and store in freezer until ready to fill profiteroles. Before serving, fill bottom half of each shell with one of the ice cream mounds, then cover mound with top half of shell. Place 6 to 8 filled profiteroles in each dessert bowl. Pour about 3 tablespoons warm Bittersweet Chocolate Sauce over puffs. Serve immediately.

Makes 4 dozen profiteroles, serves 8.

Bittersweet Chocolate Sauce

1. Combine the water and sugar in a saucepan; bring to a boil over low heat, stirring constantly until sugar dissolves. Remove from heat and cool to 120° F (test with an instant-read thermometer).

2. Combine semisweet and unsweetened chocolates in top of double boiler; place over hot (not boiling) water until chocolate is just melted. Remove from heat. Pour in sugar syrup (at 120° F) all at once. Stir until smooth.

3. Heat cream in a small saucepan over low heat to 120° F. Pour into chocolate mixture and stir until smooth and shiny.

▪ GOUGERE

In the Burgundy region of France, this cheese-flavored, seasoned cream puff pastry ring is a traditional specialty. Gruyère or Swiss cheese is mixed into the dough and sprinkled on top of each dough mound. Serve it as an appetizer or salad accompaniment.

> 2⅔ cups Cream Puff Pastry (see page 163)
> Pinch *each* cayenne pepper and
> freshly grated nutmeg
> 1 cup diced Gruyère or Swiss cheese

1. Preheat oven to 375° F. Prepare Cream Puff Pastry, stirring into mixture the cayenne and nutmeg just before adding flour. Mix in ¾ cup of the cheese after all the eggs have been added and mixture is smooth and shiny.

2. Spoon out dough to make 8 equal mounds in a circular shape on a parchment-lined or greased baking sheet. Sprinkle mounds with remaining ¼ cup cheese.

3. Bake until ring is well browned and crisp (40 to 45 minutes). Serve hot.

Makes 1 ring, serves 8.

Profiteroles are a variety of cream puff pastry petits fours. They make a stunning presentation and are sure to be the highlight of any party.

cessor or blender; for dry bread crumbs, use day-old (or older) slices and dry slowly in a 325° F oven until completely dried out (at least 15 to 20 minutes). Tear into pieces and process as for fresh crumbs. To make cracker crumbs, crush crackers with a rolling pin until of the desired coarseness or fineness (it's less messy if what is to be crushed is contained in a plastic bag or between sheets of waxed paper).

CRIMP, TO

To create a decorative pattern on the edge of a pie or pastry by using a fork or other tool such as a pastry crimper. This device resembles a pair of wide-armed tweezers, which grabs the dough between its "teeth." If a pie has two crusts or a lattice top, crimping will also join top and bottom crusts. The seal will be tighter if crusts are first bonded with water, milk, or beaten egg (egg yolk makes a stronger bond than a whole egg).

CRUMB, TO

To break up bread, crackers, or cookies into crumbs or to coat food with crumbs. Fresh, soft crumbs are made by processing pieces of bread (crusts removed) in a food pro-

CRUMBLE, TO

To break into small pieces with the fingers, as in crumbling blue cheese for use in a salad dressing.

CRUSH, TO

To reduce to crumbs (crackers or dried bread) or fine particles (peppercorns) by pounding with a mallet, rolling pin, or other device or machine (such as a food processor) or by grinding with a manual or electric mill. Garlic is crushed, typically with a garlic press or with a knife, to release as much of its flavor as possible.

CUBE, TO

A butchering term meaning to cut meats into measured cubes of even sizes (usually ½ or 1 inch) for use in stews. Vegetables cut this way are said to be diced; the pieces are usually smaller.

CUCUMBER

The cucumber is a gourd of the same family as pumpkin, zucchini, and other squashes. There are basically two types of cucumbers: pickling varieties and slicing varieties. Pickling varieties, such as the gherkin, the American dill, and the *cornichon* (small French pickle), are relatively small. The gherkin and the cornichon are rarely more than 2 inches long, the American dill rarely more than 4 inches. All of the varieties have dark green skin with knobby warts or spines.

Slicing cucumbers may be either outdoor varieties with seeds or greenhouse varieties, such as the long, thin-skinned English cucumber, which has few seeds. Outdoor varieties have a smooth, dark green skin and are usually about 8 inches long and 1½ inches wide, tapering at each end. The skin is often waxed to prolong shelf life. Greenhouse varieties, such as the English cucumber, are about 12 to 15 inches long.

Other commercially available slicing cucumbers include the round, pale yellow lemon cucumber, which has a very mild flavor, and the Japanese cucumber, a narrow, thin-skinned variety with few seeds.

Cucumbers have a crisp texture, a moist, cool flesh, and a mild flavor. Pickling cucumbers are appreciated for their crisp, firm texture, slicing varieties for their refreshing, juicy flavor.

Use Pickling cucumbers are packed in brine for use as a relish. Slicing cucumbers add crunchy texture and cool flavor to salads and sandwiches; they may also be steamed or sautéed and eaten as a vegetable. Cucumbers, hot or cold, have a particular affinity for fish and are often used to garnish salmon dishes. In Japan, cooks use cucumbers in sushi and cold salads, and in England, tea wouldn't be tea without cucumber sandwiches.

Availability Slicing cucumbers are available all year but peak season is the summer months. Most pickling cucumbers are sold only during the summer months. Many of the greenhouse varieties are wrapped in plastic to prevent dehydration.

Selection Choose firm cucumbers without soft spots. With the exception of lemon cucumbers, they should have a solid green color without signs of yellowing or puffiness.

Storage Keep cucumbers in refrigerator crisper for up to one week.

Preparation Pickling cucumbers should be scrubbed to remove loose spines. Greenhouse slicing cucumbers do not need to be peeled or seeded. Outdoor varieties may be peeled and seeded or not, as desired. Waxed cucumbers, however, should be peeled.

To seed a cucumber, slice it in half lengthwise and scrape out the seeds with a small spoon.

■ SWEET-AND-SOUR CUCUMBER SALAD

This dressing is also good with carrots, beets, cabbage, and zucchini. Also see the sour cream variation.

    ¼ cup cider vinegar
    1 teaspoon sugar
    ½ teaspoon salt
    ¼ teaspoon white pepper
    2 English cucumbers, sliced
    1 small red onion, diced

In a medium bowl whisk vinegar, sugar, salt, and pepper. Stir in cucumber slices and onion to coat with dressing. Cover and chill 2 hours.

Serves 6.

Sour Cream Cucumber Salad Stir ½ cup sour cream and 1 tablespoon dried dill into dressing.

Recipes and Related Information
Bread and Butter Pickles, 321; Cucumber-Mint Sauce, 294; Dill Spears, 322; Jam, Jelly, Preserve, and Condiment, 316; Pickle, Commercial, 430.

CUMIN

Native to the eastern Mediterranean, cumin is the tiny aromatic seed of a plant in the parsley family. The amber seed is about ⅛ to ¼ inch long and resembles caraway. Its aroma and flavor are very pungent, spicy, and sharp.

Use Cumin is widely used in Latin American cuisines and is the predominant flavor in many Latin sauces, soups, and stews. Cumin flavors Moroccan lentil soup and tomato salads, Texas chili (it is an ingredient in most chili powders), and Indian curries. The French serve cumin seed with Muenster cheese.

Availability Cumin can be purchased whole or ground, in bulk or packaged in airtight jars or tins.

Selection Packaged seasonings lose quality after a while; try to buy from a store that restocks its spice section fairly often.

Storage Keep in an airtight container in a cool, dry, dark place. Replace ground cumin every six months; cumin seed will keep indefinitely.

Preparation Freshly toasted and ground cumin seed is much more aromatic than purchased ground cumin.

Toast seeds in a skillet over low heat, shaking pan constantly, until they are aromatic and just begin to smoke; do not allow to burn. Grind in a clean coffee grinder or electric minichopper or with a mortar and pestle.

Recipes and Related Information
Cilantro Chutney, 130; Hummus, 418; Pakoras, 106.

CURDLING

This is the often undesirable state when a mixture containing egg, milk, or cream separates into solids and liquid. Curdling can be a sign of spoilage in milk, temporary or permanent failure of Hollandaise sauce, or complete failure of custards, but is the first step in making cheese and the process by which cultured crème fraîche is produced. The villain (when there is one) is usually heat or acid.

In the presence of heat, proteins in egg (and to a lesser degree in milk or cream) slowly form a gel (a semisolid network that traps liquid and serves as a thickening agent). When overheated, the gel clumps (shrinks into curds) and the liquid is squeezed out of the gel—resulting in a curdled custard or sauce. An acid acts on milk or cream in a similar manner, causing it to thicken or even produce clumps, for example, when cream and fruit are combined. Sometimes this process is intentional: crème fraîche, a French cultured cream, is purposely curdled by adding an acid-producing bacterial culture to pasteurized whipping cream. It can be made at home by adding buttermilk, an acid, to cream.

To avoid curdling, the key is control. Heat these mixtures slowly to set the protein and keep stirring to break up clumps of protein as they begin to form. You want the proteins to start to solidify—that is the thickening process—but not more than necessary. When adding eggs to a hot liquid, first mix some of the liquid slowly into the eggs to bring up their temperature; then add warmed egg mixture to hot liquid.

CURE, TO

To preserve foods, particularly meats and fish. Most curing involves a brine, which is a mixture of salt and other ingredients. By effecting chemical changes in the food, the brine protects it from harmful bacterial growth.

There are two basic types of brines, a dry and a wet. A sugar-cure is perhaps the best-known dry brine; a sugar-salt mixture is rubbed on a food, which is then packed tightly, weighted slightly, and turned every few days until the cure is completed. Prosciutto, bacon, and *gravlax,* the Scandinavian salmon dish, are sugar-cured.

A wet cure uses a brining stock made with water, salt, and flavorings; a food is covered in the brining liquid until cured. Corned beef is wet-cured. Saltpeter (sodium nitrate or potassium nitrate) is usually added to preserve color. Most smoked foods are first brined to add flavor and to help preserve them. Pickling, curing, and brining are very similar processes.

Recipes and Related Information
Beef, 39; Gravlax, 233.

CURRANT

The currant is the small round berrylike fruit of a prickly shrub. It is probably native to Scandinavia, where it is still a popular fruit; it is also much appreciated in England and Germany. Although currants have been cultivated in America, cultivation is now discouraged—and in some areas forbidden—because the shrub is host to a parasite that kills neighboring white pines.

Currants may be red, white, or black. All are tart but the former two may be eaten raw with sugar; the black variety is too bitter to eat fresh. The small, raisinlike dried Zante currant is actually a grape but is discussed here.

Use Fresh red or white currants may be eaten with cream and sugar; along with the black variety, they may be cooked with sugar and made into pie fillings, puddings, dessert sauces, jams, and jellies. Red currant jelly is stirred into Cumberland sauce, an English sauce for game. It's also used to fill jelly rolls and Danish pastry, to fill and glaze baked apples or pears, and to sweeten braised red cabbage. Black currants are made into jams and jellies; in France they are made into a nonalcoholic syrup called *sirop de cassis* and an alcohol-based liqueur called *crème de cassis,* used in French apéritifs.

Dried Zante currants add sweetness to cakes, cookies, breads, and scones. They may be used whenever raisins are called for.

Availability Fresh currants are rarely available commercially. Specialty produce markets may occasionally carry them in July and August. Currant jelly is widely sold packed in jars; whole currants packed in light syrup are available in some specialty food stores.

Fresh Zante currants are not widely distributed commercially but may be found in some specialty markets in midsummer. Dried Zante currants are available in bulk or packed in boxes.

Storage Keep fresh currants in a plastic bag in the refrigerator and use within a couple of days. They may be frozen for up to two months. Store dried Zante currants in an airtight container; they will keep indefinitely.

Preparation When using fresh currants, discard any crushed or bruised fruit, wash, dry, and remove stems.

CUSTARD

Beloved by children of all ages, custard is a mixture of eggs, milk, sugar, salt, and flavoring, either gently cooked on top of the stove until thickened but still pourable (stirred custard), or slowly baked until firm (baked custard). Although a seemingly simple food, custard is temperamental and must be assembled and cooked with great care and attention. It is such a classic dish, with so many applications, that all cooks should develop a level of comfort with its preparation.

Stirred custard, also known as *crème anglaise*, is used as a sauce, as a pastry filling, and as the base for many chilled and frozen desserts, including ice cream and Bavarian cream. Baked custard is wonderful simply garnished with fresh fruit or whipped cream, or bathed in caramelized sugar syrup as in the famous French dessert *crème caramel* and its Latin counterpart, flan.

Made properly, custard is creamy and tender, not the curdled or weepy mess that has frustrated most cooks at one time or another. Custards thicken because egg proteins jell (form a semisolid network that enmeshes liquid) in the presence of heat. As a general rule, 1 whole egg or 2 egg yolks will thicken 1 cup milk. Problems occur when mixture is cooked too quickly and at too high a temperature. Always cook custards slowly and with gentle heat.

Stirred custards usually take about 10 to 12 minutes to thicken. Don't rush the process by raising the temperature. The line between a thickened custard and a curdled one is often only a few degrees of heat. Protect stirred custards by using a double boiler over hot, but never boiling, water. Keep stirring throughout cooking time to break up and evenly disperse the gel as it forms; this action will develop a thick mixture that is not rigid or lumpy. A custard has thickened sufficiently when it leaves a velvety coat on the back of a spoon and if a track made by running a finger down the coated spoon stays clear. It will have the consistency of cream whipped to soft peaks. Remove finished custard from heat immediately as it will continue to thicken as it cools. Strain into a bowl to achieve a smooth texture (for the same reason, strain baked custards before pouring into baking dish). Set pan in a bowl of ice or ice water to stop cooking. If you think custard has overheated, add a few slivers of ice to lower temperature. If the custard starts to curdle while cooking, remove from heat immediately and beat.

Although baked custards aren't stirred, they still must be prepared with care. They need to cook in a moderate oven and should be insulated from the heat by being set in a pan of hot water (a bain-marie or hot water bath). They are done when the center still jiggles slightly and a knife inserted halfway between center and edge comes out clean. Another test is to touch the surface with your finger; if it comes away clean, custard is ready. When properly cooked, texture is smooth and fine. An overheated baked custard is watery.

■ STIRRED CUSTARD
Crème anglaise

This is the basic vanilla custard sauce. It can be used right away or held in the refrigerator. For additional flavor, add 2 tablespoons orange-flavored liqueur (or liqueur of choice) to the finished sauce.

- **2 cups milk**
- **½ vanilla bean *or* 1 teaspoon vanilla extract**
- **4 egg yolks**
- **3 tablespoons sugar**

1. If using vanilla bean, bring milk to a boil with bean in a heavy-bottomed saucepan, remove from heat, and let sit for 10 to 15 minutes to infuse milk with vanilla flavor. If using extract, it is added later; bring milk without flavoring to a boil.

2. In a medium bowl beat yolks and sugar together until thickened and lemon-colored. Add milk, stirring to combine well.

3. Turn mixture into a double boiler or return to same saucepan and cook over low heat, stirring, until it thickens and coats back of a spoon (about 10 minutes; a finger drawn across back of spoon should leave a trail). Remove custard from heat and strain through a fine sieve into a clean bowl set over ice to stop cooking; if using vanilla extract, stir in. Note that if using vanilla bean, which has now been strained out of custard, it can be put back into custard to enhance flavor further, or it can be washed, dried, and stored for later use.

4. Use custard immediately as a sauce, or refrigerate, with plastic wrap laid on surface to prevent a skin from forming, for up to 24 hours.

Makes about 2 cups.

■ BAKED CUSTARD

This is true comfort food, enriched with the addition of extra egg yolks. For a smooth consistency, remember to strain the custard before putting into the baking dish. Baked custard may be served immediately after cooking or set in the refrigerator to chill.

- **2 eggs**
- **2 egg yolks**
- **2 cups milk**
- **3 tablespoons sugar**
- **Vanilla extract or freshly grated nutmeg, to taste**

1. Preheat oven to 350° F. In a medium bowl beat eggs, egg yolks, milk, sugar, and vanilla together; strain through a sieve into a 1-quart baking dish or soufflé dish.

2. Set in a larger pan and fill pan with enough hot water to reach halfway up sides of baking dish. Bake until just set (30 to 35 minutes; center will be slightly wobbly). Serve warm, or refrigerate and serve chilled.

Serves 4 to 5.

A hot water bath (bain-marie) is used for Baked Chocolate Custard to ensure very gentle cooking and to guard against overheating.

■ BAKED CHOCOLATE CUSTARD
Petit pots de crème

Little porcelain custard pots with matching lids have given their name to the rich custard dish that is served in them. The most common flavor for this custard is chocolate, although coffee and vanilla are other popular choices. The custards must chill for several hours or overnight; they will keep up to one day, covered, in the refrigerator.

> 6 ounces semisweet chocolate, chopped
> 3 cups half-and-half
> 1 vanilla bean
> 1 egg
> 8 egg yolks
> ⅓ cup sugar
> 2 teaspoons instant coffee powder dissolved in 2 tablespoons hot water

1. Preheat oven to 325° F. Melt chocolate in a double boiler over hot, but not boiling, water. In a medium, heavy-bottomed saucepan, bring half-and-half to a boil with vanilla bean, remove from heat, and let sit for 10 to 15 minutes to let milk infuse with vanilla flavor.

2. In a medium bowl beat egg, yolks, and sugar until thickened and lemon-colored. Add milk, stirring to combine well. Add dissolved coffee and warm, melted chocolate. Stir well to combine into a creamy mixture. Strain mixture through a sieve into a pitcher and skim off any bubbles or foam from surface. Fill 7 individual molds (5 ounces each) or 8 *pots de crème;* set custards in a baking dish or pan and fill with enough hot water to reach halfway up sides of molds.

3. Bake until set (35 to 40 minutes). Remove from oven and cool to room temperature; cover and refrigerate at least 3 hours, or overnight. Serve lightly chilled.

Serves 8.

■ CREME CARAMEL

The Spanish counterpart for this satiny smooth, syrup-drenched, baked French custard is flan. Note that the dish must be prepared at least six hours in advance of serving, and preferably the day before.

> ½ cup sugar
> ¼ cup water
> Baked Custard (opposite page)

1. In a small, heavy-bottomed saucepan, dissolve sugar in the water over low heat (stir only until dissolved; do not stir while it colors). As soon as sugar is dissolved, raise heat to a boil and cook until it turns light brown (8 to 10 minutes). Remove caramel from heat and pour into a 1-quart ovenproof baking dish or soufflé dish. Set aside.

2. Prepare Baked Custard through step 1. Strain through a sieve onto reserved caramel. Bake as for Baked Custard. Cool and refrigerate for at least 6 hours, or preferably overnight (you will have more caramel syrup if you make the dish a day in advance).

Serves 4 to 5.

CREME BRULEE

This famous dessert, also known as burnt cream or Trinity cream, is a rich custard protected by a sugary crust broiled golden brown. England claims it as its own, although its lineage is often debated. It is a standard dish on the menu at celebratory dinners at Trinity College in Cambridge, where it is said to have originated.

- 3 cups whipping cream
- 1 vanilla bean, split
- 6 egg yolks
- 3 tablespoons granulated sugar
- 1½ cups superfine or brown sugar, for topping

1. *To make custard:* In a medium, heavy-bottomed saucepan, bring cream to a boil with vanilla bean, remove from heat, and let sit for 10 to 15 minutes to infuse milk with vanilla flavor.

2. In a medium bowl beat yolks and granulated sugar together until thickened and lemon-colored. Add warm cream, stirring to combine well.

3. Turn mixture into a double boiler or return to same saucepan and cook over low heat, stirring, until mixture thickens and coats back of a spoon (about 10 minutes; a finger drawn across back of spoon should leave a trail). Remove custard from heat and strain through a fine sieve into a clean bowl. (Vanilla bean can be washed, dried, and stored for later use.)

4. Pour into a 3-cup shallow baking dish or 4 individual 5-ounce molds. Chill 2 to 3 hours, or overnight.

5. *To make sugar crust:* Preheat broiler. Remove custard from refrigerator; sieve superfine sugar over custard. Brown sugar under broiler until caramelized; watch carefully so that sugar doesn't burn (to keep custards cold while they broil, set them in a tray of ice, if desired). Chill until ready to serve.

Serves 4.

Variation For a firmer custard use 2 whole eggs and 4 egg yolks instead of all yolks.

BAVARIAN CREAM

When a stirred custard is lightened with whipped cream and set with gelatin, it becomes a delightful chilled dessert called Bavarian Cream. Shape in a lightly oiled mold or use as a filling for desserts such as Charlotte Russe (at right) or Lemon Roulade Charlotte (see page 171). The filling for the Charlotte Russe is a basic vanilla Bavarian; if desired, substitute 2 tablespoons rum, orange-flavored liqueur, or other liqueur for the vanilla extract. To use by itself, spoon into a 4- to 5-cup oiled mold and chill four hours or overnight. For a fruit-flavored Bavarian cream, use the Lemon Bavarian Cream filling recipe from Lemon Roulade Charlotte and substitute an equal amount of lightly sweetened, puréed fruit for the Lemon Curd. Spoon into an oiled 4- to 5-quart mold and chill four hours, or overnight.

For a particularly effective presentation, layer two colors of Bavarian cream in one mold or marble two of contrasting colors, such as vanilla and strawberry.

CHARLOTTE RUSSE

A special tinned steel charlotte mold with flaring sides is traditional for this dish, but any ovenproof dish of the proper size will work.

- 24 to 30 ladyfingers (see page 84 and Note, below)
- 2 cups whipping cream
- 4 egg yolks
- ⅓ cup sugar
- 1 envelope unflavored gelatin
- 2 tablespoons water
- 1 tablespoon vanilla extract
- 1 cup Chantilly Cream (see page 252), for decoration
  Raspberry or Strawberry Sauce (see page 522), for accompaniment

1. Tightly line a 6-cup charlotte mold or soufflé dish with ladyfingers, standing them on end, sides touching. Cover with plastic wrap and set aside. Whip 1 cup whipping cream to soft peaks and set aside.

2. In a medium, heavy-bottomed saucepan, bring remaining cup of cream to a boil. In a medium bowl beat yolks and sugar together until thickened and lemon-colored. Add cream to yolk mixture and stir well.

3. Turn mixture into a double boiler or return to same saucepan, and cook over low heat, stirring, until mixture thickens and coats back of a spoon (about 10 minutes; a finger drawn across back of spoon should leave a trail). Remove custard from heat and strain through a fine sieve into a clean bowl set over ice to stop cooking.

4. In a small saucepan sprinkle gelatin over the water and let stand to soften; dissolve over low heat (3 to 4 minutes). Pour into warm custard and stir to blend thoroughly. Add vanilla and keep stirring until mixture is on point of setting (it will have the consistency of cream whipped to soft peaks); fold in whipped cream.

5. Pour mixture into lined mold, smooth top, cover, and refrigerate until set (2 to 4 hours). Any leftover ladyfingers can be crumbled and sprinkled over top of custard before refrigerating.

6. To serve, unmold charlotte by carefully running a knife between ladyfingers and mold. Invert onto a serving platter. Pipe rosettes of Chantilly Cream around top edge (if desired), and spoon a pool of Raspberry or Strawberry Sauce around bottom of charlotte.

Serves 6.

Note If using packaged ladyfingers that are a little sticky, sprinkle them with sugar before lining mold.

LEMON ROULADE CHARLOTTE

This is a spectacular rolled charlotte. Although the preparation takes time, so much of it can be, or needs to be, done in advance that it's actually a good party dessert. Use lemon or any flavor Bavarian cream (see opposite page) and fill with a fruit preserve instead of the Lemon Curd.

   1 **Basic Sponge Cake Roll (see page 83)**
   1 **cup Lemon Curd (see page 252)**
      Basic Glaze (use apricot preserves; see page 250), for topping
      Raspberry Sauce (see page 522), for accompaniment

Lemon Bavarian Cream

   1 **cup whipping cream**
 1½ **cups milk**
      Grated rind of 1 lemon
   4 **egg yolks**
 ⅓ **cup sugar**
   1 **envelope unflavored gelatin**
 ½ **cup fresh lemon juice**
 1½ **cups Lemon Curd (see page 252)**

1. As smoothly as possible, line a round-bottomed 1½- to 2-quart bowl or mold with aluminum foil. On flat Sponge Cake Roll, evenly spread Lemon Curd, stopping 1 inch from each edge. Gently roll up, jelly-roll fashion. Cut into ½-inch slices. Lay slices in lined mold, beginning in center and working out to make a complete, balanced shell (save any leftover slices and lay over filling). Cover and set aside.

2. Pour Lemon Bavarian Cream into cake-lined mold, cover, and refrigerate 4 hours, preferably overnight.

3. To serve, unmold by laying a serving platter on top and inverting; lift off foil-lined mold. Brush with Apricot Glaze. Serve as is or with Raspberry Sauce (if desired).

Serves 8.

Lemon Bavarian Cream

1. Whip cream to soft peaks and set aside. In a heavy-bottomed saucepan bring milk and lemon rind to a boil. In a medium bowl beat yolks and sugar together until thickened and lemon-colored; combine with milk.

2. Turn mixture into a double boiler or return to same saucepan and cook over low heat, stirring, until mixture thickens and coats back of a spoon (about 10 minutes). Remove custard from heat and strain through a fine sieve into a clean bowl set over ice to stop cooking.

3. In a small saucepan sprinkle gelatin over lemon juice and let stand to soften; dissolve over low heat (3 to 4 minutes). Pour into warm custard and stir to blend thoroughly. When custard is cool, add 1½ cups Lemon Curd, stirring continually until mixture is on point of setting (it will have the consistency of cream whipped to soft peaks); fold in whipped cream.

ZABAGLIONE

Zabaglione is an Italian wine custard; sabayon is the French counterpart. Serve the frothy whipped egg custard warm or cold with crunchy *biscotti* for textural contrast, or spoon it over sliced strawberries.

   6 **egg yolks**
 ½ **cup sugar**
 ½ **to 1 cup Marsala, sherry, or Madeira**
      Sliced strawberries, or Biscotti (see page 8), for accompaniment

1. Whisk egg yolks, sugar, and wine in a double boiler over simmering water. Whisk by hand or with electric mixer until mixture doubles in volume and is very smooth and fluffy.

2. Serve immediately with strawberries or Biscotti. Mixture is unstable and will separate if left standing. To serve it cold, set over ice and continue whisking until chilled. It will then hold for about 3 hours; serve as is, or fold in whipped cream, or gelatin and whipped cream.

Serves 4 to 6.

CUT IN, TO

To mix solid fat (butter, solid vegetable shortening, or lard, or a combination) and dry ingredients (flour, mixed with any or all of the following: salt, baking powder, baking soda, sugar) with a cutting motion. The process, used when making pastry, whittles the fat into smaller and smaller flour-coated pieces by the action of a pastry blender, two knives, a fork, the fingers, or the metal blade of a food processor, until reduced to the desired texture. *Rub in* is another recipe term that has the same meaning, but this process is done with the fingertips.

To develop flakiness, fat is left in relatively large pieces, usually described as coarse crumbs or small peas, rather than being ground so fine that it merges with the flour. As pie crust or biscuits bake, particles of fat melt and create empty spaces that fill with steam and expand. This expansion causes pie crust or biscuit to rise, and creates layers of crust or crumb called the flake. Large particles of fat leave bigger air pockets and create a lighter, more flaky pastry or biscuit; fine particles hardly leave a trace and produce a dense, sandy pastry or a biscuit that lacks characteristic texture.

Work with chilled fat and utensils (even the fingers, especially on a hot day). If fat starts to melt, briefly chill mixture; try not to heat the room with other cooking. Work quickly but gently so as not to toughen dough.

Recipes and Related Information
Biscuit, 49; Cake and Pastry Tools, 91; Pie and Tart, 431.

D&E

When deep-frying, use a wire skimmer to scoop food out of the hot fat; the open mesh lets the fat drain off the food and back into the pot. A deep-fat thermometer helps the cook monitor the temperature of the oil.

DASH

There are many arguments about what constitutes a dash. For dry seasonings such as ground cayenne pepper and chili powder, a dash is best described as a small pinch—what can be held between one finger and the thumb. For liquid seasonings, it's a few drops shaken from the bottle.

DATE

The ancient date palm, cultivated in the Sahara from Neolithic times, produces a glossy oval fruit that is as sweet as candy. Fresh dates are generally about 1 inch to 1½ inches long and ½ to ¾ inch wide. They have a thin golden skin; moist, sweet golden flesh; and a small brown pit. Most dates are marketed in their dried state, however. Dried dates are a darker brown with chewier, drier flesh and an almost candylike sweetness.

The date palm ripens fruit only in warm arid climates. Today most of the world's crop comes from Iraq, although most dates eaten in America are grown in the Coachella Valley in California. The main variety is the Deglet Noor, although the Medjool—a large and exceptionally moist variety—is increasingly grown in California.

Use   Dates may be eaten out of hand as a snack or dessert. They may be pitted and stuffed with marzipan or whole nuts; wrapped with bacon or stuffed with sausage and broiled; chopped and used to sweeten cakes, cookies, stuffings, breads, muffins, cooked cereals, and fruit salads. Moroccan cooks add dates to salads and stews.

Availability   The fresh crop is available from September through May, with peak supplies in November. Dried dates are sold the year around, in bulk or packed in plastic bags or boxes. Packaged pitted dates are also readily available.

Selection   Look for plump, lustrous dates with a rich golden brown color.

Storage   Keep soft fresh dates in the refrigerator in a plastic bag and use within one week. Dried dates will keep indefinitely if wrapped airtight and refrigerated.

Preparation   Unpitted dates are usually pitted before use, although Moroccan cooks add them whole to stews.

Recipes and Related Information
Date Filling, 627; Dried Fruit, 184.

DEEP-FRY, TO

To cook food in deep, hot fat. As down-home as crisply fried fritters, as formal as chicken Kiev, deep-fried foods have wide appeal and can assume a multitude of guises.

Most people love the crunchiness of these foods but often hesitate to prepare them at home. Yet deep-frying is neither complicated nor difficult. Fried foods have a bad name, but it is not all deserved. Improperly frying foods can cause a lot of oil absorption, making them both unappetizing and unhealthful; but good technique prevents this. The keys to good frying are the quality of the oil, its temperature, and the coating on the foods to be fried.

OIL AND TEMPERATURE CONTROL

The best oil for frying is a clear, relatively flavorless vegetable oil with a high smoke point (that is, an ability to withstand high temperatures without burning). Oil temperature is critical. For best results the oil should be between 360° and 390° F. At this temperature, the batter or other coating seals almost instantly, preventing any further oil absorption. Oil that is too hot can burn the outside of the food before the inside is fully cooked. The oil itself will begin to burn at over 400° F, giving a burnt flavor to the food. Oil that is too cool is equally bad; below 350° F, the food will absorb a lot of oil before it is cooked.

To control oil temperature, either fry in a thermostatically controlled deep-fryer or use a thermometer specially made for deep-frying and candy making (see THERMOMETER). To keep the temperature up during frying, do not try to fry too many pieces of food at a time. Watch the temperature: If it drops below 350° F and does not recover quickly, you are frying too much food for the quantity of oil. One obvious solution is to use as much oil as you can safely and conveniently. Be careful, however, to leave enough room for the oil to bubble up during frying. As a general rule, the frying container should be no more than two-thirds full of oil.

Oil can be used three or four times before it is no longer suitable for cooking. Oil will last longer if particles of food are skimmed off after each batch of food has been fried. To store, cool the oil in the pot, strain through cheesecloth, and keep in the refrigerator for up to three months. Check for rancidity before using (see RANCIDITY).

COATINGS FOR DEEP-FRIED FOODS

In general, a coating shields the food from the oil. Because deep-fried foods come into contact with more fat than foods that are sautéed or stir-fried, there is a greater chance of overabsorption of the fat. The cook can prevent overabsorption by maintaining the proper cooking temperature and by sealing the food with a protective coating. There are three basic types of coating: Flour is the simplest one and forms a thin, crisp crust; the second type, which adds extra insulation, is a dipping of food in flour, egg, and bread crumbs, which form a crunchy barrier that preserves the moistness of the food within; the third alternative, fritter batter, forms a fluffy coating.

DEEP-FRYING TECHNIQUE

Deep-frying is most suitable for pieces of chicken, seafood, and vegetables. Foods to be deep-fried must be similar in size and thickness so all will cook at the same rate. They must be dry and at room temperature. Lower food into the hot oil gently; to avoid splashing hot oil, do not drop the food from a height. A slotted spoon, wire skimmer, or basket insert is best for removing the cooked food from the pan. Hold the spoon or other utensil containing fried food over the oil for a few seconds to drain, and then transfer to a plate or tray lined with paper towels to drain further. If frying many items, transfer the cooked pieces to a low-heat oven to keep warm.

To proceed, follow the general frying guidelines outlined in FRY.

THE DEEP-FRY PANTRY

The basic requirements for deep-frying are mainly coatings and oils. If you're going to be doing a fair bit of deep-frying and have extra storage space, you may want to purchase a fry basket, a slotted spoon, a spoon rest, and a deep-fat thermometer. These tools are a help in mastering the process.

In the Refrigerator   Eggs, beer, milk, yeast.

On the Shelf   Flour; cornstarch; dry bread crumbs; baking powder; salt, pepper, and other seasonings; vegetable oil; solid vegetable shortening; wine.

Equipment   Kettle with wire basket insert and lid (the pot should have a flat bottom for stability), or an electric fryer; a deep-fat thermometer; a slotted spoon or wire skimmer; a spoon rest; paper towels.

▦ PAPER-WRAPPED CHICKEN

Bite-sized pieces of chicken fried inside a wrapper of paper or aluminum foil are a popular Chinese appetizer. Marinades for the chicken can be complicated mixtures of condiments, or a simple combination such as the following. Parchment paper suitable for cooking is available at well-stocked supermarkets and cookware stores. Note that the chicken pieces must marinate at least 30 minutes and up to several hours.

1   **chicken breast half, skinned, boned, and cut into ½-inch cubes**
1   **tablespoon *each* soy sauce and Shaoxing wine or dry sherry**
1   **tablespoon grated fresh ginger**
1   **teaspoon sesame oil**
    Oil, for deep-frying

1. Combine chicken, soy sauce, wine, ginger, and sesame oil; marinate for 30 minutes to several hours. Cut eighteen 4-inch squares of parchment paper or aluminum foil.

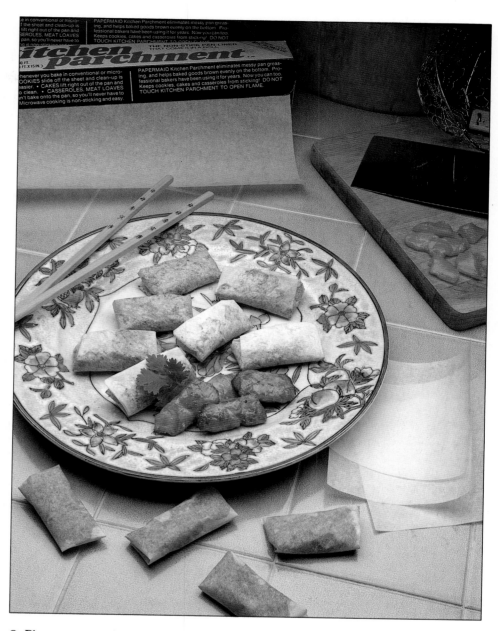

2. Place a square of paper on work surface, one corner facing you ("south"). Place 2 or 3 chicken cubes across center of square. Fold south corner over chicken to ½ inch from north corner. Crease fold. Fold in east and west corners so that they overlap each other, and crease edges. Fold whole package toward north, forming an envelope shape. Tuck north corner into envelope and crease to seal. Repeat folding procedure with remaining packages.

3. In a wok or other deep pan, heat oil to 375° F. Fry chicken packages, a few at a time, until paper turns golden brown (about 1 minute). To facilitate unwrapping, slit open each package along folded edge before serving. To undo package and eat contents, use fingers or chopsticks.

Serves 4 to 8 as an appetizer (2 to 4 pieces per serving).

Deep-fried packets of Paper-Wrapped Chicken are easily unwrapped with the fingers. Inside are juicy, tender pieces of ginger-flavored chicken breast.

HOW TO DEGLAZE

The instructions given here for making a deglazing sauce are based on Chicken Breasts With Sherry, Cream, and Mushrooms (see page 611). Sauté the lightly floured chicken breasts in the butter.

Transfer browned breasts to warmed plates. In the same skillet, sauté aromatic ingredients—mushrooms, garlic, and green onions. As they cook, scrape up any bits of chicken or flour stuck to the pan.

Add wine and boil vigorously to reduce in volume and cook away alcohol; add cream and reduce sauce again. Season to taste.

■ COUNTRY FRIED CHICKEN

This version of a classic southern preparation comes from North Carolina. The cook insists that its special flavor is the result of salting the bird a day ahead of frying.

>   2 whole frying chickens, cut up
>   Salt
>   1 cup milk
>   1 egg
>   2 cups flour
>   2 tablespoons paprika
>   2 teaspoons salt
>   1 teaspoon ground white pepper
>   Dash cayenne pepper
>   5 cups (approximately) solid vegetable
>   shortening, for frying

1. One day ahead of serving, wash chicken pieces and pat dry. Lightly salt, and refrigerate 12 to 24 hours.

2. Two hours before serving, mix together milk and egg in a small bowl. In a sturdy plastic bag sift together flour, paprika, salt, white pepper, and cayenne.

3. Dip chicken pieces in egg-milk mixture; then shake pieces in plastic bag to coat with flour; shake off excess flour. Place chicken on a rack and let stand 30 minutes to allow coating to set.

4. In a kettle or deep-fryer over medium-high heat, melt shortening and bring to 365° F (use a deep-fat thermometer).

5. Gently slip chicken into hot fat and fry until golden brown on both sides (about 15 minutes per side). With a slotted spoon remove chicken pieces from pan to a rack lined with paper towels to drain.

Serves 6 to 8.

■ FRITTO MISTO WITH CAPER MAYONNAISE

A traditional Italian Christmas Eve food, *fritto misto* means mixed fry. Use any combination of fish and shellfish and serve as part of a buffet with an assortment of salads.

>   2 cups flour
>   2 teaspoons fresh rosemary *or*
>   1 teaspoon dried rosemary
> 1¼ teaspoons salt
>   2 tablespoons dry sherry
>   2 tablespoons vegetable oil
> 1½ cups water
>   1 pound squid, cleaned
>   12 small smelt
>   ½ pound angler, cut in ¼-inch medallions
>   1 pound shrimp, cleaned
>   Salt and freshly ground pepper
>   4 to 6 tablespoons fresh lemon juice
>   Oil, for deep-frying
>   Lemon wedges (optional)

Caper Mayonnaise

>   1 cup Mayonnaise (see page 519)
>   3 tablespoons fresh lemon juice
>   ¼ cup capers, drained

1. In a large bowl combine flour, rosemary, and the 1¼ teaspoons salt. Add sherry and 2 tablespoons oil to the water. Beat water mixture into flour mixture until smooth. Cover and let batter rest 1 hour.

2. Cut bodies of squid into 1-inch circles. Leave tentacles whole. Lay squid pieces, smelt, angler, and shrimp on a platter. Sprinkle with salt, pepper, and lemon juice. Let stand for 5 minutes; then pat dry.

3. In a kettle or deep-fryer heat oil to 375° F. Dip fish and shellfish into batter, then gently slip a few pieces at a time into hot oil to deep-fry. Cook until golden. Remove with a slotted spoon and drain on paper towels. Keep pieces in a warm (200° F) oven until all are fried.

4. Serve with lemon wedges or Caper Mayonnaise.

Serves 8 to 10.

Caper Mayonnaise   Prepare Mayonnaise; whisk together with fresh lemon juice and drained capers until well blended.

> ***Recipes and Related Information***
> *Batter, 27; Cookware, 151; Fat, 216; Oil, 394.*

DEGLAZE, TO

To pour liquid—water, stock, wine, or liquor—into a pan in which food has been roasted or sautéed in order to absorb the glaze and the browned, crusty bits formed on the bottom of the pan. These concentrated, coagulated meat essences add wonderful flavor to a dish or sauce.

To deglaze, remove meat from pan. If more than a thin film of fat remains in the pan, discard excess. Pour one of the above liquids into the pan and cook over high heat, scraping bottom of pan to loosen drippings into the liquid. From this point, a sauce can be made. It can be simple—using a mix of fresh lemon juice and stock—or rich, with whipping cream and grated cheeses. A variety of flavorings, from tomatoes and fresh herbs to mustard and soy sauce, can add excitement to deglazed sauces. As you become comfortable with this method, you will be able to create your own sauces. See photographs at left.

> ***Recipes and Related Information***
> *Chicken Breasts With Sherry, Cream, and Mushrooms, 611; Drippings, 186; Sauce, 512; Stock and Soup, 558; Wine in Cooking, 608.*

DEGREASE, TO

To remove grease from roasting pans (being careful to leave the drippings in the pan), and to remove congealed fat from chilled stock, stews, or essences. Skimming fat is essentially the same as degreasing.

There are several ways to degrease a pan. *With a ladle or serving spoon:* Use a ladle for stocks and large quantities of liquid; use a spoon for sauces and small quantities. Stir the surface of the liquid to force fat to the edges of the pan; don't stir below the surface or the fat will be mixed with the other liquid. Tilting the ladle slightly, dip edge into layer of fat just enough so that fat streams into bowl of ladle or spoon. Move ladle around perimeter until full; repeat until all fat is spooned off. With a spoon, tip the pan to make a pool of fat, slide spoon in, and fill. *With a skimmer:* The wire mesh or perforated-metal skimmer is a cleanup tool used to catch any fat that remains after degreasing with a ladle or spoon. Use as you would a spoon, tipping the pan to pool the little fat that may remain. Slide skimmer into pan and trap fat. *With filter paper:* A coffee filter (or paper towel) can be used to soak up small amounts of fat. Lay paper on surface and let it absorb fat; pull away and repeat as needed. *By chilling:* Bring stock, sauce, or soup to room temperature; cover and chill until fat hardens, then carefully spoon off solid fat. See photographs at right.

Recipes and Related Information
Stew, 555; Stock and Soup, 558.

DEVEIN, TO

To remove the black intestinal vein that runs along the outside curve of a shrimp (see photograph, page 537). This often cosmetic procedure is usually unnecessary on small- or medium-sized shrimp. On larger shrimp, the vein contains grit that would interfere with the taste and should be removed. To devein, slit shrimp along the back with a sharp knife or a deveining tool and pull away vein. Sometimes the vein snaps; to remove the pieces, hold shrimp under cold running water and vein will wash away.

DICE, TO

To cut into even, tiny cubes. Dicing results in smaller pieces than does chopping but larger than with mincing. This term refers primarily to vegetables, but can apply to any food that can hold this shape. To dice a vegetable, cut first into sticks, then cut sticks into cubes. The size of the sticks and how thick you slice them control the size of the dice. See KNIFE, Cutting Techniques.

DILL

A member of the parsley family, dill is both an herb and a spice. The soft feathery leaves are harvested for use as an herb called dill weed; the small, hard, dried seeds are used as a spice. The leaves have a refreshing, cool quality; the seeds have a warm, slightly bitter pungency. Dill seed is a component of most pickling spice mixtures.

Use Dill weed is the main flavoring agent in dill pickles. It may be added to other vegetable pickles or used in salads, soups, cream sauces, vegetable sautés, and savory yeast breads. It has an affinity for cucumbers and fish. Scandinavian cooks use it to flavor salt- and sugar-cured salmon (*gravlax*); they add it to shrimp dishes, to cucumbers in sour cream, and to open-faced sandwiches. Use dill seed in breads, pickles, sauerkraut, and cole slaw.

Availability Fresh dill is sold the year around in many supermarkets, with peak supplies in summer months. Dried dill weed and dill seed are sold in bulk or packed in jars, tins, or plastic bags.

Selection Choose fresh-looking bunches without evidence of drying, wilting, or decay. Packaged seasonings lose quality after a while; try to buy from a store that restocks its spice section fairly often.

Storage Wrap fresh dill in damp paper towels, then in a plastic bag and refrigerate in crisper; use within a few days. Keep dried dill weed in an airtight container in a cool, dark, dry place and use within six months. Store dill seed in an airtight container in a cool, dark, dry place; it will keep indefinitely.

Recipes and Related Information
Bohemian Pork Goulash, 459; Dill Spears, 322; Gravlax, 233; Herb Biscuits, 49; Sour Cream Cucumber Salad, 166; Stuffed Grape Leaves, 281.

DILUTE, TO

To weaken or tone down a liquid because its flavor is too strong for a particular purpose. For example, if an oil and vinegar dressing has too much bite, it can be tamed by increasing the amount of oil in the mixture.

DISJOINT, TO

A butchering technique that means to separate at the joints, it most often refers to poultry. A joint is the point where bones connect to one another; they are held together by tendons and cartilage, which have more give than bone and are therefore easier to cut through. With some experience, your hands will learn to recognize this elastic tissue by touch.

HOW TO DEGREASE

With a ladle or serving spoon Dip edge of ladle or spoon into surface and let fat flow into bowl; repeat until all fat is spooned off. If needed, trap any remaining fat with a perforated metal or wire mesh skimmer.*

With filter paper Lay a paper coffee filter (or paper towel) on the surface of the liquid; it will absorb fat. Remove filter when saturated and repeat until all fat is absorbed. Change filter paper as needed.

By chilling When chilled, fat will harden into a solid layer and can be easily removed. Let liquid come to room temperature before placing in refrigerator; remove hardened layer with a spoon.

DISJOINTING POULTRY

With a sharp boning knife, cut with even strokes through skin between leg and breast to expose joint. Hold body with one hand and leg with other hand; lift leg up and pop the hip joint free.

Cut along remaining connective tissue with smooth, easy strokes until leg has been cut free. Hold leg up as you cut it away so weight of carcass is in counterbalance to leg; this tension will help to separate leg from body. Repeat for other leg.

To separate drumstick from thigh, if desired, rotate leg to locate joint. Lay piece right side up. At line where leg and thigh join, cut through to see joint, then cut through completely.

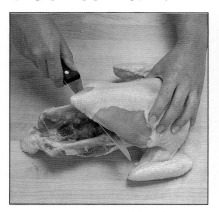

To remove breast, use rib cage as guide, cut through flap of skin just below rib cage until you hit resistance (point where rib cage begins). Pull back with hands to pop backbone; cut through tag of flesh that still holds backbone. At sides of rib cage, cut down just until you meet resistance (just below wing joint). Pull back slightly on rib cage between wing joints and cut to free wing joints on each side. Reserve back for stock.

To halve breast more easily, first remove breastbone: Turn whole breast underside up and make a slit through the white protective covering of the breastbone cartilage. Grab the breast with both hands, thumbs on either side of slit, and pull back to pop the breastbone free. With fingers, run along breastbone on both sides to loosen. Then gently but firmly pull bone to loosen further; cut away completely with a knife.

Cut through breast to wishbone. With a chef's knife or poultry shears, halve breast by cutting completely through wishbone. To remove wing, pull away from breast and cut at joint. You will now have two breast halves (with wings attached or separate), two drumsticks, two thighs, plus the back.

Disjointing is a simple, quick procedure if you know where the joints are or how to locate them, use a sharp knife and a cutting board, and have a relaxed approach to the whole process. By learning to cut up a whole bird yourself, you'll save money; poultry pieces cost more per pound because labor costs have been built in to the price. You'll also be a more confident and flexible cook, as you will have more control over food preparation even if you choose to have the butcher perform this service for you most of the time. See POULTRY, Preparation, for information on how to ready a bird for disjointing.

> ### Recipes and Related Information
> *Bone, 55; Carve, 102; Chopping and Cutting Board, 129; Knife, 328.*

DISSOLVE, TO

To add a solid to a liquid and cause it to become completely incorporated in the liquid or, in scientific terms, to pass into solution. Examples in cooking are dissolving gelatin or yeast in hot water, salt in a soup or stew, and sugar in hot cocoa. *Dissolve* also means to liquefy or melt, as when thinning honey or molasses by heating.

DOLLOP

A heap or pile of indeterminate size, *dollop* describes a generous spoonful of a semiliquid substance such as sour cream, whipped cream, or jelly added as a garnish or finish to a dish. The exact size of a dollop depends on the cook's taste.

DOT, TO

Usually part of the phrase "to dot with butter," meaning to place small bits of butter across the surface of food to be baked in the oven. The fat keeps the surface moist, adds richness, and can promote browning.

DOUGH

An uncooked mixture of flour, liquid, and often salt, eggs, sugar, fat, flavorings, and leavening, which is stiff enough to work with the hands. (Although a batter has the same basic composition, it is too wet to handle; batters are poured or dropped from a spoon.)

Doughs are classified by the ratio of dry to liquid ingredients. A soft dough, of the type used for biscuits and yeast breads, has approximately 3 parts flour to 1 part liquid. Stiff doughs, such as those for cookies and pie crusts, have more dry ingredients in proportion to liquid.

Recipes and Related Information

Batter, 27; Biscuit, 49; Cookie, 139; Cream Puff Pastry, 162; Doughnut and Fried Bread, 179; Pie and Tart, 431; Puff Pastry, 480; Quick Bread, 490; Waffle and Pancake, 598; Yeast Bread, 613.

DOUGHNUT AND FRIED BREAD

A doughnut is a small fried cake, usually ring-shaped and leavened with yeast or baking powder. Fried cakes and breads are pieces of dough cooked in hot fat. Sometimes they are glazed, filled with jelly, or dusted with sugar.

If you've grown up eating only storebought doughnuts and fried breads, you'll find your own far more flavorful and delicate. Many of the recipes take no more time to prepare than a cake batter or a batch of cookies. You can also prepare dough the day before, so it takes only a few minutes to fry a batch of fresh doughnuts.

For frying you will need a deep kettle of hot fat. Peanut oil or corn oil is better than solid shortening for frying, since either oil can be heated to a higher temperature without smoking. The oil can be used again, but no more than four or five times. After that it becomes very dark and has an unpleasant odor when heated. After each use, cool oil completely, strain through cheesecloth into a bottle, cap tightly, and refrigerate.

The frying vessel can be either a thermostatically controlled electric skillet or deep-fryer, or a small roasting pan or Dutch oven heated on the stove top. Whichever you choose, have at least 2 to 3 inches of oil in the pan. A pan measuring 9 to 10 inches in diameter needs 2 to 3 quarts of oil, for example.

Choose your favorite from this doughnut array: iced Maple Bars (see page 183), Old-fashioned Cake Doughnuts dusted with confectioners' sugar (see page 180), sugar-sprinkled Yeast-Raised Doughnuts (see page 183), and plain cake doughnuts (see page 180). Fry the cutouts for bite-sized doughnut holes.

Keep frying temperature fairly constant—although it's bound to fluctuate a few degrees while you're cooking. A deep-fat or candy thermometer (see THERMOMETER) is the best gauge. Chopsticks or knitting needles are handy tools for turning breads as they fry.

You should wrap and freeze any fried breads you won't use in a day. To reheat, brush off any ice crystals and set on a baking sheet in a 350° F oven for about 7 minutes.

■ OLD-FASHIONED CAKE DOUGHNUTS

These favorites, with a slightly crunchy outside and a soft, cakelike inside, are easy and inexpensive to make. Serve while still warm.

    1   cup sugar
    4   teaspoons baking powder
    1½ teaspoons salt
    ½   teaspoon freshly grated nutmeg
    2   eggs
    ¼   cup butter, melted
    1   cup milk
    4   to 4½ cups cake flour
        Oil, for frying

Cinnamon Sugar (optional)

    ¾   cup sugar
    1   tablespoon ground cinnamon

1. In a large bowl stir together sugar, baking powder, salt, and nutmeg to combine.

2. Add eggs, butter, and milk; beat well.

3. Add 3 cups of the flour, beating until thoroughly blended. Add 1 more cup of flour and beat well. Dough should be rather soft, sticky, and just firm enough to handle. If necessary, gradually stir in enough of the remaining flour to make a shaggy-looking, barely manageable mass.

4. Cover with plastic wrap and chill for at least 1 hour or overnight.

5. In a Dutch oven, heavy deep skillet, or other frying kettle, begin heating at least 2 inches of oil to 360° F.

6. Scrape half the chilled dough onto a floured surface, then push, pat, and roll to make a mass about ½ inch thick. Cut doughnuts with a floured doughnut cutter. Set doughnuts and their holes aside on a lightly floured baking sheet. Push scraps together, reroll, and cut again. Repeat with other half of dough.

7. Fry about 4 doughnuts and holes at a time. Gently drop them into hot fat, and flip them over as they rise to the surface and puff. Turn a few more times as they cook. They are done when they turn golden brown all over (2 to 3 minutes). Remove with a slotted spoon and drain on paper towels. While doughnuts are still warm, toss in Cinnamon Sugar (if used).

Makes about 25 doughnuts and holes.

Cinnamon Sugar   In a small bowl mix sugar and cinnamon until well combined.

Chocolate Doughnuts   Omit nutmeg. Stir ½ cup unsweetened cocoa with dry ingredients in step 1, and add 1 teaspoon baking soda. Also add 1 teaspoon vanilla extract when milk is used in step 2.

Spice Doughnuts   Add 1½ teaspoons ground cinnamon, 1 teaspoon freshly grated nutmeg, ½ teaspoon ground cloves, and ½ teaspoon ground ginger to the dry ingredients in step 1.

Whole Wheat Doughnuts   Substitute 3½ to 4 cups whole wheat flour for cake flour. Doughnuts will not be quite as light and delicate.

■ CRULLERS

Some sources say that this twisted fried doughnut was once called an Aberdeen *crulla* (small cake), perhaps the origin for the name we know it by today. Whatever you call them, these spiced, lemon-accented Crullers are delicious for dunking in tea or coffee. They are tangy and tender because of the buttermilk in the batter.

    4   cups flour
    2   teaspoons baking soda
    1   teaspoon baking powder
    ½   teaspoon ground cinnamon
    ¼   teaspoon freshly grated nutmeg
    ¾   cup butter, cut in pieces
    ½   cup sugar
    ½   teaspoon grated lemon rind
    4   eggs
    ¼   cup buttermilk
    1   teaspoon vanilla extract
        Oil, for frying
        Sugar, for dusting

1. Into a large bowl sift flour, baking soda, baking powder, cinnamon, and nutmeg. Cut in butter until mixture resembles fine crumbs; stir in sugar and lemon rind. Make a well in center and add eggs, buttermilk, and vanilla. Stir to combine ingredients; turn out onto a lightly floured surface and knead 2 to 3 minutes.

2. In a Dutch oven, heavy deep skillet, or other frying kettle, begin heating at least 2 inches of oil to 365° F.

3. Shape dough into a square, then pat or roll into a rectangle approximately 10 by 24 inches and ½ inch thick. With a sharp knife cut dough into 5-inch-long by 1-inch-wide strips. Twist 2 strips together and fry, turning once, until golden on both sides (2 to 3 minutes total). Several can be fried at a time as long as they are not crowded.

4. Remove from oil, drain on paper towels, and sprinkle with sugar. Serve warm.

Makes 24 Crullers.

BUÑUELOS

Often available in Mexican bakeries, *buñuelos* are small, round, puffy pillows of sweet dough. The hollow centers make them perfect for Jelly Doughnuts (see page 183).

¼ cup butter, softened
⅓ cup sugar
2 eggs
1 teaspoon vanilla extract
1¾ cups flour (more as needed)
2 teaspoons baking powder
1 teaspoon salt
¼ cup milk
Oil, for frying
Cinnamon Sugar (opposite page)

1. In medium bowl of electric mixer, cream butter and sugar together until blended. Add eggs and beat well. Stir in vanilla.

2. Stir and toss 1 cup of the flour with baking powder and salt. Add to first mixture and mix until blended. Beat in milk. Add remaining flour and mix to make a soft dough.

3. Turn onto a floured surface and knead 1 or 2 minutes until dough is smooth, kneading in more flour (you may need up to ½ cup more) if necessary to keep it from being too sticky.

4. Roll dough until it is about ¼ inch thick, flouring it lightly if it sticks. Cut into 3-inch rounds.

5. In a Dutch oven, heavy deep skillet, or other frying kettle, heat about 2 inches of oil to 360° F.

6. Fry about 6 Buñuelos at a time, turning them often, until they look like puffy, golden pillows (1½ to 2 minutes). Drain on paper towels and toss in Cinnamon Sugar while still warm.

Makes about 2 dozen Buñuelos.

CHURROS

Another Mexican fried bread, *churros* are made with long ropes of cream puff paste. In Mexico, the churro stand laden with these freshly cooked, golden sweet pastries is a common sight at all festivals. They should be eaten warm, when the outside is crisp and golden and the inside so puffy it's almost hollow.

1 cup water
½ teaspoon salt
1 tablespoon sugar
½ cup butter
1 cup flour
4 eggs
Oil, for frying
Cinnamon Sugar (opposite page)

1. Place the water, salt, sugar, and butter in a heavy saucepan. Heat slowly until butter melts, then bring to a full boil.

2. Add flour all at once, and beat vigorously until mixture is thick and smooth. Continue beating over medium heat for about 2 minutes, then remove.

3. Add eggs, one at a time, beating vigorously after each addition until mixture is smooth. (A handheld electric beater is useful.)

4. In a Dutch oven, heavy deep skillet, or other frying kettle, heat about 2 inches of oil to 390° F.

5. Scoop mixture into a large pastry bag fitted with a ½-inch star tip and fold down top of bag to seal. Squeeze bag over hot oil, pushing out a rope of paste 4 to 5 inches long. Cut with a knife, letting rope fall gently into oil. Rapidly form about 6 more Churros the same way. Turn them frequently until golden (about 2 minutes). Remove with a slotted spoon and drain on paper towels.

6. Fry remaining paste the same way, and while Churros are still warm, toss in Cinnamon Sugar.

Makes 3 to 4 dozen 4- to 5-inch Churros.

Churros and Buñuelos are both Mexican fried breads. Churros are ropes of cream puff paste, while Buñuelos are round, hollow, puffy pillows of dough.

Sopaipillas are light, airy puffs of deep-fried dough. Served piping hot, these weightless "pillows" are ready to receive a spoonful of honey in their hollow centers.

allow to rest at room temperature for 45 minutes, or refrigerate overnight or longer. (Dough will keep, chilled, for about 1 week. It may also be frozen for up to 2 months and defrosted in refrigerator when needed.)

2. Lightly flour a pastry board or a sheet of waxed paper. Take a lump of dough about the size of a lime or a plum and lightly sprinkle it with flour. Place dough on floured work surface and push it down with the heel of your hand so that it forms a slightly flattened round. Sprinkle flour on both sides of the round and swiftly roll out to a rough circle about 5 inches in diameter (like a small corn tortilla). As each circle is rolled out, place it on an individual sheet of lightly floured waxed paper until ready to fry. (Dough will hold up to 1 hour.)

3. In a Dutch oven, heavy deep skillet, or other frying kettle, heat oil to 375° F. Just before frying poke a small hole in the center of each round of dough. Fry rounds, one at a time, until they are browned, puffed, and crisped on the outside (about 2 minutes per side), turning with tongs halfway through cooking. Regulate heat to maintain a temperature between 350° and 370° F. Remove from oil when done and drain on paper towels. Serve hot.

Makes 8 to 10 rounds.

■ SOPAIPILLAS

Another southwestern favorite, these airy fried puffs can be served for breakfast, at dinner (in place of bread), or even for dessert.

- 2 **cups flour**
- ½ **teaspoon salt**
- 2 **teaspoons baking powder**
- 2 **teaspoons sugar**
- 2 **tablespoons lard or shortening**
- ½ **scant cup (approximately) hot tap water**
  Oil, for frying
  Confectioners' sugar, for sprinkling
- 1 **cup (approximately) honey, for accompaniment**

1. In a medium bowl sift together flour, salt, baking powder, and sugar. With a pastry blender or fingers, cut in lard to make an even, lumpy meal. Add the water, stirring with a fork, until a dough forms. Flour your hands and rapidly knead dough about 12 times. If dough sticks to your hands, sprinkle on more flour by tablespoons and knead it in until dough is easily handled. If dough is too crumbly and dry to knead, add more hot water by tablespoons. After kneading, cover dough with plastic wrap and let stand at room temperature for about 30 minutes, or refrigerate overnight.

2. Preheat oven to 325° F. In a Dutch oven, heavy deep skillet, or other frying kettle, heat at least 2 inches of oil to 375° to 380° F. Meanwhile, flour a work surface and roll out dough in a rectangle about ¼ inch thick. Cut dough into 3-inch squares. Drop squares into hot oil, a few at a time, regulating heat to maintain a temperature

■ NAVAHO FRY BREAD

This specialty of the American Southwest proves to be both simple to make and addictive to eat. The bouncy, elastic dough is very forgiving and is even more easily handled when well chilled.

- 2 **cups flour (more as needed)**
- 1 **tablespoon baking powder**
- 1 **teaspoon salt**
- 1 **tablespoon shortening or lard**
- 1 **cup boiling water**
- 2 **cups corn or peanut oil**

1. Combine flour, baking powder, and salt. Add shortening and rub mixture between your fingers until shortening is well broken up. Pour the water into flour mixture and stir with a fork until mixture forms a ball. If flour remains dry, add very hot tap water, ¼ cup at a time, and knead in with fingers. If flour becomes too wet to form a ball, add flour by tablespoons. As soon as dough forms a firm ball, cover with plastic wrap and between 360° and 385° F. The squares will fall, then rise, as they puff into little pillows. Push them down and turn often until they are golden. Remove with a slotted spoon, drain on paper towels, and keep warm in oven. Sprinkle with confectioners' sugar and serve hot with honey to spoon into the cavities.

Makes 16 puffs.

▓ YEAST-RAISED DOUGHNUTS

These doughnuts are lighter and more tender than Old-fashioned Cake Doughnuts (see page 180) because they are leavened with yeast.

   1 cup warm (105° to 115° F) milk
   1 package active dry yeast
   ½ cup sugar
   1½ teaspoons salt
   ¼ teaspoon *each* ground cinnamon and nutmeg
   2 eggs
   ¼ cup butter, melted
   3½ to 4 cups flour
      Oil, for frying
      Cinnamon Sugar, optional (see page 180)

1. Pour milk in a large mixing bowl, sprinkle on yeast, stir, and let stand a few minutes to dissolve.

2. Add sugar, salt, cinnamon, nutmeg, eggs, and melted butter, and beat vigorously until blended. Add 2 cups of the flour and beat until batter is heavy but smooth. Add 1 more cup of flour, beating well, then add enough of the remaining flour to make a soft but manageable dough.

3. Turn out onto a lightly floured surface and knead a few minutes, until dough is smooth and elastic, sprinkling on a little additional flour if necessary to keep it from being too sticky.

4. Place in a greased bowl, cover with plastic wrap, and let rise until doubled in bulk (or refrigerate and let rise overnight if you wish to make fresh doughnuts the next morning).

5. Turn dough out onto a floured surface, punch down, then roll and pat until dough is about ½ inch thick. Cut with a floured doughnut cutter and set aside on baking sheets covered with waxed paper, leaving about 1½ inches between doughnuts. Reroll scraps and continue until all dough is cut. Cover with a towel and let rise until doubled in bulk.

6. When you are almost ready to fry doughnuts, heat 2 to 3 inches of oil to 360° F in a Dutch oven, heavy frying skillet, or other frying kettle.

7. Gently drop 3 or 4 doughnuts and their holes into hot fat. Turn frequently until golden brown on both sides (2 to 3 minutes). Remove with a slotted spoon and drain on paper towels. Fry remaining doughnuts the same way and toss while warm in Cinnamon Sugar (if used).

Makes about 18 to 20 doughnuts and holes.

▓ MAPLE BARS

For authentic maple flavor, make the glaze with real maple syrup instead of an imitation product.

   1 recipe Yeast-Raised Doughnuts (at left)

Maple Glaze

   1 cup confectioners' sugar
   4 to 5 tablespoons maple syrup

1. Prepare Yeast-Raised Doughnuts through step 4. Turn dough out onto a floured surface, punch down, then press, pat, and roll to a fairly even rectangle about ½ inch thick. With a sharp knife, trim off any uneven edges. Cut into rectangles about 2 inches wide and 4 inches long. Set aside on baking sheets covered with waxed or parchment paper, cover with a towel, and let rise until doubled in bulk.

2. Fry as in Yeast-Raised Doughnuts. While still warm, brush top of each with Maple Glaze.

Makes about 15 bars.

Maple Glaze   Beat confectioners' sugar and 4 tablespoons of the syrup together until smooth. If glaze is too stiff to spread, beat in a little more syrup.

Makes about ½ cup.

▓ JELLY DOUGHNUTS

Another name for jelly doughnuts is Bismarks.

   1 recipe Old-fashioned Cake Doughnuts
      (see page 180) or Buñuelos (see page 181) or
      Yeast-Raised Doughnuts (at left)
   2 cups jelly or thick jam (do not use preserves;
      they will clog pastry bag)

1. Prepare one of these recipes, cutting cake doughnuts or raised doughnuts into rounds, not rings.

2. After pastries have cooled, use a knife point to make a small slit in the side of each pastry. Fill a pastry bag, fitted with a round tip, with about 2 cups jelly or jam. Pipe a generous tablespoon of jam or jelly into pastry.

Makes 18 to 24 doughnuts, depending upon recipe.

Recipes and Related Information
Deep-fry, 174; Fry, 254.

DRAIN, TO

To separate liquids and solids by setting both in a colander or strainer and letting the liquid pass through the holes (pasta from its cooking water), or by setting on absorbent paper (fat from fried food). This process also describes removing excess fat by pouring from the cooking pan into a receptacle, leaving only the pan juices.

DREDGE, TO

To coat food by sprinkling with a powder, for example, flour, cornstarch, or confectioners' sugar. For fried foods, a powdery coat ensures that the surface of the food will remain dry (moisture causes hot oil to sputter and drop in temperature; wet food steams instead of fries and won't brown properly). A coating of sugar sweetens fritters and other fried desserts.

DRESS, TO

The term *to dress* can refer to a number of processes. In classic French cuisine, it means the art of placing foods on a serving platter or plate in an attractive manner. It is sometimes used incorrectly to mean to eviscerate, but it can describe the preparation of meats by a butcher for retail sale.

DRIED FRUIT

Fruit may be dried by the sun or in commercial dehydrators. Valued not only for their packability and natural sweetness, dried fruits are also produced for their long shelf life and intense flavor.

Use   Dried fruits make a nutritious and convenient out-of-hand snack. Because they can be kept at room temperature for a few weeks without danger of spoilage, and because they are so light, they are an excellent energy source for backpackers and campers. Dried fruits are used in candies and confections, cookies, cakes, and breads. When used in baked goods, they are often presoaked to soften them; large ones may be cut up or minced. Dried fruits can be added to a stew or to a fruit compote. Raisins or minced dried fruits can be added to cooked or dried cereals. If plumped in beverage alcohol to keep from freezing, dried fruits can be added to ice cream or other frozen sweet desserts.

Availability   Most supermarkets carry a selection of packaged dried fruits, including raisins, prunes, apricots, and figs. Some supermarkets also carry dried fruits in bulk and mixed cut dried fruits. For a broad selection of dried fruits, both individual types and mixed, check health-food stores. The most commercially important dried fruits are discussed in this entry.

Storage   For long keeping, store all dried fruits in a plastic bag in refrigerator. Cut fruits (apples, pears, apricots, for example) may be kept for up to one year, and whole fruits (prunes and raisins) up to 18 months.

Preparation   If a recipe calls for chopped dried fruit, the fruit will be easier to chop if first tossed with oil or frozen. For 1 cup fruit, use 1 teaspoon vegetable oil. If the fruit is to be plumped, cover with very hot tap water and soak 2 to 5 minutes (longer results in flavor and nutrient loss).

CUT DRIED FRUITS

Some fruits—such as grapes, prunes, and figs—are dried whole. Others are cut and pitted or cored before drying. These include apples, apricots, pears, peaches, pineapple, papaya, mango, banana, and persimmon.

Among cut dried fruits, dried apricots are probably the most popular. Tree-ripened apricots are harvested at peak sweetness, cut in half and pitted, then placed, cut side up, on drying trays. Most apricots are then exposed to burning sulfur for several hours to prevent oxidation. They are then sun-dried and stored until shipment. When ready for shipment, they are cleaned, graded by size, and packed.

Most peaches intended for drying are freestone varieties. They are processed similarly to apricots.

Dried apples are made from mature apples that have been peeled, cored, sliced, and dried in modern dehydrators. When ready for shipment, they are graded and then packed.

Dried pears are processed similarly, although they are generally left in halves.

Cut dried fruits make a convenient and nutritious out-of-hand snack. They may be poached for a breakfast or dessert fruit compote or added to fruitcakes, quick breads, breakfast cereals, grain pilafs, steamed puddings, and stuffings. If desired, soak first in warm water to soften.

Recipes: Apricot-Almond Squares, 143; Apricot Filling, 627; Fruited Coffee Ring, 493; Your Own Bridge Mix, 59.

DRIED DATES
See DATE.

DRIED FIGS

Commercial dried figs may be sun-dried or dried in dehydrators. After drying, they are sorted and sent to processing plants, where they are inspected, graded by size, and stored until ready for shipment. Figs are packed just before shipment.

Although figs are one of the world's oldest fruits, the finest dried fig available today—the Calimyrna—is a fairly recent development. It is derived from the Turkish Smyrna fig, which was introduced to California in the late nineteenth century. It has a golden skin, a chewy moist flesh, and a particularly rich, nutlike flavor. The Black Mission fig is another fig variety that is frequently dried.

Dried figs are a delicious out-of-hand snack. They may also be poached whole for breakfast or dessert compotes. Minced figs add sweetness and chewy texture to cookies, cakes, breakfast cereals, grain dishes, steamed puddings, yeast breads, quick breads, and stuffings. Whole figs may be baked with butter and honey or steamed and dipped in chocolate for a rich dessert. See FIG.

PRUNES

Dried plums made from plum varieties that can be dried with the pit intact and without fermenting are called prunes. The fresh fruit is called a prune or a prune plum.

After harvesting, prunes are taken directly to a commercial dehydrator. After dehydrating, they are shipped to a processor or packager where they are inspected, graded by size, and stored until ready for shipment. Just before shipping, they are washed and cooked slightly to make them tender, drained, sorted again, and packed.

Prunes may be eaten out of hand as a snack or stewed and eaten cold or hot for breakfast or dessert. They make a delicious addition to fruit compotes or, when chopped, to fruit salads. Prunes add natural sweetness to savory stews and are an especially pleasing complement to rabbit, duck, chicken, and pork. Chopped prunes contribute sweetness and chewy texture to stuffings, fruit cakes, quick breads, breakfast cereals, grain dishes, cookies, and sweet fillings.

Recipes: Braised Pork With Prunes, 458; Prune Filling, 627.

RAISINS

California supplies about half the world's raisins, and about 95 percent of those are from the Thompson Seedless grape. Other grapes grown for raisins include Muscat, black Zante currant, and sultana.

To make raisins, grapes are harvested by hand at about 22 percent sugar content, laid out on paper trays between rows of vines, and sun-dried for three to five weeks. The trays are rolled and set under the vines for one to three weeks, then shipped to packing plants where they are washed, sorted, sized, packaged, and shipped.

To make golden raisins, Thompson Seedless grapes are not sun-dried, but instead are sent to the processing plant immediately after harvest. There, they are dipped in hot water and treated with sulfur dioxide to retain color, then dried in commercial dehydrators. Golden raisins are valued for their amber color and moist texture.

Muscat grapes have a distinctive perfume and flavor. The fresh grapes contain seeds, but the seeds are usually removed before the grapes are made into raisins. Raisins made from the round sultana grape have a small edible seed. Zante currants are very small, dark grapes (see CUR-RANT). Raisins made from them are correspondingly quite small and dark.

Raisins are a convenient and nutritious out-of-hand snack. They add natural sweetness and flavor to cakes, cookies, stuffings, stews, breads, muffins, breakfast cereals, grain dishes, salads, and fruit desserts. If desired, soak raisins in warm water to soften them or in brandy to flavor them before using in cakes and pastries. Sultanas and Zante currants are used in commercial baking to make a variety of cakes, steamed puddings, sweet rolls, and mincemeat.

Recipes: Biscotti, 8; Carrot and Baby Onion Stew With Raisins, 101; Carrot-Raisin Salad, 507; Cinnamon-Raisin Muffins, 375; Irish Soda Bread, 24; Lucia Buns, 99; Mincemeat Pie, 438; Nut-Currant Muffins, 375; Raisin Rice Pudding, 275; Rich Fruitcake, 88; Ricotta Cheesecake, 119; Roast Chicken With Rice, Fruit, and Almond Stuffing, 470; Rum Raisin Ice Cream, 312; Scones, 50; Sole With Almonds, Pine Nuts, and White Raisins, 533; Stuffed Grape Leaves, 281; Traditional Raisin-Oatmeal Cookies, 140; Your Own Bridge Mix, 59.

Dried fruit makes a delicious, chewy snack or a naturally sweet addition to baked goods, salads, entrées, and vegetable dishes. Pictured here are dried apples, pears, and persimmons.

Panforte is a specialty of the Tuscan city of Siena. Typical of Italian baked desserts, it is rich in nuts and dried fruit. A cup of espresso is a perfect accompaniment.

■ PANFORTE

Panforte is a nut-filled Italian confection that is a cross between a dessert and a candy. It can be served in tiny pieces accompanied by a cup of espresso after dinner. It also makes an excellent gift for those who love sweets.

½ **pound whole almonds**
½ **pound whole hazelnuts**
6 **ounces dried figs**
5 **ounces dark raisins**
5 **ounces golden raisins**
  Rind of whole orange
  Rind of whole lemon
½ **cup flour**
¼ **cup cocoa**
2 **teaspoons ground cinnamon**
⅛ **teaspoon white pepper**
⅛ **teaspoon mace**
¾ **cup honey**
½ **cup sugar**
  Juice of 1 orange
½ **cup confectioners' sugar**

1. Preheat oven to 350° F. Toast almonds and hazelnuts on baking sheet for 10 to 15 minutes. Remove from oven and cool. Reduce oven temperature to 300° F. Line an 8- by 8-inch baking pan with aluminum foil.

2. *If using a food processor:* Place figs, raisins, and orange and lemon rinds into food processor. Mix ingredients and process to purée. *If processing manually:* On a cutting board, finely chop figs, raisins, and orange and lemon rinds to a paste. Place mixture into a mixing bowl and stir to combine.

3. Sift together flour, cocoa, cinnamon, pepper, and mace. Add to dried fruit purée or mixture.

4. In a 1-quart saucepan heat honey, sugar, and orange juice until sugar dissolves. Carefully pour hot liquid into dried fruit and flour mixture. Add toasted nuts and stir to combine. Place fruit and nut mixture into prepared baking pan. Bake in preheated oven 50 to 55 minutes.

5. Cool in pan 10 minutes. While Panforte cools, dust a 12-inch square of foil with ¼ cup confectioners' sugar. Turn Panforte upside down onto coated foil and peel back foil used to line pan. Dust top with remaining ¼ cup confectioners' sugar. Cool completely.

6. Cut into 1-inch squares and serve immediately. To give as a gift, cut into quarters, cover in plastic wrap, and tie with ribbon.

Makes 32 bite-sized pieces or 4 squares for gifts.

■ WINTER FRUIT COMPOTE

This dish of dried fruits, plumped in spiced port, would be perfect for Sunday brunch.

½ **pound (about 1¼ cups) dried prunes**
1 **package (6 oz) dried apricots**
1 **stick (2 to 3 in.) cinnamon**
½ **lemon, thinly sliced**
  Juice of 1 orange
3 **tablespoons brown sugar**
¼ **cup port wine**

1. In a 2-quart saucepan combine prunes, apricots, cinnamon stick, lemon slices, and orange juice. Sprinkle with brown sugar. Add just enough water to cover fruits.

2. Bring to a boil, cover, reduce heat, and simmer until fruits are plump and tender (8 to 10 minutes).

3. Stir in port; transfer to a glass bowl. Serve fruits (with their liquid) warm, at room temperature, or chilled.

Serves 6.

DRIPPINGS

The juices that collect in the bottom of a roasting pan when meats or fowl are roasted are called drippings. After excess surface fat is removed, the drippings, full of the essences of the meat, are used as a flavoring agent, particularly for sauces and gravies.

Recipes and Related Information
Deglaze, 176; Perfect Gravy, 515.

DRIZZLE, TO

To pour a liquid such as butter or glaze in a thin stream over a surface to create a pattern of irregularly spaced, fine lines. For large amounts of food, drizzling is most effectively accomplished with a small ladle swirled in a tight circle so that the liquid just spills over the top. For smaller portions, dip a spoon in the liquid and shake lightly over food so that liquid falls in a stream.

Danish, cakes, and sweet breads are often drizzled with a confectioners' sugar icing as a final touch or with a thin crisscrossing of chocolate.

DROP, TO

To let a soft mixture fall from a spoon—such as dumpling batter into a simmering liquid or cookie dough onto a baking sheet.

DRY, TO

To remove moisture from raw foods before cooking, especially from those foods to be browned in some way, by patting with a towel. To dry also means to preserve food by drawing out its moisture. Drying can be accomplished at home in a dehydrator, in an oven, or in the sun. It is a relatively inexpensive way to preserve food. You pay only for the energy to heat the dehydrator or oven, and for the materials to make the trays.

METHODS FOR HOME DRYING: SUN, DEHYDRATOR, OVEN

There are several methods of home-drying: in the sun, in a dehydrator, or in an oven. The method you choose will depend upon the amount of time and money you wish to invest in drying and the types and quantities of food you intend to dry.

DRYING IN THE SUN

Sun-drying is by far the oldest method of preserving food. Although it takes longer than other methods—4 to 5 days of hot sun for most foods—it requires little investment. It's an ideal method in areas that have consecutive hot, dry days with temperatures in the nineties or higher, low humidity, and relatively clean air—for example, central California, the Southwest, and parts of the Midwest. Avoid sun-drying in areas where the air is dusty, animals are housed, or heavily traveled roads are nearby. People living in humid areas such as the South have had unsatisfactory results when sun-drying.

Certain fruits and vegetables are recommended for sun-drying because they won't spoil during the several-day drying period: apples, apricots, cherries, citrus peels,

---

TRAYS FOR DRYING

Drying trays can be simple cooling racks from your kitchen or elaborate home-constructed wooden models. Ultimately, your choice will depend on the drying method you select, the amount of time and money you want to invest, and the materials or equipment you have on hand.

Factory-made dehydrators usually come with trays, which are frequently made of plastic-coated or stainless steel screen embedded in a plastic or metal frame. Trays made entirely of plastic may warp and sag over time. Dehydrator trays are easy to maintain: Simply soak for a few minutes in warm water and wipe clean.

Trays for oven-drying and sun-drying are interchangeable. If you're planning to dry only a small quantity of food, rely on readily available tray materials. Cooling racks tightly covered with several layers of cheesecloth or nylon netting (available at fabric stores) work well. Secure the cheesecloth with straight pins; sew the nylon netting into a pillowcase shape and slip over each cooling rack.

If you plan to dry a large quantity of food in the oven or the sun, it's easy to make wooden trays. You'll need pieces of wood approximately the width and thickness of a stretcher for a painter's canvas, cut to appropriate lengths for the frame, kitchen string, and cheesecloth, nylon netting, or stainless steel mesh. Do not use aluminum, fiberglass, copper, or galvanized screen; all of these materials will negatively affect the quality of the dried food.

You can construct trays of any size, but keep these points in mind: For oven-drying, determine the dimensions of the trays by subtracting at least 1 inch from width and depth measurements of the interior of your oven to permit air circulation. Trays for sun-drying can be as large as you can handle comfortably; the larger the tray, the more drying space it offers.

When you have built the frame, run strings diagonally across the frame, tacking them at opposite corners, to support the cheesecloth, nylon netting, or stainless steel mesh. Stretch and tack the cheesecloth, netting, or mesh to the other side of the frame.

---

figs, grapes, nectarines, peaches, pears, plums, and pineapple among the fruits and chile peppers, lentils, peas, shell beans, sweet corn, and tomatoes among the vegetables. Meats and fish should not be sun-dried because there is a risk of spoilage. The only limit to the amount of food you can sun-dry at one time is the number of trays you have on hand. The recipe will give you specific directions for this method.

DRYING IN A DEHYDRATOR

Using a dehydrator is by far the simplest method of drying because it involves fewer variables than do sun- or oven-drying. You can dry virtually any food in a dehydrator, and, on the whole, dehydrator-dried food has a better appearance than food dried in the sun or an oven. Food also dries more evenly, and is almost impossible to scorch or overdry, in a dehydrator. The appliance can be left unattended and can be operated day and night. Finally, dehydrator-drying—unlike sun-drying—is not dependent on climatic conditions, although dehydrators perform best indoors, in a dry, well-ventilated room. Operating instructions vary from model to model, so consult the manufacturer's manual.

Dehydrators contain heating elements, which draw moisture from the food, and a fan, which blows warm air across the food to absorb the released moisture and carry it away. You can choose a ready-made dehydrator, available at department stores, hardware stores, or through mail-order catalogs, or you can construct your own.

Dried tomatoes in oil are a flavorful addition to salads or pasta, and they are not difficult to make in a dehydrator or in your oven.

DRYING IN AN OVEN

Oven-drying involves little or no investment in equipment. It is especially suited for drying a small quantity of food and for areas where sun-drying isn't possible.

Whether your oven is suitable for drying depends upon the *lowest* temperature it can achieve. Test your oven by heating it to its lowest setting, opening the door 4 to 6 inches, and measuring the temperature with an oven thermometer. The oven should maintain a temperature of 120° to 140° F. Too high a temperature will cook the food rather than dry it. Unfortunately, some older ovens offer a minimum temperature that is too high for oven-drying.

Heat should only come from the bottom of the oven. If your oven has a top heating element that gives off heat when the "bake" setting is on, remove the top element or place a large baking sheet on the top shelf as close to the heating unit as possible to deflect heat.

Options for trays to use in oven-drying are described in Trays for Drying (see page 187). Baking sheets are not recommended because they do not allow air to circulate all around the food. Tray size depends on the size of your oven. To allow air movement, trays should be at least 1 inch smaller than the inside of the oven. Use blocks or bricks to stack trays about 3 inches apart, allowing at least 3 inches of clearance at the bottom and top of the oven.

In general, to oven-dry, spread food on trays in a single layer; pieces should not touch each other. Preheat oven to 140° F; add loaded trays. Place a thermometer on the top tray toward the back of oven and monitor the temperature frequently, adjusting the oven thermostat to maintain a temperature between 120° and 140° F. To improve air circulation, prop the oven door open 4 to 6 inches and use an electric fan to keep moist air from accumulating. Place the fan on a chair or stool outside the oven. Position it to move air through the opening and across the oven, and set the fan on "low." Change the position of the fan from one side of the oven to the other every few hours.

Rotate the trays from top to bottom and from front to back every 2 to 3 hours. Turn pieces of food at least once. Food at the outer edges of the trays will dry faster, so needs removal before the inner pieces. Watch food carefully toward the end of the drying period because oven-dried foods can scorch easily when they are almost dry.

If you need the oven for cooking before food is dry, remove trays and keep in a dry spot. When you have finished cooking, allow the oven to cool to 120° to 140° F, replace the trays, and continue drying. The more frequently you remove the trays from the oven, the longer it will take the food to dry. Remember that food reabsorbs moisture at room temperature.

■ DRIED TOMATOES

The dried tomatoes will keep at room temperature for as long as the olive oil remains fresh. Refrigerate for longer storage. Add them to salads, serve as an appetizer, toss in pasta, or use to top pizza.

> **3 pounds Roma or other small pear-shaped tomatoes**
> **Salt, to taste**
> **2 or 3 cloves garlic, peeled**
> **2 or 3 small sprigs rosemary**
> **Olive oil**

1. Choose the smallest tomatoes you can find. Slice lengthwise almost in half and lay them open like a book (cut side up). Sprinkle cut surfaces lightly with salt.

2. Place tomatoes, cut side up, on drying trays. Dry in a dehydrator or the oven at 120° to 140° F: 4 hours or longer in a dehydrator or 24 hours or longer in the oven. When tomatoes are dry, they will be shriveled to small, flattish ovals and will feel dry but still pliable, not brittle.

3. Pack tomatoes, garlic, and rosemary loosely into 2 or 3 half-pint jars. Pour in enough oil to cover tomatoes completely—they may mold if exposed to air. Cap jars.

4. Let stand in a cool, dark place for 1 month for flavors to develop.

Makes 2 to 3 half pints.

DRY INGREDIENTS

This baking term refers to flour or other meal, salt, sugar, dry seasonings, and a chemical leavening such as baking powder or soda, as opposed to the liquids of a recipe—milk, water, butter, eggs, extracts, and the like.

DUMPLING

A small amount of dough cooked by boiling or steaming, a dumpling sometimes has a savory filling or is made into a sweet baked dessert of pastry-wrapped fruit. Dumplings are homey foods that are part of the culinary traditions of many cultures. Savory dumplings give substance to soup (Chinese wontons and Jewish matzo balls), can kick off a meal or be the main course (Italian *gnocchi*), and serve as a satisfying conclusion to a family supper or casual dinner party (American apple dumplings).

◼ CHICKEN SOUP WITH DUMPLINGS

In one form or another, this straightforward, satisfying soup probably nourished all of us as children. Cake flour or a mixture of half cake flour and half all-purpose flour makes a lighter dumpling. An Herbed Dumplings variation is offered at the end of this recipe as is a recipe for Matzo Balls, which are dumplings made with matzo meal (ground from unleavened bread most often eaten at Passover).

    2 cups cake flour
    4 teaspoons baking powder
    1 teaspoon salt
    2 eggs, lightly beaten
    ¾ cup milk
   16 cups Chicken Stock (see page 560)
    6 small carrots, diced
    6 stalks celery, diced
    3 onions, finely chopped

1. In a large bowl sift together flour, baking powder, and salt. In a small bowl combine eggs and milk. Make a well in center of flour; pour egg-milk mixture into well and stir until well combined. Set aside.

2. In an 8-quart stockpot or Dutch oven, bring stock to a boil. Add carrots, celery, and onions; reduce heat to medium-low and simmer 10 minutes.

3. Drop dumpling batter into simmering broth, 1 tablespoon at a time. Cover and simmer for 10 minutes without lifting lid. Serve at once.

Makes 16 cups.

Herbed Dumplings Depending on herb used, blend 1 to 2 teaspoons of crushed dried herbs in with the dry ingredients. Continue as directed in step 1.

Matzo Balls In a medium bowl beat 4 eggs and combine with ⅓ cup melted shortening, ¼ cup water, 1 teaspoon salt, and a dash of pepper; mix in 1 cup matzo meal. Chill, covered, about 20 minutes. Shape mixture (with wet hands) into golf ball–sized balls and drop in simmering salted water or stock; cover and simmer about 30 minutes. If desired, recipe can be halved; cooking time will be the same.

◼ GNOCCHI DI PATATE

Gnocchi are chewy Italian dumplings, most often made with potato as a base, although others are prepared with semolina flour or flavored with spinach. They may be served as a first course or main course, topped with butter or a sauce. Try Pesto (see page 27) or Ragù Bolognese (see page 412).

    2 pounds Idaho baking potatoes (the older
       the better), unpeeled
  1½ cups (approximately) flour
    1 teaspoon salt
    1 egg, slightly beaten (optional)
    ⅔ cup freshly grated Parmesan or
       Romano cheese, plus additional cheese
       for passing

1. Cook potatoes whole in boiling, salted water until tender. Drain and peel, then purée in a food processor or potato ricer, or put through a medium-mesh wire sieve. Place purée in a large bowl.

2. Add 1 cup of the flour, salt, and egg. Knead with fingers until smooth, adding more flour a little at a time until dough is no longer sticky.

3. Shape into long rolls about ¾ inch thick, then cut into lengths about 1¼ inches long. With your fingers, press each piece against the back of a fork so that one side will have impression of tines and the other will have a dent in the middle made by your finger. Each piece can also be rolled against the work surface with your finger to form a bow shape; set aside on lightly floured surface. Rest completed gnocchi on a lightly dusted board.

4. Cook immediately after shaping all the dough: Drop about ⅓ at a time into 4 quarts boiling, salted water. After they rise to the surface, continue to cook for 10 to 15 seconds, then remove with a slotted spoon to a heated bowl and toss in a little melted butter or some of the heated sauce in which you plan to serve them. Cover container with aluminum foil to keep warm while you cook rest of gnocchi.

5. To serve, pour selected sauce over gnocchi, add about ⅔ cup grated Parmesan cheese, and mix well. Pass additional grated cheese at the table.

Serves 6.

TIPS

PREPARING STEAMED DUMPLINGS

Light and fluffy dumplings are not difficult to make, but they are tricky enough that successful ones are applauded by appreciative guests, and failures deemed more suitable for bouncing than for eating. The secret is in what not to do. For those dumplings that are cooked covered, resist the urge to lift the lid while dumplings are steaming and you will be rewarded with an airy, tender product. When the lid is raised, steam escapes and cooking temperature lowers. In the time it takes to raise the temperature again, dumplings will overcook. Use a pan large enough to allow dumplings to expand as they steam, and keep cooking liquid at a simmer.

■ GNOCCHI VERDE

Green *gnocchi*, made with chopped spinach and green onion, can be prepared several hours ahead of time, then dropped into boiling water for cooking just before serving. (Gnocchi dough can also be frozen and used later.) Serve with the same sauces that accompany Gnocchi di Patate (see page 189) or use Tarragon Cheese Sauce, which appears at the end of this recipe. This dish can precede any roasted, grilled, or sautéed meat or fowl. Gnocchi are also delicious as garnishes for any clear soup, such as a plain consommé or a flavorful chicken stock.

  1 **pound fresh spinach, chopped,** *or*
     **1 package (10 oz) frozen chopped spinach,
     thawed completely**
1½ **cups ricotta cheese**
  1 **cup fine dry bread crumbs**
  2 **eggs, beaten**
  ¼ **cup freshly grated Parmesan cheese**
  ¼ **cup finely chopped green onion**
  ½ **teaspoon salt**
  1 **teaspoon freshly grated nutmeg**
     Flour, for coating

Tarragon Cheese Sauce

  2 **tablespoons butter**
  3 **tablespoons flour**
2½ **cups milk**
  ½ **cup homemade Chicken Stock (see page 560)
     or regular-strength canned broth**
  ½ **teaspoon dried tarragon**
     Pinch freshly grated nutmeg
     Salt and freshly ground pepper, to taste
  ½ **to ¾ cup freshly grated Parmesan cheese**

Crumb Topping

  3 **tablespoons fine white bread crumbs**
  2 **tablespoons freshly grated Parmesan cheese**

1. If you are using fresh spinach, wilt leaves for about 30 seconds in a pot of boiling, salted water. Drain spinach well by putting it in a sieve or colander and pressing with a wooden spoon. When drained, chop finely.

2. In a mixing bowl combine spinach, ricotta, bread crumbs, eggs, Parmesan, green onion, salt, and nutmeg. Blend well, cover, and refrigerate for about 2 hours to firm.

3. When chilled, form gnocchi by rolling about 1 teaspoon of the mixture between palms of your hands into small, walnut-sized balls. Roll lightly in flour. Arrange on a tray lined with waxed paper. Refrigerate until cooking time.

4. To cook gnocchi, butter a shallow, baking dish; set aside. In a large pot bring several quarts of salted water to a simmer. Drop in gnocchi a few at a time, depending on size of pot, and regulate heat so water remains at a simmer. Gnocchi are done when they rise to the surface.

5. Remove cooked dumplings to buttered baking dish, using a slotted spoon for ease in handling. Continue until all the gnocchi have been cooked.

6. Fold sauce into gnocchi in baking dish. Sprinkle on topping and place under a hot broiler for 2 to 3 minutes to melt cheese and brown bread crumbs. Serve immediately.

Serves 4.

Tarragon Cheese Sauce   Melt butter in a saucepan. When it begins to froth, add flour and stir frequently over medium heat. Meanwhile, combine milk and stock and bring to a simmer. After flour and butter mixture has cooked for 4 or 5 minutes, remove pan from heat. When cooled slightly, add simmering liquid all at once and blend with a wire whisk until smooth. Return saucepan to medium heat and stir until sauce coats a spoon lightly and flour taste disappears. Add seasonings. Taste carefully and simmer 2 to 3 minutes. Add cheese and stir until fully incorporated.

Crumb Topping   Combine bread crumbs and Parmesan cheese; toss to blend.

■ SPATZLE

A traditional favorite German side dish, these nutmeg-scented morsels of batter are quickly boiled and then sautéed in butter until golden. A metal *spätzle* maker (see page 549), which looks like a strainer with ¼-inch-diameter holes, is handy to have. It's inexpensive and can be found in cookware shops. In a pinch, however, you can force the Spätzle batter through a flat cheese grater or a colander with large holes.

  8 **cups water**
  2 **cups flour**
  ¼ **teaspoon salt**
  ¼ **teaspoon freshly grated nutmeg**
  3 **eggs, lightly beaten**
  ¾ **cup (approximately) milk**
     Butter or margarine, to taste

1. In a large saucepan bring the water to a boil.

2. Meanwhile, in a medium mixing bowl, combine flour, salt, and nutmeg.

3. Stir in eggs and gradually add enough milk to make a heavy batter.

4. Force some of the batter through holes of a spätzle maker or colander into the boiling water. Spätzle will cook quickly. As they rise to the surface, remove them with a slotted spoon to a colander. Rinse Spätzle with cold water and drain. Repeat until batter is used up.

5. Traditionally, Spätzle are sautéed in butter until golden brown. They're also good simply tossed with a little butter. Serve as a side dish with meat or poultry.

Serves 4 to 6.

Two different cooking techniques—panfrying and steaming—give Potstickers their unique combination of crisp, browned bottoms and tender tops. Try them with an assortment of fillings.

POTSTICKERS

These dumplings from northern China get their name from their method of cooking, a combination of panfrying and steaming that causes the bottoms to stick to the pan slightly. Getting just the right amount of "stick" without destroying the dumplings takes a little practice, so don't despair if the first few batches tear when you try to lift them from the pan. Practice this dish with family or not-too-fussy friends. The Pork and Shrimp Stuffing makes a delicious filling. Or, try the Pork and Cabbage Stuffing suggested for Wontons (see page 192). If you are in a hurry, use 1 pound of seasoned ground pork. Fresh pot-sticker wrappers are available at markets that specialize in Chinese foods. Well-stocked supermarkets should also carry them.

½ **pound potsticker skins**
   Oil, for frying
¾ **cup water or thin chicken stock**
   Soy sauce, chile oil, and black or rice vinegar for dipping, or one or more dipping sauces (see page 522)

Pork and Shrimp Stuffing

½ **pound boneless pork**
½ **pound shrimp, peeled and roughly chopped**
¼ **cup *each* minced green onion and water chestnuts**
4 **teaspoons minced fresh ginger**
¼ **cup finely shredded carrot**
2 **tablespoons *each* soy sauce and Shaoxing wine or sherry**
1 **teaspoon sesame oil**
1 **egg**

1. Prepare stuffing. Place 1 heaping teaspoon of stuffing across center of a skin and lightly moisten entire edge with a little water. Lift both sides of skin and pinch together in center of arc, above stuffing. Working on one side of center at a time, seal edges, making 3 or 4 pleats toward center as you work your way toward edge. Repeat on other side of center. Dumpling will naturally curl away from pleats to form a flat-bottomed crescent with a pleated ridge across top.

2. Heat a heavy, flat-bottomed skillet (nonstick or well-seasoned cast iron) with a tight-fitting lid over medium-high heat. Add enough oil to coat bottom generously. Arrange dumplings in pan in a closely packed circle, pleated sides up. Cook until edges begin to show browning on bottom. Add the water (careful—it will splatter a bit), and immediately cover pan. Reduce heat to medium and cook until dumplings are swollen and liquid is nearly evaporated (6 to 8 minutes).

3. Remove lid and increase heat to medium-high. Cook until liquid boils away and dumplings begin to sizzle in remaining oil. If oil is nearly all gone, add a little more for the final browning. Continue cooking until bottoms become crisp and golden brown. Loosen with a spatula and transfer to a serving plate. Serve one or more of the Chinese dipping sauces on page 522.

Makes 16 potstickers, 4 to 8 servings.

Pork and Shrimp Stuffing   Grind pork finely in a food processor or mince by hand to a fine texture. Combine with shrimp, green onion, water chestnuts, ginger, carrot, soy sauce, wine, sesame oil, and egg.

Makes 2 cups.

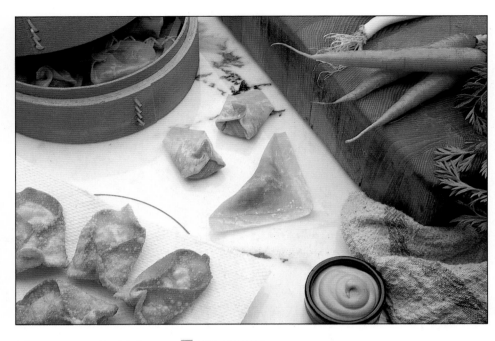

Whether steamed or fried and paired with a dipping sauce, or simmered in soup, Wontons are among the most versatile and popular of Chinese dumplings. They can be cooked immediately after assembling, or frozen uncooked for later use.

■ WONTONS

Probably the most familiar Chinese dumpling to Westerners is the wonton, a relatively large noodle skin wrapped around a small amount of stuffing. Most often served in soup, they can also be fried or steamed. Fried, they go well with tangy sweet-and-sour sauces or mustard dips; steamed, they are best with soy sauce dips. To fill the wontons, use the Pork and Cabbage Stuffing given here, the Pork and Shrimp Stuffing from Potstickers (see page 191), or 1 pound seasoned ground pork.

    1 **pound wonton skins**
       Oil, for deep-frying (optional)

Pork and Cabbage Stuffing

    ½ **cup shredded cabbage (bok choy, Chinese, or any green variety)**
    ½ **teaspoon salt**
    1 **pound boneless pork**
    ¼ **cup *each* minced green onion and bamboo shoots**
    1 **tablespoon minced fresh ginger**
    2 **tablespoons *each* soy sauce and Shaoxing wine or dry sherry**
    1 **teaspoon sesame oil**
    1 **egg**
    1 **teaspoon cornstarch**

1. Have at hand a small bowl of water with a brush for sealing edges. Peel off 2 or 3 wonton skins and place on the table, one corner "south" or toward you. Keep remaining skins covered with a towel to prevent drying.

2. Place a scant teaspoon of stuffing just south of center of skin. Brush near edges lightly with water and fold south corner over stuffing to within ½ inch of north corner. Press edges to seal. Pick up east and west corners and bring together at south end. Pinch or twist

slightly to seal corners together. Repeat with remaining skins and stuffing.

3. Keep finished Wontons covered with a towel to prevent them from drying, or freeze on a baking sheet and transfer to plastic bags when fully frozen. Boil in plain or lightly salted water before adding to soup, steam 6 to 8 minutes as a simple appetizer, or deep-fry in 375° F oil until golden brown and crisp.

Makes 60 to 70 Wontons.

Pork and Cabbage Stuffing Toss cabbage with salt and place in a colander to drain 30 minutes. Squeeze out excess moisture. Grind pork finely in a food processor or mince by hand to a fine texture. In a large bowl, combine pork, drained and squeezed cabbage, green onions, bamboo shoots, ginger, soy sauce, wine, oil, egg, and cornstarch; blend thoroughly.

Makes 2 cups.

Variation Substitute beef, lamb, or dark meat from chicken or turkey for pork.

Pork and Mushroom Stuffing Add ¼ cup soaked and minced black mushrooms (about 3 caps) to Pork and Cabbage Stuffing.

■ GOLDEN CHICKEN STEW WITH CHEESE DUMPLINGS

Choose an attractive Dutch oven in which to stew this creamy chicken dish. After the fluffy, cheese-flecked dumplings have steamed atop the bubbling chicken, the stew is served directly from the pot.

  4½ **to 5 pounds meaty chicken pieces (thighs, drumsticks, and breasts)**
       Salt, white pepper, grated nutmeg, and paprika
    2 **tablespoons butter or margarine**
    2 **shallots, finely chopped (about ¼ cup)**
    ½ **pound large mushrooms, quartered**
    1 **stalk celery, thinly sliced**
    3 **medium carrots, sliced about ⅛ inch thick**
    ½ **teaspoon dried tarragon**
    ¼ **teaspoon dried thyme**
    2 **cups water**
    ½ **cup *each* dry white wine and whipping cream**
    3 **tablespoons cornstarch, blended with 3 tablespoons cold water**
    ½ **cup shelled fresh or frozen peas**
    ¼ **cup chopped parsley**

Cheese Dumplings

    2 **cups flour**
    1 **tablespoon baking powder**
    ½ **teaspoon salt**
       Pinch freshly grated nutmeg
    ⅓ **cup grated sharp Cheddar cheese**
    ¼ **cup butter or margarine**
    1 **cup milk**

1. Sprinkle chicken pieces lightly on all sides with salt, pepper, nutmeg, and paprika. Melt butter in a 4½- to 5-quart Dutch oven over medium heat. Add chicken pieces, about half at a time, and brown lightly on all sides, removing them as they brown.

2. To the same pan add shallots and mushrooms; cook, stirring occasionally, until mushrooms brown lightly. Spoon off and discard as much fat as possible. Mix in celery and carrots. Return chicken pieces to pot. Sprinkle with tarragon and thyme. Add the water and wine. Bring to a boil, cover, reduce heat, and simmer until chicken is tender (1 to 1¼ hours).

3. Remove pot from heat. Remove and reserve chicken pieces. Skim and discard fat from cooking liquid. Blend in cream. Place over medium heat; blend in cornstarch mixture. Cook, stirring, until mixture thickens and boils. Add peas and parsley, then return chicken pieces to sauce. Reduce heat to low.

4. Using two tablespoons to shape them, drop rounded dumplings about 1 inch apart over chicken pieces. To prevent dough from sticking, dip spoons into sauce before forming next dumpling. Cover and simmer until dumplings feel firm when touched lightly (15 to 20 minutes; do not uncover until dumplings have cooked for 15 minutes). Serve directly from Dutch oven.

Serves 6 to 8.

Cheese Dumplings In a large bowl stir together flour, baking powder, salt, nutmeg, and cheese. Using two forks or a pastry blender, cut in butter until mixture resembles coarse crumbs. Add milk all at once, stirring just until ingredients are moistened and a soft dough forms.

■ **APPLE DUMPLINGS WITH NUTMEG SAUCE**
These dumplings from New England are made of whole apples wrapped in a rich biscuit dough, baked until tender and golden, and served with creamy Nutmeg Sauce. They are a perfect conclusion to a family dinner and a wonderfully homey dessert for guests. If you wish, omit the Nutmeg Sauce and serve with any remaining pan juices and a pitcher of cream or a scoop of vanilla ice cream. The amount of dough given here is generous, since it's far easier working with too much than too little.

- 6 Golden Delicious apples
- 2 tablespoons *each* sugar and butter
- 1½ cups apple juice

Biscuit Dough

- 3 cups flour
- 2 tablespoons sugar
- 4 teaspoons baking powder
- 1 teaspoon salt
- 1 cup solid vegetable shortening
- ¾ cup milk

Nutmeg Sauce

- 1 cup apple juice
- 1 cup whipping cream
- ½ teaspoon freshly grated nutmeg
- 2 tablespoons sugar
- ¼ cup butter

1. Preheat oven to 375° F. Butter a 9- by 13-inch baking dish. Peel and core apples, leaving them whole; set aside.

2. On a smooth, lightly floured surface, push, pat, and roll Biscuit Dough to a rectangle 13 by 20 inches, keeping sides as even as possible and lifting and flouring often to prevent sticking. Cut in half lengthwise, then in thirds crosswise, thus making six 6½-inch squares.

3. Place an apple in the center of each dough square. One at a time, bring the 4 corners of each square together at the top to enclose apple. Twist and pinch attached corners together to seal. If dough tears, just patch it; don't worry if it looks a little ragged.

4. Place dumplings in prepared baking dish about 1 inch apart. Sprinkle with sugar and dot with butter; pour apple juice around dumplings. Bake until dough is golden brown and apples are tender when pierced with a toothpick or skewer (about 45 minutes). If they brown too much while baking, cover loosely with foil. While apples bake, prepare Nutmeg Sauce.

5. When apples are done, remove dumplings to a platter. Pour juices remaining in baking dish into Nutmeg Sauce, reheat if necessary, and pass sauce with dumplings.

Serves 6.

Biscuit Dough In a medium bowl stir and toss together flour, sugar, baking powder, and salt. Cut in shortening until mixture resembles coarse crumbs. Pour in milk and stir with a fork just until dough holds together in a shaggy, cohesive mass. Turn onto a smooth, lightly floured surface and knead 10 times.

Nutmeg Sauce In a medium saucepan combine apple juice, whipping cream, nutmeg, and sugar. Bring to a boil and boil until reduced to about 1¼ cups (about 10 minutes). Swirl in butter and set aside.

DUST, TO

To sprinkle very lightly with a powder. Dusting implies a fine coating, as opposed to dredging, which involves covering food with a heavier layer. Greased baking pans may be dusted with flour to keep batters and doughs from sticking; cakes and pastries are often given a light dusting of confectioners' sugar, cocoa, or ground nuts as a finishing touch.

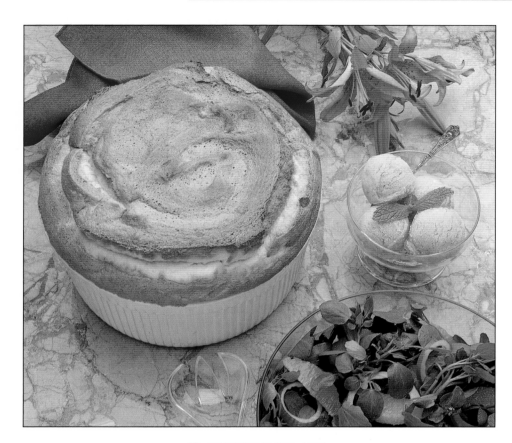

Although a baked soufflé must be served immediately, the soufflé base can be made ahead so that the only work at the last minute is beating egg whites and putting the soufflé in the oven. Soufflés make a wonderful main course for lunch or light supper, along with a salad and a fruit dessert such as the sorbet shown here.

▧ CHEESE ROULADE

The word *roulade* indicates that this cheese soufflé is baked flat and rolled. Any of the variations suggested for the Blue Cheese Soufflé (see page 205) will work for the roulade. The filling is a tasty combination of sautéed mushrooms and ricotta cheese, complemented by a seasoned, uncooked tomato sauce. This roulade is delicious served warm from the oven or chilled for a festive picnic. Parchment paper makes assembly and cleanup easier.

> 1 recipe Parmesan-Spinach Soufflé
> (see page 205)
> ½ cup freshly grated Parmesan cheese or dry bread crumbs, for dusting
> ½ pound mushrooms
> 1 tablespoon butter
> ¼ pound Monterey jack cheese, grated
> 1 clove garlic, minced
> ¼ cup snipped fresh chives
> 2 cups ricotta cheese
> 1½ teaspoons kosher salt

Tomato-Shallot Sauce

> 1 large tomato, minced
> 4 shallots, minced
> 2 tablespoons red wine vinegar
> 6 tablespoons olive oil
> 1 teaspoon oregano
> ½ teaspoon kosher salt
> ¼ teaspoon freshly ground pepper

1. Preheat oven to 350° F. Line a 10- by 15-inch jelly-roll pan with parchment paper, or grease with butter and dust with ¼ cup Parmesan cheese. Spread soufflé mixture into prepared pan and bake until puffed and golden brown (10 to 15 minutes); cool in pan 5 minutes.

2. While roulade is cooling, place a piece of parchment paper or a towel on work surface. Sprinkle with remaining ¼ cup Parmesan cheese. Loosen edges of soufflé and invert onto parchment. Roll parchment and roulade together, jelly-roll fashion, and cool completely (about 1 hour).

3. Slice mushrooms about ¼ inch thick. Heat butter and sauté mushrooms until lightly browned (12 to 15 minutes). Remove to a 3-quart mixing bowl to cool for 10 minutes.

4. Place jack cheese in bowl with mushrooms. Add garlic, chives, ricotta, and salt. Mix well to combine.

5. Carefully unroll roulade and spread with filling, leaving 1 inch uncovered around edge. Roll up again and refrigerate until serving time.

6. To serve, remove and discard parchment, and cut roulade into 2-inch-thick slices. Place on individual plates. Top pieces with Tomato-Shallot Sauce.

Serves 8.

Tomato-Shallot Sauce   In a small bowl mix together tomato, shallots, vinegar, oil, oregano, salt, and pepper. Marinate for 1 hour before serving.

Food Processor Version   Use metal blade to process Parmesan cheese (about 1 minute) and remove. Slice mushrooms with slicing disk and remove. Use shredding disk to process well-chilled Monterey jack cheese with light pressure and remove. Use metal blade for garlic and chives. Use ingredients as directed in recipe.

▧ HOT LEMON SOUFFLE

Dessert soufflés are often sprinkled with confectioners' sugar as soon as they come out of the oven. The most efficient way to do this is to put the sugar in a shaker (also called a dredger) made for this purpose. With a slight change in ingredients, this versatile base becomes the classic Grand Marnier version or the popular chocolate soufflé. See the variations at the end of the recipe.

> 1 cup milk
> 3 egg yolks
> 6 tablespoons granulated sugar
> 4 tablespoons flour
> 2 tablespoons fresh, strained lemon juice
> 4 teaspoons grated lemon rind
> 5 egg whites
> Confectioners' sugar, for dusting (optional)

1. Set aside 2 tablespoons milk. Bring remaining milk to a boil in a small, heavy-bottomed saucepan.

2. In a medium bowl whisk yolks lightly. Add 4 tablespoons granulated sugar and 2 tablespoons reserved milk and whisk until thick and smooth. Stir in flour with whisk.

3. Gradually whisk in half the hot milk. Return mixture to milk in pan and whisk. Cook over low heat, whisking, until mixture comes to a boil.

4. Remove from heat and whisk in lemon juice and rind. If not using immediately, dab mixture with a small piece of butter to prevent a skin from forming. Mixture can be kept, covered, up to 8 hours in refrigerator.

5. Preheat oven to 425° F. Generously butter a 5-cup soufflé dish.

6. Transfer lemon mixture to a heavy saucepan and whisk until smooth. Heat over low heat, whisking, until just hot. Remove from heat.

7. Beat egg whites until stiff. Add remaining granulated sugar, beating at high speed. Continue beating for about 30 seconds. Stir about one quarter of whites into lemon mixture. Spoon this mixture over remaining egg whites and fold together as gently but as quickly as possible, until just blended.

8. Transfer soufflé mixture to buttered soufflé dish and quickly smooth top with spatula. Bake until puffed and browned (about 15 minutes). When you carefully move dish, soufflé should shake very gently in center.

9. Set soufflé dish on serving platter, sprinkle soufflé with confectioners' sugar (if desired), and serve immediately. Dish up with 2 spoons so that each portion includes some soft center and some firmer crust.

Serves 4.

Chocolate Soufflé   Substitute 2 teaspoons vanilla extract and 2 ounces semisweet chocolate, melted, for lemon juice and lemon rind.

Grand Marnier Soufflé   Substitute grated orange rind for lemon rind and Grand Marnier or other orange-flavored liqueur for lemon juice.

▨ CHILLED LEMON SOUFFLE

Cold soufflés are more like mousses. Set with gelatin, they give the appearance of rising because they expand upward from their dish. Of course, this is an illusion. The sides of the mold are made taller with the use of a paper collar. Orange juice and rind can be substituted for the lemon juice, if desired.

¾   **cup fresh lemon juice**
1   **envelope unflavored gelatin**
3   **eggs, separated**
¾   **cup superfine sugar**
2   **teaspoons finely grated lemon rind**
1   **cup whipping cream**
    Pinch cream of tartar (optional)
1   **cup Chantilly Cream (see page 252),**
    for decoration

1. Wrap a 4- to 5-cup soufflé dish with a collar made from parchment paper, aluminum foil, or waxed paper. To make collar, cut a 12- by 19-inch rectangle; fold in half so that it is 6 by 19 inches. Turn folded edge up about 2 inches and tape collar around mold, with double fold hugging rim of dish. Fasten with kitchen string. Lightly oil inside of collar.

2. Place half the lemon juice in a small saucepan; sprinkle gelatin over juice and let soften (3 to 4 minutes); dissolve over low heat. Set aside.

3. In a double boiler over simmering water, whip egg yolks and sugar until thick and lemon-colored (ribbon stage); add remaining lemon juice and half the grated lemon rind.

4. Add gelatin mixture to egg-yolk–lemon mixture and continue to whip until blended. Set bowl over ice and stir until mixture is on the point of setting (it will have the consistency of cream whipped to soft peaks). In a separate bowl whip cream to soft peaks; fold into egg mixture.

5. In a copper or stainless steel bowl (add cream of tartar if not using copper bowl), whip egg whites until stiff, but not dry, peaks. Fold one third of whites into soufflé base to lighten, then fold in remaining whites and finally remaining lemon rind.

6. Pour soufflé into prepared mold and chill until set (2 to 3 hours).

7. When ready to serve, remove soufflé from refrigerator, carefully unwrap paper collar, and decorate with Chantilly Cream.

Serves 6.

Recipes and Related Information
Angel Food Cake, 82; Basic Sponge Cake, 83; Bind, 49; Cake, 77; Clarify, 131; Copper Egg-White Bowl, 155; Custard, 168; Egg and Caper Salad, 98; Egg-Preparation Equipment, 210; Egg Wash, 211; Emulsion and Emulsifier, 212; Génoise, 84; Hollandaise Sauce, 516; Mayonnaise, 519; Meringue, 359.

EGGPLANT

An ancient fruit probably native to India, the eggplant belongs to the nightshade family along with the tomato. Eggplants are cultivated in a variety of shapes, sizes, and colors. All have a thin, glossy, edible skin, a pale whitish green flesh that becomes soft and watery when cooked, and a mild flavor that combines well with oil, cheese, herbs, and other seasonings. The flesh of the large, globular Western eggplant has more moisture and is more bitter than that of the Asian varieties. To draw off some of the bitter juices, Western eggplants are often salted before cooking; Asian eggplants do not require salting.

Use Eggplants can be steamed or boiled to soften the pulp, then baked in a casserole with eggs, cheese, and bread crumbs; sliced and fried, either in flour or in batter; skewered and grilled; halved, stuffed, and baked; stewed with tomatoes and peppers or with oil and garlic; or sliced, layered with cheese and tomato sauce, and baked parmigiana. Indian cooks include eggplant in curries.

Asian cooks pickle it, braise it with pork, or fry it in tempura batter. In southern Italy, eggplant is part of pasta sauces, baked dishes, and the popular relish caponata. Greek moussaka is a baked casserole of eggplant, lamb, and cream sauce. The mild flavor of eggplant makes it a good foil for spicy sauces or highly seasoned dishes. It readily soaks up oil and seasonings.

Availability In the United States the most common variety is the large, globular, purple type, weighing about 1 pound each. The Japanese eggplant is long, slender, and deep purple; a similar Chinese variety is slightly longer, with a lavender skin. Other cultivated varieties, usually grown on farms near Asian communities, are the small, round, white Thai eggplant and the tiny, round, white Chinese variety used for pickling. Peak availability is July and August, but eggplants are available all year.

Selection Choose eggplants that feel heavy for their size. Skin should be smooth and shiny; flesh should feel firm, without bruised areas.

Storage Place eggplant in a plastic bag and refrigerate in crisper for up to four days.

Preparation Eggplants do not need to be peeled. Wash and trim stem ends. Large globe varieties may be bitter; to remove some bitterness, slice and salt eggplant liberally, then drain for one hour between sheets of paper towels weighted with a heavy plate. Pat dry.

Cooking See BRAISE, BROIL, DEEP-FRY, GRILL.

■ MEDITERRANEAN EGGPLANT SPREAD

The warm flavors of the Mediterranean come through in this coarse eggplant spread, designed to be made in a food processor. Serve it with savory crackers or wedges of pita bread before a dinner of garlicky roast lamb or chicken. It can be stored in the refrigerator for up to two weeks.

    1 eggplant (about 1 lb)
    ¼ cup olive oil
    2 red bell peppers, chopped
    2 large tomatoes, peeled, seeded, and chopped
    1 medium zucchini, chopped
    2 cloves garlic, minced
    1 teaspoon paprika (preferably Hungarian)
    1 teaspoon ground cumin
       Juice of 1 lemon
       Salt, to taste
       Crackers, pita bread wedges, or Belgian
       endive leaves, for accompaniment

1. Preheat oven to 450° F. Trim ends of eggplant; cut eggplant into lengthwise slices, about ¼ inch thick.

2. Brush a baking sheet with 2 tablespoons oil, then heat in oven 5 minutes. Place eggplant slices on heated baking sheet and bake 10 to 15 minutes. Remove from oven and let cool.

3. Place eggplant in food processor and purée coarsely, turning motor on and off rapidly. Set aside.

4. In remaining oil, sauté peppers over medium heat until soft (7 to 8 minutes). Add tomatoes, zucchini, garlic, paprika, cumin, lemon juice, and salt to taste and continue cooking 2 minutes. Remove from heat and cool slightly.

5. Combine pepper mixture and eggplant; process briefly. Spread should be very coarse. Pack into crocks and seal with a little olive oil.

6. At serving time, taste and adjust salt and lemon as necessary. Serve with crackers, warm pita bread, or leaves of Belgian endive.

Makes 2 cups.

■ EGGPLANT RELISH

Sicilians are renowned for their sweet-and-sour dishes, a particularly winning example of which is caponata. This eggplant relish of wonderfully complex flavors and textures is scooped up with hearts of lettuce or chunks of bread. Smooth and crunchy, hot and cool, sweet and tart—it's all there in this beguiling dish.

    3   large eggplants or 6 small Japanese eggplants
    1½   cups olive oil
    3   cups minced onions
    ⅓   cup minced garlic
    1   cup diced celery
    2   cups peeled, seeded, and chopped tomatoes
           (½-in. chunks)
    3   tablespoons capers
    ⅔   cup minced carrot
    ½   cup toasted pine nuts
    2   cups oil-cured black olives
    ⅓   cup sugar
    ⅔   cup red wine vinegar
    ½   teaspoon cayenne pepper, or more to taste
           Salt, to taste
    ⅔   cup minced parsley
           Olive oil, for garnish
           Minced parsley, for garnish

1. Preheat oven to 375° F. Peel eggplants and cut into ½-inch dice. Oil a large baking sheet or roasting pan with 3 tablespoons olive oil. Toss eggplant with ¾ cup olive oil to coat well, then transfer to baking sheet or pan. Bake, tossing eggplant frequently, until soft and lightly browned (about 20 minutes).

2. Heat remaining oil in a large skillet over moderate heat. Add onions and garlic and sauté until soft (7 to

10 minutes); do not allow garlic to brown. Add celery, tomatoes, capers, carrot, pine nuts, olives, sugar, vinegar, and cayenne. Simmer slowly 30 minutes. Add salt to taste. Add eggplant and cook an additional 10 minutes. Add the ⅔ cup parsley and let cool. Taste again and correct seasoning. To serve, transfer to a bowl, drizzle with olive oil, and garnish with minced parsley.

Serves 12.

Food Processor Version   Use metal blade to process parsley, onions, garlic, celery, tomatoes, and carrots to desired consistency. Process each vegetable individually. For best results, process parsley first.

■ MOUSSAKA

Plan a Greek dinner with this layered lamb and eggplant casserole as the main course. Start with a lemon and rice soup. For dessert, serve Baklava (see page 222), a sweet pastry made with tissue-thin filo dough, ground almonds, and honey.

>   1   **large eggplant (about 1½ lb)**
>   **Salt, as needed**
>   ⅓   **cup (approximately) olive or vegetable oil**
>   1   **pound ground lamb, crumbled**
>   1   **large onion, finely chopped**
>   1   **clove garlic, minced**
>   ¼   **teaspoon ground cinnamon**
>   1   **teaspoon salt**
>   ⅛   **teaspoon *each* freshly grated nutmeg and white pepper**
>   ¼   **teaspoon dried oregano**
>   ¼   **cup chopped parsley**
>   2   **tablespoons tomato paste**
>   ½   **cup dry red wine or Beef Stock (see page 560)**
>   ½   **cup freshly grated Parmesan cheese**

Cream Sauce

>   2   **tablespoons butter or margarine**
>   2   **tablespoons flour**
>   ½   **teaspoon salt**
>   **Dash *each* freshly grated nutmeg and white pepper**
>   2   **cups milk**
>   2   **eggs**
>   1   **egg yolk**

1. Preheat oven to 350° F. Cut off stem end of eggplant; cut unpeeled eggplant in half lengthwise. Cut crosswise in ½-inch slices; liberally sprinkle both sides with salt. Set in a single layer between sheets of paper towel and weight with a heavy plate; set aside for 1 hour to drain.

2. In a large frying pan, heat 1 tablespoon oil and cook lamb, stirring, until browned. Spoon off excess fat. Mix in onion and cook, stirring occasionally, until onion is tender. Mix in garlic, cinnamon, salt, nutmeg, pepper, oregano, parsley, tomato paste, and wine. Bring to a boil,

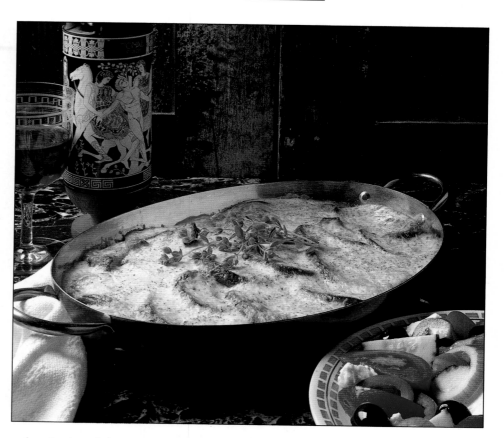

reduce heat, and simmer, covered, for 15 minutes. Uncover and continue simmering until sauce is thick (about 5 minutes).

3. Pat eggplant dry with paper towels. Arrange slices in a single layer in a large shallow pan. Brush with some of the remaining oil. Broil, about 4 inches from heat, until lightly browned (about 5 minutes). Turn, brush second sides with oil, and broil until browned (5 minutes longer).

4. To assemble, place half the eggplant slices in a single layer in an ungreased square or oval casserole of about 2-quart capacity. Top with meat sauce; sprinkle with 2 tablespoons Parmesan cheese. Cover with remaining eggplant; sprinkle with 2 more tablespoons cheese. Pour on Cream Sauce; sprinkle with remaining cheese. At this point casserole can be covered and refrigerated overnight.

5. When ready to serve, bake until top is lightly browned (45 minutes to 1 hour).

Serves 6.

Cream Sauce   Melt butter in a medium saucepan; stir in flour, salt, nutmeg, and pepper. Remove from heat and gradually stir in milk. Return to heat and cook, stirring, until thickened. In a small bowl beat eggs and egg yolk. Mix in a little of the hot sauce. Over low heat, blend egg mixture gradually into sauce and mix well.

Food Processor Version   Use metal blade to process Parmesan cheese, then parsley, onion, and finally garlic.

Moussaka, a Greek lamb and eggplant casserole, should be on everyone's list of dinner party entrées. It can be prepared up to the point of baking and then refrigerated overnight, if desired. An hour before serving, put the casserole in the oven to cook while the rest of the meal is being assembled.

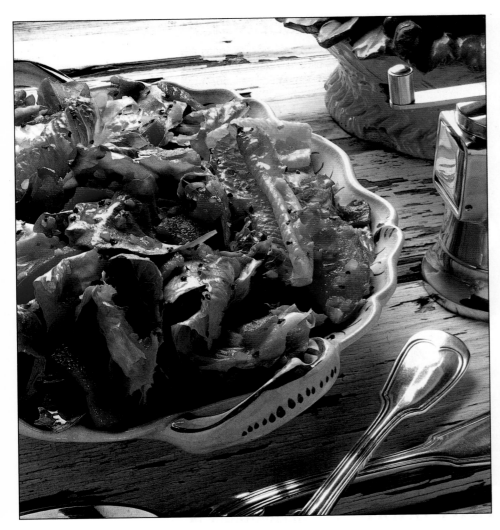

A warm, sweet-and-sour dressing softens the raw crispness of the greens in Hot Romaine and Escarole Salad. Like all wilted salads, this one should be served immediately after tossing.

EMULSION AND EMULSIFIER

When two liquids usually incapable of forming a stable mixture are in suspension, the combination is called an emulsion. What links them together is the addition of a third substance, called an emulsifier, which is compatible with both. For example, oil and water will mix when beaten, but will separate as soon as the beating stops unless stabilized with an emulsifying agent. Emulsions can be temporary (lasting a few minutes, such as an oil and vinegar salad dressing) or more permanent (lasting hours, days, or longer, such as mayonnaise).

Egg yolk is the most effective emulsifier for sauces. Other common ones are acids (lemon juice, vinegar, wine), dry and prepared (wet) mustard, and paprika, which is why these ingredients are basic to vinaigrette dressings.

Recipes and Related Information
Hollandaise Sauce, 516; Mayonnaise, 519; Vinaigrette Dressing, 520.

ENRICH, TO

To add an ingredient, known as an enrichment, to a dish to deepen its flavor and develop a luxurious finish, both visually and to the taste. Butter and cream, and sometimes egg yolks, are enrichments that are often swirled into sauces and cream soups just before serving.

ESCAROLE

A sturdy salad green of the chicory family, escarole has broad, wavy, jagged-edged green outer leaves that whiten near the core. The flavor is slightly bitter; the texture is firm and crisp.

Use An escarole salad can stand up to hot bacon dressings or assertive vinaigrettes. Wilted escarole leaves can be added to bean or vegetable soups. Just a few hearty escarole leaves contribute pleasing texture to a mixed green salad.

Availability Escarole is sporadically available throughout the year. However, it is at its best and most abundant in the winter.

Selection Leaves should be crisp and creamy inside; avoid wilted heads with browning edges.

Storage Keep escarole in a plastic bag in refrigerator crisper for up to three days.

Preparation Discard ragged or dark green outer leaves. Wash well and dry, trim core end, and tear by hand into smaller pieces.

◼ HOT ROMAINE AND ESCAROLE SALAD
This barely wilted salad combines two greens with substantial texture—romaine and escarole—in a piquant sweet-and-sour dressing with bacon and tomato.

   2 **tablespoons fresh lemon juice**
   1 **tablespoon catsup**
   1 **teaspoon *each* sugar and Dijon mustard**
  ½ **teaspoon Worcestershire sauce**
   1 **clove garlic, minced**
   6 **slices bacon**
     Vegetable oil, as needed
   1 **medium onion, finely chopped**
   6 **cups torn romaine lettuce**
   4 **cups torn escarole**
   1 **medium tomato, cut in thin wedges**
     Freshly ground pepper

1. In a small bowl mix lemon juice, catsup, sugar, mustard, Worcestershire sauce, and garlic.

2. Cut bacon crosswise into ½-inch strips. In a large frying pan, cook bacon until crisp and brown, stirring often; remove with a slotted spoon and drain.

Measure ¼ cup bacon drippings; add oil (if needed) to make ¼ cup, or discard any drippings in excess of ¼ cup. In the same pan cook onion in drippings over medium heat, stirring, for about 1 minute. Add lemon juice mixture; bring to a boil.

3. Add romaine, escarole, and tomato; immediately remove from heat. Mix lightly to coat well with dressing. Transfer to a salad bowl and sprinkle with bacon and pepper. Serve at once.

Serves 4 to 6.

■ ESCAROLE SOUP

Try this very simple soup that can be prepared and served within one hour. Fresh spinach or other greens may be substituted for escarole.

- ⅓ **cup butter**
- 1 **small onion, minced**
- 1 **head escarole, well washed and coarsely chopped**
  Salt and freshly ground pepper, to taste
- 4 **cups homemade Chicken Stock (see page 560)**
  or regular-strength canned broth
- ¼ **cup crushed vermicelli**
- ¼ **cup freshly grated Parmesan cheese, for topping**

1. In a large saucepan melt butter and sauté onion over medium heat until browned. Add escarole and salt and pepper to taste. Sauté briefly, then add stock. Cover and cook over low heat for 15 minutes. Add vermicelli and cook an additional 15 minutes.

2. Taste and season. Serve with Parmesan cheese.

Makes about 8 cups, 4 servings.

EVAPORATE, TO

To release steam from a liquid by boiling. Cooks use this principle when boiling liquids to decrease their volume and to intensify their flavor. Sauces are often thickened or reduced this way. A shallow, wide pan promotes faster evaporation than does a deep, narrow one, because the heat reaches more of the liquid at one time and the greater surface area allows water vapor to escape more quickly.

EVISCERATE, TO

To remove the internal organs from freshly killed birds, animals, and fish. Because the viscera spoil quickly and the enzymes in the digestive tract speed deterioration, evisceration is done for sanitary reasons. Also called draw and gut, it is typically done by slitting from the base of the gullet to the bottom of the belly and trimming the entrails from where they are attached to the chest cavity.

EXTRACT AND ESSENCE

The many extracts and essences used to flavor foods are derived from aromatic plant oils, from natural, nonplant ingredients, and from synthetics combined in a laboratory.

The characteristic taste and fragrance of many fruits, flowers, spices, and other plants are contained in the essential oils of the plant. Pure extracts are made by distilling these essential oils and dissolving them in alcohol or a diluted alcohol base, which keeps the oil in suspension. Pure vanilla and almond extracts, for example, are made in this fashion. Unlike extracts, flavorings—butterscotch and rum are two examples—are neither alcohol-based nor derived from plants.

Some flavors, such as maple or banana, cannot be extracted by distillation. In place of pure extracts, scientists have developed imitation and artificial flavorings. Imitation flavorings contain all or some nonnatural ingredients; artificial flavorings such as butterscotch may contain natural or synthetic flavors but do not have a natural counterpart that they are attempting to reproduce.

Use   Extracts and essences impart flavor to a given dish without adding solids or excess liquids. They are most commonly used in baking. Home cooks add vanilla, almond, lemon, and peppermint extracts and butter and rum flavorings to cakes, puddings, ice creams, custards, cookies, and candies. Rose water and orange flower water are used not only in baked goods and custards but also in savory rice dishes.

Extracts and essences are highly volatile; they dissipate rapidly in the atmosphere, even more rapidly in the presence of heat. As a result, they should be added to cool or cooling mixtures for maximum effect. When creaming butter and sugar for cakes or cookies, add extracts to the fat to slow vaporization and promote even distribution.

In general, 1 teaspoon of extract is enough to flavor 1 pint or 1 pound of food. Delicate flower waters—orange flower water and rose water—may be used more liberally.

Availability   Although many extracts and flavorings widely used in commercial food manufacturing are unavailable to the consumer, dozens of extracts and essences are packaged for consumers and are sold on spice shelves in supermarkets.

Selection   Pure extracts will give a truer, more concentrated flavor than imitation or artificial flavorings. For flavorings unavailable in pure form, such as banana or pistachio, an artificial extract will probably taste less harsh than the imitation product.

Storage   Extracts lose potency when exposed to light and heat. Stored in a cool, dark place, they will keep indefinitely.

F

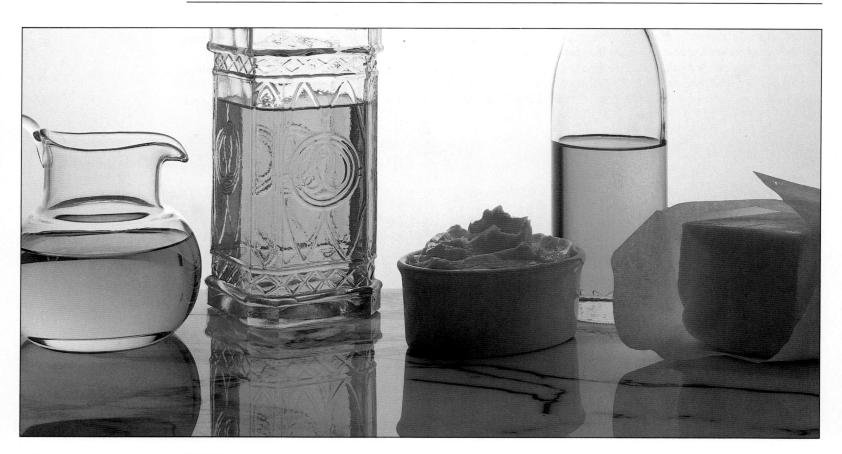

Solid cooking fats such as butter, margarine, and lard, along with liquid oils, play important culinary roles: They add tenderness, flavor, and color, keep foods from sticking to cooking pans, and add richness to sauces and dressings.

FAT

Fats and oils have similar chemical compositions. Both are made up of triglycerides (glycerol molecules with three fatty acids attached). However, fats are solid at room temperature and oils liquid because fats contain more saturated fatty acids. As a result of this difference, fats and oils have different cooking qualities.

The following section looks at the role of solid fats in cooking. Also see BUTTER; MARGARINE; PORK, About Pork Lard; and POULTRY, About Chicken Livers, Giblets, and Fat. For information on liquid fats, see OIL.

Use   To the cook, solid fats are especially important in baking, deep-frying, and sautéing. In addition, they are useful as flavor enhancers, emulsifiers, and sealants. The best fat for a particular dish depends on the flavor and texture desired.

Storage   Although the decomposition process is not entirely understood, it is known that saturated fats oxidize and turn rancid more slowly than unsaturated fats. Beef, for example, has a longer freezer life than chicken or pork because its fat is more saturated. Pastries made with lard stay fresh longer than those made with polyunsaturated oils. These facts probably have more implications for the commercial food processor than for the home cook who will choose a cooking or baking fat for its flavor and texture.

For specific storage instructions, see individual fats.

FAT IN BAKING

The primary role of fat in baking is as a shortening or tenderizing agent. When fat is combined with flour in a batter or dough, it limits development of gluten, an elastic protein network that gives a baked product its structure. If less strands of gluten are developed, the result is a more tender cake, cookie, pie dough, or loaf of bread; more gluten means baked goods will be tougher. Cookies without solid fat, such as meringues, are hard rather than tender.

Fat is also responsible for making pastry doughs flaky. In puff pastry and Danish pastry, for example, the fat content (usually butter) is extremely high. Butter is rolled between the layers of dough to make alternating layers of gluten and fat. When baked, the fat melts and generates steam, which leavens the dough and produces flaky sheets of pastry.

Fat imparts flavor and color to baked goods. An all-butter pie crust has a noticeably different flavor and color than an all-lard crust. The flavor of lard is important to Mexican and Chinese breads and pastries; the flavor of butter is important to French pastries. Although, technically, butter can be substituted for lard (or vice versa), the authentic, characteristic flavor of the product often depends on the fat used.

Some baked goods use fat as a leavening agent. When fat and sugar are creamed, the air trapped in the dough or batter adds volume to the baked product. For this reason, thorough creaming is essential to producing a cake with a light texture. Fats at room temperature cream more easily; they incorporate and hold air better (see CREAM).

Fat adds richness, smoothness, and sheen to the crumb of baked goods. High-fat breads such as brioche have a richer flavor and smoother, shinier crumb than fat-free breads such as a French-style baguette.

Fat improves the longevity of baked goods. By coating the starch granules, it slows moisture loss. Breads with fat last for several days, in contrast to the fat-free baguette, which goes stale in one day.

FAT IN DEEP-FRYING

Deep-frying requires a fat that does not burn or break down at high temperatures or in the presence of moisture. The temperature at which a fat or oil begins to deteriorate is called its smoke point. In general, saturated fats are more stable and have higher smoke points than unsaturated fats. The presence of free fatty acids in a fat, however, lowers its smoke point. Animal fats such as suet and butter have lower smoke points than vegetable oils because of their high proportion of free fatty acids. The best fat for deep-frying, then, would be a saturated (fully hydrogenated) vegetable shortening. These shortenings have a smoke point of about 460° F, compared to 320° to 330° F for butter and 340° to 350° F for lard.

Repeated use will lower the smoke point of a fat because of the moisture and the food particles left behind from previous use. To extend the life of a frying fat, carefully strain or filter it after each application, and store in a tightly capped container away from light and heat. Frying in a deep kettle, as opposed to a shallow, wide pan, exposes less of the fat to air and thus extends its life somewhat (and is safer). Fat that smokes or foams has broken down and should be discarded.

FAT IN SAUTEING

In panfrying and sautéing, the hot pan is coated with a thin layer of fat. The hot fat keeps the sautéed food from sticking to the pan and it aids in the formation of a crust, which helps to contain juices. It also imparts flavor and helps conduct heat from the pan to the item being cooked.

Although the mild flavor of butter may be desirable in sautéed items—especially in delicate foods such as fish and veal—butter burns easily. Clarified butter (see page 68) is preferred for high-heat sautéing because it has a higher smoke point than whole butter. Alternatively, adding oil to the butter in the sauté pan raises its smoke point.

OTHER USES FOR FAT

Apart from cooking, the most obvious use for fat is as a flavor enhancer. Adding butter to mashed potatoes or spreading goose fat on toast is the cook's way of taking advantage of the flavor of fat. Fat also adds what food scientists call mouthfeel to a dish, a palate sensation that largely determines whether we accept or reject a particular dish.

Fat also acts as an emulsifier in some sauces. To make a classic French beurre blanc, softened butter is whipped into a reduction of wine and shallots. The acid in the wine holds the butter in suspension and creates a filmy sauce. Whisking a few tablespoons of butter into a sauce enriches it, emulsifies it, and gives it sheen.

English potted meats and French *rillettes* (potted pork) and duck *confit* (preserved duck) are packed into jars or crocks and sealed with a layer of melted fat—usually fat rendered from the meat itself. The fat effectively keeps out moisture and air, and extends the storage life of the food. Potted meats sealed with fat will keep for several weeks under refrigeration.

Recipes and Related Information
Bard, 25; Beurre Blanc, 518; Cake, 77; Cream, 161; Cream Puff Pastry, 162; Deep-fry, 174; Emulsion and Emulsifier, 212; Fry, 254; Lard, 338; Panfry, 404; Puff Pastry, 480; Sauté, 531; Stir-fry, 557; Yeast Bread, 613.

FEIJOA

Also known as the pineapple guava, the feijoa is a small oval fruit with a smooth, gray-green skin, a creamy white flesh with a juicy, pearlike texture, and a sweet flavor reminiscent of pineapple, pear, and banana. It is native to South America but is now grown in California and throughout the South Pacific.

Use   Enjoy feijoa "on the half shell," with lime or lemon. Peel, slice, and serve with prosciutto, or use it in fruit salads, preserves and jellies, sorbets, and mousses.

Availability   The New Zealand crop is available from March through June, the California fruit from September through December.

Selection   Ripe feijoas are fragrant and give slightly to gentle pressure.

Storage   Place ripe fruit in a plastic bag in the refrigerator crisper. Underripe fruit will ripen if kept at room temperature. Use ripe fruit as soon as possible.

FENNEL

Also known as finocchio, fennel is a plant of Mediterranean origin, valued for its bulb, leaves, stems, flowers, and seeds. The greenish white bulb is made up of overlapping ribs like those of celery, broad at the bulbous base but narrowing to tubular stems. Feathery green leaves grow up from the middle of the bulb. Raw fennel has a licoricelike flavor and a crunchy, celerylike texture. Cooking mutes the flavor somewhat and softens the texture.

PREPARING FENNEL

Cut off and discard upper portion, including feathery leaves and ribs; remove bruised or discolored outer ribs; trim base.

Halve trimmed bulbs and remove a wedge of tough core from each.

Slice halves thinly lengthwise; bulbs can also be sliced crosswise, depending upon use.

Use   Fennel bulb is eaten raw or cooked. Slice thinly and add it to salads, or dress with lemon, olive oil, and freshly grated Parmesan cheese for a first course, or serve it raw with an assortment of vegetables and a dipping sauce. Bake it with butter and bread crumbs, add it to soups or stews, or steam it and dress with butter and lemon or cheese sauce. Fennel bulb is particularly compatible with white-fleshed fish and lobster.

French cooks stuff fish with feathery fennel leaves or add leaves to salads or fish soups. The edible flowers may also be added to salads. Young fennel branches may be eaten raw with oil and salt or with a dip. Adding dried fennel branches to a fire imparts a special fragrance to grilled fish.

The small, yellowish brown fennel seed adds a licorice-like flavor to fish soups, breads, sausages, pork roasts, stuffings, and apple pie. Indians often serve fennel seed after dinner as a digestive and breath freshener.

Availability   Fresh bulb fennel is sold in Italian markets and many supermarkets in fall and winter. Fennel seed is available on supermarket spice racks.

Selection   Fennel bulb should be smooth and whitish green without cracks and discoloration; leaves should look fresh and lively, not wilted. The bulb should be compact; spreading at the top indicates overmaturity. For fennel seed, remember that packaged seasonings lose quality after a while; try to buy from a store that restocks its spice section fairly often.

Storage   Keep fennel in a plastic bag in the refrigerator crisper; use within three to four days. Store fennel seed in an airtight container in a cool, dark place; it will keep indefinitely.

Preparation   Trim bulb base and cut away feathery stalks (save for other uses). Remove thick, tough outer ribs. Halve, core, and slice crosswise or lengthwise. See Preparing Fennel at left.

Cooking   See BOIL, BRAISE, GRILL, STEAM, STIR-FRY.

■ BRAISED FENNEL

This simple treatment brings out the subtle, sweet flavor of fennel. Although the fennel takes some time to tenderize, the preparation is easy and needs little attention other than occasional stirring. If desired, substitute chicken stock for the water or use a mixture of half stock and half water. If stock was used, taste the finished dish before adding salt; most stocks are already seasoned.

> **3 large fennel bulbs**
> **½ cup olive oil**
>   **Salt, to taste**

1. Remove and discard damaged or wilted outside parts of fennel, as well as tops, and cut a slice off bottom of bulbs. Cut bulbs into lengthwise slices and wash slices in cold water.

2. Place fennel slices, olive oil, and water to barely cover in a saucepan. Cook over medium heat, uncovered, until fork-tender (30 to 40 minutes), stirring occasionally. If fennel becomes dry, add a bit of hot water. Add salt to taste and serve on a preheated platter.

Serves 4.

■ FENNEL AND ARTICHOKE SALAD

The first spring artichokes are a delicious partner for the last of the fennel. Marinated in oil and lemon, then served with toast and Parmesan cheese, the two vegetables flatter each other and almost any main course. Grilled fish, roast lamb, or chicken are all fine choices.

> **1 large *or* 2 small fennel bulbs**
> **3 lemons**
> **¾ cup olive oil**
>   **Coarse salt and freshly ground pepper, to taste**
> **4 small artichokes (about 2 to 3 in. diameter)**
> **12 slices toasted baguette (see Note)**
> **¼ pound Parmesan cheese, sliced in long, thin slabs**
>   **Olive oil and freshly ground pepper, for garnish**

1. Wash fennel bulbs and remove any tough outer stalks. Halve and core them, and slice thinly lengthwise. Put fennel slices in a stainless steel, glass, or ceramic bowl. Add juice of 2 lemons, olive oil, and salt and pepper to taste. Toss to blend and set aside to marinate.

2. Remove dark green outer leaves of artichokes; cut off top third of artichokes with a serrated knife. Rub all cut surfaces with lemon. Cook in boiling, salted water until just tender (12 to 15 minutes). Drain and refresh under cold running water, then drain thoroughly and pat dry. Cut artichokes in half. Add to fennel in bowl and stir to coat with oil. Marinate an additional 30 to 45 minutes. Taste and add more salt or remaining lemon if necessary.

3. To serve, spoon a little of the marinade onto individual salad plates. Arrange fennel atop marinade. Surround with slices of baguette. Top bread with artichoke hearts. Alternate Parmesan slices with bread slices on plates and drizzle salad with a little additional olive oil. Serve immediately and pass the pepper mill.

Serves 4.

Note   If desired, brush toast with garlic oil while bread is still warm.

FENUGREEK

The small, yellowish brown seeds inside the pods of the fenugreek plant are actually legumes, like peas and beans, but they are so aromatic when dried and roasted that they're used as a spice. Fenugreek is especially important to the cuisines of India and North and East Africa.

Use Fenugreek is an important ingredient in most curry powder blends. It is also, surprisingly, used to flavor imitation maple syrup. Ethiopians eat the tiny fenugreek seeds as a vegetable, cooking them as they do peas or beans; they also use fenugreek as a spice in stews. In India, fenugreek is an ingredient in chutneys and mango pickles as well as curries; in Morocco, fenugreek is added to breads.

Availability Whole fenugreek seed can be found in Indian and Middle Eastern markets and some specialty and health-food stores, usually in bulk.

Selection Packaged seasonings lose quality after a while; try to buy from a store that restocks its spice section fairly often.

Storage Keep fenugreek in an airtight container in a cool, dark place. It will last indefinitely. Ground fenugreek quickly loses its aromatic qualities; for maximum flavor, grind whole fenugreek as needed.

Preparation The full flavor of fenugreek is brought out by roasting. Toast whole seeds in a skillet over low heat, shaking skillet often, until seeds are fragrant. Soak them in water to soften, then grind in a pepper mill, clean coffee grinder, or electric minichopper, or with a mortar and pestle.

FERMENTATION

For home cooks, the most relevant application of fermentation relates to the action of yeast in breadmaking. When yeast is mixed with sugar in a moist, warm environment (around 80° F), a chemical reaction occurs, which as a by-product gives off carbon dioxide gas—the primary leavening agent for yeast bread doughs. Sugar is introduced into these doughs directly in granulated form and indirectly as the yeast converts starch present in flour into glucose, a simple sugar. Alcohol is also released during fermentation, but evaporates during baking. The appealing, yeasty aroma of making bread is in part due to products of fermentation.

Fermentation begins when the dough is mixed. Under conditions of proper temperature and the availability of fermentable sugars, it continues until the dough heats to 138° F in the oven, a temperature that kills yeast. Many bakers believe that a more flavorful yeast dough develops from slow fermentation. Most recipes more commonly refer to this process as rising or proofing.

Fermentation is also the process by which wine is made. A yeast naturally present on the skin of grapes feeds on the sugars in the fresh, crushed fruit to produce ethyl alcohol (ethanol) and carbon dioxide gas. Vintners commonly kill most of the wild yeast at the time of crushing with sulfur dioxide, because it produces inconsistent fermentation, and then add a "pure" strain of cultured yeast with known properties.

Once yeast starter is added to grapes (or juice) in the fermenting vessel, the yeast quickly multiplies, and before long millions of yeast cells are alive in the must (unfermented juice). For several days, the must ferments rapidly, and the carbon dioxide quickly bubbles out of the fermenting tank. Gradually, as the sugar is consumed and the alcohol level rises, the yeast cells begin to die and settle to the bottom of the tank.

Left alone, the wine will ferment completely dry, that is, until all the sugar is consumed. The vintner will step in, however, to control the fermentation process by monitoring temperature and adding sulfur dioxide, and, by filtering, to achieve a desired result.

Some wines undergo a second type of fermentation, known as malolactic fermentation, after the sugar fermentation is complete. Malolactic bacteria transform one of the natural grape acids, malic acid, into the less-tart-tasting lactic acid.

Recipes and Related Information
Yeast, 613; Yeast Bread, 613.

Ripe grapes, such as those shown here entering a stemmer/crusher, can contain as much as 25 percent sugar by weight, making them among the sweetest fruits. Fermentation by microscopic yeast cells turns the sugar to alcohol, and the juice into wine.

FIDDLEHEAD FERN

The ostrich fern, which grows wild in New England and Canada, puts forth tightly curled green shoots every spring. These shoots, known as fiddlehead ferns, are gathered when they are 2 to 5 inches long and very tightly curled and are a prized wild delicacy. The texture of the shoots resembles that of string beans; the flavor is akin to asparagus and spinach. The unfurled, mature shoots are poisonous.

Use Fiddlehead ferns are eaten both raw in salads and cooked. Steamed, they are delicious hot with butter or cold with vinaigrette. Stir cooked fiddleheads into scrambled eggs or toss with pasta; try them deep-fried or stir-fried with other vegetables.

Availability Fiddlehead ferns are gathered wild in the late spring in New England and Canada. They are available fresh in some markets at that time. Some specialty shops carry frozen and canned fiddlehead ferns.

Selection Choose the smallest fiddlehead ferns with solid green color and without browning. They should look tightly curled and crisp, not wilted.

Storage Wrap in damp paper towels, then place in a plastic bag in the refrigerator for no longer than one or two days.

Preparation Rub off fuzzy scales or wash under running water to remove them. Cook whole.

Cooking See DEEP-FRY, SAUTE, STIR-FRY.

Honey-sweetened Baklava, made with layers of paper-thin filo dough and ground almonds, is a satisfying accompaniment to a cup of rich, strong coffee.

BAKLAVA

These aromatic Greek pastries make a nice addition to a dessert buffet. They also freeze well.

  ½   **pound (half package) filo dough, thawed 8 hours in refrigerator if frozen**
  2   **cups ground blanched almonds**
  ¾   **cup sugar**
  1   **teaspoon grated lemon rind**
  ¾   **teaspoon ground cinnamon**
  1   **cup unsalted butter, melted**
      Sliced almonds, for garnish

Honey and Rose Water Syrup

  ¼   **cup *each* sugar and water**
  1   **cup honey**
  1   **tablespoon rose water**

1. Unfold sheets of filo dough so they lie flat. Cover with waxed paper, then a damp towel, to prevent them from drying out.

2. Preheat oven to 325° F. In a medium bowl combine almonds, sugar, lemon rind, and cinnamon. Generously butter an 8- or 9-inch-square pan.

3. Carefully fold 2 sheets of filo to fit pan; place in pan one at a time, brushing each with butter. Sprinkle about 3 tablespoons of the almond mixture over top sheet. Fold 1 sheet of filo to fit pan; brush with butter. Sprinkle evenly with another 3 tablespoons almond mixture.

4. Continue to add layers, using 1 folded sheet of filo, a generous brushing of butter, and 3 to 4 tablespoons almond mixture for each, until nut mixture is used up (there should be about 10 nut-filled layers).

5. Fold remaining 2 to 3 sheets of filo to fit pan. Place on top, brushing each with butter before adding the next. With a very sharp knife, carefully cut diagonally across pan to make small diamond shapes—about 1½ inches on a side—cutting all the way to bottom of pan. Pour on any remaining butter.

6. Bake until golden brown (about 45 minutes). Pour warm Honey and Rose Water Syrup over top. Decorate each piece with an almond slice. Cool before serving.

Makes about 2 dozen pastries.

Honey and Rose Water Syrup   Combine sugar and the water in a 1½-quart saucepan; bring to a boil, stirring. Mix in honey and cook until syrup boils again. Remove from heat; mix in rose water.

WALNUT-APPLE STRUDEL

Strudel is a typical Hungarian dessert, which traditionally uses homemade, paper-thin dough as the wrapper. The dough is extremely time-consuming and difficult to prepare. Using frozen filo dough streamlines the process.

  6   **sheets filo dough, thawed 8 hours in refrigerator if frozen**
  ½   **cup unsalted butter**
  1   **cup soft white bread crumbs**
  ½   **cup coarsely chopped walnuts**
  2   **large baking apples, cored and coarsely chopped**
  ¼   **cup sugar**
  ¼   **cup raisins**
  1   **teaspoon ground cinnamon**

1. Unfold sheets of filo dough so they lie flat. Cover with waxed paper, then a damp towel, to prevent them from drying out. Preheat oven to 350° F. Butter a baking sheet.

2. In a small sauté pan over medium heat, melt ¼ cup butter. Add bread crumbs and sauté until golden brown (about 7 minutes); set aside.

3. In a medium bowl combine walnuts, apples, sugar, raisins, and cinnamon; toss to coat walnuts and apples thoroughly.

4. Melt remaining butter in a small saucepan; remove from heat. Spread a slightly damp cloth over work area. Stack 2 sheets filo dough on cloth. Brush top sheet with melted butter. Repeat twice, stacking 2 sheets of dough each time.

5. Spread sautéed bread crumbs on top sheet of dough, leaving a 3-inch border of dough uncovered. Cover bread crumbs with walnut-apple mixture.

6. With longer edge of dough facing you, fold nearest edge back over filling, then lift cloth and roll dough and filling like a jelly roll. Seal seam with water. Pinch edges to seal; tuck under.

7. Place on buttered baking sheet; brush top with melted butter. Set sheet on center rack of oven and bake until strudel is golden brown (25 to 35 minutes). Slice roll into individual servings about 1½ inches wide.

Serves 4 to 6.

Food Processor Version Tear slices of fresh bread into pieces and put in work bowl with metal blade. Process 15 seconds and set aside. Use shredding disk for walnuts and set aside. Put cored, quartered apples in work bowl; turn motor on and off a few times to chop.

▦ TIROPITA

Because the cheeses vary in saltiness, taste the filling first and reduce the salt, if necessary. The little triangles can be frozen up to two months and baked direct from the freezer for quick party fare.

    2 bunches green onions, minced
    ½ cup parsley, minced
    1 clove garlic, minced
    ¼ pound Monterey jack cheese, shredded
    ¼ pound feta cheese, crumbled
    2 eggs
    ¼ teaspoon salt, or to taste
       Freshly ground pepper, to taste
   12 sheets filo dough, thawed 8 hours
       in refrigerator if frozen
    ¾ cup unsalted butter, melted

1. In a medium bowl stir together green onions, parsley, garlic, jack cheese, feta cheese, eggs, and salt and pepper to taste.

2. Place filo dough on work surface. Cut into strips about 3 inches wide; cover strips with waxed paper and a damp cloth to keep from drying out. Working with one strip at a time, brush with melted butter. Place a rounded tablespoon of cheese mixture at bottom of strip. Fold on diagonal to create a triangular shape; bottom edge of filo dough will touch left side of strip. Bring bottom of triangle up against straight edge. Fold again on diagonal so that left edge now touches right side. Repeat folding to top of strip, forming an enclosed triangular pastry. Brush folded triangle with melted butter. Repeat with remaining dough and filling.

3. Preheat oven to 400° F. Bake triangles on a baking sheet until lightly browned and hot (about 20 minutes). Cool about 2 minutes before serving.

Makes 3 dozen triangles.

Food Processor Version Cut green onions into 1-inch pieces. Use metal blade to chop green onion pieces, parsley, and garlic, turning motor on and off until desired consistency is obtained. Transfer to mixing bowl and add feta, eggs, salt, and pepper. Have jack cheese well chilled; process cheese with shredding disk and add to mixing bowl. Stir to blend with other ingredients. Continue with recipe.

FINISH, TO

Adding the final touches to a dish. This can include bringing food prepared ahead of time to serving temperature, arranging the food attractively on its plate, and adding garnishes to enhance visual appeal.

The term also specifically refers to the final attention paid by the cook to a sauce before serving it: to correct seasonings; to enrich with one or more of certain ingredients (butter, sour cream or crème fraîche, cream, or essences); and, when deemed appropriate, to add a splash of liquor to heighten the aroma.

FISH

How to purchase, prepare, and cook fish could be the subject of a multivolume cookbook. The world's lakes, rivers, and oceans are full of hundreds of species, many of which are unique to each region. Indeed, some cooks will argue that a bouillabaisse is authentic only when made in or near Marseilles, France, with local fish.

Modern transportation has improved that situation somewhat, bringing fresh Dover sole to Dallas and Maryland soft-shell crab to San Francisco. However, it is still true and worth acknowledging that fish is extremely perishable, that it ships successfully only under the most carefully controlled conditions, and that the most delicious fish is the one eaten within hours of capture. Anyone who has ever panfried and eaten a trout within moments of hooking it knows that even day-old fish has a markedly different flavor and texture. Freshness in fish is the first key to enjoyment. The second is selecting the proper cooking method.

This entry includes information to help the home cook select and prepare fish successfully; also see SHELLFISH.

CATEGORIZING FISH

Despite their great diversity, fish may be readily categorized in ways helpful to the cook. The three most important distinctions are: Is the fish round or flat? Is its flesh lean or oily? Is it from salt water or fresh water? The first question affects how the fish is cut for cooking. The second affects the choice of cooking method. The third has important health and safety implications.

basted generously during cooking to keep them moist, they may also be baked, broiled, or grilled.

Oily fish contain 5 to 50 percent fat. Their flesh is stronger tasting, richer, and less white than that of lean fish. Examples of oily fish are swordfish, trout, salmon, tuna, mackerel, catfish, sturgeon, smelt, sablefish, pompano, herring, anchovy, and eel. Because of their high oil content, they stay moist when cooked with little or no added liquid or fat (grilling, baking, and broiling). Only those oily fish lowest in fat, such as salmon, are appropriate choices for poaching.

SALT WATER OR FRESH WATER

As the popularity of sushi increases in the United States, it is important that cooks be aware of some dangers regarding raw fish. Freshwater fish from lakes and streams may carry parasites harmful to humans. Consequently, freshwater fish should never be eaten raw and are never used in sushi. Cooking to doneness—by any method—will kill any parasites present.

Parasites harmful to humans cannot survive in the flesh of saltwater fish. Consequently, such saltwater fish as tuna, halibut, salmon, and shellfish of all kinds are safe to eat raw if caught in nonpolluted waters.

Use   Depending on the character of the meat, fish may be poached, steamed, baked, panfried, grilled, broiled, braised, fried, smoked, or eaten raw. Fish bones can be used to make a stock for soups and sauces. Cooked cold fish can be used in salads, chowders, sandwich fillings, layered casseroles, fried cakes, or baked loaves. Whole fish can be stuffed and baked. Delicate fillets such as sole can be stuffed and rolled before baking. Firm-fleshed fish such as halibut and swordfish can be cubed and skewered for grilling.

Availability   Fish is available fresh or frozen, with the best selection usually found at specialty fish markets. Some markets keep fish in holding tanks for live purchase. For information on the most common retail market cuts, see Roundfish or Flatfish, Lean Flesh or Oily Flesh, and photograph at left.

Selection   Some people define fresh fish as fish that has never been frozen. However, a never-frozen fish can be considerably less than fresh. A truly fresh fish should not smell fishy—a sign of age or improper handling by the fishmonger. A fresh fish has a mild odor; firm, elastic flesh that springs back when pressed; clear, protruding eyes; reddish or pink gills; and scales that are shiny, bright, and tight to the skin.

As always, there are a few exceptions. Shark, skate, and ray, primitive fish with unique metabolisms, will have an ammoniated odor when freshly killed. Soaking them in milk or lightly acidulated water eliminates the smell. Without soaking, the odor will dissipate in a day or two, making shark, skate, and ray among the few fish that are better when not quite fresh.

There are two types of whole fish: flat and round, as illustrated by the top two fish in the photograph. Starting below the flatfish and moving clockwise, the most common cuts of fish include: whole pan-dressed fish (a small fish with head and tail, scaled, fins removed, and gutted); pan-dressed body (without head and tail); steak (a cross-section of a fish); butterflied fillet (both sides of fish still connected); fillets without skin; and fillets with skin.

ROUNDFISH OR FLATFISH

Based on their skeletal structure, all fish can be classified as either round or flat. Roundfish can be cooked whole or cut off the bone into two fillets. Large roundfish, salmon for example, can be cut crosswise into steaks. The fillets of some roundfish are thick enough to slice crosswise. Flatfish, such as flounder, cannot be satisfactorily cut into steaks or slices. They are either cooked whole or cut from the bone into four fillets, two top and two bottom.

LEAN FLESH OR OILY FLESH

Leaner fish have a mild flavor and firm white flesh. The oil or fat (5 percent or less of the total body substance) is concentrated in the liver, which is removed during cleaning. Sole, halibut, flounder, snapper, sea bass, burbot, turbot, and rockfish are examples of lean fish. Because their flesh dries out readily, they are well-suited to cooking with some sort of liquid or fat (poaching, steaming, sautéing); if

Some deep-water fish may have cloudy eyes from pressure changes when raised to the surface. Also, some flatfish may have dark, muddy gills, but they should be red or pink when washed.

If the fish has been frozen, ask how long it has been defrosted. Do not buy anything that has been defrosted for more than two days. It is better to purchase frozen fish and defrost it at home. For best quality, try to find fish that were individually quick-frozen on the fishing vessel.

Fillets offer fewer clues to freshness than whole fish. Look for flesh with a natural sheen; avoid fillets that are yellowing or browning around the edges. As with whole fish, the odor should be fresh and the flesh firm. If buying packaged frozen fillets, avoid packages that look as if they may have been thawed and refrozen. The telltale signs of fish that have been thawed at least once include a misshapen package and interior ice that is bloody.

When planning a meal, choose a recipe appropriate to the fish in season. When marketing, be prepared to change the recipe if the required fish is unavailable in good condition. It is wiser to buy the freshest fish available and plan the recipe around it.

Storage   The colder the storage temperature, the less rapidly fish deteriorates. To store fresh fish, pat dry, arrange in one layer in a baking dish lined with paper towels, cover with plastic wrap, and refrigerate. If possible, set the baking dish atop crushed ice in a larger pan, making sure the melting ice cannot enter the dish. Use as soon as possible.

Store frozen fish immediately in freezer, preferably at 0° F or below. Never refreeze thawed fish. One of the best ways to freeze a whole fresh fish is to ice glaze it. First set fish on a baking sheet and freeze just until firm. Dip frozen fish in ice water; a glaze will form immediately. Return fish to freezer to solidify glaze. Repeat glazing process until fish is coated with a layer of ice at least ⅛ inch thick. Wrap in heavy-duty foil, freezer paper, or a large plastic freezer bag and freeze. To freeze fillets and steaks, wrap individually or stack between sheets of freezer wrapping material. Wrap tightly, then overwrap. Always thaw frozen fish slowly in refrigerator.

Lean fish can be frozen longer than oily fish, large fish longer than small ones, whole fish longer than steaks or fillets. Freeze whole oily fish no longer than two months, whole lean fish no longer than six months. Freeze oily fillets no longer than one month, lean fillets no longer than three months.

Preparation   Both roundfish and flatfish need to be cleaned before use, but the cleaning procedures vary. Although a fishmonger can clean and cut up fish, there are advantages to buying fish whole: You will have a better idea of how fresh the fish is; you will have the bones and trimmings for stock; and on some fish, particularly salmon, you will get a better price per pound if you cut it up yourself.

Almost all fish require scaling. Some exceptions are trout, which have scales that are an integral part of the skin, and catfish, which have tough skin that must be removed altogether. If poaching the whole unboned fish, leave the dorsal and anal fins attached; they will help hold the fish together during poaching. See Scaling and Finning, page 227.

Gutting—removing the viscera or internal organs—can be done by the fishmonger or you can do it yourself. Because the entrails contain the bacteria that start decomposition, fish should be gutted as soon as possible—ideally, the moment it is caught, or immediately after being removed from the holding tank. If you plan to bone and fillet the fish, remove the entrails by gutting through the belly. If serving the fish whole, preserve the shape by gutting through the gills. The gutting techniques for roundfish are different from those used for flatfish. See Gutting, page 227.

Though many pan-sized fish have tasty skin that enhances flavor, some fish, such as largemouth bass and butterfish, have strong-tasting skin that interferes with the flavor of a dish. Leave skin on when poaching or grilling a whole fish. See Skinning, page 227.

Fillets are pieces of boneless fish. Steaks are cross sections cut from a whole fish. Roundfish and flatfish require slightly different filleting techniques. See Cutting Fillets and Steaks, page 228.

Cooking   The type of fish determines the most suitable cooking method. Select lean fish such as cod, sole, sea bass, or snapper for moist-heat or fat-based approaches. Use dry-heat methods on oily fish such as mackerel or tuna. Lean fish may be cooked by dry-heat methods if basted during cooking to prevent drying out. Frozen whole fish may be cooked from the frozen state. Fillets may have to be thawed to separate them; otherwise, cook from the frozen state.

See BRAISE, BROIL, DEEP-FRY, GRILL, PANFRY, POACH, SAUTE, STEAM, STEW, STIR-FRY.

The Common Fresh Fish chart on page 226 indicates preferred cooking methods for the major types of fish available in this country.

DRY-HEAT COOKING

Dry-heat cooking methods include baking, broiling, and grilling. Whatever the means, the goal is the same: cooking without robbing the food of moisture. Fish with a high internal fat or oil content are especially well suited for dry-heat cooking because they baste themselves. However, most fish have little internal fat to keep them moist during cooking, so to prevent them from drying out, a variety of precautions are available: wrapping with grape leaves, leafy greens, aluminum foil, or parchment paper; covering with vegetables, cream or bread crumb topping, or another coating; marinating and basting; stuffing; and leaving the head and tail attached.

COMMON FRESH FISH

Improved transportation, refrigeration, and freezing methods have broadened the choice of fish species available to cooks across the country. This chart offers cooking information for the most commonly available fish.

Type of Fish	Source	Flesh	Cooking Method
Anchovy	Salt water	Oily	Bake, Deep-fry, Grill, Pickle
Angler (monkfish, goosefish, lotte)	Salt water	Lean	Bake, Braise, Broil, Grill, Poach, Steam, Stew
Bonito (bonita)	Salt water	Moderately oily	Bake, Broil, Grill
Butterfish (Pacific pompano on West Coast)	Salt water	Oily	Bake, Broil, Grill
Carp	Fresh water	Moderately oily	Bake, Braise, Panfry, Poach, Steam, Stew
Catfish	Fresh water	Moderately oily	Bake, Braise, Broil, Grill, Panfry, Poach, Steam, Stew
Cod	Salt water	Lean	Bake, Braise, Broil, Grill, Panfry, Poach, Steam, Stew
Corbina (corvina)	Salt water	Moderately oily	Bake, Broil, Grill, Poach, Steam
Drum (redfish)	Salt water	Lean	Bake, Broil, Grill, Poach, Steam
Eel	Fresh water and salt water	Oily	Bake, Braise, Grill, Stew
Flounder	Salt water	Lean	Bake, Broil, Grill, Poach, Sauté, Steam
Grouper	Salt water	Lean	Bake, Braise, Broil, Fry, Grill, Poach, Steam, Stew
Haddock	Salt water	Lean	Bake, Braise, Broil, Fry, Grill, Poach, Steam, Stew
Hake	Salt water	Lean	Bake, Braise, Broil, Grill, Panfry, Poach, Steam, Stew
Halibut	Salt water	Lean	Bake, Broil, Grill, Poach, Sauté, Steam
Herring	Salt water	Oily	Bake, Broil, Grill, Pickle
Lake trout	Fresh water	Oily	Bake, Broil, Grill, Poach, Sauté, Steam
Mackerel	Salt water	Oily	Bake, Braise, Broil, Grill, Pickle, Stew
Monkfish (see Angler)			
Perch	Fresh water	Lean	Bake, Braise, Broil, Grill, Panfry, Poach, Sauté, Steam, Stew
Pike	Fresh water	Lean	Bake, Braise, Broil, Grill, Panfry, Poach, Sauté, Steam, Stew
Pollock	Salt water	Lean	Bake, Braise, Broil, Grill, Poach, Sauté, Steam, Stew
Pompano (Florida pompano)	Salt water	Moderately oily	Bake, Broil, Grill, Panfry, Sauté
Porgy	Salt water	Lean	Bake, Broil, Grill, Panfry
Ray	Salt water	Lean	Bake, Braise, Poach, Sauté, Steam, Stew
Red snapper (many fish labeled "snapper" are actually rockfish)	Salt water	Lean	Bake, Braise, Broil, Grill, Panfry, Poach, Sauté, Steam, Stew
Rockfish	Salt water	Lean	Bake, Braise, Broil, Grill, Panfry, Poach, Sauté, Steam, Stew
Sablefish (fillets known as butterfish on West Coast)	Salt water	Oily	Bake, Braise, Broil, Grill, Stew
Salmon	Salt water and fresh water	Moderately oily	Bake, Broil, Grill, Poach, Sauté, Smoke, Steam
Sea bass	Salt water	Lean	Bake, Braise, Broil, Grill, Panfry, Poach, Steam, Stew
Sea trout (weakfish)	Salt water	Moderately oily	Bake, Braise, Broil, Grill, Panfry, Poach, Steam, Stew
Shad	Fresh water	Moderately oily	Bake, Braise, Broil, Grill, Stew
Shark	Salt water	Lean	Bake, Braise, Broil, Grill, Panfry, Poach, Steam, Stew
Skate (see Ray)			
Smelt (whitebait)	Salt water	Oily	Bake, Broil, Grill, Panfry
Sole (petrale sole, rex sole, lemon sole, Dover sole)	Salt water	Lean	Bake, Broil, Grill, Poach, Sauté, Steam
Striped bass	Salt water and fresh water	Moderately oily	Bake, Braise, Broil, Grill, Poach, Sauté, Steam, Stew
Sturgeon	Salt water and fresh water	Oily	Bake, Broil, Grill, Sauté, Smoke
Swordfish	Salt water	Moderately oily	Bake, Braise, Broil, Grill, Stew
Tilefish	Salt water	Lean	Bake, Braise, Broil, Fry, Grill, Poach, Sauté, Steam, Stew
Trout	Fresh water	Moderately oily	Bake, Broil, Grill, Poach, Sauté, Smoke, Steam
Tuna	Salt water	Oily	Bake, Braise, Broil, Grill, Sauté, Stew
Turbot	Salt water	Lean	Bake, Poach, Sauté, Steam
White	Salt water	Lean	Bake, Broil, Grill, Panfry, Poach, Sauté, Steam
Whitebait (see Smelt)			
Whitefish	Fresh water	Oily	Bake, Broil, Grill, Smoke

SCALING AND FINNING

Wet fish and salt hands for a better grip. With a knife or scaler, start at tail and scrape toward head. Rinse fish well.

The dorsal (back) fin can be clipped with kitchen scissors, although this leaves part of the fin connected to the fish. Cut against the grain, tail to head.

To remove the whole dorsal fin, cut along each side of fin with a filleting or boning knife and pull fin toward head to remove it. Use the same method to remove anal fin (closest to tail at bottom). Clip other fins with scissors.

GUTTING

Flatfish *To gut a flatfish, make a small cut behind gills and pull out viscera. Rinse.*

Roundfish *To gut through belly, cut off head behind gill opening. Cut open belly from head end to just above anal (tail) fin area. Remove membranes, blood veins, and viscera. Rinse.*

To gut through gills, open outer gill with thumb. Reach a finger into gill and snag inner gill. Pull gently to remove inner gill and viscera. Rinse.

SKINNING

Catfish *Cut skin just behind head all around body. Wear gloves to protect hands from whiskerlike barbels and barbed fins. Hold head firmly and use pliers to peel skin toward tail.*

Flatfish *Place dark side of fish up, and cut across skin where tail joins body. Beginning at the cut, with knife or hand, pry up a piece of skin. Grasp skin flap with one hand while anchoring fish with other hand. Pull skin away from cut and over head. Turn fish over. Holding head, pull skin down to tail.*

Roundfish *Make a slit across body just behind gills and another slit just above tail. Make another cut down back. Using a thin knife, separate skin from flesh, starting at tail. Pull (don't saw) knife toward head, holding skin firmly with other hand.*

CUTTING FILLETS AND STEAKS

To fillet a skinned flatfish *Place skinned fish on a board with eyes up. Cut through flesh to the backbone (which is in the middle of the fish) from head to tail. Insert knife blade at a shallow angle between ribs and end of the fillet close to the head. Cut down the length of a fillet on one side of the backbone and remove it. Cut remaining fillet using the same technique. Turn fish over and remove two bottom fillets; rinse fillets in cold water.*

To fillet flatfish with skin left on *Cut along line that runs along skin to expose backbone. Cut around backbone to expose ribs. Insert knife between ribs and the end of fillet close to the head. Continue as for skinned flatfish. Turn fish over, cut through line on skin, and cut back away from backbone for one fillet; repeat on other side for second fillet.*

To skin a flatfish fillet *Place fish skin side down on a board; at tail end cut down at a 45-degree angle to the skin, but not all the way through. Pick up flesh at slit to get at skin. Holding skin taut, slide knife along skin without cutting it, wiggling skin back and forth (this motion will help the knife scrape through between flesh and skin).*

To fillet a roundfish *Make a very shallow cut along either side of the backbone with the tip of a paring knife, just to release ribs from backbone; don't cut into flesh. Entering fish at dorsal fin hole, slice along backbone from hole to tail; cut across tail, reverse direction, and cut up to head, stopping at gill cut. Trim half fillet from head by cutting down through backbone.*

To remove backbone *Slip knife under backbone about half way down from head; cut back to tail; reverse and cut back to head. Pull bone up and off to head; cut away head. To remove ribs, slip knife just under rib; cut away from you to remove ribs. Use tweezers or strawberry huller to remove any fine bones that may remain.*

Cutting a steak *Using a large, sharp knife, cut off the head just behind gills. Slice the fish crosswise into steaks of the desired thickness, usually between 1 and 1½ inches.*

CLASSIC BAKED FISH

This recipe lends itself to the use of any number of sauces, which can change the flavor of the fish in a variety of interesting ways.

    1 whole fish (3 to 4 lb), cleaned
 1½ teaspoons salt
  ½ teaspoon freshly ground pepper
  ½ lemon, sliced
     Unsalted butter, for greasing
  ½ cup water

1. Preheat oven to 425° F. Rub fish with salt, pepper, and lemon slices. Generously grease a large baking dish with butter. Place fish in dish and pour in the water.

2. Grease parchment paper or foil with unsalted butter and place over fish in baking dish.

3. Bake for 20 to 35 minutes; baking time depends on thickness of fish. Serve with sauce of your choice.

Serves 4 to 6.

BROILED SALMON
WITH SOUFFLE TOPPING

If you substitute dried herbs for fresh, use whole leaves. Serve this salmon dish with Fried Green Tomatoes (see page 581).

  ¾ cup unsalted butter
    1 large shallot, minced
    2 tablespoons minced fresh tarragon *or*
       1 tablespoon dried tarragon
    1 tablespoon minced fresh dill *or*
       ½ tablespoon dried dill
    2 tablespoons snipped fresh chives
    6 salmon fillets or steaks

Soufflé Topping

 1½ cups Mayonnaise (see page 519)
    2 tablespoons minced fresh *or*
       1 tablespoon dried tarragon
    1 tablespoon minced fresh *or*
       ½ tablespoon dried dill
    2 tablespoons snipped fresh chives
    2 egg whites

1. Preheat broiler. In a small saucepan melt butter. Add shallot, tarragon, dill, and chives. Place salmon in a large, heat-resistant gratin dish, and brush fish with the herb butter. Broil until fish is cooked (about 10 minutes); broiling time depends on thickness of fish.

2. Cover salmon with Soufflé Topping. Broil until puffy and brown (2 to 3 minutes).

Serves 6.

Soufflé Topping   In a small bowl combine Mayonnaise, tarragon, dill, and chives. Mix well. Beat egg whites until stiff but not dry; fold into mayonnaise mixture.

STURGEON BROCHETTE
WITH HONEY MUSTARD SAUCE

A brochette is usually served on a bed of rice. Try delicious Onion and Rice Soubise instead.

    4 sturgeon steaks (6 oz each), cut in
       6 to 8 equal pieces
    1 cup whipping cream
    3 tablespoons dry white wine
    1 tablespoon honey
    1 tablespoon coarse-grain mustard

Onion and Rice Soubise

    2 pounds white onions
    3 tablespoons unsalted butter
  ¾ cup rice
    2 cups Fish Fumet (see page 451) or
       Chicken Stock (see page 560)
    1 teaspoon salt
  ⅓ teaspoon white pepper
  ⅓ cup whipping cream
    2 tablespoons unsalted butter

1. Preheat broiler. Place fish on metal skewers.

2. In a small saucepan over medium-high heat, reduce cream by half (watch carefully to prevent cream from boiling over). When reduced add wine, honey, and mustard. Mix well, simmer 1 minute, and remove from heat.

3. Brush sturgeon with sauce. Place fish on baking sheet and broil 2 to 3 minutes, turning once. Serve with remaining sauce on a bed of Onion and Rice Soubise.

Serves 4 to 6.

Onion and Rice Soubise   Peel and coarsely slice onions. Melt the 3 tablespoons butter in a saucepan, add onions and cook for 5 to 7 minutes. Add rice, mix well, then add fumet, salt, and pepper. Cover and simmer 30 minutes. Purée the mixture in a food processor, adding cream and the 2 tablespoons butter. Reheat over low heat. Adjust seasonings and serve.

SWORDFISH PAILLARD WITH SALSA

In this recipe, *paillard* refers to a large, thin slice of fish. Serve with tortilla chips or warm corn tortillas.

    6 swordfish steaks (each ½-inch thick)
    3 tablespoons unsalted butter, melted
    1 teaspoon salt
  ½ teaspoon freshly ground pepper
       Salsa Cruda (see page 521)

1. Preheat broiler. Brush fish with butter and sprinkle with salt and pepper.

2. Broil fish 4 inches from heat for 1½ minutes. Turning the fish is unnecessary. Serve with Salsa Cruda.

Serves 6.

COOKING IN OIL

Sautéing, stir-frying, panfrying, and deep-frying are different cooking methods that have in common their reliance on the use of fats, a term that includes oils. Sautéing uses a very small amount of fat that often becomes part of the finished dish. Deep-fried food, on the other hand, is totally immersed in fat, which is not served with the final dish. Both of these cooking processes use extremely high temperatures; this seals in the flavor and succulence of the fish. To avoid greasy fried foods, it is important to monitor the temperature of the cooking fat; if too cool, the food could absorb the fat, and if too hot, the food will burn on its surface before being done inside.

■ PAN-FRIED CATFISH

As a bottom feeder, the "wild" catfish has an uncertain culinary reputation, but the rolling green hills of Tennessee are studded with limpid freshwater ponds where catfish are carefully bred and raised. Typically, a catfish farm includes a ramshackle roadside restaurant, from which an irresistible aroma of crisp, cornmeal-coated fried catfish wafts up and down the highway. One taste is enough to improve the catfish's reputation.

    4 to 6 **small catfish (about 1 lb each)** *or*
       2 to 3 pounds thick fillets from larger catfish
    ½ **cup flour**
    1 **teaspoon salt**
    ½ **teaspoon coarsely ground pepper**
    2 **eggs**
    1 **tablespoon water**
    1 **cup white cornmeal**
       Oil, for frying

1. Rinse catfish in cold water; dry with paper towels.

2. Mix flour, salt, and pepper. Dredge fish in the mixture and shake off excess. Place fish on waxed paper. Place eggs in a pie pan, add the water, and beat lightly to combine. Spread cornmeal on a large plate.

3. Heat ¼ inch oil in a large, heavy skillet (or two skillets, to cook all the fish at once). While oil is heating, dip fish in egg mixture, then roll in cornmeal to coat thoroughly, gently pressing the cornmeal onto fish. Place each coated fish on waxed paper.

4. When oil is rippling and fragrant (350° F), gently add fish to skillet(s), using long tongs to protect against spattering oil. Fry until coating is browned and fish is cooked through, turning carefully midway through cooking. Whole fish takes about 3 minutes per side, fillets 2 minutes per side. (For fillets, check doneness by inserting a knife; flesh should flake easily. For whole fish, inspect the flesh at the opening. Catfish retains a slightly pink color when cooked, but the flesh turns opaque.) Drain fish on paper towels and keep in the oven at low heat until ready to serve.

Serves 4 to 6.

■ HOT-AND-SOUR SHARK

Shark is a wonderfully full-flavored and versatile fish that lends itself to many types of cooking. Its lean flesh makes it well-suited for cooking techniques that use fat or other liquid—here a combination of deep-frying and stir-frying. The technique of coating with egg white and partially cooking the fish is called velveting and is common in Chinese cuisine. It produces a particularly attractive, crispy finish. Serve with steamed rice. For directions on how to prepare the sticky type of rice favored by the Chinese, see About Cooking Rice, page 274.

    2 **cups water**
       Zest of 1 orange, julienned
    2 **egg whites**
    2 **tablespoons dry sherry**
    3 **tablespoons cornstarch**
    4 **tablespoons peanut oil**
    1 **teaspoon salt**
    1 **pound shark, cut in 1- by ½-inch cubes**
       Oil, for deep-frying
    ½ **cup fresh orange juice**
    ½ **cup Chicken Stock (see page 560)**
    4 **tablespoons rice vinegar**
    2 **tablespoons sugar**
    2 **tablespoons soy sauce**
    ½ **cup julienned ginger (2-in. strips)**
    2 **dried red chiles, seeded and minced**
    ½ **cup slivered green onion (3-in. strips)**
    1 **cup seeded, julienned red bell pepper**
    2 **tablespoons minced green onion**

1. In a medium saucepan bring the water to a boil over medium-high heat. Add julienned orange zest and boil 1 minute. Remove zest from saucepan with slotted spoon, drain, and reserve.

2. In a medium bowl combine egg whites, sherry, 2 tablespoons of the cornstarch, 2 tablespoons of the peanut oil, and salt. Add shark pieces to mixture and toss to coat well.

3. In a Dutch oven, heavy deep skillet, or other frying kettle, heat at least 2 inches of oil for deep-frying to 350° F. Add shark pieces and fry until golden brown on all sides (2 to 3 minutes). Remove shark and drain on paper towels. Keep warm.

4. In small bowl combine orange juice, Chicken Stock, vinegar, remaining 1 tablespoon cornstarch, sugar, and soy sauce. In wok heat remaining 2 tablespoons peanut oil. Add ginger and chiles; stir-fry 1 minute. Add the ½ cup slivered green onion and bell pepper; stir-fry 1 minute. Add orange juice mixture; stir until it thickens.

5. Transfer shark to wok, add zest, toss, and reheat. Garnish with the 2 tablespoons minced green onion and serve immediately.

Serves 4 to 6.

Fresh trout is at its best when prepared simply. Here it is sautéed quickly, then served with a sauce of butter, lemon juice, and parsley, and garnished with toasted sliced almonds.

TROUT WITH ALMONDS

Golden sautéed almonds are a crisp, flavorful contrast to the delicate trout. You can use almost any small whole fish in this recipe.

    4 medium trout, cleaned
      Fresh lemon juice
      Freshly cracked black peppercorns
    6 tablespoons butter
    2 tablespoons oil
    ½ cup sliced almonds
    ¼ cup *each* fresh lemon juice or white wine
      and minced parsley
      Lemon slices and dill sprigs, for garnish

1. Rub trout with lemon juice and pepper.

2. Warm serving platter for fish in 200° F oven.

3. In a wide frying pan large enough to hold the 4 trout (use two pans if necessary), melt 2 tablespoons of the butter with the oil over medium-high heat. Add trout and sauté until lightly browned on one side. Turn when edges become opaque and curl slightly (3 to 5 minutes). The fish is done when it flakes at the touch of a fork at the thickest portion near the backbone. Remove fish to warm platter. Wipe out pan.

4. Melt the remaining ¼ cup butter in pan. Add almonds and sauté until golden.

5. Combine lemon juice and parsley and add to almonds. Swirl and pour sauce over trout. Garnish with lemon slices and sprigs of dill.

Serves 4.

BLACKENED FISH

The technique of charring fish in a hot cast-iron skillet was created by Paul Prudhomme especially for Louisiana red-fish. It is now prepared coast to coast in Cajun and Creole restaurants. A good exhaust fan is essential because a great deal of smoke is given off during cooking. The fish cooks rapidly, so to avoid fish that are finished on the outside but underdone within, use fillets that are not more than ½ inch thick.

    ½ cup unsalted butter, melted
    4 tablespoons vegetable oil
    1 teaspoon salt
    1 teaspoon cayenne pepper
    ½ teaspoon freshly ground black pepper
    ½ teaspoon dried thyme
    ½ teaspoon paprika
    4 fish fillets (about 2 lb total), each ½ inch thick

1. Place a cast-iron skillet over high heat until white hot (about 10 minutes).

2. Combine 4 tablespoons of the butter with oil in a shallow bowl. In another small bowl mix salt, cayenne, black pepper, thyme, and paprika. Dip each fish fillet in butter-oil mixture, then sprinkle with about 1 teaspoon seasoning mixture.

3. Place fillets in hot pan for exactly 2 minutes. Turn fillets over and cook second side for exactly 2 minutes. Remove from pan and serve immediately, drizzled with remaining butter.

Serves 4.

MOIST-HEAT COOKING

Fish requires delicate cooking. Moist heat provides a gentle means of cooking that is suitable for any type of fish. Moist-heat cooking methods—poaching, steaming, braising, and stewing—use liquid as a cooking medium. The differences among these methods lie in whether the food is cooked above the liquid (steaming) or in it (poaching, braising, and stewing), and in whether the cooking liquid is served as a part of the finished dish (braising and stewing) or not (poaching and steaming).

◾ STEAMED WHOLE FISH, CHINESE-STYLE

This presentation of steamed fish is a Chinese classic. The use of more fresh onions and herbs at the finish enhances the dish. Serve with steamed or fried rice.

  1 **whole carp or sea bass, cleaned**
  2 **tablespoons soy sauce**
  2 **tablespoons dry sherry**
  ¼ **cup julienned peeled fresh ginger**
  2 **green onions, slivered (4-in. strips;**
    use part of the green)
  8 **sprigs cilantro**
    Cilantro, for garnish
    Green onion, slivered, for garnish

1. Place fish on plate in steaming rack. (If you do not have a steamer large enough, put the plate on a rack in a turkey roaster.)

2. Sprinkle soy sauce, sherry, ginger, and the 2 slivered green onions over fish. Arrange the 8 sprigs of cilantro on top of fish.

3. Pour boiling water into pan until it comes within 1 inch of fish. Cover and steam about 15 minutes (cooking time depends on the size of the fish).

4. Remove plate from steamer and serve fish directly from plate. Garnish with cilantro and green onion.

Serves 6 to 8.

◾ COLD FILLET OF SOLE WITH CILANTRO, LIME, AND POMEGRANATE

This dish makes a wonderfully cool summer lunch or a fine first course to balance a heavy entrée such as lamb. To seed a pomegranate, see page 453.

  8 **fillets sole**
  1 **teaspoon salt**
  ½ **teaspoon freshly ground pepper**
 16 **sprigs cilantro**
  2 **jalapeño or serrano chiles, seeded,**
    deveined, and minced
  6 **to 8 cups Wine Court Bouillon (page 450)**
    Cilantro leaves
    Lime juice
  8 **thin slices of lime, for garnish**
  ½ **cup pomegranate seeds, for garnish**

1. Pat fillets dry. Place outer side of fillet down and sprinkle with salt and pepper. Place 2 sprigs of cilantro and some of the minced chiles in the center of each fillet. Fold the fillets in thirds and place folded side down in a wide, shallow saucepan.

2. Pour court bouillon over fish. The fish should be completely immersed. Cover and bring to a simmer. Poach 8 to 10 minutes. Remove from heat and cool in poaching liquid. When cool, remove from liquid.

3. To serve, sprinkle fish with the cilantro leaves and fresh lime juice. Top each fillet with a slice of lime and some pomegranate seeds.

Serves 8.

◾ PORTUGUESE FISH STEW

The distinct flavors and the herbaceous quality of the kale provide a perfect foil for the fish. The original dish used salted cod instead of fresh fish; in this version the smoked ham supplies the extra flavor.

  3 **tablespoons olive oil**
  2 **pounds cod**
  ¼ **cup fruity olive oil**
  3 **pounds new potatoes, cooked, peeled,**
    and cut in ½-inch dice
  8 **cloves garlic, peeled and quartered**
  1 **pound kale, shredded in ¼-inch strips**
    Salt and freshly ground black pepper
  ¼ **pound smoked ham cut in slivers**
  1 **cup dry white wine**

1. In a large Dutch oven heat the 3 tablespoons olive oil. Add fish to pan, fry 1 minute on each side, and remove from pan.

2. Add the ¼ cup olive oil to pan. Add potatoes and toss over medium heat until coated. Add garlic and sauté 1 minute. Add kale to pan, turning to coat with oil. Cover and cook until the greens begin to wilt (2 to 3 minutes).

3. Sprinkle potatoes and greens with salt, pepper, and slivered ham. Arrange fish on top and pour in wine. Add enough water to barely reach top of greens.

4. Cover and simmer 25 to 35 minutes, shaking pan occasionally. When potatoes are done, correct seasonings and serve.

Serves 6 to 8.

OTHER WAYS WITH FISH

Not all fish is cooked in the conventional way, or even cooked at all. The recipes here are for Japanese sushi (see opposite page), which is vinegared rice garnished with raw fish and served with various condiments. Scandinavian gravlax (see opposite page) consists of raw fish in a dry, sugar-based marinade; and Latin American seviche (see page 234) uses citrus juice to firm up fish protein in much the same way that heat does.

NIGIRI SUSHI

Although it takes many years to become a full-fledged sushi chef, any cook with a sharp knife can make a modest platter of *nigiri* sushi. Nigiri are thin slices of raw fish draped across "fingers" of molded sushi rice. Tuna and shrimp both lend themselves to this treatment. See the photographs at right for guidance in making sushi. Accompany sushi with warm sake (Japanese rice wine), a dry white wine, or cocktails.

    1 tablespoon wasabi (Japanese horseradish, available powdered in Japanese markets)
    2 tablespoons rice vinegar
    1 cup water
 1½ pounds fresh tuna fillet, in one piece
    2 cups Sushi Rice (recipe follows)

Wasabi Dipping Sauce

    2 tablespoons wasabi (see note, above)
  ¼ cup soy sauce
    2 tablespoons minced green onion
    1 tablespoon rice wine

1. In a small bowl mix *wasabi* with just enough cold water to form a thick paste. Set aside. In another bowl combine rice vinegar and water. Slice fish into twenty-four 1-ounce portions.

2. Using the vinegar-water solution to keep your hands damp, pick up a small portion of rice and gently form it into a small oval. Dot the top of the oval with a little wasabi paste and place a slice of tuna on top. Repeat with remaining rice and tuna. Arrange sushi on a platter, preferably a Japanese-style lacquer or porcelain tray. Serve with dipping sauce.

Makes 2 dozen sushi.

Wasabi Dipping Sauce Combine wasabi with just enough cold water to form a thick paste. Just before serving, combine wasabi paste, soy sauce, green onions, and rice wine.

SUSHI RICE

A vinegar dressing adds flavor to this rice, which has a sticky, but not mushy, consistency.

 3⅓ cups short-grain rice
    4 cups water
    1 three-inch square of konbu (dried kelp, available in Japanese markets); optional

Vinegar Dressing

    5 to 6 tablespoons rice vinegar
    5 tablespoons sugar
    4 teaspoons salt

1. Place rice in a large bowl; cover with cold water. Run hands through rice to remove starch, until water turns cloudy; drain. Repeat until water remains clear; drain.

2. Place rice in saucepan with the 4 cups cold water. Place *konbu* (if used) on top. Cover saucepan and bring to a boil over high heat; boil 2 minutes. Reduce heat to medium and boil, covered, for 5 minutes. Reduce heat to lowest possible setting and cook until all moisture is absorbed (about 15 minutes). Uncover; place a towel over top of pot, and cover again. Let rest 15 minutes.

3. With a thin tool like a wooden spatula held vertically, cut dressing into cooked rice, being careful not to mash rice. Mix until rice is glossy and holds together but is not mushy. Rice may be kept in a cool place, covered with a damp cloth, for up to 2 days; it should not be refrigerated.

Makes about 6 cups.

Vinegar Dressing In a small saucepan over low heat, combine all ingredients and cook until sugar and salt dissolve. Cool to room temperature. Keeps indefinitely.

GRAVLAX

Salt and sugar draw out juices, while the flavors of herbs and spices are absorbed by the fish.

    1 salmon (4 lb), boned, head removed, skin intact
  ¼ cup kosher salt
  ¼ cup sugar
    1 tablespoon crushed white peppercorns
    1 cup chopped fresh dill

Mustard Sauce

    4 tablespoons Creole mustard
    1 teaspoon hot mustard
    3 tablespoons sugar
    2 tablespoons white vinegar
  ⅓ cup vegetable oil
    2 to 3 tablespoons chopped fresh dill

1. Cut salmon into 2 pieces along the backbone. Wipe dry. In a small bowl, combine salt, sugar, and peppercorns, and rub fish on both sides with mixture. In a large, deep dish, sprinkle part of salt mixture and one third of the dill. Lay one piece of fish in dish, sprinkle with one third of the dill, and some salt mixture. Lay other piece of fish on top of the first piece. Sprinkle with remaining salt mixture and dill.

2. Cover tightly with foil, place heavy book or two bricks on top of foil to press down on fish. Refrigerate. After 4 to 6 hours some liquid will leach out; discard it. Refrigerate for 3 days, turning periodically so that the salt and seasonings penetrate evenly.

3. Before serving, drain fish on towel and scrape off the marinade. Place each fillet skin side down on serving board and cut thin diagonal slices across the grain. Serve with Mustard Sauce.

Serves 10 to 12.

Mustard Sauce In a small bowl combine all ingredients. Mix well.

HOW TO MAKE NIGIRI SUSHI

Slice boned fish fillet across the grain, approximately ¼ inch thick, to fit the shape of the rice oval (see middle photograph). To butterfly shrimp, using a sharp knife, slit the shrimp down its back, being careful not to cut all the way through. Gently flatten out the shrimp, with the cut side down.

Moisten hands with mixture of rice vinegar and water (see Nigiri Sushi recipe at left). Form a small amount of Sushi Rice (see recipe at left) into an oval.

Finished Nigiri Sushi: Rice oval is topped with a dab of wasabi paste and a slice of fish or a butterflied shrimp.

Fresh cauliflower and broccoli florets can be tray-frozen (see page 242) and then packaged airtight for later use.

■ SEVICHE

Putting limes in boiling water for one minute will yield more juice, as will warming them in a microwave oven at 50 percent power for one minute.

    1½ pounds white-fleshed fish, skinned and boned
    1½ cups fresh lime juice
     1 cup vegetable oil
     1 cup fresh orange juice
     1 to 2 hot red chiles, seeded and slivered
     1 small onion, sliced paper-thin
     1 clove garlic, minced
        Kosher salt and freshly ground pepper, to taste

1. Cut fish into ½-inch cubes; place in a small glass dish and cover with lime juice. It is extremely important that lime juice covers all of the fish. Add more if necessary.

2. Cover with plastic wrap and refrigerate for 4 to 5 hours. In the meantime, combine vegetable oil, orange juice, chiles, onion, and garlic. After fish has marinated for 3 hours, add orange juice mixture. Chill at least 2 more hours. Add salt and pepper to taste.

Serves 6 to 8.

Recipes and Related Information
Alder-Grilled Salmon, 296; Bombay Tuna, 509; Cioppino, 556; Coulibiac, 377; Dry Spice Rub for Fish, 350; Fritto Misto With Caper Mayonnaise, 176; Grilled Tuna, 295; Makizushi, 392; Poached Fish Steaks With Fresh Herbs and Cream, 452; Quenelles, 241; Steamed Salmon Steaks With Black Bean Sauce, 554.

FLAMBE, TO; FLAME, TO

To ignite foods that have liquor added, done for dramatic effect and to develop a rich flavor. Cherries Jubilee (see page 315)—vanilla ice cream with a sauce of cherries, brandy, and kirsch—is finished this way. Many savory sautés are flamed to enhance the perfume of the sauce.

If using a gas burner, tip pan slightly so wafting fumes ignite. For either gas or electric burners, ignite with a long kitchen or fireplace match. Let cook until flame disappears (at this point all alcohol has burned off). To retain some alcohol for its flavor, cover flaming dish to extinguish, or snuff out by adding wine or stock.

Liquor can also be heated in a microwave oven: Set in microwave-safe dish and heat 30 to 45 seconds at 100 percent power.

Caution   Never pour liquor from a bottle into a pan that is near an open flame. The flame can follow the stream of alcohol into the bottle and cause it to explode. Remove food from heat, add liquor (from a small pan or dish; if from the bottle, remember to set bottle away from cooking area after use), and return pan to burner.

FLAVOR, TO; FLAVORING

To give or enhance taste by the addition of extra ingredients. Extracts, herbs and spices, and wines and liqueurs are commonly used for this purpose.

A flavoring is any substance that adds taste.

Recipes and Related Information
Extract and Essence, 213; Herb, 299; Spice, 549; Wine in Cooking, 608.

FLORET

These bud clusters that form the head of broccoli and cauliflower are often cut from their stalks and cooked separately. They are also called flowerets. Fresh broccoli has tightly closed flower buds, without yellowing; a head of fresh cauliflower should be creamy white and free of brown spots.

FLOUR, TO; FLOUR

To coat with flour; the finely ground meal itself. Flour is often used as a covering for foods that will be sautéed or panfried. It acts as a barrier to keep the surface of food dry (moisture causes hot oil to sputter and drop in temperature; wet foods steam instead of fry and don't brown properly). A light first layer of flour also helps batters and bread crumb coatings adhere better. Bakers often dust cake pans with flour to prevent sticking and, in some cases, to give batter something to grip as it rises. Always remove excess flour; otherwise the coat will be unpleasantly thick. To do this, lightly tap the food or pan with your hand so that the coating is even, but fine.

Flour as an ingredient is a difficult word to define precisely. Although it most commonly describes the powdery meal derived from a grain (wheat flour, rye flour), some flours (soy flour, chick-pea flour) are ground from legumes or are made from potatoes and other starchy vegetables, nuts, and carob. For clarity of presentation, the following remarks apply only to wheat flour. Other flours are discussed separately at the end of the section.

FROM GRAIN TO FLOUR: MILLING, BLEACHING, AND AGING

Milling is the process that turns whole hard grain into fine flour. Historically most grains were ground into flour between rotating stones. Although stone-ground flour is still available, especially in health-food stores, most flour today is milled between two grooved rollers.

The mechanical rollers crack the grain, allowing germ and bran to be sieved off the endosperm (the heart of the grain). The endosperm is then ground to desired size. For whole grain flours, bran and germ are then added back. The mechanical rollers generate considerable heat; if the high-fat germ and bran were left in during grinding, the heat would accelerate rancidity.

Wheat flour has a light yellow color after milling. For aesthetic reasons, some wheat flour is bleached, usually with chlorine dioxide, to turn it white quickly. If allowed to age for one or two months it would turn white naturally through oxidation. Aging improves baking qualities but takes time and space. To speed the process, both bleached and unbleached flours are chemically aged with potassium bromate or iodate.

Use Wheat flour serves as a thickener; as a coating for fried foods; as the basis for noodles; as the foundation of many batters such as those for pancakes, waffles, and fritters; and as the main ingredient in an enormous variety of baked goods, from breads, muffins, and biscuits to cakes, cookies, pies, and pastries.

Wheat flour is a protein food that is highly absorbent. When mixed with a liquid and manipulated, two of the water-soluble proteins—glutenin and gliadin—combine to form gluten. As a batter or dough is stirred, beaten, or mixed, strands of gluten develop into a cellular, elastic network that traps air and other gases released by leavening agents. In the oven, heat causes these gases to expand, which in turn stretches the gluten. This expansion creates volume and lightness in breads, cakes, pastries, and all leavened baked goods. Toward the end of the baking time, the proteins firm, giving the final product its structure. The amount of gluten that can be developed in any batter or dough is directly related to the protein content of the flour (see Availability for a discussion of the types of flour, including protein content; also see About Nonwheat Flours).

Baking Flour gives structure to an endless variety of baked goods. When a firm, sturdy texture is desired, as for breads, the dough is kneaded repeatedly to help develop gluten (see KNEAD). When a tender, crumbly texture is desired, as in cakes and pie crusts, the moistened flour is handled lightly to avoid development of gluten.

Batter Flour gives structure to batters for fritters, pancakes, waffles, and crêpes. To avoid development of gluten and to ensure a tender texture, flour should be mixed in lightly; overmixing produces a tough texture.

Coating Pan-fried foods, such as fish, veal and pork scallops, and sliced eggplant, are usually dusted with flour before cooking to prevent them from sticking. Deep-fried foods, such as chicken, fish, and onion rings, are frequently given an initial light dusting with flour to promote the formation of a protective coating that will keep moisture in.

Thickening When dissolved in a hot liquid, the starch granules in flour swell, absorbing water molecules and causing the mixture to thicken. Flour is added to sauces, stews, soups, puddings, and creams for this purpose. As a rule, using 1 tablespoon flour per cup of liquid produces a thin sauce; using 2 tablespoons per cup produces a medium-thick sauce; using 3 tablespoons per cup produces a thick sauce. In general, flour-thickened liquids should be cooked for at least several minutes after flour is added to remove any raw flour taste.

Availability The flours sold to consumers are of three basic kinds: hard-wheat, soft-wheat, and all-purpose.

All-Purpose Flour A blend of hard- and soft-wheat flours, this type is a hybrid. Its medium protein and starch content makes it acceptable for most culinary purposes. All-purpose flour can successfully be used in both bread and cake recipes, although it will not produce the superior product a specialized flour will. In most recipes that call simply for flour, use all-purpose flour.

Durum Flour Ground from durum wheat, the hardest wheat grown, durum flour makes an extremely sturdy dough and is thus the choice for commercially manufactured dried pasta. Durum flour is also known as semolina. It is coarsely ground and never bleached.

Enriched Flour When bran and germ are removed from wheat flour during milling, most of the A and B vitamins and iron are removed as well. To make enriched flour, the B vitamins and iron are added back. Some manufacturers also add calcium and vitamin D. Enrichment is not mandated at the federal level; however, 38 states require enrichment of white flour to specifications determined by each state.

Gluten Flour or High-Gluten Flour This flour is derived from hard wheat that has been treated to remove some of its starch and concentrate its protein. It contains at least 70 percent pure gluten. Gluten flour is used in special diets for people who cannot otherwise tolerate wheat flour. It can be used in combination with low-gluten flours to improve the gluten-forming abilities of a dough, or it can be combined with regular wheat flour in bread doughs in the ratio of two to one. If used this way, decrease kneading time by one fourth to avoid overdeveloping gluten. The first rising will be quicker, the second rising slower than for a regular wheat dough.

Hard-Wheat Flour (Bread Flour) This type is generally packaged as bread flour. It is ground from hard wheat—wheat with a high protein and low starch content. The relatively high quantities of glutenin and gliadin make hard-wheat flour preferable for baking bread.

Self-Rising Flour The miller has preblended chemical leavenings and salt into flour to make self-rising flour, most common in southern states. Unless self-rising flour is stored under ideal conditions and turns over quickly in the

TIPS

IS SIFTING NECESSARY?

Almost all commercial flours available to the home baker today have been sifted many times before packaging. "Presifted" commonly appears on package labels to indicate that the flour does not require sifting before use.

Technically it does not. Given modern milling practices, it is highly unlikely that home bakers will find foreign particles or coarse bits of grain in their flour; removing these undesirable additions was a primary reason for sifting. Sifting does, however, aerate flour, giving it greater volume. Because most recipes, especially older ones, are written under the assumption that cooks have sifted the flour before measuring, it is a good idea to do so whenever a recipe calls for sifted flour. Sift, then measure as directed in Preparation. The aeration provided by sifting is more important with delicate cakes that have little or no chemical leavening, such as angel food, sponge, and pound cakes. Wherever sifting is not specifically suggested, it may be omitted.

Preparation   If possible gather flowers in the early morning when dew has just dried on them. If necessary, wash gently and pat dry. If they must be held for several hours, dip in ice water to refresh them just before using. When adding flowers to a salad, incorporate them after salad has been dressed and tossed, just before serving.

■ DEEP-FRIED ZUCCHINI BLOSSOMS

Fried squash blossoms are an Italian specialty that has stimulated many creative American chefs to develop their own versions. This recipe uses zucchini blossoms, available at specialty produce markets or from a home vegetable garden. The filling is a rich, seasoned blend of mozzarella cheese and hot peppers; a variation made with goat cheese and sun-dried tomato is offered as well. Serve this dish as an appetizer or first course.

Batter

      2 **eggs, separated**
     ½ **cup water**
     ¼ **cup white wine**
      2 **tablespoons vegetable oil**
      1 **teaspoon Worcestershire sauce**
      1 **cup flour**
     ½ **teaspoon salt**

Blossoms

     ½ to ¾ **pound mozzarella cheese, cut into ½-inch cubes**
      2 to 4 **jalapeño chiles, chopped, *or* 1 can (4 oz) diced green chiles for a milder taste**
     30 **squash blossoms, flowers cleaned and stems removed**
          Oil, for frying
          Salt and freshly ground pepper

Tomato Dipping Sauce

      3 **shallots, finely chopped, *or* ½ onion, finely chopped**
      2 **tablespoons olive oil**
      3 **cloves garlic, finely chopped**
     ½ **teaspoon *each* crushed dried oregano, thyme, and basil *or* 1 teaspoon *each* chopped fresh oregano and thyme, and 1 tablespoon chopped fresh basil**
      1 **teaspoon sugar**
      1 **can (28 oz) plum tomatoes (preferably peeled, crushed, and with added purée)**
     ½ **teaspoon *each* salt and freshly ground pepper**
          Dash hot-pepper sauce, or to taste
          Dash Worcestershire sauce, or to taste

1. *For the batter:* In a blender combine egg yolks, the water, wine, oil, Worcestershire sauce, flour, and salt on high speed. Let batter stand at least 1 hour.

2. *For the blossoms:* In a medium bowl toss together mozzarella and chopped chiles (do not handle chiles with

bare hands; use a wooden spoon or wear gloves). Gently fill blossoms with cheese mixture. Twist ends of petals to enclose stuffing. (Blossoms may be prepared ahead to this point, chilled on paper towels, and brought to room temperature about 30 minutes before frying.)

3. *To cook:* In a Dutch oven, deep, heavy skillet, or other frying kettle, heat 3 to 4 inches of oil to 370° F. Beat reserved egg whites to soft peaks; fold into batter.

4. Dip blossoms into batter, making sure they are completely coated. Drop into hot oil, frying several at once, but do not crowd in pan. Fry until golden, turning occasionally. Remove from pan with a slotted spoon and drain on paper towels. Sprinkle with salt and pepper, and serve immediately accompanied with Tomato Dipping Sauce.

Makes 30 appetizers or 10 first courses.

Tomato Dipping Sauce   In a medium saucepan sauté shallots in olive oil over medium heat until softened and transparent. Add garlic and cook 30 seconds. Add oregano, thyme, basil, and sugar, then tomatoes, and bring to a boil, stirring. Reduce heat to simmer and cook, stirring occasionally to prevent scorching, until a rich sauce develops, thick enough to coat stirring spoon (about 30 minutes). Taste, add salt, pepper, hot-pepper sauce, and Worcestershire sauce; adjust seasonings if necessary. Serve hot, at room temperature, or cold. If a smoother, less chunky sauce is desired, purée in a blender or food processor, or strain through a sieve or food mill.

Makes 2 to 2½ cups.

Variation   Combine ¾ pound softened goat cheese with 6 to 8 chopped sun-dried tomatoes. Use this mixture to fill zucchini blossoms. Twist ends of petals to enclose stuffing. Proceed with step 3 in main recipe.

■ CRYSTALLIZED FLOWERS

These flowers make lovely edible decorations for elegant desserts. Choose white or brightly colored flowers (not sprayed or treated in any way) with simple petal arrangements, such as small orchids, roses, sweet peas, and violets. This treatment also works well with grapes.

Wash blossoms quickly and gently pat dry with paper towels. Place 1 egg white in a small bowl; beat until foamy. Dip flowers, one at a time, in egg white or apply egg white with a small artist's brush; cover all parts of petals. Remove excess egg white so that petals won't stick together.

Sprinkle or sift superfine sugar over petals. Cover all egg white, shaking to avoid clumping. Blow softly on flowers to remove excess sugar. Place flowers on an aluminum foil–lined baking sheet. Let dry in cool area or in refrigerator for 2 to 3 days.

Recipes and Related Information
Candy, 93; Salad, 506.

FLUFF, TO

To lighten texture and remove lumps by tossing with a fork. Rice is commonly fluffed before serving to separate the cooked grains.

FLUTE, TO

To make an attractive edge on a pie crust by pinching the pastry with thumb and index finger into interconnecting V shapes or scallops. Decorative grooves or channels are also cut into mushrooms and other vegetables and fruits.

FOLD, TO; FOLD IN, TO

To incorporate a light, aerated mixture (usually beaten egg whites or whipped cream) into a heavier mixture without deflating the lighter mixture. This can be done with your hand, a rubber spatula, or a spoon, and with a down-up-and-over motion. It is a technique that even many experienced cooks perform improperly, but one that can be mastered with some practice and an understanding of its purpose.

Folding in beaten egg whites can have two goals: to lighten the texture of a batter or cream, and to act as a leavening agent for batters. Whipped cream also lightens a mixture and is often gently blended into sauces, soufflés, and other sweet and savory dishes.

When folding, first carefully stir about one fourth to one third of the beaten whites or whipped cream into the heavier mixture to lighten it. The resulting lightened mixture is easier to blend with the remaining whites or cream because mixtures of similar consistency can be more readily folded together.

Pour remaining whites or cream on top of the heavier mixture. Cut down through the center of the mixture, then scrape across the bottom of the bowl and up one side with a single, fluid lifting motion. This brings the mixture pushed by the spatula or spoon up and over the surface. As you fold, give the bowl a quarter turn with the other hand. Repeat the motion several times just until all the ingredients are blended (some streakiness is acceptable). Work quickly but lightly, taking care not to deflate the lighter mixture and therefore decrease volume of final product.

FOOD COLORING

The composition of food coloring and food dyes is highly regulated. Approved colorings vary from country to country. They may be artificial (derived from oil) or natural (derived from vegetables, plants, or insects). In general the natural colors are weaker and less stable. Most com-

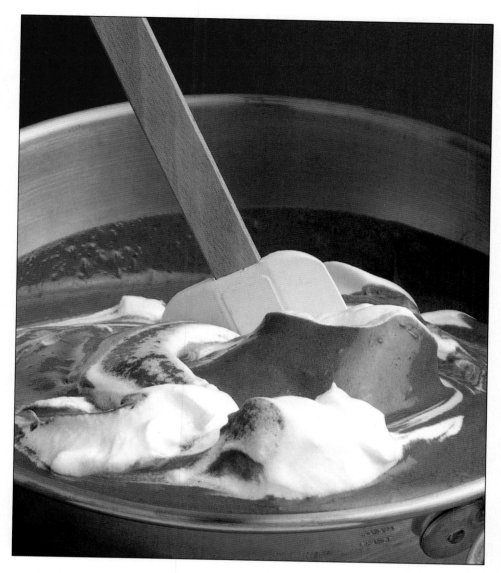

mercial food processors prefer artificial colors because they are stronger, are more heat resistant, and are less expensive.

Use Food colorings tint an enormous array of processed foods, from baked goods to salad dressings. The home cook may find them useful in tinting icings, cakes, and confections. They should be used sparingly. Liquid colorings are volatile and should be added at the end of cooking.

Availability Most food colorings sold to home cooks are packaged in liquid form. Some cookware stores and bakery suppliers offer highly concentrated food coloring pastes, which are particularly useful for icings because they mix better with fat than do liquids. Pastes also impart a darker color than liquids, which create pastel hues.

Storage Keep in a cool, dark place. Pastes will last indefinitely; liquid colorings will last three to four years.

Beaten egg whites are carefully folded into a chocolate cake batter to lighten it before baking. A large bowl, here a copper one for beating egg whites, makes the process easier.

FOOD PROCESSOR

The European-designed and manufactured food processor made its debut in the United States in the early 1970s. Although it is still not standard equipment in the majority of American kitchens, many cooks have come to consider this extremely versatile, multi-functional machine their most valuable kitchen appliance. It makes quick work out of many tedious and time-consuming culinary chores. With one machine, a cook can chop, slice, shred, mix, and purée almost instantaneously. The more powerful processors have the muscle to knead heavy bread dough with little effort.

The food processor is composed of a motor-driven shaft, a work bowl that fits over the shaft, and various blades and disks that attach to the shaft inside the work bowl and rotate at high speed when the machine is on. Food is either placed directly in the bowl or fed in through a tube on the cover of a bowl.

Full-size food processors are most efficient when used for several consecutive tasks. It's often faster and easier to do a single small job by hand—chop one clove of garlic or one tablespoon of parsley—than it is to set up the machine and have to face cleanup afterward. On the other hand, a recipe that calls for a variety of chopped vegetables—say, to be sautéed and then puréed for a soup—is perfect for the food processor.

Recognizing that consumers appreciate the speed and power of these machines, but are reluctant to dirty them for processing spoonfuls of food, manufacturers have introduced compact versions ranging from small-capacity electric chopper-grinders (electric minichoppers) to small-sized food processors. The latter have small work bowls and interchangeable blades plus a chute attachment that sends food through the work bowl for processing and out into a freestanding container. Ideal for small quantities and small households, electric minichoppers are easy to use, affordably priced, and sized to take up a minimum of space. They cannot slice or shred, however.

Food processors vary in capacity and power, from the very compact for households of one or two persons to machines intended for cooks who prepare food on a large scale. Which processor to buy depends on how often you will use the machine and the amount of food you will need to prepare at one time. A large work bowl obviously holds more—some as much as 16 cups of shredded food, or up to 7 cups of liquid. These maximum-capacity machines need a powerful motor for peak performance and are thus highest in price. With the introduction of special whisk or beater attachments, food processors are now competitive with electric mixers for whipping egg whites and cream to airy clouds, but they still cannot match the ability of the mixer to make acceptable whipped potatoes. Full-size models also cannot grind coffee beans, grains, or hard spices—tasks the minichoppers perform very well.

Standard features with most models are a large feed tube; a multipurpose steel blade for blending, mixing, and puréeing; a plastic dough blade for breads; a slicing disk; and a shredding disk. Standard on some models is a whole-bowl feed tube that accommodates larger items such as an entire tomato or onion, or several all at once. Options vary according to the manufacturer. Among the options offered are a range of slicers and shredders, including the previously mentioned whisk; a French fry cutter; an attachment for making pasta; and a citrus juicer, with strainer insert. The juicer is an automated reamer, and the strainer functions like a motorized fine-mesh sieve to create refined purées by trapping seeds, skins, peels, and fiber from fruits and vegetables.

The machine is so fast that control of its speed is critical to obtaining a quality final product. Proper technique makes the difference between finely ground nuts and nut butter, or chopped onions and onion purée. Many models have a pulse function that turns the motor on and off in bursts, letting the cook monitor the processing more accurately. For best results when chopping watery vegetables such as onions, bell peppers, or celery, it's best to turn the motor on and off (pulsing) rapidly. The same pulsing technique is used to incorporate dry ingredients into a cake batter or liquid into a pastry. When slicing or shredding foods, the amount of pressure you apply is important. Generally firm foods require firm pressure and softer foods require light to medium pressure. However, all shredded cheeses require light pressure only.

Buy a food processor that has a direct drive, rather than one that is belt-driven. Also, as with any small electrical appliance, check the warranty, customer service records, and repair policy of the food processor you have selected before you pay for it.

FORCEMEAT

Derived from the French *farce* (stuffing), this rich, savory mixture is made of finely minced, ground, pounded, or puréed raw meat, fish, fowl, or game, plus a good deal of fat, usually pork fat. Forcemeat is classically used as the filling for pâtés and terrines. Sometimes chopped vegetables and nuts are blended in for textural contrast, herbs and spices for flavor, and some sort of liquor—brandy, Cognac, or Armagnac—for depth and perfume. Eggs and often a flour-based panada, a firm paste made of bread or cooked flour soaked in milk or water, are added to bind all the ingredients together.

Forcemeats can be coarse or fine; for a more varied consistency, they can be a combination of fine pieces and a purée. To make forcemeat before the advent of the food processor, pieces of meat were fed through a meat grinder or minced by hand. If a smooth paste was desired, the meat was pounded in a mortar and then rubbed through a fine sieve. The food processor has automated and shortened this labor-intensive process, although even a processed purée should be further refined by sieving.

Seasonings vary, but generally cold forcemeat-based dishes require more generous amounts to overcome the deadening effect chilling has on flavor.

Mousseline forcemeats, which resemble a soufflé, have been lightened with cream and bound with egg white and a panada. The feather-light quenelle, a French dumpling, is made from a mousseline forcemeat. Another classic mixture consists of rolled fillets of fish lined with this airy mixture and gently poached.

QUENELLES

This classic mousseline recipe is lighter and more delicate than the flour-based panada originally used for quenelles. Without the help of a food processor, making quenelles is a laborious task. The flesh of the fish must be first pounded with a mortar and pestle, then sieved to remove the connective tissue. With the processor, the fish is easy to purée. You still need to sieve it because small amounts of invisible connective tissue may remain in the purée. Keeping the ingredients cold helps them absorb the cream and makes the quenelles light. The ramekins called for in the variation are single-serving pottery baking dishes. They are available at most cookware stores.

  1 **pound sole or other white, firm-fleshed fish,**
  cut in 1-inch pieces and chilled
  1 **egg**
  1 **egg white**
  1 **teaspoon salt**
  ½ **teaspoon white pepper**
  2 **cups whipping cream, well chilled**
  Boiling stock

1. In a food processor fitted with steel blade, purée sole. Then push purée through a sieve with a wooden spoon and return sieved purée to processor.

2. Add egg, egg white, salt, and pepper. Purée again. With machine running, slowly pour in cream and process until absorbed into fish mixture. Refrigerate the mousseline until ready for forming.

3. Use 2 tablespoons as a mold to form chilled mousseline into oval balls. As you work, dip spoons often in hot water. To form quenelles you can also use a large pastry bag with a plain tip.

4. Place formed quenelles in bottom of a large, well-buttered saucepan. Slowly pour boiling stock into pan to cover quenelles. Over low heat poach quenelles until they are firm (12 to 15 minutes).

Serves 6.

Variation Using ramekins saves the cook from having to mold the mousseline and, if you wish, serves as the vehicle for an oyster surprise. The bain-marie (hot water bath) is essential for even poaching. Preheat oven to 350° F. Heavily butter six 4-ounce ramekins. Fill halfway with mousseline. Place a small, well-drained oyster in the middle of each ramekin. Cover top with remaining mousseline mixture. Place ramekins in baking dish and surround with boiling water. Water should come up almost to top of ramekins. Bake until a knife inserted into middle of mousseline comes out clean (15 to 20 minutes).

Serves 6.

CHICKEN QUENELLES

Quenelles can be served as a main course with a sauce, as a soup dumpling, or as an accompaniment to other dishes. Using ground chicken rather than the fish of the previous recipe, this version is flecked with specks of peppery watercress and can be served with the chicken stock in which it poaches. Ask the butcher to grind the chicken for you, or you can do it yourself in a food processor.

  ½ **cup water**
  ½ **teaspoon salt**
  2 **tablespoons butter**
  ⅓ **cup flour**
  1 **egg**
  1 **egg white**
  1 **cup ground chicken**
  2 **tablespoons whipping cream**
  2 **tablespoons fresh watercress leaves**
    Salt and white pepper, to taste
  2 **cups Chicken Stock (see page 560)**

1. In a 2-quart, heavy-bottomed saucepan, combine the water, salt, and butter. Simmer over medium-low heat until butter melts.

2. With a wooden spoon, beat flour into butter-water mixture all at once. Cook over medium-high heat, beating continuously until mixture forms a ball and does not stick to sides of pan. Remove from heat.

3. Beat in egg, then egg white; set aside to cool completely.

4. In a medium bowl combine chicken, cream, watercress, and salt and pepper to taste. When flour mixture has completely cooled, blend with ground chicken mixture.

5. Simmer stock in a large, heavy-bottomed sauté pan or skillet over medium heat. Drop in quenelle batter, 1 tablespoon at a time, until pan is full. Simmer until quenelles puff and roll over easily (about 10 minutes). Remove with a slotted spoon. Repeat until all batter has been used.

Makes 20 quenelles.

G & H

Those small kitchen tools known as gadgets can be useful if they are well made, if there is room to store them, and if the cook remembers to use them. Counterclockwise from top right are: French-fry maker, melon cutters, peelers, citrus zester and stripper, bean slicer, strawberry huller, truffle slicer, crinkle-chip cutter.

GADGETS: CUTTER, PEELER, AND ZESTER

Although dismissed by overly serious chefs as novelties or even space wasters, kitchen gadgets have a purpose and will earn their keep if they are well made and therefore perform their job well. What are gadgets? They encompass all those small devices that hang from racks or fill counter bins in housewares departments. They range from the familiar, such as citrus zesters and vegetable peelers, to the unidentifiable. Many are garnishing tools—the cutters that flute, hollow, and scallop all sorts of fruits and vegetables.

As is true of all cutting tools, unless the edges are sharp they won't work. Why mention the obvious? Unfortunately, some implements on the market are dull and therefore useless. So before you buy a tool, ask the salesperson for assurance that it will work.

ASPIC-TRUFFLE CUTTER

Usually sold in sets of 12 patterns, these tinned steel cutters are so tiny that a set will nestle in a box no bigger than 2 inches in length. These miniatures are used to punch out decorative garnishes from aspic, truffles, pastry, pimientos, olives, candied fruits, and cooked egg white. The many whimsical patterns include paisleys, circles, squares, triangles, clovers, hearts, spades, clubs, crescents, and alphabet letters. Dry the cutters immediately after washing or they will rust.

BEAN SLICER

Green beans look more delicate when cut lengthwise into thin pieces. This cutter is a combination guillotine and slicer. One blade chops off the stem and blossom ends; the other creates the narrow strips. The tool is made of molded plastic with stainless steel blades.

CITRUS STRIPPER

This tool cuts a ¼-inch-wide strip of rind from a lemon or orange. Use the resulting spirals to flavor a drink or preserve them in sugar syrup for decoration. To avoid pulling away the bitter white pith with the peel, set the cutting edge against the skin and pull it around the fruit without digging too deeply. Make short strips by cutting from stem to blossom end; cut longer ones by working around the midsection of the fruit. The tool also flutes mushrooms and cuts decorative channels in cucumbers, carrots, and other vegetables; when sliced they will have scalloped edges. Measuring about 6 inches long, the stripper has a molded plastic handle and a stamped, stainless steel blade.

CITRUS ZESTER

Five little holes at the blade end of this tool cut threads of colored rind when drawn across the skin of citrus fruit. Use the long threads as is or chop fine with a chef's knife or electric minichopper. Cooks who use this method for mincing rind love it. The alternative is rubbing the fruit against a metal grater, which always takes away some knuckle and bitter citrus pith with the rind, and is difficult to clean. Lemons and oranges with the rind removed should be saved for juicing; store them in a plastic bag in the refrigerator to prevent them from drying out. Measuring about 6 inches, the citrus zester has a molded plastic or wood handle and a stamped, stainless steel blade. If storage is tight, consider a combination zester-stripper (see photograph, opposite page).

CRINKLE-CHIP CUTTER

The wavy-edged blade of this cutter slices ruffled rounds and sticks of vegetables and cheeses. It is typically used on potatoes, carrots, squash, jicama, beets, and cucumbers. The blade is stainless steel, the handle molded plastic.

FRENCH-FRY MAKER

This device cuts a potato into the familiar, even sticks used to make French fries. A chef's knife can do this chore, but it will take longer and the results won't be as uniform. Of the two basic designs, the simplest has a sharp, stainless steel grid set in a cast aluminum frame. To use, the grid is placed on an upright end of a peeled potato and then pushed through to the bottom. The other type is larger and more mechanized. A slot in the plastic housing of the cutter holds the potato in place; a push of a lever sends the potato through the metal grid. The French-fry maker also cuts carrots and other root vegetables, and can be useful when preparing ingredients of equal size to be stir-fried.

MELON BALLER

This tool forms fruits and vegetables into little balls for fruit plates or salads. It also hollows cherry tomatoes and mushrooms for stuffing. The handle is plastic or wood and the bowl is stainless steel in graduated sizes. One- and two-scoop models are sold; round bowls are most typical, but oval and fluted ones are also available.

MELON V OR U CUTTER

This garnishing tool has a V- or U-shaped, stainless steel blade that cuts a zigzag (the V) or scalloped (the U) edge. Handles are wood or molded plastic. If garnishing is important to you, these cutters give an extra, decorative touch to foods used as containers, such as watermelon baskets and melon, lemon, and orange shells. The technique is simple and the effect attractive, although this tool is certainly not a high-priority item. To make shells, insert the tool so that successive cuts touch and are continuous around the circumference of the fruit. When the last cut reaches the first, the fruit will open. To make baskets with a handle, don't cut all the way around the fruit; instead, cut almost to the center, then up and down the other side and back around. Repeat on the opposite end to finish the handle and shape the basket.

PEELER

No matter what type of cooking you do, you always have to peel an apple, pear, potato, carrot, cucumber, eggplant, asparagus, or any of numerous other fruits and vegetables. Peelers have swivel or fixed blades; buy what feels comfortable in your hand and what works best. Choose a quality peeler. The better tools will stay sharper longer; some even have replaceable blades, or blades that reverse to accommodate both right- and left-handed cooks.

Specialty peelers, designed for particular vegetables and fruits, such as asparagus, avocado, and citrus, are also available.

STRAWBERRY HULLER

Why this small device that resembles squatty, wide tweezers works as well as it does is a mystery, but it neatly plucks the stem and leaves from a strawberry in a single motion without mashing the fruit. Also use it to pick tiny bones from fish.

TRUFFLE SLICER

This relatively simple and straightforward device is made of a sheet of stainless steel and has a shape that resembles a musical instrument you can't quite identify: long neck, pinched waist, and little legs. An adjustable blade projects from the upper surface. To use, the slicer is held at a 45-degree angle, supported by the legs, and the truffle is rubbed across the blade. It can also be employed to shave chocolate.

Recipes and Related Information
Basic Aspic, 265; French-fried Potatoes, 468;
Garnish, 263; Truffle, 582.

GAME

Animals hunted for food or sport fall under the category of game. To the cook this includes both animals freshly killed by the hunter and those that are farm raised for the market. Small game animals include rabbit and hare, beaver, muskrat, raccoon, and opossum. Among the large game animals are venison (which usually refers to deer, but also includes other antlered animals such as caribou, moose, elk, and antelope), bison (American buffalo), wild boar, and bear. Duck, pheasant, and quail are some of the better-known game birds (see POULTRY). By strict definition, game also includes fish (see FISH).

Use Game furnishes some of the tastiest and most wholesome of all meat—it is rich in flavor, high in protein and minerals, and low in fat. Germans enjoy rabbit in *Hasenpfeffer*, a richly flavored stew that takes its name from the German words *Hasen*, which means hare, and *Pfeffer*, meaning pepper. Jugged hare is a Scottish rabbit

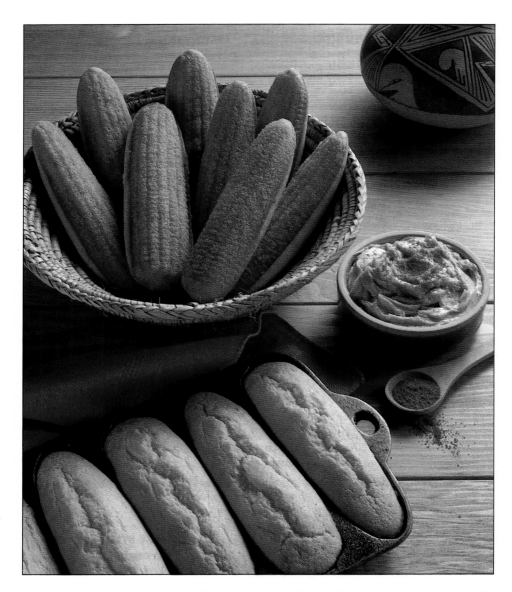

Baked in corn-shaped molds to give them their characteristic shape, corn sticks make a delicious accompaniment to hearty soups and stews.

Pearl barley is widely sold in plastic bags and in bulk. Pot barley and barley grits are sold in some health-food stores. Barley flour is also occasionally available in health-food stores.

BUCKWHEAT

Technically, buckwheat is not a cereal grain, for it is not a member of the grass family. Because it is treated as a grain in the kitchen, however, it deserves discussion here. Buckwheat has a full, nutty flavor that is even more pronounced when the grain is toasted.

Buckwheat groats add nutty flavor and texture to pilafs and stuffings; they may be mixed with rice or other grains, or with noodles. Steamed buckwheat grits make a hearty breakfast cereal. Buckwheat flour adds sturdy flavor to pancakes, Russian blini (yeast-risen pancakes), dumplings, Brittany crêpes, and breads.

Buckwheat is marketed either as whole unpolished kernels, called groats, or as ground kernels, called grits. The groats may be toasted or untoasted; the grits are usually toasted. Some supermarkets carry uncooked buckwheat groats or grits packaged as kasha (the Russian word for toasted buckwheat groats or grits). Buckwheat flour is available in health-food stores and some supermarkets.

Recipes: Blini, 602; Buckwheat Pancakes, 600.

CORN

The following section deals with dried corn and dried corn products. For information on fresh sweet corn, see CORN.

Cornmeal Cornmeal is finely ground from dried white or yellow corn. Some health-food stores sell unbolted cornmeal, which includes both bran and germ. Most supermarket cornmeal, however, is ground from the kernel with the hull and germ removed.

Boiled cornmeal is eaten as a breakfast porridge with butter and syrup, or is molded, cooled, sliced, and fried for a breakfast dish or savory side dish. Cornmeal is used in a wide variety of puddings, muffins, corn breads, fried dumplings, and pancakes. It also serves as a coating for fried foods, such as catfish and trout. Italians cook coarsely ground cornmeal, called polenta, in water or stock to make a thick cornmeal mush, also called polenta. They serve it hot with butter, cheese, meat sauces, or roast fowl. They also chill it, slice it, and fry it, or reheat it in a baking dish, layered with cheese or meat sauce.

Cornmeal is sold in bulk or packed in boxes in the supermarket. Polenta is available in Italian markets and some supermarkets. Blue cornmeal (see opposite page) is available in specialty stores and by mail order. Store unbolted cornmeal in an airtight container in the refrigerator and use within three months. Regular cornmeal can be kept in a covered container in a cool, dry place for up to one year.

■ OLD-FASHIONED BUTTERMILK CORN STICKS

Corn sticks are quick breads made in the same way as muffins. They make a flavorful accompaniment to salads, chowders and soups, casseroles, and other savory dishes. To mold them into the traditional ear-of-corn shape, use a seasoned cast-iron corn-stick pan (see page 21). Corn sticks are best when served soon after baking; they don't keep well.

  1 **cup *each* yellow cornmeal and all-purpose flour**
 ¼ **cup sugar**
  2 **teaspoons baking powder**
 ¾ **teaspoon salt**
 ½ **teaspoon baking soda**
  1 **egg**
  1 **cup buttermilk**
  2 **tablespoons vegetable oil**

1. Preheat oven to 425° F. In a large bowl blend cornmeal, flour, sugar, baking powder, salt, and baking soda.

2. In a medium bowl beat egg with buttermilk and oil. Add egg mixture to cornmeal mixture and mix just until dry ingredients are moistened.

3. Divide batter evenly into 2 well-greased corn-stick pans (or greased standard muffin pans).

4. Bake until golden brown (15 to 20 minutes). Best when served warm.

Makes 14 to 16 corn sticks or 1 dozen muffins.

■ TEXAS JALAPEÑO-CHEESE CORN BREAD

This moist, multiflavored bread is a substantial side dish (and some Texans use sour cream in place of buttermilk to make it even heavier). New Mexico's famed (and somewhat odd-looking) blue corn bread follows, with coarsely ground blue cornmeal replacing the yellow. Corn bread does not keep well. However, the batter can be prepared as much as a day ahead and refrigerated, then baked when needed and served fragrant and warm.

> 1½ **cups yellow cornmeal**
> 1½ **tablespoons flour**
> ½ **teaspoon salt**
> 2 **tablespoons sugar**
> 1 **tablespoon baking powder**
> 1 **small onion, minced (about ¾ cup)**
> 1¼ **cups buttermilk**
> 1 **can (8 oz) creamed corn** *or* **1 cup fresh corn scraped with its "cream" from cob**
> ½ **cup melted butter**
> 1 **cup grated Cheddar cheese**
> ½ **pound chorizo, fried and finely chopped (optional)**
> ¼ **to ½ cup minced canned jalapeño chiles** *or* **1 can (4 oz) diced mild chiles**

1. Preheat oven to 400° F. In a large bowl stir together cornmeal, flour, salt, sugar, and baking powder. Add onion, buttermilk, corn, and butter; mix rapidly until flour is well moistened. (Batter may be refrigerated overnight.)

2. Grease an 8-inch-square baking pan or 10-inch cast-iron skillet. Pour in half the batter. Sprinkle on half the cheese, *chorizo* (if used), chiles, and remaining cheese. Cover with remaining batter and bake until firm (45 to 50 minutes). If top is not browned, broil about 5 minutes. To serve, cut into sixteen 2-inch squares or 8 wedges.

Makes 16 squares or 8 wedges, serves 8.

Texas Jalapeño-Cheese Corn Muffins Preheat oven to 425° F. Mix cheese and chiles into batter; do not use chorizo. Pour into 12 to 16 greased muffin cups and bake 20 to 25 minutes.

Texas Jalapeño-Cheese Blue Corn Bread Preheat oven to 350° F. Substitute coarsely milled blue cornmeal for yellow cornmeal; do not use chorizo. Bake 1 hour.

Food Processor Version Use metal blade to mince onion and shredding disk to shred well-chilled cheese.

■ BASIC POLENTA

Although polenta must be watched and stirred continuously as it cooks, diligence yields delicious results: a thick, creamy, golden pudding that has inspired cooks to create countless variations. Common throughout northern Italy, polenta can be eaten hot, with butter and cheese or shaved truffles. It can also be poured into a pan, cooled until firm, and sliced, then layered with meat sauces or with mushrooms and cheese, and baked until bubbly. Often it's reheated with a mantle of grated fontina or Gorgonzola cheese. Serve this recipe hot from the saucepan, to accompany grilled sausages, chicken, or chops.

> 4 **cups water**
> 1½ **teaspoons coarse salt**
> 1 **cup polenta**
> 4 **tablespoons unsalted butter**
> ¼ **cup freshly grated Parmesan cheese**

Bring the water and salt to a boil in a heavy saucepan. Gradually add polenta, whisking constantly. Stir in half of the butter. Cook over low heat, stirring constantly with a wooden spoon, 20 minutes. Mixture will become quite thick. Stir in remaining butter and Parmesan; serve hot.

Serves 4.

■ GRILLED POLENTA

When cooled until firm, then sliced and grilled, polenta makes a great companion to dishes rich in sauce. Serve it with braised rabbit or veal stew, Ragù Bolognese (see page 412), or with plump sausages sautéed with peppers.

> 1 **recipe Basic Polenta**
> **Oil, for greasing rack**

1. Oil an 8- or 9-inch loaf pan or a 1-inch-deep cake pan and fill with hot polenta. Cool, then chill until firm.

2. Prepare a medium-hot charcoal fire. Oil grilling rack. Slice polenta ½ inch thick. Grill on both sides until hot throughout. Polenta may also be successfully cooked on an indoor griddle. Serve immediately.

Serves 4.

Recipes: Pan-fried Catfish, 230.

Dried Blue Corn This variety of field corn with blue kernels is cultivated by Pueblo and Hopi Indians in New Mexico. The dried kernels are sold whole or ground into blue cornmeal. The cornmeal is used for blue corn tortillas, corn bread, pancakes, and mush. Baked goods made with blue cornmeal have a bluish gray tinge. Dried blue corn and blue cornmeal are available in some specialty markets or from mail-order sources.

Recipes: Texas Jalapeño-Cheese Blue Corn Bread, at left.

Dried Indian Corn Multicolored Indian corn is sometimes dried on the cob and sold in supermarkets for decorative use on autumn tables.

Dried Sweet Corn Dried either on or off the cob, sweet corn is still used in Pennsylvania Dutch cookery and is available in markets that cater to a Pennsylvania Dutch clientele. It is usually reconstituted in water, then added to soups or stews or made into a side dish.

Hominy This dried field corn has been heated and soaked in a basic solution to soften its hull, then hulled and the germ removed. It is then dried and sold in bulk or plastic bags as dried whole hominy. Look for it in Latin American markets.

When heated and soaked, the hull and germ removed, and finely ground, the dried corn is known as *masa harina* and is used to make tortillas, tamales, and other basic Mexican foods. Fresh prepared *masa* (corn dough) is available in many Latin American markets.

Mexican cooks also boil whole hominy until tender, then add it to soups, such as *menudo* (tripe soup), and to stews. When fully cooked, whole hominy has a sweet flavor and a firm but creamy texture.

Whole cooked hominy, both white and yellow, is also canned and sold in supermarkets. Southern cooks add whole hominy to scrambled eggs, simmer it in cream, or bake it in puddings.

Hominy Grits When cracked, dried whole hominy is called hominy grits. Quick-cooking hominy grits are ground finer than regular grits. Instant hominy grits have been precooked and dehydrated; they can be quickly rehydrated in hot water. Hominy grits are eaten as a breakfast cereal, with butter and syrup; molded, cooled, sliced, and fried; and baked in puddings, cheese-topped casseroles, and soufflés.

■ BAKED GARLIC GRITS

Hospitable southerners who want to help their northern friends develop a taste for grits are likely to introduce them to this elaborate and delicate version, which resembles a fallen cheese soufflé. Serve baked grits for brunch (the batter can be mixed the night before) or at dinner; they are especially suited to accompany roasts and barbecues. Use Cheddar cheese if grits will be eaten with a hearty dish, Swiss cheese if with a light main course.

½ **cup milk**
3 **eggs**
½ **pound sharp Cheddar cheese or Swiss cheese, grated**
2 **tablespoons freshly grated Parmesan cheese**
8 **tablespoons unsalted butter, cut in small pieces**
2 **medium cloves garlic, minced (about 2 tsp)**
¼ **teaspoon freshly ground pepper**
1 **tablespoon snipped fresh chives or minced green onion tops**
4 **cups water**
1 **teaspoon salt**
1 **cup quick-cooking hominy grits**
1 **teaspoon butter**

1. Preheat oven to 325° F. In a medium bowl beat together milk and eggs. Add cheeses, unsalted butter, garlic, pepper, and chives. Set aside.

2. Bring the water and salt to a boil. Add grits, stir, and return to a boil. Lower heat to medium and continue cooking, stirring often, until grits are thickened (about 5 minutes). Pour out any unabsorbed water. Remove from heat, immediately pour cheese mixture into grits, and stir until cheeses and butter melt. (Grits may be prepared in advance to this point; cover and refrigerate up to one day until ready to serve.)

3. Grease a 2-quart casserole or soufflé dish with the 1 teaspoon butter. Spoon grits mixture into prepared casserole and bake until a knife inserted in center comes out clean (about 1 hour). Baked grits may be left in oven, with heat turned off, for 10 minutes before serving.

Serves 8.

Recipes: Menudo, 591.

MILLET

A small round yellow seed, millet does not require processing after harvesting. It is a common ingredient in birdseed mixtures but is otherwise used infrequently in this country. It has a crunchy texture and a flavor resembling that of corn.

Millet may be steamed and eaten as a breakfast cereal with butter, maple syrup, and cream; cooked in stock like a pilaf or baked in a pudding; or when cooked added to stuffings or breads for texture and flavor.

Millet is sold in bulk in most health-food stores and in some supermarkets.

OATS

Whole oats must be hulled before they are fit for human consumption. Hulled whole oats are also known as oat groats. Steel-cut oats are groats that have been sliced with steel blades. Rolled oats (old-fashioned oats) are groats that have been steamed and flattened by rollers into flakes. Quick-cooking rolled oats are groats that have been cut into smaller pieces before rolling, yielding thinner flakes that cook more quickly. Instant oats are made from partially cooked groat pieces rolled even thinner than quick-cooking oats. Some brands of instant oatmeal are flavored with sugar and spices; most have salt added. Regular and quick-cooking oats can be used interchangeably in recipes; using flavored instant oats alters the taste of a recipe that calls for regular or quick-cooking oats.

Apart from the morning bowl of oatmeal, oats do not figure largely in the American diet. Yet they are a flavorful and nutritious grain with several culinary uses. Although most Americans make their oatmeal from rolled oats, steel-cut oats also make a delicious cereal with chewier texture and slightly more nutritive value. Cooked whole oats can be added to soups or stews. Rolled oats are used in granola, cookies, muffins, and cakes. They can also be added, either raw or cooked, to yeast bread doughs. Cooked oatmeal contributes moisture and bulk to stuffings, breads, and meat loaves. It can also be molded, cooled, sliced, and fried like cornmeal mush. Oat groats can be ground into flour for baking.

Health-food stores generally stock oat groats, steel-cut oats, and rolled oats. Most supermarkets sell rolled, quick-cooking, and instant oats. Oat flour is available in some health-food stores.

■ OATMEAL GEMS

These chewy, slightly sweet muffins are good with soups and stews. The name *gem* refers to the old-fashioned cast-iron pans that produce a first-rate muffin with a crusty exterior and rounded top. If you don't have cast-iron gem pans, use plain muffin tins; for a similar result, try to find tins made of a heavyweight material. Leftover muffins are delicious split, toasted, and buttered. Note that the recipe calls for quick-cooking oats; however, regular oats can also be used as the two types are interchangeable in recipes.

   2 cups quick-cooking oats
1½ cups buttermilk
   ¼ cup molasses
   2 tablespoons sugar
   2 eggs
   ½ teaspoon salt
   1 cup flour
   1 teaspoon baking soda

1. Preheat oven to 400° F. Grease standard muffin pans or line with cupcake papers. Combine oats and buttermilk in a medium bowl and let stand about 15 minutes.

2. Beat in molasses, sugar, eggs, and salt. Stir together flour and baking soda, then add to oat mixture and mix just until dry ingredients are moistened.

3. Fill prepared pans two thirds full. Bake until a toothpick inserted in a muffin comes out clean (about 20 minutes). Serve warm.

Makes about 16 muffins.

QUINOA

Relatively new to the American marketplace, quinoa (pronounced keen-wa) is actually an ancient food. Native to the Andean region of South America, it was a staple of the Incan diet. Quinoa has an excellent nutritional profile, with more protein than other grains. In contrast to other grains, its protein is complete (containing all the essential amino acids).

Although, like buckwheat, quinoa isn't technically a grain, it looks, cooks, and tastes like one. It can be substituted for rice in side dishes, casseroles, salads, and stuffings. It has a notably light texture and mild flavor. Look for quinoa in health-food stores.

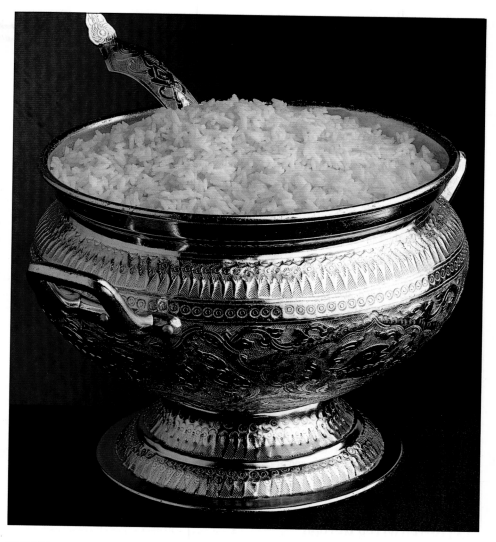

RICE

An extremely important food crop, rice provides basic sustenance to half the population of the world. The cuisines of Japan, China, India, Indonesia, and Southeast Asia are all rice-based; few meals there are served without rice or a rice dish.

Thousands of varieties of rice are cultivated, but the most important distinction from the cook's standpoint is the length of the grain. Long-grain rice has a decidedly different texture when cooked than short-grain rice and is thus better suited to certain types of dishes.

Store rice in an airtight container in a cool, dry place. It will keep indefinitely.

Some cooks insist on washing or soaking rice before use. Although washing removes external starch particles that might cause stickiness, it also washes away any vitamin or protein enrichment (see Enriched Rice). On the other hand, some cooks claim that rinsing gives the rice a cleaner, lighter taste. Whether the nutritional loss is worth the improved flavor, or whether indeed the flavor improvement is noticeable, is a matter of personal taste.

Rice fits comfortably into most meals, whether as a background for highly seasoned dishes, as a vehicle for sauces, or as a filling accompaniment to simply prepared roasted or broiled meats and poultry.

TIPS

PREPARING SKEWERS

On a single skewer combine foods that cook in the same amount of time (blanch slower-cooking elements ahead of time).

Skewers can be metal or bamboo. They should be flat sided if possible so the ingredients don't slip around when the skewer is rotated.

When you use bamboo skewers, presoak them for about 30 minutes to keep them from burning when exposed to high heat.

If all ingredients on a brochette require a relatively long cooking time, consider precooking them, then grilling or broiling as the final step to add color.

Either grilled or broiled, skewered foods usually cook in 6 to 12 minutes.

KETTLE-SHAPED GRILL

These grills are designed for cooking with the lid closed. Carefully located vents in the top and bottom provide air flow to keep the fire going while completely eliminating flare-ups. Thus, searing over a very hot fire can easily be accomplished without burning the food. If the coals are moved to each side of the kettle and a drip pan positioned in the center, food can also be cooked more slowly with the indirect-heat method of cooking. The two major drawbacks are the lack of hinged lids, which creates awkward juggling of equipment each time you open and close the grill, and the fixed grill position.

OPEN GRILL

These are not as easy to use as kettle-shaped grills, but are often less expensive. Since this type does not have a lid, the cook is likely to experience flare-ups during cooking. The best way to handle this is to use an open grill only for foods that don't have an oil-based marinade or are low in fat, such as fish or poultry. You can't use the indirect-heat method of cooking very well on an open grill because most of the heat diffuses in the air.

RECTANGULAR HINGED GRILL

Rectangular grills have the advantage of heat control because the grill can be raised or lowered. Briquettes, hardwood chips, or moistened fresh herbs can be added to the fire more easily than when using a kettle-shaped grill. A hinged lid makes opening and closing much easier. But, when it comes to heat control and evenness of cooking, kettle-shaped grills are better. The rectangular grill simply doesn't have the good heat circulation that a kettle-shaped grill does, and flare-ups are harder to control.

OTHER EQUIPMENT

Whether cooking in the kitchen or on the patio, your equipment should be close at hand and well organized. The following is considered basic for grilling.

Basting Brush   An inexpensive, twisted-wire brush works just as well as the more costly wooden-handled versions. The brush should have a long handle to keep the cook back from the fire while basting.

Charcoal Rails   Use charcoal rails to hold charcoal in even piles on each side of the drip pan for the indirect-heat method of cooking. Because the sides of the drip pan adequately perform the same function, charcoal rails are optional.

Drip Pans   These are essential for the indirect-heat method of cooking. Purchase disposable rectangular aluminum ones, 2 to 3 inches deep; because they are almost impossible to clean, they are usually used only once.

Grill Brush   There is less chance that food will stick to a clean grill. Scrub grill after each use with a special wire brush, available in hardware stores and supermarkets.

Instant-Read Thermometer   Internal temperature is an extremely accurate measure of doneness for many foods. An instant-read thermometer, well-suited for the fast pace of grill cooking, will give a very accurate reading within seconds of insertion.

Long-Handled Fork   Although long-handled forks are not recommended for turning foods (punctures will cause valuable juices to ooze out), they are very handy for removing large roasts from the fire, or for piercing food to check for doneness by looking at the color of the juices.

Mitts   Heavy-duty fireproof mitts are invaluable to protect the cook against unexpected fires. Find a pair that covers forearms as well as hands.

Roast Racks   Made of aluminum or stainless steel, V-shaped roast racks do an excellent job of holding large pieces of meat or poultry during cooking. If used with the indirect-heat method of cooking, the meat needn't be turned to cook evenly on all sides.

Skewers   Both metal and bamboo skewers are available. Metal ones can be used repeatedly; those made of bamboo are meant to be discarded after one use. Bamboo skewers need to be soaked 15 to 30 minutes so they won't flame (although even presoaked ones sometimes burn at the ends over very hot fires). If you have rosemary in your garden, strip away the needles, soak the branches for 30 minutes, and use as skewers; they imbue food with a wonderful rosemary flavor.

Spatula   Use an offset (angled-neck) stainless steel spatula with a blade that is 5 to 6 inches long. This blade will slide completely under most chops and fish fillets, preventing them from tearing and sticking to grill. Stainless steel won't rust and is easy to care for.

Spray Bottle   Always keep a spray bottle filled with water next to the grill to douse flare-ups.

Tongs   Perhaps the most useful grill tool, tongs should be at least 12 inches long and spring loaded. It's best to have two pairs—one for handling food and the other for moving hot briquettes. Tongs are preferred over long-handled forks because they don't puncture food (and allow natural juices to escape).

Wire-Hinged Baskets   These wire baskets will hold fish fillets, meat, hamburger patties, or even bread for toast between two hinged grills secured by a latch. The grills should be lightly oiled before food is set on them.

FUELS AND FRAGRANCES

Traditional hardwood briquettes now share shelf space with many other fuels. They all work well in the right situation; which fuel to use is a matter of personal preference. Many are available at well-stocked supermarkets, hardware stores, cookware stores, or can be ordered by mail through selected catalogs.

CHARCOAL BRIQUETTES

Briquettes are made from wood chips smoldered into carbon, then bound together with fillers and starch, and pressed into a uniform shape. Some brands add petroleum products to make "self-lighting" briquettes. A charcoal briquette fire is ready when the coals are completely coated with a thin layer of gray ash; at this point all of the additives have burned off. Briquettes burn evenly and consistently.

FRESH HERBS AND FRUIT RINDS

Thyme, bay, rosemary, oregano, and marjoram impart a pleasant flavor when added to the fire. Moisten fresh herbs with water (or wine or liquor) and toss them onto the coals just before the food goes on the grill. Lemon, orange, or lime rinds are other choices. Do not directly inhale the fumes of burning herbs or fruit rinds; they can be very powerful.

HARDWOOD CHARCOAL

Though not nearly as prevalent as mesquite charcoal, other hardwoods are carbonized in the same manner as mesquite into an excellent fuel. They impart a smokier flavor to food than does mesquite, but they are more costly and don't burn as hot. Using mesquite as the fuel and adding presoaked hardwood chunks as the smoke source work well.

HARDWOOD CHUNKS AND SAWDUST

Hardwood adds a unique smoky flavor to food cooked over it. Hickory, alder, mesquite, and apple wood are the most popular and available woods. For gas grills, hardwood chips work better than chunks. Use wood pieces ½ to 1 inch thick. Soak pieces in water at least 30 minutes before using. Place an old aluminum pie plate over the gas heating elements toward the back corner of the grill before turning the grill on. As the grill gets hotter, the chips will begin to smolder. With very high heat, the chips may flare up; have a spray bottle filled with water nearby.

MESQUITE CHARCOAL

Made from a Mexican hardwood, mesquite charcoal contains no additives or fillers of any kind. It burns very hot, perhaps twice as hot as charcoal briquettes and most other hardwood charcoals. This means you can use less of it and can cook at a higher temperature, which produces a tastier product. It imparts a subtle, natural flavor, which is not nearly as pronounced as fruitwoods, oak, or hickory. Mesquite coals can be used two or even three times before they need to be replaced. However, mesquite can be difficult to start, and can also emit burning embers into the air. Be careful, especially when windy outside, to avoid sending embers toward nearby trees or structures.

WOOD

You can use oak, hickory, cherry, apple wood, mesquite, or alder wood for outdoor cooking. But wood takes a very long time to burn down to usable coals and the coals are short-lived. A better use of these woods is as kindling; cut the remaining larger pieces into 1-inch chunks to add a smoky complement to your fire (see Hardwood Chunks and Sawdust, left). Never use softwood for either smoking or as a fuel. Their thick resins produce a distinctly unpleasant aftertaste. Be careful of burning any scrap wood. For instance, pressure-treated lumber (used in outdoor construction) contains chemicals that can be toxic.

The outdoor chef has many options when selecting equipment for grilling. Shown clockwise from upper left: open grill; wire-hinged basket (with hamburgers); charcoal and briquettes; charcoal chimney; kettle grill with cover; long-handled spatula, knife, and fork; aluminum drip pan; grill brush; rectangular hinged grill; basting brush; spray bottle; wire-bristle grill brush; portable gas grill; long-handled tongs.

TIPS

HOW MUCH FIRE? WHEN IS IT READY?

When determining the size of your fire, first envision the cooking surface your food will require. Spread briquettes in a single layer to an area about 1 inch past the edges of your imaginary boundaries. Adding about half again as much charcoal should provide enough for one hour's worth of fire. Usually 30 to 40 briquettes is sufficient for food for four people. If making a fire for slow cooking by the indirect-heat method, use about 25 briquettes on each side of the charcoal area, placing no charcoal directly beneath the food. Plan on adding 8 to 10 briquettes to each side per hour of additional cooking time.

A fire usually burns between 30 and 45 minutes before it is ready to be cooked over. Wait until the briquettes are covered with a light ash and are no longer flaming. Cooking over a direct flame will burn the outside of the food and leave the inside raw. Hold your hand flat over the fire at grill height. With a very hot fire, you will be able to hold your hand there for about 2 seconds; for a hot fire, about 3 to 4 seconds. If you can keep it there any longer than that, the fire has died down too much. Once the fire is ready, oil the grill and set in place to heat up for a few minutes before adding food.

STARTING THE FIRE

Whatever method you use, allow about 30 to 45 minutes for your fire to start. Have equipment and food ready.

CHARCOAL CHIMNEY

A very simple device, the charcoal chimney is an open-ended sheet-metal cylinder vented in the bottom, with a grate to hold the charcoal about 4 inches from the bottom. To use, fill chimney with charcoal, which is ignited from burning newspaper set under the grate. The coals will begin to smolder within 10 minutes; when they are ready, pour out of chimney into bottom of grill.

ELECTRIC STARTER

Check manufacturer's directions for starting a fire with an electric starter in your grill. In most cases, arrange briquettes in a pile on top of starter. Plug in starter and let it heat up. The briquettes should catch in about 10 minutes.

KINDLING

Although there are many personal styles of starting a fire with kindling, the basic method is to begin with newspaper sheets loosely crumpled or twisted into logs. Place paper logs in bottom of grill and top with a handful of dry kindling. Top with 5 or 6 briquettes and light the newspaper. If the briquettes don't light, keep adding paper and kindling until they do. Once the briquettes light, cover with more briquettes until all have caught.

LIGHTER FLUID

Follow all the manufacturer's safety precautions when using lighter fluid. Never squirt fluid directly onto a burning fire. The flame can easily travel back up the stream and ignite hand and arm. Also, never use gasoline, naphtha, paint thinner, or kerosene; they are difficult to control. Use only a product specifically labeled as lighter fluid.

PREPARING THE GRILL

Arrange the fire so that some areas of the grill do not have fire under them. If some of the foods are done more quickly than others, they can be moved to these cooler spots to keep warm while the remainder finish cooking. Also remember the following.

- Keep the grill clean. Use a wire grill brush to scrub off burned bits immediately after removing food from the grill; this avoids using soap and water, which will ruin the built-up seasoning on the grill.

- Have all tools ready and available before lighting the fire. Tongs, mitts, and a spray bottle are particularly important to have on hand. If barbecue tools are stored together in a portable bin or basket, they can be easily transported to the grill site.

- Have extra charcoal available in case the fire starts to die before the food is completely cooked.

GRILL COOKING METHODS

With the advent of covered grills, foods can be slowly cooked over indirect heat so that they become tender and stay moist during cooking. Depending on the type of food to be grilled and the desired result, grilling can be done over direct or indirect heat.

DIRECT-HEAT METHOD

Use the direct-heat method to sear foods to seal in their natural juices and to give a characteristic grilled look. For this method choose foods that are low in fat, such as poultry and fish, or that are quick-cooking—hamburgers, chops, skewered foods, vegetables, and fish fillets.

If using charcoal briquettes, start fire as described at left. When coals are covered with a light gray ash (after about 30 minutes), spread in a single layer. Place oiled grill over coals and let it heat 4 to 5 minutes. If you are using hardwood chips or chunks, spread them over coals just before cooking. They will immediately begin to smolder and smoke.

If using a kettle-shaped grill, keep lid closed for duration of cooking time; regulate heat by adjusting upper and lower vents. Lift lid only to turn the food.

If using a gas grill, turn on all three burners to high and close lid; grill should be ready in about 10 minutes. Leave burners on high, or turn one or more down, depending on the food being cooked and the desired effect.

INDIRECT-HEAT METHOD

With this method, you can now cook foods on the grill that were impossible to do even 10 years ago. Whole prime ribs, turkeys, and chickens will cook beautifully, without turning. Smaller cuts may need to be turned for even coloration and grill marks.

If using charcoal briquettes with a kettle-shaped grill, start fire as described at left. When coals are covered with a light gray ash, separate them into two piles on either side of the kettle. Place a disposable aluminum drip pan between the piles. If using hardwood chips or chunks or moistened fresh herbs, add them to the piles now. Put oiled grill in place and let it heat 4 to 5 minutes. Set food on grill directly over drip pan, close lid, and regulate temperature by adjusting the upper and lower vents. To first sear food, set directly over one pile of coals until browned, then move over drip pan.

If using a gas grill, preheat grill with all three burners on high. The grill will be ready in about 10 minutes. Turn off center burner and position disposable aluminum drip pan over it. Place oiled grill in position and let it heat 4 to 5 minutes. Set food on grill directly over drip pan; close lid and cook. Regulate temperature by adjusting the two outer burners. For a smoky complement using hardwood chips, see page 289. If using moistened fresh herbs, toss them directly onto the outside porcelain bars. These grills operate most efficiently when lid is closed. Open lid only to check on or to baste food, or to add more chips or herbs.

WHAT TO GRILL

We probably discovered by accident that fire made our food taste better. One can imagine a piece of raw meat or dry grain falling into a fire and the discovery upon its retrieval that its appearance had changed—and so had its flavor. With time, humans learned that if the meat was held a short distance from the fire, it cooked more evenly and was more digestible.

Through trial and error we not only learned techniques of open-fire cookery—how far the food should be from the flame to cook evenly and how long different foods need to cook completely—but also which foods taste best when prepared this way.

GRILLING FISH

Most fish have little internal fat to keep them moist during cooking. Care must be taken to ensure that they do not dry out on the grill. Marinades are usually unnecessary for fish. Be sure to lightly oil the grill to keep the delicate flesh of the fish from sticking to it. Avoid moving the fish too much and turn only once; excess movement will break the flesh apart. The best test for doneness is to press the flesh with your finger: Raw flesh is relatively soft and springy; properly cooked, the flesh is just firm; when overdone, it is hard and firm.

GRILLING MEATS

Most tender cuts of beef can be grilled directly over high heat. They can be cooked without a marinade, although one can be used for extra flavor. Less tender cuts should marinate to tenderize or should be grilled using the direct-heat method. Use the hand test (see When Is It Done? at right) as the best guide for doneness. A leg of lamb should marinate before grilling; lamb chops don't need further tenderizing. For skewered lamb dishes, use chunks cut from the shoulder or leg; be sure to marinate them for a tender and flavorful kabob. Pork has a tender, sweet flesh that accepts marinades beautifully, and its high internal fat content keeps the meat moist as it grills. Most cuts of pork can cook over direct heat; however, large roasts and heavily marinated cuts may cause flare-ups.

GRILLING POULTRY

Chicken is one of the most versatile foods for grilling. It accepts almost any marinade or sauce with beautiful results. Avoid boneless cuts, which tend to dry out quickly, unless skewering meat. For most recipes, use fresh fryers or broilers weighing between 3 and 4 pounds, well-sized to grill over direct heat if split. For larger birds, or to grill a whole bird, use the indirect-heat method. Poultry is done when a meat thermometer inserted in the thickest part reads 170° F, or when juices appear just slightly pink when skin is pierced. Game hens grill well also; flavor them as you would a chicken, and grill them using the direct-heat method of cooking.

GRILLING VEGETABLES

Like fish and poultry, vegetables have no way of staying moist when exposed to the high heat of a grill. They should be brushed with oil, and can be seasoned with fresh herbs or garlic. If cooked with other foods on a skewer, cut vegetables so that they will be done in the same amount of time as the other ingredients. Squash and eggplant are particularly good if sliced and grilled. Tomato, bell pepper, onion, and mushrooms are traditionally cooked on skewers. Consider blanching longer-cooking vegetables, such as carrots, before grilling so that they need less time to cook.

■ SANTA MARIA BARBECUED BEEF

The Santa Maria Valley on California's central coast has a tradition of outdoor barbecues going back to the early Spanish *rancheros*. Valley cooks have evolved a particular style—simply seasoned slabs of beef cooked over oak fires and served with a fresh tomato salsa and ham- and chile-flavored barbecue beans. (The locals insist on the pinquito bean, a small pink bean grown only in the Santa Maria Valley.) A 3-inch-thick top sirloin steak is the preferred cut of beef for a Santa Maria barbecue, but also suitable are the whole triangle tip and other small roasts from the sirloin tip. You might serve the barbecued beef with either Frijoles or Texas Jalapeño Pinto Beans (see page 35).

    1 large sirloin steak or small roast (about 3 lb)
    1 teaspoon *each* salt and garlic salt
    ½ teaspoon freshly ground pepper
    1 cup Salsa Cruda (see page 521)

1. Trim meat of excess fat and tough membranes. If using a sirloin-tip roast, remove strings and butterfly (cut across grain almost through, then open like a book). Overall thickness should be 2½ to 3 inches. Combine salt, garlic salt, and pepper; rub generously all over meat. Set aside to season at room temperature for up to 2 hours, or longer in the refrigerator.

2. Two to three hours ahead of serving: Build a fire of oak or other hardwood, then allow fire to burn down to red-hot coals. Or, build a charcoal fire 1½ hours ahead and, when most of the charcoal is burning, add small chunks of oak. Sear meat over hottest part of fire, then move to a slightly cooler part and cook to taste. Total cooking time depends on size of meat, heat of fire, and type of grill (open or covered); thinner cuts over a hot fire may be medium-rare in 8 to 10 minutes per side, but with a cooler fire or a larger piece of meat allow 15 to 20 minutes per side.

3. Carve thin slices of meat on a cutting board with grooves to catch juices. Transfer slices to a warm platter and moisten with juices. Garnish with salsa; serve immediately.

Serves 6.

TIPS

WHEN IS IT DONE?

Professional chefs rarely if ever use a meat thermometer to test food for doneness. They touch food with their fingertips, and when it feels right, it is done. Years of practice and experience in handling foods develop a very sophisticated sense of touch and timing. Until you develop your own touch, use a meat thermometer as one indication of doneness. Also get to know the following "hand test."
Rare   Let one hand dangle freely, letting it relax completely. With the forefinger of your other hand, touch the meaty area between your thumb and forefinger. This is what a rare piece of meat should feel like.
Medium   Now make a fist with your hand. Touch the same place again. This is what a medium piece of meat should feel like.
Well-Done   Now tightly clench your fist. Touch the same place again. This is what a well-done piece of meat should feel like.

RECIPE MODIFICATION FOR HIGH-ALTITUDE BAKING

Baking at altitude (above 3,000 feet) can affect ingredients, proportions, and cooking times.

Feet Above Sea Level	Reduce Each Teaspoon Baking Powder by	Reduce Each Cup Sugar by	Increase Each Cup Liquid by
3,000–5,000	⅛ teaspoon	1 tablespoon	2 tablespoons
5,000–7,000	⅛–¼ teaspoon	2 tablespoons	2–3 tablespoons
7,000–10,000	¼ teaspoon	2–3 tablespoons	3–4 tablespoons
Above 10,000	¼–½ teaspoon	2–3 tablespoons	3–4 tablespoons
Over 3,000 feet:	Increase oven temperature by 25° F. Underbeat eggs (beat whites to soft peak stage).		
Over 10,000 feet:	Add one extra egg and increase each cup flour by 1–2 tablespoons.		

HIGH-ALTITUDE COOKING

At altitudes over 3,000 feet, foods cook differently than at sea level because of lower air pressure. Water boils at a lower temperature and food takes longer to heat; liquids evaporate more quickly; leavenings expand more; sugar becomes more concentrated; and batters have a greater tendency to stick to pans.

To compensate for these differences, increase cooking time for foods that are boiled, and raise oven temperature for baked goods by 25° F. Increase liquids, decrease leavenings, underbeat eggs and egg-based batters, decrease sugar, and butter and flour pans well or line with nonstick parchment paper. For baked goods, consult the chart above for exact recipe changes. Specific information about the effect of altitude on cooking in your area is available from cooperative extension agents of the U.S. Department of Agriculture or newspaper food editors.

EFFECT OF ALTITUDE ON BOILING WATER

Above 2,000 feet, the boiling temperature of water drops, as demonstrated in this chart.

Altitude	Water Boils at
Sea level	212° F
2,000 feet	208° F
5,000 feet	203° F
7,500 feet	198° F
10,000 feet	194° F
15,000 feet	185° F
30,000 feet	158° F

HONEY

Flower nectar gathered by bees and deposited in the waxy network of cells known as a honeycomb is the source of honey. Depending on the flower from which it is derived, honey can be quite strong and dark like buckwheat honey, or pale and delicate like clover honey. Among the best-loved honeys in the world are those made from thyme, orange, heather, rosemary, acacia, sage, and tupelo.

Use   The sweetness and spreadable texture of honey make it popular as a topping for breads, toast, biscuits, and corn muffins. As an ingredient in baked goods, it adds sweetness and moisture. Cakes, cookies, and breads with honey stay moist longer than those sweetened with sugar. Honey is traditional in Greek baklava (walnut-filled pastry), Israeli honey cake, Italian *panforte,* and in many Moroccan pastries. Moroccans also use honey to glaze poultry in several savory preparations. Honey is the principal sweetener in many confections, such as Turkish halvah and nougat.

Availability   Dozens of varieties of honey are marketed in the United States, but all are of three basic kinds: comb or straight from the hive; chunk, which contains bits of honeycomb; and extracted, the most common form. Extracted honey is removed from the comb with a centrifuge, heated to destroy yeasts, strained to remove wax and debris, then filtered for clarity. Honey is generally packed in jars or plastic squeeze bottles.

Selection   As honeys vary in flavor (see introduction), select one whose character will best complement its intended use.

Storage   Honey will keep indefinitely in a cool, dark place. Store it in an airtight container to prevent the absorption of moisture from the air.

Preparation   If honey becomes crystallized on standing, reliquefy by setting jar in a pan of hot water and warming gently over low heat.

■ **SPICED FRENCH HONEY BREAD**

Classic French *pain d'épice* does not contain eggs or shortening, but gets its moist richness from the inclusion of honey and cream.

  ½ **teaspoon anise seed**
  1 **teaspoon** *each* **baking soda and ground cinnamon**
  ½ **teaspoon** *each* **ground ginger and cloves**
  ¼ **teaspoon salt**
  3 **cups flour**
  2 **tablespoons dried currants**
  ¼ **cup firmly packed brown sugar**
  ¾ **cup honey**
  ⅔ **cup whipping cream**
  ⅓ **cup milk**
  1 **teaspoon grated orange rind**

1. Preheat oven to 325° F. Lightly grease and flour a 4½- by 8½-inch loaf pan. Whirl anise seed in a clean coffee grinder or electric minichopper until powdery.

2. In a large bowl combine ground anise seed, baking soda, cinnamon, ginger, cloves, salt, flour, currants, and brown sugar.

3. In a small bowl blend honey, cream, milk, and orange rind. Add honey mixture to flour mixture, stirring just until dry ingredients are moistened. Spread in prepared loaf pan.

4. Bake until a skewer inserted in center comes out clean (1 hour and 20 minutes to 1 hour and 30 minutes). Let cool in pan 5 minutes, then turn out onto a rack to cool completely. Wrap and let stand for at least 1 day before slicing thinly to serve.

Serves 8.

Recipes and Related Information
Baklava, 222; Honeyed Chicken With Apricots, 557; Panforte, 186; Sopaipillas, 182.

HORSERADISH

Native to Eastern Europe but cultivated today in the United States, horseradish is a pungent cylindrical root in the cabbage family. It has a rough, thin, light brown skin and a white flesh that, when sliced or grated, releases an acrid oil. Its origins are unknown, but today it grows in cool regions of the United States and Europe. The plant known as Japanese horseradish (see WASABI) is botanically unrelated, although it too is valued for its pungent root.

Use Because the pungent character of horseradish is highly volatile, the root is rarely cooked. Instead it is used raw as a condiment or as an ingredient in other condiments. Grated horseradish is part of most tomato-based cocktail sauces for shellfish. Mixed with whipped cream and/or sour cream, it becomes a favorite sauce for prime rib, boiled meats, and smoked fish. It adds a lively hotness to cream dressings for beets and coleslaw. Grated horseradish is the standard accompaniment to gefilte fish, fish cakes traditional on Jewish holiday tables.

Availability Grated horseradish bottled in vinegar is sold in most supermarkets. Some varieties are colored red with beet juice. Most supermarkets also carry bottled imitation horseradish flavored with oil of horseradish. Fresh horseradish root can be found in some markets fall through spring. It is most widely available in the spring, around the time of the Jewish Passover celebration, because it has a traditional function at the holiday table. Some European specialty markets also carry dried powdered horseradish.

Selection Choose a root of fresh horseradish that is smooth and unblemished.

Storage Keep horseradish in a paper bag inside a plastic bag in the refrigerator crisper for up to one week. Freeze whole fresh horseradish up to six months (see Preparation). Bottled horseradish should be refrigerated, tightly capped, in its original container. Because it quickly loses pungency, it should be used within one month. Store dried horseradish in an airtight container in a cool, dry place; it will gradually lose pungency but should stay vigorous for up to one year.

Preparation Scrub fresh horseradish and scrape away outer skin; halve and cut out center core.

■ **HORSERADISH CREAM SAUCE**
The sharpness of horseradish livens up cool sour cream and makes a wonderful sauce for roasted meats.

    1 **cup sour cream**
    3 **tablespoons freshly grated horseradish**
    ½ **teaspoon salt**
    ⅛ **teaspoon white pepper**

Combine sour cream, horseradish, salt, and pepper. Serve chilled with hot or cold roast beef or other roasted, broiled, or grilled meats.

Makes about 1 cup.

HUCKLEBERRY

Although huckleberries resemble blueberries, they are unrelated. The huckleberry is the fruit of a native American plant of the genus *Gaylussacia*. Huckleberries are not cultivated; they grow wild, generally on low, spreading bushes, and they are generally smaller and darker than blueberries. Whereas blueberries have many tiny unnoticeable seeds, huckleberries have ten hard, rather large ones. They are also tarter than blueberries.

Use Many cooks prefer the huckleberry over the blueberry for pies because it is a tarter berry. Huckleberries can also be added to muffin and quick bread batters, or eaten fresh for breakfast with sugar and milk.

Availability Because huckleberries are not cultivated, they are generally available only to foragers.

Storage See BLUEBERRY.

Preparation Wash gently and dry quickly.

HUSK; HUSK, TO

The dry outer covering, as in the corn husk; also the act of removing the husk. Dried corn husks are the traditional wrapper for Mexican tamales.

H-L

ICE CREAM AND FROZEN DESSERT

What we now know as ice cream—at first called cream ice—was introduced by a French chef to King Charles I of England in the early seventeenth century. Initially, frozen desserts were reserved exclusively for royalty and court nobility. However, by the end of the seventeenth century commoners, too, were indulging in these confections.

Despite the rapid spread of frozen ices and ice creams throughout Europe, the enormous and widespread popularity that ice cream enjoys today is a relatively modern, and largely American, phenomenon, thanks in no small way to the development of reliable refrigeration in the twentieth century. The familiar hand-cranked ice cream churn was invented by an American in 1846, the first ice cream cone sold in St. Louis in 1904, and during the 1920s and 1930s a variety of frozen desserts were invented in rapid succession—including Eskimo Pie, the Good Humor bar, and the Popsicle.

Today, a new generation of ice cream freezers for the home—smaller, easier to use, and more efficient than earlier versions—is inspiring ice cream enthusiasts to make homemade frozen desserts on a regular basis, not just for the occasional special party as was common when freezers were far bulkier and messier. Across America thousands of electric ice cream machines and prechilled canisters stand ready to swing into action at a moment's notice.

ICE CREAM FREEZERS

Preparing ice cream to be frozen doesn't require a lot of equipment other than an ice cream churn or freezer; the bowls, spoons, and saucepans used for everyday cooking fill most needs. The following describes the four basic categories of ice cream freezers—including the strengths and weaknesses of each.

SALT AND ICE-BUCKET FREEZER

This is the traditional ice cream churn that most of us remember from childhood. It has a large bucket with a smaller canister fit into it. Originally the bucket was made of wood and needed to be soaked in water before using to prevent leaks. Today most machines use a plastic or fiberglass bucket. The canister, made of stainless steel, has a removable lid; inside is a stationary paddle called a dasher. The blades are usually wood, plastic, or another soft substance, and are positioned so that they gently scrape the inside of the canister as it turns. The canister is continuously rotated by either a hand crank or an electric motor, while a mixture of about three-fourths ice and one-fourth rock salt in the bucket freezes the ice cream inside the canister. As an added convenience, some models require only ice cubes and ordinary table salt.

The hand-cranked model is less expensive than one that is motor-driven but requires 20 to 30 minutes of cranking for each batch of ice cream. Units equipped with electric motors produce slightly better results because of their consistent speed. Both models make excellent ice cream, but they do require messing with ice and salt. Be aware that some freezers of this type won't hold whole ice cubes, so the ice must be crushed before being put into the machine. In addition, the freezer of older models must be partially disassembled to check on the ice cream, occasionally resulting in some of the brine mixture splashing into the canister. Some newer freezers have the motor under the canister, so the ice cream can be checked without taking the machine apart.

REFRIGERATOR-FREEZER UNIT

Some ice cream freezers are designed to fit inside the freezing compartment of a refrigerator, with the power cord snaking out through the closed door. An electric motor churns the ice cream mixture and drives a small fan that circulates the cold air around the canister. The canister is stationary; the dasher turns. Their major advantage

---

FROZEN DESSERTS—THE REAL SCOOP

Much confusion exists over the names and definitions of particular types of frozen desserts as they cross the boundaries of many cultures and languages. To further complicate matters, common usage varies, especially regarding sherbets and sorbets. The following are broad definitions.

Frozen Yogurt A frozen dessert with yogurt as its base, it has a smooth texture very similar to ice cream, although less creamy, and a rich, slightly acidic taste. Frozen yogurt is usually flavored with fruit.

Gelato Italian *gelato* contains less air than most French or American ice creams, making it denser and firmer. The frozen-canister-type ice cream maker, which does not incorporate much air into the base during freezing, produces an ice cream that is similar to gelato. Use any recipe adapted from French Vanilla Ice Cream Base (see page 311) to make gelato. For richer ice cream, add more egg yolks (see Custard-Based Ice Cream).

Granita The Spanish name *granita* refers to the slightly grainy, granular texture of this type of sherbet, which is frozen without constant churning. In general, granitas have less sugar than sherbets. They should be served slightly thawed and slushy. Granitas may be whipped in a food processor with a metal blade just before serving. The resulting texture is nearly as smooth as that of a churned sherbet (see Sherbet, at right).

Ice This is the generic term for a sherbet (see Sherbet, at right).

Ice Cream Egg yolks, milk, cream, sugar, and flavorings form the base of this smooth, rich, frozen dessert. U.S. Food and Drug Administration standards require that to be labeled and sold as "ice cream," it must have at least 10 percent butterfat, at least 20 percent milk solids, and not more than 50 percent air. In France it is called *glace* (see GLACE), in Italy *gelato* (see Gelato, at left). There are two general American-style types: cooked custard-based ice cream and uncooked Philadelphia-style ice cream.

Ice Milk This is the generic name for frozen desserts that cannot be labeled ice cream because they contain too much air and/or too little butterfat.

Milk Ice This is a sherbet to which a small amount of milk or cream has been added, but not enough to make it an ice cream (see Sherbet, following).

Sherbet A water ice, sherbet is usually made from pulverized fruit pulp, fruit juice, and sugar syrup. It is often called by the French name *sorbet* and sometimes by the Italian name *sorbetto*. You may also see it called ice, water ice, Italian ice, or fruit ice. To make matters a bit more confusing, in parts of the United States "sherbet" contains milk or cream and is technically a milk ice. In these places water ices are usually called sorbets. The density of the sugar syrup used greatly affects the texture and flavor of a sherbet. French sorbets, made with a fairly light syrup, are slightly grainy and have an intense fruit flavor. Italian sorbettos, made with a heavier syrup, are smoother and sweeter.

Today's ice cream freezers make it simpler than ever to prepare frozen desserts at home on a regular basis. Among the most commonly available machines are (from left to right): prechilled canister freezer, salt and bucket freezer (ice cube and table salt type), salt and bucket freezer (crushed ice and rock salt type), freezer with self-contained refrigeration.

is that they don't require salt and ice. A major disadvantage is their limited availability.

PRECHILLED CANISTER FREEZER

The newest type of ice cream machine is sometimes called a Donvier-type after the Japanese company that invented it. This machine features a sealed, hollow metal canister that is filled with a special coolant. The canister must be held at 0° F in the freezer compartment of a refrigerator for 8 hours before use. Then the canister is removed and filled with the chilled ice cream mixture; a lid with a crank and dasher assembly is placed over it. The crank is rotated by hand every 2 or 3 minutes until the mixture is frozen, which is usually 12 to 18 minutes. The major disadvantage of this type of machine is that the canister takes up a fair amount of space in the freezing compartment. The primary advantages are that it's easy to use and, because of its special coolant, it freezes quickly enough to yield a product with surprisingly good texture—if the ice cream is eaten immediately. Because little air is incorporated during the churning process, the ice cream from this type of machine becomes very hard when stored.

FREEZER WITH SELF-CONTAINED REFRIGERATION

This is the Rolls Royce of ice cream machines, complete with its own refrigeration unit. Freezing coils are wrapped around the canister and a motorized dasher mixes the ice cream as it freezes. It is the easiest machine to use: Just pour in the ice cream mixture and turn the machine on. Because it lowers the temperature of the mixture quickly, this type of machine tends to yield the smoothest texture. Its chief drawbacks are high price and amount of counter space it occupies. Try not to store a self-contained machine away from where it is used; most must stand for 24 hours to allow the refrigerant to settle before use.

OTHER ICE CREAM–MAKING EQUIPMENT

The items listed below, most of which fall into the category of ordinary kitchen equipment rather than specialty tools, are helpful but not mandatory for making ice cream and other frozen desserts.

Blender and/or Food Processor   Either machine makes it easier to purée fruit for ice creams and sherbets.

Candy Thermometer   The best way to monitor the changes sugar goes through as it is heated is with a candy thermometer. A small, instant-read thermometer can also be used (see THERMOMETER).

Ice Cream Spades and Scoops   Nonstick scoops contain a fluid antifreeze to ensure easy release of ice cream. Mechanical scoops have an arc-shaped blade that sweeps

ABOUT COOLING, FREEZING, AND STORING

Cooling an ice cream mixture thoroughly before churning is essential. It may be cooled slowly in the refrigerator or rapidly over an ice-water bath. If the mixture is warmer than 40° F when the freezing process begins, the increased churning time is likely to produce flecks of butter, especially in recipes that call for a high proportion of cream to milk. Although harmless, butter flecks are unpleasant and ruin the fine texture of homemade ice cream. (If butter forms in a batch of ice cream, allow ice cream to melt in the refrigerator. When liquid, strain the mixture through a fine sieve to remove the butter, then refreeze. The resulting ice cream will not be as smooth as if the recipe had been prepared properly, but it will be tasty and free of butter.)

EXPANSION DURING FREEZING
When filling an ice cream machine with ice cream mixture, stop at least 2 inches below the top of the canister. As ice cream freezes, it expands slightly. More important, the churning action incorporates air. This aeration, called loft or overrun, improves the texture of the finished ice cream and helps prevent it from becoming a solid block of ice.

If the freezing canister is filled two thirds and the finished ice cream reaches the top, the overrun is approximately 50 percent; if the canister is filled three quarters full and the ice cream reaches the top, the overrun is approximately 30 percent. High-quality ice cream has 20 to 50 percent overrun.

STORING AND
SERVING TEMPERATURES
Ice cream and other frozen desserts should be stored at low temperatures to prolong their shelf life and protect their texture and flavor. Between 0° and 10° F is ideal. Ice cream should be allowed to warm slightly before serving, to about 30° F for serving. If ice cream is firmly frozen, transfer it from freezer to refrigerator 20 to 30 minutes before serving, or leave at room temperature for 10 to 15 minutes. Don't let ice cream thaw too much. Repeated thawing and refreezing will destroy its texture.

Although it is best to "ripen" most homemade ice creams in the freezer for several hours, they should be eaten within one or two days. Ice cream stored for long periods develops ice crystals on its surface and acquires a heavy, undesirable texture.

---

across the interior of the bowl to release ice cream. Spades have a wide flat surface instead of a bowl-shaped one. The numbers imprinted on the handles of many scoops indicate how many scoops of that size can be removed from one quart of ice cream. Scoops come in many sizes (see SPOON, LADLE, AND SCOOP).

Mixer A hand-held or bowl mixer is useful for combining egg yolks and sugar, beating egg whites, and blending other commonly used ingredients (see MIXERS).

Molds Plastic or stainless steel molds will allow you to layer ice cream into special shapes and several flavors of ice cream or sherbet in one frozen dessert. Although some molds are made specifically for frozen desserts, any type of mold of an appropriate size will work. To unmold a frozen dessert, gently immerse the mold nearly to the top in warm water to soften the ice cream around the edges. Then place a plate or serving tray upside down over the mold, and invert them both together (see MOLD).

Stainless Steel Mixing Bowls A large stainless steel bowl with a flat bottom, set over a large kettle of boiling water, makes an excellent substitute for a double boiler, which is usually too small for the quantities involved in making ice cream. Stainless steel is better than glass or ceramic because it can be transferred from the heat to an

ice-water bath without danger of breaking. Unlike other metals, stainless steel does not react with common ice cream ingredients, such as acidic fruits; aluminum and copper tend to discolor when they come in contact with acids and can impart a metallic taste.

Stainless Steel or Wooden Spoons These types of spoons are preferred for ice cream making because they do not react with acidic ingredients and can tolerate extreme temperature changes.

Storage Containers Ice cream should always be stored in a covered, airtight container to prevent it from absorbing odors from other foods and from forming crystals (the result of free moisture) on its surface. Any plastic container with a tight-fitting lid is fine. If the container is less than half full, it is a good idea to press a sheet of plastic wrap on the surface of the ice cream to seal it from the air.

Wire Whisk In addition to performing mixing tasks when an electric mixer isn't available, a whisk is handy for stirring custard mixtures on the stove.

BASIC INGREDIENTS
For ice cream to have a smooth, creamy texture, both the water molecules and the fat globules in the mixture must be suspended evenly, so the ice crystals that form during freezing remain very small. The basic ice cream ingredients, in addition to contributing flavor, help maintain this balance.

Many commercial ice cream manufacturers use emulsifiers and stabilizers to improve the texture of their products, to mask or compensate for inferior ingredients, or to achieve an extended shelf life. Such artificial ingredients are never needed in homemade ice cream prepared in small quantities with fresh, wholesome ingredients. However, some noncommercial ice cream recipes call for such ingredients as cornstarch, instant vanilla pudding, gelatin, and flour in an attempt to simulate the texture produced by more expensive ingredients. Anyone who has tasted good homemade ice cream, made with pure, high-quality ingredients, will find it hard to offer such pseudoflavors to family and guests.

Cream The butterfat in cream is primarily responsible for providing the rich, smooth texture of ice cream. In general, the higher the proportion of butterfat, the richer and smoother the ice cream. Resist the temptation to substitute all heavy cream for light cream, half-and-half, or milk in an ice cream recipe. Too much cream greatly increases the chance of producing ice cream flecked with butter. As a general rule, do not exceed a ratio of 75 percent cream to 25 percent milk.

Eggs In many ice cream recipes egg yolks are cooked to form the custard base. They act as emulsifiers, keeping the fat globules in milk and cream from clumping together.

Fruit Most fruits used to flavor ice creams and sherbets contain naturally occurring pectin and a certain amount of fiber. Both of these substances help to keep both milk fat and water molecules in an even suspension as they freeze.

Milk The fat in milk forms small globules in the ice cream mixture and helps to keep the water molecules dispersed. The emulsifying action of the cooked egg yolks helps to keep these small fat globules from clumping together as they are churned. If they do form clumps, they will produce butter.

Sugar Water in which sugar has dissolved has a freezing point below 32° F. Because of the sugar present, not all the water in the mixture freezes. Sugar thus helps to keep the ice cream from becoming a solid block of ice.

CONTROLLING ICE CREAM TEXTURE

The texture of the finished ice cream depends on how fast it is processed. The faster the freezing process, the smoother the texture. You can control the rate of freezing by varying the amount of salt you use with the ice. Use about three fourths of a standard 26-ounce box of salt for relatively fast freezing and excellent across-the-board results. Using a whole box will shorten the freezing time, producing a finer, smoother texture; using half a box will lengthen the freezing time and give an icier texture.

CUSTARD-BASED ICE CREAM

Traditional, rich, custard-based ice cream is sometimes referred to as French custard. Egg yolks are cooked with sugar, milk, and cream to form a custard, to which flavoring is added. This method produces the richest and smoothest ice creams. The same ingredients combined in different proportions give somewhat varied results. For example, increasing the milk to 2 cups will produce a slightly lighter ice cream; adding 2 more egg yolks, for a total of 6, will make the ice cream richer. Experiment to find which combination of ingredients you prefer.

▥ FRENCH VANILLA ICE CREAM BASE
This recipe is a foundation for most flavored ice creams. It produces consistently excellent flavor and texture regardless of the ice cream machine used. The texture can be varied by combining the ingredients in different proportions (see Custard-Based Ice Cream, above). If desired, for a more intense flavor, use 2 beans or double the amount of vanilla extract. Keep in mind that vanilla beans give a richer flavor than vanilla extract (see VANILLA BEAN). A vanilla bean can be used several times; remove bean from custard by straining custard through a fine mesh sieve. Rinse bean, dry thoroughly, and store airtight. As is true of all custards, be sure to use gentle heat when cooking the egg-yolk and cream mixture or the custard will curdle.

A DICTIONARY OF ICE CREAM DESSERTS

Many ice cream concoctions go by different names in different regions. The following definitions seem to be the ones most widely held.

Banana Split Adding a banana transforms a sundae into a banana split or royale. The traditional banana split has three flavors of ice cream, three different toppings, a banana sliced lengthwise, whipped cream, chopped nuts, and maraschino cherries.

Bombe Made in a spherically shaped mold, a bombe is layered with two or more flavors of ice cream, or ice cream and sherbet; each layer forms a shell for the next layer.

Ice Cream Soda An ice cream soda is composed of three basic parts: flavoring; carbonated water, such as seltzer water or club soda; and ice cream. Whipped cream is often added as a finish. To make the "perfect" ice cream soda, choose a large glass and put in about 2 tablespoons flavored syrup (use more or less to taste). Fill glass with carbonated water to within 2 inches of the rim. Mix well. Position a scoop of ice cream on the edge of the glass, balanced so that its bottom touches the surface of the soda. If desired, add a swirl of whipped cream. Serve with a long-handled spoon and a straw. Some famous combinations include the following:
Black and White Chocolate syrup and vanilla ice cream.
Black Cow Cola and vanilla ice cream.
Brown Cow Root beer and vanilla ice cream.
Strawberry Blondie Ginger ale and strawberry ice cream.

Milk Shakes, Malteds, Floats, and Frappes A milk shake is flavored milk shaken to a thick and foamy consistency, often with ice cream added. A malted is a milk shake to which malted milk powder has been added before blending—any amount from a single teaspoon to several tablespoons is fine. A float is a combination of fruit juice or a carbonated soft drink and a scoop of ice cream. A frappe is a frozen slush mixture made without dairy products; a simple sugar syrup is mixed with fruits or flavorings and partially frozen, then processed in a blender or food processor to the desired consistency. In some parts of the country a milk shake made with ice cream is called a frappe, and in still others a frappe is carbonated water mixed with ice cream.

Parfait and Coupe As served at the soda fountain, a parfait is a layered sundae in a long, slender glass. Simple to make, it is just alternating layers of ice cream and topping. A *coupe* is ice cream served with fruit topping.

Sundae This is the most free-form soda fountain creation, limited only by the imagination of the maker and the size of the dish. A sundae can be made with a single scoop of ice cream or a mountain of different flavors. There are no hard and fast rules of sundae making. One scoop, drizzled with one sauce and crowned with whipped cream, might suffice for some ice cream lovers, while others insist on a dish overflowing with a hodgepodge of nuts, syrups, toppings, fresh fruits, crushed candies, cookies, and whipped cream.

---

    3 cups whipping cream
    1 cup milk
    ¾ cup sugar
    1 vanilla bean, split lengthwise, *or*
      1 tablespoon vanilla extract
    4 large egg yolks

1. In a heavy-bottomed, 2-quart saucepan, heat cream, milk, sugar, and vanilla bean. (If you are using vanilla extract, do not add it until step 3.) Stir occasionally until sugar is dissolved and mixture is hot but not boiling.

2. Whisk egg yolks together in a bowl. Continue whisking and very slowly pour in approximately 1 cup of cream mixture. When smooth, pour back into pan.

3. Whisk constantly over low heat until mixture thickens enough to coat back of a spoon (about 5 minutes). Do not let mixture boil or it will curdle. Custard is done if line remains when finger is drawn across back of coated spoon. Remove vanilla bean. Add vanilla extract, if used.

Makes about 1 quart.

French Vanilla Ice Cream begins with a custard base. A custard has thickened sufficiently if it coats the back of a spoon and if a line drawn through the custard with your finger remains.

■ FRENCH VANILLA ICE CREAM

True ice cream aficionados will always return to the rich flavor of vanilla ice cream. It is delicious in its basic form or in any of the variations offered at the end of the recipe.

    French Vanilla Ice Cream Base (see page 311)
 1 **vanilla bean, split lengthwise,** *or*
    1 tablespoon vanilla extract

1. Prepare French Vanilla Ice Cream Base, adding the vanilla with the vanilla in the base. Strain into a clean bowl and cool thoroughly.

2. Transfer to an ice cream machine and freeze according to manufacturer's instructions.

Makes about 1 quart.

Butter Pecan Ice Cream Prepare French Vanilla Ice Cream, but dissolve ¾ cup light brown sugar and 3 tablespoons unsalted butter in the French Vanilla Ice Cream Base instead of granulated sugar. Transfer mixture to an ice cream machine and freeze according to manufacturer's instructions; halfway through freezing process, add 1 cup chopped, toasted pecans.

Chocolate Ice Cream Prepare French Vanilla Ice Cream Base. In a double boiler melt together 3 ounces semisweet chocolate and 1 ounce unsweetened chocolate. Slowly add ½ cup of the warm ice cream base to melted chocolate; whisk constantly to keep chocolate smooth. Return mixture to ice cream base; mix well and let cool. Continue with step 2, French Vanilla Ice Cream.

Chocolate Chip Ice Cream Prepare French Vanilla Ice Cream through step 1. Transfer mixture to an ice cream machine and freeze according to manufacturer's instructions; halfway through freezing process, add 1 cup miniature chocolate chips.

Coffee Ice Cream Prepare French Vanilla Ice Cream through step 1; add 2 tablespoons instant espresso powder and whisk until it is dissolved. Continue with step 2.

Fresh Fruit Ice Cream Prepare French Vanilla Ice Cream through step 1. Peel, pit, chop, and mash 4 cups fresh fruit: peaches, nectarines, or apricots. Combine mashed fruit with ¼ to ½ cup sugar (less if fruit is very sweet, more if it is not sweet enough) and let sit 1 hour. Add fruit to strained ice cream base and continue with step 2.

Rum Raisin Ice Cream Prepare French Vanilla Ice Cream through step 1. Soak ½ cup raisins in 3 ounces dark rum for 1 hour. Transfer ice cream mixture to an ice cream machine and freeze according to manufacturer's instructions; halfway through freezing process, add raisins and rum.

Strawberry Ice Cream Prepare French Vanilla Ice Cream through step 1. Wash, hull, and mash 2 pints fresh strawberries. Combine mashed berries with ½ cup sugar and let sit 1 hour (more if berries are not sweet). Add strawberries to strained ice cream base and continue with step 2.

PHILADEPHIA-STYLE ICE CREAM

Philadelphia-style ice creams are uncooked. Some do not use eggs; others use whole eggs. Their texture is usually slightly grainier than custard-based ice creams because they lack the emulsifying action of cooked egg yolks to keep the water molecules separated as they freeze. However, bulky flavoring agents, such as significant quantities of fruit pulp or chocolate, can provide their own emulsifying action and make up for the lack of cooked egg yolks, greatly improving the texture of uncooked ice creams.

■ PHILADELPHIA-STYLE VANILLA ICE CREAM

Adding a whole egg to this recipe will give the ice cream a smoother texture.

 2 **cups whipping cream**
 2 **cups half-and-half**
 ¾ **cup sugar**
 2 **teaspoons vanilla extract**

1. Combine ingredients. Stir until sugar is dissolved.

2. Transfer to an ice cream machine and freeze according to manufacturer's instructions.

Makes about 1 quart.

■ PHILADELPHIA-STYLE CHOCOLATE ICE CREAM

Chocolate acts as a smoothing agent to give this ice cream a velvety texture.

> **8 ounces semisweet chocolate**
> **½ cup sugar**
> **1 quart half-and-half**
> **Pinch of salt**

1. In a double boiler over low heat melt chocolate; set aside. Combine sugar, half-and-half, and salt. Stir until sugar is completely dissolved. Add melted chocolate, stirring until well mixed.

2. Transfer to an ice cream machine and freeze according to manufacturer's instructions.

Makes about 1 quart.

GELATO, FROZEN YOGURT, SHERBET, AND GRANITA

Gelato contains less air than American or French ice cream. The Donvier-type ice cream machine will produce the most gelatolike product because it does not incorporate much air into the base during freezing. To make gelato, use any recipe based on French Vanilla Ice Cream Base (see page 311). For frozen yogurt, any type of yogurt can be used, but one with a higher fat content yields a creamier result. Sherbets are based on a sugar syrup, which should be well cooled, like an ice cream base, before using. They make refreshing between-course palate cleansers, as do *granitas*.

■ LEMON FROZEN YOGURT

The combined acidic flavors of yogurt and lemon make this an especially refreshing dessert.

> **4 tablespoons sugar**
> **4 containers (8 oz each) lemon-flavored yogurt**
> **Rind of 2 lemons, finely chopped**

1. Whisk sugar into yogurt until completely dissolved (about 2 minutes); stir in lemon rind.

2. Transfer to an ice cream machine and freeze according to manufacturer's instructions.

Makes about 1 quart.

■ SIMPLE SUGAR SYRUP FOR SHERBETS

This is the most traditional of syrups, somewhere between a French and an Italian type. It may be stored in the refrigerator for several weeks.

> **2 cups sugar**
> **1 cup water**

1. In a medium saucepan over high heat, cook sugar and water, stirring constantly until sugar dissolves and mixture reaches a full, rolling boil.

2. Immediately remove from heat and cool to room temperature. Strain, cover, and refrigerate until needed. Have the syrup well cooled (about 40° F) before using.

Makes about 3 cups.

■ STRAWBERRY SHERBET

This is an excellent, fresh-tasting sherbet that stores well for up to two weeks.

> **2 pints fresh strawberries *or* 12 ounces frozen strawberries, without syrup**
> **1 cup Simple Sugar Syrup for Sherbets (see left)**
> **Juice of ½ lemon**

1. Wash and hull strawberries. Purée with sugar syrup and lemon juice in a blender or food processor.

2. Transfer to an ice cream machine and freeze according to manufacturer's instructions.

Makes about 1 quart.

Fruit or Berry Sherbet Any fruit that yields a good deal of pulp when puréed may be substituted for strawberries: other berries, peaches, pears, plums, or melons. If using blackberries or boysenberries, strain the purée before freezing, as in Raspberry Sherbet (below).

Raspberry Sherbet Substitute 2 pints fresh raspberries or 12 ounces frozen raspberries for strawberries. Before freezing, seed by straining through cheesecloth or a fine sieve. If using a sieve, do not grind seeds against mesh; this will adversely affect both color and flavor.

Fresh fruits such as peaches and raspberries make super sherbets. Serve two or three flavors together for a memorable dessert.

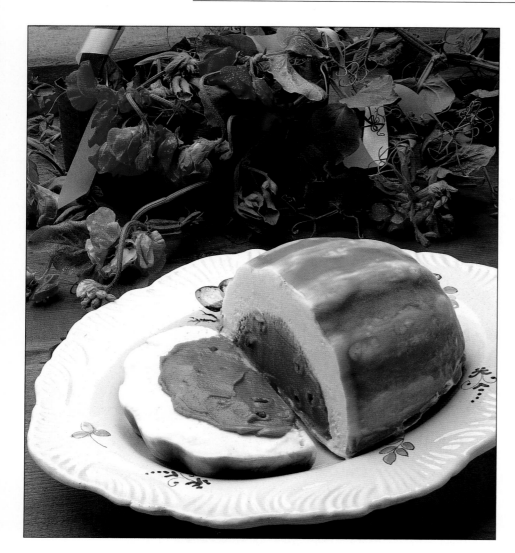

Ice cream bombes are layered desserts formed in a special melon-shaped mold. Frozen Watermelon Bombe features a vanilla ice cream "rind" with raspberry sherbet "flesh" and chocolate chip "seeds." A wash of food coloring tints the outside surface an appropriate green hue.

■ LEMON SHERBET

When fruits that provide a lot of juice but very little pulp—such as lemon, orange, grapefruit, and other citrus—are used in sherbet, the texture may become grainy because of the greater proportion of liquids to solids. The same is true of sherbets made from Champagne, wines, and liqueurs. Adding stiffly beaten egg whites to the sugar syrup base smooths the texture. The syrup base in such sherbets is called an Italian meringue (see Note).

>   2 **large egg whites**
> 2¼ **cups sugar**
>   1 **cup water**
> 1½ **cups fresh lemon juice**

1. In a large bowl beat egg whites until very stiff; set aside. In a medium saucepan over high heat, cook sugar and the water, stirring constantly until sugar dissolves and the mixture reaches a full, rolling boil. Remove from heat and slowly drizzle hot syrup into egg whites, whisking constantly until all the syrup is incorporated. Continue whisking and slowly add lemon juice. Stir over an ice-water bath or cover and refrigerate until cold.

2. Transfer to an ice cream machine and freeze according to manufacturer's instructions.

Makes about 1 quart.

Note Another technique for improving the texture of such sherbets is to increase the proportion of sugar syrup to 50 percent of the total volume of the mixture. The extra sugar helps to keep the ice crystals, which form during freezing, small.

■ WHITE ZINFANDEL GRANITA

Any dry white wine will work in this refreshing *granita,* which does not need an ice cream machine; it freezes in the freezer compartment of the refrigerator.

> 1½ **cups water**
> ¾ **cup sugar**
> 1½ **cups white Zinfandel**

1. In a medium saucepan bring the water, sugar, and half the wine to a boil, stirring constantly until sugar dissolves. Reduce heat and simmer 3 minutes without stirring.

2. Allow syrup to cool to room temperature, or cool in refrigerator. Add remaining wine to cooled syrup. Place in a shallow metal pan and freeze in freezer compartment of refrigerator.

3. Stir well every 30 minutes until firm, 3 to 4 times. Let warm slightly, and stir one final time before serving.

Makes about 1 quart.

SOME WELL-KNOWN FROZEN DESSERTS

Frozen desserts are favorite treats all over the world. Italians love *tortoni,* the French love profiteroles, and Americans love mud pie, among many others. The following recipes capture some of the distinctive flavors of a number of countries. Additional frozen desserts can be found in other entries in this book (consult Recipes and Related Information).

■ TORTONI

Your guests will never guess how simple this Italian treat is to prepare. Note that the mixture with almond-flavored liqueur must freeze at least six hours.

>   1 **cup whipping cream**
> ¼ **cup confectioners' sugar**
> ½ **cup crushed amaretti cookies or chopped, toasted almonds**
>   3 **tablespoons almond-flavored liqueur**
>   1 **large egg white, at room temperature**
>   **Crushed amaretti cookies, toasted almonds, or maraschino cherries, for garnish (optional)**

1. In a medium bowl whip the cream and sugar to soft peaks. Fold in crushed cookies and liqueur.

2. In a separate bowl beat egg white until stiff but still shiny and moist. Fold into whipped cream mixture.

3. Spoon into a 1-quart bowl, parfait glasses, or paper-lined muffin cups. Garnish (if desired). Cover tightly and freeze at least 6 hours.

Serves 8.

MUD PIE

This is a favorite among coffee and chocolate lovers.

> 1 recipe Hot Fudge Sauce (see page 522)
> 1 Chocolate Crumb Crust (see page 436)
> 1 quart Coffee Ice Cream (see page 312), softened
> ¾ cup whipping cream
> 1 teaspoon vanilla extract
> 1 tablespoon confectioners' sugar
> ⅓ cup toasted almonds, for decoration

1. Pour a thin layer of fudge sauce into the cooled Chocolate Crumb Crust and freeze until firm.

2. Spoon ice cream into the frozen crust and level the top. Press plastic wrap over ice cream and freeze at least 1½ hours.

3. Spread a generous layer of fudge sauce over ice cream. Freeze at least 30 minutes. Meanwhile, whip the cream with vanilla and sugar. Spread over the frozen pie. Decorate with almonds and freeze another 2 hours or longer.

Serves 8 to 10.

FROZEN WATERMELON BOMBE

This ice cream bombe looks like a watermelon. It's a treat for the eyes as well as the palate. The bombe must freeze in stages, so preparation must begin early the day it will be served, or the day before.

> 1 quart French Vanilla Ice Cream (see page 312), slightly softened
> ¼ cup miniature semisweet chocolate chips
> 1 quart Raspberry Sherbet (see page 313), slightly softened
> Green food coloring

1. Place an 8-cup melon-shaped mold in the freezer for at least 1 hour.

2. Line inside of mold with an even layer of Vanilla Ice Cream. Cover with plastic wrap, pressing against the ice cream to seal it tightly and fill any air pockets. Return mold to freezer for at least 4 hours.

3. Stir chocolate chips into Raspberry Sherbet to simulate watermelon seeds; remove plastic wrap from mold and fill cavity with sherbet. Top with plastic wrap and freeze until firm.

4. To unmold, dip quickly in lukewarm water and invert onto a chilled platter. Return to freezer to set exterior.

5. Paint outside of molded ice cream with green food coloring, varying shades to resemble stripes on a real watermelon. Cover well and keep frozen. Slice to serve.

Serves 8 to 10.

PEACH MELBA

The great French chef Escoffier created this dessert in honor of a popular opera singer, Nellie Melba.

> 3 cups water
> 2 cups sugar
> 4 large peaches, peeled, halved, and pitted
> 1 tablespoon vanilla extract
> 1 cup fresh raspberries
> 1 quart French Vanilla Ice Cream (see page 312)

1. In a medium saucepan combine the water and sugar; bring to a boil. Add peach halves. Lower the heat and simmer, covered, for 10 to 15 minutes. Remove from heat; let cool. Stir in vanilla, then chill.

2. In a small saucepan heat raspberries to boiling, stirring and mashing berries with a spoon; cool, then chill.

3. To serve, place prepared peach halves on chilled dessert plates. Top each half with a scoop of ice cream. Drizzle raspberry topping all over each serving.

Serves 8.

CHERRIES JUBILEE

This well-known flambéed dessert provides a colorful, dramatic ending to any dinner party.

> 2 tablespoons sugar
> 1 can (16 oz) pitted sweet or sour red cherries, with juice
> 2 tablespoons kirsch
> 1 tablespoon cornstarch
> 1 pint French Vanilla Ice Cream (see page 312)
> ½ cup brandy

1. In a small saucepan over moderate heat, warm sugar and cherries with their juice until hot but not boiling. Make a paste of kirsch and cornstarch. Whisk into cherry mixture; heat, stirring, until thickened (do not boil).

2. Scoop ice cream into dessert dishes. Pour brandy into a ladle and hold it over a medium burner or candle for a minute to warm it slightly. To serve, light a match, ignite the warmed brandy, and pour it over cherry sauce. Stir until the flame dies down. Spoon cherry sauce over ice cream and serve at once.

Serves 4 to 6.

Recipes and Related Information

Ice Cream–Filled Profiteroles, 164; Papaya Ice Cream, 405; Prickly Pear Snow, 479; Rosé Pears and Ice Cream, 612; Sauce, 522; Watermelon Sherbet, 359.

INDUCTION

This method of heating uses magnetic energy to heat cookware made of magnetic materials. For this system a special electrically powered induction cook top is needed. Energy coils located under a ceramic surface convert electric current to high-frequency alternating current. When a pan made of a magnetic metal—steel or cast iron, for example—is set on the cooking surface, energy generated by magnetic force flows through the pan and causes the molecules in the metal to move at high speed and heat up.

Induction cooking is said to be as responsive as gas to change in temperature. It is also more energy efficient than either gas or traditional electric systems because only the cookware is heated, and energy does not escape into the air. As induction stove tops lack potentially hazardous open flames or exposed coils, burns and fires are less likely to occur. Maintenance is another benefit; the smooth surface is easy to clean.

The main drawback is the need for special cookware to make the system work. Conventional aluminum, aluminum-clad, copper, ceramic, and nonmagnetic stainless steel can't be used. The material must be one a magnet will cling to: cast iron, enameled cast iron, porcelain enamel on steel, magnetic stainless steel, or pans specially designed for induction cooking.

Induction cook tops plug into regular household current and are available in single and multiple burner units.

INFUSE, TO

To permeate a liquid with the soluble essences of herbs, spices, teas, or coffee by simmering. Usually the liquid is water, although other liquids can become infusions. Some recipes for custard, for example, require milk that has been infused with vanilla flavor, accomplished by warming the milk with a vanilla bean and letting it sit for 5 to 10 minutes.

> ***Recipes and Related Information***
> *Coffee, 134; Custard, 168; Tea, 573.*

JAM, JELLY, PRESERVE, AND CONDIMENT

Making jams, preserves, and pickled foods at home is not the labor-intensive, exhaustive endeavor that it used to be, thanks to modern equipment and the knowledge available today. Grandmother's summer kitchen yielded endless jars made from quantities of homegrown produce. The modern cook puts up small batches when time permits; these smaller yields cook faster and, as a result, retain more color and flavor. Quality is not being sacrificed

to fit the needs of busy schedules, for home-canned foods far outshine expensive commercial products. Once you have begun to fill your pantry with these creations, you will no longer be satisfied with storebought preserves and pickles. You can also be confident that your jars of food contain only pure, clean, and healthful ingredients. When you have mastered the following basic recipes, you can create your own combinations.

ABOUT THE RECIPES

As a word of reassurance to those who are concerned about food contamination, this entry discusses techniques that deal with high-acid or brined foods. These fruits, pickles, and relishes can be safely canned at the boiling temperature (212° F). With this treatment, the organisms that cause spoilage and the enzymes that might deteriorate quality will be destroyed. We will not discuss the canning of meat, fish, or unbrined vegetables, which are susceptible to botulism contamination with improper handling.

BASIC EQUIPMENT

Organize supplies ahead and store them together. That way you'll be able to make up a small batch with very little effort. Most canning equipment is available at hardware stores or cookware stores. Jars and lids are also sold at well-stocked supermarkets.

Candy Thermometer   To monitor the temperature of the fruit as it cooks; a combination candy and deep-fat thermometer is the practical choice for most kitchens.

Jar Tongs   For lifting hot, filled jars from the water bath after processing.

Jelly Jars   Storage jars for jelly only; they are sealed with household paraffin rather than by water-bath processing. Fancy jars with brightly colored lids and a quilted pattern on the glass will enhance the appearance of your jellies, making them especially attractive to give as gifts. When you seal jelly with paraffin, you can use many sizes and shapes of jars and glasses, as long as they can withstand the boiling temperature needed to sterilize them.

Kettle   For cooking; choose a 6- to 8-quart, nonreactive, heavy enamel or stainless steel pot. Do not use aluminum or cast-iron pots since they may react chemically with the acids and salts in foods, thereby producing unpleasant colors and metallic flavors.

Labels   For identifying and dating jars.

Ladle   For transferring cooked food to jars.

Mason Jars   Storage jars; they are widemouthed, available in half pint, pint, or quart sizes, with two-piece dome caps. They have self-sealing lids that are held in place by a metal ring band. The lids are replaced after each use, but the ring bands may be reused if they're not rusted or bent. Named for their inventor, John Mason, the jars are manufactured by several companies.

Paraffin (Household Wax) For quick-sealing jellies that don't need to be sealed by water-bath processing.

Slotted Spoon For skimming off foam that develops on surface of cooked food; done before filling jars so product won't be cloudy.

Water-Bath Canner For processing; this pot is in addition to the cooking kettle. It has a rack that lifts the filled jars off the bottom of the pot and away from direct heat (see Useful Definitions, Water-Bath Process). Be sure to read instructions provided by manufacturer.

Widemouthed Funnel For filling jars; don't use standard, narrow-necked funnels as they will clog.

Wooden Spoon For stirring fruits or vegetables as they cook; choose ones with long handles.

USEFUL DEFINITIONS

Headspace This is the air space between the food in the jar and the lid or paraffin, commonly ⅛ to ½ inch (follow recipe directions). Headspace allows for the expansion of food while it's being processed. Insufficient headspace will cause the seal to break and the contents to seep out.

Jell Point This is the temperature at which a recipe will thicken properly. Test the jell point of a recipe with a candy thermometer or by using a frozen saucer. Jelly mixtures are ready at about 220° F, jams at 221° F to 224° F. Alternatively, drop a large spoonful of jelly or jam onto a saucer that has been kept in the freezer. The mixture will set up in 2 minutes, and you can tell how "tight" the jelly or jam will be when cooled. For convenience, you may want to keep a stack of saucers in the freezer.

Pectin All of the recipes for jams, jellies, and preserves in this entry use a combination of fruit, sugar, acid, and pectin—a jelling agent. Natural pectin is found in the seeds, skin, and flesh of fruit. Some fruits, such as apples, cranberries, and most citrus fruits, are high in pectin. Fruits low in pectin are combined with a high-pectin fruit or commercial pectin. With the right amount of pectin, recipes will jell properly. Without it, the consistency might be either too runny or too thick and unspreadable. Commercial pectin is available in powdered or liquid form. Use only the form called for in the recipe.

Sealing An airtight seal protects the processed food from airborne organisms that could cause spoilage, and ensures a long shelf life. The recipes in this section are sealed either with a layer of paraffin or, more often, with metal lids and ring bands. Lids and bands seal in the following way: During water-bath processing, the contents of the jars expand and some air is forced out of the jars. When the jars cool, the remaining air contracts, creating a partial vacuum that pulls the lids tightly against the jar rims and holds them in place. The vacuum and the sealing compound of the lid maintain the seal. As the jars cool, you may hear a loud popping noise. This is an indication that a jar has just sealed. Sealing is not always accompanied by a loud noise, however. To test for a seal, press the center of the lid of a completely cooled jar with your finger. If the lid stays down, the jar is sealed. Once jars

Making preserves doesn't require much specialty equipment. Shown from left to right are: thermometer; tongs; jar labels; widemouthed funnel; water-bath canner with rack; jars, lids, and rings; kettle; ladle; slotted spoon; wooden spoon.

PRESERVES AND CONDIMENTS: A PANTRY GUIDE

Is there a difference between jams and jellies, chutneys and relishes? Yes, sometimes only a fine one, but it might be helpful to know what each product actually is before you choose which recipes to make. Listed are definitions plus suggestions for use of each type.

Chutneys are fruits or vegetables cooked very slowly with sugar, vinegar, and spices. Uses: condiment served with Indian and Asian meals, barbecue glaze.

Conserves are two or more fruits cooked with sugar and raisins or nuts. Uses: spread, ice cream and dessert sauce, cake filling, condiment.

Fruit Butters are puréed, spiced, cooked fruit, slowly simmered in an open kettle or oven until thick and creamy. Uses: spread, meat glaze, barbecue baste.

Fruit or Herb Vinegars are flavored vinegars that sometimes steep for a number of weeks to deepen their flavor. Uses: salad dressing and pan glaze.

Jams are mashed fruits, cooked with sugar and sometimes with added pectin. Uses: spread, barbecue baste, meat glaze.

Jellies are fruit juices boiled with sugar. Fine jellies are clear and shimmering; when cut, they hold their shape. Uses: spread, cake filling (jelly rolls), meat and poultry glaze.

Marmalades are soft, clear jellies cooked with the peel and flesh of citrus. Uses: spread, ice cream topping, glaze for cheesecake.

Mustards are condiments made of mustard seed or powder. Uses: spread, dipping sauce, salad dressing.

Pickles and Relishes are fruits or vegetables pickled with vinegar or preserved with sugar. Uses: meat and sandwich condiment.

Preserves are whole or coarse fruit pieces cooked with sugar and sometimes with added pectin. *Preserves* is also a general term for several types of fruit spreads, including jams and jellies. Uses: spread, cake filling, barbecue baste, meat glaze, waffle and pancake topping.

---

have sealed, the flat lids will adhere to the jar rims, so you may remove and reuse the ring bands. If a jar fails to seal, refrigerate and eat contents within a short period. See Sealing Methods for more information.

Water-Bath Process This is a method of heat processing to inactivate the enzymes in food and kill microorganisms that cause spoilage and to ensure an airtight seal. It can be safely used for such foods as jams, fruit preserves, and brined products because their high acidity inhibits the formation of toxins. To process, hot, cooked fruit is ladled into sterilized jars and covered with sterilized lids. The jars are set on a rack in the canner and enough water is added so that the jars are covered by several inches. The water is brought to a boil, the canner covered, and the jars boiled for the time specified in the recipe (timing begins when water comes to a boil). When done, jars are removed with tongs, cooled at room temperature for at least 12 hours, then stored.

SEALING METHODS

To be fully safe when sealing jellies, jams, preserves, marmalades, conserves, and chutneys, use the water-bath method. Jellies can be safely sealed with paraffin, but many people find it convenient to process jellies. This is a matter of personal preference. Try both sealing methods and decide which works best for you. Not all products must be sealed, however. Jars can be capped and stored in the refrigerator or freezer, but will not keep as long.

WATER-BATH CANNER METHOD

1. Harvest or purchase ripe, not bruised, produce. Wash and trim.

2. Check mason jars and discard those that are cracked or chipped, which will prevent airtight seals. Wash and rinse. If ring bands have been previously used, replace them.

3. Sterilize jars: Set jars in a kettle and cover with water. Boil 15 minutes. Turn off heat and let jars sit in the hot water until they are filled. The flat caps should be covered with water in a saucepan and boiled for 5 minutes. The outside ring bands do not need to be sterilized because they never touch food.

4. Cook recipe as directed. Keep heat low and watch for scorching. Test jelly for its jell point or doneness (see Useful Definitions, Jell Point).

5. Using ladle and widemouthed funnel, fill sterilized jars with prepared recipe, leaving a ¼-inch headspace or as recipe directs. Clean any spillage from mouth of jar with dampened cloth to ensure a perfect seal. Attach sterilized metal lid with tongs. Screw on outer ring.

6. Process filled jars: Set jars in rack of water-bath canner and set filled rack in canner. Keep jars from touching one another or the sides of the canner so water can freely circulate. Add enough hot water to cover jars by 2 inches. Put on canner lid. Bring water to a full rolling boil and process according to recipe directions (processing time varies from recipe to recipe; begin counting processing time when the water boils). Remove jars from canner with jar tongs. Cool on a folded towel. The cap will pop loudly as jars cool, and lid will indent in center. This can occur anytime within a 12-hour period. Test each jar after 12 hours to make sure it has sealed (see Useful Definitions, Sealing). Label and date each jar.

7. Store in a cool, dry, dark area. Jars will keep for several years.

JELLY METHOD (PARAFFIN SEAL)

1. Sterilize jelly jars as directed in Water-Bath Canner Method, step 3.

2. Prepare jelly according to recipe. Skim off any foam from mixture with a slotted spoon.

3. Using ladle and widemouthed funnel, fill jelly jars with prepared recipe, leaving ¼-inch headspace or as recipe directs. Wipe rims with a dampened cloth. Let cool.

4. Seal with paraffin: Melt household paraffin in a mason jar or heat-resistant glass measuring cup over boiling water. (Do not use a tin can or tea kettle to melt paraffin, as many books recommend; metal gets extremely hot and becomes difficult to handle. Heat-resistant glass doesn't absorb heat as dramatically and is easy to store.)

Paraffin is highly flammable; never melt over direct heat or let the water under the melting wax boil away. Pour a thin layer (⅛ inch) of paraffin over cooled jelly. A glass measuring cup with pouring lip simplifies this step. Tilt jar to be sure that paraffin touches sides. Let paraffin harden and set. Pour on another ⅛ inch in the same manner and let this set.

For convenience, set aside a jar or measuring cup to use only for storing and melting paraffin. Don't clean the container between uses; when needed, remelt what has hardened in the jar or cup, adding more if necessary.

5. Store in a cool, dry, dark area. Jars will keep for several years.

NONSEALING METHODS: REFRIGERATOR AND FREEZER

For small batches and for products that will be eaten soon after processing, it is unnecessary to seal sterilized jars. Refrigerate when cool, and use within two to three weeks. Pickles or relishes will keep up to one year in the refrigerator and actually become more delicious, with a deeper, fuller flavor, as they age and mature.

Some jam recipes have been specially developed for freezer storage. These use commercial pectin, are not processed, and need very little cooking. The final product is a jam with a bright color but a thinner consistency. The jars can be frozen for up to eight months. Once they are opened they must be refrigerated and eaten within three weeks (see Spicy Blueberry Freezer Jam, page 321).

Water-bath processed jars may also be frozen if pantry shelf space is at a premium. Be sure to leave ½-inch headspace in the jar to allow for expansion in the freezer.

■ STRAWBERRY JAM

This old-fashioned favorite has a fresh berry flavor and a clear, bright red color. It is the perfect spread for all types of breads and rolls. Spoon it on scones, English muffins, French toast, biscuits, muffins, or toast.

2 quarts crushed strawberries
3 tablespoons fresh lemon juice
6 cups sugar

1. Measure berries and place in an 8-quart or larger pot.

2. Add lemon juice and sugar to berries; bring slowly to boiling, stirring occasionally until sugar dissolves.

3. Cook rapidly to the jell point until desired thickness is reached (about 30 minutes). As mixture thickens, stir frequently to prevent sticking.

4. When ready, remove pot from heat and skim off foam with a slotted spoon.

5. Quickly ladle into clean, hot, sterilized jars, leaving ¼-inch headspace; fasten lids.

6. Process in boiling water bath 10 minutes.

Makes about 8 half-pints.

■ SUMMER PEACH JAM

Full-flavored fresh fruit is the essence of distinctive jams, jellies, and preserves. Fresh peaches are available from about May through September, and reach the peak of their season in late summer. Be sure to select firm, fully ripe fruit that is free of blemishes and bruises. Never use overripe peaches. Note that the peaches need to be peeled before cooking: To peel, cut a small *x* in blossom end and drop whole fruit into boiling water for about 30 seconds; plunge into cold water, and slip off skin.

5 pounds (about 12 large) firm, ripe peaches
3 tablespoons fresh lemon juice
5 cups sugar

1. Wash, peel, and pit peaches. Slice peaches into small pieces. Measure 10 cups of sliced peaches.

2. Place peaches, lemon juice, and sugar in a large bowl and allow to sit for 1 hour.

3. Transfer peach mixture to an 8-quart or larger pot and simmer until sugar is dissolved. Bring to a full boil.

4. Cook rapidly to the jell point until desired thickness is reached (about 25 minutes). Stir occasionally at first and then constantly as mixture nears jell point.

5. When ready, remove pot from heat and skim off foam with a slotted spoon.

6. Quickly ladle into clean, hot, sterilized jars, leaving ¼-inch headspace; fasten lids.

7. Process in boiling water bath 10 minutes.

Makes 8 half-pints.

■ APRICOT PRESERVES

Don't miss apricots at the height of their short late spring, early summer season—May through July. Fill crêpes or smother waffles with this marvelous preserve. Note that the fruit mixture must stand 4 to 5 hours before cooking. To peel apricots, follow the directions for peeling peaches given in the introduction to Summer Peach Jam.

2 pounds firm, ripe apricots
¼ cup fresh lemon juice
4 cups sugar

1. Peel, halve, and pit apricots. You should have 5 cups.

2. Thoroughly mix fruit with lemon juice and sugar. Cover tightly; let stand 4 to 5 hours in a cool place.

3. Heat fruit mixture slowly to boiling in a 6-quart or larger pot, stirring occasionally until sugar dissolves.

4. Cook rapidly until fruit is translucent (about 30 minutes). As mixture thickens, stir frequently to prevent sticking.

5. Quickly ladle into clean, hot, sterilized jars, leaving ¼-inch headspace; fasten lids.

6. Process in boiling water bath 15 minutes.

Makes 4 half-pints.

TIPS

FOR SUCCESSFUL FRUIT PRESERVES

- *Do not substitute ingredients or your recipe won't jell properly. The chemistry will change, and a failed product result.*
- *Never double recipes that call for commercial pectin as the thickener.*
- *Read the instruction booklets that accompany mason jars and commercial pectins.*

Always a favorite, Classic Orange Marmalade is chunky with fruit and peel and permeated with a rich citrus flavor. To best show off its warm, golden color, present it at the table in a clear serving bowl.

CLASSIC ORANGE MARMALADE

Traditionally, the finest orange marmalade is made from slightly bitter Seville oranges. They are hard to come by in this country, but if you can find them, by all means use them in this recipe. If you can't find bitter oranges, substitute sweet Valencia or navel oranges. Note that the fruit must sit for two 24-hour periods to soften the peel and release the natural pectin before cooking and processing.

> 6 bitter oranges (if available) or sweet oranges
> 2 sweet oranges
> 1 lemon
> 9½ cups water
> Sugar, as needed
> 1½ tablespoons fresh lemon juice

1. Slice oranges and lemon very thinly. Remove seeds and place slices in a small bowl with ½ cup of the water; set aside.

2. Place lemon and orange slices in a large pot and cover with the remaining water. Soak 24 hours.

3. Place pot containing orange and lemon slices over medium heat and simmer until peel is tender (about 35 minutes). Remove from heat and let stand another 24 hours.

4. Measure fruits and their liquid and return them to pot, adding an equal amount of sugar. Bring to a boil, reduce heat to medium, and cook, stirring frequently, until jell point is reached (45 to 60 minutes).

5. Combine lemon juice and water strained from seeds, add to pot, and cook marmalade 10 minutes more, stirring constantly.

6. Quickly ladle into clean, hot, sterilized jars, leaving ¼-inch headspace; fasten lids.

7. Process in boiling water bath 15 minutes.

Makes 6 half-pints.

CRANBERRY CONSERVE

Modify tradition a bit this year with this cranberry conserve. It's one less thing you'll have to prepare for busy holidays, and it tastes terrific with turkey, chicken, and wild game.

> 1 unpeeled orange, very finely chopped
> 2 cups water
> 3 cups sugar
> 1 quart fresh or frozen cranberries
> 1 cup raisins
> ½ cup chopped walnuts or other nuts

1. Combine orange and the water in a 6-quart or larger pot; cook rapidly until peel is tender (about 20 minutes).

2. Add sugar, cranberries, and raisins. Bring slowly to boiling, stirring occasionally until sugar dissolves.

3. Cook rapidly until mixture starts to thicken (about 8 minutes). As mixture thickens, stir frequently to prevent sticking. Stir in nuts the last 5 minutes of cooking.

4. Quickly ladle into clean, hot, sterilized jars, leaving ¼-inch headspace; fasten lids.

5. Process in boiling water bath 15 minutes.

Makes 4 half-pints.

APPLE BUTTER

Old-fashioned apple butter is difficult to find in stores and very easy to make. It is delicious on toast and waffles, or eaten as a fruit dessert with cream.

> 6 pounds apples
> Sugar, as needed
> ½ teaspoon ground cinnamon
> ½ teaspoon ground allspice

1. Slice, peel, and core apples. Put in a large kettle and add water to halfway up amount of apples. Cook over medium heat until softened (15 to 20 minutes); cool.

2. Preheat oven to 300° F. Purée apples in a blender or food processor. Measure purée. Add ½ cup sugar for each 1 cup purée. Put sweetened purée into a shallow glass baking dish. Stir in cinnamon and allspice.

3. Bake until butter is thick but not dry (2 to 2½ hours), stirring every 15 minutes.

4. Quickly ladle into clean, hot, sterilized jars, leaving ¼-inch headspace. Process in boiling water bath 10 minutes.

Makes 6 pints.

■ MINT JELLY

Traditionalists insist that the best accompaniment to roast lamb is a dollop of mint jelly. There is no comparison between artificially flavored commercial jellies and your own version, made with fresh mint leaves and stems.

>   1 cup chopped, solidly packed mint leaves
>   and tender stems
>   1 cup water
>   ½ cup apple cider vinegar
>   3½ cups sugar
>   5 drops green food coloring (optional)
>   1 pouch (3 oz) liquid fruit pectin

1. Put chopped mint into a 6-quart pot. Add the water, vinegar, and sugar; stir well.

2. Over high heat, stirring constantly, bring quickly to a full, rolling boil that cannot be stirred down.

3. Add food coloring (if desired) and pectin.

4. Return to a full, rolling boil. Boil rapidly 30 seconds.

5. Remove from heat. Skim off foam with slotted spoon. Strain immediately through two thicknesses of damp cheesecloth.

6. Ladle jelly quickly into hot, sterilized jars, leaving ½-inch headspace; seal with paraffin.

Makes 3 to 4 half-pints.

■ SPICY BLUEBERRY FREEZER JAM

Freezer jams glisten with the natural color and flavor of fresh fruit. Thinner than traditional cooked jams, they are simple, fast, and fresh tasting.

>   2½ pints blueberries
>   1 tablespoon fresh lemon juice
>   ½ teaspoon ground cinnamon
>   ⅛ teaspoon freshly grated nutmeg
>   5 cups sugar
>   ¾ cup water
>   1 package (1¾ oz) powdered fruit pectin

1. In a large bowl crush blueberries one layer at a time (crushing too many at a time inhibits free flow of juice).

2. Measure 3 cups crushed blueberries and place in a large bowl. Stir in lemon juice, cinnamon, and nutmeg. Thoroughly mix sugar into fruit. Let stand 10 minutes.

3. Combine the water and pectin in a saucepan. Bring to a full boil and boil 1 minute, stirring constantly.

4. Stir hot pectin liquid into fruit and continue to stir vigorously for 3 minutes to distribute pectin.

5. Ladle into freezer containers, leaving ½-inch headspace. Cover with lids and let stand at room temperature until set. (It may take up to 24 hours.) Store jam in freezer up to 8 months.

Makes about 6 half-pints.

PICKLES AND RELISHES

Making pickles and relishes is as easy as preserving, and many of the same principles apply. You will use water-bath canner, mason jars, and fresh, crisp produce. Pungent spices that have not lost their zest are important. You may want to grow your own herbs for the best quality possible. Kosher salt is used for brining because it does not have additives that would cloud the brine.

Follow the directions at the beginning of the chapter for using a water-bath canner. Store pickles and relishes in a cool, dark spot. Before using, let them age at least one month to mellow their sharp flavor.

■ BREAD AND BUTTER PICKLES

Most collections of early American pickled foods will include a recipe for Bread and Butter Pickles. These are sliced cucumbers, packed with onions, green peppers, and spices in a sweet-and-sour brine.

>   8 cups sliced pickling cucumbers
>   Salt
>   2 cups sliced onions
>   4 green bell peppers (with red on them if possible)
>   2 cups distilled white vinegar
>   2 cups sugar
>   1 tablespoon salt
>   2 teaspoons dry mustard
>   2 teaspoons turmeric
>   2 teaspoons celery seed
>   1 cinnamon stick, broken

1. Sprinkle cucumber slices with salt and let soak 1 hour. Rinse with cold water and drain.

2. Cut onion slices crosswise and cut peppers (remove seeds) in about 1½-inch lengths.

3. Combine vinegar, sugar, the 1 tablespoon salt, mustard, turmeric, celery seed, and cinnamon stick in large kettle; add cucumbers, onions, and peppers. Bring to a boil; cook until cucumbers start to look glassy (3 to 5 minutes).

4. Pack pickles into clean, hot, sterilized jars, leaving ½-inch headspace; fasten lids.

5. Process in boiling water bath 5 minutes.

Makes 5 to 6 pints.

With the addition of vinegar, these cucumbers and flavorings will become delicious Dill Spears.

GINGERED PEACH PICKLES

These pickles are delicious over ice cream or served with crème fraîche.

> 8 **pounds (about 3½ qt) small peaches**
> 3 **pounds light brown sugar**
> 1 **quart cider vinegar**
>   **Fresh ginger (1-in. piece), peeled and crushed**
> 2 **tablespoons whole cloves, crushed**
> 3 **cinnamon sticks, broken up**
> 1 **whole clove per peach**
>   **Additional whole cinnamon sticks, for each jar**
> 3 **to 4 tablespoons brandy (optional)**

1. Peel peaches and treat to prevent darkening. Halve and pit or leave whole.

2. Combine sugar and vinegar in a large pot; bring to a boil over medium heat and boil 5 minutes. Tie ginger, crushed cloves, and broken cinnamon sticks loosely in cheesecloth. Add to syrup and simmer 5 minutes.

3. Stick a whole clove in each peach. Add only enough peaches to boiling syrup to fill one 1-quart jar; cook until peaches are hot but not soft (about 2 minutes). Do not overcook. Remove peaches with slotted spoon and pack tightly in a clean, hot, sterilized jar along with a small stick of cinnamon. Repeat process until all peaches are packed in jars.

4. Bring syrup to a boil; remove spice bag. Pour hot syrup over peaches in jars, leaving ½-inch headspace. Add 1 tablespoon brandy (if desired). Fasten lids.

5. Process in boiling water bath 15 minutes.

Makes 3 to 4 quarts.

CORN RELISH

Corn relish tastes good with country-style cooking such as fried chicken, baked ham, and sausages of all kinds.

> 22 **medium ears of corn (enough to make 10 cups kernels)**
> 1 **cup chopped red bell pepper (1 large pepper)**
> 1¼ **cups chopped celery**
> ¾ **cup chopped onion**
> 1½ **cups sugar**
> 2½ **cups distilled white vinegar**
> 2 **cups water**
> 1 **tablespoon salt**
> 1 **teaspoon celery seed**
> 2½ **tablespoons mustard seed**
> ½ **teaspoon turmeric**

1. Cook ears of corn in boiling salted water 3 to 5 minutes. Plunge into cold water.

2. Drain corn. Cut kernels from cob with knife or corn kernel remover. Kernels should measure 10 cups.

3. In a large pot, combine kernels with remaining ingredients in large pot and simmer 15 minutes.

DILL SPEARS

Most pickling spices use dill as a major flavoring element. Dill weed (the feathery leaves) has a refreshing, cool quality; the small, hard, dried seeds are pungently warm and slightly bitter.

> 4 **pounds pickling cucumbers, washed, blossom ends removed, and cut into spears**
> 3 **cups distilled white or apple cider vinegar**
> 3 **cups water**
> ⅓ **cup salt**
> 3 **peppercorns per quart**
> 2 **dill heads *or* 2 tablespoons dill seed per quart**
> 1 **clove garlic per quart**

1. Combine vinegar, the water, and salt in a small saucepan and bring to a boil.

2. Add peppercorns, dill (or dill seed), and garlic to each clean, hot 1-quart jar.

3. Pack cucumber spears in jars. Fill jars with boiling pickling mixture, leaving ½-inch headspace; fasten lids.

4. Process in boiling water bath 20 minutes.

Makes about 3 quarts.

4. Immediately pack into clean, hot, sterilized jars, leaving ½-inch headspace; fasten lids.

5. Process in boiling water bath 15 minutes.

Makes 5 to 6 pints.

■ APRICOT AND CURRY CHUTNEY

Mention chutney, and mouths water for spicy East Indian dishes. Chutney is equally delicious with barbecued meats, roasts, poultry, chops, or cold cuts. In India, chutney is served fresh, but here it's more often preserved.

  1½ **pounds dried apricots, chopped (4 cups chopped)**
   1 **quart water**
  1½ **cups chopped onion**
   ½ **cup sugar**
   3 **cups golden raisins**
   3 **cups distilled white vinegar**
  1½ **tablespoons grated fresh ginger**
  1½ **to 2 teaspoons curry powder**
   2 **cinnamon sticks (2 in. each)**
   ¾ **teaspoon salt**

1. Combine apricots, the water, onion, and sugar in a 6-quart pot and simmer 5 minutes, stirring occasionally. Add remaining ingredients and cook 10 minutes more.

2. Remove cinnamon sticks and ladle chutney into clean, hot, sterilized jars, leaving ½-inch headspace; fasten lids.

3. Process in boiling water bath 10 minutes.

Makes about 4 pints.

HERB AND FRUIT VINEGARS AND MUSTARDS

Flavored vinegars are effective in salads and stir-fries or as pan glazes. They add zest to food and are satisfying to make. Collect different vinegars to flavor and see which ones you enjoy. Try Chinese and Japanese rice vinegars, wine vinegars, and apple cider vinegar. Wash and store empty wine bottles for vinegars. New corks are sold at hardware stores. The simple mustard recipe always works and is a great way to start to learn about this condiment.

■ HERB VINEGAR

The following is a basic method that can be used with any herb. Use about 4 ounces of fresh herbs or 2 ounces of dried herbs per quart of vinegar. Let the flavored vinegar sit for five or six weeks to deepen its flavor before using.

  Tarragon sprigs (or other fresh herb)
  White wine vinegar or rice vinegar

1. Wash fresh tarragon and pat dry with paper towels. Place a few sprigs in each sterilized bottle.

2. Pour vinegar into bottles and cap tightly.

3. Allow herbs to steep in vinegar for 5 to 6 weeks before using.

■ FRAN'S RASPBERRY VINEGAR

Use this raspberry vinegar in salad dressings, when poaching pears or apples, or to deglaze the sauté pan in which chicken or veal has been browned. This vinegar mellows as it ages. It keeps indefinitely, improving with time. Store in a cool, dark, dry place and refrigerate after opening.

  12 **pints raspberries (6 oz each)**
   1 **cup sugar**
   2 **quarts or more good-quality red or white wine vinegar**

1. Rinse berries and place in large, clean, sterilized glass jars.

2. In a saucepan, combine sugar and vinegar, and bring to a boil, stirring until sugar dissolves.

3. Pour hot vinegar over berries. Berries must be completely covered with vinegar. Cover loosely and let stand in a cool place 3 to 4 weeks.

4. Strain mixture through a fine sieve into a saucepan, pressing gently to extract juice from berries. Bring to a boil, reduce heat, and simmer 10 minutes; skim off foam.

5. In the meantime, boil canning jars or glass bottles, completely immersed in water, for 15 minutes to sterilize. (Any type of bottle that can withstand the boiling temperature may be used.)

6. Ladle hot vinegar into hot, sterilized jars or bottles, leaving ¼-inch headspace; cap tightly.

Makes 2 quarts.

■ HOMEMADE MUSTARD

This recipe is basically foolproof. It makes the French-style wine mustard.

  ¼ **cup dry mustard**
  ¼ **cup white wine vinegar**
  ⅓ **cup dry white wine**
   1 **tablespoon sugar**
  ½ **teaspoon salt**
   3 **egg yolks**

1. Mix together all ingredients except egg yolks and allow to stand 2 hours.

2. Whisk yolks into mixture; transfer to top of a double boiler. Cook, stirring constantly, over hot, not boiling, water until mustard thickens (about 5 minutes).

3. Cool mustard. Cover and refrigerate up to 1 month.

Makes 1 cup.

Tarragon Mustard Mix in ½ teaspoon crushed dried tarragon when adding egg yolks.

Lemon or Lime Mustard Mix in ¾ teaspoon grated lemon or lime rind and 1½ teaspoons fresh lemon or lime juice when adding egg yolks.

JELLY-ROLL STYLE

This term takes its name from the dessert made from a sheet of sponge cake that is spread with jelly, rolled, and baked. When sliced, the cross section shows a spiral design of cake and filling. The term has come to mean a thin, flat piece of meat, fish, cake, bread, pastry, or other food rolled around a filling.

JERUSALEM ARTICHOKE

Also known as the sunchoke, the Jerusalem artichoke is a native American vegetable. Samuel de Champlain discovered it growing in Indian gardens in Cape Cod in 1604. Despite its name, it is not an artichoke but a tuber of a species of sunflower. The word *Jerusalem* may be derived from *girasole*, Italian for sunflower.

The fresh tubers have ivory flesh and a thin, light brown skin that may have a reddish hue. Ranging from 2 to 6 inches in length, they may be either rounded with fairly smooth skins or elongated with knobby protuberances. The tubers closely resemble fresh ginger.

When raw, the Jerusalem artichoke has a crisp texture like that of a potato and a delicate, somewhat nutty flavor. When cooked, the tuber has a texture resembling boiled turnips and a flavor reminiscent of artichoke. Most consumers are surprised to discover that the Jerusalem artichoke contains no starch.

Use   Slice or grate raw Jerusalem artichokes and add to salads, or marinate in vinaigrette and serve as a salad. Bake tubers in their skins as you would potatoes; slice and sauté or deep-fry; boil or steam, then sauté in butter, or peel and purée. Substitute for water chestnut in stir-fries. Purée for soup or preserve as relish or pickles.

Availability   Fresh Jerusalem artichokes are sold fall through winter.

Selection   Pick firm tubers without soft spots. For easy cleaning and preparation, choose those with smooth, regular shapes. Jerusalem artichokes are sold in bulk in some supermarkets; in other markets, they are scrubbed and packed in plastic bags.

Storage   If packaged in a plastic bag and kept in the refrigerator crisper, Jerusalem artichokes should remain crisp and firm for at least one week.

Preparation   Scrub well, using a stiff brush if necessary to remove dirt from knobs and crevices. Leave on skin or peel, as desired. Peeled raw Jerusalem artichokes oxidize rapidly; drop in acidulated water immediately to prevent browning. Drain just before using. The tubers are easier to peel if cooked first.

Cooking   See BOIL, DEEP-FRY, PUREE, SAUTE, STEAM.

JICAMA

The tuber of a tropical vine, jicama (pronounced *hee-ka-ma*) has long been important to Mexican cooks but only recently has been widely found in American supermarkets. It looks like a large, squat, knobby turnip with a rough earth-colored brown skin. The stark white flesh inside is as cool and crunchy as an apple and almost as sweet. Jicama is a member of the legume family and is also known as yam bean.

Use   Jicama can be eaten raw or cooked. In Mexico it is cut into slivers and served with ground chiles and lime as an appetizer. Cut into spears, it is perfect for dipping, and when dressed with citrus juice, chiles, and oil becomes a refreshing savory salad. Raw jicama adds crunchy texture and sweetness to fruit salads. Its natural sweetness and low calorie count make it an appealing dieter's snack. Substitute jicama for water chestnut in stir-fries, or prepare like a potato—boiled and mashed, or baked.

Availability   Fresh jicama appears all year in Mexican markets and some supermarkets, but peak availability is October through May. Some markets cut up large jicama and sell portions wrapped in plastic.

Selection   Jicama should be firm, without blemishes. It should feel heavy for its size.

Storage   Keep in a plastic bag in the refrigerator crisper for up to two weeks. Store small cut pieces in cold water to prevent drying out.

Preparation   Wash and peel, removing the fibrous white layer just underneath the skin.

■ JICAMA WITH CHILE AND LIME

Jicama con chile y limon is commonly sold from little carts on the streets of Mexico. The mild flavor of jicama is an excellent foil for the bite of the ground chile and salt, and the tang of the lime juice. It is a delicious, simple to prepare snack or hors d'oeuvre.

1 small jicama, peeled and cut into
    bite-sized wedges
    Salt, to taste
    Ground red chile, mild or hot, to taste
2 limes, cut into wedges

1. Place jicama wedges on toothpicks and arrange on a platter. Sprinkle with salt and ground chile.

2. Serve with lime wedges. Each person squeezes a little lime juice over jicama before eating.

Serves 6 to 8 as an appetizer.

Recipes and Related Information
Avocado, Jicama, and Grapefruit Salad, 281; Nopalito Salad, 391.

JUICE EXTRACTOR

If you want to squeeze a pitcherful of fresh orange or grapefruit juice, you would use a reamer (see CITRUS REAMER). To press out the healthful juices from hard, raw fruits and vegetables such as carrots, apples, and cabbage, juice-bar style, you need this machine. All mod-
els function essentially the same: Pulp is finely grated so that its liquid is released, and as a result of centrifugal action, the juice is passed through a strainer that traps the pulp. More expensive models have a larger capacity and are probably able to extract more juice. Some heavy-duty electric mixers and food processors have extractor attachments.

JULIENNE, TO

To cut into fine, even-sized sticks, which are also called matchsticks. These strips are used to garnish soups, stews, and salads; or, they can be steamed and served as a side dish. See KNIFE, Cutting Techniques, for information on how to julienne.

JUNIPER BERRY

A small, round, blue-black berry of an evergreen shrub native to Europe, the juniper berry is the principal flavoring in gin. It is about the size of a large pea and is extremely aromatic.

Use   Apart from its importance in making gin, juniper is employed to flavor marinades for game of all kinds, for lamb, and for the German braised meat dish, sauerbraten. It is also traditionally added to Alsatian sauerkraut.

Availability   Whole juniper berries are sold on most supermarket spice racks.

Selection   Packaged seasonings lose quality after a while; try to buy from a store that restocks its spice section fairly often.

Storage   Keep in an airtight container in a cool, dark, dry place for up to two years.

Preparation   Toasting berries briefly in a warm skillet will bring out their fragrance. Crush berries gently with a mortar and pestle for use in marinades; crush finely for stuffings or sauces. They are pungent and should be used in moderation.

KALE

The leafy green vegetable known as kale, borecole, or cow cabbage is a non-head-forming member of the cabbage family and one of the first cabbages to be cultivated. Its dark green, ruffled leaves are high in vitamin C and calcium and very low in calories. It thrives in cold climates; indeed it is said that frost increases its sweetness. Collards belong to the same family but have smooth, flat leaves. Some markets now carry an ornamental kale, also known as salad savoy, which has handsome crinkly leaves bearing shades of rose, cream, purple, and green.

Use   Because it thrives throughout cold Scottish winters, kale has long been an almost daily staple in the Scottish diet. Scotch cooks use it in colcannon (mashed potatoes with kale) and in lamb and barley soup. Portuguese cooks make a simple potato and kale soup called *caldo verde*. In the southern United States, kale is boiled with ham bone or salt pork, sometimes in conjunction with collards. Ornamental kale is edible but not choice; its best use is decorative.

Availability   Fresh kale is sold fall through spring. Frozen kale is carried by many supermarkets.

Selection   The best kale has crisp, dark leaves. Avoid bunches with limp, wilted, or yellowed leaves.

Storage   It will stay fresh for several days in a plastic bag in the refrigerator crisper.

Preparation   Wash well. Discard any limp or discolored leaves. Cut away tough stems. Shred, chop, or cook whole (cut large leaves in half).

Cooking   See BOIL, STEAM.

▨ STEAMED KALE AND PEARL ONIONS
If you've never tried kale, this simple steamed side dish would be a good introduction.

> ¼ **pound pearl onions, peeled**
> 1 **bunch kale, coarsely chopped**
>   **Lemon wedges, for garnish**

Place onions and then kale in steamer over boiling water and cook until kale is wilted (8 to 10 minutes). Serve immediately with lemon wedges.

Serves 4.

KAMPYO

Also spelled *kanpyo*, these long, buff-colored, ribbonlike strips are made from dried gourd shavings.

Use   *Kampyo* is employed in Japanese cuisine both as an edible string—to tie neat food packages—and as an ingredient in fillings for rolled sushi.

Availability Look for kampyo in Japanese markets in 1-ounce plastic packets.

Storage Leftover kampyo should be kept in a plastic bag in a cool, dry place. It will keep indefinitely.

Preparation Kampyo must be softened before use. Wash first, then massage with a generous amount of salt to break down the fibers and increase absorbency. Wash again, then boil until soft. Drain.

KATSUOBUSHI

Along with kelp, *katsuobushi* (dried bonito) is the main flavoring agent in the basic Japanese stock called *dashi* (see Miso Soup, page 562). It is almost as hard as wood and must be shaved into flakes before using. The best dashi is made from katsuobushi that is shaved with a special utensil just before use. For convenience, many Japanese cooks purchase dried bonito flakes (*hanagatsuo* or *kezuribushi*).

Use Dried bonito flakes are primarily used in dashi. They are also employed to flavor a soy-based dipping sauce for sashimi and as a garnish for some vegetable dishes such as chilled, boiled spinach.

Availability Whole dried bonito is not generally sold in this country. Pale pink, dried bonito flakes are available in Japanese markets and some supermarkets, packed in boxes or plastic bags.

Storage Leftover bonito flakes should be stored in an airtight container in a cool, dry place. Replace every six months because they lose flavor.

KIMCHEE

Almost every meal in Korea is accompanied by at least one kind of kimchee (also spelled *kimchi*), a fermented, pickled vegetable. The best-known kimchee, at least in this country, is made from cabbage, but in Korea it is also made from carrots, radishes, and other vegetables. Generally, the vegetables are grated or shredded, seasoned with salt, garlic, and red pepper, and left to stand for several days. Kimchee has a pungent fermented flavor and may be quite spicy and have a strong smell.

Use For some families in Korea, kimchee is a winter replacement for fresh vegetables that are hard to find. It is served the year around, however, in much the same way pickles are served in this country. Its crunchy texture and pungent character are refreshing and revivifying.

Availability Bottled cabbage kimchee is sold in many supermarkets; most Asian markets carry a larger variety of kimchee.

Storage Refrigerate kimchee in a covered container; it will keep indefinitely.

KIWIFRUIT

Underneath the fuzzy brown skin of the kiwifruit is a lime green flesh studded with tiny black seeds. Its texture is moist and melonlike, its flavor refreshingly tart and sweet. Kiwifruit was practically unknown in this country until the late 1950s, when it began to be exported from New Zealand. Today it is also cultivated in California. Originally known as Chinese gooseberry, the fruit was renamed by exporters to avoid confusion with the green gooseberry (to which it is not related) and to identify it more strongly with their country.

Use The delicate flavor of kiwifruit is best appreciated raw. Halve lengthwise and eat with a spoon, or peel, slice in rounds, and add to fruit salads. Sliced kiwifruit makes a striking garnish for fruit tarts and frozen desserts. It may also be puréed for sorbets or sauces. Like the papaya, the kiwifruit acts as a meat tenderizer. A halved kiwifruit can be rubbed over steaks or chops before grilling or broiling to tenderize them.

Availability Fresh kiwifruits are sold all year in most supermarkets. The California crop is marketed from November through April; New Zealand imports take their place May through October.

Selection Look for kiwifruits that are firm but not hard, with no soft spots. They should give slightly to pressure. Hard kiwifruits will ripen at room temperature if stored in a plastic bag.

Storage Refrigerate ripe kiwifruit in a plastic bag for up to two weeks.

KNEAD, TO

When making bread, to work dough with hands into a smooth and malleable mass by pressing and folding. Kneading also forms and arranges gluten (a protein substance found in wheat-flour doughs) into an elastic network that gives structure to the finished product. A heavy-duty mixer with dough hook or a food processor using the steel blade will perform this task for you, but many bakers find kneading the most enjoyable part of the whole bread-making process and are reluctant to turn this step over to a machine.

Pastry and biscuit doughs are also kneaded. Unlike bread doughs, these mixtures are worked with a light touch just until all ingredients are combined. For flaky pastry, the kneading is even briefer—just until ingredients hold together.

HAND-KNEADING BREAD DOUGH

With heel of hand, push dough away from you.

Bring end of dough back over with your fingers and give it a slight turn.

Repeat process until dough feels smooth, satiny, and elastic, and small bubbles appear just under surface of dough.

HAND-KNEADING PASTRY DOUGH

With fingertips, push the dough away from you and gently fold the top over; continue this motion just until the mass looks smooth and homogeneous.

Fraiser: Gather dough into a mound. Work small portions at a time, pushing away from you with heel of hand to smear dough across work surface.

To hand-knead rich, sticky bread doughs: For brioche, pick up, flip over, and throw back down; or pick up and slam down on surface without flipping. For very liquid doughs (baba, savarin, Kugelhopf), with the flat of your hand or a flat wooden spatula, slap the dough against the side of the bowl.

KNEADING BREAD DOUGH

Set dough on a lightly floured board; flour prevents dough from sticking. Using heel of your hand, push dough away from you; bring far end of dough back over with your fingers and give it a slight turn. Repeat the pushing, folding, and turning in a continuous, rhythmic, fluid motion until dough feels smooth, satiny, and springy, and small bubbles form just under surface. Depending on amount of flour you are working and how firmly you knead, this process can take anywhere from 8 to 15 minutes. Many bread recipes give a range for the amount of flour; use the lesser amount when mixing ingredients and add more flour as you knead if it seems appropriate. In the early stages of kneading, when dough is still sticky, you may want to sprinkle work surface occasionally with flour (taken from what is as yet unused from recipe). You also may want to scrape away any wet dough with a dough scraper before reflouring.

To knead with a heavy-duty mixer with dough hook, follow manufacturer's instructions.

KNEADING BREAD DOUGH IN A FOOD PROCESSOR

The food processor makes quick work of kneading any yeast dough. The plastic dough-kneading blade works best with more than 3 cups of dry ingredients; use the metal blade for less than 3 cups. Put all dry ingredients, including solid shortening, into work bowl. Mix all liquid ingredients together in a measuring cup. Start the motor and slowly add liquid in a stream only as fast as flour absorbs it (about 20 seconds). It is better to add more slowly than too quickly. Dough should gather into a ball and clean sides and bottom of work bowl. If dough is too dry, add more liquid by tablespoons through feed tube; if dough is too wet, add flour by tablespoons. Knead 60 to 90 seconds.

A food processor makes quick work of the usually time-consuming task of mixing and kneading yeast doughs. Use the metal blade for smaller batches, the plastic blade for larger ones.

Processor kneading not only saves time but also allows you to make moist, elastic doughs with the minimum amounts of flour. You can adapt any bread recipe to the processor without altering amounts of ingredients. Just remember to add liquid to dry ingredients as described above, and follow manufacturer's recommendations for maximum amounts.

KNEADING PASTRY, BISCUIT, AND RICH YEAST DOUGHS

For pastry such as pie and tart crusts, both the work surface and dough should be cool. With just the tips of your fingers, push dough away from you and fold top over gently. Continue this motion just until mass looks smooth and homogeneous. Biscuits require a minimum of handling—maybe only 12 to 15 turns.

Fraisage is a French term for working tart dough until pliable and blended but not tough by smearing it with the heel of the hand. To perform this technique, gather dough into a rough mound on a floured work surface. Work small portions at a time, pushing away from you. When pieces of dough are smooth, elastic, and peel away from surface in one piece, press all into a ball and shape crust as directed in recipe.

Rich yeast doughs such as brioche, *Kugelhopf,* baba, and savarin can be kneaded in a heavy-duty mixer which has both dough hook and flat paddle. For brioche, knead 5 minutes using a dough hook; for very wet and sticky baba and savarin, use the flat beater and knead 5 minutes. To hand-knead sticky doughs such as brioche, lay dough on a floured surface and pick up, flip over, and throw back down; or pick up and slam down on surface without flipping. Continue until pliable and smooth (about 10 minutes). Baba, savarin, and Kugelhopf, which have such a high proportion of liquid that they are almost like a batter, must be worked in a bowl. With the flat part of your hand or a flat wooden spatula, slap dough against side of bowl until smooth and elastic (about 5 minutes).

KNEADING PASTRY DOUGH IN A FOOD PROCESSOR

The metal blade makes pie doughs in seconds. Just follow these steps: Put flour and salt (and sugar, if called for) in work bowl. Add chilled fat cut into tablespoon-sized pieces. (Butter can be straight from the refrigerator. Vegetable shortening should be frozen.) Pulse 3 or 4 times. Add liquid through feed tube while pulsing very rapidly 20 to 30 times until just short of when dough looks like it will gather into a ball. Remove dough from work bowl and press together. Use as recipe directs.

Recipes and Related Information
Biscuit, 49; Flour, 234; Pie and Tart, 431; Yeast Bread, 613.

KNIFE

Good cooking begins with good cutting. A basic set of fine knives is probably the first purchase student chefs make. Although quality cutlery is costly, properly handled and well-maintained knives are a lifetime investment invaluable to their work. Fine knives can be sharpened to a keen, durable edge, feel better in the hand because they are well balanced, and are sturdily constructed to last for years. Professional chefs depend upon their personal collection of knives to such a degree that they rarely travel without them when they cook or teach away from their own kitchens.

Home cooks should select knives with the same discerning eye as the professional, and for the same reasons—ease of use, comfort, and value. Safety is another reason; a properly sharpened knife actually prevents accidents. Forcing a cut with a dull knife is one of the easiest ways to injure yourself.

SELECTING KNIVES

Top-quality knives are made of either carbon steel or an alloy—high-carbon stainless steel—that combines the softness of carbon steel and the rust-resistant attributes of stainless steel to produce a blade that can be honed to razor sharpness and won't discolor. Prior to the introduction of high-carbon stainless steel, carbon steel knives were long the favorite of chefs and serious home cooks because they take an edge so well, but were prone to stains and rust unless thoroughly dried immediately after washing.

The best blades are forged, or beaten into shape, by hand with anvil and hammer. Forging develops desirable characteristics in the metal impossible to obtain when shaped by machine. A handcrafted tool is also more aesthetically appealing than a machine-made product. Blades can be stamped or cut, processes that are automated and therefore less costly. Knives made by either of these methods are predictably less expensive than those that are hand-forged.

To be effective, the sharp edge of a blade must be thin enough to cut yet strong enough not to bend or ripple. It must, of course, be able to be resharpened when necessary. Grinding, the final step in the process of making a knife, imparts this strength to a very thin piece of metal. As with forging, grinding by hand produces a knife of superior quality. Hollow grinding, a machine process, produces an edge that can't be reground and is therefore best suited for serrated knives, which keep their factory-shaped edge indefinitely.

The part of the blade that extends into the handle is called the tang. A full tang extends completely into the handle and assumes the shape of the handle, adding balance and weight to a knife. This is an important feature for most tasks except some butchering and slicing procedures; knives for these tasks have partial tangs. Very heavy knives may have a rattail tang. Narrow and thin, and extending the length of the handle, this shape imparts strength but reduces heft. Better knives use metal rivets embedded in the handle on both sides rather than glue to hold the tang in place. On a riveted handle, the tang is a visible line of metal around the center of the edge of the handle. Choose a knife with a full or rattail tang, and with full rivets, not merely inlays.

A good handle is made of resin-impregnated wood so that it is smooth and waterproof. Polypropylene is another material commonly used for handles. Some companies use dense-grained natural hardwood handles that should not be cleaned in a dishwasher, but a good knife in any case should never be washed by machine because the heat will ruin its edge, as will harsh detergents and being knocked around in the utensil basket. Whatever the handle material, it should display a refined surface without crevices or recesses where food can hide and bacteria can grow. It should not have rough edges that can irritate your hand.

Before buying a knife, don't forget to pick it up to see how it feels in your hand. Due to slight differences in handle design, width, and material, knives of comparable quality may not be of comparable comfort. If you don't like to hold it, no matter how well made it may be, you won't use it and you'll have wasted your money.

As with cookware, don't feel compelled to purchase your knives in sets. While the price of a set may seem appealing, in reality there is better value in buying knives individually. That way you know you are getting only those you will use. Consider which you need based on your cooking style and storage space, then investigate what's available. Ask retailers for specific information regarding construction and quality for the brands they carry.

CARING FOR KNIVES

If you have invested in quality cutlery, take the time to care for it properly. Hard surfaces dull even the best of edges. Always cut on a surface that has some resilience. Wood is an excellent choice, as is polycarbonate, which gives much like wood. Avoid glass, metal, hard plastic, and ceramic tile (see CHOPPING AND CUTTING BOARD).

Fine knives should be washed immediately after use—don't soak—and dried thoroughly. Even if the handle is waterproof, good cutlery lasts longer and retains its appearance better when washed by hand.

Store knives in a slotted rack or drawer, or on a magnetic bar; never throw them bare-bladed into a drawer. Not only is this a safety hazard, but such cavalier treatment also damages the edges. If you want to store knives in a drawer, protect them with plastic sheaths, available at better cookware and cutlery stores.

SHARPENING KNIVES

A sharp edge is a necessity for good cutting and, again, for safety. For proper care, knives should be honed fre-quently, sharpened occasionally, and reground every one or two years, depending upon use.

SHARPENING STEEL

The easiest and best way to maintain a sharp edge on any knife is with a sharpening steel, if it is used correctly. If you don't already own a steel, buy one and learn to handle it; it will save you time, money, and frustration. The ideal steel is at least 12 inches long, not counting the handle, with a smooth or very finely ridged surface. The steel does not remove metal from the edge of a knife, as a whetstone does; rather, it realigns the cutting edge to keep it razor-sharp. If you use the steel every time you bring out your knife, it will hardly ever need to be sharpened on a stone or reground. Frequent, regular employment of a steel will maintain a good edge for up to two years.

To use a steel, hold steel in left hand, either out in front of you at chest level or vertically with tip resting on cutting board. Place heel of blade against steel near top, with blade making a 15- to 20-degree angle with steel. (Too wide an angle dulls the edge; too narrow an angle produces a brittle, fragile edge that dulls easily with use.) Maintaining gentle sideways pressure against steel, swing blade downward, drawing length of cutting edge across steel. Repeat on other side of knife. Alternate sides, making 10 or 12 strokes in all.

WHETSTONE

Eventually, even knives sharpened daily will need regrinding. The wedge-shaped edge will have worn down to such a degree that it must be re-created. A whetstone, made of an abrasive known as Carborundum, realigns the edge so that it will respond to the sharpening steel. If you haven't made a habit of using a steel regularly, a stone will bring a dull knife back to life. To use, draw the knife across the stone at the same 20-degree angle as with the steel, alternating sides, making 5 or 6 strokes on each side.

RODS

Other alternatives to the sharpening steel are ceramic or steel rods, which are available in three forms: a free rod that you use like a steel; a fixed rod on a stand that is already angled properly—to use, hold the knife perpendicular to the floor and draw across the rod; and a pair of crossed rods preset to a 20-degree angle.

AUTOMATIC HONER-SHARPENER

Until recently, electric knife sharpeners have done little more than grind away at the blade. A new machine, which uses a grinding wheel and two grinding pads studded with diamond particles, allows you to attain a sharper edge than previously possible with a home device. Magnets keep the knife at the proper angle in each slot; all you do is pull the knife through. The grinding wheel resets the edge, the coarse diamond pad sharpens, and the fine diamond pad hones. The machine uses household current.

A well-chosen selection of quality knives should last a lifetime. Shown clockwise from upper right: whetstone, automatic honer-sharpener, Asian knife, cleaver, utility and paring knives, poultry shears, kitchen scissors, chef's fork, shrimp deveiner, oyster knife, clam knife, tomato knife, avocado pitter, bread knife, ham slicer, boning knife, sandwich knife, fillet knife, chef's knife, sharpening steel.

A GUIDE TO BUYING KNIVES

Every kitchen should have at least four basic knives: a large chopping knife, a medium-sized slicing knife, a small paring knife, and a thin boning knife for delicate operations. A pair of good quality kitchen scissors will also prove invaluable. After that choose among the specialty knives as you see fit. Because good knives will last for years if well cared for, the most economical strategy in the long run is to invest in fewer knives of top quality rather than to accumulate a slew of cheaper slicers and choppers. Size is the blade measurement, excluding the handle.

Asian Knives Because of their large, rectangular blades, which look vaguely like those of Western meat cleavers, all Chinese knives, from lightweight vegetable knives to extraheavy, bone-chopping cleavers tend to be lumped together under the name Chinese cleaver. The name is misleading, however; only the heaviest of these knives are cleavers in the Western sense, that is, knives meant to chop through bones. At first you may find these large knives unwieldy, but with practice you will soon find them indispensable because they perform with such efficiency and are so versatile. These knives are numbered on the blade—the higher the number, the smaller and lighter the knife. Number 1, the heaviest, most

closely corresponds to a true cleaver. The lighter versions are strictly for vegetables and boneless meats.

A medium-weight number 3 or 4 Chinese knife and the similar Japanese type with a narrower blade are called vegetable knives. Used like French chef's knives, they are good for slicing, dicing, and mincing; crushing garlic and ginger; and carrying chopped foods from cutting surface to cooking pan. They have wooden handles that some cooks use as pestles for grinding peppercorns and other spices.

Avocado Pitter Certainly not a necessary item, but if you typically have difficulty removing the pit from an avocado, this tool will make the process go more smoothly.

Boning Knife The extra-narrow, flexible, tapered blade of a boning knife affords maximum maneuverability when separating chicken breast from bone, the most common boning procedure for home cooks. These knives are typically 5 or 6 inches long.

Chef's Fork This two-pronged heavyweight fork performs many functions: transfers whole birds and roasts from pan to carving board or platter, holds meat and fowl in place during carving, and protects fingers from hot food by doing the lifting and moving.

Chef's Knife   Serious cooks consider this knife with its wide, slightly curving blade to be the most versatile and important of all cutting tools. Although its large size and deep blade may feel unwieldy at first, you will soon find it indispensable. Its primary function is chopping, done with a rocking motion that follows the arc of the blade or with rapid up and down movements. Not only is it good for slicing, dicing, and mincing, but its broad side can be used to smash garlic cloves or to flatten chicken breasts. The blade is also handy for scooping whatever you have just cut, from a bit of minced parsley to a pile of sliced celery, and transferring it to sauté pan or mixing bowl. The best of these knives has a thickening of the blade, called the bolster, between the blade and the handle, and sometimes a metal collar that extends past the bolster to the handle. The bolster improves balance by adding weight and also serves as a barrier to keep your hand from slipping into the cutting edge. These knives range in length from 6 to 13 inches; a 6- or 8-inch blade is probably the most popular size for home cooks. Some manufacturers call this knife a cook's knife.

Clam Knife   This knife tends to have a blunt, rather than a sharp edge, because clams have a different muscle structure than other bivalves. You can use an oyster knife for clams if you want to buy only one specialty tool. The technique for opening both bivalves is basically the same (see Oyster Knife).

Filleting Knife   Don't consider this knife part of your basic set, but if you like to fillet fish yourself, then it will earn its price tag. It has a paper-thin, extremely flexible blade that maneuvers superbly between flesh and superdelicate bones and skin. Two popular sizes are 6 and 10 inches; you will also find them well suited to slicing fragile cakes and pastries.

Grapefruit Knife   Some grapefruit lovers can't imagine life without this serrated cutter. The curved blade neatly separates flesh from membrane and from outer peel. A sharp paring knife does this job almost as well.

Kitchen Scissors   A pair of durable kitchen scissors is a necessity. Use them to snip fresh herbs, cut parchment paper to fit cake pans, trim poached eggs into neat ovals, groom houseplants and trim blossoms, prepare wrapping paper, double as poultry shears for halving game hens, and perform hundreds of other jobs. Some have many functions; they open cans and bottles, as well as cut. Scissors that come apart are easier to clean.

Meat Cleaver   These are meant to chop through bone. While the blades of chopping knives have a constant taper from the top to the cutting edge, the cleaver blade tapers slowly from the top to within an inch or so of the edge, then tapers quickly to the cutting edge. The result, technically known as a roll grind, is an edge that is not as fine as that of the chef's knife, but is capable of hacking through bones without denting or cracking. A cleaver can be used for coarsely chopping meats and vegetables, but its bulkier blade makes precise work, and especially thin slicing, more difficult. Choose a large knife; with practice you will find its extra size and weight working for you.

Oyster Knife   Opening oysters takes strength. Using this specially designed knife with its short, strong blade and hand guard makes the job easier. There are as many versions of bivalve knives as there are varieties of bivalves to open. To use, top of knife is inserted into hinge of oyster shell and twisted to pry shell apart.

Paring/Utility Knife   Use this knife as an extension of your index finger to make small cuts; used with a twisting motion of your hand and wrist, it is perfect for peeling and slicing fruits and vegetables, carving out the eyes of a potato, chopping or cutting up small amounts of herbs, and sculpting garnishes. Its shape resembles that of a chef's knife, but has less of an arc; a variation has an upwardly curved blade. Midsize paring knives are also called utility knives or sandwich knives. A 3- to 4-inch blade is typical for paring knives; utility knives have blades that are 6 to 8 inches long.

Poultry Shears   Made of heavy stainless steel or chrome-plated steel, poultry shears should have a spring-lever action for extra cutting power to work through bone and cartilage. Use them to disjoint all kinds of fowl or to divide little Rock Cornish game hens. A locking hinge at the handle secures blades for safe storage. Look for shears that come apart; they are easier to clean.

Serrated Knife   A serrated edge makes a clean cut through a firm crust or skin without crushing the delicate interior crumb or flesh. Serrated slicers do an excellent job cutting bread, and halving génoise, sponge, or butter cake layers for multitiered pastries (for an even cut, use a knife longer than the diameter of the cake; see photograph, page 85). Bread knives are 8 inches. Shorter serrated blades, around 5½ inches long, breeze through tomatoes—whose skin is notoriously resistant to all but the sharpest blades—with ease. They are also better suited than the longer bread knife for slicing a thin baguette loaf and for slicing fruits without forcing out the juice in the process. Use a back-and-forth sawing motion when cutting with a serrated knife.

Shrimp Deveiner   The arc of the blade, which duplicates the curved back of the shrimp, permits you to slice the shell and remove the black vein in one operation.

Slicing/Carving Knives   Designed to cut through cooked meats of all kinds, these knives have a pointed or round tip and long blades that are either flexible or rigid, depending on the piece to be cut. Rigid, more sturdy knives work better for slicing ham and roasts; poultry requires a thinner blade that can conform somewhat to its bone structure.

CUTTING TECHNIQUES

In the following descriptions of techniques, the right hand refers to the hand holding the knife, and the left hand to the one holding the food to be cut (with an apology to left-handed cooks). A French chef's knife and an Asian vegetable knife (Chinese or Japanese) are interchangeable in this discussion.

Work slowly at first until you get the hang of each technique; speed will come naturally. It is important to learn safe and efficient cutting habits. Give yourself plenty of room to work, stand in a comfortable position, relax, and focus entirely on the task at hand; you will find yourself cutting quickly and with minimum effort. Don't try to cut too much at one time. Work with a manageable amount so that you are aware of and can control what you are doing. The following techniques are illustrated in the photographs on the opposite page.

HAND POSITION

Holding food for safe and precise cutting is mostly a matter of keeping your fingers out of the way of the blade. For most cutting tasks, this means holding food against board with the fingertips of the left hand curled back away from blade. The blade then rides against the curved knuckles to guide the cut. As long as you do not lift the blade above the level of the knuckles and do not straighten out the fingers, you can avoid cutting yourself in this position.

The position of your hand depends upon the task. For precise cutting, grip handle close to blade, with thumb and forefinger grasping blade itself. Let the knife work with you by gripping it near its balance point. To find that point, lay the knife flat across the index finger. There are two basic blade positions: resting tip of knife on board and slicing with a rocking motion, or lifting entire blade, holding edge parallel to board, and slicing with a downward and forward motion. The former method allows more control, the latter more speed. For other grips, see Chopping, Paring, and Cleaver Chopping (following).

SLICING

Hold ingredient with fingers curled back and knuckles away from blade at a distance that equals one slice. Slice with a French chef's knife or Asian vegetable knife, using knuckles to guide blade, then move fingers back along food (or push food forward with thumb) to get into position for next slice.

SHREDDING AND JULIENNE CUTTING

To cut food into fine shreds, larger pieces, or julienne (matchsticks), first cut ingredient into slices of the desired length and thickness. Carrots and other slender vegetables may have to be sliced on a slant to achieve the right length. Stack slices, overlapping them slightly like shingles, and slice down through stack lengthwise, forming squared-off sticks. Shreds are very fine julienne pieces, less than ⅛ inch thick; matchsticks are twice as thick.

To shred green onions for garnish or stir-fries, first slice them into desired length. Slit white and pale green sections lengthwise, but do not cut all the way through. Open halves like a book and cut lengthwise into thin shreds. To shred hollow green tops, bundle them together under fingertips of left hand and carefully slice bundle into fine shreds.

DICING AND MINCING

These terms describe the same process, but differ in the size of the cut: Diced means cubes of ¼ to ½ inch, minced less than ⅛ inch, and finely diced somewhere in between. First cut (using a French chef's knife or an Asian vegetable knife) ingredient into shreds or matchsticks of the desired thickness, as described at left. Then gather sticks into a bundle and cut across into uniform cubes. Always try to keep food you are cutting in a shape that works with you. Cut round objects into sections, so that they lie flat.

Garlic, onion, and shallot are diced or minced by a slightly different method. First peel, leaving root end intact, then split in half lengthwise. Place cut side down on board and, positioning knife blade horizontally, make one or more cuts parallel to cutting board, almost to root end. Make a series of vertical, lengthwise cuts almost to root end, of the desired thickness. Slice across cuts toward root end to produce cubes. Discard root end.

SMASHING AND BRUISING

When an aromatic ingredient such as garlic, ginger, or green onion is used in large pieces to flavor a food, smashing or bruising it first helps release its flavor into the food. Cut to desired size, place pieces on board, and smack them smartly with broad side of blade. Another method is to place knife flat on top of food, then pound it with your fist. Watch out for cutting edge if using this technique.

To peel garlic, lay clove on a board. Hold flat side of a chef's knife just above it. Lightly pound knife, hitting garlic and loosening its skin. Pull skin off, cutting if necessary.

CHOPPING

Although uniform cubes (dice or mince) are sometimes unnecessary, cooking or processing will be faster if hard ingredients are cut into smaller pieces. You may also need to finely chop fresh parsley or other herbs. If the foods are very large, such as carrots or onions, first roughly cut up. For herbs, remove leaves from stems. Then place these pieces or leaves on cutting board. Grip knife a little farther out on handle than for slicing. Use left hand to press tip of knife down against board and chop with a rocking motion, pivoting knife back and forth across food. Chop to desired size with a rolling, downward and forward motion (not an up-and-down chop), scraping pile together.

If you hear your knife hitting cutting board along with vegetable, half your effort isn't reaching its target. Keep pile of food high and in a neat rectangle, if possible; remember not to chop too much at one time.

CUTTING TECHNIQUES

Hand position   For safety and to keep the food anchored while cutting, hold food against cutting board with fingertips curled back away from blade.

Slicing   Hold food with knuckles away from blade at a distance that equals one slice. Slice, then move fingers back the width of another slice or push food forward that distance.

Shredding and julienne cutting   Cut ingredient into slices of desired length and thickness. Stack slices, overlapping slightly, and slice lengthwise. The result will be squared-off sticks.

Dicing and mincing   Cut food into shreds or matchsticks (see Shredding and Julienne Cutting). Gather pieces into a bundle and slice across into uniform cubes.

Dicing/mincing garlic, onion, shallot   Place peeled, halved ingredient cut side down on cutting board. Position knife horizontally and make cuts parallel to board, almost to root end. Cut vertical, lengthwise cuts of desired thickness. Slice across cuts to root end.

Smashing and bruising   Lay ingredient on cutting board and smack with broad side of knife blade or lay blade on food and pound it with fist. Use the latter technique to loosen garlic peel.

Chopping   Arrange pieces of food on board in a high, neat pile. Grip knife handle with one hand and use other to press tip of knife down against board; chop with a rocking motion across food.

Paring   Lay blade on food, angled diagonally away from you. Cut in just the thickness of peel and draw knife toward you as you rotate food in opposite direction.

Cleaver chopping   Hold cleaver with right hand well back on handle, thumb on top or on side. Swing down from wrist. Let gravity move the cleaver; lift knife and let fall.

PARING

A paring knife is used like an extension of your index finger to make small precise cuts. The action centers more on the tip and end of the knife than with other knives. Hold a paring knife so that it moves with ease—index finger resting on top of blade and thumb gripping handle and serving as a balance. To peel away skin of a fruit or vegetable, grip paring knife as follows: grasp handle so that thumb rests against one side of blade and index finger lies along other side; handle should nestle in palm between fleshy pad and base of first finger. To peel, lay blade on fruit or vegetable, angled diagonally away from you. Make a cut just the thickness of the peel and draw the knife toward you as you rotate ingredient in the opposite direction. Skin should pull away in long strips.

CLEAVER CHOPPING

With a cleaver or heavier Asian vegetable knife, it is easy to chop meats to any texture, from rough cubes to a fine paste. Start by dicing meat, then change to a chopping grip (right hand well back on handle, thumb on top or on side). Swing from wrist for maximum chopping efficiency. With a good, heavy cleaver, little downward force is required; knife is simply lifted and allowed to fall. The left hand is not involved in this type of chopping. Stop every once in a while to scrape pile of pieces back together.

To chop through bones, as in cutting a chicken into braising pieces, hold knife as above. It may be unnecessary to hold food with other hand. For safety's sake, hold food as far away from where you will cut as possible. When you get to the last couple of inches, place food on board, get your left hand out of the way, take aim, and chop.

KOHLRABI

A member of the cabbage family, kohlrabi has a flavor reminiscent of both cabbage and turnip. It is moist and crunchy when raw; when cooked, its texture is like that of broccoli. Unlike the turnip, which it resembles, it is not a root, but a swollen, bulbous stem that grows above ground. The bulb may be pale green or purple outside; both varieties are white inside. Leaf stalks with leaves like those of turnips protrude from all sides (these stalks are generally trimmed away in the supermarket).

Use   Serve kohlrabi raw, or blanched and chilled, with a dip or marinated in vinaigrette. Steam or boil and dress with butter; add to soups or stews; purée with butter and cream; or use in any recipe in place of turnip. In Italy, raw or steamed kohlrabi is sometimes served with *bagna cauda* (a hot dip of butter, oil, garlic, and anchovies).

Availability   Fresh kohlrabi is sold in many supermarkets from May through November, with peak supply in June and July.

Selection   Choose small bulbs, about the size of a large egg; larger ones may be woody. If leaves are still attached, they should look fresh and perky. Avoid bulbs with cracks or blemishes.

Storage   Keep kohlrabi in a plastic bag in the refrigerator crisper for up to one week.

Preparation   Very young bulbs do not need to be peeled, but larger bulbs should be. If leaves are still attached, cut them off and boil or steam separately like spinach.

Cooking   See BLANCH, BOIL, PUREE, STEAM.

KONBU

Sun-dried kelp, called *konbu* (also spelled *kombu*) by both Japanese and Americans, appears in the market as a stiff, gray green sheet with a powdery finish. It must be rehydrated by soaking for use in the kitchen.

Use   Konbu imparts a delicate, fresh ocean taste to foods. Its primary function is as a flavoring for dashi, the basic Japanese stock (see page 563). Softened konbu is also wrapped around raw fish for several hours as a form of marinade; it is removed before serving. Pickled konbu is sometimes offered as a relish. Shredded konbu may be deep-fried or sautéed and used as a vegetable. Save steeped konbu sheets after making dashi, store in a plastic bag in the refrigerator, and use sheets as edible wrappers for other foods.

Availability   Dried konbu sheets are sold in Japanese markets and some health-food stores, packaged in plastic. One ounce is sufficient for four servings of dashi.

Storage   Unopened konbu will keep indefinitely in a cool, dry place. After opening, store in an airtight container in a cool place; it will keep for several months.

Preparation   Do not wash konbu. Wipe clean with a damp towel. Some Japanese cooks score surface lightly to release glutamic acid; others look down on this procedure. Steep sheets according to dashi recipe.

> ### Recipes and Related Information
> *Miso Soup, 562; Sushi Rice, 233.*

KUMQUAT

Resembling a miniature egg-shaped orange, the kumquat is rarely more than an inch long. Part of the citrus family, it is native to China but is now cultivated in Florida and California. Unlike other citrus, the skin of the kumquat is sweeter than its flesh.

Use Massage kumquat between fingers to mingle sweet skin and tart flesh, then eat the whole fruit raw. It can also be sliced and added to fruit salads. Kumquats make excellent preserves, marmalades, and relishes. Cooked or preserved kumquats can be used in a sauce for roast duck, pork, and turkey. Mince preserved kumquats and add to desserts or roll in sugar and serve as a sweetmeat.

Availability Fresh kumquats are sold in many super-markets. They are stocked November through June, with peak availability from November through February. Whole kumquats preserved in syrup and bottled are carried by supermarkets and specialty stores. Preserved and sugared kumquats are found in Chinese markets during the Chinese New Year.

Selection Choose plump, firm kumquats; avoid those that look shriveled or dull.

Storage Fresh kumquats will keep in the refrigerator for up to one month. Kumquats preserved in syrup may be stored indefinitely at room temperature in the original jar; preserved and sugared kumquats will keep up to six months in a covered jar in a cool place.

LAMB

Humans learned to domesticate sheep tens of thousands of years ago. Indeed, for ancient civilizations, sheep were animals of incomparable value. Their wool provided clothing, their meat and milk sustenance. Furthermore, they were rugged animals capable of surviving extreme conditions.

The early importance of sheep and their offspring is evident in the role they played, and still play, in many religions. Lamb was the traditional sacrificial offering in early religious rites and is still part of many religious observances. Celebratory tables at the Christian Easter, the Jewish Passover, and the Muslim New Year are all traditionally graced with symbolic roast lamb.

The sheep that sustained earlier cultures was much different from modern lamb. Sheep were raised as much for their wool as for their meat and were often herded long distances in search of pasturage. By the time they were slaughtered, the meat was generally tough and had a strong flavor. Cooks developed ways to combat these two qualities. They might marinate it in acidic ingredients to tenderize it and mask its flavor; or they might stew it for several hours, often with fruits; or they might grind it and season it lightly.

Today's lamb, the result of sophisticated crossbreeding, is butchered at an early age and is mild and tender. Most lamb is slaughtered at 6 to 9 months; lamb older than 12 months cannot legally be sold as genuine lamb. If the animal were 12 to 24 months old at slaughter, the meat may be identified as yearling lamb and will be stronger in flavor. Some diners appreciate the rich, full flavor

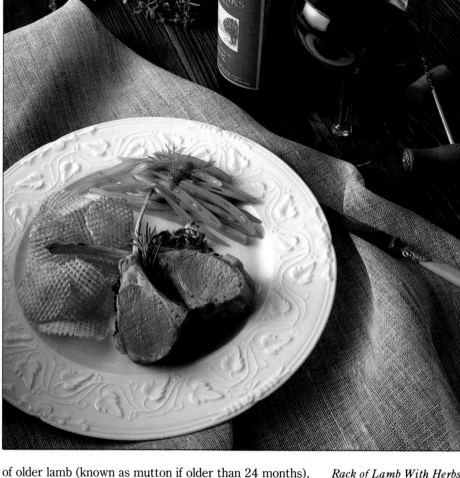

of older lamb (known as mutton if older than 24 months), but most Americans prefer the more delicate flavor of young lamb. Some specialty markets offer baby lamb, also identified as milk-fed lamb, butchered at 3 to 5 months, or hothouse lamb, butchered at 6 to 10 weeks. It is extremely tender, pale in color, and delicate in flavor.

The term *spring lamb* has no legal definition and no longer has any practical meaning. In the past, sheep gave birth in September or October and the six-month-old spring lamb was a treat looked forward to by many diners for their Easter and springtime tables. Today's modern breeding and flock management enable sheep to give birth throughout the year.

Use Lamb is most appreciated today in the regions where it was first consumed: the Middle East, North Africa, and Greece. In these areas, it is safe to say that lamb is the preferred meat. Lamb is also widely eaten in India, France, Italy, Spain, England, China, and New Zealand, the world's chief sheep-raising country. It is much less popular in the United States, Latin America, Central and Eastern Europe, and is practically unknown in Japan and Southeast Asia.

Rack of Lamb With Herbs, an international favorite, makes a perfect combination with Zinfandel, strictly an American wine. The recipe is on page 338.

CUTS OF LAMB

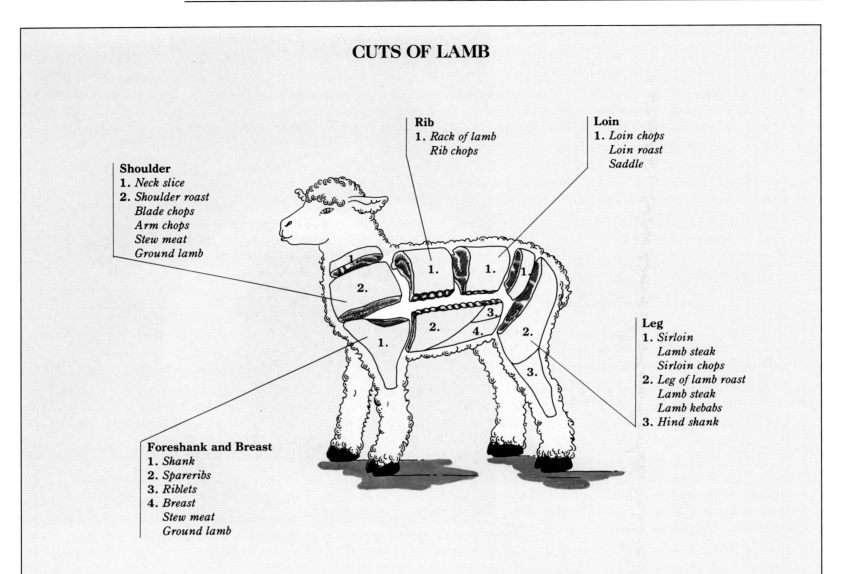

Shoulder
1. *Neck slice*
2. *Shoulder roast*
   Blade chops
   Arm chops
   Stew meat
   Ground lamb

Rib
1. *Rack of lamb*
   Rib chops

Loin
1. *Loin chops*
   Loin roast
   Saddle

Leg
1. *Sirloin*
   Lamb steak
   Sirloin chops
2. *Leg of lamb roast*
   Lamb steak
   Lamb kebabs
3. *Hind shank*

Foreshank and Breast
1. *Shank*
2. *Spareribs*
3. *Riblets*
4. *Breast*
   Stew meat
   Ground lamb

Lamb has fewer retail cuts than beef, but many of the same rules apply: The parts that do the least work are the tenderest. However, a lamb is a smaller, younger animal than a steer, and even the "tough parts" are usually more tender than the corresponding section of beef.

Shoulder   This is the hardest-working muscle of the lamb, with the most fat, and plentiful bone. It is best suited for braising or stewing. The neck section of lamb is a stewing cut taken from the front of the shoulder. Boneless shoulder is sometimes sold as a roasting cut (although it is probably better braised). Chops cut from the shoulder (including both the blade chop with a long bone down the center, and the arm chop, with a round bone near the end) are fattier than the higher-priced rib and loin chops, but can be treated much the same way (baked, broiled, or panfried).

Foreshank and Breast   Boneless rolled breast and bone-in breast are sometimes roasted (often

with a stuffing inserted in a "pocket" cut in the center) but are more often braised, since they're rather fatty and not especially tender. Shank is always cooked in liquid, at length, until the meat starts falling off the bone. Economical lamb spareribs and riblets can be barbecued or braised, and are sometimes even roasted, but they are not entirely a bargain since the buyer is paying for a great deal of bone and a very little meat. Supermarket lamb stew meat, kebabs, and ground lamb are usually cut from the shoulder; the kebabs are from leaner shoulder meat than the stew or the ground lamb. Kebabs cut from the leg are far superior in leanness and tenderness.

Loin   The whole loin roast (and the even less common whole saddle of lamb) are found at the butcher's only occasionally. Chops cut from the loin are found more frequently. These extremely tender chops can be broiled or panfried, and luxuriously sauced.

Rib   The fine rib roast is sold as rack of lamb or, when bent into a circle, as crown roast. Chops from

the rib are tender and juicy, whether left whole or, as in the case of the French chop, trimmed of the fatty meat from the end of the rib. Rib chops can be broiled or panfried, and double rib chops can be rapidly baked with a pocket cut for stuffing if desired. Like the loin, the rib portions of lamb are compatible with luxurious sauces.

Leg   The back leg of the lamb is significantly more tender than the back leg of a steer. It may be cut into a whole leg (with the sirloin attached), a short cut leg (with sirloin trimmed off), a shank portion of the leg, and a center leg roast. These cuts are used primarily for roasting and grilling, but can be butterflied for barbecuing or cut off the bone for top-quality kebabs. Lamb steaks (to broil, panfry, or barbecue) are usually cut from either the center of the leg, or from the more tender sirloin just above the leg. Occasionally, lamb sirloin roast and sirloin chops can be found; these are both lean and tender. The hind shank, like the foreshank, is braised.

Spit-roasted suckling lamb is an Easter specialty in Greece. At other times, Greek cooks roast whole legs with oregano and white wine, or cook skewered lamb with herbs and serve it with yogurt. In the Middle East, ground lamb is massaged with cracked wheat to make kibbe, served raw or cooked. Ground lamb is used to stuff eggplants or grape leaves. In Iran lamb is marinated, grilled on skewers, and served with aromatic rice.

North African cooks braise lamb shoulder with vegetables for Couscous (see page 278) or stew it in a special covered clay pot called a *tajine*, often with fruits such as quince or prunes. In India lamb is curried, braised with spinach, or rubbed with spices and roasted in a *tandoor* (clay oven).

Milk-fed Spanish lamb is cooked in hot wood-burning ovens and served with potatoes. The French rub leg of lamb with thyme and lavender, stud it with garlic, and roast it, serving it with white beans or the green beans called *flageolets*. Italian cooks roast lamb with rosemary, or coat thin young chops with egg, bread crumbs, and Parmesan, and deep-fry them.

Irish lamb stew with potatoes and carrots; shepherd's pie from England, ground lamb topped with mashed potatoes; Finnish sauna-cured leg of lamb; and Mongolian hot pot are other ways that lamb is cooked around the world.

Availability   See Cuts of Lamb (opposite page).

Selection   All lamb sold retail is inspected by state or federal authorities for wholesomeness. About two thirds of lamb sold to consumers is also graded for quality. Lamb may be graded prime, choice, or good, depending primarily on the degree of marbling (intramuscular fat). Generous marbling contributes flavor and succulence. Most lamb sold at retail is graded choice.

In general, the paler the meat, the younger the lamb. Look for lamb with dry white fat, firm meat, and moist bones. Avoid buying lamb with yellowing fat or dark, mushy meat.

Storage   The larger the cut, the longer it may be refrigerated or frozen. Whole roasts, for example, may be stored longer than ground lamb. Large cuts may be refrigerated, well wrapped, for up to four days or frozen for up to nine months. Use ground meat within two days or freeze for up to four months. Defrost frozen meat slowly in refrigerator to promote reabsorption of melting ice crystals.

Preparation   Some cuts of lamb, such as the rack and the leg, are sold with part of the fat covering intact. Lamb fat has a strong flavor and should be trimmed away. However, be careful not to remove the fell, the papery outer membrane that holds the meat in shape. Cubed lamb for stew should be carefully trimmed of excess fat.

Cooking   See BRAISE, BROIL, GRILL, PANFRY, ROAST, STEW.

▨ LEG OF LAMB WITH GARLIC, POTATOES, AND ONIONS

Garlic slivers inserted into the lamb flavor the meat, and additional chopped garlic and roasting juices from the lamb give zest to the potatoes. Use a heavy roasting pan to prevent the vegetables from burning. Accompany this dish with green beans cooked until tender-crisp.

1	leg of lamb (6 lb)
4	medium cloves garlic, peeled
6	tablespoons butter, softened
½	teaspoon dried thyme
	Salt and freshly ground pepper, to taste
2½	pounds large, all-purpose white potatoes
2	tablespoons vegetable oil
2	large onions, thinly sliced

1. Preheat oven to 450° F. Trim skin from lamb and remove as much excess fat as possible.

2. Cut 2 garlic cloves lengthwise into thin slices, then in thin slivers. Make slits in lamb about 1 inch deep with a small, sharp knife, spacing them fairly evenly. Insert garlic slivers in slits.

3. Chop remaining cloves with any remaining garlic slivers. Mix with butter, thyme, and salt and pepper to taste. Let stand at room temperature.

4. Peel potatoes, halve them lengthwise, and cut each half crosswise into slices about ¼ inch thick.

5. Set lamb on a rack in a large, heavy roasting pan. Spoon oil over lamb and sprinkle with salt and pepper. Roast 15 minutes. Reduce oven to 350° F and roast, basting lamb occasionally with juices, for 20 minutes.

6. Remove lamb and rack from pan. Put potato and onion slices in lamb juices in pan and mix well. Sprinkle with salt and pepper. Scatter garlic and butter mixture over potatoes. Replace lamb on rack in pan over vegetables.

7. Continue roasting, stirring vegetables occasionally, until lamb is done to taste (about 1 hour). To check, insert a meat thermometer into thickest part of lamb; lamb is rare at 130° to 140° F, medium at 145° F, and well-done at 160° F.

8. Transfer lamb to a carving board, cover loosely with aluminum foil, and let stand 10 minutes. Taste a relatively thick potato slice; if it is not tender, continue baking vegetables for a few minutes. Taste vegetables and add more salt and pepper, if needed.

9. Carve lamb; drain carving juices into a small saucepan and heat gently.

10. To serve, arrange lamb slices on a platter. Using a slotted spoon, transfer potato slices to platter or to separate serving dish. Pour juices remaining in roasting pan (mainly melted butter) into a small serving dish and heated carving juices into another.

Serves 10.

Meats that lack natural moisture benefit from larding, inserting strips of fat into the muscle with a special larding needle.

▦ RACK OF LAMB WITH HERBS

Rosemary, oregano, thyme, and bay leaf, either alone or in combination, are delicious with lamb. Fresh herbs have more flavor, but dried herbs can also be used. The garlic- and herb-flavored salt rub in this recipe could easily be adapted to other cuts of lamb, such as a roast leg of lamb or a boned and rolled shoulder.

> 1 **rack of lamb, 2 to 2½ pounds (see Note)**
> 2 **or 3 cloves garlic, peeled, and thinly sliced**
> 2 **tablespoons fresh herbs (see list above)** *or*
>   **1 teaspoon dried**
> 1 **teaspoon kosher salt**
> ¼ **teaspoon freshly ground pepper**

1. Preheat oven to 450° F. Remove excess fat from lamb. With tip of a knife, make several shallow incisions in meat and remaining fat, and push a slice of garlic into each cut (the garlic will infuse the meat with its flavor as the lamb roasts). If you are using fresh herbs, chop them finely together with any remaining garlic. If you are using dried herbs, crumble them finely.

2. Combine herbs, salt, and pepper; rub on lamb. Place lamb, fat side up, on a rack in a roasting pan.

3. Place lamb in oven, reduce heat to 400° F, and roast (without basting) to desired degree of doneness (about 25 minutes for medium rare; internal temperature should be about 140° F). Allow lamb to rest, loosely covered with aluminum foil, at least 10 minutes before serving. To serve, carve into chops.

Serves 2 to 4 (2 or 3 chops each).

Note   For easier carving, ask the butcher to cut through backbone between ribs. After roasting, rack can then be neatly carved into chops with single ribs.

> ### *Recipes and Related Information*
> *Butterflied Leg of Lamb With Cucumber-Mint Sauce, 294; Cassoulet, 556; Couscous, 278; Dry Spice Rub for Lamb, 350; Moussaka, 209; Russian Marinated Lamb on Skewers, 453; Spring Lamb Stew With Fresh Peas, 420.*

LARD, TO

To add fat to lean meats by running strips of pork fat, known as lardoons, through the muscles with a larding needle (see NEEDLE AND FASTENER, Larding Needles), or by piercing the flesh with a thin knife and forcing the strips of fat through. This process adds flavor and moistness by increasing fat content. As the meat cooks, the fat melts, keeping the interior from drying out. Barding is another method of basting with fat; when you bard, the fat is wrapped around the outside of a piece of meat, rather than through its mass (see BARD). Seasonings, such as fresh herbs and garlic, are also used for internal flavoring, but not as a baste as they have no fat content. To add flavor, make shallow slits evenly around the roast and fill each slit with a sliver of garlic or piece of herb.

LEAVEN, TO

To lighten the texture and increase the volume of a batter or dough by the action of a natural agent such as air beaten into egg whites or the fermentation of yeast, or by using a chemical substance such as baking powder or baking soda, or by a combination. Each leavening agent contributes gases that expand and cause the dough or batter to rise.

> ### *Recipes and Related Information*
> *Baking Powder, 23; Baking Soda, 23; Yeast, 613.*

LEEK

A mild member of the onion family much appreciated in Europe, the leek resembles a giant scallion, with overlapping green leaves and a blanched white base.

Use   Very young, pencil-thin leeks are tender enough to be sliced and eaten raw in salads. Older leeks should be poached or steamed and served hot or cold in the same way as asparagus: with vinaigrette, mayonnaise, or garnish of hard-cooked egg. Leeks add a mild onion flavor to soups, stuffings, and stews. Green leek tops add onion flavor to stocks. Whole leeks can be grilled, braised in stock, or baked and served as a side dish.

Availability   Fresh leeks are sold all year, but supplies peak in fall and spring. Although some specialty markets now carry baby leeks as thin as young asparagus, most markets offer leeks an inch or more in diameter.

Selection   Large leeks can be woody inside. Select small to medium leeks, without ragged or wilted leaves.

Storage   Refrigerate in a plastic bag and use within three to five days.

Preparation   To keep the base of the leeks white, dirt is piled up around the stalk. Although leeks are cleaned for market, dirt is often still trapped between the leaves. Wash well and remove any tough, ragged outer leaves. Trim roots from base. If cooking leeks whole, slit them lengthwise at least halfway down the stalk and run cold water between the leaves to wash away any dirt. If slicing leeks, slit them lengthwise through the base and wash well before slicing.

Cooking   See BOIL, BRAISE, GRATIN, STEAM, STIR-FRY.

> ### *Recipes and Related Information*
> *Leeks Braised With Tasso, 59; Vichyssoise, 566.*

LEGUME

Technically, legumes are plants that carry their seeds in a pod. Beans of every shape and color, peas, and peanuts are all legumes. An exceptionally nutritious component in the human diet, they have, on average twice the protein of grains and a good dose of iron and B vitamins. With some legumes, such as peanuts and mature English peas, we eat only the seeds and discard the pods. Other legumes, such as sugar snap peas or Kentucky Wonder beans, are edible in their entirety. For more information on individual legumes, see BEAN, PEA, PEANUT.

LEMON

Although lemons are too tart to eat on their own, they are probably used more than any other fruit. Their lively tartness sharpens other flavors and gives a lift to all manner of foods.

Use Lemon is the principal flavor in a variety of desserts, from lemon ice cream and sherbet to lemon curd, lemon mousse, lemon meringue pie, and lemon cake. In addition, lemon juice and grated rind are used in many other desserts—especially fruit desserts—as a subsidiary flavor.

In the savory realm, lemon adds zest to sautéed or roasted chicken and is almost always served with fish and shellfish to heighten their flavor. A squirt of lemon juice in melted butter makes a lively dressing for cooked asparagus, broccoli, spinach, potherbs, green beans, and carrots. Italians serve the best young vegetables, such as celery hearts and baby artichokes, with nothing but lemon, salt, and olive oil. Moroccan cooks preserve lemons in salt, then use them to flavor stews and salads. Avocado is unthinkable without lemon alongside. Many melons and tropical fruits are also often served with a wedge of lemon. Lemon juice takes the place of vinegar in salad dressings and marinades. The acid juice of a lemon or lime is sometimes used to "cook" fish and shellfish. Seviche is an example.

Lemon juice enlivens such beverages as lemonade, iced tea, tomato juice, fruit punches, and cocktails. It is also valuable as an antioxidant: Rubbing lemon juice on cut bananas, apples, or pears inhibits browning; soaking some of these foods in acidulated water, an acidic mixture of lemon juice or vinegar and water, has the same effect.

Availability Fresh lemons are sold all year. Bottled lemon juice is also widely available in supermarkets.

Selection Choose firm lemons that feel heavy for their size. Generally, rough-textured ones have thicker skin and less juice than fine-skinned varieties.

Storage Refrigerated, lemons should keep for up to one month.

Preparation The desirable lemon oils are stored in the yellow peel. Be sure to grate only the yellow peel; the white pith is unpleasantly bitter. For directions on removing the rind, see GADGETS. To extract more juice from a lemon, press down on it as you roll it on a countertop or table. Lemons also yield more juice when slightly warm or at room temperature. If chilled, warm in a microwave on 50 percent power 1 minute. A citrus reamer is an effective way to juice and seed a lemon (see CITRUS REAMER).

▪ LEMON CHICKEN BREASTS

This is a speedy interpretation of a popular Chinese chicken dish.

> 3 whole chicken breasts (2½ to 3 lb), halved, boned, and skinned
> 2 lemons
> 1 tablespoon *each* butter or margarine and vegetable oil
> 1 clove garlic, minced
> ⅓ cup Rich Chicken Stock (see page 560)
> 2 teaspoons *each* cornstarch and sugar
> 1 tablespoon *each* soy sauce and water
> Salt, to taste

1. Cut chicken crosswise into ½-inch-wide strips. Grate rind from 1 lemon and squeeze juice; reserve both. Halve other lemon; squeeze juice from one half and add to reserved juice. Slice remaining half lemon thinly and reserve for garnish.

2. In a large, heavy-bottomed frying pan or wok, brown chicken breast strips (about half at a time) on both sides in butter and oil over medium-high heat, removing them as they brown. When all chicken is browned, return to pan and mix in garlic.

3. Add stock and reserved lemon juice. Bring to a boil, cover, reduce heat, and simmer until chicken is just firm and opaque (5 to 6 minutes; do not overcook). In a small bowl blend cornstarch, sugar, soy sauce, and the water.

4. Add lemon rind and soy sauce mixture, bring to a boil over medium-high heat, and stir until thickened and smooth. Add salt if needed. Garnish with lemon slices.

Serves 4 to 6.

Recipes and Related Information
Asparagus With Lemon, Tomato, and Onions, 14; Chilled Lemon Soufflé, 207; Fresh Lemon Bars, 143; Hot Lemon Soufflé, 206; Lemon Chiffon Cake, 85; Lemon Chiffon Pie, 440; Lemon Crème Fraîche, 107; Lemon Curd, 252; Lemon Custard Glaze, 117; Lemon Fondant, 251; Lemon Frozen Yogurt, 313; Lemon Meringue Pie, 439; Lemon Mustard, 323; Lemon Pasta, 412; Lemon Risotto, 275; Lemon Roof-Tile Cookies, 142; Lemon Roulade Charlotte, 171; Lemon Scones, 50; Lemon Sherbet, 314; Lemon Tart, 443; Seviche, 234; Tangy Lemon Loaf, 492; Zest, 631.

LEMON BALM

This perennial herb is appreciated for its lemon-scented, toothed leaves. The leaves add a minty lemon flavor to fruit salads, compotes, and stuffings. The leaves can be infused in hot water to make lemon tisane, a refreshing beverage that some say has medicinal properties. They are also used in cosmetics and fragrances. Fresh lemon balm is sporadically available in specialty markets; look for fragrant, sprightly leaves.

LEMONGRASS

Also known as citronella, lemongrass is a stiff, tropical grass that resembles a large fibrous green onion. It has yellowish white stems, gray-green blades and a delightful lemony aroma. An essential herb in Southeast Asian cooking, it adds a lemony flavor to many Vietnamese, Burmese, Thai, and Malaysian dishes.

Use Lemongrass imparts a characteristic sourness to many Southeast Asian dishes, especially to soups and fish preparations. The gray-green blades are cut away and the stalks sliced crosswise very thinly. Generally, the large slices of lemongrass used in soup or sautés are considered flavoring agents and are not eaten. In Thailand, lemongrass is used in curry pastes and in hot and spicy shrimp soup; in Vietnam, it is part of meat stir-fries.

Availability Now widely grown by Asian farmers in warmer areas of the United States, fresh lemongrass is sold in most Asian markets throughout the year. It is also available as dried blades, which must be soaked, and as a ground powder. Some health-food stores and herb shops carry ground lemongrass for use in teas.

Selection Choose firm, unblemished stalks.

Storage Keep in the refrigerator crisper for up to two months. Store dried and powdered lemongrass in a cool, dark, dry place; use within two months.

Preparation Trim away the gray-green blades; wash stalks and slice thinly crosswise. Dried blades must be soaked for two hours in warm water before using. Most recipes call for the slices to be minced or pounded to a paste with other ingredients. Ground lemongrass can be added directly to a dish; substitute 1 teaspoon powder for each fresh stalk.

LEMON VERBENA

A woody deciduous shrub, lemon verbena has sharply lemon-scented leaves.

Use The leaves of the lemon verbena shrub are employed to flavor beverages, cakes, puddings, and fruit compotes. Both fresh and dried leaves are infused in hot water to make tisane, a relaxing drink that some claim has medicinal value.

Availability Fresh lemon verbena may occasionally be found in specialty markets. Dried lemon verbena is sold in herb stores and some health-food stores.

Selection Look for fresh and fragrant leaves.

Storage Keep fresh lemon verbena in a plastic bag in the refrigerator crisper and use within one or two days. Store dried lemon verbena in a cool, dark, dry place and use within a few months.

LETTUCE

Cultivated at least since 800 B.C., lettuce is today one of the most widely eaten vegetables in the Western world. In America and Western Europe, it is undoubtedly the major salad vegetable.

There are dozens of lettuce varieties but only four general types. Cos or romaine lettuce forms an elongated head with dark green, thickly ribbed outer leaves and a pale green inner heart. It is a sturdy lettuce that can take heavy or full-flavored dressings. Cabbagehead lettuce may be either crisphead, such as iceberg, or butterhead, such as Bibb, Boston, and limestone. Crisphead lettuces have tightly packed, solid heads with crisp, light green leaves; butterhead lettuces have soft leaves and loose, spreading heads. Looseleaf lettuce (also known as cutting lettuce or salad bowl lettuce) grows loosely from a central stem and does not form a heart. Oakleaf lettuce is a good example. The fourth type is stem lettuce, also known as celtuce or asparagus lettuce. Like romaine, it has a long edible stem and leaves; it is not commonly available commercially.

Use Lettuces appear primarily in the salad bowl. Their refreshing flavor and crisp texture are best appreciated raw; because they are mostly water, cooking greatly alters their texture. French cooks, however, make lettuce soup and often cook shredded lettuce with steamed peas.

Frilly or colorful lettuces are often used to garnish serving platters. The outer leaves of cabbagehead lettuce are used as wrappers for some Chinese dishes, such as minced squab. Lettuce adds a crisp, crunchy texture to sandwiches and tacos.

Lettuce is the main or supporting ingredient in a virtually endless collection of salads, from a simple tossed green salad to the elaborate Cobb salad with diced bacon and chicken. It is almost always served with an oil- or cream-based dressing.

Availability Stem lettuce is occasionally sold in Asian markets, but in general is not readily available commercially. The other lettuce varieties are carried in most supermarkets throughout the year.

Selection Crisphead lettuces should be firm and round, with green outer leaves that look fresh. Avoid heads with brown-tinged leaves. Heads that are especially hard, heavy, and white are probably overgrown and will have a large bitter core. Butterhead lettuces should have firm green leaves without brown edges; avoid heads with wilting or slimy leaves. Romaine lettuces should be full and compact. Avoid overly large heads, because outer leaves and ribs will be tough; reject heads with wilting leaves or rusty-looking ribs.

Storage Wash lettuce before storing. Dry thoroughly in a salad spinner or with paper towels, then wrap in paper towels, overwrap with a plastic bag, and store in refrigerator crisper. Leaf and butterhead lettuces will keep one or two days. Sturdier romaine and crisphead lettuces will keep three or four days.

Preparation Before washing lettuces, discard any wilted or bruised outer leaves. Twist out the central core, if any, or trim away base. Lettuce should be hand torn, not cut with a knife. Unless the recipe specifies otherwise, never dress a salad until just before serving; dressing makes leaves go limp and soggy.

CURRIED LETTUCE AND PEA SOUP

When fresh peas are in season, it's worth the effort of shelling them to make this piquantly seasoned soup. Otherwise, use about 2½ cups of frozen peas. When the soup is served hot, the curry flavor is assertive; chilled, the soup tastes more lemony.

> 2 pounds fresh peas in shells
> 2 medium onions, finely chopped
> 1 large clove garlic, minced
> ¼ cup butter or margarine
> 2 tablespoons vegetable oil
> 2 tablespoons curry powder
> 1 teaspoon ground turmeric
> 2 tablespoons flour
> 1 small head butterhead-type lettuce, shredded (about 4 cups, lightly packed)
> Grated rind and juice of 1 lemon
> 2 teaspoons sugar
> 4 cups Rich Chicken Stock (see page 560) or canned chicken broth
> 1 cup half-and-half
> Salt, to taste

1. Shell peas (you should have about 2½ cups). Reserve about 2 tablespoons small peas to use as garnish.

2. In a 3½- to 4-quart saucepan, cook onions and garlic in butter and oil over medium heat, stirring often, until soft but not browned. Blend in curry powder and turmeric, then flour. Add shredded lettuce, lemon rind (reserve a few threads for garnish, if desired) and juice, sugar, and peas. Remove from heat and gradually blend in stock.

3. Bring to a boil, stirring, over medium heat; then cover, reduce heat, and simmer until peas are just tender (8 to 10 minutes). Blend in half-and-half. Taste, and add salt if needed.

4. Transfer mixture, about a third at a time, to food processor or blender, and process or whirl until smooth.

5. To serve cold, cover and refrigerate until thoroughly chilled. To serve hot, return to cooking pan and heat, stirring often, until steaming hot. Serve garnished with reserved uncooked peas and reserved lemon rind (if used).

Makes about 9 cups, 6 to 8 servings.

Peas are cooked with tender lettuce and piquant seasonings to make creamy Curried Lettuce and Pea Soup, which can be enjoyed either hot or cold. Lemon zest or small peas make an appropriate garnish.

Recipes and Related Information
Caesar Salad, 506; Cream of Lettuce Soup, 563.

LIAISON

A mixture—such as a butter and flour roux, beurre manié, or beaten eggs and cream—used to thicken and enrich (add a luxurious finish to) soups, sauces, and stews is called a liaison. Other thickeners include flour, cornstarch, and even vegetable purées. Delicate egg-based thickeners must be warmed slightly before adding to hot liquid. To do this, pour a little of the hot sauce or soup into the mixture and whisk to blend. Pour back into the hot liquid and gently heat. Do not allow to boil or mixture will curdle.

LILY BUD

Also known as golden lilies or golden needles, lily buds are the dried, unopened buds of tiger lilies. They generally measure 2 to 4 inches long and are golden brown, very slender, and wrinkled. They have a chewy texture and a mild, slightly musky flavor.

Use   Chinese cooks use lily buds for texture in such dishes as Mu Shu Pork and hot and sour soup.

Availability   Dried lily buds are sold in Asian markets packed in plastic.

Storage   Dried lily buds may be kept indefinitely in an airtight container in a cool, dark, dry place.

Preparation   Soak lily buds in cool water for 20 minutes, then drain and snip off any hard stems. Use whole or halve lengthwise.

LIME

Like lemons, limes are too tart to eat on their own, but they add a refreshing tang to many sweet and savory dishes. Florida, California, and Mexico are the major regions where limes are grown for the American market, with the Persian lime the most common variety. Florida also grows a small, round variety called the Key lime, which produces the juice used in the popular Key lime pie.

Use   Limes are valued for the refreshing tartness of their juice and the aromatic oils in their skin. Lime wedges are often served with melons, and with tropical fruits such as papaya and mango. Lime juice gives a lift to a variety of cocktails, including the vodka gimlet and the daiquiri. Lime juice is added to marinades for chicken, pork, and fish. It is used extensively in Mexican cooking, in soups, salads, and fish dishes, the acidic juice "cooks" fish and shellfish, as in the popular Latin seviche. Juice and rind figure in a variety of desserts, including Key lime pie, lime curd, lime sherbet, and chiffon pie. Limes also make an excellent marmalade.

Availability   Fresh limes come to market all year. When domestic supplies are low in the spring, they are supplemented with imports from Mexico and the West Indies. Bottled lime juice is also usually available in most supermarkets.

Selection   Choose limes that are heavy for their size and that have a solid green color. Brown spots will not affect flavor, but avoid limes that are yellowish (they lack acidity) or hard and blackened (they are grainy).

Storage   Refrigerated, limes should keep for approximately one month.

Preparation   See LEMON.

▓ KEY LIME PIE

This traditional recipe from Key West, Florida, takes less than 30 minutes to prepare.

> ½ **cup (scant) fresh lime juice (from about 6 Key limes *or* 3 large, ripe regular limes)**
> 2 to 3 **teaspoons grated lime rind**
> 1 **can (14 oz) sweetened condensed milk**
> 4 **eggs, separated**
> 1 **prepared Graham Cracker Crumb Crust (see page 118) or homemade baked pastry crust**
> 5 **tablespoons sugar, or to taste**

1. Preheat oven to 400° F. Stir together lime juice, lime rind, and condensed milk until mixture thickens to the consistency of heavy pastry cream (the acid of the lime juice thickens the milk). Beat egg yolks until thick and lemon colored; add to milk mixture to make a light custard. Turn custard into pie crust.

2. Beat egg whites until soft, droopy peaks form. Add sugar, 1 tablespoon at a time. (If a very sweet meringue is desired, use additional sugar.) Continue beating until meringue is shiny and forms stiff peaks.

3. Mound meringue over top of pie. Bake just until meringue is browned but still tender (about 10 minutes). Cool, then chill before serving.

Serves 8.

Recipes and Related Information
Cold Fillet of Sole With Cilantro, Lime, and Pomegranate, 232; Elotes, 158; Jicama With Chile and Lime, 324; Lime Chiffon Pie, 440; Lime Mustard, 323; Seviche, 234.

LITCHI

Also spelled litchee, lychee, and leechee, this tropical fruit is grown in China, Mexico, and the United States. The litchi tree produces a small oval fruit with a rough-textured, strawberry red hull. Underneath the hull, milky white pulp with a grapelike texture surrounds a hard brown seed. The flesh is sweet and moist. Dried litchis, also known as litchi nuts, are brown and shriveled with a prunelike flesh and a sweet, smoky flavor.

Use   Peeled and chilled fresh litchis are eaten in fruit compotes and fruit salads. They can garnish chicken, duck, ham, or turkey salad. They are also sometimes added to stir-fried sweet-and-sour chicken or pork. Dried litchis are eaten out of hand as a snack.

Availability   Fresh litchis are sold in Asian markets in June and July. Dried litchis and peeled, pitted litchis canned in syrup are also available in Asian markets.

Selection   Select fresh litchis that look plump and firm; they should not be withered.

Storage Refrigerate fresh litchis for up to 1 month or freeze indefinitely. Keep leftover canned litchis in their syrup in an airtight, nonmetal container in the refrigerator for one week. Refrigerated or frozen, dried litchis will keep indefinitely.

Preparation Fresh litchis must be peeled and seeded; the leathery hull easily pulls away.

LOGANBERRY

A cross between the raspberry and the blackberry, the loganberry is red with a slightly elongated shape.

Use It may be used in any way that blackberries or raspberries are. See BLACKBERRY and RASPBERRY.

Availability Loganberries are found fresh in some markets in midsummer; canned loganberries are sold in some supermarkets.

Selection See BLACKBERRY.

Storage See BLACKBERRY.

LOQUAT

The fruit of a large evergreen shrub or tree often grown as an ornamental, the loquat is similar in texture and shape to the apricot and is usually 1 to 2 inches in diameter. The skin is yellowish gold; the flesh may be orange, yellow, or white, depending on variety. The loquat has large black seeds and a sweet-tart flesh that becomes sweeter as the fruit ripens. It is also known as the Japanese medlar.

Use In China and Japan, peeled loquats are eaten as dessert or cooked with chicken. They can be made into jams, jellies, and preserves or can be dried for later use. Peeled and sliced or diced, loquats are added to fruit salads or compotes or cooked with roast pork.

Availability Loquats must ripen on the tree and are too delicate to ship well. They are rarely available fresh, although some Asian markets carry them in the spring. Dried and canned loquats are sold in Asian markets.

Selection Choose firm, unblemished loquats that give slightly to pressure.

Storage In the refrigerator, loquats will last for up to two weeks. Dried loquats will keep indefinitely in the refrigerator or freezer. Leftover canned loquats may be stored in their syrup in a covered nonmetal container in the refrigerator for up to four days.

Preparation Peel before using.

LOTUS ROOT

This thick, smooth-stalked vegetable has a thin, light brown skin and grows in six-inch increments resembling a string of fat sausages that may reach up to 4 feet long. The crisp ivory flesh is perforated with large holes. When the root is peeled and sliced crosswise, the slices exhibit a lacy snowflake pattern. The flavor is somewhat sweet and starchy.

Use Lotus root may be thinly sliced, blanched, dressed, and served raw as a cold salad. Slices may also be deep-fried in tempura batter. Indian cooks incorporate lotus root in chutneys; Chinese cooks use the lacy slices to garnish platters. Because lotus root has the texture of potato, it may be substituted for potatoes in soups and stews. Lotus root starch, made from the ground root, is used as a thickener for Chinese soups and sauces and as a coating for fried foods.

Availability Fresh lotus root is sold in Asian markets from July to February. It is also marketed as dried slices, sugared slices, or canned slices.

Selection Choose firm, unblemished roots.

Storage Refrigerated lotus roots will keep two to three weeks. Dried or sugared slices will keep indefinitely in a cool, dark, dry place. Leftover canned lotus root may be stored in water in a covered nonmetal container in the refrigerator for up to one week; change the water every other day.

Preparation Lotus root discolors quickly; put peeled slices immediately in acidulated water to prevent browning. To soften dried lotus root, soak in acidulated water for one hour or until soft.

LOVAGE

The bright green leaves of this perennial herb look and taste a lot like celery. The flavor of the seeds is also celerylike.

Use Lovage adds its pungent flavor to soups, stuffings, salads, and vegetable dishes. The ground seeds may be used to season breads, soups, roasts, and cheese dishes.

Availability Fresh lovage is occasionally sold in some specialty markets. Lovage seed is carried in some specialty markets and herb stores.

Selection Look for bright green leaves with no signs of wilting.

Storage Place fresh lovage in a plastic bag and keep in the crisper; use immediately.

M

An assortment of fresh seasonal fruits macerated in sweet Muscat wine is a refreshing finish to a summer meal.

MACADAMIA NUT

Although the macadamia nut is native to Australia, most of the commercial crop now comes from Hawaii. Small and round, with a hard brown shell, the nut is almost always shelled and roasted in coconut oil before being marketed. The meat is cream colored, smooth and round, and very rich in flavor.

Use   Roasted and salted macadamia nuts are enjoyed as a cocktail snack. They can be minced and sprinkled on fish or sautéed vegetables. They are also used in desserts, including cream pies, cakes, and cookies.

Availability   Outside of their place of origin, macadamia nuts are almost always sold shelled and roasted. They are found in vacuum-packed tins or jars in most supermarkets.

Storage   Unopened tins and jars will keep indefinitely in a cool place. Once opened, the nuts should be used within one month or frozen for longer storage.

Preparation   For use in sweet dishes, salted nuts are often blanched first.

■ MACADAMIA CRISPS

Nuts of all sorts are a favorite ingredient for many kinds of cookies. These thin, crisp, buttery rounds are the perfect showcase for the rich flavor of elegant macadamia nuts. Fresh sweet cherries would be a juicy counterpoint to the crunchy texture of the cookies.

>   1 cup flour
>   ¼ teaspoon baking soda
>   ½ cup butter or margarine, softened
>   1¼ cups firmly packed brown sugar
>   1 egg
>   1 teaspoon vanilla extract
>   1 cup chopped macadamia nuts

1. In a small bowl stir together flour and baking soda to combine thoroughly; set aside.

2. Preheat oven to 375° F. In mixer bowl combine butter and brown sugar, and beat until well blended. Beat in egg until fluffy. Add vanilla and mix to blend.

3. Gradually add flour mixture until just blended. Stir in macadamia nuts.

4. Drop by rounded teaspoonfuls, placed about 1½ inches apart, onto lightly greased baking sheets. Bake until cookies are golden brown (8 to 10 minutes). Let stand briefly on baking sheets, then remove to wire racks to cool completely.

Makes about 5 dozen 2½-inch cookies.

MACE

Surrounding the shell of the nutmeg is a fragile, lacy, red skin called mace. The mace is separated from the nutmeg at harvest and then ground separately or broken into flakes called blades. The flavor of mace is related to that of nutmeg but is more pungent and less sweet.

Use   Mace contributes pungent flavor to sweet breads, pound cake, cherry pie, and puddings. It is an ingredient in Indian and Moroccan spice blends and is added to many Indonesian curries. Blade mace is often used whole in pickles and clear soups.

Availability   Ground mace is found on most supermarket spice racks. Whole dried blade mace is sold in some Asian and Caribbean markets.

Selection   Packaged seasonings lose quality after a while; try to buy from a store that restocks its spice section fairly often.

Storage   Keep ground mace in a cool, dry, dark place; it is highly perishable and should be replaced every three to four months. For longer storage keep mace in the refrigerator. Blade mace will keep for one year in a cool, dry, dark place.

Preparation Ground mace can be added directly to dishes; blade mace can be used whole, or ground just before use in a pepper mill, clean coffee grinder, or electric minichopper, or with a mortar and pestle.

> **Recipes and Related Information**
> Nutmeg, 393; Traditional Sugar-Cookie Cutouts, 149.

MACERATE, TO

To place food in a flavored liquid to improve flavor and soften texture. This is the same process as marinating, a term usually applied to meats, fish, and vegetables. Macerating has come to be associated with fruits, most often fruits soaked in spirits.

▧ FRESH FRUIT IN WINE

Marinades for fruit serve to moisten and enhance the flavor of the fruit. An assortment of seasonal fruits steeped in sweet Muscat wine makes a light, refreshing dessert. A glass of the same wine makes a good accompaniment.

Blackberries or boysenberries shouldn't be used for this dish because they tend to disintegrate and their juice stains the whole dish. Casaba melon can be too soft to hold together in the marinade and watermelon adds a lot of liquid, diluting the flavor. Try to combine tart fruits such as oranges or pineapple with low-acid types such as pears or bananas, but don't use too much tart fruit or the acidity will overpower the wine. Choose three or four of the following, depending upon what is in season. Strawberries, hulled, split if large; cantaloupe, honeydew, or other firm melon, in cubes or balls; orange or tangerine sections, all white pith removed; peaches or nectarines, unpeeled, sliced; blueberries or huckleberries; red, green, or purple grapes, especially Muscat types; mango, peeled, seeded, and cut into wedges; papaya, peeled, seeded, and diced; pears, peeled, cored, and diced; fully ripe pineapple, in chunks; bananas, peeled and sliced.

    4 cups assorted fresh fruit (see above)
    1 cup sweet Muscat Blanc, Muscat Canelli,
       or Malvasia Bianca
       Fresh lemon juice, to taste (omit if using
       citrus fruits)
       Mint leaves or borage blossoms, for garnish

1. Combine cut fruit in a large bowl, pour in wine, and toss to moisten fruit thoroughly with wine. Marinate in refrigerator 1 to 4 hours.

2. Taste a piece of the sweetest fruit and a piece of the most tart. Add lemon juice if necessary. Serve in individual bowls or from a large bowl as part of a buffet. Garnish with a sprig of fresh mint or borage blossoms.

Serves 4.

MACHE

The French name for a hardy leafy green, *mâche* is perhaps better known in the United States as corn salad or lamb's lettuce. The leaves have a mild, slightly nutty flavor. Some varieties produce leaves that are slightly cup-shaped; others produce round, flat leaves.

Use Mâche serves primarily as a salad green, either alone or in combination with other greens. The mild flavor is a good counterpoint to stronger-flavored greens, such as arugula and chicory.

Availability Mâche is not widely grown commercially but may appear in some specialty markets in spring, fall, and winter. It also grows wild in much of North America.

Selection Choose only unblemished leaves with no signs of wilting.

Storage Place greens in a plastic bag in the refrigerator crisper and use within one or two days.

Preparation Wash and dry thoroughly. Trim roots and discard blemished or yellowed leaves.

MALT

When barley, or occasionally barley and corn, has been allowed to germinate partially and then is roasted and ground, the product is malt. When powdered malt is soaked in water, then heated and reduced to a syrup, the result is malt extract. Malted milk is powdered milk containing maltose (malt sugar) and dextrin (an unfermentable sugar).

Use The primary function of malt is in the making of beer and Scotch whisky. The malt provides the sugars needed by the yeast to ferment. In addition, the degree to which the malt is roasted is a major determinant of the final flavor of both beer and Scotch.

Malt extract, also known as malt syrup, is widely employed in commercial bakeries and can be easily used in the home kitchen. Malt, being hygroscopic (it readily absorbs and holds moisture), gives breads a moist texture; it improves the rising of dough and helps give a golden color to the crust. Only a very small quantity is needed to derive these benefits. For a standard two-loaf recipe, add 1 teaspoon malt syrup to the required liquid.

Malted milk powder was originally devised as food for invalids and infants, but it is now best known as a soda fountain ingredient, used to impart a toasty flavor to milk shakes. It is also a substance in the commercial manufacture of baked goods, cake mixes, and ice cream.

Availability Malt extract in jars or cans is sold in some supermarkets, health-food stores, and stores that carry beer-making equipment.

Storage If packaged in a tightly closed jar or other airtight container in a cool, dark, dry place, malt will keep indefinitely.

Preparation Malt extract is very sticky. To make measuring easier, coat measuring spoon lightly with oil before adding malt extract. It will slip off the oiled spoon with little problem.

MANDARIN ORANGE

The mandarin orange is not one citrus fruit but many. The varieties of mandarin orange vary in size, color, flavor, and quantity of seeds. They can be as small as a golf ball or as large as a baseball. The skin can be a greenish gold or deep orange-red. The flesh can be seedless or full of seeds, and the juice sweet as honey or quite tart. What they have in common is their ease of peeling; mandarins are sometimes known as loose-skinned oranges or kid-glove oranges because they peel so readily. *Tangerine* is the name commonly used for deeply colored mandarins.

Use Mandarin oranges are commonly eaten out of hand. Because they peel easily, they are an excellent lunch-box or picnic fruit. Their refreshing flavor is especially appealing at breakfast or at the end of a winter dinner. Mandarin oranges may be sectioned and added to fruit salad, green salad, or chicken salad. Sweet varieties may be squeezed for a breakfast juice. The juice may also be used in sorbets, marinades, and dessert sauces. The grated peel can flavor cakes, muffins, quick breads, stuffings, rice, and other grain dishes. Dried tangerine peel is used in Chinese cooking to add flavor to stews, stir-fries, and smoked poultry.

Availability Mandarin oranges are in peak supply from November through March. Canned mandarin orange segments are also widely available in supermarkets. Dried tangerine peel is available in Chinese markets. Among the major mandarin orange varieties are the following:

Clementine Sweet and juicy Algerian variety that can have few or many seeds.

Dancy Small, with a rich red-orange color, a rich but acidic flavor, and many seeds.

Fairchild An early variety that is sweet and juicy but with many seeds.

Honey Exceptionally sweet, with many seeds.

Kinnow Richly flavored, with a rind that is thin and relatively difficult to peel.

Satsuma Sweet and almost seedless Japanese variety.

Tangelo Cross between a mandarin orange and a pomelo or grapefruit, a Malaysian fruit that is the ancestor of the grapefruit. Tangelos range in color from pale yellow to deep orange, in size from medium-small to medium-large, with flavors and aromas that combine the best of both parents. The best-known variety is the Minneola, a large juicy fruit with a nipple-shaped stem end and few seeds.

Selection Look for mandarins that feel heavy for their size. They should not have soft spots. Although some varieties are naturally puffy due to their loose skin, fruits that are extremely puffy may be overripe.

Storage In the refrigerator, mandarin oranges will keep for up to one month. Refrigerate leftover canned mandarin orange segments in an airtight nonmetal container for up to one week. Store dried tangerine peel airtight in a cool, dark, dry place; it will keep indefinitely.

Preparation Peel and section. Soften dried tangerine peel in cool water for about 30 minutes before using.

MANDOLINE

Before the food processor there was the mandoline. This tool for slicing, with adjustable blades, has long been used in professional kitchens to cut hard vegetables and fruits, such as carrots, cabbage, potatoes, beets, and apples, into uniform shapes. It functions like a grater or shredder—food moves over the cutting surface and the cut pieces fall through the cutting slots. With it you can shred, slice, julienne, waffle cut, and shape French fries.

Resembling an old-fashioned washboard, the mandoline is long, narrow, and rectangular, with a body made of wood, plastic, or heavyweight stainless steel for professional models. The simplest models are single bladed, designed for shredding; in fact, they are sometimes dubbed slaw slicers. Other models have two blades of different thicknesses, or adjustable blades that permit a range of thicknesses. Food is held in place by a metal carriage that has a hinged lid and knob, and glides on tracks so your hand is protected from the cutting edges. Better models have foldaway legs that diagonally prop up the device.

All of these functions can also be done with a food processor, except for the waffle or ripple cut; however, if you don't have a processor, or if you enjoy using a hand tool for certain tasks, then the mandoline, long appreciated by professionals, might suit your needs.

Recipes and Related Information
Food Processor, 240; Grater, Shredder, and Mill, 281.

MANGO

The most commonly grown fruit in India, exceeding all other fruits combined, the mango is also extremely popular in the Caribbean and Mexico. When ripe, the fruit of the mango tree has a tantalizing perfume. Under its smooth thin skin is moist, golden orange flesh with a flavor reminiscent of peach, apricot, and papaya. The flesh clings to a large flat seed in the middle and must be cut away from it. The fruit must also be peeled before eating.

Of the hundreds of mango varieties of different sizes, shapes, and colors, those most common in the United States are round to oval, weigh from 6 ounces to 1 pound each, and have a skin that may be green with red patches or yellowish green with rosy parts. As a mango ripens, the warm red, orange, and yellow shades increase and the green fades.

Use   Mangoes can be eaten raw, either alone or in combination with other fruits, often garnished with tart lemon or lime wedges. Sliced ripe mangoes may be used in many desserts, such as compotes, cakes, and tarts; puréed mangoes can form the base of sherbets, whips, ice cream, beverages, and dessert sauces. Underripe mangoes are a chief ingredient in mango chutney and mango pickle; in India, they are prepared as a savory vegetable—cubed, braised with onions and warm spices, and served over rice.

Availability   Fresh mangoes are sold in Latin American and Indian markets and in well-stocked supermarkets and specialty produce markets from May to September, with peak supplies in June. Some Latin American markets also carry canned mangoes in syrup.

Selection   The sweetest mangoes have skins with a great deal of red or orange; all-green, hard mangoes will probably never ripen properly. Avoid shriveled, overripe mangoes with black spots on the skin.

Storage   Leave underripe mangoes at room temperature until color develops; ripe mangoes are very fragrant and give gently to pressure. To speed ripening, place mangoes in a paper bag pierced with a few holes. Refrigerate ripe fruit in a plastic bag and use within two or three days. Leftover canned mango may be refrigerated in its syrup in a covered container for up to four days.

Preparation   Mango halves cannot be readily pried away from the pit. To section a mango, cut vertically all the way around the fruit with a small sharp knife. Peel skin back, then cut flesh off the pit in long vertical slices. Ripe mangoes are messy and juicy, and mango juice stains; eat with caution.

Recipes and Related Information
Fresh Fruit in Wine, 347; Mango With Prosciutto, 358; Pavlova, 362.

MARGARINE

A substitute for butter, margarine is made from hydrogenated vegetable oils, predominantly soy and corn oil. Because it is cholesterol-free, less expensive, and lower in saturated fats than is butter, margarine is the preferred solid cooking fat in many American households today. Margarine is colored (see ACHIOTE) and fortified with vitamins to increase its similarity to butter (see BUTTER). Milk solids and diacetyl, a molecule that contributes a buttery flavor, are also added. Margarine is less frequently referred to as oleomargarine.

Use   Margarine may be substituted for butter in almost all recipes, although it will not impart the same rich, nutty flavor. It may be used for sautéing, for coating vegetables or bread, and for baking. It is unsuitable for butter-based sauces, such as Hollandaise and beurre blanc.

Availability   Margarine is readily found in all supermarkets, packaged in plastic tubs or in foil-wrapped sticks overwrapped with a paper carton.

Storage   Margarine should be refrigerated. It will keep for several weeks in the refrigerator or indefinitely in the freezer.

MARINADE; MARINATE, TO

A seasoned liquid or a paste of herbs and spices is a marinade. To marinate, let food sit in a wet or dry mixture to tenderize and/or increase the flavor of a food. Meats, fish, and even vegetables and fruit benefit from this treatment. Also see MACERATE.

Typically a wet marinade contains oil, seasoning, and an acid such as lemon juice, vinegar, or wine. The acid breaks down muscle fiber for a more-tender final product, while the oil adds moisture and, along with the seasoning, increases your appreciation of the food: Studies have shown that foods containing fat have a better mouthfeel. A dry marinade—a spice rub—is massaged into the food, infusing it with a particular blend of spices and dried herbs that grows stronger as the coating remains on the food.

Foods usually sit in marinades for at least one hour, or overnight, or in some cases longer, depending upon the desired intensity of flavor and the amount of preparation time available to the cook. For a short period of time—one hour or less—marinating foods can be left out at room temperature; otherwise keep in the refrigerator. If chilled, let food warm to room temperature (about 30 minutes) before cooking.

To prepare acid-based wet marinades, always use a nonreactive container, such as one made of glass or stainless steel, or a plastic bag to prevent adverse reactions or

Use marinades and bastes to tenderize and flavor meats, fish, and vegetables.

off-colors. Marinated foods are usually cooked by broiling, grilling, or roasting. Fat may cause flare-ups on the grill or in the broiler, so before cooking, drain off the marinade and pat away excess from the food. Also, the sugars present in some marinades lower the browning temperature. Cooks must be vigilant to see that the caramelizing sugars brown and do not burn.

To prepare dry spice rubs, wash and dry all food before marinating. For cuts of beef, lamb, and poultry, lightly oil all external surfaces. For fish, lightly coat with clarified butter. Then massage spice rub over external surfaces of food. Depending on type of spice mixture, use from 1 to 2 tablespoons of marinade per pound of beef, poultry, or fish. Let stand for one hour at room temperature before cooking to allow the spices to permeate the flesh.

■ VERSATILE MARINADES AND DRY SPICE RUBS

To marinate, use a container that holds the food snugly in a single layer. Cover with plastic wrap. Leftover marinade can be refrigerated in a covered jar for several weeks.

Wet marinades can be mixed in a blender or by hand with a whisk. Make the dry spice rubs by combining all ingredients and mixing well.

Mustard and Herb Marinade
Use for lamb or chicken. Makes about 1 cup.

⅓ cup vegetable oil
¼ cup dry white wine
1 tablespoon *each* red wine vinegar and lemon juice
1 large clove garlic, minced
1½ tablespoons Dijon mustard
¼ teaspoon *each* salt and sugar
⅛ teaspoon *each* dried thyme, oregano, summer savory, and tarragon
Dash white pepper

Teriyaki Marinade
Use for beef, chicken, or fish. Makes about ¾ cup.

½ cup soy sauce
3 tablespoons sugar
2 teaspoons grated fresh ginger *or* ½ teaspoon ground ginger
1 clove garlic, minced
2 tablespoons dry sherry

Dry Spice Rub for Fish
Makes about 4 tablespoons.

2 teaspoons grated lemon rind
1 teaspoon garlic powder
1 teaspoon tarragon
1 teaspoon basil
2 teaspoons freshly ground black pepper
½ teaspoon cayenne pepper
1 tablespoon paprika
½ teaspoon salt

Dry Spice Rub for Lamb
Makes about 4 tablespoons.

1 teaspoon garlic powder
1 teaspoon fennel seed, bruised or crushed in a mortar with a pestle
½ teaspoon thyme
2 teaspoons freshly ground black pepper
½ teaspoon cayenne pepper
1 tablespoon paprika
1 teaspoon oregano
2 teaspoons rosemary
1 teaspoon basil
½ teaspoon salt

Dry Spice Rub for Meat
Makes 3 tablespoons.

> 1 teaspoon garlic powder
> 1 teaspoon fennel seed, bruised or crushed in mortar and pestle
> ½ teaspoon thyme
> 2 teaspoons freshly ground black pepper
> ½ teaspoon cayenne pepper
> 1 tablespoon paprika
> ½ teaspoon oregano
> ½ teaspoon salt

Dry Spice Rub for Poultry
Makes 3 tablespoons.

> 1 teaspoon garlic powder
> 2 teaspoons tarragon
> ½ teaspoon sage
> 1 teaspoon marjoram
> ½ teaspoon thyme
> 2 teaspoons freshly ground black pepper
> ½ teaspoon cayenne pepper
> 1 tablespoon paprika
> ½ teaspoon salt

■ TANDOORI CHICKEN

A tandoor is an Indian clay oven, but a conventional oven will work at home for this dish. The marinade and high heat turn the chicken very dark brown as it cooks. Marinating takes at least two hours, or overnight.

> 2 whole chickens (about 3 lb each), quartered
> 1½ teaspoons cumin seed
> 1 teaspoon whole coriander, crushed
> ⅛ gram saffron threads (½ vial)
> 2 tablespoons boiling water
> 2 cloves garlic, minced
> 1 teaspoon fresh ginger, minced
> 1 jalapeño chile, minced
> 1 tablespoon paprika
> 1 cup plain yogurt
> 3 tablespoons fresh lemon juice
> 6 tablespoons unsalted butter, melted

1. Score chicken pieces in diagonal cuts through meat almost to bone in 3 or 4 places.

2. In a small, dry skillet, slowly toast cumin seed and coriander until barely browned (4 to 5 minutes). In a small bowl dissolve saffron in the boiling water.

3. Stir cumin seed, coriander, garlic, ginger, chile, paprika, yogurt, lemon juice, and 3 tablespoons of the butter into saffron. Mix thoroughly. Rub marinade into chicken and let marinate in the refrigerator for 2 hours or overnight.

4. Preheat oven to 500° F. Place chicken pieces on a broiler rack set in a shallow pan and roast 30 minutes.

Baste with remaining butter and turn to brown second side, just to color (5 to 8 minutes). Serve hot from oven.
Serves 8.

> ***Recipes and Related Information***
> *Spicy Red-Wine Marinade, 610; Wine in Cooking, 608.*

MARJORAM

A perennial herb in the mint family, marjoram (also known as sweet marjoram) is often confused with oregano. It has a similar flavor and leaf shape, but is slightly milder and sweeter. The small green oval leaves are important to Mediterranean cooking.

Use Marjoram flatters many Mediterranean vegetables, such as tomatoes, beans, squash, and onions. Rub it on chicken, pork, and lamb before roasting; include it in meat loaves, sausage mixtures, and stuffings; or let it simmer in soups and tomato sauces. Because marjoram is delicate, it should be added to cooked dishes (such as soups and sauces) shortly before serving.

Availability Some specialty markets carry fresh marjoram the year around. Both whole dried leaves and ground marjoram are packed in jars and tins and are widely available on supermarket spice racks.

Selection Choose fresh leaves. Packaged seasonings lose quality after a while; try to buy from a store that restocks its spice section fairly often.

Storage Refrigerate fresh marjoram in a plastic bag and use as soon as possible. Store dried leaves or ground marjoram in a cool, dark, dry place. Replace leaves once a year, ground marjoram every six months.

Preparation Mince fresh leaves before adding to a dish. Rub dried leaves between fingers to release aromatic oils before using.

MATERIALS FOR COOKWARE

The materials used for cookware can play a role in the success or failure of the final product. Metals, glass, and ceramics each have properties that make them suitable for certain culinary jobs and undesirable for others. When choosing cooking equipment, it's as important to match the material to the task as it is to consider appropriate sizes and shapes. Use the chart on page 352 as a guide. For discussions of specific equipment, such as cookware or baking dishes, see particular entries.

COMMON MATERIALS FOR KITCHEN EQUIPMENT

For consistently successful results, choose cookware made of a material best suited for the job at hand. This chart describes the properties and suggested uses for the most common materials.

Type of Material	Advantages and Disadvantages	Care and Cleaning
Aluminum	A superior heat conductor, aluminum heats evenly and quickly. Can react with acidic foods, adversely affecting taste and color of food. Alkalies can cause pan to darken. Anodized aluminum has a fused-on coating that seals the metal, making it nonreactive and almost nonstick.	If necessary, scrub with coarse salt or mildly abrasive cleanser; rinse immediately. If darkened from oxidation, fill with water and vinegar or lemon juice, and boil 15 minutes.
Cast iron	Because cast iron absorbs heat slowly and evenly, it is good for baking and frying. Moisture can cause rusting. Seasoning before first use seals porous surface and keeps food from sticking. To season, rub inside of pan with vegetable oil; set over medium heat until oil begins to smoke (about 15 minutes); cool completely and wipe off excess oil with paper towels.	Retain seasoning by wiping clean with a paper towel; to remove food, scrub gently with a nylon pad. If used infrequently, coat cast iron with oil or wrap in plastic and store in dry place to keep rust-free and dry. Reseason when necessary.
Clad metals	These are a combination or sandwich of several metals for their best qualities: stainless steel for durability and resistance to corrosion, aluminum or copper for heat conductivity, and anodized aluminum for nonreactive and nonstick properties. Combination depends upon manufacturer.	Follow manufacturer's directions for care.
Copper	An excellent heat conductor, copper is well-suited for sauces and liquids. Copper cookware is usually lined with tin or stainless steel to prevent toxic interactions with certain foods.	Clean in hot, soapy water; dry at once. Brighten with commercial copper polish. Re-tin when necessary.
Earthenware, stoneware	Although poor heat conductors, they retain heat well and are good for baking and slow cooking. Both come glazed and unglazed. Porous unglazed clay bakers must soak in water prior to use; follow manufacturer's instructions. Stoneware is less porous and more durable than earthenware.	To clean earthenware soak in hot water, scrub with coarse salt, rinse, and air dry. Glazed stoneware is usually dishwasherproof.
Enameled metals	Cast iron or steel may be coated with a porcelain enamel that can chip and crack. Some have a dark, nonstick coating. Enameled steel is lighter than cast iron and has a thin, fragile glaze. Light-colored interiors can become stained.	Avoid knocking or hitting with metal utensils (wood utensils are preferable). Soak in hot, soapy water; avoid harsh abrasives. Follow manufacturer's directions for care.
Glass, glass-ceramic, porcelain	Poor heat conductors but good heat retainers, all are nonreactive, suitable for baking and, in a very few cases, for stove-top use; confirm at time of purchase. Glass and porcelain can crack or break if exposed to sudden changes of temperature. Glass-ceramic is impervious to sudden changes of temperature, so can go safely from freezer to oven, and sometimes to stove top.	Soak in hot, soapy water to remove any food stuck to surface. All are dishwasherproof.
Nonstick surfaces	Fused to interior of pan, nonstick surfaces permit almost fat-free cooking.	Wipe clean with a sponge and warm, soapy water; use only abrasives designed for these finishes.
Rolled steel	Appropriate for quick cooking, rolled steel absorbs heat rapidly. Often used for omelet pans, crêpe pans, and woks, it is susceptible to rust if exposed to moisture. Season and store as for cast iron.	See Cast iron.
Stainless steel	A poor heat conductor, stainless steel is best if clad with a good conductor such as copper or aluminum, or if entire pan or pan bottom contains a core of one of these metals. Stainless steel is sturdy, nonreactive, and easy to clean.	Wash in hot, soapy water; scrub with a nylon pad. Clean stubborn stains with stainless steel cleanser.

MEALY

This word is used to describe food that resembles crumbly and coarse meal. Cooked potatoes can have a mealy texture, which tastes dry and granular. The appearance of biscuit and pastry dough after the fat has been sufficiently cut into the dry ingredients is also described as mealy.

MEASURE, TO

To allot a specific quantity of food, whether dry or liquid; also, to determine the dimensions and volumes of pans, dishes, and molds.

To watch experienced cooks at work, it seems that they are casual to the point of recklessness about measuring—a pinch of this, a few splashes of that. Actually, they are more like tourists on a return visit: The recipe, like an itinerary, becomes the starting point for their explorations rather than a map to be slavishly followed. They have learned when exact measures are indispensable and when they are a matter of personal taste. Even without measuring tools, their dashes and splashes are remarkably accurate—the result of long practice.

Why measure? For one thing, measurements are a system of notation that helps ensure reproducible results. If the recipe is faithfully followed, the dish you make today should look and taste about the same as when you made it last month. If you share the recipe with grateful guests, they should rightly expect that their efforts will be as successful as yours.

Cooking is a science as well as an art. Precise measurements are sometimes critical to the success of a recipe; baking requires this type of attention. Many such recipes are balanced formulas. Amounts of ingredients are carefully chosen to interact in a specific way. Upset the balance more than just a bit or make improper substitutions and the final product will fail.

BASIC MEASURES		
1 tablespoon	=	3 teaspoons
¾ tablespoon	=	2¼ teaspoons
½ tablespoon	=	1½ teaspoons
⅓ tablespoon	=	1 teaspoon
Pinch	=	Less than ⅛ teaspoon
1 cup	=	16 tablespoons
½ cup	=	8 tablespoons
⅓ cup	=	5⅓ tablespoons
¼ cup	=	4 tablespoons
1 gallon	=	4 quarts/8 pints/16 cups
1 quart	=	2 pints/4 cups
1 pint	=	2 cups
1 pound	=	16 ounces
¾ pound	=	12 ounces
⅔ pound	=	10⅔ ounces
½ pound	=	8 ounces
⅓ pound	=	5⅓ ounces
¼ pound	=	4 ounces

WEIGHT EQUIVALENTS OF SOME COMMON FOODS

Dry ingredients have different weights per cup. Even the weight of two identical measures of the same ingredient may vary depending on how it was added to the measuring cup—with a light touch or a heavy hand, sifted or unsifted, packed down or leveled off with knife or spatula. Professional cooks, in particular bakers, prefer to measure by weight. Home cooks who bake frequently might find it useful to purchase a scale (see Measuring Cups, Spoons, Scales).

Granulated Sugar

¼ cup	=	1¾ ounces
⅓ cup	=	2¼ ounces
½ cup	=	3½ ounces
⅔ cup	=	4½ ounces
¾ cup	=	5 ounces
1 cup	=	7 ounces
1½ cups	=	10½ ounces
2 cups	=	14 ounces

Solid Fats:
Butter, Margarine, Vegetable Shortening

2 cups/4 sticks/ 32 tablespoons	= 16 ounces
1 cup/2 sticks/ 16 tablespoons	= 8 ounces
½ cup/1 stick/8 tablespoons	= 4 ounces
¼ cup/½ stick/4 tablespoons	= 2 ounces
¼ stick/2 tablespoons	= 1 ounce
⅛ stick/1 tablespoon	= ½ ounce

All-purpose Flour

	Unsifted	Sifted
2 cups	10 ounces	8½ ounces
1½ cups	7½ ounces	6¼ ounces
1 cup	5 ounces	4¼ ounces
¾ cup	3½ ounces	3 ounces
⅔ cup	3¼ ounces	2½ ounces
½ cup	2½ ounces	2 ounces
⅓ cup	1½ ounces	1¼ ounces
¼ cup	1¼ ounces	1 ounce

HOW TO MEASURE INGREDIENTS

Good cooks know not only when to measure accurately, but also how to measure correctly. When accuracy is critical, use the container that fills to the amount you need to measure—a half cup for that amount of flour, for example, instead of filling a full cup halfway. A liquid measuring cup won't be as accurate for dry ingredients because it can't be leveled off.

TO MEASURE DRY INGREDIENTS: POWDERS, CRUMBS, CHOPPED OR GRATED FOODS

Baking Powder and Baking Soda   Use a measuring spoon of the correct size; dip into container and level off with edge of package lid, or with knife or metal spatula.

Crumbs and Chopped Foods   Lightly fill measuring cup; level off with knife or spatula.

Flour   Because particles of flour tend to pack, it is impossible to give an absolute value for the weight of a cup of flour. This will vary depending upon the method used to fill the cup, and whether the flour was sifted first (see Weight Equivalents of Some Common Foods). Many cookbooks and some recipes specify how to measure flour; follow cookbook or recipe instructions for good results. If a method is not specified, for consistent results choose one of the following and use it each time. Aerate or loosen flour by fluffing with a fork, then spoon lightly into measuring cup; don't tap or bang cup, since this will pack flour. Level off with knife or spatula. Or, aerate flour with a fork, scoop it up with measuring cup, then level off. If recipe calls for *1 cup sifted flour*, sift flour, then gently fill measuring cup. If it says *1 cup flour, sifted*, measure first, then sift.

Salt and Ground Spices   Use a measuring spoon of the correct size; pour powder into spoon and level off with a knife or spatula.

Sugar   Measure granulated white sugar as for Crumbs and Chopped Foods or by weight (see Weight Equivalents of Some Common Foods). Sift confectioners' sugar first (unless directed otherwise), then measure as for flour. For brown sugar, pack firmly into measuring cup so that when turned out it retains shape of cup. If lumpy, roll before measuring.

TO MEASURE LIQUIDS, OILS

Use a liquid measuring cup with calibrations marked on the inside. Fill to desired level; set on a flat surface and check at eye level. (Don't lift cup; it will not be as steady and reading won't be as precise.)

For easier removal of sticky liquids—such as honey, molasses, and syrups—from measuring cups, lightly grease the cup first, spray with vegetable cooking spray, or use a rubber spatula to scrape out food.

U.S. MEASURE AND METRIC MEASURE CONVERSION CHART

Metric equivalents are becoming increasingly common. Use this chart to translate between U.S. and metric measurements. For convenience, rounded measures for often-used quantities are also provided.

Measure	Symbol	Formulas for Exact Measures When You Know	Multiply by	To Find	Rounded Measures for Quick Reference		
Mass (weight)	oz	Ounces	28.35	Grams	1 oz		=30 g
	lb	Pounds	0.45	Kilograms	4 oz		=115 g
	g	Grams	0.035	Ounces	8 oz		=225 g
	kg	Kilograms	2.2	Pounds	16 oz	=1 lb	=450 g
					32 oz	=2 lb	=900 g
					36 oz	=2¼ lb	=1,000 g (1 kg)
Volume	tsp	Teaspoons	4.9	Milliliters	¼ tsp	=¹⁄₂₄ oz	=1 ml
	tbsp	Tablespoons	15.0	Milliliters	½ tsp	=¹⁄₁₂ oz	=2 ml
	fl oz	Fluid ounces	29.57	Milliliters	1 tsp	=⅙ oz	=5 ml
	c	Cups	0.237	Liters	1 tbsp	=½ oz	=15 ml
	pt	Pints	0.47	Liters	1 c	=8 oz	=250 ml
	qt	Quarts	0.95	Liters	2 c (1 pt)	=16 oz	=500 ml
	gal	Gallons	3.785	Liters	4 c (1 qt)	=32 oz	=1 liter
	ml	Milliliters	0.034	Fluid ounces	4 qt (1 gal)	=128 oz	=3¾ liter
Temperature	°F	Fahrenheit	5∕9 (after subtracting 32)	Celsius	32° F	= 0° C	
					68° F	= 20° C	
	°C	Celsius	9∕5 (then add 32)	Fahrenheit	212° F	=100° C	

TO MEASURE FATS

Spoon solid vegetable shortening and softened butter into dry measuring cups; level off. Sticks of butter or margarine usually have wrappers printed with tablespoon markings. There are 8 tablespoons in a stick of butter (see Weight Equivalents of Some Common Foods). For melted fats, measure in solid form and then melt, or melt and then measure as a liquid.

MEASURING BY WEIGHT

Quantity recipes and recipes from countries outside of the United States typically state ingredients by weight. This easy method has long been used by restaurant kitchens and professional bakers because it is consistent, exact, and reliable. Some recipes give weight equivalents; to convert those that don't, weigh the foods as you use them, and record weights for future reference (see Weight Equivalents of Some Common Foods).

THE METRIC SYSTEM

This decimal system of weights and measures (in units of ten) is based on the meter (for length), the kilogram (for dry weight), and the liter (for liquids). Unlike most countries of the world, the United States does not follow this system, but it is being routinely taught in American schools. More and more frequently, measuring tools sold in the U.S. have both pound and kilogram markings. See U.S. Measure and Metric Measure Conversion Chart.

TO MEASURE
BAKING PANS AND DISHES

For best results, use the correct pan size. Recipes will describe a pan or dish in terms of shape (round, square, or rectangular), dimensions (9- by 13-inch, 8-inch), or volume (a 6-cup mold, a 2-quart dish). Many manufacturers stamp the size on the pan. If this hasn't been done, measure as follows.

Dimension   With a ruler, measure length and/or width across the top of the pan from one inside edge to the other. Measure depth from the outside, bottom to top of one side. Scratch size on the pan for future reference. See BAKING PANS.

Volume   The volume of a pan is measured by the amount of liquid it holds when filled to the rim. With a measuring cup, fill dish or pan with water; note capacity on the underside of the pan for future reference.

EQUIPMENT FOR MEASURING

Measuring tools are necessities for the cook. Buy measuring cups for liquid and dry ingredients, measuring spoons, and, if you have storage space, a scale with both American and metric weights. It makes sense to have several sets of cups and spoons—one set for liquids, the other for dry ingredients.

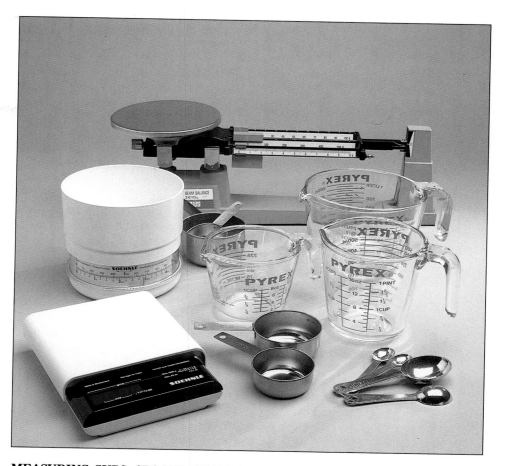

MEASURING CUPS, SPOONS, SCALES

Cups and spoons are standardized to measure liquid or dry ingredients. The standard liquid cup equals 8 fluid ounces or 236.6 milliliters. The standard dry cup equals 16 level tablespoons. The standard teaspoon equals 4.9 milliliters.

Cups for Liquids   Cups for measuring liquids have a capacity of 1 quart or less, with a pouring lip and a handle. They are marked in divisions of quarts, pints, fluid ounces, and cups. Many have metric markings in millimeters as well. Buy sturdy cups with comfortable handles in several sizes. They are available in glass and plastic; some are microwave-safe. If buying plastic cups, be sure they are dishwasher-safe.

Cups for Dry Ingredients   Made of stainless steel or plastic, these typically come in sets of 1 cup, ½ cup, ⅓ cup, ¼ cup, and sometimes ⅛ cup. Also available is a 2-cup measure that is handy for bakers. Buy several sets; if plastic, choose sturdy ones that can go in the dishwasher.

Measuring Spoons   Like cups, these are sold in sets of individual spoons, typically including 1 tablespoon, 1 teaspoon, ½ teaspoon, ¼ teaspoon, and sometimes also ⅛ teaspoon. They are made of aluminum, plastic, or stainless steel. For use with liquids, fill to rim of spoon; for dry measure, fill and level off. If a recipe calls for a rounded or heaping spoonful, do not level off after filling the measuring spoon.

Precise measurements can sometimes mean the difference between the success or failure of a recipe. Shown clockwise from top: balance beam scale, measuring cups for liquids, measuring spoons, measuring cups for dry ingredients, electronic scale, spring scale.

Scales   Whether you weigh ingredients routinely, only occasionally, or hardly ever, you will find a scale useful in the kitchen. Features to consider are capacity (how much do you need to weigh at one time?); accuracy (important for baking, but less so for estimating cooking times by weight); ability to zero out (scale can be reset to zero, which means that ingredients can be weighed one after the other in the same container, or that the reading will reflect only what's in the container and not the weight of the container as well); size (if it can sit on the counter, you will probably use it more); and readability (numbers can be seen easily).

There are three types of scales: spring, balance beam, and electronic. The spring model, the most inexpensive, is the least accurate because the spring mechanism loses elasticity over time. It usually has a plastic housing, American and metric markings, and ranges in capacity from diet portions to 6 to 10 pounds. Like the scale in a doctor's office, the balance beam scale is adjusted by weights that slide across a horizontal arm. It is very accurate, but can't zero out. Measurements are American and/or metric, and models can handle small amounts up to about 22 pounds. Materials are plastic or enameled cast iron. One manufacturer offers a balance scale with a small capacity, an adjusting wheel, and a hidden mechanism that can be reset to zero. Electronic scales need batteries and are priced to reflect their state-of-the-art status. They are the most precise, can zero out, have both American and metric measurements, and weigh diet-sized portions to about 10 pounds. Most electronic scales are plastic.

MELON

Like cucumbers and squash, melons are members of the Cucurbitaceae family, commonly known as gourds. There are dozens of melon varieties and, because they cross-pollinate readily, they are difficult to categorize. The somewhat random distinctions that taxonomists draw between melons are unimportant to the cook, who usually only wants to know how to find a ripe one. Suffice it to say that melons may be either smooth skinned or netted, hollow centered or solid fleshed, sweet or bitter.

Use   Because melons are more than 90 percent water, cooking destroys their texture; they are almost always eaten raw. Two exceptions are the Chinese bitter melon and winter melon, which are always cooked. The high water content and natural sweetness make chilled melon an especially refreshing summer fruit. Melons are among the most appealing fruits—whether served in chilled wedges for breakfast or dessert; scooped into balls with a melon baller and added to fruit salad; seeded and filled with port, yogurt, cottage cheese, or ice cream; or puréed for a beverage or sorbet.

Availability   The list below outlines some of the best-known melon varieties, their seasons, storage requirements, and recommended preparations.

Selection   With few exceptions, you can tell a ripe melon by the fragrance. Most ripe melons also give slightly to pressure at the blossom end. Avoid melons that are soft or feel wet at the stem end. A melon that sloshes when shaken is probably overripe. See individual melons for further guidance.

Storage   See individual melons.

BITTER MELON

Also known as balsam pear, the bitter melon looks like a warty cucumber. It is usually 6 to 10 inches long, light green, with bumpy ridges. The silvery green flesh is firm, with a spongy center containing pale brown seeds. Because of its high quinine content, it is indeed bitter; when presalted or parboiled and cooked, however, the bitter flesh develops more of a cool, mintlike character. It is popular in the summer for its refreshing qualities.

Chinese cooks use bitter melon in stir-fries with meats or seafood. They also steam it, stuff it with pork or shrimp, and add it to soups. Indian cooks use bitter melon as part of a spicy, mixed-vegetable preparation or stuffed with a spicy onion mixture and fried.

Fresh bitter melon is found in Asian markets from April through September. It is also available canned and dried. Choose small, firm melons with light green, shiny skin without brown spots. Refrigerate for up to one week. Leftover canned melon may be refrigerated in a nonmetal covered container for up to three days.

Most recipes call for soaking bitter melon in salt water for 30 minutes to remove bitterness. Alternatively, it may be cut up, sprinkled with salt, and allowed to drain for 30 minutes. A third method is to parboil the cut melon for 3 minutes before cooking.

CANTALOUPE

The cantaloupe is a muskmelon, a very fragrant melon with a raised netting on its skin. The netting is cream colored over a yellowish green background. The sweet, moist, orange flesh of the cantaloupe surrounds a hollow center partly filled with juice, pulp, and seeds.

Chilled cantaloupe may be halved, seeded, and eaten as is or cut into peeled wedges and draped with prosciutto (see Use, at left, for further suggestions).

Supplemented by Mexican imports in the winter, markets stock cantaloupe almost continually. Supplies peak in summer months and are lowest October through December. A ripe cantaloupe should have an enticing aroma and both ends should give slightly to pressure. Cantaloupe should have a smooth, symmetrical shallow basin at the stem end called a full slip. This indicates that the melon broke away naturally from its stem when it reached peak ripeness. Melons cut away from the stem before peak ripeness may show telltale stem fibers, scarring, or damaged tissue at the stem end; avoid these melons. Also avoid melons with pronounced yellow rind color (indicates overripeness); mold growth or moldy aroma; soft, wet tissue; or smooth spots without netting on the surface.

If melon is hard but properly colored, keep in a warm room for several days, away from sunlight, preferably in high humidity. Melons do not become sweeter after harvest, but they will soften and become juicier. When melon is aromatic and soft at stem and blossom ends, refrigerate. It will keep for up to one week.

CASABA

The round casaba melon has a golden yellow, slightly furrowed skin and creamy white to yellow flesh. Use like cantaloupe. Casabas are available from July through November, with peak supplies and peak quality in September and October.

Look for deep golden skin color and slight give at the blossom end. Casabas lack aroma. Avoid any with dark, sunken, water-soaked spots. Store like cantaloupe.

CHRISTMAS MELON

Also known as Santa Claus melon, this elongated variety resembles a small watermelon. The green skin sports yellow stripes; the flesh is creamy white to yellow and tastes like the casaba. Use like cantaloupe. Christmas melon is on the market in December, which accounts for its name.

A Christmas melon should have good aroma and give slightly at both ends. Avoid any with soft spots. Store like cantaloupe; this melon will keep up to one month under refrigeration.

CRENSHAW

Also known as Cranshaw, this melon has mottled green and yellow skin and salmon-colored flesh. It is quite large, weighing up to 9 pounds, and is highly aromatic. Its flesh has a rich, spicy taste. Use like cantaloupe. Crenshaws are available from July through October, with peak supplies in August and September.

The green skin turns yellow in parts at maturity. A ripe Crenshaw should be very aromatic and should give slightly at the blossom end. Store like cantaloupe; a Crenshaw will keep under refrigeration longer than a cantaloupe.

HONEYDEW

This large (average 6 pounds) oval melon has a smooth, creamy white to yellow-green skin and a pale green flesh. Pink-fleshed honeydew is occasionally available. The flesh is thick, juicy, and very sweet when ripe. Use like cantaloupe. Latin American imports supplement the domestic crop, making honeydew available almost all year. Peak supplies are June through October.

Look for yellowish white to creamy rind; a soft, velvety, slightly sticky feel; slight softening at blossom end; and faint, pleasant aroma. Avoid melons with flat white or greenish color, hardness, and cuts or punctures through the rind. Store like cantaloupe.

PERSIAN MELON

This melon resembles the cantaloupe but is slightly larger and rounder, with finer netting. The flesh is a delicate pink-orange and is thick, firm, and sweet. Use like cantaloupe. Persian melon is available from July through October, with peak supplies in August and September.

Choose melons with good aroma, slight give at both ends, no slick spots on the skin, and no dark or greenish black netting. Store like cantaloupe.

WATERMELON

The watermelon has solid flesh with small hard black seeds distributed evenly throughout. The hard skin is deep green and may be solid, striped, or mottled; the flesh is usually deep pink to red, although varieties with yellow flesh exist. Watermelons have an oblong shape, rather like a fat cucumber, and are generally quite large, often exceeding 30 pounds. The flesh is crisp and juicy and quite sweet when ripe. Seedless hybrids are grown commercially in some regions.

When cut into manageable wedges or rounds, watermelons can be eaten as is, for dessert or snack. Watermelon balls or cubes make a refreshing addition to fruit salads. Thick pieces of watermelon rind make excellent sweet pickles. A hollowed, scalloped shell filled with cut-up fruit is a dramatic addition to a buffet table.

In winter and spring, Mexican watermelons supplement the domestic crop, making the melons available almost continually. Domestic supplies are available June through September, with peak supplies in the hottest months. Because watermelons can be so large, they are frequently cut up by the retailer and sold in halves or quarters.

With cut melons, look for firm, juicy red flesh and dark brown or black seeds. Soft white seeds indicate immaturity. Avoid sections that are cracked or streaked with white. With uncut melons, look for a smooth and slightly dull rind (neither shiny nor very dull), filled-out and rounded ends, and a creamy underside. Store watermelons like cantaloupe.

WINTER MELON

Chinese winter melon is a very large gourd that somewhat resembles a greenish white pumpkin. Slightly more tall than wide, it has a hard ridged skin displaying a heavy white bloom. The large seed cavity contains pumpkinlike seeds. The flesh is snowy white with a delicate flavor, somewhat akin to a steamed cucumber.

Honeydew, cantaloupe, and watermelon balls make an attractive and naturally delicious salad.

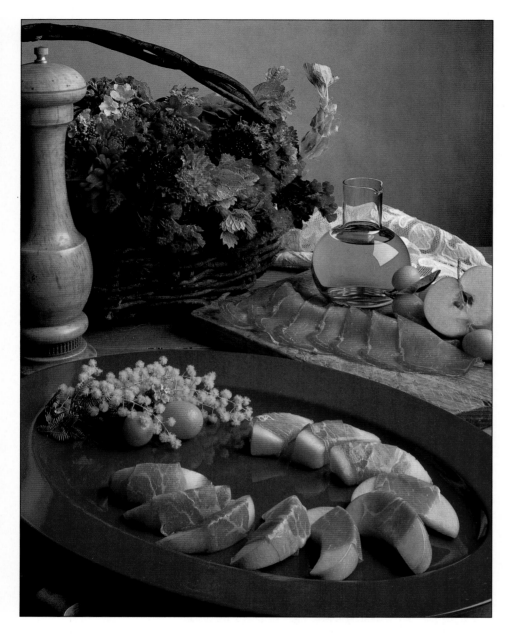

Prosciutto and melon—the prosciutto ultra-thin and the melon ripe and cool—make a refreshingly simple appetizer.

Winter melon is always cooked. The peeled and diced flesh is added to stir-fries, especially with pork, chicken, or shellfish. A half melon may be carved out, steamed, and used as a decorative container for other foods, most often for a soup made with the pulp. Sugar-glazed winter melon is eaten as candy.

Fresh winter melon is sold in Asian markets in late summer and fall. Because it is so large, many markets sell it in pieces; it should preferably be cut to order. Select uncut melon that appears plump and well shaped. Cut melon should look juicy. Cover cut surfaces with plastic wrap and refrigerate; covered and properly stored, melon will keep three to five days.

To prepare, cut away all green rind. Halve melon; scoop out and discard seeds and fibrous center. Cut up flesh as recipe directs.

■ MELON . . . OR PAPAYA . . . OR PEAR . . . OR MANGO WITH PROSCIUTTO

The combination of prosciutto and melon may be commonplace in Italian restaurants, but that doesn't mean it's dull. All that's required is paper-thin prosciutto and the sweetest, most fragrant melon you can find. The combination of salty ham with sweet, cold fruit is unforgettable. For a change of pace, or if melon is not available, substitute papaya, pear, or mango—or serve them all, complemented by a crisp, cold white wine.

  1 **large ripe, sweet melon of any variety,** *or*
    2 ripe papayas, pears, or mangoes, *or*
    any combination of these fruits
    Half a lemon
  6 **ounces prosciutto, sliced paper-thin**
    Freshly ground pepper
    Olive oil (optional)
  1 **tablespoon minced parsley, for garnish**

1. If using melon, cut away rind, then halve melon lengthwise. Scoop out seeds, then cut each half in half horizontally. Slice each quarter into pieces about ½ inch wide. If using papayas, pears, or mangoes, peel fruit, remove core or seeds, and slice into spears about ½ inch wide. Rub pears lightly with lemon to prevent browning.

2. Wrap fruit with prosciutto slices, allowing ends of fruit to show. Arrange on a serving platter. Dust with pepper, drizzle lightly with olive oil (if used), and garnish with parsley.

Serves 12.

■ WINTER MELON SOUP

This Chinese soup has gentle flavors and textures. The mild, slightly crunchy chunks of winter melon flesh absorb the flavors of a rich chicken stock, and bits of ham, ginger, and green onion provide little nuggets of stronger flavor. In a Chinese banquet, this soup is typically served inside a whole steamed winter melon, the rind of which has been decorated with carvings of dragons or other symbols of good luck. Winter melons are available at Asian markets.

  4 **cups Rich Chicken Stock (see page 561)**
  1 **ounce Smithfield ham, cut in thin slivers**
  1 **teaspoon grated fresh ginger**
    Salt and freshly ground pepper, to taste
  ½ **pound winter melon, seeded, green rind removed**
  2 **green onions, sliced**

Bring stock to a boil with ham and ginger. Season with salt and pepper. Cut winter melon flesh into wedges, and slice each wedge ¼ inch thick. Add melon and green onions to soup; simmer until melon becomes slightly translucent (about 3 minutes). Serve from pot or transfer to tureen; in either case, ham will settle to bottom, so stir soup with ladle while serving.

Serves 4 to 6.

WATERMELON SHERBET

Any of your favorite melons can be substituted for the watermelon, if desired. For a charming presentation, use this recipe instead of the Raspberry Sherbet in Frozen Watermelon Bombe, page 315. Be sure the miniature chocolate chips, which serve as "seeds," are blended into the Watermelon Sherbet as directed. For more information on making frozen desserts, see ICE CREAM AND FROZEN DESSERT.

¼ cup sugar, or more to taste
¼ teaspoon salt
1 heaping quart chilled melon chunks,
  seeds removed and juice reserved
  (the flesh from a 4-lb watermelon)
2 large egg whites

1. Sprinkle sugar and salt over watermelon chunks and mix well. Once sugar has dissolved, taste watermelon for sweetness, and add more sugar (if desired).

2. In a food processor or blender, purée melon, its juice, and egg whites. Chill well, then transfer mixture to ice cream machine and freeze according to manufacturer's instructions.

Makes about 1 quart.

Recipes and Related Information
Fresh Fruit in Wine, 347; Gadgets, 258.

MERINGUE

A meringue is a foam of beaten egg whites mixed with sugar. The term refers both to the sugar-sweetened foam and to the shells, cake layers, and other baked desserts made from it.

There are two types of meringue, soft and hard, depending on the proportion of sugar to egg whites in the mixture. The soft type has less sugar and is used as a topping for pies and baked Alaska. Hard meringue has more sugar and is shaped into containers for fruits or cream, or piped into cookie kisses and other fanciful baked confections. Versatile Italian meringue possesses the characteristics of both hard and soft meringues and is used in similar ways.

MAKING MERINGUE

When making any meringue, the two most important steps in the process are whipping the egg whites to maximum volume without overbeating and adding the sugar slowly but thoroughly at the proper time so that it is completely incorporated and dissolved. Sugar sweetens the foam and helps it set in the oven, but if added to the whites too soon, it slows their ability to froth. If you are using an electric mixer, which works so fast that the whites can be overbeaten almost before you know it, adding some sugar earlier in the whipping process will work to your advantage. Its delaying action will counteract the speed of the machine. To add sugar, beat egg whites to soft peaks, beat in approximately 1 teaspoon sugar per egg white (or as directed in recipe), beat to stiff peaks, then by hand fold in remaining sugar (in two or three batches, depending upon amount). For a complete discussion of beating egg whites, see EGG. Keep these points in mind as well.

- Eggs beat to greatest volume at room temperature, but separate easiest when cold.

- Keep all equipment—beaters and bowls—completely free of fat. Even a speck of fat can reduce the volume of beaten egg whites by as much as two thirds.

- A copper bowl and wire balloon whisk produce a superior egg white foam. If you don't use copper, add a pinch of cream of tartar to the whites just as they start to foam. A stainless steel bowl is the next best choice. Avoid these materials: aluminum, which will gray the egg whites; glass, which is slippery; and plastic, which is too difficult to clean so that it is absolutely fat-free.

- Although granulated sugar is used most often when making a soft meringue, you can, if desired, substitute superfine sugar, which is very easily incorporated and absorbs excess moisture from the whites that would otherwise bead on the surface of the meringue. Granulated sugar can be ground fine in a clean coffee grinder, electric minichopper, or food processor.

PROBLEMS AND HOW TO CORRECT THEM

Common problems with meringue are weeping (liquid oozing out of a meringue topping), beading (drops of amber sugar syrup forming on a meringue as it bakes), and an undesirable sticky, spongy texture. Weather is often the culprit. Making meringue on a humid or rainy day may cause the sugar to absorb moisture from the air. This moisture will end up as beads on the surface of the meringue or will produce a meringue that is soft and gooey. Beading is also the result of overworking the sugar in the foam or failing to dissolve it fully, not baking the meringue right away, undercooking, or baking at too high a temperature. Removing a hard meringue from the oven before it has dried out completely can give it a gummy, limp texture; it will be difficult to remove from the baking sheet. A fully cooked, properly dried out meringue will release without difficulty.

STORING MERINGUE

Once baked, meringues will stay crisp up to two weeks packaged airtight in a plastic bag and then in a sealed container. If you live in a humid climate, store them frozen. Pies don't store well; it's best to bake and serve them the same day. Let them sit out in a cool place until they are ready to eat.

HOW TO MAKE MERINGUE SHAPES

Meringue Disk   *Draw a circle the size of the disk; beginning in center, pipe meringue in a spiral to fill circle.*

Meringue Kiss   *For each kiss, point pastry bag straight down and let a small amount of meringue fall onto baking sheet. Pull back to cut off flow of meringue.*

Meringue Shell   *Hold pastry bag at an angle and squeeze out meringue to form oval of desired size.*

■ HARD MERINGUE

Swiss meringue

This is what most of us recognize as meringue. Light, delicate, and crumbly, it melts to a creamy texture when softened with a filling. This softening eases cutting and mingles the flavors, so fill about an hour or so before serving. Hard meringue is baked at very low heat, more to dry it out than actually cook it. A very white color is desirable, so don't let meringue brown.

> **4 egg whites, at room temperature**
> **Pinch cream of tartar (optional)**
> **1 cup plus 2 tablespoons sugar**

1. In a stainless steel or copper bowl, beat egg whites to soft peaks (if bowl is stainless steel, add pinch cream of tartar to whites when just foamy). Add 2 tablespoons sugar and continue to beat until stiff, glossy peaks form.

2. Gently fold in remaining sugar, taking care not to overwork meringue or it will deflate. Use immediately as directed in recipe.

Makes two 9-inch disks, five dozen kisses, or twelve to sixteen 3-inch shells.

Meringue Disks   Preheat oven to 200° F. Line two baking sheets with parchment paper. Draw a 9-inch circle on the back of each piece of parchment paper.

To make with a pastry bag: Fill pastry bag fitted with a ½-inch plain tube tip half full with meringue. Working from center of circle out, let meringue fall from bag and move in concentric rings to form two 9-inch solid disks of meringue. Refill bag as necessary.

To make by hand: With a spoon spread meringue evenly on the parchment inside of the two circles.

Bake until crisp (1 to 1½ hours; if meringues begin to brown, reduce temperature to 150° F). When done, meringues will pull away easily from parchment paper. Remove from oven and cool on paper on wire racks. To serve, sandwich layers of buttercream, whipped cream, or mousse between disks, or use as desired. If not using immediately, package in a plastic storage bag or wrap in plastic wrap and store airtight until needed.

Meringue Kisses   Preheat oven to 200° F. Line a baking sheet with parchment paper.

To make with a pastry bag: Fill pastry bag fitted with a ½-inch plain tip or number 4 rose tip half full with meringue. Hold pastry bag ½ inch above baking sheet, and with tip pointing straight down, press bag until a kiss of the desired size is formed, then pull back.

To make by hand: Drop by rounded teaspoons onto parchment-lined baking sheet. For larger kisses, use a tablespoon.

Bake until crisp (45 to 60 minutes; if meringues begin to brown, reduce temperature to 150° F). When done, meringues will pull away easily from parchment paper. Remove from oven and cool on paper on wire racks. Use

immediately, or package in a plastic storage bag or in plastic wrap and store in an airtight container until ready to use.

Meringue Shells   Resembling little eggs, these shells have an oval shape. Preheat oven to 200° F. Line a baking sheet with parchment paper.

To make with a pastry bag: Fill a pastry bag fitted with a ½- to ¾-inch plain or star tip half full with meringue. Hold pastry bag at 45-degree angle and squeeze out meringue until desired width. Continue to squeeze, drawing bag toward you to create characteristic oval shape and smooth surface; stop pressure and pull back.

To make by hand: Scoop up meringue with a soup spoon. Transfer meringue to a second spoon by sliding bowl of spoon under meringue to scoop it off first spoon. Repeat movement between spoons until desired shape. Carefully drop onto parchment-lined baking sheet. Or, for more irregularly shaped meringues, scoop up meringue with a soup spoon and drop onto parchment-lined baking sheet.

Bake until crisp (1 to 1½ hours; if meringues begin to brown, reduce temperature to 150° F). When done, meringues will pull away easily from parchment paper. Cool on paper on wire rack. To serve, sandwich two meringue shells together with whipped cream. Accompany with fresh raspberry or other fruit sauce. If not using right away, package in a plastic storage bag or wrap in plastic wrap and store in an airtight container until needed.

■ SOFT MERINGUE

This meringue is used as a topping for pies and other desserts. It is a recipe you will probably use often. Amounts are given for 8-, 9-, and 10-inch pies.

For an 8- or 9-inch pie

> **3 egg whites, at room temperature**
> **¼ teaspoon cream of tartar (optional)**
> **¼ teaspoon cornstarch**
> **4 tablespoons superfine sugar**
> **½ teaspoon vanilla extract**

For a 10-inch pie

> **5 egg whites, at room temperature**
> **½ teaspoon cream of tartar (optional)**
> **½ teaspoon cornstarch**
> **6 tablespoons superfine sugar**
> **¾ teaspoon vanilla extract**

1. In a stainless steel or copper bowl, beat egg whites until foamy. Add cornstarch (if bowl is stainless steel, also add cream of tartar) and add 1 tablespoon sugar. Continue to beat until stiff peaks form.

2. Gently fold in vanilla, then remaining sugar, taking care not to overwork meringue. Use as directed in recipe.

Makes topping for 8-, 9-, or 10-inch pie.

DACQUOISE

This is a hard Swiss meringue with ground almonds added for flavor and extra texture. You will see *dacquoise* under various names: Broyage, Progrès, Japonais, and Succès. The difference is primarily in the proportion of sugar to nuts. Almond meal made of nuts ground with their skins will be darker than meal made with ground blanched almonds.

    1½ cups ground almonds
    1½ cups sugar
     6 egg whites
     ½ teaspoon cream of tartar (optional)

1. In a small bowl combine ground almonds with all but 2 tablespoons of the sugar. Follow directions for Hard Meringue (opposite page), substituting sugar-almond mixture for plain sugar.

2. Follow directions for preparing Meringue Disks (opposite page). Use as needed.

Makes three 8-inch disks or two 9- to 10-inch disks.

ITALIAN MERINGUE

There are many ways to use this hybrid between hard and soft meringues—as a topping for baked Alaska, as a base for many frozen desserts, and as the foundation for numerous frostings. Italian meringue has the highest proportion of sugar to egg whites; it pipes very well, and holds its shape well. Anything made with Swiss meringue can be made with Italian meringue, but it will be drier, crunchier, and more powdery. This meringue is also more stable than Swiss meringue, so it needn't be used immediately, and can even be refrigerated.

    1½ cups sugar
     ½ cup water
     4 egg whites
        Pinch cream of tartar (optional)

1. In a medium, heavy-bottomed saucepan (preferably a copper sugar pot), combine sugar and the water. Cook, stirring, over low heat until all the sugar has dissolved. Cook without stirring until the soft-ball stage (238° F on a candy thermometer) is reached.

2. As sugar syrup cooks, whip egg whites to soft peaks in a stainless steel or copper bowl (if bowl is stainless steel, add cream of tartar to whites when just foamy). Time this process so that egg whites are ready when sugar reaches soft-ball stage.

3. Remove sugar from heat. With electric mixer on high or beating furiously by hand with a whisk, slowly pour onto egg whites in a thin stream. Continue to whip mixture until it cools (8 to 10 minutes). Use meringue as recipe directs.

Makes two 9-inch disks, five dozen kisses, or twelve to sixteen 3-inch shells.

ALMOND MERINGUE CAKE

Three layers of crisp almond meringue (*dacquoise*) are filled with Chocolate and Praline Buttercream or Coffee and Chocolate Buttercream (see page 248) and decorated with a border of buttercream rosettes.

    1 recipe (three 8-inch disks) Dacquoise (at left)
    3 cups Buttercream Frosting (see page 248)
       Toasted hazelnuts or almonds (optional),
       for garnish

To assemble cake: For an even-sided cake, carefully trim each of the three layers of Dacquoise to form an 8-inch circle. Use a sharp knife to avoid cracking meringue. There are two ways to fill layers with buttercream. You may either spread it on with a knife or decoratively pipe it onto each layer with a pastry bag fitted with an open-star tip. Decorate the top with stars and rosettes of buttercream. Small, whole, toasted hazelnuts or almonds can be used to decorate the center of each rosette.

Serves 8.

Variation Spread buttercream on the first two layers of meringue. Place third layer on top. Ice sides. Press toasted, chopped nuts onto sides of cake. Dust top with confectioners' sugar or decorate with rosettes.

Mousse Meringue Cake Prepare Chocolate Mousse (see page 127). Ice first two layers of meringue with mousse. Place third layer on top. Ice sides with mousse. Press chopped, toasted slivered almonds on sides of cake. Lightly dust top with confectioners' sugar. Cover and chill until ready to serve.

Layers of almond meringue separated by buttercream filling will enhance any table. For extra texture, press chopped nuts into the sides of the frosted cake.

PAVLOVA

A famous New Zealand dessert, Pavlova is said to have been created to commemorate a visit to that country by the well-known Russian ballerina, Anna Pavlova. It traditionally uses fruits from that part of the world—kiwifruit, passion fruit, bananas, and pineapple. Improved shipping has made exotic fruit more widely available in this country, but if you are unable to find the more unusual ones, any ripe fruit in season may be served. Select fruit with some acidity to balance the sweetness of the meringue. Note that the assembled Pavlova must refrigerate for at least one hour before serving, and then needs to sit out to warm to room temperature.

    1½ cups sugar
     2 tablespoons cornstarch
     6 egg whites
     ½ teaspoon cream of tartar (optional)
     1 teaspoon fresh lemon juice or vinegar
     1 teaspoon vanilla extract
     1 cup whipping cream
        Kiwifruit, passion fruit, pineapple, banana,
        mango, or other tropical fruit in season,
        prepared and attractively cut in pieces

1. Preheat oven to 250° F. Line a baking sheet with parchment paper. Draw a 6- or 7-inch circle on the paper to use as a guide. Set aside 3 tablespoons sugar. In a small bowl sift together remaining sugar and cornstarch to aerate and blend.

2. In a stainless steel or copper bowl, whip egg whites to soft peaks (if bowl is stainless steel, add cream of tartar to whites when just foamy). Add the 3 tablespoons sugar and continue to whip until stiff, glossy peaks form. Gently fold in half the sugar-cornstarch mixture. Add lemon juice, vanilla, and remaining sugar-cornstarch mixture; gently fold in.

3. Pour egg white mixture onto center of circle drawn on parchment paper. Shape meringue into a round approximately 6 to 7 inches in diameter, with sides higher than center so there is a small well in center. Bake until crisp on outside and firm to the touch (1 to 1½ hours). Let meringue shell cool on baking sheet in oven with door propped open.

4. One hour before serving, whip cream to soft peaks. Spread over center of baked shell and approximately halfway up sides. Decoratively arrange prepared fruit over whipped cream and refrigerate for at least 1 hour to let meringue soften and flavors blend. Serve at room temperature.

Serves 6.

Recipes and Related Information
Copper Egg-White Bowl, 155; Cream of Tartar, 162; Egg, 194; Whisk, 608.

MICROWAVE OVEN

The microwave oven is fast becoming America's most popular major appliance, according to manufacturers' sales figures. More than half of all homes in the U.S. have one, and the number is growing. Microwave cookery is quick, cool, and clean. Many foods cook in one fourth the time and with less energy than they would in a conventional oven or on a surface cooking unit. The microwave oven emits no heat—only the food gets hot—so the kitchen and the cook stay comfortably cool. Cleanup and maintenance are easy. Because food doesn't bake onto the dish or the oven walls, equipment and utensils wash clean with a sponge and soapy water, and the oven requires only an occasional wipe with a damp cloth to remove spills and spatters. Microwave ovens plug into regular household current and are sold in a range of sizes to fit into almost any space, so most kitchens can easily accommodate one.

HOW DOES IT WORK?

Microwaves are short, high-frequency radio waves. They are reflected by metal but pass through glass, paper, ceramic, and some plastics; they are attracted to the moisture, fat, and sugar content of food.

A magnetron tube inside each microwave oven converts electricity into high-frequency energy—the microwaves—and transmits the microwaves into the oven cavity. Because of their special properties, microwaves bounce off the metallic oven walls and are absorbed by food (they only penetrate a few inches, however). Inside the food, microwaves cause water molecules to vibrate very rapidly and rub against one another and adjoining molecules. This friction produces heat, which cooks the food as the heat travels toward the center of the food by conduction.

WHEN TO USE A MICROWAVE OVEN

The foods that do best in a microwave oven are those that are cooked in a conventional oven with moist heat. Because cooking time is brief and little water is used, vegetables retain vivid color, crisp texture, and valuable nutrients; fish is juicy, firm, and delicately flavored in minutes; and stews, casseroles, and sauced foods are done in less time and have minimal cleanup.

Microwave ovens are the ideal complement to the home freezer. With defrost capability, a microwave oven can thaw a frozen dish and then heat the food to serving temperature. Reheated foods stay fresh, with no warmed-over taste.

OTHER FACTORS TO CONSIDER

The microwave oven is a kitchen miracle worker for many tasks, but it isn't perfect. It will not brown most foods or produce a crisp crust, which limits its appropriateness for cooking meats and baking. Those baked goods that do not need a browned top—for instance, a sheet cake that will be frosted—may still not be as good when baked in a microwave oven as they would be when baked conventionally; the microwave performs best with rich batters baked in a round pan. Some dishes cook unevenly (this may be less of a problem with newer models). Bringing a liquid to a boil can take every bit as long in a microwave oven as on top of the stove, and cooking in large quantities can also negate the time savings. It's also quite easy—because of the unfamiliarity with either the oven or the recipe—to overcook foods. And it can be difficult to feel comfortable with a new cooking technology.

Enrolling in a microwave cooking class is a way to learn what the oven does best and how this appliance can be integrated into your individual cooking style. Introductory classes are sometimes offered by the retailer. Certainly read through the instruction booklet that accompanies your oven to become familiar with the features of that particular model and with microwave cooking in general.

WHICH OVEN FOR YOU?

Microwave ovens offer many options. They come full-size, midsize, and compact; portable or built-in; paired with a full-sized conventional oven in one unit, or combined with a convection oven in one unit.

For optimum benefits from the microwave, it's probably best to buy a single-purpose oven. If counter space is at a premium in your kitchen, lightweight models can be hung under a cabinet, or an oven can be set into existing cabinet space. Keep in mind, however, that smaller models usually hold less, which won't matter for one or two people, but it makes a difference when cooking for four or more. A smaller model is also less powerful—which means slower cooking.

Look for an oven with at least four power levels—High, Medium, Low, and Defrost. Some ovens have just one setting that is basically useful only for reheating; other models have as many as ten settings. Each setting corresponds to a percentage of power. Generally, High is 100 percent power, Medium is 50 percent power, and so on. Be sure to check manufacturer's instructions to learn with what percentage your oven is operating at each setting.

Most full-sized ovens feature 600 to 720 watts, and most recipes are written for ovens of this wattage. Some smaller ovens have less wattage, and therefore less power, at each setting. Recipes must be adjusted accordingly. Manufacturer's directions will guide you in making adjustments. It is increasingly common for recipes developed for the microwave oven to note the wattage required to prepare the dish in the specified amount of time.

MICROWAVE COOKING

As with most cooking, experience is the best teacher for using the microwave. The sooner you incorporate the microwave oven into your daily routine, the more quickly you will gain confidence and realize its full potential as a timesaving appliance.

Microwave cooking is based on time, not heat. To avoid overcooking, keep in mind the following variables:
- Shape of food: Thin pieces cook faster.
- Temperature at start of cooking: Chilled foods take longer to heat.
- Amount of food: When you double the quantity, the cooking time is nearly doubled.
- Composition of food: Low-moisture, high-fat, and high-sugar content foods cook faster.
- Density of food: Porous foods cook faster.
- Oven power: Ovens with higher wattage ratings cook faster at each power setting.
- Carryover cooking: Food continues to heat internally even after it is removed from the microwave, so always undercook to avoid drying out the food.

Because of all these variables, no recipe can give the exact instructions you will need for optimum results. Recipes should be considered guides to successful microwave cooking; some experimentation with your particular oven, as well as careful checking as dishes cook, will be required.

Uneven cooking—a major problem—is the result of uneven microwave penetration. Microwaves are attracted to corners and edges. In new models, stirrer fans in the oven wall help distribute the energy in a better pattern. Turntables serve the same purpose. To assure even heating, put the quickest-cooking area of the food in the center; arrange food in a circular pattern or use round dishes, if possible; rotate food during cooking time; stir food to bring cooked edges in and still-raw center portions out.

In microwave cooking, food is often covered to control moisture loss or to prevent spattering. If a recipe calls for a cover, use a tight-fitting lid or plastic wrap. For protection against spattering, use waxed paper, a paper towel, or a paper napkin. With high temperatures, pierce plastic wrap or lift a corner to allow steam to escape.

REHEATING AND DEFROSTING BAKED GOODS AT 50 PERCENT POWER

Baked goods can quickly dry out—even to the point of becoming rock hard—if overcooked. Try the shorter time first, and briefly return food to the microwave oven, if needed. Take into account that internal heat will continue to warm the food after it is removed from the microwave (carryover cooking).

Servings	Starting at Room Temperature	Starting Frozen
1	10–30 seconds	30 seconds–1 minute
2	15–40 seconds	45 seconds–1¼ minutes
3	20–50 seconds	1–1½ minutes
4	30–60 seconds	1½–2 minutes

Aside from wattage, other options include a temperature probe, dial or touch panel control, racks, turntables (developed to correct uneven cooking, they limit the size of the cooking dish to one that fits the turntable), clocks, and electronic programming, which permits multistage cooking—defrost/reheat or cook/hold, for example. The features you need will depend upon how you intend to use your oven. Some stores will allow you to exchange your oven for another model within a certain period of time if you decide that your first choice wasn't the right one.

Heating Liqueur Heat brandy or other liqueur for flamed entrées and desserts 30 to 45 seconds at 100 percent power.

Opening Bivalves: Clams, Mussels, Oysters Soak and scrub shellfish in cold water, then arrange in a circle on a paper-towel–lined glass plate. Cover tightly with plastic wrap; cook at 100 percent power until shells open slightly (half a dozen oysters or a dozen mussels or clams takes 1 to 1½ minutes). Remove from oven and finish opening by hand.

Poaching Chicken To cook chicken breasts for use in salads, soups, and fillings for entrées, microwave half of a breast in a covered casserole with ¼ cup vermouth or chicken stock and ¼ cup green onion for 8 to 10 minutes; cool and cut up.

Popcorn Regular popcorn is only moderately successful when cooked by this method, leaving many unpopped kernels. If you wish to make popcorn in the microwave oven, use popcorn specially packaged for microwave use.

Precooking The microwave oven can speed up outdoor grilling and produce more tender and juicy meats. For example, cook ribs, roasts, or fowl on 50 percent power until about half done, then transfer to the grill to finish cooking.

Reheating Foods The microwave oven is almost unsurpassed in maintaining taste and texture when reheating foods. Points to remember include the following: 1. To reheat frozen foods, first thaw in refrigerator for easier reheating; 2. to attain even results, choose a dish close to the size of the food you are reheating; 3. to avoid overheating, begin reheating on 100 percent power, then lower to 50 percent power; 4. to reheat foods that absorb water during the initial cooking process (rice, noodles, vegetables, casseroles), add more cooking liquid (2 tablespoons per cup of food) to help food reheat evenly; 5. to reheat more than one item, reheat the food that can maintain the longest standing time first, then others in descending order (for example, a casserole, then a vegetable, then breads).

Steaming Fish Steam 1 pound of fish in its own juices until moist and tender in 5 to 6 minutes. It will taste as if it were poached.

WHAT NOT TO MICROWAVE

Microwave cooking saves time and effort over conventional cooking in many cases. Some food's appearance, texture, and flavor are enhanced. However, certain dishes cannot be cooked in a microwave as successfully or as fast as with conventional methods.

Deep-fried Foods Do not attempt to deep-fry in the microwave oven; temperature cannot be controlled and fats may spatter.

Eggs in Shells Cook eggs in their shells by conventional methods; they may burst during microwave cooking.

Foods With Crisp, Browned Surfaces Crispness and browning are best accomplished with conventional cooking methods.

Home-Canned Goods Since safe internal temperatures cannot be accurately maintained, home canning should not be done in the microwave oven.

Pancakes and Crêpes Although they can be warmed in the microwave oven, these foods need surface cooking to brown and crisp properly.

Rice, Dried Beans, and Pasta Although rice cooks well in a microwave oven, no time is saved; dried beans and pasta also cook in the same amount of time as with conventional methods.

Turkey For a bird over 15 pounds, conventional cooking is easier.

MILK

In the United States, the word *milk* commonly refers to cow's milk, although goats and sheep are valuable sources of milk outside the U.S. Milk as it comes from the cow is highly nutritious. It is a good source of protein (primarily from casein, a complete protein), carbohydrates (from lactose, a milk sugar that aids mineral absorption), fats (low-fat and nonfat milk have less fat), vitamins A, D, and B-2 (riboflavin), and minerals (especially calcium and phosphorus). Because milk is so nutritious, however, it is host to many microbes and is easily contaminated. For this reason, most milk is processed further (pasteurized) before it is sold.

Use Undoubtedly a large share of the milk consumed in the U.S. is consumed as a beverage. Milk is also an ingredient of major importance to the home cook. Milk provides the base for other beverages: hot and cold cocoa, eggnog, and milk shakes, for example. It adds richness and softens bitter beverages such as coffee and tea. Milk moistens dry breakfast cereal and enriches hot cereal. It may be used in place of water or stock to give body and flavor to soups; fish chowders, for example, are usually milk based.

Milk plays a major role in the making of sauces, both sweet and savory. The classic custard sauce (*crème anglaise*) is milk based. One of the most basic savory sauces, béchamel, and its many derivatives are milk based. Milk is the primary liquid in most puddings, soufflés, and custards, including bread pudding, corn pudding, and *crème caramel*. Many ice creams, despite their name, are made with milk instead of cream; some fruit sherbets get their body from milk.

Due to its milk fat, milk adds moisture and richness to cakes, cookies, and bread doughs. It makes breads brown better, improves their keeping qualities, and gives a creamier, softer crumb. It is also the liquid of choice for most batters, including those for muffins, coffee cakes, waffles, popovers, and crêpes. Buttermilk is sometimes used for the tangy flavor it imparts to baked goods.

Milk is sometimes used as a soaking medium. Fish is dipped in milk before coating and frying in order to provide a moist surface to which the coating will adhere. Some cooks soak fish or chicken livers in milk for about an hour to rid them of strong flavors.

Poaching liquids for fish, sweetbreads, and cauliflower sometimes include milk to keep these foods white. Milk does not figure heavily in meat cookery. One exception, however, is the Italian favorite pork loin braised in milk; the milk cooks down into rich, nutty clumps that the Italians call *bruti ma buoni* (ugly but good).

Milk as it comes from the cow yields butter and cream; it is also the starting point for all yogurt and cheese.

Availability The following remarks should clarify the differences among the many milk products available on supermarket shelves.

Acidophilus Milk A cultured milk, acidophilus is pasteurized skim or low-fat milk with a bacterial culture added. The milk is immediately packaged and cooled, however, to prevent fermentation; thus it retains the flavor and texture of uncultured milk. When consumed, the bacterial culture is activated at body temperature. It is believed that these bacteria help maintain the balance of beneficial microorganisms in the intestinal tract. Acidophilus milk is often recommended for people taking antibiotics.

Buttermilk Originally, buttermilk was the milky residue from churning cream into butter. Today commercial buttermilk is made by adding bacterial cultures to pasteurized milk (usually skim milk). The cultures convert the milk sugar (lactose) into lactic acid, producing a tartness in the buttermilk. Some processors add butter flakes to approximate the buttermilk of yesteryear. Buttermilk is drunk as a beverage by those who appreciate its smooth, creamy texture and buttery flavor. It adds a rich, creamy tang to cold soups and salad dressings; it imparts flavor and tenderness to pancakes, biscuits, quick breads, and cakes.

Chocolate Milk This is pasteurized whole milk flavored with chocolate or cocoa and sweeteners. Chocolate low-fat and nonfat milks are also marketed.

Condensed Milk (also known as concentrated milk) Although similar to evaporated milk, condensed milk has usually not been heat-treated for sterilization. Sweetened condensed milk is condensed milk with sweetener (usually sugar) added. It contains 40 to 45 percent sugar and cannot be substituted for evaporated milk in recipes.

Evaporated Milk and Evaporated Skimmed Milk Both of these products have been heated to remove about 60 percent of their water, then sealed in cans and heat-treated for sterilization. One half cup of evaporated milk can be reconstituted with an equal amount of water to make 1 cup whole milk.

Extra-rich Milk This form of milk contains either slightly more milk fat or slightly more nonfat milk solids.

Homogenized Milk Most milk is homogenized after pasteurization, although homogenization is optional under federal standards. Homogenization is a method of dispersing milk fat throughout the milk to keep it from rising to the top as cream. After pasteurization, the milk is pumped at high pressure through extremely small openings and onto a hard surface. This breaks up the fat globules into such small particles that they remain dispersed in the liquid.

Low-Fat Milk Some of the milk fat has been skimmed away to produce this product; it usually retains about 2 percent milk fat.

Nonfat Dry Milk (also known as powdered milk) To make nonfat dry milk, the water is removed from pasteurized skim milk. It reconstitutes readily in warm water. Instant nonfat dry milk reconstitutes readily in cold water. These products are valued for their convenience and their long shelf life. They are also widely used in packaged mixes (such as cake and pudding mixes). Many commercial bakers find dry milk easier to work with than liquid milk.

Pasteurized Milk To destroy potentially harmful microbes and improve its keeping quality, most milk is pasteurized: It is heated to 161° F and maintained at that temperature for 15 seconds. Ultrapasteurized milk is heated to 280° F and held there for at least two seconds; this process extends the refrigerated shelf life even further. Ultra-high-temperature (UHT) processed milk is treated like ultrapasteurized milk but is then packaged in sterilized containers and aseptically sealed. It may be safely stored unrefrigerated for at least three months.

Raw Milk Milk shipped in interstate commerce must be pasteurized. Some states allow intrastate shipment of raw (unpasteurized) milk from certified herds. Because raw milk has not been pasteurized, it contains potentially disease-producing microbes and has a shorter refrigerated shelf life.

Skim or Nonfat Milk To be labeled skim or nonfat, milk must be skimmed of as much fat as possible. Milk fat content must be less than 0.5 percent.

Whole Milk To be labeled whole milk, a product must contain at least 3.5 percent milk fat and 8.6 percent solids that are not fat (proteins, carbohydrates, minerals, and vitamins).

TIPS

CALORIES IN MILK

Calorie counters may want to know that whole milk supplies about 160 calories per cup; low-fat milk, 140 calories; and skim milk, 90 calories. Because of its significantly lower fat content, skim milk cannot readily be substituted for whole milk in recipes. If calories are unimportant, 1 cup skim milk plus 1 tablespoon cream can be substituted for 1 cup whole milk in most cases.

Storage Fluid milk is highly perishable. It should be one of the last purchases in the supermarket and should be refrigerated immediately at home. Keep opened milk containers closed to prevent milk from absorbing other odors. Milk kept at room temperature for at least 30 minutes (in a milk pitcher, for example) should not be poured back into the original container. Refrigerate it in a separate container. Dry milk will keep indefinitely in a cool, dry place; store in an airtight container after opening. Reconstituted dry milk should be refrigerated. Unopened canned milk will keep indefinitely in a cool place; pour any unused canned milk into a clean container and refrigerate.

Pull Date All milk sold in interstate commerce is marked with a pull date to indicate when the product should be withdrawn from retail sale. The pull date is intentionally conservative to allow for additional storage time in the consumer's refrigerator.

Preparation Although many modern bread recipes instruct cooks to scald milk to destroy bacteria that might hamper the development of yeast, the pasteurized milk available today renders this step unnecessary. Some recipes call for heating milk for other reasons, however—dissolving sugar or melting shortening, for instance.

> **Recipes and Related Information**
> *Basic White Sauce, 513; Cheese Sauce, 513; Crème Caramel, 169; Down-Home Mashed Potatoes, 466; New England Clam Chowder, 539; Scalloped Potatoes, 465.*

MINCE, TO

Strictly defined, *mince* means to cut food into the finest dice possible, into pieces of even size. However, in common usage it has come to mean to chop very finely. Parsley is an ingredient that is typically minced.

MINT

The mint family of perennial herbs is quite large and includes such varied members as spearmint, peppermint, pineapple mint, pennyroyal, orange bergamot, and apple mint. Spearmint is most often used in cooking, although the others may be substituted. Mints have a strong aroma, a sweet, slightly hot flavor, and a cool aftertaste.

Use Whole mint leaves are often used to garnish salads or beverages; crushed mint leaves are important to some cocktails, particularly mint julep. Minced mint leaves add a cool, refreshing quality to coleslaw and fruit salads; mint also flatters peas, beets, carrots, onions, and cucumbers. Fresh mint contributes a delightful cool flavor to spicy

Thai and Vietnamese salads and is used in the filling for Vietnamese spring rolls. Indian cooks incorporate mint in chutneys and curries. Moroccans make an aromatic sweet tea with mint leaves. Crushed mint leaves are also used to make the sweet jelly served with roast lamb in many English and American homes. Italian cooks employ mint in stuffings, vegetable soups, and dried bean dishes.

Mint extract and oil of mint are ingredients in a variety of desserts and confections, including ice cream, peppermint candies, and chocolate-covered mints. Mint and chocolate are often paired in desserts and candies; mint and fruit are another compatible team.

Availability Fresh mint is sold in some markets all year, with peak supplies in summer. Dried mint leaves, packed in jars and tins, are available on most supermarket spice racks. Mint extract is also widely sold in supermarkets.

Selection Choose fresh mint that show no signs of wilting or decay. For dried mint, keep in mind that packaged seasonings lose quality after a while; try to buy from a store that restocks its spice section fairly often.

Storage Prop fresh mint in a tall glass of water, cover with a plastic bag, and refrigerate; change water daily and use within three or four days. Store dried mint in a cool, dry, dark place; replace every year.

Preparation Wash and dry fresh mint; remove leaves from stalk; use whole or minced. Rub dried mint between fingers to release aromatic oils before adding to a dish.

> **Recipes and Related Information**
> *Cucumber-Mint Sauce, 294; Mint Jelly, 321; Tabbouleh, 277.*

MIREPOIX

A combination of aromatic vegetables added to soups, stocks, braises, and roasts, *mirepoix* increases the flavor of the food but is not necessarily included as part of the final dish. Mirepoix can be strained away or later puréed, mixed with pan juices, and used as sauce. Onions, celery, carrots, leeks, and sometimes parsnips are the classic mirepoix vegetables. *Brunoise* is a similar preparation, but the vegetables are cut in finer pieces (see BRUNOISE).

MIX, TO

To combine ingredients so that the result is blended and homogenous, or so that each substance is still somewhat distinguishable from one another but evenly dispersed.

MIXERS

There is no better way to whip cream, beat egg whites, and mix up light, airy cake batters than with an electric mixer. There are two types of mixers: portable and stand. The portable or handheld version is the simplest; the cook holds the machine with the beaters

inserted into a freestanding bowl and controls the movements of the mixer.

Portable mixers differ from one another primarily in power and speed settings. The high-quality ones may also come with dough hooks for kneading, and a few can be attached to a separate base that allows the mixer to function also as a stand mixer. Handheld mixers are lightweight, easy to store, and can be moved around the kitchen. On the other hand, the cook can't do other tasks while holding the mixer, and holding it can be tiring. Some portable mixers fade when working on stiff doughs.

Stand mixers range from light to heavy-duty. Electronic controls help maintain speed as the mixture gets heavier; some also have a timer. Bowl capacity is usually around 4 quarts, but other sizes are available. Some are very versatile, with a flat, open, paddle-type beater, plus a balloon whisk for whipping and a dough hook for kneading. Among the attachments are food grinders, juicers, slicer/shredders, sausage stuffers, pasta makers, grain grinders, and ice jackets.

Serious bakers are advised to buy a quality, heavy-duty stand mixer. Otherwise, most mixing can be done with a good portable.

Even on lowest speeds, electric mixers are fast; dry ingredients can erupt in a cloud that settles on your counter or even in your face before you realize what's happening. If you are adding many ingredients at one time—liquid and dry—cover the dry with the wet. This will have a blanketing effect that contains the flour in the bowl and out of your face.

Rotary eggbeaters are essentially portable electric mixers without the electric capability; your muscle is their power. They will quickly whip cream, aerate pancake and crêpe batters, and beat eggs, but will bog down in heavy mixtures such as dense cake batters. They function like a whisk and should have thin, rather than flat, wires so that as much air as possible is incorporated. Gear-driven beaters have the smoothest action. In these days of electric-powered, multipurpose mixing and processing machines, does the mechanical eggbeater warrant a spot in your kitchen? By all means, if you like using this tool and if it works for you. Be sure to select a rotary beater with a handle that you can grip comfortably.

MIXING BOWL

Every kitchen needs a generous assortment of these very versatile, multipurpose bowls, matched in capacity, shape, and material to the tasks done most often. Tall, narrow shapes are best for creaming and beating; the high sides prevent liquids or solids from

flying out of the bowl onto counter or face when quickly mixed with spoon, beater, or whisk. Wide and shallow bowls keep all ingredients in view and within reach; nothing gets lost on the bottom. They work for stuffings, salads, and ground-meat mixtures. Bowls with smoothly rounded bottoms make the best molds. These kitchen indispensables should more aptly be called mixing-stirring-folding-tossing-storing-holding-serving-molding-beating-marinating-organizing-heating-cooling bowls. Most cooks could think of dozens more uses for them. In general, use bowls larger than seems necessary for the job; the extra capacity will help control messes and reduce cleanup. Look for containers that sit flat on the work surface, are easy to pick up, and are not too heavy to move and store.

Any bowl-shaped container can serve as a mixing bowl. Those specially manufactured as such, however, are usually more durable. Typical materials include stainless steel, glass, ceramic, melamine plastic, and copper (for beating egg whites; see COPPER EGG-WHITE BOWL), in 1-quart through 8-quart capacities, and often in sets of three or four bowls. Smaller sizes (less than 1 quart) are handy for beating or separating a few eggs, setting out ingredients for stir-fries or other preparations in which ingredients are added in stages, and storing. It is unnecessary to purchase matching bowls, but sets usually come in the most practical sizes and nest for more compact storage. Overall, stainless steel is the preferred material. It is highly durable, nonreactive (it won't discolor batters, doughs, or high-acid foods), and resistant to thermal shock (it can withstand sudden changes of temperature—setting hot custard in a bowl of ice water, for example).

MOLD, TO; MOLD

To form into a shape with the hands, or by putting in a container (a mold) and then chilling or cooking until the food takes on the contour of the container. The receptacle that holds the molded food is called a mold. Meat loaves and pâtés, gelatin-based dishes, and candies are molded.

A mold does just that—gives food shape. Whether the food can maintain that shape on its own depends not on the mold but on the recipe—if it has gelatin, eggs, or another binding ingredient. Sometimes a mold will have the same

Molds are used to shape many types of foods: ice cream, gelatin, and pâtés, for example. They can be made of a variety of materials and in many configurations. Molds shown from top left to right: round gelatin/aspic, soufflé, pudding, terrines, ice cream (bombe and bird), coeur à la crème, custard, ramekin, pâté, timbale, oval gelatin/aspic.

name as the food it is most often associated with: timbale, angel food cake, *Kugelhopf,* charlotte, soufflé, gratin, and muffin have given their names to the specific pans used to prepare them.

ASPIC AND GELATIN MOLDS

For chilled gelatin-based dishes, metal molds cool the fastest and set the dish in the least amount of time. Porcelain or glass dishes will work also. The simpler the mold, the easier it is to remove its contents. On the other hand, some modeling enhances the appeal of an otherwise simple preparation. Select a mold that is sculptured but without deeply modeled, fine detail that would trap food. Clear, well-defined, simple patterns transfer best.

Molds are sold in hundreds of designs—fish, animals, birds, hearts, rings, crowns, stars, and turbans—in individual to buffet sizes, and formed of tin, copper, stainless steel, plastic, glass, and ceramic. Special oval ramekins for Oeufs en Gelée (see page 266), a light luncheon dish of poached eggs set in aspic, can be found in better cookware stores. Buy for pattern and use; very decorative copper or porcelain dishes make attractive kitchen accessories.

COEUR A LA CREME MOLD

To make this classic chilled French cheese dessert (see page 111), cheese with soft curds is blended with confectioners' sugar and cream, spooned into a heart-shaped porcelain mold or wicker basket (*coeur* means heart in

French), and drained. Fresh berries are often served with it. The mold is pierced to allow the liquid to drain off. Both individual molds and larger dishes are available.

ICE CREAM MOLDS

For fancy molded ice creams, the classic shape is a bombe, which resembles half a football. This mold holds 1 to 1½ quarts and comes with a lid. Another classic is one shaped like an elongated cantaloupe with deep, widely spaced ribs. It also has a cover and is sized the same. Both designs are made of tinned steel and can double as pudding molds.

PATE MOLDS AND TERRINES

By definition, the classic pâté is a rich, baked mixture of ground meats, seasonings, and fats—a Gallic meat loaf—encased in a pastry crust (*pâté en croûte*). The classic terrine, on the other hand, is a sort of pâté without a crust, named for the earthenware dish it is baked in. Few people except the French make these distinctions any longer; most American restaurants and cookbooks use the words interchangeably. The molds for pâtés and terrines are made of tinned steel, enameled cast iron, porcelain, and earthenware. Molds for pâté en croûte range from simple loaf pans to elaborate affairs of tinned steel with hinges, clips, or pins, often fluted or otherwise patterned. The sides and bottom separate for easy removal of the baked pâté. Terrine molds are simple loaf pans with covers. They are country-style and are rectangular or oval in shape. Some are finished to resemble a pâté en croûte—with a golden surface that resembles a baked crust, fluted, crimped, and topped with the image of an animal or bird to suggest the type of pâté encased within; the interior is glazed. Sizes are 2 to 4 quarts.

PUDDING BASIN

The English have long been consummate makers and eaters of steamed pudding; most households have special slope-sided glazed ceramic bowls just for this purpose. A gauzy pudding cloth, used to cover these dishes as they steam, is lovingly cleaned and folded after each use and set aside until the next time pudding is made. The basin is traditionally deep, wide at the top, and narrow at the bottom, with a flat base. It is rimmed so that the pudding cloth has something to rest against. Capacities range from 1 to about 3 quarts. Also available are fancier tinned steel pudding molds with covers.

SOUFFLE MOLD, CUSTARD CUP, AND RAMEKIN

To rise, a soufflé requires a straight-sided, flat-bottomed dish made of a heat-conductive material that encourages rapid expansion of the air trapped in the beaten whites. Because a soufflé is served in its baking dish, the dish should be attractive enough to bring to the table. Soufflé dishes are typically made of porcelain with ridged sides that replicate the pleated paper collars used by French chefs for hundreds of years to extend the sides of the dish and allow the soufflé to rise above it. The molds are usually rimmed for easier handling. Other materials include heat-resistant glass and stoneware. Dishes are typically 1, 1½, or 2 quarts, and ovenproof, since soufflés are classically baked, but soufflé dishes are also suitable for cold soufflés and mousses, for any baked casserole, and for serving dishes.

CUSTARD CUP

These heatproof ramekins with sloping sides are sized for individual servings of creamy baked custard or pudding, but perform other functions as well. Use them to hold ingredients for stir-fries, for melting chocolate and butter in a microwave oven, for serving condiments, for beating an egg or two, and for storing small amounts of leftovers. Choose from cups made of porcelain, heatproof glass, or glazed earthenware; the most useful size is about 5 ounces. Have at least one half dozen.

RAMEKIN

Any baking dish designed for a single serving can be accurately called a ramekin. Typically ramekins resemble scaled-down soufflé dishes, are porcelain or earthenware, and hold about 4 ounces of food. Use them for custards and sweet and savory mousses.

TIMBALE MOLD

Also known as a dariole mold, *timbale* comes from the French word for kettledrum, an apt description of its shape. The term refers to both the baking dish and the creamy meat, fish, or vegetable mixture cooked in it. As a preparation, timbales have several forms; the filling can be cooked alone, in a pastry crust like a pâté en croûte, or in a shell of macaroni or potato. Today timbales are often vegetable custards served with a meat, fish, or poultry main course. The molds hold about ½ cup, are made of stainless steel, and are tall, narrow, and straight or slope sided. They double as baking pans for the rich yeast bread called baba.

Recipes and Related Information
Blue Cheese Soufflé, 205; Chilled Lemon Soufflé, 207; Custard, 168; Frozen Watermelon Bombe, 315; Gelatin, 264; Hot Lemon Soufflé, 206; Pâté and Terrine, 416; Spinach Timbales, 579.

MONOSODIUM GLUTAMATE

Also known as MSG, or by its most common brand name, Accent, monosodium glutamate is technically a sodium salt made from glutamic acid. Although the process is little understood, monosodium glutamate appears to heighten the flavors of other foods, perhaps by increasing receptivity in the taste buds. In its commercial form, MSG is a coarse white crystal that resembles coarse salt.

Many diners experience reactions to monosodium glutamate, especially if eaten on an empty stomach—for example, in a soup served as a first course in a Chinese restaurant. Common reactions are facial tightness or numbness, burning sensations, and a feeling of pressure in the chest. Symptoms rarely last more than one hour.

Use Monosodium glutamate serves as a flavor enhancer in much the same way that salt does. It is sprinkled on meats before cooking or added to soups and stir-fries. Initially used only in Japan, it is now widely found in Japanese and Chinese kitchens. At home it should always be used in small quantities, if at all; it may be omitted from any recipe calling for it, although the salt level may need to be adjusted.

Availability Monosodium glutamate is found in the spice section of most supermarkets. A popular Japanese variety, Aji-No-Moto, is sold in Japanese markets and is offered as a table condiment in many Japanese restaurants.

Storage Monosodium glutamate will keep indefinitely in a cool, dark, dry place.

MOUSSE

A French word, *mousse* means frothy, which aptly describes the light and spongy character of this dish. It has an appealing soft and creamy texture and can be savory or sweet, cold or hot.

The main ingredients of a savory mousse are ground or puréed fish, poultry, cheese, or vegetables, plus cream, and beaten egg whites or whipped cream. If served hot, it is baked in a bain-marie until firm. If cold, gelatin is sometimes added to set the mixture. A dessert mousse is chilled or even frozen. It is easily made from a base of puréed fruit or melted chocolate, which is lightened with whipped cream or beaten egg whites and often thickened with gelatin.

◼ CHILLED SAVORY MOUSSE

This cold mousse must be prepared at least four hours in advance of serving. Consider this a basic recipe and create your own versions by varying the main ingredients and seasonings. If desired, once the mousse has set, it can be covered with a thin layer of aspic and then chilled further until the aspic is firm. See Curried Chicken or Duck Liver Pâté in Aspic, page 416, for directions.

        1   pound cooked, puréed meat or fish (chicken,
            veal, ham, rabbit, or salmon)
        4   tablespoons butter, softened
        2   cups Basic White Sauce (see page 513),
            cooled to room temperature
        1   envelope unflavored gelatin
        ½   cup Chicken or Fish Stock (depending on
            main ingredient; see page 560 or 561)
        ½   cup whipping cream
            Salt and freshly ground black pepper, to taste
            Optional seasonings (choose any or all):
            ¼ teaspoon freshly grated nutmeg,
            ¼ teaspoon cayenne pepper, ½ teaspoon
            Worcestershire sauce
            Minced parsley or parsley sprigs, for garnish

1. In a large bowl blend together puréed meat and butter. Add cooled white sauce and mix with a wooden spoon until well combined or smooth (or mix in a food processor with a few short pulses so meat mixture doesn't become a paste).

2. In a small saucepan sprinkle gelatin over stock and let stand to soften (3 to 4 minutes). Dissolve gelatin over low heat; pour into meat mixture, and stir well. Whip cream to soft peaks and fold in. Taste and season with salt, pepper, and seasonings (if used).

3. Pour into a 5- to 6-cup soufflé or serving dish and smooth top. Cover tightly with plastic wrap and refrigerate at least 4 hours before serving to set mousse.

4. To serve, let sit out at room temperature at least 30 minutes. Decorate with minced parsley or parsley sprigs.

Serves 6 to 8 as a first course.

◼ CHICKEN OR DUCK LIVER MOUSSE

A beautifully glazed mousse adds beauty to a pâté and cheese buffet. Since the aspic and mousse must set for several hours or more, this dish should be prepared a day ahead. If desired, make flower petals from pieces of tomato skin and black olives, and from skins from chives (see Aspic Glaze).

        1   pound chicken or duck livers
        1   small onion, minced
        1   clove garlic, minced
        1   teaspoon salt
        ½   teaspoon dried thyme
        ¼   teaspoon allspice
        ¼   teaspoon white pepper
        6   tablespoons unsalted butter
        2   tablespoons brandy
        1   envelope unflavored gelatin
        1   cup whipping cream

Aspic Glaze

        1   recipe Basic Aspic (see page 265)
        1   tablespoon vegetable oil
            Tomato-skin cutouts, for garnish
            Chives, for garnish
            Black olive pieces, for garnish

1. Prepare Aspic Glaze. Pour 1 cup Basic Aspic into an 8-inch square baking pan and chill for at least 2 hours (this chilled aspic will be cubed and used to garnish mousse).

2. In a medium skillet sauté chicken livers, onion, garlic, salt, thyme, allspice, and pepper in 2 tablespoons butter over medium heat until livers are brown on the outside but remain pink on the inside (about 12 minutes). Remove to a blender or food processor. Add brandy to skillet, scraping cooked-on bits to loosen; add to liver.

3. In a small saucepan soften gelatin in ½ cup of the reserved Basic Aspic. Dissolve gelatin over low heat, stirring until liquid is clear (2 to 4 minutes). Add to liver and purée to a smooth paste. Remove to a medium bowl. Stir in remaining butter. Cool at room temperature until mixture thickens slightly (about 20 minutes).

4. Whip cream to soft peaks; fold into liver mixture. Carefully spoon into aspic-coated mold. Cover with plastic wrap to prevent the mousse from drying out. Chill until firm (about 4 hours).

5. To unmold, loosen sides of mold with a knife. Pour 1 inch hot water into a pan larger than mold. Place mold in the hot water for about 2 minutes to loosen. Place a serving plate (at least 3 inches larger in diameter than mold) over mousse, invert, and lift mold from mousse. Dice 8-inch square sheet of Basic Aspic into cubes and surround the mousse.

Serves 12 to 20 as an appetizer.

Aspic Glaze Prepare Basic Aspic; set aside until cool but still liquid and reserve 1 cup aspic for mousse and for glaze. Coat 5-cup mold with 1 tablespoon vegetable oil. Pour ½ cup of reserved aspic into mold. Arrange tomato-skin cutouts, chives, and black olives in a decorative pattern to form flowers on aspic (if desired). Chill until firm (about 2 hours).

▆ CHILLED FRUIT MOUSSE

A fruit mousse is easily made by thickening fruit purée with gelatin and enriching it with whipped cream. Reserve some of the berries for garnish. Like all cold, creamy mousses, this one is a boon to the busy cook because it can be prepared ahead of time.

> 2 **pints strawberries** *or* **1 pint raspberries**
> 2 **eggs**
> 2 **egg yolks**
> ½ **cup superfine sugar**
> 1 **envelope unflavored gelatin**
> ¼ **cup fresh lemon juice**
> 1 **cup whipping cream**

1. Rinse berries and pat dry; set aside some of the best-looking ones for garnish. If using strawberries, hull. Purée berries in a food processor or blender (to make 1 cup purée); strain through a fine sieve to remove seeds and set aside.

2. In a large bowl whip eggs, yolks, and sugar until thick, or until mixture drops off the beater in a ribbon. In a small saucepan sprinkle gelatin over lemon juice and let stand to soften (3 to 4 minutes). Dissolve over low heat. Pour in a thin stream into egg-sugar mixture; whip to combine. Add fruit purée and mix well. In a separate bowl whip cream to soft peaks and set aside.

3. Set bowl with mousse over ice and stir mixture until it is on the point of setting (it will have the consistency of cream whipped to soft peaks); remove from ice and fold in whipped cream. Pour immediately into a 6-cup mold or 6 individual ramekins. Refrigerate until set (2 to 3 hours). Serve with reserved berries.

Serves 6.

▆ CHOCOLATE MOUSSE TORTE

Everyone loves chocolate mousse, especially when it's encased in a chocolate cookie-crumb crust that sparkles with the addition of large crystals of raw sugar. The torte must chill at least four hours, or overnight, so it's an excellent dish to make ahead for a party.

> 2 **cups chocolate cookie crumbs (one 8½ oz package chocolate wafers, crushed)**
> ¼ **cup coarse sugar**
> ⅓ **cup unsalted butter, melted**
> 1 **recipe Chocolate Mousse (see page 127)**
> **Chantilly Cream (see page 252), for decoration**
> **Chocolate Curls (see page 126), for garnish**

1. Preheat oven to 350° F. In a medium bowl combine crumbs and sugar. Pour in melted butter and stir to coat crumb mixture evenly with butter. Press into an 8-inch springform pan; bake 10 minutes. Cool and refrigerate.

2. Prepare Chocolate Mousse; do not chill, but pour into chilled shell. Refrigerate pie at least 4 hours, or overnight.

3. To serve, remove from pan, pipe spirals of Chantilly Cream around edge, and sprinkle cream with some Chocolate Curls (if desired).

Serves 8 to 10.

A double shot of chocolate— in the filling and in the sugar-speckled crumb crust—makes Chocolate Mousse Torte a favorite dessert of chocoholics everywhere.

Recipes and Related Information

Gelatin, 264; Mousse Meringue Cake, 361; Ribbon, 498; Sole Mousse, 377.

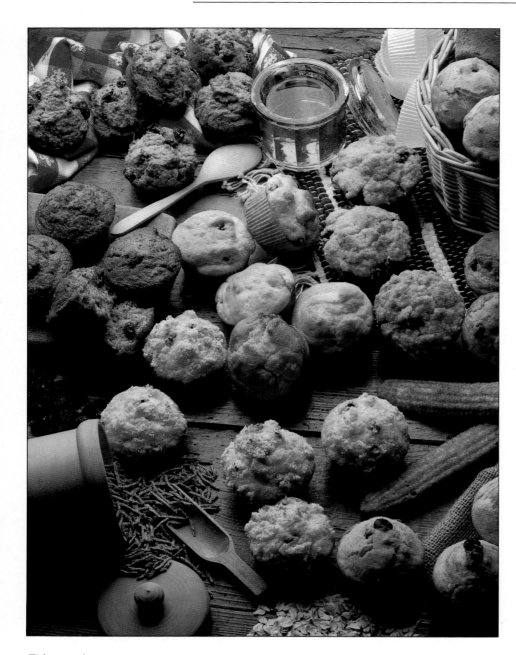

This tempting arrangement of muffins illustrates how easily this simple quick bread can be varied by changing a few ingredients.

MAKING AND BAKING MUFFINS

Mix dry ingredients thoroughly to disperse the baking powder and/or baking soda evenly. The batter should be baked as soon as liquid and dry ingredients have been combined or leavening will lose some of its punch. As a timesaver, the dry ingredients can be combined ahead of time, as can the liquids. Unless the recipe indicates that it can be prepared in advance, though, don't blend the two mixtures until you are ready to fill the muffin pan and put it in the oven.

Always grease the pan, even if it has a nonstick lining. Coat with butter, shortening, or vegetable cooking spray, or use paper cupcake liners. Buy a heavyweight muffin pan that will conduct heat well. It will last for years, and your muffins will look better because they will rise higher. Fill standard muffin cups two thirds to three fourths full (unless directed otherwise in the recipe) with a spoon or measuring cup. If there isn't enough batter to fill all the muffin cups, fill the empty ones with water so the pan won't warp. Always preheat the oven for 10 to 15 minutes, and bake on the center rack. Muffins are done when the centers spring back when pressed lightly and when a toothpick inserted in the middle comes out clean.

Turn baked muffins onto a wire rack to cool. If some stick, tap bottom of cup lightly with your knuckles. If they still won't budge, let them sit in the pan briefly; steam that develops between muffin and pan will help dislodge them. If necessary, loosen around edges with a knife.

STORING MUFFINS

Plain muffins have the shortest life span. They should be eaten soon after baking. Muffins with fruits and vegetables, and those made with oil, stay moist longer. Don't store muffins or any bread in the refrigerator; they will quickly dry out. Muffins freeze extremely well. If not eaten the day they are made, place cooled muffins in a plastic bag, seal airtight, and freeze for six to twelve months. To reheat, bake frozen muffins, wrapped in aluminum foil, at 350° F for 15 to 20 minutes, or until thawed and heated through.

MONSTER MUFFINS

Muffins have become extremely popular as a take-out breakfast bread. On the assumption that you can't have too much of a good thing, the size of muffins has risen to huge proportions. Some are as large as 4 inches across and 2 inches tall, more a minibread than a single-serving bun. Although novel, these giants are often dry, especially if they must sit on a bakery counter for any length of time. Protect oversized homemade muffins from getting stale by freezing those not eaten right away.

Any of the muffin recipes in this section may be made in giant form by filling standard muffin cups to the top and increasing the baking time to 30 to 40 minutes. This time

MUFFIN

A muffin is a quick bread made from a mixture of 2 parts flour to 1 part liquid, plus one or more eggs, sugar, and other flavoring ingredients. Baking powder or baking soda is the leavening agent.

The classic muffin has a uniform shape, large in proportion to its weight, with a gently rounded top with a surface that is pebbled, somewhat like that of a cauliflower. The crust is an even golden brown and slightly shiny. The texture should be light, moist, and evenly grained, and the flavor pleasing, without tasting of baking powder or baking soda. The standard muffin is made in a pan with cups each measuring approximately 2¾ inches wide at the top and 1½ inches deep.

is approximate; some recipes will take longer than others. Test for doneness after about 20 minutes, then every 10 minutes or so. As the muffin batter will overflow onto the top of the muffin tin, remember to grease that surface as well as the molds.

◼ BASIC MUFFINS

These basic muffins have a breadlike texture. To prepare them, the dry ingredients are typically sifted into a bowl, the liquid ingredients (including melted butter or shortening or oil) are then added together, and all are stirred just until moistened. Overbeating may cause tunnels in the muffins, which are elongated cells formed by bubbles of carbon dioxide trapped in the batter. Muffins may have peaked tops as well if overbeaten.

     2½ cups flour
      ¾ cup sugar
      1 tablespoon baking powder
         Pinch salt
      ¾ cup milk
      ½ cup unsalted butter, melted, or vegetable oil
      2 eggs

1. Preheat oven to 350° F. Sift flour, sugar, baking powder, and salt together into a large bowl; make well in center. Mix milk, melted butter, and eggs together and pour into well; stir just to combine.

2. Pour into greased 2¾-inch muffin pans, filling two thirds to three fourths full. Bake until golden brown and a toothpick inserted in center comes out clean (25 to 30 minutes). Serve warm.

Makes 12 muffins.

Blueberry Muffins Gently fold into batter 1 cup fresh or frozen blueberries.

◼ BEST CAKE MUFFINS

If a more fine-grained, cakelike, and less crumbly texture is desired, try this recipe. Sugar and butter are creamed together before the liquid and dry ingredients are added, much as you would for a shortened cake batter.

     1½ cups flour
      2 teaspoons baking powder
      ½ teaspoon baking soda
         Pinch salt
      ½ cup butter
      ¾ cup sugar
      2 eggs
      1 teaspoon vanilla extract
      ⅔ cup milk

1. Preheat oven to 350° F. Grease muffin pan and lightly dust with flour. Sift flour, baking powder, baking soda, and salt together into a medium bowl and set aside. In a medium bowl cream butter and sugar together until light, fluffy, and a pale, ivory color. Add eggs, one at a time, beating well after each addition (if mixture begins to curdle as you mix in eggs, add 1 tablespoon flour and beat on low speed until blended). Stir in vanilla and milk. Fold in dry ingredients.

2. Spoon batter into prepared 2¾-inch muffin pan, filling each mold three fourths full. Bake until golden brown and a toothpick inserted in center comes out clean (20 to 25 minutes). Serve warm.

Makes 12 muffins.

Blueberry Muffins Gently mix into batter 1 cup fresh or frozen blueberries.

Cinnamon-Raisin Muffins Sift ½ teaspoon cinnamon with dry ingredients; gently mix into batter ¾ to 1 cup dark or golden raisins.

Citrus–Poppy-Seed Muffins Mix into dry ingredients 1 tablespoon grated lemon or orange rind and ¼ cup poppy seed.

Nut-Currant Muffins Gently mix into batter ½ cup chopped walnuts or pecans and ½ cup dried currants.

◼ BRAN MUFFINS

These muffins contain banana for moistness and richness, buttermilk for tang, and raisins for natural sweetness.

     2½ cups whole wheat flour
     1⅓ cups bran
      3 tablespoons sugar
      2 teaspoons baking soda
      ½ teaspoon salt
     2½ cups buttermilk
      1 egg
      ⅓ cup molasses
      3 tablespoons butter, melted
      1 ripe banana, mashed
      2 cups raisins

Bran Topping

      2 tablespoons bran
      2 tablespoons raw sugar

1. Preheat oven to 400° F. Into a large bowl sift together flour, bran, sugar, baking soda, and salt. (Some of the flour and bran may not pass through sieve; remove what remains and add to sifted ingredients.)

2. In a medium bowl combine buttermilk, egg, molasses, melted butter, and banana. Add liquid to dry ingredients and stir just to combine. Fold in raisins.

3. Spoon into greased 2¾-inch muffin cups, filling each three fourths full. Sprinkle with Bran Topping. Bake until muffins are well browned and spring back when touched lightly (25 to 30 minutes). Serve warm.

Makes 12 muffins.

Bran Topping Combine bran and sugar in a small bowl.

NAP, TO

To barely coat with one thin sheet, usually when covering a food with its companion sauce. *To nap* implies to add sauce with a light hand, applying in such a way that it covers the food completely.

NECTARINE

As is obvious from its appearance, the nectarine is a smooth-skinned relative of the peach. When ripe, the skin is a deep yellow-gold with a red blush. The flesh is similarly colored, and is very fragrant and juicy when ripe. Some nectarine varieties are clingstone, others freestone.

Use   The nectarine is commonly eaten out of hand, as a snack or dessert. It can also be sliced and enjoyed in pies, tarts, and cobblers, in compotes or fruit salads, and on breakfast cereal. Nectarine purée can be used in sherbets and ice creams, mousses, puddings, and whips.

Availability   The season for domestic nectarines runs from late March through September, with peak supplies in July and August. Imports from the southern hemisphere are available in some markets during the domestic off-season.

Selection   Look for nectarines with good fragrance and color; they should have a deep gold skin with a red blush. Avoid hard green fruit, although a hint of green is natural in some varieties. A ripe nectarine will give slightly to pressure but should not be overly soft. To ripen mature fruit, leave at room temperature for a few days.

Storage   Refrigerate ripe nectarines and use promptly.

Preparation   Nectarines do not require peeling but may be peeled for use in more elegant desserts. Sprinkle cut fruit with lemon juice to prevent browning.

FROZEN NECTARINE TORTE

Peaches or plums also work well in this quick summer dessert, which would be a wonderful finish to a brunch.

>   2 **pounds ripe nectarines, peeled,**
>   **seeded, and chopped**
>   1 **cup sugar**
>   1 **tablespoon fresh lemon juice**
>   1 **cup whipping cream**
>   1 **cup macaroon crumbs**

In a large bowl mash nectarines with sugar and lemon juice, mixing well. Whip cream to soft peaks and fold into nectarine mixture. Sprinkle ½ cup crumbs on the bottom of a 1-quart mold. Pour in nectarine mixture and top with remaining crumbs. Freeze until firm.

Serves 8.

NEEDLE AND FASTENER

These implements perform related functions: closing a cavity or pocket to hold in a stuffing or to improve appearance (lacing pins); drawing extremities (legs, wings) of a bird close to its body to form an attractive, compact shape (trussing needle, kitchen twine); holding meats, fish, fowl, and vegetables in place as they cook on a grill or under a broiler (skewers); or inserting strips of fat into lean meats to increase flavor and moistness (larding needle).

KITCHEN TWINE

For trussing or tying up poultry and meats, with or without a needle, or tying up cheesecloth bags of herbs for bouquet garni, use a heavy-gauge, natural-fiber string that can withstand high oven heat (linen is best because it won't burn under normal usage). Coated household sewing thread will impart a waxy taste to food, and nylon thread can melt. Uncoated cotton thread is satisfactory but is thin and may cut fingers when pulled tight.

LARDING NEEDLES

Of the two types of larding needles, one has a long, slender trough (about 10 inches) attached to a wooden handle. To use, strips of pork fat are set in the trough, then the needle is inserted into the roast with the grain of the meat and is rotated as it proceeds through from one end to the other. The needle is withdrawn slowly so that the fat is not pulled out. This process is repeated at regular intervals. A shorter version (about 6 inches long) has an eye, rather than a trough, and is designed for larding a shallow surface. Both needles are stainless steel. For an illustration of larding, see photograph on page 338.

POULTRY LACERS

These short, narrow shafts, with points at one end and loops or angled heads at the other, are used for closing poultry cavities, for securing pockets of stuffed meats, and for maintaining the shape of rolled meats. Widely available, they are made of stainless steel and come in sets of six pins with twine. The pins are set in place, then the twine is crisscrossed between skewers and pulled tight like the laces on a pair of boots. The loops or bent ends make it easier to remove the pins after roasting.

SKEWERS

Flat skewers are preferable because food won't slip when skewers are turned on the grill or under the broiler. Those made of stainless steel all have a loop or decorative head at one end so chunks of food won't slide off. Always soak bamboo skewers in water for at least 15 minutes before using on a grill or under a broiler so they won't burn. These picks make good cake testers as well. Sizes range from 8 to 14 inches.

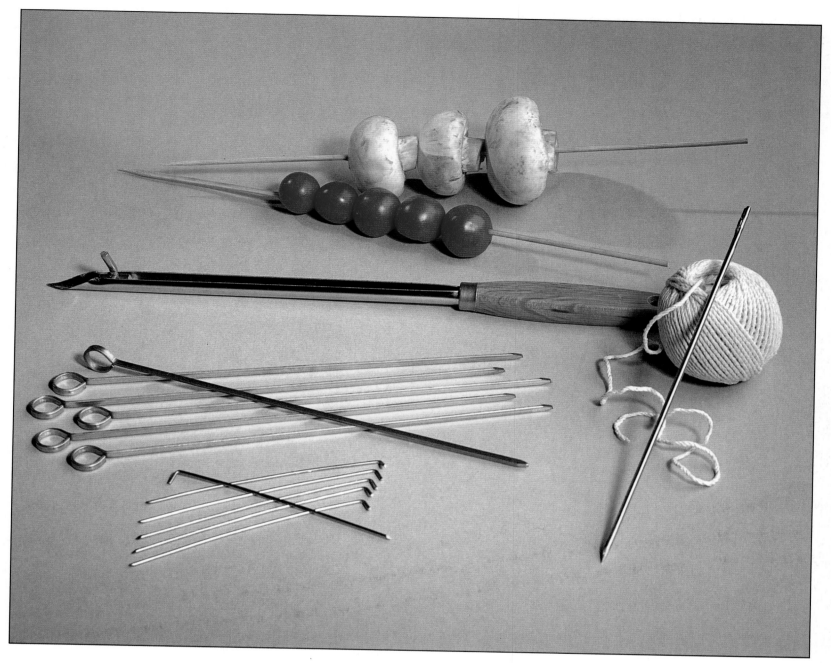

TRUSSING NEEDLE

Trussing holds the appendages of a bird together during roasting, makes a boned roast more compact so that it has a neater appearance and a more uniform shape that allows even cooking, and closes off the cavity of a bird or a pocket of stuffed meat. Trussing needles are made of stainless steel and are most commonly 8 inches long. They are used with uncoated heavyweight string made of a natural fiber (see Kitchen Twine, opposite page).

Recipes and Related Information
Bouquet Garni, 56; Lard, 338; Truss, 584.

NONREACTIVE

In the presence of an acidic food, certain metals—aluminum, cast iron, and unlined copper—produce a chemical reaction. The result is an off color or taste. When one of these foods—such as tomatoes, vinegar, lemon juice, or wine—is an ingredient in a recipe, most often you will be directed to mix or cook in a "nonreactive" or "nonaluminum" pan to avoid this undesirable reaction. Cookware made of stainless steel, enameled steel or cast iron, anodized aluminum, or a cladded metal doesn't interact with acids and is safe to use with acidic ingredients (see MATERIALS FOR COOKWARE).

Implements used by the cook to secure cavities or hold food in place include (top to bottom): bamboo skewers, larding needle, trussing needle, kitchen twine, metal skewers, poultry lacers.

An assortment of Chinese noodles of various shapes; clockwise from upper right: bean threads, two sizes of dried wheat-flour noodles, precooked rice noodles, and fresh wrappers—square for wontons and round for siu mai or potstickers.

NOODLE, ASIAN

Although many Westerners think of rice as the primary starch in Asian cuisine, noodles also play a major role. Unlike Western noodles, which are always made with wheat flour, those from Asia may have as their base wheat flour, rice flour, or vegetable starches such as yam, soybean, and potato. The best-known Asian noodle types are discussed on the following pages by country.

Due to the intertwined histories of Asian countries, noodle varieties overlap considerably throughout that part of the world. Wheat noodles (both with egg and without), rice noodles, and bean-starch or potato-starch noodles are employed in almost all these cuisines, as are small wrappers often made of rice flour. Although size and texture may vary slightly from country to country, substitutions are certainly possible and not problematic. Chinese egg noodles, for example, are widely available in supermarkets and are a fine substitute for Japanese *ramen,* Thai *bà mee,* Korean *gougsou,* or Philippine *pancit canton.*

Use   The Asian cook uses noodles in a great variety of ways. Noodles give body to soup, as in the Vietnamese *phở bo* (beef noodle soup) or the chilled Korean beef and noodle soup called *naeng myun.* Noodles are boiled and then eaten both hot and cold, with toppings or with dipping sauces. Examples include spicy *dan dan mein* (egg noodles tossed with peanut sauce, a specialty of the

Szechuan province of China) and Japanese *zaru soba* (cold buckwheat noodles accompanied with a soy-based dipping sauce). Noodles can be steamed, then stir-fried, as in the popular Thai dish called *pad Thai* (rice noodles tossed with bean sprouts, cooked egg, peanuts, and dried shrimp). Chinese cooks coil steamed vermicelli into thick pancakes, fry them on both sides until crisp, and top them with a stew or stir-fry.

Almost every Asian cuisine can boast a variety of noodle dumplings or stuffed noodle dishes. Examples include Chinese wonton and *fun* (sheets of steamed rice noodles, stuffed with shrimp and green onion), Japanese *gyoza* (pan-fried dumplings), and the Korean beef dumplings called *mandu.* In addition, noodles are used in stuffings, as in the Vietnamese *cha gio,* fried spring rolls filled with softened cellophane noodles, pork, and crab.

Availability   If you live near an Asian neighborhood, you should be able to find all sorts of fresh Asian-style noodles and wrappers. Most well-stocked supermarkets carry some varieties.

Selection   Buy fresh noodles from a market with a rapid turnover or from a store that receives fresh supplies daily.

Storage   Fresh wheat noodles should be refrigerated and used within two or three days. If truly fresh when purchased, these noodles may be wrapped with plastic wrap overwrapped with aluminum foil, and frozen for up to three months. Rice-flour noodles are often stored at room temperature in markets because they stiffen when chilled; they may be stored at room temperature for two days or kept in the refrigerator for up to one week. To soften noodles stiffened by refrigeration, steam briefly in a covered steamer just until softened, then gently run hot water over noodles and drain. If very fresh, they may also be frozen for up to two months. Dried noodles of all kinds will keep indefinitely in a cool, dry place.

Preparation   Many recipes using Asian noodles call for the noodles to be boiled prior to further treatment, whether combining with a sauce, stir-frying, or braising. If you are using homemade or packaged fresh egg noodles, fluff them a little first to loosen the clumps, then drop them into a large pot of rapidly boiling, lightly salted water. Stir immediately with long chopsticks or a spoon to separate the noodles, and begin testing them as soon as the water returns to a boil. Most will be done within a few seconds. Dried noodles take longer; follow package directions. Rice noodles generally do not need preliminary boiling if they are to be cooked in a sauce. Toss the noodles under running water by hand so you can feel when they are thoroughly cooled. Drain well and toss with a little oil to keep them from sticking. If sufficiently oiled and tightly wrapped, noodles can be kept for several hours or even overnight, covered, in the refrigerator.

CHINA

Noodles have been an important part of the Chinese diet since the Han Dynasty period (206 B.C. to A.D. 220), when the Chinese learned the technology of milling flour from an unknown neighbor to the west. Before this time, most grains were simply boiled whole, as rice is today; but finely milled flour could be combined with water, kneaded, and worked into various shapes, and cooked by various methods to produce noodles, dumplings, and breads.

Bean-Starch Noodles   Also known as bean threads, glass noodles, cellophane noodles, silver noodles, Chinese vermicelli, transparent noodles, and long rice, these threadlike noodles are made from mung bean starch. Folded into skeins about 6 inches long, they are packaged in plastic or net bags. They may be soaked in hot water until soft (about 30 seconds), then used in stir-fries, soups, and salads. The soaked noodles have a slippery texture and a glassy look. Like dried rice noodles (see below), they may also be deep-fried without presoaking.

Dried Rice Noodles   Also known as rice stick or rice vermicelli, these noodles made from rice flour are as thin as string. They are usually coiled into nests and packaged in plastic bags. Dried noodles may be deep-fried quickly in 400° F oil. They will puff dramatically into crisp, brittle white noodles, which provide the crunchy base for Chinese Chicken Salad. Dried noodles may also be soaked

in warm water until soft and slippery, then stir-fried or added to soups.

Egg Noodles   Chinese markets offer both fresh and dried egg noodles in several widths. Some supermarkets also carry fresh Chinese egg noodles. These wheat-based noodles cut in shoelace lengths are very popular in northern China, where wheat is the predominant starch. The noodles are added to soups for a quick lunch. They may also be boiled and served with meat or peanut sauce, or boiled, then fried into a crisp pancake and topped with a stew or sauce. Boiled noodles are also eaten cold dressed with oil, soy sauce, vinegar, and green onions.

Fresh Rice Noodles   Many Asian markets carry cooked fresh noodles made from rice flour, which are sold in wide sheets or cut into ¾-inch widths. Soft, smooth, flimsy, and very bland, they absorb other flavors well. These slippery noodles are used in many dim sum dishes; served both cold and hot, they may be stuffed with ground pork or simply garnished with soy sauce, shrimp, and minced green onions. Narrow rice noodles are frequently used in soups or topped with stew for a quick, nourishing lunch.

Nonegg Noodles   Chinese markets also offer both fresh and dried wheat noodles containing little or no egg. They are used in the same way as egg noodles.

Shrimp- and Crab-Flavored Noodles   These dried noodles have been flavored with the roe of shrimp or crab. They are particularly good in soup but may be used as any other dried Chinese noodle.

Wonton or Egg Roll Wrappers   The same dough in egg noodles is used for wonton skins and egg roll wrappers. These thin, square wrappers are available fresh in many supermarkets, packaged in plastic.

JAPAN

Noodles are among the most popular foods eaten in Japan, with buckwheat noodles (*soba*) more common in the north and wheat noodles (*udon*) in the south. At lunchtime, shoppers and workers throughout Japan stop for a quick bowl of noodles in one of that country's countless noodle shops. Also supplying the never-ending Japanese passion for noodles, street vendors can be found dishing up their wares at all hours of the day and late into the night. In the summer, many diners opt for chilled noodles served with a soy-based dipping sauce; in cold weather, the preference is for the warmth of noodles in steaming broth.

Harusame   Also called *saifun, harusame* are long thin noodles made of potato and cornstarch. They are used in soups and salads or deep-fried for a garnish.

Hiyamugi   These dried wheat noodles, about as long as spaghetti but slightly thicker, are packaged in bunches and tied with a cloth ribbon. They are usually eaten cold, served with garnishes and a dipping sauce.

Selection Packaged seasonings lose quality after a while; try to buy from a store that restocks its spice section fairly often.

Storage Keep both whole and ground nutmeg in a cool, dark, dry place. Whole nutmeg will stay pungent for two years; replace ground nutmeg every six months.

Preparation Grate whole nutmeg just before using; add ground nutmeg directly to dish.

■ BAKED NUTMEG DOUGHNUTS

Although these doughnut-shaped rolls are baked, not fried, they resemble a doughnut in flavor. The dough does not require kneading and is light and puffy in texture.

```
    2  packages active dry yeast
    ¼  cup warm (105° to 115° F) water
 1⅓  cups warm (105° to 115° F) milk
    ¼  cup sugar
    2  teaspoons freshly grated nutmeg
    1  teaspoon salt
    ¼  teaspoon ground cinnamon
    ⅔  cup butter
 4½  to 5 cups flour
    2  eggs
    ½  cup Vanilla Granulated Sugar (see page 585)
```

1. Sprinkle yeast over the water in large bowl of electric mixer. Let stand until soft (about 5 minutes). Stir in milk, sugar, nutmeg, salt, cinnamon, and ⅓ cup butter.

2. Add 3 cups flour. Mix to blend, then beat at medium speed until smooth and elastic (about 5 minutes). Beat in eggs, then gradually stir in about 1½ cups flour to make a soft dough.

3. Transfer to a greased bowl, cover with plastic wrap, and let rise in a warm place until doubled (about 1 hour). Stir down dough.

4. Turn dough out on a well-floured surface (use some of remaining flour), and shape with floured hands into a flattened ball. Coat well with flour. Lightly roll out about ½ inch thick. Cut with a floured 2½-inch doughnut cutter. Place doughnuts about 2 inches apart on greased baking sheets.

5. Brush lightly with some of remaining butter, melted, and let rise until nearly doubled (about 30 minutes).

6. Preheat oven to 425° F. Bake until doughnuts are golden brown (about 10 minutes). Brush warm doughnuts with remaining melted butter and roll lightly in Vanilla Granulated Sugar.

Makes 3 dozen doughnuts.

Recipes and Related Information
Apple Dumplings With Nutmeg Sauce, 193; Grate, Grater, 281; Herb and Spice Blends, 301.

OIL

The edible oils used in the kitchen are expressed from a variety of sources: seeds (such as sesame); legumes (such as peanuts and soybeans); plants (such as safflower and corn); fruits (such as olives); and nuts (such as coconuts, walnuts, and almonds).

Oils differ in both flavor and cooking qualities. Some are well suited to high-heat frying; others should be used only for salads. Selecting the right oil for the job and understanding the special requirements of an oil are an important part of even the most basic cooking.

The most common edible oils are outlined under Availability, along with specific recommendations for use and handling. The Use section below applies generally to all edible oils.

Use Oils function in the kitchen as a lubricant, an ingredient, and a cooking medium. As a lubricant, oil keeps food from sticking to a pan or baking dish. Bread pans and cake pans are often brushed with oil (or butter) to make the finished loaf or cake easy to remove. Oil is an essential ingredient in many preparations. It provides the body for salad dressings and mayonnaise, which in turn provide lubrication for lettuces, cold vegetables, and sandwiches. It is the foundation of Italian pesto, yielding a cold sauce that spreads easily over hot pasta. Other oil-based sauces such as the French aioli (garlic mayonnaise) and rouille (garlicky red pepper sauce), the Spanish *romesco* (mayonnaise with red pepper and ground almonds), and the Italian *salsa verde* (parsley, onion, and garlic sauce) are spooned on top of soups for enrichment, spread on sandwiches, and served with boiled meats or seafood.

Oil also provides the required fat in some cakes, especially moist loaf cakes such as carrot cake. It is used to enrich bread doughs and batters. Some stronger tasting oils, such as Asian sesame oil, are used as flavorings; they are rubbed over steamed chicken and drizzled over stir-fried vegetables in the same way that a Western cook would add butter to a bowl of peas.

As a cooking medium, oils are essential to frying, whether sautéing, stir-frying, or deep-frying. In sautéing and stir-frying, a thin film of oil both keeps food from sticking to the pan and transfers heat to the food being cooked. Oil also imparts flavor. Foods sautéed in olive oil have a flavor quite different from those fried in peanut oil or vegetable oil. In sautéed dishes where the flavor of butter is important, oil is often added to the butter to raise the smoke point of the butter.

Availability The following are the most often used edible oils.

Almond Oil When imported from France, almond oil has a toasty almond flavor that is pleasing in salads and cold dishes. Its flavor is destroyed by heat. Use almond oil in mayonnaise, salad dressings, and cold poultry dishes.

The domestic product is considerably paler in flavor. Refrigerated, almond oil will keep for up to one year. Look for it in specialty stores and well-stocked supermarkets.

Avocado Oil   Derived from California avocados, this mild, buttery oil has a delicate flavor suitable for mayonnaise, salad dressings, and baked goods. Because it has a high smoke point, it can be used for sautéing, stir-frying, and deep-frying.

Coconut Oil   Used as a cooking oil in India and Malaysia, coconut oil imparts a coconut flavor to foods and can be heated to high frying temperatures. It is highly saturated and is solid when cool. Coconut oil is available in markets that carry Indian or Indonesian products. Refrigerated, it will keep for up to one year.

Corn Oil   This is a bland, unsaturated oil that is excellent for frying. It is also a major component in most margarine. Because it does not contain cholesterol, it is an oil of choice for many on low-cholesterol diets. Store in a cool, dark place for up to six months or refrigerate for up to one year. It is widely available in supermarkets.

Hazelnut Oil   This very expensive French import imparts a delicious toasted hazelnut flavor to cold dishes. Heating destroys its special flavor. It is strong and should be used with restraint. Use hazelnut oil in conjunction with a milder oil in salad dressings and mayonnaise, or drizzle it over green beans, artichokes, and asparagus. Refrigerated, it will keep for up to one year. It is available in specialty stores and well-stocked supermarkets.

Olive Oil   Pressed from the fruit of the olive tree, olive oil is a prized salad and cooking oil in the Western world. Indeed, 90 percent of the world's olive crop goes to oil. It is fundamental to the cooking of the Mediterranean: Spain, Italy, southern France, Greece, and Turkey. It is not well suited to deep-frying, for it smokes at moderate temperatures. However, it is excellent for sautéing and is an ingredient used for that purpose by almost all Mediterranean cooks. Olive oil is an ingredient in salad dressings, mayonnaise, sauces, soups, marinades, and even pastries in Mediterranean countries. Italians celebrate the new crop of olive oil by drizzling it on toasted bread; they also serve olive oil as a dip for raw vegetables, along with coarse salt and lemon.

Commercial olive oil is available in several different grades according to the degree of acidity. Although oils can be deacidified chemically, the best olive oil is naturally low in acidity because it is cold-pressed. These cold-pressed, low-acid oils are termed extravirgin olive oil (although chemically deacidified oils will also qualify for this term). In increasing level of acidity, olive oil is classified as extravirgin, superfine, fine, and virgin or pure.

The first, cold pressing of the olive gives the finest, fruitiest oil. Subsequent pressings in the presence of heat yield oil of lesser quality. Because the terms on olive oil labels do not necessarily indicate quality, it is important to experiment widely and find a brand that you like. The best oils have a clear, deep green appearance, a fruity aroma, and a flavor that is clean, light, often slightly peppery, and distinctly of the olive. Avoid heavy or bitter oils. Price is also not a good indication of quality.

The best extravirgin olive oils lose their character when cooked. They should be used in cold dishes or added to hot dishes at the end of cooking. For sautéing, select a mild olive oil.

Store olive oil in a cool, dark place for up to six months or in the refrigerator for up to one year. It will cloud in the refrigerator but will clear at room temperature. Olive oils in a wide range of quality are available in supermarkets and specialty markets. France, Italy, and Spain are the major exporters.

Peanut Oil   Among Chinese cooks, peanut oil is the most popular cooking oil. It imparts a faint peanut flavor to stir-fried foods, and it may be heated to high frying temperatures. Western cooks also find it suitable for salad dressings and sautéing. It is available in all supermarkets and in Asian markets. Some health-food stores also carry a cold-pressed peanut oil that is more perishable. Peanut oil will keep for up to one year in a cool, dark place. It will cloud at refrigerator temperature but will clear again when brought to room temperature.

Safflower Oil   This flavorless cooking oil can be heated to high frying temperatures. It is excellent for deep-frying but its bland, heavy character makes it less suitable for a salad oil. It is available in many supermarkets. Store in a cool, dark place, where it will keep for up to one year.

Sesame Oil   Pressed from sesame seeds, this oil is an important adjunct to Chinese cooking. Its toasty, nutty flavor adds an intriguing note to noodle dishes, soups, stir-fries, and dipping sauces. It is often rubbed over poultry or drizzled on fish after steaming. The Chinese rarely use it for cooking as heat would alter its flavor. Chinese sesame oil is available in some supermarkets and in Asian markets, packaged in a plastic squeeze bottle. It has a deep gold color and an arresting fragrance. A Japanese version of sesame oil is slightly lighter in color and flavor. Japanese cooks add it to the cooking oil used to make tempura. A cold-pressed sesame oil, available in health-food stores, has a much more pallid flavor and is not a substitute. Store Asian sesame oil in a cool, dry place for up to six months or in the refrigerator for up to one year. Cold-pressed sesame oil is more perishable; refrigerated, it will keep for up to six months.

Soybean Oil   A major cooking oil in America, it heats to high frying temperatures and has a bland flavor. Because of its lack of flavor, it is not a superior salad oil, but it does not contain cholesterol and is thus an oil of choice for many on special diets. Soybean oil is also used in margarine. It is available in supermarkets; store in a cool, dark place for up to one year.

Oils are used in the kitchen for lubrication and cooking, and as an ingredient. Depending on their source, they can range from pale colors to deeper hues.

P

PARBOIL, TO

To cook foods partway in boiling water. This treatment is particularly helpful for stir-fries and sautés. By partially tenderizing longer-cooking ingredients such as carrots or broccoli, for example, their final cooking time will be faster and they can be combined with ingredients that finish quickly. Parboiling can be done in advance, which adds to its appeal as a time-saving preparation technique. Blanching is identical to parboiling except that foods are cooked only for a brief time (see BLANCH).

PARE, TO

In general, to remove the outer skin of a food, usually vegetables or fruits. A short-bladed paring knife or vegetable peeler is used. A narrower definition would be to trim away the irregular outer surface in order to produce pieces of uniform size that will cook at the same rate and have a more symmetrical final appearance. An example would be the classic garnish of pared nugget-shaped carrots or potatoes for roasted meats and poultry.

> ### Recipes and Related Information
> *Gadgets, 258; Knife, 328.*

PARSLEY

One of the most widely used culinary herbs, parsley is important to almost all the world's cuisines. With its fragile stems and sturdy, bright green leaves, parsley imparts a clean, fresh, slightly peppery flavor to dishes. The two main varieties are the curly-leaf type, widely available in supermarkets, and the flat-leaf Italian parsley, less common in American markets but quite common in Europe. Flat-leaf parsley is more pungent.

Use　The mild, fresh flavor of parsley harmonizes with almost all savory dishes. It is frequently mixed with other, more pungent herbs. Fines herbes (see HERB AND SPICE BLENDS) always include parsley, as does the classic bouquet garni (see BOUQUET GARNI). Minced parsley is a visually appealing garnish for soups, stews, sautés, meat loaves, and casseroles. Mixed with lemon rind and minced garlic, it becomes Gremolata, an Italian garnish for braised veal shanks (Osso Buco). Mixed with bread crumbs and minced shallots or garlic, it becomes *persillade,* which is spread on rack of lamb before roasting. It is a major component of the Italian *salsa verde* (green sauce) for boiled meats and of Middle Eastern Tabbouleh (cracked wheat, tomato, and parsley salad). Parsley sprigs can be deep-fried as a garnish for fried foods. They can be added to green salads or even lightly dressed and served as a salad on their own.

Availability　Fresh curly-leaf parsley is widely found all year in supermarkets. Flat-leaf Italian parsley is available in specialty markets and some well-stocked supermarkets. Dried parsley is sold on most supermarket spice racks. Given the ready availability and affordability of fresh parsley, there is little if any reason to use dried.

Selection　Whether curly-leaf or flat-leaf, look for bright green, vigorous bunches with a fresh, clean aroma. Avoid limp bunches with dull-looking leaves.

Storage　Wash well, shake off excess water, and wrap parsley in paper towels, then in a plastic bag. Store in refrigerator and use within three or four days.

Preparation　To mince parsley, separate leaves from stems. Finely mince leaves. Save stems to flavor stocks.

■ WARM PARSLEY SAUCE FOR SHELLFISH

Keep this sauce warm in a chafing dish and serve with chilled scallops, crab legs, or shrimp.

> 4　cups parsley, leaves only
> 2　cups whipping cream
> 2　shallots, minced
> ½　cup dry white wine
> ¼　cup cold butter, cut into 4 pieces
> 　　Salt and freshly ground pepper, to taste

1. Blanch parsley in boiling water 20 seconds; drain and transfer to a bowl of ice water to stop cooking and set color. Drain and dry thoroughly on paper towels. Chop by hand or in a food processor until almost puréed; set aside.

2. In a medium saucepan over high heat, reduce cream by half. In a medium skillet over high heat, cook shallots and wine until wine has almost evaporated. Whisk in hot reduced cream. Remove from heat and whisk in butter, one piece at a time, until incorporated. Add parsley and salt and pepper to taste.

Makes 1¾ cups.

> ### Recipes and Related Information
> *Gremolata, 58; Osso Buco, 58; Piquant Parsley Dipping Sauce, 46; Tabbouleh, 277.*

PARSNIP

It is easy to tell by sight that the parsnip is a member of the carrot family. This sweet-flavored root vegetable looks like an ivory-colored or pale yellow carrot. It is usually less uniform in thickness, however, being wider at the top and tapering to a very narrow root. Unlike carrots, parsnips are always eaten cooked; they are starchy and tough when raw. Cooked parsnips have a texture and flavor somewhere between carrots and sweet potatoes, although they remain pale yellow when cooked.

Use Parsnips are a delicious winter root vegetable. They may be peeled, sliced, and steamed like carrots, or boiled, then mashed with butter and cream. They may be cut into chunks and added to soups or stews, or baked in the oven with meat stock and butter.

Availability Parsnips are found in many supermarkets during winter months. They are sold with their tops clipped, either in bulk or in plastic bags.

Selection Look for small parsnips; larger ones may have woody cores. Avoid parsnips that are limp or shriveled or have splits or brown spots. Choose those that are reasonably uniform; misshapen ones that have to be severely trimmed are uneconomical.

Storage Keep in a plastic bag in the refrigerator crisper and use within three or four days.

Preparation Peel and trim ends.

Cooking See BOIL, BRAISE, PUREE, STEAM.

▪ PARSLEYED PARSNIPS

If you've only used parsnips to flavor soups and stocks, you may be surprised to learn that they are also delicious on their own as a side dish to a winter meal. If you prefer small parsnips, they may be used whole. Larger ones are more appealing and will cook faster if cut in pieces.

- 8 to 10 medium (1½ lb) parsnips, peeled, trimmed, and quartered
- 2 tablespoons butter
- ¼ cup minced parsley
- ½ teaspoon dried basil

In a large, covered skillet cook parsnips in boiling water to cover until tender-crisp (about 15 minutes); drain. Add butter, parsley, and basil. Toss to coat parsnips.

Serves 4.

PASSION FRUIT

Also known by its Spanish name, *granadilla,* the passion fruit supposedly owes its English name to its flowers: Their markings, some say, resemble the instruments used in the Crucifixion. The fruit itself is small and egg-shaped, with a brittle, wrinkled skin. Both skin and flesh color vary by variety, but the most commonly available variety has a dark purple skin and a deep gold flesh with small black seeds. Some Latin markets carry a Mexican variety with yellow skin and grayish flesh. All have a soft, juicy pulp that is highly aromatic.

Use Passion fruit can be halved and eaten from the shell, seeds and all. The fruit can also be squeezed for its juice and the juice strained through a sieve to remove the seeds. Seeded passion fruit pulp, puréed in a blender, is a

delicious flavor base for sorbets and ice creams, mousses, pies, and dessert sauces. Passion fruit juice adds an exotic accent to punches, cocktails, or fruit juice blends.

Availability Passion fruit is native to Brazil, but is now grown in California, Hawaii, New Zealand, and Australia. Fresh passion fruit is sold in Latin markets and some supermarkets between late February and early October. Bottled or canned passion fruit juice is sold in specialty markets, Latin markets, and some health-food stores.

Selection The skin of ripe passion fruit will be shriveled. The fruit will ripen if left at room temperature for several days.

Storage Refrigerate ripe fruit in a plastic bag and use within two or three days.

Preparation Halve and eat from the shell (the shell is not eaten); or scoop out the pulp and press it through a sieve to remove the seeds; or purée with seeds for use in ice creams, sorbets, and mousses.

Parsnips are a flavorful winter root vegetable that makes a tasty side dish when simply cooked and tossed with herbs and butter.

> ***Recipes and Related Information***
> *Ice Cream and Frozen Dessert, 308; Mousse, 372.*

▮ LASAGNE VERDI

Make your own spinach pasta for this recipe or substitute ¾ pound storebought noodles. This updated, extremely attractive version of a classic recipe is full of striking, contrasting colors and new combinations. The Lasagne With Meat Sauce variation is more traditional.

      1 recipe Spinach Pasta (see page 411)
         Olive oil, for moistening
      1 medium eggplant
      1 teaspoon kosher salt
      2 medium zucchini
     12 shiitake mushrooms *or*
         ½ pound domestic mushrooms
      3 leeks, cleaned
      1 tablespoon butter
      1 tablespoon olive oil
      3 cups Northern-Style Tomato Sauce (see page 412)
      ¾ cup freshly grated Parmesan cheese
      3 cups ricotta cheese
      ¾ cup grated Monterey jack or mozzarella cheese

1. Prepare Spinach Pasta. Cut pasta into lasagne-shaped noodles approximately 12 inches long to fit a 9- by 12-inch baking dish. Bring a large pot of salted water to a boil. Add lasagne noodles and cook until almost tender. Drain and refresh under cold water, drain again, and dry. Moisten noodles with olive oil and spread out on clean kitchen towels.

2. Preheat oven to 350° F. Slice eggplant in half. Slash ½-inch deep cuts into each half. Place halves on a towel and sprinkle with the salt. Let rest for 30 minutes. Place in colander, rinse, and pat dry. Place eggplant on a baking sheet and bake until tender (40 to 50 minutes). Cool slightly, then slice ¼ inch thick and reserve. Slice zucchini lengthwise into ⅛-inch-thick pieces and reserve.

3. Slice shiitake mushrooms about ¼ inch thick. Slice leeks into ½-inch-thick slices. In a large skillet heat butter and oil over medium heat, add leeks and mushrooms, and cook together for 10 to 12 minutes. Add tomato sauce to skillet; simmer for 15 minutes.

4. Spread one fourth of tomato-mushroom-leek sauce on bottom of baking dish. Place lasagne noodles on sauce, and cover with one third of the Parmesan cheese, half of the ricotta, and half of the Monterey jack. Cover cheeses with eggplant slices. Repeat layers using one third of the remaining sauce, one half of the lasagne noodles, half of the remaining Parmesan cheese, all of the remaining ricotta and Monterey jack cheeses, and the zucchini slices. Cover with one half of the remaining sauce and the remaining lasagne noodles. Top with remaining sauce and Parmesan cheese. Bake until warmed through and cheese is lightly browned (35 to 40 minutes). Cool 5 minutes before serving.

Serves 6.

Lasagne With Meat Sauce Substitute 3 cups Ragù Bolognese (see page 412) for Northern-Style Tomato Sauce. Omit eggplant, zucchini, and leeks. Follow directions for Lasagne Verdi; bake about 30 minutes.

Serves 6.

▮ PASTA PRIMAVERA

The typical *pasta primavera* is a veritable garden on a plate, with the most tender young vegetables tossed with herbs and thin pasta. You can readily substitute whatever is freshest in the market, but remember to aim for lively colors and contrasting textures. So that all the vegetables cook evenly, some are blanched before they are added to the other ingredients.

      1 pound sugar snap peas, strings removed, *or*
         1 cup shelled fresh peas
      1 pound fresh asparagus
      1 cup sliced slender green beans, in 2-inch lengths
      ½ cup thin carrot strips
      3 tablespoons olive oil, plus 1 tablespoon
         if using dried pasta
      2 tablespoons unsalted butter
      ½ cup diced red bell pepper
      ½ cup diced yellow bell pepper (optional)
      2 tablespoons pine nuts, toasted
      1 recipe Fresh Herb Pasta (see page 411) *or*
         ¾ pound dried spaghettini pasta
      1 cup thinly shredded romaine lettuce
      2 tablespoons snipped fresh chives
         Salt, to taste
      4 tablespoons minced parsley, for garnish
         Freshly grated Parmesan cheese

1. Bring a large pot of salted water to a rolling boil. Blanch peas, asparagus, beans, and carrots separately; when each batch is tender but crisp, remove to ice water to stop cooking. Drain well and pat dry. Save the cooking water.

2. Heat the 3 tablespoons olive oil and butter in a large, heavy-bottomed skillet over moderate heat. When butter foams, add red peppers and yellow peppers (if used) and sauté 1 minute. Add pine nuts and sauté 1 more minute. Add blanched and dried peas, asparagus, beans, and carrots, and toss until coated with butter-oil mixture and warmed through.

3. To cook pasta, bring reserved vegetable water to a rolling boil. If using dried pasta, add 1 tablespoon oil (if you are using fresh pasta, there is no need to add oil). Add pasta and cook until just done. Drain well and transfer to a warm serving bowl. Add hot vegetables to pasta with romaine and chives. Toss well, add salt to taste, then toss again. Divide pasta among warm serving plates. Garnish each portion with minced parsley; pass grated Parmesan separately.

Serves 4.

■ SPINACH RAVIOLI

Ravioli can be made with a variety of fillings and doughs. Be careful to match the dough and filling to make a compatible combination. These plump little pillows are made with a spinach dough stuffed with an unusual cheese and escarole mixture that is complemented by either tomato sauce or light Parmesan Cream Sauce. They're quite rich and should be followed with a simple main course. They can be prepared a few hours before serving and held on lightly floured baking sheets. Make sure they do not touch. Cover and refrigerate. They will freeze for up to three months; tray-freeze (see FREEZE) and wrap airtight.

    2 recipes Spinach Pasta (see page 411)
    1 recipe Northern-Style Tomato Sauce *or*
      1 recipe Parmesan Cream Sauce (see page 412)
    3 tablespoons minced parsley, for garnish
    ¼ cup freshly grated Parmesan cheese, for garnish

Cheese and Escarole Filling

    3 tablespoons minced leek or onion
    ½ tablespoon minced garlic
    3 tablespoons olive oil
    1 tablespoon butter
    1 large bunch escarole, washed and finely shredded
    1 teaspoon dried oregano
    2 tablespoons Marsala
    2 tablespoons whipping cream
    ¼ cup whole-milk ricotta cheese
    ¼ cup grated Bel Paese or
      grated mozzarella cheese
      Salt and freshly ground pepper, to taste
      Pinch freshly grated nutmeg

1. Roll dough out in sheets. Form ravioli as described in How to Make Ravioli (photographs at right).

2. Bring a large pot of salted water to a boil. Add ravioli to boiling water a few at a time; do not crowd the pot. Ravioli will sink, then float. After they begin to float, cook 2½ minutes. Remove one and taste for doneness. With a slotted spoon, remove cooked ravioli to a warm platter and keep warm in a low oven. Add remaining ravioli to boiling water in batches until all are cooked. Meanwhile, reheat tomato or cream sauce.

3. When all ravioli are on the platter, top with hot sauce. Garnish with parsley and Parmesan.

Serves 4 to 6.

Cheese and Escarole Filling   Sauté leek and garlic in oil and butter over moderate heat until leek is very soft (about 15 minutes). Add escarole and oregano and sauté 2 minutes. Add Marsala, turn heat up to high, and cook until Marsala is almost completely evaporated. Reduce heat to medium and add cream. Stir to combine; simmer until cream thickens into a sauce (2 to 3 minutes). Remove from heat and cool slightly. Stir in cheeses; season to taste with salt, pepper, and nutmeg.

■ PASTA ROLL

The pasta roll can be made early in the day. Reheat by immersing in the boiling water 8 to 10 minutes. If you don't have a pot large enough to hold the full roll, cut pasta roll in half, wrap each half separately, and then poach.

    1 bunch spinach, julienned
    1 medium onion, diced
    2 cloves garlic, minced
    2 tablespoons unsalted butter
    1 tablespoon olive oil
    ½ pound ground veal or pork
    ½ pound boneless chicken breast, finely minced
    1 pound (2 cups) whole-milk ricotta cheese
    6 to 8 sprigs parsley, minced
    ½ teaspoon freshly grated nutmeg
    ½ teaspoon salt
    ½ teaspoon dried thyme
    ¼ teaspoon white pepper
    2 egg yolks
    1 cup freshly grated Parmesan cheese
    1 egg beaten with 1 tablespoon water
    ½ pound Basic Egg Dough (see page 411),
      rolled into 2 sheets (8 by 16 in. each)
      Northern-Style Tomato Sauce, for
      accompaniment (optional, see page 412)
      Melted butter and grated Parmesan cheese,
      for accompaniment (optional)

1. In a large skillet sauté spinach, onion, and garlic in butter and oil; set aside. In a large bowl or in food processor, mix veal and chicken breast (the processor will give you a smoother mixture).

2. In a large bowl mix cooked onion mixture with veal and chicken. Stir in ricotta cheese, parsley, nutmeg, salt, thyme, pepper, egg yolks, and Parmesan cheese.

3. Place egg-water wash in a small bowl. Lay out a piece of cheesecloth (larger than 16 inches square) on work surface. Place one sheet of dough on cheesecloth. Brush one long edge of dough with egg wash. Place second sheet of dough slightly overlapping first along long edge and press length to seal.

4. Spread prepared filling on pasta. Roll up jelly-roll style. Lay pasta roll along one edge of cheesecloth and oll up. Tie ends with string. In a fish poacher or a Dutch oven large enough to hold pasta roll, bring 6 quarts water to a boil. Gently lower roll into boiling water, reduce heat, and simmer 30 minutes. Remove from water and slice into 1-inch-thick pieces. Serve with tomato sauce or melted butter and Parmesan cheese, if desired.

Serves 8 as a main course.

Recipes and Related Information
Fettuccine With White Truffles, 583; Fusilli Salad, 508; Pesto, 27; Squid Marinara, 546.

HOW TO MAKE RAVIOLI

Roll pasta dough into sheets. Place mounds of filling, about ¾ teaspoon each, at regular intervals the length of the pasta. Brush lightly with cold water between mounds.

Place another sheet of pasta over the first and use fingers to press sheets together between mounds of filling.

Cut ravioli with a pizza cutter or pastry wheel. Use a fork to crimp and seal edges.

PATCH, TO

To repair cracks or tears in pie dough after it has been rolled out by sealing with a thin piece of leftover dough. Sometimes the patch is made stronger by gluing with water. It is better to patch pastry dough than to reroll it because rerolling will toughen it.

PATE AND TERRINE

A pâté is a spreadable paste of ground meats, livers, and seasonings. Its consistency can be airy and smooth like a mousse or more coarsely textured and country style. Ingredients for pâtés can be precooked and then combined, or the mixture can be processed and then baked in a crust, or in a mold that is often lined with pork fat. Special containers called terrine molds are traditionally used for pâtés, but any loaf pan of equal volume will work just as well (see MOLD). A terrine is made in a mold of the same name and was traditionally served in its mold. The pâté was freestanding. These definitions are, however, no longer rigidly followed. You will find the terms *pâté* and *terrine* used interchangeably.

Mixtures for pâtés are called forcemeats. These are made of fish, pork, lean veal, duck, game, or fowl, plus fat and flavorings, and are bound together with a bread or flour paste (see FORCEMEAT). Multicolored vegetable pâtés are increasingly popular.

Pâtés and terrines are served as appetizers or first courses. They are much like the American meat loaf, but have a richer, more luxurious texture and flavor. They are easy to prepare, especially with a food processor, although they may require costly or hard-to-find ingredients. Pâtés and terrines are wonderful for entertaining because they can be prepared well ahead; in fact, they improve when aged for several days.

■ CURRIED CHICKEN OR DUCK LIVER PATE IN ASPIC

The glistening aspic decoration belies the easy assembly of this curried liver pâté. Be sure to use a mold that is attractive enough to bring to the table.

    1 pound chicken or duck livers
    1 tart apple, diced
    1 small onion, diced
    4 tablespoons unsalted butter
    1 tablespoon curry powder
    ¼ cup Chicken Stock (see page 560) or apple brandy
    1½ tablespoons flour
    ½ teaspoon salt
    ¼ teaspoon freshly ground pepper
    1 egg
    1 baguette, sliced, for accompaniment

Aspic Glaze (see Note)

1. Preheat oven to 350° F. In a large skillet sauté livers, apple, and onion in butter over medium-high heat until livers are brown on outside but remain pink on inside (about 12 minutes). Stir in curry powder and cook 3 to 4 minutes.

2. Remove to a blender or food processor. Pour stock into pan, scraping cooked bits to loosen. Add pan juices to liver, and purée until smooth. Add flour, salt, pepper, and egg, and purée again until smooth.

3. Pour into a 3½- to 4-cup mold. Cover with aluminum foil, and place in a baking dish filled with about 1 inch warm water. Bake until knife inserted in center comes out clean (about 45 minutes). Remove from oven and cool. Chill for 1 hour and decorate with Aspic Glaze. Serve with baguette slices.

Serves 12 to 20 as an appetizer.

Note   See Aspic Glaze, page 372; use one half recipe Basic Aspic.

■ PATE MAISON

Set out this flavorful pâté with tiny French *cornichons* (pickles), a crock of Dijon mustard, and sliced baguettes. Cold and thinly sliced on French bread, it makes a splendid sandwich the next day.

    ½ medium onion, minced
    2 tablespoons butter
    ½ cup plus 2 tablespoons Cognac or Armagnac
    1 pound ground pork
    1 pound ground veal
    1 clove garlic, minced
    2 eggs, slightly beaten
    1 teaspoon salt
    ⅛ teaspoon freshly ground pepper
    1 teaspoon dried thyme
    1 chicken breast, boned and skinned
    1 pound pork fat, cut into ⅛-inch slices
    2 ounces pistachio nuts, shelled

1. Preheat oven to 350° F. In a small skillet sauté onion in butter over medium-high heat until translucent. Pour in ½ cup of the Cognac. Cook until Cognac is absorbed into onion (mixture will measure about ⅓ cup). Remove from heat and place in a large mixing bowl.

2. Add pork, veal, garlic, eggs, salt, pepper, and thyme. Mix with hands until thoroughly blended, or blend in food processor until light in texture and well blended.

3. Cut chicken breast into ½- by 3-inch slices. Put slices in a small bowl and add the remaining 2 tablespoons Cognac.

4. Line a 2-quart terrine or loaf pan with slices of pork fat. Press one half of ground meat mixture into pan. Cover with Cognac-soaked chicken, then pistachios. Press remaining ground meat mixture on top. Cover with another layer of pork fat.

5. Cover terrine with aluminum foil. Set in a pan of boiling water. Place on rack in center of oven. Bake until juices run clear yellow and pâté has shrunk from sides of pan.

6. When pâté is done, remove terrine and set on cooling rack. Place another loaf pan on top of pâté; fill with 3 to 4 pounds of weight (canned goods or bricks work well). Let pâté cool at room temperature for several hours, then refrigerate 2 to 3 days before slicing. To serve, unmold and slice.

Serves 10 as a first course.

◼ HOT PORK AND HAM PATE IN BRIOCHE

French through and through, this hot pâté is baked inside a buttery brioche dough. The flavor of the pâté will intensify if the mixture is allowed to cure overnight in the refrigerator.

    2 tablespoons butter
    1 large onion, finely chopped
    1 clove garlic, minced
    ¼ cup brandy
    1 egg
    ½ cup soft bread crumbs
    1 pound ground pork
    2 cups ground baked ham
    ¼ cup finely chopped parsley
    ½ teaspoon *each* salt and dried thyme
    ¼ teaspoon ground allspice
    ⅛ teaspoon white pepper
    1 egg beaten with 1 teaspoon water

Brioche Dough

    1 package active dry yeast
    ¼ cup warm (105° to 115° F) water
    1 tablespoon sugar
    ½ teaspoon salt
    2 cups flour
    2 eggs
    ½ cup butter, softened

1. Prepare Brioche Dough and, while it is rising, make filling.

2. In a medium frying pan, melt butter and cook onion until soft but not browned. Mix in garlic and brandy; cook, stirring, until most of the liquid cooks away.

3. Beat the 1 egg in a large bowl. Mix in bread crumbs, then ground meats, onion mixture, parsley, salt, thyme, allspice, and white pepper. Cover and refrigerate until ready to enclose in dough.

4. Roll dough out on a generously floured board or pastry cloth to make a rectangle about 10 by 20 inches. Shape filling with your hands into a loaf about 4 by 8 inches. Place filling at one end of dough. Pinch dough to seal ends. With long sealed edge at bottom, place in a well-greased 5- by 9-inch loaf pan.

5. Cover lightly with waxed paper and let rise in a warm place until dough looks puffy (about 30 minutes); or cover and refrigerate for several hours or overnight, and let stand at room temperature until puffy looking (about 1 hour).

6. Preheat oven to 350° F. Brush dough lightly with beaten egg mixture. Bake until dough is well browned and juice runs clear when a long skewer is inserted in center (about 1½ hours).

7. Place pâté (still in pan) on a rack and let stand for about 15 minutes; then carefully remove loaf from pan and cut into 1-inch-thick slices. Serve warm.

Serves 6 to 8.

Brioche Dough   Sprinkle yeast over the water in large bowl of electric mixer; let stand for 5 minutes to soften. Mix in sugar and salt, then ½ cup flour. Beat at medium speed until elastic (about 3 minutes). Beat in eggs, one at a time, until smooth, then gradually beat in remaining flour. Add butter, 1 tablespoon at a time, beating well after each addition. Transfer to a greased bowl, cover, and let rise in a warm place until doubled (about 1½ hours). Stir dough down.

Pâtés, such as Pâté Maison, probably developed as a Gallic solution to the universal problem of what to do with leftovers.

Hoppin' John, a richly flavorful dish of black-eyed peas, is traditionally served in the Deep South on New Year's Day.

PEA

All peas are members of the legume family, plants whose seeds are borne in pods. Some varieties, such as English peas and the French *petits pois,* are valued for their seeds only and are known as shelling peas. Some of the shelling peas—English peas, for example—are usually eaten fresh; others, such as pigeon peas, field peas (which, when split, are the common green or yellow split pea), and chick-peas, are usually dried.

The other major type of pea is the edible-podded pea, eaten in its entirety before the seeds develop. The Chinese snow pea is the best-known example.

Use Depending upon their variety, peas may be used as a side dish or added to soups, salads, stews, rice and pasta dishes, and casseroles.

Availability Fresh and dried peas are found in supermarkets and specialty produce stores; some health-food stores carry a selection of dried peas. This entry discusses the most common types of fresh and dried peas.

Selection See specific peas.

Storage Keep both shelling peas (in their pods) and edible-podded peas in a plastic bag in the refrigerator crisper and use within one or two days. Dried peas will keep for up to one year in an airtight container in a cool, dry place.

Preparation Shelling peas should be shelled just before using. Open pod by removing string. Remove peas. Snow peas and sugar snap peas should be strung as well, although the pods should be left unopened. *About soaking and quick-soaking dried peas:* Most dried peas require presoaking to soften them before cooking. Cover with cold water and soak at least 8 hours or overnight. To quick-soak, cover with cold water, bring to a boil, and boil for 1 minute; cover, remove from heat, and let stand for 1 hour. Discard soaking liquid.

Cooking *Fresh Peas:* See BOIL, SAUTE, STEAM, STIR-FRY. *Dried Peas:* See BOIL. Also see specific peas.

BLACK-EYED PEA

See Cowpea.

CECI BEAN

See Chick-pea.

CHICK-PEA

Also known as garbanzo beans or ceci beans, chick-peas are a staple in India and figure prominently in the cuisines of North Africa and the Middle East. Use chick-peas in salads, soups, and stews or as a side dish. They may be roasted and served as a snack; ground for flour for use in breads and fritters; puréed and seasoned for a dip; or added to the North African stew known as Couscous. Chick-peas are occasionally available fresh in the summer; the pod is a small, fuzzy, green oval with one or two seeds inside. Dried chick-peas are packaged in plastic bags or sold in bulk. For fresh peas, select full, light green pods without signs of drying.

To prepare fresh chick-peas, open the pod and remove the beans. Simmer beans, covered, in boiling water until tender. To prepare dried chick-peas, soak overnight or quick-soak (see Preparation); then simmer, covered, in 3 parts water to 1 part peas until tender (1½ to 2 hours).

■ HUMMUS

Serve this Middle Eastern dip with fresh raw vegetables, cracker bread, or toasted pita bread. Sesame tahini has the consistency of peanut butter. It's available in many supermarkets and specialty food stores. If it has separated, stir well before using.

> 2 **cans (15 oz each) chick-peas**
> 3 **cloves garlic**
> 2 **tablespoons fresh lemon juice, or more, to taste**
> 6 **tablespoons sesame tahini** *or*
>   **2 to 3 tablespoons peanut butter**
> ¼ **teaspoon ground cumin, or to taste (optional)**
>   **Salt, to taste**
>   **Finely chopped parsley, for garnish**

1. Drain liquid from 1 can chick-peas and put beans in a food processor or blender. Add peas from remaining can with their liquid, and garlic, lemon juice, and tahini; purée until smooth.

2. Add cumin (if used) and salt to taste, and purée a few seconds more. Serve garnished with parsley.

Makes 3 cups.

CHINESE SNOW PEA

Edible-podded Chinese snow peas are delicious when stir-fried quickly in oil by themselves or with other ingredients. They should be cooked only until hot throughout (one or two minutes). They may be stir-fried with Chinese black mushrooms, water chestnuts, and bean curd, or lightly glazed with oyster sauce. Snow peas can be added to soups or stews or served as a stir-fry side dish for all manner of Western dishes—from baked fish to roast pork, chicken, or beef.

Chinese snow peas are available the year around in Asian markets and in some supermarkets, with peak supplies in spring and fall. They should be bright green, and firm. Choose ones that are small and flat, with immature seeds. Avoid those with drying along the seam.

◼ STILTON SNOW PEAS

A quick blanching highlights the color and flavor of snow peas while retaining their crispness. The filled snow peas will hold in the refrigerator for several hours if loosely covered with plastic wrap to prevent drying out.

    40 snow peas
     3 ounces Stilton cheese, at room temperature
     3 ounces cream cheese, softened
     1 teaspoon chopped parsley

1. Remove stems from snow peas. Bring 3 quarts of water to a boil. Drop in snow peas and blanch for 30 seconds. Remove with slotted spoon and immediately place in ice-cold water to stop cooking. Remove from water and pat dry with paper towels. Carefully cut a 1- to 1½-inch slit in center of curved side of each snow pea with a sharp paring knife.

2. In a small mixing bowl, mix Stilton cheese, cream cheese, and parsley. Fill each snow pea through slit, using two spoons or a pastry bag fitted with a small star tip. Chill until serving time on paper-towel–lined baking sheets covered loosely with plastic wrap. To serve, arrange in a fan shape on an attractive plate.

Makes 40 appetizers.

Recipe: Shrimp With Snow Peas and Water Chestnuts, 606.

COWPEA

Also known as crowder peas, cowpeas are widely eaten in the American South and in Africa. They have a mealy texture and an earthy flavor that is complemented by pork, especially ham. The black-eyed pea is a type of cowpea. Use cowpeas in soups, stews, and salads or as a side dish. In the summer, cowpeas are occasionally available fresh, either shelled or unshelled. If you are buying unshelled fresh peas, select those with full, moist pods. Dried black-eyed peas and cowpeas are available packaged in plastic bags or sold in bulk; they should be used within one year of purchase. Black-eyed peas may also be purchased canned and frozen.

To prepare fresh cowpeas, open pod and remove beans. Cook fresh cowpeas in boiling water, covered, until tender. To prepare dried cowpeas, soak overnight or quick-soak (see Preparation); simmer, covered, in 3 parts water to 1 part peas until tender (about one hour).

◼ HOPPIN' JOHN

In the Deep South black-eyed peas eaten on New Year's Day are supposed to bring good luck in the coming year. In some areas residents insist that the peas bestow good luck only if they're prepared in Hoppin' John and served with cooked greens, which symbolize money. This recipe uses dried black-eyed peas. Note that the peas must stand for at least one hour or as long as overnight. Accompany Hoppin' John with Country-Style Greens. That recipe appears on page 287.

  1½ cups (about ½ lb) dried black-eyed peas
  1½ teaspoons salt, plus salt to taste
    6 strips bacon, diced
    1 medium onion, chopped
    ¾ cup long-grain white rice
    2 tablespoons butter (optional)
       Salt and freshly ground pepper, to taste
       Dash of Louisiana-style hot sauce, to taste
    ½ cup minced green onions, including
       green tops, for garnish
    3 tablespoons minced parsley, for garnish

1. Rinse peas and pick them over. Cover with 3 cups cold water, add 1 teaspoon of the salt, and let stand overnight. (For a quicker soak, to serve peas the same day, see Preparation.)

2. Drain peas, discarding water, and place in a large pot. In a separate pan, sauté bacon until crisp; add it to peas, reserving rendered drippings. Add onion, remaining ½ teaspoon salt, and 2 cups water. Bring just to a boil, lower heat, and simmer until peas are tender (about 30 minutes). A small amount of cooking liquid should remain; if liquid is absorbed too quickly during cooking, add fresh water by ¼ cups.

3. In separate pot, cover rice with cold water. Bring to a boil, stir once, cover, and lower heat to the barest simmer. Simmer rice for 20 minutes.

4. When peas are tender, add cooked rice to pot. Stir in 2 tablespoons reserved bacon fat or 2 tablespoons butter (if preferred), salt, pepper, and hot sauce to taste. Cover and simmer about 15 minutes longer so flavors mingle and rice absorbs some of the remaining cooking liquid. To serve, garnish with green onions and parsley.

Serves 6 to 7.

CROWDER PEA

See Cowpea.

ENGLISH PEA

Fresh shelled peas are best when steamed briefly in a covered saucepan in a small amount of boiling water. Steamed peas are usually buttered and occasionally creamed as well. French cooks add shredded lettuce to the steaming peas; other cooks add onion or green onion. Indian cooks braise peas with spices and cubes of firm homemade cheese. Italian cooks braise peas with prosciutto. Steamed peas can be cooled, then tossed with diced ham and mayonnaise for a summer salad. They can be mixed with other vegetables, such as carrots or corn, and served hot. They can be added to soups or stews and are particularly delicious with delicate meats such as veal or veal sweetbreads.

Fresh English peas are available in supermarkets the year around, with the domestic summer crop being supplemented by imports from Mexico. The domestic crop peaks in quantity and quality in the summer months. Both English peas and the tiny French *petits pois* are available frozen and canned. Fresh shelling peas are full of sugar at harvest but begin to convert their natural sugar into starch the moment they're picked. For that reason, the sooner the pea is cooked after harvest, the better. Buy English peas from a market with rapid turnover or, better yet, buy peas at local farm stands or farmers' markets, if possible. When selecting English peas, break a pod open and taste a pea; it should be sweet, not starchy. The pods should be well filled but the seeds should not be overlarge. Look for bright green pods; avoid those that have dry seams.

■ SPRING LAMB STEW WITH FRESH PEAS

Fresh mint seasons the lamb in this glistening stew. Serve with butter-fried potatoes and a leafy green salad tossed with your favorite dressing, crusty bread and butter, and fresh strawberries for dessert.

>   3 pounds boneless lamb leg or shoulder,
>   fat trimmed and cut in 1-inch cubes
>   Salt and white pepper, to taste
>   3 tablespoons butter
>   3 tablespoons vegetable oil
>   3 shallots, finely chopped
>   1 clove garlic, minced
>   1 large carrot, cut in ¼-inch-thick slices
>   3 or 4 sprigs fresh mint
>   1 cup Rich Chicken Stock (see page 560) or
>   canned chicken broth
>   1½ cups dry white wine
>   1½ to 2 cups shelled fresh peas

1. Sprinkle lamb lightly with salt and pepper. In a large, deep frying pan or Dutch oven, melt 2 tablespoons butter with oil. Add lamb, about a third at a time. Brown well, removing lamb as it browns. When all lamb is removed from pan, add shallots, cooking and stirring until they are soft and lightly browned. Mix in garlic and carrot.

2. Return lamb to pan. Add mint, broth, and wine. Bring to a boil, cover, reduce heat, and simmer until tender (45 minutes to 1 hour).

3. Remove lamb and keep it warm. Strain cooking liquid, discarding carrot and mint. Skim and discard surface fat. Return liquid to pan and bring to a boil over high heat. Cook, stirring, until slightly reduced and syrupy. Taste, and add salt if needed. Mix in peas and cook, stirring, for 1 to 2 minutes.

4. Cut remaining butter in pieces. Off heat, stir in butter, one piece at a time, until melted.

5. Return lamb to sauce, stirring to coat well. Spoon lamb into center of each warm plate. Surround with sauce and peas and serve at once.

Serves 6 to 8.

FIELD PEA

Small round peas grown especially for drying are known as field peas; they may be green or yellow. When split, they are called split peas. Whole field peas and split peas are boiled in about 4 parts water to 1 part peas until soft (about one hour). They can be boiled further to reduce them to a purée, then seasoned with butter or spices or made into soup. Bacon, sausage, or smoked pork make a pleasing addition to dried peas and dried pea soups. Whole field peas are available in plastic packages in some supermarkets and in bulk in some health-food stores. Split peas are available in plastic packages in most supermarkets and in bulk in most health-food stores.

Recipes: Curried Lettuce and Pea Soup, 341; Split Pea Soup, Black Forest Style, 565.

GARBANZO BEAN

See Chick-pea.

PETITS POIS

See English Pea.

PIGEON PEA

Also known as *gunga, goongoo,* or congo peas, pigeon peas are native to Africa and are widely eaten today in the Caribbean, Africa, and India. The dried peas are beige or pale yellow with red mottling; they are not widely available fresh. In the Caribbean cooks make pigeon peas into soup or dumplings or serve them with rice. Look for dried pigeon peas in health-food stores and markets catering to an Indian, African, or Caribbean clientele.

SPLIT PEA

See Field Pea.

SUGAR SNAP PEA

The sugar snap pea, a relatively new variety, is a cross between a shelling pea and an edible-podded pea. Its pod is still sweet and tender when the seeds are developed. Sugar snap peas are available in spring and fall in some supermarkets and specialty markets. Sugar snap peas should be bright green and firm, not limp. They should be plump, but not filled to bursting; avoid pods that are dried around the seam. Sugar snap peas need only brief blanching—a couple of minutes in a large quantity of boiling salted water, then draining, drying, and reheating in oil or butter. They should still be crunchy when served. Sautéed sugar snap peas make an excellent side dish for fish, poultry, pork, beef, or veal.

PEACH

The sweet, juicy peaches grown today probably bear little resemblance to the earliest peaches, native to China. Until modern horticulturists developed the strains we enjoy today, most peaches were small, fairly sour, and certainly more fuzzy than modern varieties. Today, there are thousands of named peaches. Some have stones that cling to the flesh (clingstone varieties); others are freestone. Some have white or pale pink flesh; others have yellow flesh. Some have white skins with a pink blush; others have a deep yellow skin with a reddish blush. Some are firm-fleshed varieties designed for canning; others are for eating out of hand. In any case, the peach is one of America's favorite fruits and one of the country's most important fruit crops.

Use A ripe peach eaten out of hand is a delicious breakfast food or snack. Sliced peaches can be added to fruit salads and gelatin salads; they also may be poached for compotes. Sliced and sugared peaches are often spooned on top of shortcake or soaked in wine or Champagne for an easy summer dessert. They can be baked with butter and sugar and macaroon crumbs, or with a cobbler dough or a fruit-crisp topping. Peaches can be puréed for sherbet and ice cream or made into jam or preserves. They can be pickled, home-canned in sugar syrup, or made into chutney. Peach juice makes a pleasing ingredient in fruit punches or cocktails.

Availability Domestic peaches are sold from early May to mid-September. Imports from the southern hemisphere may supplement the domestic crop in some supermarkets in the winter. Frozen peaches, canned peaches, and canned peach nectar are sold in most supermarkets.

Selection An appealing fragrance is the best clue to a ripe peach. Look also for fruit that gives slightly to pressure and has a yellow or creamy background color between its blushed areas. Avoid fruit with greenish undertones and fruit that is bruised or very soft.

Storage Peaches will keep in the refrigerator crisper for up to two weeks.

Preparation Peaches eaten out of hand do not require peeling. Most peaches are peeled for use in cooked dishes, however. Very ripe peaches are usually easy to peel; others may need to be blanched first. To blanch, cut a small *x* in the rounded end opposite the stem; dip fruit in boiling water for about 30 seconds, then plunge into ice water. Skin will peel away readily. Peaches oxidize and brown when exposed to air; rub or sprinkle with lemon juice to prevent browning.

▦ NUTTY PEACH PIE

For a variation, omit the nut topping and bake as a double-crust or lattice-top pie. Serve warm or at room temperature, topped with Chantilly Cream (see page 252) or with ice cream.

    1 9-inch single-crust Nut Egg Pastry (see page 435)
    5 cups peeled, sliced freestone peaches
       (5 to 6 large peaches)
    ½ to ¾ cup granulated sugar
    2½ to 3 tablespoons cornstarch
       Dash freshly grated nutmeg
    1 tablespoon fresh lemon juice
    ⅛ teaspoon almond extract
    1 egg white, lightly beaten (optional)
    ⅓ cup firmly packed light brown sugar
    ½ cup flour
    6 tablespoons unsalted butter
    1 cup chopped nuts (mixture of almonds
       and pecans)

1. Preheat oven to 425° F. Line a 9-inch pie plate with Nut Egg Pastry. In a large bowl combine sliced peaches, ½ to ¾ cup granulated sugar (depending upon ripeness of peaches), cornstarch, and nutmeg. Allow to stand 15 minutes.

2. Stir in lemon juice and almond extract.

3. Lightly brush uncooked pie shell with a thin layer of egg white (if used) to make pie crust moistureproof. Pour filling into pie shell.

4. Mix brown sugar with flour; cut in butter until crumbly. Stir in nuts. Sprinkle mixture over peaches.

5. Bake for 15 minutes. Reduce oven to 400° F and continue baking for 35 to 40 minutes. Cover edges of crust with strips of aluminum foil, if necessary, to prevent excessive browning.

Makes one 9-inch pie.

This Nutty Peach Pie is baked in an almond pie crust and topped with an almond-pecan crumble. It's a perfect dessert for summer, when peaches are in season.

Recipes and Related Information
Ginger-Peach Upside-Down Cake, 87; Gingered Peach Pickles, 322; Peach Filling, 627; Peach Melba, 315; Summer Peach Jam, 319.

PEANUT

Actually a legume rather than a nut, the peanut has seeds that are encased in a fragile, dry pod. Like other legumes, the oval seeds may be split into two parts. The seeds are ivory-colored and covered with a papery brown skin. Peanuts have a buttery, nutty flavor that is intensified by roasting or frying.

Use   In this country half the peanut crop is made into peanut butter. Some portion of the remainder is sold in the shell; probably most of the unshelled peanuts marketed in this country are sold at sporting events. Shelled peanuts may be roasted or unroasted, salted or unsalted. They are used in candy bars and snack foods such as caramel corn, in nut mixes marketed as cocktail snacks, and in cookies. Chopped peanuts are added to salads and slaws, and to muffins and quick breads, and serve as a garnish for ice cream sundaes and sautéed vegetables. Peanuts are pressed for their oil, which is excellent for sautéing and frying and for salad dressings. Peanuts are popular in Africa, where they are known as groundnuts. African groundnut stew is a spicy chicken and tomato dish made with ground peanuts. Nigerian cooks grind peanuts into flour for bread. The Chinese eat seasoned and roasted peanuts as an hors d'oeuvre or grind them to make a sauce for noodles. Indonesian cooks make a spicy dipping sauce for skewered meats with ground peanuts, chiles, and coconut milk.

Availability   Most supermarkets carry peanuts both shelled and in the shell. Shelled peanuts are usually packed in vacuum-sealed jars or cans. Peanut butter, both smooth and chunky, is sold in all supermarkets. It may contain added sugar or preservatives. Natural peanut butter is available in most health-food stores. Chinese markets are a good source for raw peanuts.

Storage   Peanuts turn rancid quickly, shelled peanuts faster than unshelled. Store unshelled peanuts in the refrigerator or in a cool, dry, dark place for up to six months. Refrigerate shelled peanuts in an airtight container for up to three months, or freeze for up to six months. Natural peanut butter should be refrigerated after opening; it will keep for up to six months. Peanut butter containing preservatives will keep indefinitely in a cool, dry place.

Preparation   To toast peanuts, shell them, then arrange them on a baking tray and bake at 325° F until fragrant and lightly browned (8 to 10 minutes). Rub between towels to remove skins.

Recipes and Related Information
Choco–Peanut Butter Cookies, 145; Peanut Brittle, 96; Peanut Butter–Chocolate Chip Cookies, 141.

PEAR

Of unknown origin, pears today are cultivated in temperate zones all over the world. Among tree fruits grown in these zones, only the apple is more heavily planted. Of the 5,000 varieties of pears, only a few are of commercial importance in this country. Commercial varieties vary considerably in skin color, texture, and flavor. See Availability for a description of major types.

Use   Pears are probably most often eaten out of hand, as a breakfast food, dessert, or snack. Ripe pears are particularly delicious with a blue cheese such as Gorgonzola, Roquefort, or Stilton. Sliced pears are used in fruit salads and compotes. Pears may be poached, either whole or in halves, in a light wine syrup, raspberry syrup, or sugar syrup. They can be baked with butter and sugar or poached, sliced, and arranged on top of a fruit tart.

Availability   In addition to fresh pears, supermarkets also carry canned pears and canned pear nectar. The major commercial pear varieties include the following.

Anjou   This winter pear with greenish yellow skin and yellowish white flesh is globular in shape with a short neck. The Anjou is a hardy pear that ships and stores well; it holds its shape when cooked. It is available from October through May.

Bartlett   Also known as the Williams' pear, it is a popular summer pear with yellow skin and ivory flesh. There is also a variety with red flesh. It is very aromatic, very tender when ripe, with flesh that is sweet, juicy, and buttery. It is available from mid-July through November.

Bosc   This winter pear with an elongated shape and a russet brown skin has white flesh that is firm when ripe and quite sweet. Bosc pears hold their shape well when cooked and are excellent for poaching or baking.

Comice   Having perhaps the finest flavor and smoothest texture of generally available pears, this winter pear has a squat, almost neckless shape, a brownish green skin, and a white flesh. Ripe Comice are highly aromatic and fairly firm; they should not be allowed to get soft. A choice pear for eating out of hand, it has a buttery texture and a winy flavor. It also bakes well and makes fragrant sherbet. Look for Comice from October through January.

French Butter Pear   Also known as Beurre Hardy, this delicate pear does not cook well. However, it is exceptional for eating out of hand or with cheese. It has a brownish skin with a creamy flesh and a buttery texture that explains its name. It is available late summer through fall.

Seckel   This very small, brownish pear is often poached for a ham or turkey garnish or canned in a spiced syrup. It has a grainy texture and is available in some markets in late fall and winter.

Winter Nellis   This firm, spicy pear (also spelled Nelis) has a squat shape and a dull green skin with russet dots. Because it is firm, it holds its shape well when baked. It is available from late fall through spring.

Selection   Pears are one of the few fruits that won't ripen properly on the tree; for that reason, they are picked mature but hard and must be allowed to soften slightly before eating. Choose pears that are fragrant, free of blemishes, and beginning to color and soften.

Storage   Hold pears at room temperature in a warm place until they give slightly to pressure. Refrigerate and use within a few days. Pears intended for cooking should be cooked when still fairly firm.

Preparation   Pears do not require peeling for eating out of hand, although some have coarse or tannic skins that may be unpleasant. Peel as desired. Peeled pears oxidize rapidly; rub or sprinkle with lemon juice or store in acidulated water until ready to use.

■ **BAKED PEAR TART**

This tart looks especially pretty when baked in a scalloped tart band. Thinly sliced pear halves radiate from the center to form the petals of a flower.

  1   **10-inch Sweet Tart Pastry for scalloped tart tin (see page 441)**
  6   **tablespoons unsalted butter**
  1½ **large eggs (beat second egg and use half)**
  ½   **cup plus 1 tablespoon granulated sugar**
  3   **tablespoons sifted flour**
  4   **ripe pears (Anjou or Bartlett)**
  2   **tablespoons fresh lemon juice**
  ½   **cup apricot preserves**
  1   **tablespoon pear liqueur or water**
  ¼   **cup confectioners' sugar**

1. Position a 10-inch scalloped tart band on a flat baking sheet. (You may substitute a 10-inch tart tin with removable bottom or 10-inch circular tart band.) Roll out tart pastry and line tart band or tin. Trim dough even with top of tart band. Wrap and refrigerate 1 hour, or freeze for later use.

2. To make custard filling, cook butter over medium heat until butter browns. Immediately remove from heat and cool in pan 5 minutes. Place eggs in a mixing bowl and gradually whisk in granulated sugar. Whisk in flour. Whisk in melted butter and all of the browned bits that cling to bottom of pan (these give tart a delicious nutty flavor and aroma). Set aside until tart is assembled.

3. Preheat oven to 375° F. Peel pears. Cut each in half lengthwise, remove core and seeds, and place into a large bowl of cold water with lemon juice (this keeps pears white). Remove pear halves from water; dry well on paper towels. Using a sharp, thin knife held at a 45-degree angle to cutting board, slice each pear half

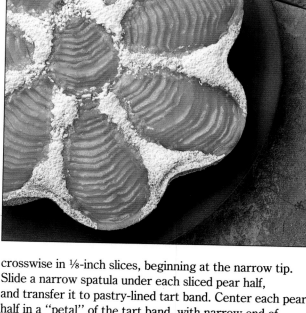

This custard-filled pear tart is baked in a scallop-edged tart band. The top is dusted with confectioners' sugar to create a delicate flower pattern.

crosswise in ⅛-inch slices, beginning at the narrow tip. Slide a narrow spatula under each sliced pear half, and transfer it to pastry-lined tart band. Center each pear half in a "petal" of the tart band, with narrow end of pear pointing toward center. Then push pear slices from narrow to wide end to fan them slightly. Trim tip off last pear half, slice, and place in center of tart. Pour custard filling in empty spaces around, but not on top of, pears. Custard should come only halfway up sides of tart.

4. Bake for 20 minutes at 375° F. Reduce oven to 350° F and bake until custard looks fully cooked (40 to 50 minutes longer). If edges of crust begin to brown too much, cover them with strips of aluminum foil. Cool completely.

5. To make glaze: Melt preserves over low heat. Strain to remove pieces of fruit; stir in pear liqueur. When tart is cool, brush pear halves with a thin coat of preserves. Then cover each pear half with an upside-down boat-shaped tartlet tin (or a cardboard pattern of the same shape). Cover center pear with an upside-down, small, round brioche tin, tartlet tin, or cardboard pattern. Sift a light layer of confectioners' sugar over tart. Carefully lift off tins.

6. Lift off tart band, slide tart onto a serving plate, and serve at room temperature.

Serves 10.

Recipes and Related Information
Pear With Prosciutto, 358; Rosé Pears in Chocolate Bath, 612.

Pralines (say praw-leens), usually associated with New Orleans, are traditionally served with strong, hot, black coffee with chicory.

PECAN

The pecan is a native American nut that is still not widely cultivated elsewhere. Most pecans today are grown in the South and Southwest, with Georgia the leading producer. Like the walnut, the pecan is a species of hickory. Its smooth, pale brown, oval shell often has black markings and is usually about an inch long. Some pecans are also dyed red to hide blemishes. The kernel is a rich, golden brown with an ivory interior; its flavor is rich and buttery, especially when toasted.

Use   Pecans are widely used in the South and Southwest in pies, cakes, ice cream, pralines, and cookies. Pecans may be shelled, buttered, and roasted for a cocktail snack, or toasted, chopped, and added to salads and sautéed vegetables.

Availability   Pecans are harvested in the fall and are available in their shells in some markets at that time. Most supermarkets and health-food stores carry shelled pecans, either in bulk or packaged, whole or chopped.

Selection   Unshelled nuts should feel heavy for their size. Shelled nuts turn rancid quickly; buy them from a market with a rapid turnover.

Storage   Because of their high oil content, pecans turn rancid quickly. Store unshelled pecans in a cool, dark, dry place and use within six months. Shelled pecans may be frozen for up to six months or refrigerated for up to three months.

Preparation   To bring out their flavor, toast pecans on a baking sheet in a preheated 350° F oven until fragrant (six to eight minutes).

▓ PRALINES

A mixture of caramelized sugar and nuts, pralines are usually crisp, but this recipe produces a softer candy. The use of buttermilk gives this version of the Louisiana classic a delicious tang. Traditionally these candies are eaten after a meal with strong black coffee.

>   2 **cups buttermilk**
>   2 **cups sugar**
>   1 **teaspoon baking soda**
>   ½ **cup unsalted butter**
>   1½ **cups coarsely chopped pecans**

1. In a heavy-bottomed, 4- to 6-quart saucepan, combine buttermilk, sugar, baking soda, and butter. Cook over medium heat, stirring frequently with a wooden spoon and monitoring temperature with a candy thermometer. First the mixture will foam, then darken as it thickens. It is done when it reaches 238° F (soft-ball stage).

2. Remove mixture from heat and stir in pecans with a wire whisk. Beat mixture until it cools to about 220° F (on a candy thermometer). While it is still soft, spoon nut mixture onto waxed paper in 1- to 2-tablespoon mounds.

As pralines cool, they will become firm and can be removed from waxed paper.

Makes 2 to 3 dozen pralines.

> ### *Recipes and Related Information*
> *Butter Pecan Ice Cream, 312; Chocolate-Pecan Waffles, 599; Pecan Applesauce Cake, 87; Pecan Buttermilk Waffles, 599; Pecan Lace Cookies, 142; Southern Pecan Pie, 439; The Stickiest Pecan Rolls, 629.*

PEEL; PEEL, TO

The skin of a fruit or vegetable, also called the rind. To remove this skin.

Peeling tools include the fingers, a sharp paring knife, and a vegetable peeler. Sometimes heating facilitates peeling. Blanching some thin-skinned fruits and vegetables, such as peaches, plums, and tomatoes, splits the skin, which then pulls away in strips. Peppers can be peeled by scorching them over a flame or under a broiler or by roasting them in a hot oven until blistered, then sweating them in a paper or plastic bag 10 to 20 minutes. The moisture causes the skin to loosen. The easiest way to peel a clove of garlic is to cut off its root end and crush the clove with the side of a chef's knife; the skin will slip off. To skin nuts, toast in the oven until fragrant, then rub in a towel.

PEPINO

Like the potato, tomato, and eggplant, the pepino is a member of the nightshade family. The heart-shaped fruit is yellow with purple markings; the yellow flesh is aromatic, with a flavor reminiscent of cantaloupe, honeydew melon, and pear. It has a small seed cavity that contains inedible seeds.

Use   Eat on the half shell with lemon or lime wedges. Add sliced, peeled pepino to fruit salads, compotes, and chutneys. Purée for sorbets. Sauté in butter to garnish duck or chicken.

Availability   Fresh California-grown pepino is available in some supermarkets from August to December. Imports from New Zealand appear in the markets from February to June.

Selection   Choose aromatic pepinos with good yellow skin color; a ripe fruit will give slightly to pressure.

Storage   If fruit is slightly underripe, store at room temperature until it colors and softens. Refrigerate up to three days in a plastic bag in the refrigerator crisper.

Preparation   Halve and remove seeds.

PEPPER

All peppers, whether sweet or hot, are members of the capsicum family and are native to the New World. The plant that produces peppercorns, *Piper nigrum,* is native to Asia and is not related.

Peppers are a rich source of vitamin C, superior even to citrus, and they contain as much vitamin A as carrots. For centuries, chiles (hot peppers) have been put to medicinal use, particularly as a topical healing agent. Even today, many commercial liniments contain oleoresin of capsicum. Ground hot peppers are said to be effective in homemade insecticides, and at least one commercial manufacturer exploits the irritative quality of hot peppers in a product designed to discourage thumb sucking. The color extracted from red pepper is used as a natural coloring agent in a variety of foodstuffs, including sausage and cheese. Similarly, some processors add pimiento to chicken feed to impart a deep yellow color to the birds' skin and fat.

Capsicum peppers range in flavor from mild and sweet to blisteringly hot. The heat comes from capsaicin, a compound found in the veins and seeds of hot peppers, but not in their walls.

Pepper nomenclature is confusing, as it varies from country to country. In the United States the mild peppers are known as sweet peppers; hot peppers are known either as hot peppers or chiles. In England all peppers are known as chiles, but hot ones are referred to as hot chiles. In Latin America hot peppers are chiles and mild peppers are pimientos. In the United States pimientos are just one variety of sweet red pepper. To add to the confusion, some varieties have several different common names.

The following discussion divides peppers into two types: sweet and hot. Although it is sometimes difficult to distinguish a sweet pepper from a hot one by sight, it is generally true that the smaller the pepper, the hotter. However, weather, soil, and degree of maturity can affect capsaicin content, making one pepper hotter than another of the same variety; even peppers on the same plant can vary in pungency. The following glossary should at least help you to distinguish mild, hot, and hotter.

SWEET PEPPERS

The most widely available sweet pepper is the bell pepper, named for its bell-like shape. Green bell peppers are the most common, but red, yellow, and even purple bells are increasingly available in specialty markets. Most green bells become red with age; red bell peppers are simply green bells that have been allowed to ripen on the vine. Consequently, red bells are sweeter than greens and are available later in the season. All bell peppers have a mild flavor and a crisp, crunchy texture.

Use   Raw bell peppers add color and crunchy texture to salads and to raw vegetable assortments served with dips. Mediterranean cooks sauté strips of sweet peppers and serve them as a side dish or a garnish for braised salt cod or lamb. In Spain, Italy, and southern France, cooks roast and peel sweet peppers and serve them cool, as a salad, with lemon and oil. Middle European cooks stuff bell peppers with meat and/or seasoned rice or stew them with veal or chicken. In Japan strips of bell peppers are dipped in tempura batter and fried. Chinese cooks add bell pepper strips to stir-fries of all kinds.

Availability   Green bell peppers are found in most markets the year around; peak season is August and September. The domestic red, yellow, and purple bells are harvested in late summer and fall, with some markets stocking imports from Mexico and Holland at other times of the year. Dehydrated bell pepper flakes are available on some supermarket spice racks.

Other sweet peppers include the following.

Bull's Horn   A long, narrow, sickle-shaped green pepper with a pointed tip. Roast and peel it, then serve it whole with olive oil, garlic, and lemon. It is available in late summer and fall in some specialty markets. Select and store as for bell peppers.

Cubanelle   A long (about 4 inches), tapered pepper that may be yellow or red. It has thick, meaty walls and is generally more flavorful than the bell pepper. Also known as the Cuban pepper, it is available sporadically in specialty markets. Select and store as for bell peppers.

Lamuyo   Also known as European sweet pepper or rouge royal; a very sweet bell-shaped pepper, longer, larger, and more slender than the standard bell. Thick-fleshed and flavorful, it comes in a range of colors. Look for it in specialty markets in late summer and fall; select, store, and use as for bell peppers.

Pimiento   A large, heart-shaped red pepper sold in some markets in late summer and fall. It has thicker, meatier flesh than the bell. Because of their thick walls, they are excellent for roasting and peeling. Bottled or canned peeled pimientos are available in most supermarkets. Select, store, and use as for bell peppers.

Sweet Banana   A long banana-shaped yellow pepper that also comes in a hot variety (see Yellow Wax Pepper). It may be stuffed or pickled.

Selection   Choose bell peppers that feel heavy for their size; they will have thick, meaty walls. Avoid any with soft spots or shriveled areas. Bell peppers should be firm and shiny.

Storage   Keep peppers in a plastic bag in the refrigerator for up to one week.

Preparation   If stuffing or slicing, ribs and seeds should be removed. To keep peppers whole for stuffing, cut about ¼ to ½ inch off top and scoop out or trim away seeds and white ribs. If peppers will be sliced, cut them in half, then trim away stem, seeds, and ribs.

TIPS

ROASTING AND PEELING PEPPERS

The directions for roasting and peeling sweet and hot peppers are the same. When handling hot peppers, use caution to prevent irritation of skin or eyes. Wear gloves and wash hands well afterwards.

Hold peppers over open gas flame or charcoal fire, or place under a broiler. Turn often until blackened on all sides. Transfer peppers into a paper or plastic bag; close and set aside until cool (15 to 20 minutes).

Peel peppers; halve; remove stem and seeds. Lay halves flat and use dull side of a small knife to scrape away any black bits of skin and stray seeds. Slice into ¼-inch strips.

Roasted Red Peppers Roast 2 red bell peppers as directed above. Put sliced peppers in a medium bowl; add 1 clove finely minced garlic, 2 tablespoons extravirgin olive oil, and 1 teaspoon minced fresh oregano. Salt to taste. Toss to blend and let marinate at room temperature for 1 hour before using.

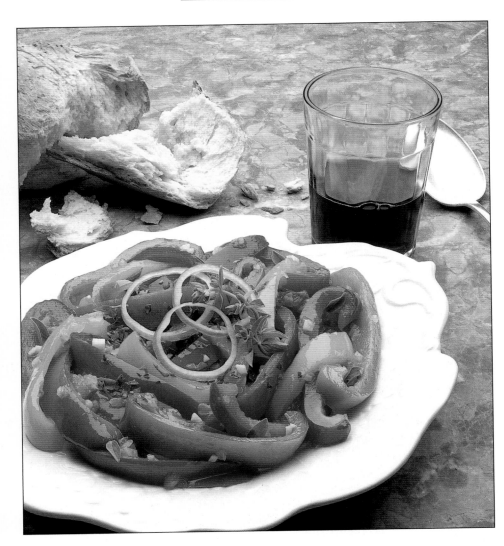

Mixed sweet peppers make tricolored Peperonata, a lively late-summer antipasto. For a more substantial first course, pair the peppers with sliced mozzarella.

■ PEPERONATA

Mixed marinated peppers

Sweet peppers stewed slowly with tomatoes, herbs, and garlic are a popular summer first course in southern Italy. Serve them with crusty bread to mop up the aromatic juices, or offer Peperonata as part of a larger antipasto platter. Select meaty peppers that feel heavy for their size.

   ½ **cup olive oil**
   2 **tablespoons minced garlic**
   ½ **yellow onion, minced**
   2 **red bell peppers**
   2 **green bell peppers**
   1 **yellow bell pepper (if unavailable, substitute another red or green pepper)**
   2 **tomatoes, peeled, seeded, and coarsely chopped**
   2 **teaspoons salt**
   ¼ **cup fresh oregano leaves**
   ½ **red onion, in paper-thin slices, for garnish**
   2 **tablespoons minced parsley, for garnish**
   2 **tablespoons fruity olive oil (optional)**

1. In a large skillet over medium heat, heat the ½ cup olive oil until it is hot but not smoking. Add garlic and onion and sauté, stirring until lightly colored (about 3 minutes).

2. Halve peppers; remove seeds and trim away white ribs. Cut lengthwise into strips ½ inch wide. Add all peppers to skillet at one time and stir to blend with garlic-onion mixture. Add tomatoes and salt and mix gently. Scatter oregano leaves across top. Cover and simmer slowly until peppers are soft (12 to 15 minutes). Remove from heat and transfer to serving bowl to cool.

3. Serve peppers at room temperature, garnishing the top with the sliced red onion and minced parsley. If desired, drizzle with the 2 tablespoons fruity olive oil just before serving.

Makes about 3½ cups.

■ STUFFED GREEN PEPPERS MEXICANA

These stuffed peppers have a sweetly spicy, south-of-the-border flavor. The peppers and filling can be cooked and the peppers stuffed ahead of time; store in refrigerator overnight, if desired, and let dish warm to room temperature before baking.

   6 **medium-sized green bell peppers (about 2 lb)**
   2 **tablespoons butter or margarine**
   ½ **cup slivered almonds**
   1 **pound ground beef, crumbled**
   1 **large onion, finely chopped**
   1 **clove garlic, mashed**
   ⅓ **cup raisins**
   1 **tablespoon cider vinegar**
   1 **teaspoon *each* sugar and ground cinnamon**
   ¾ **teaspoon salt**
   ¼ **teaspoon *each* ground cumin and cloves**
   1 **can (15 oz) tomato sauce**
  1½ **cups cooked short-grain rice**

1. Preheat oven to 350° F. Cut a thin slice from stem end of each pepper; carefully cut out seeds. Cook peppers, uncovered, in boiling salted water to cover, for 5 minutes; turn upside down to drain.

2. In a large, heavy-bottomed frying pan, heat butter over medium heat; add almonds and cook until lightly browned. Remove from pan with a slotted spoon; reserve. In the same pan cook ground beef and onion until lightly browned. Mix in garlic, raisins, vinegar, sugar, cinnamon, salt, cumin, cloves, and half of the tomato sauce. Simmer, uncovered, about 10 minutes. Mix in cooked rice and almonds.

3. Fill peppers with ground beef mixture. Arrange in an ungreased, deep, covered baking dish just large enough to hold the 6 peppers. Pour on remaining tomato sauce. (At this point peppers can be covered and refrigerated for several hours or overnight; if chilled, let dish sit out at room temperature for 30 minutes before baking.)

4. Bake, covered, for 45 minutes; uncover, spoon sauce over, and continue baking for 15 minutes.

Serves 6.

HOT PEPPERS (CHILES)

Capsaicin, a compound found in the seeds and veins but not the walls of hot peppers, gives these peppers their heat. They range from the mildly spicy *pepperoncini* to the incendiary tabasco pepper. The jalapeño pepper, a pepper most diners consider very hot, usually measures 2,500 to 4,000 in Scoville Heat Units, the accepted measurement for heat in peppers. By comparison, the tiny tabasco may weigh in at 60,000 to 80,000 units!

Use Hot peppers are one of the world's most common seasonings. They add zest to all manner of dishes and are especially appreciated in hot climates, where their consumption has a cooling effect. Minced raw hot peppers are used in Mexican *salsa cruda* (fresh salsa), the ubiquitous table relish, or in guacamole. In fact few savory dishes in Mexico are prepared without chiles in some form, either fresh or dried; egg dishes, soups, stews, and appetizers are almost always enlivened with chiles. In the Hunan and Szechuan regions of China, hot red chiles give a lift to stir-fries and dipping sauces. Southeast Asian cooks use sliced green chiles in dipping sauces and soups; Thai curries are always liberally seasoned with green or red chiles. In this country, dried tabasco peppers are used to make one of America's most famous condiments, Tabasco Sauce. The well-known Texas specialty chili takes its name from its principal incendiary seasoning.

Availability Many supermarkets today stock at least a few fresh chiles, such as jalapeño and *serrano* varieties. Dried whole red chiles are often available in jars on the spice rack. In addition, many supermarkets carry canned or bottled chiles. For a wider selection of fresh, dried, and canned or bottled chiles, seek out a Latin or Asian market or a well-stocked specialty produce market. Most fresh hot chiles are available the year around, although supply of some varieties may be sporadic.

Recognizing the various chiles takes some practice and experimentation because there are dozens of varieties of similar shape and size. Many are sold in both fresh and dried states. The following are among the most common hot peppers.

Anaheim Also known as the New Mexico pepper, Rio Grande pepper, long green chile, or California pepper. This long (6 to 8 inches), slender green pepper is one of the mildest of the hot peppers. It is the pepper used for making *chiles rellenos* (fried cheese-stuffed chiles) in the southwestern United States. The mature Anaheim, a red pepper, is dried and ground for chili powder and paprika.

Ancho The correct name for the ripened and dried *poblano* (see Poblano; some markets incorrectly identify the fresh poblano as the Ancho, too). The dried ancho is perhaps the mostly commonly used chile in Mexico. It is about 5 inches long and dark brick red. Like the poblano, it may be slightly hot to hot. It is often ground for use in cooked sauces, such as mole.

Cayenne, Chile de Arbol, Thai Pepper Although not the same, they are similar: All are small, thin peppers marketed green, red, and dried. In Asian markets, they may be identified as bird peppers. The fresh red peppers are generally hotter than the green, but all are quite hot. The dried cayenne pepper can be soaked in vinegar and salt for a few days to make a pungent, liquid hot red-pepper sauce. Thai cooks use both fresh and dried bird peppers in dipping sauces, soups, and stir-fries.

Cherry Pepper A small round pepper that is pickled and bottled. Pickled red and green cherry peppers are available in many supermarkets. Slightly piquant, they make a colorful addition to a salad, an antipasto platter, or a sandwich plate.

Jalapeño A small (about 2 inches long), smooth-skinned green chile that is popular in Mexico and the southwestern United States. It is often pickled with carrots and onions and served as a table relish. Jalapeños are minced raw and used in salsas or split, deveined, stuffed with cheese or fish, and served as an appetizer. They are frequently canned, either whole, sliced, or in seeded strips. Jalapeño slices add zest to tacos, hamburgers, cheese dishes, and pizza. When ripened and smoked, jalapeños are known as *chiles chipotles.*

Pasilla A long (about 6 inches), narrow pepper with wide shoulders. When fresh, it is dark green to near black and may be identified in Latin markets as *chile chilaca*; when dried, it is chocolate brown. It has a deep, rich flavor and is moderately hot. Fresh ones are toasted and skinned before using in recipes; often they are cut into strips for use in soups, stews, and casseroles. Dried pasilla chiles are often ground for use in table sauces or seafood dishes.

Pepperoncini The small green pepper that is packed in vinegar, bottled, and sold in Italian markets and supermarkets. It is often used to garnish green salads or antipasto platters. A yellow variety, also pickled in vinegar and bottled, is imported from Greece and is available in some markets. Both are only slightly piquant.

Poblano Also known as the *chile ancho* (see Ancho). Ranging from 2½ to 6 inches in length and from dark green to near black, Ancho chiles are wide at the shoulder but taper to a point at the bottom. Flavor ranges from slightly hot to hot. They are usually roasted and peeled before using in recipes. Widely used in Mexico, they are stuffed with cheese, coated with batter and fried to make *chiles rellenos,* or are cut into strips for use in casseroles, soups, and sauces.

Whole chiles, mild or hot, will dry in several weeks at room temperature. When they are dry, crumble or grind them for use in chili recipes and other spicy-hot dishes.

Serrano A slender, very hot green chile, usually about 2 inches long. In Mexico it is used raw in guacamole and some salsas crudas and is cooked in other salsas. Serrano chiles are also commercially pickled.

Yellow Wax Pepper Also known as the Hungarian wax pepper or *chile guero*, it is pale yellow and usually about 5 inches long. It may be used raw in salsas; toasted, seeded, and used in salads; pickled and canned; and cooked in stews. It is extremely pungent.

Selection Fresh hot chiles should have a smooth skin without dry cracks. They should feel firm and look shiny.

Storage Wrap fresh chiles in paper towels and refrigerate for up to three weeks (they will sweat and deteriorate rapidly in plastic bags). Dried red chiles are perishable. Store them in an airtight container in a cool, dark, dry place for up to three or four months; for longer storage, refrigerate.

Preparation Hot peppers require caution in handling. Some people are extremely sensitive to the capsaicin in the pepper seeds and veins. The capsaicin irritates their skin and, if hands touch tongue or eyes, the discomfort can be severe. Wear rubber gloves when handling hot peppers until you can gauge your sensitivity. Always wash hands well after handling peppers.

Fresh hot chiles are often charred and peeled before use (see Roasting and Peeling Peppers, page 425).

Because the capsaicin in peppers is in the seeds and ribs, removing these parts significantly reduces a pepper's kick. If a recipe calls for whole hot peppers, you can reduce the heat by halving the peppers and cutting away seeds and ribs.

Dried red chiles can be ground in a pepper mill, clean coffee grinder, or electric minichopper, or with a mortar and pestle. When removing lid from appliance, keep head well out of the way bacause escaping fumes can burn.

Dried chiles are sometimes soaked in warm water to soften before using. Follow recipe instructions.

◾ NACHOS

This popular translation of a traditional Mexican snack offers a balance of flavors and textures.. Beer is the perfect beverage to cool the heat of the peppers. Another way to tame their spiciness is to remove the ribs and seeds.

> 1 package (12 oz) corn tortilla chips
> ½ cup green jalapeños, minced
> ½ cup green onions, chopped
> 2¼ cups shredded Monterey jack or
>   sharp Cheddar cheese

Preheat oven to 400° F. Place tortilla chips in a single layer on 2 baking sheets. Sprinkle with jalapeños and green onions. Cover with shredded cheese. Bake until cheese melts (about 5 minutes). Serve warm from oven.

Serves 8 as an appetizer or 4 as a light lunch.

◾ CHILES RELLENOS

A classic Mexican dish, *chile relleno* is certainly a favorite in the United States. The chile relleno is a large, mild, green cooking chile that has been roasted, cleaned, and peeled; filled and dipped in batter; and fried until puffed and golden. In Mexico the chile relleno is always served in a sauce. There are three distinct schools of thought on the egg batter in which the chile is dipped: The batter may be flat, fluffy, or extra fluffy. The recipe that follows is right in the middle and the easiest to manage. If you want flatter chiles rellenos, just beat the eggs without separating them. For fluffier chiles rellenos, fold in one tablespoon flour for each egg in the recipe.

Although in Mexico the chile relleno is most often filled with a spiced shredded meat mixture, in the United States it is usually filled with cheese, as in this version. In Mexico the cheese-filled chile relleno is identified on menus as *Chile relleno con queso*. The chile relleno is usually served as a main dish but it can also be served as a vegetable side dish or as a brunch dish. For directions on how to roast chiles, see page 425.

A variation of chile relleno is *chile en nogada*, a classic in its own right that features a meat-and-fruit filling and a walnut cream sauce. The dish originated in Puebla, the walnut capital of Mexico, and is served traditionally on Mexico's two independence days.

> 6 large, mild, green chiles, roasted and peeled,
>   leaving on stems (or canned whole green chiles)
> ½ pound jack or Colby cheese, cut into strips
>   approximately ½ inch wide, 2 inches long,
>   and ¼ inch thick
>   Flour
> 4 eggs, separated
>   Oil 1 inch deep, for frying
>   Sour cream and cilantro, for garnish

Tomato Sauce

> 1 tablespoon vegetable oil
> ½ cup chopped onion
> 2 cloves garlic, crushed
> 1 can (28 oz) solid-pack tomatoes, puréed
>   briefly in blender
> 3½ cups Chicken Stock (see page 560)

1. Carefully slit each chile lengthwise along one side; remove seeds and veins. Fill each chile with several strips of cheese, roll in flour, and set aside.

2. Beat egg whites until stiff; slightly beat yolks and fold into whites. Heat oil in a large skillet to 400° F. Drop a large spoonful of egg mixture into oil; lay a chile in the middle, top with another spoonful of egg, and smooth the egg to enclose all sides. Carefully baste the top with hot oil, to set. Cook until golden on the underside (about 1 minute); turn and cook again until golden on the underside. Drain on paper towels while preparing Tomato Sauce.

3. Carefully place the rellenos into the tomato sauce and simmer gently to heat thoroughly (about 15 minutes). Do not cook too long or batter will begin to break away.

4. Serve with some of the sauce, and garnish with a dab of sour cream and a few cilantro leaves.

Serves 3 to 6.

Tomato Sauce　Heat oil in a large saucepan. Add onion and garlic and cook only until onion is soft. Add puréed tomatoes and stock, bring to a boil, reduce heat, and simmer 5 minutes.

Makes about 6 cups.

■ **PINTO BEAN CHILI**

This beef and pinto bean chili may strike you as the most traditional version.

   1　cup dried pinto beans, rinsed and drained
   3　cups water
   2　pounds boneless beef chuck, fat trimmed,
      cut in 1-inch cubes
   2　tablespoons butter or margarine
   1　large onion, finely chopped
   1　clove garlic, minced
   2　teaspoons salt
   1　teaspoon ground cumin
   1　tablespoon chili powder
   1　can (1 lb) tomatoes
   1　can (4 oz) diced green chiles
   1　can (8 oz) tomato sauce
      Shredded Cheddar cheese (optional)

1. In a large, heavy saucepan, bring beans and the water to a boil. Boil briskly for 2 minutes; then remove from heat, cover, and let stand for 1 hour.

2. In a large, deep frying pan or Dutch oven, brown beef cubes well on all sides, about half at a time, in butter over medium-high heat, removing and reserving meat as it browns. When all the beef is removed from pan, add onion to pan and cook, stirring often, until soft and lightly browned. Return beef to pan. Mix in garlic, beans and their liquid, salt, cumin, chili powder, tomatoes (coarsely chopped) and their liquid, and green chiles.

3. Bring to a boil, cover, reduce heat, and simmer until beef and beans are tender (2 to 2½ hours).

4. Mix in tomato sauce and cook, uncovered, stirring occasionally, until chili is thickened to your taste (about 15 minutes).

5. Serve bowls of hot chili with cheese for sprinkling, if desired.

Serves 6 to 8.

Recipes and Related Information
Guacamole, 15; Salsa Cruda, 521; Salsa Verde, 580.

PEPPERCORN

The *Piper nigrum* vine, native to Asia, produces the world's most-used spice. Pepper berries grow in clusters around a stem, like grapes. As they ripen, the tiny berries change from green to yellow to red. The familiar black peppercorn is picked when slightly underripe, then sun-dried until it blackens and shrivels. The white peppercorn is the same peppercorn harvested ripe and hulled; it is less pungent than the black. Green peppercorns are soft, un-dried, underripe *Piper nigrum* berries. Pink peppercorns are pungent pink berries unrelated to *Piper nigrum*.

Use　The importance of pepper to the world's cuisines and to world history cannot be underestimated. When Columbus and other explorers set off to search for trade routes to the Far East, they were hoping to find a shortcut to pepper. The pungent spice breathes life into dishes all over the world. Peppercorns are added to brines and marinades. Meats and fish are often seasoned with pepper before cooking; vegetables, soups, and salads with freshly ground black pepper. Cracked peppercorns are rubbed into the surface of a steak to make Steak au Poivre. Pepper is even used to heighten the flavor of strawberries and sweets. The milder and less visible white peppercorns are generally used with fish dishes. Green and pink peppercorns are a pungent seasoning for meats and fish.

Availability　Black and white peppercorns, whole and ground, are found in most supermarkets. Some specialty markets carry a variety of peppercorns in bulk. The best black varieties are Tellicherry, Lampong, and Allepeppy; the best white varieties are Muntok, Brazilian, and Sarawak. Green and pink peppercorns may be packed in water or vinegar or freeze-dried; they are available in some supermarkets and most specialty markets.

Selection　Packaged seasonings lose quality after a while; try to buy from a store that restocks its spice section fairly often.

Storage　Keep ground pepper in a cool, dark, dry place and replace every three months. Whole peppercorns will keep indefinitely in a cool, dark, dry place. Once opened, green peppercorns in water will last for one week refrigerated airtight; green peppercorns in brine will last for a month in their brine in an airtight container in the refrigerator. Discard green or pink peppercorns when they turn dark. Store freeze-dried green or pink peppercorns in a cool, dry, dark place for up to six months.

Preparation　Black and white peppers are most pungent when ground just before use. Keep a pepper mill on hand for easy last-minute grinding.

Recipes and Related Information
Steak au Poivre, 41; Tartar Sauce With Green Peppercorns, 520.

PERSIMMON

Of the two varieties of persimmon common in American markets, the Hachiya is the largest, weighing up to 1 pound. Its shape is like a large, elongated peach. It has a smooth, orange-red skin even before it is fully ripe. When underripe, the Hachiya is extremely tannic and unpleasant to eat. A fully ripe Hachiya persimmon has a silky flesh with the texture of pudding and a delightfully sweet flavor. Another variety, the Fuyu, is smaller, with a shape resembling a tomato. It has orange-red skin like the Hachiya and may be eaten when firm.

Use   A ripe persimmon makes a delicious breakfast food or snack, halved and eaten like a melon, with a wedge of lemon or lime. The firm Fuyu persimmon may be sliced and used in winter salads or compotes. The Hachiya can be puréed for sorbets, ice cream, steamed puddings, cookies, and quick breads. Frozen Hachiya persimmons can be whipped in a blender to make a creamy dessert resembling a mousse.

Availability   Both Hachiya and Fuyu persimmons are available from October through January. Dried persimmons are also sold in some health-food stores and Japanese markets.

Selection   Choose persimmons with good color and without bruises or splits in the skin.

Storage   Ripen Hachiyas at room temperature until as soft as a water-filled balloon; the process may take several weeks. Refrigerate and use immediately. The Fuyu persimmon should give slightly to pressure; ripen at room temperature if necessary. When ripe, refrigerate and use within a few days.

Preparation   Slice Fuyus into horizontal slices or vertical wedges; discard stem. Remove stem from Hachiyas and halve or purée. Some Hachiyas contain a few black seeds, which should be discarded.

■ PERSIMMON PUDDING

During the cool months, when persimmons are plentiful, extend their season by freezing the pulp in 1-cup batches.

1½	cups flour
1	teaspoon baking powder
1	teaspoon baking soda
1	teaspoon ground cinnamon
½	teaspoon freshly grated nutmeg
¼	teaspoon salt
3	ripe persimmons, puréed (see Note)
1	cup sugar
3	eggs
1	cup buttermilk
½	cup whipping cream
½	cup butter, melted and cooled
	Whipped cream, vanilla ice cream, or Crème Anglaise (see page 168), for accompaniment

1. Preheat oven to 350° F. Butter a 10-inch baking pan or ovenproof dish. Sift together flour, baking powder, baking soda, cinnamon, nutmeg, and salt; set aside.

2. In a large bowl combine purée, sugar, eggs, and buttermilk; beat until smooth and creamy. Add cream and melted butter and beat again until smooth.

3. Fold in sifted flour mixture and pour batter into prepared pan. Bake until set (about 1 hour). The pudding will settle upon standing. Serve warm with whipped cream, vanilla ice cream, or Crème Anglaise.

Serves 8 to 10.

Note   Persimmons must be very ripe. To remove pulp, halve fruit, discard seeds, and scoop out flesh; mash with a spoon if very soft or purée in a food processor.

PICKLE, COMMERCIAL

Although most Americans use the word *pickle* to describe a cucumber pickle, pickles may be made from a variety of fruits and vegetables. Pickles are preserved in a seasoned brine and used as a piquant condiment or counterpoint (see HERB AND SPICE BLENDS, Pickling Spice). The highly acidic brine prevents the growth of organisms that cause spoilage and gives pickles their long shelf life (see JAM, JELLY, PRESERVE, AND CONDIMENT, Pickles and Relishes). Besides cucumbers, other commonly pickled vegetables include peppers, onions, green tomatoes, green beans, red cabbage, beets, cauliflower, and okra. Commonly pickled fruits include watermelon rind, cherries, grapes, peaches, plums (popular in Japan), and melons. Other foods that are commonly pickled include ginger, pig's feet, herring, radishes, and walnuts.

Use   The tangy flavor of pickles makes them useful as a piquant condiment. In America dill pickles are often served with sandwiches. In Japan pickles are served at almost every meal—radish pickles, cabbage pickles, eggplant pickles. Indeed, rice, pickles, and tea are the trio that ends traditional Japanese meals, both formal and informal. The French serve *cornichons* (tiny pickles) with pâté. The Italians serve *giardiniera* (pickled mixed vegetables) as part of an antipasto assortment. Northern Europeans eat pickled fish and meats as a first course. The English eat pickled walnuts with cold meats and cheese. Minced pickle or pickle relish adds a sweet-tart character to egg salad and tuna salad and to such cold sauces as tartar sauce and rémoulade sauce.

Availability   Cucumber pickles are widely sold in supermarkets as dill pickles, sweet gherkins, kosher dills, sweet bread-and-butter pickles, sweet pickle relish, and dill pickle chips or slices. Some specialty markets and supermarkets carry other pickle varieties. Check specialty stores and ethnic markets for French cornichons, Italian giardiniera, Japanese pickled ginger, and pickled plums.

Bread-and-Butter-Pickles These are made from medium to large cucumbers packed in a sweet-tart brine.

Cornichons Made from tiny cucumbers, cornichons are tart French pickles usually about 1½ inches long. They are packed in a tangy brine, often with tarragon.

Dill Pickles These are tart cucumber pickles flavored with fresh dill.

Half-Sour and Sour Pickles These are garlic-flavored and prepared in a salt brine without vinegar; sour pickles develop their stronger flavor because they are left longer in the brine.

Kosher Dill Pickles Despite what their name implies, kosher dill pickles are not necessarily prepared according to Jewish dietary law unless otherwise indicated on the jar. They are dill pickles flavored with garlic.

Sweet Gherkins Quite sweet, these pickles are made with the tiny pickling cucumbers known as cornichons. They are often chopped for use in chicken or tuna salad.

Sweet Pickle Relish This is a sweet-tart mince of pickles, onions, and sweet red pepper.

Storage Unopened pickles should be kept in a cool, dark place, where they will keep for one or two years. Once opened, they should be refrigerated. Most pickles will keep for one year under refrigeration.

PIE AND TART

What makes a pie a pie and a tart a tart? You might call the tart a French cousin to the pie, for their similarities seem to put them in the same family. They both have a pastry crust and a filling and are usually served in wedges. However, while they are made from the same basic ingredients, the similarities between pies and tarts fade when you take a closer look at the nature of their crusts and the shape of the pans in which they are baked.

INGREDIENTS FOR PIES AND TARTS: WHAT EACH DOES

Pie and tart crusts have few ingredients—basically flour, fat, liquid, and some flavoring such as salt or sugar. Occasionally egg is added to impart strength and color to the crust. The proportion of these basic ingredients in the dough and how they are incorporated give a pastry a distinctive characteristic: tender or tough, crumbly or flaky.

Flour The main ingredient in a pastry dough, flour provides structure. Liquid added to flour develops a protein called gluten, which forms an elastic framework that holds the dough together and allows it to be stretched and rolled out without breaking. For pie and tart doughs, use all-purpose flour or white pastry flour (unbleached

is best). All-purpose flour is a blend of hard (high-gluten) and soft (low-gluten) white wheat flours. Pastry flour (not to be confused with cake flour) is a soft (low-gluten) flour that can be used in place of all-purpose flour; it is often difficult to find, however. Whole wheat flour adds a nutty flavor to pie and tart crusts. However, if it is used alone it produces heavy doughs that are difficult to mix and roll. A better product is a combination of all-purpose and whole wheat flours.

Fat Adding tenderness, or shortness, as well as richness to pastries, fat works by coating particles of flour to inhibit them from joining with water to produce gluten (see Flour). Pure fats, such as shortening and lard, have more shortening power than butter because, unlike butter (or margarine), they don't contain any moisture and therefore can't encourage gluten development. They produce flakier, more tender crusts. On the other hand, although a butter crust is less tender and flaky, it has a rich, buttery flavor and aroma. Sometimes the fat used is

Flour and shortening have been cut together in a bowl with a pastry blender. Ice water is waiting to be measured and added to complete the dough. In the background a glass pie plate holds an unbaked pastry crust finished with a rope edge.

an oil; the resulting pastry is crumbly, rather than flaky, because an oil has more coating power than a solid fat and so covers many more of the flour particles (rather than making layers). You can produce a good pie crust by using all shortening, all lard, all butter, or a combination of these in any of the basic pie crust recipes in this entry. Keep in mind the effect that the type of fat will have on the crust.

Liquid Some liquid, usually water, is needed in a pie or tart dough so that the flour particles can form a dough; the liquid also acts as a leavening when it converts to steam during baking. However, the minimum amount of water should be used; too much liquid will make a tough crust. It is always better to begin by adding the smaller amount of liquid suggested in the recipe. If more liquid is needed, add a few teaspoons or 1 tablespoon at a time until the desired consistency is reached. For flakiness, use ice water or ice-cold liquids so as not to melt the fat.

Acid Sometimes acidic lemon juice, vinegar, sour cream, or even crème fraîche is added to the dough to relax the gluten and tenderize the crust.

Salt When added, salt improves the flavor and color of the baked crust.

Sugar Although not all doughs contain sugar, those that do include it for the flavor and color it imparts when it caramelizes.

EQUIPMENT FOR MAKING PIES AND TARTS

It is entirely possible to make a pie crust with the fingertips and to roll it out on the countertop with a wine bottle. However, if you have some basic pastry-making equipment in your kitchen, the process will be faster and simpler. Unless you make many pies at a time, you really only need one pie plate, preferably heat-resistant glass or heavyweight aluminum; 9 inches is the standard size. For tarts, choose a fluted pan of tinned steel with a removable bottom. Miniature tinned steel tart pans are available for tartlets.

Also helpful are a pastry blender, a rolling pin (15 inches is a versatile length), a sharp knife and other cutters, a fluted pastry-cutting wheel, a ruler, aluminum foil or parchment paper, and metal or ceramic pie weights (or dried beans). Some recipes recommend that juicy pies or delicate tarts bake on a baking sheet; a heavyweight aluminum one is best. Some cooks like to use a cloth rolling pin sleeve and a pastry cloth on which to roll dough. The same results can be achieved by keeping the work surface and rolling pin lightly dusted with flour at all times when rolling out pastry.

Other equipment useful for pastry making includes kitchen staples such as wooden spoons, spatulas, measuring spoons and cups, mixing bowls, cooking racks, a quality portable or electric stand mixer with a strong motor, and a food processor with metal blade.

MAKING THE DOUGH

Pie crusts can be mixed with the fingertips, a wire pastry blender, two knives, the paddle attachment of a heavy-duty mixer, or a food processor. The process—called cutting in or rubbing in—literally whittles the fat into smaller and smaller flour-coated pieces (see CUT IN); the fineness of texture depends on the type of pastry you are making. For flaky pie crusts, the fat should be in discrete pieces that will then layer with the dough. For tarts, the fat is mixed in more uniformly.

Chill fat; when using more than one type, soften the fats, mix them together, and then chill this mixture. When using a food processor to make pastry that contains solid vegetable shortening, first measure and freeze the fat before cutting it into the flour. By doing this, the pastry will resist the heat produced by the action of the machine. If butter, margarine, or lard is used, the fat need only be chilled rather than frozen. Cut fats in quickly; overmixing results in oily pastry.

ROLLING OUT PIE AND TART PASTRY

Let chilled dough soften slightly before rolling. Place dough on lightly floured surface; sprinkle a little flour on top of dough or rub some on rolling pin. Roll out dough from center toward edge (easing pressure near edge of dough) ⅛ inch thick and 2 inches larger than the pie plate or 1½ inches larger than the tart tin. Carefully lift dough and give a quarter turn after each rolling, reflouring surfaces as needed to prevent sticking and tearing. Cupping hands slightly, occasionally reshape dough into a circle. If dough cracks or tears, brush a small flat piece of dough with water and apply as a patch (patching is preferred to rerolling, which toughens dough; see PATCH).

To Transfer Dough to Pie Plate or Tart Tin Place rolling pin just to one side of center of dough. Lightly and gently drape half of dough over rolling pin, rest dough across pie plate, and unfold dough onto pie plate. Fit dough into plate with fingertips or a small ball of dough. For tart, trim dough even with top of tart tin or band. Do not stretch dough or crust will shrink as it bakes. Pie or tart shell may be frozen at this point.

For a Single-Crust Pie Trim edge so it extends ½ inch to 1 inch beyond edge of pie plate. Fold edges of dough under. Finish edges (see opposite page). Blind bake or fill and bake.

For a Double-Crust Pie Trim lower crust even with rim of pie plate. Roll out second piece of dough (for top) slightly thinner than bottom crust. Fill pie; brush rim of bottom crust with cold water. Place top crust on pie; press edges to seal; trim edge to ½ inch from rim and finish edges (see opposite page). Cut steam vents (slits or designs) in top crust before or after crust is on pie. Bake according to recipe directions.

DECORATIVE FINISHES

The top crust of a double-crust pie can be left plain or enhanced with applied cutouts made from dough scraps. Roll out scraps as thin as possible; use cookie cutters or a knife to cut out shapes that relate to the filling—little apples and leaves or berries and vines—or design your own: stars, flowers, even initials (see Apple Pie, page 437). Brush cutouts with water and press into place on the top crust. You may brush the top crust with one of the following glazes: milk and a sprinkling of sugar, cream, or, for a shiny brown glaze, egg or egg yolks lightly beaten with a pinch of salt and 1 teaspoon of water.

A woven lattice top allows the filling to show through and is extremely attractive (see Strawberry-Rhubarb Pie, page 498). To form a lattice, line pie plate with pastry and trim bottom crust to ½ inch beyond rim. Roll out a circle of dough 2 inches larger than rim of pie plate for lattice

top; with a knife or fluted pastry wheel and a ruler, cut strips of dough ½ inch wide. Fill pie. Lay half of the strips of pastry, ¾ inches apart, across pie. Fold back every other strip at center. Lay a strip across the unfolded strips; unfold other strips over this. Fold back the alternating strips (ones that were flat the last time) and lay the next strip ¾ inch from the last. Continue until half of pie is covered with lattice pattern. Repeat this procedure on other side of pie. Trim lattice strips to match edge of bottom crust; lift lattice strips at edge and moisten rim of crust underneath; press lattice strips onto bottom crust at edge of pie. Flute edges.

To make attractive edges (see below for instructions for a variety of pastry crust edges) for single- or double-crust pies, allow pastry to extend ½ inch to 1 inch beyond rim of pie plate. Fold edge of dough under so it is even with the edge of the pie plate to create a raised, even rim.

Fork-fluted edge Trim pastry even with rim of pie plate. Firmly press tines of fork into pastry around entire rim of pie plate.

Fluted edge Place left index finger on inside of rim, pointing toward outside of shell. Pinch pastry into V shape between right index finger and thumb; repeat along entire edge. Pinch again to sharpen points.

Rope edge Press thumb at an angle into pastry and pinch pastry toward thumb with bent index finger; repeat along entire edge.

Ruffle edge Place left thumb and index finger 1 inch apart on edge of pastry, pointing toward outside of shell. Gently pull pastry between them toward outside of shell with right index finger; repeat along entire edge.

Spiral edge Trim pastry even with edge of pie plate. Brush rim with water. Cut long, straight, ¾-inch strips of pastry. Press one end of strip to rim, twist strip, and press into rim with index finger after each twist.

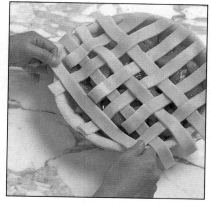

Lattice top Fold back every other strip. Lay a strip across unfolded strips; unfold strips to cover pie and fold back the strips that were at first left lying flat. Lay next strip and repeat folding and unfolding procedure.

BAKING PIES AND TARTS

Cooking time is only a general guideline as to when a pastry is ready to come out of the oven. For double-crust pies, the crust should appear golden brown, crisp, and dry; the filling should be bubbling through the steam vents. For single-crust pies and tarts, the crust edge should appear golden brown (but not burnt), crisp, and dry; the filling should be set (a knife inserted into the center comes out clean). If edges of crust begin to brown too much before pie is fully baked, cover with strips of aluminum foil.

More than one pastry can be baked in an oven at one time if there is sufficient room for air to circulate around the pans. Although experts do not recommend the microwave oven for baking pies since the crusts don't brown or become crisp, some bakers feel that the crusts are flakier than those cooked conventionally.

Crusts that may get soggy due to fillings such as custard and cream and crusts that will serve as a shell for an uncooked filling are often blind baked, which is a method used to prebake a pastry crust before it is filled. The pastry shell can be either partially baked or fully baked, depending on the way it is to be later filled. To keep the unfilled crust from puffing and distorting, it is usually lined with aluminum foil or parchment paper and then filled with dried beans or metal or ceramic pie weights and then baked. For shells to be fully baked, the weights are removed after the crust has baked for 15 to 20 minutes and has set; the crust is then pricked to allow steam to escape and baked further until golden brown. Fully baked blind-baked crusts are always cooled completely before filling (see BAKE BLIND).

Fruit tarts can get soggy from the juice exuded by the fruits. However, there are several ways to prevent soggy crusts and diluted pastry creams. After baking the crust, use a pastry brush to paint the inside of the crust with a thin layer of melted currant jelly. This will in essence waterproof the crust. Or, sprinkle crumbled vanilla wafers, ladyfingers, or stale white cake over the pastry cream before topping it with fruit. This will provide a dry barrier between the juicy fruit and the pastry cream and will help absorb the juices. Be sure to dry fruit well with paper towels before placing on tart. Assemble tart just before serving, whenever possible.

BASIC PIE CRUSTS

Pie crusts are most often a pastry of some sort, but biscuit and yeast doughs, crumbs, nuts, and meringues are used as well. Pies are known for their tender, flaky short crusts and are usually made with lard or shortening. Pie dough is easier to handle than tart pastry, and can be used to form double-crust and lattice-top pies with decoratively fluted edges. Because flaky pie crusts are fragile when baked, they must remain in the pie plate for support. A pie is served directly from the pie plate in which it is baked: a 1-inch deep plate or tin with a slanted, rimmed side.

Both Flaky Pastry (see below) and Egg Pastry (see opposite page) produce tender, flaky pie crusts and are appropriate for most single-crust, double-crust, or lattice-top pies. Flaky Pastry yields the flakiest crust, but Egg Pastry tastes buttery and is easier to handle.

Crumb crusts are just right for the chilled or frozen fillings—such as Bavarian cream, chiffon, or ice cream—of make-ahead pies and, best of all, they're easy to prepare: Just add a little sugar to the crumbs and stir in butter; press crumb crust mixture into pie plate, chill, and fill. There's no dough to roll or bake—an attractive feature during warm weather. For a crisper crumb crust, however, bake at 350° F for 10 minutes.

Cookie or cracker crumbs that are commonly used for crumb crusts include vanilla wafers, chocolate wafers, gingersnaps, dry macaroons, *amaretti* cookies, graham crackers, and zwieback or melba toast. Cracker and toast crumbs will need to be sweetened. For variety finely ground nuts, poppy seed, or sesame seed can be substituted for some of the crumbs.

Press-in crusts shortcut the process of rolling and shaping. Like nut crusts, they are quickly assembled and are essentially foolproof; the dough is set in the pie pan and worked with the fingers to cover the pan bottom and sides. They are a boon to those cooks who lack the time or the self-confidence to shape a crust by traditional methods.

◼ FLAKY PASTRY

You will use this crust over and over again. It is tender and when cut reveals thin, flaky layers, the hallmark of a classic pie crust.

Single Crust (for one 9- to 10-inch pie)

1¼	cups flour
¼	teaspoon salt
½	cup cold solid vegetable shortening
3	tablespoons ice water

Double Crust (for one 9- to 10-inch double-crust pie or two 9-inch single-crust pies)

2¼	cups flour
½	teaspoon salt
¾	cup cold solid vegetable shortening
5 to 7	tablespoons ice water

1. Sift flour and salt together; place in a medium bowl.

2. Divide shortening in half. Cut half of shortening into flour mixture with fingertips, a pastry blender, two knives, or the paddle attachment of an electric mixer until mixture resembles coarse meal. (For food processor method, see end of recipe.) Then cut in remaining shortening until mixture resembles small peas.

3. Sprinkle ice water over mixture; toss with a fork to moisten dough evenly. Use as few strokes as possible and the minimum amount of water needed. Gently press dough into a ball. (For a double crust, divide dough into two portions and form 2 balls.) Flatten ball slightly with a few strokes with the side of your hand. Wrap dough with plastic wrap and refrigerate at least 1 hour. It will keep for 2 to 3 days in refrigerator or 1 month in freezer. To roll out dough see Rolling Out Pie and Tart Pastry, page 432.

Whole Wheat Flaky Pastry *For Single-Crust Pie:* Use Flaky Pastry recipe. Substitute 1 cup all-purpose flour and ⅓ cup whole wheat flour for the 1¼ cups flour, ¼ cup cold unsalted butter and ¼ cup cold vegetable shortening for the ½ cup shortening, and increase ice water to 3 to 4 tablespoons. Proceed as for Flaky Pastry. *For Double-Crust Pie:* Use Flaky Pastry recipe. Substitute 1¾ cups all-purpose flour and ⅔ cup whole wheat flour for the 2¼ cups flour, 5 tablespoons cold unsalted butter and 5 tablespoons cold vegetable shortening for the ¾ cup shortening, and increase ice water to 7 to 8 tablespoons. Proceed as for Flaky Pastry.

Food Processor Version   Measure shortening; freeze until firm. Place flour and salt in work bowl of processor fitted with metal blade. Add half of the frozen shortening (cut into small pieces). Process with half-second pulses until mixture resembles coarse meal. Add remaining shortening; process with half-second pulses until mixture resembles small peas. Add ice water quickly through feed tube while pulsing; stop pulsing as soon as dough looks as if it will gather into a ball. Mixture should look crumbly but not dry. (Add more ice water, 1 tablespoon at a time, if necessary to moisten dough.) Gather dough into a ball, flatten slightly with side of hand, wrap, and refrigerate at least 1 hour.

■ EGG PASTRY

This pastry crust, made with butter and egg yolk, is easier to work with and tolerates handling better than does Flaky Pastry (see page 434). The butter and egg yolks lend a rich golden hue to the crust and improve the flavor. A little vinegar or lemon juice helps to soften the gluten and produce a tender crust. Egg Pastry is flaky, but somewhat sturdier than Flaky Pastry, so it's especially well suited for pies and tarts with moist custard fillings, rich pies, and certain freestanding deep-dish tarts. If you prefer, use all butter in this recipe. Nut Egg Pastry is less flaky and tender than Egg Pastry, but the nutty flavor is delicious.

Single Crust (for one 9- to 10-inch pie)

　1¼　**cups flour**
　　½　**teaspoon sugar**
　　¼　**teaspoon salt**
　　¼　**cup *each* unsalted butter and solid vegetable shortening, combined and chilled**
　　½　**teaspoon vinegar**
　　1　**egg yolk**
　　2　**to 3 tablespoons ice water**

Deep-Dish Tart (for one 9- to 10-inch tart)

　1½　**cups flour**
　　½　**teaspoon sugar**
　　¼　**teaspoon salt**
　　⅓　**cup unsalted butter *and* 3 tablespoons solid vegetable shortening, combined and chilled**
　　½　**teaspoon vinegar**
　　1　**extralarge egg yolk**
　　3　**to 5 tablespoons ice water**

Double Crust (for one 9- to 10-inch double-crust pie or two 9-inch single-crust pies)

　2¼　**cups flour**
　　1　**teaspoon sugar**
　　½　**teaspoon salt**
　　½　**cup unsalted butter *and* ¼ cup solid vegetable shortening, combined and chilled**
　　1　**teaspoon vinegar**
　　2　**large egg yolks**
　　4　**to 6 tablespoons ice water**

1. Sift together flour, sugar, and salt. Cut cold butter-shortening mixture into pieces and add to flour mixture. Cut into flour until mixture resembles coarse meal. (For food processor method, see below.)

2. Mix vinegar and egg yolk with smaller amount of ice water in a small bowl. Sprinkle liquid mixture over flour and toss with a fork to moisten dough evenly. Use as few strokes as possible and the least amount of water needed to moisten ingredients, only enough to gather dough into a ball. Add more water, 1 tablespoon at a time, if dough is too dry. Gently press dough into a ball; flatten ball with side of hand. (For a double crust, divide dough into 2 portions and form 2 balls.) Wrap dough with plastic wrap; refrigerate at least 1 hour. Dough will keep for 2 to 3 days in refrigerator or 6 to 8 weeks in freezer. To roll out dough, see Rolling Out Pie and Tart Pastry, page 432.

Nut Egg Pastry   Use Egg Pastry recipe. Substitute ¼ cup finely ground nuts (almonds, pecans, hazelnuts, or walnuts) for ¼ cup of the flour. For a sweeter crust, add 3 tablespoons sifted confectioners' sugar to the flour. Finely grated orange or lemon rind can be added if desired. Proceed as for Egg Pastry.

Food Processor Version   Mix butter and shortening together; freeze. Place flour, sugar, and salt in work bowl. Cut frozen butter-shortening mixture into pieces and add to bowl; using metal blade process with half-second pulses until mixture resembles coarse meal. Combine vinegar, egg yolk, and smaller amount of ice water and add quickly through feed tube while pulsing; stop as soon as dough looks as if it will gather into a ball. Mixture should look crumbly but not dry. (Add more water, 1 tablespoon at a time, if necessary to moisten dough.) Gather dough into a ball, flatten slightly with side of hand, wrap, and refrigerate at least 1 hour.

■ MINCEMEAT PIE

Mincemeat was originally made with minced or ground meats, usually beef or tongue, mixed with dried fruits and preserved with alcohol. Meat is absent from contemporary mincemeat recipes, although suet is used for richness. If you prefer a finer texture, grind all ingredients through the coarse disk of a meat grinder or in a food processor with metal blade, using a pulse action. The mincemeat recipe makes more than you will need for one pie, so use the leftover portion to make individual turnovers or to mix with apples for an especially flavorful apple-pie filling. To develop a rich, deep flavor, the mincemeat must be made six weeks before use. Prepared, storebought mincemeat can be substituted.

>   1   nine-inch double-crust Flaky Pastry (see page 434) or Egg Pastry (see page 435)
>   1   egg white, lightly beaten
>   2   tablespoons sugar

Mincemeat

>   1½   cups dark raisins
>   1½   cups golden raisins
>   1½   cups dried currants
>   3   apples, peeled, cored, and chopped
>   1   cup suet, finely chopped or ground by butcher
>   1   cup firmly packed brown sugar
>   1   cup candied citrus peel
>   ½   cup almonds, sliced or slivered
>   Grated rind and juice of 2 lemons
>   Grated rind and juice of 1 orange
>   ¼   teaspoon ground cinnamon
>   ¼   teaspoon freshly grated nutmeg
>   ⅛   teaspoon ground cloves
>   1   cup brandy
>   ½   cup sherry

1. Preheat oven to 400° F. Roll out pastry for bottom crust and use to line a 9-inch pie plate. Roll out remaining pastry for top crust.

2. Fill bottom crust with 3 cups mincemeat. Brush edges of crust with water; cover with top crust; press edges to seal, trim away excess dough, and finish edges as desired. Chill 10 to 15 minutes. Cut steam vents. Brush surface with egg white and sprinkle with sugar.

3. Bake 10 minutes; lower heat to 375° F and bake until golden brown (25 to 35 minutes). Serve hot, warm, or at room temperature.

Serves 6 to 8.

Mincemeat   In a large bowl combine dark raisins, golden raisins, currants, apples, suet, brown sugar, citrus peel, almonds, lemon and orange rinds and juice, cinnamon, nutmeg, and cloves; mix well. Add brandy and sherry; stir to combine (more brandy may be added, if necessary, to moisten all the ingredients). Pack into sterilized jars; cover with parchment paper or waxed paper and screw on lid to acquire a tight seal. Let mincemeat ripen in a cool, dark, dry place for at least 6 weeks before using. Mincemeat will keep several months.

Makes about 1 quart.

■ PUMPKIN PIE

For lovers of this traditional Thanksgiving dessert, all the familiar spices and the smooth, creamy texture are here. This recipe yields two pies; if you don't serve them both, you can freeze half the filling or freeze the baked pie. If pie is frozen, thaw in the refrigerator overnight; then warm in a 350° F oven 15 to 20 minutes or serve cold.

>   2   recipes 9-inch single-crust Flaky Pastry (see page 434)

Pumpkin Purée Filling

>   1   pumpkin (about 2 lb)
>   3   eggs
>   2   cups whipping cream
>   ¾   cup sugar
>   1   teaspoon ground cinnamon
>   ¾   teaspoon ground ginger
>   ½   teaspoon freshly grated nutmeg
>   ¼   teaspoon *each* ground cloves and ground allspice

1. Preheat oven to 400° F. Roll out Flaky Pastry for bottom crusts and use to line two 9-inch pie plates. Blind bake until partially baked.

2. Place pie shells on a baking sheet. Divide filling between two crusts. Bake 10 minutes; reduce heat to 350° F and bake until filling is set and a knife inserted near the center comes out clean (40 to 50 minutes). Serve warm or at room temperature.

Makes two 9-inch pies, serves 6 to 8 each.

Pumpkin Purée Filling

1. *To prepare pulp by baking:* Preheat oven to 350° F. Cut pumpkin in half. Scrape out seeds and strings. Place cut side down on a glass baking pan; add ⅛ inch water to pan. Bake until pulp is tender (1½ hours). Remove from oven and scrape pulp away from skin. *To prepare pulp by steaming:* Peel pumpkin with a sharp knife. Cut into 2-inch chunks. Place chunks in a vegetable steamer and steam until tender (20 to 30 minutes).

2. Purée pulp in food mill or food processor. Place purée in a fine-meshed sieve and drain well. Freeze purée after draining or use immediately. (If frozen, thaw purée in a fine-meshed sieve. A lot more water will drain off during the thawing process.)

3. In a medium bowl beat 2 cups cooked pumpkin purée just until smooth; add eggs, one at a time, beating well after each addition. Add cream, sugar, cinnamon, ginger, nutmeg, cloves, and allspice; beat to combine.

Makes about 2 cups.

SOUTHERN PECAN PIE

Pecan pie is a long-standing southern favorite that is generally among the most popular desserts at church suppers and elsewhere. Even the most iron-willed calorie watchers find it hard to resist this sweet seduction. Buy the freshest pecans you can find; they will be the crispest. Vanilla ice cream or whipped cream would be a good choice for an accompaniment.

    1 nine-inch single-crust Egg Pastry (see page 435)
    4 eggs, lightly beaten
    ⅔ cup firmly packed dark brown sugar
 1⅓ cup light corn syrup
    ¼ cup unsalted butter, melted
    ½ teaspoon salt
    4 teaspoons flour
    2 teaspoons vanilla extract
 1¼ cups coarsely chopped pecans

1. Roll out Egg Pastry for bottom crust and use to line a 9-inch pie plate. Blind bake until partially baked.

2. Preheat oven to 375° F. In a large bowl combine eggs, sugar, corn syrup, butter, salt, flour, and vanilla; stir to blend. Mix in pecans. Pour into partially baked pie shell.

3. Bake until filling is set (30 to 40 minutes). Cover edges of crust with strips of foil, if necessary, to prevent excessive browning. Cool on wire rack.

Serves 8.

LEMON MERINGUE PIE

This version of lemon pie filling derives its rich yellow hue from egg yolks, butter, and lemon zest—no yellow food coloring here! The quick and easy lemon curd filling can be poured piping hot directly into a fully baked shell. Almonds are a good choice if you make a nut crust.

    1 nine-inch single-crust Flaky Pastry (see
       page 434), Egg Pastry (see page 435), or
       Nut Egg Pastry (see page 435)
    4 eggs
    3 egg yolks (reserve whites for Meringue Topping)
    1 cup plus 2 tablespoons sugar
    ¾ cup fresh lemon juice
    2 teaspoons finely grated lemon rind
    9 tablespoons unsalted butter, softened

Meringue Topping

    3 egg whites (reserve yolks for filling),
       at room temperature
    ¼ teaspoon cream of tartar
    ¼ teaspoon cornstarch
    4 tablespoons superfine sugar
    ½ teaspoon vanilla extract

1. Roll out pastry for bottom crust and use to line a 9-inch pie plate. Blind bake until fully baked; let cool on a wire rack.

2. In a nonaluminum bowl combine eggs, egg yolks, sugar, lemon juice, and lemon rind. Place bowl over a pot of boiling water and whisk or stir over medium heat until mixture thickens to the consistency of mayonnaise (about 5 minutes). Do not boil or eggs will curdle.

3. Remove from heat; whisk in butter, 2 tablespoons at a time, until incorporated. Pour immediately into baked pie shell. Cool to room temperature before topping with meringue.

4. Preheat oven to 350° F. Spread meringue over pie, sealing to edges of crust all around. Bake until golden brown (10 to 15 minutes). Serve at room temperature. To cut meringue easily, dip the knife into water.

Serves 6 to 8.

Meringue Topping Beat egg whites until foamy. Add cream of tartar and cornstarch. Beat until whites form soft peaks. Add sugar, 1 tablespoon at a time, beating after each addition. Beat in vanilla and continue beating until stiff, glossy peaks form.

Two-layered Lemon Meringue Pie is a perennial favorite. To add some crunch, make an almond-based nut crust instead of the more expected flaky one.

■ CUSTARD PIE

It's best to eat a custard pie soon after it's baked. These pies typically develop a soggy shell if left to set and are prone to bacterial spoilage if not stored properly. If not eaten fairly quickly, keep in the refrigerator. However, the crust won't be as crisp.

    1 **nine-inch single-crust Flaky Pastry (see page 434) or Cream Cheese Pastry (see page 436)**
    2 **eggs**
    4 **egg yolks**
    ½ **cup sugar**
    1 **cup milk**
    1 **cup whipping cream**
    1 **tablespoon vanilla extract**
      Freshly grated nutmeg (optional)

1. Preheat oven to 325° F. Roll out Flaky Pastry for bottom crust and use to line a 9-inch pie plate. Blind bake until fully baked; cool.

2. In a medium bowl beat eggs, egg yolks, sugar, milk, cream, and vanilla until smooth and the sugar has dissolved.

3. Set baked shell on a baking sheet; strain custard into shell. Sprinkle with nutmeg, if desired. Bake until custard is set (30 to 40 minutes). Filling may be slightly wobbly in center when shaken, but will set as the pie cools.

4. Serve at room temperature or slightly chilled.

Serves 6 to 8.

Coconut Custard Pie   Follow recipe for Custard Pie. Reduce sugar to ⅓ cup and stir in ½ cup sweetened flaked coconut to custard. Ten minutes before end of cooking, sprinkle ¼ cup toasted flaked coconut over top of pie; finish baking.

■ BANANA CREAM PIE

For this classic American pie, choose bananas that are slightly firm but ripe. If you really love bananas, the filling can accommodate several more. Tossing the fruit in rum gives it a tropical accent. Cream pies are especially susceptible to spoilage if improperly stored. Refrigerate if not eaten within three hours.

    1 **nine-inch single-crust Flaky Pastry (see page 434) or Press-In Pie Crust (see page 436)**
    3 **tablespoons flour**
    3 **tablespoons cornstarch**
    ⅔ **cup sugar**
    3 **cups half-and-half or milk**
    4 **egg yolks**
    2 **teaspoons vanilla extract**
    4 **tablespoons butter**
    3 **to 4 ripe bananas**
    2 **tablespoons rum (optional)**
    1 **to 2 cups whipping cream, whipped, or Meringue Topping (see page 439), for topping**

1. Roll out pastry for bottom crust and use to line a 9-inch pie plate. Blind bake until fully baked; cool.

2. In a medium bowl sift together flour, cornstarch, and sugar. Add ½ cup of the half-and-half, the egg yolks, and vanilla; mix until smooth and creamy. In a medium, heavy-bottomed saucepan, heat remaining half-and-half and add to flour mixture, stirring until completely smooth; return to saucepan and cook over medium heat, stirring continuously. Bring to a boil and cook until starchy taste disappears (2 to 3 minutes). Pour custard into a bowl and dot with butter; set aside to cool.

3. Slice bananas and sprinkle with rum (if used). Fold into cooled custard and pour into pie shell.

4. Top with whipped cream or Meringue Topping and serve.

Serves 6 to 8.

Coconut Cream Pie   Use Coconut-Flake Crust (see page 436). For filling, reduce sugar to ½ cup. Fold 2 cups flaked coconut into custard before dotting with butter and setting aside to cool. If using Meringue Topping, sprinkle with ½ cup toasted coconut before browning.

■ LEMON OR LIME CHIFFON PIE

Chiffon pies are wonderful in a shimmery, ethereal way and make a refreshing summer dessert.

    1 **nine-inch crumb crust of Press-In Pie Crust (see page 436) or Press-In Nut Crust (see page 436)**
    1 **envelope unflavored gelatin**
    ¾ **cup fresh lemon or lime juice**
    4 **egg yolks**
    ¾ **cup sugar**
    1 **teaspoon finely grated lemon or lime rind**
    3 **egg whites**
    2 **cups Chantilly Cream (see page 252), for garnish**
      Strips of lemon or lime rind, for garnish

1. Roll out pastry for bottom crust and use to line a 9-inch pie plate. Bake as directed in recipe.

2. In a small saucepan sprinkle gelatin over ¼ cup of the lemon or lime juice and set aside to soften. In a double boiler combine egg yolks, ½ cup of the sugar, remaining ½ cup lemon juice, and grated lemon rind. Cook over medium heat, stirring constantly, until mixture thickens to consistency of whipping cream and coats the back of a spoon. Do not boil or mixture will curdle. Set aside.

3. Dissolve gelatin over low heat. Stir into lemon mixture. Set bowl over ice and stir until it is about to set (it will have the consistency of cream whipped to soft peaks). Beat whites to stiff peaks. Stir one third of whites into gelatin-lemon mixture to lighten, then fold in remaining whites. Pour into prepared pie shell, smooth top, and refrigerate until set (3 to 4 hours). Serve garnished with Chantilly Cream and rind.

Serves 6 to 8.

BASIC TART CRUSTS

A tart has a short crust made with butter and eggs and often sweetened with sugar. These ingredients make the pastry rich and crumbly rather than flaky. A tart is baked in a shallow, rimless, straight-sided tart tin with a removable bottom, or in a tart band positioned on a baking sheet. When baked, the once-fragile pastry develops enough strength to form a pastry shell that can support its filling without the help of the tart tin.

▪ SAVORY TART PASTRY
Pâte brisée

This basic French tart dough is used for quiches and other savory pies. It is tough, strong and suitable for custard fillings that would make other types of dough soggy. This dough is made without sugar. For a touch of sweetness, if desired, add 2 tablespoons sugar with the flour and salt.

For one 9½- by 1-inch tart band or tin

    1½ cups flour
    ¼   teaspoon salt
    6   tablespoons cold unsalted butter
    2   egg yolks
    3 to 4 tablespoons ice water

For one 10- by 2-inch tart band or tin

    2   cups flour
    ½   teaspoon salt
    ½   cup cold unsalted butter
    2   egg yolks
    4 to 6 tablespoons ice water

1. Sift flour and salt together onto work surface; make a well in the center.

2. Place butter, yolks, and 3 tablespoons of the water in well. Using fingertips, pinch butter to mix with the water and yolks. With a dough scraper or pastry blender, gradually work flour into yolk mixture with a cutting motion to make coarse crumbs (if mixture seems dry and crumbly, add more water).

3. Gather crumbs into a rough mound. Work small portions of the dough against the work surface with the heel of your hand (pushing away from you), so that the dough is smeared across the work area surface (this is known as *fraisage;* it distributes the ingredients evenly through the dough).

4. When pieces of dough are pliable and peel away from the surface in one piece, press into a ball. Wrap well and refrigerate until firm (about 2 hours). Use as directed.

Food Processor Version Put flour and salt in work bowl of food processor; process a few times to aerate. Add butter; process briefly to cut in. Add yolks and water and pulse rapidly just until mixture comes together. Turn out and continue with step 3.

▪ SWEET TART PASTRY
Pâte sucrée

The high percentage of butter, large amount of sugar, and viscosity of the egg yolks in Sweet Tart Pastry produce a dough that is soft, moist, and sticky. The tender, crumbly, and fragile, rather than flaky, dough is quite suitable for delicate tart shells. This pastry can be difficult to roll. If covering a large area, press into shape with fingertips rather than spreading and thinning with a rolling pin. To ease dough into corners, use a ball of scrap dough for pushing and molding. This pastry dough patches without showing repairs.

For one 9½- by 1-inch tart band or tin

    1¼ cups flour
    ⅛   teaspoon salt
    ¼   cup sugar
    2   extralarge egg yolks
    ½   teaspoon vanilla extract
    6   tablespoons cold unsalted butter

For one 10-inch scalloped tart band or one 10- by 2-inch tart tin

    1½ cups flour
    ¼   teaspoon salt
    ⅓   cup sugar
    3   large egg yolks
    ½   teaspoon vanilla extract
    ½   cup cold unsalted butter

1. Sift flour, salt, and sugar onto work surface; make a well in the center.

2. Place egg yolks and vanilla in center; mix with fork or fingertips to thoroughly blend ingredients.

3. Pound butter with rolling pin to soften; add to yolks. Using fingertips, pinch butter to mix with yolks. With a dough scraper or pastry blender, gradually work flour into yolk mixture with a cutting motion to make coarse crumbs.

4. Gather crumbs into a rough mound. Work small portions of the dough against the work surface with the heel of your hand (pushing away from you), so that the dough is smeared across the work area surface (this is known as *fraisage;* it distributes the ingredients evenly through the dough).

5. When pieces of dough are pliable and peel away from the surface in one piece, press into a ball. Wrap well and refrigerate until firm (about 2 hours). Use as directed.

Food Processor Version Place salt, sugar, egg yolks, vanilla, and cold butter in work bowl of food processor and process using four rapid (1-second) pulses. Add flour and process with six to eight rapid pulses, until dough begins to clump (but doesn't form a ball). Turn out and continue with step 4.

Hazelnuts add texture and crunch to Nut Tart. For more flavor, toast the nuts before chopping.

■ SAND PASTRY
Pâte sablée

Use this sweet, short pastry dough to make crusts for tarts and tartlets or cookies. Once baked, this pastry has a sandy, crumbly texture—from which it gets its name—and is very fragile. The dough is difficult to roll and lift and so should be pressed into the baking pan. When made with a high-quality unsalted butter, it is exceptionally flavorful. Fill tartlets with seasonal fresh fruits or lemon curd. For cookies, cut into rounds and triangles and bake in a 350° F oven until slightly colored (five to eight minutes).

    1½ cups flour
        Pinch salt
    ¾   cup cold unsalted butter
    ½   cup confectioners' sugar

1. Sift flour and salt onto work surface; make a well in the center.

2. Place butter and sugar in well. Using fingertips, pinch butter with sugar to make a smooth paste. With a dough scraper or pastry blender, gradually work flour into butter mixture with a cutting motion to make coarse crumbs.

3. Gather crumbs into a rough mound. Work small portions of the dough against the work surface with the heel of your hand (pushing away from you), so that the dough is smeared across the work surface (this is known as *fraisage;* it distributes the ingredients evenly through the dough).

4. When pieces of dough are pliable and peel away from the surface in one piece, press into a ball. Wrap well and refrigerate until firm (about 2 hours).

Makes one 8-inch tart shell or 4 to 6 tartlets.

A TART SAMPLER

Tart fillings can simply be flavored fresh fruit, fresh fruit on top of a layer of smooth pastry cream, a citrus curd, a custard with or without a fruit topping, or one similar to a pecan pie. See Baking Pies and Tarts (page 434) for suggestions on how to avoid a soggy tart crust.

■ FRESH FRUIT TART

A buttery, sweet crust, vanilla pastry cream, and fresh fruit combine to create a classic tart. Few pastries delight the eye and palate more than a tempting array of colorful fresh fruit tarts. The recipe below uses strawberries, kirsch-flavored pastry cream, and a red currant jelly glaze for a strawberry tart. When you vary the fruit, select a flavoring and glaze that will complement or heighten the characteristic taste of the fruit. When glazing the tarts, choose a jam or jelly that matches the fruit in color and flavor. Note that the pastry cream can be made up to three days ahead.

    1   Sweet Tart Pastry (9½ in.; see page 441)
    1   cup milk
    1   vanilla bean, split in half lengthwise, *or*
         1 teaspoon vanilla extract
    3   egg yolks
    ¼   cup sugar
    3   tablespoons flour
    2   tablespoons kirsch
    ½   cup stiffly whipped cream (optional)
    3½   cups hulled, halved strawberries
         (approximately two 12-oz baskets)
    1   cup red currant jelly

1. Roll out tart pastry and use to line a 9½- by 1-inch tart tin that has a removable bottom. Blind bake until fully baked; cool; reserve.

2. To make pastry cream: In a heavy-bottomed saucepan, bring milk to a boil with vanilla bean; remove from heat and allow bean to steep in milk for 10 minutes. Remove vanilla bean, rinse off, and let it dry (it can be reused one more time). If using vanilla extract, add in step 4.

3. Beat egg yolks and sugar together until thick and light. Stir in flour.

4. Reheat milk to boiling. Whisk milk into yolk mixture and return to saucepan. Whisk over low heat until mixture boils; cook gently for 2 minutes, whisking constantly. Remove from heat and stir in vanilla extract (if using instead of vanilla bean). Transfer pastry cream mixture to a small container and cover surface with a piece of buttered plastic wrap or parchment paper. Cool to room temperature and store in the refrigerator, where it will keep 2 to 3 days.

5. Stir 1 tablespoon of the kirsch into pastry cream. If pastry cream is too thick, lighten by folding in ½ cup stiffly whipped cream.

6. To assemble tart: Spread a ½-inch layer of pastry cream in bottom of fully baked tart shell. Arrange a design of strawberries over the cream in concentric circles. You may use whole, halved, or sliced berries to form your design.

7. To make glaze: Heat jelly in a saucepan over low heat until just melted and bubbly. Stir in remaining kirsch. Brush surface of strawberries with a thin layer of glaze. Reserve leftover glaze for another tart.

Serves 6 to 8.

◼ LEMON TART

This filling bears a slight resemblance to that of Lemon Meringue Pie (see page 439). Actually, it is more like a set custard than it is gelatinous and bouncy. This is an elegant, refined dessert that would look lovely garnished with piped rosettes of Chantilly Cream (see page 252) and candied violets. Check better cookware stores, and cake-decorating suppliers for candied violets.

  1 Savory Tart Pastry (9½ in., with extra
    2 tablespoons sugar; see page 441)
  3 eggs
  3 egg yolks
  ⅓ cup sugar
    Finely grated rind and juice of 3 lemons
  1 tablespoon cornstarch
  4 tablespoons butter, melted and cooled

1. Roll out tart pastry and use to line a 9½- by 1-inch tart tin that has a removable bottom. Blind bake until fully baked; cool.

2. Preheat oven to 350° F. In a medium bowl beat eggs, egg yolks, and sugar until combined; add rind and beat until mixture is smooth and light. In a separate small bowl, combine lemon juice and cornstarch and mix until smooth and well blended.

3. Combine the two mixtures; stir in butter. Pour lemon custard mixture into pie shell and bake until set and a knife inserted near center comes out clean (25 to 35 minutes). Let cool; serve at room temperature.

Serves 6 to 8.

◼ NUT TART

Chez Panisse in Berkeley, California, is known for its nut tart. This version was inspired by the one served there. While hazelnuts are called for, any nuts will work as well. The dough is frozen, rather than just chilled, to better withstand the high heat of the cooked filling.

  ¾ cup whipping cream
  ¾ cup sugar
  1 tablespoon frangelico or other hazelnut liqueur
  1 tablespoon vanilla extract
  1 cup hazelnuts, roughly chopped
  1 nine-inch frozen Flaky Pastry (see page 434)
    or Savory Tart Pastry (9½ in., see page 441)

1. Preheat oven to 400° F. In a medium, heavy-bottomed saucepan, combine cream and sugar and stir over low heat until sugar has dissolved. Increase heat to medium and cook until mixture reaches 238° F (soft-ball stage) on a candy thermometer.

2. Remove from heat and stir in liqueur and vanilla; then add the nuts. Cool at least 10 minutes, then pour into frozen pie shell.

3. Bake until filling is a golden caramel color (25 to 30 minutes). Cool. Serve at room temperature.

Serves 6 to 8.

◼ QUICHE LORRAINE

Quiche evolved in the area in eastern France that borders Germany; the word has its roots in *kuchen*, German for cake. Unlike the versions one commonly comes across in restaurants and specialty food stores today, some classic recipes for quiche Lorraine (like the version offered here) do not have cheese. The main ingredients are bacon, eggs, and cream. Pans for quiche are fluted, either metal (preferably with removable bottom) or porcelain, and are large—usually measuring 10 inches in diameter by 1½ inches deep (see BAKING PANS, FOR BATTER AND DOUGH, Quiche Pan). If a pie plate is used, only half the filling will be required; use extra filling for a second pie.

  8 ounces bacon, diced
  1 Savory Tart Pastry tart shell, partially baked
    (10 in., see page 441)
  8 eggs
  2½ cups half-and-half
  ½ cup whipping cream
  1½ teaspoons salt
  ½ teaspoon ground white pepper
  ½ teaspoon freshly grated nutmeg

1. Preheat oven to 375° F. In a medium skillet sauté bacon over medium-high heat to remove some fat (about 8 minutes). Remove with a slotted spoon to a paper-towel–lined plate; cool briefly. Sprinkle over bottom of partially baked quiche shell.

2. In a large mixing bowl beat eggs and stir in half-and-half, cream, salt, pepper, and nutmeg. Pour into shell and bake until knife inserted in center comes out clean (about 1 hour). Remove from oven and cool 30 minutes before serving. Serve at room temperature.

Serves 8 to 10.

Recipes and Related Information

Baking Pans, 18; Beef and Mushroom Piroshki, 46; Cake and Pastry Tools, 89; Deep-Dish Chicken Pie, 472; Key Lime Pie, 342; Mud Pie, 315; Nutty Peach Pie, 421; Orange Custard Tart, 401; Raspberry-Almond Tart, 496; Sour-Cherry Pie, 120; Strawberry-Rhubarb Pie, 498.

PINEAPPLE

When the early European explorers found pineapple growing in the Caribbean and in Central and South America, they were immediately seduced by its sweet flavor. Taking it with them on their ships, they spread it to Africa, Madagascar, India, China, Japan, and the Philippines. Surprisingly, it wasn't widely cultivated in Hawaii until the late 1800s, and it wasn't readily available on the mainland until well into the twentieth century, when advances in shipping made transportation of ripe pineapples possible.

Pineapples do not ripen further after harvest; they must be left on the tree until their starch is converted to sugar. However, at that point, they are extremely delicate and perishable. Until the development of rapid, refrigerated shipping and air freight, most pineapples were shipped green. Today the American consumer can enjoy fruit that is almost fully tree-ripened.

The pineapple grown in Hawaii, the Cayenne, has a cylindrical pinecone shape and long, spearlike fronds. A second variety, the Red Spanish, is grown in Florida, Puerto Rico, and Cuba; it is squarish in shape. Yet a third variety, the Sugar Loaf, is exported to the United States from Mexico; it is an extralarge pineapple, weighing from 5 to 10 pounds.

Use　Pineapple is perhaps at its best eaten raw, in slices, wedges, or cubes. It may be added to fruit salads and chicken or turkey salad. Cubed pineapple adds a sweet-tart flavor to Vietnamese fish soup and Indonesian curries. Thai cooks add pineapple to noodles in coconut milk and serve the fruit with spicy ground pork. Pineapple slices may be grilled and served with roast pork or duck, or may be baked and served with ham. Caribbean cooks bake it with brown sugar and rum for dessert. Diced pineapple may be added to gelatin salads if cooked first. (Uncooked pineapple contains an enzyme that inhibits jelling.) Diced pineapple is also used in cream pies and cakes and is puréed for sherbet and ice cream. Pineapple juice is a refreshing breakfast beverage and an ingredient in some punches and tropical cocktails.

Availability　Pineapples are sold the year around; supplies peak March through June. Canned pineapple, in rings, cubes, or dice, is widely sold in supermarkets. Canned pineapple juice is also widely available in supermarkets. Dried unsweetened pineapple slices and candied pineapple are found in some health-food stores and specialty stores.

Selection　The best indications of ripeness are a strong sweet aroma and a rich yellow color. Avoid pineapples that are too green and those that have soft spots or dried-out leaves.

Storage　Keep pineapple in a plastic bag in the refrigerator and use within three to five days, preferably as soon as possible. Store leftover canned pineapple in an airtight, nonmetal container in the refrigerator and use within a few days. Refrigerate leftover canned pineapple juice in an airtight, nonmetal container; use within one week.

Preparation　To peel and section a pineapple, slice off frond and stand pineapple on stem end. Slice in quarters lengthwise. Cut away central core. Using a large sharp knife, cut flesh of each pineapple quarter away from rind by gradually sliding knife underneath flesh from one end to other end. Cube or dice. Alternatively, to make pineapple rounds, slice off frond and stand pineapple on stem end. Using a large sharp knife, slice away rind from top to bottom. Cut into rounds; core if desired.

Recipes and Related Information
Corer, 156; Sweet-and-Sour Pineapple Pork, 460.

PINE NUT

Two types of pine nut, also known as Indian nut or piñon, are available in this country. The more delicately flavored pine nut used in Mediterranean and Middle Eastern cooking is the seed of the stone pine; it is long, slender, and pale ivory, with a faint pine flavor. The other pine nut, broader at one end than the other, is found in Chinese markets; it is less expensive, but has a strong pine flavor that is not desirable in Mediterranean dishes.

Use　Chinese cooks garnish poultry and fish dishes with pine nuts. They also dip them in honey and fry them to make a sweet or use them to garnish tea cakes and pastries. Italians use pine nuts in pasta sauces and in the classic pesto sauce. They also add them to stuffings, sautéed vegetables (especially spinach), and cookies and ricotta cheesecake. Greek cooks sometimes put pine nuts in stuffed grape leaves.

Availability　Pine nuts are sold in small packages in specialty markets and in bulk in some health-food stores. Chinese markets and some specialty markets carry the stronger-flavored triangular variety.

Selection　Buy as fresh as possible.

Storage　Pine nuts, being high in oil, quickly turn rancid. Wrap tightly and freeze for up to six months or refrigerate for up to two months.

Preparation　The flavor of pine nuts is improved with toasting. Put nuts in a cold skillet over moderately low heat and cook, shaking skillet constantly so that nuts color evenly, until pine nuts are golden.

Recipes and Related Information
Mushrooms Stuffed With Herb Cheese, 377; Pesto, 27; Pine Nut Crescents, 146; Ricotta Cheesecake, 119; Sole With Almonds, Pine Nuts, and White Raisins, 533; Your Own Bridge Mix, 59.

PISTACHIO NUT

The fruit of a tree native to the Middle East and Central Asia, the pistachio nut is usually about ½ inch long and is covered with a tan shell that splits easily in half. The shell is sometimes dyed pink to hide blemishes. Inside, the edible kernel has a paper-thin brown skin, green flesh, and a yellow interior. It has a sweet, mild flavor. Most pistachios come from Iran and Turkey, although California pistachios are increasingly common.

Use Pistachio nuts are an ingredient in both sweet and savory dishes, especially in the Middle East. The green color makes them particularly valuable as a garnish for all manner of foods. French cooks use them to stud pâtés and galantines. Turkish cooks use pistachios to garnish savory rice dishes and sweet custards. In India pistachios are used in sweet, milk-based candies; one of the most popular Indian sweets is made of grated carrot, milk, sugar, and chopped pistachios cooked until thick. The nuts may be salted and roasted and eaten as a cocktail snack. They may also be blanched, skinned, and chopped or ground for use in ice cream, soufflés, and pastries. Most commercial pistachio ice cream is artificially colored and flavored with almond extract.

Availability Unshelled pistachios are sold in many supermarkets, either raw or roasted and salted. Raw pistachios are widely available in bulk in health-food stores. Middle Eastern markets are another good source for pistachios.

Storage Keep pistachios in the refrigerator for up to three months or in the freezer for up to six months.

Preparation Shell pistachios. To blanch and peel, boil 30 seconds, then drain and wrap in a clean dish towel. Rub nuts back and forth with towel, then unwrap and remove any unloosened skins by hand. Toast nuts in a 300° F oven to dry them out (about 10 minutes).

Recipes and Related Information
Figs With Flavored Ricotta, 220; Pâté Maison, 416; Your Own Bridge Mix, 59.

PIT; PIT, TO

Both the stone, or hard, central portion of a one-seeded (drupaceous) fruit such as a cherry or a peach, and the act of removing this stone. Sometimes a pit pulls away easily; to pit a peach, simply halve and pry stone away with a knife or your finger. Cherry and olive pits are much more tenacious. For pitting in quantity, consider a cherry pitter, which punches pits out much as a hole puncher removes circles of paper (see CHERRY PITTER).

PIZZA

Food historians and pizza-loving Neapolitans, residents of the Italian city most associated with this dish, concur that the famous open pie, made of thinly rolled bread dough topped with a seasoned mixture, probably originated with the flat breads of ancient Egypt. When the Greeks colonized southern Italy, they brought these breads with them. Although this is not the only explanation for the appearance of pizza in Italy, it is a popular one. There is little agreement, however, about the origins of the word *pizza*. The dictionary states that it grew out of the Latin *pinsere*, to beat or knead. Other sources suggest that it is the Neopolitan pronunciation of the Greek word *picea*, which specifically refers to these types of breads or pies.

For those who relish the dish, it matters little where it comes from or what we call it. However, Americans who visit Italy for the first time might not recognize pizza in all the guises it assumes in its native land. The familiar doughy pie topped with tomatoes and cheese is most common in the southern part of the country. Elsewhere the dough may be thicker and less chewy and the toppings as simple as some fresh herbs, mushrooms, or a slice of ham. Or, it may be paper-thin and crisp, with any number of toppings, sometimes with cheese, sometimes without. Neapolitan-style pizza is but one of a family of Italian bread-based foods that serve as plate and topping in one.

The current culinary interest in fresh, regional ingredients has broadened our definition of what makes a pizza, just as it has changed our view of so many other foods. The variations that have evolved from experimentations by many young chefs are closer in spirit to the pizzas of Italy. Banished are bland or oversalted prepared tomato sauces and rubbery cheeses, replaced by inventive combinations of fresh vegetables and meats, unusual cheeses, and creative flavorings. The emphasis is on using what grows naturally and nearby, which is what makes Italian pizza, or any food, so delicious. Pizza has become regional. Cities have given their names to particular styles; Chicago, New York, Boston, and New Haven each have a version.

Making pizza at home is no more difficult than baking bread. All you need is a hot oven and, for best results, a baking stone and a wooden baker's peel. You can also buy square terra-cotta tile at just about any tile supply store (see BAKER'S PEEL and BAKING STONE AND TILE). The stone or tile converts an oven into a home version of the commercial stone restaurant ovens. The wooden peel is the easiest way to move pizza in and out of the oven. With some advance preparation, the cook can make pizza from scratch as easily as pulling a storebought pizza from the freezer. Yeast doughs are tolerant of cold. If the dough is prepared in the morning, or even the night before, it can wait in the refrigerator, or even in the freezer; when needed, let it warm to room temperature. Then shape it, add toppings, and bake. If you have a favorite sauce, make it in quantity and freeze in recipe-sized portions.

FOOD PROCESSOR PIZZA DOUGH

Process dough to lumpy state, not a smooth ball; do not overprocess. Finish mixing by hand, if desired. If kneading by machine, process dough until ingredients are well mixed and dough forms a ball.

Place dough on a lightly floured surface and knead until it is smooth and silky, adding more flour if necessary.

On lightly floured surface, roll dough out to an even circle, ¼ inch thick, and place on tile.

■ PIZZA MARGHERITA

This familiar red (tomatoes), white (cheese), and green (basil) pizza is said to have been named after Queen Margherita of Italy, who loved the dish because it bore her country's national colors.

> 1 cup grated whole-milk mozzarella cheese
> ½ cup whole fresh basil leaves
>   Salt and freshly ground pepper, to taste
> ¼ cup plus 2 tablespoons olive oil
>   Freshly grated Parmesan cheese
>   Pinch chopped fresh oregano
>   Cornmeal or rice flour, for dusting

Basic Pizza Dough

> 1½ teaspoons active dry yeast (½ package)
> ¾ cup warm (105° to 115° F) water
> 2 tablespoons olive oil
> 2½ cups unbleached flour or bread flour
> 1 teaspoon salt

Fresh Tomato Sauce

> 3 medium tomatoes (about 1 lb)
> 2 tablespoons olive oil
> 1 clove garlic, minced
> 1 tablespoon chopped fresh basil *or*
>   ½ teaspoon dried basil
> ¼ teaspoon salt
> ¼ cup dry white wine

1. Preheat baking stone at least 30 minutes in a 450° F oven (475° F for a crisper crust). Roll pizza dough into a square or round and place on a baker's peel or baking sheet well dusted with cornmeal or rice flour.

2. Cover surface of pizza with Fresh Tomato Sauce, then cheese, then basil. Season with salt and pepper. Drizzle with ¼ cup olive oil, then dust with Parmesan cheese and oregano.

3. Slide pizza onto heated baking stone (as described in BAKER'S PEEL) and bake until well browned and puffy (20 to 25 minutes). Brush crust with remaining 2 tablespoons olive oil. Cut into small squares or wedges and serve hot or at room temperature.

Makes 2 medium pizzas or 1 large pizza.

Basic Pizza Dough　Dissolve yeast in the warm water in a small bowl; let proof 5 minutes. Stir in olive oil. In a large bowl combine flour and salt. Add yeast mixture and stir until dough just barely holds together (see also Food Processor Pizza Dough, on page 445). Turn dough out onto a lightly floured surface and knead until soft and silky, adding a little more flour if necessary. Put dough in an oiled bowl and turn to coat surface with oil. Cover bowl with plastic wrap and let rise in a warm place until doubled (about 1 hour).

Makes 2 medium pizza crusts or 1 large pizza crust.

Fresh Tomato Sauce　Pour boiling water over tomatoes; peel, then chop finely. Heat oil in a medium saucepan over medium-high heat. Add tomatoes and garlic. Mix in basil, salt, and wine. Bring to a boil, cover, reduce heat, and simmer for 15 minutes. Uncover and cook over medium-high heat, stirring often as sauce begins to thicken, until sauce is thick and reduced to about 1 cup (15 to 20 minutes).

Makes about 1 cup.

■ PISSALADIERE

All over the French Riviera, you find "the pizza of Nice": *pissaladière*. Baked in large sheets and cut into squares while still warm, it's handed to you on a fragile tissue to munch as you go. It features a mixture of seasoned onions, anchovies, and Mediterranean black olives.

Dough

> 1½ teaspoons active dry yeast (½ package)
> ¼ cup warm (105° to 115° F) water
> ½ teaspoon sugar
> 1¼ cups flour
> ½ teaspoon salt
> ½ teaspoon olive oil
>   Cornmeal or rice flour, for dusting

Topping

> 2 tablespoons olive oil (more, if needed)
> ¼ cup unsalted butter
> 4 yellow onions, thinly sliced
> 3 cloves garlic, minced
> 1 teaspoon minced fresh thyme *or*
>   ½ teaspoon dried thyme
>   Salt and freshly ground pepper, to taste
> 1 tin (2 oz) anchovy fillets in oil
> 12 to 15 large black Greek olives, pitted
> ¼ cup minced parsley
> ¼ cup fresh basil leaves (optional)

1. *To prepare dough with electric mixer:* In a small bowl combine yeast, the water, and sugar and let proof 5 minutes. In large bowl of electric mixer, combine flour and salt. Using dough hook, begin mixing and add olive oil. Add yeast mixture and continue mixing. Dough hook will knead dough for you. Mix 5 to 7 minutes, or until dough is silky and no longer clings to sides of bowl. *To make by hand:* Put flour and salt in a large bowl, and stir in olive oil and yeast mixture by hand; knead by hand on a lightly floured surface until mixture is silky and smooth. For either method, place dough in a well-oiled bowl, turning to coat all surfaces with oil, and let rise, covered with a warm damp towel, for 1 hour.

2. To prepare topping: In a large heavy skillet over medium heat, heat olive oil and butter. Add onion and cook gently 5 minutes. Add garlic, thyme, salt, and pepper. Cook 20 minutes, or until onions are very soft but not brown. Taste; adjust seasoning if necessary. Put 2 anchovy fillets and half the olives in a blender. Add a few drops olive oil and blend. Add more oil as necessary to make a smooth paste.

3. To assemble Pissaladière: Preheat oven to 400° F. Roll dough out into a rectangle or circle. Transfer to a baking sheet well dusted with cornmeal or rice flour. Spread with anchovy and olive paste and cover with onion slices. Arrange remaining anchovies over onions in a crisscross pattern. Slice remaining olives; arrange between anchovies. Drizzle with a little olive oil and dust with 2 tablespoons each parsley and basil (if used). Bake until well browned (30 to 35 minutes). Cool slightly, then sprinkle with remaining herbs just before serving. Cut while still warm.

Makes 16 to 20 small cocktail squares or wedges.

■ DEEP-DISH PEPPERONI PIZZA

You'll need a special high-sided pan for this pizza (see BAK-ING PANS, FOR BATTER AND DOUGH, Pizza Pan). It resembles an oversized cake pan and measures about 15 inches in diameter and 2 inches deep. Once used, the pan should be wiped clean, not washed, so it will season. The dough is especially quick and easy to make because it uses quick-rise yeast (see YEAST). The dough can be mixed in a food processor as well as by hand. If you prefer, substitute browned, crumbled Italian sausage for the pepperoni.

> 3 cups (1 lb) grated whole-milk mozzarella cheese
> 1 can (2¼ oz) sliced ripe olives, well drained
> 2½ cups (about ½ lb) thinly sliced pepperoni
> 2 recipes Fresh Tomato Sauce (opposite page)
> ⅔ cup freshly grated Parmesan cheese

Deep-Dish Pizza Dough

> 3 to 3½ cups unbleached flour
> 1 package quick-rise active dry yeast
> ¾ teaspoon salt
> 1¼ cups hot (115° to 125° F) water
> 2 teaspoons honey
> 1 tablespoon olive oil

1. Preheat oven to 450° F. Grease a deep-dish pizza pan. Roll dough out on a floured surface to about a 14-inch circle. Use your hands to pat and stretch dough to fit into pan, pressing it against bottom and then up sides of pan to reach top edge.

2. Sprinkle half the mozzarella cheese over bottom of dough. Add olives in an even layer, then pepperoni. Spread evenly with sauce. Cover with remaining mozzarella cheese, then sprinkle with Parmesan cheese.

3. Bake on lowest rack of oven until crust browns well and cheese is richly browned (25 to 30 minutes). Cut in wedges and serve at once.

Makes 1 large pizza.

Deep-Dish Pizza Dough

1. In large bowl of electric mixer, combine 2½ cups of the flour, yeast, and salt. Stir to blend dry ingredients thoroughly. In a small bowl combine the hot water, honey, and oil; stir to blend well.

2. Add water mixture to flour mixture. Mix to blend, then beat at medium speed until smooth and elastic (about 5 minutes). Stir in about ½ cup more flour to make a soft dough.

3. Turn dough out onto a floured surface. Knead until dough is smooth and satiny (8 to 10 minutes), adding just enough flour (up to ½ cup) to prevent dough from being sticky.

4. Turn dough into a greased bowl. Cover with plastic wrap and a towel, and let rise in a warm place until doubled in bulk (30 to 40 minutes). Punch dough down, cover with inverted bowl, and let rest 10 minutes; use as directed in recipe.

The sunny flavors of southern France come together in Pissaladière, the earthy "street" pizza from Nice. Anchovies, garlic, onions, and olives are the soul of Pissaladière, at its best in casual settings and washed down with a sharp white wine.

A calzone is a savory Italian turnover made with a yeast dough. Fillings usually have cheese and often some type of sausage, ham, or salami.

▇ CALZONE WITH SUN-DRIED TOMATOES

According to food historian Waverley Root, this form of pizza turnover originated in Naples. Calzone is named for the trouser leg some people think it resembles.

- 1 tablespoon oil from sun-dried tomatoes
- 1 medium onion, finely chopped
- 1 clove garlic, minced
- 1 cup (8 oz) ricotta cheese
- ¼ cup chopped sun-dried tomatoes
- 2 tablespoons chopped parsley
  Deep-Dish Pizza Dough (see page 447)
- ¼ pound sliced prosciutto or dry salami, cut into strips
- 2 cups (½ lb) grated whole-milk mozzarella cheese
  Cornmeal, for dusting
  Olive oil, for coating

1. In a medium skillet heat tomato oil over moderate heat; add onion and cook, stirring often, until soft but not browned. Mix in garlic, then remove from heat.

2. In a medium bowl mix ricotta cheese with dried tomatoes and parsley; stir in cooked onion mixture.

3. Divide dough into 2 equal portions. Roll each half out on a floured surface to a 12-inch circle. Spread half of the ricotta filling over half of each circle of dough, leaving about a ½-inch margin.

4. Sprinkle half of each circle with half of the prosciutto strips and 1 cup of the mozzarella cheese. Fold circles in half over filling, moistening and pinching edges together (or pressing with tines of a fork) to seal.

5. Preheat oven to 450° F. Sprinkle a large greased baking sheet lightly with cornmeal. Place calzone well apart on prepared baking sheet. Let rise until puffy (12 to 15 minutes).

6. Bake on center rack until crust browns well (about 15 minutes). Brush tops lightly with olive oil, then serve hot.

Makes 2 calzone.

▇ STUFFED VEGETARIAN PIZZA

Students of pizza trace the concept of the stuffed pizza to Giordano's on Chicago's South Side. The idea has been carried far and wide by alumni of that restaurant's kitchen.

- 1 large onion, thinly sliced
- ½ pound mushrooms, thinly sliced
- 1 red or green bell pepper, cut in thin strips
- ¼ cup olive oil
- 2 cloves garlic, minced
- ½ teaspoon *each* salt and dried oregano
- ⅛ teaspoon *each* freshly ground pepper and dried marjoram
  Deep-Dish Pizza Dough (see page 447)
- 4 cups (1 lb) grated Monterey jack cheese
  Fresh Tomato Sauce (see page 446)
- ⅔ cup freshly grated Parmesan or Romano cheese

1. Preheat oven to 450° F. In a large skillet over medium heat, sauté onion, mushrooms, and red pepper in oil, stirring often, until onion is soft, mushrooms brown lightly, and mushroom liquid evaporates. Add garlic, salt, oregano, pepper, and marjoram; remove from heat.

2. Grease a deep-dish pizza pan. Divide dough into 2 portions, one about a third larger than the other. Roll larger portion of dough out on a floured surface to about a 14-inch circle. Use your hands to pat and stretch dough to fit into pan, pressing it against sides of pan to reach top edge.

3. Sprinkle evenly with 3 cups of the jack cheese. Spread vegetable mixture over cheese.

4. Roll out remaining dough to a 14- to 15-inch circle; place over vegetables, pressing edge against dough already in pan. Fold dough lining pan over top layer.

5. Spread tomato sauce over top layer of dough. Sprinkle evenly with the remaining 1 cup jack cheese. Top with Parmesan cheese.

6. Bake on lowest rack of oven until crust browns well and cheese is richly browned (25 to 30 minutes). Let stand for 2 to 3 minutes before cutting into wedges.

Makes 1 large pizza.

PLANTAIN

Also known as cooking banana or Adam's fig, the plantain is a member of the banana family commonly eaten in Latin America and the Caribbean. Unlike the more familiar yellow banana, the plantain must be cooked to be edible. It resembles a yellow banana but is larger and thicker skinned, with three or four well-defined sides. Plantains are green when unripe, turning yellow, then brown, then black when ripe. When cooked, they have a mildly sweet flavor comparable to winter squash.

Use   Plantains may be peeled and fried in butter or oil and served as a side dish. They may also be roasted in their skins. In Cuba and Peru, plantains are sliced like potato chips and deep-fried. Like potatoes, plantain chunks are added to soups and stews. Venezuelan cooks use plantains to make cinnamon-scented, lightly sweet cakes that are served with pot roast. Mexican cooks fry boiled, mashed plantains in oil with onions and tomatoes and serve the dish with shrimp.

Availability   Plantains are sold the year around in Latin and Caribbean markets. Some supermarkets also carry plantains.

Selection   Plantains are usually shipped green but will ripen at room temperature. When ripe, they are dark brown or black and give slightly to pressure. Black skin does not indicate blemished flesh. Some recipes call for green plantains, which have a bland, starchy flavor.

Others call for half-ripe yellow plantains, which have a flavor similar to sweet potatoes. Still other recipes call for fully ripe black plantains, which have a flavor like bananas. Choose the degree of ripeness required by the recipe, or ripen plantains at home at room temperature. A green plantain will turn yellow-brown within one week and black within another week.

Storage Wrapped in plastic, ripe plantains will keep in the refrigerator for up to three days.

Preparation Ripe plantains are easy to peel, but unripe plantains are more difficult. To peel an unripe plantain, cut a lengthwise incision, then cut around the fruit in three places. Peel back skin with fingers.

■ FRIED PLANTAIN

Plantains are available in great variety in Mexico. This Mexican dish can be served as a vegetable or snack, similar to French-fried potatoes. If plantains are unavailable, select regular bananas that are not yet ripe.

> 3 **plantains or unripe bananas**
> ½ **cup butter**
> **Salt, to taste**

1. Peel plantains and slice fruit crosswise into ½-inch-thick slices.

2. Melt half the butter in a skillet. Sauté plantain slices, a few at a time, until tender and golden brown. Add more butter as needed. Salt lightly and serve.

Serves 6.

PLUM

The plum is one of the world's preeminent fruits, second only to the peach in commercial importance and first in the breadth of its geographic dispersion. The hundreds of plum varieties vary in size, color, and flavor. California alone grows at least 11 varieties in quantity. Generally speaking, plums have a thin, smooth skin and a very soft, moist flesh. All plums have a large center seed.

Use Plums are delicious eaten out of hand as a breakfast food or snack. They may be sliced and added raw to fruit salads or warmed in fruit compotes. Plums make excellent fruit tarts, crisps, and cobblers. They may be stewed for chutney, preserves, fruit butter, and jelly. In China plums are stewed with apricots, sugar, and vinegar to make a sweet-tart sauce served with roast duck. Plums are often distilled to make plum brandies such as slivovitz, *mirabelle,* and *quetsch;* in the United States, the sloe plum is used for gin. Plum blossoms are a fragrant addition to ice cream. The "plum" used in Japan to make pickled plums and plum wine is actually a variety of apricot. Similarly, the famous English plum pudding

usually contains a generous quantity of raisins and currants but no plums.

The prune is a variety of plum that can be dried without removing the pit. (Other plums would ferment if dried with the pit intact.) Although the word *prune* is most often applied to the dried fruit (see DRIED FRUIT, Prunes), some fresh plums are also known as prunes or prune plums. There are several varieties of prune plums, but the one that accounts for about 90 percent of domestic dried prunes is the French Agen. Other prune plums, such as the Italian prune and the sugar prune, occasionally appear fresh in markets in late summer.

Availability Fresh plums are in season from mid-May to September, with different varieties ripening at different times. Early varieties include the Santa Rosa, the Beauty, and the Burmosa; midseason varieties include the El Dorado, the Tragedy, and the Simka; late-season varieties include the Late Santa Rosa, the Casselman, the Laroda, the Nubiana, and the Queen Ann. The French prune plum is generally grown to dry for prunes but is available fresh in some markets in midsummer. The greengage plum, a green-skinned European plum, is not widely available in this country. Small beach plums grow wild along the Atlantic coast but are rarely grown commercially; they make excellent preserves and jelly.

Selection Choose plums that are firm but not hard; they should give slightly to pressure. Look for plumpness and full color. Avoid plums with breaks in the skin and brownish discoloration.

Storage Let firm plums sit at room temperature for one or two days to soften them slightly. Ripe plums should be stored in the refrigerator and consumed within three to five days.

■ HOT BUTTERED PLUMS

These fresh summer plums in a tart orange sauce are good to serve from a chafing dish, either alone or as a topping for crêpes or crisp waffles.

> ¼ **cup butter or margarine**
> ½ **cup sugar**
> 2 **teaspoons cornstarch**
> ⅛ **teaspoon freshly grated nutmeg**
> 4 **cups quartered, pitted red plums**
> ½ **teaspoon vanilla extract**
> **Juice and grated rind of 1 small orange**

1. In a large frying pan, melt butter over medium heat. Stir in sugar, cornstarch, and nutmeg. Mix in plums, turning to coat with sugar mixture. Cook, stirring occasionally, until juices form a thick sauce (3 to 5 minutes).

2. Remove from heat; gently stir in vanilla and orange juice and rind. Return to heat and stir until sauce boils and thickens slightly (2 to 3 minutes). Serve hot.

Serves 6.

As a timesaver, eggs can be poached in advance and rewarmed in hot water.

◼ FRESH PLUM KUCHEN

The fresh, small blue prune plums of early autumn bake to crimson juiciness in this sugar-sprinkled dessert. The pastry is easy to prepare as it is pressed into the baking pan rather than rolled and then fit into the pan.

⅔ cup sugar
¼ teaspoon freshly grated nutmeg
3 tablespoons flour
1 tablespoon fresh lemon juice
4 cups small blue prune plums, halved and pitted
1 tablespoon butter or margarine
Sugar, for topping
Crème Fraîche (see page 161) or sour cream, for garnish

Kuchen Pastry

1½ cups flour
¼ cup sugar
½ cup cold butter or margarine
1 egg yolk
½ teaspoon vanilla extract

1. Preheat oven to 375° F. Press Kuchen Pastry into bottom and about halfway up sides of a 9-inch springform pan.

2. Mix sugar, nutmeg, and flour. Stir lemon juice into plums in a bowl, then mix lightly with sugar mixture. Arrange fruit, cut sides up, making two layers in pastry-lined pan. Sprinkle with any sugar mixture remaining in bowl. Dot with butter.

3. Bake on lowest rack of oven until pastry is well browned and plums are tender and bubbling (50 minutes to 1 hour). Sprinkle with sugar.

4. Remove pan sides and serve tart warm or cool with Crème Fraîche or sour cream spooned over each piece.

Serves 8.

Kuchen Pastry Mix flour with sugar. Cut in butter until crumbly. Beat egg yolk with vanilla. With a fork, stir egg mixture lightly into flour mixture. Using hands, press dough into smooth, flat ball.

PLUMP, TO

To soak dried fruits, particularly raisins and dried currants, in liquid to soften them, to have them absorb the liquid, and to fill out. This process is necessary only if the fruit is dry and hard. To plump raisins and dried currants, let the fruit sit in boiling water to cover for 5 minutes until softened. For a classic pairing, use rum. Alternatively, soak fruit in the liquid it will later be cooked in for at least 10 to 15 minutes, or even overnight. If plumping in alcohol, have it at room temperature, not hot.

POACH, TO

To cook food gently in liquid that is hot, but not quite boiling (about 210° F; the surface of the liquid will show some movement, with small bubbles just starting to appear). Almost any food can be poached, but the technique is particularly suited to fish, whether whole, in fillets, or in steaks; shellfish; and chicken, especially breasts. Cuts of beef and pork that require long cooking can also be poached. Eggs are poached in water and vinegar. Even fruit can be poached in syrup.

During poaching, a flavor exchange takes place between the liquid and the food. The liquid adds flavor to the food and in turn gains flavor from it. Chicken stock is the best liquid for poaching chicken, and fish stock or court bouillon—a mixture of water, wine, aromatic vegetables, and herbs—for poaching seafood. Although beef stock can be used to poach beef, it is not really necessary because the poaching meat turns water into a stock during the relatively long cooking time required for poaching.

Because the poaching liquid gains flavor from the food, it can be used to prepare an accompanying sauce. Many poaching liquids also make a good soup or broth.

Often food is poached in relatively large pieces because they remain more moist than small ones would. Many meats are poached with their bones in because the bones add flavor to both the food and the cooking liquid and help prevent the food from becoming dry.

Any good saucepan large enough to hold both food and enough liquid to cover is suitable for poaching. If you poach whole fish and have room to store a large piece of equipment, you may want to use a long, narrow fish poacher (see COOKWARE, Fish Poacher). It is best not to choose too large a pan because too much liquid would be needed to cover the food, and the liquid would lose flavor.

◼ WINE COURT BOUILLON

Both wine and vinegar court bouillon are reusable. Just strain, reboil, and add about 1 cup of water to compensate for liquid lost in cooking. Bouillons freeze well, too.

8 cups cold water
4 cups dry white wine
2 large onions, peeled and chopped
2 carrots, peeled and chopped
2 ribs celery, chopped
Bouquet garni (see page 56)
2 tablespoons salt
½ teaspoon black peppercorns

1. In a saucepan combine the water, wine, onions, carrots, celery, bouquet garni, and salt. Simmer for about 25 minutes. Add peppercorns and simmer for another 10 minutes. (Peppercorns tend to turn court bouillon bitter if they cook too long.)

2. Let liquid cool, then strain.

Makes about 10 cups.

FISH FUMET

A fish fumet, or concentrated fish stock, is richer than court bouillon and will give more flavor to bland fish. A fumet may be a water-based stock made with a few vegetables and fish carcasses, or it may be a wine or vinegar court bouillon enriched with fish trimmings. If court bouillon is destined for a fumet, reduce it to concentrate flavor.

> 2 pounds fish heads and carcasses, rinsed and broken into pieces
> 1 large onion, cut in chunks
> 1 carrot, cut in ½-inch slices
> 1 rib celery, cut in ½-inch slices
>   Bouquet garni (see page 56)
> 10 cups water
> ½ teaspoon salt
> 10 black peppercorns

1. In a large pan place fish trimmings, onion, carrot, celery, bouquet garni, the water, and salt. Bring to a boil over low heat, skimming occasionally as scum rises to surface. Simmer for about 20 minutes.

2. Add peppercorns, then continue to simmer for 10 more minutes. After 30 minutes of cooking, fish stock is done. Further cooking causes a bitter flavor.

3. Strain stock through a colander without pressing down on the mass. Pressing solids clouds stock, making it unsuitable for an aspic or a clear sauce.

Makes 8 cups.

BASIC POACHED SHELLFISH

Poaching is an easy way to cook shellfish—the shells seal in flavors and juices. Use salted water as the poaching liquid or, for more flavor, court bouillon or fumet. To best control the temperature of the poaching liquid, have the liquid cold to begin and then bring both liquid and shellfish to a gentle simmer. Accompanied with a flavorful sauce, poached shellfish make a simple, delicious main course for any luncheon or dinner.

>   Lobster, crab, shrimp, or crayfish
>   Wine Court Bouillon (see page 450), or salted water to cover

1. Add shellfish to cold poaching liquid, then bring to a simmer. (Many people still plunge lobsters directly into boiling water, but this exposure to high heat toughens them. It is also less humane. The method of slowly heating the water also slowly numbs the lobster. The anesthetized animal expires when the water reaches about 80° F.)

2. Begin calculating cooking time when fish and liquid reach a simmer. Cook shellfish about 20 minutes per pound.

3. Lobster is done when a small leg can be pulled off easily. (Or insert an instant-read thermometer into vent hole at end of tail. A 165° F reading means lobster is

---

ABOUT POACHING

Do not overcook foods that are being poached. Also keep in mind the following.

POACHING FISH

- Use a cold poaching liquid for fish and shellfish, and heat just until surface of liquid barely moves. This prevents outside of fish from cooking before inside and helps prevent fish from falling apart. Also, if a whole fish is placed directly into hot liquid, the skin will split.
- When poaching a whole fish, first wrap it in cheesecloth. The cheesecloth preserves shape of fish and facilitates removal from liquid. Remove fish pieces with a slotted spatula. Handle all poached fish as delicately as possible.
- Almost all types of fish are suitable for poaching. The exception is fish with very soft, fatty flesh, such as sablefish, which tend to fall apart in the liquid.

POACHING MEATS

- Cook meats slowly and evenly. Prolonged boiling toughens meat and clouds broth.
- Leftover liquid can be used as stock. Leftover poached meat makes a delicious salad tossed with a vinaigrette dressing.

POACHING POULTRY

- Poaching produces an especially delicate poultry flavor. Poach whole birds or breasts. Boneless breasts are done in 6 to 7 minutes; whole chickens cook anywhere from 25 minutes to 2 to 3 hours, depending upon size and age.
- Poaching time for poultry starts just after liquid starts to move and scum has been skimmed from surface of water.
- Poached poultry is excellent for salads and sandwiches, or when a light, plain flavor is desired, without the color or fatty taste developed in sautéing.

fully cooked.) Lobster is not necessarily cooked through when shell turns red. In contrast, crabs and crayfish are finished when their shells change color. Shrimp are cooked when they change color and become opaque.

PERFECTLY POACHED CHICKEN FOR SALADS AND SANDWICHES

When the cook wants an especially delicate poultry flavor, poaching is ideal. No matter how delicious the dressing or the sandwich fixings, if the chicken is dry the dish has little appeal. Poaching produces very moist meat.

> 1 chicken (fryer, roaster, capon, or stewing hen)
> 2 medium carrots, coarsely chopped
> 2 ribs celery, coarsely chopped
> 1 large onion, quartered
>   Bouquet garni (see page 56)

1. Wash chicken, remove innards, and trim away excess fat. Place in a stockpot or Dutch oven with carrots, celery, onion, and bouquet garni. Add enough cold water to cover.

2. Bring slowly to a boil, partially covered. Skim. Reduce heat to medium-low and simmer gently, covered, until bird is just tender when pierced (see About Poaching, above). Poaching time starts just after the surface of the liquid barely bubbles and the scum has been skimmed away.

3. Remove bird from pot and set aside to cool. Strain broth and save for another use. When chicken is cool, remove meat from bones.

Makes 3 to 5 cups, depending on bird used.

This moist, two-layer Poppy Seed Cake is decorated with Cream Cheese Frosting and poppy seeds. The striped effect is achieved by placing strips of paper over the top of the cake, then sprinkling the poppy seeds onto the icing. A variety of designs can be made by using different templates.

POPPY SEED

Poppy plants yield very small, edible seeds that may be white or black, depending on the poppy variety. They have a slightly sweet, nutty flavor that is appealing in pastries.

Use Black poppy seeds are often sprinkled on top of breads to add color and texture. The seeds are cooked, sweetened, and used as a filling for strudel and the triangular Jewish pastry known as *hamantaschen*. Black poppy seeds are also used in cakes and salad dressings and are sprinkled over buttered noodles. White poppy seeds are used in Indian cooking; they are usually ground, then toasted in oil with ginger or garlic and used to thicken and flavor vegetarian dishes.

Availability Most supermarkets stock black poppy seeds. Look for white poppy seeds in Indian markets. Jars or cans of black poppy seed paste or poppy seed filling are sold in Jewish delicatessens and specialty shops.

Selection Packaged spices and seasonings lose quality after a while; try to buy from a store that restocks its spice section fairly often.

Storage Poppy seeds have a high oil content and turn rancid quickly. Store airtight in a cool, dry, dark place. Use within six months; refrigerate for longer keeping. Leftover poppy seed paste should be put in a nonmetal container; it may be refrigerated for up to one month.

Preparation To bring out the flavor of poppy seed, toast in a dry skillet over low heat, shaking skillet continuously, until seeds are crisp and fragrant (5 to 8 minutes). To grind, toast, then soak overnight in milk, drain, and grind in a blender, clean coffee grinder, or electric minichopper, or with mortar and pestle.

POPPY SEED CAKE WITH CREAM CHEESE FROSTING

A moist poppy seed layer cake is delicious with a cream cheese frosting.

⅔ **cup milk**
⅓ **cup poppy seed**
2¼ **cups sifted cake flour**
1 **tablespoon baking powder**
¼ **teaspoon salt**
1¼ **cups sugar**
½ **cup butter, softened**
2 **teaspoons vanilla extract**
½ **cup milk**
3 **large egg whites**
¼ **cup sugar**
2 **tablespoons poppy seed, for decoration**

Cream Cheese Frosting

6 **ounces cream cheese, softened**
¼ **cup unsalted butter, softened**
2 **cups sifted confectioners' sugar**
1 **teaspoon fresh lemon juice**

1. Preheat oven to 350° F. Butter and flour two 8-inch-round cake pans; line bottom of each with a circle of parchment paper.

2. Bring the ⅔ cup milk to a boil. Remove from heat and stir in poppy seed; cool to room temperature.

3. Sift together flour, baking powder, and salt; set aside. Cream the 1¼ cups sugar and butter together; beat until light. Add vanilla.

4. Combine poppy seed mixture and the ½ cup milk. Add this mixture alternately with flour to creamed mixture, adding one third of each mixture at a time.

5. Beat egg whites until they hold soft peaks. Add the ¼ cup sugar, a little at a time, and beat until whites hold stiff, glossy peaks (do not overbeat). Gently fold into batter. Divide batter evenly between the two cake pans. Bake until cake draws away from sides of pans or cake tester comes out clean (about 30 minutes). Cool in pans 10 minutes, then turn out onto wire racks to finish cooling.

6. Frost with Cream Cheese Frosting. Decorate with poppy seed.

Serves 6 to 8.

Cream Cheese Frosting Cream together cream cheese and butter. Add confectioners' sugar and lemon juice; beat until creamy. If frosting is too runny, add more sugar. If it is too stiff, add a little milk.

Recipes and Related Information
Citrus–Poppy Seed Muffins, 375; Poppy Seed Filling, 627.

PORK

By most accounts, today's domesticated pig is a descendant of the wild boar. Humans began raising pigs for the table possibly as early as the Mesolithic period; today, pork is the most widely eaten meat in the world.

Historically pork has always been a mainstay of peasant diets. The animals, being scavengers, are easy to feed, they are extraordinarily prolific (producing on average 11 offspring per litter, two times a year), and they are usable down to the last hair. Not only do people make edible use of every part of the inner body, they also know how to treat the skin for leather, the hair for upholstery and insulation, and the inedible parts of the fat for lubrication.

In the days before refrigeration, much of the meat was salted or otherwise processed for long keeping. Even today, only about one third of pork meat is sold fresh. Although we no longer need to store pork for long periods, we have developed a taste for the various hams and sausages created over the years.

Because fresh and cured pork products differ greatly from a cook's standpoint, they are discussed separately in the following sections.

Use Depending on the cut, fresh pork may be roasted, broiled or grilled, panfried, poached, or braised. A fresh leg (ham), for example, may be marinated in wine and herbs, then roasted. A crown roast makes an elegant party dish, either simply roasted or roasted and stuffed. Panfried or grilled pork chops are a popular American dish, often paired with applesauce or sautéed apples. Swedish cooks stuff boneless pork loin with plumped prunes before roasting; plumped dried apricots could be substituted for the prunes. American cooks baste spareribs and baby back ribs with barbecue sauce and either roast or grill them. The Chinese consume large quantities of fresh pork: They braise slabs of fresh belly bacon in soy sauce; braise sparerib nuggets with black beans; steam pork meatballs with cabbage; roast whole pigs; and stir-fry strips of marinated pork with mushrooms, eggs, and lily buds, then wrap the mixture in thin pancakes for Mu Shu Pork. Pork is widely used in Mexico, too—as a filling for tamales, enchiladas, and tacos, and as an ingredient in hearty soups. Seasoned ground pork makes an excellent filling for stuffed cabbage leaves or savory pies. It is also the basis for countless types of sausage (see SAUSAGE).

Flavorful cured pork products are eaten alone or used as an ingredient in many types of preparations. See specific cured pork entries.

Availability Fresh pork is sold widely in all supermarkets, although most do not carry a large variety of cuts. For a larger selection, seek out Latin, German, or Asian markets or specialty butchers.

Cured pork products are widely available in supermarkets and specialty markets. The more popular of these products are described in a separate section, beginning on page 460.

Selection Fresh pork should have a pale pink to pink color (loin cuts are generally lighter than shoulder and leg cuts) and white fat. Both flesh and fat should be firm to the touch. Like all fresh meat, it should smell fresh, with no off-odor. See specific types of cured pork for selection information.

Storage Fresh pork should be kept in the coldest part of the refrigerator. Prepackaged meat may be stored in its original wrapper. Pork wrapped in butcher paper should be unwrapped, set on a plate, and covered loosely with aluminum foil or waxed paper. Refrigerate and use within two or three days. Large cuts will keep slightly longer, ground meat slightly less.

For longer storage, pork may be frozen immediately after purchase. Remove original wrapping; place in plastic wrap and overwrap with freezer paper or aluminum foil. Large cuts may be frozen for up to six months, chops or ground meat for up to three months. Thaw slowly in freezer wrapping in refrigerator.

Store leftover cooked pork, covered, in coldest part of refrigerator within two hours of cooking. Use within four to five days. For storing cured pork see specific types.

Preparation Fresh pork does not require special preparation. Extra fat may be trimmed away from roasts or chops if desired. Before cooking, some cooks prefer to brine fresh pork for several days to firm and flavor the meat. To make a brine for 6 pounds of pork, dissolve ½ cup sugar (granulated or brown) and ¼ cup salt in 2 gallons warm water. Lightly bruise herbs and spices in a mortar (bay leaf, peppercorns, juniper berries, cloves, and thyme are traditional) and add to the warm liquid. Let liquid cool completely, then pour over pork in a clean container. Keep pork submerged with a weighted plate for two to four days. Remove from brine, rinse, and pat dry.

Cooking See BRAISE, BROIL, GRILL, PANFRY, POACH, ROAST, STIR-FRY. For cooking cured pork see specific types.

FRESH PORK

Fresh pork has not been salted, brined, smoked, or otherwise cured. It has a mild, faintly sweet flavor. Recipes for fresh pork begin on page 457.

DRY-HEAT COOKING

Virtually all the major parts of the pig take to roasting and barbecuing. Pork may be roasted at a higher temperature than beef or lamb without becoming too dry because its veins of fat will baste the lean parts throughout the roasting. When grilling, however, it's best to cook slowly, so that the inside will cook through before the outside burns. Chops, cutlets, and slices are generally cooked like beef steaks—by panfrying, broiling, or grilling.

In Braised Pork With Prunes, a favorite in much of Europe, the sweetness of the prunes is a perfect accompaniment to the richness of the meat. It is best served with a simple side dish such as white rice or steamed potatoes.

prosciutto to a size slightly smaller than that of the cutlets. Top half of the cutlets with a slice of cheese and a slice of ham. Cover with remaining cutlets and pound edges lightly to seal.

2. Holding each cutlet "sandwich" together, dip both sides in egg, then into bread crumbs to coat completely. Place on waxed paper.

3. In a heavy 10-inch skillet, heat oil over high heat until rippling. Lower heat to medium-high and add cutlets (covering with a spatter shield, if desired). Cook until cooked through (about 5 minutes per side). Remove from pan with slotted spatula, draining off oil, and serve hot, garnished with lemon wedges.

Serves 4.

MOIST-HEAT COOKING

When stewed or braised, pork shows off its adaptability. The loin, fresh hams, and the juicy shoulder butt are excellent cuts for braising. If there's time, the meat benefits from a night in a marinade. It is then braised in the marinade with enough extra liquid (stock, juice, or wine) to come about two thirds of the way up the meat (see the braising variation of Marinated Fresh Ham on page 457).

■ BRAISED PORK WITH PRUNES

Rice and boiled carrots make a good accompaniment for this dish because they complement the honey-lemon sauce and the prune garnish.

> 1 **boneless pork loin roast or shoulder roast (2½ lb), rolled and tied**
> **Salt and freshly ground pepper**
> 2 **tablespoons vegetable oil**
> 1 **tablespoon butter**
> 2 **medium onions, finely chopped**
> 1 **cinnamon stick (2 in. long)**
> 1 **cup Chicken Stock (see page 560)**
> ½ **cup water**
> 1 **cup pitted prunes**
> 2 **tablespoons mild honey**
> 2 **teaspoons fresh lemon juice**

1. Pat meat dry. Season on all sides with salt and pepper.

2. In a heavy casserole brown pork on all sides in oil and butter over medium-high heat. Remove pork to a plate.

3. Reduce heat to low, stir in onions, and cook, stirring occasionally, until softened (about 5 minutes).

4. Return pork to pan and add any juices from plate. Add cinnamon, stock, and the water, pushing cinnamon stick into liquid. Bring to a boil. Reduce heat to low, cover, and simmer, turning pork over from time to time, 1½ hours.

5. Add prunes to liquid, cover, and cook until meat is very tender when pierced with a knife (meat should register an internal temperature of 150° F on a meat thermometer) and prunes are tender (about 30 minutes).

■ STUFFED PORK CUTLETS

This quick and easy recipe, common to Italy, Spain, and the Italian-speaking area of southern Switzerland, can easily be varied. For an Italian version similar to veal saltimbocca, stuff the cutlets with prosciutto and a good mozzarella (such as buffalo milk) or Bel Paese cheese. For a French-Swiss version pair packaged sliced ham with Gruyère or Emmentaler. For an all-American version use Cheddar or Monterey jack with thinly sliced Smithfield or a similar delicatessen ham.

> 8 **boneless lean pork cutlets (from loin or butt), each about ¼ inch thick**
> 4 **thick (¼ in.) slices mild cheese (4 to 6 oz)**
> 4 **thin slices prosciutto, Smithfield, or packaged ham (about 2 oz)**
> 1 **egg, lightly beaten**
> 1 **to 1½ cups Italian-style seasoned dry bread crumbs**
> ¼ **cup light olive oil or vegetable oil**
> 1 **lemon, cut in 4 wedges, for garnish**

1. Trim away any fat or connective tissues from pork. Between two sheets of waxed paper, pound each cutlet with flat end of a meat mallet (or a heavy can) until flattened to about ⅛ inch thick. Trim cheese and

6. Stir honey into pork cooking liquid and cook, uncovered, over low heat, basting pork often, for 5 minutes. Transfer meat to a plate with 2 wooden spoons, leaving as much of the chopped onions as possible in casserole. Remove prunes to a bowl with a slotted spoon.

7. Skim as much fat as possible from cooking liquid. Boil liquid over high heat, stirring often, until it thickens (about 5 minutes). Transfer pork to a carving board and discard strings. Cut pork in slices about ½ inch thick.

8. When sauce has thickened, add lemon juice. Add more salt and pepper, if needed. Discard cinnamon stick.

9. Return prunes to casserole and reheat over low heat. Set pork slices gently on top, cover, and reheat over low heat 5 minutes. Pork can be kept, covered, up to 2 days in refrigerator; reheat pork and prunes in sauce over low heat, covered.

10. Arrange pork slices on a platter or on plates, and spoon sauce and prunes over and around slices.

Serves 4 to 5.

◼ BOHEMIAN PORK GOULASH

Dill seed and caraway seed accent this traditional pork goulash. Noodles are a good foil for the creamy sauce.

- **2 pounds lean boneless pork, cut in ½- by 2-inch strips**
- **Salt and white pepper**
- **1 tablespoon *each* butter (or margarine) and vegetable oil**
- **2 medium onions, thinly sliced and separated into rings**
- **1 clove garlic, minced**
- **1 tablespoon sweet Hungarian paprika**
- **2 teaspoons caraway seed**
- **½ teaspoon dill seed**
- **1 bay leaf**
- **1 cup Beef Stock (see page 560) or Rich Chicken Stock (see page 561)**
- **⅓ cup dry white wine**
- **1½ teaspoons cornstarch blended with 1 tablespoon water**
- **⅔ cup sour cream**
- **Chopped parsley, for garnish**

1. Sprinkle pork strips on all sides with salt and pepper. In a large, heavy frying pan over medium-high heat, melt butter with oil; add pork strips, about half at a time, and brown well on all sides, removing them as they brown. When all pork is browned, spoon off all but about 2 tablespoons of the pan drippings (if necessary).

2. Add onions and cook, stirring often, until rings are soft and begin to brown. Mix in garlic, paprika, caraway seed, and dill seed. Return pork strips (along with any accumulated juices) to pan. Add bay leaf. Pour in stock and wine. Bring to a boil, cover, reduce heat, and simmer until pork is tender (45 to 50 minutes).

3. Remove and discard bay leaf. Blend in cornstarch mixture and cook, stirring, until sauce boils and thickens. Remove pan from heat and blend in sour cream.

4. Return to low heat and stir gently until heated through. Do not boil. Taste and add salt if needed. Sprinkle with parsley.

Serves 4 to 6.

OTHER WAYS WITH PORK

The following recipes show pork's versatility. Supermarket ground pork is as high in fat as sausage (about 30 percent); consumers concerned about fat and economy may want to grind their own.

◼ CAILLETTES

What the French call *caillettes* (little quail) are actually well-seasoned rounds of ground pork, rice, and spinach. Serve as individual hors d'oeuvres or pack this mixture into a bacon-lined loaf pan or terrine mold. Bake until the juices run clear, and serve with a fresh tomato sauce.

- **2 pounds chicken livers**
- **Salt and freshly ground pepper, to taste**
- **2 tablespoons flour**
- **2 tablespoons olive oil**
- **2 shallots, finely minced**
- **2 pounds lean ground pork**
- **1 cup cooked white rice**
- **1 pound fresh spinach, washed, stemmed, and chopped**
- **½ cup minced parsley**
- **2 cloves garlic, minced (optional)**
- **1½ teaspoons minced fresh thyme *or* 1 teaspoon dried thyme**
- **3 eggs, lightly beaten**
- **1 pound caul fat (available at some butcher shops) or thinly sliced bacon**

1. Preheat oven to 425° F. Trim livers of any fat or tough spots, chop them coarsely, and put in a bowl. Sprinkle with salt and pepper, to taste, and flour.

2. In a large skillet over medium heat, heat olive oil. Add shallots and sauté until they are softened but not browned (about 10 minutes). Add livers and sauté over medium-high heat 3 to 4 minutes, or until they are barely browned outside but still pink within.

3. Transfer livers to a bowl, leaving shallots in skillet. Add pork to skillet and sauté 5 minutes, or until pork loses its raw red color but is not fully cooked.

4. Mix together livers, shallots, pork, rice, spinach, parsley, garlic (if used), thyme, and eggs. Shape into 1½-inch balls. Wrap each ball in a small square of caul fat. Place on a cookie sheet and bake until crisp and golden brown (20 to 25 minutes).

Makes about 100 small Caillettes.

dry place. Once prosciutto is cut, keep exposed surface covered and use within a few weeks.

Smithfield, Virginia, and Other Country Hams These hams are usually made from corn- or peanut-fed hogs. In a typical procedure (which varies from producer to producer), the legs are salted for about four weeks, then washed, coated with peppercorns, refrigerated for about two weeks, then smoked for about 10 days. After smoking the meat is aged for 6 to 12 months. The resulting ham may be served raw like prosciutto (see page 461), in very thin slices because it is quite salty. In the South, however, it is often cooked. To cook a Smithfield ham (or similar country ham), soak the ham for 12 to 24 hours in several changes of cold water. Using a stiff brush, scrub off any surface mold. Then cover with cold water, bring to a boil, and simmer until the small bone near the shank moves easily (15 to 20 minutes per pound). Save the cooking water for cooking greens. Slice away ham rind with a sharp knife. If desired, coat fat with brown sugar and bread crumbs and bake in a hot (400° F) oven until glazed (about 20 minutes). Let cool to room temperature before slicing thinly. Country ham can be sliced, covered with gravy, and served with grits; added to bean or vegetable dishes; or served cold with hot biscuits. Smithfield hams are available from some specialty markets and mail-order sources. See Prosciutto (page 461) for storage directions.

■ CIDER-BAKED COUNTRY HAM

In this treatment the ham is baked with cider so that simmering on the stovetop is unnecessary.

> 1 **Smithfield ham or country-style ham (12 to 14 lb)**
> 4 **cups apple cider**
> ½ **cup bourbon**
> **Brown sugar, for glaze**

1. Soak ham in several changes of cold water for at least 24 hours. Scrub under cold running water with a stiff brush and wipe dry.

2. Preheat oven to 350° F. Place a long sheet of heavy aluminum foil across the bottom of a shallow roasting pan with ends of sheet extending from each side of pan (foil should be long enough to make a tent for ham). Place ham on foil, pour on cider, and seal foil around ham. Bake until ham is cooked through and tender (about 4 hours).

3. Remove ham from oven and allow to cool until it can be handled. Discard aluminum foil. Remove drippings (save fat if desired). Gently and carefully remove skin, leaving a thick layer of fat. Score fat in a diamond pattern with a sharp knife, and return ham to oven for 15 minutes to heat surface. Slide out oven shelf so that ham is fully exposed. Heat bourbon in a small saucepan and pour it over ham. Be sure that nothing flammable is near oven opening. Using a long match and exercising great caution, light bourbon. When flames die

down, spread brown sugar over fat, and slide oven shelf back in. Continue baking until sugar forms a dark melted glaze (about 15 minutes).

Serves 8 to 10.

■ COUNTRY HAM SLICES WITH RED-EYE GRAVY

All ham slices will be enlivened by this surprising sauce. The secret is black coffee.

> 4 **slices (½ in. thick) country or old-fashioned ham, cooked or uncooked (see Note)**
> 4 **tablespoons rendered drippings from baked ham or vegetable oil**
> ¼ **cup firmly packed light brown sugar**
> ½ **cup strong black brewed coffee**

1. Score through fat at edges of ham slices to keep them from curling. Heat drippings in a large, heavy skillet. Add ham and sauté over medium heat, turning several times, until lightly browned on both sides (20 to 25 minutes if using uncooked slices, about 10 minutes if cooked).

2. Remove ham and keep warm. Stir sugar into pan juices and cook at low heat, stirring constantly, until sugar dissolves. Add coffee and simmer until gravy turns rich brown (about 5 minutes); do not boil. Pour gravy over ham and serve.

Serves 4.

Note If you are using uncooked slices of a salty, dry-cured ham, add 1 cup of water to skillet along with ham. Ham will absorb all the water by the time it is cooked through; add more water if original amount is absorbed too quickly.

SALT PORK

Cut from the pork belly, salt pork is white fat streaked with lean meat. It is salted like bacon but not smoked. Most salt pork is extremely salty and should be blanched before use. Cover with cold water, bring to a boil, simmer 3 minutes, and drain. Fry a small amount and taste; if too salty, blanch again. After blanching, it can be diced, rendered (see RENDER), and used to add flavor to green beans, cabbage, or bean soups. Rendered salt pork can be added to cornbread or dumplings. It is a traditional flavoring in clam chowder and baked beans. In the American South, it is often cooked with potherbs such as collards or mustard greens.

Many supermarkets carry packaged salt pork in 6- to 8-ounce chunks. It is also available from most meat markets. Salt pork can be refrigerated, tightly wrapped, for up to a month or frozen for several months.

Recipes: Boston Baked Beans, 34; New England Clam Chowder, 539.

POTATO

Although they were introduced late, potatoes are a significant part of the American diet today and are now common on all continents. Native to Central and South America, the potato was unknown in Europe until the late sixteenth century and didn't arrive in North America until the early eighteenth century. Because it is hardy and easy to grow, it is always one of the least expensive vegetables in the market. Widespread cultivation of the potato has made it one of the world's most important food crops.

Use Because potatoes are so important to the diets of people all around the world, it is difficult to give a meaningful overview of the ways they are used. In the United States potatoes are typically boiled, mashed, baked, sautéed, or fried. Mashed potatoes may be combined with another puréed vegetable, such as celeriac, chestnuts, or parsnips. Baked potatoes are served whole, with butter and/or sour cream. Raw potatoes may be sliced thin and sautéed, or grated and sautéed to make hash browns. Cooked, cubed, and sautéed potatoes are often flavored with onion and green pepper and served with breakfast eggs. When potatoes are cut into finger-length strips and deep-fried, they are known as French fries and are a staple of the American fast-food industry, especially as the accepted companion to hamburgers.

The French slice potatoes thinly and bake them with butter and cream to make a gratin Dauphinois; when meat stock is used instead of cream and when a topping of grated Gruyère cheese is added, the dish becomes gratin Savoyard. Vichyssoise, a cold potato and leek soup, is now a classic. Italian cooks make dumplings called *gnocchi* from potatoes. Germans and Hungarians add mashed potatoes to bread for improved flavor and texture. Swedish cooks bake potato strips with cream and anchovies to make Jansson's temptation and, like the Germans, fry thin pancakes of grated potatoes. *Lefser* is a Norwegian flatbread based on potatoes and cooked on a griddle. Russian cooks add boiled potatoes to herring salad and bake grated potatoes into pudding with onions and egg. Potatoes are also distilled into vodka in the Soviet Union. In Peru, where potatoes have long been a staple, they are boiled and garnished with a spicy chile and cheese sauce. Indian cooks deep-fry potato slices in chick-pea batter, sauté them with aromatic spices, or curry them. Potatoes are not widely used in Asia, but are known there. Almost everywhere in the world, potatoes are a major food source.

Apart from their use as a food, potatoes are a good salt absorber. An oversalted soup can occasionally be salvaged by adding potato slices and simmering until the salt is sufficiently absorbed. The potatoes are discarded before serving.

Availability Potatoes are sold in supermarkets the year around. There is no peak season because crops in different areas mature at different times and potatoes

French fries are the most popular of all potato dishes. Serve them with a thick grilled steak or with fried fish in the English tradition of fish and chips. The recipe is on page 468.

store well. Potatoes are also available in the freezer case, in the form of frozen French fries, hash browns, and other precooked shapes. Canned boiled potatoes are also found in supermarkets, as are dried potato flakes and instant mashed potatoes.

The main potato varieties, and their suitability to various cooking tasks, are as follows.

Red Skinned (New) This type has a thin red skin and a crisp white flesh. It is a waxy potato, excellent for boiling in the skin and serving whole. Because it cubes neatly after boiling and absorbs dressing readily, it is good for potato salad. Red-skinned potatoes may also be rubbed with olive oil and baked whole; they will maintain their firm, waxy texture. There are several varieties of red-skinned potatoes, but they are rarely identified by variety in the supermarket.

Russet or Idaho This standard baking potato is generally 4 to 6 inches long, about 2 inches in diameter, with a rough brown skin. The ivory flesh is dry and fluffy when baked. It is a good potato for mashing and for deep-frying, as it does not readily absorb the frying oil.

White Rose A waxy potato, the White Rose is a long, white potato with a thin ivory-colored skin. It is best for boiling but may be baked or deep-fried. Like the russet, it is recommended for French fries because it does not readily absorb the frying oil.

Other potatoes that are becoming increasingly available include:

Blue Included in this category are such varieties as Blue Carib and All Blue. They have grayish blue skin and inky blue flesh. Delicate in flavor, they should simply be boiled and buttered.

Finnish Yellow Wax As its name suggest, this light-skinned variety has yellow meat and a waxy texture. Boil in the skin and dress with butter or use in potato salads.

German Fingerling This is a small, light-skinned potato with a lumpy shape and yellow flesh. It has a waxy flesh and should be boiled whole and buttered, or coated with olive oil and baked in a covered casserole until tender when pierced with a knife.

Rose Fir Small and waxy-fleshed, the Rose Fir has thin pink to red skin. It has a creamy texture and delicate flavor and is best when simply boiled and buttered.

Selection The most important distinction to draw between potato varieties is between the starchy or mealy types (best for baking) and the waxy types (best for boiling). A starchy type falls apart when boiled; a waxy type does not develop the desired dry, fluffy texture when baked. See Availability.

When selecting potatoes, look for firm specimens. New potatoes should be of a fairly uniform size to make cooking easier. Mature baking potatoes should be dry and well shaped, without sprouting. Avoid potatoes with a greenish cast. They have been exposed to too much light, either sunlight or artificial light, and may be bitter.

Storage Potatoes keep best in a cool, dark, dry place. Do not refrigerate. They should keep for two to three weeks without sprouting.

Preparation Peel if desired; otherwise, scrub skin well. Potatoes oxidize quickly; drop peeled potatoes into water immediately to slow browning.

Cooking See BAKE, BOIL, DEEP-FRY, PANFRY, PUREE, STEAM.

■ BASIC BAKED POTATO

Use russet potatoes for baking. Remember to pierce the potatoes just after removing them from the oven. Potatoes cook much faster in a microwave oven, even when you are cooking a number of them (see chart, at right). They need to be pierced before they cook.

    3 large baking potatoes (1½ to 2 lb total)
      Oil or melted butter, for coating
      Butter, sour cream, snipped fresh chives,
      crumbled cooked bacon, for garnish (optional)

1. Preheat oven to 400° F. Rub potatoes all over with oil. Set on baking sheet or directly on oven rack.

2. Bake until tender (about 45 minutes). Immediately pierce with a fork. Slit lengthwise or slice in half, and top with a pat of butter, sour cream, snipped fresh chives, or crumbled cooked bacon (if desired).

Serves 3 to 6.

POTATOES IN THE MICROWAVE OVEN

Choose whole potatoes of even size; pierce in several places with fork. Cook at 100 percent power the following times (for 6- to 8-ounce potatoes). Touch potatoes at end of cooking time. If they are very hard, cook another one or two minutes, then let them stand. They will finish cooking in the standing time.

Amount	Approximate Cooking Time	Standing Time
1	4–6 minutes	5 minutes
2	6–8 minutes	5 minutes
4	8–12 minutes	5 minutes

■ DUCHESSE POTATOES

An old-fashioned potato ricer makes quick work of mashing potatoes and eliminates offending lumps. Duchesse Potatoes are an embellished version of simple American fare.

    4 large russet or other baking potatoes
      (about 2½ lb)
    ½ teaspoon salt
    ¼ teaspoon white pepper
    6 tablespoons unsalted butter
    2 egg yolks
    1 egg beaten with 1 tablespoon water, for coating

1. Peel and coarsely dice potatoes; place in a 4-quart saucepan and cover with water. Bring to a boil, reduce heat, and simmer until tender (25 to 30 minutes); drain. Force potatoes through a ricer or mash with a potato masher. Stir in salt, pepper, 5 tablespoons butter, and egg yolks. Cool briefly.

2. Preheat oven to 400° F. Butter a baking sheet with remaining butter or line with parchment paper. Place potato mixture into a pastry bag fitted with a 1-inch open-star tip (to give a fluted design) and pipe mounds 2 inches by 2 inches in diameter onto prepared baking sheet. Alternatively, form into egg-shaped mounds with two tablespoons and place on prepared baking sheet. Brush potatoes with egg wash. Bake until golden brown and crusty (about 20 minutes).

Serves 8.

POTATO PANCAKES

Homemade applesauce and sour cream can turn this simple side dish into a satisfying meal. Shred potatoes with a grater or in a food processor fitted with a shredding disk.

3 large baking potatoes, peeled and shredded
1 small onion, minced
1 teaspoon salt
½ teaspoon freshly ground pepper
1 egg
4 tablespoons dry bread crumbs
½ cup vegetable oil, for frying
   Sour cream and applesauce, for garnish

In a large bowl, stir together shredded potatoes, onion, salt, pepper, egg, and bread crumbs. In a medium, heavy-bottomed skillet, heat oil over medium heat. For each pancake, use 2 to 3 tablespoons potato mixture; flatten in skillet to about ½ inch thick. Sauté pancakes until crisp and golden brown (12 to 15 minutes); turn and cook second side 6 minutes. Remove from pan and serve with a dollop of sour cream and a scoop of applesauce (if desired).

Serves 6.

POMMES SOUFFLES

Twice-fried Pommes Soufflés are thinly sliced potatoes that puff into little pillows during the second dip in hot oil. For a perfect result use mature, starch-filled potatoes. Be sure to keep the oil at a constant temperature. There are always some failures, which are edible, so be prepared to make extra if presentation is important. The recipe can be made partially ahead and finished just before serving.

2 large russet potatoes (about 1½ lb)
   Oil, for frying

1. Peel potatoes and cut each into a perfectly symmetrical rectangular block. Slicing along length (which is with the grain), cut perfectly uniform, ⅛-inch slices. Cut each slice in half. Trim corners, if desired, to form hexagonal shapes. Reserve in ice water for at least 15 minutes.

2. In a heavy-bottomed saucepan or wok, heat 4 inches of oil to 250° F. Remove potatoes from ice water and dry thoroughly. Immerse potato slices, one at a time, in hot oil. When slices rise, spoon hot oil over them and continue cooking until edges start to look translucent (about 6 minutes). Remove with a wire skimmer and drain on paper towels. Potatoes may be prepared ahead to this point and reserved; reserve oil in pan as well.

3. Just before serving, heat same oil to 375° F. Carefully lower partially fried potato slices into hot oil; they should puff immediately. Cook until golden brown and crisp (3 to 4 minutes). If some have not puffed, return to hot oil one more time. Remove with a wire skimmer and drain on paper towels. Serve immediately.

Serves 8.

POTATO NESTS

The nests are dramatic edible containers that can be filled with sautéed cherry tomatoes, sautéed leeks and peas, caramelized pearl onions, or even Pommes Soufflés. The nests can be prepared ahead and reheated in the oven. To shape the nests, you must use a special two-piece wire basket designed just for this preparation (see photograph, at right). Before using the potato-nest basket for the first time, it is important to season the baskets so the potatoes won't stick to them. To season, heat oil to 375° F in a heavy-bottomed kettle. Place basket in hot oil and let sit for about 5 minutes. Turn off heat and leave basket in oil about 1 hour. Remove basket from oil and wipe dry.

2 large russet potatoes (about 1½ lb)
   Oil, for frying

1. Peel potatoes, julienne, and set in bowl of cold water to keep from turning brown. In a heavy-bottomed kettle or wok, heat 4 inches of oil to 380° F. Remove one eighth of potatoes from water and thoroughly pat dry (or they won't brown properly). Place in larger basket of seasoned potato-nest fryer in a ¼-inch thick layer. Fit smaller basket over potato layer and secure tightly.

2. Hold fryer basket handle with a hot pad (wire will get too hot to hold safely in bare hand). Immerse in hot oil and deep-fry for about 4 minutes. Still protecting hand, lift fryer from oil and carefully remove small inner basket. Return potato-lined outer basket to hot oil and fry until golden brown (about 1 minute more).

3. Remove and loosen potato nest from wire basket and drain on paper towels. These may be prepared several hours ahead and reheated in a 300° F oven 5 to 8 minutes. Fill with your choice of filling and serve.

Serves 8.

SCALLOPED POTATOES

This traditional American dish is a perennial favorite accompaniment to roasts—meat or fowl. It is rich with a garlic-flavored cream sauce.

2 tablespoons unsalted butter
2½ pounds russet potatoes, peeled
2 cups whipping cream
1 cup milk
1 clove garlic, minced (optional)
1½ teaspoons salt
½ teaspoon freshly ground pepper

1. Preheat oven to 350° F. Grease a 3-quart baking dish with butter. Slice potatoes ⅛ inch thick; layer in baking dish.

2. In a medium bowl stir together cream, milk, garlic (if used), salt, and pepper. Pour over potatoes and bake until potatoes are tender when pierced with a knife (1 hour and 10 minutes). Serve hot.

Serves 8.

A basket fryer gives shape to foods such as shredded potatoes as they cook in deep fat. The resulting edible nest makes an attractive container for a variety of vegetables. See Potato Nests, at left.

Thaw poultry at room temperature only if you are able to monitor the process carefully, because bacteria that can cause food poisoning grow rapidly at this temperature. To thaw a turkey, place the unwrapped frozen bird in a double-walled brown bag or several thicknesses of newspaper. The paper keeps the surface of the bird cold while the interior thaws. Frozen small birds and frozen parts can be thawed in their wrappings. Refrigerate or cook thawed poultry as soon as possible.

Preparation All raw poultry should be cleaned and washed before cooking. Remove any clumps of visible fat around neck and tail. Remove innards (neck and giblets) from cavity. Use tweezers or fingernails to pull out any stray feathers or hairs. Wash quickly inside and out, pulling out any bloody bits from inside the bird. Pat dry with paper towels. Some whole birds are trussed, or tied together, before roasting for a more attractive appearance (see TRUSS). For a discussion about specific poultry techniques, see also BONE, CARVE, DISJOINT.

Cooking See BROIL, BRAISE, DEEP-FRY, GRILL, POACH, SAUTE, STEW, STIR-FRY, STOCK AND SOUP.

CHICKEN

As a mild-flavored meat, chicken lends itself readily to variation; in fact chicken is compatible with almost every herb, spice, and vegetable in the marketplace. When you consider the hundreds of ways that Americans prepare chicken and add to that the thousands of chicken dishes common to the rest of the world, it is clear that the options for the curious cook are virtually unlimited. As a lean, low-cholesterol meat, it is welcome in the diets of the many Americans trying to reduce their intake of fat and cholesterol.

Chicken figures in the cuisine of almost every country in the world. In this country fried chicken, roast chicken, and some form of baked chicken are in almost every cook's repertoire. Chicken is made into pot pies, stewed with dumplings, poached to make a flavorful broth that is the basis of countless soups, and chopped or sliced for a cold salad or sandwich filling.

In Mexico chicken is shredded to make fillings for tacos, enchiladas, and tamales. French cooks are famous for coq au vin (chicken in red wine). Italians roast chicken with rosemary or sauté it alla cacciatore. Spanish cooks pair chicken with rice, tomatoes, sausage, and shellfish to make paella. Chicken Kiev, deep-fried boneless breasts rolled around seasoned butter, is a Russian specialty. In Japan chicken is marinated in soy sauce, rice wine, and ginger and grilled, or steamed with cooked rice and egg to make the popular lunch dish called *donburi*. Chinese cooks stir-fry chicken with all manner of vegetables and seasonings; they also braise a whole chicken in soy sauce or smoke it over tea leaves.

In India chicken is highly spiced and braised in curries, or marinated in yogurt and spices and roasted in the tandoor (clay oven). In West Africa chicken is simmered with tomatoes and peanuts to make groundnut stew.

Both fresh and frozen chickens are widely available in supermarkets, either whole or cut into parts. Whole chickens are almost always less expensive, but some cooks prefer the convenience of precut, packaged parts. It is easy to cut up a chicken, and the method is well worth learning (see BONE, DISJOINT). The cook who buys whole chickens not only saves money but also gets the useful fat, the tasty giblets, and the bony parts for stock. Chickens may be cooked whole or cut into parts. The legs, thighs, breasts, and wings are the choice parts, with the bony wing tips, neck, and back often reserved for making stock.

Chickens are marketed in several different sizes, each with particular cooking requirements. See Which Bird to Buy? on page 469 for more information.

◼ ROAST CHICKEN WITH RICE, FRUIT, AND ALMOND STUFFING

Although roasting chickens are slightly more flavorful than frying chickens, both can be roasted. The stuffing for this chicken is a variation of rice pilaf. If you like, serve the rice as a side dish with any roast, instead of as a stuffing. In this case, cook the rice for a total of 18 minutes.

> ½ **cup slivered almonds**
> ¼ **cup vegetable oil**
> 1 **small onion, finely chopped**
> 1 **cup long-grain rice**
> 1½ **cups hot water**
> ½ **cup strained, fresh orange juice**
>   **Salt and freshly ground pepper, to taste**
> 1 **small apple, peeled, halved, and cored**
> ½ **cup raisins**
> ¼ **teaspoon ground cinnamon**
> 1 **roasting chicken (3½ to 4 lb)**

1. Preheat oven to 400° F. Toast almonds in a baking dish in oven, stirring occasionally, until lightly browned (about 5 minutes). Transfer to a bowl and let cool.

2. In a deep frying pan, heat 3 tablespoons of the oil over low heat. Add onion and cook, stirring often, until tender (about 5 minutes). Increase heat to medium, add rice, and sauté for 2 minutes. Add the hot water, orange juice, salt, and pepper; bring to a boil. Reduce heat to low, cover, and cook for 10 minutes.

3. Dice apple. After rice has cooked 10 minutes, add apple and raisins to rice and stir very lightly with a fork. Cover and cook for 5 minutes; rice will be nearly tender. Stir in cinnamon and reserved almonds. Taste and add more salt and pepper, if needed.

4. Sprinkle chicken with salt and pepper on all sides. Spoon enough rice stuffing into chicken to fill it, but do not pack it too tightly; reserve extra stuffing at room temperature.

5. Set chicken on a rack in a roasting pan and roast until juices run clear when a skewer is inserted into thickest part of leg (about 1 hour). If juices are pink, continue roasting chicken a few more minutes. Transfer chicken to a carving board. Let stand 5 to 10 minutes before carving and serving.

6. Heat the remaining 1 tablespoon oil in a frying pan over low heat. Add remaining stuffing and cook, stirring often with a fork, until rice is tender and hot (about 3 minutes). Spoon into a serving dish.

7. Serve chicken and its stuffing on a platter. Serve remaining rice separately.

Serves 4.

◼ CHICKEN KIEV

Unlike other coated foods, Chicken Kiev must be fried cold so that the butter trapped inside the chicken roll stays frozen. If allowed to thaw, the butter would leak out during frying. The herbed butter must be frozen one hour before you prepare the chicken rolls, and then the chicken rolls must chill one to two hours before they are cooked. If the rolls seem to be browning too quickly, remove them when they are golden and finish cooking in a 325° F oven 10 to 12 minutes.

   ½ **cup butter, softened**
   2 **tablespoons chopped parsley**
   1 **clove garlic, crushed**
   1 **tablespoon snipped fresh chives**
   ½ **teaspoon salt**
     Freshly ground pepper, to taste
   4 **small whole chicken breasts, halved, boned, and skinned**
   1 **egg, lightly beaten**
   2 **cups dry bread crumbs**
   4 **cups vegetable oil, for frying**
     Watercress sprigs, for garnish

Sauce Gruyère

   3 **tablespoons butter**
   3 **tablespoons flour**
   1 **cup half-and-half**
   ½ **cup grated Gruyère cheese**
     Salt and freshly ground pepper, to taste

1. In a medium bowl, using a wooden spoon, blend butter with parsley, garlic, chives, salt, and pepper (or blend mixture in food processor). Shape into a rectangular block, wrap in waxed paper, and freeze until solid (about 1 hour).

2. Wash chicken breast halves and pat dry. Pound breast halves between two pieces of waxed paper to ¼ inch thick. Cut frozen butter into eight sticks. Place one stick in the center of each half breast. Fold edges of breasts over butter and roll up tightly, completely enveloping butter with meat.

3. Brush each chicken roll with beaten egg. Put bread crumbs on a large square of waxed paper or on a plate, and coat rolls thoroughly with crumbs.

4. Transfer chicken rolls to a baking sheet, cover lightly with waxed paper, and refrigerate 1 to 2 hours to set coating.

5. In a heavy-bottomed, 3-quart saucepan, heat oil to 365° F as registered on a frying thermometer. Deep-fry rolls until golden brown all around (about 8 minutes per roll).

6. Gently remove with a slotted spoon to a baking sheet lined with paper towels. To hold, keep warm in a 200° F oven.

7. Serve Chicken Kiev with Sauce Gruyère and garnish with watercress.

Serves 8.

Sauce Gruyère In a small saucepan over medium heat, melt butter. Whisk in flour and cook briefly. Pour in half-and-half and cook until thickened. Stir in grated cheese and season with salt and pepper.

Makes about 1½ cups.

Diners delight in the burst of herbed butter released as they cut into Chicken Kiev. In the recipe at left, parsley, chives, and garlic flavor the butter; in classic versions, tarragon is the frequently used herb.

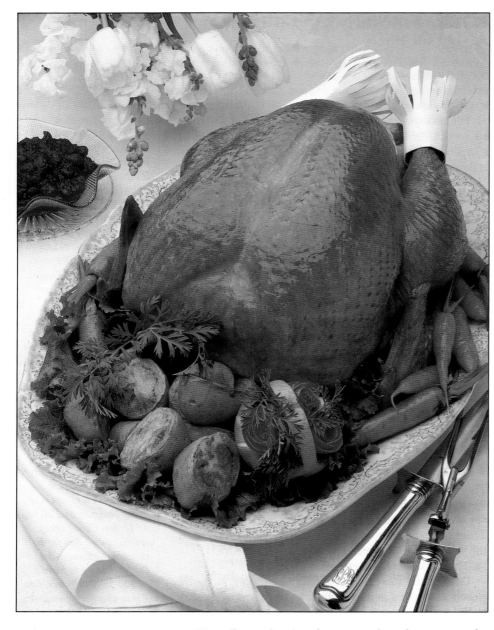

Moist and tender, a beautifully roasted turkey is the festive focus of any celebration, whether for the holidays or for another special occasion.

The efforts of turkey farmers and marketers to make turkey more than a one-season food are visible in the supermarket. Fresh whole turkeys, as well as turkey parts and processed turkey products, are now widely available the year around. The forms in which turkey, fresh or frozen, are available include: whole birds; halves and quarters; boneless roasts; bone-in and boneless whole, halved, and sliced breasts; fillets; drumsticks; wings; drummettes; thighs; and ground turkey.

Convenience options include prebasted birds, injected with natural ingredients intended to keep the bird moist (properly roasted, a bird will be moist and juicy without prebasting, however); frozen stuffed birds; and pop-up or retractable thermometers that activate when the bird has reached an internal preset temperature determined by the manufacturer.

Most turkeys are marketed as young turkeys, which means they are 14 to 22 weeks old, either female or male (see Poultry Primer, page 469). Despite a long-held belief to the contrary, there is no difference in quality between a hen and a tom; hens are merely smaller.

See Selection, Storage, and Preparation for more information.

■ ROAST TURKEY WITH GIBLET GRAVY

There are many ways to roast a turkey: plain (without a cover), in a foil tent, in a paper bag, and, according to one probably tall story, in a sleeping bag. This basic recipe recommends roasting the turkey unstuffed for an optimally moist bird. Garlic butter is rubbed under the skin to flavor the breast, and chopped onion, parsnip, and carrot are added to the pan to flavor the drippings. The recipe prepares a small turkey that will serve 10 to 15 persons. For a larger bird, cook according to the timetable on page 500; use a meat thermometer as the most accurate means of determining when the turkey is done. It is unnecessary to increase the amounts of the other ingredients when cooking a larger bird.

> 1　turkey (10 to 12 lb)
> 1　clove garlic, crushed
> 1　cup butter, softened
> 　　Salt
> 2　onions, cut in large chunks
> 2　parsnips, cut in large chunks
> 2　carrots, cut in large chunks

Giblet Gravy

> 　　Giblets and neck from turkey
> ¼　cup butter
> ¼　cup flour
> 　　Salt and freshly ground pepper

1. Preheat oven to 450° F. Remove innards from turkey and save for Giblet Gravy. Wash turkey and pat dry.

2. Gently free skin from breast meat, starting at neck end and continuing to tail.

3. Mix garlic with butter. Stuff garlic butter under breast skin. For a crisper skin, also butter outside surface. Salt turkey inside and out.

4. Truss turkey (see page 584) and set on a rack in a roasting pan. Surround with chunks of onion, parsnip, and carrot.

5. Set pan on middle rack of oven. Roast at 450° F for 30 minutes. Reduce oven to 325° F and continue to roast for another 1½ hours, or until done to suit, basting every 15 minutes.

6. When turkey is done, remove from pan and allow to rest for 20 to 30 minutes before carving. Set aside pan with drippings to make gravy.

Serves 10 to 15.

Giblet Gravy

1. Place giblets and neck from turkey in a saucepan and cover with water. Bring to a boil, then reduce heat and simmer 20 to 30 minutes. Drain giblet stock and reserve.

2. Cut giblets in small cubes and reserve.

3. When turkey is done, remove it from pan and set aside to rest while the gravy is being made. Add at least 1 cup water to roasting pan. Blend water with drippings, stirring and scraping with a wooden spoon to loosen any browned bits that may have stuck to bottom of pan. The water and pan drippings together should equal 2 cups. Reserve this liquid.

4. In a saucepan, melt butter. Whisk in flour and cook over medium heat until golden brown. Stir in reserved giblet stock and liquid from pan drippings. Stir constantly until thickened.

5. Season with salt and pepper. Stir in giblet cubes and serve with roast turkey.

Makes 2 cups.

DUCK

In its domesticated form, the dark-meated duck usually weighs about 4½ pounds. Because it is fattier and bonier than chicken or turkey, a 4½-pound duck will only feed two. Most of the meat is in the breasts, although the legs also offer enjoyable eating.

The rich meat of duck is complemented by fruit. The roasted bird is often partnered with cherries, oranges (as in duck à l'orange), figs, apples, or other fruit. Duck is almost always roasted or grilled because of its considerable fat content. Because the legs take longer to cook than the breast, some cooks remove the breast first and serve it separately; when the legs have finished cooking, they are served as a separate course, often with a green salad. Raw boneless duck breasts may be sautéed or grilled. They have a richness comparable to beef and may be served in similar fashion—with green peppercorns or red wine sauce, for example. Cold roast duck may be used in salads or sliced and served with chutney. In France duckling is considered a spring treat and is often served with spring vegetables such as peas or turnips. In China duck is a favored bird, prepared in dozens of ways. Among the many possibilities: It may be steamed, rubbed with soy sauce, and deep-fried; smoked over tea leaves; or air-dried, roasted, and served in the elaborate series of dishes that constitute Peking duck.

Inventive cooks have created uses for almost all parts of the duck. Chinese cooks braise the gelatinous duck feet. Duck fat is particularly flavorful, good for frying potatoes or omelets. Duck skin may be cut into small pieces and rendered for cracklings to sprinkle over salads. French cooks stuff the duck neck with a sausage mixture, sew it closed, and roast it. Duck liver makes a delicious pâté or may be sautéed in butter and served on toast. Duck foie gras, an expensive delicacy, is the buttery liver from specially fattened ducks. Cooked foie gras is served hot or cold, usually with toast.

Frozen duck is sold in many supermarkets. Fresh duck is available increasingly in specialty markets and is almost always available in Asian poultry markets. Imported duck foie gras is marketed in tins in specialty stores. Recently, domestic fresh duck foie gras has appeared on the market. As of this writing, it is available from specialty wholesalers catering primarily to the restaurant trade.

See Selection, Storage, and Preparation for more information.

BROILED DUCK BREASTS WITH APRICOT-MUSTARD GLAZE

Usher in the first cool night of autumn with elegant broiled duck glazed with mustard and apricot jam. To complete the menu, serve Pommes Anna (see page 466), Sautéed Cherry Tomatoes (see page 582), and Baked Pear Tart (see page 423).

> 2 whole ducks (about 4½ lb each)
> Salt and freshly ground pepper
> 1 clove garlic, slivered

Apricot-Mustard Glaze

> ½ cup apricot jam
> 3 tablespoons Dijon mustard
> 3 tablespoons soy sauce
> 3 tablespoons honey
> 1 clove garlic, minced

1. Wash ducks and pat dry. Remove innards. Bone ducks so that breasts are removed with skin attached. Reserve duck carcasses for stock and duck legs for another recipe (they can be used for Chinese Duck Salad, page 476).

2. Split duck breasts to make 4 half breasts. Remove visible fat from underside of skin. Season lightly with salt and pepper. Prick holes in skin covering breasts and insert garlic slivers.

3. Prepare Apricot-Mustard Glaze. Brush glaze on both sides of breast halves.

4. Preheat broiler. Broil breast halves, skin side down, about 6 inches from heat for 6 minutes. Turn and broil 2 to 3 minutes more. Be careful not to burn duck (if necessary, lower rack to slow cooking).

5. To serve, slice breasts on the bias and serve with remaining Apricot-Mustard Glaze.

Serves 4.

Apricot-Mustard Glaze In a small bowl or jar with a lid, thoroughly combine jam, mustard, soy sauce, honey, and minced garlic.

Makes about 1 cup.

Leftovers can be glamorous, as demonstrated by Chinese Duck Salad, served cold on a bed of shredded lettuce and puffy rice vermicelli.

1. In a large, heavy-bottomed skillet, bring stock to a boil. Add duck legs, cover, and return to a boil. Reduce heat to medium-low and simmer, covered, until cooked (about 25 minutes). Remove duck legs and cool completely. When cool, remove skin and discard. Tear meat off bones and cut into small cubes.

2. In a medium bowl combine soy sauce, ginger, and garlic. Add duck meat and toss to coat. Cover and refrigerate 8 to 24 hours.

3. When ready to assemble salad, heat oil in wok to 365° F (measure with a deep-fat thermometer). Fry rice vermicelli, a handful at a time, until it puffs (30 to 60 seconds). Be careful not to let it brown. Remove with slotted spoon and drain on paper towel. Set aside.

4. Place lettuce in a large bowl. Remove duck from marinade with slotted spoon, drain, and pat dry. Toss with lettuce, green onions, and almonds, then with Soy Dressing. Serve surrounded with rice vermicelli.

Serves 4.

Soy Dressing In a small bowl or jar with a lid, combine oil, vinegar, sugar, and soy sauce.

Makes about 2¼ cups.

Recipes: Chicken or Duck Liver Mousse, 372; Curried Chicken or Duck Liver Pâté in Aspic, 416.

■ CHINESE DUCK SALAD

Make this salad to use up the duck legs left over from Broiled Duck Breasts (see page 475). To toast almonds, cook in a small dry skillet over medium-high heat, stirring with a spoon, until golden brown (about 5 minutes).

    4   cups duck or Chicken Stock (see page 560)
    4   duck legs, washed and patted dry
    ½   cup soy sauce
    1   tablespoon minced fresh ginger
    1   clove garlic, minced
    2   cups vegetable oil
    3   ounces rice vermicelli
    1   head iceberg lettuce, washed and shredded
    2   green onions, thinly sliced
    ½   cup toasted slivered almonds

Soy Dressing

    1   cup oil
    ¾   cup rice wine vinegar
    ½   cup sugar
    2   tablespoons soy sauce

GOOSE

Like the duck, the goose is a dark-meat bird with a high proportion of bone and fat. Most of the meat is in the breast. In England, France, Scandinavia, and Germany, goose is the traditional choice for the Christmas feast. Its rich meat is flattered by the flavors of fruit such as apples, prunes, and pears. Because of its high fat content, it is almost always roasted. Some cooks prefer to put onions, apples, and bread in the cavity to flavor the bird and absorb fat; they then cook the stuffing separately to keep it from absorbing all the fat.

A whole goose offers other attractions for the cook. The long neck may be used like a sausage casing, stuffed, tied, and roasted. The fat is very flavorful, excellent for frying potatoes or eggs or for chilling and spreading on toast. In France some geese are force-fed to encourage the development of large livers; this foie gras, an expensive delicacy, resembles an extremely rich, smooth, and buttery pâté. After cooking it may be served hot or cold, usually accompanied by warm toast.

Frozen geese are available in some well-stocked supermarkets the year around. More supermarkets stock frozen geese at Christmas time. Look for fresh geese in specialty markets at Christmas time; most markets require advance ordering.

See Selection, Storage, and Preparation for more information.

▪ BRAISED GOOSE IN HARD CIDER

The hard cider in the pan juices infuses the goose with a wonderful apple flavor.

2 stalks celery, coarsely chopped
1 carrot, peeled and coarsely chopped
1 parsnip, peeled and coarsely chopped
1 medium onion, quartered
1 goose (about 14 lb)
    Salt and freshly ground pepper
4 cups hard cider

Pan Gravy

¼ cup flour
2 cups goose or Chicken Stock (see page 560)
    Salt and freshly ground pepper

1. Preheat oven to 450° F. In a large roasting pan, place celery, carrot, parsnip, and onion.

2. Remove giblets from goose. Wash goose and pat dry; remove excess fat. Pierce skin of goose several times with the tip of a knife. Sprinkle inside and out with salt and pepper. Tie legs together and set goose on vegetables in roasting pan.

3. Roast in center of middle rack of oven for 30 minutes. Reduce heat to 325° F. After roasting for an additional 1½ hours, pour hard cider into bottom of pan. Roast 1½ more hours (a total of 3½ hours), or until done to suit. Periodically skim fat from pan with a bulb baster.

4. When goose is done, remove it from oven; allow it to rest 30 minutes before carving. Serve with Pan Gravy.

Serves 10 to 12.

Pan Gravy Skim off all but ¼ cup fat from pan juices. Place roasting pan with juices over medium-high heat. Add flour and cook until golden brown, stirring constantly. Add stock, stirring and scraping with a wooden spoon to loosen any browned bits that may have stuck to bottom of pan. Cook and stir until texture of gravy is smooth and velvety. Season with salt and pepper.

Makes 3 cups.

SQUAB

The squab is a pigeon bred for the table. The dressed bird usually weighs under 1 pound and has dark meaty breasts with a rich flavor. Squabs are generally roasted or braised, with or without a stuffing. In China squab meat is minced, stir-fried, and served with lettuce wrappers; or is fried whole, carved, and served with a fragrant pepper salt. French cooks serve braised squab with spring peas.

Frozen squabs are available from some specialty markets. Fresh squab may be ordered from some butchers; some Asian poultry markets also carry fresh squab.

See Selection, Storage, and Preparation for more information.

▪ SMOKED, STUFFED SQUABS WITH CALVADOS

Smoking the squabs is easy. You will need a kettle grill with cover for this recipe, as the birds smoke while they grill. Soak apple cuttings in water mixed with apple juice for two to four hours. When the fire is hot, put the cuttings on top of the coals, place the squabs on the grill, and set the cover in place.

⅓ cup apple juice
⅓ cup Calvados or applejack
⅓ cup vegetable oil
2 squabs (about ¾ lb each)

Stuffing

¼ cup Calvados or applejack
½ pippin apple, cubed
1 shallot, minced

Calvados Sauce

½ cup apple juice
¼ cup Calvados or applejack
1 tablespoon cornstarch mixed with
    2 tablespoons water

1. Make Stuffing. Set aside.

2. In a medium bowl combine apple juice, Calvados, and vegetable oil to make marinade.

3. Wash squabs and pat dry. Set in a pan just big enough to hold both birds. Pour marinade over squabs and marinate in refrigerator for 4 hours.

4. Remove squabs from marinade, reserving marinade for basting, and pat squab dry.

5. Insert Stuffing into squabs and tie legs together with kitchen string; tuck wings under.

6. Prepare fire. When coals are ready, grill squabs 5 inches from heat, breast side down, with cover on grill so that smoke can penetrate meat.

7. After 15 minutes turn squabs breast side up. Continue grilling, basting frequently with marinade, until breast meat springs back slightly when touched (about 10 minutes).

8. To serve, snip kitchen string and remove. Spoon out Stuffing and serve on the side. Smother squabs with Calvados Sauce.

Serves 2.

Stuffing In a small bowl mix together Calvados, apple, and shallot.

Makes about ½ cup.

Calvados Sauce In a small saucepan stir together apple juice, Calvados, and cornstarch paste. Simmer until thickened.

Makes ¾ cup.

QUAIL

Small, dark-meat birds, quail weigh about ½ pound each. Most recipes call for at least two per person. The legs and wings are inconsequential; most of the meat is in the breast. Quail are almost always cooked whole, roasted, braised, panfried, or deep-fried. They may be wrapped with bacon before roasting for added flavor and moisture. They may be stuffed with fresh herbs and then roasted; deep-fried and served with Chinese roasted pepper salt; or panfried in bacon fat and served for breakfast.

Frozen quail are available from some specialty butchers, who can also provide fresh quail by special order. Some Chinese markets also carry fresh quail.

See Selection, Storage, and Preparation for more information.

■ SAUTEED QUAIL WITH RED CURRANT SAUCE

The delicate quail, in their deep red sauce, would make a romantic Valentine's Day menu. Carry out the holiday motif by serving red caviar on toast hearts as a first course.

    4 quail
       Salt
    2 tablespoons butter
    1 tablespoon vegetable oil

Red Currant Sauce

    ¼ cup red currant jelly
    ¼ cup canned gooseberries with juice
    1 tablespoon red wine vinegar
    ⅛ teaspoon *each* ground cinnamon,
       ground nutmeg, and ground ginger

1. Wash quail and pat dry; truss. Sprinkle with salt. Heat butter and oil in a medium, heavy-bottomed sauté pan or skillet over medium-high heat.

2. Add quail and sauté until golden brown on all sides (about 4 minutes). Reduce heat to medium-low, cover, and cook until tender (12 to 15 minutes). Remove quail and set aside. Leave drippings in pan for sauce.

3. To serve, discard trussing strings. Return quail to sauté pan; pour sauce over quail and warm gently over medium heat for 2 minutes. Arrange birds on serving platter and spoon sauce over.

Serves 2.

Red Currant Sauce In a small bowl combine jelly, gooseberries with juice, vinegar, and spices. Transfer to a small saucepan and cook over medium heat until jelly melts (about 3 minutes). Pour mixture into sauté pan, stirring and scraping with a wooden spoon to loosen any browned bits that may have stuck to the bottom of the pan. Cook over medium heat until heated through.

Makes about ½ cup.

POUND, TO

To flatten meat to a uniform thickness, usually about ¼ inch, for even cooking and an attractive appearance. Veal scallops are often compressed to ⅛ inch, which enables them to cook in mere seconds. Pounding also tenderizes tougher cuts by breaking down connective tissue that is difficult to chew. To prevent meat from tearing, place it between two sheets of plastic wrap. With the flat bottom of a meat pounder (not the edge, which will shred meat), pound with a downward stroke until meat is evenly flattened.

PREHEAT, TO

To warm an oven or broiler to a specified temperature before food is set in it. Heating oil or another fat in a skillet before adding food serves the same preparatory purpose as does preheating an oven, although it isn't called preheating. Foods that cook in dry heat—baked goods and roasts particularly—need that burst of hot air provided by a preheated oven before cooking or to create a crisp outer coat. Deep-fried foods will be soggy and greasy if cooked at too low a temperature. Preheating is less important for foods that use moist heat, such as stews and casseroles, or for oven-cooked foods that take several hours or more to finish. Most recipes will specify preheating, but some don't, so use your own judgment as to when the step will make a difference in the final product.

PREPARING PAN FOR BAKING

To release cooked food more easily and cleanly, baking pans, casseroles, and baking sheets are often coated with a thin layer of butter, oil, or shortening, or a light film of vegetable cooking spray as a first step. Some pans are also dusted with flour, sugar, crumbs, or grated cheeses. These coatings give batters, including sweet and savory soufflés, something to cling to as they rise. The layer of sugar, crumbs, or cheese adds a crisp coating or sandy texture as well as more flavor to the finished product.

Personal preference most often dictates which fat to use, and whether you want it to be neutral or flavored. Butter imparts a rich, distinctive taste; vegetable shortening, oils, and vegetable cooking spray do not have a flavor of their own. Applying the fat in a thin, even layer is really more important than which fat you choose. If the coating is unevenly applied, there is a chance the food will stick in the bare areas. If the layer is too thick, the food will be greasy. Liquid fats can be wiped on with a pastry brush, with your fingers, or with paper towels. Use your fingers or paper towels for solid fats.

Lining pans with parchment paper, aluminum foil, or waxed paper is another way to prevent sticking. It also facilitates cleanup. Cookies baked on parchment-lined baking sheets can be transferred to cooling racks simply by sliding the paper onto the rack. Sugar-rich meringues are easier to remove after baking if piped onto paper-covered baking sheets.

Nonstick pans should always be coated. Most recipes give instructions for preparing pans for baking. If not, experiment with different methods and use the one that works the best for you.

> **Recipes and Related Information**
> *Baking Pans, for Batter and Dough, 18; Cake, 77.*

PRICKLY PEAR

Also known as tuna, cactus pear, Indian fig, and barbary fig, the prickly pear is the fruit of the prickly pear cactus. It is an egg-shaped fruit, slightly larger than an egg, with skin that ranges from yellow to red. The skin has sharp spikes that are usually removed before it is sent to market. The sweet, moist flesh ranges from salmon or pink to magenta and contains small, hard seeds.

Use   Peel and eat raw with lemon or lime (discard seeds). Purée for sorbet, ice cream, and dessert sauce.

Availability   Fresh prickly pear can be purchased from September through December in Latin markets and some supermarkets.

Selection   Choose firm but not rock-hard fruit with a shiny appearance. Hard ones will soften at room temperature in a few days.

Storage   Refrigerate ripe prickly pears in a plastic bag and used within two or three days.

Preparation   Remove any remaining sharp spines with pliers. Cut off ends, then peel fruit back from top to bottom with a sharp knife. To remove seeds, press fruit through a sieve or pass through a food mill.

▪ PRICKLY PEAR SNOW

Prickly pear tastes like a seedy watermelon. Prickly pear syrup is delicious as a topping on ice cream, in milk shakes, and in this light, refreshing, "southwestern nouvelle cuisine" sorbet. The sorbet will keep packaged airtight in the freezer two to three weeks.

  ½ **cup sugar**
  1 **cup water**
  6 **prickly pears**
  1 **tablespoon fresh lime or lemon juice**
  2 **egg whites**
     Pinch cream of tartar
  ½ **teaspoon orange-peel liqueur**

1. Heat sugar and the water together in a heavy, 2-quart saucepan over low heat, stirring occasionally until sugar dissolves. Simmer mixture for 10 minutes until it has reduced slightly and thickened but has not yet started to color.

2. Meanwhile, wearing thick rubber or leather gloves, halve prickly pears and spoon out pulp. (Handle prickly pears with care. Even storebought ones may have a few tiny spines that will stick to fingers. Discard shells before removing gloves.) Add prickly pear pulp and lime juice to reduced sugar mixture, and simmer until fruit is mushy (about 20 minutes).

3. Briefly purée prickly pear mixture in a food processor or blender. With a wooden spoon, push purée through a strainer into a bowl. Discard seeds left in strainer. Pour syrupy purée into two pie pans and freeze until partly solid (2½ hours), stirring purée after 1 hour and again 30 minutes later.

4. Beat egg whites with cream of tartar until they are stiff but not dry. Remove frozen purée from freezer and stir again (or purée again in food processor if it has become too firm to stir). Blend in orange liqueur, then fold purée into egg whites. Place sorbet in a serving bowl, cover with plastic wrap, and return to freezer until it chills to the consistency of ice cream (3 to 4 hours). Before serving, place in refrigerator for 30 minutes to soften slightly.

Serves 6 to 8.

Variation   Use the syrup yielded at the end of step 3 as a sauce for vanilla ice cream or fresh fruit salad, or to lend a brilliant beet-red color to any fruit dessert.

PROOF, TO

A bread-baking term, *proof* is used two ways. The first meaning refers to the test for the potency of yeast: In a small bowl put ½ cup warm (about 110° F) water. Sprinkle in a pinch of sugar and 1 tablespoon active dry yeast (1 package) or 1 crumbled, compressed, small yeast cake. Stir and let sit 5 to 10 minutes to soften. If the yeast is alive, the surface of the liquid will form a thick foam. There's the proof. A lack of foam indicates that the yeast is most likely dead; discard that batch and begin again with a fresher package.

Proofing also describes the second rising of a yeast dough after it has risen, been punched down, and shaped. The dough sits in a warm spot (75° to 80° F) until it has doubled in bulk and retains the mark of your finger if pressed into it.

> **Recipes and Related Information**
> *Yeast, 613; Yeast Bread, 613.*

PREPARING BAKING PANS

To grease pan, use fingers, paper towel, or brush if using liquid fat. Apply a thin, even layer of butter, margarine, vegetable shortening, or oil, or spray with a fine mist of vegetable cooking spray. Use a light touch or surface of baked good will be gummy.

If lining pan with parchment paper, use pan as a template. Set pan on paper and trace around it with a pencil. Cut out just inside of pencil line. Set in pan and smooth to fit; remove and trim if too large.

If called for, dust pan lightly with flour, crumbs, or sugar. Hold pan at an angle over paper or sink, and tap gently to loosen excess coating. Let excess fall from pan.

PUFF PASTRY

Also called *pâte feuilletée*, puff pastry holds the distinction of being the most versatile, intriguing, and delicious of all the pastry doughs. Like conventional pie and tart pastry, puff pastry is made from very basic ingredients—flour, salt, water, and butter. The dough is much richer in butter than the others, however, and the butter is worked into the dough in a unique manner—not in one step, but repeatedly, through a series of rollings and foldings. What results are paper-thin sheets of dough separated by equally fine layers of fat. During baking the fat melts and releases steam that causes the dough to rise up to ten times its original height.

The dough is leavened solely by steam and hot air, rather than by yeast or chemical leaveners. Folding traps air within the dough. During baking the air fills the many spaces left by the butter when it melts. The air expands from the heat and puffs the pastry. Moisture from water in the dough and from the many layers of butter convert to steam when heated during baking, which also causes the dough to rise.

Close inspection of the airy, golden brown pastry reveals hundreds of separate, crispy layers, one upon the other. The estimate is that more than 700 layers are created by the time the dough and butter have been rolled and folded the traditionally recommended six turns. The flavor and aroma of puff pastry are rich and buttery.

Volumes could be written on the attributes of puff pastry and its many sweet and savory applications. It can be made into pastry cases for all sorts of fillings in many shapes and sizes, freestanding pastry decorations, applied pastry decorations, hors d'oeuvres, cookies, and wrappers for meat, fish, cheese, and fruit *en croûte*.

PUFF PASTRY BASICS

The reputation of puff pastry for being temperamental and time-consuming causes many novice bakers to shy away from attempting to make it. Admittedly, making puff pastry is not a one-step procedure. But the process is neither difficult nor time-consuming. Each step actually takes only 5 to 10 minutes to accomplish. Between steps, the dough rests in the refrigerator for about one hour. If you subtract the resting time from the total amount of time needed to make the dough, you will see that actual working time is only 30 to 40 minutes.

Puff pastry dough is made from two basic elements: (1) a smooth, elastic dough called the *détrempe* and (2) a block of butter beaten until pliable. When dough and block of butter are the same temperature and consistency, the butter is wrapped up in the dough, and this lump of dough-wrapped butter is given six turns. To give the dough a turn, it is rolled out into a rectangle, folded into thirds like a business letter, and rotated a quarter turn (90 degrees) on the work surface. Each turn is an exact repetition of this rolling, folding, and turning process.

The end product of this turning is virgin puff pastry: puff pastry that has been given six turns and has not been rolled out, cut out, or shaped in any way. Some pastries require virgin puff pastry and some pastries can be made with puff pastry trimmings and scraps.

Don't throw away the trimmings left over after virgin puff pastry is cut. Layer scraps, wrap, and refrigerate for at least one hour. (They can be stored up to two days in the refrigerator or can be frozen for up to one month.) The scraps can then be rolled out into a sheet and used. All pastries can be made with virgin puff pastry, but in some cases—where a high, puffy rising is unnecessary—the scraps will suffice. They can be used quite successfully for the following: as the base for a dessert or as one of the layers of a dessert; for *mille-feuilles* or napoleons; as pastry cases for pies (blind baked without filling) to be used as a first course, an entrée, or a dessert.

INGREDIENTS FOR PUFF PASTRY

Use the ingredients recommended in the recipe. A combination of pastry flour and all-purpose flour yields a dough that will roll out easily and has enough strength to be rolled out without tearing and baked without breaking. The resulting dough can hold its shape when baked, but remains tender. You can use 50 percent pastry flour (soft flour) and 50 percent all-purpose flour (a combination of hard and soft flours) or 75 percent pastry flour and 25 percent hard flour (bread flour high in gluten). Fresh, cold, unsalted butter and ice water are essential.

PREPARING PUFF PASTRY

To produce the characteristic layers of dough and butter, the butter should be neither too soft nor too hard. Ideally, the dough and butter should be of equal temperature and consistency, which is why the détrempe is chilled before the first rolling. Very soft butter will blend too thoroughly with the dough. The result will be crumbly rather than multilayered and flaky, much like a short pie crust. Butter that is too hard will shear through the dough, leaving holes that will allow steam and air, which leaven the dough, to escape.

The butter also should be plastic, which means that it can be manipulated. Usually, a recipe recommends that you beat the cold butter with a rolling pin to make it pliable, although not work it so much that it loses its chill.

Temperature is critical, not only for butter but for all the ingredients, the equipment, and the room you are working in. The goal is to keep everything cool enough so the layers of butter stay separate from the layers of dough. Try to make puff pastry during the coolest part of the day, and on a day when you plan to be home for several hours. On warm days, chill the work surface and rolling pin for 30 minutes. If you have room, you can chill a portable marble slab or cutting board in the refrigerator. Otherwise, place on the work surface a rimmed baking sheet filled with ice cubes.

WORKING WITH PUFF PASTRY

Roll chilled détrempe (dough) into a rounded cross shape. Work surface and rolling pin should be chilled and lightly floured. When rolling, do not press down hard on dough; use even pressure. Roll dough thinner at edges.

Place square of cold butter in center of dough cross. Wrap butter in dough as shown. If dough seems warm, return to refrigerator 10 minutes before rolling.

Complete wrap as if forming an envelope. Then for each turn, roll dough into a rectangle. Fold in thirds as if you were folding a business letter. Rotate a quarter turn clockwise (90 degrees), square edges, and either roll again or refrigerate, as directed in recipe. Remove any excess flour by brushing dough with a pastry brush before and after folding.

The dough also should chill between every two turns. This firms up the butter and relaxes the dough, making it easier to roll out without compressing the layers. The dough should also be allowed to rest in the refrigerator again just before it's baked so the baked puff pastry will maintain its original shape and size.

A marble work surface is best for puff pastry, as it is for other pastry doughs. It naturally maintains a temperature 20° F cooler than the air, and because it is nonporous, pastry won't stick to it. However, marble is expensive and quite heavy. An alternative is a cutting board made of white polycarbonate if you can find one of sufficiently large size. If you have one of these portable boards, make a lot of pastry, and have room in your refrigerator, store board on a refrigerator shelf to keep it at the proper cold temperature. Countertops made of plastic laminate are also suitable for making puff pastry. Chill when necessary with ice cubes and tray as described in Preparing Puff Pastry (see opposite page).

CUTTING PUFF PASTRY: UNBAKED AND BAKED

Always cut puff pastry dough when cold and use a sharp knife. Cut straight down into dough with a clean, sharp movement. Do not drag knife through warm dough or you will seal layers of dough together, making it difficult for them to separate and rise to their fullest volume. Always trim away folded edge of puff pastry; if left, folded edge won't rise. Large pastries like vol-au-vents (see page 483) sometimes shrink out of shape in the oven. To help them rise straight, cut them at a slight angle: Slant the knife so that the edge of the pastry is slightly wider at the bottom. Flip pastry so top is wider. As it bakes, the pastry will rise evenly.

To make rectangular puff pastry cases out of baked pastry dough, slice puff pastry horizontally with a serrated knife. This will create a case, with a top and bottom, like a box, which can be filled with your choice of filling.

To serve pastry, cut with a serrated knife held at a 45-degree angle to the pastry. Use a gentle sawing motion. Cut carefully because puff pastry is very fragile and flaky. Using a nonserrated knife may crush pastry and cause it to splinter.

REFRIGERATING OR FREEZING PUFF PASTRY

After four turns, unbaked dough may be wrapped in plastic wrap and refrigerated for two to three days, or it may be wrapped well and frozen for one month. Thaw, wrapped, in refrigerator (several hours or overnight). Before using, give pastry one more turn. It is best not to freeze pastry in a self-defrosting freezer for more than one week.

After dough is cut and shaped, let it rest for up to one hour in the refrigerator. Then it should be either baked immediately or frozen as follows: Place pastry on a tray, freeze, remove from tray, wrap well, and freeze for up to one month. Frozen puff pastry shells and other puff pastries may be blind baked without thawing; brush with egg wash and bake.

Baked pastries don't refrigerate well. To freeze, cool completely, freeze on a tray until firm, wrap well or place in freezer containers, and freeze for six to eight weeks. Loosen wrapping and thaw at room temperature. Crisp pastry in 350° F oven 5 to 10 minutes.

■ CLASSIC PUFF PASTRY
Pâte feuilletée

To keep the pastry light and puffy, don't apply too much pressure to the dough when rolling or give the dough an excessive number of turns.

> 1 cup plus 1 tablespoon unbleached
>   all-purpose flour
> 1 cup plus 1 tablespoon unbleached
>   white pastry flour
> 1 teaspoon salt
> 3½ tablespoons cold unsalted butter,
>   cut into small pieces
> ½ cup plus 1 tablespoon ice water
> 1 cup cold unsalted butter

1. *In a food processor:* Place flours, salt, and the 3½ tablespoons butter in bowl of food processor fitted with metal blade. Process with 1-second pulses until butter is cut into flour and resembles coarse meal. *To make by hand:* Combine flours and salt. Cut in butter with pastry blender or two knives.

2. Put flour mixture in a medium bowl and sprinkle with a scant ½ cup ice water; toss with fingertips to moisten. Add more water, a few drops at a time, until mixture is just moist enough to be gathered into a ball. Knead two or three times to form a soft, smooth ball of dough.

3. Cut an *x* into top of dough, ½ inch deep, with a knife; wrap well. Refrigerate until firm (2 to 3 hours). Can be refrigerated overnight.

To Wrap Butter in Détrempe and Give Dough Six Turns

1. Remove *détrempe* from refrigerator. Let sit out to warm slightly (10 minutes).

2. Place butter between two pieces of waxed paper on work surface and beat with rolling pin to soften. Beat until butter is pliable and smooth but still cold. Pat butter into a 6-inch square.

3. When détrempe and butter are the same temperature and consistency (test by inserting a finger into each), roll out détrempe into a rounded cross shape (see photographs, page 481) 12 inches in diameter on an ice-cold, lightly floured surface (marble is best). Roll edges of dough thinner than center.

4. Place square of butter in center of dough and wrap dough around it as shown (see photographs, page 481).

5. Return dough to refrigerator for 10 minutes if it has warmed up too much in wrapping process.

6. Place cool dough on a cold, lightly floured surface with vertical seam pointing toward you. Press dough down with rolling pin to flatten slightly. Begin rolling dough at end farthest from you, always rolling away from you, never sideways or toward you. Ease up on rolling pin when you come to ends of dough to avoid pushing butter out of the dough. As you roll out dough and fold it, keep sides and ends parallel and thickness even. If butter breaks through dough at any time during rolling process, dust problem areas generously with flour and then continue rolling dough.

Turn 1 Roll dough into an 8- by 18-inch rectangle, with the short side facing you. Brush dough with soft pastry brush to remove flour. Fold bottom third of rectangle up (brush away any flour with pastry brush), then fold top third down, as if it were a business letter. Dust off excess flour and rotate dough a quarter turn clockwise (90 degrees) so seam is on your left. Square up edges by tapping them with rolling pin.

Turn 2 Roll out dough as before. Fold in thirds as before (like a business letter). Square up edges of dough. Mark dough with two finger indentations to indicate number of turns. Wrap and refrigerate for 1 hour. After 1 hour proceed to turns 3 and 4. Do not store dough longer than 1 hour.

Turn 3 Remove dough from refrigerator and allow to warm slightly if very stiff and cold. Place seam on your left, and roll and fold as if for turns 1 and 2.

Turn 4 Turn dough a quarter turn clockwise (90 degrees) and roll and fold again. Mark dough with four finger indentations, wrap, and refrigerate at least 1 hour, or until ready to use. Dough can be frozen at this point or refrigerated 2 to 3 days.

Turns 5 and 6 Give dough two more turns and roll out to thickness specified in recipe. Cut or shape as directed. Rest 1 hour. Bake at 450° F unless otherwise indicated. After dough has been given six turns, it is best to roll out, shape it, and either bake it or freeze shaped dough. The best time to store unshaped puff pastry dough is after four turns.

Makes 21 ounces puff pastry.

■ QUICK AND EASY PUFF PASTRY

This quick method is like the one for Classic Puff Pastry in that it calls for repeated rolling, folding, and turning. The difference is in how the butter is incorporated into the dough. (Note that the butter must be frozen 30 minutes before using.) With this method, you can achieve very similar results with half the effort. The finished product is exceptionally light and flaky, suitable for tarts, twists, and turnovers. The dough may be frozen, well wrapped, for several months, or refrigerated for up to three days. If it is frozen, thaw in refrigerator overnight before using.

> 1⅓ cups all-purpose flour
> ⅔ cup cake or pastry flour
> 1 teaspoon salt
> 14 tablespoons unsalted butter, cut in pieces
>   and frozen 30 minutes
> ½ to ¾ cup very cold whipping cream

1. Combine flours and salt in a bowl or on a marble work surface. Cut in butter coarsely until it is reduced to ¼-inch bits. Add ½ cup cream and mix gently, adding additional cream if necessary, until mixture just forms a ball. Amount of cream will vary depending on humidity and type of flour.

2. Roll dough out on a lightly floured surface into a rectangle measuring approximately 8 by 20 inches. Fold the two 8-inch ends toward center until they meet in middle. Then fold one half over the other. Wrap in plastic and refrigerate dough 1 hour. Repeat rolling and folding process twice, refrigerating dough 1 hour after each time. Repeat rolling and folding one more time. Puff pastry is now ready to use.

Makes about 1 pound puff pastry.

■ VOL-AU-VENT

One of the classic French pastry cases for either savory or sweet fillings, a vol-au-vent looks lovely as a centerpiece for a first course or as the featured dish on a buffet table. The pastry is shaped and trimmed so that a lid is formed from the upper pastry layer. A *bouchée* is a miniature vol-au-vent. *Bouchée* is the French word for *little mouthful,* which is just what they are: little mouthfuls of flaky, filled pastry. Bouchées are a useful part of an hors d'oeuvres repertoire, for they can be partnered with just about any type of filling, including mushrooms and chopped chicken livers sautéed in wine, creamed chicken or sweetbreads, spicy curried crab or shrimp, or creamed asparagus.

Classic Puff Pastry (opposite page)
2 egg yolks, beaten with a pinch of salt

1. Roll out pastry ¼ inch thick. Using a plate as a guide, or your own pattern made of cardboard, cut out two 8-inch circles. Cover and refrigerate dough circles 30 minutes. Gather pastry scraps and reroll ⅛ inch thick; cover and refrigerate.

2. Place one circle of pastry on a parchment-lined baking sheet. With a 5-inch-diameter plate or cardboard pattern as a guide, cut a circle in center of other round of chilled dough, but do not cut through. Brush egg wash around outer 3 inches of full circle, making sure that egg does not drip down sides of dough. Cover with second circle, pressing dough just gently enough to seal two pieces together. Freeze 10 minutes. Remove rolled scraps from refrigerator and cut into fancy shapes for decorating lid of pastry.

3. When dough is chilled but not frozen, mark a chevron pattern with a very sharp knife on surface of outer rim of upper circle. Use egg wash to glue on decorative cutouts made from scraps. Freeze 20 minutes (if freezing longer, wrap well with plastic wrap).

4. Preheat oven to 425° F. Remove pastry from freezer and brush surface with beaten egg, making sure that egg does not drip down sides. Bake until golden brown and

puffy (25 to 35 minutes). If dough starts to brown too much before pastry is ready, lower temperature after about 20 minutes to 400° F.

5. Remove from oven and carefully cut around inner circle of dough with a very sharp knife and a gentle, sawing motion. Remove this lid and, with a fork or spoon, scoop out any soft, uncooked dough from inside. Cool completely and fill with desired filling.

Makes 1 Vol-au-Vent.

Bouchées Follow Vol-au-Vent recipe, but cut out rounds with a 2-inch biscuit cutter. Use a small sharp knife or a 1-inch biscuit cutter to make small lids on half of the 2-inch rounds. Brush unmarked 2-inch rounds lightly with egg. Position marked rounds directly on top. Transfer to parchment-lined baking sheets and chill or freeze 10 minutes, if desired; brush again with egg wash and bake in a preheated 475° F oven 5 minutes; reduce heat to 400° F and bake an additional 5 to 8 minutes or until done. Cool Bouchées on a rack. When cool, remove lid and scoop out the soft centers.

Makes about 12 Bouchées.

This fresh fruit tart band is filled with pastry cream, topped with peach halves and blueberries, and then glazed with apricot jam. This dessert can be made with almost any fruits in season. The recipe is on page 485.

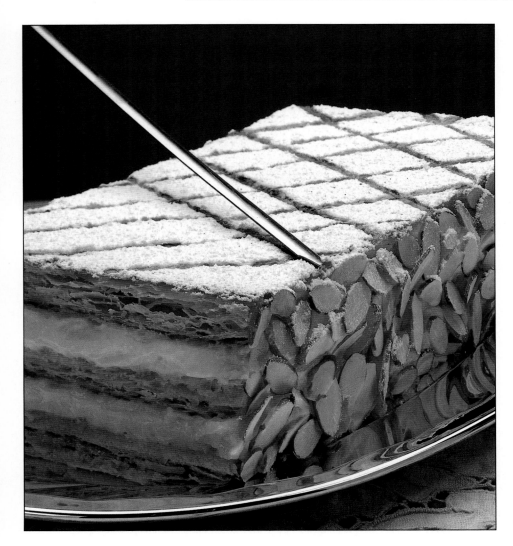

A red-hot metal skewer burns caramelized lines into the sugar on top of Mille-Feuilles. The Mille-Feuilles features three layers of puff pastry filled with vanilla pastry cream.

■ MILLE-FEUILLES

In French *mille feuilles* means *a thousand leaves,* and that is what you get—many thin, delicate leaves of puff pastry. Here they are layered with rum pastry cream to form the base for Mille-Feuilles and for napoleons. Both preparations begin with a long, narrow pastry that is either dusted with confectioners' sugar (for Mille-Feuilles) or iced with marbled glaze (napoleons). Assembled as a large pastry, it is then cut into small servings. Puff pastry is very flaky and should be cut with a serrated knife and a sawing motion. It is best when assembled just before serving. Puff pastry trimmings can be used instead of virgin puff pastry.

> 2½ cups Pastry Cream (see page 251)
>   Classic Puff Pastry with 6 turns (see page 482)
>   1 cup apricot jam, melted and sieved
>   2 teaspoons rum
>   ¼ cup whipping cream
>   1 cup toasted sliced almonds, coarsely chopped
>   ⅓ cup confectioners' sugar

1. Prepare Pastry Cream and chill.

2. Roll out Classic Puff Pastry into a 12- by 18-inch rectangle, ⅛ inch thick; chill until firm (about 20 minutes). Cut into three equal rectangles that measure 6 inches by 12 inches each. Prick each rectangle all over. Place on parchment-lined baking sheets, cover, and refrigerate 30 minutes. If you have an oven and baking sheets that will accommodate the 12- by 18-inch sheet of puff pastry, this large sheet can be pricked all over and baked whole. Then, after baking, it can be cut into three equal strips with a serrated knife.

3. Preheat oven to 425° F. Cover pastry strips or whole sheet with parchment paper. Set another baking sheet on top of each pastry layer to weight dough. Bake 10 minutes. Lift up baking sheet and parchment paper, prick dough again, replace top baking sheet and parchment, and bake 5 minutes more. Reprick dough. When pastry is browning and appears to be set, remove baking pan and parchment paper from top of pastry. When pastry is crisp, golden brown, and thoroughly baked, remove from oven. Transfer to wire racks and set aside to cool.

4. Trim pastry rectangles with a serrated knife so they are all the same size. Reserve flattest layer for top. Cut out a cardboard rectangle slightly smaller than puff pastry rectangles to use as a base for the cake. Wrap cardboard with aluminum foil.

5. Place one of the three pieces of puff pastry on the foil-wrapped cardboard. Brush this pastry with a thin layer of warm apricot jam. Stir rum into Pastry Cream. Whip cream until stiff and fold into Pastry Cream (see Note).

6. Spread half of Pastry Cream on first layer of pastry. Place second layer on top. Brush with a thin layer of jam. Spread all but ¼ cup of remaining cream on second layer. Place third layer of pastry on top with smoothest side up. Ice long sides of cake with remaining cream and press toasted almonds on sides.

7. Sift a fine layer of confectioners' sugar evenly over top of cake. Heat a long metal skewer over stove burner (gas burners work best) until red-hot. Hold skewer at a 45-degree angle to long sides of cake with point angled toward top left corner of cake. Burn lines in the confectioners' sugar 1½ inches apart on top of cake. Reheat skewer as necessary to create dark caramelized lines in the sugar. To create a crosshatch pattern, burn another set of lines beginning with skewer angled toward upper right corner of cake.

Serves 6.

Note If you must assemble cake several hours before serving, you can add a small amount of gelatin to Pastry Cream. Sprinkle 2 teaspoons gelatin over 2 tablespoons water or rum. When gelatin is spongy, place bowl over hot water (double boiler) and stir to dissolve gelatin. Cool over ice until syrupy. Stir into Pastry Cream just before folding in whipped cream.

PUFF PASTRY TART BAND

Showcase fresh seasonal fruits in a puff pastry tart band. Create colorful combinations of flavors and textures by using more than one kind of fruit on a tart. Raspberries can be combined with sliced figs or fresh poached peaches. Or arrange peach halves down the center of the band and edge with fresh blueberries. Let each peach half equal one serving. Kiwi slices look pretty with strawberries. Puff pastry scraps may be used in place of virgin puff pastry to make tart band.

> 1¼ cups Pastry Cream (see page 251)
> ½ recipe Classic Puff Pastry with 6 turns (see page 482)
> 1 egg yolk lightly beaten with 1 teaspoon water
> 1 tablespoon fruit liqueur or brandy
> ¼ cup whipping cream or Crème Fraîche (see page 161)
> 3 cups fresh raspberries, hulled, halved strawberries, or sliced fruit
> ¼ cup apricot preserves, sieved (for light-colored fruits) or currant jelly (for dark fruits)
> 1 tablespoon liqueur or brandy

1. Prepare Pastry Cream and chill.

2. To prepare tart band: Roll out Classic Puff Pastry into an 8- by 16-inch rectangle that is ⅛ thick. Cover and refrigerate until firm.

3. Cut out three cardboard templates with the following dimensions: 5 inches by 15½ inches, ⅞ inch by 15½ inches, and ⅞ inch by 3¼ inches .

4. When dough is well chilled, use cardboard templates and a long, sharp knife to cut out one 15½- by 5-inch rectangle of dough for tart base, two 15½- by ⅞-inch strips of dough for side walls of tart, and two 3¼- by ⅞-inch strips of dough for ends of tart.

5. Place large rectangle of puff pastry (base) on a parchment-lined baking sheet. Prick all over with a fork. Brush 1-inch border at edge of dough with cold water. Place thin strips of dough on moistened border to form tart walls and lightly press into place. Score edges of tart with back of a small knife, making ⅛-inch-deep marks every ¼ inch along border. Cover and refrigerate 30 minutes.

6. Preheat oven to 425° F. Brush top only of narrow strips (walls) with egg wash. Bake 20 minutes, or until tart is puffed and light brown. Lower oven to 400° F and bake until golden brown and done. Cool completely on wire rack before filling.

7. To assemble tart: Stir fruit liqueur into Pastry Cream with a wooden spoon. Stiffly whip cream into Pastry Cream. Spread a ¼-inch layer of cream on bottom of tart. Arrange fresh fruit on top of cream. Melt preserves or jelly in small saucepan until bubbly; stir in liqueur to make glaze. Brush glaze over fruit.

Serves 6 to 8.

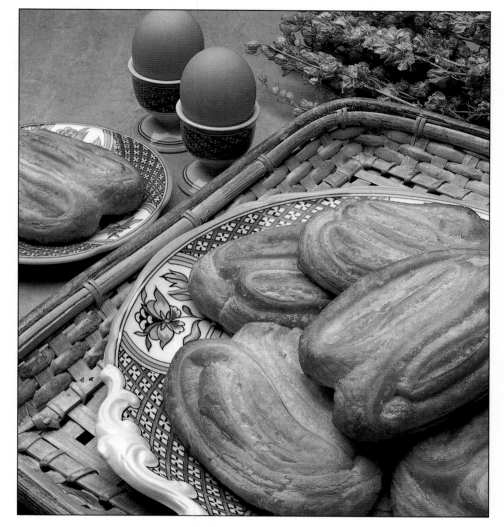

CHEESE PALMIERS

Rolled in sugar, dainty *palmiers* (palm leaves) can be eaten with dessert; rolled in salt or grated cheese, they become a savory to enjoy with cocktails or wine.

> **Quick and Easy Puff Pastry (see page 482)**
> **1½ cups freshly grated Parmesan cheese**

1. On a surface covered with grated Parmesan, roll out puff pastry dough into a rectangle 8 inches wide by 12 inches long by ⅛ inch thick.

2. Fold two 8-inch sides toward center, meeting in middle. Dust surface lightly with cheese. Then fold top half of dough down over bottom half. Dust dough with any remaining Parmesan. Chill dough, wrapped in plastic, for 1 hour.

3. Preheat oven to 350° F. Cut roll into ¼-inch widths. Place on ungreased baking sheets, widely separated. Bake until golden brown (20 to 25 minutes). Serve warm, or cool on a rack and store in an airtight container for up to 2 weeks.

Makes about 50 palmiers.

Quick puff pastry dusted with Parmesan can be turned into buttery Cheese Palmiers, to serve warm or cool with cocktails or red wine. Provide plates or large napkins: The palmiers are deliciously flaky.

To make Raspberry Feuillantines, a puff pastry rectangle is baked, then split horizontally and filled with vanilla pastry cream, raspberries, and Chantilly Cream. Use a large open-star tip to pipe the cream.

■ RASPBERRY FEUILLANTINES

Feuillantines are rectangles of puff pastry that are decorated and baked to form pastry cases. These elegant containers are a perfect pastry to follow any dinner party. Here they hold kirsch-flavored pastry cream, fresh raspberries or strawberries, and Chantilly Cream.

    1¼ cups Pastry Cream (see page 251)
         Classic Puff Pastry with 6 turns (see page 482)
    1 egg yolk lightly beaten with 1 teaspoon water
    1 tablespoon kirsch or other liqueur
    4½ cups fresh raspberries, or halved or
         quartered fresh strawberries
    2½ cups Chantilly Cream (see page 252)

1. Prepare Pastry Cream and chill.

2. To prepare feuillantines: Roll out Classic Puff Pastry into a 12- by 14-inch rectangle that is ¼ inch thick. Place on a parchment-lined baking sheet and refrigerate until very firm (about 20 minutes).

3. Meanwhile cut out a cardboard rectangle that is 2¾ inches by 5 inches to use as a pattern. Using this pattern, cut out eight rectangles of puff pastry from chilled dough with a sharp knife. Turn each rectangle of dough over and place on parchment-lined baking sheet. Cover and refrigerate 1 hour.

4. Gather scraps into a ball; chill. When scraps are firm, roll out very thin. Place on a baking sheet and freeze briefly to chill dough. Cut out small leaves, flowers, stems, and other designs from dough to decorate tops of

rectangles. Brush tops of rectangles with egg wash. Arrange cutouts decoratively on top of each rectangle. Chill 20 minutes. Rectangles may be frozen at this point. The frozen puff pastry dough may be baked unfilled and without thawing.

5. Preheat oven to 425° F. Brush top of each rectangle with egg wash. Bake 20 minutes. Lower oven to 400° F and continue baking until golden brown and puffy. Cool on wire racks. Store in dry place at room temperature until ready to fill.

6. To assemble: Split each rectangle in half horizontally with a serrated knife, creating a bottom and a top. Remove any uncooked dough from center. Place bottoms on dessert plates.

7. Stir kirsch into Pastry Cream. Spoon 2 tablespoons Pastry Cream into each bottom. Sprinkle fresh berries on top of cream.

8. Prepare Chantilly Cream. Place Chantilly Cream in a pastry bag fitted with a large, open-star tip. Pipe a layer of rosettes on top of berries. Place puff pastry tops on filled bottoms. Decorate plate with a few berries. Serve immediately while pastry is still warm.

Makes 8 pastries.

Recipes and Related Information
Brie or Camembert in Puff Pastry, 112; Cake and Pastry Tools, 89.

PUNCH DOWN, TO

A bread-making term that means to put your fist gently into risen yeast dough to deflate it. At this point the dough has lightened from a heavy mass into an inflated foam due to the action of the gases given off by yeast during fermentation. These gases are trapped by strands of gluten formed when the dough was mixed and cause this gluten network to expand.

Yeast doughs are punched down to avoid overstretching and breaking the gluten strands. This step also creates more gas bubbles, which means a wider distribution of carbon dioxide in the dough and a more even grain when the bread is baked.

Actually, you don't really have to punch the dough; if you lift it gently, it will collapse in the same way.

> ***Recipes and Related Information***
> *Yeast, 613; Yeast Bread, 613.*

PUREE, TO; PUREE

To blend, sieve, or process food into a soft, smooth consistency; the food that results from this process. A purée is a thick liquid made from finely ground, cooked vegetables, fruits, grains, or legumes. Familiar purées include applesauce, mashed potatoes, and pumpkin pie filling. Purées are the primary flavor base for many ice creams, mousses, pâtés, soups, and sauces. Purées add more nutrition when thickening a soup or sauce than do flour, fat, or dairy products.

Prepare food for puréeing by washing, trimming blemishes, and removing seeds. Skins should be scrubbed but do not always have to be removed. Hard-skinned vegetables, however, such as pumpkins and winter squash, should be peeled; peeling most other foods is a matter of personal taste. Cook food until tender in stock or water, then purée with some of the cooking liquid (for soups) or a few tablespoons of butter (for vegetables). Most fruits and vegetables purée best while still warm. Mash food with a potato masher, if desired, then purée by pressing through a fine strainer; or cut into uniform pieces and purée in a food processor or blender, or with a food mill. Although unnecessary, using a blender or food processor is the easiest method. A food mill is useful for puréeing fibrous vegetables such as celery and watercress.

Different foods can be cooked separately or combined for purées. Nonstarch foods such as beans and tomatoes produce very liquid purées, which are good for sauces. Starchy vegetables such as carrots, potatoes, and parsnips produce thicker purées.

Serve purées immediately, or store in the refrigerator for up to four days or in the freezer for up to one month. Reheat in a double boiler or in a heavy-bottomed saucepan over low heat.

In general, 1 pound of trimmed and cleaned raw fruits and vegetables makes about 2 cups of purée. Thick-skinned vegetables and pitted fruits are an exception. For these foods, about 1 pound of raw food yields 1 cup of purée. One-half pound of beans makes 2½ cups of purée. When using purée as a thickener, 1 cup of puréed potato or a similar starchy vegetable is enough to thicken 2 quarts of vegetable soup.

◼ VEGETABLE PUREES

A delicious variation for serving vegetables, purées are good with broiled, baked, or sautéed meats. Almost any vegetable is suitable; the list below gives some suggestions. If you wish to serve more than one, prepare them separately and serve them side by side or swirled together on the plate. Purées can also be made into soup (see instructions at end of recipe).

> **1 pound fresh vegetables, trimmed**
> **1 tablespoon butter or margarine**
> **¼ to ½ cup half-and-half**
> **Salt and freshly ground pepper, to taste**

1. Cut vegetables into pieces of even size. Steam until tender in a small amount of water. Drain, reserving any liquid for soups, if desired.

2. Place vegetables and butter in food processor or blender. Process until smooth.

3. With machine running, slowly add half-and-half to make a smooth, creamy purée. Season to taste with salt and pepper.

Serves 4 to 6.

Variation   Herbs and spices add another dimension to vegetable purées. Here are a few suggestions.

Broccoli   Add a pinch of cayenne pepper.

Carrots   Add fresh or dried dill to taste.

Cauliflower   Add curry powder or ½ cup shredded Swiss or Cheddar cheese. Dust with paprika or serve with a purée of contrasting color.

Parsnips   Add ground allspice or ground nutmeg to taste.

Spinach   Add ground nutmeg to taste.

Zucchini, pattypan, or crookneck squash   Add a few sprigs of dill.

Puréed Vegetable Soup   Blend vegetable purée with enough chicken or beef stock to make a soupy mixture. Gently heat in saucepan until warmed throughout.

> ***Recipes and Related Information***
> *Ice Cream and Frozen Dessert, 308; Mousse, 372; Pâté and Terrine, 416; Persimmon Pudding, 430; Pumpkin Purée Filling, 438; Sauce, 512; Stock and Soup, 558.*

Q&R

QUICK BREAD

Aptly named, quick breads are relatively fast to assemble and bake because they are made with leavenings other than yeast and therefore don't require a preliminary rising before they are put in the oven. Cream puffs, popovers, biscuits, muffins, corn bread, pancakes and waffles, sweet loaves, and quick coffee cakes are all members of this family of baked goods.

Quick breads may be grouped by the type of leavening used and/or by whether they are made from a batter or a dough. Cream puffs and popovers (and their English sibling, Yorkshire pudding) are leavened by steam. Others depend on baking powder and/or baking soda for their volume. Batter-based quick breads include popovers, pancakes, and waffles, each made from a thin, runny mixture known as a pour batter, which has an equal amount of flour and liquid. By increasing the proportion of dry to liquid ingredients, a pour batter thickens into a drop batter, used for some biscuits, corn bread, loaves, and dumplings. Even thicker are soft doughs, which have a three to one ratio of flour to liquid. They are stiff enough to be manipulated by hand. Cut biscuits, scones, and doughnuts are made from soft dough.

All quick breads have a tender, moist, and light texture. The crumb can be slightly coarse and breadlike like the classic muffin, flaky like a biscuit, or velvety like a cake, depending on how the ingredients are mixed together. For batters (muffins, sweet loaves, and corn bread), the dry ingredients are well combined and then quickly, but with a light hand, blended with the liquids. Overworking the batter may cause tunnels or other undesirable characteristics. For doughs (biscuits and scones, for example), solid shortening (butter, margarine, or vegetable shortening) is added to the dry ingredients and the mixture worked until the particles of shortening are uniformly the texture of coarse crumbs. For many fruit and/or nut loaves, fat is creamed with sugar and eggs, dry ingredients are folded in alternately with liquid, and nuts and/or fruit are added last.

Diversity, as well as fast assembly, adds to the appeal of quick breads. By experimenting with ingredients and their proportions, as well as with the way you mix and shape the batter or dough, you can produce endless variations of a basic recipe.

The following recipes are for sweet loaves. Other types of quick breads are covered elsewhere; see Recipes and Related Information on page 493.

BAKING, COOLING, AND STORING QUICK BREAD LOAVES

Sweet quick bread loaves, served with a spread such as butter, jam, or whipped cream cheese, are a delightful accompaniment to coffee or tea. They are moist, keep well if wrapped airtight, and actually improve in flavor if left to sit for a day. Like all quick breads, they can be made in minutes and generally bake in one hour or a little less.

For best results, use the pan called for in the recipe. Even if the pan has a nonstick finish, it should be greased and floured before filling. Typically, the pans used for quick bread loaves are the standard 5- by 9- by 3-inch size or the slightly smaller 4½- by 8½- by 2½-inch version. Many recipes make enough batter for two loaves; if you make these breads often, buy two pans of the same size. Some recipes, such as Boston Brown Bread, bake in coffee cans or vegetable cans. Fill pans one half to two thirds full and spread batter with a spatula to distribute it evenly. Bake in the center of a preheated oven until a wooden skewer inserted in the center comes out free of crumbs. It is usual, even characteristic, for a crack to form across the top of a quick bread loaf, so don't consider the bread a failure if this occurs.

If possible, let the cooled loaves ripen at least several hours, preferably overnight, wrapped well in plastic wrap and aluminum foil. They should stay fresh three or four days. To freeze, wrap tightly in plastic wrap and aluminum foil and label; they will maintain quality two to four months. Thaw in wrapping at room temperature. To warm, set loaf in a baking pan, cover loosely with foil, and heat in a 350° F oven about 10 minutes (longer if not at room temperature).

■ ZUCCHINI BREAD

Try this flavorful version of a favorite loaf bread to use up a bountiful zucchini crop. If possible, prepare the bread a day ahead to better develop its taste and ease of slicing.

   3 **cups flour**
   1 **tablespoon baking powder**
   1 **teaspoon salt**
  ½ **teaspoon ground cinnamon**
  ½ **teaspoon freshly grated nutmeg**
  ½ **teaspoon ground cloves**
  ¼ **teaspoon ground allspice**
  ½ **cup milk**
   2 **eggs, lightly beaten**
  ½ **cup vegetable oil**
1½ **cups firmly packed brown sugar**
2½ **cups grated zucchini**
   2 **cups chopped walnuts**

1. Preheat oven to 350° F. Grease and lightly flour two 4½- by 8½-inch loaf pans.

2. In a large bowl sift together flour, baking powder, salt, cinnamon, nutmeg, cloves, and allspice. In a small bowl combine milk, eggs, oil, and sugar; pour into dry ingredients, stirring to combine. Add zucchini and walnuts, and stir just to combine.

3. Divide batter evenly between prepared pans and bake until a wooden skewer inserted into the center comes out clean (about 1 hour). Cool in pans on wire rack 15 minutes; turn out onto wire rack to cool completely.

Makes 2 loaves.

TOASTED COCONUT-BANANA BREAD

A generous measure of coconut lends a tropical taste to this favorite fruit-nut bread. It's the perfect use for almost overripe bananas. For best flavor, wrap the cooled bread and let sit at least one day.

1 cup grated coconut
2 cups flour
1 tablespoon baking powder
1 teaspoon ground cinnamon
½ teaspoon *each* salt and baking soda
¾ cup sugar
1 cup finely chopped walnuts
1 egg
¼ cup milk
⅓ cup vegetable oil
1 teaspoon vanilla extract
2 soft, ripe bananas

1. Preheat oven to 350° F. Grease and lightly flour a 4½- by 8½-inch loaf pan. Spread coconut in a shallow pan and bake, stirring occasionally, until lightly toasted (12 to 15 minutes). Set aside to cool.

2. In a large bowl mix flour, baking powder, cinnamon, salt, baking soda, and sugar. Stir in walnuts and coconut.

3. Beat egg with milk, oil, and vanilla until well combined. Mash bananas (you should have about 1 cup); blend with egg mixture. Add banana mixture to dry ingredients, stirring just until blended.

4. Spread in prepared pan and bake until loaf is well browned and a wooden skewer inserted in the center comes out clean (50 to 60 minutes).

5. Cool in pan 15 minutes on wire rack; turn out onto wire rack to cool completely.

Makes 1 loaf.

PUMPKIN HARVEST BREAD

Spicy and moist, pumpkin bread makes a fine and somewhat unconventional accompaniment to hearty autumn fare such as bean soup or baked beans.

2 cups flour
2 teaspoons baking powder
1 teaspoon ground cinnamon
½ teaspoon freshly grated nutmeg
¼ teaspoon *each* salt, baking soda, ground ginger, and ground cloves
¼ cup granulated sugar
½ cup chopped walnuts
¼ cup raisins
2 eggs, lightly beaten
½ cup firmly packed brown sugar
1 cup canned pumpkin
½ teaspoon vanilla extract
⅓ cup butter or margarine, melted and cooled, or vegetable oil

1. Preheat oven to 350° F. Grease and lightly flour a 4½- by 8½-inch loaf pan. In a large bowl sift together flour, baking powder, cinnamon, nutmeg, salt, baking soda, ginger, cloves, and granulated sugar. Mix in walnuts and raisins.

2. In a medium bowl beat together eggs, brown sugar, pumpkin, vanilla, and butter. Add pumpkin mixture to flour mixture, stirring just until dry ingredients are moistened.

3. Spread in prepared pan and bake until loaf is well browned and a wooden skewer inserted in the center comes out clean (50 to 55 minutes).

4. Cool in pan 15 minutes on wire rack; turn out onto wire rack to cool completely.

Makes 1 loaf.

For an inviting family meal, accompany an autumn supper of baked beans with chunks of garlic sausage and slices of Pumpkin Harvest Bread.

One of the most pleasing desserts is fresh raspberries topped with a rosette of whipped cream.

crushed for use in dessert sauce, mousse, ice cream, and sherbet. Raw raspberries make a handsome tart and a colorful addition to fruit salads. Raspberries may be combined with other fruits, such as peaches or nectarines, in cobblers and crisps. In France they are distilled to make a fragrant liqueur.

Availability   Raspberries, a summer fruit, mature as early as May in some parts of the country and as late as November in others. Peak availability is in June and July. Frozen raspberries are found in most supermarket freezer cases.

Selection   Raspberries are generally packed in plastic or cardboard containers and mold quickly. Check carefully to be sure a basket does not contain moldy berries. A cardboard basket that is stained on the bottom probably includes crushed berries. Raspberries should have a full red, black, or gold color and be highly perfumed; the green caps should not be attached.

Storage   At home, invert berries onto a paper-towel–lined tray. Discard any moldy berries. Refrigerate and use within one or two days.

Preparation   Raspberries rarely require washing. If they appear dusty, rinse quickly just before using.

■ RASPBERRY-ALMOND TART

This tart can be prepared hours before serving because the crust won't get soggy if the tart must sit awhile before serving: The almond cream filling insulates the crust from the juicy berries. In addition this tart lends itself to a myriad of colorful fruit toppings including whole strawberries, blueberries, sliced persimmons, sliced poached pears or peaches, kiwifruit, fresh currants, mandarin orange segments, or poached rhubarb.

> 1 Sweet Tart Pastry (9½-inch; see page 441)
> 7 tablespoons unsalted butter, softened
> 1¼ cups sifted confectioners' sugar
> 1¼ cups finely ground blanched almonds
> 1 small egg, lightly beaten
> 1 cup red currant or red raspberry jelly
> 1 tablespoon raspberry-flavored liqueur or kirsch
> 2 to 3 cups fresh raspberries

1. Roll out tart pastry and use it to line a 9½-inch tart tin with removable bottom. Blind bake until partially baked; cool.

2. Preheat oven to 350° F. In a large bowl cream together butter and sugar. Stir in ground almonds. Add egg and stir until well mixed. Spread almond mixture evenly over bottom of partially baked tart shell. Bake for 25 to 30 minutes. Cool on wire rack.

3. In a heavy-bottomed saucepan heat jelly over low heat until just melted and bubbly. Stir in liqueur. Brush surface of tart filling with a thin layer of warm jelly just before placing fruit on tart.

4. Arrange whole raspberries very close to one another in concentric circles on top of filling. Reheat jelly-liqueur mixture and brush it lightly on tops of berries to glaze them. Carefully lift tart so that it releases from pan sides and serve.

Serves 6 to 8.

Recipes and Related Information
Fran's Raspberry Vinegar, 323; Raspberry Feuillantines, 486; Raspberry Glaze, 117; Raspberry Sauce, 522; Raspberry Sherbet, 313; Raspberry Vinegar and Shallot Dressing, 521.

RECONSTITUTE, TO

To restore a dehydrated food to liquid form or a condensed food to full strength by adding water. Also, to rebuild a sauce that has separated. For starch-bound sauces, a good whisking after heating is usually all that is needed. To reconstitute Hollandaise sauce, beat 1 egg yolk with 1 tablespoon of water in a double boiler until thick and fluffy. Then slowly add curdled sauce, beating constantly, until fully incorporated.

RED PEPPER SPICE

Spice packers market several different products made from ground dried capsicum peppers (both sweet and hot), including cayenne pepper, paprika, and ground red pepper. The varieties and combinations of peppers used in each blend vary from packer to packer. Some manufacturers do not make a distinction between cayenne pepper and ground red pepper. Others pack both, making the ground red pepper a milder blend than the cayenne pepper. Red pepper flakes—also called crushed red pepper, pizza pepper, or pepperoni *rosso*—are a product of blended dried red chiles, but are ground coarse rather than fine.

Most commercial blends of ground red pepper are indeed hot; how hot is a matter of the style of the packer. Most cayenne pepper is blended from pungent Chinese, Indian, African, and Mexican chiles. Most ground red pepper is blended from milder California, Louisiana, Carolina, and Turkish capsicums. Although brands of red pepper flakes vary in pungency, they can be extremely hot and should be used with caution.

Use   Ground red pepper adds piquancy to sauces, chili, stews, egg dishes, pizza, soups, and sausages, and to any other dish that needs a lift. Use with restraint as brands vary in pungency. Red pepper flakes are used as a table condiment to add heat to pizzas, salads, pasta, and other dishes at the discretion of the diner. In the kitchen red pepper flakes can add zest to soups, tomato sauces, steamed shellfish, and fresh sausage.

Availability Ground red pepper is sold in bulk in some health-food stores and ethnic markets; it is widely available on supermarket spice racks packed in bottles, tins, and bags. Red pepper flakes in jars and tins are found on supermarket spice racks. Some health-food stores sell red pepper flakes in bulk.

Selection Packaged seasonings lose quality after a while; try to buy from a store that restocks its spice section fairly often.

Storage Keep ground red pepper and red pepper flakes in an airtight container in a cool, dark, dry place. Replace every six months.

> ***Recipes and Related Information***
> *Cayenne Pepper, 107; Paprika, 405; Pepper, 425.*

REDUCE, TO

To boil rapidly to decrease volume and intensify flavors. As the liquid evaporates, it also thickens and concentrates the essences. The end product is called a reduction. Typically, a recipe requires that a mixture cook until one third to one half of its original volume has boiled away (*one third* usually applies to sauces, and *one half* most often refers to wine reductions). Seasoning should be added after reducing; if added at the start of cooking, these flavors also intensify and the final product might become overseasoned. The reduction process is also used to produce a sauce from a vegetable purée; the purée alone is cooked down to produce an intense, yet light, flavor.

A wide, heavy-bottomed saucepan is best for reducing. The larger the surface area of the pan, the faster the liquid can evaporate. The thick bottom permits better control of heat.

> ***Recipes and Related Information***
> *Sauce, 512; Stock and Soup, 558.*

REFRESH, TO

To plunge boiled foods—most often vegetables—immediately after cooking into cold water or an ice bath to halt the cooking process, set color, and crisp texture. It is considered by professional cooks as the sister process to blanching, the critical finish that ensures a superior final product. Food should be refreshed only briefly—just long enough to chill it completely and stop it from cooking further. It should then be drained to prevent sogginess.

> ***Recipes and Related Information***
> *Blanch, 52; Boil, 54.*

RENDER, TO

To extract an animal fat from its connective tissue by melting. Lard, from pork, and chicken fat are two rendered fats used in cooking. Rendering is a slow process, done in a heavy-bottomed pan over low heat. It continues until all the fat drains out, the tissue has turned brown and crispy, and any impurities have sunk to the bottom of the pan. The remaining clear fat is strained carefully through filter paper. The crisp bits left in the pan after the fat is strained off are considered a delicious, though rich, delicacy known as cracklings. In traditional Jewish cooking, they are called *greben*, if derived from chicken or goose fat, and are mixed into stuffings or chopped liver, as well as served as a snack.

Many bakers prefer lard for pastries because it is a pure fat, without the water or milk solids found in butter and margarine, and so has more shortening or tenderizing power than fats with moisture. Lard and rendered chicken fat have long been favorites for frying, for basting roasts, and for making sauces because they contribute rich flavor. As evidence more clearly links high intake of animal fats and certain diseases, this practice is losing favor among health-conscious cooks.

> ***Recipes and Related Information***
> *Pie and Tart, 431; Pork, 455; Poultry, 468.*

RHUBARB

Although botanically a vegetable, rhubarb is considered a fruit by most cooks and diners. Its long, celerylike stalks are edible; the leaves and roots contain oxalic acid, which is toxic. Rhubarb may be either hothouse- or field-grown. Hothouse rhubarb has pink stalks, yellow leaves, and few strings; field-grown rhubarb has red stalks and green leaves. Generally, hothouse rhubarb has a milder flavor. Rhubarb is extremely tart when cooked and is usually generously dosed with sugar.

Use Rhubarb is also commonly known as pie plant, a good clue to its most frequent use. It is excellent in pies, especially when tossed with spices and flour to thicken its abundant juices. Rhubarb is also frequently combined with strawberries or pineapple in double-crust or lattice-topped pies. It may be stewed with sugar and served warm or cold, with or without cream. To make rhubarb fool, an equal quantity of whipped cream is folded into stewed, cooled rhubarb. The vegetable makes a delicious crisp and cobbler; it is also fermented to make wine.

Availability Hothouse rhubarb is sold in some supermarkets almost all year. Field-grown rhubarb is a spring crop, harvested in April and May.

Selection Look for crisp, unblemished stalks. Avoid any that are limp or wilted.

The tart, refreshing flavor of rhubarb paired with the sweetness of strawberries makes a delicious pie. The addition of raisins and ginger gives it an unusual twist. The lattice-top crust lets the strikingly colorful filling show through.

2. In a large bowl combine strawberries, rhubarb, raisins, sugar, flour, and ginger; let stand 15 minutes.

3. Brush inside of bottom crust with egg white. Pour filling into shell. Dot with butter.

4. Moisten rim of bottom crust with water and cover with top crust or lattice top; seal and finish edges.

5. Place pie on a rimmed baking sheet and bake 20 minutes. Lower oven to 400° F and continue baking until crust is golden brown (40 minutes). Cover edges of crust with strips of aluminum foil, if necessary, to prevent excessive browning.

Serves 8.

RIB

A single branch from a head of celery is a rib or a stalk, although some books and chefs use the term *stalk* to mean the entire head. Ribs can be as much as a foot long. They were so named perhaps because they slightly resemble human ribs and because they have a stringy ribbing on their outer surface. To continue the parallel to human anatomy, the innermost celery ribs are called the heart.

RIBBON

This term is used to describe the consistency of a batter or mixture of egg and sugar beaten to the point of optimum incorporation of air. At this stage, the mixture will fall slowly from the whisk or beater and leave a ribbonlike trail on top of the mixture in the bowl. The trail remains on top for a few seconds before sinking into the rest of the mixture. This consistency applies to any air-lightened mixture, such as génoise and meringue.

> ***Recipes and Related Information***
> *Cake, 77; Egg, 194; Meringue, 359.*

Storage   Refrigerate and use within two or three days.

Preparation   Wash stalks and remove leaves. Cut stalks crosswise into ½-inch widths. Place in a saucepan with sugar (about ½ cup per pound) and a little water; cover and simmer over moderately low heat until tender.

▇ STRAWBERRY-RHUBARB PIE
For a delicious treat, raisins and ginger are added to this Strawberry-Rhubarb Pie.

      1   nine-inch double-crust Flaky Pastry (see
          page 434) or Egg Pastry (see page 435)
      2   cups washed, hulled, and halved strawberries
      4   cups sliced, young, unpeeled rhubarb stalks
     ⅓   cup raisins
    1⅓   cups sugar
      6   tablespoons flour
     ¼   teaspoon ground ginger
      1   egg white, lightly beaten
    1½   tablespoons unsalted butter

1. Preheat oven to 425° F. Roll out pastry for bottom crust and line a 9-inch pie plate. Roll out remaining pastry to form top crust or lattice top.

RICE, TO

To force cooked root vegetables—such as potatoes—through a special tool that resembles a giant garlic press. The food is extruded in little pellets resembling grains of rice. Cooks fond of mashed potatoes say the best versions—which are not pasty or lumpy—are processed with a potato ricer.

> ***Recipes and Related Information***
> *Down-Home Mashed Potatoes, 466; Grate, Grater, 281; Potato, 463.*

RIND

This is the skin or peel of a fruit; in particular citrus fruit such as lemon, orange, and grapefruit. Citrus rinds are often candied or preserved in sugar syrup, and used as decoration. The outer colored portion, also called the zest, is removed in strips, fine threads, or finely grated pieces to infuse baked goods, beverages, sauces, soups, and other dishes with its essence and perfume. Special gadgets are available to remove the zest. The citrus zester has five tiny holes that cut threads of zest when dragged across the rind; the citrus peeler cuts a single ¼-inch piece.

Recipes and Related Information
Candy, 93; Gadgets, 258; Peel, 424; Zest, 631.

ROAST, TO

To cook raw food with currents of hot, dry air in order to make food edible and more flavorful. Roasting and its twin, baking, are the same process. Generally, roasting refers to the cooking of whole meats, including poultry, often with added fat. Most other oven-cooked foods—fish, bread, or cut-up poultry, for instance—are referred to as baked. On the other hand, ham is baked and chestnuts are roasted. These distinctions are more a matter of usage than an indicator of any real difference.

A roast is a cut of meat or poultry cooked, uncovered, by dry heat (without the addition of moisture). Most roasts are cooked in a shallow pan to permit good air circulation; the result is even heat penetration. A roast is usually placed fat side up, which lets the fat that melts during cooking baste the meat as it drains. A rack or trivet in the bottom of the pan holds the meat out of the drippings.

ROASTING BASICS

Roasting is ideal for the most tender cuts of meat. Not all cuts that are labeled roast, however, are truly suitable for roasting. For beef, lamb, and pork, the rib roast (sometimes called a rack) is the most popular cut for roasting. In the case of pork and lamb, this type of roast is sometimes tied by the butcher into a crown roast. Another popular cut for this cooking method is the loin, especially of pork and veal. Leg of lamb, veal, and pork also provide excellent roasts. Roasts should be relatively large so that they remain succulent. All types of poultry can be roasted, from small Rock Cornish game hens (suitable for one or two servings) to chickens, ducks, and turkeys.

ROASTING BEEF

Ask a dozen people how to roast a cut of beef and you'll get a dozen different answers. Some advocate roasting beef at a high temperature for a short time; others advocate low temperatures and long cooking times; still others prefer moderation or a combination of the two methods, starting out at a high temperature, then reducing it. Some cooks roast beef at a very high temperature for a short time, then turn off the oven and let the roast finish cooking in the retained heat. All these methods have advantages and drawbacks, defenders and detractors. How you roast beef is largely a matter of personal preference.

Slow, even cooking will produce a roast with a uniform interior color. A medium-rare roast will be medium-rare from the interior to the exterior and from one end to the other. Another advantage of slow-cooked meat is that it shrinks less during cooking, so you get more meat for your money. However, slow-cooked roasts do not have a crisp browned crust. Also, some cooks like to have a range of doneness on one roast, which is impossible to achieve with the slow-cook method.

High-temperature roasting produces the crisp, well-browned crust preferred by many diners. Some cooks also claim that a quickly formed crust helps to lock in meat juices, yielding a juicier, more flavorful roast. However, high-temperature roasting is not recommended for large cuts such as a standing rib roast, which would burn on the outside before it cooked through in the middle. Also, high-heat roasting causes fat to spatter on oven walls, leaving a dirtier oven to clean.

ROASTING OTHER MEATS

When lamb, a lean meat, is cooked by a dry-heat method, it dries out and, when overcooked, develops strong flavors. With the exception of baby lamb, lamb should always have at least a tinge of pink in the center. The delicate flavor of baby lamb is best when the meat is well-done. Lamb roasts to a higher internal temperature than beef for comparable stages of doneness (see Guide to Internal Temperatures, page 575).

Milk-fed veal has a delicate flavor that is fully developed only when the meat is fully cooked. Cooking it to rare or medium-rare does not show veal at its best. However, its lack of internal marbling means that veal can easily dry out. The best solution is to roast it in a slow (325° F) oven and bard the roast well (cover with a thin layer of fat to add moisture; see BARD).

Pork roasts are delicious, and since they are fattier cuts than beef roasts, they are moist and juicy without additional basting. A medium oven (350° F) is appropriate for a pork roast. Many roasting timetables recommend cooking pork to an internal temperature of 170° F to ensure that potentially harmful parasites that can be present in fresh pork are killed. However, pork is safe to eat if cooked to an internal temperature of 150° F, and will still be appetizing.

Whether to roast poultry at a steady high heat or at an initial high temperature that is then reduced for the remainder of cooking is basically a matter of personal preference. Again, what is most important is to produce a roasted bird that is moist, yet cooked to the desired internal temperature. The current recommendation is to roast

ROASTING TIMETABLE

Many factors affect the cooking time of any roasted meat, including its size and shape, whether it was chilled or at room temperature when put in the oven, and the reliability of the oven. For best results use an instant-read thermometer to monitor internal temperature, a very accurate indicator of doneness. See When Is It Done, at right.

Type of Meat	Weight (Pounds)	Oven Temperature	Internal Meat Temperature
Beef			
Prime rib	6–8	325° F	125°–130° F (rare)
			140°–145° F (medium)
Rib eye (Delmonico)	4–6	350° F	125°–130° F (rare)
			140°–145° F (medium)
Tenderloin, half	2–3	425° F	125°–130° F (rare)
Tenderloin, whole	4–6	425° F	125°–130° F (rare)
Top loin (New York)	5–7	325° F	125°–130° F (rare)
			140°–145° F (medium)
Top round	8–10	325° F	125°–130° F (rare)
			140°–145° F (medium)
Top sirloin	6–8	350° F	125°–130° F (rare)
			140°–145° F (medium)
Lamb			
Leg			
Boneless	5–8	375° F	130°–145° F (rare, medium-rare)
Bone-in	10–12	375° F	130°–145° F (rare, medium-rare)
Rack	1½–3	400° F	130°–145° F (rare, medium-rare)
Shoulder			
Boneless	3–5	325° F	130°–145° F (rare, medium-rare)
Bone-in	7–10	325° F	130°–145° F (rare, medium-rare)
Pork			
Boston butt	4–6	350° F	145°–155° F (medium, medium-well)
Leg (fresh ham)			
Whole (boneless)	10–14	350° F	145°–155° F (medium, medium-well)
Whole (bone-in)	12–16	350° F	145°–155° F (medium, medium-well)
Loin			
Boneless	3–5	350° F	145°–155° F (medium, medium-well)
Center	3–5	350° F	145°–155° F (medium, medium-well)
Blade loin or sirloin	3–4	350° F	145°–155° F (medium, medium-well)
Shoulder			
Boneless	3–5	350° F	145°–155° F (medium, medium-well)
Bone-in	5–8	350° F	145°–155° F (medium, medium-well)
Spareribs	3–5	325° F	145°–155° F (medium, medium-well)
Poultry			
Under 6 pounds			
(Broiling and frying	1	425° F	170°–175° F (medium)
chicken, duck, game	1½–2	425° F	170°–175° F (medium)
hen, pheasant, poussin)	2½–3½	425° F	170°–175° F (medium)
Over 6 pounds			
(Capon, roasting	6–8	450°/325° F*	170°–175° F (medium)
chicken, turkey)	8–10	450°/325° F*	170°–175° F (medium)
	10–12	450°/325° F*	170°–175° F (medium)
	12–14	450°/325° F*	170°–175° F (medium)
	14–16	450°/325° F*	170°–175° F (medium)
	16–20	450°/325° F*	170°–175° F (medium)
	20–24	450°/325° F*	170°–175° F (medium)
Veal			
Leg, boneless	5–8	325° F	140°–145° F (medium, medium-well)
Loin, boneless	4–6	325° F	140°–145° F (medium, medium-well)

*Begin roasting in a 450° F oven for the first 30 minutes; reduce oven to 325° F for remainder of cooking.

until the breast is cooked, 170° to 175° F on a meat thermometer. The thigh joint may be pink at this stage. If this is objectionable, the bird can be carved in the kitchen and the dark meat returned to the oven to cook further. If the bird is stuffed, remember to add 20 to 30 minutes to the cooking time to be sure that the stuffing reaches a safe temperature, which is about 165° F. Or, the stuffing may be baked separately in a covered casserole.

PREPARATION

To prevent lean meats from drying out and to add extra flavor, a roast can be marinated; basted as it cooks with roasting juices, oil, melted butter, or a marinade; or covered with a layer of fat (barding) or softened butter. The liquids can be sprinkled, spooned, or brushed over the food. Barding is recommended for lean cuts of beef, veal, chicken, and small birds, such as game hen and squab, but not for duck and goose, which are already fatty. Poultry will look better if trussed before roasting (see TRUSS).

Roasts are usually set on a rack in a roasting pan; the pan should be large enough so that no part of the meat extends beyond its edge; otherwise, some meat juices will drip into the oven. If the pan is much too large, however, the juices will burn. To roast a small bird or a relatively small cut of meat, you can use a heavy, shallow baking dish instead of a roasting pan. A rack provides open space beneath the roast so that heat can reach the underside, and allows any drippings to fall to the pan below. Without a rack, the bottom of the roast will stew in the pan juices instead of staying dry and crisp. The meat is roasted uncovered so that it will be cooked by dry heat rather than by the steam that would form under a cover.

WHEN IS IT DONE?

There are two aspects to doneness. First, the roast must achieve a safe internal temperature; second, it should be done to the cook's individual taste. The Roasting Timetable at left can help you estimate how long to cook a roast in the oven. However, it should be considered only a guideline. The most reliable indicator is internal temperature (see Guide to Internal Temperatures, page 575) measured with a meat thermometer (see THERMOMETER). Bring meat to room temperature before roasting. Let roast sit out for 10 to 30 minutes (depending upon size) before carving. The meat will reabsorb juices as it rests, making it firmer and easier to slice (see CARVE).

To use a standard meat thermometer, insert in thickest part of muscle before roasting. Make sure thermometer does not touch bone. An instant-read thermometer is not set in place before roasting; it is inserted during roasting and will give an accurate reading within seconds.

Recipes and Related Information
Beef, 37; Lamb, 335; Pork, 455; Poultry, 468; Veal, 591.

ROSEMARY

A pungent herb native to the Mediterranean, rosemary has dark green, needlelike leaves with a faint camphor flavor. When used in excess, the leaves can impart an acrid taste. The rosemary plant, with its tiny blue flowers, is a hardy perennial often grown by home gardeners as an ornamental.

Use Sparingly used, rosemary flatters most meats, especially pork, lamb, veal, and chicken. Whole sprigs may be added to the fire when grilling meats or may be dipped in oil and used to baste grilling meats. Rosemary also complements potatoes, beans, and bean soups.

Availability Fresh rosemary is sold in some supermarkets and specialty markets all year. Dried rosemary is widely available on supermarket spice racks.

Selection All packaged seasonings lose quality after a while; try to buy from a store that restocks its spice section fairly often.

Storage Keep fresh rosemary in a plastic bag in the refrigerator for up to one week; frozen in plastic bags, the leaves will keep indefinitely. Store the dried herb in a cool, dark, dry place. Whole dried rosemary will keep for up to one year; ground rosemary should be discarded after about four months. Fresh rosemary sprigs can be tied in bunches and air-dried; remove dried leaves and store them as for dried whole rosemary.

Preparation Rosemary leaves should be chopped or pulverized to release their oils.

Recipes and Related Information
Dry Spice Rub for Lamb, 350; Rack of Lamb With Herbs, 338.

RUTABAGA

The yellow rutabaga is a member of the cabbage family and is, in fact, a cross between a turnip and a wild cabbage. It resembles the turnip in its round, slightly squat shape. Unlike the turnip, however, its flesh is golden yellow and its skin yellow deepening to purple at the top. When cooked, the flesh is sweet and firm.

Use Rutabaga, also known as a Swede or a Swedish turnip, is a highly underutilized vegetable in light of its appealing sweet flavor. Peeled, boiled, and buttered, it makes a delicious companion to meats, especially ham, duck, and pork. It can be added to winter soups and stews or sliced thinly and baked with stock and buttered bread crumbs. Rutabagas can be sliced and parboiled, then pan-fried with apples as a side dish for pork chops. Mashed with butter and cream or stock, rutabagas are a delightful and overlooked winter dish.

Availability Fresh rutabagas are found in some supermarkets all year but are most plentiful in fall and winter.

Selection Look for firm, unblemished roots; avoid spongy ones. They should feel heavy for their size. Small rutabagas are particularly sweet; large rutabagas may have a woody interior.

Storage Rutabagas should be stored in a cool, humid place, where they will keep for several weeks. They can also be refrigerated for at least one month.

Preparation Peel thick skin; cube, slice, or dice as recipe directs.

Cooking See BAKE, BOIL, STEAM, SAUTE, STIR-FRY.

■ SHERRIED OXTAIL SOUP

Thick, rich oxtail soup suggests a German menu. Start the meal with a creamy beet and herring salad, and accompany the soup with a wonderful homemade rye bread, sliced thickly and served slightly warm.

      3 pounds oxtails, cut into segments
        Salt, white pepper, ground allspice,
        and flour, for coating
      2 tablespoons butter
      3 onions, chopped
      3 carrots, shredded
      1 small rutabaga (about ½ lb), peeled and sliced
      1 small celeriac (about 12 oz), peeled and cubed
      5 cups water
      1 teaspoon *each* salt and paprika
      ⅛ teaspoon *each* white pepper, cayenne pepper,
        and dried thyme
      1 bay leaf
      ½ cup dry sherry

1. Sprinkle oxtails lightly with salt, white pepper, and allspice, then coat lightly with flour. Heat butter in a 5- to 6-quart saucepan or Dutch oven; brown oxtails well on all sides in heated butter, removing them as they brown. When all are browned, pour off most of the drippings. Add onions and carrots; cook, stirring occasionally, until onion is limp and lightly browned. Return oxtails to pan with rutabaga, celeriac, the water, the 1 teaspoon salt, paprika, the ⅛ teaspoon white pepper, cayenne, thyme, and bay leaf. Bring to a boil; reduce heat, cover, and simmer until meat is very tender (about 4 hours).

2. Skim off fat, then strain soup. Return liquid to kettle. Discard bay leaf. Remove meat from bones and add to broth. Purée strained vegetables in blender or food processor with a little broth. Mix puréed vegetables into broth.

3. Boil soup gently, uncovered, to reduce liquid slightly (about 20 minutes). Stir in sherry. Add salt to taste.

Serves 4 to 6.

S

Paella, a Spanish casserole of poultry, sausage, shellfish, and vegetables, uses a saffron-infused chicken stock to tint the rice a warm golden yellow.

SAFFRON

It isn't hard to understand why saffron is the most expensive spice in the world. Made from the dried yellow-orange stigmas of a species of crocus, saffron must be picked by hand. Each crocus blossom yields three stigmas; about 225,000 stigmas make 1 pound.

Fortunately, a little saffron goes a long way. Just a few threads dissolved in hot liquid can add a rich golden color to a pot of soup or rice. Its distinctive flavor and aroma are indescribable but immediately recognizable; if overused, saffron can have an unpleasant medicinal taste.

Use Saffron imparts color and flavor to many Mediterranean, North African, and Middle Eastern dishes. Paella and many other Spanish rice recipes are seasoned with saffron. It can be found in Italian *risotto alla Milanese* and Mediterranean fish soups such as bouillabaisse, and is present in most Moroccan versions of couscous, in Iranian rice dishes, and in Indian curries, tandoori dishes, and pilafs. In Sweden, Spain, and Italy, saffron is added to buns, breads, and cakes. The Pennsylvania Dutch are also great consumers of saffron, adding it to chicken and noodle dishes and soups.

Availability Saffron is packed both in thread form and as a powder. It is widely carried in supermarkets; some store it on the spice rack and others require customers to request it.

Selection Because powdered saffron quickly loses its pungency, threads are preferred. Powdered saffron is sometimes adulterated with turmeric or other powders that are less expensive.

Storage Keep saffron, whether powder or threads, in a cool, dark place and use within six months.

Preparation Saffron must be heated to release its color and flavor. To dissolve powdered saffron or saffron threads, steep for 2 minutes in a small amount of hot water or other liquid used in the recipe; add infusion directly to dish, straining out threads if desired (it is not necessary). For fullest flavor, add saffron near the end of the cooking process.

■ PAELLA

Traditionally, this rice-based Spanish dish is cooked in a shallow, wide-bottomed pan known as a paella pan.

    1   chicken (3½ lb), cut into 8 pieces
    1   teaspoon salt
    ½   teaspoon freshly ground black pepper
    1   teaspoon dried oregano
    4   cups Chicken Stock (see page 560)
    ¼   gram (1 vial) saffron threads
    4   tablespoons olive oil
    ½   pound spicy Italian or Spanish sausage
    2   onions, diced
    3   cloves garlic, diced
    4   tomatoes, diced
    1   bell pepper, diced
    2   cups uncooked long-grain rice
    1   pound fresh peas or
        1 package (10 oz) frozen tiny peas
    1   pound prawns, shelled
    ½   pound clams in the shell, scrubbed
    ½   pound mussels in the shell, scrubbed

1. Wash chicken pieces and pat dry. Season with salt, black pepper, and oregano. Let rest for 30 minutes. Meanwhile, in a medium saucepan, heat stock; add saffron, turn off heat, and let steep.

2. In a 6- to 8-quart Dutch oven, sauté chicken in oil over medium heat until golden brown (about 7 minutes). Turn and brown 5 minutes. Remove to paper-towel–lined plate and reserve. Add sausage and brown, turning to cook all sides, for about 5 minutes. Remove sausage to a paper-towel–lined plate and reserve. Cut sausage in half. Add onion and garlic to Dutch oven and sauté 5 minutes. Add tomatoes, bell pepper, rice, reserved chicken, and saffron stock to cover and simmer 20 minutes. Add halved sausages, peas, and prawns. Stir to mix well. Cover and cook 10 minutes. Add clams and mussels. Cover and cook 15 minutes. Fluff the rice and serve in casserole dish.

Serves 8.

SAGE

A member of the mint family native to the southern Mediterranean, sage is one of the more pungent herbs in the cook's pantry. Sage leaves are long, narrow, grayish green ovals with a coarse texture. They are aggressive in aroma and flavor, slightly musty or camphorlike, especially when subjected to heat.

Use   Sage is especially appreciated in Italian and English cuisines. Italians use it to flavor dried-bean dishes and pork. To make the famous saltimbocca, a whole sage leaf is sandwiched between a veal scallop and a slice of prosciutto; the "package" is skewered with toothpicks

and sautéed in butter with wine. English cooks use sage in stuffings and blend it with cream cheese or cottage cheese to make a sandwich spread. They also layer Derby cheese with the juice of fresh sage leaves to make the green-streaked Sage Derby. In America minced sage is popular as a sausage seasoning; it is also a virtual fixture in turkey stuffings. Because of its pungent character, it should be used with restraint.

Availability   Some well-stocked supermarkets and specialty markets now carry fresh sage the year around. Dried, rubbed (crumbled) sage and ground sage are sold on supermarket spice racks.

Selection   Choose fresh sage with a strong aroma and no signs of wilting. Packaged seasonings lose quality after a while; try to buy from a store that restocks its spice shelf fairly often.

Storage   Fresh sage can be stored for a few days in the refrigerator if wrapped in a paper towel and placed inside a plastic bag. It can also be preserved in salt: Wash and dry the leaves, then layer them with salt in a jar or freezer container. Cover and refrigerate or freeze indefinitely; wash salt off leaves before using. Dried, rubbed, and ground sage quickly go musty; keep in a cool, dark, dry place and replace every three months.

■ SALTIMBOCCA

This Roman dish is a good example of the Italian penchant for whimsical food names; it is so succulent it almost leaps into your mouth (*salta in bocca*). The success of the dish depends on tender, milk-fed veal and fresh sage. Serve with a light red wine or a rich Italian Chardonnay.

    1¼   pounds leg of veal, cut into 12 scallops
         Salt and freshly ground pepper
    12   fresh sage leaves
    12   paper-thin slices prosciutto
     2   tablespoons unsalted butter
     3   tablespoons dry white wine
    1½   tablespoons minced parsley, for garnish

1. Place each scallop between pieces of plastic wrap and, using a mallet or the bottom of a skillet, pound to a uniform ⅛-inch thickness. Salt and pepper scallops lightly. Put a sage leaf on each and cover with a slice of prosciutto. Secure prosciutto to scallop with toothpicks.

2. Melt 1 tablespoon of the butter in each of two large skillets. Add scallops and brown quickly on both sides. When scallops are just barely cooked, transfer them to a warmed serving platter; remove toothpicks.

3. Scrape juices and browned bits from one skillet to the other. Add wine to skillet with juices and reduce slightly over high heat. Pour sauce over scallops; garnish with parsley.

Serves 4.

TIPS

MAKE YOUR OWN CROUTONS

Making your own salad croutons is simple—all it takes are a few slices of day-old (or older) bread. Homemade croutons are much fresher and more flavorful than the packaged kind. They accent many types of salads. Once you have tasted the following, you will never again spend money on storebought croutons.

Any croutons that aren't used within a day or two should be stored in a cool place in an opaque, airtight container. They can also be frozen.

Garlic Croutons *Cut crusts from 5 slices firm white bread or 6 slices French bread. Dice bread into ½-inch cubes. In a large frying pan over medium heat, heat 2 tablespoons each butter or margarine and olive oil or vegetable oil. Mix in 1 clove garlic (minced or pressed). Add bread cubes, stirring until well coated with butter mixture. Transfer bread cubes to a rimmed baking sheet and spread in a single layer. Bake in a 300° F oven until lightly browned and crisp (25 to 30 minutes). Cool. Makes about 2 cups.*

SALAD

Interestingly, the word *salad* comes not from anything to do with the green and leafy foods we most often associate with it, but from *sal*, the Latin word for *salt*, the first salad dressing. Salt was used as an early preservative to keep herbs and other plants fresh. These salted foods could be considered the original salads.

Eventually, all manner of ingredients were added to the simple mixtures. Today a salad can consist of so many different types of ingredients and be served in so many ways that it almost resists definition, except to call it, as does the dictionary, a hodgepodge. However, whether cold or hot, appetizer, first course, main course, post-entrée refresher, all vegetable, all fruit, with meat, or meatless, most salads share a common characteristic: a sauce or dressing of some sort. After that it's up to personal taste and the creativity of the salad-maker. For salad dressing recipes, see SAUCE, Dressings.

■ CAESAR SALAD

Here is that classic, said to have been created by a hotel chef in Baja, California, in the 1920s. Some versions require merely rubbing the serving bowl with garlic; but including it in the dressing results in a more pronounced flavor. Adorning the salad with your own homemade croutons adds a special touch. The lettuce can be washed, dried, and torn in advance, then refrigerated until needed (see Leafy Green Salads, opposite page).

   1 **egg**
   8 **cups torn romaine lettuce**
   3 **tablespoons fresh lemon juice**
   1 **clove garlic, minced**
   1 **teaspoon Dijon mustard**
  ⅓ **cup olive oil**
   6 **flat anchovy fillets, drained and finely chopped**
      Freshly ground pepper
  ⅓ **cup freshly grated Parmesan cheese**
   1 **cup Garlic Croutons (at left)**

1. Place egg on a spoon and carefully lower it into a small pan of boiling water. Immediately remove pan from heat; let egg stand in water 1 minute. Remove egg and place in cold water.

2. Place romaine in a large salad bowl; if done ahead, cover and refrigerate.

3. In a medium bowl mix lemon juice, garlic, and mustard. Using a whisk or fork, gradually beat in oil. Mix in anchovies.

4. Bring to the table egg, salad bowl, dressing, pepper mill, cheese, and croutons. Grind pepper generously over greens. Add dressing to greens and mix gently. Break in prepared egg and mix well. Sprinkle with cheese and croutons and mix again. Serve at once.

Serves 4.

■ CRISPY COLESLAW

This slaw (the word *cole* comes from *Kohl,* the German word for *cabbage)* is a favorite accompaniment to hamburgers or delicatessen-style sandwiches.

  ½ **cup *each* mayonnaise and sour cream**
  ½ **teaspoon salt**
   1 **teaspoon sugar**
   2 **teaspoons mustard**
   1 **tablespoon *each* horseradish and apple cider vinegar**
   1 **medium-sized green cabbage (1½ to 2 lb), thinly shredded**
   1 **medium carrot, shredded**
   6 **green onions (tops included), thinly sliced**
  ¼ **cup chopped parsley**

1. In a medium bowl combine mayonnaise, sour cream, salt, sugar, mustard, horseradish, and vinegar; stir until well blended.

2. In a large bowl combine cabbage, carrot, green onions, and parsley. Pour dressing over vegetables; mix lightly to coat well. Cover and refrigerate to blend flavors for at least 2 hours (up to 8 hours).

Serves 6 to 8.

■ CHURCH-SOCIAL POTATO SALAD

This soulful potato salad combines elements from traditional French, German, and Creole recipes. It has green and red onions and celery for crunch and a tangy cayenne-spiked dressing for punch.

   4 **large potatoes, peeled and halved**
  ½ **cup chopped red onion**
  ¼ **cup sliced green onion**
   1 **stalk celery, chopped**
   4 **hard-cooked eggs, peeled and chopped**

Dressing

   3 **tablespoons vinegar**
1¼ **cups vegetable oil**
   2 **tablespoons Dijon mustard**
   1 **teaspoon horseradish**
   1 **teaspoon salt**
   1 **teaspoon dried tarragon**
  ½ **teaspoon cayenne pepper**
  ½ **teaspoon freshly ground black pepper**

1. Boil potatoes until tender (20 minutes), cool, and chop into chunks.

2. Combine red onion, green onion, and celery. Add to potatoes and blend gently. Add Dressing, fold in hard-cooked eggs, mix gently, and chill.

Serves 4 to 6.

Dressing Combine all ingredients and beat until smooth. Set aside.

TOMATOES WITH MOZZARELLA AND BASIL

This classic is a salad for summer, when the tomatoes and basil are at their best. Use only sweet, vine-ripened tomatoes, and visit a cheese merchant for the finest whole-milk mozzarella. A hot loaf of crusty bread should be on the table, too.

    8 ounces fresh whole-milk mozzarella or imported
      buffalo-milk mozzarella, at room temperature
    4 tomatoes, at room temperature, cored
      and thinly sliced
    ½ cup extravirgin olive oil
      Juice of 1½ large or 2 small lemons
    ¼ cup shredded fresh basil leaves
      Kosher salt and freshly ground pepper
      Additional basil sprigs, for garnish

1. Slice cheese into rounds about ⅛ inch thick. On a large serving platter or on individual salad plates, arrange alternate slices of cheese and tomato in a concentric pattern.

2. In a small bowl combine olive oil, lemon juice, and basil. Whisk well. Spoon dressing over salad. Season with salt and pepper. Garnish with basil sprigs and serve immediately.

Serves 4 as a first course.

GREEK SALAD

This leafy salad is refreshing before, with, or after a Greek-style main course. During warm weather you can make it a main dish for two or three people simply by doubling the amount of cheese. Feta cheese, made from goat's milk, is available in the refrigerator section of most supermarkets and from cheese markets.

    ½ cup Greek olives
    4 cups each torn red and green leaf lettuce
    ½ cup slivered mild red onion
    1 medium tomato, chopped
    1 small green pepper, seeded and slivered
    ½ cup crumbled feta cheese

Oregano Dressing

    1 tablespoon red wine vinegar
    2 teaspoons fresh lemon juice
    1 clove garlic, minced or pressed
    ½ teaspoon *each* salt and dried oregano
    ⅛ teaspoon coarsely ground pepper
    ¼ cup olive oil

1. In a small bowl combine dressing with olives; cover and let stand for 30 minutes at room temperature.

2. In a salad bowl combine lettuce, onion, tomato, and green pepper. Mix lightly with olives and Oregano Dressing. Sprinkle with cheese.

Serves 4 to 6.

LEAFY GREEN SALADS

The basic salad ingredient, lettuce, tastes and looks best if treated carefully between market and table. A green salad will be the most satisfying if the greens are crisp, well dried, and cold before you add dressing. If greens are too wet, the dressing will not cling to them and the flavor will be diluted.

How much can you do ahead? Greens can be torn, placed in a plastic bag or covered in the bowl in which the salad will be mixed, and refrigerated for several hours before serving. The dressing can also be made in advance. An oil and vinegar dressing can stand out at room temperature for several hours; a creamy one should be covered and refrigerated.

With the exception of shredded lettuce and cabbage for certain salads, greens will be most pleasing if torn rather than cut. In the United States lettuce is usually served in bite-sized pieces; in France the most familiar salad is made with whole leaves of butter lettuce (which are folded with the fork, never cut, to eat).

When it comes to selecting and combining greens, choose from among many available flavors and appearances. Romaine and iceberg lettuces provide crispness; butter and oakleaf lettuces contribute softness and varied shapes; the color of red-leaf lettuce and radicchio brightens the mixture. A few shredded leaves of sorrel lend a pleasant tartness; curly endive adds texture and interesting bitterness; spinach gives a coarse quality. For a sharp bite, include watercress, arugula, or Belgian endive.

The addition of herbs and flowers expands the range of ingredients even more. Nasturtiums, chrysanthemums, violas, violets, alyssum, daylilies, roses, and dianthus are just a few of the edible flowers with which you can enhance your salad (as long as they are free of chemical sprays). Herb flowers add lovely flavor and color, although the flavors of the herbs themselves are intense, so use them judiciously.

Mix the salad at the last possible moment before serving in order to prevent the lettuce from wilting. Since greens should be handled gently, the phrase *tossed salad* is a bit misleading. When mixing a salad, use two large spoons or a pair of salad servers with a light, up-and-over motion—rather like folding egg whites into a soufflé. Many professional chefs prefer to toss greens with their hands, considering that technique the least bruising.

Figure on about 8 cups of lightly packed greens for four servings of a mixed salad. For this quantity of lettuce, you will need about ⅓ cup of an oil-and-vinegar dressing or ⅓ to ½ cup of a creamy one. Too much dressing will overwhelm the greens, but too little will leave them tasteless and bland.

Oregano Dressing In a small bowl mix vinegar, lemon juice, garlic, salt, oregano, and pepper. Using a whisk or fork, gradually beat in oil until well blended.

Makes about ⅓ cup.

CARROT-RAISIN SALAD

Walnuts add texture to this longtime favorite salad. Make it at least one hour before serving so the flavors can blend.

    ½ cup mayonnaise
    2 tablespoons sour cream
    1 tablespoon cider vinegar
    ½ teaspoon sugar
    ¼ teaspoon salt
    3 large carrots, grated
    1 cup raisins
    1 cup walnuts, coarsely chopped

In a 2-quart bowl stir together mayonnaise, sour cream, cider vinegar, sugar, and salt. Toss carrots with dressing to coat well. Add raisins and walnuts. Let salad marinate for 1 hour before serving.

Serves 6 to 8.

TIPS

SEASONING WITH SALT

Always add salt in small increments, tasting as you go. An oversalted dish is difficult to salvage. To correct an oversalted soup or stew, stretch it with water if feasible or add more vegetables or bland starches. A peeled, quartered potato simmered in a salty soup for 15 minutes will absorb some of the excess salt. When making foods ahead, always recheck seasoning just before serving. Often the balance of flavors shifts and more salt is required. Perceptions are dulled when food is very hot or very cold. If you're seasoning the dish when it's warm, taste it again once it's chilled or reheated. The salt level will probably need adjusting.

it for salads and uncooked dishes because they like its texture. Others object to the texture and use it only where it will dissolve, such as in soups or water used to boil pasta or vegetables.

Pickling or Canning Salt More finely ground than table salt, pickling or canning salt has no additives that might cloud pickles.

Rock Salt Coarse-grained rock salt is crystallized salt found in rocks. It is less refined than table salt. Because it is used, along with ice, to pack around the outside of ice cream freezers to speed the rate of freezing, it is sometimes referred to as ice cream salt.

Sea Salt As its name suggests, sea salt is obtained from sea water; its texture can be coarse or fine. The best varieties come from England, France, and the United States and have a fresh, light taste.

Storage Store salt in a closed container; it will keep indefinitely.

Recipes and Related Information
Gravlax, 233; Ice Cream and Frozen Dessert, 308.

SANDWICH GRILLING IRON

The French version of a grilled cheese sandwich, *croque-monsieur* has a filling of a slice of ham topped with Swiss, Emmentaler, or Gruyère cheese; *croque-madame* uses chicken as the meat. To cook, the sandwich is sautéed in butter in a skillet or browned in

a cast-aluminum grilling iron that impresses the bread with a decorative shell pattern. The iron, which sits directly on the burner unit of a stove, consists of two plates joined with a hinge at the back. Each plate has two shell-shaped impressions. Heatproof handles allow safe movement of the iron. A version without the shell design is also available and is slightly smaller in size.

Aside from the classic sandwiches, consider these combinations, all on buttered bread: fresh peaches or other fruit; whipped cream cheese and jam; asparagus tips with basil butter; or thin slices of red onion with romaine lettuce and mayonnaise.

To use, butter the grilling-iron plates or spray them with vegetable cooking spray. Clean by washing gently and wiping dry.

SAUCE

Broadly defined, a sauce is any fluid dressing, including relishes and condiments. An exquisite sauce has always been the hallmark of fine cuisine and the test of a cook's expertise. A well-made sauce is impressive even when it may actually be easily and quickly prepared. It implies luxury and competence and mastery of a revered culinary art. Most of all, however, sauces are a treat to the palate, in both flavor and texture.

A sauce is basically a thickened liquid—usually stock, milk, cream, melted butter, or wine, but other liquids are sometimes used. The most common thickeners are flour, or other starches, and egg yolks. Some sauces contain no thickeners but gain body by being reduced or boiled until they are concentrated. Once a liquid has been thickened, it needs only seasonings to give it flavor. The preparation of a sauce usually involves the following steps: gently simmering the ingredients, skimming away any impurities that may rise to the surface, and reducing to add body and ripen the flavor.

Sauces can be thought of as belonging to groups. They are categorized according to their major ingredients and their thickening agent. The major sauce families are white and brown sauces, which are thickened with flour and made with milk or stock; tomato sauces; butter sauces; flourless cream sauces, which are thickened by reduction; and dressings.

Each family of sauces has a different use. In general the white sauces, butter sauces, and flourless cream sauces are served with seafood, light meats, and vegetables, and the brown sauces are served with dark meats. Tomato sauces are served with pasta, fish, fowl, and some light meats. Dressings, of course, are for salads. However, because saucing is such a question of taste, there are many exceptions to these guidelines.

Once you master the techniques of preparation, you can vary any sauce to suit your own preference or particular need. Remember, however, that sauces are meant to enhance, not to disguise, the flavor of food. Add new seasonings gradually and taste the sauce before adding any additional flavor.

Use heavy saucepans of good quality so that flour-thickened sauces will not stick or burn and egg yolks will not curdle. A small whisk, which can quickly and easily reach all parts of the saucepan, is also essential. A food processor or blender is an invaluable aid in making some sauces, especially those in the mayonnaise family, which otherwise require prolonged whisking.

WHITE SAUCES

The simplest of the hot sauces, white sauces are quickly made with ingredients usually at hand. This group can be subdivided: the milk-based white sauces and the stock-based, cream-colored *velouté* sauces.

The techniques for making both types are similar. Both are thickened with a light roux—a mixture of butter and flour that is cooked until bubbling and until the starchy taste of the flour has dispersed. The liquid is added only after the roux cooks long enough to toast the flour lightly. If the roux is not properly cooked, or if too much flour is used for the amount of liquid, the sauce becomes unpleasantly pasty and sticky.

Flour tends to cause lumps if not combined properly with the liquid. To avoid lumps, the liquid should be whisked into the roux rather than mixed in with a spoon. Whisking, which blends the mixture more thoroughly, should be constant while the liquid is being added and until the sauce comes to a boil.

A roux gives a creamy texture to these sauces, which are often further enriched with cream and egg yolks. With or without added enrichment, white sauces can be quite rich, although they are lower in calories than butter sauces and flourless cream sauces.

Almost all vegetables, light-meat chicken and turkey, fish, and shellfish can be served with a white sauce. For poultry and seafood, velouté is generally preferred because then the stock is related to the dish. Fish stock reinforces the fish flavor and poultry stock enhances the flavor of a chicken or turkey dish.

Almost any flavoring can be added to these basic sauces. Cheeses—from the mild Swiss cheeses to the sharper Parmesan or tangy blue cheeses—are popular additions to milk-based sauces. Fresh herbs, Dijon mustard, and spices such as curry powder and paprika also excite the palate.

White sauces can be made up to two days ahead and then refrigerated or frozen. If sauces are to be enriched with egg yolks, however, it is best to add the yolks after the sauce has been reheated. Reheat white sauces in a medium saucepan over low heat, whisking often.

■ BASIC WHITE SAUCE

Also known as béchamel, this is a classic French sauce usually made with milk (but sometimes enriched with cream) and a white roux. Sauces derived from Basic White Sauce are often served with vegetables but also accompany eggs, fish, pasta, and sometimes poultry. White sauce can also be mixed with cooked vegetables to make creamed vegetables or poured over vegetables, sprinkled with grated cheese, and baked as a gratin. Béchamel is sometimes layered in baked lasagne and is the secret to making macaroni and cheese creamy. A thicker version of the sauce, made with more flour, is the base for soufflés; a thinner version, made with less flour, is the foundation for cream soups.

> 1 cup milk
> 1½ tablespoons butter
> 1½ tablespoons flour
> Salt and white pepper, to taste
> Freshly grated nutmeg

1. In a small, heavy-bottomed saucepan, bring milk to a boil. Remove from heat. Melt butter in a small, heavy-bottomed saucepan over low heat. Whisk in flour. Cook, whisking constantly, until mixture is well blended and bubbly (about 2 minutes). Let cool slightly.

2. Gradually pour milk into flour mixture, whisking. Return pan to heat and bring to a boil over medium-high heat, whisking constantly. Add pinch of salt, pepper, and nutmeg. Reduce heat to medium-low and simmer, uncovered, whisking often, for 5 minutes.

3. Taste and add more salt, pepper, and nutmeg, if needed. If not using sauce at once, dab top with butter to prevent a skin from forming. Sauce can be refrigerated, covered, for up to 2 days or frozen. To reheat, whisk over medium heat. Serve hot.

Makes 1 cup.

Cheese Sauce Bring 1 cup Basic White Sauce to a simmer in a small, heavy-bottomed saucepan over medium heat, whisking often. Remove from heat and whisk in ¼ cup freshly grated Parmesan, Gruyère, or sharp Cheddar cheese until melted. Quickly whisk in 1 egg yolk (if sauce is to be part of a baked dish, but do not reheat sauce with yolk, which may curdle) or 2 tablespoons butter (if sauce is to be used as an accompaniment). Taste and add salt and pepper.

Cream Sauce Bring 1 cup Basic White Sauce to a simmer in a small, heavy-bottomed saucepan over medium heat, whisking often. Whisk in ¼ cup whipping cream. Simmer sauce, whisking often, until slightly thickened (about 2 minutes). Taste and add salt, pepper, and nutmeg, if needed. If desired, stir in 1 tablespoon chopped fresh chives, tarragon, parsley, or basil. Serve hot.

One of the classics of French cuisine, béchamel is the base of many sauces. Made with milk or cream, it is white, smooth, and rich enough to be pleasurable in itself—over fish, poultry, or vegetables—yet adaptable enough to accept other flavorings.

Madeira Sauce dresses up any roast, poultry, or meat. If you keep brown sauce in the freezer, it can be prepared in just a few minutes.

flour into butter. Cook, whisking constantly, until mixture turns a light beige color (about 3 minutes). Remove from heat and let cool slightly.

2. Gradually pour stock into flour mixture, whisking. Bring to a boil over medium-high heat, whisking constantly. Add pinch of salt and pepper. Reduce heat to medium-low and simmer, uncovered, whisking often, for 5 minutes.

3. Taste and add more salt and pepper, if needed. If not using sauce at once, dab top with butter to prevent a skin from forming. Sauce can be refrigerated, covered, up to 1 day or frozen.

Makes 1 cup.

Creamy Velouté Sauce   Bring Velouté Sauce to a simmer in a medium, heavy-bottomed saucepan, whisking often. Whisk in ¼ cup whipping cream and bring to a boil. Simmer, whisking occasionally, until sauce thickens slightly (about 2 minutes). If desired, stir in 1 tablespoon chopped fresh chives, tarragon, parsley, basil, or dill. Taste and add salt and white pepper, if needed.

BROWN SAUCES

Like white sauces, brown sauces are thickened with a roux of butter and flour cooked together, although the roux for brown sauces is cooked until it has just taken on some color. This roux gives color to the sauce. The liquid used in the sauce, usually beef or veal stock, also adds a warm brown appearance. Even darker is the roux used as a thickener and flavoring agent in Louisiana cooking; it deepens to a rich red-brown.

Brown sauces are served mainly with dark meats, especially beef and lamb, and with duck; they are good with roast poultry and poached eggs as well. They reinforce the taste of meat and enhance it with additional flavorings. Brown sauces are not served with seafood or vegetables, although vegetables can accompany the meats served with these sauces.

These sauces are often served on the side as an accompaniment to a beautifully browned roast or steak, so as not to hide the color of the food. Not usually thick, they moisten food without coating it or clinging to it.

A favorite flavoring for brown sauce is wine, especially a fortified wine such as port or Madeira. The flavor and color of tomatoes also complement these sauces. Fresh herbs are another popular addition. A small amount of butter can be stirred into the sauces, but often this enrichment is not necessary because the meat they accompany is rich enough.

Brown sauces can be made up to three days ahead and refrigerated or frozen. Reheat them in a heavy saucepan over medium heat, whisking often. If they contain fresh herbs or fortified wines, add more of these flavorings after reheating to compensate for flavor lost during the process of chilling and reheating.

▮ VELOUTE SAUCE

Like Basic White Sauce, Velouté Sauce is generally used as a base for other sauces served with fish, chicken, turkey, veal, and eggs. Often the fish, poultry, or meat is poached in stock, which gains more flavor and is then used to prepare the *velouté*. To vary the sauce, consider combining white wine with the stock.

    1   **cup Chicken Stock (see page 560) or Fish Stock (see page 561)**
   1½   **tablespoons butter**
   1½   **tablespoons flour**
      Salt and white pepper, to taste

1. Bring stock to a boil in a small, heavy-bottomed saucepan. Remove from heat. Melt butter in a small, heavy-bottomed saucepan over low heat. Whisk

▪ BASIC BROWN SAUCE

This rich, meat-flavored sauce is the basis for all brown sauces. It is generally not used as is, but is flavored with Madeira, mushrooms, or other ingredients. These sauces are served mainly with beef and lamb, as well as some poultry and egg dishes. Brown sauce freezes well and can be used as needed to turn any broiled, roasted, or sautéed meat into a festive dish.

> 2 tablespoons vegetable oil
> 2½ tablespoons flour
> 2 cups Beef Stock or Brown Veal Stock (see page 560)
> 1 onion, coarsely chopped
> 1 carrot, diced
> 1 tomato, diced
> 1 bay leaf
> 1 sprig fresh thyme *or* a pinch of dried thyme
> 5 parsley stems
> 2 teaspoons tomato paste
>   Salt and freshly ground pepper, to taste

1. In a medium, heavy-bottomed saucepan, heat oil over low heat; add flour and cook, whisking constantly, until mixture is golden brown. Be careful to keep it from burning. Remove from heat.

2. Gradually whisk stock into flour mixture. Add onion, carrot, tomato, bay leaf, thyme, and parsley. Bring to a boil, stirring constantly. Reduce heat to low and simmer, uncovered, stirring frequently, for 1 hour.

3. Stir tomato paste into sauce, season lightly with salt and pepper, and simmer 1 minute. Strain through a fine sieve. If not using sauce at once, dab top with butter to prevent a skin from forming. Sauce can be refrigerated, covered, up to 3 days, or frozen.

Makes about 1½ cups.

▪ MADEIRA SAUCE

Serve with grilled or sautéed steaks or with roast beef, veal, chicken, or turkey.

> 1½ cups Basic Brown Sauce (above) or Quick Brown Sauce (at right)
> 4 tablespoons Madeira
>   Salt and freshly ground pepper, to taste
> 1 tablespoon butter (optional)

1. In a medium, heavy-bottomed saucepan, bring brown sauce to a boil over medium heat, whisking often.

2. Whisk in 2 tablespoons of the Madeira, add salt and pepper, and simmer, uncovered, over medium-low heat for 10 minutes.

3. Add remaining 2 tablespoons Madeira and bring just to a simmer. Remove from heat and stir in butter, if desired. Taste and add more salt and pepper, if needed. Serve hot.

Makes about 1½ cups.

▪ QUICK BROWN SAUCE

This version of brown sauce provides a quick substitute for Basic Brown Sauce (at left), although this recipe produces a sauce that is lighter in color and texture and not quite as rich; it also includes tomatoes and tomato paste for additional flavor.

> 1 tablespoon vegetable oil
> 1 onion, diced
> 1 carrot, diced
> 2 cups Beef Stock, Brown Veal Stock, or Chicken Stock (see page 560)
> 2 ripe, medium fresh tomatoes *or* 4 drained canned plum tomatoes, diced
> 4 tablespoons cold water
> 1 tablespoon tomato paste
> 1 tablespoon potato starch or cornstarch
>   Salt and freshly ground pepper, to taste

1. In a medium, heavy-bottomed saucepan, heat oil over medium-high heat. Add onion and carrot and sauté, stirring often, until well browned. Be careful not to let vegetables burn.

2. Add stock and tomatoes to saucepan. Bring to a boil, stirring constantly. Reduce heat to very low, cover, and simmer 30 minutes.

3. In a small bowl whisk the cold water into tomato paste. Add potato starch and whisk to form a smooth paste. Gradually pour into simmering sauce, whisking constantly. Bring sauce back to a boil, whisking. Season very lightly with salt and pepper. Strain sauce, pressing on vegetables.

4. If not using sauce immediately, dab surface with a small piece of butter to prevent a skin from forming. Sauce can be refrigerated, covered, up to 3 days, or frozen.

Makes about 1½ cups.

Brown Sauce With Herbs   Bring 1 cup Quick Brown Sauce or Basic Brown Sauce (at left) to a simmer in a small, heavy-bottomed saucepan over low heat. Remove from heat and stir in 1 to 2 tablespoons chopped fresh tarragon, chives, basil, or parsley. If desired, stir in 1 tablespoon butter.

TOMATO SAUCE

Favorites in many cuisines, tomato sauces are good with almost every food, from meats to fish and pasta. The best tomato sauces are those made with fresh tomatoes, although canned ones can be used as well. In fact, when tomatoes are not plentiful, canned tomatoes may be a better choice; they will often have more flavor than what is offered fresh in the market off-season. Because tomatoes are the star ingredient and determine the final flavor of the sauce, they must be ripe. Sometimes the appearance of

---

TIPS

HOW TO MAKE PERFECT GRAVY

For many people, a beef roast or a turkey just isn't a meal without rich brown gravy. Here are some ideas for making your gravy smooth and flavorful.

- *Think of gravy as a thickened sauce. First remove the meat from the roasting pan, then pour or spoon off the fat and measure it. For each cup of gravy, measure 1 to 2 tablespoons of fat into a saucepan. Discard the rest.*

- *Loosen the drippings in the pan with liquid— beef or chicken broth, water, or red or white wine (or a combination of these). Heat and stir to loosen brown bits, and pour the liquid into a measuring cup; if there are large undissolved bits, pour liquid through a sieve. Don't add too much liquid, or the flavor will be weak.*

- *For each cup of liquid, measure 1 to 2 tablespoons flour. Stir the flour into the fat in the saucepan and heat until bubbly. Remove from heat. Using a wire whisk, gradually stir in the liquid. Return to heat and cook, stirring constantly, until mixture is thickened. Boil 3 to 5 minutes more. Salt to taste.*

- *If you prefer a creamy gravy for pork or chicken, use a liquid of about half milk, and half broth or water.*

■ BEARNAISE SAUCE

A zesty version of Hollandaise sauce, béarnaise is prepared like a Hollandaise, except the egg yolk mixture is flavored with tarragon, vinegar, wine, and shallots. Pepper is added in two forms—as cracked peppercorns that cook in the vinegar and as freshly ground pepper at the end. Serve the sauce with broiled fish, especially salmon, with steak, or with poached eggs. (For a quick version, see Quick Hollandaise Sauce, page 517. For hints on saving a separated sauce, see page 516.)

   ½ teaspoon black peppercorns
   2 tablespoons white wine vinegar
   3 tablespoons dry white wine
   2 shallots, chopped
   3 tablespoons dried tarragon
      Hollandaise Sauce (see page 516)
   1 tablespoon *each* chopped fresh tarragon leaves and chopped parsley
      Salt and freshly ground pepper, to taste

1. In a small heavy-bottomed saucepan, combine peppercorns, vinegar, wine, shallots, and dried tarragon. Bring to a boil and reduce until ingredients are barely moist. Set aside.

2. Prepare Hollandaise Sauce and then whisk in reduction. Add fresh tarragon leaves and parsley. Taste and add salt and pepper, if needed.

3. Serve sauce as soon as possible. It can be kept warm for about 15 minutes in pan if set on a rack above warm water, but it must be whisked frequently. It can also be kept warm in a thermos.

Makes about 1 cup.

■ BEURRE BLANC

This is the most popular butter sauce in modern French cooking and has become a great American favorite as well. It is a delicate sauce thickened only with butter. Although not traditional, cream is used in this recipe to allow the sauce to be held longer. Serve it with poached or steamed fish, shellfish, and vegetables. It is also good with poached chicken breasts. Leftover beurre blanc cannot be reheated because it would separate, but it can be used instead of plain butter to enrich flour-thickened sauces or stirred into hot cooked vegetables, pasta, or rice.

   2 large shallots, finely chopped
   2 tablespoons white wine vinegar
   3 tablespoons dry white wine
   2 tablespoons whipping cream
      Salt and white pepper, to taste
   1 cup softened butter, cut into 16 cubes

1. In a small, heavy-bottomed, nonreactive saucepan, combine shallots, vinegar, and wine. Bring to a boil, reduce heat to medium, and simmer mixture, uncovered, until liquid is reduced to about 2 tablespoons.

2. Whisk in cream and reduce heat to low. Simmer mixture, whisking occasionally, until liquid is reduced to about 3 tablespoons. Mixture can be prepared up to this point as much as 1 day ahead, covered, and refrigerated.

3. If chilled, simmer shallot mixture and season lightly with salt and pepper; reduce heat to low. Add one cube of butter, whisking constantly. When butter is nearly blended in, add another cube, still whisking. Continue adding one cube at a time, whisking constantly. The sauce should be pleasantly warm and should thicken. If it becomes too hot and drips of melted butter appear, remove saucepan immediately from heat and whisk sauce well; add next 3 or 4 cubes of butter off heat, whisking constantly. When temperature of sauce drops again to warm, return to low heat and continue adding butter cubes. Remove from heat as soon as last cube is added.

4. Strain sauce if desired. Taste and add salt and pepper, if needed. Serve sauce as soon as possible. It can be kept warm in saucepan if set on a rack above a pan of warm water, but it must be whisked frequently to prevent separation and the temperature must be kept constant. It can also be kept warm in a thermos.

Makes about 1 cup.

FLOURLESS CREAM SAUCE

The traditional cream sauce gets its body from flour. This type of sauce is richer than the traditional ones because reduced cream gives the sauce its body; the liquid is boiled with cream until a portion of the water evaporates and the sauce thickens naturally.

These sauces are not as thick as the white sauce; they are light in texture and are very quick to make. Nearly as rich as butter sauces, they usually contain white wine and can also be flavored with stock or with the same ingredients as any white or *velouté* sauce. Like white, velouté, and butter sauces, flourless cream sauces are good accompaniments to seafood, light meats, and vegetables.

These sauces can be made ahead and refrigerated for up to two days. Reheat them in a heavy, uncovered saucepan, whisking often.

■ MUSTARD CREAM SAUCE

Serve this sauce with broiled or sautéed fish fillets, sautéed veal scallops, chicken breasts, turkey breast slices, or pork chops. Prepare the sauce with chicken or veal stock to accompany poultry or meats and fish stock for fish.

   1 tablespoon butter
   2 shallots, finely chopped
   ¼ cup dry white wine
   ½ cup Chicken Stock (see page 560), Brown Veal Stock (see page 560), or Fish Stock (see page 561)
      Salt and freshly ground pepper, to taste
  1¼ cups whipping cream
  1½ to 2 tablespoons Dijon mustard

1. In a medium, heavy saucepan, melt butter; add shallots and cook, stirring, until softened (about 2 minutes).

2. Add wine, stock, and salt and pepper; simmer, stirring, until liquid is reduced to about 2 tablespoons. Stir in cream and bring to a boil, stirring. Reduce heat to medium and cook, stirring often, until sauce is thick enough to coat a spoon (about 7 minutes). At this point, sauce can be kept, covered, 1 day in the refrigerator.

3. Reheat sauce, if necessary, over medium heat, whisking. Reduce heat to low and whisk in 1½ table-spoons mustard. Taste and add more salt, pepper, and mustard, if needed. Serve hot.

Makes about 1 cup.

DRESSINGS

Served cold or at room temperature, dressings are sauces used on salads. The foods they accompany are also usually cold or at room temperature, although some dressings are good with hot food. Homemade dressings taste much fresher and better than commercial types and they are free of preservatives.

The two basic dressings are vinaigrette and mayon-naise. Most other dressings are variations of these. Vinai-grette is light and clear, making it ideal for greens and colorful salads, which are most appealing when the in-gredients show through the dressing. It is also good with salads containing rich ingredients such as beef or duck. Mayonnaise-based dressings are richer and creamier and complement lean ingredients such as fish and chicken

Like butter sauces, dressings are emulsified sauces or blends of fat and liquid; unlike butter sauces, dressings are not blended over heat. The ingredients are simply whisked gradually together or are whirled in a blender or a food processor. Vinaigrette is not stable and therefore must be whisked just before using. An egg yolk binds mayonnaise together, making it relatively stable.

Differing versions of both types of dressings can be produced by varying the kind of vinegar and oil used, and both benefit from the addition of chopped fresh herbs and condiments such as mustard or capers.

◼ MAYONNAISE

Mayonnaise can be prepared in a bowl, blender, or food processor. This mayonnaise made in a food processor with a whole egg will not be as rich or as thick as one made with egg yolks alone. Mayonnaise can be refrigerated, covered, for up to one week.

> 2 **egg yolks (or 1 large egg),**
>   **at room temperature (see Note)**
>   **Salt and white pepper, to taste**
> 1 **teaspoon Dijon mustard**
> 2 **tablespoons white wine vinegar or**
>   **strained fresh lemon juice**
> 1½ **cups vegetable oil, at room temperature**
> 1 **tablespoon warm water (optional)**

1. *To prepare with a whisk or mixer:* In a medium, heavy bowl, whisk egg yolks with a pinch of salt and pepper, mustard, and 1 tablespoon of the vinegar. Begin whisking or beating in oil drop by drop. When 2 or 3 tablespoons oil have been added, whisk or beat in remaining oil in a very fine stream. Stir in remaining vinegar. *To prepare with a food processor or blender:* Process 1 whole large egg with a pinch of salt and pepper, mustard, 1 tablespoon of the vinegar, and 1 tablespoon of the oil in a blender or food processor until well blended. With machine running, pour in remaining oil, about 1 teaspoon at a time. After ¼ cup oil has been added, pour in remaining oil in a fine stream, with machine still running. Add remaining tablespoon vinegar and process briefly to blend.

2. Taste and add more salt and pepper, if needed. If mayonnaise is too thick, gradually beat in 1 tablespoon warm water.

Makes about 1½ cups.

Note When preparing the mayonnaise in a blender or food processor, use 1 whole large egg instead of two yolks, if you wish. In this case, reduce the oil used to 1¼ cups.

Make perfect mayonnaise by blending fresh ingredients by hand or with a blender or food processor. The homemade flavor is worth the extra effort.

A Mexican table setting is incomplete without a bowl of salsa. The ingredients common to most red salsas are onions, garlic, tomatoes, fresh cilantro, and, of course, chiles.

■ TARTAR SAUCE WITH GREEN PEPPERCORNS

Green peppercorns give extra zip to tartar sauce, a traditional accompaniment to fried fish. The sauce is also delicious with fried vegetables, especially cauliflower, and with cold chicken or turkey. For added interest, use green peppercorn mustard or herb mustard instead of Dijon mustard.

    1 cup Mayonnaise (see page 519)
    1 tablespoon Dijon mustard
    2 tablespoons chopped parsley
    1 tablespoon chopped green onion, preferably green part
    1 hard-cooked egg, chopped
    1 tablespoon drained capers, rinsed and chopped
    2 teaspoons drained green peppercorns
    1 tablespoon chopped dill pickle
    1 teaspoon strained fresh lemon juice (optional)
    Salt and pepper, to taste

1. In a bowl mix mayonnaise and mustard until thoroughly blended. Stir in parsley, green onion, egg, capers, peppercorns, and pickle.

2. Taste and add lemon juice (if desired) and salt and pepper, if needed. Sauce can be refrigerated, covered, up to 2 days.

Makes about 1¼ cups.

■ VINAIGRETTE DRESSING

This popular salad dressing is perfect for green salad because it coats the greens lightly. It is also good with almost any salad ingredient, from raw or cooked vegetables to meats, fish, and pasta. Herb vinaigrette is especially good with seafood salads. Although vinaigrette is usually associated with cold dishes, it also makes a quick and pleasant sauce for hot food, especially fish, poultry, and meat.

There are many ways to vary the basic dressing. Replace the vegetable oil with olive, walnut, or other oil. Use white wine vinegar or red wine vinegar for dressings used every day; or try Champagne vinegar, sherry vinegar, or tarragon vinegar for special occasions.

    2 tablespoons wine vinegar or strained fresh lemon juice
    Salt and pepper, to taste
    6 tablespoons vegetable or olive oil

1. In a small bowl whisk vinegar and salt and pepper until salt dissolves.

2. Whisk in oil. Taste, and add more salt and pepper, if needed. Dressing can be refrigerated, covered, up to 1 week. Whisk before using.

Makes about ½ cup.

Caper Vinaigrette With the oil, whisk in 1 tablespoon chopped capers and 2 tablespoons chopped parsley. As capers are salty, add salt to the dressing with a light touch. This dressing flatters grilled fish and fish salads.

Herb Vinaigrette Just before using, add 1 tablespoon chopped parsley, chives, basil, or tarragon. For a more intense tarragon flavor, make the dressing with tarragon vinegar and add chopped fresh tarragon.

■ MUSTARD VINAIGRETTE

This dressing is thicker than most vinaigrettes because the oil is whisked in gradually. In addition the mustard helps to thicken it. Instead of plain Dijon mustard, you can use a grainy type or a flavored version such as herb mustard or green peppercorn mustard. If desired, add capers for more texture and flavor.

    1 teaspoon Dijon mustard
    3 tablespoons red wine vinegar
    1 clove garlic, minced
    Salt and pepper, to taste
    9 tablespoons olive oil
    1 tablespoon capers (optional)

1. Whisk mustard, vinegar, garlic, and salt and pepper together in a small bowl. Gradually pour in oil in a fine stream, whisking constantly.

2. Mix in capers, if used. Adjust seasoning, if needed. Dressing can be refrigerated, covered, up to 1 week. Whisk before using.

Makes about ¾ cup.

RASPBERRY VINEGAR AND SHALLOT DRESSING

This pink dressing has a wonderful aroma of raspberries. Use it to flavor poultry salads and to add unexpected zip to simple green salads. The dressing is made quickly in a food processor, but it can be prepared in a blender or bowl instead if the shallot is finely chopped by hand. If you are using a blender, combine the chopped shallot with the other ingredients in step 1 and continue with the rest of the recipe. If you prefer to prepare the dressing by hand, follow the procedure for Vinaigrette Dressing (opposite page), adding the chopped shallot at the beginning.

½ small shallot, peeled and halved
3 tablespoons raspberry vinegar
   Salt and pepper, to taste
½ cup plus 1 tablespoon vegetable oil

1. Chop shallot until fine by dropping pieces one by one down feed tube of a food processor while blade is turning. Add vinegar and salt and pepper; process until combined.

2. As blade is turning, gradually pour in oil. Dressing will thicken slightly. Taste and add more salt and pepper, if needed. Dressing can be refrigerated, covered, up to 2 days. Whisk before using.

Makes about ¾ cup.

OTHER SAUCES

In addition to the classic sauces, we enjoy many other types throughout a meal, as dipping sauces for hors d'oeuvres, as accompaniments to the main course, and as toppings for all kinds of desserts.

CURRY SAUCE

A smooth and silky curry dip works magic on hard-cooked eggs, boiled shrimp and crab, or a basket of snow peas and hearts of bok choy. Or, serve it with thinly sliced cold chicken, smoked turkey, roast pork, or ham. The sauce keeps up to two weeks in the refrigerator.

¼ cup honey
1 cup Chicken Stock (see page 560)
2 tablespoons hot curry powder
1 tablespoon ground coriander
½ teaspoon cayenne pepper
½ teaspoon white pepper
⅓ cup Dijon mustard
3⅓ cups Mayonnaise (see page 519)

1. In a small saucepan combine honey and stock. Heat and stir until honey dissolves. Add curry powder, coriander, cayenne, and white pepper. Continue cooking over moderate heat until mixture is reduced to ¾ cup.

2. Remove from heat and cool completely. Add mustard and Mayonnaise. Mix well.

Makes about 4 cups.

WATERCRESS DIP WITH GREEN ONIONS AND BASIL

This dip is a showstopper—a nutty, coarse-textured creation fragrant with basil and brilliantly green. Beside it arrange a basket of crudités: cherry tomatoes, cauliflower and broccoli florets, snow peas, endive leaves, zucchini and carrot spears, artichoke hearts, and radishes or fennel. The dip keeps up to 10 days in the refrigerator. To stem the watercress easily, hold the base of the watercress in one hand. With the other hand, pull along the stem. All the leaves on one stem will come off with this one movement.

3 cups watercress, stems trimmed
¾ cup fresh small basil leaves
¼ cup minced garlic
½ cup good-quality olive oil
1 cup freshly grated Parmesan cheese
¾ cup whipping cream
½ cup finely ground walnuts
¼ cup minced green onions
   Salt and freshly ground pepper, to taste
1 tablespoon milk or water (optional)

1. In a blender combine watercress, basil, garlic, olive oil, and grated Parmesan cheese. Blend until pasty. Add cream and blend only until ingredients are mixed (do not overblend).

2. Transfer mixture to a bowl and stir in walnuts and green onion. Add salt and pepper. Mixture will thicken as it stands; if desired, add milk or water to thin it out before serving.

Makes 2 cups.

SALSA CRUDA

This basic uncooked salsa is found on the tables of practically every restaurant in Mexico. It is an indispensable presence at a Mexican meal and should be a part of any repast with a Mexican theme. Set it out as a dip for fried tortilla chips or as a sauce for grilled or broiled seafood. It is delightful spooned onto raw oysters or steamed mussels on the half shell; or try it wrapped up in a warm soft tortilla with crispy *carnitas* or pork in green chile.

1 yellow onion, peeled and minced
3 fresh ripe tomatoes, peeled, seeded, and coarsely chopped
2 tablespoons minced cilantro
1 clove garlic, minced
1 small green chile, minced, or more to taste
1 tablespoon fresh lime juice
   Salt, to taste

In a small bowl combine all ingredients except salt no more than 1 hour before serving. Do not add salt until the last minute. Salsa is best when freshly made.

Makes about ¾ cup.

■ CILANTRO RAITA

While this *raita* can be made without the chiles, the zest they add is a delicious contrast to the creamy coolness of the yogurt.

    8 tablespoons cilantro
    1 clove garlic
    ½ jalapeño chile
    1 teaspoon kosher salt
    1 cup plain yogurt

Mince cilantro, garlic, and chile. Stir this mixture and salt into yogurt. Chill.

Makes 1¼ cups.

■ SOY-BASED DIPPING SAUCES

Soy sauce with a little something mixed in provides an endless variety of dipping sauces. Each of the following recipes makes an individual serving.

Shellfish Dipping Sauce   Combine 1 tablespoon soy sauce, 1 teaspoon grated fresh ginger, and ½ teaspoon rice vinegar. This sauce is especially good with steamed crab or shrimp.

Soy and Chile Oil Dipping Sauce   Combine 1 tablespoon soy and ½ teaspoon chile oil (or to taste). Use with steamed dumplings.

Soy-Ginger Dipping Sauce   Combine 1 tablespoon soy sauce, ½ teaspoon grated or finely minced ginger, and a few drops sesame oil. Use with poached or steamed chicken.

Soy and Mustard Dipping Sauce   Combine 1 tablespoon soy sauce and Dijon mustard, to taste. Use with dumplings or vegetables with pork stuffings.

■ SWEET-AND-SOUR DIPPING SAUCE

This sweet-and-sour sauce tastes good with fried appetizers, because it is not too sweet. Try it with fried shrimp or Shanghai Spring Rolls (see page 389).

    ½ cup water
    ¼ cup rice wine vinegar
    3 tablespoons brown sugar
    1 teaspoon tomato paste
    1 tablespoon minced fresh ginger
    1 clove garlic, minced
    1 teaspoon soy sauce
    1 teaspoon cornstarch

1. In a small, heavy-bottomed saucepan combine ¼ cup of the water, the vinegar, sugar, tomato paste, ginger, garlic, and soy sauce; bring to a boil. Reduce heat and simmer 5 minutes.

2. Dissolve cornstarch in remaining water and add to sauce. Simmer until glossy. Strain before serving.

Makes ⅔ cup.

■ RASPBERRY SAUCE

Perhaps no other fruit sauce better complements so many desserts than this very simple, extremely delicious raspberry purée. It is a sauce you will use over and over again.

    2 cups fresh or thawed frozen raspberries
    4 to 5 tablespoons confectioners' sugar,
       sifted (optional)
    1 to 2 tablespoons kirsch (optional)

Purée raspberries in a food processor or blender until very smooth. Strain into a bowl, pressing the purée through the mesh. If you are using fresh or unsweetened frozen berries, whisk in 4 tablespoons sugar. Taste and add more sugar, if needed. Add kirsch, if desired. Refrigerate until ready to use. Sauce can be kept, covered, up to 2 days in refrigerator.

Makes about 1 cup.

■ STRAWBERRY SAUCE

For the best natural flavor, buy strawberries in the peak of their season. Serve with pound cake, poached or raw fruit, or over ice cream.

    2 cups strawberries, chopped
    ½ cup sugar
    2 to 4 tablespoons water (optional)

In a small bowl combine strawberries and sugar; let stand about 1 hour. In a small saucepan over medium heat, cook berry mixture about 5 minutes, mashing berries as they cook. Add the water 1 tablespoon at a time if berries are not very juicy. Serve hot or cold.

Makes about 2 cups.

■ HOT FUDGE SAUCE

What would any ice cream sundae be without thick, rich, chocolatey Hot Fudge Sauce?

    6 tablespoons unsalted butter
    ½ cup water
    4 ounces unsweetened chocolate
    1 cup sugar
    3 tablespoons light corn syrup
    ⅛ teaspoon salt
    2 teaspoons vanilla extract

1. In a heavy-bottomed 1-quart saucepan, melt butter in the water over medium heat. Bring to a boil, stirring constantly.

2. Add chocolate, stirring occasionally, until it melts. (Do not worry if chocolate lumps at this point; it will smooth out later.)

3. Add sugar, corn syrup, and salt. Boil 5 minutes. Remove from heat and add vanilla. Serve hot.

Makes about 2 cups.

OLD-FASHIONED BUTTERSCOTCH SAUCE

Butter and brown sugar are the characteristic flavors paired to make butterscotch.

- ½ cup unsalted butter
- 1 cup firmly packed light brown sugar
- 3 tablespoons light corn syrup
- ½ cup whipping cream

In small, heavy-bottomed saucepan, melt butter. Stir in brown sugar, corn syrup, and cream. Bring to a boil over medium heat. Cool slightly before serving.

Makes about 1½ cups.

OLD-FASHIONED CHOCOLATE SAUCE

This sauce is the kind your mother might have made, with a slightly grainy texture.

- 8 ounces bittersweet chocolate
- ½ cup light corn syrup
- ½ cup whipping cream
- 2 teaspoons vanilla extract

In a 1-quart saucepan, melt chocolate over low heat. Add corn syrup and stir until smooth. Stir in cream and vanilla. Serve warm or at room temperature.

Makes about 1½ cups.

SAUCE AND CONDIMENT, COMMERCIAL

Today's cook faces a nearly endless range of packaged sauces and condiments. These items give characteristic flavor to many dishes or provide a piquant counterpoint to a finished dish. This section describes some of the most widely available sauces and condiments.

Use   Sauces and condiments provide the seasoning or garnishing without which many dishes would be bland or uninteresting.

Availability   Check well-stocked supermarkets, ethnic markets, and specialty stores for the more exotic sauces and condiments.

Selection   See specific sauce or condiment.

Storage   See specific sauce or condiment.

BEAN PASTE, BROWN

Asian brown bean paste is a thick sauce made from fermented yellow soybeans, flour, water, and salt. Some varieties are quite smooth; others contain some whole beans. It adds saltiness, rich flavor, and body to bland vegetable and bean curd dishes and is used to season fish, beef, pork, and duck. Brown bean paste is available in cans and jars in Asian markets and well-stocked supermarkets. Store in a covered container in the refrigerator; it will keep for up to one year. Stir in peanut or sesame oil if sauce gets too thick or stiff.

CATSUP

The word *catsup* (also spelled *ketchup)* derives from *ketsiap,* a pickled fish sauce used centuries ago in China. The word has since been altered and applied to a variety of quite different condiments. In Indonesia *kecap manis* is a sweet, soy-based condiment. Early English ketchups were fermented relishes made of walnuts or mushrooms. The modern American version is a tomato-based product, seasoned with vinegar, sugar, onion, garlic, and spices. Catsup is widely used as a condiment for hamburgers, hot dogs, and French fries. Its sweet-tart tomato flavor is important to some versions of barbecue sauce, meat loaf, baked beans, and Chinese sweet-and-sour pork.

Pakoras are deep-fried Indian vegetable fritters. The refreshing coolness of the accompanying sauce, yogurt-based Cilantro Raita, makes a good foil for the highly seasoned fritter batter. The fritter recipe can be found on page 106.

Bottled catsup is available in all supermarkets. Unopened, it will keep indefinitely in a cool pantry. Store opened catsup tightly capped in refrigerator; it will keep indefinitely.

CHILE PASTE WITH GARLIC

Made of ground red chiles, soybeans, salt, oil, and garlic, this Chinese condiment adds a full-flavored spiciness to stir-fried dishes. To use, add a small amount to the oil in the wok when stir-frying. Chile paste is packed in jars and is available in Chinese markets. Store chile paste in an airtight jar in refrigerator; it will keep indefinitely.

CHILE SAUCES

The chile sauces outlined below are moderately thick to very thick. For information on thin chile-based sauces, see Hot-Pepper Sauce.

The array of commercial chile sauces is practically infinite, varying by manufacturer and by country of origin. The following categories should be helpful in identifying chile sauces for particular needs.

American Chili Sauce Most American-style chili sauces are thick, mild, tomato-based products heightened with horseradish or chili powder. They are bottled and widely available in supermarkets. Their primary use is in cocktail sauces for shellfish.

Chinese Chile Paste With Garlic See Chile Paste With Garlic (above).

Chinese Chile Sauce Simultaneously hot, sweet, and sour, this thick sauce is made from ground red chile, apricot, lemon, and garlic. It is added in small quantities to pickled vegetables, fish dishes, and stir-fries.

Indonesian Chile Paste Sambal is the generic word for Indonesia's chile-based condiments, which range from mild to fiery hot and may be raw or cooked. The contents of bottled sambals vary, but the main varieties found in this country are *sambal ulek* (*oelek*), made of ground fresh red chiles, salt, and vinegar; *sambal bajak* (*badjak*), similar to sambal ulek but flavored with dried shrimp or with nuts and onions; and *sambal manis,* sweeter and milder, containing onions and spices. Sambals add a lift to stir-fries, noodle dishes, and dipping sauces for spring rolls or grilled meats. Look for them in Asian markets.

Thai Chile Sauce Nam prik is the generic name for Thai chile sauces, of which there are many. Some type of nam prik is almost always on the table, to be used as a dipping sauce for spring rolls or grilled meats or to perk up soups or noodles. Some cooks make their own, although bottled versions are common. Most are based on red chile, garlic, sugar, salt, and vinegar and have a catsuplike consistency. However, some Thai chile sauces also contain dried shrimp, shrimp paste, fish sauce, coconut cream, tamarind liquid, shallot, or peanut. One of the most widely distributed brands in the United States is Sriracha sauce, a smooth, pourable blend of red chile, garlic, sugar, salt, and vinegar. Sriracha sauce and other bottled Thai chile sauces are sold in Asian markets.

Tunisian Chile Paste Known as *harissa,* Tunisian chile paste is made of dried red chile, garlic, olive oil, and occasionally caraway seed. It is packed in jars, cans, and tubes and sold in Middle Eastern markets. Harissa is used to season olives and is thinned with lemon juice and oil for use as a marinade for brochettes, a dressing for salads, or a condiment for couscous.

DRIED SHRIMP PASTE

Shrimp paste in various guises is essential in several Asian cuisines. From Chinese shrimp paste (*hom har jeung*) to Thai (*kapee*), Indonesian (*trasi*), Vietnamese (*mam ruoc*), and Philippine (*bagoong*) varieties, shrimp paste imparts a pungent, salty fish flavor to many Asian dishes. In that sense, it is the Asian equivalent of Western anchovies or anchovy paste. Chinese shrimp paste is made from dried ground shrimp in brine. Many of the Southeast Asian shrimp pastes are made from salted, fermented dried shrimp or anchovies.

Chinese shrimp paste adds a lively shrimp flavor to pork, fish, bean curd, vegetable, and fried rice dishes. Thai shrimp paste is an ingredient in most Thai curries and dipping sauces. Vietnamese cooks use shrimp paste to enliven soups and sauces. Filipinos employ bagoong as a table relish, adding it to stews, grilled fish, and steamed rice. Indonesian trasi is added to fried rice and to the spicy sambals (chile sauces) used as condiments. Characteristic to all of these cuisines, shrimp paste turns up in dozens of sauces, soups, stews, noodle and rice dishes, and sautés.

All these pastes have a strong odor and should be used sparingly; however, cooking moderates both odor and flavor. Look for dried shrimp paste in ethnic markets. They are available either fresh (liquid, usually bottled) or dried (in paper-wrapped bricks, cakes, plastic tubs, or jars). They range in color and texture from the grayish pink, pourable Chinese shrimp sauce to the chocolate-brown Indonesian trasi, which is sold in firm bricks or sausagelike rolls. Dried shrimp paste can be stored, tightly wrapped, in a cool, dry place for months. Liquid shrimp pastes should be covered and refrigerated after opening.

FISH SAUCE

Pourable sauces made from salted fermented fish are an important seasoning agent in most Southeast Asian cuisines. They go by different names in Thailand (*nam pla*), Vietnam (*nuoc mam*), the Philippines (*patis*), Burma (*ngan-pya-ye* or *ngapi*), Indonesia (*petis*), and China (*yu lu* or *yu chiap*), but all have a salty and strong flavor. Although brands differ in strength, in general the Philippine fish sauce is milder than the Vietnamese and Thai varieties. These fish sauces are also referred to as fish's gravy.

Fish sauce adds a pungent, fishlike flavor to dipping sauces, soups, stir-fries, salad dressings, noodle and rice dishes, and a variety of other preparations. Like salt in Western cooking, it is used to heighten flavors, but fish sauce should not be noticeable itself. Bottled fish sauce is available in Asian markets. Opened fish sauce will keep indefinitely if tightly capped and refrigerated.

GRAVY BROWNER

Commercial gravy browner is a liquid product based on caramel and water; most brands also contain seasonings such as dried vegetables, salt, dried herbs, and spices. Gravy browner adds a rich brown color and some flavor to stews, sauces, and soups. Although it duplicates the color that roasted veal and beef bones give to stock, it does not impart the intense, meaty flavor derived from real bones. It is also used to contribute appetizing color to microwaved roasts that do not develop color from surface caramelization. Brush on a mixture of gravy browner and water for meats and gravy browner and oil for fowl. Gravy browner is available in jars in most supermarkets. Follow package directions to use.

GRENADINE SYRUP

Historically, grenadine syrup was derived from pomegranate juice. Today most bottled grenadine syrup is made with artificial flavors and colors and contains no pomegranate juice at all. The syrup has the cherry red color of pomegranate juice and a vaguely similar flavor.

Grenadine syrup figures in a variety of drinks, such as the tequila sunrise and the Shirley Temple. It can also be spooned over ice cream or added to sparkling water or lemonade for sweetness and color. Some brands of grenadine syrup contain a small amount of alcohol; check the label. Bottled grenadine is available in liquor stores and some supermarkets. Store grenadine containing alcohol in a cool place after opening; syrup without alcohol should be refrigerated after opening. Both will keep indefinitely.

HOISIN SAUCE

A sweet, jamlike sauce based on fermented soybeans, commercial *hoisin* sauce may also contain flour, sugar, chile, garlic, vinegar, and red beans. Hoisin sauce is used in Chinese cooking both as an ingredient and as a table condiment. It adds a sweet, pungent flavor to stir-fried shellfish, chicken, pork, and vegetables. It is often spread on the pancakes served with Peking duck or barbecued pork. In stir-frying, hoisin sauce is usually added to the wok before the main ingredients to give the sugars a chance to caramelize. It comes packed in cans and jars and is sold in Chinese markets. To store, transfer canned hoisin sauce to an airtight nonreactive container; bottled sauce may be kept in its bottle. Hoisin sauce will keep indefinitely in the refrigerator. If it thickens, thin with sesame or peanut oil.

HOT-PEPPER SAUCE

Most of the hot-pepper sauces available in this country are made of hot fresh or dried peppers and vinegar. Tabasco Sauce, a brand named after the region in Mexico where the peppers originated, is certainly the best known. Tabasco Sauce is made from fresh peppers that are ground, salted, and aged in oak barrels for three years before being mixed with vinegar. Several other commercial hot-pepper sauces are based on whole fresh peppers packed in vinegar or sherry.

Hot-pepper sauce adds a lift to tomato juice cocktails, gumbo, cooked greens, seafood stews, oysters, eggs, barbecue sauce, and a variety of Cajun and Creole dishes. In the American South, it is a common table condiment to be added at will to any savory dish. Brands vary considerably in pungency; it takes only a few drops of the most incendiary varieties to add zest to a dish. Tabasco Sauce is available in supermarkets. Other brands of liquid hot-pepper sauce—Crystal, Red Rooster, and Louisiana Hot Sauce—are also sold in some supermarkets and in specialty stores.

Hot-pepper sauce will keep for six months in a cool, dark place but begins to lose flavor if stored longer. Refrigerated, it will keep indefinitely. For information on thick chile-based sauces, see Chile Sauces, page 524.

MISO

Also known as soybean paste or bean paste, miso is made from boiled soybeans that are crushed and fermented. It is an extremely important part of the Japanese diet, eaten in some form almost daily. There are several varieties of miso, made by adding another grain to the soybeans. Yellow miso is made from soybeans and rice and is slightly sweet; it is good for dressings. Red miso is made from barley and soybeans; it is heartier and good in soups. A very dark, thick miso is also available, made primarily from soybeans.

In this country miso is best known as the milky ingredient in Miso Soup, a light, slightly nutty soup that often introduces a meal in a Japanese restaurant. In Japan miso soup is often served for breakfast. Miso is thinned with dashi for use as a salad dressing; it is also brushed on grilled skewered vegetables and seafood to make a category of dishes known as *dengaku*.

Most supermarkets carry at least one variety of miso and Japanese markets carry several. Miso is packed in tubs, jars, tubes, and plastic bags and is usually stocked in the refrigerated section. Refrigerate miso and use within three months; it loses flavor upon standing. Thin miso with dashi before adding to soup to ensure that it blends smoothly.

MUSTARD

See MUSTARD.

ORANGE FLOWER WATER

A highly perfumed, clear liquid, orange flower water is distilled from fresh orange blossoms. In Morocco orange flower water is sometimes used to scent the water poured over hands before dining. Middle Eastern cooks use it to scent rice dishes, puddings, cookies, cakes, and pastries. It is an ingredient in some cocktails, such as the Ramos gin fizz. The fragrance of orange flower water dissipates with air and heat; for maximum effect, add it to cooked dishes when they are cool or cooling. Orange flower water is available in liquor stores and some supermarkets. Store in a cool, dark place; it will keep for several months but will gradually lose strength.

OYSTER SAUCE

This thick, pourable brown liquid is made by fermenting dried oysters with soy sauce and brine. The best oyster sauces are fermented for several years before bottling. They are widely used in Cantonese cooking as a flavor enhancer. Chinese cooks use oyster sauce to impart richness and body to many dishes. It is added to stir-fried meats and vegetables and is offered as a table condiment for roast pork and cold chicken. Oyster sauce in bottles, jars, and cans is readily available in Asian markets. It will keep indefinitely in the refrigerator. Some brands contain cornstarch and will thicken a sauce slightly; adjust ingredients accordingly. Because oyster sauce is salty, most recipes calling for it do not require salt.

PLUM SAUCE

Made from plums, apricots, chiles, vinegar, and sugar, this thick Chinese condiment is dark amber in color, with a sweet-tart, slightly hot flavor. Also known as duck sauce, it accompanies roast duck, pork, spareribs, and egg rolls. Plum sauce is sometimes used as a basting sauce for roast duck and as a sauce enrichment in stir-fried dishes. Plum sauce, bottled or canned, is widely available in Chinese markets. Once opened, canned plum sauce should be transferred to an airtight nonreactive container; it may be refrigerated for up to one year.

ROSE WATER

A highly perfumed, clear liquid, rose water is distilled from fragrant rose petals. A more concentrated form is known as rose essence. Rose water is a popular flavoring in Middle Eastern cooking, added to orange salads, rice pudding, and custard-filled pastries. In India, where rose flavoring is also appreciated, rose essence is preferred and used in a version of ice cream, in the yogurt drink called *lassi*, in sweet carrot pudding, and in the syrup served with fried dessert dumplings. Iranian cooks make a sherbet of rose water, sugar, and water. Rose water is also required in some exotic cocktails. The essence is much stronger than the water and should be added drop by drop.

Bottled rose water is available in some supermarkets, liquor stores, and specialty markets. Rose water and rose essence are sold in Middle Eastern and Indian markets. Store rose water and rose essence in tightly closed bottles in a cool, dark place. They will keep for at least one year but lose strength with age. Because these fragrances are alcohol based, they are volatile (dissipating with heat). Add them to cooled or cooling mixtures for maximum effect.

SOY SAUCE

Essential to Chinese and Japanese cooking, soy sauce is a fermented product based on soy beans. Most brands also contain wheat. Tamari is essentially the same as soy sauce but is made without wheat (see Tamari). Although brands and styles vary in color and flavor, most soy sauce is dark brown. Japanese soy sauce has a relatively sweet flavor and is less salty than either Chinese or American varieties. Chinese soy sauce is extremely salty. Black soy sauce, specified in some recipes, has molasses added; it is richer and saltier in flavor than regular soy sauce. Most American-made soy sauce falls between the two styles. The most widely distributed brand, Kikkoman, is light bodied, light flavored, and lacks the sweetness of the Japanese brands and the saltiness of the Chinese. Synthetic soy sauces made from hydrolized soy protein, which are also manufactured in this country and have wide distribution, are a poor substitute for the real thing.

Soy sauce is used by Chinese and Japanese cooks in much the same way that Westerners use salt—as a flavor enhancer. In China it is not considered a table condiment; rather, it is added to foods before or during cooking. Soy sauce adds a distinctive fermented flavor to almost all stir-fried dishes, whether of meat, chicken, fish, or vegetables; it adds a brown gloss to steamed chicken and roast duck; it flavors noodle dishes, both hot and cold. In Japan soy sauce is on the table to be used as a dipping sauce for sushi, sashimi, and tempura; it is used in soups such as *shabu-shabu* and provides the base for dozens of basting sauces brushed on pork, seafood, or chicken while grilling.

All supermarkets stock American-made soy sauce in bottles or cans. Many also stock synthetic soy sauce and low-sodium soy sauce. Asian markets stock imported soy sauces from China and Japan. Because of its high salt content, soy sauce does not require refrigeration. It will keep indefinitely in a cool, dark place. Low-sodium soy sauce must be refrigerated.

STEAK SAUCE

Although steak sauces vary from manufacturer to manufacturer, most are liquid to semiliquid condiments with a sweet-sour-salty balance of flavors. The most popular brand in this country, A-1 Sauce, contains tomato paste, vinegar, corn syrup, raisins, orange peel, and other herbs, spices, and seasonings. Other popular brands contain chile peppers, molasses, or soy sauce.

Sprinkle steak sauce on steaks, chops, or hamburgers before or after grilling or add to barbecue sauces and marinades. Most supermarkets carry a variety of bottled steak sauces, which should be stored in the refrigerator after opening; steak sauce will keep indefinitely.

SWEET-AND-SOUR SAUCE

The contrast of sweet-and-sour flavors is important to Chinese cooking but bottled sweet-and-sour sauce was created for the American palate. Most commercial versions of this sauce are thick with cornstarch and may contain food coloring. The texture and flavor they impart are far removed from the texture and flavor of authentic Chinese sweet-and-sour dishes. In the American kitchen, the sauce can be used to glaze ham or spareribs. Bottled sweet-and-sour sauce is available in most supermarkets and some Asian markets. After opening, store lidded jar in the refrigerator; it will keep indefinitely.

TABASCO SAUCE

See Hot-Pepper Sauce.

TAMARI

A cultured and fermented liquid soybean product, tamari resembles soy sauce, but is thicker and stronger in flavor than soy. It is used in Japan as a dipping sauce and a base for basting sauces. Tamari is available in many health-food stores and Japanese markets. A salt-free tamari is also available in some markets. Refrigerate tamari after opening; it will keep indefinitely.

THAI CURRY PASTE

In Thai cooking, many dishes seasoned with a paste of herbs and spices are known as curries. The major types of curry paste in Thailand are red (based on red chile peppers), green (based on green chiles and coriander), and yellow (based on yellow chiles and turmeric). Many cooks make their own curry pastes regularly, altering them with herbs and spices to suit individual tastes. However, bottled curry pastes are widely available and are acceptable to many Thai cooks.

Check Asian markets for bottled Thai curry paste. After opening, store lidded jars in refrigerator; they will keep for several weeks.

WORCESTERSHIRE SAUCE

A liquid condiment reputedly devised by two British chemists in the nineteenth century, Worcestershire sauce today is a fixture in most American refrigerators. The exact formula is a secret, but the label lists vinegar, molasses, tamarind, anchovies, and spices. It is dark brown, with a distinctive flavor that incorporates sweet, sour, salty, and spicy elements. It can be sprinkled on hamburgers or

steaks before or after cooking; some cooks add it to barbecue sauce, marinades, and basting sauces. It is used in most renditions of Caesar salad, in cocktail dips and cheese spreads, in English steak and kidney pie, in steak tartare, Welsh rarebit, and Bloody Marys.

Bottled Worcestershire sauce is available in supermarkets. Refrigerate after opening; it will keep indefinitely.

Grilled Italian sausages and sautéed bell peppers and onions are robust accompaniments to omelets. Cook the meat outdoors on a grill or indoors in a skillet.

SAUSAGE

Highly seasoned ground pork is the basis for most of the world's sausages, although some delicious sausages are made using chicken, turkey, game birds, and even seafood. Perhaps the best definition is that sausage is made from ground meat, usually stuffed in a casing (but not necessarily), usually highly seasoned with herbs and/or spices, and frequently laced with such flavorful additions as cubes of fat, truffles, pistachios, peppercorns, wine, or chiles.

A piquant green sauce unites all elements in Boiled Dinner Bolognese (recipe is on page 530). If you wish, serve the cooking broth as a first course. Or, strain and freeze it to use later as the base for your next bollito misto.

Use Sausage is used in sandwiches, stuffings, pasta sauces, savory pies and pastries, soups, casseroles, and stews. From breakfast links to the midday hot dog to a dinner of grilled wurst and potatoes, sausage satisfies American appetites all day long.

Availability Most of the sausage available in the United States is made there or in Canada. Imported pork products must conform to extremely strict federal regulations and are, at this writing, essentially unavailable in the United States.

The major types of sausages sold in America are described in the following pages. Although supermarkets carry a variety of fresh and cured sausage, the best sausages are generally found in ethnic markets and specialty stores. Italian, German, and French markets are good sources for sausages made by traditional European methods.

Selection An off odor is the first clue to deterioration in sausage; avoid any that smell strong or sour. Fresh sausage is especially perishable and should be bought from a market with a rapid turnover.

Storage Because it is so perishable, sausage should be refrigerated and used within two or three days or it can be frozen for up to two months. If the meat has been lightly smoked, it can be refrigerated for up to one week. Cooked sausages can be kept for up to one week in the refrigerator or two months in the freezer; if vacuum-packed and unopened, they can be refrigerated longer. Semidry sausages may be kept at room temperature for two or three days; for longer keeping, refrigerate for up to three weeks. Dry sausages may be stored unsliced at cool room temperature for six weeks; after slicing, refrigerate and use within three weeks. Both semidry and dry sausages may be frozen for up to three months, but with some loss of flavor and texture.

FRESH SAUSAGE

Made from raw ground and seasoned meat, fresh sausage is often bound with eggs, bread crumbs, or cereals. It may or may not be stuffed in a casing and may or may not be smoked. It must be cooked before it is served. Some of the better-known types of fresh sausage are described below.

Bockwurst A German-style veal sausage, occasionally with pork added, *bockwurst* is usually first boiled, then grilled or panfried. It is traditionally served with potatoes, mustard, and German beer.

Chaurice See Chorizo.

Chorizo Both Mexican- and Spanish-style *chorizos* are available. The Mexican type is made from fresh pork and is highly seasoned with vinegar, chiles, garlic, and cumin. It is stuffed into casings and made into links, but most recipes call for removing the casings and crumbling and frying the chorizo. Spanish-style chorizo is usually made from smoked pork and is firmer than the Mexican version; it can be grilled in its casing and sliced for use in soups and bean dishes. *Chaurice* is the Cajun version, made of ground pork highly seasoned with garlic and hot red pepper.

Cotechino This large, Italian-style pork sausage is usually seasoned with garlic, pepper, fennel seed, and wine. The sausage is poached whole and served hot, with potato salad, lentils, or other boiled meats and vegetables as part of a *bollito misto* (mixed boil).

Crépinette A French-style sausage that is shaped into a patty and wrapped in caul fat, most *crépinettes* are made of ground pork and seasoned with herbs, although ground chicken, cooked spinach, and nuts such as pistachios and chestnuts are other common additions. They may be panfried without any fat, or brushed with butter, coated with bread crumbs, and grilled.

Italian Link Sausage Most Italian markets carry hot and sweet versions of this link sausage. Both are pork sausages seasoned with garlic, wine, and fennel, but the hot version has red pepper, too. To cook, the sausages are poached briefly, then panfried or grilled. The meat can be removed from the casings and used on pizzas or in sauces or stuffings.

Saucisson à l'Ail   This French garlic sausage is comparable to Italian *cotechino* without fennel. It is usually served with lentils, potato salad, mashed potatoes, or white beans.

Weisswurst   This white German sausage is made from veal. After steaming it can be eaten in a bun with mustard or cut up and added to stews and soups.

COOKED SAUSAGE

Although the following sausages are generally sold fully cooked and ready to eat, many taste better when hot; they are usually reheated before serving.

Andouille   Usually salted and smoked, *andouille* is a large French-style tripe sausage that is most often eaten cold in thin slices. *Andouillette* is a similar but smaller sausage, made of tripe and spices stuffed in a sausage casing; it is not usually smoked. Andouillettes are usually grilled and served hot with mashed potatoes, potato salad, or French fries.

Blood Sausage   The British call this sausage *black pudding;* the French, *boudin noir;* Cajuns, *boudin rouge;* and the Germans, *blutwurst.* It is made from pork blood, pork fat, and seasonings. French varieties usually contain bread crumbs and cream; English varieties may include barley or oatmeal; Cajun blood sausage commonly contains cayenne pepper and garlic. They are generally grilled or sautéed in butter or bacon fat and served hot with French fries, potato salad, mashed potatoes, or sauerkraut.

Bologna   Spelled baloney in American markets, *bologna* is the term applied to a large variety of lightly smoked sausages that are sliced thin and eaten cold. Bologna may be made of pork, beef, turkey, veal, ham, or a combination. It may be fine or coarse textured and lightly or richly spiced. Bologna is usually served in thin slices as an appetizer or sandwich filling.

Boudin Blanc   This smooth-textured French-style white sausage is made of pork, veal, and/or chicken, usually bound with cream, onions, and bread crumbs. *Boudin blanc* is usually panfried or grilled before serving and is often accompanied by mashed potatoes.

Bratwurst   A German-style pork or pork and veal sausage, bratwurst may be fresh or cooked. If fresh, it must be boiled first. Fresh bratwurst is often simmered in beer, then panfried or grilled, and served with sauerkraut. Cooked bratwurst is reheated—either steamed, panfried, or grilled—before serving.

Braunschweiger   See Liverwurst.

Frankfurter   Today, *frankfurter* is a generic name for a huge variety of sausages, also known as wieners or hot dogs. Frankfurters may be made of pork, beef, turkey, chicken, or a combination; kosher franks are all beef. Frankfurters range from the tiny cocktail size (24 to a pound) to foot-long dogs (4 to a pound), but most are about 4 inches long and 8 or 10 to a pound. Frankfurters are usually steamed or grilled before being served in buns with such optional accompaniments as mustard, relish, chili, and sauerkraut. Frankfurters may also be cut into chunks and added to stews or soups, such as old-fashioned split pea soup.

Head Cheese   Composed of small pieces of hog's head bound in gelatin, head cheese is usually seasoned with white wine and spices. It is sliceable and commonly served cold with vinaigrette and a salad.

Knockwurst   Similar to frankfurters, but usually thicker and more highly seasoned, knockwurst (or knackwurst) are German-style sausages that may be cooked whole and served like hot dogs or may be sliced and added to potato salad.

Liverwurst and Braunschweiger   Both variations on the same theme, these two sausages are smooth textured, spreadable, and usually made of pork liver (sometimes beef or goose liver). American-style liverwurst is usually not smoked, but German-style braunschweiger usually is. Both are served as an appetizer with crackers or as a sandwich filling.

Thuringer   Several types of German-style sausage are called Thuringer. It may be fresh, in which case it must be poached before serving, then panfried or grilled. Or it may be semidry, smoked, and ready-to-eat. The semidry type is often served as an appetizer, thinly sliced, or cut up and added to split pea or bean soups.

SEMIDRY AND DRY SAUSAGE

Semidry sausages have been smoked to remove some of the moisture. They are often called summer sausages, a legacy from prerefrigeration days. Because they were partially dried, they could be kept for some time without spoiling, even in warm weather.

Fully dry sausages may be smoked or unsmoked but have been dried from one to six months for preservation. They usually have a slightly shriveled exterior and are firm enough to slice thinly.

Cervelas   A semidry French-style pork sausage, *cervelas* is usually seasoned with garlic. To serve, it is poached, then sliced and accompanied with mustard and potato salad. It is also occasionally poached, then wrapped in brioche dough and baked.

Cervelat   The name *cervelat* is applied to a variety of Middle European–style summer sausages. Most are made of pork or beef and are smoked. They may be thinly sliced as an appetizer or diced and added to salads, soups, or bean dishes.

Kielbasa This is the Polish word for sausage, usually applied in this country to a smoked, semidry sausage seasoned highly with garlic, pepper, paprika, and herbs. Most American-made *kielbasa* is shaped into long, thick links that may weigh a pound or more. They are usually made of pork but some contain beef or veal as well. Kielbasa can be sliced and eaten cold, but it is usually poached and served with potatoes, lentils, or sauerkraut. It may also be sliced and added to soups and stews or used in recipes that call for garlic sausage.

Linguiça A Portuguese-style pork sausage seasoned with red pepper and garlic, *linguiça* is similar to chorizo but generally thinner, firmer, and milder. It is diced and scrambled with eggs or added to omelets. It may be added to soups, or cut into chunks, skewered, and grilled.

Mortadella Smooth-textured mortadella is an Italian-style pork sausage larded with cubes of fat and black peppercorns. Most domestic mortadella is about 6 inches in diameter; in Italy it can be much wider. Mortadella is thinly sliced and eaten cold as an appetizer; it may also be diced and added to stuffings.

Pepperoni Another dried type of Italian-style sausage, pepperoni is made of beef or pork, usually 1 to 1½ inches in diameter, and highly seasoned with red and black pepper. It is thinly sliced and served as an appetizer or a pizza garnish.

Salami Including a variety of dried, sliceable sausages made throughout Europe, most salami is made of raw pork or beef that is highly seasoned, stuffed into casings, and air-dried. It is usually not smoked. Popular salami made in the United States include Genoa and French Lyonnaise types, the latter identified as *saucisson sec*. Salami is usually sliced thin and served as an appetizer or sandwich filling. Jewish delicatessens often scramble eggs with sliced kosher all-beef salami.

■ HOMEMADE PORK SAUSAGE

Pork butt often contains a generous proportion of fat. Trim off some of it if you prefer a leaner sausage—but not all of it. Fat makes the sausage juicy and carries the flavors of the seasonings. Grind the meat, using a meat grinder or a food processor, then mix in savory seasonings.

   2 pounds boneless pork butt, cut in 1-inch cubes
   1 clove garlic, minced or pressed
1½ teaspoons dried sage
   1 teaspoon salt
  ½ teaspoon *each* coarsely ground black pepper and dried summer savory or marjoram
  ¼ teaspoon *each* ground allspice and dried thyme
  ⅛ teaspoon cayenne pepper

1. *To make in a meat grinder:* Using coarse blade, grind pork cubes twice. *To make in a food processor:* Spread pork cubes in a single layer on a baking sheet and place in freezer until meat is firm but not frozen (about 20 minutes). Then process, using short on-off bursts, until meat is coarsely ground.

2. Using mortar and pestle or blender, combine garlic, sage, salt, black pepper, summer savory, allspice, thyme, and cayenne thoroughly. Add to ground meat and mix well until seasonings are evenly distributed. (Use your hands, if desired.)

3. Wrap well and refrigerate for 8 hours or overnight to blend flavors.

4. Form into patties and cook in a frying pan over medium-low heat until well browned and crusty, or use in recipes as directed.

Makes 2 pounds.

■ BOILED DINNER BOLOGNESE

A dazzling array of meats and vegetables, each added at just the right stage to achieve tenderness, makes up the Italian simmered dinner known as *bollito misto*. Look for the distinctive, plump *cotechino* sausage in Italian delicatessens; if it isn't stocked regularly, perhaps the dealer can order it for you. It contributes a lot of flavor to the dish.

   1 beef rump roast (3½ to 4 lb)
 12 cups water or Beef Stock (see page 560)
   1 fresh beef tongue (2½ to 3 lb)
   1 veal shank (1 to 1½ lb), cut through bone into 3 sections
   1 large onion, finely chopped
   4 large carrots
   2 stalks celery, sliced
   5 sprigs parsley
   1 tablespoon salt
  ¼ teaspoon *each* whole allspice and black peppercorns
   1 cotechino sausage (1 to 1½ lb)
  4 to 6 leeks, well rinsed, with coarse outer leaves discarded and leafy tops trimmed to about 5 inches
 10 to 12 small red potatoes, scrubbed (unpeeled)
   1 small savoy cabbage (about 1 lb), cut into 8 wedges

Green Sauce

  ½ cup olive oil
  ¼ cup white wine vinegar
   3 green onions, coarsely chopped
   1 cup lightly packed parsley sprigs
   2 tablespoons capers
   1 clove garlic, minced
   1 tablespoon anchovy paste
      Pinch freshly ground pepper
  ¼ cup lightly packed fresh basil leaves *or* 1 tablespoon dried basil
      Salt (optional)

1. Preheat oven to 500° F. Place rump roast in a shallow, heavy roasting pan. Bake, uncovered, turning once, until meat is well browned (20 to 25 minutes). Transfer roast to a 10- to 12-quart, heavy-bottomed kettle with cover. Add a little of the water to juices left in bottom of roasting pan, stirring to loosen any brown drippings that may be stuck to pan bottom and to blend water, juices, and drippings; pour water-drippings mixture over roast in kettle.

2. To kettle add tongue, the 3 pieces of veal shank, and chopped onion. Slice one of the carrots and add it to meats with celery, parsley sprigs, salt, allspice, peppercorns, and remaining water. Bring to a boil over medium heat, cover, reduce heat, and simmer for 2 hours. Add sausage, cover again, and cook for 1 hour more until meats are tender.

3. Meanwhile, cut remaining carrots lengthwise into quarters; cut quarters crosswise into halves. Add carrot pieces to kettle with trimmed whole leeks and whole unpeeled potatoes; cook until meats and potatoes are tender (about 45 minutes).

4. With a slotted spoon remove tongue and set it aside. Remove rump roast, veal shank, and sausage to a large, heated platter. Surround with leeks, potatoes, and carrots. Cover lightly with foil and keep warm while preparing cooked tongue.

5. Cut off and discard bones and gristle at thick end of tongue. Slit the skin on the underside, and starting at the thick end, peel it off. Add tongue to meats and vegetables on platter.

6. Add cabbage wedges to gently boiling broth and cook, uncovered, until cabbage is tender when pierced with a knife and bright green (8 to 10 minutes). While cabbage cooks, prepare Green Sauce. Add cooked cabbage to meats and vegetables on platter.

7. If you wish to serve broth as a first course, strain through a wire sieve, taste and salt if needed, and serve it hot. Then carve meats and serve with vegetables and Green Sauce.

Serves 10 to 12.

Green Sauce In a food processor fitted with a metal blade or a blender, combine olive oil, wine vinegar, green onions, parsley sprigs, capers, garlic, anchovy paste, pepper, and basil. Process or whirl until smooth. Taste and add salt if needed. Serve at room temperature.

Makes about 1¼ cups.

Recipes and Related Information

Barbecued Pork Ribs and Sausages, 292;
Cassoulet, 556; Choucroute Garni, 75; Red Beans
and Rice, 32; Split Pea Soup, Black Forest Style, 565;
Stuffed Mirliton, 110.

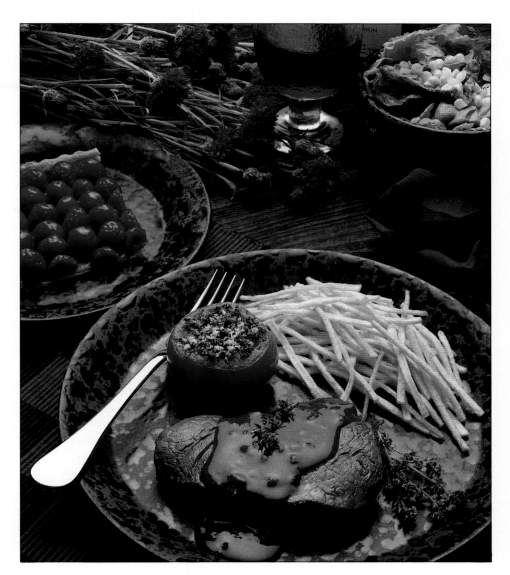

SAUTE, TO

Sautéing has been done for centuries, with the French and Chinese its most accomplished practitioners. In fact sautéing and stir-frying are the same technique (see STIR-FRY). In its strictest culinary application, sauté, from the French *sauter* (to jump), means to rapidly cook small, uniformly sized pieces of food over high heat in oil or fat in a specially designed straight-sided, shallow pan with an extralong handle. To keep the food from sticking, the pan is kept in constant motion, so the food "jumps" in the pan. More typically, sautéed food is turned, rather than tossed. Any skillet made of a material that conducts heat well can be substituted for a sauté pan.

When the food is browned on all sides, it is removed from the pan, set aside, and kept warm while the juices are made into an accompanying sauce. Deglazing removes caramelized bits of food from the bottom of the pan and incorporates them into the liquid that is the base for the sauce (see DEGLAZE).

Sautéed Beef Steaks Marchand de Vin is a beef- and red-wine-lover's dream dish—tender, aged beef and a deglazing sauce of good red wine, enriched at the last minute with a bit of butter. The recipe is on page 533.

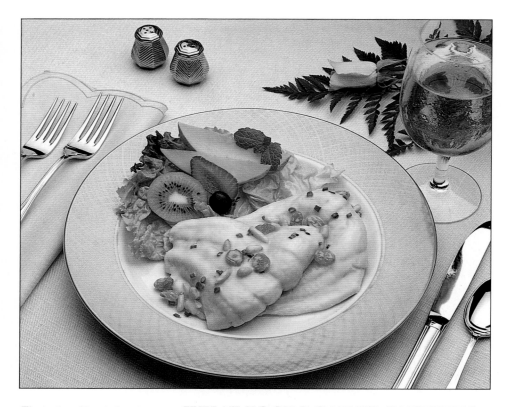

The tastes of toasted nuts and sweet raisins offer an interesting contrast to the mild-flavored fish in Sole With Almonds, Pine Nuts, and White Raisins. Sauté the nuts in clarified butter to bring out their flavor.

WHAT FOODS CAN BE SAUTEED?

Meats of the highest quality are most suitable for sautéing. Among the dark meats, thin beef steaks and relatively small lamb chops are ideal because they cook through in the time it takes to brown them. Sautéing is also a favorite way to cook chicken livers or thin slices of beef or calf's liver. It is a perfect technique for cooking slim pieces of tender light meats, such as veal chops, and slices of veal scallop, chicken breast, or turkey breast. Food should be uniform in size so the pieces cook quickly and evenly; for this reason slices of meat or poultry are often pounded before being sautéed.

Any fish fillet can be sautéed. Try to choose fillets that are relatively firm fleshed and do not appear to be falling apart. Short fish fillets are easiest to sauté because there is less chance of breakage during turning or transferring to the serving platter. Cut fillets in half before cooking them if they are too long to be handled easily. Very thin fillets such as sole require only about 2 minutes of sautéing on each side. Fish steaks up to 1 inch thick and small whole fish are suitable for sautéing, too, as are shrimp and scallops.

Almost any vegetable can be sautéed. Those that are naturally tender, such as peppers, mushrooms, and zucchini, can be cut into small pieces and sautéed. Others, such as broccoli and cauliflower, should first be blanched to soften them slightly. The blanching process is actually a timesaver: Cut vegetables in appropriately sized pieces, blanch in boiling water and refresh in cold water to stop cooking; then just before serving, sauté vegetables briefly in butter to heat and flavor them.

GETTING STARTED

A successful sauté depends upon three factors. First, the fat must be hot. If it is not hot enough, the food will stick to the pan, the outside won't be seared, and the juices will escape. Second, the food must be absolutely dry. Moisture on the food forms a layer of steam between the food and the fat that prevents searing and browning. Third—and many cooks overlook this factor—the pan must not be too crowded. Space between pieces of food is a prerequisite for thorough browning. Crowding causes steaming, rather than searing, and results in the juices escaping from the food into the pan. It is equally important not to allow too much space between pieces of food in too large of a pan (the more the food covers the fat, the less likely the fat will burn).

Oil alone, or a combination of butter and oil, is used for sautéing. Oil can withstand higher temperatures without burning than butter and is often the choice for searing meats. Butter gives a lovely flavor, but burns easily at higher temperatures; restaurant chefs often add 1 or 2 tablespoons of cooking oil to the butter to raise the temperature at which it will begin to smoke. Or, they use clarified butter (see page 68), which can heat to a higher temperature without deteriorating than unclarified butter.

To protect the delicate flesh of white meats, poultry, and fish from sticking to the pan, cooks often flour these foods lightly before sautéing. Floured meat browns more easily than uncoated meat and has an appetizing appearance. If a nonstick pan is used, these foods can be sautéed without being floured but they will not brown as well. Red meat does not require flouring because the higher fat content helps to keep it from adhering to the pan.

Although the coating has a protective function, it too should be treated with care. Floured food should not be allowed to sit for more than a few minutes because moisture from the food will make the coating gummy. For the same reason, the coated pieces of food should never be piled one on top of the other.

THE SAUTE PANTRY

If the simplicity and speed of sautéing appeal to you, consider having the following on hand as staples in the refrigerator and pantry.

In the refrigerator Butter (including clarified butter), cream or half-and-half, eggs, sauce bases, and stock. Freeze stock and sauce bases that will be held longer than a few days.

On the shelf Bread crumbs, flour, herbs and spices, oils, canned tomatoes and tomato purée, red and white wine, sherry, and brandy.

Equipment Sauté pan or skillet, wooden spoons, slotted spoons, spatula, meat pounder, and paper towels.

SOLE WITH ALMONDS, PINE NUTS, AND WHITE RAISINS

This is a variation of a Venetian dish called *sfogi in saòr*, which means savory soles.

    ¼ cup white raisins
    2 cups dry white wine
    5 tablespoons Clarified Butter (see page 68)
    ¼ cup slivered almonds
    6 sole fillets
    1 teaspoon salt
    ½ teaspoon freshly ground pepper
    4 tablespoons flour
    3 tablespoons unsalted butter
    2 tablespoons minced shallot
       Salt and freshly ground pepper, to taste
    2 tablespoons pine nuts

1. Soak raisins in white wine for 30 minutes. Remove raisins and reserve both wine and raisins.

2. In sauté pan heat the 5 tablespoons clarified butter. Add almonds to pan and sauté until they begin to color. Remove almonds with slotted spoon and drain on paper towels.

3. Sprinkle fish with the 1 teaspoon salt, ½ teaspoon pepper, and flour. Add fish to pan and sauté each side to a golden brown. Remove fish to a warm platter. Add the 3 tablespoons butter to pan. When butter has melted, add shallot and cook until soft. Add reserved wine and raisins. Cook for 2 to 3 minutes and season to taste with salt and pepper. Add pine nuts to sauce and pour over fish.

Serves 6.

SAUTEED VEGETABLE MEDLEY

This quick side dish pairs well with most roasted meats.

    ¾ pound small new potatoes, quartered
    1 large carrot, cut in sticks
    4 small white onions, peeled and halved
    2 tablespoons butter
    ½ pound (20 medium) mushrooms, halved
    1 teaspoon dried basil
       Grated Parmesan, Romano, or Sapsago cheese, for garnish (optional)

1. In a large saucepan cook potatoes in boiling salted water to cover for 10 minutes; drain and set aside. Blanch carrot and onions briefly and refresh in cold water to stop cooking.

2. Meanwhile, in a large skillet melt butter; then add mushrooms to skillet and sauté.

3. Add potatoes, carrot, and onions to skillet, and sauté briefly with mushrooms.

4. Add basil; toss vegetables to mix. Garnish with cheese, if desired.

Serves 4.

SAUTEED BEEF STEAKS MARCHAND DE VIN

This simple dish, "wine merchant style," relies on two basic ingredients: good beef and good red wine.

    1½ to 2 pounds tender beef steaks (filet mignon, strip, sirloin), ¾ to 1 inch thick
        Salt and freshly ground pepper, to taste
    2   tablespoons minced shallot
    4   tablespoons butter
    ½   cup red wine

1. In a heavy skillet over medium-high heat, rub a piece of fat trimmed from steak. Cook steaks, turning once and season after turning with salt and pepper. Test for doneness by pushing on steak with finger: A rare steak offers slight resistance; when medium-rare, it springs back lightly; when medium or beyond, it gets increasingly stiff and resistant. Remove steaks to warm plates.

2. Cook shallot in meat juices until translucent. Add a little of the butter if the pan is nearly dry. Add wine, bring to a boil, and reduce by two thirds. Remove pan from heat, swirl in butter, check seasoning, and spoon the sauce over the steaks.

Serves 4.

Recipes and Related Information

Broccoli Sautéed With Garlic, 60; Chicken Breasts With Grapes, 280; Chicken Breasts With Sherry, Cream, and Mushrooms, 611; Sautéed Cherry Tomatoes, 582; Sautéed Quail With Red Currant Sauce, 478; Trout With Almonds, 231.

SAVORY

An herb native to the Mediterranean region, savory is of two types: summer savory, an annual, and winter savory, a hardy perennial. The two have a related peppery flavor, but summer savory is milder.

Use Summer savory flatters egg dishes, fish soups, and summer vegetables. Winter savory complements dried bean dishes, meats, sausages, and stuffings.

Availability Look for dried summer and winter savory, both whole and ground, in well-stocked supermarkets. Fresh savory is carried sporadically by specialty markets.

Selection Fresh savory should be crisp and green, with no signs of wilting or decay. Packaged seasonings lose quality after a while; try to buy them from a store that restocks its spice section fairly often.

Storage Dried savory will keep one year in a cool, dark, dry place. Refrigerate fresh savory wrapped in paper towels and plastic wrap.

Sautéing is a fast-moving process in which food is cooked quickly in a shallow pan and turned frequently with a spatula.

SCALD, TO

To heat milk so that tiny bubbles form around the inside edge of the pan, although milk should not boil. To dip foods in boiling water or to pour boiling water over them (the same as blanching).

Before milk was pasteurized, scalding was a sanitary measure. Although unnecessary for sanitation today, some recipes specify scalding in order to improve flavor and shorten cooking time. Yeast bread recipes suggest scalding for outmoded reasons. Most custards use heated milk, although it's wisest to let scalded milk cool slightly before mixing with eggs to avoid curdling.

SCORE, TO

To cut shallow lines partway through the top layer of a dough to create a decorative pattern, or into meats to tenderize and allow a marinade to penetrate more fully. The lines are usually in a crisscross, diamond pattern.

SCUM

Impurities that float to the top of a stock, sauce, or other liquid are called scum. They often form a gray, filmy covering on the surface of the liquid. This layer is removed by skimming with a special long-handled spoon with a wire or perforated bowl (see SKIM).

SEAR, TO

To brown meat with intense heat in order to seal in the juices and to impart color and more flavor; this is done in a skillet or in the oven. Searing is often the first step when preparing a stew or braise.

SEED, TO; SEED

To remove, from a fruit or vegetable, the seeds, which are the portion normally capable of germination. The method of seeding depends on the size of the seed and how easy it is to access. Some seeds, such as those in watermelons and cherimoyas, are large enough to be removed by hand when you encounter them while eating or preparing fruit. Seeds that run in the core of a vegetable, such as a cucumber or zucchini, can be removed by scraping with a spoon or with a special coring tool (see CORE). Apple and pear seeds are removed through coring. Tomatoes are seeded by squeezing cut pieces gently or by being puréed and then strained. Berries can be seeded only by being puréed and then strained through a fine-mesh sieve. Citrus seeds revealed in slices and wedges get picked out with the point of a knife; when citrus fruits are juiced through a reamer with a strainer basket, the seeds are trapped by the strainer.

SEPARATE, TO

To divide a whole egg into yolk and white. Also, to become divided into two distinct parts, as when a custard curdles into liquid and gel or when the ingredients in an emulsion cease to be in suspension.

Recipes and Related Information
Curdling, 167; Custard, 168; Egg, 194; Emulsion and Emulsifier, 212.

SESAME SEED

The tiny sesame seed is the seed of an herbaceous plant native to Indonesia and East Africa. The creamy white variety is the most common, but a black variety is used in southern Indian cooking. Sesame seeds have a mildly sweet, nutty flavor that is enhanced by toasting.

Use   Sesame seeds are pressed for oil, which may be made in several different styles (see OIL). The seeds themselves are a valued cooking ingredient in the Middle East, India, China, Japan, and Korea. Middle Eastern cooks blend sesame seeds into a paste called tahini, which they use to season dressings and dipping sauces (see TAHINI). In India sesame seeds are added to pilafs, stuffings, sauces, chutneys, and candies. Chinese cooks use both black and white sesame seeds as a garnish, in candies, and as part of a coating for fried foods. In addition the Chinese use toasted white sesame seeds to make a paste that is used in salad dressings and noodle dishes. In Japan white sesame seeds are ground and added to salad dressings; black sesame seeds garnish grilled squid and hand-shaped rice balls wrapped in seaweed. Cooks in Korea use great quantities of sesame seed, sprinkling it over braised beef ribs and grilled chicken and adding it to chicken salad, meatballs, noodle dishes, and mixed vegetables.

Sesame seed is also found in confections all over the world. In the United States, for example, it is sprinkled on breads for a nutty garnish; in the south, where it is known as benne seed, it is baked into crackers.

Availability   White sesame seeds are found commonly in jars or tins on supermarket spice racks. Health-food stores often stock them in bulk. Asian, Middle Eastern, and Indian markets also carry sesame seeds, often including black as well as white varieties.

Storage Because of their high oil content, sesame seeds go rancid quickly at room temperature. However, they will keep in the refrigerator or freezer indefinitely.

Preparation Toasting brings out the full flavor of sesame seeds. To toast, cook them in a dry skillet over moderately low heat, shaking pan constantly, until they are lightly browned and fragrant (about 3 minutes).

▪ SESAME FRIED FISH FILLETS

This Chinese version of the familiar three-step batter uses sesame seeds rather than bread crumbs. If black sesame seeds are available, mix them with the white variety for an attractive and textured coating reminiscent of multicolored beach pebbles.

> 1 **pound fillet of catfish or other lean white fish**
> 2 **teaspoons minced fresh ginger**
> 2 **green onions, minced**
> 2 **tablespoons Shaoxing wine or dry sherry**
> **Pinch of salt**
> **Oil, for deep-frying**
> ¼ **cup cornstarch**
> 1 **egg, lightly beaten**
> ¾ **cup white sesame seed**
> ¼ **cup black sesame seed**
> **Soy and Mustard Dipping Sauce**
> **(see page 522), for dipping**

1. Slice fish crosswise into two-bite-sized slices, about ¼ inch thick. Place in a shallow bowl, sprinkle with ginger, green onion, wine, and salt, and marinate in refrigerator for 30 minutes to several hours.

2. In a wok or other deep pan, preheat oil to 375° F. Drain fish and pat dry with paper towels. Have cornstarch in one shallow bowl, beaten egg in another, and combined sesame seeds in a third. Dip a piece of fish in cornstarch and shake off excess; dip into egg (use a wire skimmer or tongs to avoid getting egg on hands; coating will stick to hands, rather than fish); then roll in sesame seeds until coated.

3. Fry until white sesame seeds are light tan (3 to 4 minutes). Drain on paper towels and serve with Soy and Mustard Dipping Sauce.

Serves 4 to 6 with other dishes.

SET, TO

To firm up or to solidify. Gelatin in the presence of cold, and egg protein when heated, cause foods to congeal. Also, as melted chocolate hardens, it sets.

> ### *Recipes and Related Information*
> *Chocolate, 124; Custard, 168; Egg, 194; Gelatin, 264; Mousse, 372.*

Two colors of sesame seeds— white and black—add visual interest to the coating of Sesame Fried Fish Fillets.

SHALLOT

A mild member of the onion family, shallots grow in clusters of several small bulbs, each of which is rarely larger than a walnut and may be much smaller. They are sheathed in a papery reddish brown or yellowish brown skin that is easily removed. The white flesh is tinged with red or purple.

Use Shallots are valued for their gentle onion flavor. Favored by French cooks for sauces, salad dressings, and some soups, shallots are also essential to the classic French butter sauces such as beurre blanc and its variations. They may be pickled and used as a garnish for cold meats or braised whole as part of a vegetable stew.

Availability Shallots are found in most supermarkets. In some stores they are packaged in netting or in cellophane-wrapped boxes. Many supermarkets also stock freeze-dried shallots.

Selection Select firm shallots that are not sprouting.

Storage Keep shallots in a cool, dry place with some air circulation, such as a basket. Under proper conditions, they will keep for up to one month. Store freeze-dried shallots in a cool, dark, dry place for up to six months; they lose flavor with time.

Preparation Remove papery outer skin; trim away root end. Reconstitute freeze-dried shallots according to package directions. See KNIFE, Cutting Techniques, for a description of how to mince shallots.

OPENING BIVALVES

Oysters   Wearing work gloves or using a heavy cloth, hold oyster with deep cup of oyster down. Insert tip of oyster knife into hinge and twist to open shell. Slide knife along inside of upper shell to sever muscle; slide knife under flesh to sever bottom muscle.

Clams   Refrigerate bivalves for a few hours or freeze 30 minutes; they will be easier to open. Slide blade of clam knife between the two shells. Work knife between shells toward hinge until you can pry shells apart. To sever muscles, slide blade along inside of one shell and under clam.

Mussels   Debeard by pulling out threads of tissue that protrude from the shell. Mussels die soon after debearding; prepare immediately. Open as you would a clam.

SHELL, TO

To remove the natural outer covering, or shell, of a food. Typically the term refers to nuts; eggs; seafood such as crab, mussels, and oysters; and to vegetables such as peas and beans.

SHELLFISH

All shellfish fall into one of three categories: crustaceans (crabs, shrimp, prawns, lobsters, crayfish); mollusks (including univalves such as abalone and conch, and bivalves such as mussels, clams, oysters, and scallops); and cephalopods (such as squid and octopus), which, despite being classed as shellfish, do not have shells. Even within these categories, flavors and textures vary greatly. To discuss the best ways to select, store, and prepare shellfish, it is helpful to consider the major varieties separately.

Use   Shellfish preparations are among the world's best-loved dishes. Favorites include Louisiana boiled crayfish, French steamed mussels with white wine and onion, baked clams on the half shell with buttered bread crumbs and bacon, Chinese stir-fried crab with black bean sauce, grilled lobster with drawn butter, and fried shrimp.

Availability   Shellfish are marketed fresh and frozen. The best quality and selection are usually found at a specialty fish market. Some merchants keep crabs and lobsters in holding tanks for live purchase.

Selection   Shellfish deteriorate rapidly after harvesting. Buy from a reputable dealer with a rapid turnover. Carefully frozen shellfish are preferable to "fresh" shellfish that have been out of the water too long.

Periodically during the summer months, local fish-and-game departments declare some sections of coastal waters temporarily unsafe due to the presence of toxic organisms that could be taken up by bivalves. Before harvesting bivalves from coastal waters, check with local fish-and-game authorities to make sure warnings are not in effect.

Storage   Refrigerate fresh shellfish immediately after purchase. If possible, store on a bed of ice in the refrigerator, loosely covered with a clean towel.

Preparation   See individual shellfish entries for specific preparation tips.

Cooking   See BAKE, BOIL, BRAISE, BROIL, DEEP-FRY, GRILL, SAUTE, STEAM, STIR-FRY.

ABALONE

The abalone is a univalve, its mushroom-shaped flesh hiding underneath a large, one-sided shell. The highest concentrations of abalone are found along the coasts of California, Mexico, Japan, and Australia. The flesh is very chewy and must be tenderized by pounding. The texture is silky, the flavor briny and mild.

Scaloppine-like abalone steaks are usually floured lightly and fried quickly in butter. To prepare, remove shell the same way you would shuck a clam (see Opening Bivalves, at left), then scrub off or carefully cut away the outer black skin. Cut thin steaks across the muscle or cut thin strips with the grain. Pound with a mallet or the side of a cleaver to about ¼-inch thickness. Slash meat with a sharp knife to prevent it from curling during cooking. The meat may also be finely minced or ground for use in shellfish cakes or croquettes; small tenderized (pounded) strips may be deep-fried.

The harvesting of fresh abalone in California is highly regulated. Abalone is sporadically available in the shell in the spring and autumn and is easiest to find in Asian fish markets. Some markets sell tenderized steaks. Abalone is also sold canned, dried, and frozen.

Fresh abalone should be alive when purchased; if live, the exposed muscle will react when touched. Abalone flesh should smell sweet, not fishy. Refrigerate and cook within one day. Frozen abalone may be stored in the freezer for up to three months; thaw in the refrigerator. Once opened, canned abalone should be kept covered with water in a covered container; change water every two days. Keep dried abalone tightly wrapped in a cool, dry place; it will keep indefinitely.

◼ ABALONE STEW

The classic use for abalone is as a steak quickly sautéed in butter for less than one minute on each side. This stew gives another savory use for these univalves. Fresh abalone needs to be pounded to tenderize it, but if purchased frozen or canned, that has been done.

    1 **pound abalone steaks**
    ⅓ **cup unsalted butter**
    1 **cup finely chopped onion**
    1 **large clove garlic, peeled and minced**
    ⅓ **cup finely chopped red or green bell pepper**
    1 **bay leaf**
    1 **can (8 oz) tomato sauce**
    2 **cups water**
    3 **potatoes, peeled and cut in ½-inch cubes**
    ½ **teaspoon salt**
    ⅓ **teaspoon cayenne pepper**

1. Cut abalone in ½-inch cubes; reserve. In a large saucepan over medium heat, melt butter and sauté onion, garlic, and bell pepper until onion is soft and pale gold in color (about 5 minutes). Add bay leaf, tomato sauce, the water, potatoes, salt, and cayenne.

2. Cover and simmer until potatoes are almost tender (about 15 minutes). Add abalone cubes and simmer until abalone is tender (4 to 5 minutes).

Serves 8.

PREPARING SQUID

Rinse squid in cold water. Cut off tentacles just above the eye. Squeeze the thick center part of tentacles, which pushes out the hard beak. Discard beak.

Squeeze the entrails from the body by running your fingers from the closed to the cut end. Pull out the transparent quill that protrudes from the body.

Slip a finger under the skin and peel it off. Pull off edible fins from either side and skin them.

PREPARING AMERICAN LOBSTER

Hold lobster right side up on a firm surface. With a sharp knife, pierce the shell and flesh at the center of the cross-shaped mark behind the head.

Cut in half lengthwise. Remove and discard gravel sac near the head and intestinal vein in tail. Remove the gray-green tomalley (liver) and any roe from body; reserve for flavoring sauces.

Twist off and save claws. With sharp knife, separate each of the two halves between tail and body. Slice tail between every other shell segment, leaving shell intact. Crack claws and joints, leaving shell in place.

PREPARING SHRIMP AND CRAYFISH

Shrimp Remove legs. Peel a bit of shell from head end of body. Holding the peeled section with hand, pull tail with other hand and shell will come off.

Slit shrimp down outside curve and remove the intestinal vein. On larger shrimp the intestinal vein contains grit that would interfere with the taste of the recipe. Often on medium shrimp grit is not present and the intestinal vein need not be removed before serving.

Crayfish To remove tail, hold crayfish securely on firm surface, right side up. Lift center tail flap and twist carefully to free it from body. Holding crayfish firmly with one hand, pull tail flap away from crayfish to remove intestinal vein.

PREPARING HARD-SHELL CRABS

Hold crab firmly against work surface. Kill it instantly by stabbing crab just behind the eyes with the point of a sharp knife. Turn crab over. Gently fold back and then twist or pull off apron or tail flap. The attached intestinal vein will pull out along with apron; discard both. Turn crab right side up.

With one hand, hold on to crab body where apron was removed and use other hand to pry up and tear off top shell. Discard shell. Remove gills from each side of crab and take out grayish, saclike sand bag. Pull out and discard mandibles from front of crab.

Holding body where legs are attached, apply pressure so that crab splits in half along center of body. Fold back halves and twist apart. Twist off claws and legs where they join the body. Crack them with a nutcracker and remove the meat.

PREPARING SOFT-SHELL CRABS

Cut across the eyes with kitchen shears or a sharp knife. Reach into the cut and pull out the gray saclike stomach, called the sand bag. Discard the stomach.

Turn crab over, lift up flap or apron, and fold it down away from body. Gently pull out the apron and attached intestinal vein. Discard apron and vein.

Turn crab right side up. Lift flaps at each side near the legs, then scrape off and discard the spongy gills.

CLAMS

A bivalve, the clam has edible flesh inside two hinged shells. Atlantic clams include the small soft-shell steamers and the hard-shell quahogs, which range in size from little-necks to cherrystones to large chowder clams that must be ground or minced. Pacific clams include the hard-shell littleneck, the soft-shell razor clam, and the large geoduck, which has an elephantlike trunk protruding from its shell.

With the exception of the chowder clam, Atlantic clams are often shucked and eaten on the half shell or in raw clam cocktails. Most West Coast clams are too tough to eat raw. Clams may be steamed open with wine and garlic, then eaten as is or added to chowders or pasta sauces. Clams on the half shell are often topped with a seasoned bread mixture or herb butter and baked until hot.

Fresh clams are sold in the shell or shucked. Both East and West Coast varieties are available the year around but are better in the colder months. Clams are also canned and smoked. Fresh unshelled clams should be alive when purchased; if live, the shells will be tightly closed or will close when touched. Reject any that refuse to close tightly. Store live clams in the refrigerator, covered with a damp cloth. Cook and eat within one or two days. Scrub clam shells well. To shuck, see Opening Bivalves, page 536.

■ NEW ENGLAND CLAM CHOWDER

As with any traditional clam chowder, the amount of salt you add depends on the saltiness of the clam broth and salt pork; be sure to taste before seasoning.

20 medium-sized clams, scrubbed, *or*
   1 quart shucked clams
 2 tablespoons butter
 ¼ pound salt pork, rinsed in cold water
   and diced finely
1½ cups diced onion
 8 cups clam broth, reserved from steaming clams,
   or bottled clam juice
 3 cups peeled, cubed potatoes, cooked in
   salted water
 3 cups half-and-half
   Salt and freshly ground white pepper, to taste
   Butter, for garnish
   Oyster crackers or pilot crackers,
   for accompaniment

1. If necessary, steam clams and remove and discard shells. Strain clam broth and reserve.

2. In a large kettle place the 2 tablespoons butter with salt pork. Cook over low heat to render fat and brown pork. Remove pork pieces (cracklings) with slotted spoon and reserve.

3. Add diced onions to fat and cook until they begin to soften. Add clam broth or clam juice to kettle and bring to a boil. Reduce heat and simmer for 5 minutes. Chop clams into small pieces and add to kettle along with cooked potatoes.

4. Cover and simmer for 10 minutes. Add half-and-half to kettle and heat gently. Return pork cracklings to kettle and season with salt and pepper.

5. Serve in warm bowls with a pat of butter in each bowl and plenty of freshly ground pepper. Pass the crackers.

Serves 8.

■ MANHATTAN CLAM CHOWDER

This is the red version of the well-known New England Clam Chowder, which is white. The saltiness of the clams, salt pork, and clam broth affects the amount of additional salt and pepper required.

 ¼ cup salt pork, finely diced
 1 green bell pepper, diced
 1 onion, minced
 3 medium boiling potatoes, peeled and diced
 2 cups ripe tomatoes
   (about 3 large tomatoes), diced
 ½ teaspoon dried thyme
   Salt and freshly ground black pepper, to taste
 ⅛ teaspoon cayenne pepper
 3 cups Fish Stock (see page 561) or
   bottled clam juice
 2 cups shucked steamed clams
   Crusty bread, for accompaniment

1. In a 4-quart saucepan sauté salt pork over medium heat. Add bell pepper and onion, and cook until softened (3 to 5 minutes). Stir in potatoes, tomatoes, thyme, salt, pepper, cayenne, and Fish Stock.

2. Cover and simmer 25 minutes. Add clams, and cook 10 minutes more. Serve steaming hot with crusty bread.

Serves 6 to 8.

Recipes: Cioppino, 556; Steamed Clams, 611; White Clam or Mussel Sauce, 413.

CONCH

Also known as whelk, the conch is a univalve, its sweet flesh almost completely encased in a beautiful rose-tinged, whorled shell. The flesh is tough but may be tenderized by long, slow cooking or by pounding and parboiling. In the Caribbean, conch is eaten raw in a cold cocktail with lemon, onion, and minced tomato, or minced and made into conch chowder.

The meat may be ground, bound with a fritter batter, and deep-fried. It may be sliced thin, pounded, floured, and sautéed in butter like abalone or slowly stewed with wine and herbs. Italians call it *scungilli* and braise it with marinara sauce.

Conch is harvested the year around off the coast of Florida. It is sold in the shell or shucked. A Pacific coast variety is occasionally available in Asian markets on the West Coast. Conch is also marketed frozen (both cooked and raw) and canned, especially along the Atlantic coast and in the Gulf states.

Fresh conch should smell sweet, not fishy. Refrigerate and cook within one day. After opening, canned conch should be covered with water and stored in an airtight container; refrigerate and use within three days. Store frozen conch for up to three months; thaw in the refrigerator before using.

Conch meat is difficult to extract from the convoluted conch shell. Use a hammer to knock a hole in the shell about 1 inch below the crown. With a small, sharp knife, sever the muscle where it attaches to the crown. Grasp the portion of the conch meat that protrudes from the shell and pull to extract it. Trim away the soft parts from the crown end of the meat and cut out the intestinal vein. Peel off the skin, using a knife to cut away any parts that cling. Cut away the hard, flat operculum at the foot of the meat.

CRABS

The Atlantic and Pacific coasts harbor a variety of different crabs, all of which yield sweet white meat. Crabs are eaten both cold and hot, in the shell and shelled. The Dungeness crab and blue crab have edible body and claw meat. In the Alaskan king crab and spider crab, the edible meat is concentrated in the legs and claws; in the southern Atlantic stone crab, the edible meat is only in the claws.

Crabs are often boiled or steamed and served whole. Hot, steamed crabs in the shell are usually accompanied by lemon butter. Cold crab in the shell is usually accompanied by mayonnaise or a tomato-based cocktail sauce. Crab in the shell is added to a variety of hearty soups from gumbo to Cioppino. Chinese cooks stir-fry crabs with ginger and green onion or black bean sauce. Soft-shell blue crabs—crabs that have just molted their hard shells—are entirely edible; they are generally panfried in butter and eaten shell and all.

Crabmeat is often sold cold as a first-course cocktail, with lemon, mayonnaise, or cocktail sauce. Shelled crabmeat may be baked with seasoned cracker crumbs and butter; mixed with mayonnaise and bread crumbs, formed into cakes and fried; made into stuffings for trout; creamed and served in pastry shells; added to soups; or made into cold or hot mousses. Caribbean cooks season the meat highly, stuff it back into the shell, and bake it. Crabmeat may also be used as a filling for enchiladas, tacos, quiche, or crêpes.

Pacific Dungeness crab is available fresh from Washington state to Baja, California, from October through May; it is sold either live or precooked. Fresh Dungeness crabmeat is available locally and is shipped canned or frozen to other parts of the country.

Soft-shell blue crabs from the Atlantic and Gulf coasts are available from April through September; they are airfreighted fresh to some urban markets and are widely sold frozen. Hard-shell blue crabs are available all year, with local seasons depending on water temperature. The she-crab is a female blue crab with orange roe; she-crab soup, containing both meat and roe, is popular in the southern Atlantic states. Florida stone crab claws are enjoyed fresh locally and are frozen for shipment. The legs and claws of Alaskan spider and king crabs are frozen and sold the year around. Frozen Alaskan king crab legs are available in most fish markets.

Canned crabmeat is widely available in supermarkets; most of it is from spider crabs (sometimes identified as "snow crab"), although some markets carry Alaskan king crabmeat or Dungeness crabmeat.

Fresh uncooked crabs should be alive when purchased; if they are alive, they will be active and kicking. Avoid any sluggish or still ones. Refrigerate fresh crab immediately and cook that day. Cooked crabs and crabmeat should smell sweet when they are purchased. Refrigerate and use within three days. Once opened, canned crabmeat should be stored in an airtight nonreactive container in the refrigerator and used within two days. Fresh meat may be frozen for up to three months, although there will be some loss of flavor and texture. Thaw frozen crabmeat slowly in the refrigerator. Blot dry before using to keep it from watering down the dish in which it will be used. The liquid from canned crabmeat is usually used in recipes. All crabmeat should be picked over carefully to remove any bits of shell or cartilage.

■ MARYLAND CRAB CAKES

Nothing can match the sweetness of Chesapeake Bay crab, but this dish is worth making with other types as well. The homemade Tartar Sauce that accompanies it is wholly different from the commercially bottled product.

> 1 **pound crabmeat (preferably from Maryland blue crabs)**
> 1 **cup soft bread crumbs**
> 1 **large egg, lightly beaten**
> ¼ **cup mayonnaise**
> 1 **tablespoon mustard**
> 1 **teaspoon Worcestershire sauce**
> 2 **tablespoons minced parsley**
> ¼ **teaspoon white pepper**
>   **Dash Tabasco Sauce**
>   **Oil, for frying**
>   **Lemon wedges, for accompaniment**
>   **Tartar Sauce With Green Peppercorns (see page 520), for accompaniment**

1. If you are using something other than Maryland blue crab, taste a pinch of it; if it is too salty, rinse briefly under cold running water.

2. Carefully pick over crabmeat, removing any shell and other inedible bits; leave crab in large lumps. Gently mix in bread crumbs.

3. Combine egg, mayonnaise, mustard, Worcestershire, parsley, pepper, and Tabasco. Gently blend this mixture with crabmeat.

4. Form crab mixture into six thick patties. Wrap individually in plastic wrap and refrigerate for 30 minutes to firm the mixture.

5. Pour ¼ inch of oil into a large skillet; heat until aromatic and rippling (about 350° F). Add crab cakes and fry, turning once, until golden on both sides (about 3 minutes per side). Serve immediately with lemon wedges and Tartar Sauce With Green Peppercorns.

Serves 6.

Recipes: Chilled Savory Mousse, 372; Cioppino, 556; Crab Salad Louis, 509.

CRAYFISH

The crayfish (also known as crawfish or crawdad) is a freshwater crustacean harvested from rivers and ponds. It resembles a tiny lobster and is usually about 4 inches long. The prized parts are the sweet white tail meat and the fat in the head, which adds richness to crayfish dishes.

Important to Louisiana Cajun and Creole cooking, crayfish are steamed and served in the shell, cold or hot. They are added to gumbos and jambalaya and made into stews, bisques, salads, and pies.

Crayfish are available, either live or cooked, in some markets from spring through fall. They are farmed in Louisiana in flooded fields and are airfreighted around the country and to Europe. Frozen whole crayfish or frozen tail meat is available in some markets or by mail. Uncooked crayfish should be alive when purchased; avoid any that are sluggish or still. Refrigerate immediately and cook within one day. Cooked crayfish should smell sweet when purchased. Refrigerate and use within two days. Frozen crayfish will keep for up to three months. Thaw frozen crayfish slowly in the refrigerator; do not refreeze. See Preparing Shrimp and Crayfish, page 537.

Fresh crayfish are sometimes muddy; soak in cold water for 10 minutes. Crayfish are cooked in their shells, then shelled to retrieve the tail meat.

■ BOILED SEAFOOD DINNER

The liquid prepared in step 2 constitutes a homemade crab boil. It can be reused three or four times. Refrigerate and use within a week, or freeze. If you can't find blue crabs or live crayfish, use just shrimp (about 6 pounds should be enough for 12 people).

5	pounds live crayfish
2	gallons water
2	cups salt
1	cup fresh lemon juice
½	cup cayenne pepper
¼	cup black peppercorns
2	teaspoons whole allspice
1	tablespoon whole cloves
1	tablespoon thyme
12	bay leaves
2	teaspoons whole celery seed
2	tablespoons coriander
3	heads garlic
6	onions, halved
24	small red potatoes
12	blue crabs
3	pounds shrimp
12	ears corn, cut in half widthwise

1. Purge crayfish by soaking in cold salted water. Drain and rinse; repeat this process until the soaking water is no longer muddy. Set crayfish aside.

2. In a 4- to 5-gallon pot, bring the 2 gallons water and salt to a boil over high heat. Add lemon juice, cayenne, black peppercorns, allspice, cloves, thyme, bay leaves, celery seed, and coriander; continue boiling for 20 minutes.

3. Add garlic, onions, and potatoes; boil another 10 minutes. Add crabs and boil 5 minutes. Add crayfish and continue boiling for 5 minutes. Add shrimp and corn and boil until shrimp are pink and firm (5 to 7 minutes). Drain boiled food through a colander suspended over a large pot.

4. Serve seafood and vegetables in large, shallow bowls or on platters.

Serves 12.

LOBSTER

Two varieties of lobster are taken in American waters. The spiny lobster, a warm-water crustacean found along the coasts of Florida and California and in the Gulf of Mexico, contains meat in its tail only; the American lobster, found in the Atlantic from New England to southern Canada, has edible meat in both tail and claws. The spiny lobster has a rough, reddish brown shell and no claws; the bluish black American lobster has large claws with sharp pincers. Both types turn bright red when cooked.

Lobster is usually poached, steamed, baked, or grilled and may be eaten cold or hot. Cold lobster is generally served as a first-course cocktail or in a salad with mayonnaise or vinaigrette. Hot lobster is often served in the shell with melted butter and lemon. Lobster shells are used to flavor bisques and aromatic sauces and butters. The meat is used in soups, casseroles, soufflés, and sautés, or it may be creamed and served in a pastry shell. Split lobsters are topped with buttered bread crumbs and baked. Chinese cooks stir-fry lobster meat with black bean sauce or with ginger and green onion.

This spicy boiled dinner uses three crustaceans found fresh in Louisiana: blue crabs, crayfish, and shrimp. Or, if you prefer, any of these can be used alone.

Moules Marinière is an adaptation of a classic French dish that never fails to please even the most discriminating palate. Easily prepared and economical, this recipe may well become a mainstay in your seafood repertoire.

Spiny lobsters are available live or cooked the year around in some markets. Frozen spiny lobster tails (often identified as rock lobster or *langouste*) are widely available. American lobster, also known as Maine lobster, is usually sold live from tanks and is available all year; some markets sell whole cooked American lobsters.

Live lobster should be active when taken from the tank; avoid sluggish ones. Cooked lobsters should smell sweet; their tails should be tightly curled underneath the body, a sign that they were alive when cooked. Refrigerate live lobsters and cook within one day. Cooked lobster should be eaten within two days. Frozen lobster may be stored up to three months; thaw slowly in the refrigerator.

Live lobsters are usually cooked whole. However, some recipes call for splitting and cleaning the lobster before cooking; see Preparing American Lobster, page 537. Prepare a live spiny lobster by setting it on its back on a firm surface; with a heavy, sharp knife, stab point into mouth to sever spinal cord. Turn lobster over and split in half lengthwise; use a rubber mallet, if necessary, to force knife through body. If starting with a cooked spiny lobster, begin preparation by splitting in half. With both cooked and uncooked lobsters, rinse viscera from body and intestinal vein from tail under cold running water.

◼ LOBSTER SALAD

This salad is best with your own mayonnaise, made with lemon juice instead of vinegar. Prawns and crab can be added to the salad for variety. Note that the salad should chill for two hours before serving; chilled plates keep the salad cool longer.

> 3 **cups cooked lobster meat**
> **(2 live lobsters, approximately 1½ lb each;**
> **see Basic Poached Shellfish, page 451)**
> 2 **stalks celery, diced**
> 1 **red bell pepper, diced**
> 1 **small bunch chives, snipped**
> 1 **shallot, minced**
> 1 **cup Mayonnaise (see page 519; use fresh lemon**
> **juice instead of vinegar)**
> 1 **head Bibb lettuce, separated into leaves**
> 1 **lemon, cut into 8 wedges, for garnish (optional)**
> 8 **parsley sprigs, for garnish**

1. Cube the cooked lobster into large pieces (about ¾ inch each). In a 2-quart mixing bowl, place lobster, celery, bell pepper, chives, and shallot. Add mayonnaise and stir well to combine. For best flavor chill at least 2 hours before serving.

2. To serve, wash the lettuce leaves, then pat dry. Place one leaf on each chilled salad plate. Serve about ½ cup salad on each lettuce leaf. Garnish each plate with lemon wedge and parsley sprig, if desired.

Serves 8.

Recipes: Basic Poached Shellfish, 451.

MUSSELS

Bivalves with a smooth, bluish black shell, mussels have flesh that ranges from deep yellow to orange. They are found clinging to rocks along both Atlantic and Pacific coasts and are successfully produced by aquaculture in New England. Most of the commercial harvest is from the East Coast; due to toxic substances in the water, Pacific coast mussels are usually quarantined during the summer.

Fresh mussels are steamed in the shells, usually with white wine, oil, and garlic, until they open; they are then eaten from the shell with melted butter or tossed with pasta. They may be shelled, chilled, and used in salads or shellfish cocktails. Mussels may also be grilled over coals until they open. Steamed mussels and their liquid may be made into soups or added to shellfish stews. They may also be steamed open, then dressed with butter and bread crumbs and baked on the half shell. In most recipes, mussels can be substituted for clams.

Fresh East Coast mussels are sold the year around. West Coast mussels are available from November through April. They are generally marketed live, in the shell, although some East Coast markets sell shucked mussels. Canned smoked mussels are also available in most markets. Mussels in the shell should be alive when purchased. Their shells will be tightly closed or will close when touched; discard any that refuse to close. Refrigerate, covered with a damp cloth; cook within one day. Store cooked, shucked mussels in a tightly closed container in the refrigerator; use within two days. Scrub mussel shells well with a stiff brush. See Opening Bivalves, page 536.

■ MOULES MARINIERE

This version of a classic French dish features a richly flavored cream sauce. Fennel adds a hint of licorice to the cooking stock. For directions on how to debeard a mussel, see photograph on page 536.

> **6 dozen mussels**
> **4 shallots, chopped**
> **1 bay leaf**
> **½ teaspoon fennel seed**
> **1 cup dry white wine**
> **1 cup whipping cream**
> **3 egg yolks**
>   **Juice of 1 lemon**
> **2 tablespoons unsalted butter**
>   **Salt and pepper, to taste**
>   **Chopped parsley, for garnish**

1. Scrub and debeard mussels. Soak them in a bowl of cold water or in sink for 30 minutes. Any sand will leach out and sink to bottom of bowl.

2. In a large stockpot simmer shallots, bay leaf, fennel seed, and wine for 5 minutes. Add mussels and steam for 5 minutes; all mussels should open in that time. If doubling recipe, it will take longer for mussels to open. Transfer mussels to a large bowl and keep them warm.

3. To make sauce, strain mussel stock and boil until reduced to about 1½ cups. In a medium bowl beat together cream, egg yolks, and lemon juice. Add 1 cup of mussel stock to cream mixture in a thin stream, then pour the mixture back into the remaining stock. Heat very gently, stirring constantly so that egg yolks do not scramble. Turn off the heat and stir in butter. Season with salt and pepper, if necessary.

4. Divide mussels among 6 large, shallow soup bowls. Ladle sauce over each bowl and sprinkle each with chopped parsley. Place a large bowl on the table for mussel shells.

Serves 6.

Recipes: Cioppino, 556; White Clam or Mussel Sauce, 413.

OYSTER

The oyster is a bivalve that lives in shallow, temperate, and tropical waters. Inside its rough, hard, gray shell is the soft, briny flesh that is appreciated both raw and cooked. Today, several varieties of oysters are commercially farmed on both Atlantic and Pacific coasts of the United States.

Most of the oysters of the world are probably eaten raw on the half shell, with lemon, vinegar, or cocktail sauce. However, there are also dozens of delicious ways to cook them. They may be grilled over coals until their shells open. They may be shelled, poached, and served in a cream sauce or simmered in milk or cream with butter for an oyster stew. Oysters on the half shell may be topped with herb butter or buttered bread crumbs and baked. Whole oysters may be wrapped in bacon and broiled or simmered in butter with hot-pepper sauce and served atop toast. Oysters are added to bread stuffings for turkey or fish and are baked in double-crust pies. Deep-fried cornmeal-coated oysters may be eaten hot with lemon or tucked into a loaf of French bread to make an Oyster Loaf (see page 544). Smoked oysters are usually eaten as an appetizer with crackers or mixed into cream cheese–based dipping sauces.

Most varieties of oysters are available fresh the year around but are better in the colder months. They spawn during the summer and their flesh gets fatty, making them less appealing on the half shell. Oysters are usually sold live in the shell; some varieties are also available shucked in jars or smoked and packed in tins.

Today's commercial oysters are carefully monitored for the toxin that shellfish can ingest in the summer months, and thus present no danger to diners. Unshelled oysters should be alive when purchased; if live, their shells will be tightly closed. Discard any with open shells. Store them in the refrigerator cup side down, covered with a damp towel; use within three days. Shucked oysters should be refrigerated in their liquor and used as soon as possible. See Opening Bivalves, page 536.

■ OYSTER LOAF

Food has always played a prominent role in San Francisco. During the rowdy days of the city in the late 1800s, carousing husbands often carried home an oyster loaf—not candy or flowers—after a late night out as a peace offering to their annoyed spouses. This makes an excellent first course for up to six people or dinner for two.

1	loaf French bread (about 1 lb)
8	tablespoons unsalted butter
¼	teaspoon freshly grated nutmeg
¼	teaspoon cayenne pepper
½	teaspoon freshly ground black pepper
1	teaspoon salt
½	cup flour
½	cup milk
1	egg
16	medium oysters, shucked, *or*
	2 jars (10 oz each) oysters
¾	cup dry bread crumbs (see step 1)
3	tablespoons vegetable oil, for frying
	Juice of 1 lemon
	Tartar Sauce With Green Peppercorns, for accompaniment (see page 520), optional

1. Preheat oven to 400° F. Slice top off loaf of bread. Scoop out soft center, leaving a ½-inch-thick crusty shell. Break soft bread into crumbs and place on a baking sheet. Toast 10 minutes; reserve. Coat inside of bread shell with 3 tablespoons of the butter. Place shell on baking sheet and toast in oven until golden brown (about 10 minutes); reserve.

2. In a small bowl stir together nutmeg, cayenne, pepper, salt, and flour. In another small bowl beat together milk and egg. Dip oysters in seasoned flour, then in egg-milk mixture, and finally in bread crumbs. Place on a plate and chill 1 hour.

3. In a medium skillet sauté oysters in oil and remaining butter over medium heat until golden and crusty on first side (about 4 minutes). Turn; sauté second side 2 minutes. Place cooked oysters in bread shell and pour pan juices over. Serve drizzled with lemon juice and accompanied with Tartar Sauce With Green Peppercorns (if desired).

Serves 4 to 6 as a first course, 2 as a main course.

Recipes: Hangtown Fry, 202.

SCALLOPS

The scallop is a bivalve found on the Atlantic and Gulf coasts. The edible part is the sweet white muscle that holds together the two fan-shaped, hinged shells. The larger sea scallop is about 5 inches across, with a muscle that may be 1 inch wide and ½ inch thick; it is found in water from the mid-Atlantic to the New England coast. The smaller bay scallop is about 2 inches across, with a muscle considerably smaller than that of the sea scallop. Bay scallops are found in Atlantic estuaries. The Florida calico scallop is about the same size as the bay scallop, but the calico is a deep-sea scallop.

Scallops may be baked with buttered bread crumbs or herb butter; sautéed with butter, herbs, and wine or cream sauce; added to soups, shellfish stews, and pasta sauces; floured and deep-fried; poached and eaten cold in salads; or skewered and grilled. They may be marinated for seviche or eaten raw in sushi.

Fresh sea scallops are available all year but supplies are more plentiful in summer. They are almost always sold shucked; they die quickly out of the water. However, live sea scallops are occasionally available in some markets. Bay scallops are available fresh in fall and winter on the East Coast, where they are most prevalent; they, too, are almost always sold shucked. Frozen bay and sea scallops are widely available in fish markets.

Fresh shucked scallops should smell sweet, not fishy. Refrigerate immediately and use within one or two days. Scallops may be frozen for up to three months; thaw slowly in the refrigerator.

■ COQUILLES ST. JACQUES

Scallops come in two sizes, tiny bay scallops (about 100 to the pound) and the larger and more variably sized sea scallops (from 20 to 40 per pound). The larger scallops take slightly longer to cook; if they are cut in thirds or quarters, their cooking time will match that of the smaller bay scallops.

3	shallots, minced
¼	cup parsley, minced
1	clove garlic, minced
4	tablespoons unsalted butter
¾	cup dry white wine
	Bouquet garni (see page 56)
1	pound bay scallops
½	cup soft bread crumbs
2	tablespoons freshly grated Parmesan cheese
2	tablespoons butter, melted
½	teaspoon salt
⅛	teaspoon freshly ground pepper

1. Preheat broiler. In a large, heavy-bottomed sauté pan, sauté shallots, 2 tablespoons of the parsley, and garlic in the 4 tablespoons butter over medium-low heat until soft but not browned (about 10 minutes). Add wine and bouquet garni and simmer 10 minutes.

2. Cut scallops so that all are approximately the same size. Add to pan and cook 4 to 6 minutes (scallops will appear opaque but slightly resilient when done). Remove bouquet garni and divide scallops among 4 shallow gratin dishes or shells.

3. In a small bowl stir together bread crumbs, Parmesan, melted butter, remaining parsley, salt, and pepper. Sprinkle about ¼ cup over each dish of scallops. Place on op rack of oven and broil until golden brown and slightly crisp (2 to 3 minutes).

Serves 4.

SHRIMP AND PRAWNS

Shrimp are saltwater crustaceans and prawns are found in fresh water. However, most consumers and fish markets use the word *prawn* to designate a large shrimp. Shrimp are found on all coasts: From the southern Atlantic and the Gulf of Mexico come brown, white, and pink varieties; from the California coast come spot shrimp known as Monterey prawns. The flesh is firm and white and, when cooked, has coral striations. The flavor is sweet and slightly briny.

Fresh shrimp and prawns may be cooked and served in the shell, either hot or cold. Hot shrimp in the shell are often accompanied by melted lemon butter, cold shrimp by mayonnaise or tartar sauce. Cooked peeled shrimp are used cold in salads and shellfish cocktails and hot in casseroles, crêpe fillings, curries, and fish stuffings. Shrimp may be sautéed, stir-fried, poached, grilled, or braised, either peeled or in the shell. Peeled shrimp may be battered and fried. Shrimp are an important part of Louisiana Cajun and Creole cooking, turning up in bisques, jambalaya, gumbo, and *étouffée* (stew). Crushed shrimp shells may be used to flavor sauces and butters for shellfish dishes.

Monterey prawns (spot shrimp) are available from spring through fall, either whole or with heads removed. Gulf shrimp are available the year around and are almost always sold with heads removed. Almost all shrimp have been frozen at some point in the shipping process, although they may be thawed for retail sale. Most fish markets carry cooked and peeled shrimp as well as raw shrimp in the shell. Canned and frozen shrimp are also available in most markets.

Shrimp, both raw and cooked, should feel firm and smell sweet; avoid any with an ammoniated odor. If buying thawed frozen shrimp, be sure they have not been thawed more than one or two days. Uncooked shrimp should be refrigerated immediately and cooked as soon as possible. Cooked shrimp may be refrigerated for up to three days. Shrimp may be frozen for up to three months; thaw slowly in the refrigerator.

Deveining is optional with small shrimp; with large shrimp, the black intestinal vein may be gritty and therefore should be removed. See Preparing Shrimp and Crayfish, page 537.

■ SHRIMP CREOLE

In French and in the culinary vernacular of New Orleans, *creole* means to cook with tomatoes and sweet bell peppers, and usually to accompany with rice.

    4 **tablespoons butter**
    1 **large onion, diced**
    1 **large stalk celery, diced**
    1 **large green bell pepper, diced**
    2 **cloves garlic, minced**
    ½ **teaspoon dried thyme**
    ½ **teaspoon salt**
    ½ **teaspoon white pepper**
    ½ **teaspoon cayenne pepper**
    ½ **teaspoon freshly ground black pepper**
    1 **tablespoon flour**
    ¼ **cup dry white wine**
    1 **cup peeled and diced tomatoes**
    1 **cup Chicken Stock (see page 560)**
    2 **bay leaves**
      Hot-pepper sauce, to taste (optional)
    2 **pounds shrimp (24 to 30 per lb in shells), shelled and deveined**
    6 **to 8 cups cooked rice, for accompaniment**

1. In butter in a large skillet, sauté onion, celery, bell pepper, and garlic over medium heat until lightly browned (about 6 minutes).

2. In a small bowl mix thyme, salt, white pepper, cayenne, black pepper, and flour; stir into onion mixture and cook 2 minutes. Stir in wine, tomatoes, stock, bay leaves, and hot-pepper sauce (if used). Reduce heat and simmer 20 to 25 minutes.

3. Remove bay leaves. Stir in shrimp and simmer until bright pink (3 to 4 minutes). Serve with hot rice.

Serves 6.

Recipes: Boiled Seafood Dinner, 541; Cioppino, 556; Fritto Misto With Caper Mayonnaise, 176; Pork and Shrimp Stuffing, 191; Potstickers, 191; Shellfish Bisque, 564; Shrimp-Crowned Eggs, 199; Shrimp Okra Pilau, 397; Shrimp With Snow Peas and Water Chestnuts, 606; Spinach-Shrimp Soufflé, 205; Stuffed Mirliton, 110; Tempura Batter, 28.

SQUID AND OCTOPUS

Squid and octopus are cephalopods, mollusks with a distinct head, eyes, a beak, and muscular tentacles. Both have mottled skin overlaying smooth white flesh; when cooked, both are chewy and firm. In general the octopus is tougher and requires longer, slower cooking. Both squid and octopus have a somewhat off-putting appearance, but they are inexpensive and highly versatile.

Both squid and octopus are served in Japanese sushi bars; the octopus is always boiled first. Squid may be cut into rings and sautéed, deep-fried, or added to shellfish

If you've been hesitant about trying squid, tomato-based Squid Marinara just might change your mind. Serve with a crusty bread to mop up the wonderful sauce.

soups; the rings may also be poached and served cold in a seafood salad. Whole squid bodies may be skewered and grilled teriyaki-style or stuffed and baked. Italian cooks typically use squid in pasta sauce. The black squid "ink" is used in Italy to color and flavor rice and pasta dishes. Octopus takes well to slow-cooking methods, such as braising in red wine or in tomato-based sauces. If tenderized first, it may be grilled.

Squid is found on both coasts the year around and is sold fresh and frozen, either whole or cleaned bodies (tentacles removed) only. Octopus is also sold fresh or frozen, whole or in pieces, raw or cooked. It is readily available in fish markets that cater to a Japanese clientele. Fresh squid and octopus should smell sweet, not fishy. Refrigerate and cook within one or two days. Cooked squid and octopus should be refrigerated and eaten within three days. Frozen squid or octopus may be stored for up to three months; thaw slowly in the refrigerator.

See Preparing Squid, page 537. Octopus requires tenderizing before use; simmer for 20 to 25 minutes in salted water before adding to a soup, stew, or sauce.

◼ SQUID MARINARA

This flavorful, peppery squid dish may be eaten hot or cold. It also makes a wonderful sauce for pasta. Spaghetti would be a good choice.

- 4 **pounds squid**
- ⅓ **cup fruity olive oil**
- 4 **cloves garlic, minced**
- 4 **cups crushed tomatoes in purée**
- 1 **teaspoon dried oregano oregano leaves (not powdered), crumbled**
- 1 **teaspoon dried basil *or* 6 fresh basil leaves**
  Salt and freshly ground black pepper, to taste
- ¼ **cup chopped Italian parsley**
- 1 **teaspoon red pepper flakes**

1. Clean squid (see Preparing Squid, page 537). Cut the bodies crosswise into ¾-inch-wide pieces. Also cut the tentacles if they are large.

2. In a heavy casserole or Dutch oven, heat oil. Add squid and sauté for 5 to 6 minutes. Add garlic and stir for 1 minute.

3. Add tomato, oregano, basil, salt, and pepper. Cover and cook until squid are tender (about 20 minutes). Stir in parsley and red pepper flakes. Adjust seasonings to taste. *Serves 8.*

Recipes: Cioppino, 556; Fritto Misto With Caper Mayonnaise, 176.

SHORT

Dough with a high proportion of fat to flour. Short pastry and cookie doughs are tender and crumbly. By water-proofing the flour particles, fat limits the development of gluten, a structure-building offshoot of flour proteins created when flour mixes with liquid. Without this structure, the dough is more brittle, but it tastes so rich and wonderful you hardly mind the crumbs.

> ### Recipes and Related Information
> *Classic Scotch Shortbread, 144; Sand Pastry, 442.*

SHUCK, TO

To remove the outer covering of clams, oysters, and mussels; nuts; the husk of corn; the same as *to shell* and *to husk.* For information on opening bivalves, see SHELLFISH.

SKIM, TO

To remove surface fat or other impurities from a soup, stock, stew, or sauce with a skimmer, a spoon, or a ladle.

> ### Recipes and Related Information
> *Degrease, 177; Spoon, Ladle, and Scoop, 551.*

SKIN, TO

To remove the skin of poultry, fish, or game. Particular preparations, such as boned chicken breasts and fish fillets, are traditionally served skinless for reasons of taste, digestion, or aesthetics.

SLASH, TO

To notch the fat of a steak at even intervals all the way around or to make shallow cuts in the surface of a thin piece of veal. By doing this the meat will stay flat as it cooks; otherwise it will curl as it shrinks to its final size.

SLIVER, TO; SLIVER

To cut a thin and usually short stick of food, as fine as a splinter. The term is most often used to describe garlic cut this way; the garlic pieces are inserted into slits cut into roasts, particularly lamb, in order to flavor the meat internally as it cooks.

SMOKE POINT

The temperature at which a fat decomposes and gives off smoke and an acrid gas. Different fats break down at different temperatures; it is worthwhile knowing the smoke point of common fats since it is this characteristic that determines a fat's suitability for frying. For example, cooks appreciate the delicious flavor butter imparts to food, but know that it can't reach frying temperature without burning; vegetable oils (such as safflower, corn, peanut, and grapeseed oils) stay intact at higher temperatures and are often combined with butter in order to raise the smoke point of butter. See FRY for more information about the smoke points of different fats and about frying.

SORREL

Also known as sour grass and dock, sorrel is a leafy, deep-green member of the buckwheat family. Sorrel leaves, with their slender stems, somewhat resemble spinach, but the flavor is markedly different. Cooked sorrel has a pronounced lemonlike tang that is especially appealing in cream sauces, stuffings, and soups.

Use Very young sorrel leaves may be added to salads with other greens. Otherwise, sorrel is almost always cooked. When simmered in butter and cream, it makes a delicious partner to salmon and trout. French cooks stuff whole shad with sorrel purée and make a sorrel soup thickened with eggs and cream; Eastern European Jews make a cold sorrel and sour cream soup called *schav.*

Availability Sorrel grows wild throughout North America and is cultivated commercially. Fresh sorrel is marketed sporadically in supermarkets the year around, although it is most easily found in the spring. Specialty markets also carry cooked sorrel in jars.

Selection Look for green leaves with no sign of yellowing. Sorrel wilts readily after harvesting but flavor is not compromised.

Storage Wash and dry leaves; wrap in paper towels, then enclose in a plastic bag and refrigerate for up to four days. Bottled sorrel should be refrigerated after opening and used within one week.

Preparation Remove leaves from stems.

Availability All supermarkets carry a wide assortment of spices in whole and ground forms. Health-food stores, ethnic markets, and specialty stores are another good source for spices. For information on a particular spice, see individual entries; for information on commercially prepared blends, see HERB AND SPICE BLENDS.

Selection When possible, buy spices in whole form and grind them yourself. Whole spices stay fresh much longer than ground, and freshly ground spices are far more pungent than those that are preground. Buy from a merchant who stores spices correctly: in a cool, dark, dry place.

Storage Whole spices will keep for up to two years under ideal conditions; ground spices for about six months.

Preparation Whole spices such as cloves, peppercorns, and cinnamon stick can be added directly to stews and soups and strained out before serving. For easy removal, wrap them in a cheesecloth bag tied with string or use a tea infuser. Whole spices can be ground with a mortar and pestle, or in a pepper mill, clean coffee grinder, or electric minichopper. Some recipes specify toasting spices lightly before grinding to bring out their flavor.

SPINACH

Leafy, green spinach probably originated in southwestern Asia, in the vicinity of modern-day Iran. Although introduced late to Europe, it caught on quickly. Today spinach is appreciated for its sprightly, fresh flavor and high content of vitamins A and C, iron, and folic acid.

Use Raw spinach has recently become popular as a salad green, often tossed with crumbled bacon and egg. Spinach also is wilted in butter or oil and served as a side dish; creamed and served with fish; puréed for soups, soufflés, and quiches; or minced and worked into pasta dough. Iranians enjoy *gormeh sabzi,* lamb braised with spinach and herbs; Indian cooks, using different spices, make a similar preparation called *saag gosht.* In Greece minced spinach is combined with eggs, feta cheese, and seasonings, then layered with filo dough and baked to make *spanakopita.*

Availability Fresh spinach is sold in most supermarkets the year around, with peak supplies from March through June. There are several varieties of spinach, some with flat smooth leaves, others with crinkly leaves. What appears in some markets as "New Zealand spinach" is neither spinach nor from New Zealand. Despite a fuzzy texture its leaves resemble spinach in color and flavor and can be used in its place. All supermarkets also carry canned and frozen spinach.

Selection Look for bright green leaves; avoid any that are wilted or slimy. Small, tender leaves, which impart a delicate flavor, are preferred for salads.

Storage Wrap fresh spinach in plastic and keep in the refrigerator for up to three days.

Preparation Spinach is grown in sand and can be very gritty. Wash well, in several changes of water if necessary, and remove tough stems. For salads, dry leaves thoroughly.

Cooking See SAUTE, STEAM, STIR-FRY.

◼ CHAFING DISH SPINACH SALAD

Heated just until it begins to wilt, spinach makes a dramatic first course salad to prepare at the table—if you are a bit of a culinary exhibitionist.

> 2 **bunches (about ¾ lb each) spinach**
> 1 **tablespoon olive oil**
> **Freshly ground pepper**
> 4 **slices bacon, crisply cooked, drained, and crumbled**
> 2 **hard-cooked eggs, grated**
> **Lemon wedges, for garnish**

Mustard Dressing

> 2 **tablespoons tarragon wine vinegar**
> 1 **tablespoon Dijon mustard**
> 1 **small shallot, finely chopped**
> ½ **teaspoon sugar**
> ¼ **teaspoon salt**
> ⅓ **cup vegetable oil**

1. Remove and discard stems from spinach; you should have about 15 cups leaves. If done ahead, place in a bowl, cover, and refrigerate.

2. In a deep, broad chafing dish, heat olive oil over moderately high heat. Add several grindings of pepper, then crumbled bacon. Stir to heat through.

3. Add spinach and mix lightly just until spinach begins to wilt (about 1 minute). Remove from heat at once. Mix gently but thoroughly with Mustard Dressing. Serve salad on individual plates.

4. Garnish each serving with egg and a lemon wedge.

Serves 4 to 6.

Mustard Dressing In a small bowl blend together vinegar, mustard, shallot, sugar, and salt. Using a whisk or fork, gradually beat in oil.

Makes about ½ cup.

Recipes and Related Information

Cream of Spinach Soup, 563; Ground Beef and Spinach Stuffing, 592; Parmesan-Spinach Soufflé, 205; Spinach-Ham Soufflé, 205; Spinach Omelet, 203; Spinach Pasta, 411; Spinach Ravioli, 415; Spinach-Shrimp Soufflé, 205; Spinach-Stuffed Breast of Veal, 592; Spinach Timbales, 579; Vegetable Purées, 487.

SPOON, LADLE, AND SCOOP

Spoons don't resemble your arm and hand by chance; they serve as an extension of your body to mix, beat, and otherwise move food around. You could use your hand as a spoon (and many cooks prefer to mix and toss dry ingredients, batters, and salads that way), but most cooks use a long-handled spoon to maintain clean hands and to prevent exposure to overly hot or cold foods. The ubiquitous wooden spoons and spatulas, solid and slotted cook's spoons, wire and perforated skimmers, ladles of all sizes, and multifunctional scoops and paddles are kitchen work horses and basic culinary equipment.

COOK'S SPOONS

These long-handled metal spoons are preferred to wood ones for stove-top use because they can take high heat without burning, won't absorb cooking flavors, and don't harbor bacteria. They can scratch pans, however, so are best for mixing large quantities, such as soups or stews with many ingredients, where there is less chance that the bowl of the spoon will drag against the pan's interior. Use a spoon with a solid bowl for transferring and serving, and the slotted type for removing solid foods from liquid. However, when lifting fried foods from hot fat, a wire skimmer (at right) lets more fat fall back into the pan than a slotted spoon. Choose a cook's spoon made of heavy, sturdy stainless steel, that, as a poor heat conductor, keeps the spoon from heating up when set in hot liquids. Generally, these spoons measure from 11 inches to 13 inches overall (yours should be long enough to reach into your deepest pot, or several may be preferred if a very long one seems unwieldy for most tasks).

WOODEN SPOONS AND SPATULAS

Utensils made of wood have a comfortable feel—both in your hand and against the sides of mixing bowls and cookware. A poor heat conductor, wood won't get hot or cold, so it can be held without worry. Wooden spoons and spatulas are such basic equipment that it's hard to imagine any kitchen counter without a crock filled with them in several sizes. Use them to stir, mix, and fold both hot and cold foods, and to transfer mixtures from a bowl to a pan or plate.

Do you need both spoons and spatulas? These tools function the same, although their shapes differ: Spoons tend to have rounded handles and end in a bowl; spatulas have slightly flattened handles and a flat or gently curved paddle. Some cooks prefer spatulas when folding mixtures together because of the shape. If you are curious, buy both a spoon and paddle and see which you prefer. It won't be a wasted purchase because both can be used over and over, and a collection of these wooden tools enhances your

batterie de cuisine. Overall lengths range from 8 to 16 inches; bowl shapes vary also. Buy tools that fit comfortably into your mixing bowls, saucepans, and stockpots. Those made of a hard wood such as boxwood are preferred because they won't split and are less porous, and therefore less likely to absorb food flavors. However, they shouldn't be cleaned in the dishwasher or soaked in water. After using, rinse and dry well.

SKIMMERS

Tools for removing solids from liquids, skimmers are made in several styles to suit their various purposes: for removing foods from hot fat or liquid, and spooning off the frothy scum that rises to the surface of stocks and preserves. Skimmers for transferring food are either metal perforated with many small holes or are wire. The first type has a long metal handle ending in a shallow disk. It functions like a slotted spoon in that it permits liquid to pass through its perforations; but because it has so many more holes, it won't trap unwanted fat as does a slotted spoon. Its bowl is only slightly concave so that it can pass over the surface of a stock or bubbling pot of jam and lift off only the scum. Another type of spoon for removing scum has a fine wire mesh, instead of holes, in a stainless steel frame. Skimmers for deep-fried foods have

A tangy mustard dressing coats the warm, wilted greens of Chafing Dish Spinach Salad. For a special presentation, toss the salad at the table in an attractive serving dish.

STAR ANISE

This pungent spice is a dark brown, eight-pointed star about ½ inch in diameter. Star anise is native to China.

Use Star anise lends its licoricelike flavor to Asian soups, stews, and marinades. It is one of the five components of five-spice powder. Red-cooked Chinese beef, pork, and poultry always contain star anise. The spice is included in the smoking mixture for Chinese tea-smoked chicken and duck. Peanuts and soybeans are simmered in liquids seasoned with star anise, then cooled and eaten cold as a snack. Star anise also flavors the poaching liquid used for Chinese marbleized tea eggs. Both Thai and Vietnamese versions of beef noodle soup are flavored with star anise.

Availability Star anise is available in packages in Asian markets.

Storage Keep star anise in a cool, dark, dry place for up to one year.

Preparation Many recipes call for a given number of star anise "points," which consist of both the seed and the hard seed covering. The points may be added directly to a stock or stew, but, for easy removal, wrap points in cheesecloth before adding.

Recipes and Related Information
Beef Soup With Noodles, 390; Herb and Spice Blends, 301.

STEAM, TO

To cook food by the heat of steam. Food is placed on a rack above, but not in direct contact with, boiling liquid. The rack is set in a pan that is covered, to keep the steam from escaping. Steam from boiling liquids swirls around food and cooks it with intense, moist heat.

Steaming is an excellent method in terms of nutrition. Whereas water-soluble vitamins might be washed away during boiling, steaming keeps vitamin loss to a minimum. Steamed vegetables also retain their color better than those that are boiled or cooked in oil. Steaming can also be especially efficient; with Chinese-style stacking steamers, many different foods can be cooked at once over a single heat source. But the greatest virtue of steaming is in the texture and flavor of the finished dish. There is no better way to preserve the delicate taste and texture of a perfectly fresh fish than to cook it gently with steam. This method is suitable for whole fish, fillets, and fish steaks. Scallops and shrimp also are very tender and succulent when steamed. Some holiday puddings and breads, such as plum pudding and Boston Brown Bread (see page 492), are traditionally steamed.

HOW TO STEAM

The factors that govern successful steaming are simple: The steam must circulate freely in the steamer; the liquid should never touch the steamed food; and the liquid should never boil dry. If you are using stacking steamers, the heat source must be strong enough to circulate the steam through the racks. If, upon lifting the lid, it is evident that the steam is not reaching the top rack, remove the top rack so the steaming is efficient. Keep a separate pot of water boiling in order to replenish the steaming water while maintaining the temperature of the steam.

Steaming is a cooking method done to perfection in a microwave oven. In minutes fish steams in its own juices to a moist and tender result. Vegetables cook to crisp-tender and are vibrantly colored. For more information see MICROWAVE OVEN or the manufacturer's instructions that accompany your microwave oven.

Several types of steamers are available. Chinese bamboo or metal steamers are convenient because the trays can be stacked and several foods can be steamed at once. You can make any deep saucepan into a steamer by setting a folding steamer rack inside and covering the pan tightly. To steam small amounts of food, you can improvise a steamer by setting a colander or strainer in a large saucepan and covering it tightly. See COOKWARE, Steamers, for more information.

■ STEAMED SALMON STEAKS WITH BLACK BEAN SAUCE

This recipe features some of the basic ingredients of Chinese cooking, including garlic and salted fermented black beans. Both ingredients lend themselves beautifully to braising, stir-frying, and steaming. The beans have an indefinite shelf life when stored in an airtight container. They are sold in Asian markets and are usually labeled "salted black beans." If you don't have a wok, any large pan with a domed lid will work just as well.

    4 salmon steaks (each 1 inch thick)
    1 teaspoon salt
    4 green onions, flattened with the side
       of a cleaver and cut in 2-inch-long sections,
       plus 2 green onions, shredded
    4 slices of peeled fresh ginger the size of
       a quarter coin, shredded, plus 1 teaspoon
       minced, peeled fresh ginger
    2 tablespoons salted fermented black beans,
       covered with water for 5 minutes, rinsed,
       and drained
    2 tablespoons soy sauce
    2 cloves garlic, peeled and coarsely chopped
    1 tablespoon dry sherry or dry vermouth
    ½ teaspoon sugar
    4 tablespoons peanut oil
       White pepper, to taste
       Fresh cilantro, for garnish

1. Blot salmon dry and sprinkle with salt. Place half of the 2-inch-long green onion sections and half of the shredded fresh ginger on the bottom of a shallow, heat-resistant plate. Arrange salmon steaks in a single layer on top of ginger and green onions. (Use 2 plates and 2 steamers, stacked, if necessary.) Scatter the remaining green onion sections and shredded fresh ginger over the salmon steaks.

2. Combine beans with soy sauce, garlic, sherry, sugar, and the 1 teaspoon minced ginger. Spread ingredients evenly over fish.

3. Fill a wok with boiling water to 1-inch from the bottom of a bamboo steamer. Bring the water to a boil. Put the plate of fish in the steamer, cover, and place the steamer in the wok. Steam over medium heat for 10 minutes. When done, remove from wok. Uncover steamer, tilting lid away from you.

4. In a small pan heat peanut oil until hot and almost smoking. Meanwhile, sprinkle white pepper and shredded green onions over salmon steaks set on plate in steamer. Carefully pour oil over the entire surface of each steak to coat completely. The oil should sizzle. Serve hot, garnished with fresh cilantro.

Serves 4 to 8.

STEW, TO

To cook slowly over low heat, causing a wonderful exchange of flavors among the ingredients. It is an ideal cooking method to use with inexpensive cuts of meat. The gentle cooking in moist heat tenderizes the meat and makes it succulent. Yet economy is not the only reason to prepare a stewed dish. These cuts are also most flavorful and produce the best-tasting sauces.

A stew is usually made of small pieces of meat covered completely with liquid—water, stock, wine, or a combination; usually other ingredients such as vegetables and seasonings are added for flavor. The meat may or may not be browned first, and the cooking liquid becomes the sauce, which can be thickened naturally by boiling until reduced in volume or by adding flour or another thickening agent (see SAUCE).

Stews and braises, including casseroles, ragouts, and daubes, are almost identical preparations, the main difference being the amount of liquid used and the way the meat is cut up. Braising calls for less liquid and the meat is usually whole or in large pieces. A stew has more liquid and the meat is generally in small pieces.

Stews offer considerable opportunity for the cook to be creative, as long as the ingredients have similar cooking times. Hardier root vegetables such as onions, carrots, and parsnips, prized for their sweet flavor, hold up well when cooked for a long time. More delicate additions that will lose their color when overcooked, such as mushrooms,

STEAMING BASICS

Steaming can be done over boiling water, in butter and water, and in a paper package, a technique called *en papillote*. A note of caution: Steam can cause severe burns. When removing the cover from a steaming pot, open it away from you and let the steam dissipate before you reach or look inside. Long sleeves or long oven mitts can protect your wrists from steam burns. Exercise the same care when steaming in a microwave oven: Pierce plastic wrap or lift a corner of a covered dish to allow the steam to escape.

• When steaming over water, be sure the food is at least 1 inch above the surface of the boiling water so that vigorously bubbling water cannot boil the food.

• To steam vegetables over boiling water, use a metal steamer or a colander. Place it over a few inches of water in a 2- or 3-quart saucepan with a tight-fitting lid. Bring the water to a boil, add the vegetables, and steam until crisp-tender (5 to 20 minutes).

• To butter steam vegetables, add vegetables and about ¼ inch of water to melted butter in a large skillet; cover tightly and steam over medium-high heat until tender. Butter steaming is particularly suited for long, thin vegetables such as asparagus or whole green beans; it is a very quick way to cook cut-up vegetables because the skillet offers a large surface area over which to spread them.

• Steaming food in parchment paper saves cleanup and calories: The paper encases the food, assuring flavor by sealing in natural juices and flavorings, and eliminates the need for a cooking pan. Very little, if any, fat is needed for this method. Fish is particularly well-suited for this technique, but other delicate foods, such as pieces of boned poultry, can also be prepared this way. Cook the packages in a conventional or microwave oven. Parchment paper is available in well-stocked supermarkets and better cookware stores.

potatoes, peas, and green beans, should be mixed in during the final 20 to 30 minutes. If the dish is made ahead, these more delicate vegetables go into the pot during the reheating period.

FINISHING, STORING, AND REHEATING STEWS

For even heating a heavy pan with a tight-fitting cover is necessary. It should be made from materials that are efficient heat conductors, such as enameled cast iron or clad metals (see MATERIALS FOR COOKWARE).

One of the most attractive features of stews is that, although they may take time to prepare, once done they keep well and need only to be reheated to serve.

Stews are wonderful do-ahead meals, tasting even better a day or so after cooking, when the flavors have had a chance to blend. They will keep up to one week in the refrigerator and up to two months in the freezer.

No matter when the dish is to be served, immediately or later on, any fat should be skimmed away after cooking. This is most easily accomplished when the dish has cooled and the fat has congealed on the surface. If it is to be refrigerated or frozen, cool it first at room temperature.

To reheat from the refrigerator, use a very low temperature to just warm the meat, avoiding further cooking. If raw vegetables are to be added at this point, increase the heat to medium-low and cook, covered, until the vegetables are tender and cooked through (10 to 20 minutes). To reheat from the freezer, first thaw the stew, then refrigerate until ready to reheat.

Stir-frying is an ideal way to preserve the flavor and crunchy texture of fresh asparagus. Here Beef With Asparagus makes for a springtime treat.

THE STIR-FRY PANTRY

Ingredients for stir-fried dishes are not always easy to find. Try well-stocked supermarkets or specialty food stores; they frequently have an ethnic foods section where many ingredients used for Asian cooking can be found. If you are fortunate enough to have access to Asian markets, your shopping will be simplified and the range of dishes you can prepare much expanded.

In the refrigerator Snow peas, fresh ginger, fresh garlic, green onions, chicken stock. If you wish to hold stock longer than a few days, freeze it.

On the shelf Canned bamboo shoots, canned water chestnuts, dried mushrooms, soy sauce, oyster sauce, hoisin sauce, hot-pepper sauce, peanut oil, sesame oil, rice wine, rice wine vinegar, pale dry sherry, cornstarch. (Most of these ingredients can be stored for a long time without refrigeration.)

Equipment Wok with cover, wooden spoons, chopsticks, slotted spoon.

■ BEEF WITH ASPARAGUS

When asparagus is in season, virtually every Chinese restaurant features this simple but delicious stir-fry.

 2 teaspoons minced fresh ginger
 2 tablespoons Shaoxing wine or dry sherry
 3 tablespoons dark soy sauce *or* 2 parts light
  and 1 part black soy sauce (see Note)
 ½ teaspoon sesame oil
 ½ pound lean beef, thinly sliced into strips
1½ teaspoons cornstarch
 2 to 3 tablespoons vegetable oil
 1 pound asparagus, cut diagonally
  into 2-inch pieces

1. In a medium bowl combine ginger, wine, soy sauce, and sesame oil. Toss beef strips in soy mixture; marinate for 30 minutes to several hours.

2. Drain beef well and reserve marinade. Combine marinade with enough water to make ⅓ cup. Dissolve cornstarch in this mixture.

3. Heat wok over high heat and add 1 tablespoon of the oil. Add beef to pan; stir-fry until meat loses the raw color (about 1 minute). Remove meat from pan.

4. Add remaining oil to wok. Add asparagus and stir-fry over medium heat until just heated through. Return beef to pan; add reserved marinade. Increase heat to high and cook until sauce thickens. Serve immediately.

Serves 4 to 6 with other dishes.

Variation When asparagus is not in season, sliced Chinese or Western-style broccoli can be used in its place. Blanch, if desired (see BLANCH).

Note For a richer sauce, reduce soy sauce in marinade to 1 tablespoon dark soy; add 2 tablespoons oyster sauce to pan in step 4.

Recipes and Related Information
Green Onions in Silky Beef, 285; Lemon Chicken Breasts, 339; Mu Shu Pork, 378; Shrimp With Snow Peas and Water Chestnuts, 606; Stir-Fried Noodles With Shredded Pork, 389.

STOCK AND SOUP

To the French, stocks are the foundation of all cuisine. These rich brews develop from slow-cooking meats, bones, and vegetables in liquid in order to extract their nutrients and flavor and to draw out other natural materials that add desirable body and texture. The purpose of stocks is to provide a base of flavor upon which a recipe can be built. Stock is the starting point, or critical ingredient, of a multitude of dishes, particularly soups and sauces. Beef stock has the deepest flavor and color, and is followed by chicken stock; fish stock is the lightest.

Basically, soup is a liquid that has been cooked with additions intended to impart enough flavor and nutrients so that the final product becomes an appealing food. In cooking, soups are categorized as *clear* (broths, consommés) or *thickened* (cream soups, vegetable purées), *light* (broths, consommés, bouillon, light cream soups) or *hearty* (dense vegetable soups and thick cream soups).

INGREDIENTS FOR STOCKS AND SOUPS

A stock of good quality is the offspring of an arranged marriage between mildly flavored vegetables, incorporated for their sweetness and aroma, and meat and bone, used for their flavoring and thickening properties. Water is the medium that brings these elements together.

Because the ingredients of stock are often free or cost very little, stock is economical to prepare. Beef and veal bones are available from butcher shops and at many supermarkets. Chicken wings or necks for chicken stock are found in almost every supermarket; poultry bones and carcasses left over from other preparations can be frozen for later use in a stock. Fish bones for fish stock can be obtained at seafood markets.

Although all the components of soups do not need to be crisp, fresh ingredients heighten flavor and visual appeal. This does not mean that leftovers have no place in a soup. Yesterday's cooked vegetables, steamed rice, or roast chicken, when added to a flavorful homemade stock, makes a delicious dish.

EQUIPMENT FOR MAKING STOCKS AND SOUPS

Although not a difficult process, making stock is time-consuming, so it's most practical to prepare a large quantity in one session—some to use right away and the rest to freeze. Use a large, heavy-bottomed stockpot with at least an 8-quart capacity or a Dutch oven (see COOKWARE). Also helpful, but not necessary, is a chinois, which is a conical sieve with a very fine mesh (see COLANDER, STRAINER, AND SIEVE) used to strain cooked stock. You can substitute a colander lined with several thicknesses of finely woven, dampened cheesecloth for a chinois, but do not use cloth with a loose weave.

Soup making requires little equipment other than a large saucepan and a wooden spoon. The pan should be heavy and a good heat conductor so the ingredients will cook evenly. A food processor or blender is convenient for puréeing and chopping ingredients.

PREPARATION BASICS

For stocks ingredients should always be covered with cold water, which is more effective for drawing out flavorful essences than hot water. The liquid is slowly brought to a boil and then simmered for the remainder of the cooking time. The slow simmering, as opposed to a continuous boil, allows fat and albuminous material (scum) to rise to the surface, where it can be skimmed off at regular intervals. The skimming is important to obtain a refined stock.

An especially clear stock results if the ingredients simmer uncovered. This is practical for fish stock, which is ready after only 20 minutes of simmering, but less so for the others because the liquid evaporates rapidly and water needs to be added frequently. A compromise is to cover the stock partially as it simmers so that steam can escape but the liquid does not evaporate too quickly.

Soups are so diverse in type and in composition that the best preparation is to follow the recipe as directed.

COOLING AND DEGREASING STOCK

Stock should be cooled quickly so that it can be refrigerated or frozen as soon as possible. If left too long in a warm kitchen, stock can spoil. To cool stock quickly, put bowls of strained stock in the sink and fill the sink with enough cold water to come almost to the rim of the bowls. To speed the cooling, add ice cubes to the water in the sink. Change the water when it becomes warm. Refrigerate the stock when it has cooled to room temperature.

Before using, fat should be removed so the stock will be clear and will not taste greasy. Even stocks that were skimmed frequently while they cooked will still contain some fat (except for fish stock, which contains very little fat). The easiest way to remove fat is to refrigerate the stock. As it cools, the fat solidifies on the surface and it can be scraped off with a spoon. However, if you are not planning to use the stock right away, let the layer of congealed fat sit on the chilled liquid since it acts as a shield, protecting the stock from bacterial contamination. To remove fat from hot stock, skim the fat from the surface with a spoon or wire skimmer. Then draw strips of paper towels or a paper coffee filter across the surface.

STORING AND REHEATING STOCKS AND SOUPS

Most soups and stocks can be made ahead, refrigerated or frozen, and reheated. Cool soups and stocks to room temperature before you refrigerate or freeze them; store in covered containers. Use refrigerated stocks or soups within three to five days. Stocks can be kept up to about one week if brought to a boil for 10 minutes every other day. Freeze stocks in portion-sized containers—1- or 2-cup size for sauce making, larger for soups—or in ice cube trays. Once frozen, transfer the cubes to plastic storage bags for easy access. Remember to leave an inch or so of headroom in the larger storage containers to allow for the expansion of the liquid as it freezes. Most stocks can be frozen about six months; soups will freeze for about four months. Always boil refrigerated or frozen stock before using in a recipe.

Refrigerated soups should be reheated in a saucepan over medium-low heat. Stir vegetable purée soups, cream soups, and velouté soups frequently during reheating to prevent scorching and sticking. It is best not to reheat soups containing egg yolks, which may curdle. Soups containing thickeners such as flour, potatoes, or rice thicken on standing; when reheating the soup, stir in a few tablespoons of additional liquid if necessary. Many fresh herbs lose their flavor when reheated; if the herb is already in the soup, it is good to add a little more of it after reheating. Try to defrost frozen soups before reheating.

Stock frozen in a plastic container can be defrosted quickly by the following method: Set container, uncovered, in a pan of hot water for a few minutes until the stock at the edges and bottom defrosts. Then push on the bottom of the container and slip the frozen stock into a saucepan. Cover the saucepan and heat the stock over medium-low heat until it melts and can be measured. Measure the desired amount. Freeze remaining stock immediately.

BASIC STOCK

Stock making needn't be a weekly ritual, but it is a procedure with which all good cooks should be comfortably familiar. Homemade stocks add a special dimension to cooking. A supply of the following basic stocks, stored in serving-sized portions in your freezer, will actually simplify meal preparation, as well as improve its presentation. After sautéing a chicken breast, a pan sauce can be quickly assembled from pan juices, some stock, and seasonings. Adding fresh vegetables and cooked meat to already prepared broth makes a flavorful soup.

■ BEEF STOCK

The bones and vegetables in this recipe are first roasted to give the stock a brown color and a rich flavor. For the best flavor, use knuckle bones with some meat attached. If possible, use a mixture of beef soup bones and veal knuckle bones; the combination will make a more flavorful stock, with the veal bones also serving as a natural thickener. Or, if desired, use only veal bones (see variation). Meat scraps, completely trimmed of fat, can be added to the stock during the last quarter of cooking time.

   4 **pounds beef soup bones, chopped in a few pieces by the butcher**
   2 **medium onions, unpeeled, root end cut off, quartered**
   2 **medium carrots, scrubbed but not peeled, quartered**
   2 **stalks celery, cut in approximately 2-inch pieces**
   2 **bay leaves**
  10 **stems parsley (without leaves)**
   4 **cloves garlic (unpeeled)**
  ½ **teaspoon black peppercorns**
  ½ **teaspoon dried thyme**
  16 **cups (approximately) cold water**

1. Preheat oven to 450° F. Roast bones in a roasting pan, turning occasionally with a slotted metal spatula, until they begin to brown (about 30 minutes). Add onions, carrots, and celery; roast until browned (about 30 minutes).

2. Drain off fat. With a slotted spatula, transfer bones and vegetables to a stockpot, kettle, or other large pot. To ingredients in stockpot add bay leaves, parsley stems, garlic, peppercorns, thyme, and enough of the cold water to cover.

3. Bring just to a boil. Add a little more cold water to reduce to below boiling; stir once. Bring back just to a boil and reduce heat to very low so that liquid bubbles very gently. Skim off foam that collects on surface. Partially cover and cook, skimming foam and fat occasionally, for 4 to 6 hours. During first 2 hours of cooking, add hot water occasionally to keep ingredients covered.

4. Strain stock through a colander lined with several thicknesses of dampened cheesecloth, discarding solids. If stock is not to be used immediately, cool to lukewarm. Refrigerate until fat rises to the surface and congeals (about 8 hours). If stock will be used within 3 to 5 days, leave fat; skim fat when ready to use. If stock is to be frozen, skim fat.

Makes about 8 cups.

Brown Veal Stock   Substitute veal bones, preferably knuckle bones, for the beef bones.

Glace de Viande (Meat Glaze)   Use this concentrated essence to flavor sauces and soups or to glaze meats. Boil stock, uncovered, over high heat until syrupy and reduced by about seven eighths. Let cool; it will become gelatinous. Store, covered, for 1 week in the refrigerator, or cut into tablespoon-sized cubes and freeze.

■ CHICKEN STOCK

The process for stock making is the same regardless of which bird is the main ingredient. Chicken and turkey are most common in stock, but other fowl, such as duck or pheasant, are also used. The most flavorful result is produced from an older bird such as a stewing hen. However, use whatever parts are available—carcass, cooked scraps, wing tips, giblets (excluding livers), skin, or any leftovers. For more flavor you can brown the bones, carcass, necks, and back. Cook in a 450° F oven until brown (15 to 30 minutes); watch carefully, turn occasionally, and drain off all fat.

   3 **pounds chicken wings, chicken backs, or a mixture of wings, backs, necks, and giblets (except livers)**
  16 **cups (approximately) cold water**
   2 **medium onions, peeled and quartered**
   2 **medium carrots, peeled and quartered**
   2 **bay leaves**
  10 **stems parsley (without leaves)**
  ½ **teaspoon black peppercorns**
  ½ **teaspoon dried thyme**

1. Put chicken in a stockpot, kettle, or other large pot. Add enough of the cold water to cover. Bring just to a boil. Add a little more cold water to reduce to below boiling; stir once. Bring back just to a boil and reduce heat to very low so that liquid bubbles very gently. Skim off foam that collects on surface.

2. Add onions, carrots, bay leaves, parsley stems, peppercorns, and thyme. Adjust heat to keep surface just breaking with bubbles, but not boiling. Partially cover and cook, 2 to 3 hours, skimming foam and fat occasionally.

3. Strain stock through a colander lined with several thicknesses of dampened cheesecloth, discarding solids. If stock is not to be used immediately, cool to lukewarm. Refrigerate until fat rises to surface and congeals (about 8 hours). If stock will be used within 3 to 5 days, leave fat; skim fat when ready to use or if freezing stock.

Makes about 10 cups.

Rich Chicken Stock   For a more strongly flavored stock, add beef, pork, or veal bones and trimmings. Increase the simmering time by 1 hour or more to extract additional flavor and body. Or, follow the recipe for Chicken Stock, but begin with a previous batch of stock in place of water. The resulting "double stock" will make an excellent soup. Cutting up chickens regularly is a good way to keep a batch of stock fresh, and it gets richer with each extraction. Rich stock can always be diluted with water when a basic or thin stock is needed.

■ FISH STOCK

The best bones for fish stock come from mild fish, such as sea bass or halibut. Do not use bones from strong-flavored fish, such as tuna or mackerel. If bones are not available, substitute 1½ pounds of fish pieces for chowder. Concentrated fish stock is called fumet (see page 451).

  2 **pounds fish bones, tails, and heads**
  1 **tablespoon unsalted butter**
  1 **medium onion, sliced**
 ½ **cup dry white wine**
7½ **cups cold water**
  1 **stalk celery, cut in approximately 2-inch pieces**
  1 **bay leaf**
  8 **stems parsley (without leaves)**
 ½ **teaspoon dried thyme**

1. Put fish bones in bowl in sink. Let cold water run over bones for 5 minutes.

2. Melt butter in stockpot, kettle, or large saucepan over low heat. Add onion and cook, stirring often, until soft but not brown (about 10 minutes).

3. Add fish bones, wine, the water, celery, bay leaf, parsley, and thyme. Mix well. Bring just to a boil and skim thoroughly to remove foam. Reduce heat to low and simmer, uncovered, skimming occasionally, for 20 minutes.

4. Pour contents of pot through a fine wire-mesh strainer into a bowl without pressing down on the mass; discard solids. (Pressing down on the solids will cloud the liquid, making it unsuitable for an aspic or a clear sauce.)

5. If not using immediately, cool to room temperature. Pour into 1- to 2-cup containers. Refrigerate, covered, up to 2 days or freeze up to 3 months.

Makes about 6 cups.

■ VEGETABLE STOCK

This vegetable-based stock adds a fresh flavor to other preparations, although it lacks the intensity and stick-to-the-ribs quality of broth made from chicken or beef bones. It can be used as a substitute for chicken or beef stock in recipes for puréed or cream soups, or as the cooking liquid in any full-meal soup or stew. If you follow a vegetarian diet, this stock will work well as a foundation for many nonmeat dishes.

  2 **leeks**
  2 **tablespoons vegetable oil**
  2 **yellow onions, peeled and chopped into ½-inch pieces**
  9 **small cloves garlic, coarsely chopped**
  2 **small carrots, peeled and cut into ½-inch rounds**
  1 **parsnip, peeled and cut into ½-inch rounds**
  3 **small potatoes, quartered**
  2 **stalks celery, cut into ½-inch slices**
 ½ **pound mushrooms, halved**
  1 **teaspoon dried thyme**
  1 **bay leaf**
  1 **teaspoon dried oregano**
  4 **sprigs parsley**
10 **cups cold water**
  2 **teaspoons kosher salt**
 ½ **teaspoon pepper**
  2 **tablespoons miso (see page 525)**

1. To clean leeks: Cut off hairy root ends of leeks; remove and discard coarse outer leaves. Discard green tops. Split remaining stalk lengthwise, cutting, from leafy end, to within 1 inch of root end. Soak in cold water for several minutes. Separate leaves under running water to rinse away any clinging grit. Chop leeks across width into ½-inch pieces.

2. Heat oil in a 6-quart stockpot over medium heat. Add leeks, onions, and garlic. Stir to coat with oil and cook about 5 minutes. Add remaining ingredients. Bring to a boil, skim impurities from surface, and reduce heat to low. Cook for 30 minutes. Strain into a 3-quart bowl. Discard vegetables.

3. Stock can be stored in the refrigerator in a covered container for up to 5 days or frozen in an airtight container for up to 1 month.

Makes about 10 cups.

TIPS

SOUP GARNISHES

Garnishes can be quite simple—a few spoonfuls of chopped fresh herbs or some vegetable slivers. They can also be quite elaborate and time-consuming, like delicate quenelles. Some garnishes work better for certain styles of soup than others. Use the following lists as a guide, but certainly experiment on your own.

For Thick Soups
Croutons
Grated cheese (try Parmesan or Romano)
Julienned poultry, ham, or sausage

For Cream Soups
Chopped nuts (particularly toasted slivered almonds)
Dollop of sour cream or crème fraîche

For Clear Soups
Julienned vegetables (for consommé)
Dumplings
Gnocchi
Quenelles

For All Soups
Snipped fresh chives
Thin slices of lemon
Leeks cut in rings
Fluted mushroom caps
Thin slices of mushroom
Nasturtium blossoms
Parsley sprigs or chopped parsley
Watercress leaves

A SOUP SAMPLER

Soup has a thousand faces. It can be part of a meal or the meal itself. It can be as plain as the unadorned soothing chicken broth we all sip as a tonic when we are ill or as sophisticated and stylish as a sparkling consommé or a delicate cream soup that might begin an elaborate, multi-course dinner. In between are a myriad of combinations, textures, and consistencies which make soup cookery a delightful adventure for the creative cook.

■ CLASSIC BEEF CONSOMME WITH VEGETABLE JULIENNE AND MADEIRA

This consommé provides a light first course with a con-centrated beef flavor. Made from beef stock, it is clarified by simmering with egg whites. Ground beef and chopped vegetables cook in the stock together with the whites and give the soup its rich flavor. Preparing consommé does demand patience because quite a bit of whisking is re-quired at the beginning of the clarification process.

> 1 **small leek**
> 4 **cups Beef Stock (see page 560)**
>   **Salt and freshly ground pepper**
> 3 **egg whites**
> ½ **pound very lean ground beef**
> 1 **medium carrot, quartered lengthwise and cut in thin slices**
> 1 **medium stalk celery, halved lengthwise and cut in thin slices**
> 2 **medium tomatoes, cored and diced**
> ¼ **cup Madeira**

Vegetable Julienne

> 1 **small stalk celery**
>   **Reserved white and light green part of leek (see step 1)**
> 1 **small carrot**
> 1¼ **cups Beef Stock (see page 560)**
>   **Salt and freshly ground pepper**

1. Prepare and clean leek. Use dark green part of leek for making consommé and cut it in thin slices; reserve white and light green part for vegetable julienne.

2. Skim fat thoroughly from surface of stock. In a large, heavy saucepan heat stock until warm. Remove from heat and skim off any remaining fat by quickly drawing strips of paper towel over surface. Season stock to taste with salt and pepper.

3. In a large bowl whisk egg whites lightly until foamy. Add leek, beef, carrot, celery, and tomatoes, and mix thoroughly with egg whites. Slowly ladle in about 2 cups stock, stirring well after each addition. Slowly pour in remaining stock and mix well. Return to saucepan.

4. Cook mixture over medium heat, using large whisk to stir constantly. Stop whisking as soon as mixture just begins to bubble and looks milky; mixture should reach about 180° F on a thermometer. Continue cooking 1 or 2 more minutes, until a foamy crust forms on surface of soup, indicating that filter of egg whites has risen to top.

5. Reduce heat to low. Using ladle make small hole in egg white filter near side of pan so that soup bubbles mainly in hole. Cook, uncovered, for 45 minutes without stirring mixture or moving saucepan. Remove from heat. Taste liquid for seasoning, adding more salt and pepper through hole if necessary, but do not stir.

6. Line a large strainer with several layers of dampened, wrung-out cheesecloth. Set strainer above a medium saucepan, leaving room for consommé to drip through into saucepan without coming in contact with strainer. Slowly and carefully begin to ladle consommé into strainer, beginning where hole was made. When most of consommé is ladled through, carefully slide egg white filter and remaining consommé into strainer. Let soup drip through but do not press on filter. If consommé is not very clear, strain it again through mixture in cheesecloth. Discard solids in cheesecloth.

7. Remove any remaining fat by quickly drawing strips of paper towel over surface of consommé. Soup can be prepared ahead up to this point and kept, covered, up to 2 days in refrigerator.

8. Bring consommé nearly to a boil and stir in Vegetable Julienne and Madeira. Serve hot in small soup bowls.

Makes 3½ to 4 cups, 3 to 4 servings.

Vegetable Julienne   Peel celery, using a vegetable peeler to remove strings. Cut celery, reserved white and light green part of leek, and carrot into 1½-inch-long pieces. Cut carrot pieces lengthwise into ⅛-inch-thick slices, then cut each piece again lengthwise at ⅛-inch in-tervals to make thin strips. Cut celery and leeks into thin lengthwise strips about same size as carrot strips. Put vegetable strips in medium saucepan and add Beef Stock and a pinch of salt and pepper. Bring to a boil and skim off any foam. Reduce heat to low, cover, and simmer until tender (about 8 minutes). Drain vegetables; reserve cooking liquid. (This liquid can be reused as stock. Do not add it to consommé, or consommé will cloud.)

■ MISO SOUP

Protein-rich miso soup is traditionally served as a prelude to a Japanese meal of tempura or sushi. One-half cup of cooked, diced spinach, whole bean sprouts, or cubed tofu can be added to make a more substantial offering. Dried bonito flakes (*katsuobushi*, see page 326) and strips of seaweed (*konbu*, see page 334) are made into a flavorful broth known as dashi that gives the character to this na-tional dish.

> 2 **tablespoons red miso (see page 525)**
> 1 **green onion, sliced in thin rounds**
> 2 **mushrooms, sliced thinly**
> 2 **radishes, cut in thin circles**

Dashi

- 1 ounce konbu (dried kelp)
- 1 quart cold water, plus more as needed
- 1 ounce katsuobushi (dried bonito flakes)

Bring dashi to a boil. Stir in miso to thoroughly dissolve the miso paste. Stir in green onion, mushrooms, and radishes. Boil for 5 to 8 minutes and serve in small bowls.

Makes about 4 cups, 3 to 4 first-course servings.

Dashi In medium stockpot put konbu and the 1 quart cold water. Heat slowly, just below a boil, about 10 minutes (do not boil or flavor will be too strong). At this point konbu should be soft; if not, add ¼ cup cold water and cook until soft (about 1 minute). Remove konbu with slotted spoon and set aside. Bring stock to a boil; add ¼ cup cold water and katsuobushi. Boil, then immediately remove from heat. Let flakes settle (about 1 minute), then skim off any foam and strain soup.

Makes 3 to 4 cups.

◼ CREAM OF ANY VEGETABLE SOUP

Use this creamy base to make soup from whatever vegetable is in season. Some possibilities are given here, but try your favorite vegetable or a combination. The soup can be served hot or chilled.

- ¼ cup butter
- 1 medium onion, thinly sliced, *or*
  1 bunch green onions, sliced
- 2 tablespoons *each* flour and noninstant,
  nonfat dry milk
- 1 quart whole milk, at room temperature

1. In a large pot melt butter. Add onion and sauté until softened.

2. Stir in flour and dry milk and cook until bubbly.

3. Gradually add whole milk, stirring until soup is smooth. Heat, stirring occasionally, until soup thickens. Add your choice of vegetable (see recipes below).

4. In a blender or food processor, whirl until smooth. Serve hot or chilled.

Cream of Asparagus Remove tough stem ends from 1 pound asparagus. Cut spears into 1-inch pieces. Add asparagus and ½ cup chopped celery to soup in step 3 and simmer until tender (5 to 7 minutes). After processing add dry sherry to taste (optional).

Cream of Broccoli Coarsely chop 1 pound broccoli. Add to soup in step 3 and simmer until tender (6 to 8 minutes). After processing add dry sherry to taste (optional).

Cream of Carrot Scrub 8 to 10 carrots; slice. Add to soup in step 3 and simmer until tender (10 to 12 minutes). After processing stir in 1 to 2 teaspoons dried dill.

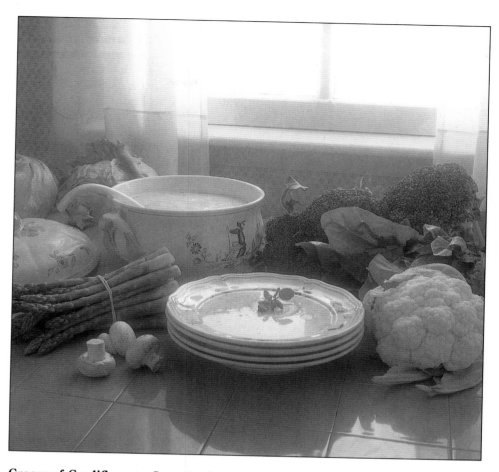

Cream of Cauliflower Coarsely chop 1 medium head cauliflower. Add to soup in step 3 and simmer just until tender (10 minutes). After processing stir in ½ cup shredded Cheddar cheese.

Cream of Lettuce In step 3 add 3 to 4 cups shredded iceberg lettuce. Cook, covered, for 3 minutes. After processing stir in dry sherry to taste (optional). Sprinkle with paprika or nutmeg.

Cream of Mushroom In the basic recipe replace 2 cups of the whole milk with 2 cups Chicken or Beef Stock (see page 560) or 1 can (14½ oz) broth. In step 3 add 1 pound (40 medium) mushrooms, sliced or chopped, and ¼ cup chopped parsley. Cook, covered, until mushrooms are soft (about 5 minutes). After processing stir in 1 cup plain yogurt or sour cream. Sprinkle with nutmeg.

Cream of Spinach Remove stems from 2 bunches fresh, cleaned spinach and coarsely chop leaves (or thaw two 10-ounce packages frozen chopped spinach). Add to soup in step 3 and simmer 3 minutes. After processing season with ¼ teaspoon dried thyme and stir in 1 cup plain yogurt. Garnish with sieved egg yolk.

Cream of Watercress Remove stalks from 3 bunches watercress. Add to soup in step 3. Cook, covered, for 3 minutes. After processing garnish each serving with a dash of nutmeg and a slice of lemon.

Low-calorie Cream of Any Vegetable Soup contains no cream—nonfat dry milk helps thicken the roux. Once the base is made, add a puréed vegetable for both color and nutrition. For the finishing touch, stir one tablespoon of Champagne or sherry into each serving.

■ GAZPACHO, UXMAL STYLE

Replete with crisp vegetables, this soup can be kept in the refrigerator for up to three days.

- 1 large can (28 oz) whole tomatoes and their liquid
- 1 tablespoon red wine vinegar
- 3 tablespoons olive oil
- 1 cup tomato juice
- 1 clove garlic, minced
- 1 teaspoon salt
- ½ teaspoon *each* sugar and dried oregano
- 1 stalk celery, finely chopped
- 1 small green chile, seeded and finely chopped *or* ⅛ teaspoon cayenne pepper
- ½ cup peeled, seeded, and chopped cucumber
- ¼ cup *each* finely chopped mild red onion and seeded green bell pepper
- ¼ cup sliced pimiento-stuffed green olives
- 1 avocado, peeled, seeded, and diced
  Lime wedges, Garlic Croutons (see page 506), sour cream, crumbled crisp bacon, and cilantro sprigs, for accompaniment

1. Reserving 2 whole tomatoes, purée remainder and liquid, vinegar, olive oil, tomato juice, garlic, salt, sugar, and oregano.

2. Pour purée into a large bowl. Finely chop reserved tomatoes and add to purée; add celery, green chile, cucumber, onion, bell pepper, and olives. Cover and chill from 8 hours to 3 days.

3. Just before serving, mix in avocado. Serve cold; pass small bowls of condiments to add to taste.

Makes about 7 cups, 6 to 8 servings.

■ VICHYSSOISE

The French name leads some to think that this classic originated in France, but it is thought to have been created in the kitchen of a New York hotel.

- 5 medium leeks (2 to 2½ lb)
- 2 tablespoons butter
- 1 small onion, finely chopped
- 3 medium smooth-skinned potatoes (1 to 1¼ lb), peeled and diced
- 2 teaspoons salt
- ⅛ teaspoon white pepper
- 4 cups boiling water or Chicken Stock (see page 560)
- 1 cup milk
- 2 cups half-and-half
- 1 cup cold whipping cream
  Salt, to taste
  Snipped fresh chives, for garnish

1. Cut off root ends and tops of leeks. Clean, drain, and slice them about ¼ inch thick.

2. In a 3- to 4-quart saucepan over medium heat, melt butter. Add leeks and onion and cook, stirring often, until soft but not browned. Mix in potatoes, salt, pepper, and the boiling water. Bring to a boil, cover, reduce heat slightly, and cook until potatoes are very tender (25 to 30 minutes).

3. Purée mixture, about half at a time, in a blender or food processor until smooth. Return to cooking pan. Blend in milk and half-and-half. Stir over medium heat until steaming hot. Strain into a large bowl. Cover and refrigerate 3 to 5 hours or overnight.

4. Using a whisk, blend in whipping cream. Taste and add salt if needed. Serve sprinkled with chives.

Makes 9 or 10 cups, 8 to 10 servings.

Recipes and Related Information

Beef Soup au Pistou, 26; Beef Soup With Noodles, 390; Budapest Borscht, 76; Chicken Quenelles, 241; Chicken Soup With Dumplings, 189; Country Watercress Soup, 607; Curried Lettuce and Pea Soup, 341; Escarole Soup, 213; Gnocchi Verde, 190; Matzo Balls, 189; Menudo, 591; Morel Soup, 379; Sherried Oxtail Soup, 501; Sorrel Soup, 548; Vegetable Purées, 487; Winter Melon Soup, 358; Wontons, 192.

STRAWBERRY

Its intense fragrance, its natural sweetness, and its brilliant red color have made the strawberry one of the world's best-loved fruits. Strawberries grow wild on several continents, including North America, and have been cultivated since at least the fifteenth century. However, it has taken years of experimentation and crossbreeding to produce a strawberry that can tolerate shipment. Today's commercial California berry, much hardier (and some say less flavorful) than its ancestors, is often shipped as far away as Europe.

Use Strawberries and cream are a marriage made in heaven, but the berries are also flattered by a sprinkling of lemon, rum, or wine. Slightly underripe berries can be sugared to bring out their sweetness. Some say that a little freshly ground black pepper also brings up the flavor of the berries. Strawberries are a favorite in ice cream, sherbet, sorbets, dessert sauces, chiffon pies, tarts, mousses, soufflés, and fruit salads. Strawberry shortcake is an American classic.

Availability When the weather cooperates, California strawberries are found from Valentine's Day through November. Elsewhere strawberries arrive on the market later and depart earlier. In most parts of the United States, supply and quality peak in May and June. Some specialty markets are beginning to offer tiny *fraises des bois* ("wood strawberries"), which have an almost candy-like flavor. They are exceedingly delicate and always expensive. Frozen strawberries are available in most supermarkets.

Selection   Ripe strawberries have a full color and fragrance. Avoid berries with white shoulders and with faint or no aroma. Berries in plastic baskets can easily bruise and mold; look the basket over carefully for decomposing berries.

Storage   Refrigerate for up to three days; berries will last longer if arranged in one layer on a paper-towel–lined tray. Wash berries just before using.

Preparation   Wash quickly and pat dry; remove hulls and inner white core with a knife or strawberry huller.

Recipes and Related Information
Berries and Cherries Rosé, 264; Berry Shortcake, 50; Chilled Fruit Mousse, 373; Dipped and Stuffed Strawberries, 128; Fresh Fruit in Wine, 347; Fresh Fruit Tart, 442; Fruit Cobbler, 51; Fruit Fondue, 254; Fruit Fool, 254; Gadgets, 259; Red Fruit Plate With Cream Cheese Dressing, 510; Strawberries in White Chocolate, 128; Strawberry Ice Cream, 312; Strawberry Jam, 319; Strawberry-Rhubarb Pie, 498; Strawberry Sauce, 522; Strawberry Sherbet, 313.

SUGAR AND SYRUP

The range of sugars and syrups employed in the kitchen is quite broad—from powdery confectioners' sugar to thick dark molasses. Each is used primarily as a sweetener, but the choice of sweetener affects texture, keeping qualities, flavor, appearance, and taste.

Use   Sugars and syrups are valued as sweeteners, but they also play other roles. In baking, sugar imparts a tender crumb and a brown crust and improves keeping qualities. Up to a point, sugar promotes yeast growth. It gives stability to whipped egg whites, creating firm meringues that can stand up to baking or poaching. Sugar is also a preservative: In sufficient quantity it slows or prevents the growth of harmful bacteria in foods. Syrups are widely used as toppings; see also specific syrups.

Availability   Granulated sugar, brown sugar, confectioners' sugar, superfine sugar, sugar subsitutes, corn syrup, honey, maple syrup, and molasses are available in all supermarkets; check health-food stores for blackstrap molasses, fructose, and turbinado sugar. Coarse sugar can be found at bakers' supply stores. Demerara sugar is more common in English markets than in American ones, but can be found in some supermarkets. Rock sugar is available in well-stocked supermarkets, Asian markets, and specialty stores.

Storage   If kept in an airtight container in a cool, dry place, all sugars will keep indefinitely. Once opened, maple syrup and molasses should be stored in the refrigerator. Store corn syrup, tightly capped, in a cool, dry, dark location.

SUGAR SYRUPS

A sugar syrup is a solution of sugar dissolved in water; it varies in concentration, depending on the ratio of water to sugar. Typically, a *simple sugar syrup* is used for poaching fruit, diluting fondant, and for adding to frostings and sherbets. To make a simple syrup, sugar and water are cooked over low heat until the granules dissolve; the heat is increased and the mixture boiled for 1 minute. For flavor, lemon or orange juice may be added to the water; extracts or liqueur may be stirred in after the syrup has boiled. A thin syrup is 3 parts water to 1 part sugar; a medium syrup is 2 parts water to 1 part sugar; a heavy syrup is equal amounts of water and sugar. A *soaking syrup* is a concentrated, flavored sugar syrup; it is used for soaking cakes and as a light glaze. If the syrup is boiled further, it begins to change character and pass through stages of concentration. See CANDY for a further discussion of these stages.

Eventually, sugar begins to change color, deepening from a pale yellow to dark brown, then rich mahogany; its flavor deepens as well. This change is called caramelization and gives its name to the chewy candy, caramel. It also adds color and flavor to such well-known dishes as *crème caramel*, crème brûlée, and pralines, and to sauces, soups, and gravies.

To caramelize sugar, cook sugar and water in a heavy-bottomed saucepan (or a special copper caramelizing pot) over low heat until sugar dissolves. The mixture can be stirred at this point (although not once the sugar dissolves or it will crystallize) and the sides of the pan should be brushed down with a damp brush to remove any sugar crystals. When sugar is dissolved, increase heat to high and cook *without stirring* until sugar deepens to the desired color. The color of the liquid changes very quickly, so monitor the process and remove from heat as soon as it is ready. To keep the color for later use, set pan in bowl of ice; this will prevent the syrup from cooking further. It will thicken as it cools; warm on stove to reliquefy.

BROWN SUGAR

A mixture of granulated sugar and molasses, brown sugar is moist and clingy when fresh. Exposure to air dries it out, but adding a slice of apple or bread to the box will restore moisture. Dark brown sugar contains more molasses than light brown sugar. Both can be substituted for granulated sugar; they will impart a slightly darker color and a subtle molasses flavor. Brown sugar tends to trap air between the crystals and should be firmly packed when measured.

CASTOR SUGAR

Also spelled *caster sugar,* castor sugar is the British equivalent of superfine sugar. The term is often encountered in old American or English recipes.

COARSE SUGAR

Also called decorator's sugar, coarse sugar is used for garnishing breads, cakes, cookies, and pastries.

CONFECTIONERS' SUGAR

Also known as powdered sugar, confectioners' sugar is made by grinding granulated sugar to a powder. Because it absorbs moisture easily, many packers add a small amount of cornstarch to prevent caking. Confectioners' sugar is most useful in uncooked dishes such as frostings and coatings because it doesn't leave a grainy texture. It should be sifted before measuring.

HOW TO CARAMELIZE SUGAR

Dissolve sugar in water over low heat in a heavy-bottomed pan. In the early stages of cooking, the liquid is nearly colorless.

Once the sugar has dissolved, increase heat to high. Do not stir or undesirable crystals will form. As the liquid cooks, it will begin to turn a golden, honey color.

Caramelized sugar is a rich, warm brown. Be sure to monitor the liquid as it cooks because the color changes occur very quickly.

CORN SYRUP

Derived from corn kernels, the thick, pourable corn syrup has certain advantages in cooking. It keeps other sugars from crystallizing, which makes it valuable in candy making. Because it is hygroscopic (it absorbs moisture), it helps keep baked goods moist. Dark corn syrup has caramel color and flavor added.

DEMERARA SUGAR

Not as highly refined as granulated white sugar, demerara sugar is a light brown or amber cane sugar that resembles light brown sugar, but is not as moist. It is common in Great Britain. Granulated or light brown sugar can be substituted for it.

FRUCTOSE

This is one of the two simple sugars (monosaccharides) that make up table sugar (sucrose). Because it is the sugar found naturally in fruits, some people believe it is less refined and more nutritious than sucrose. However, the granulated fructose in retail stores is refined from high-fructose corn syrup, not from fruit. It is sweeter than sucrose and is not directly substitutable in cooking.

GRANULATED SUGAR

Certainly granulated sugar is one of the most useful staples in the kitchen. White granulated sugar is about 99.8 percent sucrose, derived from sugarcane or sugar beets. In the United States pure cane sugar is preferred for home cooking, with beet sugar reserved for commercial food processing.

HONEY

See HONEY.

MAPLE SYRUP

Boiling the sap of maple trees produces maple syrup. The syrup is graded according to color, which is a good indication of quality. The palest, most delicate syrups are Fancy Grade. Grade A, Grade B, and Unclassified syrups have progressively darker color and stronger flavor. Maple syrup is the traditional American companion to pancakes, waffles, and corn cakes. Some people drizzle it on hot oatmeal, fried doughnuts, or cornmeal mush. It adds a delicious buttery flavor to ice cream, puddings, frostings, chiffon pies, spice cakes, and apple pies. It can be used to glaze a ham, spareribs, or cooked carrots. Pure maple syrup, imitation maple syrup, and maple-flavored syrup (with real maple flavoring) are available in most supermarkets. Some specialty stores and mail-order sources offer Fancy Grade maple syrup. Refrigerate after opening and use within a few months.

MOLASSES

The refining of cane sugar produces molasses, a by-product. Light molasses is the residue from the first boiling of sugarcane juice; the second boiling yields dark molasses. Blackstrap molasses is the very dark, strongly flavored residue of the third boiling; high in minerals, it is usually found in health-food stores. Molasses may be sulfured or unsulfured depending on whether sulfur was used in the sugar-making process.

Light molasses can be used as a topping for pancakes or hot cereal. Dark molasses is used to flavor many New England dishes. It improves the keeping qualities of breads and other baked goods and imparts a dark color and distinctive flavor to pies, breads, baked beans, and gingerbread. It adds richness and sweetness to barbecue sauce.

ROCK SUGAR

The crystallized sugar known as rock sugar may be clear or slightly amber. The Chinese use it to impart sweetness and sheen to stews and braises. It can be coarsely crushed with rolling pins and used to decorate cookies or cakes.

SUGAR SUBSTITUTES

Synthetic sugars approved for consumer use today include saccharin and aspartame. Both are sweeter than granulated sugar and are not directly substitutable in cooking.

SUPERFINE SUGAR

A fine grind of granulated sugar, superfine sugar is useful in sweetening cold beverages, raw fruits, and meringues because it dissolves so readily.

TURBINADO SUGAR

When raw sugar crystals are washed with steam in a centrifuge, they yield turbinado sugar. These coarse amber crystals have the subtle molasses flavor of brown sugar.

Recipes and Related Information
Caramels, 95; Crème Brûlée, 170; Crème Caramel, 169; Pralines, 424.

SUNFLOWER SEED

The fruit of the sunflower is a small ivory seed encased in a thin black and white shell that is soft enough to split with one's teeth.

Use Most sunflower seeds are pressed for the oil, which has industrial uses. However, the seeds themselves have a pleasant nutty flavor and crunchy texture. They can be sprinkled on salads or added to breads and granola. Unshelled seeds are roasted and salted, then eaten from the shells as a snack. Sunflower seeds are very high in protein; they can be ground to flour in a blender and then added to breads for protein enrichment.

Availability Sunflower seeds are sold roasted and unroasted (raw), salted and unsalted, in the shell and shelled. Many supermarkets carry roasted and salted sunflower seeds in packages. Check health-food stores for raw, unsalted, or shelled sunflower seeds in bulk.

Storage Keep unshelled sunflower seeds in a cool, dark, dry place; refrigerate shelled sunflower seeds. Both should be used within one month.

SWEAT, TO

To draw out the juices of a food by cooking over low heat in a fat, such as butter. At this stage, before the food has begun to brown, beads of moisture will appear on the surface. Vegetables are often given this preliminary step to remove rawness and to develop their flavor before other ingredients are added.

SWEET POTATO

A native of the New World, the sweet potato is not a potato at all but a member of the morning glory family. It has thin yellow-brown skin and golden yellow flesh. What Americans call yams (see YAM) are actually a variety of sweet potato distinguished by a copper-colored or purplish skin and deep orange flesh. American yams generally have a denser texture than sweet potatoes.

Use In the United States sweet potatoes are baked whole and eaten with butter; boiled and mashed with butter; or cubed, boiled, then glazed with butter and honey, brown sugar, or maple syrup. Sweet potatoes are present in some form on most American Thanksgiving tables. Sweetened and mashed sweet potatoes can be combined with eggs, milk, and spices and baked in a pie crust. Japanese cooks fry slices of batter-covered boiled sweet potato for tempura. In Peru chunks of boiled sweet potato are simmered in stews or served as a garnish for seviche.

Availability Sweet potatoes are sold in most supermarkets the year around, although supplies are lowest in the summer months. Canned sweet potatoes are carried by most supermarkets.

Selection Choose firm, smooth-skinned sweet potatoes without soft spots, cracks, or blemishes.

Storage Sweet potatoes are poor keepers; they may be stored in a dark, humid place for up to two weeks.

■ **MAPLE-GLAZED SWEET POTATOES**

The crusty brown slices, just slightly sweet, are good for breakfast with bacon and eggs or as a vegetable accompaniment to either poultry or ham.

> 3 to 4 (about 2 lb) medium sweet potatoes
> 6 tablespoons butter
> ¼ teaspoon *each* salt and freshly ground pepper
> ¼ cup maple syrup

1. Peel sweet potatoes, quarter them lengthwise, then cut crosswise with a sharp knife or food processor into ⅛-inch-thick slices.

2. In a large skillet over medium heat, melt butter. Add potatoes and season with salt and pepper. Toss for 1 minute or so to thoroughly coat potatoes.

3. Lower heat, cover pan, and continue to cook for about 10 minutes more. Toss occasionally to prevent sticking. Potatoes should be just tender when pierced; if not, cook a few minutes longer.

4. Add maple syrup and raise heat to medium. Cook uncovered for 5 to 10 minutes more, tossing or stirring occasionally, until potatoes are thoroughly glazed.

Serves 4 to 6.

SWISS CHARD

Also known simply as chard, Swiss chard is a variety of beet grown for its leaves rather than for its root. Two varieties are commonly cultivated: green chard, with deep green leaves and white ribs and stems, and red chard, with similar leaves and beet red ribs and stems. Both are full-flavored greens with a bitter edge.

Use Chard, both red and green, is boiled and eaten as a potherb (see GREENS). It may be seasoned with a piece of salt pork or bacon or, in the Italian fashion, with olive oil, garlic, and lemon. Italian cooks also fill raviolis with cooked and seasoned chard, add chard to soups, and bake it with Parmesan cheese.

Availability Swiss chard is most plentiful fall through spring but is available in many markets the year around.

Selection Look for crisp leaves with no browning or bruised spots.

Storage Keep in a plastic bag in the refrigerator and use within three or four days.

Preparation Because ribs take longer than leaves to cook, they should be handled individually. Cut leaves from ribs; cut ribs into smaller pieces. After cooking, combine ribs and leaves or serve separately.

Cooking See BOIL, BRAISE, STEAM, STIR-FRY.

T-Z

TAHINI

Common to Middle Eastern cooking, tahini (also spelled tahina) is an oily paste made of ground raw (untoasted) sesame seeds. A similar Chinese paste, much darker and nuttier in flavor, is made with toasted sesame seeds.

Use   Tahini seasons many well-known Middle Eastern dishes. Combined with lemon juice, garlic, minced parsley, and salt, it makes a dip known as *taratoor*. This sauce is particularly delicious with wedges of pita bread, grilled fish, or cold steamed vegetables. It may also be used as a dressing for green salads. Lebanese cooks add it to eggplant purée to make *baba ganoosh* and to chick-pea purée to make hummus. Falafel, the fried balls of cracked wheat and chick-peas popular in the Middle East, are served in pita bread with sliced tomato and a spoonful of tahini dipping sauce.

Availability   Bottled and canned tahini are sold in Middle Eastern markets, health-food stores, and some supermarkets.

Storage   Because of its high oil content, tahini turns rancid quickly. It should be refrigerated after opening and used within one or two months.

Preparation   Stir tahini well before using to reincorporate the oil floating on top.

TAMARIND

Also known as the Indian date, tamarind is the fruit of a large evergreen tree that grows in India, the East and West Indies, the Pacific islands, and the American tropics. The tree produces a brown pod in the shape of a flat snap bean, 3 to 7 inches long. As the fruit inside matures, the pod becomes very brittle. Inside the pod is a dark brown pulp surrounding firm white seeds. The pulp—the edible part of the fruit—is very sticky and both tart and sweet at the same time, resembling the taste of a sour prune.

Use   Tamarind imparts an intriguing flavor, both sweet and tart, to beverages, candies, condiments (it is an ingredient in Worcestershire sauce), marinades, and chutneys. Indian cooks make a sweet and spicy chutney from tamarind pulp. Filipino cooks add tamarind to soup broth to give it a cool, sour taste. In Indonesia chicken is marinated in tamarind-flavored water and spices before frying. In Vietnam tamarind flavors a peanut dipping sauce for grilled shrimp paste wrapped around sugarcane.

Availability   Whole tamarind pods are found in Latin American, Indonesian, Indian, and Southeast Asian markets. Most of these markets also carry tamarind pulp in firm bricks, concentrated pulp in jars, and instant powder. Dutch or Indonesian markets also offer tamarind syrup for use in beverages.

Storage   Tamarind pods, dried pulp, and instant powder can be stored indefinitely in a cool, dark, dry place. Fresh pulp or reconstituted dried pulp will keep one to two weeks in the refrigerator; freeze for longer storage. Tamarind syrup should be refrigerated after opening.

Preparation   With the exception of the instant powder, tamarind must be softened before use. To prepare whole pods, crack brittle shell and put fruit (pulp and seeds) in a bowl. Cover with water, break fruits up with fingers, and let stand overnight. Squeeze fruit with fingers to separate seeds from pulp. When pulp is very soft, press it through a sieve and discard seeds. If using tamarind pulp in blocks or tamarind concentrate, simply put a small piece in a bowl and cover with boiling water. When it is soft (30 minutes or more), press it through a sieve to separate it from seeds. Some recipes call only for the tamarind soaking liquid, not the pulp.

TAPIOCA

The starchy food known as tapioca derives from the root of the cassava, a South American and African plant.

Use   Tapioca serves both as a thickener and as a dessert in itself. Tapioca starch (also known as tapioca flour) is an excellent thickener for sauces and fruit fillings that must be frozen because it does not break down when thawed. It is also used to thicken glazes for fruit tarts because it does not cloud the glaze. Pearl tapioca, dried barley-sized balls of tapioca starch, can be made into a creamy cooked custard or baked pudding, akin to rice pudding. Pearl tapioca is occasionally used to thicken soups.

Availability   Tapioca starch is found in Latin American markets, Asian markets, and health-food stores. Pearl tapioca and instant pearl tapioca are available in most supermarkets.

Storage   Both tapioca starch and pearl tapioca will keep indefinitely in a cool, dark, dry place.

Preparation   Tapioca starch can be used as a thickener in the same manner as cornstarch. After adding it to a liquid, do not boil or tapioca may turn stringy.

■ TAPIOCA PUDDING

The tapioca pearls glisten in this soothing childhood favorite. Note that the pudding cooks slowly.

> 2 **cups half-and-half**
> 2 **cups milk**
> ⅓ **cup sugar**
> 1 **tablespoon vanilla extract**
> ½ **cup pearl tapioca**

1. Preheat oven to 300° F. Generously butter a 1½-quart ovenproof dish.

2. In a medium bowl stir together half-and-half, milk, sugar, and vanilla. Add tapioca and stir well. Pour in prepared dish and bake until a creamy, golden skin has formed on the surface (2 to 2½ hours).

3. Serve hot or warm.

Serves 4 to 6.

Recipes and Related Information
Cornstarch, 159; Pie and Tart, 436.

TARRAGON

A perennial herb, tarragon has slender, spiky green leaves rarely more than an inch long. The leaves have a pungent aroma and flavor, reminiscent of anise.

Use Tarragon is used often in French cooking, where it is considered one of the four fines herbes (sweet herbs—chervil, parsley, chives, and tarragon) added to eggs and many other dishes. It is the principal flavoring in béarnaise sauce, a relative of Hollandaise. It is particularly compatible with fish and shellfish, tomatoes, chicken, eggs, and salad greens. Tarragon is an ingredient in many recipes for green goddess dressing and tartar sauce. The whole herb is also used to flavor vinegar; tarragon vinegar is delicious in salad dressings.

Availability Fresh tarragon can be found in well-stocked supermarkets and specialty markets; it is most plentiful in the summer. Dried tarragon is found on all supermarket spice racks.

Selection Choose fresh tarragon with rich green leaves that show no signs of wilting or drying. Packaged seasonings lose quality after a while; try to buy from a store that restocks its spice section fairly often.

Storage Refrigerate fresh tarragon wrapped in damp paper towels and overwrapped in plastic; it will keep for one week. The leaves can be removed from the stems, packed tightly in a clean jar, then covered with white wine vinegar and refrigerated for up to one year. Store dried tarragon in a cool, dark, dry place, and use within one year.

Preparation Mince fresh tarragon. Tarragon packed in vinegar should be squeezed lightly to remove as much vinegar as possible before using. Dried tarragon should be crumbled between the fingers to release its essential oils when adding it to a dish.

Recipes and Related Information
Basic Single-Serving Omelet With Herbs, 203;
Béarnaise Sauce, 518; Herb, 299; Herb Vinegar, 323;
Tarragon Mustard, 323; Veal Chops With
Tarragon, 593.

TEA

Although the term *tea* traditionally refers to the leaves of the oriental shrub *Camellia sinensis*, it has come to apply to all drinks made from leaves, flowers, seeds, roots, or bark steeped in hot water. In a broad sense all teas are herbal teas since they are made from edible plant parts. Current usage, however, classifies Asian teas separately from caffeine-free herbal teas.

Use Teas may be brewed for consuming either hot or cold. They are frequently served with such optional additions as lemon, sugar, honey, or milk.

Availability Asian tea is widely sold in American supermarkets. Most supermarket tea is blended tea, packed in disposable tea bags for convenience, although some markets now stock loose tea in airtight canisters. Instant iced tea is also widely available. For a large selection of premium-quality loose teas, it may be necessary to visit a specialty store, a health-food store, or an Asian market. Many supermarkets and health-food stores now also sell a wide variety of caffeine-free herbal teas.

Selection Some of the world's most popular teas—such as English breakfast, Irish breakfast, and Earl Grey—are blends of tea leaves from various sources. Individual teas

Although paraphernalia for making coffee abounds, the preparation of tea has remained a fairly simple and straightforward process that requires little equipment. Shown clockwise from top right: teapot, sugar bowl and cream pitcher, ceramic tea infuser, tea-bag rest, metal tea infuser, cup with strainer, teapot with strainer, tin of loose tea leaves, cup with infuser.

TEATIME: IN A POT, IN A CUP, OVER ICE

To brew a pot of tea To keep the tea from cooling too quickly, warm teapot by filling it with boiling water; let stand for 1 or 2 minutes, then pour off water. Meanwhile, fill teakettle with fresh cold water from the tap. Bring water to a full, rolling boil. Put 1 teaspoon tea leaves per 6-ounce cup in the teapot. Add appropriate amount of boiling water. Cover and let steep 3 to 6 minutes for black tea, 6 to 8 minutes for green and oolong teas, and 8 to 12 minutes for herbal teas. Stir once, then pour into warm cups through a strainer (some teapots are equipped with a built-in strainer). The lengthy steeping brings out the full flavor of the tea.

To brew a cup of tea Warm a teacup by filling it with boiling water; let stand for 1 or 2 minutes, then pour off water. Bring fresh cold water to a rolling boil in a teakettle. Put 1 teaspoon of leaves in a tea ball or perforated infusing spoon. Set ball or spoon in warmed cup; pour in boiling water. Infuse 3 to 6 minutes for black tea, 6 to 8 minutes for green and oolong teas, and 8 to 12 minutes for herbal teas. Stir once with infuser, then remove infuser and serve.

To brew iced tea Make an extrastrong pot of hot tea and allow it to cool completely. Then strain tea into an ice-filled glass. This method will produce a cloudy tea. To prevent cloudiness (which does not affect flavor), make a cold-water infusion: Measure 3 tablespoons tea leaves per quart of cold water; combine in a pitcher, cover, and refrigerate for several hours, then strain over ice.

EQUIPMENT FOR BREWING TEA
The preparation of tea requires very little equipment. Select a teapot that retains heat well: Porcelain or glazed earthenware is a good choice. For catching tea leaves as you pour from teapot to teacup, you will need a strainer. The simplest ones are miniature versions of the mesh baskets used to drain cooked vegetables and pasta. More elegant strainers are chrome or even silver-plated. If brewing tea by the cup, buy an infuser. This can take the form of a mesh or perforated metal ball or a perforated spoon. The infuser is filled with tea leaves, immersed in a cup of hot water, then removed when tea has brewed to suit. Also on the market are electric teakettles imported from England; they automatically bring water to the proper boil and maintain the temperature, ever ready for that next cup of tea.

are named for their place of origin—Darjeeling, Ceylon, Keemun, and Assam, for example. Both blends and individual teas may be flavored with citrus peel, flower blossoms, or spices.

The name of a black tea sometimes reflects the size of the tea leaves. Because large leaves brew slower than small leaves, teas are usually sorted by size for more efficient brewing. Souchong (as in Lapsang souchong) denotes large leaves. Pekoe denotes medium-sized leaves. Orange pekoe teas are made of the smallest leaves.

Green tea leaves are easy to identify by their appearance. Oolong teas are also relatively easy to distinguish from black teas by their color. When in doubt, ask the merchant for guidance.

Storage Teas should be stored in an airtight container in a cool, dark, dry place. They may be kept for up to one year without loss of flavor.

Preparation Brewing tea is a simple process, but many people sidestep the few procedures necessary to brewing a superior cup of tea. See Teatime: In a Pot, In a Cup, Over Ice, above. For herbal teas, see HERB.

ASIAN TEAS

Despite their differences, the many types of Asian tea available to the consumer all come from the same plant, *Camellia sinensis*, an evergreen bush in the camellia family. The differences among teas derive from where they are grown and how they are processed. Native to Southeast Asia, the plant from which tea leaves are obtained has been cultivated in China at least since the fourth century. It thrives in tropical and subtropical climates; today most of the commercial crop comes from China, Japan, India, Indonesia, Sri Lanka, and Taiwan. The choicest teas, such as Darjeeling from the foothills of the Himalayas, are grown in high altitudes. On any given bush, the best pluck consists of the smallest leaves and the unopened leaf buds.

TYPES OF ASIAN TEAS
After plucking, the leaves are subjected to one of three different processes, depending on the type of tea desired. The countless varieties of tea are classified by their processing: fermented (black), unfermented (green), and semifermented (oolong).

Black Tea This is the type most familiar to Westerners. First the teas leaves are withered in the sun. Next, they are mechanically bruised to break their leaf cells, then left in a warm place for a few hours to ferment. This fermentation is unlike the yeast fermentation that turns grape juice into wine; the word is used in a broad sense to describe the action of enzymes on the tannin and the natural oils in the tea leaves. During this process, leaf color deepens and flavor and astringency develop. Finally, the leaves are fired to stop the fermentation process and preserve them. An expert fermentation supervisor knows just when to fire the leaves for desired color and flavor. Black teas have a rich reddish brown color and a full aroma and flavor.

Green Tea Leaves for green tea are steamed immediately after harvesting to prevent fermentation and to make them pliable. They are then rolled to crush the leaf cells. The final step is to fire or dry them with a blast of hot air. Green teas have a pale color and less aroma and flavor than black tea.

Oolong Tea To make oolong tea, the leaves are given an intermediate treatment—they are allowed to ferment partially and then are steamed to stop the process. They yield a tea somewhere between green and black tea in color, flavor, and body.

HERBAL TEAS

These teas are made from just one kind of herb or a mixture of several, with flowers and spices added. When brewed, they are sometimes known as tisanes or infusions. Popular herbal teas include chamomile, linden, jasmine, lemon verbena, hibiscus, and rose hip. The leaves and flowers of virtually any edible plant can be dried for a tisane. Most yield a pale beverage with a subtle aroma.

TEMPERATURE

The measure of the hotness or coldness of a material is its temperature. In cooking, temperature can be expressed in degrees (a 375° F oven) or with words (cook over simmering, not boiling, water). Recipes use degrees when the desired result is indicated by a particular temperature or is the product of it: "cook sugar syrup to 238° F (soft-ball stage)" or "roast for 45 minutes at 325° F." Words substitute when it's less critical to hit a temperature right on the mark: "Bring to room temperature" is a familiar cooking instruction that means to about 72° F.

Professional chefs consider internal temperature the best way to tell when food has reached a particular stage of doneness. A beef roast that is approximately 125° F in its interior will always be rare, whether cooked at 325° F or 425° F and regardless of how long it took to reach that temperature. Use the chart at right as a guide for judging when roasted, broiled, or grilled meats and poultry are done. An accurate meat thermometer or instant-read thermometer should be basic equipment in every kitchen.

TEMPERATURE EQUIVALENTS

This chart gives degrees Fahrenheit and descriptions of some common cooking temperatures.

Stage	Temperature
Freezer	0° F
Freezing	32° F (water)
Refrigerator	40° to 45° F
Cool room temperature	60° to 65° F
Room temperature	68° to 77° F
Warm room temperature	75° to 79° F
Lukewarm	98.6° F
Scalding	149° F
Simmering	210° F (water)
Boiling	212° F (water)

Oven Temperature	
Very slow	Below 300° F
Slow	300° F
Moderately slow	325° F
Moderate	350° to 375° F
Hot	400° to 425° F
Very hot	450° to 475° F
Extremely hot	500° F and above

GUIDE TO INTERNAL TEMPERATURES

Note that the internal temperature denoting a particular stage of doneness isn't the same for all types of meat. Suggested temperatures may be lower than may appear on a meat thermometer or in older recipes; the temperatures in this chart reflect the greater accuracy and reliability of home ovens and broilers today and the preference for meats that are less well-done.

Type of Meat	Rare	Medium	Well-done
Beef	125°–130° F	140°–145° F	160° F
Lamb	130°–140° F	145° F	160° F
Pork		145°–150° F	160° F
Poultry		170°–175° F	180° F
Veal		140°–145° F	160° F

THERMOMETER

Are your cookies underdone or burned? Does your frozen food lose quality sooner than expected? Is your turkey dry and tasteless, your roast medium when you really wanted rare? These can all be problems of temperature, whether of the cooking or storing environment—oven or freezer—or of the food itself. Experienced cooks know that ovens have hot and cool spots, and actual temperature can vary 25° F or more from its setting. They have learned that, for roasts, internal temperature is a better indicator of doneness than time. They also recognize that the freezing compartment in many combination refrigerator-freezers doesn't maintain the recommended setting of 0° F. Reliable thermometers are invaluable kitchen tools because their data helps the cook be more accurate and have more control over the cooking process.

TWO BASIC TYPES

Regardless of their application, thermometers are one of two types: bimetal or glass-tube.

Bimetal thermometers have a face, like a dial, and a pointer. The pointer moves by action of a spring made of two metals welded together, which react differently to heat. A change in temperature causes the spring to wind or unwind and move the pointer around the dial. Bimetal thermometers are less accurate than the glass-tube type, but the dials are easier to read and they hold a temperature reading longer. Use them when it is less critical to measure to a precise degree, such as for roasting and baking. For use in appliances, these thermometers come mounted on a stand to set on a shelf or rack and with a hook for hanging. To serve as a food probe, the dial is fastened to a stem. Select bimetal thermometers with shatter-resistant faces and clearly marked dials. Some have magnifying covers, a real advantage, or movable red arrows to mark a particular reading.

Specialized thermometers are designed for use with appliances and food. Shown top to bottom: candy and deep-fat, hydrometer, meat, instant-read, oven, refrigerator-freezer.

Instant-read thermometers are stem-type bimetal devices designed for quick response when inserted into meat, poultry, yeast doughs, and hot liquids. They have slender stainless steel shafts and a face with large numbers that register from 0° to 220° F. Unlike traditional meat thermometers that remain inserted in food throughout cooking, instant-read devices are inserted periodically, read, and removed. They will respond very quickly—in about 20 to 30 seconds. They are very versatile and highly recommended.

Glass-tube models register temperature by the expansion or contraction of a fluid—mercury or a colored liquid—trapped in a thin column of glass. The tube rests against a scale typically marked in 2°, 5°, or 10° F increments. The temperature graduations are occasionally marked on the tube itself. Glass-tube thermometers are very accurate and responsive, but are fragile and more difficult to read than a dial type. Magnifying lenses are an advantage, as are scales with dark numbers marked on a white or light background.

TO TEST FOR ACCURACY

It only makes sense that a thermometer be as accurate as possible, or why bother to use it. Use the boiling point of water, 212° F, as a reference point for probe and glass-tube stand models. Bring water to a boil, immerse either stem or entire unit (whichever is appropriate), and note the reading. If the reading is off and the model is adjustable, set it to 212° F; if you cannot reset it, note the difference, and adjust for it when you use the thermometer. For

stand thermometers with dials, set in oven, refrigerator, or freezer alongside one that you know is accurate; compare readings.

Some thermometers have a narrow temperature range that stops below the boiling point. To verify accuracy, compare with one you know to be accurate or against a laboratory model, sold at scientific equipment stores.

SPECIALTY THERMOMETERS

Some thermometers are designed for multiple uses. They usually have a wide temperature range; certain probe models are suitable for roasting, testing yeast doughs, and determining the internal temperature of foods cooked in a microwave oven. Single-application models are marked to suit their purpose. Oven thermometers begin at around 100° F and climb to about 600° F. Freezer thermometers register from -40° F to 80° F. Candy and deep-fat thermometers, often one dual-purpose device, usually start at 100° F and stop at 400° F, a range that covers all the stages of working with sugar, plus the usual frying temperature range of 365° to 390° F. Meat thermometers mark from 100° F to 220° F.

What are the benefits of specialty thermometers? Their narrow temperature range means greater accuracy. Because fewer numbers need to be indicated on the dial or scale, the markings are larger and thus clearer. Some have special adaptations, such as hooks or stands, for ease of use. As with any equipment, select the thermometers that suit your needs. A well-known brand, backed by the retailer, is always a sensible choice.

CANDY AND DEEP-FAT THERMOMETERS

When working with sugar syrups, it's critical to know the concentrations. Concentration of a sugar syrup can be measured by its appearance—threads, soft-ball stage, rigid strands, or deep brown color—or by its temperature reading on a candy thermometer. These devices are preferably glass-tube types (although bimetal ones are available and do work), and the most practical are set on a stainless steel frame with a plastic extension at the top for easy handling. They usually have a clip so that, once the sugar syrup comes to a boil, the thermometer can be attached to the side of the pan, partially immersed in the liquid, to register the temperature without the cook having to hold the device in place.

For fried foods that are neither soggy and pale from cooking at too low a temperature nor burned on the outside and underdone within from an overly high temperature, hot oil must be kept at the recommended level—usually between 350° and 400° F. Deep-fat thermometers resemble those for candy making, although the upper register is usually slightly higher.

Combination candy and deep-fat thermometers are commonly available and are a practical choice for most households. Make sure that the markings accommodate both procedures.

FREEZER THERMOMETER

Foods keep best in the freezer at 0° F. Although they are still safe to eat if stored at higher temperatures, color, flavor, and texture begin to deteriorate above 5° F. For each 10 degrees above zero, the storage life of food is cut up to half. It's a good idea to monitor the temperature of the freezer section with a freezer thermometer. Place the thermometer toward the top and front of the freezer. Leave it overnight without opening freezer door. If the temperature is above 0° F the next day, adjust the temperature control and take another reading. Freezer thermometers have hooks to hang on the front of a loaded freezer shelf.

HYDROMETER

A candy thermometer measures the concentration of sugar syrup by noting its heat. When making ice cream and sorbets, you may also want to measure density, which affects both texture and flavor—smooth and sweet, grainy and intense. The lightness or heaviness (the density or specific gravity) of a syrup, the result of how much water evaporates from cooking, is expressed in degrees Baumé (named after the French chemist who developed the scale). Taking this measure requires a hydrometer, a glass tube roughly the shape of an ordinary fever thermometer and about one third larger in size, and which is marked from 0° to 40° Baumé. To use, a solution is poured into a tall container and the hydrometer dropped in and allowed to float. The measure of density is taken at the point where the stem rises above the surface of the liquid. Hydrometers are not a usual part of a well-equipped kitchen, although they are used extensively in restaurants and commercial food preparation. You may want one if you make a lot of frozen desserts or fruit syrups. However, most recipes are designed to work without such a precise measure.

MEAT THERMOMETER

A meat thermometer measures the inside temperature of a turkey, chicken, or roast while it is in the oven. Roasting charts should be regarded as very general guidelines because there are many variables to consider—how an oven heats, the shape of the food being cooked, how often the oven door is opened, the cook's definition of doneness. Internal temperature as measured by a thermometer gives a better indication than time alone whether or not food has reached a particular stage. Meat thermometers are of two types: one that stays in food throughout cooking or the instant-read type. Cooks today tend to prefer the latter as it has a thinner shaft that won't puncture as big a hole in the food as well as a larger dial that is easier to read. Instant-read thermometers are meant for quick use so you can take a range of readings.

OVEN THERMOMETER

A variation of plus or minus 25° F from the set temperature is considered normal for even the best-quality home ovens. If you regularly use an oven thermometer, you can adjust the oven setting to match the actual heat produced and avoid guesswork and failed recipes (directions for this adjustment are in the owner's manual of your oven). Both bimetal and glass-tube stand models with hook are available. Because internal temperature can vary, place the thermometer where you will be cooking, generally on the center rack. Heat the oven to the desired temperature and check thermometer (preferably through the oven window) when oven indicates it has reached the preset temperature. If necessary, adjust oven dial, wait until the new temperature has been reached, and read thermometer again. A folding model, which uses a glass tube protected in a stainless steel case, is extremely accurate and is the instrument of choice for those who service ovens. Used for spot checks at timed intervals, it isn't left in the oven throughout the cooking period. Because of its high quality, it is considerably more expensive than other models.

Recipes and Related Information
Candy and Confection, 94; Deep-fry, 174; Freeze, 242; Ice Cream and Frozen Dessert, 308; Roast, 499; Temperature, 575.

THYME

A Mediterranean native of the mint family, thyme is one of the most widely used herbs on the pantry shelf. Its subtle aroma and flavor make it a "background" herb, rarely the major seasoning in a dish but one that gives complexity to countless culinary preparations.

Use   Thyme is a common herb throughout the Mediterranean. In southern France and Greece, it is almost always paired with lamb and often with chicken. Thyme flavors shellfish stews and chowders, gumbo, poultry stuffings, and dried bean dishes. It is often used with tomatoes and dishes with tomato sauce, as well as with eggplant, onions, or green beans. A lemon-scented variety, called lemon thyme, enhances the flavor of fish, chicken, and veal.

Availability   Some supermarkets and specialty markets sporadically offer fresh thyme, with the best availability in the summer months. Dried thyme and ground thyme are found on all supermarket spice racks.

Selection   Choose fresh herbs that have good green color; avoid those that are wilted. Packaged seasonings lose quality after a while; try to buy from a store that restocks its spice section fairly often.

Storage   Refrigerate fresh thyme in damp paper towels overwrapped in plastic; it will keep for up to one week. Store dried thyme and ground thyme in a cool, dark, dry place. Dried thyme will keep up to one year, ground thyme up to six months.

■ THYME-SCENTED CHICKEN WITH POTATOES, BACON, AND BABY ONIONS

The combination of potatoes, bacon, and baby onions is a favorite addition to braised chicken dishes in French cooking. This dish is often regarded as a symbol of good home cooking. Homemade chicken stock will produce a more flavorful, full-bodied sauce. If possible, make stock in quantity and store in the freezer.

> 1 **frying chicken (3½ lb), at room temperature**
> ¼ **pound bacon, preferably thick sliced,**
>   **cut crosswise in ¼-inch strips**
> 16 **baby onions, peeled**
>   **Salt and freshly ground pepper, to taste**
> 1 **tablespoon vegetable oil**
> 2 **tablespoons butter, at room temperature**
> 3 **tablespoons dry white wine**
> ¾ **cup Chicken Stock (see page 560)**
> 2 **sprigs fresh thyme** *or* **½ teaspoon dried thyme**
> 6 **medium-sized oval potatoes (about 1½ lb total),**
>   **peeled, halved lengthwise, and put in a bowl of**
>   **cold water**
> 2 **teaspoons flour**

1. Remove neck and giblets from chicken. Pull out fat from inside of chicken on both sides near tail. Cut off tail and wing tips. Thoroughly pat chicken dry. Sprinkle on all sides evenly with salt and pepper.

2. Heat bacon in a large, heavy, oval casserole over medium-low heat until some fat is rendered. Raise heat to medium-high. Add onions and sauté with bacon, shaking pan often. When bacon browns, transfer it to paper towels using a slotted spoon. Continue to sauté onions, turning them over carefully until they are browned on all sides. Transfer to paper towels. Discard all but 1 tablespoon fat from pan.

3. Add oil and 1 tablespoon butter to casserole and heat over medium-high heat. When foam subsides, set chicken in hot fat on its side so that leg is in contact with fat; brown side of chicken. Using two wooden spoons, turn chicken gently onto its breast and brown it. Turn chicken on other leg and brown it. Lastly, turn chicken on its back and brown it. Remove chicken from casserole.

4. Add wine, stock, and thyme to casserole, and bring to a boil, stirring to dissolve any brown bits in pan. Return chicken to casserole, placing it on its back. Reduce heat to low, cover, and simmer for 20 minutes.

5. Meanwhile, trim each potato half to an oval shape, using paring knife to round any sharp angles. Keep potatoes in bowl of cold water until ready to cook.

6. Put potatoes in large saucepan and cover with fresh water. Bring to a boil. Add pinch of salt, cover, and simmer over medium heat until nearly tender (about 20 minutes). Drain thoroughly.

7. While chicken cooks, mash remaining 1 tablespoon butter in a small bowl with a fork until softened. Mix in flour until mixture becomes a uniform paste.

8. After chicken has simmered 20 minutes, add onions, cover, and continue cooking until chicken juices run clear when thickest part of leg is pierced with a thin skewer (about 25 minutes); if juices are still pink, cook a few more minutes and test again.

9. When chicken is tender, transfer to a platter with two wooden spoons, reserving juices in casserole. Cover chicken with aluminum foil and keep it warm. If onions are tender, remove with slotted spoon; if not, cook a few more minutes until tender. Spoon onions into a bowl and add bacon.

10. Bring chicken cooking liquid to a boil. Reduce heat to low. Add potatoes, salt, and pepper; cover. Cook potatoes until they are just tender (about 10 minutes), carefully turning them often. With a slotted spoon, remove potatoes to a dish; keep warm.

11. Skim off as much fat as possible from chicken cooking liquid. Boil liquid until it is reduced to about ¾ cup; discard thyme sprigs (if used).

12. Pour liquid into a small, heavy saucepan and bring to a simmer. Gradually whisk butter-flour paste into simmering sauce, a small piece at a time, whisking constantly. Bring to a boil, whisking.

13. Return vegetables and bacon to sauce, and heat 2 minutes over low heat to blend flavors. Taste and add more salt and pepper, if needed. Discard any liquid that chicken has released onto platter. Spoon sauce and vegetable-bacon mixture around whole chicken and serve immediately. Carve chicken at the table.

Serves 4.

TIMBALE

Both the mold and the dish made in it are called a timbale. The name is French, meaning kettledrum, an apt description of its shape (see MOLD). A traditional timbale was a dish cooked in a pastry crust. Today it more often is an individually sized, custard-based vegetable or fish dish served as a first course or a side dish. The molds are small, designed for a single serving.

◼ SPINACH TIMBALES

Timbales can be baked ahead and served at room temperature, a time-saving feature a cook will appreciate. As they are prepared in individual molds, each sized for a single portion, they simplify serving. These extremely flavorful spinach molds are an excellent accompaniment to poultry.

½ cup whipping cream, warmed
1 egg
¼ teaspoon salt
⅛ teaspoon mild Hungarian paprika
  Pinch freshly grated nutmeg
½ cup cooked, chopped spinach, drained and squeezed dry
3 tablespoons freshly grated Parmesan cheese
2 tablespoons minced shallot
1 tablespoon minced parsley

1. Preheat oven to 325° F. In a medium bowl mix together cream, egg, salt, paprika, and nutmeg. Add spinach, Parmesan cheese, shallot, and parsley. Stir to blend.

2. Generously butter two 1-cup timbale or soufflé molds. Fill molds about two thirds full with mixture. Place molds in a small glass baking dish. Fill dish with hot water to reach about three fourths up sides of molds.

3. Place dish with molds in center of middle rack of oven. Bake until timbales are golden brown and a knife inserted in center comes out clean (20 to 30 minutes).

4. To unmold, run a knife around inside edge of each mold. Invert molds onto dinner plates, tap sharply with a knife, and lift off. Serve timbales hot or at room temperature.

Serves 2.

TIMER

Although most ovens these days have built-in timers, hearing them requires us to stay nearby—captive in the kitchen. Timers that we can carry with us allow us to pursue other tasks around the house while a turkey roasts, a cake bakes, or a soufflé rises. The old-fashioned hourglass still does the job, but it has become outmoded—not because it lacks trendy gears or circuits, but because it does not sound an alarm to remind us that a cooking process requires our attention. It is also unable to measure very brief units of time such as one minute or less. Timers with alarms are of two basic types: spring-action and digital.

Spring-action timers are activated by rotating a dial to the desired number of minutes; the mechanism ticks off the seconds until the dial returns to zero and then alerts you with a buzzer, beep, or bell that the time has elapsed. Battery-operated, digital timers are electronic and therefore more expensive than spring-action models. However, some can monitor four separate tasks at one time, and can measure seconds, minutes, and hours. Although most spring-action timers must be reset for more than 60 minutes, the digital timer can be programmed for almost 10 straight hours.

When deciding which timer is best for you, also consider: *Accuracy*—Some timers have play; do you need exact measurements for the type of cooking you do most frequently? *Loudness*—How loud is the alarm and how long will it ring? Will you be in the same room as the timer or will you need to hear it from some distance away? Also, some sound once for several seconds and shut off; others continue to ring until they are turned off or the battery dies. *Readability*—Are the numbers easy to read? Is the display large enough to be clear?

TOMATILLO

Despite its name and appearance, the tomatillo isn't a variety of tomato. A native of Mexico, the tomatillo is related to the ground cherry and the cape gooseberry. It resembles a small green tomato encased in a papery husk. Mexican cooks, confusingly, call it *tomate verde* (green tomato). Its texture is like that of a firm tomato; its flavor is lemony or applelike.

Use The tomatillo is rarely eaten raw in its native land, although some American diners enjoy its tart flavor in salads. In Mexican cooking, where it is an important ingredient, it is husked and simmered in water about 10 minutes to soften slightly, then puréed and used in salsas and stews. The ubiquitous *salsa verde,* a table condiment applied to tacos, enchiladas, and quesadillas, is made of ground tomatillos, onion, and chiles. Tomatillos are added to pork stews and to the several Mexican dishes cooked *en mole verde* (in green mole).

Availability   Fresh tomatillos are sold in Latin markets and some specialty markets, with peak supplies August through November. Canned, husked tomatillos are available in Latin markets.

Selection   When buying them fresh, tomatillos should be firm and unblemished. They turn yellow as they ripen, but the green ones are more desirable for their firm texture and tart flavor.

Storage   Refrigerate fresh unhusked tomatillos in a paper bag for up to three weeks. Leftover canned tomatillos should be transferred to an airtight nonmetal container and refrigerated; they will keep for up to five days.

Preparation   Husk and wash fresh tomatillos to remove the sticky residue on the surface. Simmer (do not boil) until just tender when pierced with a knife (about 10 minutes). Drain and purée or use as recipe directs.

■ SALSA VERDE

This green salsa has an unusually fresh flavor that results from the blending of tomatillos and cilantro. It is particularly good with pork, chicken, and fish dishes.

> 1   **jalapeño** *or* **2 serrano chiles, fresh or canned, chopped**
> 1   **can (12 oz) tomatillos, drained,** *or* **8 fresh tomatillos, cooked and drained**
> 2   **cloves garlic, chopped**
> 3   **tablespoons finely minced white onions** *or* **2 green onions, finely chopped**
> ¼   **cup cilantro leaves**
> ¼   **teaspoon salt**
> ¼   **cup water**

1. Place chiles, tomatillos, garlic, white or green onion, cilantro, and salt in a blender or food processor and blend briefly to a purée.

2. Add the water in small amounts and blend to desired consistency.

Makes about 1½ cups.

TOMATO

Native to the lower Andes (parts of modern Ecuador, Peru, and Bolivia), the tomato is a New World plant. The early explorers took tomato seeds back to Europe, but for many years the tomato was considered only an ornamental plant. Botanists correctly recognized it as a member of the deadly nightshade family and assumed that it was poisonous; in fact, only the leaves and stems are toxic. Up until the middle of the nineteenth century, Americans also refused to eat tomatoes. Even then, most cookbooks of the time instructed that tomatoes be cooked for three hours. The taste for raw tomatoes is primarily a phenomenon of the twentieth century.

Use   Today tomatoes are used throughout the world in countless ways, in appetizers, soups, salads, sauces, stews, and side dishes. They rarely appear at dessert, although New England cooks turn green tomatoes into a sweet green tomato pie. More typically, Americans quarter them and add them to salads, halve them and stuff them with egg salad or shrimp salad, slice them and layer them in sandwiches for moisture, and cook them with sugar and spices to make bottled catsup. Mexicans mince tomatoes with onions, cilantro, and chiles to make salsa, an everyday table condiment.

Italian cooks, famous for their tomato recipes, turn tomatoes into aromatic sauces for pasta, toppings for pizza, and luscious salads with anchovies, herbs, and olive oil. They are fundamental to the cooking of the Mediterranean region, where they figure in such famous dishes as French ratatouille, Moroccan tomato and green pepper salad, Spanish gazpacho, Greek shrimp with tomatoes and feta cheese, and Italian *pizza alla Napoletana.* Tomatoes are relatively little used throughout Asia. They are not part of the Japanese diet and were not introduced to China until the 1930s. In India tomatoes are used raw in a chopped salad and are added to a variety of stews and vegetable dishes. They appear on the Swedish smorgasbord and, in the form of tomato paste, flavor a Norwegian butter spread on grilled mackerel. South African tomatoes are, by some accounts, among the best in the world.

Even unripe tomatoes have culinary uses. In the American South, and in the upper midwestern and Plains states, green tomatoes are sliced, dipped in flour or cornmeal, and fried or simmered with onions and spices to make green tomato relish.

Availability   Fresh tomatoes are sold in most supermarkets the year around, but vine-ripened tomatoes are available only during the summer and fall. Vine-ripened tomatoes have superior flavor but are extremely fragile. For that reason, most tomatoes that must be shipped any distance are picked and shipped green and allowed to ripen in warming rooms. Hydroponic tomatoes (grown in water without soil) and greenhouse tomatoes often have a lovely appearance but generally lack flavor.

The following are popular tomatoes.

Cherry Tomato   This bite-sized, round tomato is often used as a garnish or a salad tomato.

Sauce Tomato   Also known as the plum tomato, Roma tomato, Italian tomato, or paste tomato, this egg-shaped variety has thick meat and few seeds. The meaty texture makes it excellent for sauces.

Slicing Tomato This large, slightly squat tomato is probably the most familiar, with a shape well suited to slicing. It has a large seed cavity and lots of juice, which make it better for eating raw than for cooking.

Yellow Pear Tomato A relatively recent addition to specialty markets, this tiny pear-shaped tomato is less than an inch long and is generally used in the same way as cherry tomatoes.

Supermarkets and specialty stores stock a wide variety of prepared tomato products.

Canned Tomatoes These tomatoes are available in several forms in supermarkets, such as peeled whole tomatoes, peeled and crushed tomatoes, whole tomatoes with added basil, and peeled whole plum tomatoes. In general, Italian packers pick canning tomatoes riper than American processors do; compare imported Italian canned tomatoes with American brands. Canned tomatoes are convenient for soups, sauces, casseroles, and stews. In most cooked dishes, they are preferable to unripe fresh tomatoes.

Canned Tomato Sauce Available in all supermarkets, tomato sauce is a convenience product, useful in making sauces, casseroles, and stews.

Sun-Dried Tomatoes A recent addition to most markets, sun-dried tomatoes were initially imported from Italy, but are now produced domestically as well. Sun-drying gives tomatoes a chewy texture and an almost candylike flavor. To keep them moist, they are generally packed in olive oil. Use sun-dried tomatoes as a garnish for sandwiches, pizza, salads, and soups. They add a rich tomato flavor to pasta sauces and stews. Most brands are extremely salty and should be used with restraint.

Tomato Paste Available in cans and, increasingly, in tubes, tomato paste is highly concentrated and is usually used in small amounts. Tubes of tomato paste are especially convenient because they allow the cook to use only the amount required and refrigerate the rest indefinitely.

Selection Choose fresh tomatoes by their color and aroma. Vine-ripened tomatoes have good color and a noticeable fragrance. They should be neither overly soft nor overly firm. Avoid any with blemishes or splits.

Storage Firm, underripe tomatoes can be stored in a warm, sunny spot for a few days; they will soften and improve in flavor. Ripe tomatoes can be left at room temperature for a day but should be refrigerated for longer storage; once ripe, use tomatoes within a few days. Any leftover tomato sauce should be transferred to an airtight nonmetal container, refrigerated, and used within a few days. Leftover canned tomato paste should be transferred to an airtight nonmetal container and covered with a film of olive oil to prevent oxidation. In that condition, it may be refrigerated for two weeks or frozen indefinitely.

Cover unused sun-dried tomatoes with olive oil and keep refrigerated in an airtight container; they will keep several months.

Preparation Wash and core large tomatoes. Remove caps on cherry tomatoes, if present. *To peel tomatoes:* Cut a skin-deep x in the blossom end of each tomato. Drop into boiling water and blanch 15 seconds. Lift out with a slotted spoon and drop into a bowl of ice water. Skin will slip off easily. Alternatively, spear tomatoes with a fork and hold them over a gas or charcoal flame, turning them until skin splits. *To seed tomatoes:* Halve them horizontally. Hold each tomato half over a bowl, cut side down, and squeeze to remove seeds.

▪ FRIED GREEN TOMATOES

Early cold snaps in the upper midwestern and Plains states often catch unripened tomatoes on the vine. Green tomato preserves are one way to use these tart fruits; an even faster way is to panfry them to serve as a vegetable.

    4 medium-sized green tomatoes
       Salt and freshly ground pepper, to taste
    ⅓ cup (approximately) flour
       Vegetable oil, for frying
    1 egg, lightly beaten

1. Slice tomatoes about ½ inch thick. Sprinkle lightly with salt and pepper. Dust slices with flour on all sides.

2. Pour oil into a large frying pan to a depth of about ¼ inch. Place over medium heat. While oil heats, dip tomato slices into egg to coat all sides.

3. Fry tomatoes, about half at a time, turning once, until golden brown on all sides. Serve hot.

Serves 6.

▪ TOMATOES AU GRATIN

For a more attractive presentation, halve the tomatoes with a zigzag cut. The tomatoes can broil along with salmon steaks or lamb chops.

    2 large tomatoes, halved
    2 tablespoons melted butter
    ½ cup freshly grated Parmesan or Romano cheese
    ¼ cup dry bread or cracker crumbs
    ½ teaspoon *each* paprika and dried basil
    2 tablespoons dry white wine, tomato juice,
       or chicken broth

1. Gently squeeze tomato halves to remove seeds.

2. Combine butter, cheese, crumbs, paprika, basil, and wine. Divide evenly among tomato halves, pressing lightly into tomatoes.

3. Broil on oiled aluminum foil until crumb mixture is slightly browned and tomato is warmed through (about 10 minutes).

Serves 4.

Fresh tomatoes in season have a naturally sweet flavor that needs only a simple dressing and some fresh herbs to show it off.

■ SAUTEED CHERRY TOMATOES

This is a quick summer vegetable dish that gets its flavor from fresh herbs and tomatoes in the peak of their season.

    1 tablespoon olive oil, butter, or margarine
    1 pint cherry tomatoes, stemmed
    2 to 3 tablespoons finely chopped parsley *or*
      a mixture of parsley and fresh basil, oregano,
      or thyme
      Salt and freshly ground pepper, to taste

1. Heat oil in a large skillet over medium heat. Sauté tomatoes, stirring occasionally, for 2 to 3 minutes. Cook until tomatoes are soft, but do not let them burst.

2. Sprinkle with herbs. Toss to coat. Season to taste with salt and pepper.

Serves 6.

Recipes and Related Information
Asparagus With Lemon, Tomato, and Onions, 14;
Basic Tomato Sauce, 516; Calzone With Sun-Dried
Tomatoes, 448; Dried Tomatoes, 188; Fresh Tomato
Sauce, 446; Northern-Style Tomato Sauce, 412; Okra
and Tomato Stew, 397; Tomato Dipping Sauce, 238;
Tomato Sauce, 428; Tomato-Shallot Sauce, 206;
Tomatoes With Mozzarella and Basil, 507.

TONGS

Like spatulas and knives, tongs function as extensions of your hand. They permit you to turn steaks, hamburgers, bacon, and sausages at a safe distance from heat or spattering grease, and to pluck ears of corn or other vegetables from boiling water. Tongs

can stand in as spaghetti and salad servers. Unlike a fork, tongs hold food without piercing the surface, so juices aren't lost. One type resembles heavy wire scissors and has handles and open loops for grasping. Another works like tweezers by spring action; the gripping end is wider than the shaft and sometimes has small teeth to enable a more secure hold. Made of stainless steel or chromed steel, tongs average 8 or 9 inches in length.

TOSS, TO

To mix by gently flipping or lifting food to combine or coat, as in tossing a salad. In restaurant kitchens this is often done with the hands to better feel the amount of dressing on the greens. In fact, many serious cooks do a great deal of mixing with their hands because they enjoy the tactile experience and because touch develops a more direct sensitivity to the food they are preparing.

TRUFFLE

The truffle, like the mushroom, is a fungus that grows in symbiosis with trees, specifically oak trees. Because the truffle grows underground and doesn't break the surface, it must be hunted with dogs or pigs trained to sniff it out. The impossibility of cultivation and the difficulty and unpredictability of the hunt make truffles one of the world's most expensive foods.

The two most prized varieties are the black truffle (found primarily in the Périgord and Quercy regions of France and the Umbria region of Italy) and the white truffle (found primarily in the Piedmont region of northern Italy). The black truffle has an earthy aroma and flavor that it imparts to any food it is cooked with. The white truffle is even more aromatic, with a garlicky, slightly cheesy aroma.

Use White truffles are rarely cooked; instead they are grated over hot foods as they are served. Pasta, polenta, or risotto with shaved white truffles is a great specialty of the Piedmont region. White truffles are also shaved over melted fontina cheese to make *fonduta,* the Italian version of fondue. Black truffles are used to garnish and flavor pâtés and terrines, especially those made of foie gras (fatted goose or duck liver). Black truffles flavor scrambled eggs, omelets, even mashed potatoes. Minced black truffles are added to sauces for beef, pheasant, and other rich meats and poultry.

Availability　Fresh truffles are found in late autumn to winter. In season, they are imported to the United States and are sold at specialty markets. Many specialty markets also carry canned black truffles (whole or in pieces) and tubes of truffle paste throughout the year. While they cannot match the intense aroma of the fresh item, they are more available and more affordable.

Selection　Choose aromatic, well-shaped truffles without blemishes.

Storage　Truffles are perishable and are best used immediately. To store for a few days, bury truffles in a bed of rice in a covered glass jar and refrigerate, or bury them in a basket of whole fresh eggs and refrigerate.

Preparation　Use a mushroom brush or an old toothbrush to gently clean truffles. Black truffles should be peeled (save the peel to flavor soups or sauces), then sliced paper-thin, with either a knife, vegetable peeler, or truffle slicer (see GADGETS). White truffles do not require peeling; shave them with a truffle slicer over hot food.

■ FETTUCCINE WITH WHITE TRUFFLES

This dish is delicious served as a starter for or alongside delicately flavored salmon.

> 2 tablespoons butter
> 1 tablespoon minced shallot
> 1 cup whipping cream
> 1 white truffle
> 2 ounces Italian fontina cheese
> 　Salt and freshly ground pepper, to taste
> 1 pound fettuccine, preferably fresh, cooked in lightly salted water

1. Boil water for pasta. The sauce will take about 5 minutes to make, so time pasta accordingly.

2. Melt butter in a large skillet over medium heat. Add shallot and cook until soft and translucent. Pour in cream, turn heat to high, and reduce cream by half.

3. While sauce is reducing, use a vegetable peeler or truffle slicer to shave off enough tiny slices of truffle to make about 1 tablespoon.

4. When cream begins to thicken, add cheese and stir until it is melted. Season sauce to taste, turn down heat, and keep it at a simmer until pasta is ready.

5. Drain pasta thoroughly. Add truffle shavings to sauce, then immediately toss pasta in sauce. Serve immediately on warm plates with a little freshly ground pepper.

Serves 3 or 4 as a main dish, 6 as a first course.

■ CHICKEN IN HALF-MOURNING

This classic French dish gets its name from the circles of black truffles stuffed under the skin of the chicken. They show through as black shadows when the bird is cooked.

> 1 can (25 g) black truffles *or* 1 fresh black truffle, about 1¼ inches in diameter
> 2 tablespoons Madeira (if using fresh truffle)
> 2 whole chickens (3 to 3½ lb each)
> 1 medium onion, sliced and separated into rings
> 1 medium carrot, sliced
> 1 stalk celery, sliced
> ¼ teaspoon white peppercorns
> 3 sprigs parsley
> 4 cups Rich Chicken Stock (see page 561) *or* 2 cans (14½ oz each) chicken broth and ½ cup water
> 3 tablespoons butter or margarine
> ¼ cup flour
> ½ cup whipping cream
> 2 tablespoons fresh lemon juice
> 　Salt

1. Drain and reserve liquid from canned truffles. Cut 12 thin slices from a truffle; finely chop rest of truffle(s). Place in bowl with liquid (or Madeira, if a fresh truffle).

2. Rinse chickens and pat dry; reserve giblets for another use. Remove and discard any excess fat. With two fingers, reach into each chicken from neck end and carefully loosen skin from flesh across breasts and tops of drumsticks. Using 6 truffle slices for each chicken, gently slide truffles under skin across breast and tops of drumsticks. Fasten neck and body cavities of each chicken with a skewer. Place chickens side by side in a deep, heavy Dutch oven just large enough to hold them both.

3. To chickens, add onion, carrot, celery, peppercorns, parsley, and stock. Bring stock to a boil over medium heat; then cover, reduce heat, and simmer until chickens are very tender when thighs are pierced with a fork (about 1½ hours). Remove chickens to a warm platter; cover with aluminum foil and keep warm.

4. Strain cooking liquid, discarding vegetables. Skim and discard fat. Return liquid to a boil over high heat, uncovered, until reduced to 2½ cups. Remove from heat.

5. In a 2- to 3-quart saucepan over medium heat, melt butter. Blend in flour; cook and stir until bubbly. Remove from heat; gradually blend in the 2½ cups reduced chicken broth. Cook, stirring until thickened and boiling. Blend in cream and return to a boil, stirring often. Stir in lemon juice and chopped truffles plus liquid (or Madeira). Add salt, if needed.

6. Spoon about a third of the sauce over and around chickens; serve remainder in a warm sauceboat. Use poultry shears to cut chickens into quarters to serve.

Serves 8.

TRUSSING POULTRY

Fold wing tips under ribs. Force legs down into wing joints to stabilize bird. Cut a piece of twine about four times length of bird (to measure, drape string around bird as shown above).

Lay string across and under neck opening; draw string up over wings and under drumsticks. Pull ends toward you between drumstick and breast on each side and cross over.

Bring string over ends of drumsticks, making sure it goes across end of breastbone. Take string under bird, flip bird over, and tie tightly with a half bow. Snip away extra string. Bird is now ready for cooking.

TRUSS, TO

To secure the appendages of a bird close to the body. Trussing holds the bird together during cooking so that, when finished, it has an attractive appearance and even shape. With stuffed poultry, trussing keeps the stuffing from falling out.

There are many ways to truss poultry. The simple tie method shown here is easy for the home cook to employ. If you wish, you can augment this method by closing up the cavity with small poultry skewers. It is very important to tie the bird tightly; the more tightly the string is drawn, the better and more rounded the cooked bird will be. Use a kitchen twine made of natural fiber and of as heavy a gauge as you can find. Very thin twine may cut into your hands when you are making the final pull. Some birds come with the legs held together by a metal clip, which serves the same purpose as trussing. Remove all trussing, whether by metal clip or string, before the bird is served.

> ***Recipes and Related Information***
> *Needle and Fastener, 384; Poultry, 468.*

TURMERIC

Like its relative ginger, turmeric is a rhizome—an underground stem. It resembles ginger externally, but its color and flavor are very different. Turmeric has a bright yellow-orange color and a pungent, slightly acrid flavor.

Use Because of its vibrant color, turmeric is used as a fabric dye in Asia; in this country, it is sometimes employed to color margarine and other dairy products. It adds color and flavor to American-style mustard and is a major ingredient in commercial curry powders and in many homemade Indian spice blends. Turmeric is also used to color and flavor pickles, Indonesian rice dishes, and Balinese roast pig. Slices of fresh turmeric are used by Southeast Asian cooks to flavor and color soups.

Availability Fresh turmeric is sold in a few Southeast Asian markets; dried whole turmeric is sometimes available in Indian and Southeast Asian markets. Dried ground turmeric is found on supermarket spice racks.

Selection Packaged seasonings lose quality after a while. Try to buy from a store that restocks its spice section fairly often.

Storage Ground turmeric will keep in a cool, dark, dry place for up to six months.

TURNIP

A sweet, crisp-textured root vegetable, the turnip has the squat round shape of a spinning top. Its flesh is white, its thin skin white with purple shoulders. When grown in cool climates and picked young, the turnip is mild, crisp, and sweet; turnips grown in hot weather can develop hot flavors, and older turnips can be woody inside. Turnip greens are also edible when young (see GREENS).

Use Young turnips can be peeled, sliced, and eaten raw with dips or in salads. More often, however, turnips are boiled or steamed, then tossed with butter and parsley. Turnips can also be boiled and mashed with butter and cream, puréed for soup, or added to soups. In France turnips are a sign of spring and are often paired with roast duck on spring menus.

Availability Turnips are sold in many supermarkets the year around but are best in the cool months.

Selection Turnips should be firm to the touch, not spongy or rubbery, and should feel heavy for their size. Avoid large turnips, which may be woody inside.

Storage Turnips will keep several weeks in a cool, humid place or in the refrigerator.

Preparation Wash, trim ends, and peel.

Cooking See BOIL, STEAM, STIR-FRY.

Recipes and Related Information
New England Boiled Dinner, 42; Winter Salad of Beets and Turnips, 48.

UGLI FRUIT

The ugli fruit is a cross between three citrus fruits: the grapefruit, the orange, and the tangerine. It is about the size and color of a yellow grapefruit, but its thick rind is bumpy. Its pink flesh is sweeter than both the grapefruit and the orange, and it has few seeds.

Use Ugli fruit, which is grown in Jamaica, is most often eaten out of hand like an orange. However, it may be used in any of the ways oranges and grapefruits are: in sherbets, sorbets, or fruit salads, for example.

Availability Ugli fruit is sold in some specialty produce markets in the winter.

Selection The skin of ripe ugli fruit has a hint of orange.

Storage Refrigerate and use within one week.

Preparation Ugli fruit peels easily. Peel and section as you would an orange, or halve and section as you would grapefruit.

UNMOLD, TO

Both *unmold* and *turn out* have the same meaning when used in a recipe: to remove food from its container, with the implication that the food is firm enough to hold its shape when out of the mold. *Unmold* describes removing a gelatin-based mixture from a mold. *Turn out* usually refers to removing a baked pastry from the pan in which it was baked.

Oiling mold or spraying with vegetable cooking spray will aid unmolding. The best method is to dip mold quickly into a pan of very hot water; this should take at the most 5 seconds (less for cream-based mixtures). If you notice a slight movement of the food within the mold, or a little melting at the edges as you try to slide it from side to side, you will know it is ready to be removed. Too much

time in hot water will melt some of the gelatin, destroying detail and shape.

If molding onto a serving plate, first rinse plate with cold water. The water will make the plate slick, which will allow you to center the food by sliding it gently in place. Place serving plate over mold, invert it rapidly, and give mold a firm shake or tap. Molded food should drop smoothly onto plate. Sometimes it may be necessary to slip a thin-bladed knife between food and mold to release the vacuum that holds food in place. Then, if it doesn't come right out, leave mold inverted on plate for a few minutes and let gravity do its work. If a chilled mold, return to refrigerator to firm up before serving.

Cakes, cupcakes, muffins, and loaf breads are turned out by inverting the baking pan over a wire cooling rack and lifting off the pan. Some recipes suggest letting baked product sit in its pan for 10 or 15 minutes before turning out; the steam that builds up as the food cools will help release food from pan. To remove tarts from tins with loose bottoms, push up the removable bottom and allow sides of tin to fall away from tart. For tarts baked in a tart band, lift off the ring, then slide tart onto a cooling rack.

Recipes and Related Information
Gelatin, 264; Mold, 369.

VANILLA BEAN

The vanilla bean is the pod of an orchid native to Central America. When ripe and ready for handpicking, the pod is yellow and odorless. Its characteristic aroma and dark color develop during a period of slow sunning and drying. Whole commercial vanilla bean is generally about 4 to 5 inches long and chocolate brown. Slit open lengthwise, the pod reveals hundreds of minuscule black seeds, which appear as specks in many high-quality vanilla ice creams.

Use Vanilla is prized for the flavor it imparts to other dishes, primarily sweets. It is the most popular ice cream flavor in America, and it enhances other custard desserts as well. Vanilla is almost always used to flavor flan (*crème caramel*), custard sauce (*crème anglaise*), pastry cream, and rice pudding.

Vanilla adds its intriguing taste to most cakes and cookies and is often used to flavor whipped cream. Vanilla is also appealing with many fruit desserts. Pears, peaches, apples, or apricots may be poached in a syrup flavored with vanilla beans; it is commonly added to applesauce and banana desserts. It is often paired with chocolate because it heightens the chocolate flavor. The Aztec emperor Montezuma was said to have flavored his hot chocolate with vanilla. Vanilla Sugar (see Fragrant Vanilla Sugar, at right) can be sprinkled on strawberries, pie crusts, and ricotta cheese; many cookie recipes call for rolling the finished cookies in vanilla sugar.

TIPS

FRAGRANT VANILLA SUGAR

When either granulated or confectioners' sugar is infused with the flavor and perfume of vanilla bean, the result is a delicious product that can be substituted for plain sugar.

Vanilla Granulated Sugar Split a vanilla bean in half lengthwise. Place both halves in a tall jar. Fill jar with 1 to 2 cups granulated sugar. Cover and let stand for at least 24 hours for sugar to absorb vanilla flavor. Replenish sugar as you use it. Vanilla will continue to flavor sugar for up to one year.

Stirring may dislodge some of the tiny seeds inside the split vanilla bean. They're a potent flavor as they become distributed throughout the sugar. If these tiny specks become too numerous, strain sugar through a fine sieve as you use it, returning seeds to sugar in jar.

Vanilla Confectioners' Sugar Substitute confectioners' sugar for granulated sugar in the directions given above.

Availability Whole vanilla bean is found in the spice section of most supermarkets and specialty food stores. All supermarkets carry bottled pure vanilla extract and imitation vanilla extract. Pure extract is more expensive but is far superior in flavor. Specialty stores may offer several brands of pure extract for you to choose from.

Selection Whole vanilla beans should be pliable and should have a fine white "bloom" of vanillin crystals on the outside. Avoid any that are excessively hard and dry. The best pure vanilla extract has a rich, well-balanced aroma and flavor.

Many American tourists are tempted to bring back vanilla extract from Mexico where it is inexpensive and exceptionally strong. However, some "pure" Mexican vanilla extract may be adulterated with coumarin, a plant derivative with vanilla flavor. Unfortunately, coumarin is mildly toxic. To be safe, purchase Mexican vanilla extract only from a source that can guarantee its purity.

Storage Vanilla bean can be stored for several months in a tightly covered jar in a cool place; if the bean is to be used again after cooking, rinse, wipe bean free of liquid, and store as directed. Store vanilla extract in a cool, dark place for up to one year.

Preparation Like all alcohol-based extracts, vanilla extract is highly volatile (its flavor dissipates when exposed to air and heat). For maximum effect, add it to cool or cooling liquids. Whole vanilla bean can be added to a sauce or simmering liquid, then strained out. Rinsed and dried, the bean can be reused. Alternatively, split the vanilla bean lengthwise and scrape the seeds into the simmering liquid.

Recipes and Related Information
Custard, 168; Extract and Essence, 213; Ice Cream and Frozen Dessert, 308.

VARIETY MEAT

The term *variety meats* (or *offal*) is applied to the innards and the extremities of the animals we eat. In the United States these are among the least appreciated items in the meat case, although they are also among the most affordable and most delicious. In other countries, variety meats are often highly prized; European, Latin, and Asian cooks have developed countless dishes that take advantage of the special flavors and textures of variety meats.

Use Around the world, variety meats are enjoyed in appetizers, soups, salads, and main courses. In Italy sweetbreads and kidneys are used as a garnish for pasta and risotto. Tongue is often eaten cold as a salad or sandwich filling. Brains are also occasionally eaten cold, with mayonnaise or vinaigrette. As a main course, variety meats can be sautéed, braised, grilled, or fried. Delicate

tripe is better suited to slow braising or to the hearty soups popular in Mexico and Spain. Kidneys can be grilled with bacon, and brains can be coated with batter and fried.

Availability Few American supermarkets stock fresh variety meat because the meats are highly perishable and there is not a strong demand for them. Ethnic markets and supermarkets with a large Latin, Asian, or black clientele have a larger selection of variety meats. Most butcher shops can order them for you. A discussion of the most-available variety meats follows.

Selection Because variety meats are highly perishable, freshness should be your first consideration when purchasing. It is advisable to buy from a butcher who can attest to the freshness of the meats and who will let you smell and inspect the items before buying. Freezing tends to damage the delicate texture of most variety meats. However, if they were frozen while still very fresh, were carefully wrapped, and were thawed slowly, they are a better choice than meats that are labeled fresh but are actually several days old.

Storage Again, remember that fresh variety meats are perishable and keep only a few days. If purchased fresh, variety meats should be refrigerated and used within two days. If purchased frozen, they can be kept in the freezer for up to three months; thaw slowly in the refrigerator before cooking.

Preparation See specific variety meats.

Cooking See BRAISE, FRY, GRILL, POACH, SAUTE.

BRAINS

In the United States, the brains offered on restaurant menus are almost invariably calf's brains, prized for their smooth texture and delicate flavor. However, pork, beef, and lamb brains are also available to cooks who seek them out. Check specialty butchers and ethnic markets for brains; they may have to be ordered in advance.

Brains consist of two symmetrical, ridged lobes held together by a thin membrane. They should be firm and plump, with a moist, shiny surface, and with no off-odor. Soak the brains in cold water for 30 minutes, changing the water several times, to draw out blood and make the membrane easier to remove. Peel away the membrane; soak brains an additional hour to whiten them.

Some recipes call for poaching brains in a seasoned court bouillon until firm (about 25 minutes for calf's brains). After poaching, they may be sliced and served with vinaigrette or with brown butter, coated with batter and fried, or scrambled with eggs. Other recipes call for a brief blanching (about 5 minutes) to be followed by further cooking. After blanching, they may be floured and pan-fried in butter; coated with butter and bread crumbs and baked; or sautéed with mushrooms and cream.

■ BRAINS IN BROWN BUTTER SAUCE

This is the classic recipe for brains, and for good reason—the sauce has just the right amount of tartness to give the tender unctuousness of the brains a little bite. If desired, with this recipe poaching can be omitted; the brains will be a little stronger tasting, but even more tender.

 1 pound lamb's or calf's brains, soaked, trimmed, and, if desired, poached (see page 586)
   Salt and white pepper, to taste
 ½ cup Clarified Butter (see page 68)
 1 tablespoon drained capers
 ¼ cup plus 1 tablespoon minced parsley
 ¼ cup fresh lemon juice
 ¾ cup sifted flour
 2 tablespoons unsalted butter
 1 tablespoon olive oil
 1 large lemon, cut in 8 wedges

1. Slice brains ½ inch thick. Dust lightly with salt and pepper and set aside. In a slow oven, gently warm a small, heavy bowl and a plate that will cover the bowl comfortably.

2. In a medium saucepan, heat Clarified Butter over medium heat; let darken to golden brown, then remove from heat. Stir in capers and the ¼ cup parsley; pour into warmed bowl (reserving saucepan), cover with plate, and return to oven to keep warm.

3. Pour lemon juice into saucepan used to cook butter. Over high heat, cook down lemon juice to about 1 tablespoon. Season with salt and pepper; add to warm butter mixture, cover with plate, and return to oven to keep warm.

4. Dredge brain slices in flour; shake off excess. In a large skillet, heat the 2 tablespoons unsalted butter and olive oil over medium heat. When butter stops foaming, add brains; increase heat to medium-high and brown on both sides until golden (about 3 minutes per side). Remove slices with a slotted spoon to a serving dish; pour reserved butter sauce over them, and serve garnished with 1 tablespoon parsley and lemon wedges.

Serves 4.

CHITTERLINGS

The large intestines of pigs are called chitterlings. Some markets sell whole chitterlings; others slit them and cut them into sections. Fresh chitterlings should be pinkish beige and moist; they may have a strong odor. To prepare, cut into lengths and slit open. Soak two hours in several changes of acidulated water; drain, dry, and pull off fatty inner lining.

Chitterlings may be simmered three to four hours with tomato sauce, herbs, and spices; they may be marinated or highly seasoned and stuffed into chitterling casings to make sausages. Sausages made of tripe or chitterlings are known as *andouilles* in France and are quite popular.

EARS

Fresh pig's ears should be pale pink and dry, with a smooth, not sticky, texture. To prepare, scrape ears with a small knife or stiff brush to remove any hairs; to singe off stubborn hairs, hold ear over an open flame. They should be parboiled 5 minutes, then rinsed and kept in acidulated water until ready to cook. French cooks stew pig's ears with pig's feet, vegetables, and herbs. German cooks dice the parboiled ears and braise them with peas, herbs, and potatoes. In Portugal the ears are braised whole until tender with herbs, garlic, tomatoes, and peppers.

FEET

Calf's feet are a rich source of gelatin and are often added to veal stock or a slow-cooked stew to give it body. Moroccan cooks make a highly spiced stew of calf's feet, bulgur, and chick-peas. In Germany pig's feet are stewed with sauerkraut; in France they are braised until tender, then rolled in butter and bread crumbs and broiled. In Greece,

Delicate sweetbreads are enriched with a wine-flavored sauce and fresh, sautéed mushrooms. The recipe appears on page 590.

Steak and Kidney Pie is traditional lunchtime fare in pubs throughout England. Broiled tomatoes and a hearty English beer or ale are appropriate accompaniments.

where lamb is popular, lamb's feet are simmered until tender and served with egg and lemon sauce. Chicken feet are used by cooks all over the world to give body to chicken stock. Chinese cooks braise duck feet with black beans and serve them as dim sum, a tea-house snack.

Select feet that are moist; avoid those that are sticky, dry, or blemished, or that have an off-odor. Scrape or singe off any stray hairs. Some recipes call for feet split lengthwise; a butcher can easily do this for you.

Recipes: Menudo, 591.

FRIES

The testicles of lamb, pigs, beef, and veal are known as fries. They are also sometimes referred to as mountain oysters; beef and veal fries are sometimes also known as Rocky Mountain oysters or prairie oysters. Fries should be plump and firm, with their outer skin intact. To prepare, slit the three layers of skin with a small sharp knife without slitting the flesh; pull off the skin. Soak fries in several changes of acidulated water to draw off any blood. Cover fries with cold salted water, bring to a boil, and simmer until firm (6 to 7 minutes). Drain and pat dry. They may then be sliced, coated with egg and bread crumbs, and fried; dipped in fritter batter and fried; browned slowly in butter and spices; or simmered in a highly seasoned tomato sauce. Fries are highly perishable.

GIZZARD

Chicken gizzard, the equivalent of the stomach in other animals, is tough but flavorful if properly prepared. It has a tough membrane that must be trimmed away. The gizzard may then be diced and browned slowly in butter with other giblets for giblet gravy, stuffing, or stew. Cajun cooks add finely ground cooked gizzards and black pepper to steamed rice to make dirty rice. Fresh gizzards should be plump and shiny, without an off-odor.

Recipes: Roast Turkey With Giblet Gravy, 474.

HEAD

Recipes for pig's, lamb's, goat's, or calf's head are common in many cuisines. Mexican families may roast a whole goat, including its head, as a celebration dish; Greek families do the same with goat or lamb. Whole heads may be boned, laid flat, and wrapped around a stuffing; they may be halved and baked with vegetables until tender; or they may be boned, poached, and served hot with vinaigrette, *salsa verde* (Italian parsley and caper sauce), or fresh tomato salsa and hot tortillas.

Ask the butcher to remove the eyes and to bone or split the head, as the recipe requires. Soak the head in several changes of acidulated water to draw out blood. Keep in acidulated water if cooking that day; otherwise, pat dry, wrap in plastic, and refrigerate for up to three days.

HEART

The deep-red heart muscle is richly flavored but tough if not properly handled. To prepare heart, trim away any visible fat, fibrous tissue, and tubes. Large beef hearts may be stuffed, tied, and braised whole. In Peru beef heart is served as an appetizer, after being cubed, marinated, skewered, and grilled over coals. Hearts can be braised with wine, herbs, and vegetables or cut in julienne strips and stir-fried with vegetables and soy sauce. Poultry hearts can be minced, sautéed in butter, and added to stuffings or gravy. To keep large hearts tender, they should either be sliced thinly and cooked quickly or kept whole or in large pieces for slow braising.

KIDNEY

Lamb and pork kidneys consist of a single lobe; beef and veal kidneys are multilobed. Beef, lamb, and pork kidneys are dark red; veal kidneys are slightly lighter. Kidneys have a rich flavor and firm texture and are appealing on their own or added to other dishes. English cooks have many kidney dishes in their repertoire, including the famous Steak and Kidney Pie and kidneys broiled with bacon or braised with mushrooms and cream. The English also find a place for kidneys on the breakfast table. Chinese cooks stir-fry pork kidneys with vegetables; French cooks braise kidneys with mustard or mushrooms and cream, or grill them with herb butter.

Beef, veal, and pork kidneys should be plump, firm, and encased in a shiny membrane. Lamb kidneys are often sold encased in their fat, which should be off-white. Avoid kidneys with a strong odor.

To prepare kidneys, trim away any fat and connective tissue and pull off the outer membrane. Beef and veal kidneys should be halved to allow for easier removal of fat and tissues.

■ STEAK AND KIDNEY PIE

Some of the most typical and enjoyable English foods can be found in pubs (public houses), especially at noontime. There you are likely to find well-prepared cold plates, fine cheeses, and exceptional meat pies such as this well-known preparation. The pie may be assembled in advance (through step 3), covered, and refrigerated for several hours before baking. Accompany Steak and Kidney Pie with a green vegetable and a crisp salad. The pastry is easily made from frozen puff pastry shells, available in the freezer cases of specialty food stores and well-stocked supermarkets. The frozen shells will thaw to a consistency suitable for rolling in about 20 minutes.

 6 tablespoons flour
1½ teaspoons salt
 ¼ teaspoon *each* ground pepper, dried
    thyme, chervil, marjoram, and summer savory
 2 pounds boneless top round steak, cut in
    ½-inch cubes
 ½ pound beef or lamb kidneys, sliced
 ½ pound mushrooms, quartered
 2 tablespoons butter or margarine
 ½ cup dry red wine or Beef Stock (see page 560)
    or regular-strength canned beef broth
 6 frozen puff pastry patty shells (10-oz package),
    thawed
 1 egg, beaten with 1 teaspoon water

1. Preheat oven to 325° F. In a large bowl mix flour, salt, pepper, thyme, chervil, marjoram, and savory. Mix in steak cubes and kidney slices, coating well with flour mixture.

2. Sauté mushrooms in butter until lightly browned.

3. Place half the beef and kidney mixture in a 2-quart, 2-inch-deep baking dish. Top with mushrooms, then with remaining meat. Pour on wine or stock.

4. Arrange the patty shells, overlapping slightly, on a floured board or pastry cloth. Roll out pastry into a slightly larger shape than the top of the casserole. Lay pastry over meat mixture; trim and flute edge, sealing it to baking dish. Pierce or slit top in several places to allow steam to escape. Trim with pastry scraps cut into decorative shapes, if desired.

5. Brush pastry with egg mixture. Bake until meat is tender (insert a long wooden skewer to test) and pastry is well browned (1½ to 2 hours). Serve immediately.

Serves 6 to 8.

LIVER

Appreciated by cooks throughout the world, liver has a rich flavor and smooth texture. Beef, veal, pork, lamb, duck, and chicken all have delectable livers that may be used in countless ways. Beef and veal livers can be roasted whole but they are usually sliced and pan-fried. Calf's liver with onions is a popular Venetian dish. Chicken livers can be fried with bacon and served with rice or pasta. Duck livers make an unctuous, savory mousse or a rich topping for pasta. Chopped liver, that staple of the Jewish delicatessen, is usually made with beef liver but may also contain chicken liver; it is served as an appetizer with crackers or as a sandwich filling. German cooks make delicate calf's liver dumplings to float in soup. Chinese cooks stir-fry pork liver with green onions and mushrooms. Goose liver is made into a rich, creamy spread by Middle European cooks. The famous fatted goose and duck livers of France (foie gras) are one of the world's greatest delicacies, served cold in the form of a terrine or pâté, or sliced, pan-fried, and served hot.

Liver should be firm and moist, with a shiny appearance, and without any off-odor. True calf's liver is easy to distinguish from beef liver by appearance: Calf's liver is a pale reddish brown; beef liver is a dark reddish brown that verges on purple. To prepare livers, trim away any visible fat and tough connective tissue. Calf and beef livers, if purchased whole, both have a thin exterior membrane that should be pulled off. Liver is sometimes soaked in milk for one hour before cooking to "sweeten" it. Cook liver briefly and quickly; overcooked liver is dry, tough, and disagreeable.

Recipes: Curried Chicken or Duck Liver Pâté in Aspic, 416; Chicken or Duck Liver Mousse, 372.

SWEETBREADS

The thymus glands of calves or young lambs, sweetbreads gradually shrink as the animal ages. They are delicate in taste, smooth and soft in texture, and are considered a delicacy by many diners. Calf's sweetbreads are readily available from most specialty butchers, either fresh or frozen. Lamb sweetbreads may require special ordering. Sweetbreads should be plump and firm, with the exterior membrane intact.

Soak sweetbreads in several changes of cold water for one hour to draw out any blood. Then blanch in simmering acidulated water for 3 to 5 minutes (depending on size) and plunge into cold water to firm them. When cold, drain them and trim away any membranes and connective tissues. If serving whole, chill several hours under a weight to firm and shape; otherwise, separate with hands into smaller lobes.

Sweetbreads may be braised with peas or with mushrooms and cream; wrapped in bacon, skewered, and grilled; or braised in butter and served atop spinach or sorrel purée. They are also sautéed, poached, and broiled.

■ SWEETBREADS AND MUSHROOM-MARSALA SAUCE

The exuberance of Marsala and the luxury of sautéed mushrooms unite in a light, buttery sauce that bathes sweetbreads in a warm, rich Italianate glow. Serve with French-fried potatoes to dip in the sauce, and follow with a tartly dressed green salad.

½ cup unsalted butter
1 small onion, minced
1 medium carrot, finely diced
2 tablespoons minced shallot
¼ cup finely diced mild cooked ham
½ pound mushrooms, sliced
1½ to 2 pounds sweetbreads, soaked, blanched, trimmed, weighted, and sliced if pieces are large (see page 589)
Salt and freshly ground pepper, to taste
½ cup Marsala
1 cup Beef Stock (see page 560) or canned consommé
¼ teaspoon dried marjoram
3 tablespoons minced parsley
1½ tablespoons flour

1. Preheat oven to 350° F. In a flameproof, heavy-bottomed, 2-quart casserole, melt 3 tablespoons of the butter over low heat. Add onion, carrot, shallot, and ham; cover and cook over low heat until tender (about 10 minutes). Uncover and add mushrooms and 3 more tablespoons butter. Set remaining 2 tablespoons butter aside to soften. Increase heat under casserole to medium and sauté vegetables until mushrooms darken and begin to soften.

2. Season sweetbreads with salt and pepper. Combine with vegetable mixture in casserole. Pour on Marsala and stock; add marjoram, 2 tablespoons of the parsley, and additional salt and pepper to taste. Cover and bake 45 minutes.

3. Remove casserole from oven. With a slotted spoon, remove sweetbreads and most of the vegetables to a bowl. Set a colander over bowl and invert bowl over casserole so that liquid from sweetbread mixture drains back into casserole. Set sweetbread mixture aside in bowl, covered, and keep warm.

4. Over highest heat, boil down liquid in casserole until reduced by ½ to 1 cup, stirring frequently and scraping sides and bottom of casserole. Meanwhile, work remaining 2 tablespoons butter together with flour to make beurre manié. When liquid has reduced, add beurre manié to casserole. Lower heat to medium, and cook, stirring constantly, until butter melts and sauce thickens (about 1 minute). Correct seasoning. To serve, spoon sweetbreads onto a serving dish or individual plates. Pour on sauce and garnish with remaining parsley.

Serves 4 to 6.

TAIL

Beef tails (usually identified as oxtails) and pig's tails are appreciated by many diners for their rich meat and gelatinous texture. Slow braising tenderizes them and softens the gelatinous cartilage. Both oxtails and pig's tails may be stewed in wine with herbs and aromatic vegetables. The pieces can also be braised, then coated with butter and bread crumbs and broiled.

Fresh oxtails are almost always sold pretrimmed and sliced. They should have bright red meat and white fat. Pig's tails are available from ethnic markets; the meat should be firm and rosy red, the fat creamy white.

Recipes: Sherried Oxtail Soup, 501.

TONGUE

Fresh tongue—whether beef, veal, lamb, or pork—should be firm, and with no off-odor. Tongue has a rich flavor and firm meaty texture and is appealing on its own or in combination with other foods. Small whole lamb tongues can be pickled or preserved in aspic. Whole tongue can be poached and served hot or cold with mayonnaise, vinaigrette, or *salsa verde* (Italian parsley and caper sauce); it may be braised with wine and vegetables and served hot in a rich sauce. Poached tongue may also be cubed and tossed with cold vegetables and a vinaigrette for a salad. Whole tongue may be corned or smoked, thinly sliced, and served in sandwiches, traditionally on rye bread with mustard.

Fresh tongue should be soaked in several changes of cold water for two to three hours to draw out blood before cooking. A corned tongue should then be blanched 5 minutes and rinsed to remove excess salt. Poach fresh or corned tongue in court bouillon until tender (1½ to 2 hours for beef tongue, 30 minutes for lamb tongue). Drain; when cool enough to handle, trim away fat and gristle and peel off skin, which is easier to remove while tongue is hot.

Recipes: Boiled Dinner Bolognese, 530.

TRIPE

The muscular lining from two of the four parts of a ruminant's stomach is called tripe. Beef tripe is the most common; some butchers may be able to obtain veal and lamb tripe by special order. Smooth-textured tripe comes from the first stomach; honeycomb tripe, which owes its name to its appearance, comes from the second stomach. Fresh tripe should have an ivory color and no off-odor. By the time it appears in the market, it has already been cleaned, soaked, and precooked. It should be rinsed in cold water and patted dry.

Tripe is extremely bland, which is partly its virtue. During long, slow cooking with vegetables, herbs, and gelatinous meat such as calf's feet, it absorbs their flavor and becomes tender. Tripe can be cooked as little as one or two hours, but it is often encased in a tightly sealed container and braised slowly for up to 24 hours. French cooks braise tripe with onions, carrots, and cider for at least 12 hours to make *tripe à la mode de Caen.* Spanish cooks braise tripe with tomato and sweet peppers or simmer it with chick-peas and *chorizo* to make a one-dish meal. Italian cooks braise tripe in tomato sauce and then garnish it with basil and Parmesan cheese.

■ MENUDO
Tripe soup

To hear Mexicans talk of the beneficial effects of menudo, one would expect to find it included in the pharmacopoeia, along with other medicines and remedies, instead of in a cookbook. It has the reputation for fighting the ailments of the *cruda*, or hangover, and is therefore traditionally served on New Year's Day.

- 1 calf's foot, cut into pieces
- 3 pounds tripe, washed, trimmed of fat, and cut into 1-inch squares
- 4 quarts water
- 2 teaspoons salt
- 3 ancho chiles (see Note)
- 1 fresh Anaheim chile (see Note)
- 1 large onion, chopped
- 3 cloves garlic, crushed
- 1 teaspoon freshly ground pepper
- 2 cans (29 oz each) hominy, drained, *or* 5 cups cooked hominy
- ½ cup cilantro
- Lime wedges, chopped onion, fresh mint, dried oregano, salsa, or sliced jalapeño, for garnish

1. Place calf's foot, tripe, the water, and salt in a large stockpot. Bring to a boil, reduce heat, and simmer, uncovered, for 2½ hours, skimming occasionally.

2. Remove and discard stems and seeds from chiles; crumble chiles into a blender or electric minichopper, and process until finely ground.

3. Remove calf's foot from pot. Remove any meat remaining on the bones and discard the bones. Coarsely chop meat and return it to soup. Add onion, garlic, pepper, and ground chiles, and continue to cook, uncovered, for another 2½ hours.

4. Add hominy and bring soup to a boil; reduce heat and simmer 1 to 2 hours. Soup will be finished in 1 hour, but an additional hour of cooking will improve the flavor. Stir in cilantro during the last 30 minutes of cooking.

5. Serve soup with garnishes passed separately.

Serves 8.

Note Two to three tablespoons mild ground red chile without spices may be substituted for the *ancho* and Anaheim chiles.

VEAL

The meat of young calves, usually no more than four months old, is the source of veal. (After six months, calf meat is considered beef.) The palest, most delicate veal is from milk-fed calves. Even young calves, if fed a grass diet, will develop red meat with stronger flavor. Veal is prized for its tender texture and mild flavor and subsequent versatility in the kitchen.

Use The delicate flavor of veal is appreciated by European cooks, with Italians having perhaps the widest repertoire of veal dishes: veal scaloppine (thin cutlets), veal stews and braises, stuffed whole breast of veal, and veal stuffings for pasta. French cooks also have a way with veal stews and sautés; Austrians are famous for their breaded veal cutlets. In Spain veal is stewed with sausage and peppers, and veal kidneys are cooked with sherry.

Veal bones are high in natural gelatin and are thus preferred by many cooks for making stock (see STOCK AND SOUP). A stock made with veal bones and some meaty veal pieces will have the rich body and mild flavor that is desirable in many French sauces.

Quickly cooked Veal Chops With Tarragon make a delicious foil for the subtle flavors of a Pinot Noir. An assortment of fresh vegetables will complete the meal nicely. The recipe is on page 593.

Selection Because veal comes from young animals, it lacks the extensive intramuscular fat (marbling) typical of good beef. The best indication of quality in veal is its color. Look for veal with pale meat and white fat. Its texture should be fine, not coarse.

Successful veal cookery requires selecting the right method for each cut. Despite the fact that this meat comes from animals with underdeveloped muscles, all veal is not necessarily tender. It lacks the intramuscular marbling that acts as shortening by coating the muscle fibers and making them easier to cut. In addition, some cuts of veal are high in collagen, a protein which can be softened by long, slow cooking but which toughens if improperly handled. See Cuts of Veal at left.

Storage Follow storage directions for BEEF.

Preparation Trim off or slash the membrane that surrounds each veal scallop to prevent the meat from curling in the pan. In most recipes, scallops are pounded before cooking to flatten them as thin as possible (see POUND).

Cooking Veal is generally cooked by moist-heat methods because it does not have enough natural fat to baste itself. Even when roasted, veal is either basted with a liquid or cooked in a covered pot in order to develop moisture in the form of steam. In many recipes, veal is paired with a sauce to compensate for its lack of flavorful fat. Veal chops, although lean, can be broiled or grilled; watch carefully to see that they don't overcook and get dry. Boneless roasts are braised or roasted in the oven. See BRAISE, BROIL, ROAST.

CUTS OF VEAL

The primal cuts of veal are similar to those of a full-grown beef steer (see page 38), but there are fewer of them. The rump, round, and hind shank, for instance, are all considered a part of the leg, and the breast is a single cut.

Ground veal The breast and/or the shoulder are the cuts that are ground. Unless it has been mixed with beef suet, it contains only 20 percent fat or less. If the veal has not been ground with a meat grinder, it is relatively difficult to process at home; the meat is too slippery to shred well in a food processor.

Leg of veal Most commonly, the leg is boned and sold as a roast. Butchers also divide the leg into its separate muscles and then slice the muscles thinly to make cutlets and scallops; the center cut of the leg (which is often labeled as a round) is probably the major source of these prized cuts. (More reasonably priced veal scallops can be cut at home from a boned leg.) Occasionally one finds other versions of leg of veal: Veal "round" roasts may actually be from the leg rather than the shoulder, as are bone-in rump roasts (cut from the area where the leg joins the hip). These and the center cut leg, are more tender than the shank half leg, which is occasionally sold as a roast but should really be braised.

Loin of veal The loin includes numerous smaller cuts, not all of them available from a typical meat case. Loin chops are, of course, the most familiar, and can be sautéed, broiled, braised, or baked. The next most common cut from this section is the boneless rolled loin roast. This and several cuts from the leg are perhaps the most suitable cuts of veal for genuine roasting; all require basting. The rolled loin can be unrolled, filled with stuffing, and rerolled (tied in several places with kitchen twine) for an elegant roast. A bone-in loin includes the T-bone, and is a V-shaped cut that's also suitable for roasting.

Shoulder of veal This cut is much more tender than the corresponding part of a steer, although tougher than the rib, loin, or leg. The shoulder is excellent for stewing and braising. Although this cut contains many membranes, long, slow cooking breaks down the chewiness. Boneless shoulder is often sold as a roast as well. Veal neck, a cut from the shoulder, is quite tough and must be cooked slowly by moist heat. Shoulder of veal is sometimes cut into steaks, which, despite the steak designation, should be braised, rather than grilled.

Veal breast Although tough, bony, and (for veal) rather fatty, the breast is always economical. With the bone in, the breast can be cut into riblets and grilled. More popular are boned breasts, with a pocket cut in them for stuffing. Ground veal is usually made from this cut. It is much less fatty than other ground meats.

Veal foreshank Usually this cut is sold under its Italian name, *osso buco*. Although tougher than the hind shank (which is often sold as part of the leg), and full of membranes, it is perhaps the richest-flavored cut when cooked slowly in liquid long enough to dissolve the sinews. The bones also yield delicious marrow. Veal foreshank is a common ingredient in meat stocks (and the sauces and soups based on meat stocks), yielding the gelatin that makes stocks rich and substantial. This cut is usually sold at a very reasonable price, but it has a very high ratio of bone to meat. As meat for stock, however, where the bones play a major role as a thickener, it's a superb value.

Veal rib Occasionally veal rib is sold as an entire rack or a crown roast for use as a roast. More often, the rib section is cut into tender, flavorful chops.

Veal sirloin Not common in butcher shops, veal sirloin is the portion of the loin next to the leg. It's a delicious cut, but since a calf is so much smaller than a steer, it's a bony one; as a result, this cut yields relatively little meat for its premium price. Veal sirloin chops are high-priced and delicious. Many butchers also cut the boned sirloin into veal scallops, although genuine veal scaloppine is supposed to be cut from the center portion of the leg.

■ SPINACH-STUFFED BREAST OF VEAL

Breast of veal, a large and dramatic-looking dish, is actually cooked covered for part of the time to keep the meat moist. With its meaty stuffing of ground beef, spinach, and cheese, this baked veal breast is frankly Italian. Accompanied by a salad or green vegetable, it will serve a large group economically and well.

> 1 **breast of veal (3 to 3½ lb)**
> 2 **tablespoons olive oil or vegetable oil**
> 1 **cup** *each* **Chicken Stock (see page 560) or full-strength canned chicken broth and dry white wine**

Ground Beef and Spinach Stuffing

> ½ **pound ground beef**
> 1 **medium onion, chopped**
> 1 **clove garlic, minced or pressed**
> ¼ **pound small mushrooms, thinly sliced**
> 1 **package (9 or 10 oz) frozen chopped spinach, thawed and squeezed dry**
> ½ **cup soft bread crumbs**
> 1 **cup grated Monterey jack cheese**
> 1 **egg, slightly beaten**
> ½ **teaspoon** *each* **salt and dried basil**
> ⅛ **teaspoon freshly ground pepper**

1. Have butcher cut pocket in veal breast for the stuffing. Preheat oven to 325° F.

2. Fill pocket with stuffing and fasten open end with small metal skewers. Place meat in large roasting pan. Brush with oil. Pour on ¾ cup each of the stock and the wine. Cover with foil and bake until meat is very tender (2 hours). Increase oven temperature to 350° F and continue baking, uncovered, for 25 to 30 minutes longer. Brush occasionally with pan drippings to brown meat. Remove meat to heated platter and keep warm.

3. To loosen pan drippings, add remaining ¼ cup each of broth and wine, stirring over high heat until liquid is reduced by about one third. Serve sauce separately. To carve veal, cut between rib bones.

Serves 6 to 8.

Ground Beef and Spinach Stuffing Crumble ground beef into a large frying pan and brown it in its own drippings. Mix in onion, garlic, and mushrooms. Cook, stirring occasionally, until onion is soft and begins to brown. Remove from heat; mix in spinach, then bread crumbs, grated cheese, egg, salt, basil, and pepper.

▣ BLANQUETTE DE VEAU

This is the classic French white stew. Although it appears to want color, do not leave the carrots in for the traditional presentation. The recipe can be made almost completely in advance and finished just before serving (see Note). Serve over rice pilaf or steamed potatoes.

> 1 pound mushrooms
> 2 tablespoons fresh lemon juice
> 4 tablespoons butter
> ½ teaspoon salt
> ½ teaspoon white pepper
> 3 tablespoons brandy or
>   Brown Veal Stock (see page 560)
> 5 cups Brown Veal Stock (see page 560) or
>   additional water
> 3 cups cold water
> 4 pounds veal shoulder, trimmed of fat
>   and cut into 2-inch cubes
> 2 medium onions, cut in quarters
> 6 carrots, cut in quarters
>   Bouquet garni (see page 56)
> ½ pound small onions
> 3 tablespoons flour
> ¼ cup whipping cream (optional)
> 2 egg yolks (optional)

1. Toss mushrooms with lemon juice. In a medium skillet sauté mushrooms in 2 tablespoons of the butter over medium heat 1 to 2 minutes. Season with salt and pepper. Remove mushrooms with a slotted spoon and set aside. To avoid possible flare-ups, remove pan from heat, then add brandy, stirring to remove any cooked bits. Reserve liquid.

2. In a 6-quart kettle add the 5 cups Brown Veal Stock, 2½ cups of the cold water, and cubed veal shoulder. Bring mixture to a boil; add remaining water and remove from heat. Skim away any scum that has risen to the surface and return kettle to heat; add onions, carrots, and bouquet garni. Reduce heat to low and simmer, covered, for 1½ hours.

3. Bring 1 quart of water to a boil. Blanch small onions for 1 minute. Trim the root end, slip off the skins, and cut an *x* in the root end of each onion. Heat remaining butter in a small skillet and sauté onions over low heat until barely browned (about 15 minutes); remove onions with a slotted spoon and reserve buttered skillet.

4. Remove onion and carrot pieces from stock; set aside. In the small skillet, whisk flour into melted butter and cook briefly. Whisk 1 cup of stock into flour mixture. Return flour-stock mixture to veal, stirring thoroughly to combine. Add reserved mushrooms, their cooking liquid, and small onions to veal. Simmer for 15 minutes.

5. In a small bowl stir cream and egg yolks (if used) together; whisk into veal, and cook over low heat for 1 to 2 minutes (do not allow to boil or yolks will curdle).

Serves 8.

Note The recipe can be made through step 4 up to four days ahead. Refrigerate covered. When ready to continue, bring back to a simmer and continue with step 5.

▣ VEAL CHOPS WITH TARRAGON

If pale pink, milk-fed, eastern veal is available in your area, by all means try this simple, elegant treatment. The redder, beefier-tasting veal typical of the West can be prepared the same way.

> 4 veal rib chops, ¾ to 1 inch thick
> 2 or 3 sprigs fresh tarragon, plus leaves
>   for garnish (see Note)
> 1 teaspoon kosher salt
> ¼ teaspoon freshly ground pepper
> ½ cup unsalted Chicken, Brown Veal, or Beef Stock
>   (see page 560) *or* ¼ cup canned broth mixed with
>   ¼ cup water

1. Trim excess fat from chops. Finely chop half the tarragon and combine it with the salt and pepper. Rub salt mixture over both sides of chops.

2. Heat a large skillet (nonstick or well-seasoned cast iron) over medium heat. Add chops; cook until center springs back readily when pressed with a fingertip (3 to 4 minutes per side). Remove chops to a warm platter or to individual plates.

3. Deglaze skillet with stock, scraping up any browned drippings. Add remaining tarragon leaves. Reduce sauce by half, taste for seasoning, and correct if necessary.

4. Spoon sauce over chops, decorating each with tarragon leaves.

Serves 4.

Note If fresh tarragon is unavailable, substitute 1 teaspoon crumbled dried tarragon leaves to season the chops and omit the additional tarragon from the sauce and as the garnish. Or, use tarragon leaves packed in vinegar (available at specialty shops), well drained, in place of fresh leaves.

Meats such as veal or poultry that lack natural fat are sometimes wrapped in a layer of exterior fat to keep them moist during cooking. This technique is called barding.

◼ VITELLO TONNATO

Because this dish of cold, sliced leg of veal with tuna sauce must be made in advance, it works beautifully for a buffet. To serve, fan veal slices on platter and spoon sauce over meat. The piquant, creamy sauce—sparked with anchovy, garlic, capers, and vinegar—needs to refrigerate for a day to marry the flavors and the veal also needs to chill overnight.

    1   can (6½ oz) tuna, drained
    2   anchovy fillets
    1   clove garlic, sliced
    ¼   cup olive oil
    2   tablespoons white wine vinegar
    1   tablespoon whipping cream
    1   tablespoon capers, drained
        Leg of veal (4 lb), boned and rolled

1. Preheat oven to 350° F. In a blender or food processor purée tuna, anchovies, garlic, olive oil, vinegar, and cream. Stir in capers; chill (this sauce is better when made a day in advance so flavors can blend).

2. Place veal on a rack in an 8- by 12-inch roasting pan. Roast about 45 minutes (to an internal temperature of about 140° F). Cool briefly and refrigerate overnight.

3. To serve, slice veal ¼ inch thick, arrange on a platter, and pour tuna sauce over pieces.

Serves 8 to 10.

◼ WIENER SCHNITZEL

Any thin slice of meat is a *schnitzel* in German, but veal is the meat of choice. This preparation—Viennese (Wiener) style—consists of paper-thin veal scallops coated with seasoned crumbs and sautéed until golden brown. To keep the bound coating from slipping off in the skillet, the cutlets must sit 30 minutes before cooking. See variations at end of recipe for other classic veal scallop dishes. Use milk-fed veal from the leg for these quick sautés. When pounded to an even ⅛-inch thickness, the little scallops cook through quickly and remain tender.

    2   pounds veal scallops
    1   egg
    1   tablespoon water
    1   teaspoon salt
    ½   teaspoon freshly ground pepper
    1   cup dry bread crumbs
    4   tablespoons unsalted butter
    2   tablespoons vegetable oil
    1   lemon, for garnish
        Red Cabbage With Apples (see page 75),
        for accompaniment
        Boiled parsleyed potatoes, for accompaniment

1. Lightly pound veal cutlets with a wooden mallet to tenderize and flatten to about ⅛ inch thick, or have the butcher do it for you. In a shallow, small bowl, beat egg with the water. In another shallow, small bowl, mix salt, pepper, and bread crumbs.

2. Dip veal slices in beaten egg to coat thoroughly, then dip in seasoned bread crumbs. Place on a plate and chill 30 minutes.

3. In a large skillet sauté one half of the veal in 2 tablespoons butter and 1 tablespoon oil over medium heat 2 minutes; turn and cook second side 2 minutes. Reserve in 200° F oven while preparing remaining veal with remaining butter and oil. When all are cooked, remove to a serving platter and drizzle with lemon juice. Serve with Red Cabbage With Apples and boiled parsleyed potatoes.

Serves 6.

Schnitzel à la Holstein   Prepare veal as above. Prepare Basic Poached Eggs (see page 199) or Basic Fried Eggs (see page 200) and serve on top.

Veal Marsala   Prepare as for Veal Scaloppine (below), reducing cooking time to 20 to 30 seconds on each side (they will finish cooking in the sauce). Transfer cooked veal to a plate. Add 1 tablespoon butter and 1 tablespoon finely minced garlic to skillet; sauté until fragrant, then add ¾ cup Marsala wine. Bring to a boil and reduce until about half original volume. Remove pan from heat, swirl in 3 more tablespoons butter, cut into small pieces. Season to taste with salt and pepper. Return veal to pan briefly just to warm through. Divide scallops and sauce onto dinner plates and garnish with minced parsley.

Veal Parmigiana   Prepare veal as above, adding 1 teaspoon dried basil and 1 teaspoon dried oregano to bread crumb mixture. Prepare 4 cups Basic Tomato Sauce (see page 516). Place veal on an ovenproof serving platter, coat each piece with ½ cup tomato sauce, place a 1-ounce slice mozzarella cheese on each piece, and bake in a preheated 400° F oven until cheese melts (about 3 minutes). Serve immediately.

Veal Picatta   Prepare as for Veal Scaloppine (below); reserve in a 200° F oven while preparing lemon sauce. Over very low heat, add 6 tablespoons fresh lemon juice and ¼ cup minced parsley to skillet and scrape all browned bits from sides and bottom of pan. Add 4 tablespoons butter and stir until butter melts. Remove veal to a serving platter, pour sauce over, season with salt and freshly ground black pepper to taste, and garnish with lemon slices and minced parsley.

Veal Scaloppine   Pound veal and lightly sprinkle with salt and freshly ground black pepper. Dredge veal lightly in flour, shaking off excess. Sauté in butter and oil quickly on both sides (less than 1 minute per side). Serve immediately.

Recipes and Related Information
Brown Veal Stock, 560; Osso Buco, 58; Saltimbocca, 505.

VEGETABLE

The American vegetable marketplace has expanded dramatically in the recent past. Today's supermarket stocks a much greater variety of vegetables than consumers could have imagined just 10 years ago.

The new marketplace owes its breadth in part to a curiosity about other cuisines. Many supermarkets carry a wide assortment of Chinese vegetables and Latin chiles in addition to Japanese mushrooms, Thai eggplants, and Belgian endive. Americans have also begun to demand the variety of vegetables that they find in restaurants: baby squash and squash blossoms, radicchio, and wild mushrooms. Growers, aided by progressive seed companies, have taken an interest in supplying markets and restaurants with these unusual and exotic vegetables. Another factor affecting the growth of the marketplace is the increased interest in nutrition—in reducing intake of meat, and in raising the proportion of high-fiber foods in our diet. All these recent developments provide challenge and constant delight for the curious cook.

Baby vegetables include both special miniature varieties of common vegetables and regular varieties picked when immature. Fully mature miniatures add natural sweetness and a whimsical touch to a dish; regular varieties harvested when young may or may not have fully developed flavor.

For helpful information on purchasing, storing, and preparing most of the vegetables currently available, check the individual vegetable entries in this book.

Use Although most Americans think of vegetables as secondary to meat, in many cuisines vegetables take center stage. In China vegetable stir-fries are embellished with a small amount of meat rather than the reverse. In India, even among nonvegetarians, meals based on vegetables are common.

Around the world, vegetables are appreciated at all times of the day, from breakfast through dessert. Ethiopians often eat a breakfast of boiled beans flavored with onions and tomatoes; the English enjoy baked or stewed tomatoes in the morning, and the American coffee-shop breakfast wouldn't be complete without fried potatoes. At the other end of the day are the vegetable-based desserts, ranging from carrot cake and sweet potato pie to sugar-dusted Italian squash-blossom fritters.

Vegetables are served in salads, casseroles, sautés and stir-fries, stews and braised dishes, pickles, pasta, soups, and side dishes. Some vegetables are so highly prized that they are often served as a separate course: steamed asparagus, sautéed wild mushrooms, sliced beefsteak tomatoes, whole steamed artichokes, or hot corn on the cob can launch a meal in simple but memorable style. Other vegetables are usually given a supporting role: Onions and garlic, for example, are appreciated more for the aromatic qualities they lend to other dishes than as dishes in themselves.

Baby vegetables can be used in all standard preparations; they are particularly appealing served whole.

Availability Buying vegetables in season is the best way to get superior quality. When prices are lowest, quality is usually at its best because the domestic harvest is at its peak. Vine-ripened autumn tomatoes from a local supplier have little in common with midwinter tomatoes shipped green from Mexico. Learn to enjoy vegetables to the fullest during their season and to forgo them at other times of the year. The good cook takes pleasure in following the seasons and the well-ordered parade of colors in nature. The first asparagus, June peas, and the first sweet corn of summer give way to the sunset colors of peppers and tomatoes, followed by the earthy winter comfort of mushrooms, rutabagas, and fennel.

The season for most farmed baby vegetables corresponds with the season for the regular varieties.

Selection Without exception, vegetables are best the moment they are harvested. The longer it takes to get a vegetable from the field to the market, the more flavor and texture suffer. For best quality, patronize local farmers' markets; most likely the vegetables were grown nearby and picked within the previous 24 hours. Alternatively, look for a market that knows how to care for its vegetables by keeping them cool and neatly trimmed, and by making an effort to stock locally grown produce. Fresh vegetables have good, bright color and firm texture. Carrots, celery, and root vegetables should feel firm, not spongy; leafy greens should be crisp, not wilted; asparagus and beans should be sturdy, not limp.

Crudités—raw fresh vegetables—are always welcome as part of an hors d'oeuvres buffet. Throughout the year, the produce market yields a varied palette of fresh vegetables. Choose the best the season has to offer, prepare them in bite-sized pieces, and arrange them in an eye-catching still life, with a dip or two alongside.

Storage The more quickly you use the vegetables you buy, the better. Some vegetables, such as peas and corn, quickly convert sugar to starch after harvest; they should be cooked the day they are purchased. Others, such as hard-shelled winter squash, can withstand long storage but do not improve in flavor after harvest.

Most vegetables, including baby vegetables, which are particularly perishable, should be refrigerated until use, preferably in a vegetable bin. Potatoes, garlic, onions, and shallots are exceptions, however; refrigerating them encourages rot. Store them in a cool, airy place. Hard squashes can be refrigerated but don't require it; they will keep in a cool, airy place for several months.

Preparation For most vegetables, wash and dry; peel and trim as necessary. Some baby vegetables, such as carrots and potatoes, have very delicate skins that do not require peeling.

Cooking See BLANCH, BOIL, BRAISE, BROIL, GRILL, MICRO-WAVE OVEN, PARBOIL, PUREE, STEAM, STIR-FRY.

VEGETABLE COOKING SPRAY

Most pan sprays are made of vegetable oil, alcohol, lecithin (a vegetable compound used as an emulsifier), and a propellant. They are a boon to those on low-calorie or low-cholesterol diets because they eliminate the need to grease baking pans or skillets. Most commercial brands instruct the user to apply the coating while the pan or skillet is cold.

Stored in a cool place, cooking sprays will keep indefinitely. Widely available in supermarkets, they are usually stocked next to the cooking oils.

VERTICAL ROASTER

To a great degree, food cooks by conduction—the slow, molecule-by-molecule transfer of heat from outside to center mass. If heat could somehow reach both the interior and the exterior at the same time, cooking time would be faster and food would cook more evenly. That's why dense or delicate cake batters are often baked in tube pans and why a baked potato will be done sooner with a nail tapped through the center. It's also the clever idea behind the vertical roaster for poultry.

These open, upright frames of stainless steel wire conduct heat to the internal cavity of fowl set on them. When roasted this way, poultry cooks faster and stays juicier than with conventional methods because the metal frame is an excellent heat conductor that promotes cooking from the inside as well as the outside. The frames are available for chickens and Rock Cornish game hens (see Mustard Madness, page 381).

VINEGAR

When a naturally fermented alcohol—such as sherry, wine, or apple cider—is attacked by a type of airborne bacteria called acetobacter, the alcohol is converted to acetic acid, creating vinegar. Winemakers take precautions to keep acetobacter from attacking their wine, but vinegar manufacturers take the opposite approach. Most encourage the growth of acetobacter by inoculating their base material with a starter culture. By this method, manufacturers can promote a consistent and desirable flavor.

The variety of vinegars available to consumers has increased dramatically in recent years. Formerly, distilled white vinegar, apple cider vinegar, and wine vinegar were the only readily available options. Today, well-stocked supermarkets and specialty shops offer a variety of herb-flavored vinegars, such as tarragon and dill; fruit vinegars, such as raspberry and blueberry; Champagne vinegar; sherry vinegar; Japanese rice vinegar; malt vinegar; and the famous Italian *aceto balsamico* (balsamic vinegar), made from wood-aged wine. See Availability for descriptions of specific vinegars.

The commercially available flavored vinegars are generally expensive, yet flavored vinegar is easy to make at home (see JAM, JELLY, PRESERVE, AND CONDIMENT).

Use High-quality vinegar has a fruitiness and refreshing acidity that give a lift to many dishes. Perhaps the most common use for vinegar is in salad dressing. Almost any type of salad—whether of mixed greens, cold vegetables, cold rice, or shellfish—benefits from the jolt of acidity that vinegar provides. Vinegar also acts as a tenderizer in meat marinades by denaturing the surface proteins. Vinegar in egg-poaching water (about 2 tablespoons per quart) will keep the whites from spreading and make the eggs more tender. In a Hollandaise sauce or related sauce, vinegar keeps the protein in the egg yolk from coagulating when the sauce is cooked. Vinegar acts as an antioxidant, slowing the browning of foods such as avocado and celery root, and as a preservative, preventing the growth of harmful bacteria in pickles.

The flavor of vinegar is essential to many dishes around the world. Most pickles wouldn't be pickles without the vinegar that preserves and flavors them. American diners, especially those from the Deep South, like to flavor cooked greens such as spinach with vinegar. English fish and chips are always served with strong malt vinegar as a condiment. Japanese salads get their distinctive taste in part from mild, slightly sweet rice vinegar. Italians enrich sauces with the mellow balsamic vinegar; the finest balsamic vinegar is used, drop by drop, as a table condiment. Modern French cooks add sherry vinegar to sautéed calf's liver and pair raspberry vinegar with duck livers. The basic dressing known as vinaigrette derives its name from the French word for vinegar (*vinaigre*); usually made from 3 parts oil to 1 part vinegar, this versatile sauce is used to dress green salads and salads of cold vegetables, leeks, fish, and grains. Champagne vinegar with minced shallots and black pepper is a popular condiment for raw oysters in France. In China black vinegar made from rice is used to dress cold noodle dishes and to enrich stir-fries.

Availability   The following are among the most widely used vinegars today; they are sold in supermarkets and specialty stores.

Apple Cider Vinegar   Made from the juice of apples, apple cider vinegar has an aroma and flavor that distinctly suggest the fruit. Its fruity quality is appealing in dressings for cabbage salads and fruit salads. It is also widely used in pickling.

Balsamic Vinegar   Made from the juice of a white grape, balsamic vinegar is aged for several years in wood barrels. The vinegar is dark brown, with a mellow sweet-and-sour character that is greatly appreciated by Italian cooks. In Italy balsamic vinegar enriches stews, dresses salads, and even perks up the flavor of strawberries. The finest balsamic vinegar is carefully aged for decades and is extremely expensive.

Distilled White Vinegar   The flavor of distilled white vinegar, which is made from grain alcohol, is too coarse for most salad dressings, but it is widely used in pickling.

Raspberry Vinegar   Macerating raspberries in white wine vinegar and then straining the vinegar produces raspberry vinegar. The fruit imparts a pale raspberry color and an unmistakably raspberry flavor and aroma. The fruity character is appealing when with chicken, duck, and liver, and in salads with a fruit component.

Rice Vinegar   Used in Chinese and Japanese cookery, rice vinegar is clear to pale gold in color, with a mild and subtly sweet flavor. Asian cooks use rice vinegar in noodle dishes, salad dressings, dipping sauces, and pickles.

Sherry Vinegar   A fragrant, slightly nutty vinegar made from Spanish sherry, it is best in salad dressings; with green beans, asparagus, and chicken or duck; or to deglaze the skillet after sautéing chicken or calf's liver.

Wine Vinegar   Either red or white, good-quality wine vinegar has a pleasing aroma and is pungent without being harsh. Generally, red wine vinegar is used with dark meats, in marinades, and in salads where its color is not objectionable. Use white wine vinegar with fish, in potato salads, or in pickles where a clear vinegar is preferred.

White wine vinegar is the base for many commercial herb vinegars.

Storage   Keep bottles of vinegar tightly capped; store in a cool, dark place for up to six months.

■ PORK ADOBO

The famous adobo is a classic dish of the Philippines. Like the curries of other countries, adobo probably originated as a way of preserving meat. In this case the preserving agent is vinegar, not chiles or other spices. The following version calls for boiling cubes of pork in a vinegar and garlic mixture until the liquid evaporates and the cubes begin to fry in their own rendered fat. Use pork with some visible fat, either from the shoulder or the nearby section of the loin (usually sold as "country-style spareribs").

1½	**pounds boneless pork, in 1-inch cubes**
½	**cup rice vinegar**
6	**cloves garlic, minced**
3	**tablespoons soy sauce or fish sauce**
¼	**teaspoon freshly ground pepper**
1½	**cups water**
1	**bay leaf**

1. In a bowl combine pork cubes, vinegar, garlic, soy sauce, and pepper; marinate 1 to 3 hours in the refrigerator.

2. Transfer all ingredients to a non-aluminum saucepan, add 1 cup of the water and bay leaf, and bring to a boil, uncovered. Adjust heat so meat cooks at a lively simmer but does not boil too rapidly.

3. Cook until liquid is nearly gone, then reduce heat further. Mixture will sizzle and pop as the last bits of water evaporate; then the pork cubes will begin to brown in the remaining fat. Turn cubes to brown evenly and remove from heat if mixture shows signs of scorching.

4. Remove pork cubes to serving dish. Add ½ cup of the water to pan and bring to a boil, stirring to scrape browned bits from pan. Pour over pork. Serve with rice.

Serves 4 with other dishes.

Variation   Follow Pork Adobo recipe. Use a mixture of chicken, cut into braising pieces (1 to 2 inches long with bones), and boneless pork. Cook only until liquid is reduced to ½ cup, then brown meats in a separate pan: In a large skillet add 1 to 2 tablespoons vegetable oil (enough to coat bottom of pan). Heat oil over medium-high heat and brown chicken and pork pieces well. Transfer browned meats to a warm platter and cover with sauce.

Recipes and Related Information
Fran's Raspberry Vinegar, 323; Herb Vinegar, 323; Raspberry Vinegar and Shallot Dressing, 521; Vinegar Dressing, 233.

TIPS

COOKING WITH VINEGAR

Because vinegar is highly volatile, its flavor dissipates with heat and air. To retain its pungent character in a cooked dish, add vinegar to the dish only after removing it from heat. If a less pungent flavor is desired, add the vinegar while the dish is cooking and allow vinegar to boil off slightly.

WAFFLE AND PANCAKE

A thin mixture called a pour batter—the amount of liquid and dry ingredients are about equal and are wet enough to be pourable—forms the base for waffles and all types of pancakes. Most pour batters are classified as quick breads because they use a leavening other than yeast; blini, a buckwheat pancake, is the exception since it is yeast leavened. Like all quick breads, pour batters are fast to assemble and cook. Pancakes and waffles are popular breakfast foods; crêpes and blini appear on hors d'oeuvres trays as first courses, as desserts at elegant dinners, and on the menus of the trendiest restaurants.

INGREDIENTS AND METHOD

Dry ingredients include flour, baking powder or soda, salt, sometimes sugar, and often spices. These are blended and then combined with the liquid additions: milk, oil or melted butter, and eggs. For a light and delicate finished product, the eggs can be separated into yolks and whites: The yolks are added with the liquids and the whites beaten and folded into the batter as the final step.

Frequently, the same batter can be used for either pancakes or waffles; the difference is in how the batter is cooked. For pancakes, spoonfuls of batter are dropped onto a preheated griddle or skillet and cooked on both sides until golden brown. For waffles, the batter is poured onto the grids of a preheated waffle iron and baked until crisp and golden brown. See specific recipes for information on other food products.

Although pancakes, waffles, and other types of pour-batter products cook quickly, it is important not to rush them. When underdone, they are brown on the surface and unpleasantly liquid on the inside. To cook, the pan or appliance should be preheated to the proper temperature: For nonelectric pans, a drop of water will jump when it hits the hot pan; for thermostatically controlled devices, a light signals readiness. Flip pancakes when the surface appears dry and the bubbles around the edge have set. Cook waffles until steam is no longer given off or until the indicator light on an automatic waffle maker denotes that the waffles are ready.

EQUIPMENT

Although drop batters and doughs are stiff enough to hold their shape, a pour batter requires a special pan or iron if it is to have a distinctive form or imprint (see WAFFLE IRON AND PANCAKE PAN). Otherwise, when spooned onto a flat cooking surface—a griddle or skillet—the batter will spread in a gradually widening circle until set by heat.

A new griddle or skillet should be seasoned before use (see MATERIALS FOR COOKWARE). A well-seasoned pancake griddle or waffle iron should not be washed after using. Wipe away any clinging bits with a little oil and a paper towel, and store in a dry place. If the pan you are using isn't reserved only for pancakes, and isn't seasoned, you may need to add a thin coat of oil to it during preheating; if the batter contains fat, this may not be necessary.

Other equipment useful for making pancakes, waffles, and similar products includes pancake turners, whisks or wooden spoons for mixing the batter, an electric mixer for beating egg whites, and a mixing bowl. If you make these foods often, you may want to look for a batter bowl, which is an oversized liquid measuring cup with a 2-quart capacity; it is large enough to hold the batter and has a convenient pouring lip.

■ BASIC WAFFLES

If you are using a stove-top waffle iron, cook batter at least 1 minute for crisp waffles, preferably 2 minutes, after steam stops rising from iron. The top should lift without resistance. Serve waffles immediately after cooking for best texture and flavor, accompanied with butter and maple syrup, fresh fruit, or even ice cream. If they must be held, keep them warm in a 350°F oven 3 to 5 minutes. Serve on warm plates and warm any sauce served with them as well. Don't stack waffles or they will lose their crispness and get soggy. Extra waffles can be frozen, well wrapped, and toasted, but they won't have the same crispy flavor as when freshly made.

> 1¾ cups flour
> 1 tablespoon baking powder
> Pinch salt
> 2 tablespoons sugar
> 2 cups milk
> 3 eggs, separated
> 6 tablespoons butter, melted
> Pinch cream of tartar (optional)
> Butter and warm maple syrup, for topping

1. Sift together flour, baking powder, salt, and sugar into a medium bowl. Make a well in center of mixture. In another bowl combine milk, egg yolks, and melted butter. Pour into well in flour mixture; stir until smooth and creamy. This can also be done in a blender or food processor, but don't overwork or batter will be tough.

2. Preheat waffle iron according to manufacturer's directions or until a drop of water sizzles and bounces when placed onto hot iron.

3. In another bowl beat egg whites to soft peaks (if not using a copper bowl, add cream of tartar to whites when just foamy). Fold one third of beaten whites into batter to lighten, then fold in remaining whites.

4. Pour enough batter onto lightly oiled waffle iron to spread into corners (about 1 cup batter for a 4-square waffle iron). Cook 2 minutes after moment when steam stops escaping from sides of waffle maker. When waffles are cooked sufficiently, iron should release them easily. Serve immediately with butter and syrup.

Makes 4 cups batter, four 4-square waffles.

Cornmeal Waffles Prepare Basic Waffles, but substitute ¾ cup cornmeal for 1 cup of the flour. Spread with cream cheese and chopped jalapeño chile, and serve with soup or eggs.

■ BUTTERMILK WAFFLES

This batter makes a light, tender waffle. Also try one of the variations: pecan, blueberry, or chocolate.

  1¾ **cups flour**
   1 **teaspoon baking powder**
   1 **teaspoon baking soda**
   2 **tablespoons sugar**
   2 **cups buttermilk**
  ½ **cup butter, melted**
   2 **eggs, separated**
      Pinch cream of tartar (optional)

Prepare as for Basic Waffles.

Makes 4 cups batter, four 4-square waffles.

Blueberry Buttermilk Waffles Fold 1 cup washed and dried blueberries into batter before cooking.

Chocolate-Pecan Waffles Substitute ¼ cup unsweetened cocoa powder for ¼ cup flour called for in recipe. Use a total of 6 tablespoons sugar. Mix in 1 teaspoon vanilla extract to buttermilk mixture. Fold in 1 cup chopped pecans to batter before cooking.

Pecan Buttermilk Waffles Fold 1 cup pecan pieces into batter before cooking.

■ BELGIAN WAFFLES WITH BLUEBERRY SAUCE

Yeast-leavened Belgian waffles are rectangular and have an extradeep grid made with a special waffle iron (see page 603). They can also be made in a regular waffle iron.

   1 **package active dry yeast**
  ¼ **cup warm water**
   2 **cups flour**
  ¼ **cup sugar**
  ¼ **teaspoon salt**
  ¼ **cup butter or margarine, melted and cooled**
   2 **tablespoons vegetable oil**
  1½ **cups water**
  ½ **teaspoon vanilla extract**
   2 **eggs, separated**
      Whipped cream (optional)

Blueberry Sauce

  ⅓ **cup butter**
  ⅔ **cup sugar**
   3 **tablespoons light corn syrup**
  ¼ **cup water**
   2 **tablespoons grated lemon rind**
  ¼ **teaspoon freshly grated nutmeg**
  1½ **cups fresh or frozen unsweetened blueberries**

1. Sprinkle yeast over the ¼ cup warm water in a small bowl; let stand about 5 minutes to soften. In a large bowl mix flour, sugar, and salt. Beat in butter, oil, the 1½ cups water, and vanilla until smooth. Then beat in egg yolks and yeast mixture.

2. Beat egg whites until they form soft peaks; fold gently into batter. Cover and refrigerate several hours or overnight; stir down batter.

3. Place a seasoned 6- by 7½-inch Belgian waffle iron directly over medium heat, turning it over occasionally, until a few drops of water dance on grids (or preheat an electric model). Spoon about ½ cup batter onto lightly oiled iron, spreading it just to cover grids.

4. Close iron and turn occasionally until waffle is well browned (4 to 5 minutes in all). Transfer waffles to wire rack unless served immediately.

5. If waffles are made ahead, cool, wrap in aluminum foil, and freeze. Reheat in a preheated 325° F oven, uncovered, in a single layer on baking sheets until hot and crisp (about 10 minutes).

6. Serve hot, with Blueberry Sauce. Top with whipped cream (if desired).

Makes 9 waffles.

Blueberry Sauce Combine butter, sugar, and corn syrup in a medium saucepan. Cook over medium heat, stirring, until mixture boils. Stir in the water and boil 2 minutes. Add lemon rind, nutmeg, and blueberries. Cook, stirring, until mixture boils.

Makes about 1¾ cups.

Belgian waffles have deep grids, the better to trap delicious syrups and sauces. Blueberry Sauce, shown here, is served hot and is flavored with fresh nutmeg and grated lemon rind.

■ BASIC PANCAKES

Making pancake batter yourself is almost as easy as using a mix and always tastes better. For quick breakfasts, you can have the dry ingredients combined, all ready to stir into the egg mixture. Do this while the pan is heating. If the batter thickens too much upon standing, thin with a little extra liquid. Leftover batter can be stored in the refrigerator in an airtight container overnight, but the pancakes made from it won't be as light because the baking powder will have lost some of its punch. Always preheat the skillet or griddle before pouring on the batter. Test for readiness by shaking a few drops of water on the pan surface. The pan is ready to use if the water skips, sizzles, and quickly evaporates. Pour batter onto griddle or pan, and cook until the bubbles that form begin to burst and the edges look dry. Turn and cook on the other side.

    1¾ cups flour
    ¼ cup sugar
    2 teaspoons baking powder
    ½ teaspoon salt
    2 eggs
    4 tablespoons butter, melted
    1¼ cups milk
        Butter and warm maple syrup, for topping

1. Sift flour, sugar, baking powder, and salt into a medium bowl. Add eggs, butter, and milk and beat until smooth and creamy; set aside.

2. If using an electric skillet, preheat to 350° F; preheat lightly oiled griddle or skillet over medium heat until a few drops of water dance on the surface. For each pancake pour ¼ cup batter onto hot griddle and cook on first side until bubbles that form begin to pop and edges look dry. With a spatula, turn and cook until second side is a rich, golden brown.

3. Serve at once with butter and syrup.

Makes 8 to 12 four-inch pancakes.

Buckwheat Pancakes Prepare batter with 1¼ cups all-purpose flour and ½ cup buckwheat flour.

Whole-Grain Pancakes Prepare batter with 1 cup all-purpose flour and ¾ cup whole wheat flour.

■ BUTTERMILK PANCAKES

The addition of buttermilk provides a little tang and makes these pancakes extratender.

    1 cup cake flour
    2 teaspoons sugar
    1 teaspoon baking powder
    ½ teaspoon baking soda
        Pinch salt
    1 egg
    1 cup buttermilk
    2 tablespoons butter, melted, or vegetable oil
        Butter and warm maple syrup, for topping

1. Sift flour, sugar, baking powder, baking soda, and salt into a medium bowl. Add egg, buttermilk, and butter, and beat until smooth and creamy; set aside.

2. If using an electric skillet, preheat to 350° F; preheat lightly oiled griddle or skillet over medium heat until a few drops of water dance on the surface. For each pancake pour ¼ cup batter onto hot griddle and cook on first side until bubbles that form begin to pop and edges look dry. With a spatula, turn and cook until second side is a rich, golden brown.

3. Serve at once with butter and syrup.

Makes 8 to 12 four-inch pancakes.

Blueberry Buttermilk Pancakes Fold ½ to 1 cup rinsed and dried blueberries into batter before cooking.

■ BUTTERMILK BLINTZES

Unlike crêpes, which are cooked on both sides, the pancakes for blintzes are browned on one side only. They are then wrapped around a sweetened cheese filling and fried to brown the outside. Making blintzes is a lengthy operation. If you make them ahead, you can cover and refrigerate the filled blintzes for up to 24 hours. When ready, brown quickly and serve hot. The name for this Jewish dish is from the Yiddish *blintse*, which in turn evolved from the Russian *blinets* (diminutive of *blin*, or pancake). Note that the batter must chill for one hour before using.

    ¾ cup flour
    ¾ teaspoon baking soda
    ½ teaspoon salt
    2 tablespoons sugar
    1 cup buttermilk
    ½ cup water
    3 eggs
    2 tablespoons vegetable oil
    3 to 4 tablespoons *each* butter or margarine
        and vegetable oil, for frying
        Sour cream and cherry preserves, for topping

Cheese Filling

    1 package (8 oz) cream cheese, softened
    1 egg
    2 tablespoons confectioners' sugar
    ½ teaspoon vanilla extract
    ¼ teaspoon ground cinnamon
    2 cups (1 lb) pot cheese (also called farmer cheese)

1. In blender or food processor, combine flour, soda, salt, sugar, buttermilk, the water, eggs, and the 2 tablespoons oil. Whirl or process until batter is smooth, stopping motor once or twice to scrape flour from sides of container. Cover and refrigerate for at least 1 hour before using.

2. Make blintzes in a lightly oiled 6- to 7-inch crêpe pan, but brown them on first side only and cook until top surface is dry to touch. Stack blintzes to cool.

3. To fill each blintz, place about 2 tablespoons of Cheese Filling in center of browned side of each pancake. Fold in opposite edges about 1 inch, then fold in remaining edges to enclose filling, overlapping in center to make a slightly rectangular envelope. Set blintzes aside, folded side down.

4. In a large frying pan over moderately high heat, melt 2 tablespoons butter with 2 tablespoons oil. Fry filled blintzes without crowding until golden on each side (1 to 1½ minutes on each side). Add more butter and oil to pan as needed.

5. Drain blintzes well on paper towels and serve on warm plates, topped with a dollop each of sour cream and cherry preserves.

Makes 20 to 24 blintzes.

Cheese Filling In a large bowl beat cream cheese with egg, confectioners' sugar, vanilla, and cinnamon. Then beat in pot cheese.

Makes about 3 cups.

◼ SWEDISH PANCAKES

These small, moist, delicate pancakes are traditionally made in a *plett,* a cast-iron griddle with shallow, 3-inch-diameter depressions to hold the batter (see page 604). If you don't have this pan, the pancakes will taste just as good. Serve them in the Swedish manner, with butter and lingonberry preserves, or with your favorite fruit-flavored syrup. Imported lingonberry preserves can be found at specialty food shops and well-stocked supermarkets.

  ⅔ **cup flour**
  ½ **teaspoon baking powder**
  ⅛ **teaspoon salt**
  2 **eggs, separated**
  1 **cup milk, at room temperature**
  ¼ **cup half-and-half**
  ¼ **cup butter or margarine, melted and cooled**
    Butter and lingonberry preserves or syrup, for topping

1. Sift flour, baking powder, and salt onto a square of parchment paper or waxed paper; set aside. In a large bowl beat egg yolks with milk and half-and-half. Beat in melted butter, then add flour mixture. Stir to combine.

2. Beat egg whites until stiff peaks form. Carefully fold into batter.

3. Set a lightly oiled Swedish pancake pan, griddle, or skillet over medium-low heat until a few drops of water dance on the hot surface. Use about 2 tablespoons batter for each pancake. Cook pancakes until golden brown on each side, turning once very carefully with a spatula. Serve hot with butter and lingonberry preserves or syrup.

Makes about 2 dozen 3-inch pancakes.

◼ DUTCH BABIE

This oven pancake is said to have originated at a small family restaurant in Seattle. Very similar to Yorkshire pudding, it uses eggs, flour, and milk, although the proportion of eggs is much higher. The recipe can be doubled or even tripled, as long as it is baked in a shallow pan in a 425° F oven.

  4 **eggs**
  1 **cup milk**
  1 **cup flour**
    Pinch *each* salt and sugar
  ¼ **cup butter**
    Confectioners' sugar, fresh lemon juice, and fruit in season, for garnish

1. Preheat oven to 425° F.

2. In a blender combine eggs and milk on high speed. Add flour, salt, and sugar in two batches, blending well after each addition until smooth and creamy.

3. Place butter in a 12- to 14-inch shallow ovenproof pan or skillet and set in oven to melt. Swirl pan to coat evenly with butter and pour in batter. Bake until puffy and golden brown (20 to 30 minutes).

4. Serve immediately in baking pan, dusted with confectioners' sugar and sprinkled with lemon juice. Accompany each serving with an assortment of fresh, seasonal fruit.

Serves 6 to 8.

Buttermilk Blintzes should be made, filled, and folded ahead of serving time and refrigerated. They can be browned later, and served hot with cherry preserves and sour cream.

HOW TO MAKE CREPES

Pour batter into greased pan, tilting pan so batter forms a thin, even covering over entire bottom.

Cook crêpe 45 to 60 seconds. Small holes will be visible on top side; bottom will be browned. Turn and cook other side.

Remove crêpe to a platter, board, or sheet of waxed paper to cool.

■ BLINI

Yeast-risen buckwheat pancakes were a fixture on the tables of imperial Russia, served dripping with butter and caviar, or with sour cream and smoked fish. Made in a smaller cocktail size, they are novel topped in many different ways: with sour cream and chutney, with sour-cream herring, with crème fraîche and smoked trout, with a slice of grilled sausage, with melted herb butter and tiny shrimp, or with melted butter and smoked oysters. Serve piping hot, with chilled vodka, Champagne, or cocktails. They may be made ahead of serving time.

    2 **cups all-purpose flour**
    ½ **cup buckwheat flour**
    1 **package active dry yeast**
    2 **teaspoons sugar**
    2 **egg yolks**
    3 **cups lukewarm (100° F to 105° F) milk**
    3 **egg whites**
    2 **tablespoons unsalted butter**

1. In a medium bowl sift together all-purpose and buckwheat flours. In a small bowl, dissolve yeast and sugar in ½ cup warm milk and set aside to soften a few minutes. Make a well in flour and add egg yolks. Gradually stir in yeast mixture and remaining milk, incorporating yolks and flour.

2. Cover bowl with a towel and place in a warm area. Let rise until doubled in bulk. Beat egg whites to soft peaks and fold into batter.

3. Melt butter on griddle or in large skillet. Form Blini by dropping heaping tablespoons of batter onto hot griddle. Cook on both sides until golden brown.

Makes 2 dozen Blini.

■ BASIC CREPES

In France, their country of origin, crêpes are served as a snack, a lunch or supper dish, or—depending on flavoring and embellishment—a dessert. Wrap hot-off-the-griddle crêpes around a number of mixtures: tiny shrimp warmed in a saucepan with a little sour cream, chopped tomatoes, shallots, and thyme; sausage and cheese; crumbled blue cheese and chopped walnuts; or grated Gruyère and crumbled bacon. Use cooled (but not chilled) crêpes to wrap around pencil-thin asparagus, or spread with chutney, then top with paper-thin slices of smoked ham or turkey and roll up.

    1 **cup flour**
    ¾ **cup water**
    ⅔ **cup milk**
    3 **eggs**
    2 **tablespoons vegetable oil**
    ¼ **teaspoon salt**

1. In blender or food processor, combine flour, the water, milk, eggs, oil, and salt. Whirl or process until batter is smooth, stopping motor once or twice to scrape flour from sides of container.

2. Cover and refrigerate batter for at least 1 hour. Blend batter well before making crêpes.

3. Add just enough batter to make a thin coat to a lightly oiled 6-inch pan. Cook each crêpe until set (about 60 seconds); turn and cook other side (about 45 seconds). Transfer to a sheet of parchment or waxed paper. Do not stack crêpes until they are completely cool.

Makes 16 to 20 crêpes.

Make-Ahead Tip Completely cooled crêpes may be stacked, wrapped in aluminum foil, and refrigerated for up to five days or frozen for up to two months. Thaw in cool oven.

■ CREPES SUZETTE

A quick-witted French chef transformed a failure into what has become a culinary classic—crêpes suzette. While the chef was preparing a dessert of crêpes with a liqueur sauce, the sauce caught fire. After tasting the sauce, he realized that the flames gave it extra depth. The dish was served in triumph. The batter makes enough crêpes for a double recipe. Extra pancakes can be frozen for later use. They are delicious with any fruit filling or ice cream.

    6 **eggs**
    6 **cups half-and-half**
    1 **cup water**
  1¼ **cups milk**
    2 **cups flour**
    2 **tablespoons butter, melted**
    1 **tablespoon sugar**
    1 **teaspoon salt**
    ¼ **cup brandy or Cognac**
    Additional butter, for cooking crêpes
    ½ **cup brandy**

Orange Butter Sauce

    6 **tablespoons butter**
    Grated rind of 2 oranges
    Grated rind and juice of 2 lemons
    Juice of 4 oranges
    ¼ **cup sugar**
    ½ **cup orange-flavored liqueur**

1. In a large bowl combine eggs, half-and-half, the water, milk, flour, melted butter, sugar, salt, and brandy. Whisk together well. Batter will be slightly lumpy. Transfer batter to blender in batches and blend until smooth. Let batter rest at room temperature 45 minutes or refrigerate overnight before using.

2. Heat a nonstick 7-inch skillet or crêpe pan over moderately high heat. Add 1 teaspoon butter and swirl to coat pan. When butter foams, add 3 tablespoons batter and quickly tilt pan to coat bottom of skillet thinly.

Cook crêpe until set (60 seconds); turn and cook other side (about 45 seconds). Transfer to a sheet of parchment paper or waxed paper. Continue with remaining batter.

3. To make Orange Butter Sauce: Melt butter in chafing dish or large shallow pan. Add orange and lemon rinds and juice and cook over medium-low heat until reduced by one third. Add sugar and stir to dissolve. Add orange-flavored liqueur and heat through.

4. To assemble: Reduce heat under sauce to low. Using 18 crêpes altogether and freezing remainder for another use, lay crêpes one by one in pan and coat with sauce. Fold each crêpe in half, and then in half again, making small triangles. Arrange triangles, overlapping them around edge of pan. Continue until all have been coated, folded, and arranged in pan.

5. Pour brandy over warm crêpes and carefully ignite, shaking pan to distribute sauce throughout dish. As soon as flames subside, transfer crêpes with sauce to warmed plates.

Serves 6.

Make-Ahead Tip Completely cooled crêpes may be stacked, wrapped in aluminum foil, and refrigerated for up to five days or frozen for up to two months. Thaw in cool oven.

WAFFLE IRON AND PANCAKE PAN

Some fascinating utensils have been designed to produce uncommon pancakes and waffles. If you enjoy varying your breakfast and brunch repertoire, you will probably want to purchase one or more of these. For more information on seasoning pans, see MATERIALS FOR COOKWARE.

WAFFLE IRONS

The iron in which waffles are baked and which gives them their distinctive gridlike pattern may be round, square, or rectangular. Some are electric; others are designed for use on top of the range, either gas or electric. In any case, the grids of a waffle iron—like the surface of a crêpe pan or a pancake griddle—should be seasoned well and then never washed. Season the grids before first use, as you would a cast-iron pan (see MATERIALS FOR COOKWARE), or if finished with a nonstick surface, follow the manufacturer's directions for seasoning. If you don't use the waffle iron often, brush grids lightly with vegetable oil or spray with vegetable cooking spray before heating iron.

Belgian Waffle Iron Belgian waffles, the hit of the 1964 world's fair in New York, are thick, with deep pockets. At the fair they were piled with fresh strawberries and whipped cream, but they are equally delicious with ice cream or fruit sauces. Belgian waffle irons come in stove-top and electric models, and with plain and nonstick grids. They are of cast aluminum.

Electric Waffle Makers A built-in thermostat takes the guesswork out of making waffles: It heats the unit to a predetermined temperature and signals you that it's ready to use. Pour on the batter, close the lid, wait a few minutes, and the light on the appliance will go on again when the waffle is ready to eat. The grids are made of cast aluminum, either plain or with a nonstick finish, and in regular or Belgian-waffle style. Some models feature reversible grids that become a griddle or have embossed disks for making *pizzelle*, thin, crisp Italian wafers.

Heart-Shaped Waffle Iron Like the *plett* (used to make Swedish pancakes, see page 604) this utensil is from Scandinavia. Circular, with five interlocking hearts, it is made of aluminum, usually with a nonstick finish. To use, the iron is first preheated, then the batter is poured over the grids. The iron is set on the burner of the stove to cook for several minutes, then is turned to finish on the other side.

PANCAKE PANS

Another name for pancakes is griddle cakes because they are best made on a wide shallow griddle. If you make pancakes frequently, consider buying a rectangular griddle. Its shape is well suited for making several servings of pancakes at a time instead of the one or two possible in a round frying pan (see COOKWARE). The following are pans for specialty pancakes.

Blini Pan A blini pan is so small some people mistake it for a one-egg frying pan. It has a bottom diameter of 3½ to 4 inches in order to shape the diminutive Russian pancakes. Otherwise, it is like a standard crêpe pan and should be seasoned and cared for in the same way.

Crêpe Pan Although a crêpe pan resembles an omelet pan in that it is fashioned of rolled steel, it differs in one important respect—it has a flat, well-defined bottom to give the crêpe a sharp edge. The sides of an omelet pan, on the other hand, curve gently into the bottom. Season as you would a cast-iron pan. Reserve it strictly for crêpes and you will never need to wash it. After each use, wipe away any crumbs with a paper towel dipped in a little oil; store in a dry place to prevent rust. Before the next use, rub a little oil over inside surface of sides and bottom as pan heats.

Crêpe pans range in size from 5 to 8½ inches (diameter of pan bottom, not top edge). Most recipes specify 6- to 7-inch crêpes.

A Breton crêpe griddle is notable for its larger size—11 to 15 inches in diameter. Not as deep as smaller crêpe pans, it has a shallow, upturned rim that contains the crêpe batter. Made of cast aluminum or cast iron, it also can be used as a griddle for modest conventional pancakes and grilled sandwiches.

Waffles and pancakes are made from batters that take on the shape of the cooking pan. Shown clockwise from top left: electric waffle iron with nonstick grids, stove-top heart-shaped waffle iron, stove-top Belgian waffle iron, Swedish pancake pan (plett), crêpe pan.

Swedish Pancake Pan (Plett) Designed to shape the small, delicate, eggy pancakes from Scandinavia, this pan can also be used to make blini. In one respect a *plett* is even more convenient than the standard blini pan because it can accommodate several pancakes at a time. The pan is a large (about 10 inches in diameter) cast-iron griddle containing seven shallow, 3-inch-round depressions. Season and treat it as you would any other cast-iron pan.

Recipes and Related Information
Batter, 27; Waffle and Pancake, 598.

WALNUT

The walnut is an ancient food of undetermined origin, although most scholarly speculation centers on Persia. Today, it is second only to the almond in world popularity. The edible portion of the nut is encased in a semi-hard, light brown, two-part shell. The meat inside consists of a pair of irregularly shaped halves connected, "back to back," near their midpoints. Of the several walnut species, only two are of commercial importance: the mild-flavored English walnut and the native North American black walnut, which has a stronger, richer flavor but is quite difficult to shell.

Use Toasted shelled walnuts can be served as a cocktail snack or incorporated in a cocktail mix of buttered, roasted, and salted nuts. Walnuts in the shell are a traditional after-dinner companion to port. Toasted walnuts add nutty flavor and texture to green salads, vegetable dishes, breads, cakes, pies, and cookies. In sufficient quantity and finely ground, they take the place of flour in some cakes. Italian cooks make a sauce of ground walnuts and cream for stuffed pasta squares known as *pansotti.* Turkish cooks make a smooth ground walnut sauce for cold shredded chicken. In Iran cooks stew chicken or duck in a sweet-and-sour pomegranate sauce with ground walnuts. Bulgarian cooks make a refreshing cold soup, called *taratòr,* with cucumber, ground walnuts, yogurt, garlic, and dill. In America cooks use the native black walnut in ice cream and quick breads.

Availability Fresh English walnuts in the shell are sold in many supermarkets and specialty markets in the fall. Packaged English walnut halves and walnut pieces are available in supermarkets all year; bulk shelled English walnuts are carried the year around by some supermarkets and health-food stores. Shelled black walnuts are available from mail-order sources. The difficulty of shelling them makes them hard to find commercially.

Selection Fresh walnuts in the shell should feel heavy for their size.

Storage If stored in a cool, dry place, fresh walnuts in the shell will keep for several months. Shelled walnuts should be refrigerated or frozen because they go rancid quickly. They will keep for about two months in the refrigerator, about one year in the freezer.

Preparation Toasting brings out the flavor of walnuts; for toasting directions and times, see NUT.

▣ GREEK WALNUT TORTE

A torte is a light cake, with nuts and/or crumbs substituting for part or all of the flour. Here, flour is omitted altogether, replaced by ground walnuts and dry bread crumbs. The torte is delicately scented with orange, both in the cake itself and in the whipped cream frosting. Since egg whites are the only leavening agent, it is important to beat them properly and to fold them into the batter without deflating them (see EGG, Beating Eggs, and FOLD).

    1 pound shelled walnuts
    6 tablespoons dry bread crumbs
    9 egg yolks
    ¾ cup sugar
    2 teaspoons finely grated orange rind
    2 tablespoons strained fresh orange juice
    9 egg whites
    ¼ cup sugar
    3 tablespoons orange-flavored liqueur
    1½ teaspoons finely grated orange rind
      Candied orange rind, for garnish

Chocolate Glaze

    1 to 2 ounces semisweet chocolate
    ¼ cup unsalted butter, clarified

Orange Chantilly Cream

    1 teaspoon unflavored gelatin
    2 tablespoons cold water
    1½ cups whipping cream
    ¼ cup sifted confectioners' sugar
    1 tablespoon orange-flavored liqueur

1. Preheat oven to 350° F. Butter and lightly flour two 10-inch-diameter by 2-inch-high cake pans or two 9½-inch-diameter by 3-inch-high springform pans. Line bottoms with circles of parchment or waxed paper.

2. Finely grind walnuts, 1 cup at a time, with 1 tablespoon of the bread crumbs, in food processor or small jar of blender. Bread crumbs and ground walnuts should equal 4 cups.

3. In large bowl of electric mixer, lightly beat egg yolks. Gradually add the ¾ cup sugar, and beat until mixture falls from beater in a ribbon and leaves a slowly dissolving trail on the surface (ribbon stage). Beat in orange rind and orange juice. Stir in walnut mixture.

4. In a large bowl, beat egg whites until they form peaks; gradually add the ¼ cup sugar and beat until they are stiff but still glossy. Stir one fourth of the whites into batter to lighten it. Gently fold in remaining whites. Whites should be completely incorporated but not deflated.

5. Divide batter equally between two cake pans. Bake until cake is springy to the touch and begins to pull away from sides of pan (30 to 40 minutes). Cool in pan 5 minutes, then remove sides of pans (if using springform pans) and allow to finish cooling on wire racks.

6. To assemble cake: Split each cake layer in half horizontally with a long, serrated knife. Place one layer on cake plate; brush with 2 teaspoons orange-flavored liqueur. Spread one third of Chocolate Glaze evenly over cake and sprinkle ½ teaspoon orange rind over glaze. Repeat these steps for the next two layers. Top with fourth layer of cake; brush with remaining orange-flavored liqueur. Ice sides and top of cake with Orange Chantilly Cream. Place remaining cream in a pastry bag fitted with an open-star tip. Decorate border with rosettes of cream or a chain of shells. Refrigerate until ready to serve. When ready to serve, place a 1-inch piece of candied orange rind in the center of each rosette to mark each slice.

Serves 10 to 12.

Chocolate Glaze In a double boiler melt chocolate over hot (not boiling) water. Remove from heat and stir in clarified (tepid) butter. Cool mixture to tepid (86° F).

Orange Chantilly Cream Soften gelatin in the cold water; in a double boiler stir over hot (not boiling) water until gelatin dissolves; cool until syrupy. Beat whipping cream until slightly thickened; add dissolved gelatin, confectioners' sugar, and orange-flavored liqueur. Continue beating until soft peaks form and hold their shape when beaters are lifted from bowl. Do not overbeat; cream should look soft and glossy.

Recipes and Related Information
Braised Celery With Walnuts, 109; Walnut-Apple Strudel, 222; Your Own Bridge Mix, 59.

WASABI

A variety of aquatic plant unique to Japan, *wasabi* comes from an edible root that has a tough brownish green skin and a pale green flesh. The flesh is finely grated to make a pungent condiment similar to horseradish.

Use Wasabi is most often encountered in sushi bars. Sushi chefs put a thin swipe of wasabi atop the rice and underneath the fish when making Nigiri Sushi (see page 233). They also serve a small mound of wasabi with sashimi (thinly sliced raw fish), which the diner mixes to taste with soy sauce to make a dipping sauce for the sashimi. Similarly, wasabi is often served with cold noodle dishes, to be added to the dipping sauce. Japanese cooks also pickle vegetables such as eggplant with wasabi and mustard.

Availability   Fresh wasabi is rarely if ever seen in this country. Powdered wasabi in tins is sold in many supermarkets and in all Japanese markets. Wasabi paste in tubes is available in some Japanese markets.

Storage   Powdered wasabi, stored in a cool, dry place, will keep indefinitely. Wasabi paste should be refrigerated after opening.

Preparation   For powdered wasabi, add just enough tepid water to powder to form a paste. Mix until smooth. Let stand 10 minutes to develop flavor. Paste wasabi is ready to use right from the tube.

WATER CHESTNUT

A tuber that grows in east Asian marshes, the water chestnut is now cultivated in the southeastern United States. It has a squat round shape with a pointed tip. Underneath its dark brown skin is cream-colored flesh as crisp and sweet as that of an apple. Young, fresh water chestnuts are best; flavor becomes starchy and less sweet with age.

Use   Water chestnuts, essential to Chinese cooking, add texture to countless soups, stir-fries, and stuffings. Chinese steamed dumplings are typically filled with a mixture of seasoned minced shrimp or ground pork and water chestnuts. The refreshing, clean taste and crisp texture of water chestnuts make them an appealing nibble at the start of a meal. American cooks sometimes wrap them in bacon and broil them to serve as an appetizer.

Availability   Fresh water chestnuts are occasionally available in Chinese markets. Canned water chestnuts, both whole and sliced, are sold in supermarkets and Chinese markets.

Selection   Fresh water chestnuts should feel rock hard and should have a smooth, not wrinkled, exterior.

Storage   If firm, fresh water chestnuts will keep up to two weeks refrigerated in a plastic bag. Canned water chestnuts, once opened, should be transferred to an airtight nonmetal container and covered with fresh water; they will keep for two to three weeks if the water is changed every few days.

Preparation   Fresh water chestnuts may be muddy. Rinse well just before using; peel. Unless using immediately, cover peeled water chestnuts with cold water to prevent discoloration. Canned water chestnuts can be blanched for 15 seconds in boiling water, then shocked in cold water, to rid them of their canned taste.

▉ SHRIMP WITH SNOW PEAS AND WATER CHESTNUTS

This Chinese stir-fry is a study in crisp textures and complementary colors. Splitting the shrimp lengthwise causes them to curl into spirals when cooked.

   ½   **pound shrimp, peeled and split lengthwise**
       Pinch salt
   2   **tablespoons Shaoxing wine or dry sherry**
       Oil, for stir-frying
   1   **tablespoon minced fresh ginger**
   ½   **pound snow peas, stems and strings removed**
   ½   **cup sliced water chestnuts (preferably fresh)**
   1   **tablespoon soy sauce**
   ½   **teaspoon cornstarch, dissolved in ¼ cup water**
       or stock

1. Toss shrimp with salt; add wine; marinate for 20 minutes to several hours.

2. Drain shrimp and reserve marinade. Heat wok over high heat; add oil. Add ginger, stir-fry until fragrant, and add shrimp. Stir-fry until shrimp are mostly opaque (2 to 4 minutes, depending on size).

3. Add snow peas and water chestnuts; stir-fry until just heated through. Add reserved marinade, soy sauce, and cornstarch mixture. Bring to a boil and cook until sauce thickens. Serve immediately.

Serves 4 to 6 with other dishes.

WATERCRESS

A member of the mustard family, watercress grows wild and profusely in shallow, slow-moving creeks. For the commercial market, it is cultivated in streams and harvested by waders. Watercress has small, round, dark green leaves on stems slightly thicker than parsley. The leaves and stems have a peppery taste.

Use   Watercress makes a peppery addition to green salads and sandwiches or a lively base for chicken or egg salad. In France cooks make watercress soup, thickened with potatoes and cream. The English put a sprig of watercress on dainty tea sandwiches.

Availability   Fresh watercress is sold by the bunch in most supermarkets the year around. Supplies peak in late spring and early summer.

Selection   Look for watercress with healthy green leaves; avoid any bunches with yellowing or slimy leaves.

Storage   Untie bunch at home and remove any bad sprigs; wash gently in cool water, dry thoroughly, then wrap in paper towels, overwrap in plastic, and refrigerate. Use within two to three days.

Preparation   Cut away any overly thick stems.

THE TIGER
Third sign of the zodiac
Magnetic, aggressive, adventuro

Stir-fried Shrimp With Snow Peas is even better when made with fresh water chestnuts, available in Chinese markets and some specialty markets.

■ COUNTRY WATERCRESS SOUP

This creamy soup, which can be served hot or cold, is lightly thickened with potato. Serve the soup hot with Garlic Croutons (see page 506) or cold with French bread. This soup thickens as it chills. If it becomes too thick, gradually stir in another 2 to 3 tablespoons of cream or milk just before serving.

>   2 **medium leeks**
>   2 **bunches watercress (10 oz total)**
>   1 **medium potato**
>   2 **tablespoons butter**
>   1 **medium onion, sliced**
> 1½ **cups Chicken Stock (see page 560)**
>   **Salt and white pepper, to taste**
> 1½ **cups milk**
>   ¼ **to ½ cup whipping cream**
>   **Freshly grated nutmeg**

1. Wash and trim leeks. Cut white and light green parts of leeks in thin slices; reserve dark green part for other uses. Thoroughly rinse watercress, discard large stems, and reserve only upper, leafy third of each bunch. Reserve 8 to 12 attractive watercress leaves for garnish. Plunge bunches of watercress into large saucepan of boiling water. Bring back to a boil, drain immediately, and rinse under cold running water. Drain thoroughly and squeeze dry. Peel potato and cut in thin slices.

2. Melt butter in heavy saucepan over low heat. Add onion and leeks and cook, stirring often, until soft but not brown (about 10 minutes). Add watercress bunches and cook, stirring, for 2 minutes. Add potato, stock, and a pinch of salt and pepper, and bring to a boil. Reduce heat to low, cover, and simmer, stirring occasionally, until potatoes are tender (about 20 minutes).

3. Purée soup through a food mill, or in a blender or food processor. Strain to remove stringy parts of watercress.

4. Return soup to saucepan and add milk. Bring to a boil, stirring occasionally. Add ¼ cup cream and bring again to a boil. If soup is too thick, stir in remaining cream. Add nutmeg. Taste and add salt and pepper, if needed.

5. Prepare garnish by dipping a small strainer containing reserved watercress leaves into a small saucepan of boiling water for 30 seconds. Rinse under cold water to stop cooking and drain.

6. Serve soup hot or cold. To chill hot soup, cool slightly, then cover and refrigerate until thoroughly cold (several hours or overnight). Ladle soup into bowls and garnish with blanched watercress leaves.

Makes 4 to 5 cups, serves 4.

Recipes and Related Information
Cream of Watercress, 563; Watercress Dip With Green Onions and Basil, 521.

WHIP, TO

To beat rapidly in a circular motion in order to increase the volume of a mixture by incorporating air into it; done with a whisk, rotary beater, or electric mixer. The action is vigorous—the whisk doesn't move around the mixture, but enters and leaves it so as to pull in the maximum amount of air.

Essentially, whipping is stirring; instead of using a single spoon, however, you use a beater or whisk consisting of 12 to 25 wires bent into a bulbous shape. Therefore, each stir represents a dozen or more stirs. The whisk has become such a standard tool for this procedure that the term *to whisk* has come to mean *to whip*.

> ### Recipes and Related Information
> *Cream, 160; Egg, 194; Whisk, 608.*

WHISK, TO; WHISK

To beat rapidly to incorporate air into a mixture (see WHIP); also the utensil used to perform this task. Like spoons and spatulas, whisks are beating tools, used to smoothly incorporate ingredients. Unlike them, however, whisks perform an additional function—that of

incorporating air, which causes a mixture to lighten or expand. Whisks are made of stainless steel wires in a range of thicknesses, shapes, and sizes depending on how they will be used. They are traditionally an integral part of the French chef's *batterie de cuisine;* in American home kitchens the electric mixer and food processor have taken over many of their functions—particularly for beating egg whites and whipping cream. However, the open design of the whisk is still invaluable for mixing sauces, batters, and dressings. Although using a whisk is more labor-intensive, many cooks prefer to whip egg whites and cream by hand. Studies indicate that egg whites whipped in a copper bowl with a balloon whisk produce the greatest volume and the finest, most stable foam.

Whisks are available with wires that are flexible or rigid, thin or heavy-gauge, and gathered in an open, elongated, or flat shape; match the whisk to your purpose. As a guideline, use a balloon whisk, which resembles an oversized light bulb and has anywhere from 12 to 25 thin, flexible wires, when you want to incorporate as much air as possible—as when beating egg whites and whipping cream. For blending, use one with a less open shape. Thinner wires work well for light mixtures and for aerating flours and other powders; heavier wires will stand up in denser batters and sauces. A flat whisk, which looks like a

standard whisk cut in cross section, is angled for mixing in shallow dishes or pans, and is particularly useful for beating eggs and reaching around the edges of a saucepan to draw any lumpy portions of a sauce into the mixture.

Don't use a fine-gauge whisk or one with wires joined close together for heavy batters; they lack the strength to move easily through a thick liquid, and the wires will trap the batter inside the whisk. Check construction to make sure that food can't collect where wires and handle meet. A whisk with a stainless steel handle can go in the dishwasher; one with a wooden handle must be washed by hand, but tends to be more comfortable to hold.

> ### Recipes and Related Information
> *Copper Egg-White Bowl, 155; Egg, 194.*

WINE IN COOKING

Apart from its pleasure as a beverage, wine has an important place in the pantry. Wherever wine is enjoyed at the table, cooks have learned to take advantage of its special properties in the kitchen. White or red, sweet or dry, wine can enhance a range of different dishes.

Use   Wine has three main uses in the kitchen: as a marinade ingredient, as a cooking liquid, and as a flavoring in a finished dish.

Selection   So-called cooking wines sold in stores are unsuitable for most culinary purposes. They have been salted to the point that they are unfit to drink so that they may be sold in stores without liquor licenses or in dry states or localities. It is far better to use an unadulterated table wine or a fortified wine (such as sherry or Madeira).

Storage   All wines should be stored in a cool, dark, well-ventilated place with moderate humidity. They should preferably be stored on their sides to keep the cork moist; a dry cork will shrink and allow air to enter. Ideal storage conditions are less important if the wine will be used within a few weeks; the longer you plan to keep the wine before using, the more important it is to store it properly.

Leftover table wines can be refrigerated and used for cooking if held for only one or two weeks. If you have at least a half bottle of wine left over, pour it off into a clean half bottle, cork it, and store in the refrigerator. Without air space at the top, the rebottled wine will keep for up to one month.

WINE AS A MARINADE

Marinating food—especially meat and poultry—in wine contributes flavor and tenderness. As well as adding a flavor of its own, wine helps food absorb the flavors of herbs, vegetables, or spices. The moderate acidity of wine also helps penetrate and tenderize meats.

Both red and white wines are suitable for marinades. It's unnecessary to use a fine wine, although you should use a well-flavored wine you wouldn't hesitate to drink. Dry wines are traditional for savory marinades, but a sweet wine can add an appealing flavor to game birds, such as squab or quail.

Wine is also used as a marinade in fruit desserts. In this context, fruits are said to macerate in wine. Peaches macerated in red wine or strawberries macerated in sparkling wine make refreshing summer desserts. Generally superfine sugar is added to taste in order to balance the acidity of the wine (see MACERATE).

WINE AS A COOKING LIQUID

Cooking directly in wine adds flavor and necessary moisture. Fish poached in white wine or chicken braised in red wine are just two examples among many of wine as a cooking medium. Poaching in wine is ideal for delicate foods, such as fish. The poaching liquid may be a simple court bouillon of wine and water flavored with aromatics or a fumet, a wine-based fish stock. Fruits, too, are often poached in a wine syrup, made by boiling wine and water with sugar and such flavorings as cinnamon or vanilla bean. Wine syrups can also be drizzled over whole just-baked cakes as a flavoring and glaze.

Steaming in wine is a technique most often used with shellfish. Clams or mussels are put into a pot with white wine, shallots or onions, and herbs; the pot is covered and the liquid brought to a boil. The shellfish open as they steam in the wine and are imbued with its flavor.

Braising meats and poultry in wine—first browning the meat or poultry in oil or fat, then adding wine and cooking slowly in a covered pan—is a technique common to some of the world's most satisfying dishes. Not only does the wine moisten and tenderize tougher cuts of meat, but its distinctive flavor also enhances the sauce. The long, slow cooking and the typical final reduction of the sauce concentrate the flavors of the wine.

This concentration, however, can be a mixed blessing. Red wines, especially, can dominate a sauce and should be used with caution. Sometimes a concentrated flavor is desirable, as in the classic Burgundian coq au vin or in dishes made with game or red meats. But with other braised dishes, even if you plan to serve a red wine, cooking with a white wine may produce the best flavors.

WINE AS A FLAVORING

Fortified wines such as sherry and Madeira are often stirred into soups at the last moment or even at the table. A spoonful of sherry or a dash of Madeira are the classic finishing touches for some consommés and cream soups. Usually the soup is not cooked further after the wine is added to avoid dissipating the flavor of the wine.

Wine is also used to deglaze a roasting pan or a skillet in which foods have been roasted or sautéed. Deglazing is

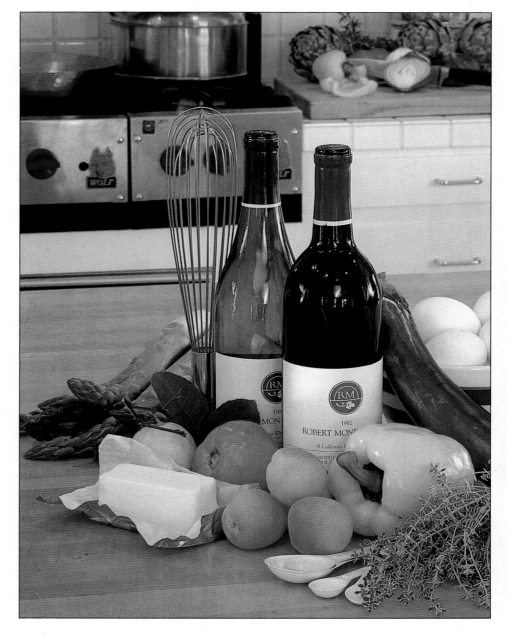

the first step in creating a delicious assortment of sauces. Whether you are working with a beef roast, pan-fried chicken, or sautéed fish fillets, the deglazing procedure is the same: Pour off excess fat, add aromatics if desired (herbs, onions, garlic), then add wine and bring it to a boil, scraping drippings loose from bottom of pan. After alcohol has boiled out of wine, other liquids such as cream or stock may be added and reduced to make a sauce.

Most recipes for wine sauces call for reducing, which simply means boiling down the sauces until the volume has been cut by about half. Reducing is an essential technique to many great sauces. Reducing a wine-based sauce eliminates the alcohol while it concentrates the flavor of the wine. Such sauces must be made with care. Reducing a wine sauce too far can make it too acidic and boil away most of the flavor.

Good cooking begins with the best ingredients. Good, inexpensive wine from a high-quality winery is an important pantry item.

Sautéed Chicken Breasts With Sherry, Cream, and Mushrooms (see page 611) is a fine complement to Chardonnay or other full-flavored white wines. The sauce lends itself to endless variations; in place of the mushrooms, try almonds or other nuts, artichoke hearts, or even a mixture of raisins and unsweetened coconut.

■ SPICY RED-WINE MARINADE

This recipe, similar to the white-wine marinade (at right), but based on a red wine, is especially good for roasted, broiled, or grilled poultry. For a sweeter taste, use ruby port instead of a dry wine.

> ½ teaspoon *each* whole coriander, fennel, black pepper, and juniper berries
> ¾ cup dry red wine
> 2 tablespoons red wine vinegar
> ½ onion, sliced
> 2 or 3 cloves garlic, minced
> 1 tablespoon minced fresh ginger *or* ½ teaspoon ground ginger

1. Grind coriander, fennel, pepper, and juniper berries together in a clean coffee grinder, electric minichopper, or with a mortar and pestle.

2. Combine ground spices, wine, vinegar, onion, garlic, and ginger in a glass, ceramic, or stainless steel bowl large enough to hold poultry.

3. Marinate whole or cut-up birds in refrigerator, covered, overnight, or for up to three days. Turn birds frequently to marinate them evenly.

4. Remove birds from refrigerator 30 minutes before cooking. Drain thoroughly and discard marinade. Roast, grill, or broil (stuffed or unstuffed) according to any standard recipe.

Makes about 1 cup (enough for a whole fryer or duck or for 2 or 3 Rock Cornish game hens).

■ PORK ROAST WITH WHITE-WINE MARINADE

Two days of marinating in a mixture of white wine, spices, and herbs gives roast pork a little of the flavor of wild boar. Be sure to marinate the pork in a nonaluminum container such as stainless steel, ceramic, or glass.

> 1 teaspoon fennel seed
> 2 teaspoons coriander seed
> 1 teaspoon black peppercorns
> 1 teaspoon salt
> ¼ teaspoon ground ginger
> 1 pork loin roast (about 3½ lb with bones)
> 1 cup Gewürztraminer or Sauvignon Blanc
> 1 large sprig fresh sage *or* ½ teaspoon dried sage
> 1 large sprig fresh thyme *or* ½ teaspoon dried thyme
> 1 bay leaf
> 8 small new potatoes

1. Two days ahead: Coarsely grind fennel, coriander, and pepper in a clean coffee grinder, electric minichopper, or with a mortar and pestle. Combine ground spices with salt and ginger. Rub this mixture all over pork roast. Put roast in a stainless steel, ceramic, or glass bowl, pour in wine, and crumble herbs into bowl. Marinate roast in refrigerator, turning it several times a day to marinate it evenly.

2. On cooking day: Remove roast from refrigerator at least 1 hour before cooking. Preheat oven to 450° F. Drain roast thoroughly and discard marinade.

3. Pat roast dry with paper towels and place it, fat side up, on a rack in a roasting pan. Put roast in hot oven, reduce heat to 325° F, and roast to an internal temperature of 170° F (25 to 30 minutes per pound). Add potatoes to roasting pan for the last 30 minutes to roast in drippings.

4. Let roast rest about 15 minutes before carving into ½-inch slices. Serve with roast potatoes and a full-flavored dry white wine or a lighter red wine.

Serves 4.

STEAMED CLAMS

When simply steamed in a seasoned broth, clams, mussels, or oysters make a tasty first course. Serve in shallow bowls with crusty bread to scoop up the juices. Steam the clams (or other shellfish) in a nonreactive saucepan so the acid in the wine will not impart a metallic flavor.

   4 pounds (about 32 medium) clams
   8 cloves garlic, minced
   2 large shallots, minced
   ½ teaspoon salt
   1 cup dry white wine
   6 to 8 sprigs parsley, minced, for garnish

1. Wash clams, scrubbing exterior, to remove any sand. Place clams in a deep, 4-quart, nonreactive saucepan. Add minced garlic and shallots to saucepan with clams. Sprinkle with salt and add wine.

2. Bring to a boil, reduce heat, and simmer for 2 minutes. Discard any clams that fail to open. Garnish with parsley.

Serves 4.

BEEF BRAISED IN RED WINE

This is not a dish for subtle wines; it works best with a full-flavored wine with ample acidity. A Petite Sirah or a Zinfandel with plenty of character will fill the bill nicely. Serve the same type of wine as a beverage. Although braised beef can be cooked on top of the stove, it is easier to maintain the slight simmer in a low oven. A slow cooker or other covered electric cooker also works well, but you will still need to do steps 1 through 3 on top of the stove.

   2½ pounds boneless chuck roast
   1 tablespoon oil or chicken or duck fat
   ⅓ pound shallots, peeled and left whole
   ½ bottle dry red wine
       Bouquet garni of parsley, bay leaf, thyme,
       and celery leaves
   ½ teaspoon salt
   ½ teaspoon freshly ground pepper
   4 dried tomato halves, chopped, *or*
       8 dry-cured olives, pitted and chopped

1. Preheat oven to 225° F. Cut meat into large cubes (2 to 2½ inches), trimmed of excess fat and gristle. Dry cubes of meat with a paper towel. (This allows them to brown more easily.)

2. Heat oil in an ovenproof casserole over medium heat. Brown cubes of meat a few at a time. (Don't try to brown too many at a time or they will stew rather than brown.) Transfer cubes to a plate as they brown and add more as space allows.

3. When all meat has been browned, brown shallots in the same fat. Pour out any fat remaining in pan. Add wine, bring to a boil, and reduce heat to a simmer. Return meat cubes to pan. Add bouquet garni, salt, pepper, and tomatoes.

4. Cover pan and place it in oven. Bake 3½ to 4 hours, adjusting heat, if necessary, so sauce barely simmers. Meat should be very tender and should absorb flavor of sauce.

5. Turn off oven. Remove cooked meat and shallots to a serving platter and return them to oven to keep warm. Discard bouquet garni and bring sauce to a boil on top of stove. Reduce sauce by a third. Taste and correct seasoning.

6. Pour sauce over meat and serve with buttered noodles, steamed potatoes, or polenta.

Serves 6.

CHICKEN BREASTS WITH SHERRY, CREAM, AND MUSHROOMS

If you are serving a first course before this dish, you can cook the chicken breasts first, then hold them in the oven for 15 minutes or so. The sauce will only take about five minutes to prepare, so you will be able to sit down and enjoy the first course before serving the entrée.

   4 chicken breast halves, boned and skinned
   ¼ cup flour
   ½ teaspoon salt
   ½ teaspoon pepper
   2 to 4 tablespoons butter
   2 tablespoons vegetable oil
   ¼ pound mushrooms, sliced
   1 tablespoon chopped garlic
   1 green onion, chopped
   ¼ cup dry sherry
   ½ cup whipping cream

1. Preheat oven to 200° F. Trim all bits of fat and membrane from chicken breasts. In a shallow bowl combine flour, salt, and pepper. Dredge breasts in seasoned flour and shake off excess. Have a warm, ovenproof plate ready.

2. In a large skillet over medium heat, heat butter and oil together. Add chicken breasts and cook just until the thickest part springs back when pressed (about 3 minutes per side). Remove to warm plate, cover loosely with aluminum foil, and keep warm in oven while you prepare sauce. (Recipe may be prepared to this point up to 15 minutes ahead of serving time.)

3. If butter has browned, pour it out and add another 2 tablespoons butter to pan. Add mushrooms, garlic, and green onion, turn heat to high, and sauté until mushrooms begin to soften. Add sherry, bring to a boil, and reduce by half. Add cream, bring to a boil, and reduce to a thick sauce. Taste for seasoning and correct if necessary.

4. Return chicken breasts to skillet to coat them with sauce. Serve topped with mushrooms and sauce.

Serves 4.

TIPS

COOKING WITH WINE

Wine can be used in place of part or all of the cooking or marinating liquid in countless recipes as long as you remember the following.

• *Boiling down wine concentrates its flavors, including acidity and sweetness. Be careful not to use too much or the finished dish may be excessively sweet or sour, or taste too strongly of wine.*

• *Whether quickly making a deglazing sauce or simmering a dish over a long period, allow enough cooking time after adding the wine for the alcohol to evaporate. Boiling a sauce rapidly in a shallow pan will cook off the alcohol in 1 or 2 minutes, but slow simmering in a deeper pan may take 15 minutes or more. Taste sauce before serving to be sure. Avoid adding wine to a sauce just before serving, or the dish may taste unpleasantly alcoholic. The last-minute addition of wine to some soups (see Wine as a Flavoring, page 609) is one delicious exception.*

• *Remember that wine does not belong in every dish. More than one wine-based sauce in a single meal can be monotonous. Use wine in cooking only when it has something to contribute to the finished dish.*

The elegant appearance of Rosé Pears in Chocolate Bath belies its ease of preparation.

■ ROSE PEARS IN CHOCOLATE BATH

Poach the pears and mix the sauce ahead of time; then assemble this elegant dessert just before serving.

> 2½   **cups red table wine**
> ⅓   **cup sugar**
> ½   **cinnamon stick, broken**
> ⅛   **teaspoon ground coriander**
> 3   **whole cloves**
>   **Grated rind of ½ orange**
>   **Grated rind of 1 lemon**
> 4   **Bartlett pears, peeled**
> 1   **cup Old-fashioned Chocolate Sauce (double recipe; see page 523)**
> 2   **to 3 tablespoons Cognac, orange-flavored liqueur, or almond-flavored liqueur**
>   **Mint sprigs, kiwifruit slices, or candied violets, for garnish**

1. In a medium saucepan combine wine, sugar, cinnamon, coriander, cloves, and orange and lemon rinds. Bring to a boil. Add pears, reduce heat, and simmer just until tender (8 to 10 minutes).

2. With a slotted spoon remove pears. Halve and core if desired. Place one pear upright in each of 4 champagne or sherbet glasses.

3. Mix chocolate sauce and Cognac. Pour around pears and garnish as desired.

Serves 4.

Nut-Filled Pears in Chocolate Bath   Poach pears as directed in steps 1 and 2. Halve pears horizontally, cutting in a sawtooth pattern to flute. Core, and stuff each half with a mixture of chopped nuts, raisins, dried dates, and dried apricots. Reassemble pears and surround each one with Old-fashioned Chocolate Sauce.

Rosé Pears and Ice Cream   Poach pears as directed in steps 1 and 2. Halve vertically and core. Place a scoop of ice cream, sherbet, or frozen yogurt in each of 4 champagne or sherbet glasses. Lean 2 pear halves against each scoop.

Rosé Pears in Vanilla Cream   Poach pears as directed in steps 1 and 2. Mix 1 to 2 tablespoons Cognac into 1 cup Stirred Custard (see page 168). Whip 1 cup whipping cream and fold into custard. Place cream in bottom of serving glasses. Add pears and garnish with mint.

Recipes and Related Information
Boeuf Bourguignonne, 43; Cheese, 110; Choucroute Garni, 75; Classic Beef Consommé With Vegetable Julienne and Madeira, 562; Fresh Fruit in Wine, 347; Game Hens Coq au Vin, 58; Marinade, 349; Stilton Crock With Port Wine, 114; Sweetbreads and Mushroom-Marsala Sauce, 590; Veal Marsala, 594; Wine Court Bouillon, 450; Winter Fruit Compote, 186.

WORK, TO

To stir or knead a mixture; implies manipulation and resistance. This is a common term used in recipes for bread doughs: "Work the flour into the dough" is a typical instruction. Although it most often refers to hands-on processes, it more generally can mean any vigorous blending of somewhat stiff, resistant mixtures whether by hand or by machine.

Recipes and Related Information
Knead, 326; Yeast Bread, 613.

YAM

The true yam, *Dioscorea,* is a tuber cultivated in Africa and Asia. (For information on the vegetable Americans call yam, see SWEET POTATO.) There are several varieties of *Dioscorea* in various shapes, sizes, and colors, but all have a high starch content. The Japanese mountain yam looks like a large old bone. It is usually peeled, grated, and eaten raw; when grated, it has a gluey consistency and mild flavor. The African giant yam or white yam may grow to weigh 100 pounds. It has a barklike skin, a white flesh, and a mild, starchy flavor.

Use   The Japanese yam serves as a binder in some processed foods and as a garnish for noodle dishes and rice. The giant yam is a staple in Africa. In West Africa it is pounded into a paste called Fufu, which may be made into dumplings or used as a thickener for soups and stews. African cooks also slice yams and deep-fry them like potato chips, boil them in milk, or slice and bake them like potatoes with sliced onions, bread crumbs, and cheese. In the Caribbean, yams may be simply steamed and buttered, or grated, bound with egg, and fried in oil.

Availability   True yams are occasionally found in Japanese, African, or Latin markets in this country. Some African and Latin markets also stock canned white yams from West Africa.

Selection   Yams should be firm, unblemished, and unwrinkled. Smaller ones are preferable.

Storage   Keep in a cool place or in the refrigerator for up to one week.

Preparation   The Japanese yam should be peeled and finely grated. The yam may be irritating to sensitive skin; wear gloves while peeling or peel under cold running water. African or Caribbean varieties should be peeled and cooked. Cut peeled yam into chunks or slices and add to stews or boil in salted water until tender.

Cooking   See BOIL, DEEP-FRY, STEAM.

YEAST

Although wild yeasts have existed since the origins of civilization, their actions were not fully understood until the work of Louis Pasteur in the 1850s. Pasteur's studies of fermentation made it possible for scientists to cultivate yeasts. Today cultivated yeast strains are made and marketed expressly for breads, wines, and beers.

Use Yeast makes bread rise and is responsible for the fermentation of grape juice into wine and barley mash into beer. The yeast feed on the sugars in the dough or the juice, converting the sugars to carbon dioxide and alcohol. In the case of bread, the carbon dioxide gas is trapped within the dough and makes it rise. In the case of wine, the carbon dioxide escapes but the alcohol remains. In beer making, trapped carbon dioxide provides natural carbonation. For the home cook, the principal value of yeast is as a leavening agent in breads.

Availability Yeast for baking is widely stocked in supermarkets, packaged either as active dry yeast or as fresh yeast in moist cakes. One yeast cake is equivalent to one ¼-ounce package active dry yeast (1 tablespoon dry yeast). Some health-food stores also carry active dry yeast in bulk. Recently available in the market is quick-rise yeast, a high-activity yeast strain that makes doughs rise up to 50 percent faster than regular yeast does.

Selection Check expiration date on package.

Storage Fresh yeast is more perishable than dry; refrigerate and use within three weeks of purchase. Bulk dry yeast should be stored airtight in a covered container. Both packaged and bulk dry yeast should be kept in a cool, dark, dry place and used within six months.

Preparation To activate dry yeast, sprinkle it over a bowl of warm (about 110° F) liquid; let soften 1 minute. Stir with a fork to dissolve yeast. Set aside to proof 5 to 10 minutes. Proofing verifies that yeast is still active. Within 10 minutes, yeast should produce a foamy layer on surface of water. If not, discard yeast and liquid, and begin again with a fresh package. To activate fresh cake yeast, place it in a bowl of warm (about 110° F) liquid; mash with a fork to blend and stir until smooth. Set aside to proof 10 minutes. Discard if yeast does not begin foaming within 10 minutes.

About Proofing: In the days when the effectiveness of commercial yeast was less predictable, proofing was essential. However, the baker's yeast produced today is extremely reliable and, if used before the expiration date on the package, should not require proofing. Indeed, many modern recipes call for adding dry yeast directly to bread dough.

Recipes and Related Information
Fermentation, 219; Leaven, 338; Proof, 479.

YEAST BREAD

Making fresh yeast-leavened bread at home is a pleasure that, if planned, can fit into most schedules. The rewards are many: the warm, relaxed kneading and shaping; the wonderful yeasty aroma that permeates the air during baking; and finally, the delight of biting into a fresh, full-tasting bread.

The world of bread is a temptingly varied one, and is much more inviting than the standard sliced white loaf frequently associated with the word *bread*. The slender, crusty French baguette and rich brioche, the dark, fragrant German rye, and the simple, chewy Italian loaf are just a few of the forms that bread takes in other cultures.

TYPES OF YEAST BREADS

All yeast breads are made from a soft dough; approximately 3 parts flour to 1 part liquid is the usual ratio. This proportion can vary somewhat as flours differ in their capacities to absorb liquid, which is why most bread recipes give a range for the amount of flour. At its most basic, bread is a combination of flour, yeast, salt, and a liquid. With the addition of eggs, sugar, milk, butter, spices, nuts, raisins, and other ingredients, the basic dough becomes richer, sweeter, and more cakelike. Flours ground from grains other than wheat also impart a special characteristic to a bread; rye, cornmeal, and oats add texture and distinctive flavor to the dough.

Examples of a straightforward yeast bread are the familiar white or whole-grain loaf. Brioche is a golden bread rich in eggs and butter and a favorite for breakfast when spread with more butter and homemade preserves. Babas and savarins also are abundantly buttery and are so sweet that they are served as a dessert, drenched in liqueur. Croissants, Danish pastries, sweet rolls, babas, and savarins are yeast leavened, but because of the high proportion of butter to flour in their doughs, they are as much a pastry as a bread.

Breads vary in shape as well—from the familiar loaf to free-form rounds and braids, to those molded in special fluted or flared tins. What these varied breads have in common is that they use yeast as a leavener. In a dough, yeast gives off carbon dioxide gas, which, along with the steam produced by liquid ingredients, causes the dough to expand and rise. Quick breads are leavened chemically; they use either baking powder or baking soda (or a combination of the two) rather than yeast (see QUICK BREAD).

INGREDIENTS FOR BREADS: WHAT EACH DOES

Most bread recipes call for the same few basic ingredients—flour, liquid, yeast, and salt—often plus shortening, eggs, and sugar or other sweetener. The nature of the ingredients, their proportion, and the way they are combined make all the difference in the final product.

The ingredients that go into a loaf of bread are simple—flour, other grains and cereals, yeast, eggs, milk, and sugar and honey. But their combined effect is wonderfully complex.

Flour This is the fundamental component—the foundation—of most breads. Wheat flours have the ability to make gluten, an elastic protein that gives structure to breads and all baked goods. Gluten is formed when liquid combines with two of the proteins contained in wheat flour. Beating, stirring, or kneading develops the gluten further into a strong cellular network to hold the gases and steam that are given off during the bread making and baking processes and inflate the finished product and make it light. Nonwheat flours have little or no gluten and produce breads that are dense and low rising; they are often combined with wheat flour for best results. See FLOUR and GRAIN.

Liquid In some form, liquid is present in most breads. It helps to distribute the yeast evenly in the flour and is a medium in which sugar and salt can dissolve. Doughs made with water generally yield crisper breads with more crust than doughs made with milk. Used in yeast breads, milk adds richness, makes a bread with a finer crumb and softer crust, and can help retard staling. Before pasteurization, milk used in a bread recipe was first scalded; this was thought to destroy some enzymes that adversely affected bread quality. However, scalding isn't necessary with pasteurized milk (see MILK).

Yeast When fed the correct amounts of food, moisture, and warmth, yeast, which are tiny plants, multiply rapidly. A small amount of sugar supports the growth of yeast, but too much sugar slows the rate. For this reason, rich doughs with a high proportion of sugar take longer to rise than leaner ones. Yeast is sold in two forms: cake (compressed) and active dry yeast (standard and quick-rise). Yeast is very heat sensitive: Too little heat and it will not multiply; too much and it will die. The optimum temperature varies according to the type of yeast. Both cake yeast and active dry yeast are most effective at about 110° F. Quick-rise active dry yeast will tolerate a range of temperatures from 90° to 115° F. See YEAST.

Salt In addition to flavoring bread, salt also helps to control the rate of fermentation of yeast breads and to make the dough easier to handle. In very hot weather, an environment that may cause a yeast dough to rise too rapidly, the addition of extra salt will slow down the reaction.

Sugar From sugar, a yeast dough gets sweetness and an immediate source of food for the yeast; sugar also imparts tenderness to the crumb and color to the crust.

Fat Butter, margarine, shortening, and oil are the usual forms fat takes in a yeast dough, although their addition is optional. Fat helps produce a tender loaf with a nice, brown crust.

Eggs A dough made with one or more eggs has a rich flavor and color.

BREAD-BAKING EQUIPMENT

The *batterie de cuisine* for baking bread ranges from the simplest baking sheet or loaf pan to a sleek heavy-duty mixer. Here are some of the basic tools many bakers use regularly.

Food Processor This appliance is good for mixing and kneading dough. More and more bread recipes are offering a variation for preparing doughs this way. Check the instructions for your machine to determine the capacity for heavy dough. Placing too much dough in the machine can damage the motor.

Measuring Utensils Have both liquid and dry measuring cups, and two sets of measuring spoons (one for liquids and one for powders). A spatula will come in handy to level off dry ingredients or to loosen baked breads from pans. A dough thermometer (also called an instant-read thermometer; see THERMOMETER) is helpful to determine that the liquid used in a yeast bread is at the proper temperature.

Mixer A heavy-duty mixer takes much of the work out of the labor-intensive task of making bread. Its strong motor can beat a fairly heavy dough to develop sufficient elasticity so that the dough requires less kneading later. These mixers often are equipped with a special dough hook, designed for yeast breads; many practiced bread makers use the dough hook of the mixer to knead the dough until it is almost ready to set aside to rise, then finish the job with a minute or two of hand-kneading to be sure the dough feels just right.

Molds Breads can be baked in a variety of pans, including the traditional loaf pans and fluted brioche molds, or they can be shaped by hand and set on a flat baking sheet. As with other cookware, a heavy metal pan made of a material that will absorb and hold heat well, will produce the best product. Clay is also well-suited for baking bread; some baking surfaces are soaked in water before baking so that the steam released in the oven will produce a crisp crust. For more information, see BAKING PANS.

Other Utensils A pastry brush is useful for applying glazes, wire racks are necessary for cooling the finished bread, and a serrated knife is the proper tool for making clean slices without tearing the crumb.

PREPARING YEAST DOUGHS

All ingredients should be at or near room temperature, about 72° F, since yeast thrives in a warm environment. The liquid is usually somewhat warmer, 105° to 115° F. On a cold day, rising time may be speeded if the mixing bowl is warmed in a low oven before use.

Often the first step in a recipe is to soften the yeast in warm water with some sugar; the yeast sits for about 5 minutes and then other ingredients are added. Some recipes specify proofing the yeast by leaving it longer, for 10 to 15 minutes; if within 10 minutes the surface bubbles and foams, the yeast is alive and can be used successfully. If a reaction fails to occur, the yeast and liquid should be discarded, and the process repeated with a fresh package. However, commercial yeast is reliable enough that, if a package is used before the marked expiration date, proofing shouldn't be necessary. Some recipes mix in the yeast directly with the dry ingredients.

KNEADING THE DOUGH

Flour is added last and then the dough is manipulated by hand, with a wooden spoon, in a heavy-duty electric mixer, or in the work bowl of a food processor. Working the dough disperses the ingredients and develops a strong network of gluten. Kneading continues until the dough takes on a silken elasticity and fine bubbles or blisters can be discerned just below the surface. More flour is added to bring the dough to a workable consistency. See KNEAD for a further discussion of this technique and information on using a food processor for making yeast doughs.

THE RISING PERIOD

When the dough has been sufficiently kneaded, it is set aside to rise. Confusingly, this stage is also called proofing (see PROOF). During rising the yeast continues to grow, giving off carbon dioxide gas that gently and slowly expands the dough. The first rising takes 1 to 1½ hours; during that time the dough generally doubles in bulk. The second and third risings, if called for, are for shorter periods. Some recipes have only one rise. However, flavor improves and a finer texture results if the dough has several long, slow risings.

For rising, the dough is shaped into a ball and placed in a lightly oiled bowl, then turned to coat the entire surface. This light covering of oil keeps the dough moist and prevents it from forming a skin that will inhibit expansion. The bowl is covered with plastic wrap or a clean kitchen towel and set in a warm, draft-free place, the environment needed for yeast doughs to rise to maximum volume (usually about 80° to 85° F). Commercial bakeries have special proofing ovens; at home doughs rise nicely in a gas oven warmed by a pilot light or in an electric oven that has been turned on at 200° F for 1 minute, then turned off. As a test to determine if the dough has risen sufficiently, dent it gently with your index finger. If the dent remains, the dough is ready. If the depression fills up and nearly disappears, the dough needs more time.

SHAPING THE DOUGH

When the dough has doubled, it is punched down or deflated by hitting it with your fist or by gently picking it up and setting back down into the bowl. This step keeps the dough from overstretching and subsequently breaking the gluten network and creates a bread with a more even grain by widely distributing the bubbles of carbon dioxide that developed during the rising period. The dough is then shaped (see Shaping Loaves and Rolls at right), set in a pan or on a baking sheet, and usually left to rise a second time. Baking pans and baking sheets should be well greased; they also may be lightly dusted with flour or sprinkled with cornmeal. After rising and before baking, loaves are sometimes slashed with a sharp knife or a razor blade, or snipped with scissors. This is done both for decorative effect and to allow excess gas, which would otherwise cause the dough to tear, to escape during baking.

BAKING, COOLING, AND STORING YEAST BREADS

Within minutes after being placed in a preheated oven, a yeast dough rises dramatically. This expansion, called oven spring, continues until the yeast is killed by the heat and the structure of the bread sets; some doughs may increase in volume by almost 80 percent during this time. A light, crispy bread can be produced by baking directly on a high-fire baking stone or on an unglazed quarry tile, the home version of a commercial brick oven (see BAKING STONE). Commercial bakery ovens produce breads with superior crusts by injecting a fine spray of water into the oven cavity. Home bakers can approximate this mechanism by setting a pan filled with hot water on the floor of a gas oven or on the lowest shelf of an electric oven. In addition, spray the oven interior several times during the first 10 minutes or so of baking with a fine mist of water. Remove the pan of water toward the end of baking time in order to allow the bread to dry and brown.

SHAPING LOAVES AND ROLLS

Forming a standard loaf Shape dough into a rectangle that is as long as the loaf pan and slightly less than twice as wide as it is long. At narrow end, roll dough tightly, jelly-roll style. Pinch ends and seam to seal; turn ends under, if necessary.

Making a braid Place ropes across baking sheet. Braid, tapering to a rounded point at both ends. Pinch ends to seal; turn ends under, if necessary.

Shaping rolls Bowknots: Tie strands of dough loosely into knots. *Cloverleaf Rolls:* Arrange 3 balls of dough in each cup of muffin pan. *Fantans:* Lay stacks of dough strips horizontally in each cup of muffin pan as shown here or vertically as shown in photograph, page 618. *Parker House Rolls:* Fold circles of dough in half.

TIPS

YEAST BREADS AND THE MICROWAVE OVEN

Rising time for yeast doughs can be shortened if done in a microwave oven that can operate at 10 percent power. See Micro-Rise Method, page 364.

Yeast breads baked in a microwave oven are pale, low in volume, and tough. However, already baked breads and rolls can be defrosted and reheated in seconds in a microwave. The secret is to reheat bread only until it's warm. Overheating will cook the bread, and it will come out of the microwave oven hard and tough. See Reheating and Defrosting Baked Goods at 50 Percent Power (page 363) for specific times.

The bread is done when it has developed a beautiful golden color and sounds hollow when tapped; however, color and touch are not always reliable indicators of doneness, so use baking time as well. Typically, a loaf of bread needs 40 minutes to 1 hour to bake.

Remove baked bread from pan or baking sheet immediately and cool on a wire rack to prevent bottom from getting soggy. If serving, slice with a serrated bread knife and a sawing motion. After the bread is completely cool, store at room temperature, tightly wrapped in plastic wrap, aluminum foil, or an airtight plastic bag. Unless you live in an environment of exceptionally high humidity, storing bread in the refrigerator will cause it to dry out more quickly than it will at room temperature. Breads enriched with eggs, butter, and fruit such as raisins keep longer than plain breads because of their higher fat and moisture contents. Home-baked yeast breads also freeze beautifully.

Freezing bread shortly after it has cooled is the best way to preserve it in peak condition. Choose a freezer wrapping that is both moistureproof and vaporproof in order to keep the bread from drying out or absorbing other flavors and odors. The wrapping should be sturdy enough not to tear when freezer packages are shifted. Use frozen breads within four to six months of baking.

Do not glaze, ice, or sugar-dust coffee cakes and rolls that you plan to freeze. Add these decorations after thawing and shortly before serving. Remove frozen breads several hours before (or the night before) you serve them. Let them thaw at room temperature, then serve as is or warm in the oven. A microwave oven is ideal for thawing or reheating breads; see Reheating and Defrosting Baked Goods at 50 Percent Power (page 363). However, breads heated in the microwave steam rather than bake, and will not be crisp.

■ OVERNIGHT WHITE BREAD

These homey loaves rest—shaped and ready to bake—in the refrigerator until the next day.

    2 packages active dry yeast
    ½ cup warm (105° to 115° F) water
    2 tablespoons honey
    1⅔ cups warm (105° to 115° F) milk
    1½ teaspoons salt
    2 tablespoons butter or margarine
    5½ to 6 cups flour
       Oil, for greasing
    1 teaspoon butter or margarine, softened (optional)

1. In a large bowl of electric mixer, sprinkle yeast over the warm water. Add 1 teaspoon of the honey. Let stand until soft (about 5 minutes).

2. Stir in milk, remaining honey, salt, and the 2 tablespoons butter.

3. Add 3 cups flour. Blend, then beat at medium speed until smooth and elastic (about 5 minutes). Stir in about 2 cups more flour to make a soft dough.

4. Turn dough out onto a board or pastry cloth coated with some of the remaining ½ to 1 cup flour. Knead until dough is smooth and satiny and small bubbles form just under surface (10 to 15 minutes), adding just enough flour to prevent dough from being sticky.

5. Cover ball of kneaded dough with plastic wrap and a kitchen towel; let rest for 30 minutes.

6. Punch dough down and divide into two equal portions. Shape each into a loaf (see photograph, page 615). Place shaped loaves in greased 4½- by 8½-inch loaf pans. Brush lightly with oil.

7. Cover with plastic wrap and refrigerate for at least 3 hours (up to 24 hours). During this time, dough should nearly double in bulk.

8. Remove from refrigerator and let stand at room temperature for 1 hour.

9. Preheat oven to 375° F. Bake until loaves are well browned and sound hollow when tapped (35 to 40 minutes). Remove loaves from pans and cool on wire racks. Rub ½ teaspoon of the soft butter (if desired) over top crust of each loaf while warm.

Makes 2 loaves.

■ QUICK-MIX HONEYED WHEAT BREAD

Using quick-rise active dry yeast, you can produce a light, fine-textured whole wheat bread that is faster to make than most yeast breads for several reasons. You mix the yeast with the other dry ingredients without first softening it in hot water; the dough needs only one rising and it rises faster than most whole-grain breads.

    5¼ to 5¾ cups all-purpose flour
    2 cups whole wheat flour
    2 packages quick-rise active dry yeast
    2 teaspoons salt
    2 cups milk
    ½ cup water
    ½ cup honey
    2 tablespoons vegetable oil, plus oil for greasing

1. In large bowl of electric mixer, combine 4 cups all-purpose flour, whole wheat flour, yeast, and salt; stir to blend dry ingredients thoroughly.

2. In a 1½- to 2-quart saucepan, combine milk, the water, honey, and oil; place over medium heat, stirring to blend well, until hot to touch (110° to 115° F).

3. Add milk mixture to flour mixture. Mix to blend, then beat at medium speed until smooth and elastic (about 5 minutes). Stir in about ¾ cup of the remaining all-purpose flour to make a soft dough.

4. Turn dough out onto a board or pastry cloth coated with some of the remaining ½ to 1 cup flour. Knead until dough is smooth and satiny and small bubbles form just under surface (about 10 minutes), adding just enough flour to prevent dough from being sticky.

5. Cover dough and let rest for 10 minutes.

6. Divide dough into two equal portions. Shape each into a loaf (see photograph, page 615). Place shaped loaves in greased 4½- by 8½-inch loaf pans. Cover lightly with waxed paper or plastic wrap. Let rise in a warm place until doubled in bulk (40 to 45 minutes).

7. Preheat oven to 375° F. Bake until loaves are well browned and sound hollow when tapped (30 to 45 minutes). Remove loaves from pans and let cool on wire racks.

Makes 2 loaves.

■ BRAIDED EGG BREAD
Poppy or sesame seed speckles the crust of this traditional Jewish bread, *challah*. It is a wonderful bread for sandwiches and makes delicious French toast. For an illustration of shaping a braided loaf, see photographs, Shaping Loaves and Rolls, page 615.

   3 **packages active dry yeast**
   3 **tablespoons sugar**
   1 **cup warm (105° to 115° F) water**
   5 **cups flour**
   1 **tablespoon salt**
   ½ **cup warm (105° to 115° F) milk**
   ¼ **cup butter, softened**
   3 **eggs**
     Oil, for greasing
   2 **egg yolks**
   1 **tablespoon water**
     Pinch salt
     Poppy or sesame seed, for sprinkling

1. In a small bowl dissolve yeast and sugar in the warm water and set aside a few minutes to soften. Sift flour and the 1 tablespoon salt and set aside.

2. In a large bowl combine milk, butter, and the 3 eggs; stir in yeast mixture. Slowly add flour, one cup at a time, to make a soft dough. Turn out onto a lightly floured surface and knead until dough is smooth, satiny, and elastic. (The mixing and about 5 minutes of kneading can be done in a heavy-duty electric mixer; finish kneading by hand.)

3. Turn dough in a lightly oiled bowl. Cover and let rise in a warm place until doubled in bulk (about 1 hour). Punch down, knead lightly, and divide dough into 6 portions.

4. Roll each portion of dough into an 18-inch-long strand. Place 3 strands side by side diagonally across a large, greased baking sheet. Braid, being careful not to overstretch dough. Pinch ends of braid and tuck under to seal. Repeat for second loaf.

5. Let rise until almost doubled in bulk (about 45 minutes). Preheat oven to 400° F. Combine egg yolks, the 1 tablespoon water, and salt; brush lightly over braids. Sprinkle evenly with seeds.

6. Bake until loaves are golden brown and sound hollow when tapped lightly (35 to 40 minutes).

Makes 2 braided loaves.

■ FRENCH BAGUETTES
This recipe contains no fat of any kind and only a little sugar, so the bread it produces is very lean. It will taste best when it's freshly baked (within 1 hour or less of baking). To freshen it, sprinkle with a little water and reheat in the oven. Or, freeze bread as soon as it has fully cooled; to reheat, let it stand at room temperature for about 15 minutes, then warm it in a 350° F oven. Special black steel or stainless steel baguette pans, which typically hold two loaves, are available at better cookware stores.

   1 **package active dry yeast**
   2 **cups warm (105° to 115° F) water**
   1 **teaspoon sugar**
   2 **teaspoons salt**
  5½ **to 6 cups unbleached flour**
     Oil, for greasing

1. In large bowl of electric mixer, sprinkle yeast over ¼ cup of the warm water. Add sugar. Let stand until yeast is soft (about 5 minutes).

2. Stir in the remaining 1¾ cups water and salt. Add 4 cups of the flour. Mix to blend, then beat at medium speed until smooth and elastic (about 5 minutes).

3. Gradually beat in about 1 cup more flour to make a soft dough.

4. Turn dough out onto a board or pastry cloth floured with some of the remaining ½ to 1 cup flour. Knead until dough is springy and small bubbles form just under surface (10 to 15 minutes), adding just enough flour to prevent dough from being sticky.

5. Turn dough in a greased bowl. Cover with plastic wrap and a towel; let rise in a warm place until doubled in bulk (about 1 hour).

6. Punch down dough; knead dough lightly into a ball on a floured surface. Cover with inverted bowl and let rest for 10 minutes.

7. Divide dough into 3 equal portions. Shape each into a slender oval loaf 16 to 18 inches long by rolling the ball of dough under palms of hands to elongate it. Place in greased baguette pans or well apart on a large, greased baking sheet. Let rise until puffy but not quite doubled (20 to 25 minutes). Preheat oven to 450° F. With a razor blade make 3 diagonal slashes, about ½ inch deep, down center of each loaf.

8. Before baking use an atomizer filled with cold water to spray shaped loaves with a fine film of moisture. Place in oven, then spray twice more at 3-minute intervals. Bake until bread is well browned (25 to 30 minutes in all). Slide onto wire racks to cool.

Makes 3 loaves.

TIPS

SPECIAL FINISHES

Although the natural, brown mat surface of a freshly baked loaf is extremely appealing, the appearance may be further enhanced by brushing the crust with a glaze or sprinkling the bread with seeds, spices, or herbs to develop textural interest. For shine, brush with an egg wash (see page 211). For a soft crust, brush with milk, buttermilk, cream, melted butter, or margarine. For a sweet glaze, brush with honey or a sugar syrup. Sesame seeds, poppy seeds, caraway seeds, fennel seeds, or finely chopped garlic or onion are a few topping suggestions; try mixing several herbs and spices for a fuller, more complex taste.

The dough for Golden Dinner Rolls can be shaped in a variety of ways. Shown here are Bowknots, Parker House Rolls, Cloverleaf Rolls, and Fantans.

1. In large bowl of electric mixer, sprinkle yeast over the water. Add 1 tablespoon of the sugar. Let stand until yeast is soft (about 5 minutes).

2. Add remaining sugar, milk, salt, and softened butter.

3. Mix in 2½ cups of the flour; beat until smooth and elastic (about 5 minutes). Beat in eggs, one at a time. Then stir in about 2 cups more flour to make a soft dough.

4. Turn dough out onto a board or pastry cloth coated with some of the remaining ½ to 1 cup flour. Knead until dough is smooth and satiny and small bubbles form just under surface (8 to 10 minutes), adding just enough flour to prevent dough from being sticky.

5. Turn dough in a greased bowl. Cover with plastic wrap and a towel. Let rise in a warm place until doubled in bulk (about 1 hour), or refrigerate (6 hours to 2 days).

6. Punch down dough. On a lightly floured surface, knead into a smooth ball; cover with inverted bowl and let rest for 10 minutes. Shape into one or more of the types of rolls shown in photograph at left and in Shaping Loaves and Rolls on page 615 (directions for specific rolls given below). Place on baking sheets or in baking pans as directed.

7. Let rise until almost doubled in bulk (30 to 45 minutes; 1 to 1¼ hours if dough has been refrigerated). Preheat oven to 400° F.

8. Brush rolls lightly with melted butter. Bake until golden brown (12 to 15 minutes). Transfer to wire racks to cool. If you wish, brush warm rolls with a little more melted butter for a softer crust.

Makes about 2 dozen rolls.

Bowknots   Divide dough into 24 equal portions; roll each portion with your hands on a lightly floured surface to make a strand 6 inches long. Tie loosely into a knot. Place on greased baking sheets.

Cloverleaf Rolls   Pinch off small pieces of dough and shape into smooth 1-inch balls. Dip into melted butter, then place three balls in each cup of a greased standard muffin pan.

Fantans   Roll dough out to about ⅛-inch thickness on a lightly floured surface. Brush with melted butter. Cut dough into strips 1 inch wide. Stack 6 strips on top of one another; cut stacked strips into 1½-inch pieces. Place each stack horizontally (as shown on page 615 or vertically, as shown in photograph on this page) in cup of greased standard muffin pan.

Parker House Rolls   On a lightly floured surface, roll dough out to ¼-inch thickness. Brush with melted butter. Cut into 2½- to 3-inch circles. Use handle of a wooden spoon to make a depression just off center across each circle. Fold along depression and place on greased baking sheets with larger portion on top.

■ GOLDEN DINNER ROLLS

One basic dough can be formed into four varieties. Shape all the rolls alike, or try two or three different kinds. The finished rolls are pictured in the above photograph. Shaping Loaves and Rolls, page 615, illustrates how to form the dough into each type of roll.

- 2 **packages active dry yeast**
- ½ **cup warm (105° to 115° F) water**
- ⅓ **cup sugar**
- ¾ **cup warm (105° to 115° F) milk**
- 1 **teaspoon salt**
- ¼ **cup butter or margarine, softened, plus melted butter or margarine for brushing**
- 5 **to 5½ cups flour**
- 2 **eggs**
  Oil, for greasing

■ SOURDOUGH STARTER

If you are using a dry starter mix, prepare it according to package directions. Most starters require several days to establish, so plan ahead. Once you have an established starter—whether you began with dry mix or with a borrowed starter—each time you bake with it, the first step is to combine the starter with flour and water and let the mixture ferment overnight. This procedure, which replenishes the basic starter and provides the additional quantity for baking, is given in the following recipe.

Sourdough starters should be stored only in glass, ceramic, or food-grade plastic containers. Never use metal containers, which might react chemically with the starter. Caps should also be nonreactive. A glass jar or ceramic crock with a clamp top and a rubber gasket is ideal. From time to time, when the starter is being replenished, the container should be washed.

If the starter will not be used for more than one week, it should be replenished by the process given here, and the excess discarded.

1 cup sourdough starter
Equal parts warm (105° to 115° F) water
and flour (at least 1 cup each)

1. Combine starter and the water in a large bowl. Stir in flour and beat to a smooth batter.

2. Cover bowl with plastic wrap and set aside in a warm (about 75° F) place. Let mixture stand until it is bubbly and sour, and a clear liquid begins to collect on surface (6 to 12 hours depending on liveliness of starter).

3. Stir starter, scoop out 1 cup of sponge, and place it in storage container; refrigerate until next use.

■ SAN FRANCISCO SOURDOUGH FRENCH BREAD

Even if you do not live near the Golden Gate, you can make a delicious sourdough bread. However, it takes time for the dough to get really sour. Try it on a weekend or some other time when you can let the dough ferment and rise at a leisurely pace. The traditional shapes for San Francisco sourdough bread are a long, oval French loaf and a 12-inch round, 3 to 4 inches thick.

1 cup sourdough starter
(see Sourdough Baking, above)
3 cups warm (105° to 115° F) water
6½ to 7 cups bread flour
1 tablespoon salt
Oil, for greasing
1 package active dry yeast
Cornmeal, for dusting
1 egg, beaten with ¼ cup milk or water (optional)

1. Two nights ahead: Follow the procedure in step 1 of Sourdough Starter (above), adding 2½ cups of the warm water and 2½ cups of the flour to the 1 cup of starter. Mixture should sit 8 to 12 hours.

SOURDOUGH BAKING

A sourdough starter is a living culture of yeast cells and leavening bacteria. It must be replenished regularly by the addition of more flour. The easiest way to do this is the way pioneers of the Old West did daily: They mixed the starter with additional flour and water and then allowed the whole mixture to ferment overnight. Some of it was ladled back into the crock to form the starter for the next day, and the rest was used for pancakes, breads, and other baked goods.

Now that reliable dry yeasts are available, cooks do not need to keep a starter alive in order to bake bread. However, the characteristic flavor of sourdough has remained popular. Although it is possible to make sourdough breads by using only the starter for leavening, this technique results in a dense bread. Most commercial sourdough is made with a combination of starter and another leavener, either yeast or baking soda.

The easiest way to make a sourdough starter is from a commercial packaged mix, available in many specialty shops and supermarkets. Of course, if you know someone who has a good starter, perhaps you can borrow a cup or so. Once established, a starter can be kept alive indefinitely.

---

2. Next day: Return 1 cup sponge to storage container. To remaining sponge add salt and 2½ cups flour. Stir until dough is too stiff to work. Spread 1 cup flour on board, turn out dough onto board, and knead until dough is smooth and resilient (8 to 10 minutes). Add more flour as necessary to keep dough from sticking; knead until flour is thoroughly incorporated.

3. Place dough ball in lightly oiled bowl and turn to oil all surfaces. Cover bowl with plastic wrap and let rise 4 to 6 hours in a warm place. Punch down dough, cover again, and refrigerate overnight.

4. On day of baking: Remove dough from refrigerator and allow to return to room temperature. In a large bowl warmed with hot water, dissolve yeast in ½ cup warm water (105° to 115° F). Add dough and knead to incorporate yeast mixture. Add ½ cup flour and knead in bowl until surface is not too sticky, then turn dough out onto a floured surface and knead until smooth, adding additional flour as needed.

5. Return dough to oiled bowl and let rise, covered, until doubled in bulk (about 1 hour). Punch down and let rise again if time allows; otherwise, proceed to form loaves.

6. Preheat oven to 350° F. Punch down dough after rising. Form into loaves and place on baking sheets dusted with cornmeal; allow room between loaves for rising. Cover with a towel and let dough rise until nearly doubled in bulk. If desired, brush tops lightly with egg mixture. Slash tops making shallow cuts with a sharp knife or razor blade (lengthwise or diagonal on long loaves, crosshatched on round loaves). Bake on lowest shelf of oven until crust is golden brown and loaves sound hollow when tapped on bottom (about 1 hour). Cool on wire racks.

Makes two 16-inch loaves or 12-inch rounds or four baguettes.

Note For a more substantial crust, see Baking, Cooling, and Storing Yeast Breads, page 615.

The Italian flat bread called focaccia is a popular children's snack but it can also accompany a meal. Serve this onion-and-herb version with soup or salad for a casual lunch.

■ FOCACCIA

By most accounts, *focaccia* is reckoned to be Italy's oldest bread—a simple yeast dough flattened and baked on a stone slab in a wood-fired hearth. Quite likely, it's the grandfather of the famous Neapolitan pizza. Today's cooks can easily make this versatile country bread at home, even without the stone and the hearth. Garnished as you like— here, with sautéed onions and basil—it can partner salads and soups, sliced tomatoes and cheese, or cocktails.

> 1¼ cups warm (105° to 115° F) water
> ¾ teaspoon sugar
> 1 package active dry yeast
> 2¾ cups unbleached flour
> 3 tablespoons unsalted butter
> ½ cup minced onion
> ⅓ cup minced fresh basil
> 1½ teaspoons coarse salt
> ½ teaspoon freshly ground pepper
> 2 tablespoons olive oil, plus olive oil for greasing and drizzling
> Cornmeal, for dusting

1. In a large bowl combine ½ cup of the water, sugar, and yeast. Set aside 10 minutes to let yeast soften. Stir in ¾ cup flour, cover, and let rise 2½ hours.

2. While dough is rising, heat butter in a skillet over low heat. Add onion and sauté until onion is soft but not browned (about 15 minutes). Remove from heat and stir in basil, ½ teaspoon of the salt, and pepper. Reserve.

3. Mix in remaining 2 cups flour to dough. Combine the 2 tablespoons olive oil and the remaining ¾ cup warm water; add to dough. Beat until dough forms a mass. Turn out onto a lightly floured surface and knead until dough is shiny and smooth (8 to 10 minutes). Transfer dough to a lightly oiled bowl and turn to coat all sides with oil. Cover and let rise until doubled in bulk (about 1½ hours).

4. Preheat oven to 450° F. Punch dough down into a 13- by 15-inch rectangle. Transfer to a baking sheet sprinkled with cornmeal. Spread top with onion mixture. Drizzle with additional olive oil. Sprinkle with remaining coarse salt and bake until golden (about 15 minutes). Cool slightly on a rack; serve warm.

Makes one 13- by 15-inch rectangle.

■ PUMPERNICKEL

Dark and hearty, this free-form loaf makes wonderful sandwiches and provides a filling and satisfying accompaniment to robust soups.

> 2 packages active dry yeast
> 2 tablespoons sugar
> ½ cup warm (105° to 115° F) water
> 4 to 5 cups dark rye flour
> 2 cups whole wheat flour
> 1 teaspoon salt
> 2 cups warm (105° to 115° F) milk
> Oil, for greasing
> 2 tablespoons butter, melted

1. In a small bowl dissolve yeast and sugar in the warm water and set aside to soften a few minutes. Sift together 4 cups rye flour, whole wheat flour, and salt; set aside.

2. In a large bowl combine milk and yeast; add flour mixture, one cup at a time, until a smooth dough forms (add additional rye flour, if needed, to make smooth dough). Turn out onto a lightly floured surface and knead until smooth, satiny, and elastic (10 to 12 minutes), or dough can be kneaded in a heavy-duty electric mixer.

3. Place dough in a lightly oiled bowl, brush with melted butter, cover with plastic wrap, and let rise in a warm place until almost doubled in bulk (about 1 hour). Punch down and knead lightly 2 minutes. Divide dough in half and shape into two free-form loaves. Set loaves on a greased or parchment-lined baking sheet, brush again with melted butter, and let rise until almost doubled in bulk (about 45 minutes).

4. Preheat oven to 375° F. Bake loaves until they are well browned and sound hollow when tapped (about 30 minutes). Cool on wire racks.

Makes 2 loaves.

SWEDISH RYE BREAD

This dark, fragrant rye bread from Sweden is perfumed with orange, fennel seed, and honey.

 2 packages active dry yeast
 ½ cup warm (105° to 115° F) water
 4 to 5 cups all-purpose flour
 2½ cups rye flour
 1 tablespoon salt
 2 cups warm (105° to 115° F) milk
 ¼ cup honey or molasses
 ¼ cup firmly packed brown sugar
 ¼ cup unsalted butter, softened
 Finely grated rind and juice of 2 large oranges (approximately ¾ cup juice)
 1 tablespoon fennel seed
 Oil, for greasing

1. In a large bowl of a heavy-duty electric mixer, combine yeast and the water and set aside to soften a few minutes. Sift together 4 cups all-purpose flour, rye flour, and salt; set aside.

2. Stir milk, honey, brown sugar, butter, orange rind and juice, and fennel seed into yeast mixture. Add flour mixture, one cup at a time, to yeast mixture, mixing well after each addition, to make a soft, pliable dough (add additional all-purpose flour, if needed, to make a soft dough). Knead 5 minutes in mixer or by hand on a lightly floured surface until smooth, satiny, and elastic (10 to 12 minutes). If prepared completely in mixer, turn out and knead 1 to 2 minutes. Place dough in a lightly oiled bowl, cover with plastic wrap, and let rise in a warm place until doubled in bulk (about 1 hour).

3. Punch down dough; turn out onto a lightly floured surface and knead gently 1 minute. Divide dough in half and shape into 2 round loaves. Set loaves on greased or parchment-lined baking sheets. With a sharp knife or razor blade, slash a cross about ¼ to ½ inch deep on surface of each loaf. Let rise until almost doubled in bulk (35 to 45 minutes).

4. Preheat oven to 350° F. Bake bread until it is golden and sounds hollow when tapped (50 to 60 minutes).

Makes 2 loaves.

BATTER BREAD

Batter breads are among the simplest to prepare because they aren't shaped. Instead, they bake in a pan.

 1 package active dry yeast
 ½ cup sugar
 ½ cup warm (105° to 115° F) water
 4 cups flour
 1 teaspoon salt
 ½ cup warm (105° to 115° F) milk
 ¼ cup unsalted butter, softened
 3 eggs
 Oil, for greasing

1. In a small bowl dissolve yeast and sugar in the warm water and set aside to soften a few minutes. Sift together flour and salt; set aside.

2. In a large bowl combine milk, butter, and eggs; stir in yeast mixture. Slowly add flour, one cup at a time, until a soft dough forms. Turn out onto a lightly floured surface and knead for at least 5 minutes by lifting and throwing the dough down as for brioche (see KNEAD), or use a heavy-duty electric mixer.

3. Place dough in a lightly oiled bowl, cover with plastic wrap, and let rise in a warm place until doubled in bulk (about 1 hour).

4. Generously butter an 8- or 9-inch round cake pan. Punch down dough, knead lightly, and place in pan. Let rise until almost doubled in bulk (35 to 45 minutes).

5. Preheat oven to 375° F. Bake until bread is golden and sounds hollow when tapped (50 to 60 minutes).

Makes 1 loaf.

BEER BREAD

Beer in the dough acts as an additional leavening agent; use dark beer for a bread with a greater depth of flavor.

 2 packages active dry yeast
 1 teaspoon sugar
 ½ cup warm (105° to 115° F) water
 4 to 5 cups all-purpose flour
 3 cups whole wheat flour
 2 cups beer (Guinness or other dark beer)
 ⅓ cup molasses
 4 tablespoons butter, melted
 2 teaspoons salt
 Oil, for greasing bowl and baking sheet
 3 tablespoons warm water, for brushing

1. In a small bowl dissolve yeast and sugar in the warm water and let soften briefly. Sift together 4 cups all-purpose flour and whole wheat flours.

2. In a large bowl combine beer, molasses, butter, and salt; stir in yeast mixture. Add flour, one cup at a time, to make a soft dough (add more all-purpose flour, if needed, to make a soft dough). Turn out onto a lightly floured surface and knead until smooth, satiny, and elastic (5 to 10 minutes). Or, mix and knead 5 minutes in a heavy-duty electric mixer, and then finish kneading by hand.

3. Place dough in a lightly oiled bowl, cover, and let rise in a warm place until doubled in bulk (about 1 hour). Punch down, knead lightly, divide, and shape into two loaves; set on greased baking sheet. Brush lightly with warm water and let rise until almost doubled in bulk (about 45 minutes).

4. Preheat oven to 400° F. Bake until loaves are well browned and sound hollow when tapped (30 to 35 minutes).

Makes 2 loaves.

◼ CLASSIC BRIOCHE

Here is a good brioche: It is fine textured, light, and tastes of butter and eggs. It can be baked as a loaf or in small brioche molds. After the first rising, you can also use this dough to make delicious raised doughnuts (see page 183). Brioche dough is sticky and can be difficult to knead. Try the method suggested in the recipe, or the one described in KNEAD, Kneading Pastry, Biscuit, and Rich Yeast Doughs. Like all breads, brioche can be made to suit your schedule. After the dough has had its first rise, you can punch it down and refrigerate it for up to a few days before forming and baking, if desired.

      1 package active dry yeast
      2 tablespoons sugar
    ½ cup warm (105° to 115° F) milk
    1½ teaspoons salt
      2 eggs
      2 egg yolks
    3¼ to 3½ cups flour
    12 tablespoons butter (softened if mixing
         by hand, chilled otherwise)
      1 egg mixed with 2 teaspoons water, for glaze
         Oil, for greasing

To Mix by Hand

1. In a large bowl sprinkle yeast and sugar over warm milk, stir, and let stand a few minutes to dissolve.

2. Add salt, eggs, and egg yolks and mix well.

3. Add 2 cups of the flour and beat vigorously until batter is smooth and heavy. Drop in softened butter, 1 table-spoon at a time, and beat after each addition until incorporated. If some tiny lumps of butter remain, don't worry; they will blend in later.

4. Add 1 cup of the remaining flour and mix well until a rough mass forms, then scrape out onto a lightly floured surface. Knead for a couple of minutes, sprinkling on a little more flour as necessary to keep dough from being too sticky. Stop kneading and let rest for about 5 to 10 minutes. Continue kneading for a few minutes more, until dough is smooth and elastic.

5. Place in a greased bowl, cover, and let rise until dough is puffy and slightly more than doubled in bulk (about 1 hour).

6. Punch down dough. Cover and refrigerate for one or two days at this point, if desired. (The dough will continue to rise until it is thoroughly chilled; just punch it down every hour or so.)

7. *To make brioches:* Cut dough in half, and on a lightly floured surface shape each piece into an even rope about 10 inches long. Cut each rope into 7 pieces, each about 1½ inches long. Plump each piece of dough into a smooth ball by holding it in one hand as you tuck the edges underneath with the fingers of your other hand, thus forming a tight round with a seam on the bottom.

Cover with a towel and let rest for 10 minutes. To form brioches, generously butter 14 brioche molds or muffin tins. Pick up a piece of dough and pinch it with your fingertips, gently stretching the ball to elongate it slightly as you pull away a marble-sized piece of dough—but don't detach it completely. To form the topknot, place dough on floured surface, lay your index finger on top of the stretched portion, then roll your finger back and forth, to pull out the small end of dough about another inch. Twist the topknot 3 or 4 times and press it firmly back into the larger base. The final shape resembles a tiny snowman with a fat body and a tiny head. Place in one of the prepared molds, pressing down firmly around the edges. Form the remaining balls the same way. Place filled molds on a baking sheet, cover loosely with a towel, and let rise until a little more than doubled in bulk and puffed well over the tops of the molds.
To make a loaf: Butter a 9- by 5-inch loaf pan. Form dough into a smooth loaf and place it in pan. Cover and let rise until doubled in bulk (about 1 hour). After rising, use a sharp, pointed knife or razor blade to make a ½-inch-deep slash lengthwise down the center.

8. Preheat oven to 375° F. Before baking, paint top of each brioche (or the loaf) with egg glaze, taking care not to let it run down into molds.

9. Bake small brioches (on a baking sheet) for about 20 minutes, turning pan once or twice during baking if they brown unevenly. Bake loaf for about 50 minutes; if it browns too much, cover loosely with a tent of foil for the remainder of the baking time.

10. Remove from oven and turn out onto racks (if any stick, pry them out with a knife point) to cool completely before wrapping for storage or freezing. To reheat, place on a baking sheet in a 350° F oven for about 10 minutes.

To Mix With a Processor

1. In a small bowl sprinkle yeast and sugar over warm milk, stir, and let stand a few minutes to dissolve.

2. Pour yeast mixture into bowl of a food processor fitted with steel blade. Add salt, eggs, and egg yolks and whirl for a few seconds.

3. Add 2 cups of the flour and process again until smooth. While blade is turning, drop in chilled butter, 2 table-spoons at a time. Continue to process until smooth.

4. Add another 1½ cups of the flour. Process again until dough comes together and forms a rough ball that revolves around the bowl; process for 30 seconds more. Continue with step 5 of To Mix by Hand for the rising and forming. (Some food processors tend to strain while kneading a dough. If yours labors or stalls, remove dough and continue kneading by hand.)

Makes fourteen 3-inch brioches, or 1 loaf.

SAVARIN

This wonderfully rich yeast cake was said to be named for the French gastronome, Brillat-Savarin. It is prepared in a ring mold, soaked with sugar syrup, and served with the center filled with whipped cream and fresh fruit. Cubes of fresh pineapple are suggested here, but any seasonal fruit will be equally flavorful and attractive. Babas au Rhum (see variation) are almost identical to a savarin, but have currants mixed into the dough, are made in special cup-shaped molds, and receive a special drenching in rum. Be sure to butter the molds well.

1 package active dry yeast
¼ cup warm (105° to 115° F) water
¼ cup sugar
1⅔ cup flour
1 teaspoon salt
3 eggs
½ cup unsalted butter, softened, plus butter for greasing
¼ cup rum, plus rum for sprinkling
1 cup whipping cream, whipped, for accompaniment
1 cup fresh pineapple cubes or other fresh fruit in season

Soaking Syrup

2 cups sugar
2 cups water

1. In a small bowl dissolve yeast and sugar in warm water and set aside to soften 5 minutes. Sift together flour and salt; set aside.

2. In a large bowl combine eggs, butter, and the ¼ cup rum. Add yeast mixture, then slowly add flour, 1 cup at a time; mix to a smooth batter. Knead by slapping dough against side of bowl with hand (see KNEAD, Kneading Pastry, Biscuit, and Rich Yeast Doughs), or with a heavy-duty electric mixer and flat beater attachment. Cover batter with plastic wrap and let rise in a warm place until doubled in bulk (about 1 hour).

3. Preheat oven to 375° F. Generously butter a 10-inch savarin mold. Punch down dough, knead lightly, then place in prepared mold. Let rise again until almost doubled in bulk (30 to 40 minutes). Bake until golden brown and high (30 to 40 minutes).

4. Let cool in pan on wire rack 10 minutes; turn out from pan onto a rimmed plate or large, square baking dish. Pour hot Soaking Syrup over bread; sprinkle with rum to taste. Pour off any excess syrup. To transfer to a serving plate, cover bread with savarin mold and invert. Lay serving plate on surface of bread and invert; bread will drop out onto plate.

5. Fill center of Savarin with whipped cream and fresh fruit. Serve at room temperature or chilled.

Serves 6 to 8.

Soaking Syrup   Place sugar and water in a medium, heavy-bottomed saucepan. Dissolve sugar in water over low heat, stirring; increase heat to medium-high and boil 3 minutes.

Babas au Rhum   Prepare Savarin up through kneading dough, step 2. Mix 1 cup currants into dough, cover with plastic wrap, and let rise until doubled. Punch down and divide dough among 10 to 12 well-buttered baba molds, filling each approximately two thirds full. Let rise until dough fills mold (25 to 30 minutes). Bake in a 375° F oven until golden brown and high (about 20 minutes). Cool in molds 10 minutes, invert, and soak with hot Soaking Syrup. Cool, then sprinkle with rum, to taste; drain off excess syrup and serve at room temperature or slightly chilled.

Makes 10 to 12 Babas.

Rich, cakelike brioche display their characteristic topknots. Shown are four stages of individual brioches: balls of dough; dough elongated to form topknots; unbaked brioches with topknots in place; and baked brioches.

Flaky croissants are shaped from triangles of butter-flecked dough that are rolled from the wide end toward the point, then curved into a crescent.

◼ CROISSANTS

With so many steps, croissant making might seem like quite a difficult task at first glance—but it's really not hard, perhaps just a bit time-consuming. The technique of building thin layers of butter between layers of yeast dough will be familiar if you have ever made puff pastry, and even if you haven't, instructions are detailed enough for beginning bakers. Follow directions carefully and you should not have any trouble producing the lightest, flakiest croissants you've ever had.

> 1 **package active dry yeast**
> 1¼ **cups warm (105° to 115° F) milk**
> 2 **teaspoons sugar**
> 1½ **teaspoons salt**
> 2¾ **cups flour**
> 1 **egg mixed with 1 teaspoon water**

Butter Mixture

> 1¼ **cups cold butter**
> 3 **tablespoons flour**

1. In a large bowl sprinkle yeast over warm milk, add sugar, stir, and let stand for a few minutes to dissolve. Add salt and flour, then mix vigorously but briefly, just until you have a rough, sticky dough that holds together. Set aside for about 5 minutes while preparing Butter Mixture.

2. Wipe work surface clean, sprinkle it generously with flour, and turn dough out onto it. Flour the dough, which is quite soft, and push, pat, and roll it into a rectangle about 10 by 14 inches. Unwrap Butter Mixture and place it on bottom half of dough, leaving about a 1-inch border on 3 sides. Lift up the top of the dough, working it loose with a spatula or scraper if it sticks to work surface, and flip it over the butter. Pinch edges to seal. Give the dough a quarter turn, so sealed flap is to your right.

3. Using smooth, even strokes, roll to a 9- by 17-inch rectangle. Check to see if it is sticking and sprinkle with flour if necessary—don't be afraid to pick it up and look. Fold bottom third of dough up over the middle, then flip top third down to cover it. Turn again so flap is to your right and roll out again to 9 by 17 inches. Fold in thirds as before, flour lightly, wrap in plastic wrap, place in a plastic bag, and chill for about 30 minutes. At this point, the first two turns are finished.

4. Roll chilled dough again to 9 by 17 inches, fold in thirds, wrap in plastic wrap and a plastic bag, and refrigerate for 45 minutes. (If at any time dough becomes soft and resists rolling out, or if butter breaks through in large, smeary patches, stop working, dust dough with flour, then slide onto a baking sheet and chill for about 20 minutes.)

5. Roll out and fold dough again, thus completing four turns. Wrap and chill for at least 1 hour (or for a few hours or overnight if it's more convenient) before forming croissants.

6. Roll dough out to 10 by 20 inches, keeping sides as even as possible. With a sharp knife, cut in half lengthwise, then cut each half into four 5-inch squares. Cut each square in half diagonally to make 2 triangles.

7. Working with one triangle at a time, pick up the 2 closest points, at the base, and gently stretch them out to about 7 inches. Hold these 2 points down with one hand and use the other hand to wiggle and stretch the other, farthest point out to about 7 inches or more. Starting at the base, roll up stretched dough just like a crescent roll. Pull points down, toward one another, to form a crescent shape.

8. Place croissants about 2 inches apart on baking sheets. Cover with a towel and let rise until puffy and doubled in size (about 1½ hours). If you've used 2 baking sheets and your oven can hold only 1 sheet on the same rack, chill 1 sheet for the first hour or so, to slow rising, so baking times are staggered.

9. Preheat oven to 425° F and place a rack on middle level. Brush each risen croissant with egg mixture and bake until well browned and puffy (12 to 15 minutes). If they are not browning evenly, quickly turn pan around from front to back once or twice during baking. If some are done before others, just remove them with a spatula. Transfer croissants to a rack to cool for a few minutes before serving. Wrap and freeze what you won't use in a day. (To reheat, unwrap and set on a baking sheet, still frozen, and place in a 400° F oven for about 7 minutes.)

Makes sixteen 4-inch Croissants.

Butter Mixture   Cut butter into tablespoon-sized bits, dropping them onto work surface, then sprinkle with flour. Tear off two good-sized sheets of waxed paper and set aside. Begin mashing butter and flour together by smearing across work surface with the heel of your hand; gather butter mixture into a pile with a spatula or pastry scraper, then repeat smearing a couple of times, until butter is smooth and workable, but still cold. With floured hands form butter into a small, rough rectangle and place it between sheets of waxed paper. Roll and pat butter into a larger, 6- by 8-inch rectangle, keeping sides as even as possible. Set aside while you roll out yeast dough.

■ DANISH PASTRY DOUGH

Danish pastry dough is slightly richer than croissant dough because it contains eggs and a little more sugar.

> 2 **packages active dry yeast**
> 1 **cup warm (105° to 115° F) milk**
> 2 **eggs, at room temperature**
> 2 **teaspoons salt**
> ¼ **cup sugar**
> 3¼ **cups all-purpose flour**

Butter Mixture

> 1½ **cups cold butter**
> ¼ **cup all-purpose flour**

1. In a large bowl sprinkle yeast over warm milk, stir, and let stand a few minutes to soften. Add eggs, salt, and sugar and mix well. Pour in flour and mix briefly, just until you have a rough, sticky dough that holds together. Set aside for about 5 minutes while preparing Butter Mixture.

2. Scrape clean surface of work area used for Butter Mixture, sprinkle it generously with flour, and turn yeast dough out onto it (dough will be quite soft). Sprinkle top of dough with flour, then roll and pat into a 10- by 14-inch rectangle. Unwrap Butter Mixture and set it on bottom half of dough, leaving a 1-inch border on 3 sides. Gently lift up unbuttered top flap and flip it down over butter. Pinch the edges to seal, then use a wide spatula or scraper to help lift dough package and give it a quarter turn, so the sealed flap is to your right.

3. To roll out and fold dough, follow steps 3, 4, and 5 of Croissants (see page 624), except roll out Danish dough a little larger, to an 8- by 20-inch rectangle, since you are working with more dough. After you've completed all the turns, form and bake the pastries (see A Variety of Danish Shapes and Fillings, page 626)—or if it is more convenient, wrap dough in plastic wrap and a plastic bag, and refrigerate overnight before forming and baking.

Makes about 2 dozen pastries, depending on shapes.

Butter Mixture   Cut cold butter into tablespoon-sized chunks, dropping chunks onto work surface. Sprinkle butter pieces with flour. Blend butter and flour by smearing them out in front of you with the heel of your hand; gather up the mixture and smear again three or four times until butter is perfectly smooth and workable but still cold. Flour your hands and pat mixture into a rectangle about 4 by 5 inches. Place between two sheets of waxed paper or plastic wrap and pat and roll into a larger, 7- by 9-inch rectangle, keeping edges as even as possible. Set aside for a moment.

Danish pastries are the flakiest and most buttery of all sweet rolls. Shown here are icing-topped Cinnamon Rolled Danish. The recipe appears on page 626.

A VARIETY OF DANISH SHAPES AND FILLINGS

The recipe for Danish Pastry Dough makes about two dozen pastries, and each shape (directions follow) requires half the dough. For variety, make two different shapes and at least two fillings. After you cut the dough in half, wrap and chill the piece you are not working on.

Fillings can be made a day ahead since they all keep well if covered and refrigerated (or frozen). Use the leftovers as cake or cookie fillings, and serve fillings made with fruit over ice cream or puddings.

If you need to use two baking sheets when baking the Danish and can't fit both pans on the same oven rack, refrigerate one rack after forming and let the other batch rise at room temperature. The chilled batch will rise more slowly, so baking times will be staggered.

If you're going to freeze a Danish, omit any icing called for after baking. Ice the pastries after reheating in a 400° F oven for about 5 minutes and they'll look and taste freshly made.

The amount of filling used in each Danish may not look generous, but it's better to have too little than too much, which would bubble up and leak out during baking. Be sure to press very firmly when sealing the edges of unbaked pastries, using your fingertips or the tines of a fork so that the pastries don't pop open in the oven (although this happens occasionally despite all precautions).

◼ CINNAMON ROLLED DANISH

   ½ **cup dried currants**
   ½ **recipe Danish Pastry Dough (see page 625)**
   4 **tablespoons melted butter**
   ½ **cup Cinnamon Sugar (see page 145)**
   ½ **cup chopped walnuts or pecans**
   1 **egg beaten with 1 teaspoon water**
      Glacé Icing (see page 250)

1. In a small bowl pour boiling water over currants and set aside while you roll out dough.

2. On a floured surface roll dough into an 11- by 17-inch rectangle. Brush with melted butter, then sprinkle evenly with Cinnamon Sugar. Sprinkle on nuts. Drain currants and pat them dry with paper towels, then distribute them over dough. Press ingredients into the dough with your fingertips. Starting with a long side, roll into a tight cylinder, like a jelly roll. Cut into 1-inch slices and place about 2 inches apart on baking sheets. Cover with a towel and let rise until puffy and almost doubled in bulk (45 minutes to 1 hour). Brush each slice with some of the egg mixture.

3. Preheat oven to 400° F. Bake until well browned (12 to 14 minutes). Transfer to wire racks to cool; brush with Glacé Icing while still warm.

Makes about 18 rolls.

◼ TURNOVERS

   ½ **recipe Danish Pastry Dough (see page 625)**
   1 **egg beaten with 1 teaspoon water**
   1 **cup Prune, Date, Apricot, or Apple Filling (see page 627)**
      Glacé Icing (see page 250)

1. Roll dough on a lightly floured surface into a 12- by 16-inch rectangle. Cut lengthwise into three strips, 4 by 16 inches, then cut each strip into four 4-inch squares.

2. Brush the edges of each square with some of the egg mixture, then place a generous tablespoonful of the filling in the center of each. Fold the squares in half diagonally, to make triangular-shaped turnovers, and press the edges firmly with your fingers to seal. Place about 2 inches apart on baking sheets, cover with a towel, and let rise until puffy and nearly doubled in bulk (about 45 minutes). Brush with remaining egg mixture.

3. Preheat oven to 400° F. Bake until golden brown and puffy (12 to 15 minutes).

4. Cool on racks and brush with icing while still warm.

Makes 1 dozen Turnovers.

◼ BEAR CLAWS

   ½ **recipe Danish Pastry Dough (see page 625)**
   1 **egg beaten with 1 teaspoon water**
   1 **cup Date, Poppy Seed, or Nut Filling (see page 627)**
      Glacé Icing (see page 250)

1. On a lightly floured surface, roll dough into a 12- by 16-inch rectangle. Cut lengthwise into three strips, 4 by 16 inches, then cut each strip into four 4-inch squares.

2. Brush edges of each square with some egg mixture. Place about 1 tablespoon of filling in the center of each, spreading it slightly down toward bottom and across center. Fold top half of dough down to cover filling and press edges firmly to seal. Make about seven ½-inch-long cuts across long, sealed edge of each rectangle, spacing cuts about ½ inch apart. Gently bend each rectangle into a curve, so cuts open slightly, forming claws. Place about 2 inches apart on baking sheets. Cover with a towel and let rise until almost doubled in bulk (about 45 minutes or a little longer). Brush each pastry with some of the remaining egg mixture.

3. Preheat oven to 400° F. Bake until puffy and well browned (12 to 14 minutes). Cool Bear Claws on wire racks and brush each with a little icing while still warm.

Makes 1 dozen Bear Claws.

Pain au Chocolat   Omit filling. Finely chop 6 ounces semisweet chocolate. Brush edges of squares with beaten egg; sprinkle the center of each with 1 tablespoon chopped chocolate. Fold over and pinch the edges to seal but do not make any cuts (shapes should be rectangular). Let rise; bake and ice as directed for Bear Claws.

PINWHEELS

½ recipe Danish Pastry Dough (see page 625)
1 cup Prune, Nut, or Apple Filling (below and right)
1 egg beaten with 1 teaspoon water
Glacé Icing (see page 250)

1. On a lightly floured surface, roll dough into a 12- by 16-inch rectangle. Cut lengthwise into three strips, 4 by 16 inches, then cut each strip into four 4-inch squares.

2. Separate squares. With a small, sharp knife, make diagonal cuts at corners of each, cutting in from corner to about ½ inch from center. Place a generous tablespoon of filling in middle of each. One by one, fold over alternating points from edge to center, overlapping them a bit. Wet overlapping points with drops of egg mixture, then pinch firmly together so they stick. Place about 2 inches apart on baking sheets, cover with a towel, and let rise until almost doubled in bulk (45 minutes to 1 hour). Brush with some of the egg mixture.

3. Preheat oven to 400° F. Bake until puffy and golden brown (12 to 14 minutes). Transfer to racks to cool and brush each with icing while still warm.

Makes 1 dozen Pinwheels.

APPLE FILLING

4 medium-sized apples, peeled and cored
⅓ cup sugar
2 tablespoons dried currants
2 tablespoons chopped walnuts
1 teaspoon fresh lemon juice

Shred apples on the coarse side of a grater into a bowl. Mix in sugar, currants, walnuts, and lemon juice.

Makes about 1½ cups.

APRICOT FILLING

1 cup (6 oz) finely chopped dried apricots
3 tablespoons sugar
¼ cup chopped almonds

Put apricots in a small saucepan, cover them with water, and simmer over moderate heat until tender. Drain thoroughly. Purée apricots in a food processor or pass through a food mill, then beat in sugar and almonds.

Makes about 1¼ cups.

Peach Filling   Substitute 1 cup (6 oz) coarsely chopped dried peaches for the apricots.

CHEESE FILLING

1 cup cottage cheese
2 tablespoons sugar
3 tablespoons flour
1 egg yolk
2 teaspoons grated orange rind
¼ cup dried currants (optional)

Press cottage cheese through a strainer or food mill 2 or 3 times, until it is fairly smooth, or simply whirl for several seconds in a food processor. Add sugar, flour, egg yolk, orange rind, and currants (if used); mix thoroughly.

Makes about 1¼ cups.

DATE FILLING

1 cup (8 oz) finely cut pitted dates
½ cup water
¼ cup firmly packed brown sugar
2 teaspoons grated orange rind

In a small, heavy saucepan, combine dates, the water, brown sugar, and orange rind. Cook over low heat, stirring frequently, until mixture is thick enough to hold a shape and dates have absorbed the water.

Makes about 1½ cups.

Fig Filling   Substitute 1 cup (8 oz) finely cut dried figs for the dates and reduce the sugar to 2 tablespoons.

NUT FILLING

1 cup walnuts, hazelnuts, or almonds
¼ cup sugar
1 egg white
1 tablespoon butter, softened

By hand or in a food processor, chop nuts into very fine pieces—about ⅛ inch, or the size of coarse bread crumbs. Combine with sugar, egg white, and butter, and beat until blended.

Makes about ¾ cup.

POPPY SEED FILLING

½ cup poppy seed
1 egg
1 egg white
5 tablespoons confectioners' sugar
¼ cup dry bread crumbs

Combine poppy seed, egg, egg white, confectioners' sugar, and bread crumbs and mix until thoroughly combined. Set aside for 20 minutes or so before using.

Makes about ¾ cup.

PRUNE FILLING

1 cup (8 oz) finely cut pitted prunes
⅓ cup water
¼ cup firmly packed brown sugar
1 tablespoon fresh lemon juice

In a small, heavy-bottomed saucepan, combine prunes, water, and sugar. Simmer gently for several minutes, stirring frequently, until mass is thick enough to hold a shape and prunes have absorbed the water. Stir in lemon juice.

Makes about 1½ cups.

CHRISTMAS PANETTONE

Legend has it that this Milanese bread has a lofty dome to honor the *duomo* or cathedral in many a Lombardian town. Food historian Waverley Root relates that it's a custom for the children of Milan to leave a bowl of panettone soaked in water on windowsills on New Year's Eve for the camels of the bearers of gifts to the Christ Child.

> 2 packages active dry yeast
> ½ cup warm (105° to 115° F) water
> ⅓ cup sugar
> ¼ cup warm (105° to 115° F) milk
> ½ teaspoon salt
> ¼ teaspoon freshly grated nutmeg
> ⅔ cup butter or margarine, softened
> 2 teaspoons grated orange rind
> 1 teaspoon vanilla extract
> 3¾ cups flour
> 2 eggs
> 2 egg yolks
> Oil, for greasing
> ¼ cup Marsala
> ½ cup golden raisins
> ⅓ cup *each* slivered candied cherries and diced mixed candied fruits
> ¼ cup pine nuts or slivered almonds
> Confectioners' sugar

1. In large bowl of an electric mixer, sprinkle yeast over the warm water; add 1 teaspoon of the sugar. Let stand until yeast is soft (about 5 minutes).

2. Add remaining sugar, warm milk, salt, nutmeg, butter, orange rind, and vanilla. Add 2 cups of the flour; mix to blend, then beat until smooth and elastic (about 5 minutes).

3. Beat in eggs and egg yolks, one at a time. Gradually beat in remaining 1¾ cups flour; when all has been added, beat at medium speed until batter is elastic (about 3 minutes).

4. Transfer batter to a greased bowl. Cover and let rise in a warm place until bubbly (about 1 hour). While batter is rising, pour Marsala over raisins in a small bowl; set aside.

5. Stir batter down; then stir in raisin mixture, cherries, candied fruits, and pine nuts until well distributed.

6. Spread batter in a well-greased, lightly floured, 9½- to 10-cup charlotte mold (about 7½ inches in diameter and 4 inches deep) or panettone pan. Let rise until doubled (30 to 45 minutes). Preheat oven to 325° F.

7. Bake until bread is well browned and a skewer inserted in center comes out clean (1 to 1¼ hours). Let stand in pan on wire rack for about 15 minutes, then remove pan and transfer to rack to cool (rounded side up). Dust with confectioners' sugar while warm.

Serves 10 to 12.

STOLLEN

During the Christmas holidays German bakeries are full of these light, fruit-filled loaves.

> 1 package active dry yeast
> ½ cup sugar
> ¼ cup warm (105° to 115° F) water
> 1 cup warm (105° to 115° F) milk
> ½ cup butter, melted
> 1 egg
> Grated rind of 1 lemon
> ½ teaspoon salt
> 4 to 5 cups flour
> ½ cup dark raisins
> ½ cup golden raisins
> ½ cup slivered almonds
> ½ cup candied peel
> Oil, for greasing
> 2 tablespoons butter, melted
> Glacé Icing (see page 250)

1. In a small bowl dissolve yeast and 2 tablespoons of sugar in the warm water; set aside briefly to soften.

2. In a large bowl combine milk, butter, egg, lemon rind, salt, and the remaining sugar; add yeast mixture. Add 4 cups flour, one cup at a time, to make a soft dough (add more flour, if needed, to get texture). In a heavy-duty mixer with dough hook or by hand on a floured surface, knead dough until smooth, satiny, and elastic (at least 5 minutes). Knead in raisins, almonds, and candied peel.

3. Place dough in a lightly oiled bowl, cover, and let rise until doubled in bulk (about 1 hour). Punch down and knead briefly. Halve dough; shape each piece into an oval; fold each oval in half along the long side. Place on a greased baking sheet, brush with melted butter, and let rise until almost doubled in bulk (about 45 minutes); brush again with butter. Preheat oven to 350° F.

4. Bake loaves until golden and hollow when tapped (about 30 minutes); cool. Drizzle with Glacé Icing.

Makes 2 loaves.

KUGELHOPF

This Alsatian specialty originated in Austria, where it is known as *gugelhopf*.

> 2 packages active dry yeast
> 1 teaspoon sugar
> ½ cup warm (105° to 115° F) water
> 2½ cups flour
> 1 teaspoon salt
> 3 eggs
> ½ cup butter, softened
> Oil, for greasing
> ½ cup whole blanched almonds
> ½ cup dried currants
> ½ cup golden raisins
> Confectioners' sugar, for dusting

1. In a small bowl dissolve yeast and sugar in the warm water and set aside a few minutes to soften. Sift together flour and salt and set aside.

2. In a large bowl beat together eggs and butter; add yeast mixture, then slowly add flour, one cup at a time, to make a soft dough. On a lightly floured surface, knead slowly (see page 327) at least 5 minutes (or use a heavy-duty electric mixer).

3. Place dough in a lightly oiled bowl, cover, and let rise until doubled in bulk (about 1 hour). Generously butter a 9-cup Kugelhopf mold or other tube pan; arrange almonds decoratively around sides of mold (butter will cause nuts to adhere to pan sides). Punch down dough, add currants and raisins, and knead lightly to mix in; set in mold. Let rise until almost doubled in bulk (about 45 minutes).

4. Preheat oven to 375° F. Bake until golden brown (40 to 50 minutes). Cool 10 minutes in pan on wire rack, then turn out of pan onto wire rack and cool completely. To serve, dust with confectioners' sugar.

Serves 10 to 12.

THE STICKIEST PECAN ROLLS
Wonderfully gooey through and through, these rolls are at their most appealing served warm.

> 2 packages active dry yeast
> ½ cup warm (105° to 115° F) water
> ¾ cup granulated sugar
> ½ cup warm (105° to 115° F) milk
> 1 teaspoon salt
> 2 teaspoons grated orange rind
> ½ cup butter or margarine, softened, plus
>   ½ cup butter or margarine, melted
> 4½ to 5 cups all-purpose flour
> 2 eggs
> ½ cup whole wheat flour
>   Oil, for greasing
> 1 cup firmly packed brown sugar
> 1 cup pecan halves
> 1 cup coarsely chopped pecans

Cinnamon Filling

> 1 cup sugar
> 1½ teaspoons ground cinnamon

1. In large bowl of electric mixer, sprinkle yeast over the water. Add 1 tablespoon granulated sugar. Let stand until yeast is soft (about 5 minutes).

2. Add remaining granulated sugar, milk, salt, orange rind, and softened butter.

3. Add 3 cups all-purpose flour. Mix to blend, then beat at medium speed until smooth and elastic (about 5 minutes). Add eggs, one at a time, beating until smooth after each addition. Stir in whole wheat flour, then about 1½ cups more all-purpose flour to make a soft dough.

4. Turn dough out onto a board or pastry cloth coated with some of the remaining ½ cup all-purpose flour. Knead until dough is smooth and satiny and small bubbles form just under surface (12 to 15 minutes), adding just enough flour to prevent dough from being sticky.

5. Turn dough in a greased bowl. Cover with plastic wrap and a towel; let rise in a warm place until doubled in bulk (1¼ to 1½ hours).

6. While dough rises, prepare baking pan. Pour ¼ cup of the melted butter into a 9- by 13-inch baking pan; tip and tilt to coat pan evenly. Sprinkle evenly with brown sugar, then with pecan halves.

7. Punch dough down. Cover with inverted bowl and let rest for 10 minutes. Roll dough out on a floured surface into an 18-inch square. Brush with remaining melted butter. Sprinkle with Cinnamon Filling, then with chopped pecans. Starting from an 18-inch side, roll dough jelly-roll fashion; moisten long edge and pinch to seal. Cut into 12 equal slices.

8. Arrange slices, cut sides down, in prepared baking pan. Cover lightly with waxed paper. Let rise until doubled in bulk (about 1 hour). Preheat oven to 350° F.

9. Bake until well browned (30 to 35 minutes). Let stand in pan on rack for 1 minute; then invert carefully onto a serving tray. Let stand with pan in place for 30 seconds, then remove pan. Serve warm.

Makes 1 dozen rolls.

Cinnamon Filling   In a small bowl mix together sugar and cinnamon.

These are The Stickiest Pecan Rolls you'll ever taste, with nuts both inside and out and a hint of orange in the dough.

Enjoy Chocolate-Swirled Babkas, a sweet yeast bread, with afternoon coffee or tea.

■ CHOCOLATE-SWIRLED BABKAS

Topped with streusel and bursting with fudgy cocoa filling, these rich, sweet loaves are a New York bakery favorite.

> 2 packages active dry yeast
> ½ cup warm water (105° to 115° F) water
> ⅓ cup sugar
> ⅔ cup warm (105° to 115° F) milk
> ½ teaspoon *each* salt and vanilla extract
> 3 tablespoons butter or margarine, softened,
>   plus 3 tablespoons butter or margarine, melted
> 4½ to 5 cups flour
> 3 eggs
>   Oil, for greasing
> 1 cup coarsely chopped walnuts

Cocoa Filling

> ⅓ cup unsweetened cocoa
> ⅔ cup sugar

Streusel Topping

> 2 tablespoons butter or margarine, softened
> ¼ teaspoon ground cinnamon
> ⅓ cup confectioners' sugar
> ¼ cup flour

1. In large bowl of electric mixer, sprinkle yeast over the water. Add 1 teaspoon sugar. Let stand until yeast is soft (about 5 minutes).

2. Mix in remaining sugar, milk, salt, vanilla, and softened butter.

3. Add 2½ cups flour. Mix to blend, then beat at medium speed until smooth and elastic (about 5 minutes). Separate one of the eggs; reserve white for glaze. Beat in egg yolk and remaining whole eggs, one at a time. Stir in about 1½ cups more flour to make a soft dough.

4. Turn dough out onto a board or pastry cloth coated with some of the remaining ½ to 1 cup flour. Knead until dough is smooth and satiny and small bubbles form just under surface (10 to 12 minutes), adding just enough flour to prevent dough from being sticky.

5. Turn dough in a greased bowl. Cover with plastic wrap and a towel; let rise in a warm place until doubled in bulk (45 minutes to 1 hour).

6. Place dough on a floured surface and punch down. Cover with inverted bowl and let rest for 10 minutes.

7. Divide dough in half. Roll out each half on floured surface to a 10- by 20-inch rectangle. Brush 1½ tablespoons of the melted butter over each rectangle, leaving about a ½-inch margin on all edges. Sprinkle half of the Cocoa Filling over buttered surface of each rectangle, then sprinkle each rectangle with ½ cup walnuts.

8. Starting with a 20-inch side, roll each rectangle of dough tightly, jelly-roll style. Pinch edge to seal.

9. Zigzag each roll back and forth to fit into a well-greased 4½- by 8½-inch loaf pan.

10. Let rise until almost doubled in bulk (35 to 45 minutes). Preheat oven to 350° F. Beat reserved egg white with 1 teaspoon water; brush egg white mixture over loaves. Sprinkle each loaf with half of the Streusel Topping.

11. Bake until coffee cakes are well browned (30 to 35 minutes). Carefully remove loaves from pans and let cool on wire racks.

Makes 2 coffee cakes.

Cocoa Filling   In a small bowl mix cocoa and sugar until well combined and no lumps remain.

Streusel Topping   In a medium bowl beat butter with cinnamon until fluffy; gradually beat in sugar, then mix in flour until crumbly and uniformly combined.

■ VANILLA FRENCH TOAST

French toast is a delicious way to finish yesterday's loaf. Use any type of slightly stale, dense-textured bread (bakery or homemade). Allow thicker slices to sit in the dipping liquid for a while, or they will be dry in the middle.

> 4 eggs
> 1 cup milk
> 1 teaspoon vanilla extract
> 8 slices day-old bread (preferably a dense-textured rather than an airy commercial type)
> ¼ cup butter (preferably clarified)
>   Confectioners' sugar, Cinnamon Sugar (see page 145), or warmed syrup, for accompaniment

1. In a shallow dish beat eggs and milk together with vanilla.

2. Dip bread into this mixture. In a large frying pan or on a griddle fry dipped bread in 2 tablespoons butter until well browned and crisp on each side, turning once (add remaining butter as needed).

3. Serve hot, sprinkled with confectioners' sugar or Cinnamon Sugar, or drizzled with syrup.

Serves 4.

YOGURT

When milk is held for several hours at a temperature of about 110° F, lactic acid–producing bacteria will grow and cause the milk to coagulate. The result is yogurt, a fermented milk product with a thick, creamy texture and a tangy flavor. Although the earliest yogurt was probably made by accident—perhaps when a desert nomad put milk in a goatskin bag and hung it next to the warm body of a camel—today's commercial yogurt is made under strictly controlled conditions.

Use Widespread acceptance of yogurt is fairly recent in this country, although it has been popular throughout the world for hundreds of years. In Greece yogurt is eaten as a breakfast food with the aromatic local honey. Throughout the eastern Mediterranean and the Middle East, yogurt is used as a dipping sauce, a basting medium, a condiment, a soup base, and a dessert. Middle Eastern cooks often mix yogurt with garlic and dill or mint and serve it as a sauce for grilled lamb or fish. Indian cooks incorporate yogurt in marinades and stews; tandoori dishes (baked in a clay oven) are marinated first in yogurt and aromatic spices. Indians also make *lassi,* a cold yogurt drink, which may be either sweet or salty. *Tzatziki,* chopped cucumber and garlic in yogurt, is a popular Greek appetizer. In Iran grated cucumbers are combined with yogurt, raisins, onions, and salt to make a cold soup.

In America yogurt is also eaten at breakfast, as a quick lunch or snack, or as a dessert with fruit. It may be used as a substitute for sour cream—for example, a salad dressing, dip, soup garnish, or baked potato topping. Frozen yogurt is a popular snack food.

Availability Yogurt is available in plain and flavored styles, made with whole milk, low-fat milk, or nonfat milk. Many of the flavored versions are fruit-based, containing fruit purée or fruit preserves. Some fruit yogurts have the fruit on the bottom of the container; others are Swiss style, with the fruit dispersed throughout. Other flavors, such as coffee and vanilla, are also popular.

Some snack shops and restaurants also sell frozen yogurt, which usually contains added sugar, stabilizers, and extra nonfat milk solids. Some soft-serve yogurt is made by blending yogurt in equal parts with ice cream.

Storage Refrigerate both commercial and homemade yogurt and use within one to two weeks. Commercial yogurt containing preservatives can be stored longer.

COOKING WITH YOGURT

Yogurt will curdle if exposed to excessive heat. When used in sauces and other cooked dishes, it is generally added at the last minute, with the pan removed from the heat. Alternatively, yogurt can be stabilized by adding 2 teaspoons of cornstarch per cup. The stabilized yogurt can be brought to a boil, but should not be cooked more than one or two minutes.

■ HOMEMADE YOGURT

High-quality yogurt is easy to make at home and has the benefit of being extremely fresh and flavored to your liking. An electric yogurt maker is helpful for maintaining a warm temperature but is unnecessary. The heat of the pilot light in a gas oven is usually sufficient. You can also place the containers in a warm water bath and change the water as it cools.

> 1 **quart milk (whole, low-fat, or nonfat; see Note)**
> 1 **rounded tablespoon plain yogurt**
>   **(commercial or homemade)**

1. In a medium saucepan heat milk just to boiling; remove from heat and let stand, covered, until temperature drops 100° F.

2. Stir in 1 rounded tablespoon of plain commercial unpasteurized yogurt or yogurt from a previous homemade batch. Pour into five 8-ounce containers with lids. Cover and set in a warm place (115° F to 120° F) until mixture coagulates (8 to 10 hours).

3. Refrigerate until cold. Serve as is or with fruit, or use as required in other recipes.

Makes 1 quart.

Note For creamier texture, add ⅓ cup nonfat dry milk per quart of milk.

ZEST

The colored, outermost layer of the skin of citrus fruits, as opposed to the bitter white pith and the flesh itself, is the zest. It contains the essential oils that carry the flavor of the fruit; when grated or pared away in fine strips and chopped, it is often used to flavor baked goods, sauces, and sautés. Any of the citrus zests can be used with great success as a seasoning or as a replacement for salt. See GADGETS for directions on how to remove and chop zest.

Recipes and Related Information
Lemon, 339; Rind, 499.

Ribbons of bright yellow lemon zest may be used to flavor many foods. An easy way to remove the zest in strips is with a citrus stripper, as shown here.